ALMANAC OF BUSINESS AND INDUSTRIAL FINANCIAL RATIOS

2013 EDITION

LEO TROY, Ph.D.

.CCH

a Wolters Kluwer business

Editorial Staff

Production .... Christopher Zwirek
Design .... Craig Arritola

This publication is designed to provide accurate and authoritative information in regard to the subject matter covered. It is sold with the understanding that the publisher is not engaged in rendering legal, accounting, or other professional service and that the author is not offering such advice in this publication. If legal advice or other professional assistance is required, the services of a competent professional person should be sought.

ISBN: 978-0-8080-3087-4

© 2012, CCH. All Rights Reserved.
4025 W. Peterson Avenue
Chicago, IL 60646-6085
800 248 3248
CCHGroup.com

Printed in the United States of America

Dedicated

To Alexander, Suzannah, Dale, Ariel Sarah Troy, Abigayle Hannah Troy, and Rachel Ilana Troy

Preface

Now in its 44th Edition, the *Almanac of Business and Industrial Financial Ratios* provides a precise benchmark for evaluating an individual company's financial performance. The performance data is derived from the latest available IRS figures on U.S. and international companies, and tracks 50 operating and financial factors in nearly 200 industries. The *Almanac* provides competitive norms in actual dollar amounts for revenue and capital factors, as well as important average operating costs in percent of net sales. It also provides other critical financial factors in percentage, including debt ratio, return on assets, return on equity, profit margin, and more. Beyond its reliable insights into corporate behavior, the *Almanac* can be used by other countries looking to model their economies on American performance.

Also included with the text, in a special pocket provided in the inside cover of the book, is a CD-ROM that contains all the materials found in the book including the explanatory discussion, the data tables, and the supporting index. Also included on the CD, but not in the book itself, is a special template that allows the reader to add individual company data of interest to compare and contrast with data from the book.

2013 Edition Highlights

The 2013 Edition of the *Almanac of Business and Industrial Financial Ratios* has been updated to include the following:

- **Broad scope:** *2013 Almanac* features the North American Industry Classification System (NAICS), so you can benchmark or analyze results consistently with corporations in the United States, Canada, and Mexico.

- **Most industry types:** *2013 Almanac* highlights most industry types, including industries with advanced technologies and newly emerging industries such as paging and wireless communications.

- **A truer picture** of corporate financial performance, since the data isn't based on a mixed bag of averages that might include partnerships or sole proprietors. *2013 Almanac* features a homogeneous universe of American corporate financial performance.

- **Many classifications:** *2013 Almanac* analyzes 195 industries with 50 financial performance items.

- **Benchmarks:** *2013 Almanac* provides 13 benchmarks, including such critical measures as Receipts to Cash Flow, Debt to Total Assets, and Return on Equity both before and after taxes.

- **Analytical tables:** *Table I, Corporations with and without Net Income (All Corporations), and Table II, Corporations with Net Income.*

- **Easier apples-to-apples comparisons:** Each table is divided into 13 asset sizes.

- **More comprehensive:** Total receipts of all corporations covered by *2013 Almanac* is $24.8 trillion, making the *Almanac* the Anatomy of American Corporate Capitalism.

Leo Troy, Ph. D.

October 2012

About the Author

Dr. Leo Troy is Professor of Economics at Rutgers University. He has been a faculty member of Rutgers for 50 years. In addition to authoring the widely praised *Almanac*, he has written many other books and articles published in leading journals. Professor Troy has been the recipient of numerous awards including two from the National Science Foundation, and two Fulbright grants. In addition, he has received numerous awards from private foundations. Dr. Troy received his Ph.D. from Columbia University and is a member of Phi Beta Kappa. He is a veteran of World War II with three battle stars and the combat infantry badge. He is the father of two children and is also a grandfather of three girls, including twins.

Acknowledgments

I wish to acknowledge the contributions of five people in particular for the development of the 44th Edition of the *Almanac:* Phil Wilson, Alan Kovar of Brighton Best, Lawrence R. Chodor, CPA, CVA, Wiss & Company, Marvin Sunshine, and Karen Kane.

Philip is responsible for the programming, which dealt with a very large amount of data, covering both the current and trend information. Alan, drawing upon his knowledge and experience as a CPA and Partner of Wiss and Company of Livingston, N.J., contributed significantly to the new content of the book. To Marvin Sunshine, Esq, my appreciation for actions and support that helped make the *Almanac* a continuing publication. Karen Kane is acknowledged for her contributions to the graphics of this issue.

Special acknowledgement is due my late friends and colleagues, Stan Katz, CPA, and Professor Emeritus of Accounting, Rutgers University, John Gilmour. I thank, too, Professor of Accounting, Rutgers University, David Zaumeyer, Ph.D., CPA, for recommending several ratios that continue to be included in the *Almanac*. I thank Mr. Ka-Neng Au, Business Librarian, Rutgers University, for significant contributions to the *Almanac*.

I wish to recognize, too, the cooperation of members of the Statistics of Income Division of the Internal Revenue Service—in particular, Ken Szeflinksi, Martha A. Harris, and Phyllis J. Whiles of the Corporation Returns Analysis Section. Without their data and its reliability, the Almanac would not be possible. Responsibility for the use of their facts and figures is, of course, solely my own. In this regard, I recall the valuable assistance I received from Barry Rosenstein, MBA, CPA, in checking procedures, in earlier editions, and which have continued into the current one. Finally, I wish to recognize the help of Suzannah B. Troy in bringing about the 44th annual edition of the *Almanac*. I anticipate continuation of her valuable assistance in subsequent editions.

INTRODUCTION

QUESTIONS, ANSWERS AND COMMENTS ON THE *ALMANAC*
Some users have requested further information on the use of the *Almanac's* ratios and statistics. This Q & A addition to the *Almanac* is in response to that demand.

1. What are the general purposes of the Almanac?

The goal of the *Almanac* is to provide users with a reliable and comprehensive source of standard financial ratios and financial statistics on all corporations, public and private, including those filing 1120S returns in the United States. Excluded are all individual proprietorships and partnerships. The *Almanac* makes available key business and financial statistics, which are consistent and neutral (unbiased by any commercial publisher or trade association).

2. What is the source and reliability of the Almanac's results?

The *Almanac's* results are computed from the Department of the Treasury, Internal Revenue Service's statistical sampling of the tax returns of all corporations. Dividends received from foreign corporations are included in total receipts of those corporations affected. The statistics apply to the company rather than the establishment.

3. Are international comparisons available?

Yes. Because of the adoption of a common system of industrial classification by the U.S., Canada and Mexico, known as the North American Industrial Classification System of industries (NAICS), under the North American Free Trade Agreement, users in Canada and Mexico can compare and contrast their results with those corporations in the United States.

4. What about comparisons within the U.S?

These are the most important applications of the *Almanac*. Results are available for each and every corporation within the U.S., whether public or private, and include small business corporations, those which file the 1120S tax return. Therefore, users can compare their corporate performance with that of their industry and asset size group of corporate enterprise in the United States.

5. How many corporations are covered in the Almanac?

The *Almanac's* results are derived from more than 5.8 million corporation tax returns. Furthermore, the user can easily determine the number of enterprises for the total of each industry and by each of the 12 asset size groups. This makes for a total of 13 asset size comparisons.

6. What about differences in the size of corporations?

In addition to the results for each industry, the *Almanac* displays 12 columns of performance by the size of assets. Again, this makes for a total of 13 asset size comparisons.

7. Does the Almanac distinguish between the profitability of corporations?

In a word, yes. Each industry is divided between two tables: Table I reports the results of all corporations in an industry, that is, those with and without net income. It is followed by a second table for the same industry, Table II, which reports only those corporations with net income.

8. How many items of information are there for each industry?

There are 50 indicators of corporate performance in each table and each industry and for all asset size groups, except where the IRS' data sample is too small, or it does not supply the necessary information.

9. Who are the users of the Almanac?

Accountants, corporate managers, business consultants, investors evaluating a corporate takeover, entrepreneurs considering new businesses, lawyers, and students of accounting, business, and management.

10. What accounting time period is covered?

The Internal Revenue Service provides the most recent statistics publicly available for the *Almanac*. For the 2013 *Almanac*, these statistics apply to the accounting period from July 2009 through June 2010.

WHAT'S NEW IN THIS EDITION

Beginning with the year 2002, the *Almanac of Business and Industrial Financial Ratios* began using the North American Industry Classification System (NAICS). NAICS replaces the Internal Revenue Service's own system, which it had used for many years, an adaptation of Standard Industrial Classification (SIC); all previous *Almanacs* had used that adaptation.

The new industrial classification system is the product of the North American Free Trade Agreement (NAFTA), and it replaces the existing classification systems not only of the United States but also of Canada and Mexico. Hence, the new system applies uniformly to the three countries, and users of the *Almanac 2013*, utilizing the new international industrial classification system, can now compare their results with corporations in all three nations.

In the United States, the new manual was created by the Office of Management and Budget (OMB). The NAICS system gives special attention to industries producing and furnishing advanced technologies, new and emerging industries, as well as service industries in general. NAICS divides the economy into 21 sectors, five in the predominantly goods-producing area, and 16 in the service producing area.

INDUSTRY SECTORS

In 2007, NAICS was revised and reorganized; several of those changes apply to the *Almanac 2013*. The Real Estate Investment Trust category (525930) was deleted. In its place, Mortgage REIT's were reclassified to Other Financial Vehicles (525995) while Equity REIT's were reclassified either to Lessors of Buildings (531115) or Lessors of Miniwarehouses, Self-Storage Units and other Real Estate (531135), depending on the content of the REIT portfolio.

The other major changes were in the information sector. The Internet Publishing and Broadcasting category (516100) was deleted and reclassified with Other Information Services (519100). Internet Service Providers (518115) were reclassified to Telecommunications (517000). Web Search Portals (also part of 518115) were reclassified to the expanded category, Other Information Services (519100). The remainder of the 518115 category was reorganized as Data processing, Hosting and Related Services (518210).

The source of the IRS's data are the tax returns of all *active* public and private corporations. Because the *Almanac's* data are derived only from corporate tax returns, there is a mixture of corporate with the financial performance of partnerships and individual proprietorships; the *Almanac's* information constitutes a **homogeneous universe**. The tax returns are classified by the IRS on the basis of the business activity which accounts for a corporation's largest percentage of total receipts. Large corporations with dissimilar business activities are included in only one industry, despite operations that are unrelated to the industry in which they are grouped.

The data developed by the IRS are derived from a stratified probability sample of corporation income tax returns. Where the sample data from the sample are small and should those numbers be used in a denominator, the result is reported as a dot (·) in the *Almanac*. Returns of the largest corporations are generally in the sample from year to year, but comparability can be affected by consolidations and mergers, changes in the law and the tax forms, and changes in the industrial classification system used over the years.

REPRESENTATIVE INDUSTRIES

The *Almanac* reports on nearly 200 industries. Minor industries are denoted by a six-digit code; major industries are designated by a three-digit industry code; industrial sectors by a two-digit code; and industrial divisions by a two-digit code. When the data are the same for minor, major, sector, and industrial division, the IRS reports only the industrial division, and similarly for other identities applicable to the major and sectoral industries; the *Almanac* follows this procedure.

Almanac 2013 continues the previous coverage of reporting information: for all industries, **Table I, Corporations with and without Net Income** (that is, the entire universe of active reporting corporations), and **Table II, Corporations with Net Income**, a subset of the universe. In the *Almanac 2013*, Table I covers over 5.8 million enterprises (corporations), and Table II covers 3.1 million corporations with net income. This implies that 2.7 million corporations reported deficits. The IRS defines net income (or deficit) as the companies' net profit or loss from taxable sources of income reduced by allowable deductions. Total receipts of the 5.8 million corporations reported in *Almanac 2013* was $24.8 trillion, down by $3.8 trillion.

The *Almanac* continues to report performance results not only by the total for each industry, but by 12 other asset size groups (a total of 13 asset size groups), providing 50 items of data and/or ratios on corporate performance:

Total

Zero
$1 to $500,000
$500,001 to $1,000,000
$1,000,001 to $5,000,000
$5,000,001 to $10,000,000
$10,000,001 to $25,000,000
$25,000,001 to $50,000,000
$50,000,001 to $100,000,000
$100,000,001 to $250,000,000
$250,000,001 to $500,000,000
$500,000,001 to $2,500,000,000
$2,500,000,001 or more

All data in Tables I and II cover an accounting period identified on all tables and are the most recent information available from the IRS. For the *Almanac 2013*, the accounting period is July 2009 through June 2010. The dating of the data is counterbalanced by the most extensive industrial coverage available in any report on financial performance, the number of items of corporate performance, and their availability in thirteen asset size groups. Moreover, the timing of the data are also counterbalanced by the stability of the *Almanac's* values as past trends have indicated. Therefore, the *Almanac's* financial results are reliable in assessing current corporate performance.

Beyond its reliable insights into corporate behavior on a micro basis, its comprehensive and detailed coverage make the *Almanac* the **Anatomy of American Corporate Capitalism**. In this macro sense, it constitutes **the** example to those countries desirous of modeling their economies on the American performance.

HOW TO USE THE ALMANAC

On the micro level, the *Almanac* multiplies manyfold the power of financial analysis to evaluate an individual company's financial performance: In contrast to many standard reports, the *Almanac* gives management, and analysts independent of any company, more of the fundamental analytical tools needed to compare their company with companies in the same industry and of the same asset size. The *Almanac* can enhance the value of any company's annual report because it affords the analyst and the stockholder detailed background of financial information for comparison.

All items and ratios are listed in Both Table I and Table II. No figures are reported in the *Almanac* when the IRS has either suppressed the underlying data, or the sample size, or other reasons affecting a calculated result, and where the ratio/item was not applicable to an industry. The 50 tax-based items that provide that financial analysis are as follows:

1. Number of Enterprises

These are the count of corporate tax returns filed by active corporations on one of the Form 1120-series returns.

> SPECIAL NOTE: Net Sales is used to compute the percentage of items 3 to 7 to Net Sales for all industries, except Finance, Insurance, and Real Estate (FIRE). For the FIRE industries, Total Receipts are used to compute the percentage of items 3 to 7.

REVENUES ($ IN THOUSANDS), ITEMS 2 TO 9

2. Operating Income (Net Sales)

This is the IRS item Business Receipts, the gross operating receipts reduced by the cost of returned goods and allowances.

3. Interest

Taxable interest includes interest on U.S. Government obligations, loans, notes, mortgages, arbitrage bonds, nonexempt private activity bonds, corporate bonds, bank deposits, and tax refunds; interest received from tax-exempt state or local municipal bonds and ESOP loans are not included in this item.

4. Rents

These are the gross amounts received from the use or occupancy of property by corporations whose principal activities did not involve operating rental properties.

5. Royalties

These are gross payments received for the use of property rights before taking deductions.

6. Other Portfolio Income

These consist of cash, notes, and accounts receivable, less allowance for bad debts and inventories.

7. Other Receipts

These receipts include such items as income from minor operations, cash discounts, claims, license rights, judgments, and joint ventures.

8. Total Receipts

Total receipts are the sum of ten items: 1. Business receipts; 2. Interest; 3. Interest on government obligations: state and local; 4. Rents; 5. Royalties; 6. Net capital gains (excluding long-term gains from regulated investment companies); 7. Net gain, noncapital assets; 8. Dividends received from domestic corporations; 9. Dividends received from foreign corporations; 10. Other receipts.

9. Average Total Receipts

Total receipts divided by the number of enterprises.

OPERATING COSTS/OPERATING INCOME, ITEMS 10 TO 22

10. Cost of Operations

This is the IRS's Costs of Goods Sold; it consists of the costs incurred in producing the goods or furnishing the services that generated the corporations' business receipts.

11. Salaries and Wages

These include the amount of salaries and wages paid as well as bonuses and director's fees, but no contributions to pension plans (see item 16) nor compensation of officers (see item 20).

12. Taxes Paid

Excludes Federal Income Taxes; they are the amounts paid for ordinary state and local taxes, social security, payroll taxes, unemployment insurance taxes, excise taxes, import and tariff duties, and business license and privilege taxes.

13. Interest Paid

These amounts consist of interest paid on all business indebtedness.

14. Depreciation

The charges allowed are governed principally by the IRS rules in effect in 1997, basically enacted in 1986, but also include other modifications. Hence, depreciation could represent amounts computed by different sets of rules.

15. Amortization and Depletion

Most amortization is calculated on a straight-line basis. Depletion is allowed for the exhaustion of natural deposits and timber.

16. Pensions, Profit-Sharing, Stock Bonus, and Annuity Plans

These are amounts deducted during the current year for qualified pension, profit-sharing, or other funded deferred compensation plans.

17. Employee Benefits

These are employer contributions to death benefit, insurance, health, accident, and sickness, and other welfare plans.

18. Advertising

Amounts include promotion and publicity expenses.

19. Other Expenses

These include expenses for repairs, bad debts, rent paid on business property, domestic production activities, contributions and gifts, and expenses not allocable to specific deductible items.

20. Officers' Compensation

Salaries, wages, stock bonuses, bonds, and other forms of compensation are included in this item.

21. Operating Margin

This is the net income after all operating costs have been deducted.

22. Operating Margin Before Officers' Compensation

This measure takes into account the effect of Officers' Compensation on the operating margin.

Selected Average Balance Sheet Items ($ in thousands) Items 23 to 29

23. *Average Net Receivables*

The total of Notes and Accounts Receivable, less Allowance for Bad Debts, divided by the number of enterprises. Notes and Accounts Receivable are the gross amounts arising from business sales or services to customers on credit in the course of ordinary trade or business. This includes commercial paper, charge accounts, current intercompany receivables, property investment loans, and trade acceptances.

24. *Average Inventories*

Total inventories are divided by the number of enterprises. Inventories include finished goods, partially finished goods, new materials and supplies acquired for sale, merchandise on hand or in transit, and growing crops reported as assets by agricultural enterprises.

25. *Average Net Property, Plant and Equipment*

This includes depreciable assets less accumulated depreciation, depletable assets less accumulated depletion, and land; the sum is divided by the number of enterprises. Depreciable assets consist of end-of-year balance sheet tangible property, such as buildings and equipment used in trade or business, or held for the production of income, and that has a useful life of one year or more. The amount of accumulated depreciation represents the portion written off in the current year, as well as in prior years. Depletable assets represent the end-of-year value of mineral property, oil and gas wells, and other natural resources; standing timber; intangible development and drilling costs capitalized; and leases and leaseholds, subject to depletion. Accumulated depletion represents the cumulative adjustment of these assets.

26. *Average Total Assets*

Total Assets (and Total Liabilities) are amounts reported in the end-of-year balance sheet. Total Assets are net amounts after reduction from accumulated depreciation, accumulated amortization, accumulated depletion, and the reserve for bad debts. Total Liabilities include the claims of creditors and stockholders' equity, and were net after reduction by the cost of treasury stock. The average of total assets was obtained by dividing it by the number of enterprises.

27. *Average of Notes and Loans Payable, and Mortgages*

These liabilities were separated on the balance sheet according to the time to maturity of the obligations. Time to maturity was based on the date of the balance sheet, rather than the date of issue of the obligations. The total was divided by the number of enterprises.

28. *Average of All Other Liabilities*

These included accounts payable, and other liabilities including other current liabilities. The total was divided by the number of enterprises.

29. *Average Net Worth*

Net Worth represents the stockholders' equity in the corporation (total assets minus the claims of creditors). It consists of Capital Stock, Paid-In Capital Surplus, Retained Earnings Appropriated, Retained Earnings Unappropriated, less cost of treasury stock.

SELECTED FINANCIAL RATIOS, NUMBER OF TIMES TO ONE, RATIOS 30 TO 44

30. Current Ratio

The items that used Current Assets for this ratio are Cash; Notes and Accounts Receivable, Less: Allowance for Bad Debts; Inventories; Government Obligations; Tax-Exempt Securities; and Other Current Assets. For Current Liabilities, the following items were included: Accounts Payable; Mortgages and Notes Maturing in Less than 1 Year; and Other Current Liabilities.

This ratio, rated highest by CPAs as a measure of liquidity, gauges the ability of a company to meet its short-term financial obligations should it be compelled to liquidate its assets. However, it is not an absolute measure of the company's ability to meet its obligations. It is obtained by dividing current assets by current liabilities. The standard guideline has been a ratio of 2 to 1; however, some companies have found that in their experience, a ratio less than 2 to 1 is adequate, while others consider a larger one to be necessary. The ratio is affected by the method of valuation of inventory (LIFO or FIFO) and by inflation. The *Almanac* provides measures that can be treated as standards by size of asset.

31. Quick Ratio

This ratio is also known as the "Acid Test Ratio" because it is often used to estimate a company's general liquidity. There is some disagreement about the inclusion of inventory in the numerator because it may be slow moving, obsolete, or pledged to specific creditors, and, therefore, not be readily convertible into cash. The *Almanac* adopts a conservative approach and does not include the item in calculating the ratio. Excluding inventories and other current assets, the numerator is the same as that used in determining current assets. The denominator, current liabilities, is unchanged. The ratio of 1 to 1 has been considered a reasonable standard, but it is jeopardized because accounts and notes receivable may not be convertible into cash at face value and at short notice. The *Almanac* provides measures that can be treated as standards by size of asset.

32. Net Sales to Working Capital

This is an efficiency, or turnover, ratio that measures the rate at which current assets less current liabilities (Working Capital) is used in making sales. (In industries in Finance, Insurance, and Real Estate, total receipts rather than net sales is used.) A low ratio indicates a less efficient (profitable) use of working capital in making sales. The *Almanac* provides measures that can be treated as standards by size of asset. Working Capital is the difference between current assets and current liabilities.

33. Coverage Ratio

This ratio measures the number of times all interest paid by the company is covered by earnings before interest charges and taxes (EBIT). For that reason, the ratio is also known as the "times interest earned ratio." The ratio indicates the company's ability to service its debt based on its income.

34. Total Asset Turnover

The ratio is an efficiency ratio because it indicates the effectiveness of the company's use of its total assets in generating sales. It is measured by dividing net sales by total assets.

35. *Inventory Turnover*

Inventory turnover measures the liquidity of the inventory. It is computed by dividing the cost of goods sold by the average inventory. The result shows the number of times that the average inventory can be converted into receivables or cash. The ratio reflects both on the quality of the inventory and the efficiency of management. Typically, the higher the turnover rate, the more likely profits will be higher.

SPECIAL NOTE: Inventory turnover is not computed for industries in Finance, Insurance, and Real Estate.

36. *Receivables Turnover*

This ratio measures the liquidity of accounts receivable. It indicates the average collection period throughout the year. It is obtained by dividing sales average by net receivables. It is not computed in the Finance, Insurance, and Real Estate industries (although it is calculated for all other industries even though conventional analysis typically omits it) for many of the industries in the *Almanac*.

37. *Total Liabilities to Net Worth*

This ratio indicates the extent to which the company's funds are supplied by short- and long-term creditors compared to its owners. It is an indicator of the company's long-term debt paying ability. The ratio is one of the most important bearing on the company's capital structure. Net worth is defined in ratio 29.

38. *Current Assets to Working Capital*

The dependence of Working Capital in part on current assets is important to understanding this part of the source of Working Capital. Current Assets are defined in ratio 30 and Working Capital is defined in ratio 32.

39. *Current Liabilities to Working Capital*

The dependence of Working Capital in part on current liabilities is important to understanding this part of the source of Working Capital. Current Liabilities are defined in ratio 30 and Working Capital is defined in ratio 32.

40. *Working Capital to Net Sales or Total Receipts*

The purpose of this ratio is to determine the working capital needed in relation to projected sales or receipts. Working Capital is defined in ratio 32.

41. *Inventory to Working Capital*

This ratio, by showing the proportion of Working Capital invested in Inventory, indicates the part of Current Assets that are least liquid. Inventories which exceed working capital indicate that current liabilities exceed liquid current assets. Working Capital is defined in ratio 32.

42. *Total Receipts to Cash Flow*

Cash Flow is the difference between cash receipts and cash disbursements. The ratio of total receipts to cash flow could suggest steps which management might take to improve the company's cash position.

43. Cost of Goods to Cash Flow

This ratio can be the basis for projections of cash requirements needed to fund projected costs of production. Cash flow is defined in ratio 42.

44. Cash Flow to Total Debt

This ratio indicates the extent to which a company could service its total debt from cash flow. It is analogous to the coverage ratio; refer to ratio 33. Cash flow is defined in ratio 42.

SELECTED FINANCIAL FACTORS (IN PERCENTAGES), ITEMS 45 TO 50

45. Debt Ratio (Total Liabilities to Total Assets)

This ratio indicates the company's ability to pay all its debts. It measures the creditors' and owners' of the company's ability to withstand losses. It is an indicator of the long-run solvency of the firm.

46. Return on Total Assets

The ratio combines the turnover and profit ratios (Sales/Total Assets x [times] Profit/Sales) and yields the return on investment (Total Assets). The result is the end product of the DuPont System of financial analysis. The system takes into account both operating income and operating assets. In Table I of each industry, the Return on Investment (ROI) is net income less deficit before income taxes divided by total assets. In Table II of each industry, the ROI is net income before income taxes divided by Total Assets. Total Assets are used because management has discretion in the investment of the resources provided by both the creditors and owners.

47. Return on Equity Before Income Taxes

This ratio measures the profitability of the company's operations to owners, before income taxes. For Table I this is net income, less deficit before income taxes and before credits. For Table II this is net income minus income tax before credits.

48. Return on Equity After Income Taxes

This ratio measures the profitability of the company's operations to owners, after income taxes. For Table I this is net income, less deficit and minus income tax before credits. For Table II this is net income minus income tax and before credits.

49. Profit Margin (Before Income Tax)

This is net income before income tax divided by net sales (or total receipts) and indicates the contribution of sales to the profitability of the company. Competition, capital structure, and operating characteristics cause the margin to vary within and among industries. For Table I, net income less deficit and before income taxes is the numerator; for Table II it is net income before tax.

50. Profit Margin (After Income Tax)

This ratio is the same as ratio 49 except that income taxes are taken into account.

Table of Contents

Page references to tables for industries with net income are in italic

PRINCIPAL BUSINESS ACTIVITY (BASED ON NAICS)

ALMANAC
of Business and Industrial
FINANCIAL RATIOS

44th ANNUAL EDITION
2013

Table I

Corporations with and without Net Income

AGRICULTURAL PRODUCTION

MONEY AMOUNTS AND SIZE OF ASSETS IN THOUSANDS OF DOLLARS

Item Description for Accounting Period 7/09 Through 6/10		Total	Zero Assets	Under 500	500 to 1,000	1,000 to 5,000	5,000 to 10,000	10,000 to 25,000	25,000 to 50,000	50,000 to 100,000	100,000 to 250,000	250,000 to 500,000	500,000 to 2,500,000	2,500,000 and over
Number of Enterprises	1	100645	9484	57651	16116	15313	•	586	169	87	61	14	•	0
Revenues ($ in Thousands)														
Net Sales	2	102607632	1999826	12873271	7487984	23302451	•	7484932	4266118	6971944	10472689	4793187	•	0
Interest	3	243507	1847	26267	37228	81686	•	15667	12497	4980	12145	7613	•	0
Rents	4	884882	30331	170066	207081	274453	•	16858	13548	13010	54720	12656	•	0
Royalties	5	70923	1	2705	11002	19593	•	704	4171	0	20042	0	•	0
Other Portfolio Income	6	1257685	115452	261538	153166	275974	•	141078	20574	32391	118571	25336	•	0
Other Receipts	7	12292419	133977	3333271	2927345	3574704	•	547472	296735	133073	259450	24752	•	0
Total Receipts	8	117357048	2281434	16667118	10823806	27528861	•	8206711	4613643	7155398	10937617	4863544	•	0
Average Total Receipts	9	1166	241	289	672	1798	•	14005	27300	82246	179305	347396	•	•
Operating Costs/Operating Income (%)														
Cost of Operations	10	50.0	72.0	17.4	21.3	34.0	•	62.9	69.3	66.5	75.9	72.6	•	•
Salaries and Wages	11	7.9	3.1	10.2	11.7	10.2	•	8.4	7.0	5.5	4.4	4.1	•	•
Taxes Paid	12	2.0	1.2	2.9	3.4	2.8	•	1.8	1.7	1.2	1.3	1.7	•	•
Interest Paid	13	2.6	3.9	3.3	3.3	3.3	•	1.8	2.5	1.4	1.2	1.2	•	•
Depreciation	14	6.4	5.3	9.1	13.8	8.7	•	4.6	4.6	3.4	3.2	4.4	•	•
Amortization and Depletion	15	0.3	0.1	0.1	0.2	0.1	•	0.1	0.3	0.9	0.2	1.0	•	•
Pensions and Other Deferred Comp.	16	0.2	0.0	0.2	0.1	0.1	•	0.1	0.2	0.2	0.2	0.4	•	•
Employee Benefits	17	1.0	1.1	1.3	1.2	1.0	•	0.9	0.5	0.5	0.8	0.8	•	•
Advertising	18	0.3	0.0	0.4	0.3	0.2	•	0.4	0.4	0.2	0.3	0.2	•	•
Other Expenses	19	41.3	34.5	80.9	84.3	54.4	•	27.0	22.0	21.5	13.7	14.0	•	•
Officers' Compensation	20	1.8	1.5	4.2	4.7	2.2	•	1.5	0.8	0.9	0.7	0.5	•	•
Operating Margin	21	•	•	•	•	•	•	•	•	•	•	•	•	•
Operating Margin Before Officers' Comp.	22	•	•	•	•	•	•	•	•	•	•	•	•	•

Selected Average Balance Sheet ($ in Thousands)

Net Receivables 23	95	0	3	21	72	•	1577	5388	8989	21282	51852	•
Inventories 24	115	0	10	36	159	•	2198	3975	10765	23700	74939	•
Net Property, Plant and Equipment 25	501	0	88	405	1059	•	6261	12323	29203	57613	153665	•
Total Assets 26	1089	0	176	705	1985	•	14717	33550	68773	153292	330801	•
Notes and Loans Payable 27	611	0	181	383	1249	•	6900	16119	28336	55116	113398	•
All Other Liabilities 28	163	0	16	48	194	•	2361	5123	9651	27143	62529	•
Net Worth 29	314	0	-21	273	542	•	5457	12308	30786	71034	154874	•

Selected Financial Ratios (Times to 1)

Current Ratio 30	1.4	•	1.1	1.5	1.4	•	1.3	1.6	1.6	1.6	1.9	•
Quick Ratio 31	0.7	•	0.8	0.9	0.7	•	0.6	0.9	0.8	0.8	0.8	•
Net Sales to Working Capital 32	11.0	•	52.1	9.4	11.3	•	11.1	4.7	7.8	6.6	4.9	•
Coverage Ratio 33	1.2	•	0.8	1.1	1.4	•	1.1	0.5	1.4	3.0	1.6	•
Total Asset Turnover 34	0.9	•	1.3	0.7	0.8	•	0.9	0.8	1.2	1.1	1.0	•
Inventory Turnover 35	4.4	•	4.1	2.8	3.3	•	3.7	4.4	4.9	5.5	3.3	•
Receivables Turnover 36	11.1	•	99.2	16.0	23.0	•	7.8	6.2	8.6	8.1	6.0	•
Total Liabilities to Net Worth 37	2.5	•	•	1.6	2.7	•	1.7	1.7	1.2	1.2	1.1	•
Current Assets to Working Capital 38	3.8	•	11.2	3.1	3.7	•	4.4	2.6	2.6	2.6	2.1	•
Current Liabilities to Working Capital 39	2.8	•	10.2	2.1	2.7	•	3.4	1.6	1.6	1.6	1.1	•
Working Capital to Net Sales 40	0.1	•	0.0	0.1	0.1	•	0.1	0.2	0.1	0.2	0.2	•
Inventory to Working Capital 41	1.2	•	1.8	0.7	1.3	•	1.7	0.8	0.9	0.9	1.0	•
Total Receipts to Cash Flow 42	3.2	6.5	1.8	1.6	2.5	•	4.9	5.8	5.2	7.1	8.5	•
Cost of Goods to Cash Flow 43	1.6	4.7	0.3	0.3	0.8	•	3.1	4.0	3.4	5.4	6.2	•
Cash Flow to Total Debt 44	0.4	•	0.6	0.7	0.4	•	0.3	0.2	0.4	0.3	0.2	•

Selected Financial Factors (in Percentages)

Debt Ratio 45	71.2	•	111.9	61.2	72.7	•	62.9	63.3	55.2	53.7	53.2	•
Return on Total Assets 46	2.8	•	3.5	2.3	3.5	•	1.6	0.9	2.2	4.2	2.0	•
Return on Equity Before Income Taxes 47	1.3	•	6.3	0.4	3.7	•	0.3	•	1.5	6.0	1.7	•
Return on Equity After Income Taxes 48	•	•	11.3	•	2.7	•	•	•	0.7	3.4	0.8	•
Profit Margin (Before Income Tax) 49	0.4	•	•	0.2	1.3	•	0.1	•	0.6	2.5	0.8	•
Profit Margin (After Income Tax) 50	•	•	•	•	0.9	•	•	•	0.3	1.4	0.4	•

Table II

Corporations with Net Income

AGRICULTURAL PRODUCTION

MONEY AMOUNTS AND SIZE OF ASSETS IN THOUSANDS OF DOLLARS

Item Description for Accounting Period 7/09 Through 6/10		Total	Zero Assets	Under 500	500 to 1000	1,000 to 5,000	5,000 to 10,000	10,000 to 25,000	25,000 to 50,000	50,000 to 100,000	100,000 to 250,000	250,000 to 500,000	500,000 to 2,500,000	2,500,000 and over
Number of Enterprises	1	50259	3747	26993	9364	9133	572	277	•	48	•	•	8	0
Revenues ($ in Thousands)														
Net Sales	2	61967938	261462	8328632	4092605	16761060	4740309	3716989	•	5114470	•	•	5159890	0
Interest	3	162838	1076	17426	24979	60781	16610	11057	•	2389	•	•	9725	0
Rents	4	633610	12903	116864	185181	211256	24119	11324	•	12946	•	•	277	0
Royalties	5	48685	0	2508	5719	19144	2714	4	•	0	•	•	0	0
Other Portfolio Income	6	808347	114207	145049	100995	190381	25068	88993	•	18478	•	•	5865	0
Other Receipts	7	9428499	132570	2660133	1972203	2574671	967585	443183	•	120897	•	•	142298	0
Total Receipts	8	73049917	522218	11270612	6381682	19817293	5776405	4271550	•	5269180	•	•	5318055	0
Average Total Receipts	9	1453	139	418	682	2170	10099	15421	•	109775	•	•	664757	•
Operating Costs/Operating Income (%)														
Cost of Operations	10	45.1	6.6	15.3	20.1	30.5	37.1	57.8	•	64.4	•	•	60.6	•
Salaries and Wages	11	7.6	7.1	7.6	7.3	9.6	13.0	6.7	•	5.5	•	•	7.3	•
Taxes Paid	12	2.1	6.0	2.5	3.6	2.5	2.3	2.0	•	1.2	•	•	0.8	•
Interest Paid	13	1.7	2.5	2.0	2.8	2.0	1.7	1.5	•	1.0	•	•	1.7	•
Depreciation	14	6.3	7.4	8.5	15.7	8.1	5.8	4.2	•	3.1	•	•	3.5	•
Amortization and Depletion	15	0.4	•	0.1	0.2	0.0	0.1	0.2	•	1.1	•	•	2.0	•
Pensions and Other Deferred Comp.	16	0.2	•	0.1	0.2	0.1	0.0	0.2	•	0.2	•	•	0.4	•
Employee Benefits	17	1.0	1.5	1.0	1.6	1.0	0.8	0.9	•	0.4	•	•	2.6	•
Advertising	18	0.3	•	0.3	0.1	0.2	0.3	0.4	•	0.2	•	•	0.6	•
Other Expenses	19	41.4	74.7	77.4	83.0	52.7	51.1	26.9	•	20.1	•	•	18.6	•
Officers' Compensation	20	1.9	1.6	4.3	5.5	1.9	1.5	2.0	•	0.7	•	•	0.4	•
Operating Margin	21	•	•	•	•	•	•	•	•	2.1	•	•	1.7	•
Operating Margin Before Officers' Comp.	22	•	•	•	•	•	•	•	•	2.8	•	•	2.2	•

Selected Average Balance Sheet ($ in Thousands)

Net Receivables 23	89	0	3	19	81	340	2193	11132	•	44380
Inventories 24	113	0	8	28	164	762	2084	10867	•	72847
Net Property, Plant and Equipment 25	497	0	82	372	1012	3516	5652	27150	•	142257
Total Assets 26	1138	0	179	716	1930	6638	15493	69924	•	690691
Notes and Loans Payable 27	467	0	107	260	881	4233	4819	25703	•	241368
All Other Liabilities 28	137	0	10	31	174	628	2455	9754	•	125262
Net Worth 29	533	0	62	425	876	1776	8219	34467	•	324061

Selected Financial Ratios (Times to 1)

Current Ratio 30	1.7	•	2.0	2.1	1.4	1.2	1.8	1.7	•	2.0
Quick Ratio 31	0.9	•	1.6	1.4	0.7	0.7	1.0	0.9	•	0.7
Net Sales to Working Capital 32	8.0	•	11.1	5.3	12.2	24.9	4.8	7.9	•	5.2
Coverage Ratio 33	6.9	37.4	9.0	6.7	5.7	5.8	9.1	6.0	•	4.1
Total Asset Turnover 34	1.1	•	1.7	0.6	1.0	1.2	0.9	1.5	•	0.9
Inventory Turnover 35	4.9	•	6.3	3.2	3.4	4.0	3.7	6.3	•	5.4
Receivables Turnover 36	14.4	•	109.4	14.4	31.9	28.1	6.2	•	•	10.6
Total Liabilities to Net Worth 37	1.1	•	1.9	0.7	1.2	2.7	0.9	1.0	•	1.1
Current Assets to Working Capital 38	2.5	•	2.0	1.9	3.6	6.2	2.2	2.4	•	2.0
Current Liabilities to Working Capital 39	1.5	•	1.0	0.9	2.6	5.2	1.2	1.4	•	1.0
Working Capital to Net Sales 40	0.1	•	0.1	0.2	0.1	0.0	0.2	0.1	•	0.2
Inventory to Working Capital 41	0.8	•	0.2	0.4	1.2	2.2	0.6	0.8	•	0.7
Total Receipts to Cash Flow 42	2.5	0.7	1.4	1.4	2.1	1.9	3.2	4.4	•	4.7
Cost of Goods to Cash Flow 43	1.1	0.0	0.2	0.3	0.7	0.7	1.9	2.8	•	2.8
Cash Flow to Total Debt 44	0.8	•	1.9	1.1	0.8	0.9	0.6	0.7	•	0.4

Selected Financial Factors (in Percentages)

Debt Ratio 45	53.1	•	65.4	40.6	54.6	73.2	46.9	50.7	•	53.1
Return on Total Assets 46	12.4	•	31.6	11.3	11.0	12.4	11.7	9.3	•	6.3
Return on Equity Before Income Taxes 47	22.6	•	81.0	16.2	20.0	38.3	19.6	15.8	•	10.1
Return on Equity After Income Taxes 48	20.6	•	78.0	15.0	19.0	35.0	18.1	14.6	•	7.3
Profit Margin (Before Income Tax) 49	9.8	91.9	16.2	15.8	9.5	8.2	12.0	5.1	•	5.1
Profit Margin (After Income Tax) 50	8.9	80.6	15.6	14.6	9.0	7.5	11.1	4.7	•	3.7

Table I

Corporations with and without Net Income

FORESTRY AND LOGGING

MONEY AMOUNTS AND SIZE OF ASSETS IN THOUSANDS OF DOLLARS

Item Description for Accounting Period 7/09 Through 6/10		Total	Zero Assets	Under 500	500 to 1,000	1,000 to 5,000	5,000 to 10,000	10,000 to 25,000	25,000 to 50,000	50,000 to 100,000	100,000 to 250,000	250,000 to 500,000	500,000 to 2,500,000	2,500,000 and over
Number of Enterprises	1	10393	2244	5655	1244	1022	•	71	29	9	0	3	•	0
Revenues ($ in Thousands)														
Net Sales	2	9653771	590951	1564844	2043066	2159276	•	767274	542772	171977	0	927063	•	0
Interest	3	71691	2928	2040	17	2945	•	1149	52	9265	0	3379	•	0
Rents	4	36133	18765	9	495	6090	•	4932	635	380	0	4742	•	0
Royalties	5	4864	0	0	1420	0	•	219	0	0	0	1973	•	0
Other Portfolio Income	6	206565	2132	18032	7441	54129	•	33489	1691	33690	0	19250	•	0
Other Receipts	7	77104	2646	1070	39166	10520	•	33572	-5896	-4137	0	70759	•	0
Total Receipts	8	10050128	617422	1585995	2091605	2232960	•	840635	539254	211175	0	1027166	•	0
Average Total Receipts	9	967	275	280	1681	2185	•	11840	18595	23464	•	342389	•	•
Operating Costs/Operating Income (%)														
Cost of Operations	10	54.8	27.0	36.3	36.0	48.0	•	90.2	93.8	83.3	•	85.9	•	•
Salaries and Wages	11	9.6	4.8	12.7	11.8	13.8	•	3.4	1.8	3.9	•	5.4	•	•
Taxes Paid	12	2.6	0.7	2.9	2.1	4.0	•	1.9	1.6	5.0	•	1.1	•	•
Interest Paid	13	3.4	3.5	3.0	2.4	2.3	•	1.8	1.6	16.3	•	0.6	•	•
Depreciation	14	6.7	1.8	12.0	9.1	7.5	•	1.0	1.3	6.5	•	1.6	•	•
Amortization and Depletion	15	0.4	0.2	0.0	•	0.0	•	0.5	0.8	2.9	•	2.5	•	•
Pensions and Other Deferred Comp.	16	0.2	0.2	0.1	0.0	0.2	•	0.2	0.1	0.3	•	0.9	•	•
Employee Benefits	17	1.5	0.1	2.6	1.2	2.0	•	0.8	0.3	1.5	•	1.7	•	•
Advertising	18	0.1	0.1	0.1	0.1	0.1	•	0.1	0.0	0.1	•	0.2	•	•
Other Expenses	19	24.1	69.2	30.1	31.1	23.9	•	7.0	6.4	21.0	•	6.7	•	•
Officers' Compensation	20	2.5	1.6	4.6	2.3	3.4	•	2.3	0.6	2.2	•	0.9	•	•
Operating Margin	21	•	•	•	4.0	•	•	•	•	•	•	•	•	•
Operating Margin Before Officers' Comp.	22	•	•	0.3	6.3	•	•	•	•	•	•	•	•	•

Selected Average Balance Sheet ($ in Thousands)

Net Receivables 23	60	0	3	36	103	•	640	939	3892	•	48091	•	•
Inventories 24	56	0	2	48	116	•	3345	3077	3670	•	4693	•	•
Net Property, Plant and Equipment 25	760	0	66	523	981	•	7619	23848	35681	•	111509	•	•
Total Assets 26	1325	0	98	684	1819	•	16151	38501	92872	•	344645	•	•
Notes and Loans Payable 27	648	0	99	646	1349	•	4404	8219	30055	•	54961	•	•
All Other Liabilities 28	70	0	6	40	91	•	958	1632	13240	•	81345	•	•
Net Worth 29	608	0	-7	-2	379	•	10789	28649	49577	•	208339	•	•

Selected Financial Ratios (Times to 1)

Current Ratio 30	0.9	2.2	1.3	2.0	•	4.2	6.1	1.7	•	1.3	•	•	
Quick Ratio 31	0.5	1.9	0.5	1.2	•	1.6	3.0	0.6	•	0.9	•	•	
Net Sales to Working Capital 32	•	22.2	38.3	9.6	•	2.8	3.0	1.7	•	18.3	•	•	
Coverage Ratio 33	0.4	0.0	3.7	0.2	•	1.2	•	•	•	6.1	•	•	
Total Asset Turnover 34	0.7	2.8	2.4	1.2	•	0.7	0.5	0.2	•	0.9	•	•	
Inventory Turnover 35	9.1	45.1	12.3	8.7	•	2.9	5.7	4.3	•	56.6	•	•	
Receivables Turnover 36	16.8	110.0	57.6	19.9	•	16.2	19.8	6.6	•	6.2	•	•	
Total Liabilities to Net Worth 37	1.2	•	•	3.8	•	0.5	0.3	0.9	•	0.7	•	•	
Current Assets to Working Capital 38	•	1.8	4.6	2.0	•	1.3	1.2	2.4	•	4.7	•	•	
Current Liabilities to Working Capital 39	•	0.8	3.6	1.0	•	0.3	0.2	1.4	•	3.7	•	•	
Working Capital to Net Sales 40	•	0.0	0.0	0.1	•	0.4	0.3	0.6	•	0.1	•	•	
Inventory to Working Capital 41	•	0.2	1.1	0.5	•	0.8	0.5	0.4	•	0.3	•	•	
Total Receipts to Cash Flow 42	6.1	4.6	3.3	6.5	•	40.8	•	•	1.6	14.0	•	•	
Cost of Goods to Cash Flow 43	3.3	1.7	1.2	3.1	•	36.8	•	0.4	•	12.1	•	•	
Cash Flow to Total Debt 44	0.2	0.6	0.7	0.2	•	0.0	•	•	•	0.2	•	•	

Selected Financial Factors (in Percentages)

Debt Ratio 45	54.1	106.7	100.3	79.2	•	33.2	25.6	46.6	•	39.5	•	•	
Return on Total Assets 46	1.0	0.0	21.0	0.5	•	1.5	•	•	•	3.4	•	•	
Return on Equity Before Income Taxes 47	•	124.0	•	•	•	0.4	•	•	•	4.7	•	•	
Return on Equity After Income Taxes 48	•	124.5	•	•	•	0.4	•	•	•	3.3	•	•	
Profit Margin (Before Income Tax) 49	•	•	6.3	•	•	0.4	•	•	•	3.2	•	•	
Profit Margin (After Income Tax) 50	•	•	6.3	•	•	•	•	•	•	2.2	•	•	

Table II

Corporations with Net Income

FORESTRY AND LOGGING

MONEY AMOUNTS AND SIZE OF ASSETS IN THOUSANDS OF DOLLARS

Item Description for Accounting Period 7/09 Through 6/10		Total	Zero Assets	Under 500	500 to 1,000	1,000 to 5,000	5,000 to 10,000	10,000 to 25,000	25,000 to 50,000	50,000 to 100,000	100,000 to 250,000	250,000 to 500,000	500,000 to 2,500,000	2,500,000 and over
Number of Enterprises	1	4490	472	2697	911	320	50	30	•	•	•	0	0	0
Revenues ($ in Thousands)														
Net Sales	2	5728824	383005	622981	1712730	764617	515582	458331	•	•	•	•	0	0
Interest	3	65954	0	1267	17	1047	37	1149	•	•	•	•	0	0
Rents	4	10013	16	0	4	78	85	4932	•	•	•	•	0	0
Royalties	5	3443	0	0	0	0	1251	219	•	•	•	•	0	0
Other Portfolio Income	6	152486	1435	13291	6109	46617	115	32352	•	•	•	•	0	0
Other Receipts	7	146212	0	514	38989	2648	2063	30371	•	•	•	•	0	0
Total Receipts	8	6106932	384456	638053	1757849	815007	519133	527354	•	•	•	•	0	0
Average Total Receipts	9	1360	815	237	1930	2547	10383	17578	•	•	•	•	•	•
Operating Costs/Operating Income (%)														
Cost of Operations	10	52.4	1.5	47.3	33.0	38.0	68.2	87.6	•	•	•	•	•	•
Salaries and Wages	11	10.6	5.2	8.5	13.9	22.2	9.6	4.0	•	•	•	•	•	•
Taxes Paid	12	2.2	0.2	2.9	2.1	3.0	3.5	2.6	•	•	•	•	•	•
Interest Paid	13	1.7	0.0	1.7	1.6	2.3	0.9	0.6	•	•	•	•	•	•
Depreciation	14	5.2	0.1	7.4	7.0	8.3	8.3	1.0	•	•	•	•	•	•
Amortization and Depletion	15	0.5	0.0	•	•	0.0	0.0	0.8	•	•	•	•	•	•
Pensions and Other Deferred Comp.	16	0.2	•	•	0.0	0.4	0.1	0.2	•	•	•	•	•	•
Employee Benefits	17	1.3	•	3.5	1.3	0.7	0.8	1.3	•	•	•	•	•	•
Advertising	18	0.1	0.0	0.1	0.1	0.1	0.1	0.0	•	•	•	•	•	•
Other Expenses	19	22.9	88.1	11.5	33.6	21.4	5.4	8.6	•	•	•	•	•	•
Officers' Compensation	20	2.2	•	7.6	1.5	3.4	1.4	2.1	•	•	•	•	•	•
Operating Margin	21	0.7	4.9	9.5	6.0	•	1.6	•	•	•	•	•	•	•
Operating Margin Before Officers' Comp.	22	2.9	4.9	17.1	7.5	3.4	3.0	•	•	•	•	•	•	•

Selected Average Balance Sheet ($ in Thousands)

Net Receivables 23	58	0	0	46	17	198	920
Inventories 24	42	0	2	33	32	99	966
Net Property, Plant and Equipment 25	390	0	27	476	631	5280	9041
Total Assets 26	1124	0	59	664	1402	6394	17096
Notes and Loans Payable 27	640	0	52	569	1028	1960	2520
All Other Liabilities 28	81	0	5	48	33	93	1250
Net Worth 29	402	0	2	47	341	4341	13325

Selected Financial Ratios (Times to 1)

Current Ratio 30	0.5	•	6.2	1.3	1.2	2.3	3.2
Quick Ratio 31	0.3	•	5.7	0.5	1.0	1.8	2.4
Net Sales to Working Capital 32	•	•	10.7	31.0	71.2	17.7	6.2
Coverage Ratio 33	5.3	350.2	7.9	6.5	3.8	3.6	11.8
Total Asset Turnover 34	1.1	•	3.9	2.8	1.7	1.6	0.9
Inventory Turnover 35	16.1	•	47.2	18.8	28.0	70.9	13.9
Receivables Turnover 36	23.1	•	1242.2	52.0	51.7	84.6	22.2
Total Liabilities to Net Worth 37	1.8	•	38.3	13.1	3.1	0.5	0.3
Current Assets to Working Capital 38	•	•	1.2	4.3	6.0	1.8	1.5
Current Liabilities to Working Capital 39	•	•	0.2	3.3	5.0	0.8	0.5
Working Capital to Net Sales 40	•	•	0.1	0.0	0.0	0.1	0.2
Inventory to Working Capital 41	•	•	0.1	1.1	0.4	0.3	0.3
Total Receipts to Cash Flow 42	4.1	1.1	4.9	2.9	5.7	16.4	14.3
Cost of Goods to Cash Flow 43	2.2	0.0	2.3	1.0	2.1	11.2	12.5
Cash Flow to Total Debt 44	0.4	•	0.8	1.0	0.4	0.3	0.3

Selected Financial Factors (in Percentages)

Debt Ratio 45	64.2	•	97.5	92.9	75.7	32.1	22.1
Return on Total Assets 46	10.2	•	53.3	28.8	15.2	5.2	6.2
Return on Equity Before Income Taxes 47	23.2	•	1828.4	343.3	45.9	5.5	7.3
Return on Equity After Income Taxes 48	20.6	•	1824.0	343.1	34.8	5.2	5.7
Profit Margin (Before Income Tax) 49	7.3	5.3	11.9	8.6	6.6	2.3	6.3
Profit Margin (After Income Tax) 50	6.5	5.3	11.9	8.6	5.0	2.2	5.0

SUPPORT ACTIVITIES AND FISHING, HUNTING AND TRAPPING

Table I

Corporations with and without Net Income

MONEY AMOUNTS AND SIZE OF ASSETS IN THOUSANDS OF DOLLARS

Item Description for Accounting Period 7/09 Through 6/10	Total	Zero Assets	Under 500	500 to 1,000	1,000 to 5,000	5,000 to 10,000	10,000 to 25,000	25,000 to 50,000	50,000 to 100,000	100,000 to 250,000	250,000 to 500,000	500,000 to 2,500,000	2,500,000 and over
Number of Enterprises **1**	27755	5057	18188	2214	1783	311	135	53	8	6	0	0	0
Revenues ($ in Thousands)													
Net Sales **2**	28444978	237241	6015806	3024386	7662283	3526399	3020811	2349844	495464	2112744	0	0	0
Interest **3**	20989	2	879	486	11648	1782	4622	1132	6	432	0	0	0
Rents **4**	25361	205	903	395	13235	4343	5679	587	0	14	0	0	0
Royalties **5**	4344	0	0	0	848	871	0	1891	0	735	0	0	0
Other Portfolio Income **6**	155637	11521	30548	22833	38183	2484	19364	25636	802	4268	0	0	0
Other Receipts **7**	1145288	6	248236	84643	413955	59875	100001	164035	11634	62898	0	0	0
Total Receipts **8**	29796597	248975	6296372	3132743	8140152	3595754	3150477	2543125	507906	2181091	0	0	0
Average Total Receipts **9**	1074	49	346	1415	4565	11562	23337	47983	63488	363515	•	•	•
Operating Costs/Operating Income (%)													
Cost of Operations **10**	63.8	31.6	43.0	27.1	76.7	72.8	74.5	85.6	61.0	78.4	•	•	•
Salaries and Wages **11**	8.6	8.1	10.0	9.2	8.7	11.8	5.8	4.0	13.5	6.2	•	•	•
Taxes Paid **12**	1.9	2.8	2.5	2.0	1.7	1.8	1.6	0.9	1.6	2.2	•	•	•
Interest Paid **13**	0.8	0.2	1.0	0.4	0.6	1.1	1.1	0.6	1.7	1.2	•	•	•
Depreciation **14**	3.4	4.5	3.5	4.1	3.5	2.7	3.3	2.1	3.8	3.7	•	•	•
Amortization and Depletion **15**	0.1	•	0.1	0.0	0.1	0.2	0.0	0.0	0.5	0.2	•	•	•
Pensions and Other Deferred Comp. **16**	0.2	•	0.1	0.1	0.2	0.2	0.1	0.5	0.1	0.1	•	•	•
Employee Benefits **17**	0.8	3.5	0.9	0.7	0.4	1.2	0.5	0.5	2.1	1.6	•	•	•
Advertising **18**	0.3	0.0	1.0	0.1	0.1	0.2	0.2	0.1	1.1	0.2	•	•	•
Other Expenses **19**	17.9	33.3	29.7	47.5	10.0	9.1	10.6	9.2	8.0	6.4	•	•	•
Officers' Compensation **20**	2.9	6.8	7.2	1.2	1.9	1.4	2.1	2.1	1.4	0.4	•	•	•
Operating Margin **21**	•	9.3	0.9	7.5	•	•	0.4	•	5.1	•	•	•	•
Operating Margin Before Officers' Comp. **22**	2.2	16.1	8.2	8.7	•	•	2.4	•	6.6	•	•	•	•

Selected Average Balance Sheet ($ in Thousands)

Net Receivables 23	79	0	7	17	260	1461	2792	8125	12885	33954
Inventories 24	65	0	5	40	166	549	3302	3251	14353	73926
Net Property, Plant and Equipment 25	174	0	36	246	606	2816	3984	9279	12836	88668
Total Assets 26	548	0	97	702	1962	7486	14072	34880	72102	289860
Notes and Loans Payable 27	225	0	77	225	906	2480	5241	10582	21264	87002
All Other Liabilities 28	126	0	25	47	368	2125	3891	10946	17075	63766
Net Worth 29	197	0	-5	430	688	2880	4940	13352	33764	139092

Selected Financial Ratios (Times to 1)

Current Ratio 30	1.7	•	2.2	2.9	2.3	1.3	1.5	1.4	1.5	1.8
Quick Ratio 31	1.1	•	1.8	2.0	1.5	0.9	0.9	1.0	0.7	0.8
Net Sales to Working Capital 32	8.8	•	15.7	5.7	7.9	14.8	8.4	8.8	6.0	5.2
Coverage Ratio 33	5.8	78.8	6.3	26.2	5.1	0.6	5.2	4.9	5.5	3.2
Total Asset Turnover 34	1.9	•	3.4	1.9	2.2	1.5	1.6	1.3	0.9	1.2
Inventory Turnover 35	10.0	•	30.4	9.3	19.9	15.0	5.0	11.7	2.6	3.7
Receivables Turnover 36	13.5	•	61.7	50.4	17.5	8.8	6.8	6.9	4.3	10.0
Total Liabilities to Net Worth 37	1.8	•	•	0.6	1.9	1.6	1.8	1.6	1.1	1.1
Current Assets to Working Capital 38	2.4	•	1.9	1.5	1.8	4.9	3.1	3.4	3.1	2.3
Current Liabilities to Working Capital 39	1.4	•	0.9	0.5	0.8	3.9	2.1	2.4	2.1	1.3
Working Capital to Net Sales 40	0.1	•	0.1	0.2	0.1	0.1	0.1	0.1	0.2	0.2
Inventory to Working Capital 41	0.5	•	0.2	0.2	0.3	0.5	1.0	0.7	1.3	1.1
Total Receipts to Cash Flow 42	5.6	2.5	3.6	1.9	11.4	16.5	8.4	10.8	8.0	13.3
Cost of Goods to Cash Flow 43	3.6	0.8	1.5	0.5	8.7	12.0	6.3	9.2	4.9	10.4
Cash Flow to Total Debt 44	0.5	•	0.9	2.6	0.3	0.1	0.3	0.2	0.2	0.2

Selected Financial Factors (in Percentages)

Debt Ratio 45	64.1	•	105.1	38.8	64.9	61.5	64.9	61.7	53.2	52.0
Return on Total Assets 46	9.2	•	22.5	22.4	6.4	0.9	9.1	4.0	8.0	4.6
Return on Equity Before Income Taxes 47	21.3	•	•	35.2	14.7	•	21.0	8.4	14.0	6.6
Return on Equity After Income Taxes 48	19.8	•	•	35.2	13.0	•	17.4	7.2	13.4	6.2
Profit Margin (Before Income Tax) 49	4.1	14.2	5.6	11.1	2.4	•	4.6	2.5	7.6	2.6
Profit Margin (After Income Tax) 50	3.8	14.0	5.4	11.1	2.1	•	3.9	2.2	7.3	2.4

Table II

Corporations with Net Income

SUPPORT ACTIVITIES AND FISHING, HUNTING AND TRAPPING

MONEY AMOUNTS AND SIZE OF ASSETS IN THOUSANDS OF DOLLARS

Item Description for Accounting Period 7/09 Through 6/10	Total	Zero Assets	Under 500	500 to 1,000	1,000 to 5,000	5,000 to 10,000	10,000 to 25,000	25,000 to 50,000	50,000 to 100,000	100,000 to 250,000	250,000 to 500,000	500,000 to 2,500,000	2,500,000 and over
Number of Enterprises 1	15255	3264	8697	1840	1144	162	105	33	•	•	0	0	0
Revenues ($ in Thousands)													
Net Sales 2	20320831	221084	4765751	2730139	4514041	2070083	2736341	1973650	•	•	0	0	0
Interest 3	14296	2	593	100	6599	1498	3941	1125	•	•	0	0	0
Rents 4	15885	0	113	49	9823	4029	1469	388	•	•	0	0	0
Royalties 5	4344	0	0	0	848	871	0	1891	•	•	0	0	0
Other Portfolio Income 6	142657	10339	29837	16418	35348	2222	18290	25422	•	•	0	0	0
Other Receipts 7	834532	7	163658	83713	216012	68360	100765	152962	•	•	0	0	0
Total Receipts 8	21332545	231432	4959952	2830419	4782671	2147063	2860806	2155438	•	•	0	0	0
Average Total Receipts 9	1398	71	570	1538	4181	13253	27246	65316	•	•	•	•	•
Operating Costs/Operating Income (%)													
Cost of Operations 10	57.8	31.7	40.9	27.9	67.2	64.6	72.6	87.8	•	•	•	•	•
Salaries and Wages 11	9.8	8.6	9.5	8.6	13.1	15.6	6.3	3.6	•	•	•	•	•
Taxes Paid 12	2.0	1.8	2.3	1.8	2.4	2.2	1.6	0.7	•	•	•	•	•
Interest Paid 13	0.6	0.2	0.6	0.2	0.5	0.6	1.0	0.5	•	•	•	•	•
Depreciation 14	2.7	3.9	2.3	3.6	3.1	2.0	3.2	1.0	•	•	•	•	•
Amortization and Depletion 15	0.1	•	0.1	•	0.0	0.0	0.0	0.0	•	•	•	•	•
Pensions and Other Deferred Comp. 16	0.2	•	0.1	0.1	0.3	0.3	0.1	0.2	•	•	•	•	•
Employee Benefits 17	0.8	3.8	1.0	0.5	0.6	1.1	0.5	0.6	•	•	•	•	•
Advertising 18	0.3	0.0	0.9	0.1	0.2	0.0	0.2	0.1	•	•	•	•	•
Other Expenses 19	18.5	25.1	25.8	46.5	9.7	8.7	10.9	8.9	•	•	•	•	•
Officers' Compensation 20	3.3	6.6	8.1	1.2	2.4	2.0	2.2	0.5	•	•	•	•	•
Operating Margin 21	4.0	18.3	8.3	9.5	0.7	2.8	1.3	•	•	•	•	•	•
Operating Margin Before Officers' Comp. 22	7.2	24.9	16.5	10.7	3.1	4.8	3.6	•	•	•	•	•	•

Selected Average Balance Sheet ($ in Thousands)

Net Receivables 23	116	0	12	12	298	2561	3165	11196
Inventories 24	85	0	3	39	202	583	3706	4404
Net Property, Plant and Equipment 25	167	0	35	207	515	2179	4049	5870
Total Assets 26	646	0	129	715	2011	8195	14439	32793
Notes and Loans Payable 27	161	0	40	226	338	1719	4880	6220
All Other Liabilities 28	166	0	23	44	483	2782	4378	12447
Net Worth 29	320	0	66	445	1190	3695	5182	14126

Selected Financial Ratios (Times to 1)

Current Ratio 30	1.8	•	3.1	3.1	2.1	1.7	1.4	1.4
Quick Ratio 31	1.3	•	2.7	2.1	1.4	1.5	0.8	1.0
Net Sales to Working Capital 32	8.1	•	12.7	5.3	7.1	6.2	9.6	10.0
Coverage Ratio 33	15.8	118.2	22.5	55.7	15.1	11.1	6.8	11.6
Total Asset Turnover 34	2.1	•	4.2	2.1	2.0	1.6	1.8	1.8
Inventory Turnover 35	9.0	•	69.6	10.6	13.1	14.2	5.1	11.9
Receivables Turnover 36	12.1	•	74.3	66.1	16.6	5.6	6.9	6.8
Total Liabilities to Net Worth 37	1.0	•	0.9	0.6	0.7	1.2	1.8	1.3
Current Assets to Working Capital 38	2.3	•	1.5	1.5	1.9	2.5	3.4	3.5
Current Liabilities to Working Capital 39	1.3	•	0.5	0.5	0.9	1.5	2.4	2.5
Working Capital to Net Sales 40	0.1	•	0.1	0.2	0.1	0.2	0.1	0.1
Inventory to Working Capital 41	0.4	•	0.1	0.2	0.3	0.2	1.2	0.7
Total Receipts to Cash Flow 42	4.3	2.2	3.1	1.9	8.1	8.1	7.5	8.5
Cost of Goods to Cash Flow 43	2.5	0.7	1.3	0.5	5.4	5.3	5.5	7.5
Cash Flow to Total Debt 44	0.9	•	2.8	2.9	0.6	0.3	0.4	0.4

Selected Financial Factors (in Percentages)

Debt Ratio 45	50.5	•	48.5	37.8	40.8	54.9	64.1	56.9
Return on Total Assets 46	19.6	•	55.2	27.8	13.9	11.2	12.5	10.6
Return on Equity Before Income Taxes 47	37.2	•	102.4	44.0	21.9	22.6	29.6	22.4
Return on Equity After Income Taxes 48	35.6	•	100.9	43.9	20.4	20.8	25.2	20.6
Profit Margin (Before Income Tax) 49	8.9	23.0	12.4	13.2	6.6	6.5	5.9	5.3
Profit Margin (After Income Tax) 50	8.5	22.8	12.2	13.2	6.1	6.0	5.0	4.9

6

Table I

Corporations with and without Net Income

OIL AND GAS EXTRACTION

MONEY AMOUNTS AND SIZE OF ASSETS IN THOUSANDS OF DOLLARS

Item Description for Accounting Period 7/09 Through 6/10		Total	Zero Assets	Under 500	500 to 1,000	1,000 to 5,000	5,000 to 10,000	10,000 to 25,000	25,000 to 50,000	50,000 to 100,000	100,000 to 250,000	250,000 to 500,000	500,000 to 2,500,000	2,500,000 and over
Number of Enterprises	1	21383	4402	11815	1735	1702	708	478	201	102	104	46	53	36
Revenues ($ in Thousands)														
Net Sales	2	152811669	1347724	4593948	1356150	2129001	3918328	1988866	2394172	1547567	4670260	4325974	13945256	110594425
Interest	3	1802448	10744	4794	1987	18494	7200	27182	13238	6981	43267	46724	161635	1460202
Rents	4	415019	6	0	130249	15074	36794	42586	2549	16868	5277	650	2769	162196
Royalties	5	968890	11650	18571	3830	46288	39333	96871	21887	19249	28635	3951	35159	643466
Other Portfolio Income	6	6646801	86544	20651	22447	135916	33469	157546	272934	55199	211134	535600	252897	4862467
Other Receipts	7	15508073	305640	147042	21058	164001	315661	256883	186901	286296	781197	391384	2642860	10009147
Total Receipts	8	178152900	1762308	4785006	1535721	2508774	4350785	2569934	2891681	1932160	5739770	5304283	17040576	127731903
Average Total Receipts	9	8332	400	405	885	1474	6145	5376	14386	18943	55190	115310	321520	3548108
Operating Costs/Operating Income (%)														
Cost of Operations	10	51.2	3.9	58.9	35.2	33.7	46.2	27.7	32.0	22.4	41.4	35.4	30.7	57.0
Salaries and Wages	11	5.2	4.3	4.4	8.9	17.7	8.9	14.2	8.7	11.8	10.7	4.3	5.8	4.2
Taxes Paid	12	2.6	2.2	2.3	4.0	4.4	4.2	5.9	4.6	6.4	3.4	2.6	4.2	2.1
Interest Paid	13	5.7	2.9	0.5	1.9	2.5	0.7	3.3	7.7	5.3	6.5	6.4	9.5	5.7
Depreciation	14	10.2	13.1	2.2	4.6	7.7	4.0	14.5	12.9	20.6	11.4	12.2	15.9	9.7
Amortization and Depletion	15	9.1	6.6	1.7	1.7	5.4	1.1	8.3	9.7	14.1	14.5	17.3	26.3	7.2
Pensions and Other Deferred Comp.	16	0.5	0.3	0.7	0.2	0.3	0.7	0.6	0.4	0.3	0.9	0.3	0.2	0.5
Employee Benefits	17	0.5	0.6	0.2	0.6	1.7	1.0	1.6	0.8	1.7	0.9	0.9	0.4	0.4
Advertising	18	0.0	0.0	0.2	0.3	0.3	0.0	0.3	0.1	0.1	0.0	0.0	0.0	0.0
Other Expenses	19	32.3	45.9	24.6	39.3	45.1	27.1	46.7	63.9	52.2	45.4	27.7	38.9	29.9
Officers' Compensation	20	1.4	0.8	6.1	6.2	9.1	2.9	4.5	2.9	4.1	2.9	1.6	1.0	0.8
Operating Margin	21	•	19.6	•	•	•	3.2	•	•	•	•	•	•	•
Operating Margin Before Officers' Comp.	22	•	20.4	4.4	3.4	6.1	6.1	•	•	•	•	•	•	•

Selected Average Balance Sheet ($ in Thousands)

Net Receivables 23	2173	0	18	62	295	1388	1612	3112	5175	14111	36841	72885	991678
Inventories 24	253	0	3	43	13	70	206	374	824	1842	3633	7801	116402
Net Property, Plant and Equipment 25	12277	0	52	125	552	1609	5082	15083	29633	79402	185744	722573	5445123
Total Assets 26	22920	0	138	738	2442	7110	16034	35805	71280	162237	354058	1144159	10057817
Notes and Loans Payable 27	6055	0	68	308	604	1017	2794	11678	19921	52476	90421	372978	2535741
All Other Liabilities 28	6343	0	18	187	1041	1992	3498	7047	12455	35732	70702	236841	3000872
Net Worth 29	10523	0	52	242	797	4101	9741	17080	38904	74029	192935	534340	4521204

Selected Financial Ratios (Times to 1)

Current Ratio 30	1.4	•	2.3	2.1	0.9	1.7	1.7	1.1	1.8	1.3	1.8	1.5	1.3
Quick Ratio 31	1.0	•	2.0	1.2	0.7	1.4	1.3	0.9	1.4	0.9	1.4	1.0	1.0
Net Sales to Working Capital 32	6.7	•	8.8	3.5	•	3.5	1.5	21.6	1.7	4.6	2.5	4.2	8.9
Coverage Ratio 33	0.9	18.6	6.3	6.3	•	21.1	1.4	•	•	•	3.2	•	1.0
Total Asset Turnover 34	0.3	•	2.8	1.1	0.5	0.8	0.3	0.3	0.2	0.3	0.3	0.2	0.3
Inventory Turnover 35	14.5	•	82.1	6.4	32.0	36.8	5.6	10.2	4.1	10.1	9.2	10.4	15.0
Receivables Turnover 36	3.7	•	29.5	8.5	4.5	5.3	2.5	4.0	2.1	3.4	2.5	3.9	3.6
Total Liabilities to Net Worth 37	1.2	•	1.6	2.0	2.1	0.7	0.6	1.1	0.8	1.2	0.8	1.1	1.2
Current Assets to Working Capital 38	3.7	•	1.8	1.9	•	2.5	2.4	17.0	2.2	4.3	2.2	3.1	4.2
Current Liabilities to Working Capital 39	2.7	•	0.8	0.9	•	1.5	1.4	16.0	1.2	3.3	1.2	2.1	3.2
Working Capital to Net Sales 40	0.1	•	0.1	0.3	•	0.3	0.7	0.0	0.6	0.2	0.4	0.2	0.1
Inventory to Working Capital 41	0.3	•	0.1	0.2	•	0.1	0.1	0.4	0.1	0.1	0.1	0.1	0.4
Total Receipts to Cash Flow 42	3.8	1.3	4.0	2.9	4.8	2.7	2.9	13.5	3.3	4.2	3.4	4.1	3.9
Cost of Goods to Cash Flow 43	1.9	0.1	2.3	1.0	1.6	1.3	0.8	4.3	0.7	1.7	1.2	1.2	2.2
Cash Flow to Total Debt 44	0.2	•	1.1	0.5	0.2	0.7	0.2	0.0	0.1	0.1	0.2	0.1	0.1

Selected Financial Factors (in Percentages)

Debt Ratio 45	54.1	•	62.1	67.2	67.4	42.3	39.2	52.3	45.4	54.4	45.5	53.3	55.0
Return on Total Assets 46	1.5	•	8.4	13.0	•	11.6	1.2	•	•	•	5.4	•	1.7
Return on Equity Before Income Taxes 47	•	•	18.7	33.4	•	19.2	0.5	•	•	•	6.8	•	•
Return on Equity After Income Taxes 48	•	•	17.9	32.8	•	18.6	•	•	•	•	3.4	•	•
Profit Margin (Before Income Tax) 49	•	50.4	2.5	10.4	•	14.2	1.3	•	•	•	14.0	•	•
Profit Margin (After Income Tax) 50	•	30.6	2.4	10.2	•	13.8	•	•	•	•	7.1	•	•

Table II

Corporations with Net Income

OIL AND GAS EXTRACTION

MONEY AMOUNTS AND SIZE OF ASSETS IN THOUSANDS OF DOLLARS

Item Description for Accounting Period 7/09 Through 6/10		Total	Zero Assets	Under 500	500 to 1,000	1,000 to 5,000	5,000 to 10,000	10,000 to 25,000	25,000 to 50,000	50,000 to 100,000	100,000 to 250,000	250,000 to 500,000	500,000 to 2,500,000	2,500,000 and over
Number of Enterprises	1	12063	1996	7230	1035	825	452	293	86	41	51	20	18	16
Revenues ($ in Thousands)														
Net Sales	2	90006768	1152390	1740403	942149	914680	3027937	1421826	1513589	797758	3136420	3162700	5545416	66651501
Interest	3	929593	8866	3826	1256	8752	1495	6842	5855	3430	24777	37488	7034	819972
Rents	4	226992	0	0	130249	13193	36525	8649	310	14967	1940	18	0	21140
Royalties	5	848166	7340	3079	107	27395	17975	85038	19500	16138	17474	2183	10928	641008
Other Portfolio Income	6	5724386	29945	9720	21960	114561	30179	98218	107895	31440	200532	435688	61535	4582710
Other Receipts	7	7415040	172122	149725	20901	127936	226882	218532	139975	147750	542756	207107	859479	4601879
Total Receipts	8	105150945	1370663	1906753	1116622	1206517	3340993	1839105	1787124	1011483	3923899	3845184	6484392	77318210
Average Total Receipts	9	8717	687	264	1079	1462	7392	6277	20781	24670	76939	192259	360244	4832388
Operating Costs/Operating Income (%)														
Cost of Operations	10	53.8	1.9	25.2	23.8	16.8	43.0	24.0	31.8	22.4	45.2	39.6	20.7	62.2
Salaries and Wages	11	4.2	0.7	4.6	9.8	9.5	7.4	11.1	6.8	7.5	10.0	2.2	3.4	3.5
Taxes Paid	12	2.6	1.5	3.7	3.8	4.1	4.5	5.2	4.4	5.9	3.6	1.7	4.1	2.2
Interest Paid	13	3.6	1.5	0.5	0.3	1.1	0.5	1.6	1.1	1.6	2.5	2.6	5.5	4.0
Depreciation	14	8.9	10.9	4.0	3.1	5.5	3.0	10.9	8.9	13.4	8.3	6.8	13.5	9.1
Amortization and Depletion	15	5.0	1.4	1.2	1.5	6.0	1.2	6.0	3.9	5.3	6.6	8.1	13.6	4.5
Pensions and Other Deferred Comp.	16	0.5	0.3	1.6	0.3	0.2	0.7	0.4	0.3	0.4	0.9	0.3	0.2	0.5
Employee Benefits	17	0.4	0.2	0.3	0.6	2.6	1.0	1.1	0.6	1.6	0.6	0.7	0.3	0.3
Advertising	18	0.0	0.0	0.3	0.1	0.2	0.0	0.0	0.1	0.1	0.0	0.0	0.0	0.0
Other Expenses	19	22.3	16.4	31.5	40.6	30.2	21.7	28.6	30.5	30.0	22.4	20.2	31.8	20.7
Officers' Compensation	20	1.4	0.6	10.9	7.7	8.8	2.0	3.9	2.2	2.9	2.8	0.8	1.2	0.9
Operating Margin	21	•	64.6	16.1	8.2	15.0	14.9	7.1	9.3	9.1	•	16.8	5.7	•
Operating Margin Before Officers' Comp.	22	•	65.1	27.0	15.9	23.8	16.9	11.0	11.6	12.0	•	17.7	6.9	•

Selected Average Balance Sheet ($ in Thousands)

Net Receivables 23	2313	0	28	39	357	1274	1403	2689	3298	18194	59939	94981	1385962
Inventories 24	268	0	5	37	11	50	206	610	1200	2481	6371	9897	158318
Net Property, Plant and Equipment 25	10093	0	55	105	418	1653	3356	12687	21469	60698	171608	731939	6093464
Total Assets 26	20037	0	162	741	2146	7078	15551	36073	70044	164438	354260	1186015	11715281
Notes and Loans Payable 27	3544	0	49	62	194	987	1969	5049	8918	38883	54468	354036	1931346
All Other Liabilities 28	5692	0	13	134	545	1774	2798	6251	8378	33040	84873	261640	3586858
Net Worth 29	10800	0	100	544	1408	4316	10784	24772	52749	92515	214919	570338	6197077

Selected Financial Ratios (Times to 1)

Current Ratio 30	1.8	•	3.6	2.8	2.2	1.7	2.1	2.1	3.8	2.1	2.8	1.7	1.7
Quick Ratio 31	1.4	•	3.0	1.6	1.7	1.5	1.6	1.8	2.9	1.5	2.2	1.2	1.4
Net Sales to Working Capital 32	4.1	•	3.2	3.0	1.7	4.4	1.3	3.3	1.1	2.0	2.1	2.9	5.2
Coverage Ratio 33	5.4	54.9	51.4	93.2	42.2	51.6	23.5	25.1	23.8	9.8	15.7	5.0	3.7
Total Asset Turnover 34	0.4	•	1.5	1.2	0.5	0.9	0.3	0.5	0.3	0.4	0.4	0.3	0.4
Inventory Turnover 35	15.0	•	13.3	5.9	17.6	57.3	5.7	9.2	3.6	11.2	9.8	6.4	16.4
Receivables Turnover 36	3.2	•	11.6	7.7	3.0	7.0	3.0	5.1	2.1	3.9	2.8	3.1	3.0
Total Liabilities to Net Worth 37	0.9	•	0.6	0.4	0.5	0.6	0.4	0.5	0.3	0.8	0.6	1.1	0.9
Current Assets to Working Capital 38	2.2	•	1.4	1.6	1.8	2.5	1.9	1.9	1.4	1.9	1.6	2.5	2.4
Current Liabilities to Working Capital 39	1.2	•	0.4	0.6	0.8	1.5	0.9	0.9	0.4	0.9	0.6	1.5	1.4
Working Capital to Net Sales 40	0.2	•	0.3	0.3	0.6	0.2	0.7	0.3	0.9	0.5	0.5	0.4	0.2
Inventory to Working Capital 41	0.1	•	0.1	0.0	0.0	0.0	0.1	0.1	0.0	0.1	0.1	0.1	0.2
Total Receipts to Cash Flow 42	3.0	1.1	1.8	2.1	1.5	2.2	1.7	2.0	1.6	2.6	2.3	1.9	3.8
Cost of Goods to Cash Flow 43	1.6	0.0	0.5	0.5	0.3	0.9	0.4	0.6	0.4	1.2	0.9	0.4	2.3
Cash Flow to Total Debt 44	0.3	•	2.1	2.2	1.0	1.1	0.6	0.8	0.7	0.3	0.5	0.3	0.2

Selected Financial Factors (in Percentages)

Debt Ratio 45	46.1	•	38.4	26.5	34.4	39.0	30.7	31.3	24.7	43.7	39.3	51.9	47.1
Return on Total Assets 46	7.3	•	38.8	33.2	24.8	24.3	11.7	13.9	10.6	9.1	18.4	7.2	5.3
Return on Equity Before Income Taxes 47	11.1	•	61.8	44.7	37.0	39.1	16.1	19.4	13.4	14.5	28.4	12.1	7.4
Return on Equity After Income Taxes 48	8.9	•	61.1	44.2	33.9	38.3	14.9	18.1	12.4	12.7	21.5	10.2	5.4
Profit Margin (Before Income Tax) 49	16.1	83.5	25.6	26.7	46.9	25.2	35.9	27.3	36.4	21.9	38.6	22.3	10.9
Profit Margin (After Income Tax) 50	12.8	60.3	25.3	26.4	43.1	24.7	33.1	25.4	33.7	19.1	29.2	19.0	8.0

Table I

Corporations with and without Net Income

COAL MINING

MONEY AMOUNTS AND SIZE OF ASSETS IN THOUSANDS OF DOLLARS

Item Description for Accounting Period 7/09 Through 6/10	Total	Zero Assets	Under 500	500 to 1,000	1,000 to 5,000	5,000 to 10,000	10,000 to 25,000	25,000 to 50,000	50,000 to 100,000	100,000 to 250,000	250,000 to 500,000	500,000 to 2,500,000	2,500,000 and over
Number of Enterprises 1	1150	15	543	303	39	146	46	17	14	12	0	9	6
Revenues ($ in Thousands)													
Net Sales 2	30461943	916444	514089	765674	224145	1533070	1352639	625897	1204547	1630493	0	6304384	15390562
Interest 3	152113	3126	211	0	532	28795	638	5167	812	1554	0	31019	80259
Rents 4	43323	639	0	0	37859	40	26	0	0	25	0	2518	2215
Royalties 5	259895	5463	0	0	5153	0	0	0	2607	9648	0	23804	213221
Other Portfolio Income 6	153763	47056	7	0	5576	4356	140	7479	2895	1140	0	17600	67511
Other Receipts 7	2233025	61117	10841	1422	-14253	9112	6449	8697	14334	34102	0	656202	1445004
Total Receipts 8	33304062	1033845	525148	767096	259012	1575373	1359892	647240	1225195	1676962	0	7035527	17198772
Average Total Receipts 9	28960	68923	967	2532	6641	10790	29563	38073	87514	139747	•	781725	2866462
Operating Costs/Operating Income (%)													
Cost of Operations 10	63.4	58.2	99.4	1.3	83.6	66.9	71.7	78.6	62.6	65.0	•	69.3	61.1
Salaries and Wages 11	2.1	9.1	•	12.5	0.9	1.3	2.5	1.1	2.6	4.1	•	2.0	1.2
Taxes Paid 12	6.0	10.4	2.3	2.2	8.5	6.6	3.5	2.8	4.1	4.1	•	3.8	7.6
Interest Paid 13	3.3	3.8	0.7	0.0	8.8	0.4	1.8	0.9	4.1	1.4	•	5.5	3.3
Depreciation 14	6.3	9.3	0.2	1.6	5.3	4.8	4.3	7.5	8.2	9.2	•	7.6	5.9
Amortization and Depletion 15	6.0	5.3	0.1	•	0.0	0.2	3.7	3.2	5.9	3.6	•	4.6	8.4
Pensions and Other Deferred Comp. 16	1.1	1.4	•	3.5	0.0	0.1	0.1	0.5	0.2	0.2	•	0.4	1.6
Employee Benefits 17	3.8	3.6	0.9	1.8	0.3	0.7	2.0	2.5	1.6	3.7	•	4.7	4.4
Advertising 18	0.1	0.0	•	•	•	0.0	0.0	0.2	0.0	0.0	•	0.0	0.1
Other Expenses 19	12.4	14.0	6.1	43.3	10.4	22.6	13.1	3.6	8.4	16.9	•	8.7	11.5
Officers' Compensation 20	0.7	0.5	•	12.0	0.5	0.8	0.6	0.9	0.7	0.4	•	0.4	0.3
Operating Margin 21	•	•	•	21.9	•	•	•	•	1.7	•	•	•	•
Operating Margin Before Officers' Comp. 22	•	•	•	33.9	•	•	•	•	2.4	•	•	•	•

Selected Average Balance Sheet ($ in Thousands)

Net Receivables 23	21096	0	0	153	435	383	3168	11313	3794	20079	78902	3799819
Inventories 24	1382	0	0	0	50	266	930	1826	2323	6944	42669	159603
Net Property, Plant and Equipment 25	21448	0	5	169	761	1625	6274	8543	26736	86828	554342	2917494
Total Assets 26	62381	0	83	682	2142	7295	16976	41089	65311	167713	1151754	9260847
Notes and Loans Payable 27	12258	0	7	0	2865	1106	8132	7640	23130	45213	445614	1406476
All Other Liabilities 28	35006	0	91	62	1015	1137	5535	9878	11649	39687	470290	5781407
Net Worth 29	15117	0	-15	620	-1737	5053	3309	23571	30532	82814	235850	2072964

Selected Financial Ratios (Times to 1)

Current Ratio 30	1.0	•	0.9	8.3	0.9	2.1	1.0	2.2	1.2	1.2	1.0	1.0
Quick Ratio 31	0.9	•	0.7	8.2	0.8	1.5	0.8	1.8	1.0	0.9	0.7	0.9
Net Sales to Working Capital 32	25.6	•	•	5.6	•	10.7	210.9	4.0	25.3	19.7	947.2	24.8
Coverage Ratio 33	2.3	0.3	•	2726.2	0.7	•	•	2.7	1.8	•	1.8	3.0
Total Asset Turnover 34	0.4	•	11.4	3.7	2.7	1.4	1.7	0.9	1.3	0.8	0.6	0.3
Inventory Turnover 35	12.1	•	•	•	95.6	26.4	22.7	15.8	23.2	12.7	11.4	9.8
Receivables Turnover 36	1.5	2310.5	•	•	3.3	•	12.3	3.2	13.2	5.7	8.1	0.8
Total Liabilities to Net Worth 37	3.1	•	0.1	•	•	0.4	4.1	0.7	1.1	1.0	3.9	3.5
Current Assets to Working Capital 38	25.6	•	1.1	•	•	1.9	44.0	1.8	5.4	6.3	305.3	42.9
Current Liabilities to Working Capital 39	24.6	•	0.1	•	•	0.9	43.0	0.8	4.4	5.3	304.3	41.9
Working Capital to Net Sales 40	0.0	•	0.2	•	•	0.1	0.0	0.3	0.0	0.1	0.0	0.0
Inventory to Working Capital 41	1.4	•	•	•	•	0.3	8.6	0.2	0.7	1.0	71.7	1.6
Total Receipts to Cash Flow 42	7.6	17.3	•	1.5	24.2	7.9	15.1	26.7	11.6	14.4	9.3	6.8
Cost of Goods to Cash Flow 43	4.8	10.1	•	0.0	20.2	5.3	10.8	21.0	7.3	9.3	6.5	4.2
Cash Flow to Total Debt 44	0.1	•	26.7	•	0.1	0.6	0.1	0.1	0.2	0.1	0.1	0.1

Selected Financial Factors (in Percentages)

Debt Ratio 45	75.8	118.5	9.1	81.8	181.1	30.7	80.5	42.6	53.3	50.6	79.5	77.6
Return on Total Assets 46	3.2	•	•	16.1	•	•	•	2.2	9.8	•	6.1	2.7
Return on Equity Before Income Taxes 47	7.3	•	467.8	89.9	9.3	•	•	2.4	9.6	•	13.5	8.0
Return on Equity After Income Taxes 48	5.8	•	467.8	89.9	15.6	•	•	2.0	8.9	•	13.3	6.2
Profit Margin (Before Income Tax) 49	4.2	•	•	22.1	•	•	•	1.6	3.4	•	4.6	6.5
Profit Margin (After Income Tax) 50	3.3	•	•	22.1	•	•	•	1.3	3.2	•	4.5	5.0

Table II

Corporations with Net Income

COAL MINING

MONEY AMOUNTS AND SIZE OF ASSETS IN THOUSANDS OF DOLLARS

Item Description for Accounting Period 7/09 Through 6/10	Total	Zero Assets	Under 500	500 to 1,000	1,000 to 5,000	5,000 to 10,000	10,000 to 25,000	25,000 to 50,000	50,000 to 100,000	100,000 to 250,000	250,000 to 500,000	500,000 to 2,500,000	2,500,000 and over
Number of Enterprises 1	466	10	•	303	22	78	20	10	9	•	0	•	•
Revenues ($ in Thousands)													
Net Sales 2	20344346	149026	•	765674	6679	1131815	478823	472268	896018	•	0	•	•
Interest 3	113606	0	•	0	463	28620	638	5167	252	•	0	•	•
Rents 4	39266	0	•	0	37859	40	26	0	0	•	0	•	•
Royalties 5	190244	0	•	0	5153	0	0	0	0	•	0	•	•
Other Portfolio Income 6	92654	14228	•	0	5576	4197	116	7474	1003	•	0	•	•
Other Receipts 7	1949729	3965	•	1422	1513	279	4827	5193	5466	•	0	•	•
Total Receipts 8	22729845	167219	•	767096	57243	1164951	484430	490102	902739	•	0	•	•
Average Total Receipts 9	48776	16722	•	2532	2602	14935	24222	49010	100304	•	•	•	•
Operating Costs/Operating Income (%)													
Cost of Operations 10	56.7	5.0	•	1.3	28.5	68.5	50.2	78.2	55.7	•	•	•	•
Salaries and Wages 11	2.4	35.1	•	12.5	31.4	1.3	5.3	0.9	2.9	•	•	•	•
Taxes Paid 12	6.0	2.5	•	2.2	11.4	7.3	1.8	2.8	4.1	•	•	•	•
Interest Paid 13	3.4	0.1	•	0.0	294.6	0.6	1.4	0.9	1.2	•	•	•	•
Depreciation 14	5.8	2.1	•	1.6	121.2	2.7	5.9	4.7	8.1	•	•	•	•
Amortization and Depletion 15	6.8	1.1	•	•	0.9	0.2	3.9	3.9	7.2	•	•	•	•
Pensions and Other Deferred Comp. 16	1.3	0.0	•	3.5	•	0.0	0.1	0.6	0.2	•	•	•	•
Employee Benefits 17	4.1	4.2	•	1.8	9.9	1.0	1.4	1.7	1.0	•	•	•	•
Advertising 18	0.1	•	•	•	•	0.0	0.0	0.2	0.0	•	•	•	•
Other Expenses 19	14.2	38.6	•	43.3	94.2	14.2	24.7	3.5	7.5	•	•	•	•
Officers' Compensation 20	0.9	3.0	•	12.0	18.2	0.3	1.3	0.4	0.6	•	•	•	•
Operating Margin 21	•	8.2	•	21.9	•	3.9	3.9	2.1	11.5	•	•	•	•
Operating Margin Before Officers' Comp. 22	•	11.2	•	33.9	•	4.2	5.2	2.5	12.1	•	•	•	•

Selected Average Balance Sheet ($ in Thousands)

Net Receivables 23	47736	0	•	153	561	430	4599	16162	5754
Inventories 24	1998	0	•	0	89	199	1303	1486	1881
Net Property, Plant and Equipment 25	32681	0	•	169	659	1128	3681	8152	28886
Total Assets 26	115528	0	•	682	2594	7381	16559	43120	66874
Notes and Loans Payable 27	23165	0	•	0	5077	1391	7830	9053	9211
All Other Liabilities 28	69424	0	•	62	856	1157	3204	9748	11683
Net Worth 29	22939	0	•	620	-3340	4834	5526	24320	45980

Selected Financial Ratios (Times to 1)

Current Ratio 30	1.0	•	•	8.3	0.9	1.4	2.7	3.8	1.9
Quick Ratio 31	0.9	•	•	8.2	0.8	0.9	2.2	3.0	1.6
Net Sales to Working Capital 32	17.2	•	•	5.6	•	28.8	4.2	3.1	10.0
Coverage Ratio 33	4.1	201.5	•	2726.2	1.8	13.2	4.6	7.9	10.8
Total Asset Turnover 34	0.4	•	•	3.7	0.1	2.0	1.4	1.1	1.5
Inventory Turnover 35	12.4	•	•	•	1.0	50.1	9.2	24.9	29.5
Receivables Turnover 36	1.7	•	•	•	0.2	57.0	9.3	3.7	12.2
Total Liabilities to Net Worth 37	4.0	•	•	0.1	•	0.5	2.0	0.8	0.5
Current Assets to Working Capital 38	22.7	•	•	1.1	•	3.3	1.6	1.4	2.1
Current Liabilities to Working Capital 39	21.7	•	•	0.1	•	2.3	0.6	0.4	1.1
Working Capital to Net Sales 40	0.1	•	•	0.2	•	0.0	0.2	0.3	0.1
Inventory to Working Capital 41	1.1	•	•	•	•	0.8	0.2	0.2	0.3
Total Receipts to Cash Flow 42	4.7	2.0	•	1.5	0.4	6.0	4.1	12.9	5.9
Cost of Goods to Cash Flow 43	2.7	0.1	•	0.0	0.1	4.1	2.1	10.1	3.3
Cash Flow to Total Debt 44	0.1	•	•	26.7	0.1	0.9	0.5	0.2	0.8

Selected Financial Factors (in Percentages)

Debt Ratio 45	80.1	•	•	9.1	228.8	34.5	66.6	43.6	31.2
Return on Total Assets 46	5.2	•	•	81.8	63.4	14.5	9.5	7.4	20.1
Return on Equity Before Income Taxes 47	19.7	•	•	89.9	•	20.4	22.2	11.4	26.5
Return on Equity After Income Taxes 48	17.3	•	•	89.9	•	17.5	21.8	10.7	25.8
Profit Margin (Before Income Tax) 49	10.3	20.4	•	22.1	246.8	6.8	5.1	5.9	12.2
Profit Margin (After Income Tax) 50	9.1	19.6	•	22.1	182.8	5.8	5.0	5.5	11.9

Table I

Corporations with and without Net Income

METAL ORE MINING

MONEY AMOUNTS AND SIZE OF ASSETS IN THOUSANDS OF DOLLARS

Item Description for Accounting Period 7/09 Through 6/10	Total	Zero Assets	Under 500	500 to 1,000	1,000 to 5,000	5,000 to 10,000	10,000 to 25,000	25,000 to 50,000	50,000 to 100,000	100,000 to 250,000	250,000 to 500,000	500,000 to 2,500,000	2,500,000 and over
Number of Enterprises **1**	1560	6	1163	123	118	48	19	30	10	14	8	11	10
Revenues ($ in Thousands)													
Net Sales **2**	40435619	0	3000	1187	5100	43941	379439	73775	151920	271353	790987	4362196	34352722
Interest **3**	588888	0	16	620	673	2969	160	946	2160	2580	1667	38745	538351
Rents **4**	51118	0	19397	0	1385	8	0	0	0	93	201	34	30000
Royalties **5**	322108	0	0	0	0	96	0	26	0	96	0	87868	234022
Other Portfolio Income **6**	2223067	0	1684	0	15617	0	0	42	3324	859	124683	58896	2017963
Other Receipts **7**	1326953	0	18261	901	31428	1548	29074	5487	4285	146190	19121	102130	968526
Total Receipts **8**	44947753	0	42358	2708	54203	48562	408673	80276	161689	421171	936659	4649869	38141584
Average Total Receipts **9**	28813	0	36	22	459	1012	21509	2676	16169	30084	117082	422715	3814158
Operating Costs/Operating Income (%)													
Cost of Operations **10**	49.1	•	2.4	•	19.0	0.6	97.1	14.4	75.1	62.6	61.3	67.4	45.8
Salaries and Wages **11**	2.1	•	•	•	215.8	26.0	2.8	54.8	4.5	11.1	0.8	0.8	2.1
Taxes Paid **12**	1.8	•	192.7	0.7	46.9	3.0	0.3	3.5	0.5	2.9	1.5	1.6	1.8
Interest Paid **13**	3.8	•	63.5	80.7	229.2	11.1	•	0.8	0.9	3.4	1.2	1.9	4.2
Depreciation **14**	6.1	•	56.4	49.6	179.0	8.4	0.6	14.0	8.0	13.2	15.0	6.8	5.7
Amortization and Depletion **15**	12.2	•	48.0	76.6	212.6	29.2	1.3	23.2	10.9	19.4	7.8	11.3	12.4
Pensions and Other Deferred Comp. **16**	0.3	•	•	•	•	•	0.1	0.4	0.5	0.2	•	0.8	0.3
Employee Benefits **17**	1.0	•	101.4	69.3	4.7	0.6	0.4	4.5	4.5	1.2	3.5	0.1	1.0
Advertising **18**	0.0	•	•	•	1.2	0.0	0.0	0.9	0.0	0.1	•	0.0	0.0
Other Expenses **19**	17.3	•	1499.6	2398.0	1208.4	224.4	7.7	95.0	40.6	47.6	8.8	4.7	18.0
Officers' Compensation **20**	0.5	•	691.2	•	36.0	27.0	2.3	2.0	3.4	1.5	1.2	0.4	0.3
Operating Margin **21**	5.7	•	•	•	•	•	•	•	•	•	•	4.1	8.3
Operating Margin Before Officers' Comp. **22**	6.2	•	•	•	•	•	•	•	•	•	0.2	4.5	8.7

Selected Average Balance Sheet ($ in Thousands)

Net Receivables 23	20411	0	0	0	1	83	2094	256	1920	3012	4702	77218	3084165
Inventories 24	4571	0	0	0	10	89	175	135	6500	16597	14970	86736	574798
Net Property, Plant and Equipment 25	21957	0	16	263	676	4123	3316	11814	20518	41976	181075	542538	2529846
Total Assets 26	96198	0	87	645	2097	7843	14525	33500	77700	141804	338269	1180753	12952685
Notes and Loans Payable 27	13954	0	20	575	1189	4782	8510	12672	47530	37134	82277	106976	1793286
All Other Liabilities 28	37129	0	77	453	2263	3868	3500	3113	11930	53924	80079	274086	5263412
Net Worth 29	45115	0	-10	-384	-1355	-807	2514	17715	18240	50746	175913	799691	5895987

Selected Financial Ratios (Times to 1)

Current Ratio 30	1.8	•	1.6	45.6	0.6	0.4	2.5	1.0	4.2	2.2	2.4	1.7	1.8
Quick Ratio 31	1.4	•	1.4	29.7	0.4	0.1	1.8	0.9	2.4	1.1	1.7	1.0	1.4
Net Sales to Working Capital 32	1.8	•	0.1	0.0	•	•	5.2	•	0.7	1.0	1.5	3.7	1.7
Coverage Ratio 33	5.7	•	•	•	•	•	•	•	•	•	16.0	7.1	6.0
Total Asset Turnover 34	0.3	•	0.0	0.0	0.1	0.1	1.4	0.1	0.2	0.1	0.3	0.3	0.3
Inventory Turnover 35	2.8	•	•	•	0.9	0.1	111.1	2.6	1.8	0.7	4.0	3.1	2.7
Receivables Turnover 36	1.3	42.3	•	3.2	•	•	11.2	15.0	4.2	4.7	20.6	6.1	1.1
Total Liabilities to Net Worth 37	1.1	•	•	•	•	•	4.8	0.9	3.3	1.8	0.9	0.5	1.2
Current Assets to Working Capital 38	2.3	2.6	1.0	•	•	•	1.7	•	1.3	1.8	1.7	2.5	2.3
Current Liabilities to Working Capital 39	1.3	1.6	0.0	•	•	•	0.7	•	0.3	0.8	0.7	1.5	1.3
Working Capital to Net Sales 40	0.6	6.8	28.8	•	•	•	0.2	•	1.5	1.0	0.7	0.3	0.6
Inventory to Working Capital 41	0.3	•	•	•	•	•	•	•	0.3	0.4	0.4	0.9	0.3
Total Receipts to Cash Flow 42	3.1	2.4	•	•	2.7	•	48.1	•	•	2.9	4.8	6.8	2.8
Cost of Goods to Cash Flow 43	1.5	0.1	•	•	0.5	•	46.7	•	•	1.8	2.9	4.6	1.3
Cash Flow to Total Debt 44	0.2	0.0	•	•	0.0	•	0.0	•	•	0.1	0.1	0.2	0.2

Selected Financial Factors (in Percentages)

Debt Ratio 45	53.1	•	111.2	159.5	164.6	110.3	82.7	47.1	76.5	64.2	48.0	32.3	54.5
Return on Total Assets 46	5.9	•	•	•	•	•	•	•	•	•	5.4	4.5	6.6
Return on Equity Before Income Taxes 47	10.4	•	344.1	61.5	34.8	249.4	•	•	•	•	9.8	5.7	12.0
Return on Equity After Income Taxes 48	5.3	•	344.1	61.6	34.8	249.4	•	•	•	•	7.9	3.7	6.4
Profit Margin (Before Income Tax) 49	18.1	•	•	•	•	•	•	•	•	•	17.4	11.5	20.7
Profit Margin (After Income Tax) 50	9.3	•	•	•	•	•	•	•	•	•	14.1	7.5	10.9

Table II

Corporations with Net Income

METAL ORE MINING

MONEY AMOUNTS AND SIZE OF ASSETS IN THOUSANDS OF DOLLARS

Item Description for Accounting Period 7/09 Through 6/10	Total	Zero Assets	Under 500	500 to 1,000	1,000 to 5,000	5,000 to 10,000	10,000 to 25,000	25,000 to 50,000	50,000 to 100,000	100,000 to 250,000	250,000 to 500,000	500,000 to 2,500,000	2,500,000 and over
Number of Enterprises 1	980	0	•	•	18	0	9	0	0	•	•	•	•

Revenues ($ in Thousands)

	Total	Zero Assets	Under 500	500 to 1,000	1,000 to 5,000	5,000 to 10,000	10,000 to 25,000	25,000 to 50,000	50,000 to 100,000	100,000 to 250,000	250,000 to 500,000	500,000 to 2,500,000	2,500,000 and over
Net Sales 2	31531721	0	•	•	5100	0	441496	0	0	•	•	•	•
Interest 3	474735	0	•	•	39	0	50	0	0	•	•	•	•
Rents 4	28493	0	•	•	0	0	0	0	0	•	•	•	•
Royalties 5	285586	0	•	•	0	0	0	0	0	•	•	•	•
Other Portfolio Income 6	2010487	0	•	•	1333	0	12	0	0	•	•	•	•
Other Receipts 7	1037260	0	•	•	12178	0	32116	0	0	•	•	•	•
Total Receipts 8	35536282	0	•	•	18650	0	473674	0	0	•	•	•	•
Average Total Receipts 9	36090	•	•	•	1036	•	52630	•	•	•	•	•	•

Operating Costs/Operating Income (%)

	Total	Zero Assets	Under 500	500 to 1,000	1,000 to 5,000	5,000 to 10,000	10,000 to 25,000	25,000 to 50,000	50,000 to 100,000	100,000 to 250,000	250,000 to 500,000	500,000 to 2,500,000	2,500,000 and over
Cost of Operations 10	41.1	•	•	•	19.0	•	84.7	•	•	•	•	•	•
Salaries and Wages 11	2.3	•	•	•	146.6	•	6.3	•	•	•	•	•	•
Taxes Paid 12	2.1	•	•	•	25.2	•	0.7	•	•	•	•	•	•
Interest Paid 13	3.7	•	•	•	1.5	•	0.1	•	•	•	•	•	•
Depreciation 14	6.5	•	•	•	18.9	•	1.2	•	•	•	•	•	•
Amortization and Depletion 15	13.5	•	•	•	•	•	•	•	•	•	•	•	•
Pensions and Other Deferred Comp. 16	0.4	•	•	•	•	•	0.2	•	•	•	•	•	•
Employee Benefits 17	0.8	•	•	•	•	•	1.0	•	•	•	•	•	•
Advertising 18	0.0	•	•	•	0.0	•	0.0	•	•	•	•	•	•
Other Expenses 19	10.5	•	•	•	34.9	•	6.2	•	•	•	•	•	•
Officers' Compensation 20	0.4	•	•	•	•	•	1.9	•	•	•	•	•	•
Operating Margin 21	18.7	•	•	•	•	•	•	•	•	•	•	•	•
Operating Margin Before Officers' Comp. 22	19.1	•	•	•	•	•	•	•	•	•	•	•	•

Selected Average Balance Sheet ($ in Thousands)

Net Receivables 23	25991	0	5168
Inventories 24	5899	0	254
Net Property, Plant and Equipment 25	25664	1871	2576
Total Assets 26	122148	2563	18976
Notes and Loans Payable 27	14511	0	9989
All Other Liabilities 28	45587	66	3565
Net Worth 29	62049	2497	5422

Selected Financial Ratios (Times to 1)

Current Ratio 30	2.1	6.8	2.8
Quick Ratio 31	1.7	6.7	2.6
Net Sales to Working Capital 32	1.5	1.3	7.6
Coverage Ratio 33	9.6	79.1	103.5
Total Asset Turnover 34	0.3	0.1	2.6
Inventory Turnover 35	2.2	•	163.4
Receivables Turnover 36	1.1	•	11.9
Total Liabilities to Net Worth 37	1.0	0.0	2.5
Current Assets to Working Capital 38	1.9	1.2	1.6
Current Liabilities to Working Capital 39	0.9	0.2	0.6
Working Capital to Net Sales 40	0.7	0.8	0.1
Inventory to Working Capital 41	0.3	•	0.0
Total Receipts to Cash Flow 42	2.5	0.8	12.5
Cost of Goods to Cash Flow 43	1.0	0.2	10.6
Cash Flow to Total Debt 44	0.2	5.3	0.3

Selected Financial Factors (in Percentages)

Debt Ratio 45	49.2	2.6	71.4
Return on Total Assets 46	9.5	13.4	13.4
Return on Equity Before Income Taxes 47	16.7	13.6	46.4
Return on Equity After Income Taxes 48	10.9	13.6	36.2
Profit Margin (Before Income Tax) 49	32.2	119.5	5.1
Profit Margin (After Income Tax) 50	21.0	119.5	4.0

Table I

Corporations with and without Net Income

NONMETALLIC MINERAL MINING AND QUARRYING

MONEY AMOUNTS AND SIZE OF ASSETS IN THOUSANDS OF DOLLARS

Item Description for Accounting Period 7/09 Through 6/10	Total	Zero Assets	Under 500	500 to 1,000	1,000 to 5,000	5,000 to 10,000	10,000 to 25,000	25,000 to 50,000	50,000 to 100,000	100,000 to 250,000	250,000 to 500,000	500,000 to 2,500,000	2,500,000 and over
Number of Enterprises **1**	3939	82	2374	171	843	188	162	50	31	23	6	10	0
Revenues ($ in Thousands)													
Net Sales **2**	22979684	45804	226037	244623	3420152	1352386	1865786	1299636	1451135	2854820	1835146	8384159	0
Interest **3**	39567	42	456	0	5644	3580	1803	2981	2599	4501	1034	16927	0
Rents **4**	38463	0	0	0	1355	352	707	2168	496	1817	265	31302	0
Royalties **5**	76045	192	50959	0	1	0	0	340	28	39	3474	21012	0
Other Portfolio Income **6**	338209	74788	2108	0	25185	3075	6626	10475	8143	52485	3489	151836	0
Other Receipts **7**	294091	2167	14709	76	28004	2560	24787	3333	44137	16815	12309	145194	0
Total Receipts **8**	23766059	122993	294269	244699	3480341	1361953	1899709	1318933	1506538	2930477	1855717	8750430	0
Average Total Receipts **9**	6034	1500	124	1431	4129	7244	11727	26379	48598	127412	309286	875043	•
Operating Costs/Operating Income (%)													
Cost of Operations **10**	63.4	34.8	44.7	67.7	64.4	63.3	63.4	69.7	69.8	65.5	68.6	59.5	•
Salaries and Wages **11**	5.0	21.4	11.2	0.6	4.6	4.8	5.7	4.1	5.3	3.4	5.4	5.4	•
Taxes Paid **12**	2.5	23.3	4.8	4.2	3.4	2.4	2.6	2.3	1.6	1.5	1.3	2.6	•
Interest Paid **13**	3.1	18.4	2.4	3.6	1.4	2.8	1.7	2.1	1.9	1.7	3.3	4.9	•
Depreciation **14**	7.9	14.9	6.9	10.4	5.0	4.7	8.8	9.6	6.5	8.1	5.8	9.8	•
Amortization and Depletion **15**	2.6	5.6	•	0.3	0.2	1.6	2.3	2.5	1.4	2.8	3.2	3.8	•
Pensions and Other Deferred Comp. **16**	1.2	•	•	0.0	0.6	0.8	0.5	0.6	0.6	0.8	0.9	2.3	•
Employee Benefits **17**	2.4	1.0	0.0	2.3	1.6	3.1	2.3	1.5	2.3	2.2	1.4	3.1	•
Advertising **18**	0.3	0.4	0.6	0.2	0.2	0.9	0.2	0.3	0.2	0.1	0.2	0.2	•
Other Expenses **19**	10.8	68.0	49.6	11.9	11.4	9.6	9.4	7.7	10.8	9.6	7.2	11.3	•
Officers' Compensation **20**	1.5	8.2	2.3	3.4	2.2	3.1	3.2	1.9	1.3	1.4	1.0	0.6	•
Operating Margin **21**	•	•	•	•	5.0	3.0	•	•	•	3.0	1.6	•	•
Operating Margin Before Officers' Comp. **22**	0.9	•	•	•	7.2	6.1	3.0	•	4.4	2.7	•	•	•

Selected Average Balance Sheet ($ in Thousands)

Item	1	2	3	4	5	6	7	8	9	10	11	12
Net Receivables 23	761	0	6	531	785	1627	3846	5951	18909	40102	107246	•
Inventories 24	732	0	3	180	656	1762	4448	6343	15747	31482	95064	•
Net Property, Plant and Equipment 25	3896	0	24	569	1120	3280	7962	14467	28593	63562	187730	814284
Total Assets 26	10012	81	736	2691	6809	17196	36326	67297	162266	370126	2293015	•
Notes and Loans Payable 27	3243	23	737	788	3997	4820	9441	19156	39719	137657	758992	•
All Other Liabilities 28	2224	35	16	309	967	2357	4629	12913	28598	71717	613002	•
Net Worth 29	4545	22	-17	1593	1845	10018	22255	35227	93949	160751	921021	•

Selected Financial Ratios (Times to 1)

Item	1	2	3	4	5	6	7	8	9	10	11	12
Current Ratio 30	1.9	•	2.1	3.5	3.2	2.2	2.5	2.5	2.4	2.5	1.3	•
Quick Ratio 31	1.1	•	1.8	2.2	2.7	1.1	1.4	1.6	1.4	1.4	0.6	•
Net Sales to Working Capital 32	5.2	•	4.9	14.9	4.2	3.4	3.7	3.3	3.5	4.8	10.0	•
Coverage Ratio 33	1.9	5.0	4.2	•	5.8	2.3	0.7	2.1	4.3	1.9	1.2	•
Total Asset Turnover 34	0.6	•	1.2	1.9	1.5	2.3	0.7	0.7	0.8	0.8	0.4	•
Inventory Turnover 35	5.1	•	14.7	17.8	14.5	6.9	4.1	5.1	5.2	6.7	5.2	•
Receivables Turnover 36	7.5	•	31.3	30.8	8.7	7.0	6.0	7.6	6.7	7.7	10.5	•
Total Liabilities to Net Worth 37	1.2	•	2.6	•	0.7	2.7	0.6	0.9	0.7	1.3	1.5	•
Current Assets to Working Capital 38	2.1	•	1.9	1.4	1.5	1.8	1.8	1.7	1.7	1.7	4.2	•
Current Liabilities to Working Capital 39	1.1	•	0.9	0.4	0.5	0.8	0.8	0.7	0.7	0.7	3.2	•
Working Capital to Net Sales 40	0.2	•	0.2	0.1	0.2	0.2	0.3	0.3	0.3	0.2	0.1	•
Inventory to Working Capital 41	0.7	•	0.1	0.4	0.2	0.6	0.5	0.5	0.4	0.5	1.6	•
Total Receipts to Cash Flow 42	11.1	0.8	3.0	15.5	7.4	9.2	13.2	10.0	8.0	13.4	17.5	•
Cost of Goods to Cash Flow 43	7.0	0.3	1.3	10.5	4.8	5.8	8.3	6.9	5.2	9.2	10.4	•
Cash Flow to Total Debt 44	0.1	0.5	0.5	0.1	0.5	0.2	0.1	0.1	0.2	0.1	0.0	•

Selected Financial Factors (in Percentages)

Item	1	2	3	4	5	6	7	8	9	10	11	12
Debt Ratio 45	54.6	•	72.5	102.3	40.8	72.9	41.7	47.7	42.1	56.6	59.8	•
Return on Total Assets 46	3.5	•	11.7	•	12.3	6.9	2.2	2.8	5.5	5.1	2.2	•
Return on Equity Before Income Taxes 47	3.8	•	32.4	392.5	17.1	14.5	1.9	2.8	7.3	5.4	1.1	•
Return on Equity After Income Taxes 48	2.6	•	32.4	399.4	16.8	13.9	1.7	2.6	4.0	3.5	0.1	•
Profit Margin (Before Income Tax) 49	3.0	72.6	7.6	•	6.7	3.7	1.6	2.1	5.5	2.8	1.2	•
Profit Margin (After Income Tax) 50	2.0	41.0	7.6	•	6.6	3.6	1.5	1.9	3.0	1.8	0.1	•

Table II

Corporations with Net Income

NONMETALLIC MINERAL MINING AND QUARRYING

MONEY AMOUNTS AND SIZE OF ASSETS IN THOUSANDS OF DOLLARS

Item Description for Accounting Period 7/09 Through 6/10		Total	Zero Assets	Under 500	500 to 1,000	1,000 to 5,000	5,000 to 10,000	10,000 to 25,000	25,000 to 50,000	50,000 to 100,000	100,000 to 250,000	250,000 to 500,000	500,000 to 2,500,000	2,500,000 and over
Number of Enterprises	1	2042	76	1016	•	536	97	81	28	14	17	•	6	0
Revenues ($ in Thousands)														
Net Sales	2	15136927	43679	70189	•	3108797	925477	1215423	931733	1015666	2498306	•	3895040	0
Interest	3	22549	42	389	•	1161	3076	1216	414	1116	4435	•	10413	0
Rents	4	24401	0	0	•	105	50	187	1054	177	1817	•	20900	0
Royalties	5	65424	192	50959	•	1	0	0	107	0	39	•	14127	0
Other Portfolio Income	6	141285	74788	2108	•	25185	2599	2531	5963	4612	8862	•	12547	0
Other Receipts	7	160277	2278	14346	•	24865	1090	15194	6576	27966	24083	•	36023	0
Total Receipts	8	15550863	120979	137991	•	3160114	932292	1234551	945847	1049537	2537542	•	3989050	0
Average Total Receipts	9	7616	1592	136	•	5896	9611	15241	33780	74967	149267	•	664842	•
Operating Costs/Operating Income (%)														
Cost of Operations	10	63.4	36.5	30.4	•	64.3	59.7	60.9	71.4	72.5	65.4	•	58.1	•
Salaries and Wages	11	4.1	21.2	19.4	•	4.7	4.8	5.5	3.3	3.9	3.0	•	3.5	•
Taxes Paid	12	2.3	23.7	9.4	•	3.4	1.7	2.1	2.3	1.3	1.3	•	2.2	•
Interest Paid	13	2.2	18.2	3.3	•	1.4	1.6	1.4	1.3	1.0	0.9	•	4.5	•
Depreciation	14	7.2	15.0	10.5	•	4.6	3.5	7.7	7.7	5.1	7.1	•	10.0	•
Amortization and Depletion	15	2.3	5.9	•	•	0.2	1.5	2.6	1.7	1.4	2.5	•	4.4	•
Pensions and Other Deferred Comp.	16	0.7	•	•	•	0.6	1.1	0.5	0.5	0.3	0.9	•	0.8	•
Employee Benefits	17	2.0	1.0	0.1	•	1.4	3.4	2.3	1.8	1.0	2.2	•	2.5	•
Advertising	18	0.3	0.4	0.8	•	0.2	1.2	0.2	0.4	0.1	0.1	•	0.4	•
Other Expenses	19	8.8	41.4	72.4	•	10.4	9.0	7.4	6.0	7.8	7.4	•	9.1	•
Officers' Compensation	20	1.6	8.4	5.4	•	1.6	3.8	3.0	1.7	1.2	1.4	•	0.9	•
Operating Margin	21	5.1	•	•	•	7.3	8.7	6.5	1.9	4.5	7.8	•	3.7	•
Operating Margin Before Officers' Comp.	22	6.7	•	•	•	8.8	12.5	9.5	3.5	5.7	9.1	•	4.6	•

Selected Average Balance Sheet ($ in Thousands)

				•							•	
Net Receivables 23	984	0	0	•	716	1318	2052	4097	8812	21702	•	99556
Inventories 24	916	0	0	•	217	821	1581	6455	7045	13561	•	151198
Net Property, Plant and Equipment 25	3687	20	0	•	1390	1930	8085	14982	32207	67942	•	515605
Total Assets 26	9708	112	0	•	3164	7150	19109	34054	69285	164163	•	1611309
Notes and Loans Payable 27	2965	23	0	•	798	2814	4069	8772	15601	21163	•	599972
All Other Liabilities 28	2210	13	0	•	398	812	2546	4076	9902	30468	•	496707
Net Worth 29	4534	77	0	•	1968	3524	12494	21206	43782	112532	•	514630

Selected Financial Ratios (Times to 1)

				•							•	
Current Ratio 30	2.5	13.9	•	•	2.8	3.1	2.6	3.1	2.7	3.0	•	2.1
Quick Ratio 31	1.5	12.2	•	•	2.3	1.9	1.7	1.6	1.6	1.6	•	1.1
Net Sales to Working Capital 32	4.1	1.5	•	•	5.9	4.8	3.1	3.5	4.3	3.2	•	3.6
Coverage Ratio 33	4.5	14.6	6.8	•	7.3	6.9	6.9	3.7	9.2	11.3	•	2.4
Total Asset Turnover 34	0.8	0.6	•	•	1.8	1.3	0.8	1.0	1.0	0.9	•	0.4
Inventory Turnover 35	5.1	•	•	•	17.2	6.9	5.8	3.7	7.5	7.1	•	2.5
Receivables Turnover 36	6.9	•	•	•	8.8	5.9	6.7	7.9	8.3	7.8	•	5.1
Total Liabilities to Net Worth 37	1.1	0.5	•	•	0.6	1.0	0.5	0.6	0.6	0.5	•	2.1
Current Assets to Working Capital 38	1.7	1.1	•	•	1.5	1.5	1.6	1.5	1.6	1.5	•	1.9
Current Liabilities to Working Capital 39	0.7	0.1	•	•	0.5	0.5	0.6	0.5	0.6	0.5	•	0.9
Working Capital to Net Sales 40	0.2	0.7	•	•	0.2	0.2	0.3	0.3	0.2	0.3	•	0.3
Inventory to Working Capital 41	0.5	•	•	•	0.2	0.5	0.4	0.6	0.5	0.4	•	0.8
Total Receipts to Cash Flow 42	7.9	0.7	1.1	•	6.8	6.3	8.0	14.2	7.7	7.0	•	10.6
Cost of Goods to Cash Flow 43	5.0	0.3	0.4	•	4.4	3.7	4.9	10.1	5.5	4.6	•	6.2
Cash Flow to Total Debt 44	0.2	•	1.7	•	0.7	0.4	0.3	0.2	0.4	0.4	•	0.1

Selected Financial Factors (in Percentages)

				•							•	
Debt Ratio 45	53.3	31.5	•	•	37.8	50.7	34.6	37.7	36.8	31.5	•	68.1
Return on Total Assets 46	7.7	29.7	•	•	18.9	14.7	7.3	4.5	9.2	9.1	•	4.4
Return on Equity Before Income Taxes 47	12.8	40.3	•	•	26.3	25.6	9.6	5.3	12.9	12.1	•	8.0
Return on Equity After Income Taxes 48	10.6	40.3	•	•	25.8	25.0	9.3	4.8	12.5	8.3	•	5.2
Profit Margin (Before Income Tax) 49	7.8	44.8	105.2	•	8.9	9.4	8.0	3.4	7.8	9.2	•	6.4
Profit Margin (After Income Tax) 50	6.5	44.8	72.0	•	8.8	9.2	7.7	3.0	7.5	6.4	•	4.1

Table I

Corporations with and without Net Income

SUPPORT ACTIVITIES FOR MINING

MONEY AMOUNTS AND SIZE OF ASSETS IN THOUSANDS OF DOLLARS

Item Description for Accounting Period 7/09 Through 6/10		Total	Zero Assets	Under 500	500 to 1,000	1,000 to 5,000	5,000 to 10,000	10,000 to 25,000	25,000 to 50,000	50,000 to 100,000	100,000 to 250,000	250,000 to 500,000	500,000 to 2,500,000	2,500,000 and over
Number of Enterprises	1	10316	500	7502	810	1121	110	98	61	37	23	13	25	18
Revenues ($ in Thousands)														
Net Sales	2	68418785	2270172	3671770	862362	3293290	838757	1347648	2450152	1899865	2034908	1371181	11672409	36706271
Interest	3	869665	52607	41	2076	4598	2860	2915	6343	4504	6703	9432	84462	693124
Rents	4	2321298	2131	913	0	4326	23139	2244	3476	454	351	26191	145985	2112087
Royalties	5	252354	3942	22	271	9	28922	3725	12	366	123	194	8552	206215
Other Portfolio Income	6	1061972	23061	1587	5427	81515	11405	13641	21538	9658	60648	18250	129053	686187
Other Receipts	7	2347474	39194	46682	2621	57688	4756	49839	6927	78893	427	49875	517672	1492905
Total Receipts	8	75271548	2391107	3721015	872757	3441426	909839	1420012	2488448	1993740	2103160	1475123	12558133	41896789
Average Total Receipts	9	7297	4782	496	1077	3070	8271	14490	40794	53885	91442	113471	502325	2327599
Operating Costs/Operating Income (%)														
Cost of Operations	10	48.7	58.4	15.1	16.9	42.0	35.0	52.3	49.2	54.7	58.9	58.6	49.7	51.4
Salaries and Wages	11	11.7	13.8	24.3	18.8	10.0	20.2	14.6	13.3	13.1	10.7	12.4	11.9	9.8
Taxes Paid	12	2.1	0.9	4.0	2.6	2.8	3.6	4.6	3.1	3.0	2.6	3.0	2.5	1.5
Interest Paid	13	5.4	3.6	0.9	0.7	1.5	1.2	0.9	2.8	3.9	4.3	6.5	4.9	7.1
Depreciation	14	15.8	19.8	4.5	4.3	7.5	9.2	7.9	7.2	11.5	16.1	23.6	24.0	16.1
Amortization and Depletion	15	0.9	0.2	0.1	1.5	0.2	0.0	0.3	0.7	0.6	2.5	0.8	1.8	0.7
Pensions and Other Deferred Comp.	16	1.3	1.4	0.9	0.4	0.8	0.3	0.3	0.5	0.2	0.3	0.7	0.3	2.0
Employee Benefits	17	2.5	1.5	0.6	1.1	1.3	2.7	0.8	3.7	1.6	1.7	3.8	1.8	3.1
Advertising	18	0.1	0.1	0.4	0.3	0.3	0.4	0.2	0.1	0.2	0.3	0.1	0.1	0.1
Other Expenses	19	19.4	14.7	25.7	31.8	23.6	28.1	19.8	18.6	16.1	14.1	19.1	21.3	18.1
Officers' Compensation	20	1.6	1.5	8.6	5.3	7.0	6.9	1.7	1.2	1.3	1.1	1.4	0.9	0.5
Operating Margin	21	•	•	15.0	16.3	2.9	•	•	•	•	•	•	•	•
Operating Margin Before Officers' Comp.	22	•	•	23.6	21.6	9.9	•	0.7	0.7	•	•	•	•	•

Selected Average Balance Sheet ($ in Thousands)

Net Receivables 23	1850	0	10	89	252	1087	2498	7227	9935	22307	79921	103449	741135
Inventories 24	527	0	1	26	281	705	1077	2380	4295		29012	25953	222356
Net Property, Plant and Equipment 25	5382	0	36	216	520	1745	4772	10004	23974	68428	99784	625999	1878945
Total Assets 26	13857	0	117	703	1807	6456	14664	33482	67899	167319	366210	1223478	5199079
Notes and Loans Payable 27	4270	0	69	309	545	1222	2040	14470	18618	60815	79869	288524	1728630
All Other Liabilities 28	3076	0	13	259	198	1677	3808	6630	23990	30666	81159	282126	1140862
Net Worth 29	6512	0	35	135	1064	3557	8816	12382	25291	75838	205182	652827	2329587

Selected Financial Ratios (Times to 1)

Current Ratio 30	2.3	•	3.5	1.8	2.4	3.3	2.7	2.0	1.6	2.8	2.4	2.3	2.3
Quick Ratio 31	1.6	•	3.1	1.6	2.1	2.7	1.9	1.5	1.2	2.1	1.5	1.4	1.6
Net Sales to Working Capital 32	2.8	•	9.5	6.9	4.1	4.4	2.9	5.8	5.6	3.0	1.1	3.4	2.2
Coverage Ratio 33	1.2	•	20.1	24.7	1.8	6.1	3.2	1.4	0.7	•	•	•	1.7
Total Asset Turnover 34	0.5	•	4.2	1.5	1.2	1.6	0.9	1.2	0.8	0.5	0.3	0.4	0.4
Inventory Turnover 35	6.1	•	70.0	7.0	9.5	56.1	10.2	18.4	11.8	12.1	2.1	8.9	4.7
Receivables Turnover 36	3.3	•	48.6	11.3	6.2	8.6	3.8	5.0	5.5	3.2	1.1	3.8	2.6
Total Liabilities to Net Worth 37	1.1	•	2.3	4.2	0.8	0.7	0.7	1.7	1.7	1.2	0.8	0.9	1.2
Current Assets to Working Capital 38	1.7	•	1.4	2.2	1.7	1.4	1.6	2.0	2.7	1.6	1.7	1.8	1.7
Current Liabilities to Working Capital 39	0.7	•	0.4	1.2	0.7	0.4	0.6	1.0	1.7	0.6	0.7	0.8	0.7
Working Capital to Net Sales 40	0.4	•	0.1	0.1	0.2	0.2	0.3	0.2	0.2	0.3	0.9	0.3	0.5
Inventory to Working Capital 41	0.2	•	0.0	0.1	0.2	0.0	0.0	0.2	0.2	0.2	0.5	0.2	0.2
Total Receipts to Cash Flow 42	8.6	•	2.8	2.2	4.7	4.0	6.2	7.1	8.1	•	•	31.4	8.6
Cost of Goods to Cash Flow 43	4.2	•	0.4	0.4	1.7	1.7	3.2	3.5	4.4	•	•	15.6	4.4
Cash Flow to Total Debt 44	0.1	•	2.2	0.8	0.6	1.0	0.4	0.3	0.1	•	•	0.0	0.1

Selected Financial Factors (in Percentages)

Debt Ratio 45	53.0	•	69.8	80.8	41.1	44.9	39.9	63.0	62.8	54.7	44.0	46.6	55.2
Return on Total Assets 46	3.2	•	72.4	27.6	14.5	2.5	2.6	4.6	2.0	•	•	•	4.7
Return on Equity Before Income Taxes 47	1.3	•	227.6	137.8	20.5	2.0	3.0	•	•	•	•	•	4.3
Return on Equity After Income Taxes 48	•	•	223.9	137.8	18.9	0.6	1.9	•	•	•	•	•	0.7
Profit Margin (Before Income Tax) 49	1.2	•	16.4	17.5	7.4	0.9	1.9	1.9	•	•	•	•	4.9
Profit Margin (After Income Tax) 50	•	•	16.1	17.5	6.9	0.3	1.2	0.6	•	•	•	•	0.8

15

Table II
Corporations with Net Income

SUPPORT ACTIVITIES FOR MINING

MONEY AMOUNTS AND SIZE OF ASSETS IN THOUSANDS OF DOLLARS

Item Description for Accounting Period 7/09 Through 6/10		Total	Zero Assets	Under 500	500 to 1,000	1,000 to 5,000	5,000 to 10,000	10,000 to 25,000	25,000 to 50,000	50,000 to 100,000	100,000 to 250,000	250,000 to 500,000	500,000 to 2,500,000	2,500,000 and over
Number of Enterprises	1	5673	51	4324	410	708	48	52	33	17	10	4	3	13
Revenues ($ in Thousands)														
Net Sales	2	38401932	642586	3364817	522603	2330224	491305	949090	1556966	1212661	774227	397516	2251291	23908644
Interest	3	491392	817	41	125	1810	849	995	3304	1107	5285	5297	3777	467985
Rents	4	2062001	0	0	0	4034	13962	1407	327	324	205	3649	1077	2037015
Royalties	5	199714	740	0	0	0	0	0	12	226	0	194	8430	190112
Other Portfolio Income	6	817583	13152	55	3776	80418	9588	12877	19125	5491	37586	8187	56435	570894
Other Receipts	7	1515886	12366	44540	1183	15799	2691	53219	1267	72626	1400	42668	85292	1182837
Total Receipts	8	43348508	669661	3409453	527687	2432285	518395	1017588	1581001	1292435	818703	457511	2406302	28357487
Average Total Receipts	9	7666	13131	788	1287	3435	10800	19569	47909	76026	81870	114378	802101	2181345
Operating Costs/Operating Income (%)														
Cost of Operations	10	48.9	65.2	15.8	12.5	44.2	20.1	51.1	61.0	56.8	49.7	67.2	59.1	52.4
Salaries and Wages	11	8.1	7.0	23.5	13.4	6.2	23.2	11.5	5.1	6.4	13.4	13.0	3.7	6.1
Taxes Paid	12	2.1	0.7	3.8	2.6	2.4	3.1	5.1	3.4	2.9	2.9	2.5	1.2	1.6
Interest Paid	13	3.5	0.1	0.9	0.7	1.2	1.5	0.4	1.3	3.0	3.1	0.5	1.6	4.8
Depreciation	14	11.0	1.0	3.7	2.3	3.9	10.1	5.4	5.3	6.7	8.8	10.6	13.1	13.8
Amortization and Depletion	15	0.7	0.1	0.1	•	0.0	0.1	0.1	0.3	0.1	3.6	0.3	2.3	0.8
Pensions and Other Deferred Comp.	16	1.1	3.1	1.0	0.2	1.0	0.3	0.4	0.6	0.2	0.7	1.9	0.6	1.2
Employee Benefits	17	2.1	0.6	0.5	1.0	1.3	2.7	0.9	4.3	1.0	1.9	2.6	1.2	2.4
Advertising	18	0.1	0.1	0.3	0.1	0.3	0.2	0.1	0.1	0.2	0.7	0.1	0.0	0.1
Other Expenses	19	17.8	15.2	22.9	28.6	21.4	26.0	17.4	8.0	14.5	10.0	4.9	14.0	18.0
Officers' Compensation	20	2.0	1.4	8.2	1.6	7.5	9.6	1.0	0.7	1.3	2.2	1.8	1.1	0.6
Operating Margin	21	2.8	5.6	19.2	37.0	10.5	3.2	6.5	9.8	6.9	3.0	•	2.1	•
Operating Margin Before Officers' Comp.	22	4.8	7.0	27.3	38.6	18.0	12.8	7.5	10.6	8.1	5.2	•	3.3	•

Selected Average Balance Sheet ($ in Thousands)

Net Receivables 23	2262	0	11	35	298	1070	2819	8824	14078	24606	188442	194201	788502
Inventories 24	687	0	2	17	19	290	1268	1173	3966	4686	23519	78997	155954
Net Property, Plant and Equipment 25	4732	0	52	199	373	2177	3939	7214	17104	57302	40636	553343	1772324
Total Assets 26	13682	0	164	747	1611	6705	15477	33879	66563	173969	356878	1241909	5014602
Notes and Loans Payable 27	3215	0	70	105	231	1816	1159	8641	16500	54592	27390	221962	1207244
All Other Liabilities 28	2934	0	13	283	259	1352	2861	4904	29737	22764	127302	340680	1050049
Net Worth 29	7533	0	81	359	1121	3537	11457	20334	20326	96613	202186	679268	2757309

Selected Financial Ratios (Times to 1)

Current Ratio 30	2.5	•	3.9	1.5	2.8	2.5	4.3	2.5	3.6	2.1	1.8	2.5
Quick Ratio 31	1.8	•	3.5	1.5	2.3	2.1	3.0	2.1	3.0	1.7	1.0	1.8
Net Sales to Working Capital 32	2.4	102.5	10.2	9.3	5.1	4.1	2.8	4.8	2.2	0.7	4.6	1.9
Coverage Ratio 33	6.0	102.5	24.8	58.4	13.6	7.0	39.9	9.5	3.8	21.2	8.1	4.9
Total Asset Turnover 34	0.5	•	4.7	1.7	2.0	1.5	1.2	1.4	0.4	0.3	0.6	0.4
Inventory Turnover 35	4.8	•	78.1	9.5	77.4	7.1	7.4	24.5	8.2	2.8	5.6	6.2
Receivables Turnover 36	2.3	•	90.5	18.0	7.5	5.9	3.7	4.3	2.0	0.4	•	0.8
Total Liabilities to Net Worth 37	0.8	•	1.0	1.1	0.4	0.9	0.4	0.7	0.8	0.8	0.8	0.8
Current Assets to Working Capital 38	1.7	•	1.3	2.9	1.6	1.6	1.3	1.7	1.4	1.9	2.3	1.6
Current Liabilities to Working Capital 39	0.7	•	0.3	1.9	0.6	0.6	0.3	0.7	0.4	0.9	1.3	0.6
Working Capital to Net Sales 40	0.4	•	0.1	0.1	0.2	0.2	0.4	0.2	0.4	1.5	0.2	0.5
Inventory to Working Capital 41	0.2	•	0.0	0.1	0.0	0.2	0.1	0.1	0.1	0.2	0.5	0.2
Total Receipts to Cash Flow 42	4.2	7.2	2.6	1.6	3.3	3.7	3.9	5.9	6.5	8.1	5.7	4.7
Cost of Goods to Cash Flow 43	2.1	4.7	0.4	0.2	1.5	0.7	2.0	3.6	3.2	5.4	3.4	2.5
Cash Flow to Total Debt 44	0.3	•	3.7	2.0	2.0	0.9	1.2	0.6	0.2	0.1	0.2	0.2

Selected Financial Factors (in Percentages)

Debt Ratio 45	44.9	•	50.5	52.0	30.4	47.3	26.0	40.0	44.5	43.3	45.3	45.0
Return on Total Assets 46	10.2	•	101.2	66.0	32.8	15.5	16.6	17.7	5.2	2.8	7.8	8.6
Return on Equity Before Income Taxes 47	15.5	•	196.0	135.0	43.6	25.2	21.9	26.4	7.0	4.8	12.5	12.4
Return on Equity After Income Taxes 48	11.5	•	193.2	135.0	41.2	22.0	20.4	24.7	6.3	4.1	8.1	8.2
Profit Margin (Before Income Tax) 49	17.2	9.8	20.5	38.0	14.8	8.7	13.7	11.4	8.7	9.7	11.3	18.6
Profit Margin (After Income Tax) 50	12.8	7.3	20.2	38.0	14.0	7.6	12.8	10.6	7.9	8.3	7.4	12.2

Table I

Corporations with and without Net Income

ELECTRIC POWER GENERATION, TRANSMISSION AND DISTRIBUTION

MONEY AMOUNTS AND SIZE OF ASSETS IN THOUSANDS OF DOLLARS

Item Description for Accounting Period 7/09 Through 6/10	Total	Zero Assets	Under 500	500 to 1,000	1,000 to 5,000	5,000 to 10,000	10,000 to 25,000	25,000 to 50,000	50,000 to 100,000	100,000 to 250,000	250,000 to 500,000	500,000 to 2,500,000	2,500,000 and over
Number of Enterprises 1	1092	87	444	207	120	28	35	16	27	28	20	32	49
Revenues ($ in Thousands)													
Net Sales 2	304106339	1534387	131220	56854	126384	81126	219120	2026130	1935966	2330481	1855762	11156655	282652254
Interest 3	436656	4261	239327	1404	58	250	1874	4576	38300	37156	32526	217352	3759571
Rents 4	1199870	11772	0	0	0	1338	0	1213	3443	573	14019	10618	1156894
Royalties 5	46133	0	0	0	0	0	0	0	76	0	0	23834	22224
Other Portfolio Income 6	203296	14607	9189	0	303	0	62439	5319	8380	85669	7178	170073	1670140
Other Receipts 7	11800149	121084	2160	0	1462	2275	1271	62030	49197	160792	80338	1019496	10300044
Total Receipts 8	323522443	1686111	381896	58258	128207	84989	284704	2099268	2035362	2614671	1989823	12598028	299561127
Average Total Receipts 9	296266	19381	860	281	1068	3035	8134	131204	75384	93381	99491	393688	6113492
Operating Costs/Operating Income (%)													
Cost of Operations 10	54.8	30.3	92.2	•	63.1	26.9	54.9	94.3	58.8	67.2	75.8	56.2	54.3
Salaries and Wages 11	3.5	1.4	6.5	1.6	18.4	17.2	12.7	0.7	4.9	2.7	3.9	5.0	3.5
Taxes Paid 12	4.0	1.9	1.9	21.4	2.0	6.2	3.4	0.3	1.2	1.4	2.0	2.8	4.1
Interest Paid 13	7.2	32.9	171.9	1.5	3.9	6.2	13.5	0.5	1.9	4.2	8.8	6.3	7.1
Depreciation 14	12.1	18.7	0.3	4.9	7.5	10.9	14.8	0.9	2.7	6.5	10.4	15.1	12.2
Amortization and Depletion 15	1.7	11.0	0.2	•	0.7	2.3	2.0	0.1	1.0	0.8	0.5	1.7	1.6
Pensions and Other Deferred Comp. 16	1.2	0.1	•	•	•	0.8	1.3	•	1.5	0.3	0.4	0.7	1.3
Employee Benefits 17	1.2	0.1	0.5	•	1.5	2.3	1.7	0.2	1.5	0.7	0.9	1.0	1.2
Advertising 18	0.1	0.0	0.0	0.0	0.6	0.1	1.0	0.2	0.1	0.2	0.1	0.1	0.1
Other Expenses 19	23.1	30.9	38.2	51.7	94.1	110.9	23.9	6.6	28.3	20.5	23.1	38.1	22.5
Officers' Compensation 20	0.3	0.2	•	34.3	7.0	3.3	2.6	0.1	1.0	0.4	0.6	0.6	0.3
Operating Margin 21	•	•	•	18.8								•	•
Operating Margin Before Officers' Comp. 22	•	•	•									•	•

Selected Average Balance Sheet ($ in Thousands)

Net Receivables 23	56591	0	0	0	950	741	790	6531	20167	9211	16644	71801	1185656
Inventories 24	14340	0	51	0	19	268	1318	238	1430	2899	8273	33380	290307
Net Property, Plant and Equipment 25	467004	0	0	147	457	3087	6935	10956	16437	63915	154151	659471	9856301
Total Assets 26	838255	0	19	756	2797	6637	18105	37213	64694	158629	388139	1164329	17599925
Notes and Loans Payable 27	343954	0	0	11	974	3548	5674	25719	40455	72773	188736	520269	7167665
All Other Liabilities 28	283472	0	74	153	986	1123	5803	39003	22604	25592	144243	353793	5979125
Net Worth 29	210829	0	-55	592	837	1966	6628	-27509	1635	60263	55160	290266	4450135

Selected Financial Ratios (Times to 1)

Current Ratio 30	1.1	•	0.3	4.0	2.7	1.9	2.1	0.4	2.0	1.8	1.0	1.1	1.1
Quick Ratio 31	0.6	•	0.2	3.1	2.1	1.4	1.2	0.3	1.6	1.3	0.6	0.8	0.6
Net Sales to Working Capital 32	23.7	•	•	0.6	0.9	3.1	2.1	•	4.4	7.0	•	19.3	24.4
Coverage Ratio 33	0.6	0.5	0.9	•	•	•	0.9	0.6	2.2	2.8	•	•	0.7
Total Asset Turnover 34	0.3	•	15.8	0.4	0.4	0.4	0.3	3.4	1.1	0.5	0.2	0.3	0.3
Inventory Turnover 35	10.6	•	5.3	•	35.6	2.9	2.6	500.8	29.5	19.3	8.5	5.9	10.8
Receivables Turnover 36	4.9	•	14.2	•	2.0	2.1	3.1	8.5	4.4	6.5	5.5	4.1	4.9
Total Liabilities to Net Worth 37	3.0	•	•	0.3	2.3	2.4	1.7	•	38.6	1.6	6.0	3.0	3.0
Current Assets to Working Capital 38	11.8	•	•	1.3	1.6	2.2	1.9	•	2.0	2.3	•	12.8	12.1
Current Liabilities to Working Capital 39	10.8	•	•	0.3	0.6	1.2	0.9	•	1.0	1.3	•	11.8	11.1
Working Capital to Net Sales 40	0.0	•	•	1.7	1.1	0.3	0.5	•	0.2	0.1	•	0.1	0.0
Inventory to Working Capital 41	1.3	•	•	•	0.0	0.4	0.6	•	0.0	0.1	•	1.2	1.4
Total Receipts to Cash Flow 42	6.7	8.4	•	4.8	•	77.1	19.4	21.9	3.8	4.7	472.9	6.2	6.7
Cost of Goods to Cash Flow 43	3.7	2.5	•	8.6	•	20.8	10.7	20.7	2.2	3.1	358.5	3.5	3.6
Cash Flow to Total Debt 44	0.1	•	•	0.4	0.3	0.0	0.0	0.1	0.3	0.2	0.0	0.1	0.1

Selected Financial Factors (in Percentages)

Debt Ratio 45	74.8	•	397.5	21.7	70.1	70.4	63.4	173.9	97.5	62.0	85.8	75.1	74.7
Return on Total Assets 46	1.5	•	2396.9	•	•	•	4.0	1.2	4.6	6.0	•	•	1.6
Return on Equity Before Income Taxes 47	109.5	•	•	•	•	•	•	0.9	100.6	10.2	•	•	•
Return on Equity After Income Taxes 48	•	•	110.4	•	•	•	•	1.6	53.0	9.1	•	•	•
Profit Margin (Before Income Tax) 49	•	•	•	•	•	•	•	•	2.3	•	•	•	7.4
Profit Margin (After Income Tax) 50	•	•	•	•	•	•	•	•	1.2	•	•	•	6.6

17

Table II
Corporations with Net Income

ELECTRIC POWER GENERATION, TRANSMISSION AND DISTRIBUTION

MONEY AMOUNTS AND SIZE OF ASSETS IN THOUSANDS OF DOLLARS

Item Description for Accounting Period 7/09 Through 6/10	Total	Zero Assets	Under 500	500 to 1,000	1,000 to 5,000	5,000 to 10,000	10,000 to 25,000	25,000 to 50,000	50,000 to 100,000	100,000 to 250,000	250,000 to 500,000	500,000 to 2,500,000	2,500,000 and over
Number of Enterprises 1	575	49	425	0	0	21	12	•	13	15	6	•	16
Revenues ($ in Thousands)													
Net Sales 2	123492758	81159	8531	0	0	66783	196367	•	1441032	2001702	407126	•	116289413
Interest 3	1938892	103	239263	0	0	2	281	•	2806	30051	9114	•	1580582
Rents 4	437456	19	0	0	0	1338	0	•	2783	107	13831	•	416801
Royalties 5	36251	0	0	0	0	0	0	•	76	0	0	•	12342
Other Portfolio Income 6	546051	14607	0	0	0	0	61918	•	84	85655	5908	•	370422
Other Receipts 7	8704540	4	472	0	0	1069	190	•	16966	145943	33275	•	7554603
Total Receipts 8	135155948	95892	248266	0	0	69192	258756	•	1463747	2263458	469254	•	126224163
Average Total Receipts 9	235054	1957	584	•	•	3295	21563	•	112596	150897	78209	•	7889010
Operating Costs/Operating Income (%)													
Cost of Operations 10	52.1	2.4	78.3	•	•	29.8	55.3	•	73.4	70.5	63.7	•	51.2
Salaries and Wages 11	3.3	3.9	•	•	•	3.7	6.2	•	5.9	2.0	1.6	•	3.2
Taxes Paid 12	3.6	7.0	0.7	•	•	6.9	2.6	•	1.3	1.2	0.9	•	3.6
Interest Paid 13	7.6	31.0	2545.2	•	•	7.5	14.2	•	1.1	2.8	9.0	•	7.6
Depreciation 14	10.2	25.4	•	•	•	12.1	10.3	•	1.0	2.3	8.2	•	10.4
Amortization and Depletion 15	1.4	4.4	•	•	•	•	0.2	•	0.7	0.5	0.6	•	1.4
Pensions and Other Deferred Comp. 16	1.3	0.6	•	•	•	1.0	1.5	•	2.0	0.2	0.3	•	1.3
Employee Benefits 17	0.9	0.0	•	•	•	1.9	1.2	•	2.0	0.4	0.9	•	0.9
Advertising 18	0.1	•	•	•	•	•	0.7	•	0.1	0.2	0.0	•	0.1
Other Expenses 19	22.0	25.9	8.6	•	•	38.5	10.9	•	5.5	19.3	17.8	•	22.1
Officers' Compensation 20	0.3	0.7	•	•	•	•	1.4	•	1.0	0.3	0.5	•	0.3
Operating Margin 21	•	•	•	•	•	•	•	•	6.2	0.2	•	•	•
Operating Margin Before Officers' Comp. 22	•	•	•	•	•	•	•	•	7.2	0.6	•	•	•

Selected Average Balance Sheet ($ in Thousands)

Net Receivables 23	40199	0	0	•	551	827	•	13951	13198	10244	•	1325856
Inventories 24	15388	0	0	•	182	2421	•	1083	3747	8371	•	524007
Net Property, Plant and Equipment 25	337042	0	0	•	4081	6225	•	17710	47760	167181	•	11596318
Total Assets 26	624535	0	13	•	5989	18036	•	61340	163516	406314	•	21328348
Notes and Loans Payable 27	268156	0	0	•	3935	6079	•	17241	75280	159646	•	9172506
All Other Liabilities 28	214599	0	0	•	1084	8867	•	28211	34667	186730	•	7402129
Net Worth 29	141779	0	13	•	970	3090	•	15888	53569	59937	•	4753712

Selected Financial Ratios (Times to 1)

Current Ratio 30	1.2	•	352.6	•	1.1	4.7	•	1.7	2.1	3.1	•	1.2
Quick Ratio 31	0.7	•	336.2	•	0.8	2.8	•	1.2	1.5	2.1	•	0.6
Net Sales to Working Capital 32	10.0	•	1.5	•	28.5	2.4	•	8.3	6.8	1.6	•	11.1
Coverage Ratio 33	1.9	1.5	1.1	•	1.3	2.9	•	8.4	5.7	2.2	•	1.9
Total Asset Turnover 34	0.3	•	1.5	•	0.5	0.9	•	1.8	0.8	0.2	•	0.3
Inventory Turnover 35	7.3	•	•	•	5.2	3.7	•	75.1	25.1	5.2	•	7.1
Receivables Turnover 36	4.4	•	•	•	2.1	19.5	•	10.9	11.2	3.4	•	4.5
Total Liabilities to Net Worth 37	3.4	•	0.0	•	5.2	4.8	•	2.9	2.1	5.8	•	3.5
Current Assets to Working Capital 38	5.4	•	1.0	•	10.3	1.3	•	2.5	1.9	1.5	•	5.9
Current Liabilities to Working Capital 39	4.4	•	0.0	•	9.3	0.3	•	1.5	0.9	0.5	•	4.9
Working Capital to Net Sales 40	0.1	•	0.7	•	0.0	0.4	•	0.1	0.1	0.6	•	0.1
Inventory to Working Capital 41	0.7	•	•	•	2.0	0.4	•	0.1	0.1	0.8	•	0.8
Total Receipts to Cash Flow 42	4.1	3.5	0.3	•	2.5	4.7	•	8.3	3.9	3.8	•	4.1
Cost of Goods to Cash Flow 43	2.1	0.1	0.3	•	0.7	2.6	•	6.1	2.8	2.4	•	2.1
Cash Flow to Total Debt 44	0.1	•	1524.4	•	0.3	0.2	•	0.3	0.3	0.1	•	0.1

Selected Financial Factors (in Percentages)

Debt Ratio 45	77.3	•	0.3	•	83.8	82.9	•	74.1	67.2	85.2	•	77.7
Return on Total Assets 46	4.9	•	4268.6	•	5.2	37.6	•	15.9	13.2	3.3	•	4.8
Return on Equity Before Income Taxes 47	10.3	•	420.6	•	7.2	144.4	•	54.0	33.1	12.4	•	9.9
Return on Equity After Income Taxes 48	7.3	•	416.8	•	7.1	139.4	•	43.8	30.8	9.5	•	6.9
Profit Margin (Before Income Tax) 49	6.8	16.9	277.4	•	2.2	27.3	•	7.7	13.3	10.9	•	6.5
Profit Margin (After Income Tax) 50	4.8	12.9	274.8	•	2.2	26.3	•	6.3	12.4	8.4	•	4.5

18

Table I

Corporations with and without Net Income

NATURAL GAS DISTRIBUTION

MONEY AMOUNTS AND SIZE OF ASSETS IN THOUSANDS OF DOLLARS

Item Description for Accounting Period 7/09 Through 6/10	Total	Zero Assets	Under 500	500 to 1,000	1,000 to 5,000	5,000 to 10,000	10,000 to 25,000	25,000 to 50,000	50,000 to 100,000	100,000 to 250,000	250,000 to 500,000	500,000 to 2,500,000	2,500,000 and over
Number of Enterprises 1	856	•	311	55	135	9	22	•	•	11	9	9	14
Revenues ($ in Thousands)													
Net Sales 2	71496639	•	25174	55101	168089	142877	302077	•	•	2603852	5435501	16705264	45342270
Interest 3	427382	•	27	356	511	54	9036	•	•	682	17537	12018	385148
Rents 4	55883	•	0	3062	0	127	0	•	•	2019	4102	2622	43935
Royalties 5	4828	•	0	0	0	0	0	•	•	3854	721	0	230
Other Portfolio Income 6	164377	•	0	0	0	5	7454	•	•	625	195	38491	86626
Other Receipts 7	2857530	•	267	1494	241	2207	1557	•	•	4263	122599	161206	2471634
Total Receipts 8	75006639	•	25468	60013	168841	145270	320124	•	•	2615295	5580655	16919601	48329843
Average Total Receipts 9	87625	•	82	1091	1251	16141	14551	•	•	237754	620073	1879956	3452132
Operating Costs/Operating Income (%)													
Cost of Operations 10	73.2	•	84.4	75.1	60.8	86.2	81.2	•	•	89.8	86.3	87.6	65.4
Salaries and Wages 11	3.1	•	•	•	8.2	0.9	2.1	•	•	1.6	2.4	1.6	3.8
Taxes Paid 12	2.4	•	1.7	0.4	2.0	0.4	1.3	•	•	0.6	0.9	1.5	3.0
Interest Paid 13	3.6	•	•	0.0	1.9	0.3	1.2	•	•	0.7	3.0	0.9	5.0
Depreciation 14	7.4	•	•	•	8.4	8.1	4.2	•	•	1.9	1.4	2.6	10.3
Amortization and Depletion 15	0.7	•	•	•	0.1	0.2	0.3	•	•	0.1	0.7	0.2	0.9
Pensions and Other Deferred Comp. 16	0.4	•	•	•	2.1	•	0.3	•	•	0.2	0.0	0.4	0.5
Employee Benefits 17	0.8	•	•	•	0.6	1.8	0.5	•	•	0.2	0.4	0.4	1.1
Advertising 18	0.1	•	•	•	0.0	0.2	0.1	•	•	0.1	0.1	0.0	0.1
Other Expenses 19	13.3	•	53.7	28.7	18.8	6.6	10.6	•	•	3.2	10.1	3.1	17.8
Officers' Compensation 20	0.4	•	•	5.0	6.0	2.1	0.1	•	•	0.3	0.4	0.3	0.4
Operating Margin 21	•	•	•	•	•	•	•	•	•	1.3	•	1.3	•
Operating Margin Before Officers' Comp. 22	•	•	•	•	•	•	•	•	•	1.6	•	1.6	•

Selected Average Balance Sheet ($ in Thousands)

Net Receivables 23	15462	74	•	106	125	3911	•	26644	63594	138986	774245
Inventories 24	6446	0	•	16	0	935	•	9231	37310	142892	264001
Net Property, Plant and Equipment 25	96677	10	•	359	5572	4947	•	58006	59021	655783	5369044
Total Assets 26	196234	88	608	2648	7988	12936	•	137089	339505	1374297	10674686
Notes and Loans Payable 27	92410	8	613	925	1050	3525	•	30113	150731	413890	5235838
All Other Liabilities 28	76067	174	1	1065	2857	2810	•	53349	183092	498517	3093449
Net Worth 29	27756	-94	-6	658	4082	6601	•	53627	5683	461889	2345399

Selected Financial Ratios (Times to 1)

Current Ratio 30	1.1	0.6	•	0.6	2.8	0.9	1.8	1.4	1.4	1.3	1.0
Quick Ratio 31	0.6	0.6	•	0.6	2.8	0.7	1.3	1.0	0.7	0.6	0.6
Net Sales to Working Capital 32	43.4	•	1.6	2.2	2.2	•	4.0	15.5	12.0	21.6	•
Coverage Ratio 33	0.9	•	•	•	•	•	4.5	3.5	•	3.7	0.7
Total Asset Turnover 34	0.4	0.9	1.6	0.5	1.6	2.0	1.1	1.7	1.8	1.4	0.3
Inventory Turnover 35	9.5	•	•	46.5	•	•	11.9	23.0	14.0	11.4	8.0
Receivables Turnover 36	4.3	2.2	4.6	6.9	78.2	•	2.7	8.8	12.5	12.9	3.2
Total Liabilities to Net Worth 37	6.1	•	3.0	1.0	•	1.0	2.2	1.6	58.7	2.0	3.6
Current Assets to Working Capital 38	17.4	•	•	1.0	1.5	2.2	3.7	3.7	3.5	4.7	•
Current Liabilities to Working Capital 39	16.4	•	•	0.5	0.5	1.2	2.7	2.7	2.5	3.7	•
Working Capital to Net Sales 40	0.0	0.6	•	0.6	0.5	0.3	0.1	0.1	0.0	•	0.0
Inventory to Working Capital 41	2.5	•	•	0.0	0.0	0.2	•	0.3	0.9	1.5	•
Total Receipts to Cash Flow 42	10.1	9.6	5.5	13.8	108.2	8.2	•	22.6	15.0	20.3	8.2
Cost of Goods to Cash Flow 43	7.4	8.1	4.1	8.4	93.3	6.7	•	20.3	13.0	17.8	5.4
Cash Flow to Total Debt 44	0.0	0.0	0.3	0.0	0.0	0.3	•	0.1	0.1	0.1	0.0

Selected Financial Factors (in Percentages)

Debt Ratio 45	85.9	207.1	•	101.0	75.1	48.9	49.0	60.9	98.3	66.4	78.0
Return on Total Assets 46	1.3	•	•	•	•	•	5.6	4.3	•	4.8	1.0
Return on Equity Before Income Taxes 47	33.2	50.8	•	50.8	•	•	8.5	7.8	•	10.4	•
Return on Equity After Income Taxes 48	34.0	50.8	•	50.8	•	•	4.6	6.4	•	6.8	•
Profit Margin (Before Income Tax) 49	1.8	•	•	•	•	•	4.1	1.8	•	2.6	•
Profit Margin (After Income Tax) 50	1.4	•	•	•	•	•	2.2	1.4	•	1.7	•

Table II

Corporations with Net Income

NATURAL GAS DISTRIBUTION

MONEY AMOUNTS AND SIZE OF ASSETS IN THOUSANDS OF DOLLARS

Item Description for Accounting Period 7/09 Through 6/10	Total	Zero Assets	Under 500	500 to 1,000	1,000 to 5,000	5,000 to 10,000	10,000 to 25,000	25,000 to 50,000	50,000 to 100,000	100,000 to 250,000	250,000 to 500,000	500,000 to 2,500,000	2,500,000 and over
Number of Enterprises **1**	584	•	254	0	25	0	9	•	•	•	•	•	8
Revenues ($ in Thousands)													
Net Sales **2**	54497945	•	23638	0	68813	0	241986	•	•	•	•	•	30071734
Interest **3**	194779	•	0	0	340	0	111	•	•	•	•	•	181697
Rents **4**	39880	•	0	0	0	0	0	•	•	•	•	•	35451
Royalties **5**	4079	•	0	0	0	0	0	•	•	•	•	•	201
Other Portfolio Income **6**	126653	•	0	0	0	0	868	•	•	•	•	•	83633
Other Receipts **7**	2175487	•	0	0	43	0	992	•	•	•	•	•	1994223
Total Receipts **8**	57038823	•	23638	0	69196	0	243957	•	•	•	•	•	32366939
Average Total Receipts **9**	97669	•	93	•	2768	•	27106	•	•	•	•	•	4045867
Operating Costs/Operating Income (%)													
Cost of Operations **10**	75.2	•	89.9	•	40.8	•	87.0	•	•	•	•	•	64.9
Salaries and Wages **11**	2.9	•	•	•	8.0	•	0.8	•	•	•	•	•	3.9
Taxes Paid **12**	2.0	•	0.9	•	3.0	•	0.6	•	•	•	•	•	2.6
Interest Paid **13**	2.9	•	•	•	4.4	•	0.4	•	•	•	•	•	4.7
Depreciation **14**	6.5	•	•	•	16.2	•	1.2	•	•	•	•	•	10.2
Amortization and Depletion **15**	0.5	•	•	•	0.1	•	0.3	•	•	•	•	•	0.9
Pensions and Other Deferred Comp. **16**	0.4	•	•	•	•	•	0.2	•	•	•	•	•	0.5
Employee Benefits **17**	0.8	•	•	•	1.4	•	0.3	•	•	•	•	•	1.1
Advertising **18**	0.0	•	•	•	•	•	0.0	•	•	•	•	•	0.0
Other Expenses **19**	10.8	•	0.9	•	8.4	•	2.2	•	•	•	•	•	16.7
Officers' Compensation **20**	0.3	•	•	•	8.0	•	0.1	•	•	•	•	•	0.3
Operating Margin **21**	•	•	8.4	•	9.6	•	6.8	•	•	•	•	•	•
Operating Margin Before Officers' Comp. **22**	•	•	8.4	•	17.6	•	7.0	•	•	•	•	•	•

Selected Average Balance Sheet ($ in Thousands)

	1	2	3	4	5	6
Net Receivables **23**	20467	0	427	2567	•	1241797
Inventories **24**	6646	0	0	2096	•	181272
Net Property, Plant and Equipment **25**	103626	0	1543	2331	•	6765108
Total Assets **26**	225587	0	3232	13457	•	14610739
Notes and Loans Payable **27**	110598	0	2248	3220	•	7576462
All Other Liabilities **28**	68314	0	264	3341	•	4249307
Net Worth **29**	46676	0	719	6896	•	2784970

Selected Financial Ratios (Times to 1)

	1	2	3	4	5	6
Current Ratio **30**	1.0	•	2.7	6.4	•	1.0
Quick Ratio **31**	0.7	•	1.6	6.4	•	0.7
Net Sales to Working Capital **32**	53.9	•	4.7	1.9	•	1.4
Coverage Ratio **33**	1.8	•	19.8	3.3	•	1.4
Total Asset Turnover **34**	0.4	•	2.0	0.9	•	0.3
Inventory Turnover **35**	10.6	•	•	11.2	•	13.5
Receivables Turnover **36**	3.8	•	5.2	7.1	•	•
Total Liabilities to Net Worth **37**	3.8	•	1.0	3.5	•	4.2
Current Assets to Working Capital **38**	21.3	•	1.6	1.2	•	•
Current Liabilities to Working Capital **39**	20.3	•	0.6	0.2	•	•
Working Capital to Net Sales **40**	0.0	•	0.2	0.5	•	•
Inventory to Working Capital **41**	3.0	•	•	0.3	•	•
Total Receipts to Cash Flow **42**	9.0	10.8	6.3	10.2	•	6.4
Cost of Goods to Cash Flow **43**	6.7	9.7	2.6	8.9	•	4.2
Cash Flow to Total Debt **44**	0.1	•	0.4	0.2	•	0.0

Selected Financial Factors (in Percentages)

	1	2	3	4	5	6
Debt Ratio **45**	79.3	•	77.8	48.8	•	80.9
Return on Total Assets **46**	2.2	•	12.5	15.7	•	1.7
Return on Equity Before Income Taxes **47**	4.7	•	39.0	29.1	•	2.5
Return on Equity After Income Taxes **48**	3.1	•	38.1	20.1	•	1.4
Profit Margin (Before Income Tax) **49**	2.3	8.4	10.2	7.5	•	1.9
Profit Margin (After Income Tax) **50**	1.5	7.4	9.9	5.1	•	1.0

Table I

Corporations with and without Net Income

WATER, SEWAGE AND OTHER SYSTEMS

MONEY AMOUNTS AND SIZE OF ASSETS IN THOUSANDS OF DOLLARS

Item Description for Accounting Period 7/09 Through 6/10		Total	Zero Assets	Under 500	500 to 1,000	1,000 to 5,000	5,000 to 10,000	10,000 to 25,000	25,000 to 50,000	50,000 to 100,000	100,000 to 250,000	250,000 to 500,000	500,000 to 2,500,000	2,500,000 and over
Number of Enterprises	1	4086	656	2341	493	351	146	43	25	10	6	5	7	3
Revenues ($ in Thousands)														
Net Sales	2	8201254	163153	520710	434640	350511	425953	229891	156382	86819	212585	452526	1459559	3708524
Interest	3	27863	78	496	850	1689	156	873	3741	238	1192	4105	4485	9960
Rents	4	20421	34	391	0	1931	17	390	1833	162	1060	819	9416	4369
Royalties	5	51	0	0	0	0	4	0	48	0	0	0	0	0
Other Portfolio Income	6	115487	14925	31329	44	0	0	315	49772	45	322	3897	11588	3250
Other Receipts	7	184640	43	5534	1423	6275	26401	3518	1912	716	4206	5352	12972	116287
Total Receipts	8	8549716	178233	558460	436957	360406	452531	234987	213688	87980	219365	466699	1498020	3842390
Average Total Receipts	9	2092	272	239	886	1027	3100	5465	8548	8798	36561	93340	214003	1280797
Operating Costs/Operating Income (%)														
Cost of Operations	10	31.3	2.6	11.6	14.3	26.5	39.7	48.8	27.3	26.3	24.0	30.7	43.9	31.5
Salaries and Wages	11	8.9	1.7	10.6	24.3	7.5	8.6	9.7	6.0	18.6	8.6	13.4	4.8	8.3
Taxes Paid	12	6.9	2.7	3.0	5.2	2.8	6.8	4.9	14.9	7.1	7.4	6.7	6.1	8.3
Interest Paid	13	8.7	1.1	2.6	0.7	5.0	3.5	5.3	6.4	11.2	8.2	8.3	11.0	11.3
Depreciation	14	17.3	1.9	6.8	5.2	12.3	13.8	10.3	12.0	15.3	25.3	16.1	18.3	21.7
Amortization and Depletion	15	1.0	0.6	0.0	•	0.2	0.2	0.8	1.1	6.1	0.2	2.5	0.4	1.5
Pensions and Other Deferred Comp.	16	2.2	0.4	2.5	0.2	0.4	0.3	1.3	0.9	0.7	2.9	1.8	2.8	2.8
Employee Benefits	17	3.0	0.6	2.4	0.7	0.8	2.1	5.9	5.5	3.2	2.5	2.4	3.0	3.5
Advertising	18	0.2	0.1	0.1	0.3	0.0	0.1	0.1	0.1	0.1	•	0.1	0.1	0.2
Other Expenses	19	23.1	79.4	46.8	30.8	37.7	24.6	19.6	27.7	64.6	14.5	24.1	9.4	19.7
Officers' Compensation	20	2.6	42.4	7.2	4.9	3.3	3.4	3.1	10.1	1.2	3.9	1.4	1.0	0.2
Operating Margin	21	•	•	6.3	13.4	3.5	•	•	•	•	2.4	•	•	•
Operating Margin Before Officers' Comp.	22	•	8.8	13.5	18.3	6.8	0.2	•	•	•	6.3	0.2	0.2	•

Selected Average Balance Sheet ($ in Thousands)

Net Receivables 23	239	0	7	83	33	453	922	656	2626	3714	12785	18879	180399
Inventories 24	59	0	3	25	32	26	54	206	45	761	1220	14159	16218
Net Property, Plant and Equipment 25	6403	0	117	314	1556	4496	12053	19839	37451	157357	314204	675760	5299808
Total Assets 26	8746	0	157	648	2598	6599	17026	32363	68699	186056	392286	1053656	6830715
Notes and Loans Payable 27	3382	0	77	144	1749	2804	4747	5263	21625	46264	144134	409015	2709594
All Other Liabilities 28	2668	0	39	53	200	2592	7292	12850	18539	69116	157530	328088	2005087
Net Worth 29	2696	0	40	451	649	1204	4986	14250	28535	70676	90602	316554	2116034

Selected Financial Ratios (Times to 1)

Current Ratio 30	0.9	•	0.9	8.6	2.4	1.3	1.3	1.1	0.7	1.9	0.8	0.4	1.0
Quick Ratio 31	0.6	•	0.8	6.3	2.3	0.9	1.1	0.8	0.5	1.5	0.6	0.2	0.5
Net Sales to Working Capital 32	•	•	•	3.3	2.3	13.6	7.8	16.9	•	4.8	•	•	•
Coverage Ratio 33	0.9	•	6.3	21.2	2.3	1.9	•	4.8	•	1.7	0.5	1.2	0.5
Total Asset Turnover 34	0.2	•	1.4	1.4	0.4	0.4	0.3	0.2	0.1	0.2	0.2	0.2	0.2
Inventory Turnover 35	10.7	•	7.7	5.0	8.3	45.1	48.5	8.3	50.9	11.2	22.8	6.5	24.0
Receivables Turnover 36	7.7	•	23.4	7.1	18.7	8.0	3.9	6.0	•	•	9.9	•	6.5
Total Liabilities to Net Worth 37	2.2	•	2.9	0.4	3.0	4.5	2.4	1.3	1.4	1.6	3.3	2.3	2.2
Current Assets to Working Capital 38	•	•	•	1.1	1.7	4.9	4.1	7.8	•	2.1	•	•	•
Current Liabilities to Working Capital 39	•	•	•	0.1	0.7	3.9	3.1	6.8	•	1.1	•	•	•
Working Capital to Net Sales 40	•	•	•	0.3	0.4	0.1	0.1	0.1	•	0.2	•	•	•
Inventory to Working Capital 41	•	•	•	0.2	0.0	0.2	0.1	0.1	•	0.1	•	•	•
Total Receipts to Cash Flow 42	6.9	2.1	2.4	2.4	2.6	5.6	13.8	4.4	4.4	6.0	6.9	13.8	17.1
Cost of Goods to Cash Flow 43	2.1	0.1	0.3	0.2	0.7	2.2	6.7	1.2	1.2	1.4	2.1	6.1	5.4
Cash Flow to Total Debt 44	0.0	•	1.9	0.2	0.1	0.0	0.0	0.1	0.1	0.1	0.0	0.0	0.0

Selected Financial Factors (in Percentages)

Debt Ratio 45	69.2	•	74.4	30.4	75.0	81.8	70.7	56.0	58.5	62.0	76.9	70.0	69.0
Return on Total Assets 46	1.8	•	22.9	19.9	4.4	2.9	•	6.0	2.6	2.6	0.9	2.6	1.0
Return on Equity Before Income Taxes 47	•	•	75.1	27.3	9.8	7.4	•	10.8	•	2.8	•	1.2	•
Return on Equity After Income Taxes 48	•	•	75.1	27.2	8.6	7.4	•	7.9	•	1.5	0.3	0.3	•
Profit Margin (Before Income Tax) 49	•	•	13.6	14.0	6.3	3.1	•	24.6	•	5.5	1.9	1.9	•
Profit Margin (After Income Tax) 50	•	•	13.6	13.9	5.6	3.1	•	18.0	•	2.9	0.0	0.5	•

21

Table II

Corporations with Net Income

WATER, SEWAGE AND OTHER SYSTEMS

MONEY AMOUNTS AND SIZE OF ASSETS IN THOUSANDS OF DOLLARS

Item Description for Accounting Period 7/09 Through 6/10	Total	Zero Assets	Under 500	500 to 1,000	1,000 to 5,000	5,000 to 10,000	10,000 to 25,000	25,000 to 50,000	50,000 to 100,000	100,000 to 250,000	250,000 to 500,000	500,000 to 2,500,000	2,500,000 and over
Number of Enterprises 1	1402	•	841	215	220	64	21	19	•	•	•	•	0
Revenues ($ in Thousands)													
Net Sales 2	3813047	•	303486	257937	276883	356300	48490	137882	•	•	•	•	0
Interest 3	12092	•	372	71	1086	55	100	3596	•	•	•	•	0
Rents 4	7691	•	0	0	0	17	306	1034	•	•	•	•	0
Royalties 5	0	•	0	0	0	0	0	0	•	•	•	•	0
Other Portfolio Income 6	110927	•	31329	44	0	0	0	49449	•	•	•	•	0
Other Receipts 7	92775	•	448	447	2184	13040	2381	1761	•	•	•	•	0
Total Receipts 8	4036532	•	335635	258499	280153	369412	51277	193722	•	•	•	•	0
Average Total Receipts 9	2879	•	399	1202	1273	5772	2442	10196	•	•	•	•	•
Operating Costs/Operating Income (%)													
Cost of Operations 10	31.8	•	14.8	9.0	24.4	41.4	9.3	31.0	•	•	•	•	•
Salaries and Wages 11	8.3	•	12.9	31.5	8.2	6.6	6.6	6.4	•	•	•	•	•
Taxes Paid 12	6.5	•	2.2	5.3	2.8	6.5	11.0	14.9	•	•	•	•	•
Interest Paid 13	6.2	•	2.0	0.2	4.8	2.2	9.5	6.6	•	•	•	•	•
Depreciation 14	16.9	•	7.8	2.5	11.3	11.1	21.0	11.9	•	•	•	•	•
Amortization and Depletion 15	0.5	•	0.0	•	0.2	0.3	0.8	1.3	•	•	•	•	•
Pensions and Other Deferred Comp. 16	2.0	•	•	0.0	0.5	0.3	1.4	1.0	•	•	•	•	•
Employee Benefits 17	2.0	•	•	0.3	0.5	1.9	3.9	6.2	•	•	•	•	•
Advertising 18	0.0	•	0.1	0.0	•	0.2	•	0.1	•	•	•	•	•
Other Expenses 19	17.8	•	36.4	20.3	35.2	19.7	28.6	20.9	•	•	•	•	•
Officers' Compensation 20	2.1	•	•	5.5	3.3	3.2	4.0	11.4	•	•	•	•	•
Operating Margin 21	5.7	•	23.7	25.3	8.8	6.7	4.1	•	•	•	•	•	•
Operating Margin Before Officers' Comp. 22	7.9	•	23.7	30.8	12.2	9.9	8.0	•	•	•	•	•	•

Selected Average Balance Sheet ($ in Thousands)

Net Receivables 23	252	5	97	26	909	337	793
Inventories 24	42	6	2	29	100	56	109
Net Property, Plant and Equipment 25	7384	104	408	1230	3465	13394	22762
Total Assets 26	10036	158	702	2727	6588	17340	33195
Notes and Loans Payable 27	3301	56	21	2139	2325	4130	5700
All Other Liabilities 28	3350	9	10	270	1049	6598	14850
Net Worth 29	3385	94	671	318	3214	6612	12845

Selected Financial Ratios (Times to 1)

Current Ratio 30	0.8	4.8	25.0	2.3	1.4	1.0	1.0
Quick Ratio 31	0.6	4.5	24.2	2.2	1.0	0.9	0.6
Net Sales to Working Capital 32	•	10.1	4.3	2.2	10.5	•	5.3
Coverage Ratio 33	2.9	18.2	145.9	3.1	5.7	2.0	5.3
Total Asset Turnover 34	0.3	2.3	1.7	0.5	0.8	0.1	0.2
Inventory Turnover 35	20.4	9.1	64.3	10.4	23.0	3.9	20.6
Receivables Turnover 36	7.8	26.1	10.4	29.7	7.7	1.5	6.8
Total Liabilities to Net Worth 37	2.0	0.7	0.0	7.6	1.0	1.6	1.6
Current Assets to Working Capital 38	•	1.3	1.0	1.8	3.7	•	•
Current Liabilities to Working Capital 39	•	0.3	0.0	0.8	2.7	•	•
Working Capital to Net Sales 40	•	0.1	0.2	0.5	0.1	•	•
Inventory to Working Capital 41	•	•	0.0	0.0	0.2	•	•
Total Receipts to Cash Flow 42	4.4	1.9	2.2	2.5	5.1	3.3	6.2
Cost of Goods to Cash Flow 43	1.4	0.3	0.2	0.6	2.1	0.3	1.9
Cash Flow to Total Debt 44	0.1	2.9	17.4	0.2	0.3	0.1	0.1

Selected Financial Factors (in Percentages)

Debt Ratio 45	66.3	40.6	4.4	88.3	51.2	61.9	61.9
Return on Total Assets 46	4.8	82.7	44.0	6.8	10.6	2.6	7.7
Return on Equity Before Income Taxes 47	9.3	131.6	45.7	39.6	17.9	3.4	16.4
Return on Equity After Income Taxes 48	7.9	131.6	45.6	35.9	17.9	3.4	12.2
Profit Margin (Before Income Tax) 49	11.6	34.3	25.6	10.0	10.4	9.8	28.6
Profit Margin (After Income Tax) 50	9.9	34.3	25.5	9.1	10.4	9.6	21.2

Table I

Corporations with and without Net Income

COMBINATION GAS AND ELECTRIC

MONEY AMOUNTS AND SIZE OF ASSETS IN THOUSANDS OF DOLLARS

Item Description for Accounting Period 7/09 Through 6/10	Total	Zero Assets	Under 500	500 to 1,000	1,000 to 5,000	5,000 to 10,000	10,000 to 25,000	25,000 to 50,000	50,000 to 100,000	100,000 to 250,000	250,000 to 500,000	500,000 to 2,500,000	2,500,000 and over
Number of Enterprises **1**	37	•	0	0	0	0	0	•	•	0	0	5	25
Revenues ($ in Thousands)													
Net Sales **2**	186834583	•	•	•	•	0	0	•	•	0	0	8113378	177724308
Interest **3**	1019249	•	•	•	•	0	0	•	•	0	0	9834	1009052
Rents **4**	931929	•	•	•	•	0	0	•	•	0	0	7941	923984
Royalties **5**	2179	•	•	•	•	0	0	•	•	0	0	0	2179
Other Portfolio Income **6**	4443497	•	•	•	•	0	0	•	•	0	0	4657	4438637
Other Receipts **7**	4738215	•	•	•	•	0	0	•	•	0	0	34890	4681894
Total Receipts **8**	197969652	•	•	•	•	0	0	•	•	0	0	8170700	188780054
Average Total Receipts **9**	5350531	•	•	•	•	•	•	•	•	•	•	1634140	7551202
Operating Costs/Operating Income (%)													
Cost of Operations **10**	55.4	•	•	•	•	•	•	•	•	•	•	80.8	54.1
Salaries and Wages **11**	6.3	•	•	•	•	•	•	•	•	•	•	2.1	6.5
Taxes Paid **12**	4.1	•	•	•	•	•	•	•	•	•	•	0.8	4.2
Interest Paid **13**	4.8	•	•	•	•	•	•	•	•	•	•	1.7	4.9
Depreciation **14**	11.5	•	•	•	•	•	•	•	•	•	•	2.5	11.9
Amortization and Depletion **15**	0.6	•	•	•	•	•	•	•	•	•	•	0.6	0.6
Pensions and Other Deferred Comp. **16**	1.8	•	•	•	•	•	•	•	•	•	•	0.4	1.9
Employee Benefits **17**	1.8	•	•	•	•	•	•	•	•	•	•	0.5	1.9
Advertising **18**	0.1	•	•	•	•	•	•	•	•	•	•	0.3	0.1
Other Expenses **19**	16.5	•	•	•	•	•	•	•	•	•	•	11.8	16.7
Officers' Compensation **20**	0.2	•	•	•	•	•	•	•	•	•	•	0.3	0.2
Operating Margin **21**	•	•	•	•	•	•	•	•	•	•	•	•	•
Operating Margin Before Officers' Comp. **22**	•	•	•	•	•	•	•	•	•	•	•	•	•

Selected Average Balance Sheet ($ in Thousands)

Net Receivables	23	673862	82162	976193
Inventories	24	302894	24973	444432
Net Property, Plant and Equipment	25	658186	535894	9634588
Total Assets	26	11759516	1256295	17129982
Notes and Loans Payable	27	3950001	533270	5728585
All Other Liabilities	28	4744404	272363	6957515
Net Worth	29	3065111	450662	4443882

Selected Financial Ratios (Times to 1)

Current Ratio	30	1.1	1.3	1.1
Quick Ratio	31	0.6	0.4	0.6
Net Sales to Working Capital	32	41.8	20.0	44.0
Coverage Ratio	33	1.6	0.4	1.6
Total Asset Turnover	34	0.4	1.3	0.4
Inventory Turnover	35	9.2	52.5	8.7
Receivables Turnover	36	8.2	•	8.0
Total Liabilities to Net Worth	37	2.8	1.8	2.9
Current Assets to Working Capital	38	14.5	4.3	15.6
Current Liabilities to Working Capital	39	13.5	3.3	14.6
Working Capital to Net Sales	40	0.0	0.1	0.0
Inventory to Working Capital	41	2.5	0.3	2.8
Total Receipts to Cash Flow	42	7.1	10.5	7.0
Cost of Goods to Cash Flow	43	3.9	8.5	3.8
Cash Flow to Total Debt	44	0.1	0.2	0.1

Selected Financial Factors (in Percentages)

Debt Ratio	45	73.9	64.1	74.1
Return on Total Assets	46	3.3	0.9	3.3
Return on Equity Before Income Taxes	47	4.7	•	4.9
Return on Equity After Income Taxes	48	2.0	•	2.1
Profit Margin (Before Income Tax)	49	2.9	•	3.0
Profit Margin (After Income Tax)	50	1.2	•	1.3

Table II

Corporations with Net Income

COMBINATION GAS AND ELECTRIC

MONEY AMOUNTS AND SIZE OF ASSETS IN THOUSANDS OF DOLLARS

Item Description for Accounting Period 7/09 Through 6/10		Total	Zero Assets	Under 500	500 to 1,000	1,000 to 5,000	5,000 to 10,000	10,000 to 25,000	25,000 to 50,000	50,000 to 100,000	100,000 to 250,000	250,000 to 500,000	500,000 to 2,500,000	2,500,000 and over
Number of Enterprises	1	18	•	0	0	0	0	0	•	0	•	0	0	11
Revenues ($ in Thousands)														
Net Sales	2	93380192	•	0	0	0	0	0	•	0	•	0	0	91695700
Interest	3	381143	•	0	0	0	0	0	•	0	•	0	0	380405
Rents	4	676763	•	0	0	0	0	0	•	0	•	0	0	676708
Royalties	5	2128	•	0	0	0	0	0	•	0	•	0	0	2128
Other Portfolio Income	6	4173781	•	0	0	0	0	0	•	0	•	0	0	4173361
Other Receipts	7	3539586	•	0	0	0	0	0	•	0	•	0	0	3522702
Total Receipts	8	102153593	•	0	0	0	0	0	•	0	•	0	0	100451004
Average Total Receipts	9	5675200	•	•	•	•	•	•	•	•	•	•	•	9131909
Operating Costs/Operating Income (%)														
Cost of Operations	10	59.7	•	•	•	•	•	•	•	•	•	•	•	59.6
Salaries and Wages	11	5.8	•	•	•	•	•	•	•	•	•	•	•	5.8
Taxes Paid	12	4.0	•	•	•	•	•	•	•	•	•	•	•	4.0
Interest Paid	13	4.3	•	•	•	•	•	•	•	•	•	•	•	4.3
Depreciation	14	10.2	•	•	•	•	•	•	•	•	•	•	•	10.4
Amortization and Depletion	15	0.8	•	•	•	•	•	•	•	•	•	•	•	0.8
Pensions and Other Deferred Comp.	16	1.6	•	•	•	•	•	•	•	•	•	•	•	1.6
Employee Benefits	17	1.5	•	•	•	•	•	•	•	•	•	•	•	1.5
Advertising	18	0.1	•	•	•	•	•	•	•	•	•	•	•	0.1
Other Expenses	19	11.5	•	•	•	•	•	•	•	•	•	•	•	11.4
Officers' Compensation	20	0.3	•	•	•	•	•	•	•	•	•	•	•	0.3
Operating Margin	21	0.3	•	•	•	•	•	•	•	•	•	•	•	0.3
Operating Margin Before Officers' Comp.	22	0.6	•	•	•	•	•	•	•	•	•	•	•	0.6

Selected Average Balance Sheet ($ in Thousands)

Net Receivables 23	588297	945157
Inventories 24	318839	472386
Net Property, Plant and Equipment 25	5816060	9449541
Total Assets 26	10891864	17691180
Notes and Loans Payable 27	3375628	5452400
All Other Liabilities 28	4352732	7090659
Net Worth 29	3163504	5148121

Selected Financial Ratios (Times to 1)

Current Ratio 30	1.5	1.5
Quick Ratio 31	0.8	0.8
Net Sales to Working Capital 32	9.6	9.4
Coverage Ratio 33	3.3	3.3
Total Asset Turnover 34	0.5	0.5
Inventory Turnover 35	9.7	10.5
Receivables Turnover 36	8.1	•
Total Liabilities to Net Worth 37	2.4	2.4
Current Assets to Working Capital 38	2.9	2.9
Current Liabilities to Working Capital 39	1.9	1.9
Working Capital to Net Sales 40	0.1	0.1
Inventory to Working Capital 41	0.5	0.5
Total Receipts to Cash Flow 42	6.1	6.1
Cost of Goods to Cash Flow 43	3.6	3.6
Cash Flow to Total Debt 44	0.1	0.1

Selected Financial Factors (in Percentages)

Debt Ratio 45	71.0	70.9
Return on Total Assets 46	6.7	6.7
Return on Equity Before Income Taxes 47	16.1	16.1
Return on Equity After Income Taxes 48	10.7	10.7
Profit Margin (Before Income Tax) 49	9.8	9.9
Profit Margin (After Income Tax) 50	6.5	6.6

Table I

Corporations with and without Net Income

CONSTRUCTION OF BUILDINGS

MONEY AMOUNTS AND SIZE OF ASSETS IN THOUSANDS OF DOLLARS

Item Description for Accounting Period 7/09 Through 6/10	Total	Zero Assets	Under 500	500 to 1,000	1,000 to 5,000	5,000 to 10,000	10,000 to 25,000	25,000 to 50,000	50,000 to 100,000	100,000 to 250,000	250,000 to 500,000	500,000 to 2,500,000	2,500,000 and over
Number of Enterprises **1**	221037	49840	126638	17948	20264	3508	1998	422	•	112	32	•	•
Revenues ($ in Thousands)													
Net Sales **2**	442404266	8266167	51852253	30065516	81527726	40925937	53379606	24246729	•	29436796	16350561	•	•
Interest **3**	962388	5306	11228	17858	53324	23608	26947	16506	•	22281	76479	•	•
Rents **4**	508548	10424	30585	36734	64541	37215	39746	23372	•	31271	62749	•	•
Royalties **5**	22093	0	936	0	0	0	162	0	•	7000	105	•	•
Other Portfolio Income **6**	727726	44068	48700	26068	92007	39609	45321	45145	•	24457	29251	•	•
Other Receipts **7**	5129724	98667	648298	205183	683466	406269	34798	180273	•	354803	335979	•	•
Total Receipts **8**	449754745	8424632	52592000	30351359	82421064	41432638	53526580	24512025	•	29876608	16855124	•	•
Average Total Receipts **9**	2035	169	415	1691	4067	11811	26790	58085	•	266755	526723	•	•
Operating Costs/Operating Income (%)													
Cost of Operations **10**	86.5	67.8	69.4	80.0	86.1	87.6	88.9	90.5	•	91.5	89.1	•	•
Salaries and Wages **11**	3.9	5.6	6.6	5.6	3.4	2.8	2.7	2.6	•	2.6	3.8	•	•
Taxes Paid **12**	1.0	1.4	1.8	1.7	1.2	0.7	0.7	0.7	•	0.6	0.9	•	•
Interest Paid **13**	0.9	1.6	0.6	0.7	0.6	0.5	0.5	0.6	•	0.6	1.4	•	•
Depreciation **14**	0.7	1.0	1.1	0.8	0.6	0.5	0.5	0.4	•	0.6	0.6	•	•
Amortization and Depletion **15**	0.1	0.3	0.0	0.0	0.0	0.0	0.0	•	•	0.2	0.1	•	•
Pensions and Other Deferred Comp. **16**	0.2	0.1	0.1	0.2	0.2	0.2	0.2	0.2	•	0.2	0.1	•	•
Employee Benefits **17**	0.6	0.4	0.9	0.9	0.7	0.7	0.7	0.5	•	0.4	0.5	•	•
Advertising **18**	0.3	0.4	0.6	0.3	0.2	0.2	0.2	0.2	•	0.1	0.2	•	•
Other Expenses **19**	6.7	29.0	13.2	7.9	5.1	4.3	3.3	3.8	•	3.6	5.2	•	•
Officers' Compensation **20**	2.1	3.5	5.2	3.7	2.3	2.1	1.6	1.5	•	0.8	0.8	•	•
Operating Margin **21**	•	•	0.6	•	•	0.4	0.7	•	•	•	•	•	•
Operating Margin Before Officers' Comp. **22**	•	•	5.8	2.1	1.8	2.5	2.3	0.7	•	•	•	•	•

Selected Average Balance Sheet ($ in Thousands)

Net Receivables 23	284	0	11	119	409	1640	4060	8521	•	41350	97542
Inventories 24	278	0	13	157	537	1676	3319	8969	•	29488	56623
Net Property, Plant and Equipment 25	151	0	25	155	312	842	1965	3930	•	21781	45448
Total Assets 26	1312	0	90	730	2177	6849	15167	33883	•	151560	355894
Notes and Loans Payable 27	507	0	58	377	917	2461	5138	11975	•	48321	121458
All Other Liabilities 28	488	0	25	215	772	2584	6020	14018	•	64722	132418
Net Worth 29	316	0	7	137	488	1803	4009	7890	•	38518	102018

Selected Financial Ratios (Times to 1)

Current Ratio 30	1.6	•	1.5	1.7	1.5	1.6	1.5	1.4	•	1.5	1.6
Quick Ratio 31	0.9	•	0.9	0.8	0.7	0.9	0.9	0.9	•	0.9	1.1
Net Sales to Working Capital 32	6.1	•	21.3	8.2	7.3	5.7	6.9	7.9	•	7.5	5.8
Coverage Ratio 33	•	•	4.4	0.0	2.0	4.5	3.0	1.4	•	1.7	1.2
Total Asset Turnover 34	1.5	•	4.5	2.3	1.8	1.7	1.8	1.7	•	1.7	1.4
Inventory Turnover 35	6.2	•	21.4	8.5	6.5	6.1	7.2	5.8	•	8.2	8.0
Receivables Turnover 36	6.3	•	32.7	17.1	9.1	7.1	5.4	5.1	•	5.1	4.7
Total Liabilities to Net Worth 37	3.1	•	11.8	4.3	3.5	2.8	2.8	3.3	•	2.9	2.5
Current Assets to Working Capital 38	2.8	•	2.9	2.4	2.9	2.6	2.9	3.4	•	3.2	2.6
Current Liabilities to Working Capital 39	1.8	•	1.9	1.4	1.9	1.6	1.9	2.4	•	2.2	1.6
Working Capital to Net Sales 40	0.2	•	0.0	0.1	0.1	0.2	0.1	0.1	•	0.1	0.2
Inventory to Working Capital 41	0.7	•	0.6	0.7	0.8	0.6	0.7	0.8	•	0.6	0.5
Total Receipts to Cash Flow 42	26.3	6.0	7.8	19.5	23.5	21.0	30.4	35.1	•	30.7	21.7
Cost of Goods to Cash Flow 43	22.8	4.1	5.4	15.6	20.2	18.4	27.0	31.8	•	28.1	19.4
Cash Flow to Total Debt 44	0.1	•	0.6	0.1	0.1	0.1	0.1	0.1	•	0.1	0.1

Selected Financial Factors (in Percentages)

Debt Ratio 45	75.9	•	92.2	81.2	77.6	73.7	73.6	76.7	•	74.6	71.3
Return on Total Assets 46	•	•	11.8	0.0	2.4	3.6	2.6	1.3	•	1.7	2.5
Return on Equity Before Income Taxes 47	•	•	116.9	5.3	10.6	6.6	1.7	•	•	2.7	1.5
Return on Equity After Income Taxes 48	•	•	114.6	4.3	9.5	5.8	0.6	•	•	1.8	0.2
Profit Margin (Before Income Tax) 49	•	•	2.0	0.6	1.6	1.0	0.2	•	•	0.4	0.3
Profit Margin (After Income Tax) 50	•	•	2.0	0.5	1.5	0.9	0.1	•	•	0.3	0.0

Table II

Corporations with Net Income

CONSTRUCTION OF BUILDINGS

MONEY AMOUNTS AND SIZE OF ASSETS IN THOUSANDS OF DOLLARS

Item Description for Accounting Period 7/09 Through 6/10		Total	Zero Assets	Under 500	500 to 1,000	1,000 to 5,000	5,000 to 10,000	10,000 to 25,000	25,000 to 50,000	50,000 to 100,000	100,000 to 250,000	250,000 to 500,000	500,000 to 2,500,000	2,500,000 and over
Number of Enterprises	1	114237	19940	71615	8751	10178	2106	1152	250	140	65	19	20	0
Revenues ($ in Thousands)														
Net Sales	2	312106286	3451594	37349124	18358591	55949013	32146716	43314375	20314865	24950870	24177244	13334336	38759559	0
Interest	3	216150	927	7319	10776	33716	21302	19671	12108	5157	15467	26410	63298	0
Rents	4	249066	0	18056	24722	14054	17106	27064	17705	18931	13563	34357	63507	0
Royalties	5	12023	0	0	0	0	0	0	0	8	0	105	11910	0
Other Portfolio Income	6	480379	22889	40182	17528	62507	23068	24522	28683	11453	18298	8968	222284	0
Other Receipts	7	2778543	41809	273283	78901	385606	326924	-20095	190108	138993	309103	183759	870149	0
Total Receipts	8	315842447	3517219	37687964	18490518	56444896	32535116	43365537	20563469	25125412	24533675	13587935	39990707	0
Average Total Receipts	9	2765	176	526	2113	5546	15449	37644	82254	179467	377441	715154	1999535	•
Operating Costs/Operating Income (%)														
Cost of Operations	10	84.0	43.3	66.6	77.2	84.6	86.1	87.1	89.0	90.8	90.1	90.8	88.5	•
Salaries and Wages	11	3.1	3.4	5.7	4.7	2.8	2.3	2.4	2.3	2.1	2.0	3.5	3.7	•
Taxes Paid	12	0.9	0.9	1.7	1.3	1.0	0.7	0.6	0.5	0.5	0.5	0.9	0.7	•
Interest Paid	13	0.3	0.3	0.5	0.4	0.4	0.3	0.2	0.2	0.1	0.2	0.5	0.2	•
Depreciation	14	0.6	0.9	1.0	0.6	0.5	0.4	0.4	0.3	0.4	0.5	0.5	0.6	•
Amortization and Depletion	15	0.0	•	0.0	0.0	0.0	0.0	0.0	0.0	0.0	0.0	0.1	0.0	•
Pensions and Other Deferred Comp.	16	0.2	0.0	0.1	0.2	0.2	0.2	0.2	0.2	0.2	0.2	0.1	0.4	•
Employee Benefits	17	0.6	0.3	0.9	0.8	0.6	0.6	0.7	0.5	0.5	0.4	0.4	0.5	•
Advertising	18	0.2	0.4	0.4	0.3	0.2	0.2	0.2	0.1	0.1	0.1	0.1	0.1	•
Other Expenses	19	4.5	35.3	11.8	6.3	3.9	3.7	2.8	2.5	1.6	2.8	1.6	2.6	•
Officers' Compensation	20	2.0	4.6	4.9	3.5	2.1	2.1	1.6	1.6	0.9	0.8	0.9	0.7	•
Operating Margin	21	3.6	10.7	6.4	4.8	3.8	3.4	3.8	2.8	2.8	2.5	0.5	2.0	•
Operating Margin Before Officers' Comp.	22	5.6	15.3	11.2	8.2	5.8	5.5	5.4	4.4	3.7	3.3	1.4	2.8	•

Selected Average Balance Sheet ($ in Thousands)

Net Receivables 23	325	0	11	119	488	1862	5381	12394	28946	59888	117486	346067	•
Inventories 24	127	0	10	126	451	971	1853	4738	3764	4192	34172	33997	•
Net Property, Plant and Equipment 25	123	0	22	185	236	806	1242	1780	5047	13525	31475	130744	•
Total Assets 26	1099	0	85	738	2242	6977	15268	34427	70796	148389	339350	1165484	•
Notes and Loans Payable 27	210	0	42	245	685	1586	2584	3717	6767	19268	56365	66379	•
All Other Liabilities 28	510	0	22	202	853	2981	7720	17975	43294	87041	162787	586456	•
Net Worth 29	380	0	21	291	704	2410	4964	12735	20736	42080	120198	512649	•

Selected Financial Ratios (Times to 1)

Current Ratio 30	1.5	•	1.6	2.0	1.6	1.7	1.5	1.6	1.4	1.3	1.5	1.4	•
Quick Ratio 31	1.1	•	1.2	1.2	0.8	1.0	1.1	1.2	1.1	1.1	1.2	1.1	•
Net Sales to Working Capital 32	9.6	•	28.0	8.7	7.8	6.8	9.0	7.7	10.9	14.6	8.9	9.3	•
Coverage Ratio 33	17.8	43.9	15.6	14.8	14.1	18.9	18.9	25.1	36.7	24.5	5.7	28.0	•
Total Asset Turnover 34	2.5	•	6.2	2.8	2.5	2.2	2.5	2.4	2.5	2.5	2.1	1.7	•
Inventory Turnover 35	18.1	•	33.3	12.8	10.3	13.5	17.7	15.3	43.0	79.9	18.7	50.4	•
Receivables Turnover 36	6.6	•	41.2	18.1	9.0	7.5	5.3	4.9	5.2	•	4.8	•	•
Total Liabilities to Net Worth 37	1.9	•	3.0	1.5	2.2	1.9	2.1	1.7	2.4	2.5	1.8	1.3	•
Current Assets to Working Capital 38	2.9	•	2.6	2.0	2.6	2.4	3.0	2.8	3.7	4.6	3.0	3.5	•
Current Liabilities to Working Capital 39	1.9	•	1.6	1.0	1.6	1.4	2.0	1.8	2.7	3.6	2.0	2.5	•
Working Capital to Net Sales 40	0.1	•	0.0	0.1	0.1	0.1	0.1	0.1	0.1	0.1	0.1	0.1	•
Inventory to Working Capital 41	0.4	•	0.3	0.4	0.6	0.4	0.4	0.4	0.2	0.2	0.3	0.2	•
Total Receipts to Cash Flow 42	12.3	2.2	6.0	9.8	13.4	13.7	17.3	17.7	22.2	16.7	30.6	15.3	•
Cost of Goods to Cash Flow 43	10.3	0.9	4.0	7.6	11.3	11.8	15.0	15.7	20.2	15.0	27.8	13.5	•
Cash Flow to Total Debt 44	0.3	•	1.4	0.5	0.3	0.2	0.2	0.2	0.2	0.2	0.1	0.2	•

Selected Financial Factors (in Percentages)

Debt Ratio 45	65.5	•	75.2	60.5	68.6	65.5	67.5	63.0	70.7	71.6	64.6	56.0	•
Return on Total Assets 46	12.6	•	47.9	16.7	12.3	10.7	10.1	9.9	9.1	10.2	6.1	8.9	•
Return on Equity Before Income Taxes 47	34.3	•	180.4	39.5	36.4	29.2	29.3	25.7	30.2	34.4	14.1	19.5	•
Return on Equity After Income Taxes 48	32.6	•	179.0	38.8	35.0	27.9	28.3	24.5	29.5	33.1	12.1	16.2	•
Profit Margin (Before Income Tax) 49	4.8	12.6	7.3	5.5	4.7	4.6	3.9	4.0	3.5	3.9	2.4	5.2	•
Profit Margin (After Income Tax) 50	4.5	12.5	7.2	5.4	4.5	4.4	3.7	3.8	3.4	3.7	2.1	4.3	•

Table I

Corporations with and without Net Income

HEAVY AND CIVIL ENGINEERING CONSTRUCTION

MONEY AMOUNTS AND SIZE OF ASSETS IN THOUSANDS OF DOLLARS

Item Description for Accounting Period 7/09 Through 6/10	Total	Zero Assets	Under 500	500 to 1,000	1,000 to 5,000	5,000 to 10,000	10,000 to 25,000	25,000 to 50,000	50,000 to 100,000	100,000 to 250,000	250,000 to 500,000	500,000 to 2,500,000	2,500,000 and over
Number of Enterprises **1**	25559	2572	12900	2963	4237	1500	838	305	128	72	22	17	4
Revenues ($ in Thousands)													
Net Sales **2**	192818494	2809312	9685856	6034973	20391955	21849481	24320700	20112645	14062934	13732124	10243665	18543567	31031284
Interest **3**	240878	6847	11731	6370	35760	11529	13896	9395	14914	13368	6486	49059	61522
Rents **4**	116313	0	6640	9917	17818	1783	16587	21571	15520	6620	178	12313	7364
Royalties **5**	76808	0	0	0	0	425	660	421	17569	7	935	19223	37569
Other Portfolio Income **6**	1196466	232101	68259	68064	207537	58806	78526	71512	67730	58046	33384	177464	75039
Other Receipts **7**	3481374	93673	140203	36715	205432	63225	175998	148339	39464	498376	134193	396260	1549495
Total Receipts **8**	197930333	3141933	9912689	6156039	20858502	21985249	24606367	20363883	14218131	14308541	10418841	19197886	32762273
Average Total Receipts **9**	7744	1222	768	2078	4923	14657	29363	66767	111079	198730	473584	1129287	8190568
Operating Costs/Operating Income (%)													
Cost of Operations **10**	77.2	71.7	53.5	68.5	69.2	78.1	79.9	80.6	79.2	77.6	77.4	78.7	85.1
Salaries and Wages **11**	3.9	2.4	9.3	5.5	5.1	3.2	3.2	2.9	3.1	4.1	4.5	3.7	3.4
Taxes Paid **12**	1.7	1.1	2.9	2.1	2.2	1.6	1.5	1.2	1.2	1.4	1.1	3.0	1.1
Interest Paid **13**	0.6	0.6	1.1	1.0	0.7	0.6	0.5	0.5	0.4	0.7	0.6	1.1	0.4
Depreciation **14**	3.4	2.4	3.2	3.3	5.2	3.7	3.4	3.3	3.2	3.9	4.0	3.7	1.6
Amortization and Depletion **15**	0.2	0.2	0.5	0.0	0.0	0.0	0.0	0.1	0.1	0.3	0.3	0.7	0.4
Pensions and Other Deferred Comp. **16**	0.4	0.1	0.2	0.1	0.5	0.8	0.4	0.3	0.5	0.5	0.2	0.2	0.1
Employee Benefits **17**	1.0	0.7	1.1	1.1	1.2	0.9	1.2	1.3	1.3	1.1	1.2	1.2	0.3
Advertising **18**	0.1	0.1	0.6	0.2	0.2	0.1	0.1	0.1	0.1	0.1	0.0	0.3	0.0
Other Expenses **19**	7.5	16.9	18.6	15.1	11.8	7.2	4.7	5.4	5.1	6.6	5.2	6.0	5.6
Officers' Compensation **20**	2.2	0.7	8.1	4.4	4.7	2.4	2.2	1.7	1.5	1.4	1.4	0.5	0.8
Operating Margin **21**	1.7	3.1	0.9	•	•	1.4	2.8	2.6	4.3	2.3	4.1	0.9	1.1
Operating Margin Before Officers' Comp. **22**	4.0	3.8	9.0	3.1	4.0	3.9	5.1	4.3	5.7	3.8	5.4	1.4	1.9

Selected Average Balance Sheet ($ in Thousands)

Net Receivables 23	1034	0	38	104	603	1779	4683	9888	16424	28314	73716	150980	1288564
Inventories 24	122	0	2	31	55	171	382	993	2250	6250	9735	38976	67845
Net Property, Plant and Equipment 25	1184	0	71	347	752	1944	3842	8777	17550	34231	94505	277458	1207419
Total Assets 26	4631	0	195	710	2368	6921	15232	34289	69740	145226	349852	930552	6805697
Notes and Loans Payable 27	861	0	117	325	609	1730	2779	6659	10810	25476	57768	232271	393556
All Other Liabilities 28	1568	0	35	170	600	2090	4927	11407	23642	45366	122085	349041	2729367
Net Worth 29	2202	0	43	215	1158	3101	7526	16222	35289	74383	169999	349241	3682774

Selected Financial Ratios (Times to 1)

Current Ratio 30	1.5	•	1.8	1.1	1.9	1.8	1.8	1.7	1.7	1.8	1.8	1.2	1.0
Quick Ratio 31	1.2	•	1.5	0.9	1.6	1.5	1.5	1.4	1.4	1.3	1.3	0.8	0.7
Net Sales to Working Capital 32	9.5	•	17.4	107.9	7.2	7.4	6.8	7.2	6.1	5.7	5.4	13.6	•
Coverage Ratio 33	8.0	25.1	4.1	1.7	3.1	4.4	9.0	8.4	13.7	10.1	11.3	5.2	17.9
Total Asset Turnover 34	1.6	•	3.9	2.9	2.0	2.1	1.9	1.9	1.6	1.3	1.3	1.2	1.1
Inventory Turnover 35	47.7	•	166.6	45.8	60.5	66.5	60.7	53.5	38.7	23.7	37.0	22.0	97.3
Receivables Turnover 36	6.6	•	21.6	17.2	7.8	7.3	5.6	6.3	5.6	5.5	6.9	6.5	5.2
Total Liabilities to Net Worth 37	1.1	•	3.5	2.3	1.0	1.2	1.0	1.1	1.0	1.0	1.1	1.7	0.8
Current Assets to Working Capital 38	2.9	•	2.3	16.6	2.1	2.2	2.3	2.4	2.4	2.3	2.3	5.0	•
Current Liabilities to Working Capital 39	1.9	•	1.3	15.6	1.1	1.2	1.3	1.4	1.4	1.3	1.3	4.0	•
Working Capital to Net Sales 40	0.1	•	0.1	0.0	0.1	0.1	0.1	0.1	0.2	0.2	0.2	0.1	•
Inventory to Working Capital 41	0.2	•	0.0	1.4	0.1	0.1	0.1	0.1	0.1	0.2	0.1	0.7	•
Total Receipts to Cash Flow 42	11.6	3.9	6.4	11.4	10.9	17.9	16.0	15.3	13.0	9.6	11.8	13.1	9.7
Cost of Goods to Cash Flow 43	8.9	2.8	3.4	7.8	7.6	14.0	12.8	12.4	10.3	7.4	9.1	10.3	8.2
Cash Flow to Total Debt 44	0.3	•	0.8	0.4	0.4	0.2	0.2	0.2	0.2	0.3	0.2	0.1	0.3

Selected Financial Factors (in Percentages)

Debt Ratio 45	52.4	•	77.9	69.7	51.1	55.2	50.6	52.7	49.4	48.8	51.4	62.5	45.9
Return on Total Assets 46	8.3	•	16.6	4.8	4.6	5.6	8.5	8.3	9.1	9.5	8.3	6.4	8.9
Return on Equity Before Income Taxes 47	15.3	•	56.7	6.6	6.4	9.7	15.4	15.5	16.6	16.6	15.6	13.8	15.5
Return on Equity After Income Taxes 48	13.2	•	56.3	4.7	5.1	8.1	14.5	14.3	15.1	15.0	14.6	10.7	12.6
Profit Margin (Before Income Tax) 49	4.5	14.9	3.3	0.7	1.5	2.1	4.0	3.8	5.3	6.5	5.7	4.4	7.4
Profit Margin (After Income Tax) 50	3.8	10.4	3.2	0.5	1.2	1.7	3.8	3.5	4.9	5.9	5.3	3.4	6.0

Table II

Corporations with Net Income

HEAVY AND CIVIL ENGINEERING CONSTRUCTION

MONEY AMOUNTS AND SIZE OF ASSETS IN THOUSANDS OF DOLLARS

Item Description for Accounting Period 7/09 Through 6/10		Total	Zero Assets	Under 500	500 to 1,000	1,000 to 5,000	5,000 to 10,000	10,000 to 25,000	25,000 to 50,000	50,000 to 100,000	100,000 to 250,000	250,000 to 500,000	500,000 to 2,500,000	2,500,000 and over
Number of Enterprises	1	13481	1097	6509	1347	2480	1017	592	240	105	•	18	•	•
Revenues ($ in Thousands)														
Net Sales	2	159719220	2092114	7188104	4393201	12913071	15812504	18031009	17013498	12114970	•	9109588	•	•
Interest	3	202917	6105	4076	4525	29272	9209	9857	7489	8755	•	3222	•	•
Rents	4	88849	0	6015	8694	11797	264	6779	20993	11554	•	178	•	•
Royalties	5	75591	0	0	0	0	410	660	153	17569	•	0	•	•
Other Portfolio Income	6	953320	226435	49106	65114	96874	38273	59825	47773	42345	•	32471	•	•
Other Receipts	7	3325363	100991	120117	35588	165586	59729	153559	122475	24185	•	132023	•	•
Total Receipts	8	164365260	2425645	7367418	4507122	13216600	15920389	18261689	17212381	12219378	•	9277482	•	•
Average Total Receipts	9	12192	2211	1132	3346	5329	15654	30847	71718	116375	•	515416	•	•
Operating Costs/Operating Income (%)														
Cost of Operations	10	77.1	74.2	53.2	71.8	63.1	76.3	77.2	80.2	78.3	•	81.8	•	•
Salaries and Wages	11	3.6	2.7	8.5	4.2	5.6	3.0	3.2	2.4	3.0	•	2.1	•	•
Taxes Paid	12	1.6	1.3	2.6	1.5	2.2	1.5	1.5	1.2	1.2	•	0.9	•	•
Interest Paid	13	0.5	0.5	1.0	0.4	0.5	0.4	0.4	0.4	0.3	•	0.3	•	•
Depreciation	14	2.9	2.0	1.9	1.9	4.9	2.5	3.0	2.8	3.0	•	3.9	•	•
Amortization and Depletion	15	0.2	0.3	0.1	0.0	0.0	0.0	0.1	0.1	0.1	•	0.2	•	•
Pensions and Other Deferred Comp.	16	0.4	0.1	0.3	0.1	0.5	0.9	0.5	0.3	0.5	•	0.2	•	•
Employee Benefits	17	0.9	0.8	1.2	0.9	0.9	0.9	1.1	1.3	1.2	•	0.8	•	•
Advertising	18	0.1	0.0	0.4	0.1	0.2	0.0	0.1	0.1	0.1	•	0.0	•	•
Other Expenses	19	6.6	7.2	15.6	12.7	11.4	7.1	4.7	4.9	4.6	•	3.2	•	•
Officers' Compensation	20	2.1	0.5	8.4	2.8	5.3	2.4	2.4	1.7	1.5	•	1.3	•	•
Operating Margin	21	4.0	10.3	6.9	3.6	5.4	4.9	5.9	4.5	6.2	•	5.1	•	•
Operating Margin Before Officers' Comp.	22	6.1	10.8	15.4	6.3	10.7	7.3	8.3	6.3	7.7	•	6.4	•	•

Selected Average Balance Sheet ($ in Thousands)

	•	•	•	•	•	•	•	•	•	•
Net Receivables 23	1566	0	29	104	567	1774	4750	10001	16864	72379
Inventories 24	197	0	2	40	68	234	374	877	2235	10640
Net Property, Plant and Equipment 25	1712	0	49	258	797	1547	3513	7874	16727	100644
Total Assets 26	7201	0	203	771	2437	6834	15461	34235	69714	336177
Notes and Loans Payable 27	1049	0	104	209	502	1228	2200	5265	8454	38078
All Other Liabilities 28	2489	0	41	252	504	2265	4900	11659	22887	104977
Net Worth 29	3663	0	58	310	1431	3342	8361	17311	38373	193122

Selected Financial Ratios (Times to 1)

	•	•	•	•	•	•	•	•	•	•
Current Ratio 30	1.6	•	1.7	1.2	2.5	1.9	2.0	1.8	2.0	2.0
Quick Ratio 31	1.2	•	1.4	1.0	2.1	1.5	1.6	1.5	1.6	1.6
Net Sales to Working Capital 32	9.1	•	24.5	40.2	6.2	6.9	6.1	6.9	5.2	5.1
Coverage Ratio 33	14.9	50.8	10.7	15.6	16.0	14.6	19.8	15.6	23.4	24.2
Total Asset Turnover 34	1.6	•	5.4	4.2	2.1	2.3	2.0	2.1	1.7	1.5
Inventory Turnover 35	46.3	•	287.8	58.4	48.4	50.7	62.9	64.8	40.4	38.9
Receivables Turnover 36	6.6	•	48.1	24.6	8.3	7.0	5.6	6.8	5.7	6.8
Total Liabilities to Net Worth 37	1.0	•	2.5	1.5	0.7	1.0	0.8	1.0	0.8	0.7
Current Assets to Working Capital 38	2.8	•	2.5	5.3	1.7	2.1	2.1	2.2	2.0	2.0
Current Liabilities to Working Capital 39	1.8	•	1.5	4.3	0.7	1.1	1.1	1.2	1.0	1.0
Working Capital to Net Sales 40	0.1	•	0.0	0.0	0.2	0.1	0.2	0.1	0.2	0.2
Inventory to Working Capital 41	0.2	•	0.0	0.5	0.1	0.1	0.1	0.1	0.1	0.1
Total Receipts to Cash Flow 42	9.5	3.8	5.2	8.4	6.6	11.4	10.9	12.6	11.0	12.2
Cost of Goods to Cash Flow 43	7.4	2.8	2.8	6.0	4.1	8.7	8.4	10.1	8.7	10.0
Cash Flow to Total Debt 44	0.4	•	1.5	0.8	0.8	0.4	0.4	0.3	0.3	0.3

Selected Financial Factors (in Percentages)

	•	•	•	•	•	•	•	•	•	•
Debt Ratio 45	49.1	•	71.5	59.8	41.3	51.1	45.9	49.4	45.0	42.6
Return on Total Assets 46	12.4	•	56.7	27.9	17.7	13.5	14.8	12.5	12.1	10.8
Return on Equity Before Income Taxes 47	22.8	•	180.6	65.0	28.2	25.8	26.1	23.2	21.0	18.1
Return on Equity After Income Taxes 48	20.4	•	180.0	62.2	26.5	23.6	24.9	21.8	19.4	17.0
Profit Margin (Before Income Tax) 49	7.0	26.1	9.4	6.2	7.8	5.5	7.2	5.7	7.0	6.9
Profit Margin (After Income Tax) 50	6.3	20.2	9.4	5.9	7.3	5.1	6.8	5.3	6.4	6.5

28

Table I

Corporations with and without Net Income

LAND SUBDIVISION

MONEY AMOUNTS AND SIZE OF ASSETS IN THOUSANDS OF DOLLARS

Item Description for Accounting Period 7/09 Through 6/10		Total	Zero Assets	Under 500	500 to 1,000	1,000 to 5,000	5,000 to 10,000	10,000 to 25,000	25,000 to 50,000	50,000 to 100,000	100,000 to 250,000	250,000 to 500,000	500,000 to 2,500,000	2,500,000 and over
Number of Enterprises	1	37928	4291	17631	3855	9578	1469	713	231	84	44	17	14	0
Revenues ($ in Thousands)														
Net Sales	2	19637902	950155	2565460	660705	6159147	1441062	1791885	1795201	913553	1322345	1042652	995736	0
Interest	3	158638	3217	2310	4310	9109	8611	2247	8775	13435	12830	32281	61513	0
Rents	4	310937	33441	8223	2991	12924	33715	48962	9308	27086	65354	3567	65368	0
Royalties	5	18154	0	0	274	1474	71	15199	606	0	446	0	85	0
Other Portfolio Income	6	107932	2873	1979	1398	23645	15887	7677	25538	5780	8962	1745	12448	0
Other Receipts	7	773189	103287	144751	107933	86611	76563	63093	4905	61494	102348	60255	-38054	0
Total Receipts	8	21006752	1092973	2722723	777611	6292910	1575909	1929063	1844333	1021348	1512285	1140500	1097096	0
Average Total Receipts	9	554	255	154	202	657	1073	2706	7984	12159	34370	67088	78364	•
Operating Costs/Operating Income (%)														
Cost of Operations	10	83.3	143.2	64.3	79.7	80.8	97.0	99.8	78.3	80.2	75.1	44.3	107.4	•
Salaries and Wages	11	9.3	1.2	19.2	3.7	6.6	3.6	6.8	11.3	8.8	9.5	19.9	10.5	•
Taxes Paid	12	3.6	1.5	3.5	2.9	2.6	2.9	3.3	3.3	2.9	3.7	12.5	5.5	•
Interest Paid	13	6.8	4.0	3.1	8.0	4.0	9.5	8.4	6.1	8.5	6.4	13.1	23.2	•
Depreciation	14	3.1	2.0	2.2	0.9	2.8	1.7	3.0	3.0	4.5	5.1	5.4	4.8	•
Amortization and Depletion	15	0.3	1.8	0.0	0.0	0.0	0.1	0.3	0.1	0.4	0.4	0.6	1.0	•
Pensions and Other Deferred Comp.	16	0.4	•	•	0.1	0.7	0.1	0.2	0.2	0.1	1.0	0.9	0.2	•
Employee Benefits	17	0.9	0.0	2.3	0.0	0.5	0.2	0.6	0.6	0.9	1.5	0.6	1.8	•
Advertising	18	0.7	0.2	0.2	0.5	0.8	0.4	0.6	1.1	0.8	1.0	1.8	0.7	•
Other Expenses	19	21.9	33.4	22.3	39.5	12.7	10.8	23.0	16.9	22.8	25.4	30.5	64.6	•
Officers' Compensation	20	2.7	0.7	5.6	1.7	2.9	1.1	2.3	1.6	3.5	2.8	0.5	2.2	•
Operating Margin	21	•	•	•	•	•	•	•	•	•	•	•	•	•
Operating Margin Before Officers' Comp.	22	•	•	•	•	•	•	•	•	•	•	•	•	•

Selected Average Balance Sheet ($ in Thousands)

Net Receivables 23	131	0	7	29	127	106	994	2497	4053	13514	44412	28110
Inventories 24	640	0	24	312	498	2894	5250	8967	24544	34724	99750	180864
Net Property, Plant and Equipment 25	632	0	39	114	631	1851	4310	9496	16897	45698	88236	278308
Total Assets 26	2167	0	129	710	2106	6818	15124	34187	67679	153324	354731	703129
Notes and Loans Payable 27	1446	0	122	491	1483	5108	11479	20792	44332	85268	202864	369523
All Other Liabilities 28	314	0	26	79	205	869	1683	5862	9710	32588	78929	125292
Net Worth 29	407	0	-19	140	418	841	1963	7533	13637	35467	72938	208314

Selected Financial Ratios (Times to 1)

Current Ratio 30	2.4	•	2.3	4.2	2.4	2.9	2.1	1.8	3.7	1.8	3.4	1.9
Quick Ratio 31	0.5	•	0.7	0.8	0.5	0.2	0.4	0.5	0.7	0.6	1.0	0.6
Net Sales to Working Capital 32	0.8	•	3.5	0.5	1.1	0.4	0.6	1.1	0.4	1.0	0.5	0.5
Coverage Ratio 33	•	•	•	•	•	•	•	•	•	•	•	•
Total Asset Turnover 34	0.2	•	1.1	0.2	0.3	0.1	0.2	0.2	0.2	0.2	0.2	0.1
Inventory Turnover 35	0.7	•	3.9	0.4	1.0	0.3	0.5	0.7	0.4	0.7	0.3	0.4
Receivables Turnover 36	3.6	•	23.0	7.4	4.5	7.5	2.9	2.7	2.1	2.0	1.1	2.4
Total Liabilities to Net Worth 37	4.3	•	•	4.1	4.0	7.1	6.7	3.5	4.0	3.3	3.9	2.4
Current Assets to Working Capital 38	1.7	•	1.7	1.3	1.7	1.5	1.9	2.2	1.4	2.2	1.4	2.1
Current Liabilities to Working Capital 39	0.7	•	0.7	0.3	0.7	0.5	0.9	1.2	0.4	1.2	0.4	1.1
Working Capital to Net Sales 40	1.2	•	0.3	2.0	0.9	2.7	1.7	0.9	2.4	1.0	2.1	1.9
Inventory to Working Capital 41	0.9	•	0.6	0.8	0.9	1.1	1.2	1.1	0.8	1.0	0.7	1.0
Total Receipts to Cash Flow 42	•	•	77.5	5.4	•	•	•	•	•	20.8	16.2	•
Cost of Goods to Cash Flow 43	•	•	49.8	4.3	•	•	•	•	•	15.6	7.2	•
Cash Flow to Total Debt 44	•	•	0.0	0.1	•	•	•	•	•	0.0	0.0	•

Selected Financial Factors (in Percentages)

Debt Ratio 45	81.2	•	114.9	80.2	80.2	87.7	87.0	78.0	79.9	76.9	79.4	70.4
Return on Total Assets 46	•	•	•	•	•	•	•	•	•	•	•	•
Return on Equity Before Income Taxes 47	•	•	126.5	•	•	•	•	•	•	•	•	•
Return on Equity After Income Taxes 48	•	•	126.5	•	•	•	•	•	•	•	•	•
Profit Margin (Before Income Tax) 49	•	•	•	•	•	•	•	•	•	•	•	•
Profit Margin (After Income Tax) 50	•	•	•	•	•	•	•	•	•	•	•	•

Table II

Corporations with Net Income

LAND SUBDIVISION

MONEY AMOUNTS AND SIZE OF ASSETS IN THOUSANDS OF DOLLARS

Item Description for Accounting Period 7/09 Through 6/10	Total	Zero Assets	Under 500	500 to 1,000	1,000 to 5,000	5,000 to 10,000	10,000 to 25,000	25,000 to 50,000	50,000 to 100,000	100,000 to 250,000	250,000 to 500,000	500,000 to 2,500,000	2,500,000 and over
Number of Enterprises **1**	9486	635	3938	1405	2895	428	102	50	19	6	4	3	0
Revenues ($ in Thousands)													
Net Sales **2**	8119684	32943	791875	304264	3430316	822436	633809	704355	378902	730257	228553	61974	0
Interest **3**	94196	287	2027	4062	6794	5570	784	1319	12315	542	30734	29762	0
Rents **4**	143732	5953	110	0	2722	23289	31708	2126	24579	3017	592	49637	0
Royalties **5**	15221	0	0	274	0	0	14947	0	0	0	0	0	0
Other Portfolio Income **6**	31330	137	0	1370	4496	595	1102	18070	1658	374	1587	1944	0
Other Receipts **7**	728413	51224	11636	185004	149261	54420	23140	14410	47215	117616	60028	14456	0
Total Receipts **8**	9132576	90544	805648	494974	3593589	906310	705490	740280	464669	851806	321494	157773	0
Average Total Receipts **9**	963	143	205	352	1241	2118	6917	14806	24456	141968	80374	52591	•
Operating Costs/Operating Income (%)													
Cost of Operations **10**	71.4	114.7	64.7	54.2	77.1	77.3	65.7	68.1	63.0	73.7	35.9	66.1	•
Salaries and Wages **11**	5.1	1.2	4.5	5.4	2.4	3.6	5.5	7.9	6.4	7.0	34.6	12.0	•
Taxes Paid **12**	2.3	9.5	1.4	1.9	2.1	2.1	3.9	1.6	2.8	2.1	2.5	11.2	•
Interest Paid **13**	2.7	5.2	1.8	1.2	2.1	3.4	3.0	2.5	4.4	0.8	2.5	56.7	•
Depreciation **14**	2.7	4.2	5.2	0.2	2.3	2.0	3.5	0.8	1.4	2.1	6.1	23.3	•
Amortization and Depletion **15**	0.1	0.1	•	0.0	0.0	0.1	0.6	0.0	0.1	0.0	0.1	0.9	•
Pensions and Other Deferred Comp. **16**	0.3	•	•	0.2	0.0	0.1	0.2	0.3	0.0	1.5	3.3	•	•
Employee Benefits **17**	0.5	0.3	0.0	0.0	0.3	0.3	0.6	0.4	0.8	1.5	1.2	3.1	•
Advertising **18**	0.4	0.1	0.4	0.9	0.3	0.1	0.2	0.5	0.4	0.1	4.5	0.8	•
Other Expenses **19**	11.5	19.7	10.3	54.7	6.7	8.5	9.9	8.7	25.2	5.7	37.0	57.9	•
Officers' Compensation **20**	2.0	•	3.6	3.4	1.3	1.7	2.9	1.7	2.9	3.5	0.6	•	•
Operating Margin **21**	1.1	8.0	•	•	5.3	0.9	4.1	7.7	•	1.8	•	•	•
Operating Margin Before Officers' Comp. **22**	3.1	11.6	•	•	6.5	2.6	6.9	9.3	•	5.3	•	•	•

Selected Average Balance Sheet ($ in Thousands)

Net Receivables 23	155	0	20	19	107	163	1668	3445	5769	37311	63829	16832	•
Inventories 24	612	0	29	299	516	3411	6581	7851	22366	16291	129710	68744	•
Net Property, Plant and Equipment 25	694	0	44	195	677	2416	5005	9379	12912	30410	91748	456931	•
Total Assets 26	2065	0	116	675	2101	7059	15562	33399	67978	166942	361068	696560	•
Notes and Loans Payable 27	1164	0	87	487	1203	5267	9533	15108	30712	75608	155208	296298	•
All Other Liabilities 28	252	0	23	45	138	1038	1365	7501	8271	41717	35335	111488	•
Net Worth 29	650	0	6	143	760	754	4664	10791	28995	49617	170524	288774	•

Selected Financial Ratios (Times to 1)

Current Ratio 30	2.6	•	1.9	5.4	2.6	3.5	1.9	1.6	7.6	1.2	8.8	1.6
Quick Ratio 31	0.8	•	1.0	1.8	0.7	0.3	0.6	0.6	2.0	1.1	2.8	0.2
Net Sales to Working Capital 32	1.4	•	6.0	0.9	1.8	0.7	1.9	2.3	0.6	11.2	0.3	0.3
Coverage Ratio 33	6.0	24.2	6.3	35.0	5.9	4.3	6.2	6.0	4.5	24.1	6.0	1.4
Total Asset Turnover 34	0.4	•	1.7	0.3	0.6	0.3	0.4	0.4	0.3	0.7	0.2	0.0
Inventory Turnover 35	1.0	•	4.4	0.4	1.8	0.4	0.6	1.2	0.6	5.5	0.2	0.2
Receivables Turnover 36	4.8	•	13.7	18.4	7.5	14.6	3.7	3.1	3.8	2.9	0.8	1.2
Total Liabilities to Net Worth 37	2.2	•	17.0	3.7	1.8	8.4	2.3	2.1	1.3	2.4	1.1	1.4
Current Assets to Working Capital 38	1.6	•	2.1	1.2	1.6	1.4	2.1	2.6	1.2	5.3	1.1	2.8
Current Liabilities to Working Capital 39	0.6	•	1.1	0.2	0.6	0.4	1.1	1.6	0.2	4.3	0.1	1.8
Working Capital to Net Sales 40	0.7	•	0.2	1.1	0.5	1.4	0.5	0.4	1.5	0.1	3.7	3.6
Inventory to Working Capital 41	0.8	•	0.9	0.6	0.8	1.0	1.2	1.2	0.6	0.0	0.6	0.2
Total Receipts to Cash Flow 42	4.3	0.7	6.1	1.1	6.4	5.5	4.5	5.4	2.7	4.5	2.2	1.3
Cost of Goods to Cash Flow 43	3.1	0.8	4.0	0.6	5.0	4.2	3.0	3.7	1.7	3.3	0.8	0.9
Cash Flow to Total Debt 44	0.1	•	0.3	0.4	0.1	0.1	0.1	0.1	0.2	0.2	0.1	0.0

Selected Financial Factors (in Percentages)

Debt Ratio 45	68.6	•	94.4	78.8	63.8	89.3	70.0	67.7	57.3	70.3	52.8	58.5
Return on Total Assets 46	6.7	•	20.1	13.4	6.8	3.9	7.3	6.2	5.8	14.0	2.4	2.3
Return on Equity Before Income Taxes 47	17.7	•	304.3	61.4	15.7	28.3	20.5	15.9	10.5	45.2	4.2	1.6
Return on Equity After Income Taxes 48	17.0	•	304.1	60.9	15.1	27.4	19.0	15.2	9.7	45.2	3.3	1.1
Profit Margin (Before Income Tax) 49	13.5	119.8	9.7	40.5	10.0	11.1	15.4	12.1	15.3	18.4	12.4	22.6
Profit Margin (After Income Tax) 50	12.9	114.8	9.7	40.1	9.7	10.8	14.2	11.7	14.2	18.4	9.7	15.5

30

Table I
Corporations with and without Net Income

ELECTRICAL CONTRACTORS

MONEY AMOUNTS AND SIZE OF ASSETS IN THOUSANDS OF DOLLARS

Item Description for Accounting Period 7/09 Through 6/10	Total	Zero Assets	Under 500	500 to 1,000	1,000 to 5,000	5,000 to 10,000	10,000 to 25,000	25,000 to 50,000	50,000 to 100,000	100,000 to 250,000	250,000 to 500,000	500,000 to 2,500,000	2,500,000 and over
Number of Enterprises 1	55921	8149	40197	3231	3170	796	258	63	•	14	•	0	•
Revenues ($ in Thousands)													
Net Sales 2	82832395	811117	19371464	6542218	15799288	13289023	9443268	5205257	•	3571282	•	0	•
Interest 3	40536	119	4406	2870	12308	5888	7390	1933	•	762	•	0	•
Rents 4	15218	4	4411	581	3020	1694	441	4065	•	313	•	0	•
Royalties 5	0	0	0	0	0	0	0	0	•	0	•	0	•
Other Portfolio Income 6	109058	17976	39602	2626	7973	8777	3017	10991	•	8189	•	0	•
Other Receipts 7	895476	617	21359	-7648	24634	40423	38718	13124	•	41549	•	0	•
Total Receipts 8	83892683	829833	19441242	6540647	15847223	13345805	9492834	5235370	•	3622095	•	0	•
Average Total Receipts 9	1500	102	484	2024	4999	16766	36794	83101	•	258721	•	•	•
Operating Costs/Operating Income (%)													
Cost of Operations 10	66.5	40.7	52.5	65.7	69.9	68.6	72.7	77.5	•	74.0	•	•	•
Salaries and Wages 11	7.0	4.1	8.6	5.8	6.1	8.2	5.5	4.6	•	7.7	•	•	•
Taxes Paid 12	2.3	3.6	3.1	2.4	2.4	2.2	1.8	1.5	•	2.1	•	•	•
Interest Paid 13	0.4	1.5	0.5	0.4	0.3	0.3	0.3	0.3	•	0.6	•	•	•
Depreciation 14	1.3	2.0	1.3	1.3	1.2	1.5	0.9	1.0	•	1.2	•	•	•
Amortization and Depletion 15	0.1	0.1	0.0	0.1	0.1	0.0	0.0	0.1	•	0.3	•	•	•
Pensions and Other Deferred Comp. 16	0.9	0.3	1.2	0.4	0.5	1.9	0.7	0.4	•	0.5	•	•	•
Employee Benefits 17	2.7	0.3	1.3	2.5	3.4	3.8	3.6	2.2	•	1.1	•	•	•
Advertising 18	0.2	0.7	0.5	0.3	0.2	0.2	0.2	0.1	•	0.1	•	•	•
Other Expenses 19	9.6	36.8	16.5	13.4	7.0	6.4	5.2	4.1	•	5.5	•	•	•
Officers' Compensation 20	5.1	8.8	9.7	6.4	4.1	3.0	4.0	2.7	•	2.4	•	•	•
Operating Margin 21	3.7	1.0	4.8	1.2	4.9	3.9	5.1	5.7	•	4.6	•	•	•
Operating Margin Before Officers' Comp. 22	8.9	9.8	14.5	7.6	9.0	6.9	9.2	8.4	•	7.0	•	•	•

Selected Average Balance Sheet ($ in Thousands)

Net Receivables 23	211	0	25	251	711	2735	6974	16850	•	57166
Inventories 24	27	0	11	74	98	218	602	550	•	1739
Net Property, Plant and Equipment 25	88	0	23	115	238	782	1472	3301	•	11651
Total Assets 26	621	0	99	738	1912	6866	15951	36184	•	145982
Notes and Loans Payable 27	99	0	45	165	253	907	2073	3189	•	20869
All Other Liabilities 28	223	0	23	245	684	2690	6494	16942	•	72749
Net Worth 29	299	0	31	329	976	3270	7385	16054	•	52364

Selected Financial Ratios (Times to 1)

Current Ratio 30	1.9	•	1.9	1.9	2.1	1.8	2.0	1.8	•	1.5
Quick Ratio 31	1.5	•	1.4	1.5	1.7	1.5	1.6	1.6	•	1.3
Net Sales to Working Capital 32	7.1	•	16.0	7.7	6.5	7.1	5.4	6.3	•	7.5
Coverage Ratio 33	13.2	3.2	10.6	3.9	17.4	14.3	20.1	23.7	•	11.2
Total Asset Turnover 34	2.4	•	4.9	2.7	2.6	2.4	2.3	2.3	•	1.7
Inventory Turnover 35	37.0	•	22.7	18.0	35.4	52.6	44.2	116.3	•	108.6
Receivables Turnover 36	6.1	•	23.4	8.2	5.9	5.4	•	4.5	•	4.6
Total Liabilities to Net Worth 37	1.1	•	2.2	1.2	1.0	1.1	1.2	1.3	•	1.8
Current Assets to Working Capital 38	2.1	•	2.2	2.1	1.9	2.3	2.0	2.2	•	3.0
Current Liabilities to Working Capital 39	1.1	•	1.2	1.1	0.9	1.3	1.0	1.2	•	2.0
Working Capital to Net Sales 40	0.1	•	0.1	0.1	0.2	0.1	0.2	0.2	•	0.1
Inventory to Working Capital 41	0.1	•	0.4	0.3	0.1	0.1	0.1	0.0	•	0.1
Total Receipts to Cash Flow 42	8.2	2.8	5.3	8.5	10.0	10.8	11.5	11.9	•	11.3
Cost of Goods to Cash Flow 43	5.4	1.1	2.8	5.6	7.0	7.4	8.4	9.2	•	8.4
Cash Flow to Total Debt 44	0.6	•	1.3	0.6	0.5	0.4	0.4	0.3	•	0.2

Selected Financial Factors (in Percentages)

Debt Ratio 45	52.0	•	68.7	55.4	49.0	52.4	53.7	55.6	•	64.1
Return on Total Assets 46	12.9	•	27.6	4.3	14.4	11.3	13.6	14.9	•	11.5
Return on Equity Before Income Taxes 47	24.9	•	80.0	7.2	26.6	22.1	27.9	32.2	•	29.1
Return on Equity After Income Taxes 48	22.9	•	79.0	6.4	24.4	20.3	26.1	30.0	•	23.2
Profit Margin (Before Income Tax) 49	5.0	3.3	5.1	1.2	5.2	4.3	5.6	6.3	•	6.0
Profit Margin (After Income Tax) 50	4.6	3.3	5.1	1.0	4.8	4.0	5.3	5.8	•	4.8

Table II

Corporations with Net Income

ELECTRICAL CONTRACTORS

MONEY AMOUNTS AND SIZE OF ASSETS IN THOUSANDS OF DOLLARS

Item Description for Accounting Period 7/09 Through 6/10	Total	Zero Assets	Under 500	500 to 1,000	1,000 to 5,000	5,000 to 10,000	10,000 to 25,000	25,000 to 50,000	50,000 to 100,000	100,000 to 250,000	250,000 to 500,000	500,000 to 2,500,000	2,500,000 and over
Number of Enterprises **1**	33713	3145	25523	1994	2114	608	221	60	•	10	•	0	0
Revenues ($ in Thousands)													
Net Sales **2**	64316859	393907	13835378	3643607	12593084	10149287	8406226	5123276	•	2883147	•	0	0
Interest **3**	23095	0	1099	1824	6138	4954	2819	1921	•	530	•	0	0
Rents **4**	8308	4	0	0	1245	1694	439	4065	•	313	•	0	0
Royalties **5**	0	0	0	0	0	0	0	0	•	0	•	0	0
Other Portfolio Income **6**	85264	17976	24616	2230	3110	8122	2800	9221	•	7712	•	0	0
Other Receipts **7**	892190	458	18992	12661	20234	38903	32014	13018	•	40095	•	0	0
Total Receipts **8**	65325716	412345	13880085	3660322	12623811	10202960	8444298	5151501	•	2941797	•	0	0
Average Total Receipts **9**	1938	131	544	1836	5972	16781	38209	85858	•	294180	•	•	•
Operating Costs/Operating Income (%)													
Cost of Operations **10**	66.7	31.2	53.2	56.0	68.3	69.2	72.2	77.7	•	75.6	•	•	•
Salaries and Wages **11**	5.8	1.5	6.3	5.3	5.8	5.9	5.3	4.4	•	6.2	•	•	•
Taxes Paid **12**	2.2	1.9	3.0	2.0	2.3	2.1	1.8	1.5	•	2.3	•	•	•
Interest Paid **13**	0.3	0.8	0.4	0.3	0.3	0.4	0.2	0.3	•	0.1	•	•	•
Depreciation **14**	1.2	1.8	1.0	1.3	1.1	0.8	0.9	0.9	•	1.0	•	•	•
Amortization and Depletion **15**	0.1	•	0.0	0.0	0.0	0.0	0.0	0.0	•	0.1	•	•	•
Pensions and Other Deferred Comp. **16**	0.6	•	0.3	0.6	0.6	0.9	0.5	0.4	•	0.5	•	•	•
Employee Benefits **17**	2.6	0.6	1.3	3.2	3.0	4.4	3.2	2.2	•	0.7	•	•	•
Advertising **18**	0.2	0.7	0.4	0.3	0.2	0.1	0.2	0.1	•	0.0	•	•	•
Other Expenses **19**	8.4	32.5	14.6	12.8	6.7	6.6	4.9	4.0	•	4.6	•	•	•
Officers' Compensation **20**	5.2	5.5	10.1	8.7	4.1	3.1	4.2	2.7	•	2.8	•	•	•
Operating Margin **21**	6.7	23.4	9.4	9.5	7.7	6.4	6.5	5.9	•	6.1	•	•	•
Operating Margin Before Officers' Comp. **22**	11.9	28.9	19.5	18.2	11.8	9.5	10.8	8.6	•	8.9	•	•	•

Selected Average Balance Sheet ($ in Thousands)

Net Receivables 23	286	0	30	251	753	2997	7136	17417	•	62260
Inventories 24	32	0	12	78	103	248	586	532	•	1271
Net Property, Plant and Equipment 25	103	0	23	100	260	602	1489	3048	•	9814
Total Assets 26	812	0	108	734	2048	7040	16217	36228	•	137055
Notes and Loans Payable 27	87	0	30	85	221	737	1733	3026	•	13377
All Other Liabilities 28	292	0	22	181	627	3246	6647	17515	•	76411
Net Worth 29	432	0	56	467	1200	3057	7836	15687	•	47267

Selected Financial Ratios (Times to 1)

Current Ratio 30	2.1	•	2.4	2.9	2.5	1.7	2.0	1.9	•	1.6
Quick Ratio 31	1.7	•	2.0	2.3	2.1	1.4	1.7	1.6	•	1.4
Net Sales to Working Capital 32	6.2	•	12.5	4.6	6.0	6.9	5.3	6.2	•	7.0
Coverage Ratio 33	26.3	35.4	26.0	34.1	32.1	19.9	30.9	25.9	•	56.5
Total Asset Turnover 34	2.4	•	5.0	2.5	2.9	2.4	2.3	2.4	•	2.1
Inventory Turnover 35	39.5	•	24.1	13.2	39.5	46.5	46.9	124.7	•	172.0
Receivables Turnover 36	5.7	•	22.0	8.4	6.4	4.7	3.9	4.6	•	•
Total Liabilities to Net Worth 37	0.9	•	0.9	0.6	0.7	1.3	1.1	1.3	•	1.9
Current Assets to Working Capital 38	1.9	•	1.7	1.5	1.7	2.4	2.0	2.2	•	2.7
Current Liabilities to Working Capital 39	0.9	•	0.7	0.5	0.7	1.4	1.0	1.2	•	1.7
Working Capital to Net Sales 40	0.2	•	0.1	0.2	0.2	0.1	0.2	0.2	•	0.1
Inventory to Working Capital 41	0.1	•	0.3	0.2	0.1	0.1	0.1	0.0	•	0.0
Total Receipts to Cash Flow 42	6.9	1.7	4.6	5.0	8.0	8.3	10.1	11.7	•	10.1
Cost of Goods to Cash Flow 43	4.6	0.5	2.5	2.8	5.4	5.8	7.3	9.1	•	7.7
Cash Flow to Total Debt 44	0.7	•	2.3	1.4	0.9	0.5	0.4	0.4	•	0.3

Selected Financial Factors (in Percentages)

Debt Ratio 45	46.7	•	47.8	36.3	41.4	56.6	51.7	56.7	•	65.5
Return on Total Assets 46	20.1	•	50.7	25.5	23.9	17.2	16.9	15.8	•	16.7
Return on Equity Before Income Taxes 47	36.3	•	93.4	38.9	39.5	37.7	33.9	35.1	•	47.5
Return on Equity After Income Taxes 48	34.1	•	92.6	37.9	36.9	35.2	32.0	32.7	•	38.3
Profit Margin (Before Income Tax) 49	8.2	28.1	9.7	9.9	8.0	6.9	7.0	6.5	•	7.8
Profit Margin (After Income Tax) 50	7.7	28.0	9.6	9.7	7.4	6.4	6.6	6.0	•	6.3

Table I

Corporations with and without Net Income

PLUMBING, HEATING, AND AIR-CONDITIONING CONTRACTORS

MONEY AMOUNTS AND SIZE OF ASSETS IN THOUSANDS OF DOLLARS

Item Description for Accounting Period 7/09 Through 6/10	Total	Zero Assets	Under 500	500 to 1,000	1,000 to 5,000	5,000 to 10,000	10,000 to 25,000	25,000 to 50,000	50,000 to 100,000	100,000 to 250,000	250,000 to 500,000	500,000 to 2,500,000	2,500,000 and over
Number of Enterprises **1**	79643	9843	61464	3495	3781	568	380	75	•	7	•	•	•
Revenues ($ in Thousands)													
Net Sales **2**	107059187	1044417	31417574	8658374	23719360	10905000	12958076	5772235	•	1953699	•	•	•
Interest **3**	39533	398	3895	5669	12099	5378	4778	2405	•	748	•	•	•
Rents **4**	9500	6	1693	351	1153	80	5415	0	•	12	•	•	•
Royalties **5**	640	0	0	0	640	0	0	0	•	0	•	•	•
Other Portfolio Income **6**	91186	8271	44046	10605	12335	4477	6453	1704	•	296	•	•	•
Other Receipts **7**	368143	18090	121106	19552	97603	42851	11663	22981	•	6079	•	•	•
Total Receipts **8**	107568189	1071182	31588314	8694551	23843190	10957786	12986385	5799325	•	1960834	•	•	•
Average Total Receipts **9**	1351	109	514	2488	6306	19292	34175	77324	•	280119	•	•	•
Operating Costs/Operating Income (%)													
Cost of Operations **10**	65.9	40.2	50.2	60.9	70.4	74.7	75.8	78.3	•	78.6	•	•	•
Salaries and Wages **11**	8.6	8.7	13.3	10.7	6.5	7.6	5.6	4.2	•	5.3	•	•	•
Taxes Paid **12**	2.5	3.4	3.2	2.5	2.4	1.7	2.1	1.4	•	3.7	•	•	•
Interest Paid **13**	0.4	0.6	0.7	0.3	0.4	0.3	0.4	0.1	•	0.7	•	•	•
Depreciation **14**	1.1	1.7	1.8	1.0	0.9	0.8	0.6	0.5	•	0.5	•	•	•
Amortization and Depletion **15**	0.1	0.2	0.1	0.0	0.0	0.1	0.0	0.0	•	0.5	•	•	•
Pensions and Other Deferred Comp. **16**	0.5	0.6	0.3	0.7	0.6	0.4	0.9	0.6	•	0.3	•	•	•
Employee Benefits **17**	1.9	0.2	1.5	2.1	2.4	1.7	2.5	2.6	•	0.8	•	•	•
Advertising **18**	0.7	1.9	1.1	1.4	0.9	0.4	0.2	0.1	•	0.5	•	•	•
Other Expenses **19**	9.7	37.7	16.0	11.3	8.4	5.7	4.8	4.0	•	3.1	•	•	•
Officers' Compensation **20**	5.1	4.9	8.9	6.2	4.4	3.7	2.5	2.4	•	1.5	•	•	•
Operating Margin **21**	3.4	•	3.1	2.8	2.6	2.9	4.7	5.7	•	4.5	•	•	•
Operating Margin Before Officers' Comp. **22**	8.5	4.7	11.9	9.0	6.9	6.6	7.2	8.2	•	5.9	•	•	•

Selected Average Balance Sheet ($ in Thousands)

Net Receivables 23	167	0	19	214	886	3053	6942	14627	•	46562
Inventories 24	24	0	7	61	178	380	408	1883	•	723
Net Property, Plant and Equipment 25	55	0	26	121	264	698	1042	2147	•	6019
Total Assets 26	447	0	95	683	2299	6799	14369	32543	•	145030
Notes and Loans Payable 27	98	0	58	102	529	826	1707	1330	•	8199
All Other Liabilities 28	182	0	23	210	873	2996	6976	17189	•	99598
Net Worth 29	167	0	15	370	897	2977	5685	14024	•	37233

Selected Financial Ratios (Times to 1)

Current Ratio 30	1.7	•	1.8	2.2	1.9	1.9	1.7	1.6	•	1.2
Quick Ratio 31	1.4	•	1.4	1.9	1.5	1.5	1.4	1.4	•	1.0
Net Sales to Working Capital 32	9.4	•	20.4	8.6	7.6	7.3	6.9	7.5	•	13.8
Coverage Ratio 33	9.8	4.7	6.2	11.3	8.6	14.6	14.4	65.2	•	7.8
Total Asset Turnover 34	3.0	•	5.4	3.6	2.7	2.8	2.4	2.4	•	1.9
Inventory Turnover 35	36.5	•	35.0	24.8	24.9	37.7	63.4	32.0	•	303.6
Receivables Turnover 36	7.0	•	23.0	10.1	6.2	5.5	•	4.1	•	5.6
Total Liabilities to Net Worth 37	1.7	•	5.5	0.8	1.6	1.3	1.5	1.3	•	2.9
Current Assets to Working Capital 38	2.4	•	2.3	1.8	2.1	2.2	2.5	2.6	•	5.7
Current Liabilities to Working Capital 39	1.4	•	1.3	0.8	1.1	1.2	1.5	1.6	•	4.7
Working Capital to Net Sales 40	0.1	•	0.0	0.1	0.1	0.1	0.1	0.1	•	0.1
Inventory to Working Capital 41	0.2	•	0.3	0.2	0.2	0.1	0.1	0.1	•	0.0
Total Receipts to Cash Flow 42	8.8	•	5.9	8.4	11.0	14.3	11.9	11.0	•	15.1
Cost of Goods to Cash Flow 43	5.8	2.9	3.0	5.1	7.7	10.7	9.0	8.6	•	11.9
Cash Flow to Total Debt 44	0.5	1.2	1.1	0.9	0.4	0.4	0.3	0.4	•	0.2

Selected Financial Factors (in Percentages)

Debt Ratio 45	62.7	•	84.5	45.8	61.0	56.2	60.4	56.9	•	74.3
Return on Total Assets 46	13.0	•	23.2	12.9	9.5	10.4	12.5	14.9	•	10.7
Return on Equity Before Income Taxes 47	31.2	•	126.2	21.7	21.6	22.1	29.4	34.0	•	36.3
Return on Equity After Income Taxes 48	29.1	•	123.3	20.5	20.0	20.7	27.9	33.0	•	36.3
Profit Margin (Before Income Tax) 49	3.9	2.4	3.6	3.2	3.1	3.4	4.9	6.2	•	4.8
Profit Margin (After Income Tax) 50	3.6	2.0	3.5	3.1	2.9	3.2	4.6	6.0	•	4.8

Table II
Corporations with Net Income

PLUMBING, HEATING, AND AIR-CONDITIONING CONTRACTORS

MONEY AMOUNTS AND SIZE OF ASSETS IN THOUSANDS OF DOLLARS

Item Description for Accounting Period 7/09 Through 6/10	Total	Zero Assets	Under 500	500 to 1,000	1,000 to 5,000	5,000 to 10,000	10,000 to 25,000	25,000 to 50,000	50,000 to 100,000	100,000 to 250,000	250,000 to 500,000	500,000 to 2,500,000	2,500,000 and over
Number of Enterprises 1	47240	5262	35573	2684	2788	491	339	71	•	•	•	•	•
Revenues ($ in Thousands)													
Net Sales 2	89342887	686074	22618116	6746500	19816538	10219402	11953339	5239845	•	•	•	•	•
Interest 3	29639	368	2079	5442	9317	4357	2319	1666	•	•	•	•	•
Rents 4	8199	6	877	250	781	80	5415	0	•	•	•	•	•
Royalties 5	0	0	0	0	0	0	0	0					
Other Portfolio Income 6	67606	528	37211	6710	9774	4397	5570	1655	•	•	•	•	•
Other Receipts 7	329757	17354	113742	11390	75848	42524	18076	22148	•	•	•	•	•
Total Receipts 8	89778088	704330	22772025	6770292	19912258	10270760	11984719	5265314	•	•	•	•	•
Average Total Receipts 9	1900	134	640	2522	7142	20918	35353	74159	•	•	•	•	•
Operating Costs/Operating Income (%)													
Cost of Operations 10	66.7	39.0	49.7	59.0	70.3	73.9	75.2	78.2	•	•	•	•	•
Salaries and Wages 11	7.8	7.1	12.6	10.2	6.0	7.6	5.6	3.9	•	•	•	•	•
Taxes Paid 12	2.4	2.9	3.1	2.5	2.2	1.7	2.1	1.5	•	•	•	•	•
Interest Paid 13	0.3	0.7	0.5	0.3	0.3	0.3	0.3	0.1	•	•	•	•	•
Depreciation 14	1.0	1.7	1.6	0.9	0.8	0.8	0.6	0.5	•	•	•	•	•
Amortization and Depletion 15	0.1	0.0	0.0	0.0	0.0	0.1	0.0	0.0	•	•	•	•	•
Pensions and Other Deferred Comp. 16	0.5	•	0.3	0.8	0.7	0.4	0.9	0.6	•	•	•	•	•
Employee Benefits 17	1.8	0.3	1.6	1.9	2.1	1.7	2.4	2.6	•	•	•	•	•
Advertising 18	0.7	1.8	1.1	1.3	0.9	0.4	0.1	0.1	•	•	•	•	•
Other Expenses 19	8.7	32.4	14.6	11.2	8.3	5.7	4.7	3.7	•	•	•	•	•
Officers' Compensation 20	4.6	5.8	8.1	6.5	4.1	3.7	2.5	2.6	•	•	•	•	•
Operating Margin 21	5.4	8.4	6.9	5.5	4.2	3.8	5.5	6.4	•	•	•	•	•
Operating Margin Before Officers' Comp. 22	10.0	14.1	14.9	12.0	8.3	7.4	8.1	8.9	•	•	•	•	•

Selected Average Balance Sheet ($ in Thousands)

Net Receivables 23	243	0	18	198	977	3300	7193	14399
Inventories 24	31	0	6	54	196	411	379	1887
Net Property, Plant and Equipment 25	68	0	27	107	248	735	1050	2013
Total Assets 26	618	0	98	682	2408	6990	14455	32659
Notes and Loans Payable 27	105	0	51	80	441	947	1497	1233
All Other Liabilities 28	263	0	24	180	969	3241	7132	17056
Net Worth 29	251	0	23	423	998	2803	5826	14370

Selected Financial Ratios (Times to 1)

Current Ratio 30	1.7	•	1.7	2.6	1.9	1.7	1.7	1.6
Quick Ratio 31	1.5	•	1.5	2.2	1.5	1.4	1.4	1.4
Net Sales to Working Capital 32	9.2	•	27.0	7.6	7.6	8.3	6.9	7.0
Coverage Ratio 33	18.4	17.2	15.2	22.8	14.9	17.2	23.5	95.1
Total Asset Turnover 34	3.1	•	6.5	3.7	3.0	3.0	2.4	2.3
Inventory Turnover 35	40.2	•	49.1	27.5	25.5	37.5	69.9	30.6
Receivables Turnover 36	6.7	•	26.3	11.3	6.4	5.6	4.2	3.9
Total Liabilities to Net Worth 37	1.5	•	3.2	0.6	1.4	1.5	1.5	1.3
Current Assets to Working Capital 38	2.3	•	2.4	1.6	2.1	2.3	2.4	2.6
Current Liabilities to Working Capital 39	1.3	•	1.4	0.6	1.1	1.3	1.4	1.6
Working Capital to Net Sales 40	0.1	•	0.0	0.1	0.1	0.1	0.1	0.1
Inventory to Working Capital 41	0.1	•	0.2	0.2	0.2	0.1	0.1	0.1
Total Receipts to Cash Flow 42	8.1	2.5	5.1	7.0	9.5	12.8	10.9	10.4
Cost of Goods to Cash Flow 43	5.4	1.0	2.5	4.1	6.7	9.4	8.2	8.2
Cash Flow to Total Debt 44	0.6	•	1.7	1.4	0.5	0.4	0.4	0.4

Selected Financial Factors (in Percentages)

Debt Ratio 45	59.4	•	76.2	38.0	58.6	59.9	59.7	56.0
Return on Total Assets 46	18.9	•	52.6	22.6	14.7	13.5	14.7	15.6
Return on Equity Before Income Taxes 47	44.0	•	206.0	34.8	33.2	31.8	35.0	35.2
Return on Equity After Income Taxes 48	41.6	•	202.9	33.5	31.2	30.0	33.3	34.1
Profit Margin (Before Income Tax) 49	5.8	11.0	7.6	5.9	4.7	4.3	5.8	6.8
Profit Margin (After Income Tax) 50	5.5	10.5	7.4	5.6	4.4	4.0	5.5	6.6

Table I

Corporations with and without Net Income

OTHER SPECIALTY TRADE CONTRACTORS

MONEY AMOUNTS AND SIZE OF ASSETS IN THOUSANDS OF DOLLARS

Item Description for Accounting Period 7/09 Through 6/10		Total	Zero Assets	Under 500	500 to 1,000	1,000 to 5,000	5,000 to 10,000	10,000 to 25,000	25,000 to 50,000	50,000 to 100,000	100,000 to 250,000	250,000 to 500,000	500,000 to 2,500,000	2,500,000 and over
Number of Enterprises	1	322348	61245	228677	15158	14086	1777	1061	208	80	35	13	8	0
Revenues ($ in Thousands)														
Net Sales	2	312369965	7454748	107897059	28239907	67808010	26568123	32161108	13139279	10050719	7167731	6687413	5195868	0
Interest	3	131659	382	17059	12302	35113	12045	15032	6755	7775	4503	6192	14501	0
Rents	4	298523	401	38619	2102	23004	5201	10761	8279	4310	550	0	205297	0
Royalties	5	6591	0	0	0	0	139	0	2912	10	2	852	2677	0
Other Portfolio Income	6	786863	40723	189976	111093	202885	90541	46142	29630	20727	30187	6925	18034	0
Other Receipts	7	1455451	-72851	210015	79031	451461	150264	185335	103895	139716	47666	123470	37447	0
Total Receipts	8	315049052	7423403	108352728	28444435	68520473	26826313	32418378	13290750	10223257	7250639	6824852	5473824	0
Average Total Receipts	9	977	121	474	1877	4864	15096	30555	63898	127791	207161	524989	684228	•
Operating Costs/Operating Income (%)														
Cost of Operations	10	63.6	36.4	52.3	56.7	68.5	77.0	75.3	77.4	76.8	74.0	74.7	78.2	•
Salaries and Wages	11	7.9	6.1	11.1	10.3	6.6	4.8	4.5	4.4	5.4	6.2	5.4	6.1	•
Taxes Paid	12	2.2	2.5	2.8	2.6	2.0	1.5	1.7	1.5	1.4	1.5	1.3	1.8	•
Interest Paid	13	0.7	0.8	0.6	0.8	0.7	0.5	0.4	0.6	0.7	1.3	1.3	4.3	•
Depreciation	14	2.2	1.5	2.1	2.4	2.3	1.8	2.1	2.7	2.0	3.6	2.5	3.5	•
Amortization and Depletion	15	0.1	0.0	0.1	0.1	0.0	0.0	0.1	0.2	0.4	0.5	0.5	1.7	•
Pensions and Other Deferred Comp.	16	0.4	0.0	0.3	0.5	0.4	0.3	0.6	0.3	0.3	0.3	0.5	0.2	•
Employee Benefits	17	1.7	1.7	1.7	1.4	1.7	1.8	2.5	1.8	1.6	1.1	0.3	1.6	•
Advertising	18	0.5	0.7	0.8	0.7	0.2	0.1	0.2	0.2	0.1	0.1	0.1	0.1	•
Other Expenses	19	13.6	41.1	18.2	17.5	11.6	7.1	6.9	7.4	8.3	5.6	7.1	6.1	•
Officers' Compensation	20	4.7	6.4	6.8	5.5	4.5	2.8	2.4	1.7	2.1	1.9	1.1	1.0	•
Operating Margin	21	2.4	4.0	3.1	1.5	1.4	2.2	3.5	1.8	1.0	3.9	5.3	•	•
Operating Margin Before Officers' Comp.	22	7.1	10.4	9.9	7.1	5.9	5.0	5.8	3.5	3.1	5.9	6.4	•	•

Selected Average Balance Sheet ($ in Thousands)

Net Receivables 23	111	0	12	151	757	2889	5949	12274	24161	41723	95506	177687	•
Inventories 24	17	0	5	39	111	348	538	1041	1962	4660	6279	27183	•
Net Property, Plant and Equipment 25	83	0	28	189	483	1183	2759	7398	11772	30652	66187	138362	•
Total Assets 26	367	0	85	687	2141	6767	15265	34741	72694	154994	334529	904026	•
Notes and Loans Payable 27	117	0	50	230	603	1511	2680	7729	12345	32357	93084	483188	•
All Other Liabilities 28	113	0	22	159	647	2363	5596	12399	29247	61503	107063	167890	•
Net Worth 29	137	0	13	298	891	2893	6988	14613	31102	61134	134383	252948	•

Selected Financial Ratios (Times to 1)

Current Ratio 30	1.7	•	1.4	2.1	1.8	1.7	1.8	1.7	1.6	1.7	1.7	1.4	•
Quick Ratio 31	1.4	•	1.1	1.6	1.5	1.4	1.5	1.4	1.3	1.4	1.4	1.1	•
Net Sales to Working Capital 32	10.3	•	39.9	8.8	7.3	6.9	6.3	7.1	6.8	5.3	7.1	8.6	•
Coverage Ratio 33	5.5	4.8	6.4	4.0	4.7	7.2	10.5	5.6	4.8	4.9	6.8	1.2	•
Total Asset Turnover 34	2.6	•	5.5	2.7	2.2	2.2	2.0	1.8	1.7	1.3	1.5	0.7	•
Inventory Turnover 35	36.6	•	46.9	26.9	29.8	33.1	42.4	47.0	49.2	32.5	61.2	18.7	•
Receivables Turnover 36	7.8	•	38.3	11.4	5.9	4.7	4.4	4.2	4.4	4.0	4.5	•	•
Total Liabilities to Net Worth 37	1.7	•	5.4	1.3	1.4	1.3	1.2	1.4	1.3	1.5	1.5	2.6	•
Current Assets to Working Capital 38	2.4	•	3.5	1.9	2.2	2.4	2.3	2.5	2.7	2.5	2.4	3.7	•
Current Liabilities to Working Capital 39	1.4	•	2.5	0.9	1.2	1.4	1.3	1.5	1.7	1.5	1.4	2.7	•
Working Capital to Net Sales 40	0.1	•	0.0	0.1	0.1	0.2	0.2	0.1	0.1	0.2	0.1	0.1	•
Inventory to Working Capital 41	0.2	•	0.4	0.2	0.1	0.1	0.1	0.1	0.1	0.1	0.1	0.4	•
Total Receipts to Cash Flow 42	7.5	2.5	5.5	6.7	9.7	14.3	12.3	13.7	11.7	13.5	9.1	24.5	•
Cost of Goods to Cash Flow 43	4.8	0.9	2.9	3.8	6.6	11.0	9.2	10.6	9.0	10.0	6.8	19.2	•
Cash Flow to Total Debt 44	0.6	•	1.2	0.7	0.4	0.3	0.3	0.2	0.3	0.2	0.3	0.0	•

Selected Financial Factors (in Percentages)

Debt Ratio 45	62.7	•	84.3	56.7	58.4	57.3	54.2	57.9	57.2	60.6	59.8	72.0	•
Return on Total Assets 46	10.4	•	23.1	8.1	7.0	8.1	9.3	6.4	5.8	8.4	13.3	3.7	•
Return on Equity Before Income Taxes 47	22.9	•	124.7	14.1	13.3	16.3	18.4	12.5	10.7	17.0	28.2	2.1	•
Return on Equity After Income Taxes 48	21.6	•	122.7	13.2	12.3	14.8	17.4	11.6	7.9	15.4	26.0	2.0	•
Profit Margin (Before Income Tax) 49	3.2	3.2	3.5	2.3	2.5	3.1	4.3	2.9	2.7	5.1	7.4	0.8	•
Profit Margin (After Income Tax) 50	3.1	3.1	3.5	2.1	2.3	2.9	4.0	2.7	2.0	4.6	6.8	0.8	•

35

Table II

Corporations with Net Income

OTHER SPECIALTY TRADE CONTRACTORS

MONEY AMOUNTS AND SIZE OF ASSETS IN THOUSANDS OF DOLLARS

Item Description for Accounting Period 7/09 Through 6/10	Total	Zero Assets	Under 500	500 to 1,000	1,000 to 5,000	5,000 to 10,000	10,000 to 25,000	25,000 to 50,000	50,000 to 100,000	100,000 to 250,000	250,000 to 500,000	500,000 to 2,500,000	2,500,000 and over
Number of Enterprises 1	203374	39133	143408	9298	9280	1206	809	144	60	22	•	•	0
Revenues ($ in Thousands)													
Net Sales 2	227269906	5487453	76074239	20682307	47094735	19870292	26526913	9889078	8136323	5171667	•	•	0
Interest 3	80004	1	6272	9610	20369	9073	11846	5339	7038	2223	•	•	0
Rents 4	37195	0	3963	1009	11026	3279	6028	7547	4115	227	•	•	0
Royalties 5	1003	0	0	0	0	139	0	0	10	2	•	•	0
Other Portfolio Income 6	445960	6086	123600	65462	102547	49183	36198	14765	19205	22942	•	•	0
Other Receipts 7	1152668	20268	147237	63579	315672	105969	118682	78733	133419	24340	•	•	0
Total Receipts 8	228986736	5513808	76355311	20821967	47544349	20037935	26699667	9995462	8300110	5221401	•	•	0
Average Total Receipts 9	1126	141	532	2239	5123	16615	33003	69413	138335	237336	•	•	•
Operating Costs/Operating Income (%)													
Cost of Operations 10	62.4	29.2	51.4	54.5	66.6	74.2	74.9	75.8	76.5	71.9	•	•	•
Salaries and Wages 11	7.3	5.2	10.0	10.8	6.3	4.8	4.2	4.0	4.7	5.5	•	•	•
Taxes Paid 12	2.1	2.4	2.7	2.5	1.9	1.5	1.6	1.5	1.3	1.6	•	•	•
Interest Paid 13	0.5	0.5	0.6	0.6	0.5	0.3	0.3	0.3	0.4	0.3	•	•	•
Depreciation 14	1.7	1.2	1.6	1.8	1.9	1.5	1.6	2.1	1.5	2.9	•	•	•
Amortization and Depletion 15	0.1	0.0	0.1	0.1	0.0	0.0	0.0	0.0	0.1	0.1	•	•	•
Pensions and Other Deferred Comp. 16	0.4	0.0	0.2	0.3	0.5	0.4	0.7	0.3	0.3	0.3	•	•	•
Employee Benefits 17	1.6	0.4	1.5	1.3	1.5	1.9	2.6	1.8	1.3	1.1	•	•	•
Advertising 18	0.4	0.7	0.8	0.7	0.2	0.2	0.2	0.2	0.1	0.1	•	•	•
Other Expenses 19	12.5	40.5	17.1	16.1	10.6	6.7	5.8	7.1	7.0	5.1	•	•	•
Officers' Compensation 20	4.4	6.1	6.3	5.0	4.4	3.2	2.5	1.8	2.0	2.2	•	•	•
Operating Margin 21	6.6	13.7	7.8	6.4	5.6	5.3	5.7	5.1	4.9	9.2	•	•	•
Operating Margin Before Officers' Comp. 22	11.1	19.8	14.1	11.3	10.0	8.5	8.2	6.9	6.9	11.3	•	•	•

Selected Average Balance Sheet ($ in Thousands)

Net Receivables 23	124	0	12	154	773	2753	6360	13336	24398	48270
Inventories 24	18	0	5	32	98	437	545	1113	1794	3623
Net Property, Plant and Equipment 25	75	0	27	157	425	1076	2290	6517	10148	27405
Total Assets 26	380	0	90	692	2075	6569	15470	34981	71887	158858
Notes and Loans Payable 27	88	0	40	193	453	1002	2094	5284	6393	14032
All Other Liabilities 28	119	0	20	151	599	2193	5673	13055	31255	63609
Net Worth 29	174	0	29	348	1023	3374	7703	16641	34238	81218

Selected Financial Ratios (Times to 1)

Current Ratio 30	1.9	•	1.6	2.3	2.2	2.0	1.9	1.7	1.7	1.8
Quick Ratio 31	1.6	•	1.2	1.8	1.8	1.6	1.6	1.5	1.5	1.6
Net Sales to Working Capital 32	9.3	•	33.1	9.5	6.3	6.4	5.9	6.7	6.5	4.7
Coverage Ratio 33	16.0	27.5	15.8	12.4	14.5	19.2	21.7	20.1	19.7	39.2
Total Asset Turnover 34	2.9	•	5.9	3.2	2.4	2.5	2.1	2.0	1.9	1.5
Inventory Turnover 35	39.6	•	52.6	38.4	34.7	28.0	45.1	46.8	57.8	46.7
Receivables Turnover 36	7.7	•	47.1	13.3	6.0	4.8	4.3	3.7	4.2	•
Total Liabilities to Net Worth 37	1.2	•	2.1	1.0	1.0	0.9	1.0	1.1	1.1	1.0
Current Assets to Working Capital 38	2.1	•	2.7	1.8	1.9	2.0	2.1	2.4	2.5	2.3
Current Liabilities to Working Capital 39	1.1	•	1.7	0.8	0.9	1.0	1.1	1.4	1.5	1.3
Working Capital to Net Sales 40	0.1	•	0.0	0.1	0.2	0.2	0.2	0.1	0.2	0.2
Inventory to Working Capital 41	0.1	•	0.3	0.2	0.1	0.1	0.1	0.1	0.1	0.1
Total Receipts to Cash Flow 42	6.0	2.0	4.5	5.4	7.2	10.7	10.4	9.9	8.3	8.3
Cost of Goods to Cash Flow 43	3.7	0.6	2.3	2.9	4.8	7.9	7.8	7.5	6.3	6.0
Cash Flow to Total Debt 44	0.9	•	1.9	1.2	0.7	0.5	0.4	0.4	0.4	0.4

Selected Financial Factors (in Percentages)

Debt Ratio 45	54.3	•	67.7	49.8	50.7	48.6	50.2	52.4	52.4	48.9
Return on Total Assets 46	23.2	•	51.7	24.5	17.3	16.2	14.1	12.7	13.6	15.4
Return on Equity Before Income Taxes 47	47.5	•	150.3	44.9	32.7	29.9	27.0	25.4	27.1	29.3
Return on Equity After Income Taxes 48	45.9	•	148.8	43.7	31.4	28.1	25.8	24.2	23.8	27.3
Profit Margin (Before Income Tax) 49	7.4	14.2	8.2	7.0	6.6	6.1	6.4	6.2	6.9	10.1
Profit Margin (After Income Tax) 50	7.1	14.1	8.1	6.8	6.3	5.7	6.0	5.9	6.0	9.4

Table I

Corporations with and without Net Income

ANIMAL FOOD AND GRAIN AND OILSEED MILLING

MONEY AMOUNTS AND SIZE OF ASSETS IN THOUSANDS OF DOLLARS

Item Description for Accounting Period 7/09 Through 6/10	Total	Zero Assets	Under 500	500 to 1,000	1,000 to 5,000	5,000 to 10,000	10,000 to 25,000	25,000 to 50,000	50,000 to 100,000	100,000 to 250,000	250,000 to 500,000	500,000 to 2,500,000	2,500,000 and over
Number of Enterprises **1**	1851	12	1193	0	323	121	81	55	23	28	5	5	5
Revenues ($ in Thousands)													
Net Sales **2**	117809850	509382	144597	0	3488474	3685934	2980295	5106440	4023724	8276587	1430135	4272022	8389260
Interest **3**	292907	0	323	0	1668	174	2016	2100	2063	12276	7141	7104	258042
Rents **4**	207988	0	0	0	1087	0	0	515	258	332	214	525	205058
Royalties **5**	412751	0	0	0	0	0	0	0	311	1885	486	58295	351774
Other Portfolio Income **6**	260539	4835	0	0	690	88	1070	1140	980	6123	36875	24270	184469
Other Receipts **7**	1717106	22692	0	0	3687	2458	32529	57276	30918	45429	6360	-86761	1602514
Total Receipts **8**	120701141	536909	144920	0	3495606	3688654	3015910	5167471	4058254	8342632	1481211	4275455	8649417
Average Total Receipts **9**	65209	44742	121	•	10822	30485	37233	93954	176446	297951	296242	855091	17298823
Operating Costs/Operating Income (%)													
Cost of Operations **10**	80.0	77.6	66.0	•	80.9	82.7	80.9	82.8	81.1	80.8	73.8	78.2	79.7
Salaries and Wages **11**	2.9	4.5	5.1	•	3.6	4.2	4.1	3.5	3.5	2.7	5.8	2.8	2.6
Taxes Paid **12**	0.6	0.9	8.1	•	0.6	0.6	0.5	0.7	0.7	0.8	1.0	0.6	0.6
Interest Paid **13**	1.5	1.9	0.4	•	0.5	0.2	0.4	0.5	0.5	1.0	3.3	1.5	1.7
Depreciation **14**	1.9	1.8	1.7	•	1.3	1.7	1.6	2.4	1.9	2.6	4.6	4.6	1.7
Amortization and Depletion **15**	0.2	0.1	0.2	•	0.0	0.0	0.0	0.1	0.1	0.3	1.1	0.7	0.2
Pensions and Other Deferred Comp. **16**	0.5	0.4	•	•	0.0	0.1	0.2	0.3	0.4	0.3	0.4	0.5	0.5
Employee Benefits **17**	0.8	0.8	4.2	•	0.5	0.6	0.5	0.7	0.7	0.8	1.3	0.9	0.8
Advertising **18**	5.1	0.1	0.1	•	1.5	0.1	0.5	0.5	0.5	0.3	1.0	1.2	6.9
Other Expenses **19**	4.8	5.7	22.5	•	6.8	8.2	4.6	5.2	5.7	5.2	7.5	6.0	4.4
Officers' Compensation **20**	0.4	1.9	9.4	•	1.5	0.1	1.2	0.9	0.6	0.9	1.0	1.0	0.2
Operating Margin **21**	1.3	4.2	•	•	2.8	1.5	5.4	2.3	4.4	4.4	•	2.2	0.6
Operating Margin Before Officers' Comp. **22**	1.7	6.1	•	•	4.3	1.6	6.6	3.2	5.0	5.3	0.3	3.1	0.8

Selected Average Balance Sheet ($ in Thousands)

Net Receivables 23	3713	0	3	•	767	2393	4050	6664	16833	25943	51254	63097	790474
Inventories 24	5177	0	7	•	1131	677	3350	7754	18741	30285	40744	71329	1318017
Net Property, Plant and Equipment 25	9298	0	10	•	735	2377	4344	12339	22779	49565	91253	346470	2308515
Total Assets 26	42269	0	29	6.2	2987	7052	14512	34289	72949	155801	381663	842578	12232972
Notes and Loans Payable 27	17258	0	108	•	1913	1850	2594	9403	15768	36888	120287	234160	5416045
All Other Liabilities 28	12309	0	18	•	876	3138	3385	10247	18949	38627	87543	184540	3677049
Net Worth 29	12702	0	-96	•	197	2065	8533	14639	38231	80285	173832	423877	3139878

Selected Financial Ratios (Times to 1)

Current Ratio 30	1.3	•	0.9	•	1.2	1.0	2.0	1.7	1.9	1.9	1.8	1.9	1.2
Quick Ratio 31	0.6	•	0.4	•	0.5	0.8	1.3	0.8	1.0	1.0	1.2	0.8	0.4
Net Sales to Working Capital 32	19.2	•	•	•	28.7	•	8.5	12.2	8.7	8.9	4.6	9.3	26.9
Coverage Ratio 33	4.0	6.2	•	•	6.5	9.8	17.3	7.9	12.5	6.2	1.9	2.7	3.7
Total Asset Turnover 34	1.5	•	4.2	•	3.6	4.3	2.5	2.7	2.4	1.9	0.7	1.0	1.4
Inventory Turnover 35	9.8	•	10.8	•	7.7	37.2	8.9	9.9	7.6	7.9	5.2	9.4	10.2
Receivables Turnover 36	17.9	•	37.2	•	16.3	16.1	8.0	14.0	9.9	10.8	5.9	11.6	23.2
Total Liabilities to Net Worth 37	2.3	•	•	•	14.1	2.4	0.7	1.3	0.9	0.9	1.2	1.0	2.9
Current Assets to Working Capital 38	3.9	•	•	•	5.7	•	2.0	2.5	2.1	2.1	2.2	2.1	5.2
Current Liabilities to Working Capital 39	2.9	•	•	•	4.7	•	1.0	1.5	1.1	1.1	1.2	1.1	4.2
Working Capital to Net Sales 40	0.1	•	•	•	0.0	•	0.1	0.1	0.1	0.1	0.2	0.1	0.0
Inventory to Working Capital 41	1.6	•	•	•	3.2	•	0.7	1.1	0.8	0.9	0.6	0.8	2.2
Total Receipts to Cash Flow 42	14.3	7.1	30.4	•	11.9	15.4	9.9	13.6	10.5	10.8	11.7	15.4	15.5
Cost of Goods to Cash Flow 43	11.5	5.5	20.1	•	9.6	12.7	8.0	11.3	8.5	8.8	8.7	12.1	12.4
Cash Flow to Total Debt 44	0.2	•	0.0	•	0.3	0.4	0.6	0.3	0.4	0.5	0.1	0.1	0.1

Selected Financial Factors (in Percentages)

Debt Ratio 45	70.0	•	429.7	•	93.4	70.7	41.2	57.3	47.6	48.5	54.5	49.7	74.3
Return on Total Assets 46	9.0	•	•	•	12.7	7.5	17.8	10.9	13.7	11.7	4.8	4.0	8.8
Return on Equity Before Income Taxes 47	22.4	•	22.1	•	162.1	23.1	28.6	22.3	24.1	19.1	5.1	4.9	24.9
Return on Equity After Income Taxes 48	15.8	•	22.2	•	160.0	19.3	27.4	21.4	20.7	15.7	4.3	3.7	16.1
Profit Margin (Before Income Tax) 49	4.5	9.6	•	•	3.0	1.6	6.6	3.5	5.3	5.2	3.1	2.4	4.7
Profit Margin (After Income Tax) 50	3.1	8.0	•	•	2.9	1.3	6.4	3.4	4.5	4.3	2.6	1.8	3.0

Table II
Corporations with Net Income

ANIMAL FOOD AND GRAIN AND OILSEED MILLING

MONEY AMOUNTS AND SIZE OF ASSETS IN THOUSANDS OF DOLLARS

Item Description for Accounting Period 7/09 Through 6/10	Total	Zero Assets	Under 500	500 to 1,000	1,000 to 5,000	5,000 to 10,000	10,000 to 25,000	25,000 to 50,000	50,000 to 100,000	100,000 to 250,000	250,000 to 500,000	500,000 to 2,500,000	2,500,000 and over
Number of Enterprises **1**	910	•	347	0	320	62	68	47	•	24	•	•	•
Revenues ($ in Thousands)													
Net Sales **2**	108361973	•	144358	0	3488474	1535457	2521249	3893163	•	6622519	•	•	•
Interest **3**	283115	•	323	0	1668	174	1832	1294	•	8690	•	•	•
Rents **4**	207041	•	0	0	1087	0	0	26	•	17	•	•	•
Royalties **5**	410127	•	0	0	0	0	0	0	•	1885	•	•	•
Other Portfolio Income **6**	257030	•	0	0	690	88	252	678	•	5889	•	•	•
Other Receipts **7**	1793625	•	1	0	3687	447	32409	45919	•	40197	•	•	•
Total Receipts **8**	111312911	•	144682	0	3495606	1536166	2555742	3941080	•	6679197	•	•	•
Average Total Receipts **9**	122322	•	417	•	10924	24777	37584	83853	•	278300	•	•	•
Operating Costs/Operating Income (%)													
Cost of Operations **10**	79.8	•	66.0	•	80.9	89.1	79.4	80.7	•	79.1	•	•	•
Salaries and Wages **11**	2.8	•	5.1	•	3.6	2.5	4.0	3.7	•	2.7	•	•	•
Taxes Paid **12**	0.7	•	7.9	•	0.6	0.5	0.5	0.7	•	0.7	•	•	•
Interest Paid **13**	1.5	•	0.4	•	0.5	0.1	0.2	0.4	•	0.9	•	•	•
Depreciation **14**	1.8	•	0.3	•	1.3	0.4	1.6	2.8	•	2.6	•	•	•
Amortization and Depletion **15**	0.2	•	•	•	0.0	•	0.0	0.2	•	0.3	•	•	•
Pensions and Other Deferred Comp. **16**	0.5	•	•	•	0.0	0.2	0.2	0.3	•	0.3	•	•	•
Employee Benefits **17**	0.8	•	4.2	•	0.5	0.2	0.5	0.8	•	1.0	•	•	•
Advertising **18**	5.5	•	0.1	•	1.5	0.1	0.5	0.6	•	0.4	•	•	•
Other Expenses **19**	4.6	•	4.7	•	6.1	2.4	4.2	4.9	•	5.1	•	•	•
Officers' Compensation **20**	0.4	•	9.4	•	1.5	0.3	1.2	1.1	•	1.0	•	•	•
Operating Margin **21**	1.6	•	1.9	•	3.4	4.1	7.6	3.7	•	5.9	•	•	•
Operating Margin Before Officers' Comp. **22**	2.0	•	11.3	•	4.9	4.4	8.8	4.8	•	6.9	•	•	•

Selected Average Balance Sheet ($ in Thousands)

Net Receivables 23	6759	11	774	2721	4021	6307	26612
Inventories 24	9690	25	1122	1043	2989	7003	26854
Net Property, Plant and Equipment 25	16803	19	742	742	4347	12453	47927
Total Assets 26	77329	83	3006	6343	14897	34544	158390
Notes and Loans Payable 27	32824	18	1189	522	2172	9208	32672
All Other Liabilities 28	23181	61	849	2156	3021	9879	39373
Net Worth 29	21324	5	968	3664	9703	15458	86346

Selected Financial Ratios (Times to 1)

Current Ratio 30	1.4	0.9	2.1	2.3	2.1	1.8	2.0
Quick Ratio 31	0.6	0.4	0.8	1.8	1.4	0.9	1.1
Net Sales to Working Capital 32	17.7		9.7	7.8	7.7	10.1	8.0
Coverage Ratio 33	4.4	6.6	7.6	67.3	39.8	12.1	8.2
Total Asset Turnover 34	1.5	5.0	3.6	3.9	2.5	2.4	1.7
Inventory Turnover 35	9.8	10.8	7.9	21.2	9.9	9.5	8.1
Receivables Turnover 36	18.3	37.1	17.1	10.0	8.8	14.2	10.6
Total Liabilities to Net Worth 37	2.6	17.0	2.1	0.7	0.5	1.2	0.8
Current Assets to Working Capital 38	3.6		1.9	1.8	1.9	2.3	2.0
Current Liabilities to Working Capital 39	2.6		0.9	0.8	0.9	1.3	1.0
Working Capital to Net Sales 40	0.1		0.1	0.1	0.1	0.1	0.1
Inventory to Working Capital 41	1.5		1.1	0.4	0.6	1.1	0.8
Total Receipts to Cash Flow 42	13.6	19.3	11.9	16.8	8.3	11.6	9.1
Cost of Goods to Cash Flow 43	10.9	12.7	9.6	15.0	6.6	9.3	7.2
Cash Flow to Total Debt 44	0.2	0.3	0.4	0.5	0.9	0.4	0.4

Selected Financial Factors (in Percentages)

Debt Ratio 45	72.4	94.4	67.8	42.2	34.9	55.3	45.5
Return on Total Assets 46	10.1	12.6	15.0	16.5	22.8	12.9	13.4
Return on Equity Before Income Taxes 47	28.4	192.8	40.6	28.1	34.2	26.5	21.5
Return on Equity After Income Taxes 48	20.4	183.8	40.2	23.9	32.9	25.4	17.9
Profit Margin (Before Income Tax) 49	5.1	2.1	3.6	4.2	8.9	4.9	6.7
Profit Margin (After Income Tax) 50	3.6	2.0	3.6	3.5	8.6	4.7	5.6

Table I

Corporations with and without Net Income

SUGAR AND CONFECTIONERY PRODUCT

MONEY AMOUNTS AND SIZE OF ASSETS IN THOUSANDS OF DOLLARS

Item Description for Accounting Period 7/09 Through 6/10		Total	Zero Assets	Under 500	500 to 1,000	1,000 to 5,000	5,000 to 10,000	10,000 to 25,000	25,000 to 50,000	50,000 to 100,000	100,000 to 250,000	250,000 to 500,000	500,000 to 2,500,000	2,500,000 and over
Number of Enterprises	1	1096	8	719	166	86	45	25	15	18	0	3	7	4
Revenues ($ in Thousands)														
Net Sales	2	55604824	0	649773	250007	258038	613175	1301689	901388	2576060	0	1838723	5630890	41585080
Interest	3	129522	165	0	1	22	767	290	628	298	0	108	8497	118747
Rents	4	47731	0	0	0	0	378	3	4025	1627	0	5	26468	15225
Royalties	5	338003	0	0	0	0	0	10669	1254	0	0	2749	4333	318998
Other Portfolio Income	6	494967	2	0	0	0	8	355	142	7078	0	210	7467	479703
Other Receipts	7	121591	0	3	843	1870	753	2182	3518	11761	0	1359	11423	87882
Total Receipts	8	56736638	167	649776	250851	259930	615081	1315188	910955	2596824	0	1843154	5689078	42605635
Average Total Receipts	9	51767	21	904	1511	3022	13668	52608	60730	144268	•	614385	812725	10651409
Operating Costs/Operating Income (%)														
Cost of Operations	10	54.2	•	66.3	62.1	59.9	66.0	78.1	81.7	69.1	•	71.4	71.9	48.3
Salaries and Wages	11	6.2	•	12.0	13.1	8.3	7.4	3.2	2.8	7.2	•	5.3	2.8	6.7
Taxes Paid	12	1.1	•	5.6	1.5	1.9	1.8	1.1	0.9	1.0	•	1.1	0.8	1.1
Interest Paid	13	5.0	•	0.3	1.2	0.5	0.9	0.4	0.7	1.3	•	1.3	1.2	6.3
Depreciation	14	3.1	•	0.5	2.3	0.8	2.0	1.1	3.7	2.3	•	3.2	4.9	3.1
Amortization and Depletion	15	1.5	•	•	•	•	0.3	0.0	0.1	1.4	•	0.0	1.1	1.8
Pensions and Other Deferred Comp.	16	0.7	•	•	3.4	0.7	0.7	0.5	0.1	0.6	•	0.5	1.4	0.6
Employee Benefits	17	1.2	•	•	•	1.8	1.1	0.3	0.2	2.0	•	0.9	1.0	1.3
Advertising	18	5.1	•	2.0	0.3	0.1	1.7	0.5	0.5	2.6	•	3.5	0.4	6.4
Other Expenses	19	19.1	•	17.5	11.6	12.6	9.8	8.9	8.2	10.9	•	9.0	11.3	21.9
Officers' Compensation	20	0.8	•	1.1	4.9	11.3	3.1	2.7	1.5	1.2	•	0.7	0.4	0.6
Operating Margin	21	1.9	•	•	•	1.9	5.1	3.2	•	0.6	•	3.1	3.0	1.9
Operating Margin Before Officers' Comp.	22	2.7	•	•	4.4	13.3	8.2	5.9	0.9	1.8	•	3.8	3.5	2.5

Selected Average Balance Sheet ($ in Thousands)

Net Receivables 23	5743	0	39	200	499	1390	3129	5976	15194	•	66587	96340	1203155
Inventories 24	4496	0	70	330	338	1020	6774	7996	22782	•	151433	97229	731750
Net Property, Plant and Equipment 25	10257	0	3	222	208	2836	5033	16866	22099	•	141650	279931	1973937
Total Assets 26	81955	0	126	867	1301	7687	16911	34259	89370	•	412615	864398	19824078
Notes and Loans Payable 27	42286	0	87	484	253	1821	4858	7525	53164	•	190757	163499	10797763
All Other Liabilities 28	22762	0	47	235	274	1487	4825	7653	32676	•	146000	267585	5412253
Net Worth 29	16907	0	-8	147	775	4380	7228	19081	3530	•	75858	433314	3614062

Selected Financial Ratios (Times to 1)

Current Ratio 30	0.7	•	0.9	2.0	2.6	2.6	1.8	1.5	0.8	•	1.9	1.4	0.6
Quick Ratio 31	0.3	•	0.4	0.9	1.7	1.8	0.8	0.8	0.4	•	0.8	0.5	0.3
Net Sales to Working Capital 32	•	•	•	4.8	4.5	6.1	11.4	10.9	•	•	4.8	9.6	•
Coverage Ratio 33	2.4	•	•	0.9	6.9	7.1	11.7	1.7	3.0	•	3.5	4.6	2.4
Total Asset Turnover 34	0.6	•	7.2	1.7	2.3	1.8	3.1	1.8	1.6	•	1.5	0.9	0.5
Inventory Turnover 35	6.1	•	8.5	2.8	5.3	8.8	6.0	6.1	4.3	•	2.9	5.9	6.9
Receivables Turnover 36	9.1	•	•	6.3	6.3	•	14.3	9.5	10.1	•	7.1	11.7	8.7
Total Liabilities to Net Worth 37	3.8	•	•	4.9	0.7	1.3	1.3	0.8	24.3	•	4.4	1.0	4.5
Current Assets to Working Capital 38	•	•	2.0	2.0	1.6	2.2	3.0	•	•	•	2.1	3.6	•
Current Liabilities to Working Capital 39	•	•	•	1.0	0.6	1.2	2.0	0.1	•	•	1.1	2.6	•
Working Capital to Net Sales 40	•	•	•	0.2	0.2	0.2	0.1	0.2	0.1	•	0.2	0.1	•
Inventory to Working Capital 41	•	•	•	1.1	0.5	1.1	0.1	1.3	•	•	1.2	1.4	•
Total Receipts to Cash Flow 42	4.7	•	17.5	13.2	8.7	8.3	9.0	14.2	9.7	•	9.5	8.0	4.0
Cost of Goods to Cash Flow 43	2.5	•	11.6	8.2	5.2	5.5	7.0	11.6	6.7	•	6.8	5.8	1.9
Cash Flow to Total Debt 44	0.2	•	0.4	0.2	0.7	0.5	0.6	0.3	0.2	•	0.2	0.2	0.2

Selected Financial Factors (in Percentages)

Debt Ratio 45	79.4	•	106.3	83.0	40.5	43.0	57.3	44.3	96.1	•	81.6	49.9	81.8
Return on Total Assets 46	7.5	•	•	1.9	7.2	11.2	14.1	2.2	6.3	•	6.8	4.9	7.8
Return on Equity Before Income Taxes 47	21.4	•	593.5	•	10.4	16.9	30.2	1.6	107.3	•	26.6	7.7	24.4
Return on Equity After Income Taxes 48	13.9	•	593.6	•	8.1	12.7	27.7	1.0	93.8	•	21.7	4.4	15.8
Profit Margin (Before Income Tax) 49	7.1	•	•	•	2.7	5.4	4.2	0.5	2.6	•	3.3	4.2	8.5
Profit Margin (After Income Tax) 50	4.6	•	•	•	2.1	4.1	3.8	0.3	2.3	•	2.7	4.2	5.5

Table II

Corporations with Net Income

SUGAR AND CONFECTIONERY PRODUCT

MONEY AMOUNTS AND SIZE OF ASSETS IN THOUSANDS OF DOLLARS

Item Description for Accounting Period 7/09 Through 6/10	Total	Zero Assets	Under 500	500 to 1,000	1,000 to 5,000	5,000 to 10,000	10,000 to 25,000	25,000 to 50,000	50,000 to 100,000	100,000 to 250,000	250,000 to 500,000	500,000 to 2,500,000	2,500,000 and over
Number of Enterprises **1**	681	0	397	•	86	36	20	7	14	3	0	4	•
Revenues ($ in Thousands)													
Net Sales **2**	50313560	0	12160	•	258038	540518	1146606	402930	1989322	1555971	0	3926397	•
Interest **3**	109679	0	0	•	22	767	290	615	140	206	0	8158	•
Rents **4**	45188	0	0	•	0	378	3	3267	1627	5	0	24683	•
Royalties **5**	261472	0	0	•	0	0	10669	1254	0	0	0	1795	•
Other Portfolio Income **6**	493732	0	0	•	0	8	352	72	7078	210	0	6308	•
Other Receipts **7**	104757	0	0	•	1870	753	2883	886	10225	435	0	-176	•
Total Receipts **8**	51328388	0	12160	•	259930	542424	1160803	409024	2008392	1556827	0	3967165	•
Average Total Receipts **9**	75372	•	31	•	3022	15067	58040	58432	143457	518942	0	991791	•
Operating Costs/Operating Income (%)													
Cost of Operations **10**	53.1	•	36.9	•	59.9	66.5	79.6	74.7	70.1	77.1	•	71.7	•
Salaries and Wages **11**	6.1	•	1.9	•	8.3	7.0	2.5	2.7	7.2	3.5	•	2.2	•
Taxes Paid **12**	1.1	•	1.9	•	1.9	1.8	0.8	0.9	1.1	1.0	•	0.8	•
Interest Paid **13**	5.2	•	0.2	•	0.5	0.9	0.2	1.0	0.8	1.2	•	0.7	•
Depreciation **14**	2.9	•	1.3	•	0.8	2.3	1.0	4.1	2.2	2.2	•	2.6	•
Amortization and Depletion **15**	1.2	•	•	•	•	•	0.0	0.2	0.2	0.1	•	0.4	•
Pensions and Other Deferred Comp. **16**	0.7	•	•	•	0.7	0.8	0.3	0.2	0.6	0.6	•	1.8	•
Employee Benefits **17**	1.2	•	•	•	1.8	1.3	0.3	0.2	2.4	1.1	•	1.0	•
Advertising **18**	5.5	•	5.6	•	0.1	1.9	0.5	0.5	1.2	1.8	•	0.1	•
Other Expenses **19**	19.3	•	34.2	•	12.6	8.0	7.6	9.1	10.2	5.1	•	11.4	•
Officers' Compensation **20**	0.8	•	14.4	•	11.3	3.4	2.9	1.5	1.1	1.0	•	0.5	•
Operating Margin **21**	3.0	•	3.7	•	1.9	6.4	4.4	4.8	3.0	5.3	•	6.8	•
Operating Margin Before Officers' Comp. **22**	3.7	•	18.1	•	13.3	9.8	7.3	6.3	4.1	6.3	•	7.3	•

Selected Average Balance Sheet ($ in Thousands)

Net Receivables 23	8550	•	2	499	1280	3330	5409	15736	45963
									138578
Inventories 24	5822	•	0	282	1271	4646	10400	23517	141208
									127085
Net Property, Plant and Equipment 25	14032	•	2	208	2446	4825	18558	21292	87815
									233909
Total Assets 26	122448	•	7	1301	8020	15864	38553	80043	325545
									958670
Notes and Loans Payable 27	62485	•	0	253	2154	3342	8449	17233	149759
									153588
All Other Liabilities 28	34262	•	5	274	1305	4078	8218	23923	121038
									271372
Net Worth 29	25701	•	3	775	4561	8444	21886	38887	54748
									533709

Selected Financial Ratios (Times to 1)

Current Ratio 30	0.7	0.9	2.6	3.8	2.5	1.9	1.7	1.9	1.5
Quick Ratio 31	0.3	0.8	1.7	2.5	1.3	1.0	0.7	0.7	0.6
Net Sales to Working Capital 32	•	•	4.5	5.0	9.7	6.3	7.4	4.8	7.7
Coverage Ratio 33	2.6	20.3	6.9	8.5	24.8	7.1	6.3	5.3	12.2
Total Asset Turnover 34	0.6	4.1	2.3	1.9	3.6	1.5	1.8	1.6	1.0
Inventory Turnover 35	6.7	64.6	6.4	7.8	9.8	4.1	4.2	2.8	5.5
Receivables Turnover 36	9.1	20.5	8.3	•	22.7	6.4	10.0	22.6	•
Total Liabilities to Net Worth 37	3.8	1.7	0.7	0.8	0.9	0.8	1.1	4.9	0.8
Current Assets to Working Capital 38	•	•	1.6	1.4	1.7	2.1	2.5	2.1	3.1
Current Liabilities to Working Capital 39	•	•	0.6	0.4	0.7	1.1	1.5	1.1	2.1
Working Capital to Net Sales 40	•	•	0.2	0.2	0.1	0.2	0.1	0.2	0.1
Inventory to Working Capital 41	•	•	0.5	0.4	0.7	0.9	1.2	1.3	1.0
Total Receipts to Cash Flow 42	4.4	3.1	8.7	8.5	8.5	7.0	8.3	10.2	6.1
Cost of Goods to Cash Flow 43	2.3	1.2	5.2	5.6	6.8	5.3	5.8	7.9	4.4
Cash Flow to Total Debt 44	0.2	2.1	0.7	0.5	0.9	0.5	0.4	0.2	0.4

Selected Financial Factors (in Percentages)

Debt Ratio 45	79.0	62.7	40.5	43.1	46.8	43.2	51.4	83.2	44.3
Return on Total Assets 46	8.2	15.9	7.2	14.4	21.3	11.0	8.4	10.6	8.9
Return on Equity Before Income Taxes 47	24.1	40.5	10.4	22.4	38.3	16.7	14.6	51.0	14.7
Return on Equity After Income Taxes 48	16.2	40.0	8.1	17.4	35.6	15.4	13.9	41.4	9.9
Profit Margin (Before Income Tax) 49	8.4	3.7	2.7	6.8	5.6	6.3	4.0	5.4	8.0
Profit Margin (After Income Tax) 50	5.7	3.6	2.1	5.3	5.2	5.9	3.8	4.4	5.4

Table I

Corporations with and without Net Income

FRUIT AND VEGETABLE PRESERVING AND SPECIALTY FOOD

MONEY AMOUNTS AND SIZE OF ASSETS IN THOUSANDS OF DOLLARS

Item Description for Accounting Period 7/09 Through 6/10	Total	Zero Assets	Under 500	500 to 1,000	1,000 to 5,000	5,000 to 10,000	10,000 to 25,000	25,000 to 50,000	50,000 to 100,000	100,000 to 250,000	250,000 to 500,000	500,000 to 2,500,000	2,500,000 and over
Number of Enterprises **1**	890	408	7	0	242	20	101	46	28	16	8	7	6
Revenues ($ in Thousands)													
Net Sales **2**	49006400	154845	13431	0	1854831	370686	2800591	2476371	3416349	3853699	4461307	9466106	20138184
Interest **3**	116586	9	0	0	1	11	1162	1252	1199	1159	26389	9001	76403
Rents **4**	15968	0	0	0	2381	0	16	321	2840	1410	844	1934	6222
Royalties **5**	254678	0	0	0	24	0	0	0	0	0	0	375	254279
Other Portfolio Income **6**	473153	0	0	0	181	0	473	3710	258	218	1662	9028	457622
Other Receipts **7**	1213281	27565	6	0	160	8318	11769	18451	22105	18694	13005	89149	1004059
Total Receipts **8**	51080066	182419	13437	0	1857578	379015	2814011	2500105	3442751	3875180	4503207	9575593	21936769
Average Total Receipts **9**	57393	447	1920	•	7676	18951	27861	54350	122955	242199	562901	1367942	3656128
Operating Costs/Operating Income (%)													
Cost of Operations **10**	65.4	88.9	194.4	•	78.3	77.3	72.5	74.2	79.2	75.9	73.6	60.2	58.0
Salaries and Wages **11**	4.5	4.8	17.7	•	2.3	5.9	5.2	4.0	2.8	4.3	3.0	7.2	4.0
Taxes Paid **12**	1.0	0.9	3.8	•	1.3	1.3	1.2	1.1	0.9	1.0	1.6	1.5	0.6
Interest Paid **13**	2.0	1.3	1.8	•	1.5	0.3	1.2	0.9	1.1	0.7	1.5	1.7	2.9
Depreciation **14**	2.7	7.2	2.0	•	1.9	1.9	2.8	3.0	2.7	2.2	2.8	2.8	2.8
Amortization and Depletion **15**	1.0	0.5	•	•	0.5	0.6	0.2	0.1	0.3	0.1	0.2	1.0	1.8
Pensions and Other Deferred Comp. **16**	1.0	0.1	•	•	0.4	•	0.3	0.1	0.2	0.3	0.2	0.3	2.2
Employee Benefits **17**	1.2	0.2	0.1	•	0.7	1.3	0.7	0.7	1.1	1.2	1.4	2.1	0.8
Advertising **18**	2.9	0.4	0.1	•	0.3	0.7	1.2	1.8	0.5	0.3	1.8	6.6	3.0
Other Expenses **19**	15.6	11.9	15.5	•	5.5	9.7	10.3	8.7	7.3	7.1	8.5	13.2	23.9
Officers' Compensation **20**	0.7	3.7	1.2	•	3.5	0.3	1.4	1.4	0.7	1.0	0.2	0.6	0.3
Operating Margin **21**	2.0	•	•	•	3.8	0.6	3.0	4.1	3.1	5.8	5.0	2.7	•
Operating Margin Before Officers' Comp. **22**	2.6	•	•	•	7.2	0.9	4.3	5.4	3.8	6.9	5.3	3.3	0.0

Selected Average Balance Sheet ($ in Thousands)

Net Receivables 23	6647	0	36	474	1059	2916	5732	10478	21661	33492	109201	591453
Inventories 24	8294	0	86	494	1587	4540	9697	26982	67164	78443	194207	408013
Net Property, Plant and Equipment 25	10225	0	137	1035	2106	4155	11030	20540	38189	101698	253507	684293
Total Assets 26	72959	307	2812	8423	14624	35764	70687	142497	309160	968510	7907952	
Notes and Loans Payable 27	17608	3774	1071	1429	5257	12318	26220	39277	67726	380400	1615314	
All Other Liabilities 28	15614	40	570	1758	4852	7233	15526	32712	97794	238781	1581307	
Net Worth 29	39738	-3507	1171	5237	4516	16213	28942	70507	143640	349329	4711331	

Selected Financial Ratios (Times to 1)

Current Ratio 30	1.6	4.1	1.3	1.6	1.8	1.6	2.3	1.7	1.7	2.5	1.3
Quick Ratio 31	0.7	1.4	0.7	0.6	0.8	0.7	0.6	0.6	0.5	1.0	0.7
Net Sales to Working Capital 32	7.9	14.9	26.9	14.0	6.4	8.3	4.5	7.9	8.1	5.4	11.3
Coverage Ratio 33	4.3	•	3.6	9.4	6.4	3.8	9.8	4.9	4.4	3.4	4.2
Total Asset Turnover 34	0.8	6.2	2.7	2.2	1.5	1.9	1.7	1.8	1.7	1.4	0.4
Inventory Turnover 35	4.3	43.6	12.2	9.0	4.1	4.4	3.6	5.2	2.7	4.2	4.8
Receivables Turnover 36	9.5	•	17.1	10.5	10.0	9.9	10.4	17.6	13.0	1.8	7.4
Total Liabilities to Net Worth 37	0.8	0.6	1.4	0.6	1.2	2.2	1.4	1.0	1.2	1.8	0.7
Current Assets to Working Capital 38	2.7	1.3	4.4	2.7	2.3	2.7	2.7	1.8	2.5	1.7	4.1
Current Liabilities to Working Capital 39	1.7	0.3	3.4	1.7	1.3	1.7	1.7	0.8	1.5	0.7	3.1
Working Capital to Net Sales 40	0.1	0.1	0.0	0.1	0.2	0.1	0.1	0.2	0.1	0.2	0.1
Inventory to Working Capital 41	1.3	0.7	1.8	1.2	1.2	1.5	1.6	1.2	1.3	0.9	1.5
Total Receipts to Cash Flow 42	5.2	•	12.4	10.0	8.8	9.0	10.6	9.1	7.7	6.8	3.4
Cost of Goods to Cash Flow 43	3.4	•	9.7	7.8	6.5	6.5	8.4	6.9	5.7	4.1	2.0
Cash Flow to Total Debt 44	0.3	•	0.4	0.6	0.3	0.3	0.3	0.2	0.4	0.3	0.3

Selected Financial Factors (in Percentages)

Debt Ratio 45	45.5	1240.8	58.4	37.8	69.1	54.7	59.1	50.5	53.5	63.9	40.4
Return on Total Assets 46	6.4	•	14.7	7.1	8.9	9.0	8.6	12.2	13.6	7.7	5.2
Return on Equity Before Income Taxes 47	9.0	74.7	25.6	10.2	21.2	16.7	16.3	22.2	23.2	15.0	6.7
Return on Equity After Income Taxes 48	6.5	74.8	24.2	10.2	20.5	14.5	12.8	19.7	18.5	10.8	4.3
Profit Margin (Before Income Tax) 49	6.5	•	3.9	2.9	3.5	5.0	3.9	6.5	6.8	3.9	9.4
Profit Margin (After Income Tax) 50	4.7	•	3.7	2.9	3.3	4.4	3.0	5.8	4.8	2.8	6.1

Table II

Corporations with Net Income

FRUIT AND VEGETABLE PRESERVING AND SPECIALTY FOOD

MONEY AMOUNTS AND SIZE OF ASSETS IN THOUSANDS OF DOLLARS

Item Description for Accounting Period 7/09 Through 6/10	Total	Zero Assets	Under 500	500 to 1,000	1,000 to 5,000	5,000 to 10,000	10,000 to 25,000	25,000 to 50,000	50,000 to 100,000	100,000 to 250,000	250,000 to 500,000	500,000 to 2,500,000	2,500,000 and over
Number of Enterprises 1	401	•	•	•	236	15	57	31	23	•	•	•	7
Revenues ($ in Thousands)													
Net Sales 2	44701156	•	•	•	1815776	327719	1901112	1835762	3092324	•	•	•	9466106
Interest 3	89795	•	•	•	1	0	157	1144	1165	•	•	•	9001
Rents 4	14465	•	•	•	2299	0	16	190	2754	•	•	•	1934
Royalties 5	254617	•	•	•	24	0	0	0	0	•	•	•	375
Other Portfolio Income 6	472545	•	•	•	181	0	182	3444	258	•	•	•	9028
Other Receipts 7	1196056	•	•	•	138	8227	6277	15465	16313	•	•	•	89149
Total Receipts 8	46728634	•	•	•	1818419	335946	1907744	1856005	3112814	•	•	•	9575593
Average Total Receipts 9	116530	•	•	•	7705	22396	33469	59871	135340	•	•	•	1367942
Operating Costs/Operating Income (%)													
Cost of Operations 10	64.2	•	•	•	78.2	78.4	72.7	71.7	78.8	•	•	•	60.2
Salaries and Wages 11	4.6	•	•	•	2.1	3.3	4.5	3.7	2.9	•	•	•	7.2
Taxes Paid 12	1.0	•	•	•	1.3	1.3	1.1	1.2	0.9	•	•	•	1.5
Interest Paid 13	1.7	•	•	•	0.9	0.3	0.9	0.6	0.9	•	•	•	1.7
Depreciation 14	2.7	•	•	•	1.9	1.7	2.1	2.4	2.4	•	•	•	2.8
Amortization and Depletion 15	0.9	•	•	•	0.5	0.2	0.2	0.0	0.2	•	•	•	1.0
Pensions and Other Deferred Comp. 16	1.1	•	•	•	0.4	•	0.4	0.2	0.2	•	•	•	0.3
Employee Benefits 17	1.2	•	•	•	0.7	1.4	0.7	0.7	1.1	•	•	•	2.1
Advertising 18	3.0	•	•	•	0.3	0.2	1.3	2.2	0.5	•	•	•	6.6
Other Expenses 19	16.2	•	•	•	5.0	5.5	7.3	9.0	6.9	•	•	•	13.2
Officers' Compensation 20	0.7	•	•	•	3.5	0.2	1.3	1.6	0.7	•	•	•	0.6
Operating Margin 21	2.7	•	•	•	5.2	7.4	7.6	6.7	4.6	•	•	•	2.7
Operating Margin Before Officers' Comp. 22	3.4	•	•	•	8.6	7.7	8.9	8.3	5.3	•	•	•	3.3

Selected Average Balance Sheet ($ in Thousands)

Net Receivables 23	13626	480	1193	2858	6616	10941	109201
Inventories 24	16239	477	4218	4988	11036	27899	217716
Net Property, Plant and Equipment 25	20097	1057	2227	4228	9922	20329	253507
Total Assets 26	145696	2815	9002	15552	35644	70416	968510
Notes and Loans Payable 27	29343	1056	1654	4274	10463	23665	380400
All Other Liabilities 28	31358	553	1909	4308	6527	15599	238781
Net Worth 29	84996	1206	5438	6970	18654	31152	349329

Selected Financial Ratios (Times to 1)

Current Ratio 30	1.6	1.3	1.7	2.0	2.4	1.7	2.5
Quick Ratio 31	0.8	0.7	0.5	0.8	1.2	0.6	1.0
Net Sales to Working Capital 32	7.8	28.1	13.4	6.8	4.5	7.5	5.4
Coverage Ratio 33	5.5	7.1	39.8	10.0	13.5	7.1	3.4
Total Asset Turnover 34	0.8	2.7	2.4	2.1	1.7	1.9	1.4
Inventory Turnover 35	4.4	12.6	4.1	4.9	3.8	3.8	3.7
Receivables Turnover 36	9.5	17.5	4.8	14.2	9.3	10.4	
Total Liabilities to Net Worth 37	0.7	1.3	0.7	1.2	0.9	1.3	1.8
Current Assets to Working Capital 38	2.6	4.5	2.4	2.0	1.7	2.3	1.7
Current Liabilities to Working Capital 39	1.6	3.5	1.4	1.0	0.7	1.3	0.7
Working Capital to Net Sales 40	0.1	0.0	0.1	0.1	0.2	0.1	0.2
Inventory to Working Capital 41	1.2	1.8	1.1	1.1	0.8	1.4	0.9
Total Receipts to Cash Flow 42	4.8	11.2	7.3	7.4	6.9	9.6	6.8
Cost of Goods to Cash Flow 43	3.1	8.7	5.7	5.4	5.0	7.5	4.1
Cash Flow to Total Debt 44	0.4	0.4	0.8	0.5	0.5	0.4	0.3

Selected Financial Factors (in Percentages)

Debt Ratio 45	41.7	57.2	39.6	55.2	47.7	55.8	63.9
Return on Total Assets 46	7.1	17.0	24.8	18.9	13.9	11.7	7.7
Return on Equity Before Income Taxes 47	9.9	34.0	40.0	37.9	24.6	22.8	15.0
Return on Equity After Income Taxes 48	7.3	32.6	40.0	37.1	21.8	18.8	10.8
Profit Margin (Before Income Tax) 49	7.6	5.3	10.0	7.9	7.8	5.3	3.9
Profit Margin (After Income Tax) 50	5.6	5.1	10.0	7.8	6.9	4.4	2.8

Table I

Corporations with and without Net Income

DAIRY PRODUCT

MONEY AMOUNTS AND SIZE OF ASSETS IN THOUSANDS OF DOLLARS

Item Description for Accounting Period 7/09 Through 6/10	Total	Zero Assets	Under 500	500 to 1,000	1,000 to 5,000	5,000 to 10,000	10,000 to 25,000	25,000 to 50,000	50,000 to 100,000	100,000 to 250,000	250,000 to 500,000	500,000 to 2,500,000	2,500,000 and over
Number of Enterprises 1	1193	•	•	0	120	•	54	33	18	13	6	9	0
Revenues ($ in Thousands)													
Net Sales 2	40169945	•	•	0	1301236	•	2307545	3082244	2629073	3249452	3596383	23016641	0
Interest 3	21152	•	•	0	813	•	1682	2414	4403	1692	107	8644	0
Rents 4	7141	•	•	0	0	•	1498	123	1506	120	2345	1495	0
Royalties 5	58584	•	•	0	0	•	0	1683	2785	0	45852	8265	0
Other Portfolio Income 6	24794	•	•	0	0	•	15603	2180	2195	1011	521	3252	0
Other Receipts 7	222100	•	•	0	1834	•	9832	5844	32429	37174	7911	112405	0
Total Receipts 8	40503716	•	•	0	1303883	•	2336160	3094488	2672391	3289449	3653119	23150702	0
Average Total Receipts 9	33951	•	•	•	10866	•	43262	93772	148466	253035	608853	2572300	•
Operating Costs/Operating Income (%)													
Cost of Operations 10	74.7	•	•	•	76.2	•	77.5	75.0	73.8	74.2	70.6	75.1	•
Salaries and Wages 11	5.3	•	•	•	4.1	•	5.4	5.5	5.7	3.4	5.6	5.6	•
Taxes Paid 12	1.1	•	•	•	1.6	•	1.2	1.1	1.2	0.9	1.1	1.1	•
Interest Paid 13	1.4	•	•	•	0.6	•	0.9	0.4	0.9	0.8	1.3	1.8	•
Depreciation 14	3.4	•	•	•	2.0	•	2.9	2.3	3.5	4.0	2.8	3.6	•
Amortization and Depletion 15	0.5	•	•	•	0.0	•	0.2	0.2	0.2	0.1	0.7	0.8	•
Pensions and Other Deferred Comp. 16	0.5	•	•	•	0.3	•	0.3	0.6	0.3	0.4	0.7	0.6	•
Employee Benefits 17	0.9	•	•	•	1.0	•	0.8	1.1	1.2	1.1	1.5	0.7	•
Advertising 18	1.6	•	•	•	0.2	•	0.5	0.5	0.5	2.3	2.1	1.9	•
Other Expenses 19	8.1	•	•	•	6.1	•	5.6	8.5	9.5	6.8	8.5	8.2	•
Officers' Compensation 20	1.6	•	•	•	3.0	•	3.3	1.0	0.9	0.7	0.7	1.8	•
Operating Margin 21	0.7	•	•	•	4.9	•	1.5	3.9	2.3	5.3	4.4	•	•
Operating Margin Before Officers' Comp. 22	2.4	•	•	•	8.0	•	4.8	4.9	3.3	6.0	5.1	0.6	•

Selected Average Balance Sheet ($ in Thousands)

Net Receivables 23	2637	766	4467	6430	12777	17595	42125	202316
Inventories 24	2211	829	2971	4884	13021	24587	51299	142020
Net Property, Plant and Equipment 25	6703	1055	5990	11911	28371	59935	115990	555153
Total Assets 26	19408	3266	15771	35428	78060	169222	323386	1634158
Notes and Loans Payable 27	7797	929	5422	7794	17934	70205	96198	733413
All Other Liabilities 28	5677	777	3582	9762	20022	29742	82715	536357
Net Worth 29	5934	1560	6767	17871	40104	69276	144472	364388

Selected Financial Ratios (Times to 1)

Current Ratio 30	1.5	1.7	2.1	1.9	1.6	2.1	1.9	1.4
Quick Ratio 31	0.7	0.9	1.3	1.0	0.8	1.1	0.9	0.6
Net Sales to Working Capital 32	13.9	12.1	9.1	10.5	11.0	7.5	10.3	20.0
Coverage Ratio 33	2.1	9.0	4.1	11.5	5.5	8.7	5.5	0.7
Total Asset Turnover 34	1.7	3.3	2.7	2.6	1.9	1.5	1.9	1.6
Inventory Turnover 35	11.4	10.0	11.1	14.3	8.3	7.5	8.3	13.5
Receivables Turnover 36	12.7	15.3	11.8	14.2	10.6	12.7	14.7	12.5
Total Liabilities to Net Worth 37	2.3	1.1	1.3	1.0	0.9	1.4	1.2	3.5
Current Assets to Working Capital 38	2.9	2.4	1.9	2.2	2.7	1.9	2.1	3.8
Current Liabilities to Working Capital 39	1.9	1.4	0.9	1.2	1.7	0.9	1.1	2.8
Working Capital to Net Sales 40	0.1	0.1	0.1	0.1	0.1	0.1	0.1	0.1
Inventory to Working Capital 41	0.9	1.0	0.6	0.6	0.9	0.8	1.0	1.1
Total Receipts to Cash Flow 42	12.8	11.3	14.4	9.0	8.4	8.1	7.9	17.9
Cost of Goods to Cash Flow 43	9.6	8.6	11.1	6.8	6.2	6.0	5.6	13.4
Cash Flow to Total Debt 44	0.2	0.6	0.3	0.6	0.5	0.3	0.4	0.1

Selected Financial Factors (in Percentages)

Debt Ratio 45	69.4	52.2	57.1	49.6	48.6	59.1	55.3	77.7
Return on Total Assets 46	5.2	19.2	9.7	12.4	9.0	10.8	13.5	1.9
Return on Equity Before Income Taxes 47	8.9	35.8	17.2	22.5	14.4	23.4	24.7	•
Return on Equity After Income Taxes 48	7.3	33.7	15.6	21.0	11.7	21.9	24.1	•
Profit Margin (Before Income Tax) 49	1.6	5.2	2.7	4.3	4.0	6.5	6.0	•
Profit Margin (After Income Tax) 50	1.3	4.9	2.5	4.0	3.2	6.1	5.8	•

Table II

Corporations with Net Income

DAIRY PRODUCT

MONEY AMOUNTS AND SIZE OF ASSETS IN THOUSANDS OF DOLLARS

Item Description for Accounting Period 7/09 Through 6/10	Total	Zero Assets	Under 500	500 to 1,000	1,000 to 5,000	5,000 to 10,000	10,000 to 25,000	25,000 to 50,000	50,000 to 100,000	100,000 to 250,000	250,000 to 500,000	500,000 to 2,500,000	2,500,000 and over
Number of Enterprises **1**	560	•	•	0	103	33	38	27	14	•	•	5	0

Revenues ($ in Thousands)

	Total	Zero Assets	Under 500	500 to 1,000	1,000 to 5,000	5,000 to 10,000	10,000 to 25,000	25,000 to 50,000	50,000 to 100,000	100,000 to 250,000	250,000 to 500,000	500,000 to 2,500,000	2,500,000 and over
Net Sales **2**	30641636	•	•	0	1212242	576516	1823728	2506103	2016241	•	•	16200751	0
Interest **3**	15577	•	•	0	660	289	1470	2037	4111	•	•	5263	0
Rents **4**	4600	•	•	0	0	52	764	103	496	•	•	720	0
Royalties **5**	58417	•	•	0	0	0	0	1683	2785	•	•	8098	0
Other Portfolio Income **6**	20735	•	•	0	0	33	15602	2078	1817	•	•	5	0
Other Receipts **7**	140043	•	•	0	1834	14489	7389	3004	13921	•	•	54612	0
Total Receipts **8**	30881008	•	•	0	1214736	591379	1848953	2515008	2039371	•	•	16269449	0
Average Total Receipts **9**	55145	•	•	•	11794	17921	48657	93148	145669	•	•	3253890	•

Operating Costs/Operating Income (%)

	Total	Zero Assets	Under 500	500 to 1,000	1,000 to 5,000	5,000 to 10,000	10,000 to 25,000	25,000 to 50,000	50,000 to 100,000	100,000 to 250,000	250,000 to 500,000	500,000 to 2,500,000	2,500,000 and over
Cost of Operations **10**	72.4	•	•	•	76.7	79.7	76.9	73.8	72.1	•	•	72.0	•
Salaries and Wages **11**	5.8	•	•	•	3.8	2.4	5.1	5.8	6.2	•	•	6.4	•
Taxes Paid **12**	1.2	•	•	•	1.5	0.9	1.2	1.1	1.2	•	•	1.2	•
Interest Paid **13**	1.7	•	•	•	0.6	0.2	0.8	0.3	0.8	•	•	2.4	•
Depreciation **14**	3.0	•	•	•	1.9	1.8	2.6	2.1	3.2	•	•	3.3	•
Amortization and Depletion **15**	0.6	•	•	•	0.0	•	0.0	0.1	0.2	•	•	1.0	•
Pensions and Other Deferred Comp. **16**	0.5	•	•	•	0.3	0.3	0.2	0.5	0.3	•	•	0.5	•
Employee Benefits **17**	1.0	•	•	•	0.9	1.2	0.6	0.9	1.2	•	•	0.9	•
Advertising **18**	1.9	•	•	•	0.3	1.4	0.5	0.5	0.4	•	•	2.5	•
Other Expenses **19**	8.3	•	•	•	5.5	6.7	4.6	8.6	8.4	•	•	8.9	•
Officers' Compensation **20**	0.8	•	•	•	3.0	3.9	3.9	1.1	1.1	•	•	0.1	•
Operating Margin **21**	2.8	•	•	•	5.5	1.3	3.7	5.3	4.9	•	•	0.8	•
Operating Margin Before Officers' Comp. **22**	3.6	•	•	•	8.5	5.3	7.6	6.4	6.0	•	•	0.9	•

Selected Average Balance Sheet ($ in Thousands)

Net Receivables 23	4357	•	892	1139	5033	6515	11912	•	•	269080
Inventories 24	3765	•	770	1464	3149	4740	11254	•	•	150030
Net Property, Plant and Equipment 25	9828	•	844	2165	5843	9475	26770	•	•	628024
Total Assets 26	30815	•	3229	6716	14994	33459	76746	•	•	2069589
Notes and Loans Payable 27	13943	•	900	1065	4481	6867	15475	•	•	1156070
All Other Liabilities 28	8539	•	811	1448	4011	8897	20736	•	•	630223
Net Worth 29	8333	•	1518	4203	6501	17695	40535	•	•	283296

Selected Financial Ratios (Times to 1)

Current Ratio 30	1.5	•	2.0	2.1	1.9	1.9	1.6	•	•	1.2
Quick Ratio 31	0.8	•	1.1	1.0	1.4	1.0	0.7	•	•	0.6
Net Sales to Working Capital 32	15.6	•	10.4	9.4	11.4	9.5	11.2	•	•	37.8
Coverage Ratio 33	3.1	•	9.9	18.9	7.3	20.8	8.3	•	•	1.5
Total Asset Turnover 34	1.8	•	3.6	2.6	3.2	2.8	1.9	•	•	1.6
Inventory Turnover 35	10.5	•	11.7	9.5	11.7	14.4	9.2	•	•	15.5
Receivables Turnover 36	11.9	•	16.5	17.2	11.2	15.7	11.9	•	•	•
Total Liabilities to Net Worth 37	2.7	•	1.1	0.6	1.3	0.9	0.9	•	•	6.3
Current Assets to Working Capital 38	3.0	•	2.0	1.9	2.1	2.1	2.8	•	•	6.4
Current Liabilities to Working Capital 39	2.0	•	1.0	0.9	1.1	1.1	1.8	•	•	5.4
Working Capital to Net Sales 40	0.1	•	0.1	0.1	0.1	0.1	0.1	•	•	0.0
Inventory to Working Capital 41	1.0	•	0.8	0.9	0.5	0.5	1.0	•	•	1.8
Total Receipts to Cash Flow 42	10.0	•	11.3	10.6	12.1	8.1	7.8	•	•	12.3
Cost of Goods to Cash Flow 43	7.2	•	8.6	8.5	9.3	6.0	5.6	•	•	8.9
Cash Flow to Total Debt 44	0.2	•	0.6	0.7	0.5	0.7	0.5	•	•	0.1

Selected Financial Factors (in Percentages)

Debt Ratio 45	73.0	•	53.0	37.4	56.6	47.1	47.2	•	•	86.3
Return on Total Assets 46	9.3	•	23.1	10.8	18.7	16.3	12.9	•	•	5.8
Return on Equity Before Income Taxes 47	23.5	•	44.1	16.3	37.3	29.3	21.5	•	•	14.2
Return on Equity After Income Taxes 48	21.2	•	41.6	14.8	34.9	27.5	18.0	•	•	10.9
Profit Margin (Before Income Tax) 49	3.6	•	5.7	3.9	5.1	5.6	6.1	•	•	1.2
Profit Margin (After Income Tax) 50	3.2	•	5.4	3.5	4.7	5.2	5.1	•	•	1.0

Table I

Corporations with and without Net Income

MEAT AND SEAFOOD PROCESSING

MONEY AMOUNTS AND SIZE OF ASSETS IN THOUSANDS OF DOLLARS

Item Description for Accounting Period 7/09 Through 6/10		Total	Zero Assets	Under 500	500 to 1,000	1,000 to 5,000	5,000 to 10,000	10,000 to 25,000	25,000 to 50,000	50,000 to 100,000	100,000 to 250,000	250,000 to 500,000	500,000 to 2,500,000	2,500,000 and over
Number of Enterprises	1	3220	25	2197	114	541	91	95	74	34	27	11	6	4
Revenues ($ in Thousands)														
Net Sales	2	114523892	184268	1830949	200006	3863470	5538984	4931513	8047411	6888240	11049126	7376910	10556054	54056961
Interest	3	104448	36	1	356	1450	133	2202	1947	429	10255	5649	23044	58946
Rents	4	23428	0	0	194	779	683	997	1131	290	945	6594	280	11535
Royalties	5	4930	0	0	0	0	0	0	0	0	0	0	151	4778
Other Portfolio Income	6	268142	1238	0	991	23630	58	490	2155	7774	18917	22640	34046	156200
Other Receipts	7	605790	8113	36	178	27898	24473	31636	24899	18844	54227	47764	105550	262174
Total Receipts	8	115530630	193655	1830986	201725	3917227	5564331	4966838	8077543	6915577	11133470	7459557	10719125	54550594
Average Total Receipts	9	35879	7746	833	1770	7241	61146	52283	109156	203399	412351	678142	1786521	13637648
Operating Costs/Operating Income (%)														
Cost of Operations	10	85.7	86.2	71.2	70.4	72.9	81.7	83.4	82.3	82.1	84.2	80.1	84.6	90.0
Salaries and Wages	11	2.8	•	7.2	5.4	6.0	7.4	3.8	3.7	3.2	2.4	2.8	2.4	1.9
Taxes Paid	12	0.6	1.6	1.2	2.9	1.7	0.8	0.8	0.7	0.7	0.7	1.0	0.7	0.4
Interest Paid	13	1.0	0.1	0.4	0.0	0.8	0.1	0.4	0.5	0.7	0.5	1.5	1.1	1.3
Depreciation	14	2.0	0.3	0.8	1.6	2.8	0.8	1.7	1.7	2.5	2.2	2.4	3.5	1.6
Amortization and Depletion	15	0.2	•	0.4	•	0.0	0.1	0.1	0.1	0.2	0.1	0.5	0.9	0.2
Pensions and Other Deferred Comp.	16	0.4	•	0.0	0.1	0.5	0.1	0.2	0.2	0.2	0.2	0.2	0.2	0.6
Employee Benefits	17	0.6	0.2	0.2	0.8	1.4	1.1	0.7	0.6	1.1	0.8	0.9	1.0	0.3
Advertising	18	0.6	0.4	1.1	1.5	0.4	0.1	0.2	0.9	2.0	0.6	0.8	0.5	0.4
Other Expenses	19	4.6	12.9	12.7	13.3	9.5	7.3	5.9	6.0	4.7	4.6	7.0	4.1	3.1
Officers' Compensation	20	0.4	1.9	1.6	4.4	2.8	0.5	1.1	0.6	0.5	0.3	0.4	0.2	0.1
Operating Margin	21	1.0	3.1	3.1	•	1.1	0.2	1.8	2.6	2.0	3.3	2.5	0.7	0.1
Operating Margin Before Officers' Comp.	22	1.4	4.8	4.8	4.0	3.9	0.7	2.9	3.2	2.6	3.7	2.8	0.9	0.2

Selected Average Balance Sheet ($ in Thousands)

Net Receivables 23	2060	0	13	122	644	2859	3125	7469	11657	25853	57050	92158	714046
Inventories 24	3087	0	2	43	266	938	2663	7693	17420	37330	89665	213043	1253404
Net Property, Plant and Equipment 25	4603	0	21	103	1195	1844	5095	11299	31064	62761	91792	339518	1708308
Total Assets 26	15604	0	90	810	3041	8872	14156	35051	71600	169219	358585	1150735	6428423
Notes and Loans Payable 27	4960	0	42	7	2045	1576	3986	12645	21346	53323	146446	313841	1913679
All Other Liabilities 28	3823	0	12	47	754	1482	2877	7479	16101	40603	104920	209274	1713362
Net Worth 29	6821	0	35	756	242	5814	7293	14926	34154	75292	107219	627620	2801382

Selected Financial Ratios (Times to 1)

Current Ratio 30	2.0	•	0.8	5.7	1.6	2.9	2.1	1.6	1.4	1.7	1.4	2.1	2.3
Quick Ratio 31	0.8	•	0.6	5.1	1.1	2.0	1.2	0.8	0.7	0.8	0.6	0.3	1.1
Net Sales to Working Capital 32	9.6	•	•	8.0	12.5	18.4	13.2	15.0	19.3	11.8	14.4	4.8	8.5
Coverage Ratio 33	3.0	22.7	9.4	16.6	4.2	7.1	6.6	6.5	4.5	9.0	3.5	3.2	1.8
Total Asset Turnover 34	2.3	•	9.3	2.2	2.3	6.9	3.7	3.1	2.8	2.4	1.9	1.5	2.1
Inventory Turnover 35	9.9	•	246.5	29.0	19.5	53.0	16.3	11.6	9.5	9.2	6.0	7.0	9.7
Receivables Turnover 36	17.6	•	62.0	14.8	15.5	27.4	14.0	16.7	15.5	15.7	11.4	22.5	18.5
Total Liabilities to Net Worth 37	1.3	•	1.6	0.1	11.6	0.5	0.9	1.3	1.1	1.2	2.3	0.8	1.3
Current Assets to Working Capital 38	2.0	•	•	1.2	2.7	1.5	1.9	2.7	3.2	2.4	3.7	1.9	1.8
Current Liabilities to Working Capital 39	1.0	•	•	0.2	1.7	0.5	0.9	1.7	2.2	1.4	2.7	0.9	0.8
Working Capital to Net Sales 40	0.1	•	•	0.1	0.1	0.1	0.1	0.1	0.1	0.1	0.1	0.2	0.1
Inventory to Working Capital 41	0.8	•	•	0.1	0.6	0.4	0.5	1.2	1.5	1.0	1.8	0.6	0.7
Total Receipts to Cash Flow 42	18.2	7.7	9.0	11.2	11.9	16.2	13.7	12.5	16.2	13.3	10.4	20.0	28.4
Cost of Goods to Cash Flow 43	15.6	6.7	6.4	7.9	8.7	13.2	11.4	10.3	13.3	11.2	8.4	16.9	25.6
Cash Flow to Total Debt 44	0.2	•	1.7	2.9	0.2	1.2	0.6	0.4	0.3	0.3	0.3	0.2	0.1

Selected Financial Factors (in Percentages)

Debt Ratio 45	56.3	•	61.1	6.7	92.1	34.5	48.5	57.4	52.3	55.5	70.1	45.5	56.4
Return on Total Assets 46	6.7	•	32.4	0.4	7.6	5.6	10.7	11.0	8.8	11.1	9.5	5.4	4.8
Return on Equity Before Income Taxes 47	10.2	•	74.5	0.5	72.9	7.3	17.6	21.9	14.4	22.1	22.8	6.8	4.9
Return on Equity After Income Taxes 48	8.6	•	74.2	0.3	71.9	6.9	15.6	19.9	13.2	20.8	20.8	4.7	3.3
Profit Margin (Before Income Tax) 49	2.0	1.6	3.1	0.2	2.5	0.7	2.5	3.0	2.4	4.1	3.6	2.4	1.0
Profit Margin (After Income Tax) 50	1.6	0.7	3.1	0.1	2.4	0.7	2.2	2.7	2.2	3.8	3.3	1.7	0.7

Table II

Corporations with Net Income

MEAT AND SEAFOOD PROCESSING

MONEY AMOUNTS AND SIZE OF ASSETS IN THOUSANDS OF DOLLARS

Item Description for Accounting Period 7/09 Through 6/10		Total	Zero Assets	Under 500	500 to 1,000	1,000 to 5,000	5,000 to 10,000	10,000 to 25,000	25,000 to 50,000	50,000 to 100,000	100,000 to 250,000	250,000 to 500,000	500,000 to 2,500,000	2,500,000 and over
Number of Enterprises	1	1709	18	1064	58	337	35	66	63	25	•	•	6	•
Revenues ($ in Thousands)														
Net Sales	2	93217145	184268	1324723	160548	2944300	986749	3513144	7038470	5468286	•	•	10556054	•
Interest	3	66786	36	0	46	1404	122	617	1939	132	•	•	23044	•
Rents	4	18959	0	0	0	779	0	147	1131	242	•	•	280	•
Royalties	5	651	0	0	0	0	0	0	0	0	•	•	151	•
Other Portfolio Income	6	174882	1238	0	2	23590	58	390	1910	5997	•	•	34046	•
Other Receipts	7	482621	428	0	178	27214	11353	30871	22192	19820	•	•	105550	•
Total Receipts	8	93961044	185970	1324723	160774	2997287	998282	3545169	7065642	5494477	•	•	10719125	•
Average Total Receipts	9	54980	10332	1245	2772	8894	28522	53715	112153	219779	•	•	1786521	•
Operating Costs/Operating Income (%)														
Cost of Operations	10	86.1	86.2	80.1	77.5	75.2	82.0	82.7	81.9	82.4	•	•	84.6	•
Salaries and Wages	11	2.3	•	0.7	1.7	5.0	3.0	3.5	3.1	2.4	•	•	2.4	•
Taxes Paid	12	0.6	1.6	0.6	1.8	1.3	0.7	0.7	0.7	0.7	•	•	0.7	•
Interest Paid	13	0.8	0.1	0.3	0.0	0.6	0.3	0.4	0.5	0.5	•	•	1.1	•
Depreciation	14	1.9	0.3	0.8	1.5	1.6	0.9	1.2	1.7	2.3	•	•	3.5	•
Amortization and Depletion	15	0.2	•	0.6	•	0.0	0.0	0.1	0.1	0.0	•	•	0.9	•
Pensions and Other Deferred Comp.	16	0.4	•	•	0.2	0.7	0.3	0.2	0.1	0.2	•	•	0.2	•
Employee Benefits	17	0.5	0.2	0.0	1.0	1.7	0.8	0.9	0.7	1.3	•	•	1.0	•
Advertising	18	0.5	0.4	1.4	1.8	0.3	0.0	0.2	0.9	2.3	•	•	0.5	•
Other Expenses	19	4.1	7.5	9.6	11.5	6.5	5.1	4.8	6.0	4.1	•	•	4.1	•
Officers' Compensation	20	0.4	1.9	0.7	2.6	2.9	1.8	1.4	0.6	0.6	•	•	0.2	•
Operating Margin	21	2.1	1.9	5.1	0.5	4.2	5.1	3.9	3.5	3.1	•	•	0.7	•
Operating Margin Before Officers' Comp.	22	2.5	3.8	5.8	3.1	7.1	6.9	5.3	4.1	3.6	•	•	0.9	•

Selected Average Balance Sheet ($ in Thousands)

Net Receivables 23	3212	0	0	240	886	1921	3116	7959	12924	92158
Inventories 24	3864	0	0	68	348	665	2907	7551	15663	234419
Net Property, Plant and Equipment 25	6947	0	15	160	1089	1418	4413	11000	31302	339518
Total Assets 26	22883	0	122	740	3536	8095	13942	35125	72161	1150735
Notes and Loans Payable 27	6563	0	19	15	1225	1787	2986	12412	19931	313841
All Other Liabilities 28	5667	0	16	55	884	1271	2831	6518	17478	209274
Net Worth 29	10653	0	87	670	1427	5037	8124	16195	34752	627620

Selected Financial Ratios (Times to 1)

Current Ratio 30	1.9	•	0.8	7.8	2.0	2.3	2.6	1.8	1.4	2.1
Quick Ratio 31	0.9	•	0.3	7.0	1.4	1.7	1.6	0.9	0.7	0.3
Net Sales to Working Capital 32	9.8	•	•	7.4	8.2	13.5	10.9	12.4	20.9	4.8
Coverage Ratio 33	4.5	40.2	19.9	39.6	11.0	19.2	14.2	8.3	7.8	3.2
Total Asset Turnover 34	2.4	•	10.2	3.7	2.5	3.5	3.8	3.2	3.0	1.5
Inventory Turnover 35	12.2	•	2764.4	31.4	18.9	34.8	15.1	12.1	11.5	6.4
Receivables Turnover 36	19.1	•	13381.0	11.8	14.4	•	14.4	17.2	16.5	38.2
Total Liabilities to Net Worth 37	1.1	•	0.4	0.1	1.5	0.6	0.7	1.2	1.1	0.8
Current Assets to Working Capital 38	2.1	•	•	1.1	2.0	1.8	1.6	2.3	3.4	1.9
Current Liabilities to Working Capital 39	1.1	•	•	0.1	1.0	0.8	0.6	1.3	2.4	0.9
Working Capital to Net Sales 40	0.1	•	•	0.1	0.1	0.1	0.1	0.1	0.0	0.2
Inventory to Working Capital 41	0.8	•	•	0.1	0.4	0.3	0.4	1.0	1.4	0.6
Total Receipts to Cash Flow 42	16.5	11.4	13.5	10.1	10.3	11.5	11.2	14.5		20.0
Cost of Goods to Cash Flow 43	14.2	9.8	8.1	10.4	7.6	8.5	9.5	9.2	12.0	16.9
Cash Flow to Total Debt 44	0.3	•	3.5	2.9	0.4	0.9	0.8	0.5	0.4	0.2

Selected Financial Factors (in Percentages)

Debt Ratio 45	53.4	•	28.8	9.5	59.7	37.8	41.7	53.9	51.8	45.5
Return on Total Assets 46	9.1	•	54.2	2.3	16.4	23.1	19.8	13.9	12.3	5.4
Return on Equity Before Income Taxes 47	15.1	•	72.3	2.5	37.0	35.2	31.5	26.5	22.3	6.8
Return on Equity After Income Taxes 48	13.1	•	72.1	2.1	36.7	34.0	29.0	24.4	20.7	4.7
Profit Margin (Before Income Tax) 49	3.0	2.8	5.1	0.6	6.0	6.3	4.8	3.8	3.5	2.4
Profit Margin (After Income Tax) 50	2.6	1.9	5.0	0.5	6.0	6.1	4.4	3.5	3.3	1.7

Table I

Corporations with and without Net Income

BAKERIES AND TORTILLA

MONEY AMOUNTS AND SIZE OF ASSETS IN THOUSANDS OF DOLLARS

Item Description for Accounting Period 7/09 Through 6/10	Total	Zero Assets	Under 500	500 to 1,000	1,000 to 5,000	5,000 to 10,000	10,000 to 25,000	25,000 to 50,000	50,000 to 100,000	100,000 to 250,000	250,000 to 500,000	500,000 to 2,500,000	2,500,000 and over
Number of Enterprises **1**	3956	272	3014	0	391	88	100	34	25	12	6	11	3
Revenues ($ in Thousands)													
Net Sales **2**	45985669	41004	1213412	0	1775981	1485449	3084078	1967765	3097411	2968478	4365440	11204892	14781759
Interest **3**	67994	0	97	0	268	89	2653	235	1605	1186	2640	31854	27367
Rents **4**	9785	0	15	0	855	0	286	827	180	481	19	5432	1690
Royalties **5**	52845	0	0	0	0	0	0	0	6490	23326	4508	9532	8990
Other Portfolio Income **6**	380069	0	2664	0	672	187	1725	268	4414	163	883	1091	368000
Other Receipts **7**	361880	0	4881	0	5924	3929	5585	2605	19875	8306	19864	93797	197115
Total Receipts **8**	46858242	41004	1221069	0	1783700	1489654	3094327	1971700	3129975	3001940	4393354	11346598	15384921
Average Total Receipts **9**	11845	151	405	•	4562	16928	30943	57991	125199	250162	732226	1031509	5128307
Operating Costs/Operating Income (%)													
Cost of Operations **10**	62.4	76.0	51.9	•	60.5	70.8	68.6	61.6	62.4	66.4	70.8	58.6	61.0
Salaries and Wages **11**	7.2	7.2	16.2	•	7.8	4.9	5.3	6.7	10.2	7.5	6.6	7.7	6.2
Taxes Paid **12**	1.9	2.7	4.6	•	1.7	1.9	1.8	1.4	1.9	1.7	1.2	2.2	1.9
Interest Paid **13**	1.8	5.4	1.1	•	0.7	0.6	1.0	1.4	1.3	1.3	1.3	1.5	2.9
Depreciation **14**	3.3	7.1	3.0	•	3.1	3.4	4.0	4.7	4.0	3.9	2.3	3.0	3.1
Amortization and Depletion **15**	0.6	1.9	0.3	•	0.3	0.0	0.3	0.5	0.5	0.5	0.7	0.6	0.8
Pensions and Other Deferred Comp. **16**	1.4	0.0	0.0	•	0.3	0.1	0.1	0.8	1.4	1.4	0.6	1.4	2.3
Employee Benefits **17**	3.2	0.8	0.1	•	0.9	1.2	1.6	1.4	3.6	3.0	1.1	4.3	4.4
Advertising **18**	2.0	0.6	0.7	•	0.9	0.1	0.4	0.6	1.0	1.1	1.6	2.4	3.3
Other Expenses **19**	12.6	46.1	23.5	•	17.0	8.7	8.6	11.3	9.1	10.9	8.8	15.3	12.6
Officers' Compensation **20**	1.1	0.9	4.3	•	5.1	1.5	2.1	2.8	2.1	0.8	0.4	0.4	0.3
Operating Margin **21**	2.5	•	•	•	1.6	6.7	6.2	6.9	2.5	1.5	4.6	2.7	1.2
Operating Margin Before Officers' Comp. **22**	3.6	•	•	•	6.7	8.2	8.3	9.6	4.5	2.3	5.0	3.1	1.5

Selected Average Balance Sheet ($ in Thousands)

Net Receivables 23	1146	0	16	•	332	1347	1820	3775	8579	22503	56567	155693	463418
Inventories 24	554	0	6	•	172	944	1871	3333	4607	12289	57322	67168	251829
Net Property, Plant and Equipment 25	2486	0	35	•	704	3302	6629	15894	25598	72930	97130	241671	1068509
Total Assets 26	8798	0	93	•	2022	6548	14850	36262	69750	146582	382180	894322	4935583
Notes and Loans Payable 27	2649	0	128	•	753	4146	5346	15099	21001	34370	115341	179386	1594650
All Other Liabilities 28	2603	0	18	•	378	3234	3141	9235	15146	47182	80475	375751	1206861
Net Worth 29	3546	0	-53	•	890	-832	6363	11928	33603	65029	186364	339185	2134072

Selected Financial Ratios (Times to 1)

Current Ratio 30	1.3	•	1.8	•	2.4	0.6	1.4	1.6	1.6	1.1	1.9	1.2	1.4
Quick Ratio 31	0.9	•	1.2	•	1.4	0.4	0.9	0.9	1.1	0.7	1.2	0.9	0.9
Net Sales to Working Capital 32	18.1	•	22.4	•	7.4	•	16.7	14.6	14.5	42.3	8.6	23.0	17.7
Coverage Ratio 33	4.4	•	•	•	3.9	13.5	6.0	7.5	3.6	3.0	5.1	3.6	4.6
Total Asset Turnover 34	1.3	•	4.3	•	2.2	2.6	1.6	2.1	1.8	1.7	1.9	1.1	1.0
Inventory Turnover 35	13.1	•	32.2	•	16.0	12.7	10.7	11.3	16.8	13.4	9.0	8.9	11.9
Receivables Turnover 36	11.4	•	41.0	•	17.4	12.3	14.8	12.7	13.7	11.7	7.6	6.8	21.3
Total Liabilities to Net Worth 37	1.5	•	•	•	1.3	•	2.0	1.3	1.1	1.3	1.1	1.6	1.3
Current Assets to Working Capital 38	3.9	•	2.2	•	1.7	•	3.2	2.7	2.7	8.6	2.1	6.4	3.3
Current Liabilities to Working Capital 39	2.9	•	1.2	•	0.7	•	2.2	1.7	1.7	7.6	1.1	5.4	2.3
Working Capital to Net Sales 40	0.1	•	0.0	•	0.1	•	0.1	0.1	0.1	0.0	0.1	0.0	0.1
Inventory to Working Capital 41	0.9	•	0.4	•	0.4	•	0.9	0.8	0.5	2.4	0.6	0.9	0.9
Total Receipts to Cash Flow 42	7.5	•	11.6	•	6.8	7.8	6.2	7.7	10.7	9.0	8.1	6.1	7.8
Cost of Goods to Cash Flow 43	4.7	•	6.0	•	4.1	5.5	3.8	5.3	6.6	6.0	5.7	3.6	4.8
Cash Flow to Total Debt 44	0.3	•	0.2	•	0.6	0.3	0.4	0.5	0.3	0.3	0.5	0.3	0.2

Selected Financial Factors (in Percentages)

Debt Ratio 45	59.7	•	156.9	•	56.0	112.7	67.1	57.2	51.8	55.6	51.2	62.1	56.8
Return on Total Assets 46	10.4	•	•	•	6.2	19.5	13.5	15.6	8.6	6.6	12.4	6.2	13.3
Return on Equity Before Income Taxes 47	19.9	•	38.9	•	10.4	•	34.3	31.6	12.9	9.9	20.4	11.8	24.0
Return on Equity After Income Taxes 48	14.5	•	39.1	•	8.5	•	32.6	28.2	10.1	8.3	17.1	7.9	16.1
Profit Margin (Before Income Tax) 49	6.1	•	•	•	2.0	7.0	7.1	6.5	3.5	2.6	5.2	3.9	10.4
Profit Margin (After Income Tax) 50	4.4	•	•	•	1.7	6.8	6.7	5.8	2.7	2.2	4.4	2.6	7.0

Table II

Corporations with Net Income

BAKERIES AND TORTILLA

MONEY AMOUNTS AND SIZE OF ASSETS IN THOUSANDS OF DOLLARS

Item Description for Accounting Period 7/09 Through 6/10		Total	Zero Assets	Under 500	500 to 1,000	1,000 to 5,000	5,000 to 10,000	10,000 to 25,000	25,000 to 50,000	50,000 to 100,000	100,000 to 250,000	250,000 to 500,000	500,000 to 2,500,000	2,500,000 and over
Number of Enterprises	1	1198	0	•	0	184	78	82	25	18	•	6	7	3
Revenues ($ in Thousands)														
Net Sales	2	39295562	0	•	0	1245234	1336815	2605486	1481976	2703606	•	4365440	7621727	14781759
Interest	3	54110	0	•	0	166	87	1593	15	751	•	2640	21057	27367
Rents	4	8863	0	•	0	855	0	0	230	158	•	19	5432	1690
Royalties	5	46355	0	•	0	0	0	0	0	0	•	4508	9532	8990
Other Portfolio Income	6	373937	0	•	0	671	187	1613	127	1245	•	883	1067	368000
Other Receipts	7	341120	0	•	0	2879	3929	3339	1837	13428	•	19864	88995	197115
Total Receipts	8	40119947	0	•	0	1249805	1341018	2612031	1484185	2719188	•	4393354	7747810	15384921
Average Total Receipts	9	33489	•	•	•	6792	17193	31854	59367	151066	•	732226	1106830	5128307
Operating Costs/Operating Income (%)														
Cost of Operations	10	62.1	•	•	•	53.6	70.3	68.0	60.7	62.1	•	70.8	57.5	61.0
Salaries and Wages	11	6.7	•	•	•	6.6	5.1	4.8	6.1	10.4	•	6.6	6.5	6.2
Taxes Paid	12	1.8	•	•	•	1.4	1.8	1.8	1.1	1.9	•	1.2	2.0	1.9
Interest Paid	13	1.6	•	•	•	0.7	0.5	0.8	0.8	0.6	•	1.3	0.6	2.9
Depreciation	14	3.3	•	•	•	3.7	2.8	3.7	5.6	3.3	•	2.3	3.7	3.1
Amortization and Depletion	15	0.6	•	•	•	0.1	0.0	0.0	0.1	0.3	•	0.7	0.8	0.8
Pensions and Other Deferred Comp.	16	1.4	•	•	•	0.3	0.1	0.2	0.9	1.6	•	0.6	0.9	2.3
Employee Benefits	17	2.9	•	•	•	0.9	1.4	1.5	1.1	3.9	•	1.1	2.2	4.4
Advertising	18	2.1	•	•	•	1.0	0.1	0.4	0.4	1.0	•	1.6	2.5	3.3
Other Expenses	19	12.4	•	•	•	14.9	7.3	7.9	9.4	8.7	•	8.8	17.4	12.6
Officers' Compensation	20	1.0	•	•	•	5.5	1.6	2.4	3.4	1.3	•	0.4	0.6	0.3
Operating Margin	21	4.2	•	•	•	11.4	9.0	8.5	10.4	4.7	•	4.6	5.4	1.2
Operating Margin Before Officers' Comp.	22	5.1	•	•	•	16.9	10.6	10.9	13.8	6.0	•	5.0	6.0	1.5

Selected Average Balance Sheet ($ in Thousands)

Net Receivables 23	2661	476	1346	1960	3679	10735	56567	82640	463418
Inventories 24	1530	216	1047	1717	2460	5248	57322	85953	251829
Net Property, Plant and Equipment 25	7039	921	3118	6549	19860	27407	97130	286134	1068509
Total Assets 26	24087	2461	6510	14331	35494	71158	382180	853706	4935583
Notes and Loans Payable 27	6898	572	2393	4001	12672	17496	115341	150855	1594650
All Other Liabilities 28	6044	572	3228	3253	6086	17844	80475	234581	1206861
Net Worth 29	11145	1317	889	7077	16736	35818	186364	468269	2134072

Selected Financial Ratios (Times to 1)

Current Ratio 30	1.5	1.9	1.0	1.7	1.5	1.5	1.9	1.4	1.4
Quick Ratio 31	0.9	1.5	0.6	1.0	1.0	1.1	1.2	0.9	0.9
Net Sales to Working Capital 32	15.9	11.0	•	12.6	14.8	15.2	8.6	19.6	17.7
Coverage Ratio 33	6.1	17.8	20.5	12.3	13.8	9.3	5.1	13.3	4.6
Total Asset Turnover 34	1.4	2.7	2.6	2.2	1.7	2.1	1.9	1.3	1.0
Inventory Turnover 35	13.3	16.8	11.5	12.6	14.6	17.8	9.0	7.3	11.9
Receivables Turnover 36	13.2	18.8	•	13.8	20.9	13.9	7.6	8.3	21.3
Total Liabilities to Net Worth 37	1.2	0.9	6.3	1.0	1.1	1.0	1.1	0.8	1.3
Current Assets to Working Capital 38	3.1	2.1	•	2.5	2.9	2.8	2.1	3.6	3.3
Current Liabilities to Working Capital 39	2.1	1.1	•	1.5	1.9	1.8	1.1	2.6	2.3
Working Capital to Net Sales 40	0.1	0.1	•	0.1	0.1	0.1	0.1	0.1	0.1
Inventory to Working Capital 41	0.8	0.5	•	0.7	0.8	0.6	0.6	0.8	0.9
Total Receipts to Cash Flow 42	6.6	4.6	7.1	6.6	5.4	9.1	8.1	4.6	7.8
Cost of Goods to Cash Flow 43	4.1	2.5	5.0	4.5	3.3	5.7	5.7	2.7	4.8
Cash Flow to Total Debt 44	0.4	1.3	0.4	0.7	0.6	0.5	0.5	0.6	0.2

Selected Financial Factors (in Percentages)

Debt Ratio 45	53.7	46.5	86.3	50.6	52.8	49.7	51.2	45.1	56.8
Return on Total Assets 46	13.3	34.2	25.6	21.1	19.0	12.4	12.4	9.8	13.3
Return on Equity Before Income Taxes 47	24.1	60.3	178.6	39.2	37.3	21.9	20.4	16.5	24.0
Return on Equity After Income Taxes 48	18.5	57.5	175.1	35.5	35.7	19.7	17.1	12.0	16.1
Profit Margin (Before Income Tax) 49	8.2	11.7	9.3	8.7	10.5	5.2	5.2	7.1	10.4
Profit Margin (After Income Tax) 50	6.3	11.2	9.1	7.9	10.1	4.7	4.4	5.2	7.0

Table I

Corporations with and without Net Income

OTHER FOOD

MONEY AMOUNTS AND SIZE OF ASSETS IN THOUSANDS OF DOLLARS

Item Description for Accounting Period 7/09 Through 6/10		Total	Zero Assets	Under 500	500 to 1,000	1,000 to 5,000	5,000 to 10,000	10,000 to 25,000	25,000 to 50,000	50,000 to 100,000	100,000 to 250,000	250,000 to 500,000	500,000 to 2,500,000	2,500,000 and over
Number of Enterprises	1	3075	•	181	490	•	171	59	41	29	13	11	3
Revenues ($ in Thousands)													
Net Sales	2	115850113	•	206086	2380724	•	6122456	4193283	5140567	7211478	6143765	12193760	69321972
Interest	3	2364180	•	0	936	•	1026	2176	4436	8112	2189	38615	2305038
Rents	4	90271	•	0	100	•	941	342	2329	6640	9769	2445	67281
Royalties	5	980897	•	0	0	•	0	198	1119	20730	43	718	946804
Other Portfolio Income	6	229775	•	218	495	•	33355	3314	4649	11169	22369	24855	128046
Other Receipts	7	966483	•	0	14984	•	43067	16925	62004	50520	17005	314747	428289
Total Receipts	8	120481719	•	206304	2397239	•	6200845	4216238	5215104	7308649	6195140	12575140	73197430
Average Total Receipts	9	39181	•	1140	4892	•	36262	71462	127198	252022	476549	1143195	24399143
Operating Costs/Operating Income (%)													
Cost of Operations	10	67.7	•	19.3	64.2	•	73.7	75.7	65.4	69.9	66.4	72.2	66.5
Salaries and Wages	11	5.7	•	16.5	11.0	•	6.4	4.3	7.0	6.6	7.0	5.1	5.2
Taxes Paid	12	1.3	•	5.0	1.7	•	1.1	0.8	1.4	1.4	1.0	1.1	1.3
Interest Paid	13	4.1	•	0.1	0.8	•	0.6	0.8	1.5	1.2	1.6	2.6	5.8
Depreciation	14	2.4	•	2.1	2.0	•	2.2	2.8	3.1	2.9	3.1	3.5	2.0
Amortization and Depletion	15	0.4	•	0.1	0.1	•	0.0	0.2	1.0	0.4	0.5	1.0	0.3
Pensions and Other Deferred Comp.	16	1.1	•	•	0.1	•	0.3	0.3	0.3	0.5	0.5	0.8	1.5
Employee Benefits	17	1.3	•	1.0	0.9	•	1.2	1.5	1.1	1.9	1.1	1.4	1.2
Advertising	18	3.0	•	1.3	1.1	•	0.8	1.1	2.8	1.2	4.1	0.8	4.0
Other Expenses	19	11.6	•	24.5	13.7	•	8.1	7.6	11.5	8.5	8.6	9.5	12.8
Officers' Compensation	20	0.5	•	15.8	3.3	•	1.1	1.1	1.2	1.1	0.7	0.5	0.1
Operating Margin	21	0.9	•	14.1	1.0	•	4.4	3.8	3.8	4.4	5.3	1.5	•
Operating Margin Before Officers' Comp.	22	1.4	•	29.9	4.3	•	5.5	4.9	5.0	5.5	6.0	2.0	•

Selected Average Balance Sheet ($ in Thousands)

Net Receivables 23	96716	•	•	0	324	•	3230	7548	10324	22274	44773	113971	97718695
Inventories 24	2952	•	•	27	643	•	4069	11962	13941	30345	60388	110941	1231652
Net Property, Plant and Equipment 25	6090	•	•	576	531	•	5167	9311	23639	41309	87940	240743	3555382
Total Assets 26	157744	•	963	2014	•	16389	38892	77806	148941	306286	1026395	151669818
Notes and Loans Payable 27	14850	•	110	857	•	5455	10673	30124	53018	105637	438543	11404265
All Other Liabilities 28	107517	•	81	366	•	3795	12215	19693	44139	75690	226302	107739332
Net Worth 29	35377	•	773	791	•	7139	16004	27989	51785	124959	361550	32526221

Selected Financial Ratios (Times to 1)

Current Ratio 30	1.0	•	4.7	2.6	•	2.1	1.6	1.9	1.7	1.9	1.6	1.0
Quick Ratio 31	0.9	•	4.3	1.3	•	1.1	0.7	0.9	0.8	0.9	0.7	0.9
Net Sales to Working Capital 32	•	•	3.8	6.1	•	7.2	8.1	7.8	8.2	7.6	7.5	•
Coverage Ratio 33	2.3	•	113.2	3.1	•	10.1	6.6	4.6	5.7	4.8	2.8	1.9
Total Asset Turnover 34	0.2	•	1.2	2.4	•	2.2	1.8	1.6	1.7	1.5	1.1	0.2
Inventory Turnover 35	8.6	•	8.2	4.9	•	6.5	4.5	5.9	5.7	5.2	7.2	12.5
Receivables Turnover 36	0.4	•	31.4	9.9	•	10.6	8.8	12.1	10.9	9.4	10.4	0.2
Total Liabilities to Net Worth 37	3.5	•	0.2	1.5	•	1.3	1.4	1.8	1.9	1.5	1.8	3.7
Current Assets to Working Capital 38	•	•	1.3	1.6	•	1.9	2.7	2.2	2.3	2.1	2.6	•
Current Liabilities to Working Capital 39	•	•	0.3	0.6	•	0.9	1.7	1.2	1.3	1.1	1.6	•
Working Capital to Net Sales 40	•	•	0.3	0.2	•	0.1	0.1	0.1	0.1	0.1	0.1	•
Inventory to Working Capital 41	•	•	0.1	0.6	•	0.8	1.4	0.9	0.9	0.8	0.8	•
Total Receipts to Cash Flow 42	6.8	•	4.0	9.0	•	8.9	9.6	6.9	8.1	8.1	8.2	6.2
Cost of Goods to Cash Flow 43	4.6	•	0.8	5.8	•	6.5	7.2	4.5	5.7	5.4	5.9	4.1
Cash Flow to Total Debt 44	0.0	•	1.5	0.4	•	0.4	0.3	0.4	0.3	0.3	0.2	0.0

Selected Financial Factors (in Percentages)

Debt Ratio 45	77.6	•	19.8	60.8	•	56.4	58.9	64.0	65.2	59.2	64.8	78.6
Return on Total Assets 46	2.2	•	16.9	6.1	•	13.7	9.4	10.8	11.6	12.0	7.8	1.7
Return on Equity Before Income Taxes 47	5.5	•	20.9	10.4	•	28.4	19.3	23.6	27.6	23.3	14.3	3.8
Return on Equity After Income Taxes 48	4.0	•	20.9	7.6	•	27.6	18.0	19.0	21.8	19.2	9.2	2.5
Profit Margin (Before Income Tax) 49	5.2	•	14.2	1.7	•	5.7	4.3	5.3	5.8	6.2	4.6	5.4
Profit Margin (After Income Tax) 50	3.7	•	14.2	1.2	•	5.5	4.1	4.2	4.5	5.1	3.0	3.5

49

Table II
Corporations with Net Income

OTHER FOOD

MONEY AMOUNTS AND SIZE OF ASSETS IN THOUSANDS OF DOLLARS

Item Description for Accounting Period 7/09 Through 6/10		Total	Zero Assets	Under 500	500 to 1,000	1,000 to 5,000	5,000 to 10,000	10,000 to 25,000	25,000 to 50,000	50,000 to 100,000	100,000 to 250,000	250,000 to 500,000	500,000 to 2,500,000	2,500,000 and over
Number of Enterprises	1	1506	14	660	181	327	72	131	48	•	23	10	•	3
Revenues ($ in Thousands)														
Net Sales	2	108779700	878228	267955	206086	2212305	1275301	5267797	3672952	•	6215301	4862663	•	69321972
Interest	3	2358427	861	11	0	878	360	893	1571	•	7465	1804	•	2305038
Rents	4	83818	129	0	0	100	296	816	342	•	595	9769	•	67281
Royalties	5	978635	11251	0	0	0	0	0	198	•	19362	43	•	946804
Other Portfolio Income	6	218912	0	0	218	273	123	33329	3225	•	6721	18798	•	128046
Other Receipts	7	807451	5572	1	0	10560	8390	41216	16074	•	31676	14365	•	428289
Total Receipts	8	113226943	896041	267967	206304	2224116	1284470	5344051	3694362	•	6281120	4907442	•	73197430
Average Total Receipts	9	75184	64003	406	1140	6802	17840	40794	76966	•	273092	490744	•	24399143
Operating Costs/Operating Income (%)														
Cost of Operations	10	67.4	56.6	23.0	19.3	65.4	71.5	72.5	75.3	•	69.6	69.4	•	66.5
Salaries and Wages	11	5.4	6.1	12.7	16.5	10.1	5.6	6.0	4.4	•	5.9	4.5	•	5.2
Taxes Paid	12	1.2	0.5	2.0	5.0	1.7	0.9	1.0	0.9	•	1.3	0.9	•	1.3
Interest Paid	13	4.2	1.5	3.3	0.1	0.5	0.5	0.5	0.6	•	1.1	1.3	•	5.8
Depreciation	14	2.2	2.3	5.5	2.1	1.8	2.2	1.9	2.2	•	2.7	2.5	•	2.0
Amortization and Depletion	15	0.3	0.6	0.7	0.1	0.1	0.0	0.0	0.1	•	0.3	0.4	•	0.3
Pensions and Other Deferred Comp.	16	1.1	0.0	•	0.1	0.0	0.4	0.3	0.4	•	0.5	0.4	•	1.5
Employee Benefits	17	1.3	3.2	0.0	1.0	1.0	0.6	1.3	1.6	•	2.0	0.6	•	1.2
Advertising	18	3.1	2.4	5.7	1.3	0.9	0.3	0.8	0.9	•	1.3	4.3	•	4.0
Other Expenses	19	11.6	25.1	36.3	24.5	9.7	7.8	8.0	7.3	•	7.9	7.2	•	12.8
Officers' Compensation	20	0.5	0.9	7.4	15.8	3.3	2.3	1.1	1.2	•	1.1	0.5	•	0.1
Operating Margin	21	1.6	0.7	3.6	14.1	5.4	7.8	6.6	5.3	•	6.3	7.9	•	•
Operating Margin Before Officers' Comp.	22	2.0	1.6	11.0	29.9	8.7	10.1	7.7	6.4	•	7.4	8.4	•	•

Selected Average Balance Sheet ($ in Thousands)

Net Receivables 23	197019	0	21	0	466	1490	3313	7818	24456	50248	• 97718695
Inventories 24	5117	0	7	27	798	1928	4135	11421	29472	48196	• 1163884
Net Property, Plant and Equipment 25	10962	0	123	576	616	1717	5149	9182	40402	76888	• 3555382
Total Assets 26	317322	0	224	963	2321	7411	16374	37641	149886	298741	•151669818
Notes and Loans Payable 27	27920	0	184	110	644	1891	4267	9840	53391	91142	• 11404265
All Other Liabilities 28	218164	0	42	81	405	1896	3491	11056	42582	62821	•107739332
Net Worth 29	71237	0	-2	773	1273	3624	8617	16745	53913	144778	• 32526221

Selected Financial Ratios (Times to 1)

Current Ratio 30	1.0	•	1.0	4.7	2.9	2.2	2.3	1.8	1.9	2.1	1.0
Quick Ratio 31	1.0	•	0.7	4.3	1.4	1.5	1.3	0.8	0.9	1.1	0.9
Net Sales to Working Capital 32	•	•	837.4	3.8	6.4	7.2	7.2	7.2	7.4	7.0	•
Coverage Ratio 33	2.4	2.8	2.1	113.2	11.8	18.1	18.5	11.1	8.0	7.9	1.9
Total Asset Turnover 34	0.2	•	1.8	1.2	2.9	2.4	2.5	2.0	1.8	1.6	0.2
Inventory Turnover 35	9.5	•	13.0	8.2	5.5	6.6	7.0	5.0	6.4	7.0	13.2
Receivables Turnover 36	0.4	•	25.9	31.7	10.3	8.5	10.9	9.4	12.2	9.4	3.7
Total Liabilities to Net Worth 37	3.5	•	•	0.2	0.8	1.0	0.9	1.2	1.8	1.1	3.7
Current Assets to Working Capital 38	•	•	85.0	1.3	1.5	1.8	1.7	2.3	2.2	1.9	•
Current Liabilities to Working Capital 39	•	•	84.0	0.3	0.5	0.8	0.7	1.3	1.2	0.9	•
Working Capital to Net Sales 40	•	•	0.0	0.3	0.2	0.1	0.1	0.1	0.1	0.1	•
Inventory to Working Capital 41	•	•	26.0	0.1	0.6	0.6	0.7	1.1	0.9	0.6	•
Total Receipts to Cash Flow 42	6.4	4.0	3.6	4.0	8.2	6.8	7.3	8.4	7.4	7.0	6.2
Cost of Goods to Cash Flow 43	4.3	2.3	0.8	0.8	5.3	4.9	5.3	6.3	5.2	4.9	4.1
Cash Flow to Total Debt 44	0.0	•	1.5	0.8	0.8	0.7	0.7	0.4	0.4	0.4	0.0

Selected Financial Factors (in Percentages)

Debt Ratio 45	77.6	•	100.9	19.8	45.2	51.1	47.4	55.5	64.0	51.5	78.6
Return on Total Assets 46	2.3	•	12.5	16.9	18.8	21.6	20.8	13.1	15.2	16.4	1.7
Return on Equity Before Income Taxes 47	6.0	•	•	20.9	31.4	41.7	37.4	26.9	37.0	29.6	3.8
Return on Equity After Income Taxes 48	4.4	•	•	20.9	28.7	38.1	36.5	25.3	29.9	25.0	2.5
Profit Margin (Before Income Tax) 49	6.0	2.7	3.6	14.2	5.9	8.5	8.0	5.9	7.4	8.8	5.4
Profit Margin (After Income Tax) 50	4.4	2.0	2.8	14.2	5.4	7.8	7.8	5.5	6.0	7.4	3.5

Table I

Corporations with and without Net Income

SOFT DRINK AND ICE

MONEY AMOUNTS AND SIZE OF ASSETS IN THOUSANDS OF DOLLARS

Item Description for Accounting Period 7/09 Through 6/10	Total	Zero Assets	Under 500	500 to 1,000	1,000 to 5,000	5,000 to 10,000	10,000 to 25,000	25,000 to 50,000	50,000 to 100,000	100,000 to 250,000	250,000 to 500,000	500,000 to 2,500,000	2,500,000 and over
Number of Enterprises 1	284	•	0	129	•	•	16	25	16	11	8	4	6
Revenues ($ in Thousands)													
Net Sales 2	55143130	•	0	209765	•	•	610463	1896847	2100177	2930277	283146	4280424	39887620
Interest 3	372127	•	0	38	•	•	24	900	1426	3666	4299	1781	320448
Rents 4	55171	•	0	0	•	•	242	0	24	541	14801	0	39326
Royalties 5	1443558	•	0	0	•	•	0	0	0	0	10990	0	1431373
Other Portfolio Income 6	1831495	•	0	1	•	•	103	616	543	18878	3873	2001	1781578
Other Receipts 7	1768171	•	0	3	•	•	15045	6633	28576	37927	38504	-281785	1884225
Total Receipts 8	60613652	•	0	209807	•	•	625877	1904996	2130746	2991289	2903613	4002421	45344570
Average Total Receipts 9	213428	•	•	1626	•	•	39117	76200	133172	271935	362952	1000605	7557428
Operating Costs/Operating Income (%)													
Cost of Operations 10	51.5	•	•	66.4	•	•	77.1	71.9	60.9	71.1	58.9	48.5	47.8
Salaries and Wages 11	11.8	•	•	1.7	•	•	6.1	6.5	11.4	7.6	12.7	15.4	12.0
Taxes Paid 12	1.8	•	•	2.1	•	•	1.2	1.3	1.3	1.2	2.4	2.0	1.8
Interest Paid 13	3.1	•	•	0.7	•	•	0.9	0.7	1.1	0.7	2.4	3.7	3.5
Depreciation 14	4.5	•	•	1.7	•	•	1.8	3.0	3.2	3.5	5.0	4.5	4.8
Amortization and Depletion 15	1.1	•	•	0.2	•	•	0.9	0.1	0.5	0.8	1.5	0.8	1.3
Pensions and Other Deferred Comp. 16	1.0	•	•	1.3	•	•	0.3	0.5	0.2	0.5	0.4	0.5	1.3
Employee Benefits 17	2.2	•	•	0.7	•	•	1.1	2.0	1.7	2.3	2.0	2.5	2.2
Advertising 18	7.9	•	•	2.3	•	•	2.2	6.5	3.7	2.2	2.7	0.5	10.0
Other Expenses 19	15.2	•	•	24.4	•	•	6.0	4.7	7.6	8.3	10.4	13.8	17.0
Officers' Compensation 20	0.3	•	•	8.6	•	•	1.1	1.5	0.9	0.4	0.6	0.4	0.1
Operating Margin 21	•	•	•	•	•	•	1.4	1.4	7.5	1.4	1.0	7.3	•
Operating Margin Before Officers' Comp. 22	•	•	•	•	•	•	2.5	2.9	8.4	1.8	1.7	7.8	•

Selected Average Balance Sheet ($ in Thousands)

Net Receivables 23	25018	116	2676	6050	17558	22199	29112	124866	934777
Inventories 24	9490	241	3209	4574	5739	13301	29274	39560	307115
Net Property, Plant and Equipment 25	49113	27	3834	9174	24493	54766	98317	274650	1777408
Total Assets 26	256090	678	15230	36741	74500	170215	344630	736432	10403052
Notes and Loans Payable 27	121012	416	3902	16562	21859	28744	128553	513483	4993358
All Other Liabilities 28	71420	74	2076	13761	18631	39442	99817	269773	2857398
Net Worth 29	63659	188	9252	6419	34010	102029	116260	-46824	2552296

Selected Financial Ratios (Times to 1)

Current Ratio 30	0.9	1.4	2.6	1.3	2.3	2.0	1.3	1.3	0.9
Quick Ratio 31	0.6	0.7	1.5	0.8	1.6	1.4	0.8	1.0	0.6
Net Sales to Working Capital 32	•	10.9	11.3	21.7	7.5	8.8	16.0	21.6	•
Coverage Ratio 33	4.7	2.4	5.2	3.6	8.9	6.0	2.4	1.2	5.3
Total Asset Turnover 34	0.8	2.4	2.5	2.1	1.8	1.6	1.0	1.5	0.6
Inventory Turnover 35	10.5	4.5	9.2	11.9	13.9	14.2	7.1	13.1	10.3
Receivables Turnover 36	7.0	11.7	8.7	11.7	8.7	11.5	9.5	8.9	6.3
Total Liabilities to Net Worth 37	3.0	2.6	0.6	1.2	0.7	0.7	2.0	•	3.1
Current Assets to Working Capital 38	•	3.2	1.6	4.5	1.8	2.0	4.2	4.4	•
Current Liabilities to Working Capital 39	•	2.2	0.6	3.5	0.8	1.0	3.2	3.4	•
Working Capital to Net Sales 40	•	0.1	0.1	0.0	0.1	0.1	0.1	0.0	•
Inventory to Working Capital 41	•	1.6	0.6	1.4	0.3	0.5	1.2	0.8	•
Total Receipts to Cash Flow 42	4.5	13.5	10.9	20.0	6.8	10.4	9.8	8.5	3.8
Cost of Goods to Cash Flow 43	2.3	9.0	8.4	14.4	4.2	7.4	5.8	4.1	1.8
Cash Flow to Total Debt 44	0.2	0.2	0.6	0.1	0.5	0.4	0.2	0.2	0.2

Selected Financial Factors (in Percentages)

Debt Ratio 45	75.1	72.2	39.3	82.5	54.3	40.1	66.3	106.4	75.5
Return on Total Assets 46	11.2	5.2	12.1	5.2	17.8	6.6	6.1	6.5	11.8
Return on Equity Before Income Taxes 47	35.4	21.3	16.1	21.3	34.5	9.1	10.7	•	39.0
Return on Equity After Income Taxes 48	23.0	18.6	15.5	18.6	33.8	6.2	8.4	•	24.9
Profit Margin (Before Income Tax) 49	11.6	1.8	3.9	1.8	8.9	3.5	3.5	0.8	15.0
Profit Margin (After Income Tax) 50	7.5	1.6	3.8	1.6	8.8	2.7	2.7	0.5	9.6

Table II

Corporations with Net Income

SOFT DRINK AND ICE

MONEY AMOUNTS AND SIZE OF ASSETS IN THOUSANDS OF DOLLARS

Item Description for Accounting Period 7/09 Through 6/10	Total	Zero Assets	Under 500	500 to 1000	1,000 to 5,000	5,000 to 10,000	10,000 to 25,000	25,000 to 50,000	50,000 to 100,000	100,000 to 250,000	250,000 to 500,000	500,000 to 2,500,000	2,500,000 and over
Number of Enterprises **1**	139	0	0	56	7	•	9	•	•	8	•	•	•
Revenues ($ in Thousands)													
Net Sales **2**	39253751	0	0	182146	98510	•	452768	•	•	2669193	•	•	•
Interest **3**	332074	0	0	11	30	•	16	•	•	3660	•	•	•
Rents **4**	50775	0	0	0	0	•	0	•	•	541	•	•	•
Royalties **5**	1442362	0	0	0	0	•	0	•	•	0	•	•	•
Other Portfolio Income **6**	1827633	0	0	1	18698	•	75	•	•	18840	•	•	•
Other Receipts **7**	1724965	0	0	3	508	•	14601	•	•	42465	•	•	•
Total Receipts **8**	44631560	0	0	182161	117746	•	467460	•	•	2764699	•	•	•
Average Total Receipts **9**	321090	•	•	3253	16821	•	51940	•	•	345587	•	•	•
Operating Costs/Operating Income (%)													
Cost of Operations **10**	48.4	•	•	65.1	43.3	•	80.9	•	•	70.8	•	•	•
Salaries and Wages **11**	10.0	•	•	0.3	2.2	•	4.0	•	•	7.5	•	•	•
Taxes Paid **12**	1.7	•	•	1.7	1.5	•	0.9	•	•	1.2	•	•	•
Interest Paid **13**	2.8	•	•	0.8	1.6	•	•	•	•	0.4	•	•	•
Depreciation **14**	4.3	•	•	1.7	1.3	•	1.3	•	•	2.6	•	•	•
Amortization and Depletion **15**	1.0	•	•	0.3	0.0	•	0.1	•	•	0.7	•	•	•
Pensions and Other Deferred Comp. **16**	0.7	•	•	1.5	0.1	•	0.3	•	•	0.5	•	•	•
Employee Benefits **17**	1.8	•	•	0.2	•	•	0.8	•	•	2.3	•	•	•
Advertising **18**	10.8	•	•	1.7	4.8	•	2.6	•	•	2.3	•	•	•
Other Expenses **19**	17.6	•	•	20.7	20.1	•	5.5	•	•	7.4	•	•	•
Officers' Compensation **20**	0.4	•	•	2.8	2.5	•	0.9	•	•	0.4	•	•	•
Operating Margin **21**	0.6	•	•	3.4	22.5	•	2.7	•	•	4.0	•	•	•
Operating Margin Before Officers' Comp. **22**	1.0	•	•	6.2	25.0	•	3.6	•	•	4.3	•	•	•

Selected Average Balance Sheet ($ in Thousands)

Net Receivables 23	42127	234	441	3327	23592
Inventories 24	14034	379	511	3559	13984
Net Property, Plant and Equipment 25	66226	50	872	3623	56546
Total Assets 26	374963	805	3350	13553	179569
Notes and Loans Payable 27	179333	354	0	0	23639
All Other Liabilities 28	117725	134	208	1618	48691
Net Worth 29	77905	317	3141	11934	107240

Selected Financial Ratios (Times to 1)

Current Ratio 30	0.9	5.4	7.1	5.2	1.9
Quick Ratio 31	0.6	2.4	5.8	3.0	1.3
Net Sales to Working Capital 32	•	5.5	11.0	9.0	11.1
Coverage Ratio 33	7.2	5.4	27.3	•	15.8
Total Asset Turnover 34	0.8	4.0	4.2	3.7	1.9
Inventory Turnover 35	9.7	5.6	11.9	11.4	17.1
Receivables Turnover 36	6.2	•	9.7	10.0	13.7
Total Liabilities to Net Worth 37	3.8	1.5	0.1	0.1	0.7
Current Assets to Working Capital 38	•	1.2	1.2	1.2	2.1
Current Liabilities to Working Capital 39	•	0.2	0.2	0.2	1.1
Working Capital to Net Sales 40	•	0.2	0.1	0.1	0.1
Inventory to Working Capital 41	•	0.6	0.1	0.5	0.5
Total Receipts to Cash Flow 42	3.4	5.6	2.5	8.9	8.7
Cost of Goods to Cash Flow 43	1.7	3.6	1.1	7.2	6.1
Cash Flow to Total Debt 44	0.3	1.2	26.6	3.5	0.5

Selected Financial Factors (in Percentages)

Debt Ratio 45	79.2	60.6	6.2	11.9	40.3
Return on Total Assets 46	15.2	17.1	183.0	22.0	12.8
Return on Equity Before Income Taxes 47	63.0	35.4	188.0	25.0	20.1
Return on Equity After Income Taxes 48	42.4	26.9	173.6	24.1	16.2
Profit Margin (Before Income Tax) 49	17.4	3.5	42.0	5.9	6.4
Profit Margin (After Income Tax) 50	11.7	2.6	38.7	5.7	5.2

Table I

Corporations with and without Net Income

BREWERIES

MONEY AMOUNTS AND SIZE OF ASSETS IN THOUSANDS OF DOLLARS

Item Description for Accounting Period 7/09 Through 6/10		Total	Zero Assets	Under 500	500 to 1,000	1,000 to 5,000	5,000 to 10,000	10,000 to 25,000	25,000 to 50,000	50,000 to 100,000	100,000 to 250,000	250,000 to 500,000	500,000 to 2,500,000	2,500,000 and over
Number of Enterprises	1	348	0	91	0	221	0	15	10	3	5	0	0	3

Revenues ($ in Thousands)

		Total	Zero Assets	Under 500	500 to 1,000	1,000 to 5,000	5,000 to 10,000	10,000 to 25,000	25,000 to 50,000	50,000 to 100,000	100,000 to 250,000	250,000 to 500,000	500,000 to 2,500,000	2,500,000 and over
Net Sales	2	21109001	0	28541	0	624739	0	349613	425162	329189	1249510	0	0	18102247
Interest	3	48359	0	0	0	0	0	39	12	10	297	0	0	48000
Rents	4	21495	0	0	0	0	0	495	0	0	178	0	0	20822
Royalties	5	309852	0	0	0	0	0	0	0	0	0	0	0	309852
Other Portfolio Income	6	1828613	0	0	0	0	0	29	25	4	2084	0	0	1826471
Other Receipts	7	723137	0	1408	0	2825	0	411	445	6583	7443	0	0	704024
Total Receipts	8	24040457	0	29949	0	627564	0	350587	425644	335786	1259512	0	0	21011416
Average Total Receipts	9	69082	•	329	•	2840	•	23372	42564	111929	251902	•	•	7003805

Operating Costs/Operating Income (%)

		Total	Zero Assets	Under 500	500 to 1,000	1,000 to 5,000	5,000 to 10,000	10,000 to 25,000	25,000 to 50,000	50,000 to 100,000	100,000 to 250,000	250,000 to 500,000	500,000 to 2,500,000	2,500,000 and over
Cost of Operations	10	38.8	•	83.9	•	47.8	•	58.5	58.4	60.0	56.4	•	•	36.0
Salaries and Wages	11	9.9	•	•	•	5.1	•	9.2	6.5	4.9	6.2	•	•	10.5
Taxes Paid	12	12.3	•	1.5	•	3.2	•	2.9	2.9	4.8	5.6	•	•	13.7
Interest Paid	13	8.8	•	•	•	1.6	•	1.3	1.8	1.2	0.8	•	•	10.1
Depreciation	14	4.0	•	•	•	16.6	•	5.1	7.5	5.6	3.6	•	•	3.4
Amortization and Depletion	15	1.4	•	53.5	•	0.0	•	0.0	0.1	0.3	0.5	•	•	1.5
Pensions and Other Deferred Comp.	16	0.8	•	•	•	•	•	0.5	0.2	0.4	0.4	•	•	0.9
Employee Benefits	17	1.7	•	•	•	0.5	•	0.9	1.4	1.0	1.1	•	•	1.8
Advertising	18	4.3	•	•	•	1.2	•	2.3	2.2	1.2	4.5	•	•	4.6
Other Expenses	19	14.9	•	0.1	•	12.2	•	10.8	6.2	10.5	11.7	•	•	15.6
Officers' Compensation	20	0.4	•	•	•	3.2	•	1.9	1.9	0.9	0.6	•	•	0.3
Operating Margin	21	2.6	•	•	•	8.6	•	6.6	10.8	9.2	8.8	•	•	1.7
Operating Margin Before Officers' Comp.	22	3.1	•	•	•	11.8	•	8.5	12.7	10.1	9.3	•	•	1.9

Selected Average Balance Sheet ($ in Thousands)

Net Receivables 23	14873	0	63	1843	3194	13488	27377	1650945
Inventories 24	2679	37	223	1757	3420	10159	5549	253289
Net Property, Plant and Equipment 25	24377	0	1103	8578	22576	71101	37295	2472545
Total Assets 26	269923	31	1864	14537	35373	201455	77926	30568552
Notes and Loans Payable 27	114139	0	1167	5115	14236	23082	18297	13024358
All Other Liabilities 28	57019	-25	325	2907	3846	40539	30142	6466000
Net Worth 29	98765	56	372	6514	17291	137834	29487	11078194

Selected Financial Ratios (Times to 1)

Current Ratio 30	2.6	•	•	1.6	1.7	2.3	2.3	2.7
Quick Ratio 31	2.2	•	•	0.8	0.9	1.9	1.9	2.3
Net Sales to Working Capital 32	2.5	10.2	12.8	11.9	11.9	4.8	5.1	2.3
Coverage Ratio 33	3.2	•	6.8	6.1	7.0	13.0	10.6	3.1
Total Asset Turnover 34	0.2	10.2	1.5	1.6	1.2	1.2	1.4	0.2
Inventory Turnover 35	8.8	7.2	6.1	7.8	7.3	13.9	11.9	8.6
Receivables Turnover 36	6.5	9.1	63.3	14.2	7.9	19.9	8.0	5.9
Total Liabilities to Net Worth 37	1.7	•	4.0	1.2	1.0	0.5	1.6	1.8
Current Assets to Working Capital 38	1.6	1.0	2.7	2.8	2.4	1.8	1.8	1.6
Current Liabilities to Working Capital 39	0.6	•	1.7	1.8	1.4	0.8	0.8	0.6
Working Capital to Net Sales 40	0.4	0.1	0.1	0.1	0.1	0.2	0.2	0.4
Inventory to Working Capital 41	0.1	•	1.2	0.9	1.0	0.1	0.3	0.1
Total Receipts to Cash Flow 42	3.8	•	6.8	7.2	6.6	5.0	4.9	3.6
Cost of Goods to Cash Flow 43	1.5	•	3.3	4.2	3.8	2.8	3.0	1.3
Cash Flow to Total Debt 44	0.1	4.3	0.3	0.4	0.4	0.8	0.5	0.1

Selected Financial Factors (in Percentages)

Debt Ratio 45	63.4	•	80.0	55.2	51.1	62.2	31.6	63.8
Return on Total Assets 46	6.4	•	16.2	13.1	15.3	17.5	12.7	6.2
Return on Equity Before Income Taxes 47	12.1	•	68.9	24.5	26.9	41.8	17.1	11.7
Return on Equity After Income Taxes 48	8.2	•	68.9	23.0	26.2	41.8	14.6	7.8
Profit Margin (Before Income Tax) 49	19.7	•	9.1	6.8	10.9	11.2	9.4	21.5
Profit Margin (After Income Tax) 50	13.4	•	9.1	6.4	10.7	11.2	8.1	14.2

Table II
Corporations with Net Income

BREWERIES

MONEY AMOUNTS AND SIZE OF ASSETS IN THOUSANDS OF DOLLARS

Item Description for Accounting Period 7/09 Through 6/10	Total	Zero Assets	Under 500	500 to 1,000	1,000 to 5,000	5,000 to 10,000	10,000 to 25,000	25,000 to 50,000	50,000 to 100,000	100,000 to 250,000	250,000 to 500,000	500,000 to 2,500,000	2,500,000 and over
Number of Enterprises **1**	133	0	0	0	102	0	•	•	0	5	0	0	3
Revenues ($ in Thousands)													
Net Sales **2**	20652785	0	0	0	342488	0	•	•	0	1249510	0	0	18102247
Interest **3**	48348	0	0	0	0	0	•	•	0	297	0	0	48000
Rents **4**	21495	0	0	0	0	0	•	•	0	178	0	0	20822
Royalties **5**	309852	0	0	0	0	0	•	•	0	0	0	0	309852
Other Portfolio Income **6**	1828613	0	0	0	0	0	•	•	0	2084	0	0	1826471
Other Receipts **7**	720916	0	0	0	2826	0	•	•	0	7443	0	0	704024
Total Receipts **8**	23582009	0	0	0	345314	0	•	•	0	1259512	0	0	21011416
Average Total Receipts **9**	177308	•	•	•	3385	•	•	•	•	251902	•	•	7003805
Operating Costs/Operating Income (%)													
Cost of Operations **10**	38.2	•	•	•	34.0	•	•	•	•	56.4	•	•	36.0
Salaries and Wages **11**	10.0	•	•	•	8.7	•	•	•	•	6.2	•	•	10.5
Taxes Paid **12**	12.6	•	•	•	3.4	•	•	•	•	5.6	•	•	13.7
Interest Paid **13**	8.9	•	•	•	0.6	•	•	•	•	0.8	•	•	10.1
Depreciation **14**	3.7	•	•	•	8.9	•	•	•	•	3.6	•	•	3.4
Amortization and Depletion **15**	1.4	•	•	•	•	•	•	•	•	0.5	•	•	1.5
Pensions and Other Deferred Comp. **16**	0.8	•	•	•	•	•	•	•	•	0.4	•	•	0.9
Employee Benefits **17**	1.7	•	•	•	0.9	•	•	•	•	1.1	•	•	1.8
Advertising **18**	4.4	•	•	•	2.2	•	•	•	•	4.5	•	•	4.6
Other Expenses **19**	15.0	•	•	•	12.9	•	•	•	•	11.7	•	•	15.6
Officers' Compensation **20**	0.4	•	•	•	4.6	•	•	•	•	0.6	•	•	0.3
Operating Margin **21**	2.9	•	•	•	23.8	•	•	•	•	8.8	•	•	1.7
Operating Margin Before Officers' Comp. **22**	3.3	•	•	•	28.5	•	•	•	•	9.3	•	•	1.9

Selected Average Balance Sheet ($ in Thousands)

Net Receivables 23	38821	89	13488	1650945
Inventories 24	6713	365	10998	242240
Net Property, Plant and Equipment 25	61822	570	71101	2472545
Total Assets 26	703353	1346	201455	30568552
Notes and Loans Payable 27	296826	735	23082	13024358
All Other Liabilities 28	148620	119	40539	6466000
Net Worth 29	257907	491	137834	11078194

Selected Financial Ratios (Times to 1)

Current Ratio 30	2.7	3.1	2.3	2.7
Quick Ratio 31	2.3	1.7	1.9	2.3
Net Sales to Working Capital 32	2.5	6.5	4.8	2.3
Coverage Ratio 33	3.3	41.0	13.0	3.1
Total Asset Turnover 34	0.2	2.5	1.2	0.2
Inventory Turnover 35	8.8	3.1	12.8	9.0
Receivables Turnover 36	6.8	46.2	•	7.3
Total Liabilities to Net Worth 37	1.7	1.7	0.5	1.8
Current Assets to Working Capital 38	1.6	1.5	1.8	1.6
Current Liabilities to Working Capital 39	0.6	0.5	0.8	0.6
Working Capital to Net Sales 40	0.4	0.2	0.2	0.4
Inventory to Working Capital 41	0.1	0.7	0.2	0.1
Total Receipts to Cash Flow 42	3.7	3.3	5.0	3.6
Cost of Goods to Cash Flow 43	1.4	1.1	2.8	1.3
Cash Flow to Total Debt 44	0.1	1.2	0.8	0.1

Selected Financial Factors (in Percentages)

Debt Ratio 45	63.3		63.5	63.8
Return on Total Assets 46	6.5		63.0	6.2
Return on Equity Before Income Taxes 47	12.3		168.4	11.7
Return on Equity After Income Taxes 48	8.4		168.4	7.8
Profit Margin (Before Income Tax) 49	20.3	24.6	9.4	21.5
Profit Margin (After Income Tax) 50	13.9	24.6	8.1	14.2

Table I

Corporations with and without Net Income

WINERIES AND DISTILLERIES

MONEY AMOUNTS AND SIZE OF ASSETS IN THOUSANDS OF DOLLARS

Item Description for Accounting Period 7/09 Through 6/10	Total	Zero Assets	Under 500	500 to 1,000	1,000 to 5,000	5,000 to 10,000	10,000 to 25,000	25,000 to 50,000	50,000 to 100,000	100,000 to 250,000	250,000 to 500,000	500,000 to 2,500,000	2,500,000 and over
Number of Enterprises **1**	1339	•	0	314	•	•	55	39	19	13	0	5	4
Revenues ($ in Thousands)													
Net Sales **2**	22641889	•	0	264735	•	•	508513	747413	883291	1502899	0	2928160	15300432
Interest **3**	99088	•	0	0	•	•	674	304	2361	1036	0	14506	78989
Rents **4**	11821	•	0	0	•	•	0	141	908	316	0	515	9536
Royalties **5**	441579	•	0	0	•	•	0	3120	0	0	0	14	438445
Other Portfolio Income **6**	236510	•	0	885	•	•	243	1309	3763	346	0	11186	216827
Other Receipts **7**	623594	•	0	482	•	•	8455	11192	6792	14836	0	14115	520457
Total Receipts **8**	24054481	•	0	266102	•	•	517885	763479	897115	1519433	0	2968496	16564686
Average Total Receipts **9**	17965	•	•	847	•	•	9416	19576	47217	116879	•	593699	4141172
Operating Costs/Operating Income (%)													
Cost of Operations **10**	54.6	•	•	50.7	•	•	49.2	44.0	59.3	68.0	•	52.5	54.5
Salaries and Wages **11**	6.2	•	•	2.1	•	•	14.6	10.7	8.0	5.1	•	5.1	5.7
Taxes Paid **12**	11.0	•	•	6.9	•	•	4.8	3.2	8.6	5.0	•	13.1	12.2
Interest Paid **13**	5.5	•	•	5.1	•	•	2.7	2.9	1.8	2.7	•	2.7	6.7
Depreciation **14**	3.5	•	•	3.1	•	•	5.3	7.5	5.9	4.0	•	4.7	2.6
Amortization and Depletion **15**	1.9	•	•	0.3	•	•	0.2	0.2	0.9	1.1	•	0.6	2.5
Pensions and Other Deferred Comp. **16**	0.8	•	•	•	•	•	0.2	0.4	0.5	0.7	•	0.3	1.0
Employee Benefits **17**	1.2	•	•	1.5	•	•	0.8	1.4	0.8	0.9	•	1.0	1.3
Advertising **18**	5.3	•	•	3.5	•	•	1.1	2.3	1.6	1.9	•	4.2	6.4
Other Expenses **19**	8.6	•	•	12.2	•	•	15.1	19.1	8.3	5.9	•	9.7	7.2
Officers' Compensation **20**	1.0	•	•	14.6	•	•	2.3	3.0	1.7	0.7	•	0.4	0.6
Operating Margin **21**	0.4	•	•	0.1	•	•	3.7	5.2	2.4	3.7	•	5.5	•
Operating Margin Before Officers' Comp. **22**	1.5	•	•	14.7	•	•	6.0	8.2	4.1	4.4	•	5.9	•

Selected Average Balance Sheet ($ in Thousands)

Net Receivables 23	2986	12	1043	2659	5725	12273	68457	792418
Inventories 24	6136	541	5752	9698	21359	49632	297586	1082216
Net Property, Plant and Equipment 25	4661	275	4741	14954	29691	45966	207331	658254
Total Assets 26	25936	907	14308	34634	69437	160944	828239	5875941
Notes and Loans Payable 27	12689	615	5222	10693	23638	62737	294920	3194712
All Other Liabilities 28	5296	23	3116	6235	10826	39572	178765	1227796
Net Worth 29	7951	269	5969	17706	34974	58636	354555	1453433

Selected Financial Ratios (Times to 1)

Current Ratio 30	2.5	7.1	2.1	2.3	2.2	2.1	2.7	2.5
Quick Ratio 31	0.8	0.7	0.4	0.7	0.6	0.4	0.5	1.0
Net Sales to Working Capital 32	2.8	1.6	2.1	2.1	3.1	2.4	2.2	3.3
Coverage Ratio 33	2.3	1.1	3.1	3.5	3.2	2.8	3.5	2.3
Total Asset Turnover 34	0.7	0.9	0.6	0.6	0.7	0.7	0.7	0.7
Inventory Turnover 35	1.5	0.8	0.8	0.9	1.3	1.6	1.0	1.9
Receivables Turnover 36	6.2	•	9.9	6.5	7.9	11.4	17.1	5.3
Total Liabilities to Net Worth 37	2.3	2.4	1.4	1.0	1.0	1.7	1.3	3.0
Current Assets to Working Capital 38	1.7	1.2	1.9	1.7	1.9	1.9	1.6	1.7
Current Liabilities to Working Capital 39	0.7	0.2	0.9	0.7	0.9	0.9	0.6	0.7
Working Capital to Net Sales 40	0.4	0.6	0.5	0.5	0.3	0.4	0.5	0.3
Inventory to Working Capital 41	1.0	1.0	1.4	1.1	1.3	1.3	1.1	0.9
Total Receipts to Cash Flow 42	7.8	9.6	6.0	4.4	9.8	10.5	7.5	7.9
Cost of Goods to Cash Flow 43	4.3	4.9	2.9	1.9	5.8	7.2	3.9	4.3
Cash Flow to Total Debt 44	0.1	0.1	0.2	0.3	0.1	0.1	0.2	0.1

Selected Financial Factors (in Percentages)

Debt Ratio 45	69.3	70.3	58.3	48.9	49.6	63.6	57.2	75.3
Return on Total Assets 46	8.3	5.2	5.3	5.7	3.9	5.4	6.8	9.8
Return on Equity Before Income Taxes 47	15.5	1.8	8.6	8.0	5.3	9.5	11.3	22.3
Return on Equity After Income Taxes 48	10.8	1.8	7.8	7.5	5.0	8.6	9.5	14.5
Profit Margin (Before Income Tax) 49	7.3	0.6	5.6	7.4	4.0	4.8	6.9	8.5
Profit Margin (After Income Tax) 50	5.1	0.6	5.0	6.9	3.8	4.4	5.7	5.5

Table II

Corporations with Net Income

WINERIES AND DISTILLERIES

MONEY AMOUNTS AND SIZE OF ASSETS IN THOUSANDS OF DOLLARS

Item Description for Accounting Period 7/09 Through 6/10	Total	Zero Assets	Under 500	500 to 1,000	1,000 to 5,000	5,000 to 10,000	10,000 to 25,000	25,000 to 50,000	50,000 to 100,000	100,000 to 250,000	250,000 to 500,000	500,000 to 2,500,000	2,500,000 and over
Number of Enterprises 1	490	•	0	181	149	•	40	25	13	9	0	•	4
Revenues ($ in Thousands)													
Net Sales 2	21454589	•	0	117832	155322	•	427027	645362	764714	1384938	0	•	15300432
Interest 3	93989	•	0	0	438	•	65	245	1526	169	0	•	78989
Rents 4	10538	•	0	0	0	•	0	141	559	295	0	•	9536
Royalties 5	441579	•	0	0	0	•	0	3120	0	0	0	•	438445
Other Portfolio Income 6	231683	•	0	0	71	•	139	1196	987	295	0	•	216827
Other Receipts 7	599931	•	0	481	29780	•	5608	8864	5496	9109	0	•	520457
Total Receipts 8	22832309	•	0	118313	185611	•	432839	658928	773282	1394806	0	•	16564686
Average Total Receipts 9	46597	•	•	654	1246	•	10821	26357	59483	154978	•	•	4141172
Operating Costs/Operating Income (%)													
Cost of Operations 10	55.1	•	•	40.6	33.0	•	47.4	44.9	56.6	69.8	•	•	54.5
Salaries and Wages 11	5.9	•	•	•	9.8	•	14.7	8.5	8.4	4.7	•	•	5.7
Taxes Paid 12	11.2	•	•	5.3	4.0	•	4.1	2.8	9.4	4.1	•	•	12.2
Interest Paid 13	5.4	•	•	9.0	1.0	•	2.5	1.2	1.5	1.3	•	•	6.7
Depreciation 14	2.9	•	•	2.4	5.6	•	4.7	5.8	5.0	3.1	•	•	2.6
Amortization and Depletion 15	1.9	•	•	0.6	•	•	0.1	0.1	0.6	1.2	•	•	2.5
Pensions and Other Deferred Comp. 16	0.8	•	•	•	0.1	•	0.2	0.4	0.5	0.7	•	•	1.0
Employee Benefits 17	1.2	•	•	•	3.1	•	0.5	1.5	0.7	0.8	•	•	1.3
Advertising 18	5.5	•	•	4.2	1.3	•	1.3	2.0	1.8	2.0	•	•	6.4
Other Expenses 19	7.6	•	•	7.3	36.8	•	15.1	19.3	7.7	5.2	•	•	7.2
Officers' Compensation 20	1.0	•	•	25.9	15.4	•	1.9	2.9	1.8	0.7	•	•	0.6
Operating Margin 21	1.4	•	•	4.6	•	•	7.5	10.7	5.9	6.4	•	•	•
Operating Margin Before Officers' Comp. 22	2.4	•	•	30.5	5.3	•	9.5	13.6	7.7	7.1	•	•	•

Selected Average Balance Sheet ($ in Thousands)

	1	2	3	4	5	6	7	8
Net Receivables 23	7998	6	57	1260	3473	7324	16029	792418
Inventories 24	13492	438	562	6400	11651	18209	78571	1022919
Net Property, Plant and Equipment 25	9872	338	395	4441	11818	22045	40525	658254
Total Assets 26	63717	869	1634	14739	34293	68947	161997	5875941
Notes and Loans Payable 27	31176	878	548	5558	6428	21151	49223	3194712
All Other Liabilities 28	13447	10	348	4043	7783	11299	4199	1227796
Net Worth 29	19094	-19	739	5138	20082	36496	71575	1453433

Selected Financial Ratios (Times to 1)

	1	2	3	4	5	6	7	8
Current Ratio 30	2.5	4.1	2.4	2.0	2.4	2.0	2.4	2.5
Quick Ratio 31	0.9	0.4	0.5	0.4	0.8	0.6	0.5	1.0
Net Sales to Working Capital 32	3.0	1.8	1.9	2.4	2.3	3.6	2.5	3.3
Coverage Ratio 33	2.6	1.6	9.9	4.6	11.7	5.6	6.3	2.3
Total Asset Turnover 34	0.7	0.7	0.6	0.7	0.8	0.9	0.9	0.7
Inventory Turnover 35	1.8	0.6	0.6	0.8	1.0	1.8	1.4	2.0
Receivables Turnover 36	6.3	•	24.4	9.6	6.8	9.6	•	3.0
Total Liabilities to Net Worth 37	2.3	•	1.2	1.9	0.7	0.9	1.3	3.0
Current Assets to Working Capital 38	1.7	1.3	1.7	2.0	1.7	2.0	1.7	1.7
Current Liabilities to Working Capital 39	0.7	0.3	0.7	1.0	0.7	1.0	0.7	0.7
Working Capital to Net Sales 40	0.3	0.6	0.5	0.4	0.4	0.3	0.4	0.3
Inventory to Working Capital 41	1.0	1.2	1.3	1.4	1.0	1.4	1.3	0.9
Total Receipts to Cash Flow 42	7.5	10.1	2.8	5.1	3.5	7.8	8.9	7.9
Cost of Goods to Cash Flow 43	4.1	4.1	0.9	2.4	1.6	4.4	6.2	4.3
Cash Flow to Total Debt 44	0.1	0.1	0.4	0.2	0.5	0.2	0.2	0.1

Selected Financial Factors (in Percentages)

	1	2	3	4	5	6	7	8
Debt Ratio 45	70.0	102.2	54.8	65.1	41.4	47.1	55.8	75.3
Return on Total Assets 46	9.5	10.5	6.6	8.2	10.5	7.3	8.0	9.8
Return on Equity Before Income Taxes 47	19.4	•	13.2	18.5	16.4	11.3	15.3	22.3
Return on Equity After Income Taxes 48	14.0	•	12.1	17.1	15.7	10.9	14.2	14.5
Profit Margin (Before Income Tax) 49	8.5	5.0	9.3	8.9	12.8	7.0	7.1	8.5
Profit Margin (After Income Tax) 50	6.1	5.0	8.6	8.3	12.2	6.8	6.6	5.5

Table I

Corporations with and without Net Income

TOBACCO MANUFACTURING

MONEY AMOUNTS AND SIZE OF ASSETS IN THOUSANDS OF DOLLARS

Item Description for Accounting Period 7/09 Through 6/10		Total	Zero Assets	Under 500	500 to 1,000	1,000 to 5,000	5,000 to 10,000	10,000 to 25,000	25,000 to 50,000	50,000 to 100,000	100,000 to 250,000	250,000 to 500,000	500,000 to 2,500,000	2,500,000 and over
Number of Enterprises	1	33	0	0	0	0	0	15	8	4	0	0	4	3
Revenues ($ in Thousands)														
Net Sales	2	47760378	0	0	0	0	0	809532	829184	645292	0	0	3619279	41857090
Interest	3	46795	0	0	0	0	0	1534	0	182	0	0	17400	27679
Rents	4	1372531	0	0	0	0	0	0	0	0	0	0	178	1372353
Royalties	5	8470	0	0	0	0	0	0	0	3052	0	0	22	5397
Other Portfolio Income	6	1677882	0	0	0	0	0	997	299	46	0	0	223447	1453094
Other Receipts	7	309818	0	0	0	0	0	352	1530	10372	0	0	24085	273478
Total Receipts	8	51175874	0	0	0	0	0	812415	831013	658944	0	0	3884411	44989091
Average Total Receipts	9	1550784	•	•	•	•	•	54161	103877	164736	•	•	971103	14996364
Operating Costs/Operating Income (%)														
Cost of Operations	10	40.0	•	•	•	•	•	28.6	76.0	44.4	•	•	32.4	40.1
Salaries and Wages	11	3.3	•	•	•	•	•	3.6	2.6	3.5	•	•	4.5	3.2
Taxes Paid	12	27.2	•	•	•	•	•	53.7	17.0	32.6	•	•	32.0	26.4
Interest Paid	13	3.3	•	•	•	•	•	0.2	0.4	1.7	•	•	2.6	3.5
Depreciation	14	1.6	•	•	•	•	•	1.2	0.3	0.3	•	•	1.2	1.7
Amortization and Depletion	15	0.9	•	•	•	•	•	0.0	•	0.5	•	•	4.3	0.7
Pensions and Other Deferred Comp.	16	1.2	•	•	•	•	•	0.3	0.0	0.2	•	•	0.9	1.3
Employee Benefits	17	1.7	•	•	•	•	•	0.5	0.2	0.5	•	•	0.5	1.9
Advertising	18	1.0	•	•	•	•	•	0.7	0.5	0.8	•	•	1.0	1.0
Other Expenses	19	8.4	•	•	•	•	•	8.0	2.9	9.5	•	•	8.6	8.5
Officers' Compensation	20	0.6	•	•	•	•	•	3.6	0.9	0.8	•	•	1.6	0.5
Operating Margin	21	10.8	•	•	•	•	•	•	•	5.2	•	•	10.5	11.4
Operating Margin Before Officers' Comp.	22	11.4	•	•	•	•	•	3.1	0.2	6.0	•	•	12.1	11.8

Selected Average Balance Sheet ($ in Thousands)

Net Receivables 23	15018	4586	1099	7832	15367	108409
Inventories 24	120917	3692	10097	26983	247406	932010
Net Property, Plant and Equipment 25	127598	2123	1843	2535	71886	1288824
Total Assets 26	1883812	12865	28606	75018	1352268	18678273
Notes and Loans Payable 27	574800	1054	8426	51154	458194	5615926
All Other Liabilities 28	922324	5675	17199	21327	285159	9662679
Net Worth 29	386688	6137	2980	2537	608914	3399668

Selected Financial Ratios (Times to 1)

Current Ratio 30	1.0	1.9	1.4	1.7	1.5	1.0
Quick Ratio 31	0.5	1.2	0.4	0.6	0.5	0.5
Net Sales to Working Capital 32	•	11.5	14.4	9.0	11.3	•
Coverage Ratio 33	6.5	0.3	•	5.2	7.9	6.4
Total Asset Turnover 34	0.8	4.2	3.6	2.2	0.7	0.7
Inventory Turnover 35	4.8	4.2	7.8	2.7	1.2	6.0
Receivables Turnover 36	60.7	18.9	36.3	41.2	20.0	80.3
Total Liabilities to Net Worth 37	3.9	1.1	8.6	28.6	1.2	4.5
Current Assets to Working Capital 38	•	2.2	3.4	2.4	2.9	•
Current Liabilities to Working Capital 39	•	1.2	2.4	1.4	1.9	•
Working Capital to Net Sales 40	•	0.1	0.1	0.1	0.1	•
Inventory to Working Capital 41	•	0.8	0.8	1.5	1.6	•
Total Receipts to Cash Flow 42	4.2	13.5	109.1	6.4	5.3	4.0
Cost of Goods to Cash Flow 43	1.7	3.9	82.9	2.8	1.7	1.6
Cash Flow to Total Debt 44	0.2	0.6	0.0	0.4	0.2	0.2

Selected Financial Factors (in Percentages)

Debt Ratio 45	79.5	52.3	89.6	96.6	55.0	81.8
Return on Total Assets 46	16.6	0.2	•	19.4	13.6	17.0
Return on Equity Before Income Taxes 47	68.4	•	•	464.6	26.3	78.9
Return on Equity After Income Taxes 48	45.6	•	•	454.3	19.3	52.1
Profit Margin (Before Income Tax) 49	18.3	•	•	7.3	17.7	19.2
Profit Margin (After Income Tax) 50	12.2	•	•	7.1	13.0	12.7

Table II

Corporations with Net Income

TOBACCO MANUFACTURING

MONEY AMOUNTS AND SIZE OF ASSETS IN THOUSANDS OF DOLLARS

Item Description for Accounting Period 7/09 Through 6/10	Total	Zero Assets	Under 500	500 to 1,000	1,000 to 5,000	5,000 to 10,000	10,000 to 25,000	25,000 to 50,000	50,000 to 100,000	100,000 to 250,000	250,000 to 500,000	500,000 to 2,500,000	2,500,000 and over
Number of Enterprises **1**	28	0	0	0	0	0	•	•	•	0	0	4	3
Revenues ($ in Thousands)													
Net Sales **2**	47397278	0	0	0	0	0	•	•	•	0	0	3619279	41857090
Interest **3**	46621	0	0	0	0	0	•	•	•	0	0	17400	27679
Rents **4**	1372531	0	0	0	0	0	•	•	•	0	0	178	1372353
Royalties **5**	8470	0	0	0	0	0	•	•	•	0	0	22	5397
Other Portfolio Income **6**	1677071	0	0	0	0	0	•	•	•	0	0	223447	1453094
Other Receipts **7**	309080	0	0	0	0	0	•	•	•	0	0	24085	273478
Total Receipts **8**	50811051	0	0	0	0	0	•	•	•	0	0	3884411	44989091
Average Total Receipts **9**	1814680	•	•	•	•	•	•	•	•	•	•	971103	14996364
Operating Costs/Operating Income (%)													
Cost of Operations **10**	39.9	•	•	•	•	•	•	•	•	•	•	32.4	40.1
Salaries and Wages **11**	3.3	•	•	•	•	•	•	•	•	•	•	4.5	3.2
Taxes Paid **12**	27.1	•	•	•	•	•	•	•	•	•	•	32.0	26.4
Interest Paid **13**	3.3	•	•	•	•	•	•	•	•	•	•	2.6	3.5
Depreciation **14**	1.6	•	•	•	•	•	•	•	•	•	•	1.2	1.7
Amortization and Depletion **15**	1.0	•	•	•	•	•	•	•	•	•	•	4.3	0.7
Pensions and Other Deferred Comp. **16**	1.2	•	•	•	•	•	•	•	•	•	•	0.9	1.3
Employee Benefits **17**	1.7	•	•	•	•	•	•	•	•	•	•	0.5	1.9
Advertising **18**	1.0	•	•	•	•	•	•	•	•	•	•	1.0	1.0
Other Expenses **19**	8.4	•	•	•	•	•	•	•	•	•	•	8.6	8.5
Officers' Compensation **20**	0.6	•	•	•	•	•	•	•	•	•	•	1.6	0.5
Operating Margin **21**	11.0	•	•	•	•	•	•	•	•	•	•	10.5	11.4
Operating Margin Before Officers' Comp. **22**	11.6	•	•	•	•	•	•	•	•	•	•	12.1	11.8

Selected Average Balance Sheet ($ in Thousands)

Net Receivables 23	17490	15367	108409
Inventories 24	141209	247406	932010
Net Property, Plant and Equipment 25	150202	71886	1288824
Total Assets 26	2213558	1352268	18678273
Notes and Loans Payable 27	674512	458194	5615926
All Other Liabilities 28	1082682	285159	9662679
Net Worth 29	456363	608914	3399668

Selected Financial Ratios (Times to 1)

Current Ratio 30	1.0	1.5	1.0
Quick Ratio 31	0.5	0.5	0.5
Net Sales to Working Capital 32	•	11.3	•
Coverage Ratio 33	6.5	7.9	6.4
Total Asset Turnover 34	0.8	0.7	0.7
Inventory Turnover 35	4.8	1.2	6.0
Receivables Turnover 36	61.2	20.0	80.3
Total Liabilities to Net Worth 37	3.9	1.2	4.5
Current Assets to Working Capital 38	•	2.9	•
Current Liabilities to Working Capital 39	•	1.9	•
Working Capital to Net Sales 40	•	0.1	•
Inventory to Working Capital 41	•	1.6	•
Total Receipts to Cash Flow 42	4.2	5.3	4.0
Cost of Goods to Cash Flow 43	1.7	1.7	1.6
Cash Flow to Total Debt 44	0.2	0.2	0.2

Selected Financial Factors (in Percentages)

Debt Ratio 45	79.4	55.0	81.8
Return on Total Assets 46	16.7	13.6	17.0
Return on Equity Before Income Taxes 47	68.6	26.3	78.9
Return on Equity After Income Taxes 48	45.9	19.3	52.1
Profit Margin (Before Income Tax) 49	18.5	17.7	19.2
Profit Margin (After Income Tax) 50	12.4	13.0	12.7

Table I

Corporations with and without Net Income

TEXTILE MILLS

MONEY AMOUNTS AND SIZE OF ASSETS IN THOUSANDS OF DOLLARS

Item Description for Accounting Period 7/09 Through 6/10	Total	Zero Assets	Under 500	500 to 1,000	1,000 to 5,000	5,000 to 10,000	10,000 to 25,000	25,000 to 50,000	50,000 to 100,000	100,000 to 250,000	250,000 to 500,000	500,000 to 2,500,000	2,500,000 and over
Number of Enterprises **1**	1514	4	•	231	184	54	69	12	16	6	4	•	0
Revenues ($ in Thousands)													
Net Sales **2**	9726351	0	•	189389	428200	587526	1465172	495375	1476273	1370169	1466450	•	0
Interest **3**	45979	12	•	3	2232	846	3488	22	1863	1378	2866	•	0
Rents **4**	4023	0	•	0	0	699	7	702	125	0	979	•	0
Royalties **5**	34179	0	•	0	0	0	0	0	8	5748	1893	•	0
Other Portfolio Income **6**	75389	0	•	0	4226	48	3658	1999	29810	3126	6443	•	0
Other Receipts **7**	96549	298	•	-1855	829	396	11410	3128	14624	8133	28811	•	0
Total Receipts **8**	9982470	310	•	187537	435487	589515	1483735	501226	1522703	1388554	1507442	•	0
Average Total Receipts **9**	6593	78	•	812	2367	10917	21503	41769	95169	231426	376860	•	•
Operating Costs/Operating Income (%)													
Cost of Operations **10**	73.4	•	•	72.0	65.8	78.3	78.1	77.3	74.9	76.6	78.7	•	•
Salaries and Wages **11**	6.3	•	•	2.7	6.2	4.8	5.2	4.8	6.7	5.1	5.5	•	•
Taxes Paid **12**	1.7	•	•	3.6	2.3	2.9	1.2	1.2	1.6	1.0	2.0	•	•
Interest Paid **13**	2.7	•	•	2.1	0.5	1.0	2.1	0.6	0.8	2.4	3.7	•	•
Depreciation **14**	3.4	•	•	0.5	1.0	2.1	4.2	3.6	2.7	6.5	3.4	•	•
Amortization and Depletion **15**	0.7	•	•	•	•	0.2	0.2	0.6	0.2	0.2	0.3	•	•
Pensions and Other Deferred Comp. **16**	0.6	•	•	0.0	0.1	0.2	0.0	0.2	0.9	0.4	1.1	•	•
Employee Benefits **17**	1.5	•	•	0.1	3.2	1.0	1.0	0.8	1.1	1.2	0.5	•	•
Advertising **18**	0.3	•	•	0.1	0.4	0.0	0.3	0.2	0.7	0.0	0.5	•	•
Other Expenses **19**	10.5	•	•	14.4	14.8	10.7	6.9	3.8	8.3	7.3	11.5	•	•
Officers' Compensation **20**	1.6	•	•	7.0	3.7	1.3	1.8	0.2	1.5	0.8	1.6	•	•
Operating Margin **21**	•	•	•	•	1.9	•	•	6.8	0.6	•	•	•	•
Operating Margin Before Officers' Comp. **22**	•	•	•	4.4	5.6	•	0.7	7.0	2.1	•	•	•	•

Selected Average Balance Sheet ($ in Thousands)

Net Receivables 23	904	0	•	78	281	1549	3669	5897	9804	27824	62514
Inventories 24	1057	0	•	29	470	2662	3338	8291	16852	27618	83154
Net Property, Plant and Equipment 25	1460	0	•	23	405	1331	4883	15133	19933	67167	98384
Total Assets 26	6649	0	•	659	2115	7137	16978	35198	70514	158362	418994
Notes and Loans Payable 27	2109	0	•	22	219	2209	9879	12736	9560	78937	113682
All Other Liabilities 28	1568	0	•	66	447	2296	1974	7323	20058	32848	124382
Net Worth 29	2971	0	•	571	1449	2633	5124	15139	40895	46576	180930

Selected Financial Ratios (Times to 1)

Current Ratio 30	1.6	•	•	7.4	6.7	2.2	2.6	1.4	2.2	2.3	1.3
Quick Ratio 31	0.8	•	•	1.0	4.1	1.1	1.4	0.7	1.0	1.3	0.6
Net Sales to Working Capital 32	6.3	•	•	1.5	1.9	4.0	3.4	8.8	4.9	5.5	11.0
Coverage Ratio 33	1.0	•	•	•	7.9	•	1.1	14.2	5.9	0.9	•
Total Asset Turnover 34	1.0	•	•	1.2	1.1	1.5	1.3	1.2	1.3	1.4	0.9
Inventory Turnover 35	4.5	•	•	20.2	3.3	3.2	5.0	3.8	4.1	6.3	3.5
Receivables Turnover 36	6.5	•	•	12.3	8.2	6.6	5.9	7.3	9.4	7.3	5.2
Total Liabilities to Net Worth 37	1.2	•	•	0.2	0.5	1.7	2.3	1.3	0.7	2.4	1.3
Current Assets to Working Capital 38	2.6	•	•	1.2	1.2	1.8	1.6	3.2	1.8	1.8	4.3
Current Liabilities to Working Capital 39	1.6	•	•	0.2	0.2	0.8	0.6	2.2	0.8	0.8	3.3
Working Capital to Net Sales 40	0.2	•	•	0.7	0.5	0.2	0.3	0.1	0.2	0.2	0.1
Inventory to Working Capital 41	1.0	•	•	0.1	0.3	0.9	0.6	1.3	0.8	0.7	2.0
Total Receipts to Cash Flow 42	13.5	•	•	19.0	6.6	18.2	18.9	10.2	12.0	19.9	30.4
Cost of Goods to Cash Flow 43	9.9	•	•	13.7	4.3	14.3	14.8	7.9	9.0	15.2	23.9
Cash Flow to Total Debt 44	0.1	•	•	0.5	0.5	0.1	0.1	0.2	0.3	0.1	0.1

Selected Financial Factors (in Percentages)

Debt Ratio 45	55.3	•	•	13.4	31.5	63.1	69.8	57.0	42.0	70.6	56.8
Return on Total Assets 46	2.5	•	•	•	4.6	•	2.7	10.1	5.9	3.0	•
Return on Equity Before Income Taxes 47	•	•	•	5.8	•	0.6	0.6	21.8	8.4	•	•
Return on Equity After Income Taxes 48	•	•	•	5.6	•	•	0.5	18.1	7.1	•	•
Profit Margin (Before Income Tax) 49	•	•	•	3.6	•	0.1	0.1	8.0	3.7	•	•
Profit Margin (After Income Tax) 50	•	•	•	3.5	•	•	0.1	6.6	3.2	•	•

Table II

Corporations with Net Income

TEXTILE MILLS

MONEY AMOUNTS AND SIZE OF ASSETS IN THOUSANDS OF DOLLARS

Item Description for Accounting Period 7/09 Through 6/10		Total	Zero Assets	Under 500	500 to 1,000	1,000 to 5,000	5,000 to 10,000	10,000 to 25,000	25,000 to 50,000	50,000 to 100,000	100,000 to 250,000	250,000 to 500,000	500,000 to 2,500,000	2,500,000 and over
Number of Enterprises	1	614	0	425	•	59	26	31	5	12	0	•	0	0
Revenues ($ in Thousands)														
Net Sales	2	4753732	0	134270	•	207235	383967	894848	380002	1535854	0	•	0	0
Interest	3	3434	0	23	•	21	1	0	22	197	0	•	0	0
Rents	4	2850	0	0	•	0	677	0	702	0	0	•	0	0
Royalties	5	1	0	0	•	0	0	0	0	0	0	•	0	0
Other Portfolio Income	6	40736	0	930	•	4226	12	0	1898	29410	0	•	0	0
Other Receipts	7	40480	0	5	•	424	212	5372	2393	9484	0	•	0	0
Total Receipts	8	4841233	0	135228	•	211906	384869	900220	385017	1574945	0	•	0	0
Average Total Receipts	9	7885	•	318	•	3592	14803	29039	77003	131245	•	•	•	•
Operating Costs/Operating Income (%)														
Cost of Operations	10	67.5	•	14.9	•	59.8	74.8	75.0	75.3	72.8	•	•	•	•
Salaries and Wages	11	7.4	•	23.3	•	4.8	6.2	6.5	4.5	5.8	•	•	•	•
Taxes Paid	12	1.8	•	3.2	•	1.7	3.4	1.1	1.4	1.3	•	•	•	•
Interest Paid	13	0.8	•	1.7	•	0.2	0.9	0.8	0.5	0.6	•	•	•	•
Depreciation	14	3.2	•	1.5	•	1.0	2.0	1.4	2.4	5.5	•	•	•	•
Amortization and Depletion	15	0.3	•	0.1	•	•	0.4	0.0	0.0	0.2	•	•	•	•
Pensions and Other Deferred Comp.	16	0.6	•	•	•	0.1	0.1	0.0	0.1	0.4	•	•	•	•
Employee Benefits	17	1.6	•	•	•	4.1	0.6	1.0	0.8	0.9	•	•	•	•
Advertising	18	0.3	•	0.1	•	0.0	0.0	0.5	0.1	0.5	•	•	•	•
Other Expenses	19	10.2	•	50.4	•	18.3	9.8	5.5	2.5	6.4	•	•	•	•
Officers' Compensation	20	1.4	•	5.0	•	1.4	0.2	1.6	0.3	1.2	•	•	•	•
Operating Margin	21	5.0	•	•	•	8.4	1.5	6.4	12.1	4.5	•	•	•	•
Operating Margin Before Officers' Comp.	22	6.4	•	4.9	•	9.8	1.7	8.1	12.4	5.7	•	•	•	•

Selected Average Balance Sheet ($ in Thousands)

Net Receivables 23	955	17	674	1981	3664	9814	14656
Inventories 24	1177	13	785	3233	4127	10910	15556
Net Property, Plant and Equipment 25	1468	19	934	1070	3503	14054	35948
Total Assets 26	7048	44	3112	7420	15919	39299	93704
Notes and Loans Payable 27	1185	66	85	2775	6021	7410	18163
All Other Liabilities 28	1623	18	857	3682	1928	10856	21833
Net Worth 29	4240	-40	2170	963	7971	21033	53708

Selected Financial Ratios (Times to 1)

Current Ratio 30	2.1	1.2	8.4	1.6	2.3	2.1	2.3
Quick Ratio 31	1.0	1.2	3.8	0.6	1.1	1.0	1.2
Net Sales to Working Capital 32	5.2	80.4	2.1	7.1	4.5	6.2	5.2
Coverage Ratio 33	9.2	1.3	50.4	2.9	9.3	28.9	12.2
Total Asset Turnover 34	1.1	7.1	1.1	2.0	1.8	1.9	1.4
Inventory Turnover 35	4.4	3.7	2.7	3.4	5.2	5.2	6.0
Receivables Turnover 36	7.3	4.4	5.9	•	9.2	9.4	10.8
Total Liabilities to Net Worth 37	0.7	•	0.4	6.7	1.0	0.9	0.7
Current Assets to Working Capital 38	2.0	5.5	1.1	2.7	1.8	1.9	1.7
Current Liabilities to Working Capital 39	1.0	4.5	0.1	1.7	0.8	0.9	0.7
Working Capital to Net Sales 40	0.2	0.0	0.5	0.1	0.2	0.2	0.2
Inventory to Working Capital 41	0.7	•	0.4	1.6	0.7	0.8	0.7
Total Receipts to Cash Flow 42	7.4	4.0	4.2	11.8	9.3	7.0	9.4
Cost of Goods to Cash Flow 43	5.0	0.6	2.5	8.8	7.0	5.3	6.8
Cash Flow to Total Debt 44	0.4	0.9	0.9	0.2	0.4	0.6	0.3

Selected Financial Factors (in Percentages)

Debt Ratio 45	39.8	189.4	30.3	87.0	49.9	46.5	42.7
Return on Total Assets 46	8.4	15.5	12.2	5.3	14.3	26.9	10.4
Return on Equity Before Income Taxes 47	12.5	•	17.2	26.9	25.5	48.6	16.7
Return on Equity After Income Taxes 48	11.3	•	16.8	25.0	25.4	42.1	15.4
Profit Margin (Before Income Tax) 49	6.8	0.5	10.6	1.8	7.0	13.4	7.0
Profit Margin (After Income Tax) 50	6.2	0.5	10.4	1.6	7.0	11.7	6.5

Table I

Corporations with and without Net Income

TEXTILE PRODUCT MILLS

MONEY AMOUNTS AND SIZE OF ASSETS IN THOUSANDS OF DOLLARS

Item Description for Accounting Period 7/09 Through 6/10	Total	Zero Assets	Under 500	500 to 1,000	1,000 to 5,000	5,000 to 10,000	10,000 to 25,000	25,000 to 50,000	50,000 to 100,000	100,000 to 250,000	250,000 to 500,000	500,000 to 2,500,000	2,500,000 and over
Number of Enterprises 1	2457	468	•	309	453	40	67	30	10	7	9	•	0
Revenues ($ in Thousands)													
Net Sales 2	19121482	0	•	487063	1568478	508955	2538099	1441024	1145610	1449794	3972400	•	0
Interest 3	14434	0	•	7	185	2474	132	230	577	447	6088	•	0
Rents 4	6478	0	•	0	0	716	0	1183	121	4096	99	•	0
Royalties 5	29522	0	•	0	0	0	0	0	80	504	9988	•	0
Other Portfolio Income 6	59962	0	•	105	19	1020	2039	1682	427	3401	26468	•	0
Other Receipts 7	278083	0	•	4635	7993	1797	7481	19457	7394	6542	94853	•	0
Total Receipts 8	19509961	0	•	491810	1576675	514962	2547751	1463576	1154209	1464784	4109896	•	0
Average Total Receipts 9	7941	0	•	1592	3481	12874	38026	48786	115421	209255	456655	•	•
Operating Costs/Operating Income (%)													
Cost of Operations 10	69.1	•	•	58.8	57.0	66.1	81.0	77.9	72.9	76.4	77.8	•	•
Salaries and Wages 11	10.6	•	•	9.3	12.2	7.9	4.7	6.7	7.0	5.6	6.7	•	•
Taxes Paid 12	1.7	•	•	3.4	2.3	2.5	0.7	1.4	1.6	1.2	1.4	•	•
Interest Paid 13	1.8	•	•	1.5	1.2	4.3	0.6	1.6	2.2	0.7	2.2	•	•
Depreciation 14	3.4	•	•	2.3	3.3	1.4	1.3	2.5	1.9	2.4	2.6	•	•
Amortization and Depletion 15	0.6	•	•	0.0	0.1	5.8	0.2	0.5	0.4	0.1	0.8	•	•
Pensions and Other Deferred Comp. 16	0.7	•	•	0.3	0.1	0.5	0.2	0.3	0.4	0.7	0.6	•	•
Employee Benefits 17	1.6	•	•	3.2	1.4	0.3	1.2	1.0	1.5	1.5	1.8	•	•
Advertising 18	0.6	•	•	0.4	0.6	1.1	0.2	0.4	0.6	0.2	0.8	•	•
Other Expenses 19	11.3	•	•	16.9	20.3	6.7	8.4	6.8	8.3	7.7	8.3	•	•
Officers' Compensation 20	1.7	•	•	9.6	2.7	9.2	1.3	1.4	0.7	1.5	0.7	•	•
Operating Margin 21	•	•	•	•	•	•	0.1	•	2.5	1.9	•	•	•
Operating Margin Before Officers' Comp. 22	•	•	•	3.9	1.4	3.3	1.4	1.0	3.2	3.5	•	•	•

Selected Average Balance Sheet ($ in Thousands)

	•	•	•	•	•	•	•	•	•	•	•
Net Receivables 23	802	0	•	173	447	1053	3259	7987	15523	32048	62599
Inventories 24	1392	0	•	180	673	2793	7397	11507	19444	33696	67451
Net Property, Plant and Equipment 25	1212	0	•	188	622	926	2444	8539	13133	35956	53974
Total Assets 26	6877	0	•	747	2200	7527	16088	34361	71927	146014	364291
Notes and Loans Payable 27	2445	0	•	526	751	4856	3296	8967	25133	33552	162463
All Other Liabilities 28	2076	0	•	189	2646	1143	4863	8728	19963	32290	104364
Net Worth 29	2355	0	•	31	-1198	1527	7928	16667	26832	80172	97464

Selected Financial Ratios (Times to 1)

	•	•	•	•	•	•	•	•	•	•	•
Current Ratio 30	1.4	•	•	1.0	2.1	2.4	1.5	1.5	2.5	1.7	1.5
Quick Ratio 31	0.7	•	•	0.4	0.8	1.0	0.8	0.8	1.3	0.8	0.8
Net Sales to Working Capital 32	8.8	•	•	•	•	3.7	5.5	8.1	4.2	6.2	7.6
Coverage Ratio 33	0.4	•	•	0.4	•	1.8	2.4	1.7	2.5	5.2	1.0
Total Asset Turnover 34	1.1	•	•	2.1	1.6	1.7	2.4	1.4	1.6	1.4	1.2
Inventory Turnover 35	3.9	•	•	5.1	2.9	3.0	4.1	3.3	4.3	4.7	5.1
Receivables Turnover 36	9.0	•	•	16.4	6.7	10.6	10.4	5.2	7.2	7.8	7.9
Total Liabilities to Net Worth 37	1.9	•	•	22.8	•	3.9	1.0	1.1	1.7	0.8	2.7
Current Assets to Working Capital 38	3.3	•	•	•	•	1.9	1.7	3.1	1.7	2.4	3.0
Current Liabilities to Working Capital 39	2.3	•	•	•	•	0.9	0.7	2.1	0.7	1.4	2.0
Working Capital to Net Sales 40	0.1	•	•	•	•	0.3	0.2	0.1	0.2	0.2	0.1
Inventory to Working Capital 41	1.4	•	•	•	•	0.9	0.9	1.2	0.8	1.1	1.1
Total Receipts to Cash Flow 42	13.4	•	•	•	12.9	6.1	16.8	16.3	10.9	10.9	16.9
Cost of Goods to Cash Flow 43	9.2	•	•	•	7.6	3.5	13.6	12.7	7.9	8.3	13.2
Cash Flow to Total Debt 44	0.1	•	•	•	0.2	0.2	0.3	0.2	0.2	0.3	0.1

Selected Financial Factors (in Percentages)

	•	•	•	•	•	•	•	•	•	•	•
Debt Ratio 45	65.8	•	•	95.8	154.4	79.7	50.7	51.5	62.7	45.1	73.2
Return on Total Assets 46	0.9	•	•	•	•	0.7	2.7	3.7	8.7	5.2	2.5
Return on Equity Before Income Taxes 47	•	•	•	•	•	•	2.1	2.4	3.1	14.0	7.6
Return on Equity After Income Taxes 48	•	•	•	•	•	•	2.5	0.5	2.3	14.0	6.5
Profit Margin (Before Income Tax) 49	•	•	•	•	•	•	•	0.5	1.1	3.3	3.0
Profit Margin (After Income Tax) 50	•	•	•	•	•	•	•	0.1	0.8	3.3	2.5

Table II

Corporations with Net Income

TEXTILE PRODUCT MILLS

MONEY AMOUNTS AND SIZE OF ASSETS IN THOUSANDS OF DOLLARS

Item Description for Accounting Period 7/09 Through 6/10	Total	Zero Assets	Under 500	500 to 1,000	1,000 to 5,000	5,000 to 10,000	10,000 to 25,000	25,000 to 50,000	50,000 to 100,000	100,000 to 250,000	250,000 to 500,000	500,000 to 2,500,000	2,500,000 and over
Number of Enterprises **1**	484	0	160	66	157	23	41	19	6	•	•	0	0
Revenues ($ in Thousands)													
Net Sales **2**	10578316	0	279721	139396	926313	314242	1821507	989396	809621	•	•	0	0
Interest **3**	4232	0	199	4	108	743	101	167	0	•	•	0	0
Rents **4**	2625	0	0	0	0	716	0	884	0	•	•	0	0
Royalties **5**	13692	0	0	0	0	0	0	0	0	•	•	0	0
Other Portfolio Income **6**	51767	0	0	105	19	0	1895	1284	171	•	•	0	0
Other Receipts **7**	168404	0	11	285	6038	1666	5604	11535	4037	•	•	0	0
Total Receipts **8**	10819036	0	279931	139790	932478	317367	1829107	1003266	813829	•	•	0	0
Average Total Receipts **9**	22353	•	1750	2118	5939	13799	44612	52803	135638	•	•	•	•
Operating Costs/Operating Income (%)													
Cost of Operations **10**	71.4	•	70.7	71.6	52.2	56.1	79.7	76.8	74.2	•	•	•	•
Salaries and Wages **11**	7.4	•	4.8	8.0	15.4	6.3	3.8	5.6	6.2	•	•	•	•
Taxes Paid **12**	1.4	•	0.9	1.6	2.0	3.1	0.8	1.4	1.7	•	•	•	•
Interest Paid **13**	1.2	•	0.0	0.7	0.5	3.4	0.4	0.7	1.1	•	•	•	•
Depreciation **14**	2.4	•	0.5	0.2	2.8	1.0	0.8	2.0	1.9	•	•	•	•
Amortization and Depletion **15**	0.6	•	•	•	•	8.9	0.2	0.1	0.2	•	•	•	•
Pensions and Other Deferred Comp. **16**	0.5	•	0.0	•	0.1	0.4	0.2	0.3	0.4	•	•	•	•
Employee Benefits **17**	1.6	•	0.5	0.6	1.7	0.3	1.2	1.4	0.9	•	•	•	•
Advertising **18**	0.6	•	1.3	0.0	0.9	0.5	0.3	0.2	0.6	•	•	•	•
Other Expenses **19**	9.2	•	15.7	11.1	21.5	6.5	5.7	6.7	5.0	•	•	•	•
Officers' Compensation **20**	1.5	•	3.4	6.1	1.3	13.1	1.4	0.8	0.8	•	•	•	•
Operating Margin **21**	2.1	•	2.1	•	1.6	0.3	5.6	4.0	7.1	•	•	•	•
Operating Margin Before Officers' Comp. **22**	3.6	•	5.5	6.1	2.9	13.5	7.0	4.8	7.9	•	•	•	•

Selected Average Balance Sheet ($ in Thousands)

Net Receivables 23	2917	179	181	760	1336	3922	9481	16275
Inventories 24	3295	136	227	1329	3304	7270	12132	24583
Net Property, Plant and Equipment 25	2489	10	41	388	1114	2269	6789	12269
Total Assets 26	15444	408	504	2310	6543	17120	37782	71578
Notes and Loans Payable 27	4306	25	337	593	4376	2592	6569	9971
All Other Liabilities 28	4310	313	109	745	1334	4580	6562	20926
Net Worth 29	6828	70	58	972	833	9949	24651	40681

Selected Financial Ratios (Times to 1)

Current Ratio 30	1.9	1.3	1.1	2.0	2.0	2.8	2.2	3.0
Quick Ratio 31	1.0	0.7	0.5	0.9	0.5	1.1	1.2	1.5
Net Sales to Working Capital 32	5.1	20.4	48.0	6.4	5.2	5.5	4.4	3.9
Coverage Ratio 33	4.4	375.8	1.4	5.2	1.4	14.4	8.6	7.7
Total Asset Turnover 34	1.4	4.3	4.2	2.6	2.1	2.6	1.4	1.9
Inventory Turnover 35	4.7	9.1	6.7	2.3	2.3	4.9	3.3	4.1
Receivables Turnover 36	7.1	10.7	•	5.3	7.5	10.4	4.9	7.9
Total Liabilities to Net Worth 37	1.3	4.8	7.7	1.4	6.9	0.7	0.5	0.8
Current Assets to Working Capital 38	2.2	4.7	10.5	2.0	2.0	1.5	1.9	1.5
Current Liabilities to Working Capital 39	1.2	3.7	9.5	1.0	1.0	0.5	0.9	0.5
Working Capital to Net Sales 40	0.2	0.0	0.0	0.2	0.2	0.2	0.2	0.3
Inventory to Working Capital 41	0.8	1.9	5.2	1.0	1.2	0.9	0.8	0.7
Total Receipts to Cash Flow 42	8.7	7.2	11.5	4.9	16.8	9.7	9.9	9.6
Cost of Goods to Cash Flow 43	6.2	5.1	8.2	2.6	9.4	7.8	7.6	7.1
Cash Flow to Total Debt 44	0.3	0.7	0.4	0.9	0.1	0.6	0.4	0.5

Selected Financial Factors (in Percentages)

Debt Ratio 45	55.8	82.8	88.5	57.9	87.3	41.9	34.8	43.2
Return on Total Assets 46	7.8	9.2	3.9	7.3	9.8	16.7	8.3	16.4
Return on Equity Before Income Taxes 47	13.5	53.5	9.5	14.0	21.7	26.8	11.2	25.2
Return on Equity After Income Taxes 48	11.7	41.7	8.0	12.5	20.3	24.3	10.4	25.2
Profit Margin (Before Income Tax) 49	4.2	2.1	0.3	2.3	1.3	6.0	5.3	7.6
Profit Margin (After Income Tax) 50	3.7	1.7	0.2	2.1	1.2	5.4	4.9	7.6

Table I

Corporations with and without Net Income

APPAREL KNITTING MILLS

MONEY AMOUNTS AND SIZE OF ASSETS IN THOUSANDS OF DOLLARS

Item Description for Accounting Period 7/09 Through 6/10	Total	Zero Assets	Under 500	500 to 1,000	1,000 to 5,000	5,000 to 10,000	10,000 to 25,000	25,000 to 50,000	50,000 to 100,000	100,000 to 250,000	250,000 to 500,000	500,000 to 2,500,000	2,500,000 and over
Number of Enterprises 1	175	0	0	102	21	16	22	•	3	•	0	0	•

Revenues ($ in Thousands)

Item Description for Accounting Period 7/09 Through 6/10	Total	Zero Assets	Under 500	500 to 1,000	1,000 to 5,000	5,000 to 10,000	10,000 to 25,000	25,000 to 50,000	50,000 to 100,000	100,000 to 250,000	250,000 to 500,000	500,000 to 2,500,000	2,500,000 and over
Net Sales 2	7097799	0	0	249686	25712	238782	512103	•	228473	•	0	0	•
Interest 3	4196	0	0	8	2295	0	841	•	251	•	0	0	•
Rents 4	142	0	0	17	89	0	15	•	21	•	0	0	•
Royalties 5	53305	0	0	0	0	0	0	•	8010	•	0	0	•
Other Portfolio Income 6	81793	0	0	729	0	81	5771	•	1870	•	0	0	•
Other Receipts 7	4139	0	0	929	0	360	-1591	•	524	•	0	0	•
Total Receipts 8	7241374	0	0	251369	28096	239223	517139	•	239149	•	0	0	•
Average Total Receipts 9	41379	•	•	2464	1338	14951	23506	•	79716	•	•	•	•

Operating Costs/Operating Income (%)

Item Description for Accounting Period 7/09 Through 6/10	Total	Zero Assets	Under 500	500 to 1,000	1,000 to 5,000	5,000 to 10,000	10,000 to 25,000	25,000 to 50,000	50,000 to 100,000	100,000 to 250,000	250,000 to 500,000	500,000 to 2,500,000	2,500,000 and over
Cost of Operations 10	75.7	•	•	71.5	76.3	60.8	80.1	•	77.3	•	•	•	•
Salaries and Wages 11	6.6	•	•	4.0	3.2	6.8	6.6	•	7.2	•	•	•	•
Taxes Paid 12	1.3	•	•	6.2	1.7	2.3	1.2	•	1.9	•	•	•	•
Interest Paid 13	2.8	•	•	0.1	0.7	0.7	0.6	•	1.1	•	•	•	•
Depreciation 14	1.1	•	•	0.3	0.2	1.7	0.7	•	1.6	•	•	•	•
Amortization and Depletion 15	0.3	•	•	0.1	•	•	0.0	•	0.1	•	•	•	•
Pensions and Other Deferred Comp. 16	0.2	•	•	0.3	0.0	0.1	0.1	•	0.6	•	•	•	•
Employee Benefits 17	1.3	•	•	0.6	0.8	1.1	0.5	•	0.5	•	•	•	•
Advertising 18	3.0	•	•	0.2	7.0	0.2	0.1	•	1.5	•	•	•	•
Other Expenses 19	8.1	•	•	14.8	16.0	12.4	6.1	•	10.5	•	•	•	•
Officers' Compensation 20	1.0	•	•	8.1	5.9	1.5	1.4	•	1.4	•	•	•	•
Operating Margin 21	•	•	•	•	•	12.3	2.5	•	•	•	•	•	•
Operating Margin Before Officers' Comp. 22	•	•	•	2.0	•	13.8	3.9	•	•	•	•	•	•

Selected Average Balance Sheet ($ in Thousands)

Net Receivables	23	4256	•	•	173	120	2418	3959	•	9983
Inventories	24	8154	•	•	204	121	1562	1646	•	16630
Net Property, Plant and Equipment	25	2507	•	•	45	56	734	1417	•	14678
Total Assets	26	27877	•	•	621	2617	6461	15237	•	74514
Notes and Loans Payable	27	13998	•	•	17	10	1827	2570	•	12814
All Other Liabilities	28	11767	•	•	100	314	1042	1870	•	14367
Net Worth	29	2111	•	•	505	2293	3592	10797	•	47333

Selected Financial Ratios (Times to 1)

Current Ratio	30	1.9	•	5.7	1.4	2.1	2.9	•	2.1
Quick Ratio	31	0.7	•	3.4	0.9	1.1	2.3	•	0.9
Net Sales to Working Capital	32	6.1	•	5.2	10.8	5.2	3.8	•	4.0
Coverage Ratio	33	1.3	•	•	•	17.6	6.5	•	1.8
Total Asset Turnover	34	1.5	•	3.9	0.5	2.3	1.5	•	1.0
Inventory Turnover	35	3.8	•	8.6	7.7	5.8	11.3	•	3.5
Receivables Turnover	36	9.3	•	21.6	10.0	9.7	6.4	•	7.6
Total Liabilities to Net Worth	37	12.2	•	0.2	0.1	0.8	0.4	•	0.6
Current Assets to Working Capital	38	2.1	•	1.2	3.8	1.9	1.5	•	1.9
Current Liabilities to Working Capital	39	1.1	•	0.2	2.8	0.9	0.5	•	0.9
Working Capital to Net Sales	40	0.2	•	0.2	0.1	0.2	0.3	•	0.3
Inventory to Working Capital	41	1.1	•	0.5	1.1	0.9	0.3	•	1.0
Total Receipts to Cash Flow	42	16.3	•	19.7	24.4	4.8	12.4	•	9.9
Cost of Goods to Cash Flow	43	12.3	•	14.1	18.6	2.9	9.9	•	7.7
Cash Flow to Total Debt	44	0.1	•	1.1	0.2	1.1	0.4	•	0.3

Selected Financial Factors (in Percentages)

Debt Ratio	45	92.4	•	18.8	12.4	44.4	29.1	•	36.5
Return on Total Assets	46	5.2	•	•	•	30.5	6.1	•	1.9
Return on Equity Before Income Taxes	47	13.8	•	•	•	51.7	7.3	•	1.3
Return on Equity After Income Taxes	48	6.6	•	•	•	51.6	6.8	•	0.6
Profit Margin (Before Income Tax)	49	0.7	•	•	•	12.4	3.4	•	0.8
Profit Margin (After Income Tax)	50	0.3	•	•	•	12.4	3.2	•	0.4

63

Table II

Corporations with Net Income

APPAREL KNITTING MILLS

MONEY AMOUNTS AND SIZE OF ASSETS IN THOUSANDS OF DOLLARS

Item Description for Accounting Period 7/09 Through 6/10	Total	Zero Assets	Under 500	500 to 1,000	1,000 to 5,000	5,000 to 10,000	10,000 to 25,000	25,000 to 50,000	50,000 to 100,000	100,000 to 250,000	250,000 to 500,000	500,000 to 2,500,000	2,500,000 and over
Number of Enterprises 1	74	0	0	37	0	•	11	•	0	•	0	0	0
Revenues ($ in Thousands)													
Net Sales 2	2515167	0	0	159088	0	•	460575	•	0	•	0	0	0
Interest 3	702	0	0	0	0	•	68	•	0	•	0	0	0
Rents 4	16	0	0	0	0	•	0	•	0	•	0	0	0
Royalties 5	2120	0	0	0	0	•	0	•	0	•	0	0	0
Other Portfolio Income 6	5646	0	0	0	0	•	5553	•	0	•	0	0	0
Other Receipts 7	4607	0	0	26	0	•	707	•	0	•	0	0	0
Total Receipts 8	2528258	0	0	159114	0	•	466903	•	0	•	0	0	0
Average Total Receipts 9	34166	•	•	4300	•	•	42446	•	•	•	•	•	•
Operating Costs/Operating Income (%)													
Cost of Operations 10	74.4	•	•	61.7	•	•	81.0	•	•	•	•	•	•
Salaries and Wages 11	5.1	•	•	1.1	•	•	6.2	•	•	•	•	•	•
Taxes Paid 12	1.6	•	•	5.4	•	•	1.1	•	•	•	•	•	•
Interest Paid 13	1.0	•	•	0.0	•	•	0.3	•	•	•	•	•	•
Depreciation 14	1.3	•	•	0.3	•	•	0.8	•	•	•	•	•	•
Amortization and Depletion 15	0.3	•	•	•	•	•	0.0	•	•	•	•	•	•
Pensions and Other Deferred Comp. 16	0.3	•	•	0.4	•	•	0.0	•	•	•	•	•	•
Employee Benefits 17	1.2	•	•	0.8	•	•	0.5	•	•	•	•	•	•
Advertising 18	1.5	•	•	0.0	•	•	0.1	•	•	•	•	•	•
Other Expenses 19	7.5	•	•	9.9	•	•	5.3	•	•	•	•	•	•
Officers' Compensation 20	1.2	•	•	7.2	•	•	0.9	•	•	•	•	•	•
Operating Margin 21	4.6	•	•	13.1	•	•	3.7	•	•	•	•	•	•
Operating Margin Before Officers' Comp. 22	5.8	•	•	20.3	•	•	4.6	•	•	•	•	•	•

Selected Average Balance Sheet ($ in Thousands)

Net Receivables 23	4160	281	6399
Inventories 24	12861	279	1790
Net Property, Plant and Equipment 25	2794	123	2330
Total Assets 26	18349	761	17826
Notes and Loans Payable 27	5121	6	2909
All Other Liabilities 28	3985	259	3083
Net Worth 29	9244	496	11834

Selected Financial Ratios (Times to 1)

Current Ratio 30	3.0	2.5	2.5
Quick Ratio 31	1.4	2.2	2.1
Net Sales to Working Capital 32	4.1	11.4	5.0
Coverage Ratio 33	6.1	2325.3	15.7
Total Asset Turnover 34	1.9	5.7	2.3
Inventory Turnover 35	2.0	9.5	18.9
Receivables Turnover 36	4.9	20.0	6.8
Total Liabilities to Net Worth 37	1.0	0.5	0.5
Current Assets to Working Capital 38	1.5	1.7	1.7
Current Liabilities to Working Capital 39	0.5	0.7	0.7
Working Capital to Net Sales 40	0.2	0.1	0.2
Inventory to Working Capital 41	0.7	0.2	0.3
Total Receipts to Cash Flow 42	9.4	6.0	11.2
Cost of Goods to Cash Flow 43	7.0	3.7	9.1
Cash Flow to Total Debt 44	0.4	2.7	0.6

Selected Financial Factors (in Percentages)

Debt Ratio 45	49.6	34.8	33.6
Return on Total Assets 46	11.6	74.4	12.3
Return on Equity Before Income Taxes 47	19.2	113.9	17.3
Return on Equity After Income Taxes 48	15.3	75.6	16.5
Profit Margin (Before Income Tax) 49	5.2	13.1	4.9
Profit Margin (After Income Tax) 50	4.2	8.7	4.7

Table I

Corporations with and without Net Income

CUT AND SEW APPAREL CONTRACTORS AND MFRS.

MONEY AMOUNTS AND SIZE OF ASSETS IN THOUSANDS OF DOLLARS

Item Description for Accounting Period 7/09 Through 6/10		Total	Zero Assets	Under 500	500 to 1,000	1,000 to 5,000	5,000 to 10,000	10,000 to 25,000	25,000 to 50,000	50,000 to 100,000	100,000 to 250,000	250,000 to 500,000	500,000 to 2,500,000	2,500,000 and over
Number of Enterprises	1	6148	1992	2662	487	669	131	123	•	20	•	6	6	•
Revenues ($ in Thousands)														
Net Sales	2	34319228	110392	1041649	625543	3440844	1949370	4505761	•	2211481	•	2582416	12875093	•
Interest	3	50666	8	80	5	2425	891	1385	•	1707	•	103	41840	•
Rents	4	14227	0	0	0	104	77	0	•	2447	•	0	10751	•
Royalties	5	877492	0	23	0	140	560	0	•	690	•	3242	867402	•
Other Portfolio Income	6	70787	10920	0	5180	86	2626	261	•	1059	•	386	43479	•
Other Receipts	7	508679	1145	4164	110	11762	51171	41757	•	37479	•	32082	274943	•
Total Receipts	8	35841079	122465	1045916	630838	3455361	2004695	4549164	•	2254863	•	2618229	14113508	•
Average Total Receipts	9	5830	61	393	1295	5165	15303	36985	•	112743	•	436372	2352251	•
Operating Costs/Operating Income (%)														
Cost of Operations	10	62.9	60.0	46.8	57.6	66.3	72.0	75.8	•	65.6	•	57.9	57.6	•
Salaries and Wages	11	10.0	1.4	6.6	13.1	10.0	10.6	5.5	•	11.6	•	11.1	11.3	•
Taxes Paid	12	2.1	1.5	1.3	2.3	2.5	2.2	2.8	•	2.1	•	2.4	1.7	•
Interest Paid	13	1.8	0.8	0.1	1.2	1.3	1.1	1.0	•	0.7	•	2.1	2.8	•
Depreciation	14	1.3	0.5	1.0	2.3	0.5	0.3	0.5	•	1.5	•	2.7	1.7	•
Amortization and Depletion	15	0.6	0.2	0.0	•	0.1	0.1	0.0	•	0.3	•	0.5	1.3	•
Pensions and Other Deferred Comp.	16	0.9	0.0	•	0.3	0.3	0.1	0.1	•	0.8	•	0.4	2.0	•
Employee Benefits	17	1.0	0.5	0.4	0.8	0.8	0.3	0.4	•	1.2	•	1.4	1.1	•
Advertising	18	2.3	0.0	0.1	1.1	1.3	2.3	0.6	•	2.3	•	4.0	3.3	•
Other Expenses	19	14.3	27.4	42.0	22.1	10.2	10.3	8.0	•	9.7	•	12.7	18.0	•
Officers' Compensation	20	2.0	8.9	1.6	7.0	5.0	1.6	3.2	•	2.2	•	1.5	0.9	•
Operating Margin	21	0.8	•	•	•	1.8	•	2.0	•	1.9	•	3.3	•	•
Operating Margin Before Officers' Comp.	22	2.8	7.7	1.5	•	6.8	0.7	5.2	•	4.1	•	4.8	•	•

Selected Average Balance Sheet ($ in Thousands)

	•	•	•	•	•	•	•	•	•	•
Net Receivables 23	630	0	27	109	386	1668	3408	10732	49791	300087
Inventories 24	921	0	23	147	1009	2670	6043	21396	116284	292620
Net Property, Plant and Equipment 25	418	0	12	151	216	632	1244	8907	55714	197822
Total Assets 26	3983	0	80	779	2484	7362	15414	68928	387148	2094672
Notes and Loans Payable 27	1161	0	77	629	823	2546	4184	13070	77934	589477
All Other Liabilities 28	1235	0	44	106	785	1880	4602	16430	96259	735202
Net Worth 29	1587	0	-41	45	876	2936	6629	39428	212956	769992

Selected Financial Ratios (Times to 1)

	•	•	•	•	•	•	•	•	•	•
Current Ratio 30	2.0	•	1.3	1.6	2.2	1.6	1.7	3.0	3.2	1.7
Quick Ratio 31	0.9	•	0.8	0.9	0.8	0.6	0.7	1.4	1.4	1.0
Net Sales to Working Capital 32	5.3	•	29.0	8.5	4.3	7.3	7.2	3.7	2.9	6.6
Coverage Ratio 33	4.1	13.5	3.6	•	2.8	2.9	4.0	6.1	3.3	4.3
Total Asset Turnover 34	1.4	•	4.9	1.6	2.1	2.0	2.4	1.6	1.1	1.0
Inventory Turnover 35	3.8	•	7.8	5.0	3.4	4.0	4.6	3.4	2.1	4.2
Receivables Turnover 36	7.2	•	16.3	14.0	16.1	7.6	10.1	9.1	7.6	5.0
Total Liabilities to Net Worth 37	1.5	•	•	16.5	1.8	1.5	1.3	0.7	0.8	1.7
Current Assets to Working Capital 38	2.0	•	4.4	2.6	1.8	2.7	2.3	1.5	1.5	2.4
Current Liabilities to Working Capital 39	1.0	•	3.4	1.6	0.8	1.7	1.3	0.5	0.5	1.4
Working Capital to Net Sales 40	0.2	•	0.0	0.1	0.2	0.1	0.1	0.3	0.3	0.2
Inventory to Working Capital 41	0.8	•	1.4	1.2	0.9	1.3	1.1	0.6	0.7	0.7
Total Receipts to Cash Flow 42	6.3	6.2	2.6	11.3	10.7	9.7	10.8	10.0	7.8	4.6
Cost of Goods to Cash Flow 43	4.0	3.7	1.2	6.5	7.1	7.0	8.1	6.5	4.5	2.7
Cash Flow to Total Debt 44	0.4	1.2	0.2	0.3	0.3	0.3	0.4	0.4	0.3	0.3

Selected Financial Factors (in Percentages)

	•	•	•	•	•	•	•	•	•	•
Debt Ratio 45	60.2	150.5	94.3	•	64.7	60.1	57.0	42.8	45.0	63.2
Return on Total Assets 46	10.3	2.5	•	•	7.3	6.2	9.5	7.4	7.6	12.1
Return on Equity Before Income Taxes 47	19.6	•	•	•	13.3	10.2	16.5	10.8	9.5	25.3
Return on Equity After Income Taxes 48	14.9	•	•	•	13.0	9.8	15.8	9.4	7.6	16.5
Profit Margin (Before Income Tax) 49	5.6	9.8	0.4	•	2.3	2.0	3.0	3.8	4.7	9.1
Profit Margin (After Income Tax) 50	4.2	6.3	0.4	•	2.2	1.9	2.9	3.3	3.8	5.9

Table II

Corporations with Net Income

CUT AND SEW APPAREL CONTRACTORS AND MFRS.

MONEY AMOUNTS AND SIZE OF ASSETS IN THOUSANDS OF DOLLARS

Item Description for Accounting Period 7/09 Through 6/10	Total	Zero Assets	Under 500	500 to 1,000	1,000 to 5,000	5,000 to 10,000	10,000 to 25,000	25,000 to 50,000	50,000 to 100,000	100,000 to 250,000	250,000 to 500,000	500,000 to 2,500,000	2,500,000 and over
Number of Enterprises 1	2372	763	•	136	460	68	80	31	11	•	•	6	0
Revenues ($ in Thousands)													
Net Sales 2	28636945	97350	•	287254	2605285	731110	3434183	2176627	1331397	•	•	12875093	0
Interest 3	47818	8	•	5	1109	141	1335	1340	1236	•	•	41840	0
Rents 4	13185	0	•	0	0	77	0	0	2240	•	•	10751	0
Royalties 5	875844	0	•	0	0	0	0	1718	403	•	•	867402	0
Other Portfolio Income 6	63875	10920	•	0	74	1212	46	478	980	•	•	43479	0
Other Receipts 7	439535	1146	•	111	11498	17870	37494	29810	23370	•	•	274943	0
Total Receipts 8	30077202	109424	•	287370	2617966	750410	3473058	2209973	1359626	•	•	14413508	0
Average Total Receipts 9	12680	143	•	2113	5691	11035	43413	71289	123602	•	•	2352251	•
Operating Costs/Operating Income (%)													
Cost of Operations 10	61.3	66.6	•	54.3	66.7	69.2	75.4	66.0	64.9	•	•	57.6	•
Salaries and Wages 11	9.6	1.5	•	12.9	7.6	5.9	5.2	9.0	11.0	•	•	11.3	•
Taxes Paid 12	2.1	1.7	•	1.4	2.2	1.9	3.4	2.0	2.3	•	•	1.7	•
Interest Paid 13	1.9	0.9	•	0.2	1.2	1.0	0.7	1.0	0.6	•	•	2.8	•
Depreciation 14	1.3	0.6	•	0.7	0.5	0.6	0.4	0.7	1.3	•	•	1.7	•
Amortization and Depletion 15	0.7	0.2	•	0.0	0.0	0.4	0.0	0.1	0.1	•	•	1.3	•
Pensions and Other Deferred Comp. 16	1.1	0.0	•	•	0.3	0.2	0.0	0.4	0.6	•	•	2.0	•
Employee Benefits 17	1.0	0.6	•	0.2	0.5	0.6	0.4	0.9	1.2	•	•	1.1	•
Advertising 18	2.3	0.1	•	0.7	1.5	0.4	0.5	1.2	1.3	•	•	3.3	•
Other Expenses 19	14.4	15.7	•	21.1	8.5	8.9	6.4	9.6	6.5	•	•	18.0	•
Officers' Compensation 20	1.8	6.9	•	2.0	4.0	2.1	3.4	1.6	2.7	•	•	0.9	•
Operating Margin 21	2.5	5.2	•	6.6	6.9	8.8	4.1	7.4	7.6	•	•	•	•
Operating Margin Before Officers' Comp. 22	4.4	12.1	•	8.6	11.0	10.9	7.5	9.1	10.3	•	•	•	•

Selected Average Balance Sheet ($ in Thousands)

Net Receivables 23	1376	0	•	154	476	902	4017	6637	12497	•	300087
Inventories 24	1630	0	•	304	1015	3242	4865	6289	21739	•	239081
Net Property, Plant and Equipment 25	921	0	•	53	243	1040	1055	2740	9203	•	197822
Total Assets 26	8910	0	•	780	2855	7177	15306	34019	70316	•	2094672
Notes and Loans Payable 27	2389	0	•	145	863	1511	3690	6692	7649	•	589477
All Other Liabilities 28	2865	0	•	106	860	2582	4851	7505	18055	•	735202
Net Worth 29	3655	0	•	530	1132	3084	6765	19822	44612	•	769992

Selected Financial Ratios (Times to 1)

Current Ratio 30	2.0	•	3.1	2.5	1.2	1.9	2.5	3.7	•	1.7
Quick Ratio 31	1.0	•	1.3	1.0	0.4	0.9	1.0	1.9	•	1.0
Net Sales to Working Capital 32	5.3	•	4.5	3.7	18.6	7.2	4.8	3.5	•	6.6
Coverage Ratio 33	5.3	20.9	45.1	7.5	12.5	8.0	10.1	17.5	•	4.3
Total Asset Turnover 34	1.4	•	2.7	2.0	1.5	2.8	2.1	1.7	•	1.0
Inventory Turnover 35	4.5	•	3.8	3.7	2.3	6.7	7.4	3.6	•	5.2
Receivables Turnover 36	8.5	•	26.7	15.8	4.7	11.7	15.6	8.0	•	•
Total Liabilities to Net Worth 37	1.4	•	0.5	1.5	1.3	1.3	0.7	0.6	•	1.7
Current Assets to Working Capital 38	2.0	•	1.5	1.7	7.4	2.1	1.7	1.4	•	2.4
Current Liabilities to Working Capital 39	1.0	•	0.5	0.7	6.4	1.1	0.7	0.4	•	1.4
Working Capital to Net Sales 40	0.2	•	0.2	0.3	0.1	0.1	0.2	0.3	•	0.2
Inventory to Working Capital 41	0.7	•	0.9	0.7	3.0	0.8	0.6	0.5	•	0.7
Total Receipts to Cash Flow 42	5.4	5.7	4.2	7.1	5.5	9.9	6.0	7.6	•	4.6
Cost of Goods to Cash Flow 43	3.3	3.8	2.3	4.7	3.8	7.5	4.0	5.0	•	2.7
Cash Flow to Total Debt 44	0.4	•	2.0	0.5	0.5	0.5	0.8	0.6	•	0.3

Selected Financial Factors (in Percentages)

Debt Ratio 45	59.0	•	32.1	60.4	57.0	55.8	41.7	36.6	•	63.2
Return on Total Assets 46	13.4	•	18.3	17.0	18.6	16.7	20.5	17.7	•	12.1
Return on Equity Before Income Taxes 47	26.6	•	26.4	37.2	39.9	33.1	31.7	26.3	•	25.3
Return on Equity After Income Taxes 48	21.2	•	26.4	36.8	39.1	31.9	30.8	24.1	•	16.5
Profit Margin (Before Income Tax) 49	8.0	17.6	6.6	7.4	11.4	5.2	9.0	9.7	•	9.1
Profit Margin (After Income Tax) 50	6.4	13.6	6.6	7.4	11.2	5.0	8.7	8.9	•	5.9

66

Table I

Corporations with and without Net Income

APPAREL ACCESSORIES AND OTHER APPAREL

MONEY AMOUNTS AND SIZE OF ASSETS IN THOUSANDS OF DOLLARS

Item Description for Accounting Period 7/09 Through 6/10	Total	Zero Assets	Under 500	500 to 1,000	1,000 to 5,000	5,000 to 10,000	10,000 to 25,000	25,000 to 50,000	50,000 to 100,000	100,000 to 250,000	250,000 to 500,000	500,000 to 2,500,000	2,500,000 and over
Number of Enterprises **1**	3942	1154	2085	102	465	56	51	•	7	•	0	0	0
Revenues ($ in Thousands)													
Net Sales **2**	9767400	797471	1145824	132561	1627863	980985	1447229	•	754842	•	•	0	0
Interest **3**	4257	103	476	2	1679	0	289	•	245	•	0	0	0
Rents **4**	620	123	0	0	0	0	4	•	237	•	0	0	0
Royalties **5**	1560	0	0	0	0	0	878	•	667	•	0	0	0
Other Portfolio Income **6**	2160	216	0	0	1296	487	15	•	19	•	0	0	0
Other Receipts **7**	64518	8644	5913	0	6261	469	12354	•	3219	•	0	0	0
Total Receipts **8**	9840515	806557	1152213	132563	1637099	981941	1460769	•	759229	•	•	0	0
Average Total Receipts **9**	2496	699	553	1300	3521	17535	28643	•	108461	•	•	•	•
Operating Costs/Operating Income (%)													
Cost of Operations **10**	63.4	48.2	61.5	76.2	65.9	74.7	66.7	•	69.9	•	•	•	•
Salaries and Wages **11**	10.5	22.8	9.6	9.3	4.7	13.5	11.5	•	9.0	•	•	•	•
Taxes Paid **12**	2.6	1.5	2.0	2.8	3.0	1.5	1.7	•	1.1	•	•	•	•
Interest Paid **13**	1.7	0.3	0.2	1.4	0.9	1.0	2.1	•	0.9	•	•	•	•
Depreciation **14**	0.9	0.2	0.2	2.4	0.5	0.4	1.4	•	0.9	•	•	•	•
Amortization and Depletion **15**	0.5	0.0	0.2	1.0	0.1	0.3	0.5	•	0.2	•	•	•	•
Pensions and Other Deferred Comp. **16**	0.4	0.3	0.0	•	1.6	0.0	0.6	•	0.0	•	•	•	•
Employee Benefits **17**	0.9	0.1	0.3	1.0	1.4	0.6	1.1	•	0.4	•	•	•	•
Advertising **18**	1.4	3.3	0.8	1.8	0.7	0.1	1.2	•	0.6	•	•	•	•
Other Expenses **19**	13.5	16.2	20.8	15.3	10.1	5.8	10.0	•	11.0	•	•	•	•
Officers' Compensation **20**	3.2	6.7	6.4	0.6	7.5	0.6	1.8	•	1.8	•	•	•	•
Operating Margin **21**	1.0	0.3	•	•	3.6	1.5	1.5	•	4.2	•	•	•	•
Operating Margin Before Officers' Comp. **22**	4.2	7.0	4.4	•	11.2	2.1	3.3	•	6.0	•	•	•	•

Selected Average Balance Sheet ($ in Thousands)

Net Receivables 23	246	0	31	72	393	2307	3513	18865
Inventories 24	445	0	71	533	558	1284	6938	21835
Net Property, Plant and Equipment 25	131	0	3	81	280	295	1545	5819
Total Assets 26	1368	0	173	623	1922	5764	15572	73165
Notes and Loans Payable 27	569	0	122	933	361	1301	5738	23552
All Other Liabilities 28	436	0	59	140	399	3546	3576	35420
Net Worth 29	363	0	-8	-450	1162	916	6257	14193

Selected Financial Ratios (Times to 1)

Current Ratio 30	1.6	•	2.5	2.5	3.1	1.2	1.9	1.9
Quick Ratio 31	0.7	•	1.4	0.6	2.1	0.6	0.7	0.8
Net Sales to Working Capital 32	7.5	•	5.7	5.5	4.1	18.3	5.5	4.4
Coverage Ratio 33	2.0	5.3	•	•	5.7	2.6	2.2	6.6
Total Asset Turnover 34	1.8	•	3.2	2.1	1.8	3.0	1.8	1.5
Inventory Turnover 35	3.5	•	4.7	1.9	4.1	10.2	2.7	3.5
Receivables Turnover 36	9.1	•	20.7	13.3	7.9	13.4	7.6	5.8
Total Liabilities to Net Worth 37	2.8	•	•	•	0.7	5.3	1.5	4.2
Current Assets to Working Capital 38	2.6	•	1.7	1.7	1.5	5.1	2.2	2.1
Current Liabilities to Working Capital 39	1.6	•	0.7	0.7	0.5	4.1	1.2	1.1
Working Capital to Net Sales 40	0.1	•	0.2	0.2	0.2	0.1	0.2	0.2
Inventory to Working Capital 41	1.2	•	0.7	1.2	0.4	2.5	1.2	0.9
Total Receipts to Cash Flow 42	8.4	7.8	7.1	•	8.2	18.6	9.3	6.9
Cost of Goods to Cash Flow 43	5.3	3.8	4.4	•	5.4	13.9	6.2	4.9
Cash Flow to Total Debt 44	0.3	•	0.4	•	0.6	0.2	0.3	0.3

Selected Financial Factors (in Percentages)

Debt Ratio 45	73.5	•	104.4	172.3	39.5	84.1	59.8	80.6
Return on Total Assets 46	6.2	•	•	•	9.3	8.1	8.3	8.4
Return on Equity Before Income Taxes 47	11.7	•	98.0	34.4	12.7	30.9	11.2	36.9
Return on Equity After Income Taxes 48	9.6	•	98.1	34.4	11.9	30.9	10.8	25.5
Profit Margin (Before Income Tax) 49	1.7	1.5	•	•	4.2	1.6	2.5	4.9
Profit Margin (After Income Tax) 50	1.4	1.5	•	•	3.9	1.6	2.4	3.4

Table II

Corporations with Net Income

APPAREL ACCESSORIES AND OTHER APPAREL

MONEY AMOUNTS AND SIZE OF ASSETS IN THOUSANDS OF DOLLARS

Item Description for Accounting Period 7/09 Through 6/10	Total	Zero Assets	Under 500	500 to 1,000	1,000 to 5,000	5,000 to 10,000	10,000 to 25,000	25,000 to 50,000	50,000 to 100,000	100,000 to 250,000	250,000 to 500,000	500,000 to 2,500,000	2,500,000 and over
Number of Enterprises **1**	1822	•	•	66	405	•	37	•	7	0	0	0	0
Revenues ($ in Thousands)													
Net Sales **2**	7033235	•	•	126101	1358062	•	1329122	•	1187889	0	0	0	0
Interest **3**	2218	•	•	0	1652	•	44	•	445	0	0	0	0
Rents **4**	417	•	•	0	0	•	0	•	237	0	0	0	0
Royalties **5**	1560	•	•	0	0	•	878	•	667	0	0	0	0
Other Portfolio Income **6**	1927	•	•	0	1296	•	0	•	19	0	0	0	0
Other Receipts **7**	35549	•	•	0	5958	•	8618	•	2630	0	0	0	0
Total Receipts **8**	7074906	•	•	126101	1366968	•	1338662	•	1191887	0	0	0	0
Average Total Receipts **9**	3883	•	•	1911	3375	•	36180	•	170270	•	•	•	•
Operating Costs/Operating Income (%)													
Cost of Operations **10**	63.9	•	•	70.1	62.8	•	66.1	•	62.1	•	•	•	•
Salaries and Wages **11**	9.8	•	•	8.4	3.7	•	11.3	•	7.6	•	•	•	•
Taxes Paid **12**	2.5	•	•	2.6	2.4	•	1.5	•	5.0	•	•	•	•
Interest Paid **13**	1.1	•	•	1.5	0.9	•	1.6	•	1.2	•	•	•	•
Depreciation **14**	0.6	•	•	2.5	0.4	•	1.2	•	0.8	•	•	•	•
Amortization and Depletion **15**	0.1	•	•	0.0	0.0	•	0.2	•	0.2	•	•	•	•
Pensions and Other Defered Comp. **16**	0.5	•	•	•	1.9	•	0.4	•	0.1	•	•	•	•
Employee Benefits **17**	0.9	•	•	1.0	1.4	•	1.0	•	1.2	•	•	•	•
Advertising **18**	1.5	•	•	0.1	0.7	•	1.2	•	2.3	•	•	•	•
Other Expenses **19**	10.4	•	•	10.9	10.1	•	8.6	•	9.1	•	•	•	•
Officers' Compensation **20**	3.5	•	•	•	8.2	•	1.7	•	1.8	•	•	•	•
Operating Margin **21**	5.1	•	•	2.8	7.6	•	5.1	•	8.6	•	•	•	•
Operating Margin Before Officers' Comp. **22**	8.6	•	•	2.8	15.7	•	6.9	•	10.4	•	•	•	•

Selected Average Balance Sheet ($ in Thousands)

Net Receivables 23	402	104	265	4436	20428
Inventories 24	614	631	350	8149	28579
Net Property, Plant and Equipment 25	159	123	292	1713	7438
Total Assets 26	1696	661	1816	16312	108957
Notes and Loans Payable 27	513	962	359	5968	25860
All Other Liabilities 28	441	183	409	4245	20778
Net Worth 29	742	-484	1048	6099	62320

Selected Financial Ratios (Times to 1)

Current Ratio 30	2.1	3.3	2.7	1.8	2.6
Quick Ratio 31	1.0	0.9	1.8	0.7	1.1
Net Sales to Working Capital 32	5.8	5.2	4.8	6.0	3.7
Coverage Ratio 33	6.2	2.9	10.2	4.7	8.2
Total Asset Turnover 34	2.3	2.9	1.8	2.2	1.6
Inventory Turnover 35	4.0	2.1	6.0	2.9	3.7
Receivables Turnover 36	9.2	13.0	•	7.7	•
Total Liabilities to Net Worth 37	1.3	•	0.7	1.7	0.7
Current Assets to Working Capital 38	1.9	1.4	1.6	2.2	1.6
Current Liabilities to Working Capital 39	0.9	0.4	0.6	1.2	0.6
Working Capital to Net Sales 40	0.2	0.2	0.2	0.2	0.3
Inventory to Working Capital 41	0.8	1.0	0.5	1.2	0.6
Total Receipts to Cash Flow 42	7.2	12.5	6.1	7.8	5.9
Cost of Goods to Cash Flow 43	4.6	8.7	3.8	5.2	3.7
Cash Flow to Total Debt 44	0.6	0.1	0.7	0.4	0.6

Selected Financial Factors (in Percentages)

Debt Ratio 45	56.2	173.2	42.3	62.6	42.8
Return on Total Assets 46	15.6	12.3	16.8	16.4	15.9
Return on Equity Before Income Taxes 47	29.9	•	26.3	34.4	24.3
Return on Equity After Income Taxes 48	27.7	•	25.3	33.9	19.1
Profit Margin (Before Income Tax) 49	5.7	2.8	8.2	5.8	8.9
Profit Margin (After Income Tax) 50	5.3	2.8	7.9	5.8	7.0

Table I

Corporations with and without Net Income

LEATHER AND ALLIED PRODUCT MANUFACTURING

MONEY AMOUNTS AND SIZE OF ASSETS IN THOUSANDS OF DOLLARS

Item Description for Accounting Period 7/09 Through 6/10	Total	Zero Assets	Under 500	500 to 1,000	1,000 to 5,000	5,000 to 10,000	10,000 to 25,000	25,000 to 50,000	50,000 to 100,000	100,000 to 250,000	250,000 to 500,000	500,000 to 2,500,000	2,500,000 and over
Number of Enterprises **1**	1351	227	933	0	130	11	26	7	9	4	0	4	0
Revenues ($ in Thousands)													
Net Sales **2**	6996433	211920	353741	0	445368	97885	729531	403580	1020287	1245444	0	2488677	0
Interest **3**	8152	0	0	0	308	32	752	273	865	3115	0	2807	0
Rents **4**	445	40	0	0	5	6	5	0	0	372	0	17	0
Royalties **5**	143541	23394	0	0	0	0	0	0	3096	1564	0	115488	0
Other Portfolio Income **6**	202750	144706	868	0	1140	255	0	0	28	9744	0	46008	0
Other Receipts **7**	72121	-9795	26	0	15	73	1176	3580	16647	13038	0	47361	0
Total Receipts **8**	7423442	370265	354635	0	446836	98251	731464	407433	1040923	1273277	0	2700358	0
Average Total Receipts **9**	5495	1631	380	•	3437	8932	28133	58205	115658	318319	•	675090	•
Operating Costs/Operating Income (%)													
Cost of Operations **10**	63.2	67.8	30.6	•	68.5	61.4	67.4	77.0	64.4	64.3	•	62.2	•
Salaries and Wages **11**	11.4	11.6	23.9	•	7.8	4.5	10.9	5.1	9.4	10.4	•	13.2	•
Taxes Paid **12**	1.7	2.0	0.7	•	2.4	1.5	1.8	2.4	1.6	1.6	•	1.5	•
Interest Paid **13**	0.8	8.5	1.4	•	0.0	0.6	0.6	0.4	1.0	0.3	•	0.4	•
Depreciation **14**	1.8	3.4	1.8	•	0.2	1.8	1.1	2.4	1.3	2.7	•	1.7	•
Amortization and Depletion **15**	0.4	1.5	0.1	•	•	0.0	0.1	0.0	0.9	0.1	•	0.6	•
Pensions and Other Deferred Comp. **16**	0.3	•	0.0	•	0.0	0.1	0.4	0.0	0.3	0.6	•	0.4	•
Employee Benefits **17**	1.2	3.6	5.2	•	0.2	1.7	1.5	1.1	1.2	0.9	•	0.7	•
Advertising **18**	3.3	3.2	5.9	•	0.6	0.2	2.1	0.9	2.7	2.2	•	5.0	•
Other Expenses **19**	13.7	35.9	25.5	•	17.2	15.5	9.4	7.2	12.9	11.6	•	13.2	•
Officers' Compensation **20**	1.8	1.4	3.8	•	2.6	4.9	2.8	1.3	1.6	1.3	•	1.3	•
Operating Margin **21**	0.4	•	1.1	•	0.3	7.8	1.9	2.1	2.7	3.9	•	•	•
Operating Margin Before Officers' Comp. **22**	2.1	•	4.9	•	2.9	12.7	4.7	3.4	4.3	5.3	•	1.1	•

Selected Average Balance Sheet ($ in Thousands)

	•	•	•	•	•	•	•	•	•	•	•
Net Receivables 23	1396	0	0	•	269	933	3932	6520	15365	46792	•	341884
Inventories 24	939	0	44	•	546	1399	5634	14368	22732	58403	•	115940
Net Property, Plant and Equipment 25	411	0	5	•	139	1368	1491	4658	7832	34262	•	59589
Total Assets 26	4543	0	94	•	1786	6665	16322	33187	79070	234520	•	859445
Notes and Loans Payable 27	570	0	103	•	18	1254	1582	6096	16107	32509	•	74908
All Other Liabilities 28	1730	0	1	•	950	495	2781	6722	15204	66032	•	421744
Net Worth 29	2243	0	-10	•	818	4916	11959	20369	47760	135978	•	362794

Selected Financial Ratios (Times to 1)

Current Ratio 30	1.8	•	2.4	•	1.6	3.6	3.7	3.0	4.3	2.1	•	1.5
Quick Ratio 31	1.1	•	0.2	•	0.7	1.0	2.1	1.6	2.3	1.3	•	1.0
Net Sales to Working Capital 32	3.5	•	18.9	•	5.8	2.5	3.0	3.7	2.5	4.4	•	3.0
Coverage Ratio 33	10.2	6.1	2.0	•	13.4	15.3	4.7	8.3	5.6	22.6	•	22.7
Total Asset Turnover 34	1.1	•	4.0	•	1.9	1.3	1.7	1.7	1.4	1.3	•	0.7
Inventory Turnover 35	3.5	•	2.6	•	4.3	3.9	3.4	3.1	3.2	3.4	•	3.3
Receivables Turnover 36	4.0	•	18.2	•	21.4	19.1	7.8	4.7	7.8	6.1	•	2.1
Total Liabilities to Net Worth 37	1.0	•	•	•	1.2	0.4	0.4	0.6	0.7	0.7	•	1.4
Current Assets to Working Capital 38	2.2	•	1.7	•	2.6	1.4	1.4	1.5	1.3	1.9	•	3.1
Current Liabilities to Working Capital 39	1.2	•	0.7	•	1.6	0.4	0.4	0.5	0.3	0.9	•	2.1
Working Capital to Net Sales 40	0.3	•	0.1	•	0.2	0.4	0.3	0.3	0.4	0.2	•	0.3
Inventory to Working Capital 41	0.5	•	1.6	•	0.9	0.4	0.5	0.7	0.5	0.7	•	0.5
Total Receipts to Cash Flow 42	6.4	21.8	4.0	•	7.2	4.6	10.0	10.3	6.6	7.0	•	5.3
Cost of Goods to Cash Flow 43	4.0	14.8	1.2	•	4.9	2.8	6.7	7.9	4.3	4.5	•	3.3
Cash Flow to Total Debt 44	0.4	•	0.9	•	0.5	1.1	0.6	0.4	0.5	0.5	•	0.2

Selected Financial Factors (in Percentages)

Debt Ratio 45	50.6	•	110.4	•	54.2	26.2	26.7	38.6	39.6	42.0	•	57.8
Return on Total Assets 46	9.1	•	11.1	•	0.9	11.7	4.8	6.0	8.3	9.5	•	7.1
Return on Equity Before Income Taxes 47	16.6	•	•	•	1.9	14.8	5.2	8.7	11.3	15.6	•	16.1
Return on Equity After Income Taxes 48	13.4	•	•	•	0.8	14.8	3.7	8.7	9.2	12.3	•	11.7
Profit Margin (Before Income Tax) 49	7.2	43.1	1.4	•	0.4	8.2	2.2	3.1	4.7	6.8	•	9.4
Profit Margin (After Income Tax) 50	5.8	43.1	1.4	•	0.2	8.2	1.6	3.1	3.9	5.4	•	6.8

Table II

Corporations with Net Income

LEATHER AND ALLIED PRODUCT MANUFACTURING

MONEY AMOUNTS AND SIZE OF ASSETS IN THOUSANDS OF DOLLARS

Item Description for Accounting Period 7/09 Through 6/10	Total	Zero Assets	Under 500	500 to 1,000	1,000 to 5,000	5,000 to 10,000	10,000 to 25,000	25,000 to 50,000	50,000 to 100,000	100,000 to 250,000	250,000 to 500,000	500,000 to 2,500,000	2,500,000 and over
Number of Enterprises 1	979	227	699	0	15	5	15	•	5	•	0	•	0
Revenues ($ in Thousands)													
Net Sales 2	5972928	211920	341779	0	148792	85279	335542	•	730506	•	0	•	0
Interest 3	6724	0	0	0	0	32	719	•	119	•	0	•	0
Rents 4	434	40	0	0	0	6	0	•	0	•	0	•	0
Royalties 5	142906	23394	0	0	0	0	0	•	2461	•	0	•	0
Other Portfolio Income 6	193085	144706	868	0	0	255	0	•	4	•	0	•	0
Other Receipts 7	61081	-9795	0	0	0	18	66	•	12538	•	0	•	0
Total Receipts 8	6377158	370265	342647	0	148792	85590	336327	•	745628	•	0	•	0
Average Total Receipts 9	6514	1631	490	•	9919	17118	22422	•	149126	•	•	•	•
Operating Costs/Operating Income (%)													
Cost of Operations 10	62.3	67.8	27.6	•	77.6	59.8	64.0	•	62.1	•	•	•	•
Salaries and Wages 11	11.5	11.6	24.7	•	1.4	4.4	9.0	•	9.5	•	•	•	•
Taxes Paid 12	1.5	2.0	0.7	•	0.4	1.3	1.7	•	1.6	•	•	•	•
Interest Paid 13	0.7	8.5	1.4	•	•	0.4	0.9	•	0.7	•	•	•	•
Depreciation 14	1.9	3.4	1.8	•	0.0	2.0	1.8	•	1.1	•	•	•	•
Amortization and Depletion 15	0.4	1.5	0.1	•	•	0.0	0.3	•	0.2	•	•	•	•
Pensions and Other Deferred Comp. 16	0.3	•	•	•	•	0.0	0.6	•	0.1	•	•	•	•
Employee Benefits 17	1.1	3.6	5.4	•	•	1.7	0.1	•	0.9	•	•	•	•
Advertising 18	3.6	3.2	6.1	•	0.0	0.0	2.8	•	2.9	•	•	•	•
Other Expenses 19	13.1	35.9	24.3	•	18.1	12.9	8.1	•	10.2	•	•	•	•
Officers' Compensation 20	1.6	1.4	3.9	•	0.1	5.0	4.0	•	1.4	•	•	•	•
Operating Margin 21	1.8	•	4.0	•	2.4	12.4	6.8	•	9.2	•	•	•	•
Operating Margin Before Officers' Comp. 22	3.4	•	7.9	•	2.5	17.4	10.7	•	10.6	•	•	•	•

Selected Average Balance Sheet ($ in Thousands)

Net Receivables 23	1810	0	0	2134	1705	2422	19618
Inventories 24	1065	0	26	1635	2348	7063	25291
Net Property, Plant and Equipment 25	495	0	6	24	2882	1729	7531
Total Assets 26	4814	0	104	4072	7819	15069	82389
Notes and Loans Payable 27	615	0	80	0	2003	2309	13252
All Other Liabilities 28	1627	0	0	1292	900	2134	18430
Net Worth 29	2572	0	23	2780	4915	10626	50707

Selected Financial Ratios (Times to 1)

Current Ratio 30	2.0	•	1.6	3.1	2.3	4.0	4.1
Quick Ratio 31	1.4	•	0.1	2.2	1.0	2.2	2.0
Net Sales to Working Capital 32	3.4	•	55.3	3.6	6.1	2.5	3.0
Coverage Ratio 33	13.9	6.1	4.0	•	29.8	9.1	16.6
Total Asset Turnover 34	1.3	•	4.7	2.4	2.2	1.5	1.8
Inventory Turnover 35	3.6	•	5.1	4.7	4.3	2.0	3.6
Receivables Turnover 36	3.7	•	37975.4	8.3	20.0	6.8	9.3
Total Liabilities to Net Worth 37	0.9	•	3.5	0.5	0.6	0.4	0.6
Current Assets to Working Capital 38	2.0	•	2.8	1.5	1.8	1.3	1.3
Current Liabilities to Working Capital 39	1.0	•	1.8	0.5	0.8	0.3	0.3
Working Capital to Net Sales 40	0.3	•	0.0	0.3	0.2	0.4	0.3
Inventory to Working Capital 41	0.5	•	2.5	0.4	0.8	0.5	0.6
Total Receipts to Cash Flow 42	5.9	21.8	3.8	5.0	4.1	7.6	5.2
Cost of Goods to Cash Flow 43	3.7	14.8	1.0	3.9	2.5	4.8	3.2
Cash Flow to Total Debt 44	0.5	•	1.6	1.5	1.4	0.7	0.9

Selected Financial Factors (in Percentages)

Debt Ratio 45	46.6	•	77.8	31.7	37.1	29.5	38.5
Return on Total Assets 46	12.8	•	26.6	5.7	28.8	11.7	21.3
Return on Equity Before Income Taxes 47	22.3	•	90.0	8.4	44.3	14.7	32.5
Return on Equity After Income Taxes 48	18.5	•	90.0	5.7	44.2	11.8	29.1
Profit Margin (Before Income Tax) 49	9.4	43.1	4.2	2.4	12.8	7.0	11.3
Profit Margin (After Income Tax) 50	7.8	43.1	4.2	1.6	12.7	5.6	10.1

Table I

Corporations with and without Net Income

WOOD PRODUCT MANUFACTURING

MONEY AMOUNTS AND SIZE OF ASSETS IN THOUSANDS OF DOLLARS

Item Description for Accounting Period 7/09 Through 6/10	Total	Zero Assets	Under 500	500 to 1,000	1,000 to 5,000	5,000 to 10,000	10,000 to 25,000	25,000 to 50,000	50,000 to 100,000	100,000 to 250,000	250,000 to 500,000	500,000 to 2,500,000	2,500,000 and over
Number of Enterprises 1	11552	1125	6481	1287	1774	477	225	70	53	33	13	14	0
Revenues ($ in Thousands)													
Net Sales 2	59679713	749557	3347939	2736213	7836769	5559818	5085027	3269095	3875527	4463335	4727159	17989273	0
Interest 3	217254	67839	37	211	6331	2279	2726	3171	11165	24758	36063	62675	0
Rents 4	30192	0	0	344	3288	416	777	1660	4741	3069	4338	11559	0
Royalties 5	18661	0	0	0	16	0	101	563	126	64	0	17793	0
Other Portfolio Income 6	931151	18299	110068	10772	6085	25524	9548	28506	29599	47632	10060	635058	0
Other Receipts 7	713165	18465	13882	1832	32182	30817	29882	8556	28727	211120	55405	282295	0
Total Receipts 8	61590136	854160	3471926	2749372	7884671	5658854	5128061	3311551	3949885	4749978	4833025	18998653	0
Average Total Receipts 9	5332	759	536	2136	4445	11863	22791	47308	74526	143939	371771	1357047	•
Operating Costs/Operating Income (%)													
Cost of Operations 10	77.2	82.0	58.8	64.3	70.0	78.5	77.7	81.4	83.4	84.7	81.1	79.9	•
Salaries and Wages 11	7.3	5.5	11.7	10.6	8.9	5.9	5.1	4.3	4.8	5.6	5.4	8.3	•
Taxes Paid 12	1.7	1.0	2.9	2.4	2.3	1.6	2.1	2.2	1.4	1.5	1.3	1.3	•
Interest Paid 13	2.8	14.7	1.3	1.2	0.9	1.0	1.4	0.9	1.8	4.7	2.1	4.9	•
Depreciation 14	4.1	6.6	2.8	1.8	2.4	3.3	4.0	3.8	4.2	5.6	5.7	4.9	•
Amortization and Depletion 15	0.5	2.1	0.2	0.1	0.1	0.0	0.1	0.2	0.6	0.6	0.5	1.1	•
Pensions and Other Deferred Comp. 16	0.8	0.0	0.0	0.2	0.2	0.1	0.5	0.2	0.1	0.4	0.4	2.1	•
Employee Benefits 17	1.6	1.9	1.5	1.0	1.2	2.2	1.1	1.3	1.6	2.0	0.7	2.0	•
Advertising 18	0.6	0.5	0.9	0.3	0.3	0.5	0.2	0.2	0.5	0.3	1.4	0.9	•
Other Expenses 19	9.9	17.7	17.8	13.5	11.1	7.4	6.4	7.5	7.6	12.1	9.2	9.3	•
Officers' Compensation 20	1.6	1.3	4.6	5.2	3.2	1.3	1.8	1.2	1.1	0.8	0.5	0.4	•
Operating Margin 21	•	•	•	•	•	•	•	•	•	•	•	•	•
Operating Margin Before Officers' Comp. 22	•	2.0	4.5	2.7	1.4	•	•	•	•	•	•	•	•

Selected Average Balance Sheet ($ in Thousands)

Net Receivables **23**	602	0	19	110	517	1167	2268	6514	7372	13861	39616	206525	•
Inventories **24**	634	0	13	243	523	1980	3922	8113	13306	20720	47370	114026	•
Net Property, Plant and Equipment **25**	2043	0	55	183	669	2413	6421	12292	27222	67984	177260	883989	•
Total Assets **26**	5035	0	139	777	2143	6940	15280	35110	69172	149615	376694	2125136	•
Notes and Loans Payable **27**	1945	0	141	460	976	2596	5837	9538	22330	61437	126908	797066	•
All Other Liabilities **28**	1092	0	38	159	366	1046	2157	5296	11183	33428	92094	518939	•
Net Worth **29**	1998	0	-39	159	802	3298	7285	20276	35659	54750	157693	809131	•

Selected Financial Ratios (Times to 1)

Current Ratio **30**	1.9	•	1.0	2.1	2.1	2.0	1.9	2.1	2.0	1.8	1.4	2.1	•
Quick Ratio **31**	0.9	•	0.7	1.0	1.2	0.8	0.9	1.2	0.9	0.9	0.6	1.0	•
Net Sales to Working Capital **32**	5.9	•	•	8.2	6.7	6.1	6.4	4.7	5.2	5.5	10.8	4.2	•
Coverage Ratio **33**	•	0.3	1.9	0.8	1.2	0.3	1.3	•	1.1	•	•	•	•
Total Asset Turnover **34**	1.0	•	3.7	2.7	2.1	1.7	1.5	1.3	1.1	0.9	1.0	0.6	•
Inventory Turnover **35**	6.3	•	23.8	5.6	5.9	4.7	4.5	4.7	4.6	5.5	6.2	9.0	•
Receivables Turnover **36**	9.5	•	28.5	15.7	8.1	10.8	9.0	7.1	9.8	9.5	8.2	8.7	•
Total Liabilities to Net Worth **37**	1.5	•	•	3.9	1.7	1.1	1.1	0.7	0.9	1.7	1.4	1.6	•
Current Assets to Working Capital **38**	2.1	•	•	1.9	1.9	2.0	2.1	1.9	2.0	2.2	3.6	1.9	•
Current Liabilities to Working Capital **39**	1.1	•	0.9	0.9	0.9	1.0	1.1	0.9	1.0	1.2	2.6	0.9	•
Working Capital to Net Sales **40**	0.2	•	•	0.1	0.2	0.2	0.2	0.2	0.2	0.2	0.1	0.2	•
Inventory to Working Capital **41**	0.7	•	•	0.9	0.7	1.1	1.0	0.8	0.9	0.7	1.2	0.4	•
Total Receipts to Cash Flow **42**	70.7	•	7.7	13.6	11.8	21.4	19.4	28.9	247.8	•	69.8	•	•
Cost of Goods to Cash Flow **43**	54.6	•	4.5	8.7	8.3	16.8	15.1	23.6	206.6	•	56.6	•	•
Cash Flow to Total Debt **44**	0.0	•	0.4	0.3	0.3	0.2	0.1	0.1	0.0	•	0.0	•	•

Selected Financial Factors (in Percentages)

Debt Ratio **45**	60.3	•	128.2	79.6	62.6	52.5	52.3	42.3	48.4	63.4	58.1	61.9	•
Return on Total Assets **46**	•	•	9.2	2.5	2.1	0.5	2.6	•	•	•	•	•	•
Return on Equity Before Income Taxes **47**	•	•	•	•	0.8	•	1.3	•	•	•	•	•	•
Return on Equity After Income Taxes **48**	•	•	•	•	0.1	•	0.3	•	•	•	•	•	•
Profit Margin (Before Income Tax) **49**	•	•	1.2	•	-0.2	•	0.4	•	•	•	•	•	•
Profit Margin (After Income Tax) **50**	•	•	1.1	•	0.0	•	0.1	•	•	•	•	•	•

Table II

Corporations with Net Income

WOOD PRODUCT MANUFACTURING

MONEY AMOUNTS AND SIZE OF ASSETS IN THOUSANDS OF DOLLARS

Item Description for Accounting Period 7/09 Through 6/10		Total	Zero Assets	Under 500	500 to 1,000	1,000 to 5,000	5,000 to 10,000	10,000 to 25,000	25,000 to 50,000	50,000 to 100,000	100,000 to 250,000	250,000 to 500,000	500,000 to 2,500,000	2,500,000 and over
Number of Enterprises	1	6012	598	3266	723	984	259	120	31	18	9	0	4	0
Revenues ($ in Thousands)														
Net Sales	2	29031239	119227	2543470	1995793	5237686	4011161	3237160	1714562	1516815	1884785	0	6770581	0
Interest	3	29727	75	1	4	4745	1390	1523	1851	7284	9695	0	3158	0
Rents	4	7519	0	0	344	2606	130	675	273	1145	1064	0	1281	0
Royalties	5	8615	0	0	0	16	0	63	562	112	0	0	7862	0
Other Portfolio Income	6	236260	18299	107769	5844	4951	22854	7944	26306	2229	36577	0	3486	0
Other Receipts	7	332161	3210	5379	186	19966	23304	15791	9628	16689	156870	0	81141	0
Total Receipts	8	29645521	140811	2656619	2002171	5269970	4058839	3263156	1753182	1544274	2088991	0	6867509	0
Average Total Receipts	9	4931	235	813	2769	5356	15671	27193	56554	85793	232110	•	1716877	•
Operating Costs/Operating Income (%)														
Cost of Operations	10	70.0	67.8	58.7	58.5	68.8	79.1	74.1	75.9	80.9	72.8	•	66.4	•
Salaries and Wages	11	7.8	0.9	13.2	12.0	7.3	5.5	4.8	4.7	3.4	7.4	•	9.7	•
Taxes Paid	12	1.8	2.4	2.6	2.4	1.9	1.3	2.0	1.6	1.1	1.9	•	1.7	•
Interest Paid	13	0.9	3.2	0.7	0.6	0.6	0.6	1.0	0.6	1.6	1.7	•	1.3	•
Depreciation	14	2.7	13.6	2.2	1.6	1.9	2.0	3.3	2.8	2.8	4.2	•	3.1	•
Amortization and Depletion	15	0.4	0.4	0.0	0.1	0.0	0.0	0.0	0.1	0.3	0.2	•	1.3	•
Pensions and Other Deferred Comp.	16	0.5	0.0	0.3	0.3	0.2	0.1	0.5	0.1	0.2	0.3	•	1.5	•
Employee Benefits	17	1.4	0.2	0.8	1.2	1.1	1.5	1.0	1.1	0.8	0.3	•	2.8	•
Advertising	18	0.7	0.3	1.1	0.3	0.4	0.5	0.1	0.2	0.3	1.8	•	1.1	•
Other Expenses	19	9.1	20.2	13.9	14.1	9.3	6.6	5.2	8.7	5.3	15.0	•	8.2	•
Officers' Compensation	20	1.9	1.7	2.9	5.2	3.3	0.8	1.9	1.3	1.0	1.1	•	0.6	•
Operating Margin	21	2.8	•	3.9	3.7	5.3	2.0	5.9	2.9	2.4	•	•	2.3	•
Operating Margin Before Officers' Comp.	22	4.7	•	6.8	8.9	8.6	2.8	7.8	4.2	3.4	•	•	2.9	•

Selected Average Balance Sheet ($ in Thousands)

Net Receivables 23	434	0	26	129	558	1534	2958	9692	6901	19337	132834	•
Inventories 24	569	0	10	176	549	2895	3332	8795	14416	29179	194004	•
Net Property, Plant and Equipment 25	796	0	59	178	611	2127	6026	9705	20619	61136	341820	•
Total Assets 26	2848	0	156	801	2278	7116	15583	35351	66832	187105	1523959	•
Notes and Loans Payable 27	851	0	156	338	555	2195	5015	6828	15409	74398	371572	•
All Other Liabilities 28	603	0	51	111	315	1113	2432	5555	11553	42647	430849	•
Net Worth 29	1394	0	-51	353	1408	3809	8136	22967	39871	70060	721538	•

Selected Financial Ratios (Times to 1)

Current Ratio 30	2.0	•	1.0	3.7	2.7	2.2	1.9	2.5	2.9	2.2	1.3	•
Quick Ratio 31	1.0	•	0.7	2.3	1.6	0.9	1.1	1.5	1.3	1.0	0.6	•
Net Sales to Working Capital 32	7.4	•	4296.4	6.9	5.9	6.2	6.9	4.1	4.1	4.9	16.0	•
Coverage Ratio 33	6.3	3.3	12.5	7.8	11.7	6.7	7.6	9.8	3.7	3.5	3.9	
Total Asset Turnover 34	1.7	•	5.0	3.4	2.3	2.2	1.7	1.6	1.3	1.1	1.1	•
Inventory Turnover 35	5.9	•	44.6	9.2	6.7	4.2	6.0	4.8	4.7	5.2	5.8	•
Receivables Turnover 36	10.7	•	33.9	19.2	9.0	9.7	8.8	6.1	12.2	10.5	11.7	•
Total Liabilities to Net Worth 37	1.0	•	•	1.3	0.6	0.9	0.9	0.5	0.7	1.7	1.1	•
Current Assets to Working Capital 38	2.0	•	477.3	1.4	1.6	1.9	2.1	1.7	1.5	1.8	4.1	•
Current Liabilities to Working Capital 39	1.0	•	476.3	0.4	0.6	0.9	1.1	0.7	0.5	0.8	3.1	•
Working Capital to Net Sales 40	0.1	•	0.0	0.1	0.2	0.2	0.1	0.2	0.2	0.2	0.1	•
Inventory to Working Capital 41	0.8	•	59.0	0.5	0.6	1.0	0.8	0.6	0.8	0.7	1.6	•
Total Receipts to Cash Flow 42	8.7	4.4	5.6	8.5	7.9	12.4	9.8	9.1	12.8	6.6	9.5	
Cost of Goods to Cash Flow 43	6.1	3.0	3.3	5.0	5.4	9.8	7.2	6.9	10.4	4.8	6.3	
Cash Flow to Total Debt 44	0.4	•	0.7	0.7	0.8	0.4	0.4	0.5	0.2	0.3	0.2	•

Selected Financial Factors (in Percentages)

Debt Ratio 45	51.0	•	132.6	56.0	38.2	46.5	47.8	35.0	40.3	62.6	52.7	•
Return on Total Assets 46	10.0	•	45.1	15.7	15.1	8.1	13.4	8.9	7.3	6.6	5.6	•
Return on Equity Before Income Taxes 47	17.2	•	•	31.1	22.4	12.9	22.2	12.4	8.9	8.9	12.7	•
Return on Equity After Income Taxes 48	16.2	•	•	31.0	21.6	12.3	20.5	10.6	8.1	8.1	11.3	•
Profit Margin (Before Income Tax) 49	5.0	7.4	8.3	4.0	5.9	3.2	6.7	5.1	4.2	4.2	3.8	•
Profit Margin (After Income Tax) 50	4.7	6.3	8.2	4.0	5.7	3.0	6.2	4.4	3.8	3.8	3.5	•

72

Table I

Corporations with and without Net Income

PULP, PAPER, AND PAPERBOARD MILLS

MONEY AMOUNTS AND SIZE OF ASSETS IN THOUSANDS OF DOLLARS

Item Description for Accounting Period 7/09 Through 6/10	Total	Zero Assets	Under 500	500 to 1,000	1,000 to 5,000	5,000 to 10,000	10,000 to 25,000	25,000 to 50,000	50,000 to 100,000	100,000 to 250,000	250,000 to 500,000	500,000 to 2,500,000	2,500,000 and over
Number of Enterprises **1**	390	5	56	0	212	21	20	19	11	12	8	18	8
Revenues ($ in Thousands)													
Net Sales **2**	72333591	180278	131037	0	697589	90689	540990	960555	1833042	1645910	2879388	18415253	44958860
Interest **3**	1029044	80	70	0	107	5	311	160	1387	9640	4520	118361	894403
Rents **4**	19856	0	0	0	0	0	0	55	142	2	3394	7140	9121
Royalties **5**	86824	0	0	0	0	0	0	0	0	0	0	25601	61223
Other Portfolio Income **6**	456159	0	0	0	0	186	93	328	4303	808	931	92568	356941
Other Receipts **7**	1397334	-50909	0	0	4551	8612	1347	2945	10595	43289	25153	577011	774743
Total Receipts **8**	75322808	129449	131107	0	702247	99492	542741	964043	1849469	1699649	2913386	19235934	47055291
Average Total Receipts **9**	193135	25890	2341	•	3312	4738	27137	50739	168134	141637	364173	1068663	5881911
Operating Costs/Operating Income (%)													
Cost of Operations **10**	72.1	95.4	38.1	•	74.8	91.0	75.7	76.2	82.9	80.6	73.3	74.3	70.2
Salaries and Wages **11**	4.9	0.8	8.0	•	1.8	9.7	7.4	5.4	3.6	2.8	8.4	3.9	5.2
Taxes Paid **12**	1.3	0.3	1.9	•	0.9	1.5	1.3	1.6	1.0	0.8	1.3	1.1	1.4
Interest Paid **13**	5.3	0.9	0.0	•	1.2	1.9	1.2	0.9	0.4	3.5	3.3	3.4	6.7
Depreciation **14**	6.2	0.0	1.1	•	0.7	7.6	2.6	2.5	2.6	4.1	7.2	7.8	5.9
Amortization and Depletion **15**	0.6	•	•	•	0.9	0.1	0.1	0.1	0.2	0.4	0.8	0.4	0.8
Pensions and Other Deferred Comp. **16**	1.5	•	11.7	•	•	0.6	0.2	1.9	0.5	0.8	1.2	1.0	1.8
Employee Benefits **17**	2.9	0.3	3.1	•	0.4	1.4	2.1	1.9	2.0	2.0	2.4	2.2	3.4
Advertising **18**	0.2	•	0.2	•	0.3	0.0	0.0	0.1	0.3	0.4	0.3	0.3	0.2
Other Expenses **19**	10.4	2.2	11.9	•	17.7	16.3	9.8	6.0	8.9	5.0	4.5	6.4	12.7
Officers' Compensation **20**	0.3	•	22.2	•	0.9	0.8	1.0	1.0	0.3	0.7	0.5	0.5	0.1
Operating Margin **21**	•	0.0	2.0	•	0.4	•	•	2.4	•	•	•	•	•
Operating Margin Before Officers' Comp. **22**	•	0.0	24.1	•	1.3	•	•	3.3	•	•	•	•	•

Selected Average Balance Sheet ($ in Thousands)

Net Receivables 23	43008	0	159	281	900	3435	6059	12794	11607	54179	197560	1529049
Inventories 24	21031	0	60	153	1748	3817	3950	16709	18871	45821	130841	606553
Net Property, Plant and Equipment 25	91074	0	5	93	3720	4586	12309	25682	47982	150152	555200	2880289
Total Assets 26	308133	0	351	1230	6506	15122	34673	75369	154618	407154	1181765	11447521
Notes and Loans Payable 27	124014	0	0	588	4166	5858	11831	22571	50052	164028	350285	4918134
All Other Liabilities 28	98976	0	298	80	2127	4338	19699	26599	37876	119950	390932	3664729
Net Worth 29	85143	0	53	561	213	4927	3143	26200	66690	123177	440547	2864658

Selected Financial Ratios (Times to 1)

Current Ratio 30	1.0	•	0.7	9.0	1.3	1.3	1.0	1.8	1.7	2.0	1.9	0.8
Quick Ratio 31	0.7	•	0.5	7.2	0.4	0.7	0.5	0.9	0.8	0.9	1.1	0.6
Net Sales to Working Capital 32	305.8	•	•	5.1	6.1	13.9	109.0	10.3	8.8	4.7	5.0	•
Coverage Ratio 33	0.7	•	527.0	1.9	•	0.2	3.9	•	1.6	0.4	1.9	0.4
Total Asset Turnover 34	0.6	•	6.7	2.7	0.7	1.8	1.5	2.2	0.9	0.9	0.9	0.5
Inventory Turnover 35	6.4	•	14.7	16.1	2.2	5.4	9.8	8.3	5.9	5.8	5.8	6.5
Receivables Turnover 36	4.0	•	29.5	11.9	•	5.7	7.5	12.4	12.5	6.0	6.1	3.3
Total Liabilities to Net Worth 37	2.6	•	5.6	1.2	29.5	2.1	10.0	1.9	1.3	2.3	1.7	3.0
Current Assets to Working Capital 38	128.2	•	•	1.1	4.0	4.5	35.7	2.3	2.5	2.0	2.2	•
Current Liabilities to Working Capital 39	127.2	•	•	0.1	3.0	3.5	34.7	1.3	1.5	1.0	1.2	•
Working Capital to Net Sales 40	0.0	•	•	0.2	0.2	0.1	0.0	0.1	0.1	0.2	0.2	•
Inventory to Working Capital 41	29.9	•	•	0.2	2.5	1.4	8.9	1.1	1.1	0.5	0.6	•
Total Receipts to Cash Flow 42	15.6	•	12.9	10.5	•	17.3	13.0	27.7	16.5	182.6	13.6	15.1
Cost of Goods to Cash Flow 43	11.3	•	4.9	7.8	•	13.1	9.9	23.0	13.3	133.9	10.1	10.6
Cash Flow to Total Debt 44	0.1	•	0.6	0.5	•	0.2	0.1	0.1	0.1	0.0	0.1	0.0

Selected Financial Factors (in Percentages)

Debt Ratio 45	72.4	•	84.9	54.3	96.7	67.4	90.9	65.2	56.9	69.7	62.7	75.0
Return on Total Assets 46	2.2	•	13.4	5.9	•	0.3	5.3	•	5.0	1.0	5.6	1.5
Return on Equity Before Income Taxes 47	•	•	88.4	6.1	•	•	43.6	•	4.2	•	7.1	•
Return on Equity After Income Taxes 48	•	•	75.1	6.1	•	•	41.8	•	2.6	•	3.9	•
Profit Margin (Before Income Tax) 49	•	•	2.0	1.0	•	•	2.7	•	2.1	•	3.0	•
Profit Margin (After Income Tax) 50	•	•	1.7	1.0	•	•	2.6	•	1.3	•	1.7	•

Table II

Corporations with Net Income

PULP, PAPER, AND PAPERBOARD MILLS

Money Amounts and Size of Assets in Thousands of Dollars

Item Description for Accounting Period 7/09 Through 6/10	Total	Zero Assets	Under 500	500 to 1,000	1,000 to 5,000	5,000 to 10,000	10,000 to 25,000	25,000 to 50,000	50,000 to 100,000	100,000 to 250,000	250,000 to 500,000	500,000 to 2,500,000	2,500,000 and over
Number of Enterprises 1	223	•	•	0	113	0	11	9	6	•	0	15	0

Revenues ($ in Thousands)

Item Description for Accounting Period 7/09 Through 6/10	Total	Zero Assets	Under 500	500 to 1,000	1,000 to 5,000	5,000 to 10,000	10,000 to 25,000	25,000 to 50,000	50,000 to 100,000	100,000 to 250,000	250,000 to 500,000	500,000 to 2,500,000	2,500,000 and over
Net Sales 2	40764037	•	•	0	560193	0	372402	402809	911473	•	0	3591144	0
Interest 3	906491	•	•	0	107	0	0	0	425	•	0	903824	0
Rents 4	6247	•	•	0	0	0	0	0	142	•	0	5866	0
Royalties 5	63003	•	•	0	0	0	0	0	0	•	0	63003	0
Other Portfolio Income 6	340390	•	•	0	0	0	0	309	127	•	0	339459	0
Other Receipts 7	621791	•	•	0	0	0	85	2548	2652	•	0	555693	0
Total Receipts 8	42701959	•	•	0	560300	0	372487	405666	914819	•	0	37786989	•
Average Total Receipts 9	191489	•	•	•	4958	•	33862	45074	152470	•	•	2519133	•

Operating Costs/Operating Income (%)

Item Description for Accounting Period 7/09 Through 6/10	Total	Zero Assets	Under 500	500 to 1,000	1,000 to 5,000	5,000 to 10,000	10,000 to 25,000	25,000 to 50,000	50,000 to 100,000	100,000 to 250,000	250,000 to 500,000	500,000 to 2,500,000	2,500,000 and over
Cost of Operations 10	65.3	•	•	•	80.1	•	68.5	65.5	72.1	•	•	64.0	•
Salaries and Wages 11	5.5	•	•	•	2.3	•	7.9	5.4	4.9	•	•	5.7	•
Taxes Paid 12	1.5	•	•	•	0.4	•	1.4	2.4	1.0	•	•	1.6	•
Interest Paid 13	5.0	•	•	•	0.6	•	0.8	0.8	0.5	•	•	5.4	•
Depreciation 14	6.3	•	•	•	0.2	•	2.8	2.3	2.4	•	•	6.7	•
Amortization and Depletion 15	0.5	•	•	•	•	•	•	0.1	0.2	•	•	0.5	•
Pensions and Other Deferred Comp. 16	2.3	•	•	•	•	•	0.1	2.6	0.7	•	•	2.5	•
Employee Benefits 17	2.0	•	•	•	0.4	•	1.5	0.8	2.6	•	•	2.1	•
Advertising 18	0.2	•	•	•	0.2	•	0.0	0.1	0.5	•	•	0.2	•
Other Expenses 19	9.7	•	•	•	12.1	•	9.9	10.0	9.0	•	•	10.0	•
Officers' Compensation 20	0.4	•	•	•	0.9	•	0.6	1.8	0.4	•	•	0.2	•
Operating Margin 21	1.3	•	•	•	2.7	•	6.6	8.1	5.6	•	•	1.0	•
Operating Margin Before Officers' Comp. 22	1.6	•	•	•	3.6	•	7.2	10.0	6.1	•	•	1.2	•

Selected Average Balance Sheet ($ in Thousands)

Net Receivables 23	39225	423	4623	5546	17281	547719
Inventories 24	21070	137	4209	4220	18075	140274
Net Property, Plant and Equipment 25	88318	102	5888	18055	21516	1244355
Total Assets 26	336317	1398	15324	38440	75534	4778664
Notes and Loans Payable 27	130376	379	5709	8755	14921	1875669
All Other Liabilities 28	99183	1	4529	12074	20665	1414646
Net Worth 29	106757	1017	5086	17611	39948	1488349

Selected Financial Ratios (Times to 1)

Current Ratio 30	1.0	979.4	1.4	1.5	2.0	1.0
Quick Ratio 31	0.7	772.9	0.8	0.8	1.1	0.6
Net Sales to Working Capital 32	111.1	4.0	12.7	9.5	6.9	•
Coverage Ratio 33	2.2	5.3	9.2	11.9	12.1	2.2
Total Asset Turnover 34	0.5	3.5	2.2	1.2	2.0	0.5
Inventory Turnover 35	5.7	29.1	5.5	6.9	6.1	10.9
Receivables Turnover 36	4.0	12.3	6.8	8.2	9.1	7.9
Total Liabilities to Net Worth 37	2.2	0.4	2.0	1.2	0.9	2.2
Current Assets to Working Capital 38	44.7	1.0	3.4	3.0	2.0	•
Current Liabilities to Working Capital 39	43.7	0.0	2.4	2.0	1.0	•
Working Capital to Net Sales 40	0.0	0.2	0.1	0.1	0.1	•
Inventory to Working Capital 41	11.2	0.2	1.4	1.0	0.8	•
Total Receipts to Cash Flow 42	7.7	9.7	7.7	5.4	7.6	7.5
Cost of Goods to Cash Flow 43	5.0	7.8	5.2	3.6	5.5	4.8
Cash Flow to Total Debt 44	0.1	1.3	0.4	0.4	0.6	0.1

Selected Financial Factors (in Percentages)

Debt Ratio 45	68.3	27.2	66.8	54.2	47.1	68.9
Return on Total Assets 46	6.1	12.1	16.4	11.2	13.3	5.9
Return on Equity Before Income Taxes 47	10.5	13.4	43.9	22.3	23.0	10.1
Return on Equity After Income Taxes 48	8.2	13.4	43.9	21.6	18.3	7.8
Profit Margin (Before Income Tax) 49	6.1	2.8	6.6	8.8	6.1	6.3
Profit Margin (After Income Tax) 50	4.8	2.8	6.6	8.5	4.8	4.8

74

Table I
Corporations with and without Net Income

CONVERTED PAPER PRODUCT

Money Amounts and Size of Assets in Thousands of Dollars

Item Description for Accounting Period 7/09 Through 6/10	Total	Zero Assets	Under 500	500 to 1,000	1,000 to 5,000	5,000 to 10,000	10,000 to 25,000	25,000 to 50,000	50,000 to 100,000	100,000 to 250,000	250,000 to 500,000	500,000 to 2,500,000	2,500,000 and over
Number of Enterprises 1	2449	144	741	259	857	145	146	72	37	21	8	10	8
Revenues ($ in Thousands)													
Net Sales 2	84697672	428500	777327	610882	5518487	2503246	5055041	4576349	4176470	5470049	4143646	8598461	42839213
Interest 3	744773	0	533	28	160	1756	1111	2964	3286	6893	571	16532	710939
Rents 4	21754	0	0	0	31	286	524	1181	1725	74	455	11456	6022
Royalties 5	1876447	0	0	895	0	0	279	2339	709	2021	5462	6026	1858714
Other Portfolio Income 6	1416387	589	21464	2	12033	6990	5792	6123	9436	44529	2717	76938	1229772
Other Receipts 7	1178595	69531	1920	24630	5337	20510	29843	34530	23688	10429	-14257	31666	940773
Total Receipts 8	89935628	498620	801244	636437	5536048	2532788	5092590	4623486	4215314	5533995	4138594	8741079	47585433
Average Total Receipts 9	36723	3463	1081	2457	6460	17468	34881	64215	113927	263524	517324	874108	5948179
Operating Costs/Operating Income (%)													
Cost of Operations 10	68.2	65.6	73.2	60.8	67.5	77.7	73.2	76.3	79.2	70.5	77.8	73.1	63.0
Salaries and Wages 11	9.0	7.4	3.6	8.5	10.4	4.7	5.8	6.8	5.3	6.5	6.0	7.3	11.0
Taxes Paid 12	1.3	2.0	2.5	1.5	1.9	1.7	1.8	1.4	0.9	1.6	1.8	1.3	1.1
Interest Paid 13	3.1	6.9	0.4	0.1	0.9	0.9	1.2	0.8	1.8	1.1	3.3	3.9	4.3
Depreciation 14	4.3	4.1	0.9	2.0	1.9	1.7	3.3	4.2	3.4	3.3	2.9	4.1	5.3
Amortization and Depletion 15	0.6	0.1	•	0.0	0.2	0.1	0.1	0.1	0.4	0.4	1.1	0.6	0.9
Pensions and Other Deferred Comp. 16	1.8	0.2	0.2	0.0	0.5	0.2	0.2	0.5	0.5	0.6	0.7	0.6	3.0
Employee Benefits 17	1.9	3.3	0.9	2.2	2.2	0.8	1.3	1.7	1.3	1.5	2.4	1.9	2.2
Advertising 18	0.7	0.3	0.1	0.1	0.2	0.1	0.1	0.2	0.2	0.7	0.1	0.3	1.1
Other Expenses 19	8.8	9.8	14.7	11.1	9.7	7.6	8.4	5.6	6.3	8.8	5.7	6.6	9.9
Officers' Compensation 20	0.8	2.1	1.8	5.1	2.9	2.4	1.7	1.2	0.9	0.7	0.5	0.4	0.3
Operating Margin 21	•	•	1.7	9.9	1.8	2.1	2.8	1.3	•	4.3	•	•	•
Operating Margin Before Officers' Comp. 22	0.3	0.3	3.5	15.1	4.7	4.5	4.6	2.5	0.6	5.0	•	0.2	•

Selected Average Balance Sheet ($ in Thousands)

Net Receivables 23	5864	61	205	744	1755	3432	7506	14065	35056	58253	142948	1146971
Inventories 24	3167	31	41	456	1110	3611	6817	14750	25086	59393	89889	459595
Net Property, Plant and Equipment 25	9158	33	93	705	2004	5928	14691	20188	53428	128049	297836	1711146
Total Assets 26	55703	269	792	2221	7121	15632	36646	72229	168936	370206	912848	13730748
Notes and Loans Payable 27	18712	74	482	1246	2946	5359	11896	26916	39923	119498	490146	4352587
All Other Liabilities 28	13349	79	210	769	1771	4182	8564	22223	43429	150269	251926	3122458
Net Worth 29	23642	116	100	206	2403	6091	16186	23091	85584	100439	170776	6255703

Selected Financial Ratios (Times to 1)

Current Ratio 30	1.2	•	2.3	3.2	1.1	1.8	1.7	1.6	1.4	1.8	1.6	1.1
Quick Ratio 31	0.8	•	1.3	2.9	0.8	1.1	0.9	0.9	0.7	1.0	0.8	0.8
Net Sales to Working Capital 32	17.0	•	8.1	5.0	60.4	9.9	9.9	9.3	11.9	8.1	9.9	24.0
Coverage Ratio 33	3.7	3.1	13.8	175.6	3.4	4.8	3.9	3.8	1.4	6.4	0.4	4.3
Total Asset Turnover 34	0.6	•	3.9	3.0	2.9	2.4	2.2	1.7	1.6	1.5	1.4	0.4
Inventory Turnover 35	7.4	•	24.5	34.7	9.5	12.1	7.0	7.1	6.1	7.3	6.8	7.3
Receivables Turnover 36	6.4	•	14.8	•	7.5	•	9.1	7.8	8.7	8.0	9.9	5.5
Total Liabilities to Net Worth 37	1.4	•	1.3	6.9	9.8	2.0	1.6	1.3	2.1	1.0	2.7	1.2
Current Assets to Working Capital 38	5.9	•	1.8	1.5	13.1	2.2	2.5	2.6	3.7	2.3	2.7	10.1
Current Liabilities to Working Capital 39	4.9	•	0.8	0.5	12.1	1.2	1.5	1.6	2.7	1.3	1.7	9.1
Working Capital to Net Sales 40	0.1	•	0.1	0.2	0.0	0.1	0.1	0.1	0.1	0.1	0.1	0.0
Inventory to Working Capital 41	1.5	•	0.2	0.1	3.4	0.6	0.9	0.9	1.5	0.8	1.1	2.0
Total Receipts to Cash Flow 42	8.7	4.4	10.0	4.9	13.6	12.7	10.9	17.7	20.1	8.2	93.4	6.4
Cost of Goods to Cash Flow 43	5.9	2.9	7.3	3.0	9.2	9.9	8.0	13.5	15.9	5.8	72.7	4.0
Cash Flow to Total Debt 44	0.1	•	0.7	0.7	0.2	0.3	0.2	0.1	0.1	0.4	0.0	0.1

Selected Financial Factors (in Percentages)

Debt Ratio 45	57.6	•	56.9	87.4	90.7	66.2	61.0	55.8	68.0	49.3	72.9	54.4
Return on Total Assets 46	7.1	•	20.2	42.2	8.6	10.0	10.7	5.4	3.9	10.9	1.6	7.1
Return on Equity Before Income Taxes 47	12.2	•	43.4	332.2	66.1	23.5	20.5	9.0	3.2	18.1	•	11.9
Return on Equity After Income Taxes 48	8.5	•	43.1	330.7	66.0	20.9	19.1	7.6	1.8	15.9	•	7.9
Profit Margin (Before Income Tax) 49	8.3	14.5	4.8	14.1	2.1	3.3	3.6	2.3	0.6	5.9	•	14.0
Profit Margin (After Income Tax) 50	5.8	14.5	4.7	14.0	2.1	2.9	3.4	1.9	0.4	5.2	•	9.3

Table II

Corporations with Net Income

CONVERTED PAPER PRODUCT

MONEY AMOUNTS AND SIZE OF ASSETS IN THOUSANDS OF DOLLARS

Item Description for Accounting Period 7/09 Through 6/10	Total	Zero Assets	Under 500	500 to 1,000	1,000 to 5,000	5,000 to 10,000	10,000 to 25,000	25,000 to 50,000	50,000 to 100,000	100,000 to 250,000	250,000 to 500,000	500,000 to 2,500,000	2,500,000 and over
Number of Enterprises **1**	1498	•	•	•	505	93	118	43	21	•	3	7	•
Revenues ($ in Thousands)													
Net Sales **2**	70992904	•	•	•	4165087	1926571	4128091	3057382	2536530	•	1302277	4950281	•
Interest **3**	733960	•	•	•	17	1501	933	1944	1954	•	309	12714	•
Rents **4**	12343	•	•	•	31	13	520	1060	214	•	55	4354	•
Royalties **5**	1870385	•	•	•	0	0	0	0	0	•	2858	5897	•
Other Portfolio Income **6**	1388004	•	•	•	3784	6960	5736	1019	8670	•	408	66858	•
Other Receipts **7**	1123987	•	•	•	3616	18557	12881	18667	13978	•	-16362	29012	•
Total Receipts **8**	76053583	•	•	•	4172535	1953602	4148161	3080072	2561346	•	1289545	5069116	•
Average Total Receipts **9**	50770	•	•	•	8262	21006	35154	71630	121969	•	429848	724159	•
Operating Costs/Operating Income (%)													
Cost of Operations **10**	66.7	•	•	•	66.8	78.8	72.4	74.5	77.9	•	76.6	71.7	•
Salaries and Wages **11**	9.3	•	•	•	10.5	3.6	6.0	6.6	5.1	•	8.7	7.0	•
Taxes Paid **12**	1.3	•	•	•	1.8	1.9	1.5	1.4	0.8	•	2.1	1.2	•
Interest Paid **13**	3.1	•	•	•	0.3	0.9	1.2	0.5	1.6	•	1.6	3.5	•
Depreciation **14**	4.4	•	•	•	1.4	1.5	3.0	3.0	2.8	•	2.6	4.4	•
Amortization and Depletion **15**	0.7	•	•	•	0.0	0.2	0.1	0.1	0.4	•	0.5	0.7	•
Pensions and Other Deferred Comp. **16**	2.0	•	•	•	0.6	0.2	0.2	0.5	0.3	•	0.5	1.1	•
Employee Benefits **17**	1.9	•	•	•	1.7	0.4	1.3	1.3	1.3	•	2.3	1.7	•
Advertising **18**	0.8	•	•	•	0.0	0.1	0.1	0.1	0.1	•	0.2	0.5	•
Other Expenses **19**	8.8	•	•	•	8.5	6.5	7.7	6.1	6.3	•	1.3	6.5	•
Officers' Compensation **20**	0.8	•	•	•	3.2	2.0	1.9	1.3	0.9	•	0.6	0.6	•
Operating Margin **21**	0.3	•	•	•	5.1	4.0	4.7	4.6	2.5	•	2.9	1.2	•
Operating Margin Before Officers' Comp. **22**	1.1	•	•	•	8.3	6.0	6.6	5.9	3.4	•	3.5	1.8	•

Selected Average Balance Sheet ($ in Thousands)

Net Receivables 23	8420	744	1997	3418	7846	14817	54082	134593
Inventories 24	4034	581	1619	3286	6967	16292	87858	69942
Net Property, Plant and Equipment 25	12884	762	2082	5748	11643	16877	154875	278321
Total Assets 26	84931	2470	7617	15435	34759	72824	335345	872846
Notes and Loans Payable 27	27330	588	3414	5248	7849	26162	71988	415405
All Other Liabilities 28	19647	725	1692	4130	7384	18437	77101	233226
Net Worth 29	37954	1157	2510	6057	19525	28225	186256	224214

Selected Financial Ratios (Times to 1)

Current Ratio 30	1.2	1.7	2.3	1.6	2.0	1.6	2.3	0.9
Quick Ratio 31	0.8	1.1	1.4	0.9	1.2	0.8	1.1	0.6
Net Sales to Working Capital 32	16.4	12.4	8.2	10.9	7.6	9.2	5.3	•
Coverage Ratio 33	4.4	17.2	7.2	5.5	11.1	3.1	2.5	2.1
Total Asset Turnover 34	0.6	3.3	2.7	2.3	2.0	1.7	1.3	0.8
Inventory Turnover 35	7.8	9.5	10.1	7.7	7.6	5.8	3.8	7.2
Receivables Turnover 36	6.4	8.0	9.9	9.5	8.2	8.5	6.5	•
Total Liabilities to Net Worth 37	1.2	1.1	2.0	1.5	0.8	1.6	0.8	2.9
Current Assets to Working Capital 38	5.9	2.5	1.8	2.6	2.0	2.8	1.8	•
Current Liabilities to Working Capital 39	4.9	1.5	0.8	1.6	1.0	1.8	0.8	•
Working Capital to Net Sales 40	0.1	0.1	0.1	0.1	0.1	0.1	0.2	•
Inventory to Working Capital 41	1.4	0.7	0.5	1.0	0.6	1.1	0.8	•
Total Receipts to Cash Flow 42	7.4	10.2	10.6	9.7	10.9	13.2	91.6	12.7
Cost of Goods to Cash Flow 43	5.0	6.8	8.4	7.0	8.1	10.3	70.2	9.1
Cash Flow to Total Debt 44	0.1	0.6	0.4	0.4	0.4	0.2	0.0	0.1

Selected Financial Factors (in Percentages)

Debt Ratio 45	55.3	53.2	67.0	60.8	43.8	61.2	44.5	74.3
Return on Total Assets 46	7.7	18.9	17.1	14.4	12.0	8.2	5.3	5.9
Return on Equity Before Income Taxes 47	13.3	38.0	44.7	30.1	19.5	14.5	5.8	11.8
Return on Equity After Income Taxes 48	9.5	38.0	40.9	28.4	17.6	12.5	5.2	9.4
Profit Margin (Before Income Tax) 49	10.6	5.3	5.4	5.2	5.4	3.4	2.5	3.7
Profit Margin (After Income Tax) 50	7.6	5.3	5.0	4.9	4.8	2.9	2.2	3.0

76

Table I

Corporations with and without Net Income

PRINTING AND RELATED SUPPORT ACTIVITIES

MONEY AMOUNTS AND SIZE OF ASSETS IN THOUSANDS OF DOLLARS

Item Description for Accounting Period 7/09 Through 6/10	Total	Zero Assets	Under 500	500 to 1,000	1,000 to 5,000	5,000 to 10,000	10,000 to 25,000	25,000 to 50,000	50,000 to 100,000	100,000 to 250,000	250,000 to 500,000	500,000 to 2,500,000	2,500,000 and over
Number of Enterprises 1	29444	5103	19619	1513	2316	465	269	84	30	16	16	12	0
Revenues ($ in Thousands)													
Net Sales 2	73980225	821888	8759284	3396346	12439096	6446854	7519563	3804933	2220392	2509155	6211174	19851541	0
Interest 3	200948	934	1144	55	9045	2872	8765	2615	10929	1017	9561	154011	0
Rents 4	30676	0	80	5353	5265	379	3686	908	108	2547	1383	10966	0
Royalties 5	50001	0	1160	0	460	673	4069	151	0	6785	7211	29494	0
Other Portfolio Income 6	406369	5300	18622	1369	102389	17103	5333	11711	3822	37786	146183	56749	0
Other Receipts 7	259621	6886	38063	35441	103855	17872	63270	113066	-398466	18571	46459	214603	0
Total Receipts 8	74927840	835008	8818353	3438564	12660110	6485753	7604686	3933384	1836785	2575861	6421971	20317364	0
Average Total Receipts 9	2545	164	449	2273	5466	13948	28270	46826	61226	160991	401373	1693114	•
Operating Costs/Operating Income (%)													
Cost of Operations 10	61.3	38.9	48.3	51.6	63.0	66.7	68.7	68.5	72.6	68.9	62.9	59.8	•
Salaries and Wages 11	11.3	10.9	12.7	18.0	11.4	11.0	9.9	10.5	11.3	7.4	12.7	10.4	•
Taxes Paid 12	2.3	3.3	2.7	2.4	2.5	1.9	1.9	1.9	2.1	1.5	1.9	2.4	•
Interest Paid 13	2.4	1.5	1.0	0.8	1.1	0.7	1.4	2.6	4.8	3.5	4.5	3.9	•
Depreciation 14	3.9	3.4	2.4	1.8	3.4	3.3	4.1	4.7	5.2	4.4	4.3	4.9	•
Amortization and Depletion 15	0.8	1.3	0.1	0.1	0.2	0.1	0.3	0.5	0.8	1.6	1.4	1.6	•
Pensions and Other Deferred Comp. 16	0.4	0.1	0.3	0.0	0.2	0.3	0.3	0.4	0.4	0.3	1.3	0.4	•
Employee Benefits 17	1.9	1.5	1.1	1.0	1.4	1.8	1.8	2.3	2.8	1.3	3.1	2.4	•
Advertising 18	0.9	1.1	0.5	1.0	0.5	0.3	0.3	0.9	3.7	1.8	0.2	1.5	•
Other Expenses 19	12.7	22.9	24.9	16.8	11.1	10.7	9.2	10.1	11.0	8.7	10.6	10.9	•
Officers' Compensation 20	2.9	10.4	8.1	4.7	4.8	2.2	2.6	1.9	2.8	1.3	0.7	0.4	•
Operating Margin 21	•	4.8	•	1.7	0.4	1.0	•	•	•	•	•	1.3	•
Operating Margin Before Officers' Comp. 22	2.2	15.2	5.9	6.5	5.2	3.2	1.9	•	•	0.6	•	1.7	•

Selected Average Balance Sheet ($ in Thousands)

Net Receivables 23	345	0	26	219	609	1882	4455	7800	12829	21581	50963	302415	•
Inventories 24	138	0	7	72	211	1050	1933	4168	7537	12578	26751	67160	•
Net Property, Plant and Equipment 25	496	0	38	203	724	2382	5835	10406	19157	33786	73990	502001	•
Total Assets 26	1903	0	107	724	2170	7864	16859	35739	67869	161934	372120	2169528	•
Notes and Loans Payable 27	802	0	80	295	1009	2146	6869	12982	31262	64896	172283	882027	•
All Other Liabilities 28	548	0	37	188	541	2325	4253	7167	23740	33951	103890	678166	•
Net Worth 29	552	0	-11	241	621	3392	5737	15590	12866	63087	95946	609335	•

Selected Financial Ratios (Times to 1)

Current Ratio 30	1.5	•	1.3	2.1	1.6	1.5	1.6	1.9	1.0	1.4	1.3	1.4	•
Quick Ratio 31	1.0	•	1.1	1.5	1.2	0.9	1.1	1.4	0.7	0.9	0.9	1.0	•
Net Sales to Working Capital 32	11.6	•	32.6	9.8	12.6	10.1	8.9	5.5	88.1	10.2	14.5	10.5	•
Coverage Ratio 33	1.3	5.2	•	4.9	2.9	3.3	1.3	0.7	•	1.6	1.1	2.0	•
Total Asset Turnover 34	1.3	•	4.2	3.1	2.5	1.8	1.7	1.3	1.1	1.0	1.0	0.8	•
Inventory Turnover 35	11.1	•	32.7	16.2	16.1	8.8	9.9	7.4	7.1	8.6	9.1	14.7	•
Receivables Turnover 36	6.3	•	16.3	8.0	9.0	7.8	6.5	4.6	5.8	7.2	6.9	6.7	•
Total Liabilities to Net Worth 37	2.4	•	•	2.0	2.5	1.3	1.9	1.3	4.3	1.6	2.9	2.6	•
Current Assets to Working Capital 38	3.2	•	4.2	1.9	2.8	3.0	2.8	2.1	38.0	3.5	4.0	3.4	•
Current Liabilities to Working Capital 39	2.2	•	3.2	0.9	1.8	2.0	1.8	1.1	37.0	2.5	3.0	2.4	•
Working Capital to Net Sales 40	0.1	•	0.0	0.1	0.1	0.1	0.1	0.2	0.0	0.1	0.1	0.1	•
Inventory to Working Capital 41	0.6	•	0.4	0.3	0.5	0.8	0.6	0.4	8.6	0.8	0.9	0.5	•
Total Receipts to Cash Flow 42	11.4	4.4	6.4	8.8	10.9	12.1	15.6	15.2	12.6	12.6	19.4	8.8	•
Cost of Goods to Cash Flow 43	7.0	1.7	3.1	4.5	6.9	8.1	10.7	10.4	8.6	8.6	12.2	5.3	•
Cash Flow to Total Debt 44	0.2	0.6	0.6	0.5	0.3	0.3	0.2	0.1	0.0	0.1	0.1	0.1	•

Selected Financial Factors (in Percentages)

Debt Ratio 45	71.0	•	110.1	66.7	71.4	56.9	66.0	56.4	81.0	61.0	74.2	71.9	•
Return on Total Assets 46	4.0	•	•	11.6	8.1	4.1	3.1	2.3	5.6	5.6	4.9	6.0	•
Return on Equity Before Income Taxes 47	2.9	•	67.0	27.8	18.6	6.5	2.4	•	5.6	5.6	0.9	10.8	•
Return on Equity After Income Taxes 48	0.1	•	68.1	27.6	17.6	6.5	0.5	•	•	3.3	•	6.7	•
Profit Margin (Before Income Tax) 49	0.6	6.4	•	3.0	2.1	1.6	0.5	•	•	0.9	0.2	4.0	•
Profit Margin (After Income Tax) 50	0.0	6.2	•	3.0	2.0	1.6	0.1	•	•	1.3	•	2.5	•

Table II

Corporations with Net Income

PRINTING AND RELATED SUPPORT ACTIVITIES

MONEY AMOUNTS AND SIZE OF ASSETS IN THOUSANDS OF DOLLARS

Item Description for Accounting Period 7/09 Through 6/10	Total	Zero Assets	Under 500	500 to 1,000	1,000 to 5,000	5,000 to 10,000	10,000 to 25,000	25,000 to 50,000	50,000 to 100,000	100,000 to 250,000	250,000 to 500,000	500,000 to 2,500,000	2,500,000 and over
Number of Enterprises **1**	14273	2145	8915	1044	1591	336	154	43	18	12	7	8	0
Revenues ($ in Thousands)													
Net Sales **2**	47454582	417494	4237425	2956031	8281203	3998391	4280483	1917553	1565708	1875356	2372420	15552519	0
Interest **3**	159711	36	687	8	6714	1428	3049	626	968	1008	2895	142293	0
Rents **4**	23422	0	0	5353	4193	379	294	239	108	2547	650	9658	0
Royalties **5**	49072	0	1160	0	460	673	3991	151	0	6785	6359	29494	0
Other Portfolio Income **6**	377040	2996	15719	457	100609	13406	3644	432	3145	37786	145659	53188	0
Other Receipts **7**	503535	6589	3690	34754	98581	13072	45384	93196	21839	17011	26235	143179	0
Total Receipts **8**	48567362	427115	4258681	2996603	8491760	4027349	4336845	2012197	1591768	1940493	2554218	15930331	0
Average Total Receipts **9**	3403	199	478	2870	5337	11986	28161	46795	88432	161708	364888	1991291	•
Operating Costs/Operating Income (%)													
Cost of Operations **10**	59.0	35.2	38.6	49.7	63.2	63.6	65.3	67.9	70.8	67.4	61.9	58.0	•
Salaries and Wages **11**	10.6	3.5	10.8	19.1	10.0	9.3	9.9	10.5	7.1	7.6	11.4	10.7	•
Taxes Paid **12**	2.3	1.8	2.7	2.4	2.1	2.1	1.8	1.6	1.9	1.2	2.3	2.5	•
Interest Paid **13**	2.2	0.8	0.7	0.7	0.8	0.7	0.9	1.7	1.3	2.8	2.2	4.4	•
Depreciation **14**	3.5	1.9	2.2	1.3	2.4	3.3	3.3	3.4	4.4	3.7	5.2	4.6	•
Amortization and Depletion **15**	0.6	0.0	0.0	0.1	0.2	0.1	0.3	0.3	0.4	1.4	1.1	1.3	•
Pensions and Other Deferred Comp. **16**	0.3	0.1	0.5	0.0	0.1	0.4	0.3	0.3	0.5	0.3	0.6	0.3	•
Employee Benefits **17**	1.9	0.3	1.3	1.0	1.4	1.7	1.6	2.0	2.1	1.3	3.1	2.6	•
Advertising **18**	0.8	0.9	0.6	0.9	0.6	0.2	0.5	1.6	0.4	2.4	0.1	1.0	•
Other Expenses **19**	12.4	11.1	28.3	15.9	11.7	12.2	9.3	6.6	6.7	8.7	9.9	10.9	•
Officers' Compensation **20**	2.8	12.9	8.8	4.5	4.3	2.5	2.7	2.2	2.3	1.4	1.3	0.3	•
Operating Margin **21**	3.6	31.4	5.6	4.4	2.9	3.9	4.1	2.0	2.1	1.8	1.0	3.3	•
Operating Margin Before Officers' Comp. **22**	6.4	44.2	14.4	8.9	7.3	6.4	6.8	4.1	4.4	3.2	2.3	3.6	•

Selected Average Balance Sheet ($ in Thousands)

Net Receivables 23	456	0	10	274	562	1652	4225	7218	14373	20307	41274	366776
Inventories 24	173	0	7	55	226	1173	2070	5127	7735	13996	26910	69533
Net Property, Plant and Equipment 25	624	0	32	180	615	2238	4757	8563	16770	28622	92602	537893
Total Assets 26	2661	0	90	698	2114	7911	16642	35419	66713	173641	345115	2579084
Notes and Loans Payable 27	950	0	45	310	662	2202	3871	9147	18079	55158	89286	1055021
All Other Liabilities 28	748	0	28	220	473	2468	3948	5689	16369	37744	73909	812623
Net Worth 29	962	0	17	169	979	3241	8823	20583	32265	80739	181921	711441

Selected Financial Ratios (Times to 1)

Current Ratio 30	1.6	•	2.2	2.1	2.1	1.5	2.0	2.6	2.1	1.5	1.9	1.3
Quick Ratio 31	1.1	•	1.7	1.6	1.5	0.9	1.4	1.8	1.5	1.0	1.3	0.9
Net Sales to Working Capital 32	9.3	•	18.6	11.2	8.1	8.8	6.2	4.4	4.8	8.5	6.6	14.0
Coverage Ratio 33	3.8	40.9	10.3	9.2	7.8	7.4	7.2	5.1	3.9	3.0	5.2	2.4
Total Asset Turnover 34	1.2	•	5.3	4.1	2.5	1.5	1.7	1.3	1.3	0.9	1.0	0.8
Inventory Turnover 35	11.3	•	25.3	25.6	14.6	6.5	8.8	5.9	8.0	7.5	7.8	16.2
Receivables Turnover 36	7.5	•	23.8	8.7	9.3	6.7	6.2	3.7	7.1	7.3	7.9	6.6
Total Liabilities to Net Worth 37	1.8	•	4.3	3.1	1.2	1.4	0.9	0.7	1.1	1.2	0.9	2.6
Current Assets to Working Capital 38	2.6	•	1.9	1.9	1.9	3.1	2.1	1.6	1.9	3.1	2.2	4.5
Current Liabilities to Working Capital 39	1.6	•	0.9	0.9	0.9	2.1	1.1	0.6	0.9	2.1	1.2	3.5
Working Capital to Net Sales 40	0.1	•	0.1	0.1	0.1	0.1	0.2	0.2	0.2	0.1	0.2	0.1
Inventory to Working Capital 41	0.5	•	0.3	0.2	0.4	0.9	0.5	0.4	0.4	0.8	0.5	0.7
Total Receipts to Cash Flow 42	7.2	2.4	3.7	7.6	7.8	8.1	8.6	9.1	12.1	9.0	8.9	7.6
Cost of Goods to Cash Flow 43	4.2	0.8	1.4	3.8	5.0	5.1	5.6	6.2	8.6	6.1	5.5	4.4
Cash Flow to Total Debt 44	0.3	1.7	0.7	0.6	0.3	0.4	0.3	0.2	0.2	0.2	0.2	0.1

Selected Financial Factors (in Percentages)

Debt Ratio 45	63.8	•	81.0	75.8	53.7	59.0	47.0	41.9	51.6	53.5	47.3	72.4
Return on Total Assets 46	10.4	•	35.7	26.3	15.5	7.9	10.4	10.8	6.5	7.5	11.4	8.0
Return on Equity Before Income Taxes 47	21.2	•	169.4	96.9	29.2	16.7	16.9	14.9	10.1	10.8	17.4	16.8
Return on Equity After Income Taxes 48	17.8	•	168.0	96.6	28.3	16.6	14.8	13.7	8.4	8.4	11.8	11.5
Profit Margin (Before Income Tax) 49	6.1	33.7	6.1	5.8	5.5	4.5	5.4	6.9	3.7	5.6	9.4	6.2
Profit Margin (After Income Tax) 50	5.2	33.4	6.1	5.8	5.3	4.5	4.7	6.3	3.1	4.3	6.4	4.2

Table I

Corporations with and without Net Income

PETROLEUM REFINERIES (INCLUDING INTEGRATED)

MONEY AMOUNTS AND SIZE OF ASSETS IN THOUSANDS OF DOLLARS

Item Description for Accounting Period 7/09 Through 6/10		Total	Zero Assets	Under 500	500 to 1,000	1,000 to 5,000	5,000 to 10,000	10,000 to 25,000	25,000 to 50,000	50,000 to 100,000	100,000 to 250,000	250,000 to 500,000	500,000 to 2,500,000	2,500,000 and over
Number of Enterprises	1	241	•	0	0	157	0	30	0	10	•	0	11	•
Revenues ($ in Thousands)														
Net Sales	2	1379953840	•	0	0	156	0	476278	0	1041340	•	0	28542470	•
Interest	3	11432234	•	0	0	73	0	661	0	3492	•	0	57053	•
Rents	4	1440766	•	0	0	0	0	885	0	51	•	0	20993	•
Royalties	5	951741	•	0	0	0	0	0	0	0	•	0	26667	•
Other Portfolio Income	6	45263023	•	0	0	199	0	931	0	1257	•	0	12962	•
Other Receipts	7	28868544	•	0	0	66228	0	8502	0	19509	•	0	445901	•
Total Receipts	8	1467910148	•	0	0	66656	0	487257	0	1065649	•	0	29106046	•
Average Total Receipts	9	6090913	•	•	•	425	•	16242	•	106565	•	•	2646004	•
Operating Costs/Operating Income (%)														
Cost of Operations	10	89.9	•	•	•	48.7	•	70.0	•	96.7	•	•	89.3	•
Salaries and Wages	11	1.8	•	•	•	389.1	•	8.4	•	1.6	•	•	2.4	•
Taxes Paid	12	1.7	•	•	•	242.3	•	2.1	•	0.6	•	•	1.3	•
Interest Paid	13	1.2	•	•	•	3355.1	•	1.6	•	0.7	•	•	1.4	•
Depreciation	14	1.3	•	•	•	50.6	•	3.7	•	2.7	•	•	3.0	•
Amortization and Depletion	15	0.5	•	•	•	•	•	0.1	•	0.0	•	•	0.8	•
Pensions and Other Deferred Comp.	16	0.3	•	•	•	•	•	0.3	•	0.2	•	•	0.1	•
Employee Benefits	17	0.3	•	•	•	•	•	1.3	•	0.7	•	•	0.3	•
Advertising	18	0.1	•	•	•	•	•	0.0	•	0.0	•	•	0.1	•
Other Expenses	19	4.6	•	•	•	3096.8	•	19.3	•	3.9	•	•	4.4	•
Officers' Compensation	20	0.1	•	•	•	1111.5	•	3.9	•	0.3	•	•	0.3	•
Operating Margin	21	•	•	•	•	•	•	•	•	•	•	•	•	•
Operating Margin Before Officers' Comp.	22	•	•	•	•	•	•	•	•	•	•	•	•	•

Selected Average Balance Sheet ($ in Thousands)

Net Receivables 23	2487776	4	1945	11071	157806
Inventories 24	140183	5	1332	4668	182357
Net Property, Plant and Equipment 25	1063090	46	4270	28002	660338
Total Assets 26	7736202	2053	14563	77951	1390056
Notes and Loans Payable 27	1566559	206	4498	15083	433905
All Other Liabilities 28	2804547	-2	1929	28204	454604
Net Worth 29	3385096	1849	8137	34664	501546

Selected Financial Ratios (Times to 1)

Current Ratio 30	1.2	63.2	1.3	0.8	1.8
Quick Ratio 31	1.1	36.4	0.9	0.6	0.8
Net Sales to Working Capital 32	11.3	0.0	10.3		10.5
Coverage Ratio 33	6.9	11.3			0.0
Total Asset Turnover 34	0.7	0.0	1.1	1.3	1.9
Inventory Turnover 35	36.7	0.1	8.3	21.6	12.7
Receivables Turnover 36	2.2	0.0	8.4	11.0	17.5
Total Liabilities to Net Worth 37	1.3	0.1	0.8	1.2	1.8
Current Assets to Working Capital 38	5.7	1.0	4.2		2.2
Current Liabilities to Working Capital 39	4.7	0.0	3.2		1.2
Working Capital to Net Sales 40	0.1	410.3	0.1		0.1
Inventory to Working Capital 41	0.3	0.0	1.0		0.8
Total Receipts to Cash Flow 42	12.0	0.0	11.3	54.6	54.6
Cost of Goods to Cash Flow 43	10.8	0.0	7.9	48.7	48.7
Cash Flow to Total Debt 44	0.1	1.8	0.2		0.1

Selected Financial Factors (in Percentages)

Debt Ratio 45	56.5	9.9	44.1	55.5	63.9
Return on Total Assets 46	6.1	18.3			0.1
Return on Equity Before Income Taxes 47	11.9	18.5			
Return on Equity After Income Taxes 48	7.5	16.2			
Profit Margin (Before Income Tax) 49	7.0	34434.0			
Profit Margin (After Income Tax) 50	4.4	30084.6			

Table II
Corporations with Net Income

PETROLEUM REFINERIES (INCLUDING INTEGRATED)

MONEY AMOUNTS AND SIZE OF ASSETS IN THOUSANDS OF DOLLARS

Item Description for Accounting Period 7/09 Through 6/10	Total	Zero Assets	Under 500	500 to 1,000	1,000 to 5,000	5,000 to 10,000	10,000 to 25,000	25,000 to 50,000	50,000 to 100,000	100,000 to 250,000	250,000 to 500,000	500,000 to 2,500,000	2,500,000 and over
Number of Enterprises **1**	159	•	0	0	•	0	13	0	3	•	0	5	10

Revenues ($ in Thousands)

	Total	Zero Assets	Under 500	500 to 1,000	1,000 to 5,000	5,000 to 10,000	10,000 to 25,000	25,000 to 50,000	50,000 to 100,000	100,000 to 250,000	250,000 to 500,000	500,000 to 2,500,000	2,500,000 and over
Net Sales **2**	927726731	•	0	0	•	0	386686	0	804424	•	0	8496958	91180664
Interest **3**	10313562	•	0	0	•	0	530	0	665	•	0	35908	10272263
Rents **4**	1126351	•	0	0	•	0	598	0	51	•	0	16012	1109528
Royalties **5**	832996	•	0	0	•	0	0	0	0	•	0	26165	806829
Other Portfolio Income **6**	44570779	•	0	0	•	0	0	0	44	•	0	9837	44476695
Other Receipts **7**	26423207	•	0	0	•	0	1855	0	263	•	0	203528	26128217
Total Receipts **8**	1010993626	•	0	0	•	0	389669	0	805447	•	0	8788408	99397420
Average Total Receipts **9**	6358450	•			•		29975		268482	•		1757682	9939742

Operating Costs/Operating Income (%)

	Total	Zero Assets	Under 500	500 to 1,000	1,000 to 5,000	5,000 to 10,000	10,000 to 25,000	25,000 to 50,000	50,000 to 100,000	100,000 to 250,000	250,000 to 500,000	500,000 to 2,500,000	2,500,000 and over
Cost of Operations **10**	87.2	•	•	•	•	•	73.5	•	95.6	•	•	81.9	87.1
Salaries and Wages **11**	2.3	•	•	•	•	•	6.3	•	1.1	•	•	3.5	2.3
Taxes Paid **12**	2.1	•	•	•	•	•	1.3	•	0.4	•	•	3.6	2.1
Interest Paid **13**	1.5	•	•	•	•	•	0.4	•	0.1	•	•	1.0	1.5
Depreciation **14**	1.3	•	•	•	•	•	2.2	•	0.5	•	•	2.5	1.3
Amortization and Depletion **15**	0.6	•	•	•	•	•		•	0.0	•	•	0.0	0.6
Pensions and Other Deferred Comp. **16**	0.3	•	•	•	•	•	0.2	•	0.1	•	•	0.2	0.6
Employee Benefits **17**	0.3	•	•	•	•	•	1.3	•	0.5	•	•	0.4	0.3
Advertising **18**	0.1	•	•	•	•	•	0.0	•	0.0	•	•	0.1	0.1
Other Expenses **19**	5.3	•	•	•	•	•	6.9	•	0.7	•	•	4.6	5.3
Officers' Compensation **20**	0.1	•	•	•	•	•	2.8	•	0.1	•	•	0.5	0.1
Operating Margin **21**	•	•	•	•	•	•	5.0	•	0.9	•	•	1.5	•
Operating Margin Before Officers' Comp. **22**	•	•	•	•	•	•	7.8	•	1.1	•	•	2.0	•

Selected Average Balance Sheet ($ in Thousands)

Net Receivables 23	3667636	2545	15033	173650	58202569
Inventories 24	172171	2599	7484	210322	2639157
Net Property, Plant and Equipment 25	1271205	2481	36239	404585	19979676
Total Assets 26	10378236	15844	78791	1245221	164225469
Notes and Loans Payable 27	1944203	988	11586	309319	30741774
All Other Liabilities 28	3905355	2381	27117	316476	61892312
Net Worth 29	4528678	12474	40088	619426	71591384

Selected Financial Ratios (Times to 1)

Current Ratio 30	1.3	4.1	1.7	2.5	1.3
Quick Ratio 31	1.2	2.8	1.4	1.0	1.2
Net Sales to Working Capital 32	6.6	4.1	16.7	5.6	6.6
Coverage Ratio 33	8.5	17.4	11.4	5.8	8.5
Total Asset Turnover 34	0.6	1.9	3.4	1.4	0.6
Inventory Turnover 35	29.5	8.4	34.2	6.6	30.1
Receivables Turnover 36	1.5	10.5	14.4	•	1.5
Total Liabilities to Net Worth 37	1.3	0.3	1.0	1.0	1.3
Current Assets to Working Capital 38	4.6	1.3	2.5	1.7	4.7
Current Liabilities to Working Capital 39	3.6	0.3	1.5	0.7	3.7
Working Capital to Net Sales 40	0.2	0.2	0.1	0.2	0.2
Inventory to Working Capital 41	0.2	0.4	0.3	0.7	0.2
Total Receipts to Cash Flow 42	8.3	8.9	72.3	12.1	8.2
Cost of Goods to Cash Flow 43	7.2	6.5	69.1	9.9	7.1
Cash Flow to Total Debt 44	0.1	1.0	0.1	0.2	0.1

Selected Financial Factors (in Percentages)

Debt Ratio 45	56.4	21.3	49.1	50.3	56.4
Return on Total Assets 46	7.1	11.5	3.9	8.2	7.1
Return on Equity Before Income Taxes 47	14.4	13.8	7.1	13.6	14.4
Return on Equity After Income Taxes 48	9.5	13.0	5.4	9.7	9.5
Profit Margin (Before Income Tax) 49	11.2	5.8	1.1	5.0	11.3
Profit Margin (After Income Tax) 50	7.4	5.4	0.8	3.5	7.4

Table I

Corporations with and without Net Income

ASPHALT PAVING, ROOFING, OTHER PETROLEUM AND COAL PRODUCTS

MONEY AMOUNTS AND SIZE OF ASSETS IN THOUSANDS OF DOLLARS

Item Description for Accounting Period 7/09 Through 6/10		Total	Zero Assets	Under 500	500 to 1,000	1,000 to 5,000	5,000 to 10,000	10,000 to 25,000	25,000 to 50,000	50,000 to 100,000	100,000 to 250,000	250,000 to 500,000	500,000 to 2,500,000	2,500,000 and over
Number of Enterprises	1	1195	•	679	132	229	62	47	•	11	•	3	3	•
Revenues ($ in Thousands)														
Net Sales	2	13503361	•	136723	459286	920570	1185077	1390262	•	1493615	•	1545998	2964022	•
Interest	3	13819	•	0	109	572	648	564	•	377	•	374	5859	•
Rents	4	3860	•	0	430	0	1752	0	•	5	•	123	0	•
Royalties	5	540	•	0	0	0	0	0	•	439	•	0	0	•
Other Portfolio Income	6	29928	•	0	4	8935	3608	154	•	317	•	96	12	•
Other Receipts	7	132487	•	0	201	18130	3159	3556	•	6056	•	8970	-3674	•
Total Receipts	8	13683995	•	136723	460030	948207	1194244	1394536	•	1500809	•	1555561	2966219	•
Average Total Receipts	9	11451	•	201	3485	4141	19262	29671	•	136437	•	518520	988740	•
Operating Costs/Operating Income (%)														
Cost of Operations	10	66.7	•	61.0	74.6	70.9	65.6	73.8	•	78.4	•	57.3	51.0	•
Salaries and Wages	11	5.6	•	9.4	2.5	11.4	9.3	3.3	•	3.5	•	7.5	5.2	•
Taxes Paid	12	1.1	•	1.5	2.4	1.8	1.4	1.0	•	0.9	•	1.3	0.8	•
Interest Paid	13	2.1	•	0.4	0.1	1.8	1.6	0.5	•	1.1	•	0.1	6.6	•
Depreciation	14	2.9	•	5.9	2.4	0.9	3.1	3.2	•	2.9	•	3.0	3.5	•
Amortization and Depletion	15	0.2	•	0.0	0.0	0.0	0.2	0.0	•	0.4	•	0.1	0.1	•
Pensions and Other Deferred Comp.	16	0.3	•	•	0.0	0.6	0.1	0.1	•	0.3	•	1.5	0.0	•
Employee Benefits	17	0.9	•	•	1.9	0.2	1.0	1.2	•	0.8	•	1.4	1.3	•
Advertising	18	1.1	•	1.5	1.0	0.2	3.4	2.6	•	0.3	•	0.5	0.6	•
Other Expenses	19	11.1	•	32.1	6.5	8.4	11.4	6.7	•	4.3	•	5.1	24.5	•
Officers' Compensation	20	1.5	•	•	8.8	2.9	3.7	1.3	•	1.4	•	1.0	0.3	•
Operating Margin	21	6.4	•	•	•	0.7	•	6.3	•	5.6	•	21.1	6.2	•
Operating Margin Before Officers' Comp.	22	7.9	•	•	8.6	3.6	2.8	7.6	•	7.0	•	22.1	6.5	•

Selected Average Balance Sheet ($ in Thousands)

Net Receivables 23	1295	•	0	200	748	1575	3012	15864	50603	100137	•
Inventories 24	1042	•	0	76	226	1392	3566	14537	36580	115210	•
Net Property, Plant and Equipment 25	2152	•	10	434	624	2910	4498	16243	89622	337891	•
Total Assets 26	9597	•	11	842	2207	7847	15244	67735	314868	1861171	•
Notes and Loans Payable 27	2422	•	86	174	3167	5031	3363	14866	6377	275371	•
All Other Liabilities 28	4723	•	0	234	2265	2146	2463	17723	89508	1291079	•
Net Worth 29	2452	•	-75	433	-3225	670	9418	35145	218983	294720	•

Selected Financial Ratios (Times to 1)

Current Ratio 30	1.3	•	•	1.3	0.7	1.2	2.7	2.8	2.5	0.9	•
Quick Ratio 31	0.9	•	•	1.0	0.6	0.6	1.7	2.0	0.8	0.6	•
Net Sales to Working Capital 32	11.2	•	237.0	43.4	•	26.4	5.0	4.9	5.3	•	•
Coverage Ratio 33	4.6	•	•	1.1	3.1	0.9	15.2	6.6	280.5	2.0	•
Total Asset Turnover 34	1.2	•	17.6	4.1	1.8	2.4	1.9	2.0	1.6	0.5	•
Inventory Turnover 35	7.2	•	•	34.2	12.6	9.0	6.1	7.3	8.1	4.4	•
Receivables Turnover 36	8.7	•	•	18.0	5.5	11.3	6.7	7.7	20.4	9.1	•
Total Liabilities to Net Worth 37	2.9	•	•	0.9	10.7	0.6	0.9	0.4	•	5.3	•
Current Assets to Working Capital 38	4.1	•	1.0	4.9	6.4	5.4	3.9	1.6	1.7	•	•
Current Liabilities to Working Capital 39	3.1	•	•	3.9	5.4	0.6	0.6	0.7	•	•	•
Working Capital to Net Sales 40	0.1	•	0.0	0.0	0.0	0.0	0.2	0.2	0.2	•	•
Inventory to Working Capital 41	0.8	•	•	0.9	2.0	0.6	0.4	0.4	•	•	•
Total Receipts to Cash Flow 42	6.1	•	15.8	18.4	11.0	10.9	8.3	11.4	3.9	3.8	•
Cost of Goods to Cash Flow 43	4.1	•	9.7	13.7	7.8	7.2	6.2	8.9	2.2	1.9	•
Cash Flow to Total Debt 44	0.3	•	0.1	0.5	0.1	0.2	0.6	0.4	1.4	0.2	•

Selected Financial Factors (in Percentages)

Debt Ratio 45	74.5	•	753.9	48.5	246.1	91.5	38.2	48.1	30.5	84.2	•
Return on Total Assets 46	11.6	•	•	0.6	10.1	3.7	13.7	14.3	35.6	6.9	•
Return on Equity Before Income Taxes 47	35.6	•	31.5	0.1	•	•	20.8	23.4	51.1	21.1	•
Return on Equity After Income Taxes 48	31.0	•	31.5	•	•	•	20.0	18.0	50.0	18.0	•
Profit Margin (Before Income Tax) 49	7.7	•	0.0	•	0.0	3.7	6.6	6.1	21.7	6.3	•
Profit Margin (After Income Tax) 50	6.7	•	•	•	2.8	6.4	4.7	•	21.3	5.4	•

Table II
Corporations with Net Income

ASPHALT PAVING, ROOFING, OTHER PETROLEUM AND COAL PRODUCTS

MONEY AMOUNTS AND SIZE OF ASSETS IN THOUSANDS OF DOLLARS

Item Description for Accounting Period 7/09 Through 6/10	Total	Zero Assets	Under 500	500 to 1,000	1,000 to 5,000	5,000 to 10,000	10,000 to 25,000	25,000 to 50,000	50,000 to 100,000	100,000 to 250,000	250,000 to 500,000	500,000 to 2,500,000	2,500,000 and over
Number of Enterprises 1	282	0	0	66	•	40	40	•	8	•	•	0	0
Revenues ($ in Thousands)													
Net Sales 2	11721506	0	0	259291	•	755990	1364670	•	1082207	•	•	0	0
Interest 3	10723	0	0	40	•	648	45	•	280	•	•	0	0
Rents 4	3430	0	0	0	•	1752	0	•	5	•	•	0	0
Royalties 5	100	0	0	0	•	0	0	•	0	•	•	0	0
Other Portfolio Income 6	17199	0	0	4	•	3000	154	•	238	•	•	0	0
Other Receipts 7	114788	0	0	1	•	2317	3555	•	5436	•	•	0	0
Total Receipts 8	11867746	0	0	259336	•	763707	1368424	•	1088166	•	•	0	0
Average Total Receipts 9	42084	•	•	3929	•	19093	34211	•	136021	•	•	•	•
Operating Costs/Operating Income (%)													
Cost of Operations 10	65.8	•	•	68.9	•	61.7	74.0	•	78.3	•	•	•	•
Salaries and Wages 11	5.5	•	•	3.2	•	7.0	2.9	•	3.6	•	•	•	•
Taxes Paid 12	1.0	•	•	1.4	•	1.2	1.0	•	1.1	•	•	•	•
Interest Paid 13	1.6	•	•	0.0	•	1.4	0.4	•	0.3	•	•	•	•
Depreciation 14	2.6	•	•	3.5	•	3.5	3.2	•	2.2	•	•	•	•
Amortization and Depletion 15	0.1	•	•	•	•	0.0	0.0	•	0.1	•	•	•	•
Pensions and Other Deferred Comp. 16	0.3	•	•	•	•	0.0	0.1	•	0.3	•	•	•	•
Employee Benefits 17	0.9	•	•	1.0	•	0.7	1.2	•	0.6	•	•	•	•
Advertising 18	1.2	•	•	0.1	•	5.2	2.6	•	0.3	•	•	•	•
Other Expenses 19	10.9	•	•	8.4	•	12.9	5.8	•	4.0	•	•	•	•
Officers' Compensation 20	1.4	•	•	12.6	•	3.4	1.3	•	0.8	•	•	•	•
Operating Margin 21	8.6	•	•	0.9	•	2.8	7.5	•	8.4	•	•	•	•
Operating Margin Before Officers' Comp. 22	10.0	•	•	13.5	•	6.2	8.8	•	9.1	•	•	•	•

Selected Average Balance Sheet ($ in Thousands)

Net Receivables 23	4262	310	1605	3146	17586
Inventories 24	3407	0	1655	3522	16585
Net Property, Plant and Equipment 25	6244	340	2690	4564	13479
Total Assets 26	30214	776	7846	15911	68064
Notes and Loans Payable 27	4770	61	4714	3441	7601
All Other Liabilities 28	15561	448	1285	2642	19612
Net Worth 29	9883	267	1848	9828	40852

Selected Financial Ratios (Times to 1)

Current Ratio 30	1.6	1.0	2.2	2.5	3.0
Quick Ratio 31	1.0	1.0	1.0	1.5	2.2
Net Sales to Working Capital 32	7.4	7.3	7.3	5.7	4.0
Coverage Ratio 33	7.3	110.4	3.7	21.4	26.9
Total Asset Turnover 34	1.4	5.1	2.4	2.1	2.0
Inventory Turnover 35	8.0		7.0	7.2	6.4
Receivables Turnover 36	10.1	11.5	9.9	9.2	7.4
Total Liabilities to Net Worth 37	2.1	1.9	3.2	0.6	0.7
Current Assets to Working Capital 38	2.7		1.9	1.6	1.5
Current Liabilities to Working Capital 39	1.7		0.9	0.6	0.5
Working Capital to Net Sales 40	0.1		0.1	0.2	0.2
Inventory to Working Capital 41	0.5		0.5	0.6	0.4
Total Receipts to Cash Flow 42	5.4	11.8	6.7	8.0	9.0
Cost of Goods to Cash Flow 43	3.5	8.1	4.1	5.9	7.0
Cash Flow to Total Debt 44	0.4	0.7	0.5	0.7	0.6

Selected Financial Factors (in Percentages)

Debt Ratio 45	67.3	65.5	76.5	38.2	40.0
Return on Total Assets 46	15.8	4.7	12.7	17.5	18.4
Return on Equity Before Income Taxes 47	41.6	13.6	39.1	26.9	29.4
Return on Equity After Income Taxes 48	36.7	11.6	31.2	26.1	23.1
Profit Margin (Before Income Tax) 49	9.9	0.9	3.8	7.8	8.9
Profit Margin (After Income Tax) 50	8.7	0.8	3.1	7.5	7.0

Table I

Corporations with and without Net Income

BASIC CHEMICAL

MONEY AMOUNTS AND SIZE OF ASSETS IN THOUSANDS OF DOLLARS

Item Description for Accounting Period 7/09 Through 6/10	Total	Zero Assets	Under 500	500 to 1,000	1,000 to 5,000	5,000 to 10,000	10,000 to 25,000	25,000 to 50,000	50,000 to 100,000	100,000 to 250,000	250,000 to 500,000	500,000 to 2,500,000	2,500,000 and over
Number of Enterprises **1**	1376	18	630	265	129	44	98	59	32	24	17	35	25
Revenues ($ in Thousands)													
Net Sales **2**	143444007	497664	117109	633120	365312	487586	2482226	2807695	2880799	5755691	5883953	22816894	98715958
Interest **3**	2393258	79	0	6	493	1402	752	3099	1754	2938	12177	151884	2218674
Rents **4**	183122	0	0	0	0	0	1415	721	1376	6514	2759	6247	164090
Royalties **5**	2816569	0	0	0	4825	0	12	0	845	14135	26057	118890	2651805
Other Portfolio Income **6**	2990087	0	0	0	2354	10000	1382	13305	1038	95886	40340	168778	2657007
Other Receipts **7**	4722135	772	0	9481	5584	2757	16137	17264	23832	179591	61424	595092	3810198
Total Receipts **8**	156549178	498515	117109	642607	378568	501745	2501924	2842084	2909644	6054755	6026710	23857785	110217732
Average Total Receipts **9**	113771	27695	186	2425	2935	11403	25530	48171	90926	252281	354512	681651	4408709
Operating Costs/Operating Income (%)													
Cost of Operations **10**	73.8	86.6	75.7	72.1	56.5	76.4	65.1	70.4	76.7	83.4	75.1	74.1	73.3
Salaries and Wages **11**	6.9	3.3	3.7	5.6	10.8	4.5	7.8	7.6	6.0	5.0	6.3	5.5	7.4
Taxes Paid **12**	1.0	0.1	2.4	0.8	2.5	1.6	1.7	1.2	1.2	0.8	0.8	0.9	1.0
Interest Paid **13**	5.9	0.0	0.0	0.2	1.1	0.6	0.5	1.1	3.3	1.6	1.7	4.0	7.3
Depreciation **14**	4.6	3.0	1.0	0.6	3.2	3.2	2.7	3.2	9.9	4.4	4.6	5.5	4.3
Amortization and Depletion **15**	1.3	2.9	0.0	•	0.5	0.3	0.2	0.5	7.3	0.6	0.8	1.1	1.3
Pensions and Other Deferred Comp. **16**	1.2	•	0.0	•	0.6	0.1	0.3	0.8	0.5	0.2	1.0	0.9	1.4
Employee Benefits **17**	1.8	1.1	2.5	1.0	1.4	1.3	1.4	1.7	1.3	0.6	1.6	2.0	1.8
Advertising **18**	0.4	0.0	0.0	0.1	0.3	0.0	0.3	0.2	0.1	0.1	0.2	0.2	0.5
Other Expenses **19**	10.7	7.4	20.0	6.8	47.3	9.3	10.1	8.6	23.8	8.0	10.2	9.8	10.7
Officers' Compensation **20**	0.5	2.0	5.5	2.2	10.1	3.5	3.0	1.9	1.6	1.1	0.5	0.5	0.3
Operating Margin **21**	•	•	•	10.8	•	•	7.0	3.0	•	•	•	•	•
Operating Margin Before Officers' Comp. **22**	•	•	•	12.9	•	2.7	9.9	4.9	•	•	•	•	•

Selected Average Balance Sheet ($ in Thousands)

Net Receivables 23	55596	0	25	289	678	1556	3341	7233	11739	29883	81603	137636	2728018
Inventories 24	12701	0	21	81	355	689	3757	7292	10199	20022	48201	97248	461525
Net Property, Plant and Equipment 25	36887	0	2	131	306	1592	3953	10505	22788	51584	116280	252415	1473004
Total Assets 26	292924	0	70	668	2417	7367	14838	33069	68761	167060	373811	1110577	13894658
Notes and Loans Payable 27	111836	0	30	95	526	2193	4171	7451	36774	54389	120526	443036	5311669
All Other Liabilities 28	89713	0	16	90	409	1418	2712	8076	21243	65894	113581	246113	4389934
Net Worth 29	91375	0	25	483	1482	3756	7955	17543	10743	46776	139705	421428	4193056

Selected Financial Ratios (Times to 1)

Current Ratio 30	1.0	•	1.4	3.7	2.9	3.5	2.8	2.4	1.4	1.3	1.5	1.6	1.0
Quick Ratio 31	0.8	•	0.9	2.3	1.9	1.8	1.6	1.5	0.9	0.8	0.9	1.0	0.8
Net Sales to Working Capital 32	34.3	•	9.8	6.2	2.7	3.4	4.0	4.6	9.3	13.9	6.8	4.9	•
Coverage Ratio 33	1.4	•	•	60.7	•	4.7	16.1	4.8	•	0.6	0.9	1.1	1.6
Total Asset Turnover 34	0.4	•	2.7	3.6	1.2	1.5	1.7	1.4	1.3	1.4	0.9	0.6	0.3
Inventory Turnover 35	6.1	•	6.8	21.2	4.5	12.3	4.4	4.6	6.8	10.0	5.4	5.0	6.3
Receivables Turnover 36	2.0	•	9.8	9.7	3.7	3.9	7.2	6.0	7.4	9.2	4.0	4.6	1.6
Total Liabilities to Net Worth 37	2.2	•	1.9	0.4	0.6	1.0	0.9	0.9	5.4	2.6	1.7	1.6	2.3
Current Assets to Working Capital 38	28.1	•	3.4	1.4	1.5	1.4	1.5	1.7	3.4	4.3	3.0	2.6	•
Current Liabilities to Working Capital 39	27.1	•	2.4	0.4	0.5	0.4	0.5	0.7	2.4	3.3	2.0	1.6	•
Working Capital to Net Sales 40	0.0	•	0.1	0.2	0.4	0.3	0.3	0.2	0.1	0.1	0.1	0.2	•
Inventory to Working Capital 41	3.9	•	1.1	0.2	0.3	0.2	0.6	0.6	0.9	1.2	0.8	0.7	•
Total Receipts to Cash Flow 42	11.8	105.1	•	5.5	•	10.3	6.5	9.4	•	25.6	13.9	13.8	10.1
Cost of Goods to Cash Flow 43	8.7	91.0	•	3.9	•	7.8	4.2	6.6	•	21.3	10.4	10.2	7.4
Cash Flow to Total Debt 44	0.0	•	•	2.4	•	0.3	0.6	0.3	•	0.1	0.1	0.1	0.0

Selected Financial Factors (in Percentages)

Debt Ratio 45	68.8	•	64.9	27.7	38.7	49.0	46.4	47.0	84.4	72.0	62.6	62.1	69.8
Return on Total Assets 46	3.0	•	•	44.5	•	4.1	14.1	7.6	•	1.5	1.4	2.6	3.3
Return on Equity Before Income Taxes 47	2.8	•	•	60.6	•	6.3	24.7	11.3	•	•	•	0.7	3.9
Return on Equity After Income Taxes 48	1.2	•	•	60.4	•	4.6	21.4	9.6	•	•	•	•	2.4
Profit Margin (Before Income Tax) 49	2.5	•	•	12.3	•	2.1	7.7	4.2	•	•	•	0.5	4.2
Profit Margin (After Income Tax) 50	1.1	•	•	12.2	•	1.5	6.7	3.5	•	•	•	•	2.6

Table II
Corporations with Net Income

BASIC CHEMICAL

MONEY AMOUNTS AND SIZE OF ASSETS IN THOUSANDS OF DOLLARS

Item Description for Accounting Period 7/09 Through 6/10		Total	Zero Assets	Under 500	500 to 1,000	1,000 to 5,000	5,000 to 10,000	10,000 to 25,000	25,000 to 50,000	50,000 to 100,000	100,000 to 250,000	250,000 to 500,000	500,000 to 2,500,000	2,500,000 and over
Number of Enterprises	1	620	•	•	•	116	27	81	49	18	13	11	19	20
Revenues ($ in Thousands)														
Net Sales	2	11441710	•	•	•	357510	433485	2224645	2528644	1945598	3620536	4950168	10432646	87258196
Interest	3	2056883	•	•	•	237	252	695	2977	1011	2015	11698	44566	1993347
Rents	4	170730	•	•	•	0	0	1415	624	911	654	2759	3981	160385
Royalties	5	2422707	•	•	•	4825	0	12	0	0	14135	25230	45055	2333449
Other Portfolio Income	6	2672658	•	•	•	2354	10000	1367	13305	1006	82530	40325	91439	2430336
Other Receipts	7	4096179	•	•	•	677	2202	7195	7899	14933	112581	64930	213077	3662417
Total Receipts	8	125838867	•	•	•	365603	445939	2235329	2553449	1963459	3832451	5095110	10830764	97838130
Average Total Receipts	9	202966	•	•	•	3152	16516	27597	52111	109081	294804	463192	570040	4891906
Operating Costs/Operating Income (%)														
Cost of Operations	10	72.1	•	•	•	56.4	77.0	63.8	71.5	70.8	84.9	73.9	66.1	72.5
Salaries and Wages	11	7.5	•	•	•	8.5	3.3	7.1	5.8	5.1	3.5	7.1	7.6	7.8
Taxes Paid	12	1.0	•	•	•	2.2	1.4	1.7	1.0	1.3	0.8	0.8	1.1	1.0
Interest Paid	13	5.0	•	•	•	0.8	0.4	0.5	0.8	0.9	1.0	1.1	3.2	6.0
Depreciation	14	4.3	•	•	•	2.4	3.5	2.4	2.5	3.5	2.0	4.0	4.9	4.5
Amortization and Depletion	15	1.1	•	•	•	0.2	0.1	0.1	0.5	0.7	0.3	0.4	1.1	1.2
Pensions and Other Deferred Comp.	16	1.3	•	•	•	0.6	0.1	0.3	0.8	0.7	0.3	0.9	1.1	1.4
Employee Benefits	17	1.9	•	•	•	1.2	1.0	1.3	1.4	1.2	0.4	1.8	2.8	1.9
Advertising	18	0.5	•	•	•	0.3	0.0	0.3	0.1	0.1	0.1	0.2	0.2	0.5
Other Expenses	19	9.6	•	•	•	16.1	5.5	9.4	7.8	7.8	5.7	7.7	8.9	10.1
Officers' Compensation	20	0.5	•	•	•	9.1	2.6	3.1	2.0	2.0	1.3	0.5	0.5	0.3
Operating Margin	21	•	•	•	•	2.1	5.0	10.1	5.7	6.0	•	1.6	2.5	•
Operating Margin Before Officers' Comp.	22	•	•	•	•	11.2	7.6	13.2	7.7	8.0	1.0	2.1	2.9	•

Selected Average Balance Sheet ($ in Thousands)

Net Receivables 23	115493	745	2221	3719	7320	15644	27304	107737	143319	3308913
Inventories 24	19702	324	938	4084	7001	12267	20945	48270	97079	429648
Net Property, Plant and Equipment 25	65282	191	2128	3583	9128	20712	44182	114981	202289	1678389
Total Assets 26	532707	2325	7996	15119	32052	66185	177836	385268	938243	15062630
Notes and Loans Payable 27	212194	411	3079	3529	6729	15623	45186	76227	321888	6148272
All Other Liabilities 28	129214	380	1877	2668	7509	16605	48365	126313	250223	3616934
Net Worth 29	191300	1535	3040	8922	17814	33958	84285	182728	366132	5297425

Selected Financial Ratios (Times to 1)

Current Ratio 30	1.0	3.3	2.5	3.2	2.6	1.9	1.8	2.2	1.8	1.0
Quick Ratio 31	0.8	2.1	2.0	1.8	1.6	1.1	1.2	1.4	1.2	0.8
Net Sales to Working Capital 32	36.8	2.7	6.0	3.7	4.7	6.2	8.1	4.2	4.0	•
Coverage Ratio 33	2.4	6.2	21.9	24.1	8.9	8.6	6.4	5.4	3.1	2.1
Total Asset Turnover 34	0.3	1.3	2.0	1.8	1.6	1.6	1.6	1.2	0.6	0.3
Inventory Turnover 35	6.8	5.4	13.2	4.3	5.3	6.2	11.3	6.9	3.7	7.4
Receivables Turnover 36	1.8	4.1	3.5	7.2	7.0	7.1	10.0	4.5	3.2	1.5
Total Liabilities to Net Worth 37	1.8	0.5	1.6	0.7	0.8	0.9	1.1	1.1	1.6	1.8
Current Assets to Working Capital 38	32.7	1.4	1.7	1.4	1.6	2.1	2.2	1.8	2.3	•
Current Liabilities to Working Capital 39	31.7	0.4	0.7	0.4	0.6	1.1	1.2	0.8	1.3	•
Working Capital to Net Sales 40	0.0	0.4	0.2	0.3	0.2	0.2	0.1	0.2	0.3	•
Inventory to Working Capital 41	4.1	0.2	0.3	0.5	0.6	0.7	0.5	0.5	0.6	•
Total Receipts to Cash Flow 42	8.3	6.4	8.2	5.6	8.0	7.8	13.3	9.7	8.5	8.3
Cost of Goods to Cash Flow 43	6.0	3.6	6.3	3.6	5.7	5.5	11.3	7.1	5.6	6.0
Cash Flow to Total Debt 44	0.1	0.6	0.4	0.8	0.5	0.4	0.2	0.2	0.1	0.1

Selected Financial Factors (in Percentages)

Debt Ratio 45	64.1	34.0	62.0	41.0	44.4	48.7	52.6	52.6	61.0	64.8
Return on Total Assets 46	4.0	6.9	16.5	20.1	12.1	13.1	10.3	6.8	5.8	3.7
Return on Equity Before Income Taxes 47	6.5	8.8	41.3	32.6	19.3	22.5	18.3	11.7	10.1	5.5
Return on Equity After Income Taxes 48	4.8	6.4	37.8	29.1	17.2	18.5	15.2	8.3	7.3	4.0
Profit Margin (Before Income Tax) 49	6.7	4.4	7.8	10.6	6.7	7.1	5.5	4.8	6.8	6.7
Profit Margin (After Income Tax) 50	5.0	3.2	7.2	9.4	6.0	5.8	4.6	3.4	4.9	4.9

Table I

Corporations with and without Net Income

RESIN, SYNTHETIC RUBBER AND FIBERS AND FILAMENTS

MONEY AMOUNTS AND SIZE OF ASSETS IN THOUSANDS OF DOLLARS

Item Description for Accounting Period 7/09 Through 6/10	Total	Zero Assets	Under 500	500 to 1,000	1,000 to 5,000	5,000 to 10,000	10,000 to 25,000	25,000 to 50,000	50,000 to 100,000	100,000 to 250,000	250,000 to 500,000	500,000 to 2,500,000	2,500,000 and over
Number of Enterprises **1**	618	4	321	0	177	17	39	13	14	15	8	6	4
Revenues ($ in Thousands)													
Net Sales **2**	38950313	445382	74931	0	846252	92580	816471	630154	1049657	3100426	3815661	5884754	22194044
Interest **3**	465488	232	0	0	30	4635	385	753	1118	2354	13874	14955	427151
Rents **4**	66538	0	0	0	0	0	0	0	0	168	755	4411	61204
Royalties **5**	723433	1	0	0	0	0	0	220	46	3396	6636	12550	700583
Other Portfolio Income **6**	209776	160	0	0	0	16196	76	176	947	82757	35079	1791	72597
Other Receipts **7**	1509778	3478	0	0	564	6099	3796	1686	5144	17148	123823	23716	1324323
Total Receipts **8**	41925326	449253	74931	0	846846	119510	820728	632989	1056912	3206249	3995828	5942177	24779902
Average Total Receipts **9**	67840	112313	233	•	4784	7030	21044	48691	75494	213750	499478	990363	6194976
Operating Costs/Operating Income (%)													
Cost of Operations **10**	72.3	73.6	68.7	•	65.7	57.3	71.3	80.5	72.6	80.2	83.6	78.3	67.8
Salaries and Wages **11**	3.0	9.0	•	•	5.7	4.1	5.2	3.5	5.0	4.2	4.4	2.9	2.2
Taxes Paid **12**	0.7	1.3	1.5	•	1.1	1.1	1.3	1.0	1.9	0.9	0.5	0.7	0.5
Interest Paid **13**	2.9	1.4	•	•	3.2	0.8	1.4	1.1	2.0	1.5	1.7	2.2	3.6
Depreciation **14**	7.0	2.2	3.2	•	2.6	2.8	5.6	4.6	4.1	4.3	3.1	8.1	8.3
Amortization and Depletion **15**	0.6	0.5	0.2	•	•	0.0	0.5	0.3	0.7	0.5	0.3	0.2	0.8
Pensions and Other Deferred Comp. **16**	1.7	0.8	•	•	1.7	0.1	0.2	0.5	0.6	0.3	0.4	0.9	2.6
Employee Benefits **17**	2.4	1.0	4.3	•	4.0	1.3	1.5	0.9	1.0	1.0	1.9	1.5	3.0
Advertising **18**	0.2	0.0	0.0	•	0.2	0.1	0.7	0.4	0.3	0.1	0.1	0.0	0.3
Other Expenses **19**	17.1	12.1	17.7	•	10.6	30.0	10.1	6.4	7.8	6.9	6.5	3.1	25.4
Officers' Compensation **20**	0.6	0.2	8.3	•	4.4	3.8	2.2	0.9	0.7	0.9	2.2	0.3	0.1
Operating Margin **21**	•	•	•	•	0.9	•	0.0	0.1	3.1	•	•	1.8	•
Operating Margin Before Officers' Comp. **22**	•	•	4.3	•	5.3	2.5	2.2	1.0	3.9	0.1	2.1	2.1	•

Selected Average Balance Sheet ($ in Thousands)

Net Receivables 23	12608	0	51	•	599	4655	2534	7242	13826	32386	97162	134114	1283968
Inventories 24	8817	0	9	•	681	607	2235	8026	12499	21930	44346	134850	859695
Net Property, Plant and Equipment 25	31587	0	41	•	641	273	6034	15625	18351	67354	85777	534023	3448387
Total Assets 26	135120	0	117	•	2722	6579	15434	36275	72980	172575	384597	1151640	17050634
Notes and Loans Payable 27	37648	0	44	•	596	1622	4333	5807	28038	40013	127244	458920	4527666
All Other Liabilities 28	69300	0	42	•	227	1463	4914	16056	16493	55591	154051	334548	9510999
Net Worth 29	28172	0	31	•	1899	3495	6187	14412	28448	76972	103302	358172	3011968

Selected Financial Ratios (Times to 1)

Current Ratio 30	1.6	•	1.6	•	3.9	4.3	1.4	1.6	1.8	2.1	1.9	2.6	1.5
Quick Ratio 31	1.0	•	1.3	•	2.1	4.1	0.7	0.8	1.0	1.1	1.3	1.4	1.0
Net Sales to Working Capital 32	5.3	•	9.1	•	4.9	1.1	10.8	8.1	4.6	4.7	5.6	4.4	5.6
Coverage Ratio 33	0.9	0.1	•	•	1.3	34.8	1.4	1.5	2.9	3.4	1.0	2.3	0.4
Total Asset Turnover 34	0.5	•	2.0	•	1.8	0.8	1.4	1.3	1.0	1.2	1.2	0.9	0.3
Inventory Turnover 35	5.2	•	18.8	•	4.6	5.1	6.7	4.9	4.4	7.6	9.0	5.7	4.4
Receivables Turnover 36	5.5	•	5.0	•	7.9	2.0	7.1	6.2	4.9	7.6	5.3	9.1	4.7
Total Liabilities to Net Worth 37	3.8	•	2.7	•	0.4	0.9	1.5	1.5	1.6	1.2	2.7	2.2	4.7
Current Assets to Working Capital 38	2.6	•	2.7	•	1.3	1.3	3.8	2.8	2.2	1.9	2.1	1.6	3.1
Current Liabilities to Working Capital 39	1.6	•	1.7	•	0.3	0.3	2.8	1.8	1.2	0.9	1.1	0.6	2.1
Working Capital to Net Sales 40	0.2	•	0.1	•	0.2	0.9	0.1	0.1	0.2	0.2	0.2	0.2	0.2
Inventory to Working Capital 41	0.7	•	0.4	•	0.6	0.0	1.1	1.2	0.7	0.5	0.5	0.5	0.9
Total Receipts to Cash Flow 42	7.4	10.6	11.2	•	12.7	2.4	13.8	16.5	9.6	12.6	22.4	20.8	5.3
Cost of Goods to Cash Flow 43	5.4	7.8	7.7	•	8.3	1.4	9.8	13.3	6.9	10.1	18.7	16.3	3.6
Cash Flow to Total Debt 44	0.1	•	0.2	•	0.5	0.7	0.2	0.1	0.2	0.2	0.1	0.1	0.1

Selected Financial Factors (in Percentages)

Debt Ratio 45	79.2	•	73.3	•	30.2	46.9	59.9	60.3	61.0	55.4	73.1	68.9	82.3
Return on Total Assets 46	1.2	•	•	•	7.3	23.6	2.7	2.2	6.0	6.2	2.2	4.3	0.5
Return on Equity Before Income Taxes 47	•	•	•	•	2.3	43.2	1.9	1.8	10.1	9.7	0.1	7.7	•
Return on Equity After Income Taxes 48	•	•	•	•	2.3	42.8	1.8	•	5.6	7.2	•	5.2	•
Profit Margin (Before Income Tax) 49	•	•	•	•	0.9	27.7	0.6	0.5	3.8	3.6	•	2.8	•
Profit Margin (After Income Tax) 50	•	•	•	•	0.9	27.5	0.5	•	2.1	2.7	•	1.9	•

Table II
Corporations with Net Income

RESIN, SYNTHETIC RUBBER AND FIBERS AND FILAMENTS

MONEY AMOUNTS AND SIZE OF ASSETS IN THOUSANDS OF DOLLARS

Item Description for Accounting Period 7/09 Through 6/10	Total	Zero Assets	Under 500	500 to 1,000	1,000 to 5,000	5,000 to 10,000	10,000 to 25,000	25,000 to 50,000	50,000 to 100,000	100,000 to 250,000	250,000 to 500,000	500,000 to 2,500,000	2,500,000 and over
Number of Enterprises **1**	252	•	0	0	173	17	21	7	•	10	3	•	0
Revenues ($ in Thousands)													
Net Sales **2**	15304060	•	0	0	844264	92580	533512	467760	•	2098544	1097068	•	•
Interest **3**	41152	•	0	0	0	4635	11	464	•	364	1261	•	•
Rents **4**	45549	•	0	0	0	0	0	0	•	0	666	•	•
Royalties **5**	15594	•	0	0	0	0	0	0	•	3042	0	•	•
Other Portfolio Income **6**	102419	•	0	0	0	16196	76	176	•	82757	519	•	•
Other Receipts **7**	80063	•	0	0	563	6099	1552	-75	•	5500	7367	•	•
Total Receipts **8**	15588837	•	0	0	844827	119510	535151	468325	•	2190207	1106881	•	•
Average Total Receipts **9**	61860	•	•	•	4883	7030	25483	66904	•	219021	368960	•	•
Operating Costs/Operating Income (%)													
Cost of Operations **10**	77.6	•	•	•	65.7	57.3	73.1	77.9	•	80.1	65.9	•	•
Salaries and Wages **11**	3.3	•	•	•	5.4	4.1	4.4	2.1	•	4.5	5.6	•	•
Taxes Paid **12**	0.8	•	•	•	1.1	1.1	1.1	0.9	•	1.0	0.9	•	•
Interest Paid **13**	1.5	•	•	•	3.0	0.8	1.2	0.6	•	1.0	0.7	•	•
Depreciation **14**	5.5	•	•	•	2.6	2.8	2.7	2.8	•	2.9	3.0	•	•
Amortization and Depletion **15**	0.4	•	•	•	•	0.0	0.6	0.2	•	0.1	0.3	•	•
Pensions and Other Deferred Comp. **16**	0.7	•	•	•	1.7	0.1	0.2	0.5	•	0.3	0.0	•	•
Employee Benefits **17**	1.5	•	•	•	4.0	1.3	1.7	1.1	•	1.1	3.0	•	•
Advertising **18**	0.1	•	•	•	0.1	0.1	1.0	0.4	•	0.1	0.1	•	•
Other Expenses **19**	5.0	•	•	•	9.9	30.0	7.0	5.7	•	5.0	16.0	•	•
Officers' Compensation **20**	0.7	•	•	•	4.3	3.8	1.5	0.7	•	1.0	0.2	•	•
Operating Margin **21**	3.1	•	•	•	2.1	•	5.5	7.3	•	2.7	4.3	•	•
Operating Margin Before Officers' Comp. **22**	3.7	•	•	•	6.4	2.5	7.0	7.9	•	3.7	4.5	•	•

Selected Average Balance Sheet ($ in Thousands)

Net Receivables 23	8000	613	4655	3732	10402	37314	78018
Inventories 24	12550	565	500	2948	8404	21034	50858
Net Property, Plant and Equipment 25	30568	655	273	5180	18159	55816	98939
Total Assets 26	66341	2755	6579	16266	38476	165477	382021
Notes and Loans Payable 27	21359	610	1622	5633	4480	21565	90578
All Other Liabilities 28	16551	180	1463	5102	13351	53095	86612
Net Worth 29	28432	1965	3495	5531	20645	90817	204831

Selected Financial Ratios (Times to 1)

Current Ratio 30	2.3	3.8	4.3	1.4	1.6	2.9	3.4
Quick Ratio 31	1.3	2.1	4.1	0.9	1.0	1.7	2.4
Net Sales to Working Capital 32	4.8	5.0	1.1	10.5	8.8	3.6	2.8
Coverage Ratio 33	4.4	1.7	34.8	6.0	14.0	9.7	8.6
Total Asset Turnover 34	0.9	1.8	0.8	1.6	1.7	1.3	1.0
Inventory Turnover 35	3.8	5.7	6.2	6.3	6.2	8.0	4.7
Receivables Turnover 36	4.3		2.2	5.7	6.5	7.4	4.5
Total Liabilities to Net Worth 37	1.3	0.4	0.9	1.9	0.9	0.8	0.9
Current Assets to Working Capital 38	1.8	1.4	1.3	3.4	2.6	1.5	1.4
Current Liabilities to Working Capital 39	0.8	0.4	0.3	2.4	1.6	0.5	0.4
Working Capital to Net Sales 40	0.2	0.2	0.9	0.1	0.1	0.3	0.4
Inventory to Working Capital 41	0.5	0.6	0.0	1.2	0.9	0.4	0.3
Total Receipts to Cash Flow 42	11.6	11.9	2.4	9.9	8.2	8.9	5.5
Cost of Goods to Cash Flow 43	9.0	7.8	1.4	7.3	6.4	7.1	3.6
Cash Flow to Total Debt 44	0.1	0.5	0.7	0.2	0.5	0.3	0.4

Selected Financial Factors (in Percentages)

Debt Ratio 45	57.1	28.7	46.9	66.0	46.3	45.1	46.4
Return on Total Assets 46	6.1	9.3	23.6	10.9	13.8	11.9	5.6
Return on Equity Before Income Taxes 47	11.0	5.4	43.2	26.7	23.9	19.5	9.2
Return on Equity After Income Taxes 48	8.2	5.4	42.8	26.5	17.1	16.3	7.3
Profit Margin (Before Income Tax) 49	5.2	2.2	27.7	5.8	7.4	8.4	5.1
Profit Margin (After Income Tax) 50	3.8	2.2	27.5	5.8	5.3	7.0	4.1

Table I

Corporations with and without Net Income

PHARMACEUTICAL AND MEDICINE

MONEY AMOUNTS AND SIZE OF ASSETS IN THOUSANDS OF DOLLARS

Item Description for Accounting Period 7/09 Through 6/10		Total	Zero Assets	Under 500	500 to 1,000	1,000 to 5,000	5,000 to 10,000	10,000 to 25,000	25,000 to 50,000	50,000 to 100,000	100,000 to 250,000	250,000 to 500,000	500,000 to 2,500,000	2,500,000 and over
Number of Enterprises	1	1264	332	275	19	39	228	116	81	47	48	16	30	31
Revenues ($ in Thousands)														
Net Sales	2	332210280	19516857	139285	34150	94370	2488708	1792376	2929525	2498805	5197002	3200052	24643155	269677994
Interest	3	3432120	449365	7	0	454	3445	3574	8135	17165	25703	15185	45069	2864017
Rents	4	143953	7532	842	0	0	115	858	655	968	1563	1339	11635	118445
Royalties	5	28105918	2517385	0	0	3403	1199	5907	24143	102792	59600	134125	617490	24639872
Other Portfolio Income	6	50810602	31711063	0	650	18805	762	79474	1833	29315	46036	6203	80541	18835918
Other Receipts	7	28835217	4097346	15950	39	13604	15310	44512	50900	164572	74434	112163	1820498	22425897
Total Receipts	8	443538090	58299548	156084	34839	130636	2509539	1926701	3015191	2811617	5404338	3469067	27218388	338562143
Average Total Receipts	9	350900	175601	568	1834	3350	11007	16609	37225	59822	112590	216817	907280	10921359
Operating Costs/Operating Income (%)														
Cost of Operations	10	51.1	41.1	50.0	•	38.2	64.1	64.6	62.2	49.0	47.5	37.3	49.1	52.0
Salaries and Wages	11	13.6	19.7	19.4	2.6	27.7	8.0	14.0	10.7	19.4	15.1	13.4	11.5	13.3
Taxes Paid	12	1.7	2.8	1.6	0.5	4.0	2.2	2.1	2.7	2.3	2.0	2.1	1.6	1.6
Interest Paid	13	4.4	4.1	3.7	4.2	6.3	1.3	1.5	2.7	2.3	1.8	2.0	2.3	4.8
Depreciation	14	3.1	2.6	4.3	0.4	3.5	2.9	5.2	3.8	4.6	3.7	4.3	2.1	3.2
Amortization and Depletion	15	1.8	2.4	0.4	•	22.1	0.9	1.0	2.8	1.7	2.3	3.9	1.7	1.7
Pensions and Other Deferred Comp.	16	1.9	4.9	•	•	0.4	0.6	0.4	0.9	0.6	0.6	0.4	0.4	2.0
Employee Benefits	17	2.6	1.4	0.3	0.1	3.2	2.3	1.5	1.9	2.3	2.5	1.8	1.7	2.7
Advertising	18	4.1	7.3	9.0	•	1.6	0.6	1.4	1.2	0.9	3.2	1.0	2.4	4.2
Other Expenses	19	26.2	33.8	47.5	14.6	186.0	13.0	21.1	20.7	28.7	24.2	26.0	27.2	25.7
Officers' Compensation	20	0.5	1.4	10.8	•	13.4	5.4	3.9	3.0	2.2	2.0	2.2	1.1	0.2
Operating Margin	21	•	•	•	77.6	•	•	•	•	•	•	5.5	•	•
Operating Margin Before Officers' Comp.	22	•	•	•	77.6	4.3	•	•	•	•	7.7	•	•	•

Selected Average Balance Sheet ($ in Thousands)

Net Receivables **23**	59719	0	147	1	201	1251	2567	5437	9303	18824	33586	106229	2237029
Inventories **24**	33538	0	32	0	883	1484	2542	4824	8753	16424	22875	138496	1148504
Net Property, Plant and Equipment **25**	58538	0	58	7	584	2726	4345	8530	13739	28879	55902	127987	2108753
Total Assets **26**	745299	0	275	588	2769	8062	14909	35783	74571	156820	325117	1023440	28660002
Notes and Loans Payable **27**	245493	0	71	3089	1145	1617	4506	12262	19321	35059	70289	231362	9601246
All Other Liabilities **28**	221262	0	61	465	2136	1648	4516	13007	23483	44225	86768	252313	8562233
Net Worth **29**	278544	0	142	-2966	-511	4797	5887	10513	31767	77536	168060	539766	10496523

Selected Financial Ratios (Times to 1)

Current Ratio **30**	1.0	•	2.9	0.4	0.6	3.0	1.6	1.5	2.3	2.3	2.9	2.0	1.0
Quick Ratio **31**	0.4	•	2.4	0.4	0.4	1.8	1.1	0.9	1.2	1.4	1.8	1.0	0.4
Net Sales to Working Capital **32**	49.9	•	3.9	•	•	3.6	4.4	5.0	2.3	2.6	1.9	3.8	•
Coverage Ratio **33**	6.9	46.4	•	19.9	•	0.8	•	•	0.3	0.6	8.1	5.1	4.7
Total Asset Turnover **34**	0.4	•	1.8	3.1	0.9	1.4	1.0	1.0	0.7	0.7	0.6	0.8	0.3
Inventory Turnover **35**	4.0	•	7.9	•	1.0	4.7	3.9	4.7	3.0	3.1	3.3	2.9	3.9
Receivables Turnover **36**	3.7	•	6.0	2732.0	3.7	10.3	5.5	7.0	5.9	6.2	5.8	7.4	3.2
Total Liabilities to Net Worth **37**	1.7	•	0.9	•	0.7	0.7	1.5	2.4	1.3	1.0	0.9	0.9	1.7
Current Assets to Working Capital **38**	34.8	•	1.5	•	•	1.5	2.6	3.0	1.8	1.8	1.5	2.0	•
Current Liabilities to Working Capital **39**	33.8	•	0.5	•	•	0.5	1.6	2.0	0.8	0.8	0.5	1.0	•
Working Capital to Net Sales **40**	0.0	•	0.3	•	•	0.3	0.2	0.2	0.4	0.4	0.5	0.3	•
Inventory to Working Capital **41**	6.2	•	0.3	•	•	0.6	0.7	0.8	0.4	0.4	0.3	0.7	•
Total Receipts to Cash Flow **42**	2.3	0.5	•	•	1.1	10.4	11.3	14.6	4.4	5.1	2.7	2.9	2.9
Cost of Goods to Cash Flow **43**	1.2	0.2	•	•	•	6.7	7.3	9.1	2.2	2.4	1.0	1.4	1.5
Cash Flow to Total Debt **44**	0.2	•	•	•	0.5	0.3	0.2	0.1	0.3	0.3	0.5	0.6	0.2

Selected Financial Factors (in Percentages)

Debt Ratio **45**	62.6	•	48.3	118.5	604.2	40.5	60.5	70.6	57.4	50.6	48.3	47.3	63.4
Return on Total Assets **46**	10.8	•	•	•	256.1	1.4	•	•	0.5	0.7	9.8	9.4	6.9
Return on Equity Before Income Taxes **47**	24.7	•	•	795.1	•	•	•	•	•	•	16.6	14.3	14.9
Return on Equity After Income Taxes **48**	16.2	•	•	•	8172.2	•	•	•	•	•	12.2	9.7	10.0
Profit Margin (Before Income Tax) **49**	26.2	186.3	•	79.6	•	•	•	•	•	•	13.9	9.4	18.0
Profit Margin (After Income Tax) **50**	17.2	121.8	•	79.6	•	•	•	•	•	•	10.3	6.4	12.1

87

Table II

Corporations with Net Income

PHARMACEUTICAL AND MEDICINE

MONEY AMOUNTS AND SIZE OF ASSETS IN THOUSANDS OF DOLLARS

Item Description for Accounting Period 7/09 Through 6/10	Total	Zero Assets	Under 500	500 to 1,000	1,000 to 5,000	5,000 to 10,000	10,000 to 25,000	25,000 to 50,000	50,000 to 100,000	100,000 to 250,000	250,000 to 500,000	500,000 to 2,500,000	2,500,000 and over
Number of Enterprises **1**	732	315	•	19	22	175	53	30	24	28	11	24	•
Revenues ($ in Thousands)													
Net Sales **2**	314900698	19278226	•	34150	89008	2252709	1105677	1729910	1655239	4082455	2395418	23412492	•
Interest **3**	3208314	449331	•	0	37	2474	1284	3571	7109	15324	8908	24077	•
Rents **4**	141672	7532	•	0	0	0	858	429	966	1175	1320	10948	•
Royalties **5**	27485861	2517385	•	0	1995	0	0	3221	101627	58048	79279	608994	•
Other Portfolio Income **6**	50803597	31709266	•	650	18791	636	77642	21	28370	45647	6203	80470	•
Other Receipts **7**	28165345	4090726	•	39	14702	13396	3569	3816	78863	50096	69088	1466607	•
Total Receipts **8**	424705487	58052466	•	34839	124533	2269215	1189030	1740968	1872174	4252745	2560216	25603588	•
Average Total Receipts **9**	580199	184294	•	1834	5661	12967	22435	58032	78007	151884	232747	1066816	•
Operating Costs/Operating Income (%)													
Cost of Operations **10**	51.1	40.6	•	•	37.0	64.4	60.7	58.9	46.1	47.1	28.8	50.2	•
Salaries and Wages **11**	13.4	19.6	•	2.6	15.6	5.5	7.5	7.0	16.1	12.7	15.0	10.5	•
Taxes Paid **12**	1.7	2.8	•	0.5	2.1	1.9	1.4	1.9	2.2	1.7	2.0	1.5	•
Interest Paid **13**	4.3	4.1	•	4.2	2.0	0.9	0.6	1.0	1.8	0.8	0.9	2.0	•
Depreciation **14**	3.0	2.5	•	0.4	1.9	2.5	4.0	3.7	3.7	2.8	3.5	2.0	•
Amortization and Depletion **15**	1.7	2.4	•	•	0.0	0.5	0.1	0.1	0.9	1.9	3.0	1.4	•
Pensions and Other Deferred Comp. **16**	1.9	4.9	•	•	0.4	0.6	0.4	0.9	0.7	0.6	0.3	0.4	•
Employee Benefits **17**	2.6	1.4	•	0.1	1.5	2.2	1.0	1.4	1.7	1.9	1.9	1.7	•
Advertising **18**	4.2	7.3	•	•	0.1	0.6	1.2	1.6	1.0	2.7	1.3	2.3	•
Other Expenses **19**	25.9	33.9	•	14.6	14.2	8.4	11.6	10.9	18.8	17.7	27.1	25.3	•
Officers' Compensation **20**	0.4	1.3	•	•	2.0	4.7	3.5	1.6	2.1	2.2	1.0	•	•
Operating Margin **21**	•	•	•	77.6	23.2	7.8	8.1	11.1	5.1	8.5	14.0	1.7	•
Operating Margin Before Officers' Comp. **22**	•	•	•	77.6	25.1	12.6	11.7	12.6	7.1	10.1	16.2	2.7	•

Selected Average Balance Sheet ($ in Thousands)

Net Receivables	23	98822	0	1	287	1448	3536	7069	13899	23464	31881	124036	•
Inventories	24	52640	0	0	609	1639	2854	5867	10896	21335	21756	150584	•
Net Property, Plant and Equipment	25	93912	0	7	987	3071	4032	9801	12469	30796	49056	122887	•
Total Assets	26	1237485	0	588	2924	8529	14702	36733	73853	154498	334327	1032541	•
Notes and Loans Payable	27	405857	0	3089	916	1423	2461	9058	15233	24659	49269	199795	•
All Other Liabilities	28	366831	0	465	404	1193	5021	9585	14608	37754	95261	267576	•
Net Worth	29	464796	0	-2966	1604	5913	7220	18091	44012	92086	189797	565170	•

Selected Financial Ratios (Times to 1)

Current Ratio	30	1.0	•	0.4	3.2	3.8	2.1	2.1	2.5	2.0	3.3	1.9	•
Quick Ratio	31	0.4	•	0.4	1.4	2.1	1.5	1.2	1.5	1.2	2.0	0.9	•
Net Sales to Working Capital	32	52.3	•	•	4.1	3.7	3.8	4.9	2.7	3.8	1.8	4.8	•
Coverage Ratio	33	7.6	46.8	19.9	32.5	10.8	28.5	12.5	10.8	16.2	23.9	6.8	•
Total Asset Turnover	34	0.3	•	3.1	1.4	1.5	1.4	1.6	0.9	0.9	0.7	0.9	•
Inventory Turnover	35	4.2	•	•	2.5	5.1	4.4	5.8	2.9	3.2	2.9	3.3	•
Receivables Turnover	36	3.7	•	2732.0	•	10.4	5.9	7.6	5.0	6.9	•	7.9	•
Total Liabilities to Net Worth	37	1.7	•	0.8	0.8	0.4	1.0	1.0	0.7	0.7	0.8	0.8	•
Current Assets to Working Capital	38	36.5	•	1.5	1.5	1.4	1.9	1.9	1.7	2.0	1.4	2.2	•
Current Liabilities to Working Capital	39	35.5	•	0.5	0.5	0.4	0.9	0.9	0.7	1.0	0.4	1.2	•
Working Capital to Net Sales	40	0.0	•	0.2	0.2	0.3	0.3	0.2	0.4	0.3	0.6	0.2	•
Inventory to Working Capital	41	6.4	•	0.6	0.6	0.5	0.5	0.6	0.4	0.6	0.2	0.8	•
Total Receipts to Cash Flow	42	2.2	0.5	1.1	1.9	6.8	4.0	5.0	3.0	3.7	2.2	2.9	•
Cost of Goods to Cash Flow	43	1.1	0.2	•	0.7	4.4	2.4	3.0	1.4	1.8	0.6	1.5	•
Cash Flow to Total Debt	44	0.3	•	0.5	1.6	0.7	0.7	0.6	0.8	0.6	0.7	0.7	•

Selected Financial Factors (in Percentages)

Debt Ratio	45	62.4	•	604.2	45.1	30.7	50.9	50.8	40.4	40.4	43.2	45.3	•
Return on Total Assets	46	11.4	•	256.1	90.0	14.3	23.0	20.0	18.7	12.9	14.2	12.5	•
Return on Equity Before Income Taxes	47	26.4	•	•	159.1	18.7	45.2	37.4	28.5	20.3	24.0	19.4	•
Return on Equity After Income Taxes	48	17.7	•	•	146.6	16.7	43.0	30.0	22.8	14.5	18.4	13.9	•
Profit Margin (Before Income Tax)	49	28.5	189.3	79.6	63.1	8.6	15.6	11.7	18.2	12.8	20.9	11.2	•
Profit Margin (After Income Tax)	50	19.1	124.0	79.6	58.1	7.7	14.9	9.4	14.5	9.2	16.1	8.1	•

Table I

Corporations with and without Net Income

PAINT, COATING, AND ADHESIVE

MONEY AMOUNTS AND SIZE OF ASSETS IN THOUSANDS OF DOLLARS

Item Description for Accounting Period 7/09 Through 6/10		Total	Zero Assets	Under 500	500 to 1,000	1,000 to 5,000	5,000 to 10,000	10,000 to 25,000	25,000 to 50,000	50,000 to 100,000	100,000 to 250,000	250,000 to 500,000	500,000 to 2,500,000	2,500,000 and over
Number of Enterprises	1	1445	•	•	•	587	88	71	22	17	9	8	6	7
Revenues ($ in Thousands)														
Net Sales	2	45387905	•	•	•	2913111	975578	1928656	978615	1411634	1137109	2430794	4840510	27488043
Interest	3	359592	•	•	•	197	23	599	330	779	1934	14846	46219	294466
Rents	4	28986	•	•	•	0	1572	1624	1250	0	59	1684	6883	15619
Royalties	5	322098	•	•	•	0	0	0	127	1191	0	2657	41757	276367
Other Portfolio Income	6	492289	•	•	•	1775	0	5961	4431	596	5	3315	57571	418625
Other Receipts	7	706844	•	•	•	19358	1940	11119	5208	18388	3314	47397	23106	575135
Total Receipts	8	47297714	•	•	•	2934441	979113	1947959	989961	1432588	1142421	2500693	5016046	29068255
Average Total Receipts	9	32732	•	•	•	4999	11126	27436	44998	84270	126936	312587	836008	4152608
Operating Costs/Operating Income (%)														
Cost of Operations	10	62.7	•	•	•	62.2	63.6	66.4	72.2	65.5	56.5	68.4	63.0	62.1
Salaries and Wages	11	10.2	•	•	•	6.8	8.3	10.1	8.3	8.7	18.1	9.8	10.7	10.2
Taxes Paid	12	1.7	•	•	•	1.8	4.9	1.5	1.5	1.7	1.6	1.9	1.7	1.6
Interest Paid	13	2.8	•	•	•	0.3	1.3	0.9	0.6	1.2	0.7	3.1	2.4	3.6
Depreciation	14	2.5	•	•	•	0.6	2.2	1.5	1.8	2.7	4.2	2.3	3.3	2.6
Amortization and Depletion	15	0.9	•	•	•	0.3	0.1	0.2	0.3	1.2	0.9	2.4	1.8	0.9
Pensions and Other Deferred Comp.	16	1.8	•	•	•	0.5	0.0	0.7	0.4	0.7	1.4	0.9	3.7	2.0
Employee Benefits	17	2.1	•	•	•	0.9	1.3	1.0	1.7	2.0	2.0	1.6	2.5	2.3
Advertising	18	1.7	•	•	•	1.8	0.3	0.5	0.2	0.6	0.4	0.6	0.4	2.4
Other Expenses	19	13.3	•	•	•	12.0	12.9	12.2	9.1	11.7	11.8	10.1	13.0	14.1
Officers' Compensation	20	1.5	•	•	•	8.1	4.3	3.0	2.0	1.9	1.7	0.8	0.8	0.4
Operating Margin	21	•	•	•	•	4.7	0.9	1.9	2.1	2.1	0.6	•	•	•
Operating Margin Before Officers' Comp.	22	0.2	•	•	•	12.8	5.2	4.9	4.0	4.0	2.3	•	•	•

Selected Average Balance Sheet ($ in Thousands)

Net Receivables 23	4496	494	1667	3658	6256	12569	24043	37075	104250	591379
Inventories 24	3050	474	1207	3247	7713	10297	21608	27577	106572	345770
Net Property, Plant and Equipment 25	5809	231	1027	2455	5691	19068	32920	43090	231743	783466
Total Assets 26	35547	2050	5719	14955	32115	72686	129746	383980	1184119	4995855
Notes and Loans Payable 27	12510	413	2224	5009	15587	38942	118806	288570		1948159
All Other Liabilities 28	13493	383	2725	4623	6607	15933	22568	119539	312487	2161515
Net Worth 29	9544	1255	770	5323	20293	41166	68236	145634	583061	886182

Selected Financial Ratios (Times to 1)

Current Ratio 30	1.1	3.1	1.0	1.8	2.4	1.6	1.9	1.7	1.1	0.9
Quick Ratio 31	0.6	2.1	0.6	1.1	1.3	1.0	1.5	0.6	0.8	0.5
Net Sales to Working Capital 32	38.4	4.9	155.9	6.3	5.0	7.1	4.3	4.4	19.3	•
Coverage Ratio 33	2.2	17.7	2.0	4.1	6.4	4.3	2.7	1.3	1.2	2.2
Total Asset Turnover 34	0.9	2.4	1.9	1.8	1.4	1.1	1.0	0.8	0.7	0.8
Inventory Turnover 35	6.5	6.5	5.8	5.6	4.2	5.3	3.3	7.5	4.8	7.0
Receivables Turnover 36	8.0	11.2	7.8	8.8	6.3	6.6	4.2	16.4	7.0	7.9
Total Liabilities to Net Worth 37	2.7	0.6	6.4	1.8	0.6	0.8	0.9	1.6	1.0	4.6
Current Assets to Working Capital 38	14.0	1.5	50.2	2.2	1.7	2.8	2.1	2.3	8.9	•
Current Liabilities to Working Capital 39	13.0	0.5	49.2	1.2	0.7	1.8	1.1	1.3	7.9	•
Working Capital to Net Sales 40	0.0	0.2	0.0	0.2	0.2	0.1	0.2	0.2	0.1	•
Inventory to Working Capital 41	3.8	0.5	17.4	0.8	0.7	0.8	0.5	0.4	2.1	•
Total Receipts to Cash Flow 42	7.5	6.9	11.0	8.0	9.4	7.2	10.2	11.7	8.8	6.8
Cost of Goods to Cash Flow 43	4.7	4.3	7.0	5.3	6.8	4.7	5.8	8.0	5.6	4.2
Cash Flow to Total Debt 44	0.2	0.9	0.2	0.4	0.4	0.4	0.2	0.1	0.2	0.1

Selected Financial Factors (in Percentages)

Debt Ratio 45	73.2	38.8	86.5	64.4	36.8	43.4	47.4	62.1	50.8	82.3
Return on Total Assets 46	5.5	13.8	4.9	6.9	5.3	5.7	1.8	3.2	2.1	6.2
Return on Equity Before Income Taxes 47	11.2	21.3	18.2	14.6	7.1	7.7	2.2	2.0	0.8	19.1
Return on Equity After Income Taxes 48	8.2	20.9	16.3	12.8	5.5	5.8	1.0	0.3	0.3	13.6
Profit Margin (Before Income Tax) 49	3.4	5.4	1.3	2.9	3.2	3.8	1.2	1.0	0.6	4.3
Profit Margin (After Income Tax) 50	2.5	5.3	1.1	2.5	2.5	2.9	0.6	0.2	0.2	3.1

Table II
Corporations with Net Income

PAINT, COATING, AND ADHESIVE

MONEY AMOUNTS AND SIZE OF ASSETS IN THOUSANDS OF DOLLARS

Item Description for Accounting Period 7/09 Through 6/10		Total	Zero Assets	Under 500	500 to 1,000	1,000 to 5,000	5,000 to 10,000	10,000 to 25,000	25,000 to 50,000	50,000 to 100,000	100,000 to 250,000	250,000 to 500,000	500,000 to 2,500,000	2,500,000 and over
Number of Enterprises	1	987	•	0	•	349	68	56	15	13	•	•	3	•
Revenues ($ in Thousands)														
Net Sales	2	31409067	•	0	•	2461314	766787	1584379	860561	1178474	•	•	3519581	•
Interest	3	180993	•	0	•	35	23	598	311	303	•	•	12598	•
Rents	4	12939	•	0	•	0	1572	1571	1250	0	•	•	3890	•
Royalties	5	297437	•	0	•	0	0	0	0	162	•	•	26504	•
Other Portfolio Income	6	370680	•	0	•	1397	0	5961	20	319	•	•	39342	•
Other Receipts	7	566956	•	0	•	7428	1680	10075	5073	15984	•	•	8862	•
Total Receipts	8	32838072	•	0	•	2470174	770062	1602584	867215	1195242	•	•	3610777	•
Average Total Receipts	9	33271	•	•	•	7078	11324	28618	57814	91942	•	•	1203592	•
Operating Costs/Operating Income (%)														
Cost of Operations	10	62.1	•	•	•	61.7	63.9	61.2	72.6	64.4	•	•	63.7	•
Salaries and Wages	11	9.9	•	•	•	5.8	5.9	11.4	7.2	8.5	•	•	8.6	•
Taxes Paid	12	1.8	•	•	•	1.7	6.0	1.6	1.4	1.5	•	•	1.4	•
Interest Paid	13	2.5	•	•	•	0.1	1.6	0.8	0.5	1.1	•	•	2.9	•
Depreciation	14	2.5	•	•	•	0.4	2.2	1.4	1.4	2.3	•	•	3.5	•
Amortization and Depletion	15	0.8	•	•	•	0.0	0.1	0.0	0.2	0.8	•	•	1.3	•
Pensions and Other Deferred Comp.	16	2.1	•	•	•	0.6	0.0	0.7	0.3	0.7	•	•	2.5	•
Employee Benefits	17	1.7	•	•	•	0.9	1.1	1.0	1.4	1.7	•	•	2.0	•
Advertising	18	1.3	•	•	•	2.0	0.1	0.6	0.2	0.8	•	•	0.2	•
Other Expenses	19	12.2	•	•	•	11.0	11.2	13.0	9.0	11.6	•	•	13.6	•
Officers' Compensation	20	1.9	•	•	•	8.4	5.4	3.0	2.1	1.8	•	•	0.8	•
Operating Margin	21	1.3	•	•	•	7.4	2.5	5.1	3.6	4.9	•	•	•	•
Operating Margin Before Officers' Comp.	22	3.2	•	•	•	15.8	7.9	8.1	5.7	6.7	•	•	0.3	•

Selected Average Balance Sheet ($ in Thousands)

Net Receivables 23	4747	676	1732	3911	8003	11432	157320
Inventories 24	3369	635	1116	2745	9350	8787	145077
Net Property, Plant and Equipment 25	5238	207	1064	2695	6976	15399	367067
Total Assets 26	34470	2260	5695	15923	32213	73597	1441497
Notes and Loans Payable 27	12975	321	2832	4432	6100	13442	464335
All Other Liabilities 28	12864	540	1364	3483	8466	16701	318963
Net Worth 29	8631	1399	1500	8008	17646	43453	658200

Selected Financial Ratios (Times to 1)

Current Ratio 30	1.2	2.9	1.4	2.3	2.2	1.6	1.1
Quick Ratio 31	0.6	1.9	0.9	1.4	1.2	1.0	0.7
Net Sales to Working Capital 32	18.3	5.3	11.6	4.8	5.4	7.0	24.1
Coverage Ratio 33	3.6	65.1	2.9	8.9	9.9	6.9	1.9
Total Asset Turnover 34	0.9	3.1	2.0	1.8	1.8	1.2	0.8
Inventory Turnover 35	5.9	6.9	6.5	6.3	4.5	6.6	5.1
Receivables Turnover 36	7.3	11.4	13.0	10.1	7.1	9.8	•
Total Liabilities to Net Worth 37	3.0	0.6	2.8	1.0	0.8	0.7	1.2
Current Assets to Working Capital 38	6.9	1.5	3.7	1.8	1.9	2.7	9.7
Current Liabilities to Working Capital 39	5.9	0.5	2.7	0.8	0.9	1.7	8.7
Working Capital to Net Sales 40	0.1	0.2	0.1	0.2	0.2	0.1	0.0
Inventory to Working Capital 41	1.8	0.5	1.2	0.6	0.8	0.8	3.0
Total Receipts to Cash Flow 42	6.6	6.1	11.1	5.8	8.4	6.1	7.0
Cost of Goods to Cash Flow 43	4.1	3.8	7.1	3.5	6.1	3.9	4.5
Cash Flow to Total Debt 44	0.2	1.3	0.2	0.6	0.5	0.5	0.2

Selected Financial Factors (in Percentages)

Debt Ratio 45	75.0	38.1	73.7	49.7	45.2	41.0	54.3
Return on Total Assets 46	8.3	24.4	8.9	12.5	8.7	9.1	4.5
Return on Equity Before Income Taxes 47	24.2	38.8	22.0	22.0	14.3	13.2	4.7
Return on Equity After Income Taxes 48	19.2	38.2	20.7	20.4	11.5	10.9	3.8
Profit Margin (Before Income Tax) 49	6.6	7.7	2.9	6.2	4.4	6.3	2.6
Profit Margin (After Income Tax) 50	5.2	7.6	2.8	5.8	3.5	5.2	2.1

Table I

Corporations with and without Net Income

SOAP, CLEANING COMPOUND, AND TOILET PREPARATION

MONEY AMOUNTS AND SIZE OF ASSETS IN THOUSANDS OF DOLLARS

Item Description for Accounting Period 7/09 Through 6/10	Total	Zero Assets	Under 500	500 to 1,000	1,000 to 5,000	5,000 to 10,000	10,000 to 25,000	25,000 to 50,000	50,000 to 100,000	100,000 to 250,000	250,000 to 500,000	500,000 to 2,500,000	2,500,000 and over
Number of Enterprises 1	2205	680	718	177	403	86	72	20	13	11	5	9	10
Revenues ($ in Thousands)													
Net Sales 2	90606563	19562	389851	319949	2503846	1346846	2279990	1059233	1168570	2207606	2706128	9118079	67486903
Interest 3	406180	6	52	17	379	223	1119	2823	1198	7339	1429	17207	374389
Rents 4	30425	16	0	0	2483	1472	3284	106	249	671	0	5275	16870
Royalties 5	3643128	0	0	0	8670	0	2682	332	487	1467	1184	203836	3424470
Other Portfolio Income 6	6320487	0	196	2	2566	807	470	7409	474	13702	353	203255	6091256
Other Receipts 7	2179045	36	180	1505	13632	8756	10082	11579	39854	35346	9320	117446	1931303
Total Receipts 8	103185828	19620	390279	321473	2531576	1358104	2297627	1081482	1210832	2266131	2718414	9665098	79325191
Average Total Receipts 9	46796	29	544	1816	6282	15792	31911	54074	93141	206012	543683	1073900	7932519
Operating Costs/Operating Income (%)													
Cost of Operations 10	42.8	78.3	69.1	71.2	60.3	44.9	61.0	64.7	62.3	57.8	59.0	49.6	38.5
Salaries and Wages 11	9.4	4.3	6.7	8.2	13.6	25.8	12.9	11.1	9.8	9.3	7.8	10.7	8.7
Taxes Paid 12	2.0	7.4	3.4	3.0	2.1	0.5	1.8	1.9	1.7	1.5	1.0	3.6	1.9
Interest Paid 13	3.6	1.6	•	1.1	0.5	0.3	0.6	0.9	1.7	3.2	1.1	4.0	4.1
Depreciation 14	2.7	1.0	0.8	1.8	0.4	3.0	2.7	1.8	3.4	2.2	2.4	2.2	2.9
Amortization and Depletion 15	1.7	3.0	0.0	0.0	0.0	0.3	0.1	0.6	2.0	1.5	0.7	0.8	2.1
Pensions and Other Deferred Comp. 16	2.4	0.0	0.3	0.6	0.9	0.9	0.2	0.2	0.2	0.3	0.8	0.6	3.0
Employee Benefits 17	1.8	0.7	0.3	1.6	1.4	0.1	1.4	1.0	2.1	0.2	2.4	1.8	1.9
Advertising 18	7.6	0.1	10.5	1.0	1.9	0.6	2.6	2.4	0.8	8.4	6.2	7.7	8.3
Other Expenses 19	19.2	31.0	14.9	11.7	14.6	14.6	11.1	12.5	14.7	15.3	9.8	18.4	20.6
Officers' Compensation 20	1.0	0.3	12.5	7.2	5.1	2.6	2.1	2.2	2.9	1.1	1.1	1.5	0.6
Operating Margin 21	5.6	•	•	•	•	6.4	3.4	0.6	•	•	7.7	•	7.4
Operating Margin Before Officers' Comp. 22	6.6	•	•	•	4.4	9.0	5.5	2.8	1.3	0.1	8.8	0.5	7.9

Selected Average Balance Sheet ($ in Thousands)

Net Receivables 23	15302	0	70	172	510	1395	4384	8675	15320	32212	66613	106599	3099918
Inventories 24	4321	0	31	138	534	1710	3287	6652	14474	27221	50888	137933	676546
Net Property, Plant and Equipment 25	6531	0	15	99	335	3120	3901	5835	12781	24653	90666	123016	1157308
Total Assets 26	111566	0	209	776	2624	7243	15503	35528	66289	166249	350922	1232304	22667271
Notes and Loans Payable 27	27540	0	72	558	521	553	3870	10120	46123	73950	105916	584496	5263359
All Other Liabilities 28	29120	0	21	112	431	2600	5011	9828	18415	47746	115828	370396	5854231
Net Worth 29	54906	0	116	107	1672	4090	6622	15580	1751	44553	129178	277412	11549682

Selected Financial Ratios (Times to 1)

Current Ratio 30	1.0	•	9.0	2.7	2.3	1.6	1.5	2.0	1.5	1.6	1.3	1.6	0.9
Quick Ratio 31	0.7	•	6.8	1.5	1.0	0.7	0.9	1.1	0.8	0.9	0.8	0.7	0.6
Net Sales to Working Capital 32	•	•	3.2	4.6	6.5	13.3	10.1	5.2	8.2	7.4	14.4	7.0	•
Coverage Ratio 33	7.2	•	•	1.7	22.9	7.7	4.1	1.5	2.2	1.6	8.3	2.4	8.1
Total Asset Turnover 34	0.4	•	2.6	2.3	2.4	2.2	2.0	1.5	1.4	1.2	1.5	0.8	0.3
Inventory Turnover 35	4.1	•	12.1	9.3	7.0	4.1	5.9	5.2	3.9	4.3	6.3	3.6	3.8
Receivables Turnover 36	2.8	•	9.2	13.5	13.2	9.1	8.3	6.8	3.9	5.8	7.9	11.3	2.2
Total Liabilities to Net Worth 37	1.0	•	0.8	6.3	0.6	0.8	1.3	1.3	36.9	2.7	1.7	3.4	1.0
Current Assets to Working Capital 38	•	•	1.1	1.6	1.7	2.7	3.1	2.0	2.9	2.7	4.3	2.7	•
Current Liabilities to Working Capital 39	•	•	0.1	0.6	0.7	1.7	2.1	1.0	1.9	1.7	3.3	1.7	•
Working Capital to Net Sales 40	•	•	0.3	0.2	0.2	0.1	0.1	0.2	0.1	0.1	0.1	0.1	•
Inventory to Working Capital 41	•	•	0.2	0.4	0.6	1.3	1.1	0.7	0.9	0.9	1.3	0.9	•
Total Receipts to Cash Flow 42	3.0	50.3	•	66.2	8.7	5.3	7.4	7.8	6.8	6.7	6.1	5.1	2.5
Cost of Goods to Cash Flow 43	1.3	39.4	•	47.2	5.2	2.4	4.5	5.1	4.2	3.9	3.6	2.5	1.0
Cash Flow to Total Debt 44	0.2	•	•	0.0	0.8	0.9	0.5	0.3	0.2	0.2	0.4	0.2	0.2

Selected Financial Factors (in Percentages)

Debt Ratio 45	50.8	•	44.5	86.3	36.3	43.5	57.3	56.1	97.4	73.2	63.2	77.5	49.0
Return on Total Assets 46	9.6	•	•	•	1.9	16.4	9.8	5.4	5.2	6.1	14.3	8.0	9.8
Return on Equity Before Income Taxes 47	16.9	•	•	•	1.2	27.7	20.0	9.3	107.9	8.2	34.2	20.8	16.9
Return on Equity After Income Taxes 48	11.0	•	•	•	0.1	27.4	16.4	7.0	61.6	5.6	29.7	11.9	11.0
Profit Margin (Before Income Tax) 49	22.5	•	•	•	0.3	7.2	4.2	2.7	2.1	1.8	8.2	5.7	28.8
Profit Margin (After Income Tax) 50	14.7	•	•	•	0.0	7.1	3.4	2.1	1.2	1.2	7.1	3.3	18.8

91

Table II

Corporations with Net Income

SOAP, CLEANING COMPOUND, AND TOILET PREPARATION

MONEY AMOUNTS AND SIZE OF ASSETS IN THOUSANDS OF DOLLARS

Item Description for Accounting Period 7/09 Through 6/10	Total	Zero Assets	Under 500	500 to 1,000	1,000 to 5,000	5,000 to 10,000	10,000 to 25,000	25,000 to 50,000	50,000 to 100,000	100,000 to 250,000	250,000 to 500,000	500,000 to 2,500,000	2,500,000 and over
Number of Enterprises **1**	571	0	102	133	157	75	60	14	6	7	•	•	6
Revenues ($ in Thousands)													
Net Sales **2**	79818836	0	114395	212946	1262953	1295245	2141317	793271	648688	1523944	•	•	6228142
Interest **3**	320439	0	43	17	58	218	1119	2745	61	187	•	•	16604
Rents **4**	27822	0	0	0	674	1472	3284	106	201	361	•	•	5049
Royalties **5**	3436381	0	0	0	8670	0	2682	214	0	1467	•	•	87758
Other Portfolio Income **6**	6260214	0	0	0	1194	807	470	3931	474	7208	•	•	196568
Other Receipts **7**	2060707	0	0	11	73	7479	3480	11442	7534	27421	•	•	113827
Total Receipts **8**	91924399	0	114438	212974	1273622	1305221	2152352	811709	656958	1560588	•	•	6647948
Average Total Receipts **9**	160988	•	1122	1601	8112	17403	35873	57979	109493	222941	•	•	1107991
Operating Costs/Operating Income (%)													
Cost of Operations **10**	41.1	•	73.0	67.7	72.5	44.4	59.8	61.6	59.7	60.6	•	•	42.8
Salaries and Wages **11**	9.0	•	7.0	4.0	5.4	26.3	12.9	11.4	6.3	10.8	•	•	11.8
Taxes Paid **12**	1.9	•	1.4	2.6	1.5	0.4	1.7	1.8	2.0	1.5	•	•	2.0
Interest Paid **13**	3.5	•	•	0.5	0.3	0.3	0.6	0.8	1.0	2.7	•	•	3.8
Depreciation **14**	2.7	•	2.3	1.8	0.3	3.0	2.6	2.0	3.4	2.2	•	•	1.9
Amortization and Depletion **15**	1.7	•	•	0.0	0.0	0.1	0.1	0.4	0.5	1.6	•	•	0.8
Pensions and Other Deferred Comp. **16**	2.3	•	0.9	0.9	1.3	0.1	0.2	0.3	0.1	0.2	•	•	0.8
Employee Benefits **17**	1.7	•	0.3	2.4	1.9	1.0	1.5	1.1	2.0	0.1	•	•	1.9
Advertising **18**	7.7	•	0.0	0.1	0.2	0.1	2.8	2.4	1.4	1.1	•	•	6.5
Other Expenses **19**	19.8	•	8.2	10.5	10.5	13.7	11.1	12.3	14.2	14.5	•	•	22.7
Officers' Compensation **20**	0.8	•	3.7	7.0	2.8	2.2	2.1	2.4	3.9	1.0	•	•	1.7
Operating Margin **21**	7.8	•	3.3	2.4	3.3	8.3	4.5	3.6	5.6	3.6	•	•	3.3
Operating Margin Before Officers' Comp. **22**	8.6	•	6.9	9.3	6.0	10.5	6.6	6.1	9.5	4.6	•	•	5.0

Selected Average Balance Sheet ($ in Thousands)

Net Receivables 23	53600	100	136	765	1368	3745	9489	21363	38587	66472
Inventories 24	15119	55	96	1038	1700	3423	6363	20208	30035	139949
Net Property, Plant and Equipment 25	22504	7	79	483	3550	4016	6091	16316	23612	118234
Total Assets 26	394448	493	726	2887	7374	15674	35254	68588	177287	1142144
Notes and Loans Payable 27	96070	0	149	356	564	4123	10095	20362	88222	503450
All Other Liabilities 28	99785	29	54	582	2469	4620	10659	20998	36639	316685
Net Worth 29	198593	464	523	1949	4341	6932	14500	27228	52426	322009

Selected Financial Ratios (Times to 1)

Current Ratio 30	1.0	16.4	8.3	3.3	1.6	1.6	1.9	1.6	1.5	2.0
Quick Ratio 31	0.7	14.4	4.8	1.6	0.7	0.9	1.0	1.0	1.0	0.7
Net Sales to Working Capital 32	213.9	2.5	3.0	5.2	13.6	10.5	6.1	7.6	7.9	5.3
Coverage Ratio 33	8.5	•	5.6	14.7	35.4	9.6	8.8	8.3	3.3	3.9
Total Asset Turnover 34	0.4	2.3	2.2	2.8	2.3	2.3	1.6	1.6	1.2	0.9
Inventory Turnover 35	3.8	14.9	11.3	5.6	4.5	6.2	5.5	3.2	4.4	3.2
Receivables Turnover 36	2.6	11.9	16.1	8.8	9.8	9.9	7.2	3.8	5.3	•
Total Liabilities to Net Worth 37	1.0	0.1	0.4	0.5	0.7	1.3	1.4	1.5	2.4	2.5
Current Assets to Working Capital 38	129.3	1.1	1.1	1.4	2.6	2.8	2.1	2.8	2.9	2.0
Current Liabilities to Working Capital 39	128.3	0.1	0.1	0.4	1.6	1.8	1.1	1.8	1.9	1.0
Working Capital to Net Sales 40	0.0	0.4	0.3	0.2	0.1	0.1	0.2	0.1	0.1	0.2
Inventory to Working Capital 41	25.2	0.1	0.2	0.6	1.3	1.1	0.8	0.9	0.9	0.7
Total Receipts to Cash Flow 42	2.7	11.7	11.0	9.8	5.0	7.0	6.2	5.2	5.5	3.5
Cost of Goods to Cash Flow 43	1.1	8.6	7.4	7.1	2.2	4.2	3.8	3.1	3.3	1.5
Cash Flow to Total Debt 44	0.3	3.2	0.7	0.9	1.1	0.6	0.4	0.5	0.3	0.4

Selected Financial Factors (in Percentages)

Debt Ratio 45	49.7	6.0	28.0	32.5	41.1	55.8	58.9	60.3	70.4	71.8
Return on Total Assets 46	10.6	7.6	6.4	12.3	21.8	12.7	10.8	12.4	10.7	13.5
Return on Equity Before Income Taxes 47	18.5	8.0	7.3	17.0	35.9	25.8	23.3	27.5	24.9	35.6
Return on Equity After Income Taxes 48	12.3	8.0	6.1	14.6	35.5	21.7	19.7	21.0	21.5	24.1
Profit Margin (Before Income Tax) 49	26.3	3.3	2.4	4.1	9.0	5.0	6.0	6.9	6.0	11.0
Profit Margin (After Income Tax) 50	17.4	3.3	2.0	3.5	8.9	4.2	5.0	5.3	5.2	7.5

Table I

Corporations with and without Net Income

CHEMICAL PRODUCT AND PREPARATION

MONEY AMOUNTS AND SIZE OF ASSETS IN THOUSANDS OF DOLLARS

Item Description for Accounting Period 7/09 Through 6/10	Total	Zero Assets	Under 500	500 to 1,000	1,000 to 5,000	5,000 to 10,000	10,000 to 25,000	25,000 to 50,000	50,000 to 100,000	100,000 to 250,000	250,000 to 500,000	500,000 to 2,500,000	2,500,000 and over
Number of Enterprises 1	1754	•	•	•	197	160	116	84	42	25	14	12	11
Revenues ($ in Thousands)													
Net Sales 2	74935495	•	•	•	961537	1702939	3118062	4224195	4183336	4402293	4550362	11709835	38012221
Interest 3	496955	•	•	•	1626	1165	4067	2909	4135	10099	6313	52867	413326
Rents 4	38843	•	•	•	428	3960	48	111	27	301	993	2059	28452
Royalties 5	471425	•	•	•	0	1	0	13015	1304	42333	6792	20809	387171
Other Portfolio Income 6	770766	•	•	•	97	1454	2902	1371	3699	10131	25096	376824	347363
Other Receipts 7	1422186	•	•	•	30119	10832	38114	30867	22278	41670	27104	441113	744751
Total Receipts 8	78135670	•	•	•	993807	1720351	3163193	4272468	4214779	4506827	4616660	12603507	39933284
Average Total Receipts 9	44547	•	•	•	5045	10752	27269	50863	100352	180273	329761	1050292	3630299
Operating Costs/Operating Income (%)													
Cost of Operations 10	68.1	•	•	•	56.6	63.4	67.0	68.1	77.1	66.3	72.3	65.9	68.4
Salaries and Wages 11	7.1	•	•	•	8.5	9.8	8.5	8.0	6.5	8.3	6.1	5.8	7.1
Taxes Paid 12	1.3	•	•	•	2.1	1.9	1.6	1.5	1.2	1.5	1.3	1.6	1.0
Interest Paid 13	3.0	•	•	•	2.4	1.1	0.7	1.2	1.3	2.0	2.1	2.0	4.2
Depreciation 14	3.7	•	•	•	1.5	2.6	2.0	2.8	2.5	3.9	4.6	3.7	4.2
Amortization and Depletion 15	1.2	•	•	•	1.4	0.1	0.2	0.4	0.4	0.9	1.2	0.8	1.7
Pensions and Other Deferred Comp. 16	0.6	•	•	•	0.5	0.6	0.4	0.3	0.5	0.9	0.3	1.6	0.4
Employee Benefits 17	1.1	•	•	•	2.4	1.8	0.8	0.7	1.1	1.4	1.4	2.0	0.9
Advertising 18	0.6	•	•	•	0.1	2.2	0.9	0.6	0.5	0.6	0.3	1.6	0.2
Other Expenses 19	11.0	•	•	•	34.5	12.5	11.9	14.0	7.4	11.0	9.3	11.5	10.2
Officers' Compensation 20	0.9	•	•	•	5.6	3.5	2.1	2.2	1.3	1.2	0.7	1.0	0.2
Operating Margin 21	1.4	•	•	•	•	0.6	3.8	0.3	0.2	2.1	0.5	2.5	1.5
Operating Margin Before Officers' Comp. 22	2.3	•	•	•	•	4.2	5.9	2.4	1.5	3.3	1.2	3.5	1.7

Selected Average Balance Sheet ($ in Thousands)

Net Receivables 23	8301	520	1354	3630	6693	14932	24837	76773	140723	833440
Inventories 24	6289	672	1095	3442	5598	14847	31925	56746	164298	505266
Net Property, Plant and Equipment 25	10315	485	1620	3496	8433	15278	39190	85243	236706	990286
Total Assets 26	62609	2214	6912	15355	35292	71853	174085	350356	1230659	6915852
Notes and Loans Payable 27	17886	975	2695	2662	10738	21764	52851	131228	368248	1907399
All Other Liabilities 28	19315	558	1488	3916	9723	18506	46188	93134	392422	2207170
Net Worth 29	25407	681	2728	8777	14830	31584	75047	125994	469988	2801283

Selected Financial Ratios (Times to 1)

Current Ratio 30	1.3	2.9	1.9	2.3	1.9	2.1	1.4	1.5	1.3	1.2
Quick Ratio 31	0.7	1.8	1.0	1.3	1.1	1.1	0.7	0.9	0.8	0.6
Net Sales to Working Capital 32	7.3	4.7	6.0	4.6	5.0	4.4	7.6	7.0	8.9	8.2
Coverage Ratio 33	3.1	*	2.6	8.5	2.2	1.8	3.5	2.0	6.2	2.7
Total Asset Turnover 34	0.7	2.2	1.5	1.8	1.4	1.4	1.0	0.9	0.8	0.5
Inventory Turnover 35	4.6	4.1	6.2	5.2	6.1	5.2	3.7	4.1	3.9	4.7
Receivables Turnover 36	5.2	5.3	10.1	7.0	8.9	7.4	7.0	3.7	6.1	4.3
Total Liabilities to Net Worth 37	1.5	2.2	1.5	0.7	1.4	1.3	1.3	1.8	1.6	1.5
Current Assets to Working Capital 38	3.9	1.5	2.2	1.8	2.1	1.9	3.7	3.2	4.0	5.3
Current Liabilities to Working Capital 39	2.9	0.5	1.2	0.8	1.1	0.9	2.7	2.2	3.0	4.3
Working Capital to Net Sales 40	0.1	0.2	0.2	0.2	0.2	0.2	0.1	0.1	0.1	0.1
Inventory to Working Capital 41	1.0	0.5	0.8	0.6	0.7	0.6	1.3	1.0	1.1	1.2
Total Receipts to Cash Flow 42	7.1	17.2	8.2	6.5	7.6	14.6	7.3	11.2	5.4	7.0
Cost of Goods to Cash Flow 43	4.8	9.7	5.2	4.4	5.2	11.3	4.8	8.1	3.6	4.8
Cash Flow to Total Debt 44	0.2	0.2	0.3	0.6	0.3	0.2	0.2	0.1	0.2	0.1

Selected Financial Factors (in Percentages)

Debt Ratio 45	59.4	69.2	60.5	42.8	58.0	56.0	56.9	64.0	61.8	59.5
Return on Total Assets 46	6.2	*	4.2	10.4	3.7	3.3	7.0	3.8	10.1	5.7
Return on Equity Before Income Taxes 47	10.3	*	6.5	16.1	4.8	3.4	11.6	5.3	22.3	8.9
Return on Equity After Income Taxes 48	6.4	*	4.8	13.4	1.3	*	8.8	1.0	14.6	5.5
Profit Margin (Before Income Tax) 49	6.1	*	1.7	5.2	1.4	1.1	4.9	2.1	10.7	7.2
Profit Margin (After Income Tax) 50	3.8	*	1.2	4.4	0.4	*	3.8	0.4	7.0	4.5

93

Table II

Corporations with Net Income

CHEMICAL PRODUCT AND PREPARATION

MONEY AMOUNTS AND SIZE OF ASSETS IN THOUSANDS OF DOLLARS

Item Description for Accounting Period 7/09 Through 6/10	Total	Zero Assets	Under 500	500 to 1,000	1,000 to 5,000	5,000 to 10,000	10,000 to 25,000	25,000 to 50,000	50,000 to 100,000	100,000 to 250,000	250,000 to 500,000	500,000 to 2,500,000	2,500,000 and over
Number of Enterprises **1**	1403	•	•	227	161	116	96	46	•	•	7	•	8
Revenues ($ in Thousands)													
Net Sales **2**	6241106	•	•	164714	778450	1340378	2707953	2981670	•	•	2697086	•	33288239
Interest **3**	422722	•	•	47	667	963	3585	880	•	•	4098	•	369337
Rents **4**	36860	•	•	2049	428	3960	48	81	•	•	513	•	27507
Royalties **5**	433453	•	•	0	0	0	0	0	•	•	421	•	383350
Other Portfolio Income **6**	746228	•	•	1667	7	1085	972	996	•	•	18288	•	341424
Other Receipts **7**	1123768	•	•	1092	578	2315	43702	20184	•	•	9220	•	550295
Total Receipts **8**	65174137	•	•	169569	780130	1348701	2756260	3003811	•	•	2729626	•	34960152
Average Total Receipts **9**	46453	•	•	747	4846	11627	28711	65300	•	•	389947	•	4370019
Operating Costs/Operating Income (%)													
Cost of Operations **10**	67.2	•	•	60.3	52.7	65.1	65.0	65.2	•	•	67.1	•	68.6
Salaries and Wages **11**	6.9	•	•	5.7	5.9	7.6	7.9	7.3	•	•	7.7	•	6.9
Taxes Paid **12**	1.3	•	•	1.7	1.8	1.7	1.5	1.3	•	•	1.6	•	1.1
Interest Paid **13**	2.4	•	•	1.6	0.3	0.7	0.5	0.5	•	•	1.0	•	3.4
Depreciation **14**	3.4	•	•	0.6	1.3	1.5	1.9	2.2	•	•	3.4	•	4.0
Amortization and Depletion **15**	1.0	•	•	•	0.1	0.0	0.2	0.1	•	•	1.0	•	1.4
Pensions and Other Deferred Comp. **16**	0.6	•	•	1.9	0.6	0.6	0.5	0.4	•	•	0.2	•	0.3
Employee Benefits **17**	1.1	•	•	1.0	2.5	1.3	0.6	0.5	•	•	1.2	•	0.9
Advertising **18**	0.6	•	•	0.7	0.1	2.7	0.9	0.4	•	•	0.2	•	0.2
Other Expenses **19**	10.6	•	•	19.7	22.7	9.5	11.6	14.0	•	•	9.1	•	9.8
Officers' Compensation **20**	0.8	•	•	6.4	4.5	3.9	2.0	1.7	•	•	0.6	•	0.1
Operating Margin **21**	4.2	•	•	0.4	7.6	5.2	7.4	6.4	•	•	6.9	•	3.3
Operating Margin Before Officers' Comp. **22**	5.0	•	•	6.7	12.1	9.1	9.4	8.1	•	•	7.5	•	3.4

Selected Average Balance Sheet ($ in Thousands)

Net Receivables 23	8907	177	573	1165	3743	7487	87171	1067110
Inventories 24	6184	158	716	960	3239	5989	64520	575060
Net Property, Plant and Equipment 25	9919	36	575	1561	3566	8758	99389	1094195
Total Assets 26	63365	783	2314	6989	15272	35887	346840	8119174
Notes and Loans Payable 27	13572	152	144	1519	2580	7372	99765	1600030
All Other Liabilities 28	20338	52	487	1001	3685	11009	91801	2722350
Net Worth 29	29455	578	1683	4469	9007	17506	155274	3796794

Selected Financial Ratios (Times to 1)

Current Ratio 30	1.4	4.1	3.0	2.1	2.8	1.8	1.4	1.3
Quick Ratio 31	0.8	2.5	1.7	1.2	1.6	1.0	0.8	0.7
Net Sales to Working Capital 32	6.8	1.9	4.6	6.4	4.3	6.5	8.9	6.3
Coverage Ratio 33	4.9	3.0	31.5	9.1	18.5	14.6	9.5	3.7
Total Asset Turnover 34	0.7	0.9	2.1	1.7	1.8	1.8	1.1	0.5
Inventory Turnover 35	4.8	2.8	3.6	7.8	5.7	7.1	4.0	5.0
Receivables Turnover 36	5.2	6.9	4.6	12.2	7.7	10.6	3.7	4.3
Total Liabilities to Net Worth 37	1.2	0.4	0.4	0.6	0.7	1.0	1.2	1.1
Current Assets to Working Capital 38	3.6	1.3	1.5	1.9	1.6	2.2	3.7	4.2
Current Liabilities to Working Capital 39	2.6	0.3	0.5	0.9	0.6	1.2	2.7	3.2
Working Capital to Net Sales 40	0.1	0.5	0.2	0.2	0.2	0.2	0.1	0.2
Inventory to Working Capital 41	0.9	0.5	0.6	0.7	0.5	0.7	1.1	0.9
Total Receipts to Cash Flow 42	6.0	5.1	3.7	7.0	5.3	5.2	6.8	6.4
Cost of Goods to Cash Flow 43	4.0	3.1	1.9	4.5	3.4	3.4	4.6	4.4
Cash Flow to Total Debt 44	0.2	0.7	2.1	0.7	0.9	0.7	0.3	0.2

Selected Financial Factors (in Percentages)

Debt Ratio 45	53.5	26.1	27.3	36.1	41.0	51.2	55.2	53.2
Return on Total Assets 46	8.1	4.6	16.9	10.9	17.9	13.8	10.3	6.3
Return on Equity Before Income Taxes 47	13.9	4.2	22.5	15.2	28.7	26.3	20.6	9.9
Return on Equity After Income Taxes 48	9.6	3.7	16.7	13.8	25.6	21.0	13.6	6.4
Profit Margin (Before Income Tax) 49	9.2	3.3	7.8	5.9	9.2	7.1	8.3	9.0
Profit Margin (After Income Tax) 50	6.3	3.0	5.8	5.3	8.2	5.7	5.5	5.8

Table I

Corporations with and without Net Income

PLASTICS PRODUCT

MONEY AMOUNTS AND SIZE OF ASSETS IN THOUSANDS OF DOLLARS

Item Description for Accounting Period 7/09 Through 6/10		Total	Zero Assets	Under 500	500 to 1,000	1,000 to 5,000	5,000 to 10,000	10,000 to 25,000	25,000 to 50,000	50,000 to 100,000	100,000 to 250,000	250,000 to 500,000	500,000 to 2,500,000	2,500,000 and over
Number of Enterprises	1	9438	1382	3517	944	2174	631	353	185	104	92	21	30	4
Revenues ($ in Thousands)														
Net Sales	2	98413876	2179006	1748436	1627706	9945701	7393391	9067741	9080078	9739960	15284537	7306047	18012621	7028653
Interest	3	213423	369	320	1269	14928	2742	2627	11194	19706	39291	15047	88772	17159
Rents	4	33493	11	0	212	1398	4742	1198	3412	1701	4339	5225	11255	0
Royalties	5	149573	0	0	0	96	64	246	615	7980	5455	45640	64314	25163
Other Portfolio Income	6	511508	16794	3193	19577	7081	2374	37837	4783	36090	55656	134652	175099	18370
Other Receipts	7	774492	3897	36755	4052	91161	21163	85853	37208	56326	189243	58030	175616	15187
Total Receipts	8	100096365	2200077	1788704	1652816	10060365	7424476	9195502	9137290	9861763	15578521	7564641	18527677	7104532
Average Total Receipts	9	10606	1592	509	1751	4628	11766	26050	49391	94825	169332	360221	617589	1776133
Operating Costs/Operating Income (%)														
Cost of Operations	10	71.1	90.3	55.7	64.4	67.3	68.4	69.6	70.3	70.9	72.8	71.4	74.8	68.4
Salaries and Wages	11	5.8	2.3	7.2	7.7	5.8	7.1	6.8	6.9	6.9	5.0	6.0	4.6	4.9
Taxes Paid	12	1.5	0.9	2.5	3.0	2.0	1.7	1.6	1.6	1.3	1.4	1.4	1.2	0.6
Interest Paid	13	2.5	0.9	1.1	0.7	1.1	0.9	1.8	1.5	1.7	2.3	4.0	4.1	6.1
Depreciation	14	4.3	0.9	3.2	3.7	3.0	3.4	3.8	4.5	3.8	4.7	4.5	5.6	4.5
Amortization and Depletion	15	0.7	0.2	1.0	0.0	0.4	0.2	0.4	0.6	0.8	0.7	1.0	0.9	1.0
Pensions and Other Deferred Comp.	16	0.4	0.0	0.1	0.1	0.4	0.5	0.3	0.4	0.4	0.4	0.7	0.4	0.6
Employee Benefits	17	1.7	0.4	1.5	1.3	1.4	1.5	1.7	1.9	1.8	1.8	2.2	1.3	3.3
Advertising	18	0.4	0.1	0.6	0.5	0.3	0.6	0.3	0.4	0.6	0.4	0.3	0.3	0.1
Other Expenses	19	9.5	6.2	25.3	17.4	11.9	10.5	9.2	8.5	9.3	8.7	10.0	7.4	9.2
Officers' Compensation	20	1.7	0.7	5.8	6.1	5.4	3.2	2.0	1.3	0.9	0.8	0.9	0.5	0.2
Operating Margin	21	0.4	•	•	•	0.9	2.0	2.6	2.1	1.6	0.8	•	•	1.0
Operating Margin Before Officers' Comp.	22	2.1	•	1.9	1.3	6.3	5.2	4.6	3.4	2.5	1.6	•	•	1.2

Selected Average Balance Sheet ($ in Thousands)

Net Receivables 23	1451	0	50	176	548	1468	3391	6526	13418	21100	41184	114639	297169
Inventories 24	1222	0	18	127	491	1234	3445	6212	13010	22552	41373	71904	170073
Net Property, Plant and Equipment 25	2351	0	35	169	551	2146	5156	12050	19006	45455	91193	169453	535873
Total Assets 26	10093	0	210	775	2089	6839	15713	35358	70270	147766	341631	828137	4980506
Notes and Loans Payable 27	4002	0	94	418	970	1991	5314	10777	22149	52707	123349	369201	2247111
All Other Liabilities 28	2427	0	50	191	528	1681	5519	9791	15700	35178	99120	229088	689912
Net Worth 29	3664	0	67	165	591	3167	4880	14790	32420	59880	119162	229848	2043483

Selected Financial Ratios (Times to 1)

Current Ratio 30	1.6	•	1.2	2.1	1.8	1.7	1.4	1.7	1.9	1.7	1.9	1.4	1.4
Quick Ratio 31	0.9	•	0.8	1.5	1.1	1.0	0.8	0.9	1.0	0.9	1.0	0.9	0.7
Net Sales to Working Capital 32	7.7	22.3	6.3	7.8	7.7	9.9	7.1	5.9	6.9	6.7	8.2	7.5	
Coverage Ratio 33	1.9	•	•	2.8	3.8	3.3	2.9	2.7	2.2	1.6	1.6	1.3	
Total Asset Turnover 34	1.0	•	2.4	2.2	2.2	1.7	1.6	1.4	1.3	1.1	1.0	0.7	0.4
Inventory Turnover 35	6.1	•	15.4	8.8	6.3	6.5	5.2	5.6	5.1	5.4	6.0	6.2	7.1
Receivables Turnover 36	7.0	•	13.4	7.8	7.7	6.9	7.0	7.6	6.6	7.1	8.4	5.2	7.7
Total Liabilities to Net Worth 37	1.8	•	2.2	3.7	2.5	2.3	2.4	1.4	1.2	1.5	1.9	2.6	1.4
Current Assets to Working Capital 38	2.7	•	5.3	1.9	2.3	2.4	3.4	2.5	2.1	2.5	2.1	3.5	3.6
Current Liabilities to Working Capital 39	1.7	•	4.3	0.9	1.3	1.4	2.4	1.5	1.1	1.5	1.5	2.5	2.6
Working Capital to Net Sales 40	0.1	•	0.0	0.2	0.1	0.8	0.1	0.1	0.2	0.1	0.1	0.1	0.1
Inventory to Working Capital 41	0.9	•	0.8	0.5	0.8	1.2	0.9	0.7	0.9	0.7	1.0	0.8	
Total Receipts to Cash Flow 42	11.2	77.8	6.7	18.9	10.4	9.9	9.5	11.3	10.0	10.7	12.9	13.5	11.2
Cost of Goods to Cash Flow 43	8.0	70.2	3.7	12.2	7.0	6.8	6.6	8.0	7.1	7.8	9.2	10.1	7.7
Cash Flow to Total Debt 44	0.1	•	0.5	0.1	0.3	0.3	0.2	0.2	0.2	0.2	0.1	0.1	0.1

Selected Financial Factors (in Percentages)

Debt Ratio 45	63.7	•	68.3	78.7	71.7	53.7	68.9	58.2	53.9	59.5	65.1	72.2	59.0
Return on Total Assets 46	5.1	•	•	•	7.1	5.8	9.4	5.9	6.2	5.6	6.5	4.7	2.9
Return on Equity Before Income Taxes 47	6.7	•	•	•	16.1	9.1	20.9	9.2	8.6	7.4	7.0	6.1	1.8
Return on Equity After Income Taxes 48	5.1	•	•	•	14.8	8.2	19.0	7.6	7.0	5.6	3.6	4.2	1.1
Profit Margin (Before Income Tax) 49	2.4	•	•	•	2.1	2.5	4.0	2.8	3.0	2.7	2.4	2.3	2.1
Profit Margin (After Income Tax) 50	1.8	•	•	•	1.9	2.2	3.6	2.3	2.4	2.0	1.2	1.6	1.3

Table II
Corporations with Net Income

PLASTICS PRODUCT

MONEY AMOUNTS AND SIZE OF ASSETS IN THOUSANDS OF DOLLARS

Item Description for Accounting Period 7/09 Through 6/10	Total	Zero Assets	Under 500	500 to 1,000	1,000 to 5,000	5,000 to 10,000	10,000 to 25,000	25,000 to 50,000	50,000 to 100,000	100,000 to 250,000	250,000 to 500,000	500,000 to 2,500,000	2,500,000 and over
Number of Enterprises 1	5761	187	2452	619	1644	358	225	117	73	54	10	•	
Revenues ($ in Thousands)													
Net Sales 2	68010298	377048	1328476	850556	7565518	4417921	6307871	6589635	7255795	9740266	3976944	•	•
Interest 3	76962	43	9	812	2705	2479	1651	5933	6582	12057	9469	•	•
Rents 4	25109	11	0	212	0	4365	460	2071	779	1211	4988	•	•
Royalties 5	105742	0	0	0	0	0	0	570	7729	992	28624		
Other Portfolio Income 6	447411	13409	1372	19577	5587	359	14458	2625	34838	40285	130359	•	•
Other Receipts 7	468788	1209	34814	4484	20753	8583	48859	20969	44928	141906	32388	•	•
Total Receipts 8	69134310	391720	1364671	875641	7594563	4433707	6373299	6621803	7350651	9936717	4182772	•	•
Average Total Receipts 9	12000	2095	557	1415	4620	12385	28326	56597	100694	184013	418277	•	•
Operating Costs/Operating Income (%)													
Cost of Operations 10	68.8	62.9	54.0	52.5	66.0	65.8	68.4	67.5	69.5	71.1	69.9	•	•
Salaries and Wages 11	5.6	6.3	6.2	8.7	5.1	5.7	6.2	7.0	6.8	4.9	7.0	•	•
Taxes Paid 12	1.5	4.0	2.8	2.9	2.1	1.7	1.4	1.5	1.2	1.5	1.5	•	•
Interest Paid 13	2.1	0.6	0.4	1.0	0.6	0.9	1.1	1.0	1.2	1.7	2.8	•	•
Depreciation 14	4.0	3.5	3.6	5.1	1.8	4.1	3.3	3.5	3.6	4.4	4.2	•	•
Amortization and Depletion 15	0.5	0.0	0.2	0.0	0.1	0.1	0.2	0.2	0.5	0.6	0.9	•	•
Pensions and Other Deferred Comp. 16	0.4	0.2	0.1	0.1	0.4	0.7	0.3	0.5	0.4	0.4	0.5	•	•
Employee Benefits 17	1.8	1.2	0.8	2.2	1.3	1.6	1.6	1.9	1.6	1.6	2.8	•	•
Advertising 18	0.3	0.1	0.2	0.6	0.3	0.3	0.3	0.5	0.5	0.5	0.1	•	•
Other Expenses 19	8.5	17.1	20.2	15.4	9.8	9.0	8.1	8.3	8.6	7.1	9.7	•	•
Officers' Compensation 20	1.8	0.7	4.2	10.5	5.7	3.0	2.1	1.4	1.0	0.8	0.7	•	•
Operating Margin 21	4.8	3.4	7.4	1.0	6.7	7.2	7.1	6.8	5.1	5.3	•	•	•
Operating Margin Before Officers' Comp. 22	6.6	4.1	11.6	11.5	12.4	10.2	9.1	8.2	6.1	6.1	0.7	•	•

Selected Average Balance Sheet ($ in Thousands)

Net Receivables 23	1552	0	61	134	560	1340	3638	6964	14159	23311	50667
Inventories 24	1227	0	13	91	501	1251	3403	6980	12818	21021	36523
Net Property, Plant and Equipment 25	2468	0	46	168	423	2659	4790	11549	19033	45088	84838
Total Assets 26	10519	0	259	759	1994	6951	15746	35769	70018	146320	326849
Notes and Loans Payable 27	4123	0	67	139	611	1774	4469	8678	16557	46353	101217
All Other Liabilities 28	2465	0	55	127	508	1541	3598	7786	15207	35226	84482
Net Worth 29	3931	0	138	494	875	3636	7679	19306	38254	64741	141149

Selected Financial Ratios (Times to 1)

Current Ratio 30	1.8	•	2.0	3.6	2.1	1.9	2.1	2.3	2.0	2.0	1.9
Quick Ratio 31	1.1	•	1.5	2.8	1.3	1.1	1.2	1.3	1.1	1.1	1.1
Net Sales to Working Capital 32	6.2	•	7.8	3.8	6.4	7.5	5.8	5.1	5.8	5.6	6.1
Coverage Ratio 33	4.2	12.2	28.0	5.0	13.3	9.3	8.1	8.3	6.6	5.4	3.7
Total Asset Turnover 34	1.1	•	2.1	1.8	2.3	1.8	1.8	1.6	1.4	1.2	1.2
Inventory Turnover 35	6.6	•	22.3	7.9	6.1	6.5	5.6	5.4	5.4	6.1	7.6
Receivables Turnover 36	7.8	•	•	6.3	7.3	7.6	7.4	7.9	7.4	•	8.9
Total Liabilities to Net Worth 37	1.7	•	0.9	0.5	1.3	0.9	1.1	0.9	0.8	1.3	1.3
Current Assets to Working Capital 38	2.2	•	2.0	1.4	1.9	2.1	1.9	1.8	2.0	2.0	2.1
Current Liabilities to Working Capital 39	1.2	•	1.0	0.4	0.9	1.1	0.9	0.8	1.0	1.0	1.1
Working Capital to Net Sales 40	0.2	•	0.1	0.3	0.2	0.1	0.2	0.2	0.2	0.2	0.2
Inventory to Working Capital 41	0.7	•	0.2	0.3	0.6	0.7	0.7	0.6	0.7	0.7	0.6
Total Receipts to Cash Flow 42	8.1	6.6	4.6	9.6	7.4	7.2	7.1	7.6	7.6	7.9	9.7
Cost of Goods to Cash Flow 43	5.5	4.1	2.5	5.0	4.9	4.7	4.9	5.1	5.3	5.6	6.8
Cash Flow to Total Debt 44	0.2	1.0	0.5	0.5	0.6	0.5	0.5	0.5	0.4	0.3	0.2

Selected Financial Factors (in Percentages)

Debt Ratio 45	62.6	•	46.8	35.0	56.1	47.7	51.2	46.0	45.4	55.8	56.8
Return on Total Assets 46	9.8	•	22.0	8.9	17.6	15.0	16.5	12.9	10.9	11.0	12.5
Return on Equity Before Income Taxes 47	20.0	•	39.9	11.0	37.1	25.6	29.7	21.1	17.0	20.3	21.0
Return on Equity After Income Taxes 48	17.6	•	39.8	9.5	36.0	24.2	27.7	19.1	15.1	17.4	15.0
Profit Margin (Before Income Tax) 49	6.6	7.2	10.1	4.0	7.1	7.6	8.1	7.2	6.5	7.3	7.4
Profit Margin (After Income Tax) 50	5.8	6.2	10.1	3.4	6.8	7.1	7.6	6.6	5.8	6.2	5.3

Table I

Corporations with and without Net Income

RUBBER PRODUCT

MONEY AMOUNTS AND SIZE OF ASSETS IN THOUSANDS OF DOLLARS

Item Description for Accounting Period 7/09 Through 6/10	Total	Zero Assets	Under 500	500 to 1,000	1,000 to 5,000	5,000 to 10,000	10,000 to 25,000	25,000 to 50,000	50,000 to 100,000	100,000 to 250,000	250,000 to 500,000	500,000 to 2,500,000	2,500,000 and over
Number of Enterprises 1	916	27	495	48	158	69	59	13	22	9	3	10	3
Revenues ($ in Thousands)													
Net Sales 2	44356456	363872	189947	140709	595742	1334416	1488069	710059	1940705	1124024	1341506	10334694	24792714
Interest 3	216221	863	0	47	1127	388	517	675	2125	3848	1508	39819	165304
Rents 4	14386	0	0	0	0	0	103	179	2824	504	645	1863	8268
Royalties 5	455664	0	0	0	0	0	0	1372	1	3942	1015	46776	402559
Other Portfolio Income 6	618540	24978	0	0	1023	248	28907	3373	3917	923	5734	225536	323900
Other Receipts 7	232297	11138	0	297	1860	12952	15099	1243	6717	7369	3710	26247	145664
Total Receipts 8	45893564	400851	189947	141053	599752	1348004	1532695	716901	1956289	1140610	1354118	10674935	25838409
Average Total Receipts 9	50102	14846	384	2939	3796	19536	25978	55146	88922	126734	451373	1067494	8612803
Operating Costs/Operating Income (%)													
Cost of Operations 10	69.0	68.5	75.4	76.3	69.0	69.7	69.5	71.6	73.6	70.8	68.2	74.5	66.0
Salaries and Wages 11	6.6	6.1	7.8	5.9	6.9	9.1	6.9	7.9	7.0	6.5	4.3	5.0	7.2
Taxes Paid 12	1.6	0.6	1.6	1.7	1.9	1.7	2.1	1.7	1.6	1.5	2.7	0.6	1.9
Interest Paid 13	1.8	1.6	1.9	0.2	2.8	0.3	0.9	2.6	2.3	3.2	1.0	2.1	1.7
Depreciation 14	3.7	5.7	1.2	0.8	2.9	0.7	5.1	3.1	3.6	5.4	1.1	3.5	3.9
Amortization and Depletion 15	1.0	1.1	•	0.0	0.0	0.0	0.3	1.0	1.0	1.9	1.2	0.7	1.2
Pensions and Other Deferred Comp. 16	2.4	0.3	•	0.0	0.3	0.4	0.3	0.2	0.7	1.0	0.9	1.9	3.4
Employee Benefits 17	3.7	1.9	0.4	1.7	2.2	1.7	2.4	2.3	2.6	1.7	1.3	4.0	4.3
Advertising 18	1.3	0.6	1.1	0.0	0.3	2.2	0.5	0.1	0.5	0.1	1.3	0.8	1.7
Other Expenses 19	10.8	28.0	13.3	9.4	14.9	5.5	8.2	7.7	6.8	9.4	9.1	8.4	12.5
Officers' Compensation 20	0.6	•	2.2	2.8	2.9	5.8	1.8	1.4	1.0	0.5	0.8	0.4	0.1
Operating Margin 21	•	•	•	1.1	•	2.8	1.0	1.3	0.3	•	8.0	•	•
Operating Margin Before Officers' Comp. 22	•	•	•	3.9	•	8.7	2.9	2.7	1.3	•	8.7	•	•

Selected Average Balance Sheet ($ in Thousands)

Net Receivables 23	6613	0	22	300	787	1929	4151	8492	11217	17246	65608	147856	1113865
Inventories 24	7712	0	11	883	1008	1279	3326	11220	11989	22398	70164	138601	1454891
Net Property, Plant and Equipment 25	10039	0	73	121	425	1349	4294	10269	19880	34347	39065	236462	1792760
Total Assets 26	45185	0	280	997	2247	6296	15012	41296	69949	157878	305244	1251225	7534330
Notes and Loans Payable 27	14351	0	83	116	1176	1168	2690	25126	30365	52446	59764	394446	2361073
All Other Liabilities 28	20569	0	104	229	796	1783	5296	9548	16684	47592	147698	441176	4147640
Net Worth 29	10265	0	92	652	274	3345	7027	6623	22900	57839	97781	415602	1025617

Selected Financial Ratios (Times to 1)

Current Ratio 30	1.4	•	1.7	2.5	1.8	2.6	2.3	1.1	2.0	1.4	1.3	1.0	1.5
Quick Ratio 31	0.8	•	1.5	1.0	0.9	1.7	1.4	0.6	1.0	0.6	0.7	0.6	0.8
Net Sales to Working Capital 32	10.6	•	14.4	5.5	4.7	6.8	4.7	26.0	5.7	9.1	11.7	57.0	9.1
Coverage Ratio 33	1.7	•	•	6.7	•	15.6	5.5	1.9	1.5	1.1	9.5	2.3	1.1
Total Asset Turnover 34	1.1	•	1.4	2.9	1.7	3.1	1.7	1.3	1.3	0.8	1.5	0.8	1.1
Inventory Turnover 35	4.3	•	26.2	2.5	2.6	10.5	5.3	3.5	5.4	3.9	4.3	5.6	3.8
Receivables Turnover 36	6.5	•	24.4	7.6	3.1	13.4	6.2	5.5	7.2	4.9	7.5	7.6	6.1
Total Liabilities to Net Worth 37	3.4	•	2.0	0.5	7.2	0.9	1.1	5.2	2.1	1.7	2.1	2.0	6.3
Current Assets to Working Capital 38	3.7	•	2.5	1.6	2.2	1.6	1.8	9.4	2.0	3.5	3.9	23.2	3.0
Current Liabilities to Working Capital 39	2.7	•	1.5	0.6	1.2	0.6	0.8	8.4	1.0	2.5	2.9	22.2	2.0
Working Capital to Net Sales 40	0.1	•	0.1	0.2	0.2	0.1	0.2	0.0	0.2	0.1	0.1	0.0	0.1
Inventory to Working Capital 41	1.4	•	0.3	0.9	0.9	0.5	0.6	4.2	0.7	1.0	1.7	7.3	1.3
Total Receipts to Cash Flow 42	11.8	7.6	18.5	18.9	12.2	12.3	10.9	13.3	16.7	14.7	5.9	12.2	11.9
Cost of Goods to Cash Flow 43	8.1	5.2	14.0	14.4	8.4	8.6	7.5	9.5	12.3	10.4	4.0	9.1	7.9
Cash Flow to Total Debt 44	0.1	•	0.1	0.4	0.2	0.5	0.3	0.1	0.1	0.1	0.4	0.1	0.1

Selected Financial Factors (in Percentages)

Debt Ratio 45	77.3	•	67.0	34.6	87.8	46.9	53.2	84.0	67.3	63.4	68.0	66.8	86.4
Return on Total Assets 46	3.3	•	•	4.7	•	12.7	8.2	6.4	4.3	2.7	14.6	3.9	2.1
Return on Equity Before Income Taxes 47	5.9	•	•	6.1	•	22.3	14.4	18.5	4.3	0.4	40.8	6.5	1.8
Return on Equity After Income Taxes 48	4.1	•	•	5.1	•	18.2	14.0	6.6	2.5	•	39.0	4.8	0.3
Profit Margin (Before Income Tax) 49	1.3	•	•	1.3	•	3.9	4.0	2.2	1.1	0.2	8.9	2.6	0.2
Profit Margin (After Income Tax) 50	0.9	•	•	1.1	•	3.1	3.9	0.8	0.7	•	8.5	1.9	0.0

97

Table II
Corporations with Net Income

RUBBER PRODUCT

MONEY AMOUNTS AND SIZE OF ASSETS IN THOUSANDS OF DOLLARS

Item Description for Accounting Period 7/09 Through 6/10	Total	Zero Assets	Under 500	500 to 1,000	1,000 to 5,000	5,000 to 10,000	10,000 to 25,000	25,000 to 50,000	50,000 to 100,000	100,000 to 250,000	250,000 to 500,000	500,000 to 2,500,000	2,500,000 and over
Number of Enterprises 1	343	3	55	•	88	65	47	9	12	5	3	•	0

Revenues ($ in Thousands)

	Total	Zero Assets	Under 500	500 to 1,000	1,000 to 5,000	5,000 to 10,000	10,000 to 25,000	25,000 to 50,000	50,000 to 100,000	100,000 to 250,000	250,000 to 500,000	500,000 to 2,500,000	2,500,000 and over
Net Sales 2	29749802	40865	123151	•	318164	1118700	1255459	535142	1244540	639400	1341506	•	0
Interest 3	111316	0	0	•	3	388	303	72	855	1051	1508	•	0
Rents 4	12974	0	0	•	0	0	103	0	1905	228	645	•	0
Royalties 5	76763	0	0	•	0	0	0	1372	1	0	1015	•	0
Other Portfolio Income 6	414884	5854	•	•	0	176	19994	3044	3558	529	5734	•	0
Other Receipts 7	199608	911	0	•	129	12697	1292	414	3362	6932	3710	•	0
Total Receipts 8	30565347	47630	123151	•	318296	1131961	1277151	540044	1254221	648140	1354118	•	0
Average Total Receipts 9	89112	15877	2239	•	3617	17415	27173	60005	104518	129628	451373	•	•

Operating Costs/Operating Income (%)

	Total	Zero Assets	Under 500	500 to 1,000	1,000 to 5,000	5,000 to 10,000	10,000 to 25,000	25,000 to 50,000	50,000 to 100,000	100,000 to 250,000	250,000 to 500,000	500,000 to 2,500,000	2,500,000 and over
Cost of Operations 10	67.5	76.9	91.4	•	65.1	68.0	67.4	72.3	69.8	68.6	68.2	•	•
Salaries and Wages 11	6.2	0.8	4.9	•	6.1	9.5	6.9	6.6	6.6	6.8	4.3	•	•
Taxes Paid 12	1.5	1.6	0.6	•	1.9	1.8	1.8	1.5	1.5	1.7	2.7	•	•
Interest Paid 13	1.2	0.9	0.0	•	2.5	0.3	0.7	1.5	1.9	2.8	1.0	•	•
Depreciation 14	3.4	1.5	0.1	•	1.2	0.7	5.1	2.6	3.6	3.4	1.1	•	•
Amortization and Depletion 15	0.3	0.0	•	•	0.0	0.0	0.2	0.6	1.2	1.6	1.2	•	•
Pensions and Other Deferred Comp. 16	2.3	•	•	•	0.2	0.5	0.3	0.2	1.1	0.9	0.9	•	•
Employee Benefits 17	3.4	0.1	•	•	2.1	1.7	2.0	2.0	3.1	2.3	1.3	•	•
Advertising 18	1.5	•	0.0	•	0.4	0.0	0.5	0.1	0.5	0.0	1.3	•	•
Other Expenses 19	10.7	16.5	2.3	•	12.6	5.5	7.1	7.5	6.2	8.9	9.1	•	•
Officers' Compensation 20	0.7	•	0.3	•	3.6	6.7	1.7	1.2	0.9	0.5	0.8	•	•
Operating Margin 21	1.3	1.7	0.5	•	4.3	5.1	6.3	4.0	3.7	2.6	8.0	•	•
Operating Margin Before Officers' Comp. 22	2.0	1.7	0.8	•	7.9	11.9	8.0	5.2	4.5	3.0	8.7	•	•

Selected Average Balance Sheet ($ in Thousands)

Net Receivables 23	15523	0	184	•	600	1972	4425	9628	11925	17410	65608
Inventories 24	8888	0	29	•	1259	1278	3364	9221	11209	12405	64988
Net Property, Plant and Equipment 25	16313	0	1	•	215	1117	4208	9613	21782	21672	39065
Total Assets 26	77742	0	223	•	2162	6189	14602	39501	77778	168035	305244
Notes and Loans Payable 27	19135	0	3	•	864	1240	2435	13213	30993	47546	59764
All Other Liabilities 28	36254	0	227	•	845	1476	3391	8649	18318	56949	147698
Net Worth 29	22354	0	-8	•	453	3473	8776	17639	28466	63539	97781

Selected Financial Ratios (Times to 1)

Current Ratio 30	1.3	•	1.0	•	2.0	3.2	2.5	1.7	2.1	1.1	1.3
Quick Ratio 31	0.7	•	0.8	•	0.7	2.1	1.6	0.8	1.2	0.5	0.7
Net Sales to Working Capital 32	11.9	•	•	•	3.8	5.3	4.8	7.0	6.3	28.2	11.7
Coverage Ratio 33	4.7	20.7	106.0	•	2.7	20.9	12.0	4.4	3.3	2.8	9.5
Total Asset Turnover 34	1.1	•	10.0	•	1.7	2.8	1.8	1.5	1.3	0.8	1.5
Inventory Turnover 35	6.6	•	71.2	•	1.9	9.2	5.4	4.7	6.5	7.1	4.7
Receivables Turnover 36	8.4	•	•	•	2.7	12.1	6.3	7.5	9.6	•	13.6
Total Liabilities to Net Worth 37	2.5	•	•	•	3.8	0.8	0.7	1.2	1.7	1.6	2.1
Current Assets to Working Capital 38	4.5	•	•	•	2.0	1.5	1.7	2.5	2.0	10.4	3.9
Current Liabilities to Working Capital 39	3.5	•	•	•	1.0	0.5	0.7	1.5	1.0	9.4	2.9
Working Capital to Net Sales 40	0.1	•	•	•	0.3	0.2	0.2	0.1	0.2	0.0	0.1
Inventory to Working Capital 41	1.7	•	•	•	1.1	0.4	0.6	1.2	0.7	2.7	1.7
Total Receipts to Cash Flow 42	8.4	3.2	52.2	•	7.3	9.5	8.4	10.3	11.3	9.4	5.9
Cost of Goods to Cash Flow 43	5.7	2.5	47.7	•	4.8	6.5	5.7	7.5	7.9	6.5	4.0
Cash Flow to Total Debt 44	0.2	0.2	•	•	0.3	0.7	0.5	0.3	0.2	0.1	0.4

Selected Financial Factors (in Percentages)

Debt Ratio 45	71.2	•	103.4	•	79.1	43.9	39.9	55.3	63.4	62.2	68.0
Return on Total Assets 46	6.3	•	5.2	•	11.4	18.4	15.9	9.6	8.5	5.9	14.6
Return on Equity Before Income Taxes 47	17.3	•	•	•	34.6	31.3	24.3	16.6	16.2	10.0	40.8
Return on Equity After Income Taxes 48	15.1	•	•	•	33.3	27.0	24.0	10.1	13.5	7.1	39.0
Profit Margin (Before Income Tax) 49	4.5	18.2	0.5	•	4.3	6.3	8.0	4.9	4.4	5.0	8.9
Profit Margin (After Income Tax) 50	3.9	12.0	0.5	•	4.2	5.4	7.9	3.0	3.7	3.5	8.5

Table I

Corporations with and without Net Income

CLAY, REFRACTORY AND OTHER NONMETALLIC MINERAL PRODUCT

MONEY AMOUNTS AND SIZE OF ASSETS IN THOUSANDS OF DOLLARS

Item Description for Accounting Period 7/09 Through 6/10	Total	Zero Assets	Under 500	500 to 1,000	1,000 to 5,000	5,000 to 10,000	10,000 to 25,000	25,000 to 50,000	50,000 to 100,000	100,000 to 250,000	250,000 to 500,000	500,000 to 2,500,000	2,500,000 and over
Number of Enterprises **1**	2132	12	1424	360	207	12	51	23	16	14	6	8	0
Revenues ($ in Thousands)													
Net Sales **2**	15052652	426232	907736	691453	1094009	302825	982471	744286	977410	1512739	1787611	5625881	0
Interest **3**	68175	5289	742	49	548	6	362	189	1094	3472	3333	53092	0
Rents **4**	3388	0	0	0	0	0	47	95	42	268	99	2835	0
Royalties **5**	46527	0	0	0	0	0	607	101	141	1756	822	43100	0
Other Portfolio Income **6**	110916	34703	33	1126	668	0	221	239	558	863	1460	71046	0
Other Receipts **7**	313307	14592	2679	11452	284	654	16055	1677	9148	9808	24719	222237	0
Total Receipts **8**	15594965	480816	911190	704080	1095509	303485	999763	746587	988393	1528906	1818044	6018191	0
Average Total Receipts **9**	7315	40068	640	1956	5292	25290	19603	32460	61775	109208	303007	752274	•
Operating Costs/Operating Income (%)													
Cost of Operations **10**	67.3	72.1	53.1	52.9	69.9	76.8	69.9	67.3	69.3	65.1	70.2	68.9	•
Salaries and Wages **11**	7.8	6.6	8.3	6.4	7.2	4.2	5.9	8.8	8.3	9.9	7.4	8.0	•
Taxes Paid **12**	1.8	2.1	2.9	3.0	2.3	2.5	1.8	2.3	1.5	1.8	0.9	1.5	•
Interest Paid **13**	2.0	2.6	0.5	0.2	0.5	0.4	0.9	1.5	2.1	1.6	2.2	3.0	•
Depreciation **14**	5.1	18.3	2.7	0.5	1.8	1.2	4.0	6.7	5.5	5.5	3.6	6.3	•
Amortization and Depletion **15**	0.6	0.8	•	0.3	0.1	0.0	0.9	0.6	0.6	0.3	0.6	0.8	•
Pensions and Other Deferred Comp. **16**	1.1	0.3	5.4	0.4	0.1	0.6	0.3	0.6	0.4	0.6	0.7	1.3	•
Employee Benefits **17**	1.6	0.9	0.1	1.9	0.7	0.4	1.5	1.4	1.3	3.0	1.7	1.8	•
Advertising **18**	0.9	1.1	0.2	1.1	0.0	0.0	0.9	0.3	0.5	1.1	0.9	1.2	•
Other Expenses **19**	11.6	8.8	19.2	15.9	14.1	3.8	9.6	10.2	11.4	11.0	12.3	10.5	•
Officers' Compensation **20**	2.2	1.3	7.8	12.7	3.2	2.6	3.1	2.3	1.1	1.2	0.4	0.7	•
Operating Margin **21**	•	•	•	4.7	0.0	7.6	1.1	•	•	•	•	•	•
Operating Margin Before Officers' Comp. **22**	0.3	•	7.6	17.4	3.2	10.2	4.2	0.2	•	0.3	•	•	•

Selected Average Balance Sheet ($ in Thousands)

Net Receivables 23	866	0	5	165	459	3144	2431	5749	12773	15747	56715	78143	•
Inventories 24	1333	0	38	192	498	1673	4274	10324	16827	36058	51200	132372	•
Net Property, Plant and Equipment 25	2662	0	39	153	747	2220	5253	13795	25287	48981	88959	396608	•
Total Assets 26	9096	0	160	688	2441	8553	14747	35798	74725	141270	312659	1460548	•
Notes and Loans Payable 27	3144	0	69	79	1254	2097	4999	12712	26265	27715	89256	550238	•
All Other Liabilities 28	2833	0	35	69	918	2371	3871	7498	21134	31868	85205	510181	•
Net Worth 29	3119	0	56	541	270	4084	5877	15587	27326	81687	138198	400129	•

Selected Financial Ratios (Times to 1)

Current Ratio 30	2.1	•	3.0	5.4	1.5	2.5	2.0	2.1	2.1	2.8	2.9	1.8	•
Quick Ratio 31	1.0	•	2.3	4.1	1.0	1.7	0.9	1.1	1.0	1.2	1.5	0.8	•
Net Sales to Working Capital 32	4.3	•	8.3	5.0	10.9	6.8	5.2	4.3	3.3	2.4	3.0	4.6	•
Coverage Ratio 33	1.9	0.2	1.3	36.4	1.4	22.9	4.3	•	0.6	1.1	1.6	2.1	
Total Asset Turnover 34	0.8	•	4.0	2.8	2.2	3.0	1.3	0.9	0.8	0.8	1.0	0.5	•
Inventory Turnover 35	3.6	•	8.9	5.3	7.4	11.6	3.2	2.1	2.5	1.9	4.1	3.7	•
Receivables Turnover 36	6.8	•	135.1	9.9	10.2	13.9	6.4	4.3	4.9	5.7	6.3	6.0	•
Total Liabilities to Net Worth 37	1.9	•	1.9	0.3	8.1	1.1	1.5	1.3	1.7	0.7	1.3	2.7	•
Current Assets to Working Capital 38	1.9	•	1.5	1.2	3.0	1.7	2.0	1.9	1.9	1.6	1.5	2.2	•
Current Liabilities to Working Capital 39	0.9	•	0.5	0.2	2.0	0.7	1.0	0.9	0.9	0.6	0.5	1.2	•
Working Capital to Net Sales 40	0.2	•	0.1	0.2	0.1	0.1	0.2	0.2	0.3	0.4	0.3	0.2	•
Inventory to Working Capital 41	0.7	•	0.3	0.3	0.8	0.5	1.1	0.8	0.8	0.6	0.6	0.7	•
Total Receipts to Cash Flow 42	10.0	27.3	8.6	5.4	8.6	9.1	9.9	15.5	13.6	11.1	8.8	10.6	
Cost of Goods to Cash Flow 43	6.8	19.7	4.6	2.8	6.0	7.0	6.9	10.4	9.4	7.3	6.2	7.3	
Cash Flow to Total Debt 44	0.1	•	0.7	2.4	0.3	0.6	0.2	0.1	0.1	0.2	0.2	0.1	•

Selected Financial Factors (in Percentages)

Debt Ratio 45	65.7	•	64.9	21.5	89.0	52.2	60.1	56.5	63.4	42.2	55.8	72.6	•
Return on Total Assets 46	3.0	•	2.4	18.7	1.4	24.2	4.9	•	1.0	1.4	3.3	3.0	•
Return on Equity Before Income Taxes 47	4.2	•	1.6	23.2	3.5	48.5	9.3	•	•	0.2	2.6	5.7	•
Return on Equity After Income Taxes 48	2.6	•	1.6	22.9	2.5	45.4	8.3	•	•	•	1.9	3.6	•
Profit Margin (Before Income Tax) 49	1.8	•	0.1	6.5	0.2	7.8	2.9	•	•	0.2	1.2	3.3	•
Profit Margin (After Income Tax) 50	1.1	•	0.1	6.4	0.1	7.4	2.5	•	•	•	0.9	2.0	•

Table II

Corporations with Net Income

CLAY, REFRACTORY AND OTHER NONMETALLIC MINERAL PRODUCT

MONEY AMOUNTS AND SIZE OF ASSETS IN THOUSANDS OF DOLLARS

Item Description for Accounting Period 7/09 Through 6/10	Total	Zero Assets	Under 500	500 to 1,000	1,000 to 5,000	5,000 to 10,000	10,000 to 25,000	25,000 to 50,000	50,000 to 100,000	100,000 to 250,000	250,000 to 500,000	500,000 to 2,500,000	2,500,000 and over
Number of Enterprises 1	1005	9	362	360	202	•	29	10	7	7	•	4	0
Revenues ($ in Thousands)													
Net Sales 2	10189901	130	277293	691453	1083548	•	696838	408558	590046	823220	•	4312445	0
Interest 3	37627	12	667	49	548	•	227	173	832	1630	•	32225	0
Rents 4	2886	0	0	0	0	•	47	15	42	268	•	2414	0
Royalties 5	41330	0	0	0	0	•	207	101	141	0	•	40609	0
Other Portfolio Income 6	92371	33161	0	1126	668	•	148	191	25	798	•	54794	0
Other Receipts 7	257760	14020	283	11452	243	•	14223	1381	2388	4856	•	204965	0
Total Receipts 8	10621875	47323	278243	704080	1085007	•	711690	410419	593474	830772	•	4647452	0
Average Total Receipts 9	10569	5258	769	1956	5371	•	24541	41042	84782	118682	•	1161863	•
Operating Costs/Operating Income (%)													
Cost of Operations 10	65.8	23.8	22.0	52.9	69.8	•	66.8	71.0	65.7	68.9	•	67.9	•
Salaries and Wages 11	7.3	52.3	11.6	6.4	7.2	•	5.7	6.1	6.6	7.3	•	7.9	•
Taxes Paid 12	1.9	0.8	4.5	3.0	2.3	•	1.9	1.9	1.6	1.9	•	1.5	•
Interest Paid 13	1.8	8.5	0.9	0.2	0.5	•	0.8	1.0	0.8	0.7	•	3.2	•
Depreciation 14	4.1	•	7.0	0.5	1.8	•	3.7	4.7	3.1	3.0	•	5.1	•
Amortization and Depletion 15	0.5	•	•	0.3	0.0	•	1.0	0.3	0.3	0.5	•	0.5	•
Pensions and Other Deferred Comp. 16	0.8	•	0.0	0.4	0.1	•	0.4	0.8	0.5	0.8	•	1.2	•
Employee Benefits 17	1.4	•	•	1.9	0.7	•	1.3	1.5	1.1	2.5	•	1.4	•
Advertising 18	0.9	•	0.3	1.1	0.0	•	1.1	0.4	0.5	1.2	•	1.4	•
Other Expenses 19	10.0	473.8	34.0	15.9	13.1	•	8.7	6.2	8.5	8.1	•	8.1	•
Officers' Compensation 20	2.3	•	8.3	12.7	3.2	•	3.1	3.1	1.1	1.2	•	0.5	•
Operating Margin 21	3.2	•	11.4	4.7	1.3	•	5.5	3.1	10.1	4.0	•	1.2	•
Operating Margin Before Officers' Comp. 22	5.5	•	19.7	17.4	4.4	•	8.6	6.2	11.3	5.3	•	1.7	•

Selected Average Balance Sheet ($ in Thousands)

Net Receivables 23	1022	0	0	165	464	•	2749	7339	19960	16800	•	74896
Inventories 24	1526	0	39	191	310	•	5141	15368	12417	32089	•	133409
Net Property, Plant and Equipment 25	3769	0	125	153	741	•	5516	14807	18270	40099	•	578688
Total Assets 26	12539	0	222	688	2463	•	16341	37659	75958	157000	•	1987704
Notes and Loans Payable 27	3383	0	135	79	1275	•	3554	5701	14416	26191	•	606649
All Other Liabilities 28	3106	0	15	69	847	•	2822	6588	11940	24452	•	552921
Net Worth 29	6050	0	72	541	341	•	9964	25370	49602	106357	•	828134

Selected Financial Ratios (Times to 1)

Current Ratio 30	2.2	•	5.6	5.4	1.6	•	2.4	3.6	4.0	3.2	•	1.6
Quick Ratio 31	1.1	•	3.8	4.1	1.2	•	1.1	2.0	2.5	1.6	•	0.7
Net Sales to Working Capital 32	5.0	•	11.2	5.0	9.2	•	4.5	3.1	2.7	2.2	•	8.4
Coverage Ratio 33	5.3	4236.9	14.0	36.4	3.9	•	9.9	4.6	14.3	7.8	•	3.9
Total Asset Turnover 34	0.8	•	3.5	2.8	2.2	•	1.5	1.1	1.1	0.7	•	0.5
Inventory Turnover 35	4.4	•	4.3	5.3	12.1	•	3.1	1.9	4.5	2.5	•	5.5
Receivables Turnover 36	7.5	•	12056.2	10.2	12.3	•	6.2	3.2	•	7.2	•	7.7
Total Liabilities to Net Worth 37	1.1	•	2.1	0.3	6.2	•	0.6	0.5	0.5	0.5	•	1.4
Current Assets to Working Capital 38	1.8	•	1.2	1.2	2.6	•	1.7	1.4	1.3	1.5	•	2.7
Current Liabilities to Working Capital 39	0.8	•	0.2	0.2	1.6	•	0.7	0.4	0.3	0.5	•	1.7
Working Capital to Net Sales 40	0.2	•	0.1	0.2	0.1	•	0.2	0.3	0.4	0.5	•	0.1
Inventory to Working Capital 41	0.7	•	0.4	0.3	0.7	•	0.9	0.6	0.4	0.5	•	1.2
Total Receipts to Cash Flow 42	7.1	0.0	3.4	5.4	7.9	•	7.1	11.1	5.7	8.7	•	7.9
Cost of Goods to Cash Flow 43	4.7	0.0	0.7	2.8	5.5	•	4.7	7.9	3.7	6.0	•	5.4
Cash Flow to Total Debt 44	0.2	•	1.5	2.4	0.3	•	0.5	0.3	0.6	0.3	•	0.1

Selected Financial Factors (in Percentages)

Debt Ratio 45	51.8	•	67.5	21.5	86.2	•	39.0	32.6	34.7	32.3	•	58.3
Return on Total Assets 46	7.6	•	43.7	18.7	4.1	•	12.4	4.9	12.8	4.3	•	6.8
Return on Equity Before Income Taxes 47	12.8	•	125.1	23.2	21.9	•	18.3	5.7	18.2	5.5	•	12.2
Return on Equity After Income Taxes 48	11.1	•	125.0	22.9	21.1	•	17.2	4.2	13.4	5.0	•	10.1
Profit Margin (Before Income Tax) 49	7.7	35842.3	11.8	6.5	1.4	•	7.6	3.5	10.7	5.0	•	9.4
Profit Margin (After Income Tax) 50	6.6	35840.8	11.8	6.4	1.3	•	7.1	2.6	7.9	4.5	•	7.8

Table I

Corporations with and without Net Income

GLASS AND GLASS PRODUCT

MONEY AMOUNTS AND SIZE OF ASSETS IN THOUSANDS OF DOLLARS

Item Description for Accounting Period 7/09 Through 6/10	Total	Zero Assets	Under 500	500 to 1,000	1,000 to 5,000	5,000 to 10,000	10,000 to 25,000	25,000 to 50,000	50,000 to 100,000	100,000 to 250,000	250,000 to 500,000	500,000 to 2,500,000	2,500,000 and over
Number of Enterprises 1	1903	330	1086	47	290	101	16	10	5	8	0	6	3
Revenues ($ in Thousands)													
Net Sales 2	20630264	4767	543542	55818	1129898	1311810	664775	353189	375906	1610072	0	4295166	10285320
Interest 3	69973	18	0	148	951	67	465	598	1288	3194	0	25260	37983
Rents 4	5493	0	0	0	0	292	575	163	480	6	0	660	3316
Royalties 5	903681	0	0	0	0	0	0	0	0	12	0	12899	890770
Other Portfolio Income 6	310475	0	0	0	161	5	1066	1179	182	21864	0	17733	268281
Other Receipts 7	328969	0	2477	35	1704	3914	3462	1595	1508	39222	0	172426	102632
Total Receipts 8	22248855	4785	546019	56001	1132714	1316088	670343	356724	379364	1674370	0	4524144	11588302
Average Total Receipts 9	11691	14	503	1192	3906	13031	41896	35672	75873	209296	•	754024	3862767
Operating Costs/Operating Income (%)													
Cost of Operations 10	67.7	•	42.0	29.9	64.8	65.1	81.8	77.5	66.2	72.4	•	74.1	65.3
Salaries and Wages 11	5.9	•	14.9	33.5	9.0	6.4	4.0	4.7	5.4	7.0	•	6.0	4.8
Taxes Paid 12	1.7	0.2	3.1	5.0	1.7	2.7	1.8	2.2	2.0	1.5	•	1.6	1.6
Interest Paid 13	2.4	•	0.4	2.4	1.1	0.8	0.8	3.0	3.5	4.3	•	2.5	2.6
Depreciation 14	4.4	•	0.4	1.2	2.4	4.4	2.5	3.9	3.1	5.5	•	7.5	3.6
Amortization and Depletion 15	0.9	•	•	0.2	0.0	0.0	0.1	0.3	0.6	1.1	•	0.5	1.5
Pensions and Other Deferred Comp. 16	1.9	•	•	•	0.0	0.1	0.1	0.2	0.4	0.2	•	1.2	3.2
Employee Benefits 17	2.5	•	0.3	5.1	1.0	1.5	2.0	0.7	3.6	1.9	•	2.5	3.0
Advertising 18	0.3	4.7	2.2	•	0.1	0.0	0.1	0.3	0.2	0.4	•	0.1	0.3
Other Expenses 19	16.9	388.3	20.2	15.0	13.0	14.6	5.5	12.5	8.4	9.3	•	9.4	22.8
Officers' Compensation 20	1.5	•	14.0	8.3	6.0	2.2	1.4	1.9	1.0	0.7	•	0.9	0.6
Operating Margin 21	•	•	2.5	•	0.7	2.1	•	•	5.6	•	•	•	•
Operating Margin Before Officers' Comp. 22	•	•	16.5	7.8	6.7	4.3	1.2	•	6.6	•	•	•	•

Selected Average Balance Sheet ($ in Thousands)

Net Receivables 23	2622	0	24	101	780	1291	4160	6872	15532	35533	76108	1216289
Inventories 24	1482	0	104	634	527	1465	4298	6975	15272	25441	199823	424099
Net Property, Plant and Equipment 25	4470	0	11	181	341	2466	5931	7944	20182	69635	307828	1819249
Total Assets 26	33169	0	172	606	1912	6608	15795	35708	79258	239169	956632	17674543
Notes and Loans Payable 27	5484	0	350	253	1090	5034	4125	11950	41666	118436	266743	2092826
All Other Liabilities 28	6218	0	45	143	243	1673	5547	9312	11805	83531	299858	2943056
Net Worth 29	21466	0	-223	210	578	-99	6123	14445	25788	37203	390031	12638661

Selected Financial Ratios (Times to 1)

Current Ratio 30	1.2	•	3.5	1.3	4.1	1.3	1.2	1.6	2.5	1.2	1.4	1.1
Quick Ratio 31	0.8	•	1.3	0.8	2.9	0.5	0.9	0.9	1.6	0.7	0.6	0.8
Net Sales to Working Capital 32	11.6	•	4.4	12.5	3.2	15.7	27.4	4.8	2.9	16.6	10.7	21.3
Coverage Ratio 33	1.8	•	9.2	0.9	1.9	3.9	1.8	•	2.9	0.9	0.6	2.5
Total Asset Turnover 34	0.3	•	2.9	2.0	2.0	2.0	2.6	1.0	0.9	0.8	0.7	0.2
Inventory Turnover 35	5.0	•	2.0	0.6	4.8	5.8	7.9	3.9	3.3	5.7	2.7	5.3
Receivables Turnover 36	5.9	•	21.0	2.8	5.4	10.9	7.3	5.5	5.1	6.6	5.9	5.6
Total Liabilities to Net Worth 37	0.5	•	•	1.9	2.3	•	1.6	1.5	2.1	5.4	1.5	0.4
Current Assets to Working Capital 38	6.4	•	1.4	4.5	1.3	4.5	5.7	2.6	1.7	7.5	3.8	15.5
Current Liabilities to Working Capital 39	5.4	•	0.4	3.5	0.3	3.5	4.7	1.6	0.7	6.5	2.8	14.5
Working Capital to Net Sales 40	0.1	•	0.2	0.1	0.3	0.1	0.0	0.2	0.3	0.1	0.1	0.0
Inventory to Working Capital 41	1.5	•	0.9	0.5	0.4	2.3	1.4	0.8	0.6	2.7	1.5	2.6
Total Receipts to Cash Flow 42	6.7	1.0	6.3	10.4	11.2	8.9	22.9	25.2	7.9	20.6	15.4	4.5
Cost of Goods to Cash Flow 43	4.5	•	2.6	3.1	7.3	5.8	18.8	19.5	5.2	14.9	11.4	2.9
Cash Flow to Total Debt 44	0.1	•	0.2	0.3	0.3	0.2	0.2	0.1	0.2	0.0	0.1	0.2

Selected Financial Factors (in Percentages)

Debt Ratio 45	35.3	•	229.6	65.4	69.7	101.5	61.2	59.5	67.5	84.4	59.2	28.5
Return on Total Assets 46	1.4	•	9.6	4.3	4.2	6.3	3.8	•	9.4	3.3	1.1	1.2
Return on Equity Before Income Taxes 47	1.0	•	•	•	6.5	•	4.2	•	19.0	•	•	1.0
Return on Equity After Income Taxes 48	0.8	•	•	•	5.2	•	•	•	15.4	•	•	0.9
Profit Margin (Before Income Tax) 49	1.9	•	2.9	1.0	1.0	2.4	0.6	•	6.5	•	•	3.9
Profit Margin (After Income Tax) 50	1.5	•	2.9	0.8	0.8	2.3	•	•	5.3	•	•	3.4

Table II

Corporations with Net Income

GLASS AND GLASS PRODUCT

MONEY AMOUNTS AND SIZE OF ASSETS IN THOUSANDS OF DOLLARS

Item Description for Accounting Period 7/09 Through 6/10	Total	Zero Assets	Under 500	500 to 1000	1,000 to 5,000	5,000 to 10,000	10,000 to 25,000	25,000 to 50,000	50,000 to 100,000	100,000 to 250,000	250,000 to 500,000	500,000 to 2,500,000	2,500,000 and over
Number of Enterprises **1**	1099	•	478	0	161	•	16	0	•	5	0	6	0
Revenues ($ in Thousands)													
Net Sales **2**	15410744	•	203665	0	796535	•	759283	0	•	999871	0	11042332	0
Interest **3**	38128	•	0	0	950	•	342	0	•	2816	0	32704	0
Rents **4**	2375	•	0	0	0	•	575	0	•	6	0	1033	0
Royalties **5**	830780	•	0	0	0	•	0	0	•	0	0	830780	0
Other Portfolio Income **6**	274874	•	0	0	107	•	1064	0	•	8516	0	264999	0
Other Receipts **7**	197787	•	0	0	260	•	3676	0	•	37152	0	153256	0
Total Receipts **8**	16754688	•	203665	0	797852	•	764940	0	•	1048361	0	12325104	0
Average Total Receipts **9**	15245	•	426	•	4956	•	47809	•	•	209672	•	2054184	•
Operating Costs/Operating Income (%)													
Cost of Operations **10**	66.0	•	51.2	•	67.0	•	81.7	•	•	68.4	•	65.1	•
Salaries and Wages **11**	5.6	•	10.2	•	10.5	•	2.8	•	•	6.8	•	5.2	•
Taxes Paid **12**	1.5	•	2.0	•	1.7	•	1.6	•	•	1.3	•	1.3	•
Interest Paid **13**	1.8	•	0.7	•	0.8	•	0.5	•	•	3.4	•	1.9	•
Depreciation **14**	4.4	•	0.3	•	2.3	•	2.5	•	•	5.3	•	4.7	•
Amortization and Depletion **15**	1.1	•	•	•	0.0	•	0.1	•	•	1.2	•	1.5	•
Pensions and Other Deferred Comp. **16**	2.3	•	•	•	0.0	•	0.1	•	•	0.3	•	3.1	•
Employee Benefits **17**	2.2	•	0.8	•	1.0	•	1.6	•	•	2.7	•	2.4	•
Advertising **18**	0.3	•	3.5	•	0.2	•	0.0	•	•	0.5	•	0.3	•
Other Expenses **19**	16.8	•	11.4	•	8.6	•	3.8	•	•	9.0	•	19.6	•
Officers' Compensation **20**	1.3	•	11.5	•	6.1	•	1.2	•	•	0.9	•	0.8	•
Operating Margin **21**	•	•	8.4	•	1.9	•	4.1	•	•	0.2	•	•	•
Operating Margin Before Officers' Comp. **22**	•	•	20.0	•	7.9	•	5.3	•	•	1.1	•	•	•

Selected Average Balance Sheet ($ in Thousands)

Net Receivables 23	3919	14	712	4985		43423		620532
Inventories 24	1634	15	495	3426		27167		206349
Net Property, Plant and Equipment 25	6060	3	372	6363		62937		983739
Total Assets 26	49854	86	2326	18490		273022		8635721
Notes and Loans Payable 27	5806	5	1081	4607		114118		835287
All Other Liabilities 28	8119	45	241	6880		107030		1334750
Net Worth 29	35929	36	1004	7004		51874		6465684

Selected Financial Ratios (Times to 1)

Current Ratio 30	1.2	1.8	5.0	1.2		1.0		1.1
Quick Ratio 31	0.8	1.7	3.3	0.7		0.7		0.8
Net Sales to Working Capital 32	11.2	11.2	3.9	26.1		83.9		11.9
Coverage Ratio 33	4.2	13.1	3.7	11.7		2.5		4.2
Total Asset Turnover 34	0.3	4.9	2.1	2.6		0.7		0.2
Inventory Turnover 35	5.7	15.0	6.7	11.3		5.0		5.8
Receivables Turnover 36	5.7	14.5	6.7	9.1				5.2
Total Liabilities to Net Worth 37	0.4	1.4	1.3	1.6		4.3		0.3
Current Assets to Working Capital 38	6.6	2.2	1.3	6.0		42.8		8.3
Current Liabilities to Working Capital 39	5.6	1.2	0.3	5.0		41.8		7.3
Working Capital to Net Sales 40	0.1	0.1	0.3	0.0		0.0		0.1
Inventory to Working Capital 41	1.4	0.2	0.4	2.1		11.4		1.5
Total Receipts to Cash Flow 42	5.2	6.8	13.5	13.6		8.8		4.4
Cost of Goods to Cash Flow 43	3.4	3.5	9.0	11.1		6.0		2.9
Cash Flow to Total Debt 44	0.2	1.2	0.3	0.3		0.1		0.2

Selected Financial Factors (in Percentages)

Debt Ratio 45	27.9	58.2	56.8	62.1		81.0		25.1
Return on Total Assets 46	2.1	45.1	5.9	13.6		6.2		1.7
Return on Equity Before Income Taxes 47	2.2	99.6	10.0	32.8		19.6		1.8
Return on Equity After Income Taxes 48	2.0	99.3	8.6	25.3		17.1		1.6
Profit Margin (Before Income Tax) 49	5.7	8.4	2.0	4.8		5.1		6.2
Profit Margin (After Income Tax) 50	5.1	8.4	1.8	3.7		4.4		5.6

Table I

Corporations with and without Net Income

CEMENT, CONCRETE, LIME AND GYPSUM PRODUCT

MONEY AMOUNTS AND SIZE OF ASSETS IN THOUSANDS OF DOLLARS

Item Description for Accounting Period 7/09 Through 6/10	Total	Zero Assets	Under 500	500 to 1,000	1,000 to 5,000	5,000 to 10,000	10,000 to 25,000	25,000 to 50,000	50,000 to 100,000	100,000 to 250,000	250,000 to 500,000	500,000 to 2,500,000	2,500,000 and over
Number of Enterprises 1	4357	825	1392	509	1102	280	122	44	31	18	7	18	9
Revenues ($ in Thousands)													
Net Sales 2	53665699	589627	770194	808152	3967039	3081000	2406950	1802655	1856129	2707728	2112314	8820437	24743473
Interest 3	408294	1920	456	731	6841	3574	3076	1147	1898	4110	4311	120757	259474
Rents 4	53622	529	0	0	3838	986	2277	898	1316	214	8133	12147	23284
Royalties 5	33782	353	0	0	0	0	3	89	1090	469	629	9883	21266
Other Portfolio Income 6	443744	32832	384	19	44957	3500	15051	24965	3135	4684	10068	116073	188078
Other Receipts 7	761392	8208	6909	5678	33560	25546	16249	8349	43409	9491	-20128	142642	481477
Total Receipts 8	55366533	633469	777943	814580	4056235	3114606	2443606	1838103	1906977	2726696	2115327	9221939	25717052
Average Total Receipts 9	12707	768	559	1600	3681	11124	20030	41775	61515	151483	302190	512330	2857450
Operating Costs/Operating Income (%)													
Cost of Operations 10	69.9	75.6	41.5	59.1	66.1	65.3	69.0	69.9	71.7	69.9	76.3	68.7	71.9
Salaries and Wages 11	6.5	2.2	21.7	9.2	6.8	4.9	7.8	6.7	5.6	6.1	3.5	4.8	7.1
Taxes Paid 12	2.2	2.7	5.0	2.2	2.4	2.0	2.5	2.4	1.9	2.5	1.7	1.7	2.3
Interest Paid 13	4.9	4.8	0.9	0.7	1.5	1.6	1.2	1.7	2.1	2.0	1.8	5.8	7.2
Depreciation 14	8.2	15.0	5.3	3.1	3.1	5.5	5.5	7.4	10.2	6.2	4.9	13.1	8.4
Amortization and Depletion 15	1.5	3.3	0.1	0.0	0.1	0.0	0.4	0.6	1.0	0.6	1.0	3.0	1.9
Pensions and Other Deferred Comp. 16	0.8	0.0	0.2	0.6	0.3	0.4	0.6	0.3	0.7	0.6	0.8	1.0	0.9
Employee Benefits 17	2.4	4.2	1.3	2.2	1.8	1.5	2.0	1.7	2.3	3.0	1.8	2.4	2.7
Advertising 18	0.4	0.1	0.2	1.2	1.3	0.2	0.6	0.5	0.5	0.4	1.0	0.2	0.3
Other Expenses 19	12.8	16.3	21.3	13.4	11.8	14.7	11.9	9.2	10.1	8.6	6.4	10.9	14.5
Officers' Compensation 20	1.3	1.1	10.0	4.4	4.5	4.4	2.0	2.3	1.3	0.9	0.8	0.5	0.3
Operating Margin 21	•	•	•	3.6	0.2	•	•	•	•	•	•	•	•
Operating Margin Before Officers' Comp. 22	•	•	2.4	8.0	4.7	3.8	•	•	•	•	0.7	•	•

Selected Average Balance Sheet ($ in Thousands)

Net Receivables **23**	2051	0	30	183	395	2090	2564	6277	10204	21513	42706	109958	467446
Inventories **24**	1548	0	20	88	294	941	2264	4901	7895	14547	33130	72323	394867
Net Property, Plant and Equipment **25**	10657	0	73	263	698	3111	6253	16341	38942	62568	152617	599573	3208925
Total Assets **26**	26526	0	171	680	2163	7592	15344	34738	72896	152013	342438	1161343	8753778
Notes and Loans Payable **27**	12704	0	115	162	1105	3329	4106	11635	26541	43264	74823	349713	4836405
All Other Liabilities **28**	6976	0	65	104	353	1773	2395	5447	12259	33205	58471	274922	2499793
Net Worth **29**	6846	0	-9	414	705	2490	8843	17656	34095	75544	209143	536708	1417580

Selected Financial Ratios (Times to 1)

Current Ratio **30**	1.5	•	1.0	3.6	2.4	1.2	2.0	2.2	1.7	2.2	2.5	1.8	1.3
Quick Ratio **31**	0.9	•	0.7	2.8	1.5	0.9	1.3	1.4	1.1	1.4	1.7	1.0	0.7
Net Sales to Working Capital **32**	7.0	•	9508.6	5.8	5.3	16.7	5.2	4.9	6.0	4.5	3.9	4.3	10.9
Coverage Ratio **33**	•	•	•	7.4	2.6	1.3	•	0.6	•	0.9	1.0	•	•
Total Asset Turnover **34**	0.5	•	3.2	2.3	1.7	1.4	1.3	1.2	0.8	1.0	0.9	0.4	0.3
Inventory Turnover **35**	5.6	•	11.3	10.7	8.1	7.6	6.0	5.8	5.4	7.2	6.9	4.7	5.0
Receivables Turnover **36**	5.0	•	13.2	8.0	8.2	5.4	6.4	5.8	4.9	6.2	5.1	4.8	4.3
Total Liabilities to Net Worth **37**	2.9	•	•	0.6	2.1	2.0	0.7	1.0	1.1	1.0	0.6	1.2	5.2
Current Assets to Working Capital **38**	2.9	•	1333.7	1.4	1.7	5.4	2.0	1.8	2.5	1.8	1.7	2.2	4.6
Current Liabilities to Working Capital **39**	1.9	•	1332.7	0.4	0.7	4.4	1.0	0.8	1.5	0.8	0.7	1.2	3.6
Working Capital to Net Sales **40**	0.1	•	0.0	0.2	0.2	0.1	0.2	0.2	0.2	0.2	0.3	0.2	0.1
Inventory to Working Capital **41**	0.8	•	329.5	0.3	0.4	1.3	0.6	0.5	0.7	0.4	0.3	0.6	1.4
Total Receipts to Cash Flow **42**	75.6	•	9.8	8.0	9.6	9.2	15.7	23.7	40.5	16.5	23.0	•	•
Cost of Goods to Cash Flow **43**	52.8	•	4.1	4.7	6.4	6.0	10.8	16.6	29.0	11.6	17.5	•	•
Cash Flow to Total Debt **44**	0.0	•	0.3	0.7	0.3	0.2	0.2	0.1	0.0	0.1	0.1	•	•

Selected Financial Factors (in Percentages)

Debt Ratio **45**	74.2	•	105.5	39.1	67.4	67.2	42.4	49.2	53.2	50.3	38.9	53.8	83.8
Return on Total Assets **46**	•	•	•	11.9	6.6	3.0	•	1.2	•	1.9	1.7	•	•
Return on Equity Before Income Taxes **47**	•	•	387.0	16.8	12.4	2.2	•	•	•	•	•	•	•
Return on Equity After Income Taxes **48**	•	•	391.7	16.6	11.6	1.4	•	•	•	•	0.1	•	•
Profit Margin (Before Income Tax) **49**	•	•	•	4.4	2.4	0.5	•	•	•	•	•	•	•
Profit Margin (After Income Tax) **50**	•	•	•	4.3	2.3	0.3	•	•	•	•	0.1	•	•

Table II
Corporations with Net Income

CEMENT, CONCRETE, LIME AND GYPSUM PRODUCT

MONEY AMOUNTS AND SIZE OF ASSETS IN THOUSANDS OF DOLLARS

Item Description for Accounting Period 7/09 Through 6/10		Total	Zero Assets	Under 500	500 to 1,000	1,000 to 5,000	5,000 to 10,000	10,000 to 25,000	25,000 to 50,000	50,000 to 100,000	100,000 to 250,000	250,000 to 500,000	500,000 to 2,500,000	2,500,000 and over
Number of Enterprises	1	2006	•	693	413	631	159	53	22	•	10	•	7	0
Revenues ($ in Thousands)														
Net Sales	2	15438719	•	436752	623123	2291669	2303625	1277634	1045546	•	1707455	•	3563581	0
Interest	3	66331	•	88	175	4479	2251	864	740	•	3371	•	49791	0
Rents	4	14674	•	0	0	633	923	1711	725	•	177	•	2121	0
Royalties	5	7433	•	0	0	0	0	3	0	•	399	•	6036	0
Other Portfolio Income	6	160010	•	384	0	43161	2802	9948	21770	•	914	•	72530	0
Other Receipts	7	146466	•	2185	4698	27816	18407	4954	995	•	3942	•	42263	0
Total Receipts	8	15833633	•	439409	627996	2367758	2328008	1295114	1069776	•	1716258	•	3736322	0
Average Total Receipts	9	7893	•	634	1521	3752	14642	24436	48626	•	171626	•	533760	•
Operating Costs/Operating Income (%)														
Cost of Operations	10	64.6	•	37.1	55.6	61.0	61.8	70.3	67.1	•	69.0	•	63.6	•
Salaries and Wages	11	5.7	•	20.1	8.6	5.5	5.2	6.1	7.7	•	5.3	•	4.9	•
Taxes Paid	12	1.9	•	4.0	2.4	2.0	1.8	1.9	2.7	•	2.5	•	1.1	•
Interest Paid	13	2.4	•	1.3	0.6	0.7	1.8	0.9	0.7	•	1.1	•	6.7	•
Depreciation	14	5.5	•	6.7	3.7	2.7	4.3	3.8	4.6	•	6.0	•	8.6	•
Amortization and Depletion	15	0.7	•	0.0	0.0	0.1	0.0	0.1	0.3	•	0.6	•	2.1	•
Pensions and Other Deferred Comp.	16	0.6	•	•	0.4	0.4	0.4	0.6	0.4	•	0.6	•	0.8	•
Employee Benefits	17	1.7	•	1.1	2.9	2.1	1.7	1.8	1.9	•	2.8	•	0.9	•
Advertising	18	0.7	•	0.1	1.3	2.0	0.2	0.6	0.4	•	0.4	•	0.3	•
Other Expenses	19	10.3	•	24.8	15.7	10.7	16.2	8.7	7.1	•	6.1	•	8.4	•
Officers' Compensation	20	2.5	•	3.8	3.3	5.4	4.3	2.2	2.5	•	0.6	•	0.8	•
Operating Margin	21	3.4	•	0.9	5.3	7.4	2.5	3.0	4.6	•	5.0	•	1.8	•
Operating Margin Before Officers' Comp.	22	5.9	•	4.8	8.7	12.8	6.8	5.2	7.1	•	5.6	•	2.6	•

Selected Average Balance Sheet ($ in Thousands)

Net Receivables 23	989	1	184	348	2266	2910	7184	25320	61314
Inventories 24	1248	14	77	218	1001	2266	6025	16276	211682
Net Property, Plant and Equipment 25	3722	111	258	514	3326	5412	13714	69141	588919
Total Assets 26	8347	178	675	1850	7737	14507	36793	160629	1175425
Notes and Loans Payable 27	2150	125	147	445	4234	3512	5599	28844	305996
All Other Liabilities 28	1994	6	70	331	1699	2934	5326	29218	357637
Net Worth 29	4203	47	457	1074	1803	8061	25868	102566	511792

Selected Financial Ratios (Times to 1)

Current Ratio 30	2.2	1.7	5.1	3.4	1.1	1.8	3.5	2.5	2.0
Quick Ratio 31	1.4	1.1	4.1	2.5	0.8	1.2	2.5	1.7	0.9
Net Sales to Working Capital 32	4.7	43.6	5.0	4.4	31.7	6.6	3.3	3.7	4.0
Coverage Ratio 33	3.6	2.2	11.0	15.8	2.9	5.9	11.1	6.1	2.2
Total Asset Turnover 34	0.9	3.5	2.2	2.0	1.9	1.7	1.3	1.1	0.4
Inventory Turnover 35	4.0	16.3	10.9	10.2	8.9	7.5	5.3	7.2	1.5
Receivables Turnover 36	4.8	194.2	8.9	10.6	6.9	5.9	6.5	•	2.5
Total Liabilities to Net Worth 37	1.0	2.8	0.5	0.7	3.3	0.8	0.4	0.6	1.3
Current Assets to Working Capital 38	1.9	2.5	1.2	1.4	8.7	2.2	1.4	1.7	2.0
Current Liabilities to Working Capital 39	0.9	1.5	0.2	0.4	7.7	1.2	0.4	0.7	1.0
Working Capital to Net Sales 40	0.2	0.0	0.2	0.2	0.0	0.2	0.3	0.3	0.3
Inventory to Working Capital 41	0.5	0.8	0.2	0.3	2.4	0.6	0.3	0.4	0.6
Total Receipts to Cash Flow 42	7.8	5.1	6.7	6.0	6.8	9.4	10.7	10.2	7.8
Cost of Goods to Cash Flow 43	5.1	1.9	3.7	3.6	4.2	6.6	7.2	7.1	4.9
Cash Flow to Total Debt 44	0.2	0.9	1.0	0.8	0.4	0.4	0.4	0.3	0.1

Selected Financial Factors (in Percentages)

Debt Ratio 45	49.6	73.6	32.2	42.0	76.7	44.4	29.7	36.1	56.5
Return on Total Assets 46	8.0	9.9	15.1	22.5	10.0	8.7	9.9	7.0	6.3
Return on Equity Before Income Taxes 47	11.5	20.3	20.2	36.4	28.2	12.9	12.8	9.1	7.8
Return on Equity After Income Taxes 48	9.5	18.4	20.0	35.5	26.8	11.6	10.5	7.4	5.2
Profit Margin (Before Income Tax) 49	6.3	1.5	6.1	10.8	3.5	4.3	6.9	5.5	7.8
Profit Margin (After Income Tax) 50	5.2	1.4	6.1	10.5	3.3	3.9	5.7	4.4	5.2

Table I

Corporations with and without Net Income

IRON, STEEL MILLS AND STEEL PRODUCT

MONEY AMOUNTS AND SIZE OF ASSETS IN THOUSANDS OF DOLLARS

Item Description for Accounting Period 7/09 Through 6/10		Total	Zero Assets	Under 500	500 to 1,000	1,000 to 5,000	5,000 to 10,000	10,000 to 25,000	25,000 to 50,000	50,000 to 100,000	100,000 to 250,000	250,000 to 500,000	500,000 to 2,500,000	2,500,000 and over
Number of Enterprises	1	4172	365	2444	279	602	162	160	58	36	29	14	10	13
Revenues ($ in Thousands)														
Net Sales	2	87881164	63077	2142451	259324	2378462	2085366	3878620	2831688	3594585	5948173	4174053	9960884	50564482
Interest	3	513451	1397	0	313	303	827	1632	7286	2797	25563	21911	23140	428281
Rents	4	49010	0	0	0	0	0	1703	172	905	1834	9862	4744	29790
Royalties	5	142529	0	0	0	0	0	2188	0	1049	247	1817	3425	133803
Other Portfolio Income	6	474537	10053	9903	785	2287	2229	11645	7691	7668	6320	114585	36074	265297
Other Receipts	7	939744	21092	16673	598	27024	884	24148	16400	26988	47877	33137	309550	415372
Total Receipts	8	90000435	95619	2169027	261020	2408076	2089306	3919936	2863237	3663992	6030014	4355365	10337817	51837025
Average Total Receipts	9	21572	262	887	936	4000	12897	24500	49366	100944	207932	311098	1033782	3987463
Operating Costs/Operating Income (%)														
Cost of Operations	10	84.1	39.7	45.3	62.6	75.9	78.5	77.2	77.5	84.5	82.9	92.7	80.3	87.5
Salaries and Wages	11	3.8	8.7	22.6	2.7	7.5	4.6	4.4	5.0	3.9	3.7	2.8	5.0	2.6
Taxes Paid	12	1.1	6.4	2.3	2.4	2.0	1.5	1.4	1.5	0.9	1.1	0.9	0.9	1.1
Interest Paid	13	2.7	14.3	0.6	1.0	0.9	0.6	0.9	2.1	1.1	1.7	1.9	1.4	3.6
Depreciation	14	5.1	7.6	2.7	4.0	3.6	1.8	3.1	3.8	3.1	3.6	4.7	4.2	6.1
Amortization and Depletion	15	0.7	0.6	0.1	0.0	0.0	0.0	0.2	0.4	0.2	0.2	0.5	2.3	0.6
Pensions and Other Deferred Comp.	16	0.8	0.0	0.2	0.5	0.1	0.4	0.6	0.5	0.8	0.4	0.5	1.1	0.9
Employee Benefits	17	2.1	0.3	3.0	3.9	2.3	1.6	1.7	2.1	2.1	1.6	1.3	1.6	2.4
Advertising	18	0.1	0.4	0.1	0.3	0.1	0.1	0.3	0.2	0.1	0.1	0.1	0.1	0.0
Other Expenses	19	7.5	50.3	17.6	22.4	9.7	4.3	6.6	6.7	5.3	6.2	3.6	8.0	7.6
Officers' Compensation	20	0.9	1.0	6.4	3.6	4.4	2.9	2.1	1.3	1.1	0.8	0.7	0.6	0.3
Operating Margin	21	•	•	•	•	•	3.6	1.6	•	•	•	•	•	•
Operating Margin Before Officers' Comp.	22	•	5.7	•	0.2	•	6.5	3.7	0.1	•	•	•	•	•

Selected Average Balance Sheet ($ in Thousands)

Net Receivables 23	3091	0	50	92	436	1486	3319	7288	12489	28704	47303	119020	627249
Inventories 24	4302	0	24	113	738	2108	3479	10354	19856	45161	91060	230922	792942
Net Property, Plant and Equipment 25	8406	0	61	146	594	2110	4334	10333	17008	50168	100889	327083	2010574
Total Assets 26	27400	0	160	755	2237	7243	15609	35411	67650	162277	334039	1126890	6426925
Notes and Loans Payable 27	9762	0	98	235	1077	1418	3504	17070	17963	42178	113916	193527	2507143
All Other Liabilities 28	7775	0	91	72	442	1860	3832	9651	25721	56508	97423	324537	1791008
Net Worth 29	9862	0	-29	448	718	3964	8273	8690	23967	63592	122701	608826	2128775

Selected Financial Ratios (Times to 1)

Current Ratio 30	1.9	•	1.0	2.8	2.0	2.5	1.8	1.8	1.6	2.4	2.0	1.6	2.0
Quick Ratio 31	1.0	•	0.6	1.5	1.0	1.3	1.0	0.8	0.8	1.3	0.8	0.8	1.1
Net Sales to Working Capital 32	4.3	•	•	5.4	5.1	4.5	6.0	5.5	6.8	3.7	3.5	6.0	3.8
Coverage Ratio 33	•	2.6	2.0	•	•	7.6	4.1	1.0	•	0.5	•	•	•
Total Asset Turnover 34	0.8	•	5.5	1.2	1.8	1.8	1.6	1.4	1.5	1.3	0.9	0.9	0.6
Inventory Turnover 35	4.1	•	16.5	5.1	4.1	4.8	5.4	3.7	4.3	3.8	3.0	3.5	4.3
Receivables Turnover 36	5.5	•	23.1	4.2	8.0	7.1	6.4	6.3	7.0	6.7	5.6	5.7	5.0
Total Liabilities to Net Worth 37	1.8	•	•	0.7	2.1	0.8	0.9	3.1	1.8	1.6	1.7	0.9	2.0
Current Assets to Working Capital 38	2.1	•	•	1.5	2.0	1.7	2.2	2.2	2.8	1.7	2.0	2.6	2.0
Current Liabilities to Working Capital 39	1.1	•	•	0.5	1.0	0.7	1.2	1.2	1.8	0.7	1.0	1.6	1.0
Working Capital to Net Sales 40	0.2	•	•	0.2	0.2	0.2	0.2	0.2	0.1	0.3	0.3	0.2	0.3
Inventory to Working Capital 41	0.7	•	•	0.7	1.0	0.7	0.8	1.0	1.1	0.7	0.8	0.9	0.6
Total Receipts to Cash Flow 42	•	•	1.5	7.4	9.6	59.7	14.9	14.8	19.8	46.5	26.8	21.2	•
Cost of Goods to Cash Flow 43	•	•	0.6	3.4	6.0	45.3	11.7	11.4	15.3	39.3	22.2	17.0	•
Cash Flow to Total Debt 44	•	•	0.6	•	0.3	0.0	0.2	0.1	0.0	0.1	0.1	0.1	•

Selected Financial Factors (in Percentages)

Debt Ratio 45	64.0	117.9	40.7	67.9	45.3	47.0	75.5	60.8	64.6	63.3	46.0	66.9	•
Return on Total Assets 46	•	5.9	•	•	7.7	5.5	2.9	1.1	•	•	•	•	•
Return on Equity Before Income Taxes 47	•	•	•	•	12.2	7.8	•	•	•	•	•	•	•
Return on Equity After Income Taxes 48	•	•	•	•	11.1	6.0	•	•	•	•	•	•	•
Profit Margin (Before Income Tax) 49	22.4	0.5	•	•	3.8	2.7	•	•	•	•	•	•	•
Profit Margin (After Income Tax) 50	22.4	0.5	•	•	3.4	2.1	•	•	•	•	•	•	•

Table II

Corporations with Net Income

IRON, STEEL MILLS AND STEEL PRODUCT

MONEY AMOUNTS AND SIZE OF ASSETS IN THOUSANDS OF DOLLARS

Item Description for Accounting Period 7/09 Through 6/10	Total	Zero Assets	Under 500	500 to 1,000	1,000 to 5,000	5,000 to 10,000	10,000 to 25,000	25,000 to 50,000	50,000 to 100,000	100,000 to 250,000	250,000 to 500,000	500,000 to 2,500,000	2,500,000 and over
Number of Enterprises 1	1815	•	1196	157	•	116	117	22	18	14	7	•	0
Revenues ($ in Thousands)													
Net Sales 2	26110323	•	943494	168292	•	1683717	3024175	1511450	1736353	3139147	2242524	•	0
Interest 3	52116	•	0	313	•	749	864	631	2375	5174	18898	•	0
Rents 4	14524	•	0	0	•	0	1703	142	21	1486	9862	•	0
Royalties 5	6540	•	0	0	•	0	2188	0	985	48	0	•	0
Other Portfolio Income 6	184702	•	518	310	•	1776	10735	1889	7437	4111	112265	•	0
Other Receipts 7	463591	•	6718	595	•	3176	21778	10524	15805	43950	16320	•	0
Total Receipts 8	26831796	•	950730	169510	•	1689418	3061443	1524636	1762976	3193916	2399869	•	0
Average Total Receipts 9	14783	•	795	1080	•	14564	26166	69302	97943	228137	342838	•	•
Operating Costs/Operating Income (%)													
Cost of Operations 10	75.0	•	32.0	61.0	•	76.0	74.0	76.9	78.4	78.4	84.6	•	•
Salaries and Wages 11	5.6	•	25.1	1.1	•	4.8	4.2	4.1	4.7	3.5	1.7	•	•
Taxes Paid 12	1.2	•	3.3	3.5	•	1.5	1.3	1.5	1.0	1.1	1.0	•	•
Interest Paid 13	0.9	•	0.8	0.5	•	0.4	0.6	1.1	0.6	0.6	1.2	•	•
Depreciation 14	3.2	•	1.9	4.8	•	1.4	2.6	2.3	2.1	3.3	3.7	•	•
Amortization and Depletion 15	0.5	•	•	•	•	0.0	0.0	0.4	0.1	0.1	0.2	•	•
Pensions and Other Deferred Comp. 16	0.7	•	•	0.8	•	0.5	0.6	0.2	0.9	0.3	0.9	•	•
Employee Benefits 17	1.8	•	3.3	5.7	•	1.6	1.6	2.0	1.8	1.5	1.0	•	•
Advertising 18	0.1	•	0.0	0.5	•	0.0	0.3	0.3	0.1	0.1	0.1	•	•
Other Expenses 19	7.2	•	20.9	15.9	•	4.1	5.8	6.2	4.9	5.9	2.8	•	•
Officers' Compensation 20	1.4	•	6.0	5.3	•	3.0	2.2	0.8	1.2	0.8	1.0	•	•
Operating Margin 21	2.4	•	6.6	1.0	•	6.7	6.7	4.3	4.2	4.3	1.8	•	•
Operating Margin Before Officers' Comp. 22	3.8	•	12.6	6.3	•	9.7	8.9	5.1	5.4	5.1	2.9	•	•

Selected Average Balance Sheet ($ in Thousands)

Net Receivables 23	1930	4	114	•	1599	3557	9196	14672	30250	55832
Inventories 24	5656	20	63	•	1847	3661	16108	24128	63568	138113
Net Property, Plant and Equipment 25	2949	51	216	•	1980	4123	7467	11223	44119	62907
Total Assets 26	10331	62	699	•	7333	15668	36930	65938	160904	336072
Notes and Loans Payable 27	2222	78	89	•	1027	2596	15371	9955	25302	48613
All Other Liabilities 28	3073	40	85	•	1298	3912	10982	20850	41270	103648
Net Worth 29	5035	-56	526	•	5008	9160	10577	35134	94332	183811

Selected Financial Ratios (Times to 1)

Current Ratio 30	1.9	0.2	2.6	•	3.8	1.9	1.8	2.1	2.9	2.1
Quick Ratio 31	1.1	0.1	1.6	•	2.0	1.1	0.9	1.3	1.8	1.0
Net Sales to Working Capital 32	5.4	•	5.6	•	3.9	6.2	7.2	4.1	3.5	3.1
Coverage Ratio 33	6.5	9.9	4.7	•	17.0	15.1	5.8	11.2	10.3	8.4
Total Asset Turnover 34	1.4	12.7	1.5	•	2.0	1.6	1.9	1.5	1.4	1.0
Inventory Turnover 35	1.9	12.7	10.4	•	6.0	5.2	3.3	3.1	2.8	2.0
Receivables Turnover 36	2.6	35.1	3.2	•	8.6	6.0	5.0	4.7	5.0	3.8
Total Liabilities to Net Worth 37	1.1	•	0.3	•	0.5	0.7	2.5	0.9	0.7	0.8
Current Assets to Working Capital 38	2.1	•	1.6	•	1.4	2.2	2.3	1.9	1.5	1.9
Current Liabilities to Working Capital 39	1.1	•	0.6	•	0.4	1.2	1.3	0.9	0.5	0.9
Working Capital to Net Sales 40	0.2	•	0.2	•	0.3	0.2	0.1	0.2	0.3	0.3
Inventory to Working Capital 41	0.7	•	0.5	•	0.6	0.7	1.0	0.6	0.5	0.6
Total Receipts to Cash Flow 42	9.7	4.4	7.7	•	10.4	8.6	10.3	10.7	10.1	13.0
Cost of Goods to Cash Flow 43	7.3	1.4	4.7	•	7.9	6.4	7.9	8.4	7.9	11.0
Cash Flow to Total Debt 44	0.3	1.5	0.8	•	0.6	0.5	0.3	0.3	0.3	0.2

Selected Financial Factors (in Percentages)

Debt Ratio 45	51.3	190.9	24.8	•	31.7	41.5	71.4	46.7	41.4	45.3
Return on Total Assets 46	8.6	104.6	3.4	•	14.7	14.0	11.7	9.6	9.3	9.6
Return on Equity Before Income Taxes 47	14.9	•	3.5	•	20.3	22.3	33.7	16.5	14.3	15.4
Return on Equity After Income Taxes 48	12.2	•	3.4	•	19.0	20.1	31.6	12.0	12.6	11.2
Profit Margin (Before Income Tax) 49	5.2	7.4	1.7	•	7.0	7.9	5.2	6.0	6.0	8.8
Profit Margin (After Income Tax) 50	4.3	7.4	1.7	•	6.6	7.1	4.9	4.4	5.3	6.4

Table I

Corporations with and without Net Income

NONFERROUS METAL PRODUCTION AND PROCESSING

MONEY AMOUNTS AND SIZE OF ASSETS IN THOUSANDS OF DOLLARS

Item Description for Accounting Period 7/09 Through 6/10	Total	Zero Assets	Under 500	500 to 1,000	1,000 to 5,000	5,000 to 10,000	10,000 to 25,000	25,000 to 50,000	50,000 to 100,000	100,000 to 250,000	250,000 to 500,000	500,000 to 2,500,000	2,500,000 and over
Number of Enterprises 1	676	6	•	9	•	47	123	55	27	18	16	22	5
Revenues ($ in Thousands)													
Net Sales 2	73177511	263011	•	75282	•	1261962	5591789	4859880	2303461	4485870	6910416	24599072	21066298
Interest 3	1525186	944	•	0	•	158	941	6804	6258	6646	19852	154372	1329134
Rents 4	40848	0	•	87	•	117	1203	228	889	30	16333	2328	16769
Royalties 5	69280	0	•	0	•	0	192	0	4942	735	458	2365	60586
Other Portfolio Income 6	302321	0	•	18055	•	1014	1496	971	5669	19993	20252	12201	222148
Other Receipts 7	1071538	-1820	•	554	•	3965	11092	11445	24877	58809	71333	302667	608778
Total Receipts 8	76186684	262135	•	93978	•	1267216	5606713	4879328	2346096	4572083	7038644	25073005	23303713
Average Total Receipts 9	112702	43689	•	10442	•	26962	45583	88715	86892	254005	439915	1139682	4660743
Operating Costs/Operating Income (%)													
Cost of Operations 10	85.1	74.8	•	111.8	•	85.7	88.9	87.5	76.6	87.4	84.0	85.0	85.0
Salaries and Wages 11	3.5	7.0	•	3.4	•	2.6	2.4	2.8	5.0	1.9	3.2	3.5	4.5
Taxes Paid 12	0.7	0.9	•	2.9	•	0.7	0.7	0.7	1.0	0.6	0.6	0.7	0.5
Interest Paid 13	4.5	4.7	•	4.3	•	0.8	0.5	0.7	1.0	1.6	2.1	4.0	9.2
Depreciation 14	3.2	2.1	•	7.6	•	1.2	1.6	1.5	2.5	1.6	2.5	2.9	5.3
Amortization and Depletion 15	0.6	0.3	•	0.5	•	0.1	0.0	0.2	0.3	0.6	0.3	0.5	1.3
Pensions and Other Deferred Comp. 16	0.5	0.2	•	•	•	0.3	0.2	0.4	0.3	1.1	0.4	0.5	0.3
Employee Benefits 17	1.2	0.6	•	•	•	1.0	0.8	1.0	0.6	1.5	1.5	1.2	1.3
Advertising 18	0.1	0.4	•	•	•	0.1	0.1	0.1	0.1	0.0	0.0	0.1	0.1
Other Expenses 19	6.6	18.3	•	21.7	•	4.1	4.1	3.3	7.6	4.9	9.9	6.6	7.1
Officers' Compensation 20	0.5	1.1	•	2.5	•	1.8	1.0	1.1	1.7	0.4	0.3	0.4	0.0
Operating Margin 21	•	•	•	•	•	1.6	•	0.7	3.3	•	•	•	•
Operating Margin Before Officers' Comp. 22	•	•	•	•	•	3.4	0.6	1.8	5.0	•	•	•	•

Selected Average Balance Sheet ($ in Thousands)

Net Receivables 23	76206	0	•	141	1105	4417	8559	11871	29832	67174	158294	8976709
Inventories 24	12663	0	•	0	2528	3188	10218	12260	38589	80252	139662	380839
Net Property, Plant and Equipment 25	28942	0	•	92	1751	4420	8475	15148	32076	95497	252611	2061466
Total Assets 26	235633	0	•	636	7161	16003	33782	67680	159032	367326	1171767	23617369
Notes and Loans Payable 27	83454	0	•	3464	2574	5484	11084	18999	45022	128229	477329	8155386
All Other Liabilities 28	67834	0	•	1425	3191	4514	10892	14583	76777	123042	348443	6572158
Net Worth 29	84344	0	•	-4253	1396	6005	11807	34098	37233	116055	345995	8889826

Selected Financial Ratios (Times to 1)

Current Ratio 30	1.2	•	0.1	1.3	2.1	1.5	2.6	1.4	1.5	1.5	1.1
Quick Ratio 31	1.0	•	0.0	0.6	1.2	0.8	1.5	0.6	0.7	0.8	1.0
Net Sales to Working Capital 32	6.7	•	•	21.8	8.6	11.6	3.7	9.8	6.7	7.0	5.3
Coverage Ratio 33	0.6	•	•	3.5	1.0	2.7	6.2	1.2	•	0.2	0.6
Total Asset Turnover 34	0.5	•	13.1	3.7	2.8	2.6	1.3	1.6	1.2	1.0	0.2
Inventory Turnover 35	7.3	•	•	9.1	12.7	7.6	5.3	5.6	4.5	6.8	9.4
Receivables Turnover 36	1.4	•	118.9	18.8	12.5	11.1	6.7	9.1	6.4	7.1	0.5
Total Liabilities to Net Worth 37	1.8	•	•	4.1	1.7	1.9	1.0	3.3	2.2	2.4	1.7
Current Assets to Working Capital 38	6.3	•	•	4.2	1.9	2.8	1.6	3.3	3.0	2.9	12.4
Current Liabilities to Working Capital 39	5.3	•	•	3.2	0.9	1.8	0.6	2.3	2.0	1.9	11.4
Working Capital to Net Sales 40	0.1	•	•	0.0	0.1	0.1	0.3	0.1	0.1	0.1	0.2
Inventory to Working Capital 41	0.7	•	•	2.0	0.7	1.2	0.6	1.8	1.3	0.8	0.4
Total Receipts to Cash Flow 42	37.1	22.5	•	19.0	32.9	29.3	9.3	22.5	19.1	50.7	328.2
Cost of Goods to Cash Flow 43	31.5	16.9	•	16.3	29.2	25.6	7.1	19.7	16.0	43.1	279.0
Cash Flow to Total Debt 44	0.0	•	•	0.2	0.1	0.1	0.3	0.1	0.1	0.0	0.0

Selected Financial Factors (in Percentages)

Debt Ratio 45	64.2	•	768.5	80.5	62.5	65.1	49.6	76.6	68.4	70.5	62.4
Return on Total Assets 46	1.2	•	•	10.5	1.5	4.7	7.8	3.0	•	0.8	1.1
Return on Equity Before Income Taxes 47	•	•	58.2	38.5	0.1	8.4	12.9	1.9	•	•	•
Return on Equity After Income Taxes 48	•	•	58.2	38.2	•	6.8	8.7	•	•	•	•
Profit Margin (Before Income Tax) 49	•	•	•	2.0	0.0	1.1	5.2	0.3	•	•	•
Profit Margin (After Income Tax) 50	•	•	•	2.0	•	0.9	3.5	•	•	•	•

Table II

Corporations with Net Income

NONFERROUS METAL PRODUCTION AND PROCESSING

MONEY AMOUNTS AND SIZE OF ASSETS IN THOUSANDS OF DOLLARS

Item Description for Accounting Period 7/09 Through 6/10	Total	Zero Assets	Under 500	500 to 1,000	1,000 to 5,000	5,000 to 10,000	10,000 to 25,000	25,000 to 50,000	50,000 to 100,000	100,000 to 250,000	250,000 to 500,000	500,000 to 2,500,000	2,500,000 and over
Number of Enterprises 1	484	•	0	0	•	25	66	28	19	•	5	13	0
Revenues ($ in Thousands)													
Net Sales 2	37904800	•	0	0	•	1034486	3470933	3086470	1630707	•	3757079	19526189	0
Interest 3	84246	•	0	0	•	104	426	475	3776	•	4329	70987	0
Rents 4	5759	•	0	0	•	0	927	0	253	•	24	1660	0
Royalties 5	26491	•	0	0	•	0	0	0	4767	•	441	20688	0
Other Portfolio Income 6	42088	•	0	0	•	33	801	952	777	•	8355	29305	0
Other Receipts 7	434889	•	0	0	•	2238	4873	2440	15776	•	44346	334359	0
Total Receipts 8	38498273	•	0	0	•	1036861	3477960	3090337	1656056	•	3814574	19983188	0
Average Total Receipts 9	79542	•	•	•	•	41474	52696	110369	87161	•	762915	1537168	•
Operating Costs/Operating Income (%)													
Cost of Operations 10	82.5	•	•	•	•	84.5	89.0	87.0	69.9	•	87.2	80.3	•
Salaries and Wages 11	3.0	•	•	•	•	2.5	2.3	2.2	5.3	•	2.1	3.7	•
Taxes Paid 12	0.7	•	•	•	•	0.4	0.6	0.6	1.3	•	0.5	0.8	•
Interest Paid 13	1.2	•	•	•	•	0.1	0.2	0.3	0.8	•	0.7	1.7	•
Depreciation 14	3.2	•	•	•	•	0.5	0.8	1.3	2.1	•	0.8	5.1	•
Amortization and Depletion 15	0.3	•	•	•	•	0.0	0.0	0.1	0.1	•	0.0	0.6	•
Pensions and Other Deferred Comp. 16	0.5	•	•	•	•	0.1	0.1	0.1	0.4	•	0.2	0.6	•
Employee Benefits 17	1.0	•	•	•	•	0.5	0.5	0.4	0.7	•	0.7	1.2	•
Advertising 18	0.1	•	•	•	•	0.1	0.1	0.1	0.1	•	0.0	0.1	•
Other Expenses 19	5.2	•	•	•	•	2.3	3.0	3.2	8.6	•	7.5	5.6	•
Officers' Compensation 20	0.6	•	•	•	•	1.8	0.8	1.0	2.3	•	0.2	0.3	•
Operating Margin 21	1.6	•	•	•	•	7.3	2.5	3.8	8.4	•	•	0.1	•
Operating Margin Before Officers' Comp. 22	2.2	•	•	•	•	9.1	3.3	4.7	10.7	•	0.1	0.3	•

Selected Average Balance Sheet ($ in Thousands)

Line	1	2	3	4	5		6	7
Net Receivables 23	13154	957	4855	7784	11631	•	121217	339027
Inventories 24	11285	2626	3409	12365	12182	•	158593	186681
Net Property, Plant and Equipment 25	17874	1501	3353	8247	14389	•	72075	541458
Total Assets 26	68900	7767	15741	34044	69501	•	411523	1951430
Notes and Loans Payable 27	18272	652	3236	7765	16667	•	61985	537208
All Other Liabilities 28	19897	2457	3621	8366	11223	•	242485	507927
Net Worth 29	30731	4658	8884	17912	41612	•	107053	906296

Selected Financial Ratios (Times to 1)

Line	1	2	3	4	5		6	7
Current Ratio 30	1.7	2.1	2.5	2.2	3.8	•	1.5	1.6
Quick Ratio 31	1.1	0.9	1.7	1.2	2.2	•	0.6	1.1
Net Sales to Working Capital 32	6.5	12.6	7.9	8.7	2.8	•	7.0	5.8
Coverage Ratio 33	3.8	76.2	12.9	12.7	14.0	•	3.0	2.5
Total Asset Turnover 34	1.1	5.3	3.3	3.2	1.2	•	1.8	0.8
Inventory Turnover 35	5.7	13.3	13.7	7.8	4.9	•	4.1	6.5
Receivables Turnover 36	1.5	32.8	11.5	13.4	7.1	•	•	5.9
Total Liabilities to Net Worth 37	1.2	0.7	0.8	0.9	0.7	•	2.8	1.2
Current Assets to Working Capital 38	2.5	1.9	1.7	1.8	1.4	•	2.9	2.8
Current Liabilities to Working Capital 39	1.5	0.9	0.7	0.8	0.4	•	1.9	1.8
Working Capital to Net Sales 40	0.2	0.1	0.1	0.1	0.4	•	0.1	0.2
Inventory to Working Capital 41	0.8	1.0	0.5	0.8	0.5	•	1.5	0.6
Total Receipts to Cash Flow 42	14.3	10.5	20.0	17.1	6.2	•	13.9	15.7
Cost of Goods to Cash Flow 43	11.8	8.9	17.9	14.9	4.3	•	12.1	12.6
Cash Flow to Total Debt 44	0.1	1.3	0.4	0.4	0.5	•	0.2	0.1

Selected Financial Factors (in Percentages)

Line	1	2	3	4	5		6	7
Debt Ratio 45	55.4	40.0	43.6	47.4	40.1	•	74.0	53.6
Return on Total Assets 46	5.1	40.8	9.7	13.7	13.2	•	4.1	3.3
Return on Equity Before Income Taxes 47	8.3	67.1	15.9	23.9	20.5	•	10.6	4.2
Return on Equity After Income Taxes 48	7.0	66.9	14.1	22.1	15.6	•	7.9	3.3
Profit Margin (Before Income Tax) 49	3.3	7.6	2.7	3.9	9.9	•	1.5	2.5
Profit Margin (After Income Tax) 50	2.8	7.5	2.4	3.6	7.6	•	1.1	2.0

Table I

Corporations with and without Net Income

FOUNDRIES

MONEY AMOUNTS AND SIZE OF ASSETS IN THOUSANDS OF DOLLARS

Item Description for Accounting Period 7/09 Through 6/10	Total	Zero Assets	Under 500	500 to 1,000	1,000 to 5,000	5,000 to 10,000	10,000 to 25,000	25,000 to 50,000	50,000 to 100,000	100,000 to 250,000	250,000 to 500,000	500,000 to 2,500,000	2,500,000 and over
Number of Enterprises **1**	1158	10	•	0	•	79	46	13	11	5	9	5	0
Revenues ($ in Thousands)													
Net Sales **2**	18918407	126395	•	0	•	782613	1036767	627173	751696	1103911	3684145	8820570	0
Interest **3**	13855	318	•	0	•	723	559	194	133	44	4839	4877	0
Rents **4**	4059	0	•	0	•	0	1204	7	24	0	526	921	0
Royalties **5**	11722	0	•	0	•	0	0	4	0	0	0	11718	0
Other Portfolio Income **6**	41670	17276	•	0	•	359	52	7790	3007	3	788	10976	0
Other Receipts **7**	292054	69122	•	0	•	7444	5164	11417	44503	9112	21624	80015	0
Total Receipts **8**	19281767	213111	•	0	•	791139	1043746	646585	799363	1113070	3711922	8929077	0
Average Total Receipts **9**	16651	21311	•	•	•	10014	22690	49737	72669	222614	412436	1785815	•
Operating Costs/Operating Income (%)													
Cost of Operations **10**	72.8	88.8	•	•	•	76.0	75.5	78.6	74.8	66.3	82.2	70.5	•
Salaries and Wages **11**	5.1	6.4	•	•	•	3.9	5.1	1.3	6.4	10.0	4.7	4.4	•
Taxes Paid **12**	1.6	2.0	•	•	•	2.1	1.7	1.8	1.9	0.7	1.2	1.6	•
Interest Paid **13**	1.5	2.9	•	•	•	1.8	1.2	3.4	1.9	2.8	2.3	1.0	•
Depreciation **14**	4.0	4.4	•	•	•	3.0	4.4	5.2	6.8	3.5	4.8	3.9	•
Amortization and Depletion **15**	0.8	1.4	•	•	•	•	0.1	0.6	0.7	1.7	0.3	1.2	•
Pensions and Other Deferred Comp. **16**	1.2	2.6	•	•	•	0.7	0.5	0.2	0.7	2.8	0.3	1.8	•
Employee Benefits **17**	2.0	5.9	•	•	•	3.5	2.5	2.3	6.5	2.3	1.3	1.7	•
Advertising **18**	0.1	0.0	•	•	•	0.3	0.1	0.0	0.4	0.0	0.2	0.1	•
Other Expenses **19**	7.0	90.5	•	•	•	4.0	5.4	6.4	6.1	16.5	4.5	4.8	•
Officers' Compensation **20**	1.7	1.3	•	•	•	2.7	4.5	1.2	1.5	0.6	0.4	0.9	•
Operating Margin **21**	2.1	•	•	•	•	2.0	•	•	•	•	•	8.2	•
Operating Margin Before Officers' Comp. **22**	3.8	•	•	•	•	4.7	3.4	0.0	•	•	•	9.1	•

Selected Average Balance Sheet ($ in Thousands)

Net Receivables **23**	2251	0	•	•	2309	2587	7931	9228	28649	58657	230048	•
Inventories **24**	2698	0	•	•	1937	3030	10902	9467	34807	41614	370652	•
Net Property, Plant and Equipment **25**	3923	0	•	•	2259	5708	15507	24678	51204	135884	398226	•
Total Assets **26**	16454	0	•	•	7575	15454	36631	69508	157878	376570	2284709	•
Notes and Loans Payable **27**	2935	0	•	•	3589	3860	14960	13500	56896	89816	256684	•
All Other Liabilities **28**	4048	0	•	•	1658	2890	13715	9779	50591	152725	463931	•
Net Worth **29**	9471	0	•	•	2328	8704	7956	46230	50390	134029	1564094	•

Selected Financial Ratios (Times to 1)

Current Ratio **30**	2.1	•	•	•	2.8	2.4	1.1	2.8	1.5	1.7	2.5	•
Quick Ratio **31**	1.1	•	•	•	1.5	1.5	0.6	1.9	0.8	1.1	1.0	•
Net Sales to Working Capital **32**	4.8	•	•	•	3.1	4.4	23.4	2.8	10.7	6.1	4.2	•
Coverage Ratio **33**	3.8	•	•	•	2.7	0.6	1.7	0.0	•	0.3	10.3	•
Total Asset Turnover **34**	1.0	•	•	•	1.3	1.5	1.3	1.0	1.4	1.1	0.8	•
Inventory Turnover **35**	4.4	•	•	•	3.9	5.6	3.5	5.4	4.2	8.1	3.4	•
Receivables Turnover **36**	6.6	•	•	•	4.3	6.8	4.5	6.2	5.2	8.6	6.9	•
Total Liabilities to Net Worth **37**	0.7	•	•	•	2.3	0.8	3.6	0.5	2.1	1.8	0.5	•
Current Assets to Working Capital **38**	1.9	•	•	•	1.6	1.7	8.3	1.6	3.1	2.5	1.7	•
Current Liabilities to Working Capital **39**	0.9	•	•	•	0.6	0.7	7.3	0.6	2.1	1.5	0.7	•
Working Capital to Net Sales **40**	0.2	•	•	•	0.3	0.2	0.0	0.4	0.1	0.2	0.2	•
Inventory to Working Capital **41**	0.7	•	•	•	0.7	0.6	3.1	0.3	1.1	0.7	0.9	•
Total Receipts to Cash Flow **42**	11.2	23.7	•	•	15.5	29.5	17.5	28.3	15.5	83.3	7.7	•
Cost of Goods to Cash Flow **43**	8.2	21.0	•	•	11.8	22.3	13.8	21.2	10.3	68.5	5.4	•
Cash Flow to Total Debt **44**	0.2	•	•	•	0.1	0.1	0.1	0.1	0.1	0.0	0.3	•

Selected Financial Factors (in Percentages)

Debt Ratio **45**	42.4	•	•	•	69.3	43.7	78.3	33.5	68.1	64.4	31.5	•
Return on Total Assets **46**	5.5	•	•	•	6.4	1.1	7.8	0.1	•	0.9	8.1	•
Return on Equity Before Income Taxes **47**	7.0	•	•	•	13.1	•	15.2	•	•	10.6	•
Return on Equity After Income Taxes **48**	4.3	•	•	•	11.9	•	9.4	•	•	7.3	•
Profit Margin (Before Income Tax) **49**	4.1	•	•	•	3.1	•	2.5	•	•	9.4	•
Profit Margin (After Income Tax) **50**	2.5	•	•	•	2.8	•	1.5	•	•	6.4	•

109

Table II

Corporations with Net Income

FOUNDRIES

MONEY AMOUNTS AND SIZE OF ASSETS IN THOUSANDS OF DOLLARS

Item Description for Accounting Period 7/09 Through 6/10		Total	Zero Assets	Under 500	500 to 1,000	1,000 to 5,000	5,000 to 10,000	10,000 to 25,000	25,000 to 50,000	50,000 to 100,000	100,000 to 250,000	250,000 to 500,000	500,000 to 2,500,000	2,500,000 and over
Number of Enterprises	1	794	0	444	0	237	71	17	7	6	•	5	•	0
Revenues ($ in Thousands)														
Net Sales	2	14796477	0	341920	0	1561055	681741	452162	323996	434522	•	2131285	•	0
Interest	3	9645	0	0	0	2167	653	251	169	29	•	4066	•	0
Rents	4	3764	0	0	0	1376	0	1204	7	0	•	454	•	0
Royalties	5	1376	0	0	0	0	0	0	4	0	•	0	•	0
Other Portfolio Income	6	23682	0	0	0	1419	359	3	7768	2504	•	651	•	0
Other Receipts	7	136429	0	0	0	43539	7368	667	781	4749	•	14866	•	0
Total Receipts	8	14971373	0	341920	0	1609556	690121	454287	332725	441804	•	2151322	•	0
Average Total Receipts	9	18856	•	770	•	6791	9720	26723	47532	73634	•	430264	•	•
Operating Costs/Operating Income (%)														
Cost of Operations	10	71.5	•	49.3	•	65.0	76.1	73.2	76.4	72.1	•	80.4	•	•
Salaries and Wages	11	4.3	•	11.6	•	6.4	3.4	4.8	1.1	6.8	•	2.9	•	•
Taxes Paid	12	1.6	•	4.7	•	2.0	2.2	1.8	1.7	1.7	•	0.9	•	•
Interest Paid	13	1.0	•	0.1	•	0.5	2.0	0.6	4.0	0.3	•	1.6	•	•
Depreciation	14	3.5	•	1.3	•	1.8	2.9	4.3	4.0	4.4	•	2.9	•	•
Amortization and Depletion	15	0.7	•	•	•	•	•	0.3	0.6	0.0	•	0.1	•	•
Pensions and Other Deferred Comp.	16	1.3	•	•	•	0.4	0.7	0.5	0.4	0.9	•	0.4	•	•
Employee Benefits	17	1.5	•	0.7	•	1.9	3.0	1.1	2.0	0.9	•	0.5	•	•
Advertising	18	0.1	•	0.2	•	0.2	0.3	0.0	0.0	0.7	•	0.2	•	•
Other Expenses	19	5.9	•	12.5	•	13.5	3.9	4.9	3.4	5.0	•	6.6	•	•
Officers' Compensation	20	1.7	•	3.2	•	7.0	2.5	1.8	0.9	1.8	•	0.4	•	•
Operating Margin	21	7.0	•	16.4	•	1.4	2.9	6.7	5.5	5.3	•	3.1	•	•
Operating Margin Before Officers' Comp.	22	8.6	•	19.7	•	8.5	5.4	8.5	6.4	7.1	•	3.5	•	•

Selected Average Balance Sheet ($ in Thousands)

Net Receivables 23	2592	40	1041	2405	2712	8498	10297	65124
Inventories 24	3176	16	643	1660	5504	14714	9809	45235
Net Property, Plant and Equipment 25	4015	23	602	2181	4860	12055	15346	115041
Total Assets 26	19491	162	3253	7442	16418	33324	69812	385918
Notes and Loans Payable 27	2534	10	518	3872	2597	12323	8475	61828
All Other Liabilities 28	4794	12	969	1706	2718	7994	9841	187337
Net Worth 29	12163	140	1766	1863	11103	13008	51496	136753

Selected Financial Ratios (Times to 1)

Current Ratio 30	2.3	11.4	2.3	2.8	5.0	1.4	4.9	1.4
Quick Ratio 31	1.1	10.3	1.7	1.5	3.2	0.9	3.6	0.9
Net Sales to Working Capital 32	4.6	6.0	5.0	3.0	3.1	10.2	1.8	8.7
Coverage Ratio 33	9.1	219.8	10.8	3.1	13.1	3.3	20.4	3.5
Total Asset Turnover 34	1.0	4.7	2.0	1.3	1.6	1.4	1.0	1.1
Inventory Turnover 35	4.2	24.3	6.7	4.4	3.5	2.4	5.3	7.6
Receivables Turnover 36	6.5	6.4	6.1	4.7	4.1	3.3	6.0	•
Total Liabilities to Net Worth 37	0.6	0.2	0.8	3.0	0.5	1.6	0.4	1.8
Current Assets to Working Capital 38	1.8	1.1	1.8	1.6	1.3	3.4	1.3	3.5
Current Liabilities to Working Capital 39	0.8	0.1	0.8	0.6	0.3	2.4	0.3	2.5
Working Capital to Net Sales 40	0.2	0.2	0.2	0.3	0.3	0.1	0.6	0.1
Inventory to Working Capital 41	0.8	0.0	0.4	0.7	0.4	1.1	0.2	0.9
Total Receipts to Cash Flow 42	8.0	4.0	7.4	13.3	9.8	9.1	8.9	10.4
Cost of Goods to Cash Flow 43	5.7	2.0	4.8	10.1	7.1	6.9	6.4	8.3
Cash Flow to Total Debt 44	0.3	8.5	0.6	0.1	0.5	0.3	0.4	0.2

Selected Financial Factors (in Percentages)

Debt Ratio 45	37.6	13.8	45.7	75.0	32.4	61.0	26.2	64.6
Return on Total Assets 46	8.8	78.3	9.9	7.8	12.6	18.7	7.1	6.2
Return on Equity Before Income Taxes 47	12.5	90.5	16.6	21.1	17.2	33.6	9.1	12.5
Return on Equity After Income Taxes 48	9.4	90.5	16.3	19.4	13.8	27.0	8.1	9.8
Profit Margin (Before Income Tax) 49	8.2	16.4	4.4	4.1	7.2	9.4	6.5	4.0
Profit Margin (After Income Tax) 50	6.1	16.4	4.4	3.8	5.8	7.6	5.8	3.2

Table I
Corporations with and without Net Income

FORGING AND STAMPING

MONEY AMOUNTS AND SIZE OF ASSETS IN THOUSANDS OF DOLLARS

Item Description for Accounting Period 7/09 Through 6/10	Total	Zero Assets	Under 500	500 to 1,000	1,000 to 5,000	5,000 to 10,000	10,000 to 25,000	25,000 to 50,000	50,000 to 100,000	100,000 to 250,000	250,000 to 500,000	500,000 to 2,500,000	2,500,000 and over
Number of Enterprises **1**	1899	52	573	442	528	108	113	40	24	16	4	0	0
Revenues ($ in Thousands)													
Net Sales **2**	14270861	595382	180820	473068	2191252	1266767	2410913	1797988	1587863	2376846	1389960	0	0
Interest **3**	31659	0	45	106	697	441	800	66	431	981	28092	0	0
Rents **4**	2693	9	0	166	124	0	107	101	168	1759	259	0	0
Royalties **5**	7	0	0	0	6	0	0	1	0	0	0	0	0
Other Portfolio Income **6**	41686	32177	0	337	759	160	1226	3004	1335	2633	56	0	0
Other Receipts **7**	157675	235	1	4719	4510	18535	12217	20240	13783	77818	5619	0	0
Total Receipts **8**	14504581	627803	180866	478396	2197348	1285903	2425263	1821400	1603580	2460037	1423986	0	0
Average Total Receipts **9**	7638	12073	316	1082	4162	11907	21463	45535	66816	153752	355996	•	•
Operating Costs/Operating Income (%)													
Cost of Operations **10**	73.0	77.5	55.2	65.7	68.7	72.9	74.2	75.9	77.2	72.6	72.8	•	•
Salaries and Wages **11**	5.1	3.4	2.3	1.8	6.4	5.0	5.1	5.6	6.3	4.2	4.4	•	•
Taxes Paid **12**	1.6	0.9	3.7	2.3	2.5	2.0	1.2	1.6	1.7	1.4	0.9	•	•
Interest Paid **13**	1.7	1.7	0.1	0.7	1.2	0.8	0.8	1.1	2.1	1.8	6.1	•	•
Depreciation **14**	4.0	1.2	1.9	0.8	3.7	2.6	3.5	4.1	5.5	6.2	3.6	•	•
Amortization and Depletion **15**	0.3	0.3	0.0	•	0.1	0.4	0.1	0.5	0.7	0.3	0.6	•	•
Pensions and Other Deferred Comp. **16**	0.7	0.1	0.5	0.7	1.0	0.5	0.5	0.2	0.5	0.6	1.9	•	•
Employee Benefits **17**	2.6	0.2	3.2	1.8	3.6	2.7	2.7	2.6	2.5	3.2	0.7	•	•
Advertising **18**	0.2	0.0	•	0.4	0.2	0.6	0.2	0.1	0.1	0.1	0.1	•	•
Other Expenses **19**	7.6	8.2	17.4	18.6	9.6	12.8	6.6	6.5	5.3	4.3	5.4	•	•
Officers' Compensation **20**	3.2	9.4	11.4	9.3	6.2	3.0	3.4	1.0	1.7	1.5	0.4	•	•
Operating Margin **21**	0.1	•	4.5	•	•	•	1.9	0.9	•	3.8	3.3	•	•
Operating Margin Before Officers' Comp. **22**	3.3	6.4	15.9	7.3	3.0	•	5.3	1.9	•	5.3	3.7	•	•

Selected Average Balance Sheet ($ in Thousands)

Net Receivables 23	1106	0	49	156	558	1447	2918	7562	11614	25703	57280
Inventories 24	1195	0	29	191	598	1440	3007	6231	9759	28850	102957
Net Property, Plant and Equipment 25	1705	0	6	35	731	1512	3750	11290	22069	44034	139871
Total Assets 26	6729	0	148	645	2426	7596	12860	33350	68656	152437	858198
Notes and Loans Payable 27	2058	0	19	114	988	2318	2979	9740	25061	41211	272029
All Other Liabilities 28	1645	0	16	118	1039	1183	3218	6511	15611	33029	214713
Net Worth 29	3026	0	113	413	400	4096	6662	17099	27985	78198	371456

Selected Financial Ratios (Times to 1)

Current Ratio 30	1.9	•	8.8	3.3	1.5	1.8	2.2	1.8	1.8	2.0	1.9
Quick Ratio 31	1.1	•	5.5	2.1	0.9	1.1	1.4	1.2	1.1	1.2	0.9
Net Sales to Working Capital 32	5.3	•	2.5	2.9	8.0	8.0	4.9	5.6	5.2	4.2	4.1
Coverage Ratio 33	2.0	2.5	52.4	•	•	•	4.4	3.0	•	5.0	1.9
Total Asset Turnover 34	1.1	•	2.1	1.7	1.7	1.5	1.7	1.3	1.0	1.0	0.4
Inventory Turnover 35	4.6	•	6.0	3.7	4.8	5.9	5.3	5.5	5.2	3.7	2.5
Receivables Turnover 36	6.1	•	5.3	7.9	7.0	7.3	6.4	6.1	5.6	5.1	4.5
Total Liabilities to Net Worth 37	1.2	•	0.3	0.6	5.1	0.9	0.9	1.0	1.5	0.9	1.3
Current Assets to Working Capital 38	2.1	•	1.1	1.4	3.1	2.3	1.8	2.2	2.2	2.0	2.1
Current Liabilities to Working Capital 39	1.1	•	0.1	0.4	2.1	1.3	0.8	1.2	1.2	1.0	1.1
Working Capital to Net Sales 40	0.2	•	0.4	0.3	0.1	0.1	0.2	0.2	0.2	0.2	0.2
Inventory to Working Capital 41	0.7	•	0.2	0.5	1.2	0.8	0.6	0.7	0.8	0.7	0.9
Total Receipts to Cash Flow 42	17.7	53.5	7.6	9.7	•	18.4	16.7	17.4	95.4	9.6	9.7
Cost of Goods to Cash Flow 43	12.9	41.5	4.2	6.4	•	13.4	12.4	13.2	73.6	7.0	7.1
Cash Flow to Total Debt 44	0.1	•	1.2	0.5	0.2	0.2	0.2	0.2	0.0	0.2	0.1

Selected Financial Factors (in Percentages)

Debt Ratio 45	55.0	•	23.4	36.0	83.5	46.1	48.2	48.7	59.2	48.7	56.7
Return on Total Assets 46	3.8	•	9.9	•	•	•	5.6	4.3	•	8.8	4.8
Return on Equity Before Income Taxes 47	4.2	•	12.7	•	•	•	8.4	5.5	•	13.8	5.4
Return on Equity After Income Taxes 48	3.4	•	12.3	•	•	•	7.4	5.0	•	12.5	5.1
Profit Margin (Before Income Tax) 49	1.7	2.5	4.6	•	•	•	2.6	2.1	•	7.3	5.7
Profit Margin (After Income Tax) 50	1.4	2.5	4.4	•	•	•	2.3	1.9	•	6.6	5.4

Table II

Corporations with Net Income

FORGING AND STAMPING

MONEY AMOUNTS AND SIZE OF ASSETS IN THOUSANDS OF DOLLARS

Item Description for Accounting Period 7/09 Through 6/10		Total	Zero Assets	Under 500	500 to 1,000	1,000 to 5,000	5,000 to 10,000	10,000 to 25,000	25,000 to 50,000	50,000 to 100,000	100,000 to 250,000	250,000 to 500,000	500,000 to 2,500,000	2,500,000 and over
Number of Enterprises	1	1140	•	480	145	309	36	68	25	13	•	•	•	0
Revenues ($ in Thousands)														
Net Sales	2	9204005	•	119574	194754	1220826	493370	1621875	1203185	1050126	•	•	•	0
Interest	3	1763	•	29	0	247	410	92	43	175	•	•	•	0
Rents	4	398	•	0	166	0	0	107	0	84	•	•	•	0
Royalties	5	6	•	0	0	6	0	0	0	0	•	•	•	0
Other Portfolio Income	6	13011	•	0	337	256	160	563	2227	1063	•	•	•	0
Other Receipts	7	107043	•	0	3876	2932	1965	10290	4094	8614	•	•	•	0
Total Receipts	8	9326226	•	119603	199133	1224267	495905	1632927	1209549	1060062	•	•	•	•
Average Total Receipts	9	8181	•	249	1373	3962	13775	24014	48382	81543	•	•	•	•
Operating Costs/Operating Income (%)														
Cost of Operations	10	69.9	•	48.3	60.7	63.6	71.9	68.9	73.1	75.2	•	•	•	•
Salaries and Wages	11	5.6	•	2.1	2.8	8.0	4.9	6.5	5.7	5.7	•	•	•	•
Taxes Paid	12	1.6	•	4.9	3.2	2.5	1.7	1.3	1.2	1.5	•	•	•	•
Interest Paid	13	0.9	•	0.1	0.6	0.8	0.5	0.6	1.1	0.6	•	•	•	•
Depreciation	14	3.7	•	2.4	1.0	3.4	2.0	2.7	3.8	3.9	•	•	•	•
Amortization and Depletion	15	0.2	•	•	•	0.0	0.4	0.1	0.7	0.1	•	•	•	•
Pensions and Other Deferred Comp.	16	0.8	•	•	1.6	1.4	0.9	0.6	0.3	0.5	•	•	•	•
Employee Benefits	17	2.6	•	4.4	1.5	3.6	2.0	3.0	2.0	2.8	•	•	•	•
Advertising	18	0.2	•	•	0.1	0.2	1.1	0.3	0.1	0.1	•	•	•	•
Other Expenses	19	5.3	•	16.5	20.5	4.7	4.7	5.9	5.3	5.2	•	•	•	•
Officers' Compensation	20	3.1	•	11.2	9.0	7.5	2.1	2.4	0.9	1.9	•	•	•	•
Operating Margin	21	6.0	•	10.1	•	4.1	7.8	7.9	5.8	2.5	•	•	•	•
Operating Margin Before Officers' Comp.	22	9.2	•	21.3	8.0	11.6	9.9	10.2	6.7	4.4	•	•	•	•

Selected Average Balance Sheet ($ in Thousands)

Net Receivables 23	1100	•	35	159	469	2221	3293	7362	14543
Inventories 24	1385	•	16	164	468	1960	3629	7868	11460
Net Property, Plant and Equipment 25	1583	•	4	56	523	1881	2888	9016	23116
Total Assets 26	5942	•	123	722	1918	8483	12255	35086	67674
Notes and Loans Payable 27	1305	•	21	171	549	1136	2733	8203	17129
All Other Liabilities 28	1108	•	12	170	321	1847	2697	5575	14854
Net Worth 29	3530	•	90	381	1047	5500	6826	21308	35690

Selected Financial Ratios (Times to 1)

Current Ratio 30	2.5	•	10.3	2.2	2.9	4.0	2.8	2.8	2.2
Quick Ratio 31	1.5	•	6.5	1.2	2.2	2.6	1.7	1.9	1.4
Net Sales to Working Capital 32	4.2	•	2.3	4.7	4.3	3.0	4.4	3.8	4.2
Coverage Ratio 33	9.1	•	76.3	3.1	6.5	17.2	16.4	6.7	6.3
Total Asset Turnover 34	1.4	•	2.0	1.9	2.1	1.6	1.9	1.4	1.2
Inventory Turnover 35	4.1	•	7.7	5.0	5.4	5.0	4.5	4.5	5.3
Receivables Turnover 36	5.9	•	5.0	9.5	6.2	•	6.2	5.3	•
Total Liabilities to Net Worth 37	0.7	•	0.4	0.9	0.8	0.5	0.8	0.6	0.9
Current Assets to Working Capital 38	1.7	•	1.1	1.8	1.5	1.3	1.6	1.6	1.8
Current Liabilities to Working Capital 39	0.7	•	0.1	0.8	0.5	0.3	0.6	0.6	0.8
Working Capital to Net Sales 40	0.2	•	0.4	0.2	0.2	0.3	0.2	0.3	0.2
Inventory to Working Capital 41	0.5	•	0.2	0.8	0.4	0.4	0.5	0.4	0.6
Total Receipts to Cash Flow 42	9.7	•	4.8	8.2	26.5	9.6	8.2	10.5	13.5
Cost of Goods to Cash Flow 43	6.8	•	2.3	5.0	16.9	6.9	5.7	7.7	10.2
Cash Flow to Total Debt 44	0.3	•	1.6	0.5	0.2	0.5	0.5	0.3	0.2

Selected Financial Factors (in Percentages)

Debt Ratio 45	40.6	•	26.9	47.3	45.4	35.2	44.3	39.3	47.3
Return on Total Assets 46	11.2	•	20.7	3.4	10.6	14.2	18.2	10.0	4.7
Return on Equity Before Income Taxes 47	16.8	•	28.0	4.3	16.5	20.6	30.7	14.0	7.5
Return on Equity After Income Taxes 48	15.7	•	27.5	3.8	15.6	17.4	29.1	13.3	7.1
Profit Margin (Before Income Tax) 49	7.3	•	10.1	1.2	4.4	8.3	8.8	6.2	3.3
Profit Margin (After Income Tax) 50	6.9	•	9.9	1.1	4.1	7.0	8.3	5.9	3.1

Table I

Corporations with and without Net Income

CUTLERY, HARDWARE, SPRING AND WIRE MACHINE SHOPS, NUT, BOLT

MONEY AMOUNTS AND SIZE OF ASSETS IN THOUSANDS OF DOLLARS

Item Description for Accounting Period 7/09 Through 6/10	Total	Zero Assets	Under 500	500 to 1,000	1,000 to 5,000	5,000 to 10,000	10,000 to 25,000	25,000 to 50,000	50,000 to 100,000	100,000 to 250,000	250,000 to 500,000	500,000 to 2,500,000	2,500,000 and over
Number of Enterprises **1**	21498	3343	12546	2123	2461	553	329	64	36	17	15	7	3
Revenues ($ in Thousands)													
Net Sales **2**	57979020	324698	4791045	3466449	8478509	6442294	7017234	3256601	2763474	2402292	4459208	4663901	9913314
Interest **3**	1902312	31	2263	2015	9541	6063	3028	10748	6219	5149	3574	9037	1844644
Rents **4**	20334	0	0	0	2734	605	4447	59	613	6824	480	2929	1644
Royalties **5**	104183	0	0	0	28	0	97	75	1228	2195	8411	1864	90284
Other Portfolio Income **6**	353415	128	872	70962	11567	3014	33214	3875	44093	5666	69148	22464	88415
Other Receipts **7**	817778	7447	13227	50769	36976	11559	24069	22456	17926	-1442	188843	107197	338748
Total Receipts **8**	61177042	332304	4807407	3590195	8539355	6463535	7082089	3293814	2833553	2420684	4729664	4807392	12277049
Average Total Receipts **9**	2846	99	383	1691	3470	11688	21526	51466	78710	142393	315311	686770	4092350
Operating Costs/Operating Income (%)													
Cost of Operations **10**	63.8	22.7	56.9	58.2	62.9	64.6	68.2	69.9	72.8	73.1	73.9	63.4	56.4
Salaries and Wages **11**	7.5	17.0	6.6	6.0	8.3	6.5	6.4	6.3	6.0	6.6	8.4	8.4	9.0
Taxes Paid **12**	2.1	3.1	3.0	3.1	3.0	2.0	1.9	1.8	1.6	1.8	1.5	1.5	1.4
Interest Paid **13**	5.8	2.5	1.2	1.4	1.7	0.5	1.6	0.9	1.5	1.5	5.3	2.4	25.5
Depreciation **14**	3.3	10.4	1.9	4.8	3.6	2.8	4.4	5.2	3.9	3.8	3.2	3.3	1.9
Amortization and Depletion **15**	1.0	•	0.2	0.1	0.1	0.1	0.3	0.3	0.5	0.6	1.5	1.4	3.6
Pensions and Other Deferred Comp. **16**	0.6	10.8	0.1	0.5	0.4	0.5	0.5	0.4	0.4	0.7	0.5	0.7	1.1
Employee Benefits **17**	2.3	0.9	1.6	2.6	2.4	2.2	2.2	2.1	1.8	1.8	2.5	2.2	3.2
Advertising **18**	0.8	0.1	0.6	0.1	0.3	0.6	0.8	0.5	0.7	0.6	0.8	1.7	1.5
Other Expenses **19**	11.6	30.2	18.0	13.1	9.4	8.2	8.9	7.7	7.9	8.1	8.2	12.1	17.8
Officers' Compensation **20**	3.8	14.0	8.5	10.2	6.6	5.0	2.6	1.8	1.9	0.9	0.8	0.7	1.2
Operating Margin **21**	•	•	1.5	•	1.4	7.1	2.1	3.3	1.0	0.6	•	2.1	•
Operating Margin Before Officers' Comp. **22**	1.2	2.2	10.0	10.2	8.0	12.1	4.8	5.2	2.9	1.5	•	2.8	•

Selected Average Balance Sheet ($ in Thousands)

Net Receivables 23	382	0	20	202	464	1347	2864	7200	11026	20431	67526	79171	646927
Inventories 24	372	0	18	63	412	1812	4158	10065	15796	30530	51179	204881	210399
Net Property, Plant and Equipment 25	431	0	31	215	625	1702	4686	9557	17455	29262	48417	144472	308982
Total Assets 26	5561	0	126	656	2325	7411	15738	34874	66161	152744	344357	948346	27519510
Notes and Loans Payable 27	2144	0	77	344	1065	991	5458	7703	22839	37498	181928	262172	10972371
All Other Liabilities 28	2039	0	32	211	532	1177	2793	7668	17716	31193	81284	171120	12006417
Net Worth 29	1378	0	16	101	728	5243	7487	19504	25605	84053	81144	515054	4540722

Selected Financial Ratios (Times to 1)

Current Ratio 30	2.0	•	2.6	1.3	1.7	3.5	2.1	2.6	2.0	2.4	2.2	3.0	1.3
Quick Ratio 31	1.2	•	1.8	1.0	1.0	2.0	1.1	1.3	0.9	1.2	1.3	1.7	1.0
Net Sales to Working Capital 32	4.9	•	8.2	19.4	6.6	3.4	4.5	3.8	4.5	3.5	4.1	2.5	8.8
Coverage Ratio 33	1.6	•	2.5	3.6	2.2	15.6	2.9	6.2	3.3	2.0	0.9	3.1	1.2
Total Asset Turnover 34	0.5	•	3.0	2.5	1.5	1.6	1.4	1.5	1.2	0.9	0.9	0.7	0.1
Inventory Turnover 35	4.6	•	12.0	15.0	5.3	4.2	3.5	3.5	3.5	3.4	4.3	2.1	8.9
Receivables Turnover 36	6.2	•	15.9	9.6	7.1	9.1	6.9	6.8	6.6	4.9	4.7	1.9	10.2
Total Liabilities to Net Worth 37	3.0	•	6.7	5.5	2.2	0.4	1.1	0.8	1.6	0.8	3.2	0.8	5.1
Current Assets to Working Capital 38	2.0	•	1.6	4.7	2.5	1.4	1.9	1.6	2.0	1.7	1.8	1.5	3.9
Current Liabilities to Working Capital 39	1.0	•	0.6	3.7	1.5	0.4	0.9	0.6	1.0	0.7	0.8	0.5	2.9
Working Capital to Net Sales 40	0.2	•	0.1	0.1	0.2	0.3	0.2	0.3	0.2	0.3	0.2	0.4	0.1
Inventory to Working Capital 41	0.6	•	0.4	0.7	0.8	0.6	0.8	0.7	0.9	0.6	0.6	0.4	0.6
Total Receipts to Cash Flow 42	8.7	8.9	7.0	8.8	12.8	8.1	11.0	9.7	12.0	13.0	18.3	6.5	5.7
Cost of Goods to Cash Flow 43	5.6	2.0	4.0	5.1	8.0	5.2	7.5	6.8	8.7	9.5	13.5	4.1	3.2
Cash Flow to Total Debt 44	0.1	•	0.5	0.3	0.2	0.7	0.2	0.3	0.2	0.2	0.1	0.2	0.0

Selected Financial Factors (in Percentages)

Debt Ratio 45	75.2	•	87.0	84.6	68.7	29.3	52.4	44.1	61.3	45.0	76.4	45.7	83.5
Return on Total Assets 46	4.6	•	9.3	12.2	5.7	12.5	6.3	7.8	5.9	2.7	4.2	5.2	3.8
Return on Equity Before Income Taxes 47	7.2	•	43.3	57.2	10.0	16.5	8.7	11.7	10.7	2.4	•	6.5	4.3
Return on Equity After Income Taxes 48	5.5	•	39.2	54.6	8.4	15.0	7.4	9.2	7.1	1.1	•	4.2	2.8
Profit Margin (Before Income Tax) 49	3.7	•	1.9	3.5	2.1	7.4	3.1	4.5	3.6	1.4	•	5.0	5.9
Profit Margin (After Income Tax) 50	2.8	•	1.7	3.4	1.8	6.7	2.6	3.5	2.4	0.7	•	3.2	3.9

Table II
Corporations with Net Income

CUTLERY, HARDWARE, SPRING AND WIRE MACHINE SHOPS, NUT, BOLT

MONEY AMOUNTS AND SIZE OF ASSETS IN THOUSANDS OF DOLLARS

Item Description for Accounting Period 7/09 Through 6/10	Total	Zero Assets	Under 500	500 to 1,000	1,000 to 5,000	5,000 to 10,000	10,000 to 25,000	25,000 to 50,000	50,000 to 100,000	100,000 to 250,000	250,000 to 500,000	500,000 to 2,500,000	2,500,000 and over
Number of Enterprises 1	11572	1663	6590	1311	1234	472	210	44	24	•	7	•	•
Revenues ($ in Thousands)													
Net Sales 2	42104763	236065	2764155	1948958	5521209	5637916	5264203	2445895	1897652	•	1610967	•	•
Interest 3	1880654	31	1950	1346	6286	3430	2058	10196	5577	•	601	•	•
Rents 4	17353	0	0	0	2624	605	3789	19	553	•	199	•	•
Royalties 5	97039	0	0	0	28	0	51	67	1228	•	3454	•	•
Other Portfolio Income 6	323975	0	872	70755	9279	2488	31583	2537	42530	•	48537	•	•
Other Receipts 7	755328	6970	4808	49077	18678	9415	17878	19850	14093	•	165302	•	•
Total Receipts 8	45179112	243066	2771785	2070136	5558104	5653854	5319562	2478564	1961633	•	1829060	•	•
Average Total Receipts 9	3904	146	421	1579	4504	11979	25331	56331	81735	•	261294	•	•
Operating Costs/Operating Income (%)													
Cost of Operations 10	61.8	26.5	55.4	59.6	60.5	63.6	66.2	67.2	70.3	•	70.7	•	•
Salaries and Wages 11	7.4	13.7	5.0	2.7	8.4	6.2	6.3	6.7	6.5	•	12.0	•	•
Taxes Paid 12	1.9	2.4	2.6	2.7	2.9	1.9	1.7	1.6	1.7	•	1.4	•	•
Interest Paid 13	7.0	1.0	0.7	1.2	1.4	0.4	1.3	0.7	1.3	•	6.6	•	•
Depreciation 14	2.7	9.0	1.5	3.6	2.6	2.7	3.3	2.9	3.1	•	3.2	•	•
Amortization and Depletion 15	1.0	•	0.0	0.0	0.1	0.0	0.2	0.2	0.3	•	1.2	•	•
Pensions and Other Deferred Comp. 16	0.6	0.0	0.1	0.1	0.5	0.4	0.5	0.3	0.5	•	1.2	•	•
Employee Benefits 17	2.3	1.0	0.8	2.6	1.8	2.1	1.8	2.1	1.4	•	3.5	•	•
Advertising 18	0.8	0.1	0.7	0.2	0.3	0.6	1.0	0.4	0.8	•	0.5	•	•
Other Expenses 19	11.6	26.4	15.4	14.3	7.9	7.6	8.7	8.2	7.5	•	7.8	•	•
Officers' Compensation 20	3.5	11.7	6.9	8.6	7.1	5.3	2.5	2.0	1.9	•	1.0	•	•
Operating Margin 21	•	8.1	10.9	4.3	6.6	9.1	6.6	7.8	4.8	•	•	•	•
Operating Margin Before Officers' Comp. 22	2.9	19.9	17.9	13.0	13.7	14.4	9.1	9.8	6.7	•	•	•	•

Selected Average Balance Sheet ($ in Thousands)

Net Receivables 23	535	0	19	181	638	1342	3362	7644	10869	78638
Inventories 24	487	0	20	60	506	1744	4137	11958	17704	47361
Net Property, Plant and Equipment 25	513	0	37	171	607	1591	4340	7149	15400	42789
Total Assets 26	9201	0	122	662	2382	7491	16254	34155	67646	336215
Notes and Loans Payable 27	3466	0	50	371	1100	753	4768	5659	14918	208717
All Other Liabilities 28	3486	0	21	140	465	1106	2940	6323	16481	73514
Net Worth 29	2249	0	52	151	817	5631	8545	22174	36246	53984

Selected Financial Ratios (Times to 1)

Current Ratio 30	2.2	•	3.8	1.4	2.3	3.8	2.6	3.4	2.5	2.3
Quick Ratio 31	1.4	•	2.7	1.1	1.5	2.2	1.4	1.6	1.1	1.5
Net Sales to Working Capital 32	4.4	•	7.4	11.7	5.1	3.3	4.1	3.4	3.7	3.2
Coverage Ratio 33	2.1	11.9	17.0	10.0	6.3	24.8	6.9	14.8	7.4	1.8
Total Asset Turnover 34	0.4	•	3.4	2.2	1.9	1.6	1.5	1.6	1.2	0.7
Inventory Turnover 35	4.6	•	11.6	14.8	5.4	4.4	4.0	3.1	3.1	3.4
Receivables Turnover 36	5.7	•	15.9	8.0	6.3	9.4	7.3	6.5	6.4	2.7
Total Liabilities to Net Worth 37	3.1	•	1.4	3.4	1.9	0.3	0.9	0.5	0.9	5.2
Current Assets to Working Capital 38	1.8	•	1.4	3.4	1.8	1.4	1.6	1.4	1.7	1.8
Current Liabilities to Working Capital 39	0.8	•	0.4	2.4	0.8	0.4	0.6	0.4	0.7	0.8
Working Capital to Net Sales 40	0.2	•	0.1	0.1	0.2	0.3	0.2	0.3	0.3	0.3
Inventory to Working Capital 41	0.5	•	0.2	0.5	0.5	0.5	0.6	0.7	0.7	0.5
Total Receipts to Cash Flow 42	6.5	3.8	4.6	5.5	8.5	7.3	7.3	6.5	8.1	9.9
Cost of Goods to Cash Flow 43	4.0	1.0	2.5	3.2	5.1	4.7	4.8	4.4	5.7	7.0
Cash Flow to Total Debt 44	0.1	•	1.3	0.5	0.3	0.9	0.4	0.7	0.3	0.1

Selected Financial Factors (in Percentages)

Debt Ratio 45	75.6	•	57.6	77.1	65.7	24.8	47.4	35.1	46.4	83.9
Return on Total Assets 46	5.9	•	40.7	26.3	16.2	15.6	13.8	16.0	11.2	7.9
Return on Equity Before Income Taxes 47	12.7	•	90.4	103.7	39.8	19.9	22.4	22.9	18.0	21.3
Return on Equity After Income Taxes 48	10.7	•	88.0	101.0	37.0	18.2	20.6	19.8	14.2	16.4
Profit Margin (Before Income Tax) 49	7.8	11.1	11.2	10.6	7.3	9.4	7.6	9.2	8.3	5.0
Profit Margin (After Income Tax) 50	6.6	11.1	10.9	10.3	6.8	8.6	7.0	7.9	6.5	3.8

Table I

Corporations with and without Net Income

ARCHITECTURAL AND STRUCTURAL METALS

MONEY AMOUNTS AND SIZE OF ASSETS IN THOUSANDS OF DOLLARS

Item Description for Accounting Period 7/09 Through 6/10	Total	Zero Assets	Under 500	500 to 1,000	1,000 to 5,000	5,000 to 10,000	10,000 to 25,000	25,000 to 50,000	50,000 to 100,000	100,000 to 250,000	250,000 to 500,000	500,000 to 2,500,000	2,500,000 and over
Number of Enterprises **1**	7569	512	3648	752	2057	223	246	76	25	15	7	9	0

Revenues ($ in Thousands)

	Total	Zero Assets	Under 500	500 to 1,000	1,000 to 5,000	5,000 to 10,000	10,000 to 25,000	25,000 to 50,000	50,000 to 100,000	100,000 to 250,000	250,000 to 500,000	500,000 to 2,500,000	2,500,000 and over
Net Sales **2**	40823108	24346	2439413	1080638	8451872	3331377	6123548	3885560	2355603	3167702	2528345	7434705	0
Interest **3**	96160	1454	250	1076	3447	830	4670	3446	3273	5179	19650	52885	0
Rents **4**	48754	0	0	0	542	320	1629	238	562	392	38755	6315	0
Royalties **5**	29208	0	0	0	1688	0	290	75	0	210	98	26847	0
Other Portfolio Income **6**	190173	841	6699	650	23318	8153	4375	2464	413	728	694	141842	0
Other Receipts **7**	338580	151	-5998	269	75763	18466	25186	29854	28106	18171	54926	93681	0
Total Receipts **8**	41525983	26792	2440364	1082633	8556630	3359146	6159698	3921637	2387957	3192382	2642468	7756275	0
Average Total Receipts **9**	5486	52	669	1440	4160	15063	25039	51600	95518	212825	377495	861808	•

Operating Costs/Operating Income (%)

	Total	Zero Assets	Under 500	500 to 1,000	1,000 to 5,000	5,000 to 10,000	10,000 to 25,000	25,000 to 50,000	50,000 to 100,000	100,000 to 250,000	250,000 to 500,000	500,000 to 2,500,000	2,500,000 and over
Cost of Operations **10**	70.7	63.1	67.8	68.2	67.6	74.2	71.0	73.8	72.7	68.1	79.1	69.7	•
Salaries and Wages **11**	7.2	0.2	4.5	8.9	7.7	5.3	6.7	7.1	6.8	9.5	5.0	8.7	•
Taxes Paid **12**	1.8	3.4	1.7	2.3	2.4	2.1	1.8	1.5	1.3	1.8	1.2	1.8	•
Interest Paid **13**	2.0	0.1	0.5	0.3	0.8	0.5	0.8	1.7	1.1	1.7	7.7	4.6	•
Depreciation **14**	2.9	10.1	1.2	2.1	1.8	2.4	2.0	2.6	2.2	2.6	4.4	5.6	•
Amortization and Depletion **15**	0.3	•	0.0	0.0	0.1	0.0	0.3	0.3	0.4	0.6	1.1	0.6	•
Pensions and Other Deferred Comp. **16**	0.9	•	1.5	0.0	0.4	0.8	0.5	0.3	0.3	0.7	3.8	1.3	•
Employee Benefits **17**	2.3	0.3	0.9	4.0	3.2	1.2	1.9	1.7	1.7	3.1	0.7	3.0	•
Advertising **18**	0.6	0.0	0.4	0.9	0.4	0.4	0.2	0.4	0.8	0.8	0.2	1.4	•
Other Expenses **19**	10.0	95.7	14.3	13.4	12.0	9.1	7.2	6.9	8.1	8.3	8.4	11.6	•
Officers' Compensation **20**	2.6	0.1	9.1	5.6	4.5	3.1	2.3	1.3	1.3	0.5	1.2	0.5	•
Operating Margin **21**	•	•	•	•	•	0.9	5.5	2.5	3.3	2.3	•	•	•
Operating Margin Before Officers' Comp. **22**	1.3	•	7.1	•	•	3.6	4.0	7.8	3.8	4.6	2.9	•	•

Selected Average Balance Sheet ($ in Thousands)

Item	1	2	3	4	5	6	7	8	9	10	11	
Net Receivables 23	842	0	172	696	1647	3688	7662	14239	29103	48135	178877	•
Inventories 24	593	0	153	350	1403	2947	6588	14780	23423	34163	121307	•
Net Property, Plant and Equipment 25	1015	0	133	511	1944	3180	7051	14656	43508	88950	334046	•
Total Assets 26	4327	0	729	2207	7642	14638	34314	73079	165828	313563	1392318	•
Notes and Loans Payable 27	1580	0	110	714	1371	3229	10100	18188	71189	155423	613125	•
All Other Liabilities 28	1032	0	214	527	1722	3542	9526	18503	43987	112873	274901	•
Net Worth 29	1715	0	405	966	4549	7868	14689	36389	50652	45268	504293	•

Selected Financial Ratios (Times to 1)

Item	1	2	3	4	5	6	7	8	9	10	11	
Current Ratio 30	1.9	•	1.2	2.9	2.3	2.4	2.3	1.9	2.0	2.0	1.4	•
Quick Ratio 31	1.2	•	0.9	2.1	1.7	1.7	1.6	1.2	1.2	1.2	0.9	•
Net Sales to Working Capital 32	5.4	•	26.3	3.7	4.7	4.8	4.6	5.3	4.8	5.6	6.8	•
Coverage Ratio 33	1.4	•	•	1.5	4.1	9.0	3.0	5.1	2.9	•	0.6	•
Total Asset Turnover 34	1.2	•	3.4	2.0	1.9	2.0	1.7	1.5	1.3	1.2	0.6	•
Inventory Turnover 35	6.4	•	24.6	6.4	7.9	7.9	6.0	5.7	4.6	6.1	4.7	•
Receivables Turnover 36	5.7	•	11.3	8.3	5.7	5.9	4.8	5.5	8.0	4.4	5.2	•
Total Liabilities to Net Worth 37	1.5	•	6.5	0.8	1.3	0.7	0.9	1.3	1.0	2.3	1.8	•
Current Assets to Working Capital 38	2.1	•	5.5	1.5	1.8	1.7	1.8	2.1	2.0	2.2	3.4	•
Current Liabilities to Working Capital 39	1.1	•	4.5	0.5	0.7	0.8	0.8	1.1	1.0	1.2	2.4	•
Working Capital to Net Sales 40	0.2	•	0.0	0.3	0.2	0.2	0.2	0.2	0.6	0.2	0.1	•
Inventory to Working Capital 41	0.5	•	0.8	0.4	0.4	0.5	0.5	0.6	0.6	0.3	0.9	•
Total Receipts to Cash Flow 42	14.0	3.8	25.3	48.2	11.9	11.1	9.0	12.2	8.8	10.9	26.3	•
Cost of Goods to Cash Flow 43	9.9	2.4	17.1	32.9	8.0	8.2	6.4	9.0	6.4	7.4	18.3	•
Cash Flow to Total Debt 44	0.1	•	0.2	0.1	0.3	0.4	0.4	0.2	0.6	0.2	0.0	•

Selected Financial Factors (in Percentages)

Item	1	2	3	4	5	6	7	8	9	10	11	
Debt Ratio 45	60.4	•	86.8	44.5	56.2	40.5	46.3	57.2	50.2	69.5	85.6 / 63.8	•
Return on Total Assets 46	3.5	•	2.1	4.3	7.6	11.7	7.5	6.1	•	•	1.6	•
Return on Equity Before Income Taxes 47	2.5	•	1.6	5.5	11.7	19.3	12.1	12.9	•	•	•	•
Return on Equity After Income Taxes 48	0.9	•	1.0	4.4	9.9	17.5	10.3	10.6	•	•	•	•
Profit Margin (Before Income Tax) 49	0.8	•	0.4	1.7	3.4	6.1	4.7	3.1	•	•	•	•
Profit Margin (After Income Tax) 50	0.3	•	0.2	1.3	2.8	5.5	4.0	2.6	•	•	•	•

115

Table II
Corporations with Net Income

ARCHITECTURAL AND STRUCTURAL METALS

MONEY AMOUNTS AND SIZE OF ASSETS IN THOUSANDS OF DOLLARS

Item Description for Accounting Period 7/09 Through 6/10	Total	Zero Assets	Under 500	500 to 1,000	1,000 to 5,000	5,000 to 10,000	10,000 to 25,000	25,000 to 50,000	50,000 to 100,000	100,000 to 250,000	250,000 to 500,000	500,000 to 2,500,000	2,500,000 and over
Number of Enterprises 1	3713	•	2156	220	935	115	200	52	18	10	•	•	0
Revenues ($ in Thousands)													
Net Sales 2	23484386	•	973583	277619	4259121	2031901	5366613	2566204	1833611	2286308	•	•	0
Interest 3	51792	•	236	488	1968	354	4489	2372	2289	4554	•	•	0
Rents 4	4684	•	0	0	542	0	1548	205	533	236	•	•	0
Royalties 5	11466	•	0	0	1688	0	290	1	0	210	•	•	0
Other Portfolio Income 6	54532	•	6696	0	552	7738	3683	531	266	655	•	•	0
Other Receipts 7	182429	•	4505	208	65886	15378	23520	25723	24320	11544	•	•	0
Total Receipts 8	23789289	•	985020	278315	4329757	2055371	5400143	2595036	1861019	2303507	•	•	0
Average Total Receipts 9	6407	•	457	1265	4631	17873	27001	49905	103390	230351	•	•	•
Operating Costs/Operating Income (%)													
Cost of Operations 10	68.9	•	51.5	62.7	64.6	69.7	70.7	71.9	73.0	66.7	•	•	•
Salaries and Wages 11	6.4	•	5.5	8.1	6.7	5.9	6.0	6.1	6.2	9.2	•	•	•
Taxes Paid 12	1.6	•	2.2	2.7	2.0	1.9	1.7	1.6	1.3	1.9	•	•	•
Interest Paid 13	0.9	•	0.8	0.0	0.3	0.2	0.6	0.9	0.6	1.1	•	•	•
Depreciation 14	2.4	•	2.6	1.7	1.5	1.8	1.8	2.5	2.1	2.4	•	•	•
Amortization and Depletion 15	0.2	•	0.0	•	0.0	0.0	0.1	0.1	0.4	0.1	•	•	•
Pensions and Other Deferred Comp. 16	0.7	•	1.5	0.1	0.6	1.2	0.5	0.3	0.3	0.7	•	•	•
Employee Benefits 17	2.0	•	1.8	3.8	2.5	0.7	1.8	1.6	1.5	3.1	•	•	•
Advertising 18	0.4	•	0.6	1.9	0.3	0.4	0.2	0.4	0.3	1.0	•	•	•
Other Expenses 19	8.2	•	19.0	11.0	11.0	8.2	6.7	5.1	5.2	8.2	•	•	•
Officers' Compensation 20	2.6	•	11.4	6.4	4.7	2.8	2.3	1.5	1.2	0.4	•	•	•
Operating Margin 21	5.7	•	3.1	1.7	5.7	7.2	7.6	7.9	7.9	5.2	•	•	•
Operating Margin Before Officers' Comp. 22	8.3	•	14.5	8.0	10.4	10.0	9.9	9.4	9.1	5.6	•	•	•

Selected Average Balance Sheet ($ in Thousands)

Net Receivables 23	918	38	161	659	1272	3863	7921	15029	26443
Inventories 24	730	15	124	360	1673	2926	7307	12365	24475
Net Property, Plant and Equipment 25	882	47	93	386	1940	3206	6213	15322	34898
Total Assets 26	4564	189	617	1962	8190	14818	33867	71232	162984
Notes and Loans Payable 27	1042	134	133	299	923	2680	6914	8024	36267
All Other Liabilities 28	1083	24	190	501	1450	3478	8882	18034	46239
Net Worth 29	2439	31	294	1161	5817	8660	18071	45174	80478

Selected Financial Ratios (Times to 1)

Current Ratio 30	2.2	•	1.0	3.1	3.5	2.7	2.1	2.6	2.0
Quick Ratio 31	1.5	•	0.7	2.4	2.8	1.9	1.4	1.7	1.3
Net Sales to Working Capital 32	4.6	•	•	2.7	4.4	4.1	4.7	3.8	5.3
Coverage Ratio 33	9.6	6.3	2651.0	23.2	38.8	15.2	10.6	15.6	6.3
Total Asset Turnover 34	1.4	2.4	2.0	2.3	2.2	1.8	1.5	1.4	
Inventory Turnover 35	6.0	15.5	6.4	8.2	7.4	6.5	4.9	6.0	6.2
Receivables Turnover 36	4.9	9.2	8.0	4.8	4.7	5.2	4.6	•	1.0
Total Liabilities to Net Worth 37	0.9	5.1	1.1	0.7	0.4	0.7	0.9	0.6	1.0
Current Assets to Working Capital 38	1.8	•	1.1	1.5	1.4	1.6	1.9	1.6	2.0
Current Liabilities to Working Capital 39	0.8	•	0.1	0.5	0.4	0.6	0.9	0.6	1.0
Working Capital to Net Sales 40	0.2	•	0.4	0.2	0.2	0.2	0.2	0.3	0.2
Inventory to Working Capital 41	0.4	•	0.3	0.3	0.2	0.4	0.5	0.5	0.6
Total Receipts to Cash Flow 42	8.0	8.4	15.0	6.9	6.3	7.8	8.2	7.6	8.5
Cost of Goods to Cash Flow 43	5.5	4.3	9.4	4.5	4.4	5.5	5.9	5.5	5.7
Cash Flow to Total Debt 44	0.4	0.3	0.3	0.8	1.2	0.6	0.4	0.5	0.3

Selected Financial Factors (in Percentages)

Debt Ratio 45	46.6	83.5	52.4	40.8	29.0	41.6	46.6	36.6	50.6
Return on Total Assets 46	11.8	12.2	3.9	17.8	18.4	15.9	14.5	14.3	9.9
Return on Equity Before Income Taxes 47	19.8	62.2	8.2	28.8	25.3	25.5	24.6	21.1	16.8
Return on Equity After Income Taxes 48	17.5	60.1	6.8	27.6	23.6	23.5	22.4	19.1	14.7
Profit Margin (Before Income Tax) 49	7.6	4.3	1.9	7.3	8.3	8.2	9.0	9.4	5.9
Profit Margin (After Income Tax) 50	6.7	4.2	1.6	7.0	7.8	7.6	8.2	8.5	5.2

Table I

Corporations with and without Net Income

BOILER, TANK, AND SHIPPING CONTAINER

MONEY AMOUNTS AND SIZE OF ASSETS IN THOUSANDS OF DOLLARS

Item Description for Accounting Period 7/09 Through 6/10		Total	Zero Assets	Under 500	500 to 1,000	1,000 to 5,000	5,000 to 10,000	10,000 to 25,000	25,000 to 50,000	50,000 to 100,000	100,000 to 250,000	250,000 to 500,000	500,000 to 2,500,000	2,500,000 and over
Number of Enterprises	1	587	21	0	184	269	4	58	19	12	7	5	4	3
Revenues ($ in Thousands)														
Net Sales	2	23067540	759185	0	168198	940219	55122	1510379	1046826	900039	910097	1397852	4215356	11164266
Interest	3	56535	683	0	0	6	6	965	41	436	2766	4009	2609	45013
Rents	4	24557	0	0	0	2352	0	586	0	22	0	9633	9021	2944
Royalties	5	134088	0	0	0	0	0	0	0	517	17	132	21352	112070
Other Portfolio Income	6	76112	622	0	408	0	0	127	2433	967	2451	6686	2292	60125
Other Receipts	7	199969	6842	0	1477	330	8	3701	2752	4163	6833	13022	24649	136193
Total Receipts	8	23558801	767332	0	170083	942907	55136	1515758	1052052	906144	922164	1431334	4275279	11520611
Average Total Receipts	9	40134	36540	•	924	3505	13784	26134	55371	75512	131738	286267	1068820	3840204
Operating Costs/Operating Income (%)														
Cost of Operations	10	77.6	77.4	•	51.4	74.5	68.2	75.9	73.2	71.8	68.6	72.8	75.4	81.6
Salaries and Wages	11	3.9	11.6	•	13.9	11.5	9.0	5.4	4.6	7.6	4.9	5.8	2.8	2.0
Taxes Paid	12	1.0	1.9	•	3.7	1.4	2.3	1.5	1.7	1.4	1.5	1.5	1.1	0.6
Interest Paid	13	3.1	11.2	•	1.0	0.3	0.0	0.6	1.6	0.9	4.2	4.4	2.6	3.5
Depreciation	14	3.6	2.6	•	1.8	1.4	0.5	1.9	2.3	4.2	4.2	3.9	5.8	3.3
Amortization and Depletion	15	1.0	0.6	•	•	•	•	0.1	0.5	1.0	0.7	1.1	0.5	1.4
Pensions and Other Deferred Comp.	16	1.1	0.0	•	1.0	0.4	0.3	0.7	0.4	0.2	0.4	0.1	2.9	0.9
Employee Benefits	17	1.6	2.3	•	0.4	4.3	1.0	1.4	2.0	2.2	1.3	0.8	0.6	1.8
Advertising	18	0.2	0.0	•	0.8	0.3	0.2	1.5	0.4	0.4	0.1	0.2	0.1	0.0
Other Expenses	19	5.3	7.7	•	11.0	9.2	5.7	6.7	6.2	6.7	6.8	7.4	3.5	4.7
Officers' Compensation	20	1.0	0.3	•	8.0	3.3	2.9	1.5	1.9	1.4	0.7	2.5	0.2	0.6
Operating Margin	21	0.6	•	•	7.0	•	9.8	2.7	5.3	2.3	6.8	•	4.4	•
Operating Margin Before Officers' Comp.	22	1.5	•	•	15.0	•	12.7	4.2	7.2	3.8	7.4	2.0	4.6	0.1

Selected Average Balance Sheet ($ in Thousands)

Net Receivables 23	3411	110	0	2261	396	3729	8905	10934	23739	61667	77335	188720
Inventories 24	4596	113	0	1096	498	3599	7926	11475	15263	71826	247642	389954
Net Property, Plant and Equipment 25	7417	346	0	703	193	3199	6866	16659	40130	37560	232498	773512
Total Assets 26	42966	788	0	8328	1479	16698	34474	65970	174118	396427	968310	5051865
Notes and Loans Payable 27	18977	136	0	86	2230	2650	10660	21862	69000	134091	343332	2456376
All Other Liabilities 28	11457	55	0	6919	392	4079	10145	16133	37757	181148	221242	1301439
Net Worth 29	12531	597	0	1324	-1143	9969	13669	27975	67362	81188	403736	1294050

Selected Financial Ratios (Times to 1)

Current Ratio 30	1.4	•	5.6	2.0	1.0	3.6	2.2	1.1	1.5	1.2	2.1	1.0
Quick Ratio 31	0.7	•	4.0	1.0	0.4	2.2	1.3	0.7	0.8	0.5	1.2	0.3
Net Sales to Working Capital 32	12.2	•	2.5	6.5	•	3.2	4.2	25.4	5.7	9.7	6.0	•
Coverage Ratio 33	1.9	•	8.8	•	5443.0	6.4	4.8	4.2	3.0	1.5	3.3	1.8
Total Asset Turnover 34	0.9	•	1.2	2.4	1.7	1.6	1.6	1.1	0.7	0.7	1.1	0.7
Inventory Turnover 35	6.6	•	4.2	5.2	8.6	5.5	5.1	4.7	5.8	2.8	3.2	7.8
Receivables Turnover 36	10.2	•	6.1	9.9	3.5	7.0	6.0	6.2	5.0	4.8	5.1	39.4
Total Liabilities to Net Worth 37	2.4	•	0.3	•	5.3	0.7	1.5	1.4	1.6	3.9	1.4	2.9
Current Assets to Working Capital 38	3.6	•	1.2	2.0	•	1.4	1.9	10.5	2.9	6.3	1.9	•
Current Liabilities to Working Capital 39	2.6	•	0.2	1.0	•	0.4	0.9	9.5	1.9	5.3	0.9	•
Working Capital to Net Sales 40	0.1	•	0.4	0.2	•	0.3	0.2	0.0	0.2	0.1	0.2	•
Inventory to Working Capital 41	1.5	•	0.3	0.9	•	0.5	0.6	3.2	0.5	2.9	0.7	•
Total Receipts to Cash Flow 42	15.2	•	10.4	6.5	•	12.0	9.1	12.6	7.4	13.0	13.2	15.8
Cost of Goods to Cash Flow 43	11.8	•	5.3	4.4	•	9.1	6.7	9.0	5.0	9.4	10.0	12.9
Cash Flow to Total Debt 44	0.1	•	0.5	0.3	•	0.3	0.3	0.2	0.2	0.1	0.1	0.1

Selected Financial Factors (in Percentages)

Debt Ratio 45	70.8	•	24.3	177.3	84.1	40.3	60.3	57.6	61.3	79.5	58.3	74.4
Return on Total Assets 46	5.4	•	10.6	•	16.3	5.7	11.9	4.4	9.2	4.5	9.1	4.6
Return on Equity Before Income Taxes 47	8.6	•	12.4	19.2	102.8	8.0	23.6	7.9	15.7	7.2	15.2	7.8
Return on Equity After Income Taxes 48	6.0	•	12.4	20.8	102.8	6.4	21.7	5.8	13.1	6.5	9.9	6.2
Profit Margin (Before Income Tax) 49	2.7	•	8.1	•	9.9	3.1	5.9	2.9	8.1	2.1	5.8	2.7
Profit Margin (After Income Tax) 50	1.9	•	8.1	•	9.9	2.4	5.4	2.2	6.8	1.9	3.8	2.1

Table II

Corporations with Net Income

BOILER, TANK, AND SHIPPING CONTAINER

MONEY AMOUNTS AND SIZE OF ASSETS IN THOUSANDS OF DOLLARS

Item Description for Accounting Period 7/09 Through 6/10	Total	Zero Assets	Under 500	500 to 1,000	1,000 to 5,000	5,000 to 10,000	10,000 to 25,000	25,000 to 50,000	50,000 to 100,000	100,000 to 250,000	250,000 to 500,000	500,000 to 2,500,000	2,500,000 and over
Number of Enterprises **1**	435	•	0	184	164	0	46	15	•	•	•	•	0
Revenues ($ in Thousands)													
Net Sales **2**	17723911	•	0	168198	692571	0	1301403	844259	•	•	•	•	0
Interest **3**	48418	•	0	0	6	0	692	0	•	•	•	•	0
Rents **4**	13456	•	0	0	2352	0	586	0	•	•	•	•	0
Royalties **5**	131784	•	0	0	0	0	0	0	•	•	•	•	0
Other Portfolio Income **6**	67372	•	0	408	0	0	80	2322	•	•	•	•	0
Other Receipts **7**	156729	•	0	1477	0	0	2662	1013	•	•	•	•	0
Total Receipts **8**	18141670	•	0	170083	694929	0	1305423	847594	•	•	•	•	0
Average Total Receipts **9**	41705	•	•	924	4237	•	28379	56506	•	•	•	•	•
Operating Costs/Operating Income (%)													
Cost of Operations **10**	77.7	•	•	51.4	69.2	•	74.1	71.7	•	•	•	•	•
Salaries and Wages **11**	3.2	•	•	13.9	9.0	•	5.2	4.0	•	•	•	•	•
Taxes Paid **12**	1.0	•	•	3.7	1.5	•	1.6	1.7	•	•	•	•	•
Interest Paid **13**	2.8	•	•	1.0	0.4	•	0.4	0.7	•	•	•	•	•
Depreciation **14**	3.2	•	•	1.8	1.5	•	1.8	2.0	•	•	•	•	•
Amortization and Depletion **15**	0.5	•	•	•	•	•	0.0	0.0	•	•	•	•	•
Pensions and Other Deferred Comp. **16**	1.3	•	•	1.0	0.6	•	0.5	0.5	•	•	•	•	•
Employee Benefits **17**	1.2	•	•	0.4	3.1	•	1.2	2.4	•	•	•	•	•
Advertising **18**	0.2	•	•	0.8	0.4	•	1.7	0.4	•	•	•	•	•
Other Expenses **19**	4.7	•	•	11.0	6.1	•	7.9	5.3	•	•	•	•	•
Officers' Compensation **20**	1.1	•	•	8.0	4.5	•	1.4	2.1	•	•	•	•	•
Operating Margin **21**	3.0	•	•	7.0	3.8	•	4.1	9.3	•	•	•	•	•
Operating Margin Before Officers' Comp. **22**	4.1	•	•	15.0	8.3	•	5.5	11.4	•	•	•	•	•

Selected Average Balance Sheet ($ in Thousands)

Net Receivables 23	3270	110	432	4134	8072
Inventories 24	5107	113	609	3499	7619
Net Property, Plant and Equipment 25	7381	346	254	3220	6511
Total Assets 26	41257	788	1519	16627	33023
Notes and Loans Payable 27	18250	136	330	1964	4962
All Other Liabilities 28	12101	55	360	3629	10998
Net Worth 29	10906	597	829	11034	17063

Selected Financial Ratios (Times to 1)

Current Ratio 30	1.5	5.6	2.1	3.5	2.1
Quick Ratio 31	0.7	4.0	1.1	2.3	1.4
Net Sales to Working Capital 32	10.4	2.5	6.5	3.5	4.6
Coverage Ratio 33	2.9	8.8	11.4	12.6	15.3
Total Asset Turnover 34	1.0	1.2	2.8	1.7	1.7
Inventory Turnover 35	6.2	4.2	4.8	6.0	5.3
Receivables Turnover 36	11.4	6.1	12.4	7.7	7.0
Total Liabilities to Net Worth 37	2.8	0.3	0.8	0.5	0.9
Current Assets to Working Capital 38	3.2	1.2	1.9	1.4	1.9
Current Liabilities to Working Capital 39	2.2	0.2	0.9	0.4	0.9
Working Capital to Net Sales 40	0.1	0.4	0.2	0.3	0.2
Inventory to Working Capital 41	1.3	0.3	0.8	0.4	0.5
Total Receipts to Cash Flow 42	11.4	10.4	14.4	9.0	7.0
Cost of Goods to Cash Flow 43	8.9	5.3	9.9	6.7	5.1
Cash Flow to Total Debt 44	0.1	0.5	0.4	0.6	0.5

Selected Financial Factors (in Percentages)

Debt Ratio 45	73.6	24.3	45.5	33.6	48.3
Return on Total Assets 46	8.1	10.6	12.5	8.1	17.8
Return on Equity Before Income Taxes 47	20.3	12.4	20.9	11.3	32.1
Return on Equity After Income Taxes 48	16.3	12.4	17.4	9.4	30.1
Profit Margin (Before Income Tax) 49	5.4	8.1	4.1	4.4	9.7
Profit Margin (After Income Tax) 50	4.4	8.1	3.4	3.7	9.1

Table I
Corporations with and without Net Income

COATING, ENGRAVING, HEAT TREATING, AND ALLIED ACTIVITIES

MONEY AMOUNTS AND SIZE OF ASSETS IN THOUSANDS OF DOLLARS

Item Description for Accounting Period 7/09 Through 6/10	Total	Zero Assets	Under 500	500 to 1,000	1,000 to 5,000	5,000 to 10,000	10,000 to 25,000	25,000 to 50,000	50,000 to 100,000	100,000 to 250,000	250,000 to 500,000	500,000 to 2,500,000	2,500,000 and over
Number of Enterprises 1	3999	296	2433	346	704	133	49	19	8	7	0	4	0
Revenues ($ in Thousands)													
Net Sales 2	11647794	102016	1152222	352862	2800123	1800220	986955	778362	905676	599181	0	2170178	0
Interest 3	25776	1004	402	2	2434	1119	554	754	783	5005	0	13720	0
Rents 4	11114	0	1071	0	3118	640	672	771	3676	0	0	1165	0
Royalties 5	21567	16	0	0	0	0	0	673	717	12816	0	7345	0
Other Portfolio Income 6	104815	387	52054	0	525	2944	23458	37	1947	6245	0	17219	0
Other Receipts 7	106099	963	41267	353	26680	4672	1427	3482	3764	3916	0	19574	0
Total Receipts 8	11917165	104386	1247016	353217	2832880	1809595	1013066	784079	916563	627163	0	2229201	0
Average Total Receipts 9	2980	353	513	1021	4024	13606	20675	41267	114570	89595	•	557300	•
Operating Costs/Operating Income (%)													
Cost of Operations 10	62.5	47.4	35.4	61.3	54.5	67.8	66.3	71.4	75.2	75.2	•	70.1	•
Salaries and Wages 11	8.5	18.0	14.1	4.8	10.0	6.8	7.0	6.2	6.5	6.9	•	8.1	•
Taxes Paid 12	2.5	2.6	4.5	1.0	3.6	1.8	2.7	2.3	2.0	0.7	•	1.7	•
Interest Paid 13	8.3	8.1	0.5	1.7	0.6	33.3	1.9	1.5	1.1	8.2	•	11.0	•
Depreciation 14	3.9	6.5	2.0	1.4	3.0	2.9	5.0	5.3	4.9	8.9	•	4.3	•
Amortization and Depletion 15	0.5	1.0	•	•	0.0	0.0	0.1	0.3	1.5	2.1	•	1.4	•
Pensions and Other Deferred Comp. 16	0.6	0.9	0.2	0.8	1.1	0.6	0.8	0.3	0.4	0.6	•	0.4	•
Employee Benefits 17	2.2	0.9	1.3	5.1	3.3	0.7	1.9	2.7	2.2	2.1	•	2.3	•
Advertising 18	0.2	0.2	0.0	0.7	0.2	0.1	0.2	0.1	0.1	0.4	•	0.1	•
Other Expenses 19	12.3	31.3	30.6	7.0	13.9	10.5	7.7	5.7	4.5	5.1	•	11.9	•
Officers' Compensation 20	5.0	3.1	13.5	5.3	9.1	3.9	4.0	1.4	1.3	0.7	•	0.7	•
Operating Margin 21	•	•	•	10.9	0.8	•	2.2	2.8	0.2	•	•	•	•
Operating Margin Before Officers' Comp. 22	•	•	11.3	16.2	9.9	•	6.2	4.3	1.5	•	•	•	•

Selected Average Balance Sheet ($ in Thousands)

Net Receivables 23	410	0	36	82	471	1901	3207	6305	11725	18044	110388
Inventories 24	327	0	7	103	136	375	1417	3441	7467	20631	192272
Net Property, Plant and Equipment 25	694	0	74	282	592	2083	6246	12679	33145	46702	166743
Total Assets 26	2807	178	673	1887	7718	15484	33296	77365	159829		1269316
Notes and Loans Payable 27	1377	175	405	449	7658	6551	8130	18515	63548		634257
All Other Liabilities 28	531	38	114	306	3033	2484	6953	17674	38631		176153
Net Worth 29	900	-36	154	1132	-2973	6449	18213	41176	57650		458906

Selected Financial Ratios (Times to 1)

Current Ratio 30	1.7	•	1.5	2.4	2.8	0.9	2.1	1.8	1.6	2.4	1.8
Quick Ratio 31	1.2	•	1.3	1.6	2.2	0.7	1.5	1.3	1.0	1.6	0.9
Net Sales to Working Capital 32	7.5	•	17.6	4.4	6.1	•	6.1	6.6	5.5	5.4	5.0
Coverage Ratio 33	0.5	•	12.9	7.5	4.3	0.2	3.5	3.4	2.3	0.2	0.2
Total Asset Turnover 34	1.0	•	2.7	1.5	2.1	1.8	1.3	1.2	1.5	0.5	0.4
Inventory Turnover 35	5.6	•	23.9	6.0	15.9	24.5	9.4	8.5	11.4	3.1	2.0
Receivables Turnover 36	5.6	•	11.6	7.0	7.6	7.7	5.8	7.4	8.1	3.4	2.8
Total Liabilities to Net Worth 37	2.1	•	•	3.4	0.7	•	1.4	0.8	0.9	1.8	1.8
Current Assets to Working Capital 38	2.3	•	3.2	1.7	1.6	1.9	1.9	2.3	1.7	2.8	2.3
Current Liabilities to Working Capital 39	1.3	•	2.2	0.7	0.6	0.9	0.9	1.3	0.7	1.8	1.3
Working Capital to Net Sales 40	0.1	•	0.1	0.2	0.2	0.2	0.2	0.2	0.2	0.2	0.2
Inventory to Working Capital 41	0.5	•	0.3	0.5	0.2	0.3	0.3	0.5	0.5	0.8	0.7
Total Receipts to Cash Flow 42	23.6	15.4	3.9	5.8	8.7	9.9	9.9	13.3	32.0	•	234.3
Cost of Goods to Cash Flow 43	14.8	7.3	1.4	3.6	4.7	6.6	6.6	9.5	24.0	•	164.3
Cash Flow to Total Debt 44	0.1	•	0.6	0.3	0.6	0.2	0.2	0.2	0.1	•	0.0

Selected Financial Factors (in Percentages)

Debt Ratio 45	67.9	•	120.0	77.1	40.0	138.5	58.4	45.3	46.8	63.9	63.8
Return on Total Assets 46	4.1	•	17.5	19.3	5.4	9.4	8.8	6.3	3.8	1.0	0.8
Return on Equity Before Income Taxes 47	•	•	•	73.1	6.9	127.5	15.1	8.1	4.0	•	•
Return on Equity After Income Taxes 48	•	•	•	73.0	6.9	128.1	14.2	7.5	0.8	•	•
Profit Margin (Before Income Tax) 49	•	•	6.1	11.0	2.0	•	4.8	3.6	1.5	•	•
Profit Margin (After Income Tax) 50	•	•	6.0	11.0	2.0	•	4.5	3.3	0.3	•	•

Table II

Corporations with Net Income

COATING, ENGRAVING, HEAT TREATING, AND ALLIED ACTIVITIES

MONEY AMOUNTS AND SIZE OF ASSETS IN THOUSANDS OF DOLLARS

Item Description for Accounting Period 7/09 Through 6/10		Total	Zero Assets	Under 500	500 to 1,000	1,000 to 5,000	5,000 to 10,000	10,000 to 25,000	25,000 to 50,000	50,000 to 100,000	100,000 to 250,000	250,000 to 500,000	500,000 to 2,500,000	2,500,000 and over
Number of Enterprises	1	2639	293	1637	243	306	104	32	15	5	4	0	0	0
Revenues ($ in Thousands)														
Net Sales	2	6461542	45307	824760	176669	1248881	1516036	821357	655587	577843	595103	0	0	0
Interest	3	11650	112	83	2	813	921	551	565	262	8341	0	0	0
Rents	4	5106	0	0	0	487	0	672	771	3175	0	0	0	0
Royalties	5	13117	0	0	0	0	0	0	673	0	12444	0	0	0
Other Portfolio Income	6	83326	0	51622	0	108	2937	23430	32	0	5201	0	0	0
Other Receipts	7	74777	868	39925	4	21290	2072	1978	2851	2302	3482	0	0	0
Total Receipts	8	6649518	46287	916390	176675	1271579	1521966	847988	660479	583582	624571	0	0	0
Average Total Receipts	9	2520	158	560	727	4155	14634	26500	44032	116716	156143	•	•	•
Operating Costs/Operating Income (%)														
Cost of Operations	10	59.6	39.3	28.0	60.8	53.4	67.7	67.4	72.5	74.5	57.7	•	•	•
Salaries and Wages	11	6.8	2.3	12.9	0.3	7.4	6.6	5.7	6.1	4.9	4.5	•	•	•
Taxes Paid	12	2.2	2.0	3.4	0.8	3.2	1.5	2.7	2.0	1.4	1.3	•	•	•
Interest Paid	13	1.6	1.2	0.4	0.1	0.3	1.5	1.4	1.6	0.7	8.4	•	•	•
Depreciation	14	3.0	4.1	1.9	1.2	2.9	2.3	2.5	4.7	4.6	3.6	•	•	•
Amortization and Depletion	15	0.3	0.3	•	•	0.0	0.0	0.1	0.4	0.5	1.9	•	•	•
Pensions and Other Deferred Comp.	16	0.5	•	0.1	1.6	1.4	0.0	0.9	0.3	0.2	0.4	•	•	•
Employee Benefits	17	1.5	0.4	0.4	0.1	2.2	0.4	1.8	2.1	1.9	3.0	•	•	•
Advertising	18	0.2	0.4	0.0	0.0	0.3	0.1	0.3	0.1	0.1	0.3	•	•	•
Other Expenses	19	11.8	36.9	31.5	5.2	10.6	10.3	6.5	5.3	5.0	11.9	•	•	•
Officers' Compensation	20	4.8	1.5	15.3	2.7	7.8	2.3	3.1	1.1	1.1	1.4	•	•	•
Operating Margin	21	7.7	11.6	6.2	27.3	10.5	7.3	7.7	3.9	5.1	5.5	•	•	•
Operating Margin Before Officers' Comp.	22	12.5	13.0	21.5	30.0	18.3	9.6	10.8	5.0	6.2	6.9	•	•	•

Selected Average Balance Sheet ($ in Thousands)

Net Receivables **23**	313	0	28	59	397	2182	4074	6405	9522	35827
Inventories **24**	354	0	4	87	151	219	1505	2427	8766	25297
Net Property, Plant and Equipment **25**	427	0	81	175	638	1522	4108	11400	28728	38133
Total Assets **26**	1907	0	165	539	1971	7476	14401	33535	74158	478904
Notes and Loans Payable **27**	447	0	53	42	343	2676	4922	8547	6023	95922
All Other Liabilities **28**	288	0	15	8	209	1365	2835	6688	14129	66396
Net Worth **29**	1172	0	98	489	1418	3435	6644	18299	54006	316587

Selected Financial Ratios (Times to 1)

Current Ratio **30**	2.4	•	3.9	17.0	3.4	1.4	2.8	1.7	3.0	2.5
Quick Ratio **31**	1.8	•	3.5	13.8	2.8	1.2	2.1	1.2	2.0	1.6
Net Sales to Working Capital **32**	6.0	•	8.8	2.1	5.9	17.1	5.0	7.0	4.8	2.7
Coverage Ratio **33**	7.4	12.4	47.8	212.5	36.5	6.2	8.6	3.9	9.8	2.3
Total Asset Turnover **34**	1.3	•	3.0	1.3	2.1	1.9	1.8	1.3	1.6	0.3
Inventory Turnover **35**	4.1	•	35.8	5.1	14.4	45.0	11.5	13.1	9.8	3.4
Receivables Turnover **36**	4.3	•	18.0	4.2	5.8	7.0	5.8	9.3	•	4.6
Total Liabilities to Net Worth **37**	0.6	•	0.7	0.1	0.4	1.2	1.2	0.8	0.4	0.5
Current Assets to Working Capital **38**	1.7	•	1.3	1.1	1.4	3.3	1.5	2.3	1.5	1.7
Current Liabilities to Working Capital **39**	0.7	•	0.3	0.1	0.4	2.3	0.5	1.3	0.5	0.7
Working Capital to Net Sales **40**	0.2	•	0.1	0.5	0.2	0.1	0.2	0.1	0.2	0.4
Inventory to Working Capital **41**	0.3	•	0.1	0.2	0.1	0.3	0.2	0.6	0.4	0.5
Total Receipts to Cash Flow **42**	5.2	2.6	2.7	3.1	4.8	6.6	6.5	11.8	10.5	4.7
Cost of Goods to Cash Flow **43**	3.1	1.0	0.8	1.9	2.6	4.5	4.4	8.6	7.9	2.7
Cash Flow to Total Debt **44**	0.6	•	2.8	4.7	1.5	0.5	0.5	0.2	0.5	0.2

Selected Financial Factors (in Percentages)

Debt Ratio **45**	38.5	•	41.0	9.2	28.0	54.0	53.9	45.4	27.2	33.9
Return on Total Assets **46**	15.7	•	53.7	37.0	26.2	17.9	22.0	8.1	10.6	5.9
Return on Equity Before Income Taxes **47**	22.1	•	89.1	40.6	35.4	32.7	42.2	11.0	13.1	4.9
Return on Equity After Income Taxes **48**	21.1	•	88.8	40.5	35.3	32.1	40.7	10.5	9.2	3.9
Profit Margin (Before Income Tax) **49**	10.6	13.7	17.3	27.3	12.3	7.7	10.9	4.6	6.1	10.5
Profit Margin (After Income Tax) **50**	10.1	9.2	17.2	27.3	12.3	7.6	10.5	4.4	4.3	8.3

Table I

Corporations with and without Net Income

OTHER FABRICATED METAL PRODUCT

MONEY AMOUNTS AND SIZE OF ASSETS IN THOUSANDS OF DOLLARS

Item Description for Accounting Period 7/09 Through 6/10		Total	Zero Assets	Under 500	500 to 1,000	1,000 to 5,000	5,000 to 10,000	10,000 to 25,000	25,000 to 50,000	50,000 to 100,000	100,000 to 250,000	250,000 to 500,000	500,000 to 2,500,000	2,500,000 and over
Number of Enterprises	1	16648	1636	9231	1299	3098	730	336	149	81	47	17	18	7
Revenues ($ in Thousands)														
Net Sales	2	102932042	441279	4067730	1970062	11929779	8195433	8224669	7839322	7839804	6732664	5942721	13551781	26196797
Interest	3	726125	1502	2361	1466	4767	3576	3309	2512	6467	17123	9573	100191	573279
Rents	4	42755	186	934	4536	79	410	2467	1555	3862	381	572	5151	22622
Royalties	5	465714	0	0	0	0	1083	4915	369	13591	13248	386	25533	406589
Other Portfolio Income	6	1167056	4055	23366	1073	42687	10055	5028	10403	83486	26627	18432	51305	890541
Other Receipts	7	1283362	29653	30326	9258	69102	31755	48841	40154	33008	71028	31872	396122	492239
Total Receipts	8	106617054	476675	4124717	1986395	12046414	8242312	8289229	7894315	7980218	6861071	6003556	14130083	28582067
Average Total Receipts	9	6404	291	447	1529	3888	11291	24670	52982	98521	145980	353150	785005	4083152
Operating Costs/Operating Income (%)														
Cost of Operations	10	68.2	65.9	63.5	52.2	65.6	64.3	69.0	68.1	70.4	65.5	71.2	71.8	69.9
Salaries and Wages	11	7.7	7.2	6.6	14.1	6.6	8.1	7.3	8.0	7.1	8.9	9.0	6.5	8.1
Taxes Paid	12	1.9	2.2	3.7	2.8	2.4	2.1	1.6	1.6	1.5	1.9	1.6	1.9	1.7
Interest Paid	13	2.7	1.6	1.2	1.5	1.2	0.7	0.9	1.0	1.2	2.4	0.9	4.3	5.4
Depreciation	14	2.8	4.8	1.6	2.4	3.2	2.3	3.2	2.8	3.1	3.6	3.2	3.5	2.1
Amortization and Depletion	15	1.2	0.8	0.1	0.4	0.0	0.0	0.3	0.3	0.3	1.0	0.5	1.4	3.3
Pensions and Other Deferred Comp.	16	1.1	1.0	0.2	0.8	0.5	0.4	0.6	0.5	0.6	0.9	0.9	1.6	2.2
Employee Benefits	17	2.1	1.4	1.2	2.0	1.8	1.7	1.9	1.5	2.1	2.2	1.9	2.2	2.6
Advertising	18	0.8	0.3	0.3	0.4	1.0	0.3	0.5	0.6	0.6	0.6	0.9	0.3	1.5
Other Expenses	19	9.5	31.9	15.3	14.1	12.0	9.1	8.7	8.8	8.2	8.0	7.1	9.0	8.9
Officers' Compensation	20	2.4	5.3	8.8	9.9	5.9	4.3	2.8	2.0	1.7	1.3	0.8	0.7	0.4
Operating Margin	21	•	•	•	•	•	6.7	3.3	4.8	3.0	3.6	1.9	•	•
Operating Margin Before Officers' Comp.	22	1.9	•	6.3	9.3	5.7	11.0	6.0	6.8	4.7	4.9	2.7	•	•

Selected Average Balance Sheet ($ in Thousands)

Net Receivables 23	454102	118916	52896	18914	12505	7663	3298	1469	448	190	25	0	800
Inventories 24	553614	155944	66243	28400	15822	10183	4524	1830	529	135	29	0	1014
Net Property, Plant and Equipment 25	651764	144944	74103	32243	17316	9132	3890	1465	580	147	43	0	1049
Total Assets 26	27937801	1147503	348837	152836	70074	36229	15468	6743	2161	695	154	0	15590
Notes and Loans Payable 27	12030980	467590	54616	41665	15890	9365	3446	1404	770	424	121	0	6273
All Other Liabilities 28	2637601	296119	82019	41191	20434	8604	3269	1244	540	108	55	0	2065
Net Worth 29	13269219	383795	212202	69980	33750	18261	8753	4095	851	162	-22	0	7251

Selected Financial Ratios (Times to 1)

Current Ratio 30	1.5	2.0	3.1	2.3	1.8	2.3	2.7	3.3	2.0	2.3	1.2	•	2.0
Quick Ratio 31	0.5	1.0	1.5	1.2	1.0	1.1	1.5	1.8	1.3	1.6	0.6	•	0.9
Net Sales to Working Capital 32	5.0	3.6	2.9	3.4	5.4	4.0	3.8	3.5	5.5	6.6	32.9	•	4.4
Coverage Ratio 33	2.0	1.3	4.1	3.4	5.3	6.6	5.5	11.8	1.6	1.2	0.1	•	2.4
Total Asset Turnover 34	0.1	0.7	1.0	0.9	1.4	1.5	1.6	1.7	1.8	2.2	2.9	•	0.4
Inventory Turnover 35	4.7	3.5	3.8	3.3	4.3	3.5	3.7	3.9	4.8	5.9	9.7	•	4.2
Receivables Turnover 36	5.0	6.0	6.1	6.8	7.4	7.0	6.6	7.5	6.8	7.1	13.1	•	6.3
Total Liabilities to Net Worth 37	1.1	2.0	0.6	1.2	1.1	1.0	0.8	0.6	1.5	3.3	•		1.1
Current Assets to Working Capital 38	2.9	2.0	1.5	1.8	2.2	1.8	1.6	1.4	2.0	1.8	6.3	•	2.0
Current Liabilities to Working Capital 39	1.9	1.0	0.5	0.8	1.2	0.8	0.6	0.4	1.0	0.8	5.3	•	1.0
Working Capital to Net Sales 40	0.2	0.3	0.3	0.3	0.2	0.2	0.3	0.3	0.2	0.2	0.0	•	0.2
Inventory to Working Capital 41	0.5	0.6	0.5	0.6	0.9	0.8	0.6	0.6	0.7	0.5	2.2	•	0.6
Total Receipts to Cash Flow 42	10.0	11.8	12.2	8.8	8.8	8.2	9.7	7.1	11.5	11.0	11.8	10.9	9.8
Cost of Goods to Cash Flow 43	7.0	8.5	8.7	5.7	6.2	5.6	6.7	4.6	7.5	5.7	7.5	7.2	6.7
Cash Flow to Total Debt 44	0.0	0.1	0.2	0.2	0.3	0.4	0.4	0.6	0.3	0.3	0.2	•	0.1

Selected Financial Factors (in Percentages)

Debt Ratio 45	52.5	66.6	39.2	54.2	51.8	49.6	43.4	39.3	60.6	76.7	114.1	•	53.5
Return on Total Assets 46	1.5	3.6	3.9	7.6	8.7	9.5	7.9	13.2	3.5	3.9	0.4	•	2.6
Return on Equity Before Income Taxes 47	1.6	2.4	4.8	11.6	14.7	16.0	11.4	19.9	3.4	2.9	22.2	•	3.3
Return on Equity After Income Taxes 48	0.9	•	2.6	8.5	11.5	14.3	10.0	18.4	2.4	0.2	23.6	•	2.2
Profit Margin (Before Income Tax) 49	5.6	1.2	2.9	5.7	5.1	5.6	4.1	7.2	0.7	0.3	•	•	3.8
Profit Margin (After Income Tax) 50	3.2	•	1.6	4.1	4.0	5.0	3.6	6.7	0.5	0.0	•	•	2.6

Table II
Corporations with Net Income

OTHER FABRICATED METAL PRODUCT

Money Amounts and Size of Assets in Thousands of Dollars

Item Description for Accounting Period 7/09 Through 6/10	Total	Zero Assets	Under 500	500 to 1,000	1,000 to 5,000	5,000 to 10,000	10,000 to 25,000	25,000 to 50,000	50,000 to 100,000	100,000 to 250,000	250,000 to 500,000	500,000 to 2,500,000	2,500,000 and over
Number of Enterprises 1	8749	415	4835	782	1586	656	239	113	•	36	12	12	•
Revenues ($ in Thousands)													
Net Sales 2	77497776	130451	1775025	1269746	7529934	7540037	6255324	6424230	•	5533567	3705734	10074668	•
Interest 3	542353	485	329	1308	3551	2229	2452	1552	•	14720	8304	59601	•
Rents 4	37197	186	0	4375	9	410	2415	1351	•	374	250	4846	•
Royalties 5	442823	0	0	0	0	0	9	301	•	13248	361	24491	•
Other Portfolio Income 6	1078322	31	13473	40	5683	4033	4774	8764	•	25337	15668	51172	•
Other Receipts 7	1052217	7344	10286	5146	47342	31433	30284	34421	•	65509	36210	371099	•
Total Receipts 8	80650688	138497	1799113	1280615	7586519	7578142	6295258	6470619	•	5652755	3766527	10585877	•
Average Total Receipts 9	9218	334	372	1638	4783	11552	26340	57262	•	157021	313877	882156	•
Operating Costs/Operating Income (%)													
Cost of Operations 10	65.8	40.4	51.0	45.2	61.4	63.3	66.6	65.7	•	63.2	64.5	71.3	•
Salaries and Wages 11	7.7	12.7	6.4	16.8	5.7	7.9	7.1	7.9	•	9.1	8.9	6.9	•
Taxes Paid 12	1.9	3.8	3.1	2.6	2.3	2.1	1.7	1.7	•	2.0	1.7	2.0	•
Interest Paid 13	2.2	1.6	0.4	1.0	0.7	0.6	0.7	0.8	•	1.4	1.1	3.4	•
Depreciation 14	2.4	0.5	1.2	1.9	2.7	2.1	2.7	2.2	•	3.4	3.7	3.1	•
Amortization and Depletion 15	1.3	•	0.0	0.0	0.0	0.0	0.1	0.2	•	0.4	0.5	1.1	•
Pensions and Other Deferred Comp. 16	1.1	•	0.1	0.9	0.5	0.4	0.6	0.5	•	0.9	1.1	1.6	•
Employee Benefits 17	1.8	0.1	0.6	1.6	1.3	1.7	1.7	1.5	•	2.0	1.6	1.8	•
Advertising 18	0.9	•	0.4	0.4	1.0	0.2	0.4	0.6	•	0.7	1.0	0.3	•
Other Expenses 19	9.3	18.1	16.4	15.9	11.6	8.8	7.9	9.0	•	8.1	8.2	7.7	•
Officers' Compensation 20	2.4	15.9	10.0	11.0	6.3	4.4	3.0	2.1	•	1.3	1.0	0.7	•
Operating Margin 21	3.1	7.0	10.3	2.7	6.4	8.4	7.5	7.9	•	7.4	6.7	•	•
Operating Margin Before Officers' Comp. 22	5.5	23.0	20.3	13.7	12.7	12.9	10.5	10.0	•	8.7	7.6	0.7	•

Selected Average Balance Sheet ($ in Thousands)

		•	•	•	•	•	•	•	•	•	•	•
Net Receivables	23	1116	0	15	204	523	1502	3613	8044	18929	52304	121476
Inventories	24	1538	0	17	134	644	1836	5150	11056	31454	63162	178410
Net Property, Plant and Equipment	25	1325	0	52	151	482	1311	3308	7434	30989	74485	143315
Total Assets	26	26031	0	109	624	2257	6689	15081	36109	153240	344794	1025171
Notes and Loans Payable	27	10895	0	45	250	641	1117	2774	7870	34050	53137	439327
All Other Liabilities	28	2395	0	18	102	514	1128	3317	8988	29582	78084	276133
Net Worth	29	12741	0	46	272	1103	4444	8990	19251	89607	213573	309712

Selected Financial Ratios (Times to 1)

		•	•	•	•	•	•	•	•	•	•	•
Current Ratio	30	2.0	•	2.5	2.3	2.8	3.7	3.0	2.7	2.6	3.4	2.2
Quick Ratio	31	0.9	•	1.8	1.8	1.8	2.1	1.8	1.3	1.3	1.6	1.2
Net Sales to Working Capital	32	4.4	•	11.4	7.3	4.5	3.3	3.6	3.6	3.2	2.4	3.9
Coverage Ratio	33	4.6	9.2	27.3	4.7	10.9	16.4	13.0	11.7	8.1	8.8	2.5
Total Asset Turnover	34	0.3	•	3.4	2.6	2.1	1.7	1.7	1.6	1.0	0.9	0.8
Inventory Turnover	35	3.8	•	10.8	5.5	4.5	4.0	3.4	3.4	3.1	3.2	3.4
Receivables Turnover	36	5.8	•	12.7	6.3	6.3	7.6	6.2	7.1	6.8	5.6	5.9
Total Liabilities to Net Worth	37	1.0	•	1.3	1.3	1.0	0.5	0.7	0.9	0.7	0.6	2.3
Current Assets to Working Capital	38	2.0	•	1.7	1.8	1.6	1.4	1.5	1.6	1.6	1.4	1.9
Current Liabilities to Working Capital	39	1.0	•	0.7	0.8	0.6	0.4	0.5	0.6	0.6	0.4	0.9
Working Capital to Net Sales	40	0.2	•	0.1	0.1	0.2	0.3	0.3	0.3	0.3	0.4	0.3
Inventory to Working Capital	41	0.6	•	0.2	0.4	0.5	0.6	0.6	0.7	0.6	0.5	0.5
Total Receipts to Cash Flow	42	7.0	3.6	4.6	7.1	6.5	6.5	7.2	6.5	6.5	6.8	8.9
Cost of Goods to Cash Flow	43	4.6	1.4	2.3	3.2	4.0	4.1	4.8	4.3	4.1	4.4	6.3
Cash Flow to Total Debt	44	0.1	•	1.3	0.7	0.6	0.8	0.6	0.5	0.4	0.3	0.1

Selected Financial Factors (in Percentages)

		•	•	•	•	•	•	•	•	•	•	•
Debt Ratio	45	51.1	•	57.4	56.4	51.2	33.6	40.4	46.7	41.5	38.1	69.8
Return on Total Assets	46	3.5	•	40.7	11.9	16.5	16.3	15.3	14.9	11.2	8.5	7.1
Return on Equity Before Income Taxes	47	5.7	•	92.1	21.4	30.7	23.1	23.7	25.6	16.8	12.1	14.1
Return on Equity After Income Taxes	48	4.5	•	90.8	18.9	29.2	21.6	21.7	23.4	13.6	8.9	9.3
Profit Margin (Before Income Tax)	49	8.2	13.2	11.7	3.6	7.1	8.9	8.1	8.7	9.8	8.4	5.2
Profit Margin (After Income Tax)	50	6.5	12.1	11.5	3.2	6.8	8.4	7.5	7.9	7.9	6.2	3.4

122

Table I

Corporations with and without Net Income

AGRICULTURE, CONSTRUCTION, AND MINING MACHINERY

MONEY AMOUNTS AND SIZE OF ASSETS IN THOUSANDS OF DOLLARS

Item Description for Accounting Period 7/09 Through 6/10		Total	Zero Assets	Under 500	500 to 1,000	1,000 to 5,000	5,000 to 10,000	10,000 to 25,000	25,000 to 50,000	50,000 to 100,000	100,000 to 250,000	250,000 to 500,000	500,000 to 2,500,000	2,500,000 and over
Number of Enterprises	1	3324	•	•	•	987	175	109	54	34	24	13	12	11
Revenues ($ in Thousands)														
Net Sales	2	108889146	•	•	•	3700252	1628757	2206693	2354285	2774063	3749602	3521761	13179580	74484758
Interest	3	3084851	•	•	•	662	836	21595	2823	3656	6305	20624	43882	2984285
Rents	4	1251555	•	•	•	1620	688	7188	84	789	6459	1598	59433	1173519
Royalties	5	653034	•	•	•	0	0	251	0	636	3119	0	40080	608949
Other Portfolio Income	6	770492	•	•	•	34319	13872	35195	3521	2673	13810	23884	55123	587735
Other Receipts	7	2619820	•	•	•	34300	13124	20561	9686	23065	45793	76121	284884	2106465
Total Receipts	8	117068898	•	•	•	3771153	1657277	2291483	2370399	2804882	3825088	3643988	13662982	81945711
Average Total Receipts	9	35219	•	•	•	3821	9470	21023	43896	82497	159379	280307	1138582	7449610
Operating Costs/Operating Income (%)														
Cost of Operations	10	72.7	•	•	•	67.0	67.4	72.0	69.9	68.3	69.3	70.9	76.1	73.2
Salaries and Wages	11	8.3	•	•	•	9.2	9.8	8.8	6.8	7.8	7.8	8.5	5.7	8.7
Taxes Paid	12	0.9	•	•	•	1.6	1.9	2.0	1.2	1.4	1.8	1.4	1.1	0.7
Interest Paid	13	4.0	•	•	•	1.1	1.1	1.6	1.0	1.5	1.5	2.8	2.2	5.0
Depreciation	14	4.6	•	•	•	5.4	4.7	2.5	2.1	2.8	3.5	2.9	3.4	5.2
Amortization and Depletion	15	0.5	•	•	•	0.1	0.1	0.2	0.3	0.5	0.6	1.1	0.4	0.5
Pensions and Other Deferred Comp.	16	1.6	•	•	•	0.3	0.1	0.4	1.0	0.8	0.7	0.5	0.8	2.0
Employee Benefits	17	2.1	•	•	•	1.0	1.5	2.7	2.0	1.9	1.3	1.8	1.1	2.4
Advertising	18	0.4	•	•	•	0.7	2.0	0.8	0.6	0.7	0.7	0.6	0.6	0.2
Other Expenses	19	10.6	•	•	•	8.5	11.4	7.1	8.4	8.0	9.9	10.2	8.6	11.2
Officers' Compensation	20	0.6	•	•	•	3.7	2.6	2.4	2.0	1.6	0.9	1.0	0.3	0.2
Operating Margin	21	•	•	•	•	1.4	•	•	4.7	4.6	2.0	•	•	•
Operating Margin Before Officers' Comp.	22	•	•	•	•	5.1	1.8	1.8	6.7	6.3	2.9	•	•	•

Selected Average Balance Sheet ($ in Thousands)

Net Receivables 23	14715	239	1289	3160	6854	10401	31216	64288	154310	3989184
Inventories 24	5963	532	2219	4832	10859	21131	46604	69512	196349	1140057
Net Property, Plant and Equipment 25	6412	508	1343	2450	6123	11996	28937	44547	210458	1426277
Total Assets 26	57838	1923	6207	14103	33533	70499	161242	339889	1244130	14524498
Notes and Loans Payable 27	24986	879	1681	4553	9468	16698	38772	82639	306822	6761041
All Other Liabilities 28	17382	268	1915	4425	6746	19317	49351	106947	358177	4426187
Net Worth 29	15470	776	2611	5125	17320	34484	73119	150303	579130	3337269

Selected Financial Ratios (Times to 1)

Current Ratio 30	1.8	2.5	1.5	1.9	2.4	2.1	1.8	2.0	1.6	1.7
Quick Ratio 31	1.1	1.2	0.6	0.9	1.1	1.0	0.8	1.0	0.7	1.2
Net Sales to Working Capital 32	2.9	5.8	6.3	4.2	3.2	3.7	3.6	3.0	6.9	2.4
Coverage Ratio 33	1.6	4.0	0.0	3.0	6.3	4.9	3.8	1.7	3.2	1.4
Total Asset Turnover 34	0.6	1.9	1.5	1.4	1.3	1.2	1.0	0.8	0.9	0.5
Inventory Turnover 35	4.0	4.7	2.8	3.0	2.8	2.6	2.3	2.8	4.3	4.3
Receivables Turnover 36	2.1	13.0	8.3	5.9	6.5	5.9	5.4	3.7	6.4	1.6
Total Liabilities to Net Worth 37	2.7	1.5	1.4	1.8	0.9	1.0	1.2	1.3	1.1	3.4
Current Assets to Working Capital 38	2.3	1.7	3.0	2.1	1.7	1.9	2.3	2.0	2.8	2.3
Current Liabilities to Working Capital 39	1.3	0.7	2.0	1.1	0.7	0.9	1.3	1.0	1.8	1.3
Working Capital to Net Sales 40	0.3	0.2	0.2	0.2	0.3	0.3	0.3	0.3	0.1	0.4
Inventory to Working Capital 41	0.5	0.9	1.6	1.0	0.8	0.9	1.0	0.7	1.2	0.4
Total Receipts to Cash Flow 42	9.7	10.2	13.8	14.2	8.2	8.1	8.3	10.6	9.6	9.8
Cost of Goods to Cash Flow 43	7.1	6.9	9.3	10.3	5.7	5.5	5.7	7.5	7.3	7.2
Cash Flow to Total Debt 44	0.1	0.3	0.2	0.2	0.3	0.3	0.2	0.1	0.2	0.1

Selected Financial Factors (in Percentages)

Debt Ratio 45	73.3	59.6	57.9	63.7	48.4	51.1	54.7	55.8	53.5	77.0
Return on Total Assets 46	3.6	8.5	0.1	6.8	8.2	8.4	5.5	3.8	6.3	3.1
Return on Equity Before Income Taxes 47	5.2	15.8	•	12.6	13.3	13.7	9.0	3.7	9.3	3.6
Return on Equity After Income Taxes 48	2.4	14.9	•	9.0	10.8	11.2	5.8	1.0	5.5	1.0
Profit Margin (Before Income Tax) 49	2.5	3.3	•	3.2	5.3	5.8	4.2	2.0	4.9	1.8
Profit Margin (After Income Tax) 50	1.2	3.1	•	2.3	4.3	4.7	2.7	0.6	2.9	0.5

Table II

Corporations with Net Income

AGRICULTURE, CONSTRUCTION, AND MINING MACHINERY

MONEY AMOUNTS AND SIZE OF ASSETS IN THOUSANDS OF DOLLARS

Item Description for Accounting Period 7/09 Through 6/10	Total	Zero Assets	Under 500	500 to 1,000	1,000 to 5,000	5,000 to 10,000	10,000 to 25,000	25,000 to 50,000	50,000 to 100,000	100,000 to 250,000	250,000 to 500,000	500,000 to 2,500,000	2,500,000 and over
Number of Enterprises **1**	2483	•	•	201	632	51	84	39	23	14	9	•	6
Revenues ($ in Thousands)													
Net Sales **2**	70983541	•	•	467423	2973993	673638	1803538	1709303	2208848	2660642	2504484	•	42930539
Interest **3**	2001911	•	•	20	654	780	21255	2078	2204	2508	7471	•	1936984
Rents **4**	737427	•	•	177	1620	688	7188	29	544	6213	1170	•	660365
Royalties **5**	209162	•	•	0	0	0	251	0	636	1713	0	•	180498
Other Portfolio Income **6**	601870	•	•	359	34111	13427	34384	3136	2491	13547	18498	•	454845
Other Receipts **7**	1186660	•	•	4108	29014	7852	21611	4926	19798	19258	64802	•	739067
Total Receipts **8**	75720571	•	•	472087	3039392	696385	1888227	1719472	2234521	2703881	2596425	•	46902298
Average Total Receipts **9**	30496	•	•	2349	4809	13655	22479	44089	97153	193134	288492	•	7817050
Operating Costs/Operating Income (%)													
Cost of Operations **10**	73.3	•	•	59.0	69.2	70.4	68.9	66.7	67.4	66.8	67.5	•	74.3
Salaries and Wages **11**	7.9	•	•	12.3	6.4	5.6	8.2	6.7	7.0	7.3	8.0	•	8.8
Taxes Paid **12**	0.8	•	•	2.2	1.1	1.7	1.9	1.1	1.3	1.5	1.4	•	0.5
Interest Paid **13**	3.1	•	•	1.1	0.2	0.9	1.5	0.6	0.6	0.9	2.4	•	4.4
Depreciation **14**	4.1	•	•	2.2	4.4	7.1	2.6	2.2	2.1	3.1	2.6	•	4.9
Amortization and Depletion **15**	0.4	•	•	•	0.1	0.0	0.1	0.0	0.2	0.4	1.5	•	0.3
Pensions and Other Deferred Comp. **16**	1.2	•	•	0.2	0.4	0.3	0.3	1.0	0.7	0.9	0.4	•	1.5
Employee Benefits **17**	1.9	•	•	1.1	0.6	0.9	2.8	2.3	1.5	1.4	1.7	•	2.3
Advertising **18**	0.4	•	•	1.3	0.8	0.3	0.9	0.5	0.7	0.8	0.6	•	0.1
Other Expenses **19**	7.0	•	•	14.4	6.7	8.2	8.2	7.5	7.2	8.6	9.9	•	6.3
Officers' Compensation **20**	0.7	•	•	2.2	3.7	1.0	2.5	2.2	1.8	0.8	1.1	•	0.2
Operating Margin **21**	•	•	•	4.0	6.3	3.7	2.0	9.2	9.5	7.5	3.0	•	•
Operating Margin Before Officers' Comp. **22**	0.1	•	•	6.3	10.0	4.7	4.5	11.5	11.3	8.3	4.1	•	•

Selected Average Balance Sheet ($ in Thousands)

Net Receivables 23	14319	105	301	1179	3333	7802	12060	28112	62595	5279814
Inventories 24	6304	137	437	2565	4016	9969	21518	49855	58571	1714910
Net Property, Plant and Equipment 25	4656	170	469	1825	2553	5083	10306	25986	42096	1321628
Total Assets 26	42124	837	2107	7004	13918	31520	69951	162517	353243	13399869
Notes and Loans Payable 27	16097	301	446	2419	4447	6344	11507	26937	94226	5728211
All Other Liabilities 28	11204	151	256	1336	4004	5705	19760	49037	103603	3493852
Net Worth 29	14823	385	1404	3249	5467	19472	38683	86543	155414	4177806

Selected Financial Ratios (Times to 1)

Current Ratio 30	2.7	2.9	4.4	1.9	2.1	3.0	2.3	1.7	1.9	3.1
Quick Ratio 31	1.9	1.9	2.6	0.7	1.1	1.5	1.2	0.8	1.1	2.2
Net Sales to Working Capital 32	1.8	6.3	5.0	5.7	3.9	2.8	3.7	4.5	3.4	1.3
Coverage Ratio 33	3.3	5.5	40.0	9.0	5.5	17.0	18.5	11.2	4.0	2.5
Total Asset Turnover 34	0.7	2.8	2.2	1.9	1.5	1.4	1.4	1.2	0.8	0.5
Inventory Turnover 35	3.3	10.0	7.5	3.6	3.7	2.9	3.0	2.5	3.2	3.1
Receivables Turnover 36	1.6	26.1	12.6	10.4	6.3	•	6.3	6.2	4.2	1.1
Total Liabilities to Net Worth 37	1.8	1.2	0.5	1.2	1.5	0.6	0.8	0.9	1.3	2.2
Current Assets to Working Capital 38	1.6	1.5	1.3	2.1	1.9	1.5	1.7	2.4	2.1	1.5
Current Liabilities to Working Capital 39	0.6	0.5	0.3	1.1	0.9	0.5	0.7	1.4	1.1	0.5
Working Capital to Net Sales 40	0.5	0.2	0.2	0.2	0.3	0.4	0.3	0.2	0.3	0.8
Inventory to Working Capital 41	0.3	0.5	0.5	1.2	0.8	0.6	0.7	1.1	0.6	0.2
Total Receipts to Cash Flow 42	9.0	6.2	7.4	7.6	8.5	6.3	6.0	6.2	7.2	10.3
Cost of Goods to Cash Flow 43	6.6	3.6	5.1	5.4	5.8	4.2	4.0	4.1	4.9	7.7
Cash Flow to Total Debt 44	0.1	0.8	0.9	0.5	0.3	0.6	0.5	0.4	0.2	0.1

Selected Financial Factors (in Percentages)

Debt Ratio 45	64.8	54.0	33.4	53.6	60.7	38.2	44.7	46.7	56.0	68.8
Return on Total Assets 46	6.9	17.0	19.4	14.9	12.6	14.3	15.6	12.1	7.5	5.9
Return on Equity Before Income Taxes 47	13.6	30.3	28.4	28.6	26.2	21.9	26.7	20.6	12.8	11.6
Return on Equity After Income Taxes 48	9.7	23.9	27.6	24.6	21.8	18.8	23.4	16.0	9.2	7.7
Profit Margin (Before Income Tax) 49	7.1	5.0	8.5	7.0	6.7	9.7	10.8	9.4	7.1	6.8
Profit Margin (After Income Tax) 50	5.0	4.0	8.2	6.0	5.5	8.3	9.4	7.3	5.1	4.5

124

Table I

Corporations with and without Net Income

INDUSTRIAL MACHINERY

MONEY AMOUNTS AND SIZE OF ASSETS IN THOUSANDS OF DOLLARS

Item Description for Accounting Period 7/09 Through 6/10	Total	Zero Assets	Under 500	500 to 1,000	1,000 to 5,000	5,000 to 10,000	10,000 to 25,000	25,000 to 50,000	50,000 to 100,000	100,000 to 250,000	250,000 to 500,000	500,000 to 2,500,000	2,500,000 and over
Number of Enterprises 1	3667	295	1695	320	699	357	136	66	38	33	13	9	5
Revenues ($ in Thousands)													
Net Sales 2	40870245	138384	523246	538266	3451265	2942380	2920549	2787033	2431523	3896126	4328608	7749967	9162897
Interest 3	156180	428	0	118	1034	1405	5013	5938	6952	18401	9974	39650	67268
Rents 4	93736	1572	0	0	352	163	2563	6031	1177	18991	48788	6782	7318
Royalties 5	139460	2	0	0	0	1066	52	1040	179	9941	37626	25278	64276
Other Portfolio Income 6	457541	20	0	1514	608	9475	5883	8767	5566	14052	62347	92818	256489
Other Receipts 7	449008	45556	0	5533	36947	33231	21607	16867	24182	31704	52095	109557	71732
Total Receipts 8	42166170	185962	523246	545431	3490206	2987720	2955667	2825676	2469579	3989215	4539438	8024052	9629980
Average Total Receipts 9	11499	630	309	1704	4993	8369	21733	42813	64989	120885	349188	891561	1925996
Operating Costs/Operating Income (%)													
Cost of Operations 10	66.4	82.1	43.7	63.9	60.5	68.0	71.5	72.1	70.3	65.7	67.8	66.9	64.1
Salaries and Wages 11	10.8	16.0	4.3	5.4	12.4	10.3	11.3	8.9	10.0	12.6	9.2	9.0	13.2
Taxes Paid 12	1.6	1.3	1.0	1.4	2.4	2.0	1.7	1.6	1.9	1.6	1.1	1.6	1.2
Interest Paid 13	2.0	1.3	0.9	1.2	1.0	1.1	0.7	1.5	2.1	1.5	2.4	2.5	3.0
Depreciation 14	2.8	4.0	1.0	3.5	1.6	2.7	1.9	3.8	2.1	2.5	2.6	3.1	3.5
Amortization and Depletion 15	1.1	1.3	•	0.1	0.1	0.3	0.3	0.9	1.2	1.3	1.6	1.4	1.5
Pensions and Other Deferred Comp. 16	1.0	0.9	0.7	0.4	0.6	0.5	0.8	0.4	0.9	0.7	1.3	1.8	1.0
Employee Benefits 17	2.6	6.7	4.3	2.9	2.8	3.2	2.4	1.9	1.9	2.5	2.9	2.0	2.9
Advertising 18	0.5	0.3	0.5	2.5	0.3	0.5	0.6	0.6	0.5	0.4	0.3	0.6	0.6
Other Expenses 19	11.5	105.7	29.8	7.3	7.4	8.6	9.4	9.5	7.7	11.3	9.8	10.2	15.8
Officers' Compensation 20	1.9	2.0	8.7	8.6	4.9	4.1	2.8	1.9	1.6	1.4	0.7	0.7	0.6
Operating Margin 21	•	•	5.1	2.8	6.0	•	•	•	•	•	0.3	0.2	•
Operating Margin Before Officers' Comp. 22	•	•	13.8	11.4	10.9	2.8	•	•	1.3	•	1.0	0.9	•

Selected Average Balance Sheet ($ in Thousands)

Net Receivables 23	3949	0	15	233	778	967	2914	7523	12928	25049	79534	164170	1754108
Inventories 24	2068	0	38	217	610	2247	4494	8692	12030	20055	68141	117339	394683
Net Property, Plant and Equipment 25	1759	0	23	60	572	1686	2264	7286	10751	20158	45598	139768	335734
Total Assets 26	17472	0	154	650	2656	6961	15424	34361	71856	147521	355730	1061276	6623815
Notes and Loans Payable 27	3787	0	53	425	690	3249	2785	9782	20829	35008	104788	307627	983272
All Other Liabilities 28	5422	0	41	52	603	1382	5784	14909	19590	34557	132513	404791	1971922
Net Worth 29	8264	0	60	174	1363	2330	6855	9669	31437	77956	118429	348858	3668621

Selected Financial Ratios (Times to 1)

Current Ratio 30	1.6	•	2.9	10.7	2.6	2.2	1.8	2.0	1.9	2.0	1.8	1.3	1.5
Quick Ratio 31	1.1	•	0.4	7.2	1.5	1.0	0.9	1.2	1.1	1.2	1.0	0.8	1.2
Net Sales to Working Capital 32	3.5	•	3.6	3.2	4.4	3.7	4.7	3.8	3.7	3.0	3.9	9.1	2.0
Coverage Ratio 33	2.0	•	6.6	4.4	8.5	1.2	•	1.2	1.6	1.6	3.7	3.2	0.9
Total Asset Turnover 34	0.6	•	2.0	2.6	1.9	1.2	1.4	1.2	0.9	0.8	0.9	0.8	0.3
Inventory Turnover 35	3.6	•	3.5	4.9	4.9	2.5	3.4	3.5	3.7	3.9	3.3	4.9	3.0
Receivables Turnover 36	2.9	•	18.1	6.0	6.8	5.8	6.2	5.4	4.2	4.3	3.8	4.1	1.2
Total Liabilities to Net Worth 37	1.1	•	1.6	2.7	0.9	2.0	1.3	2.6	1.3	0.9	2.0	2.0	0.8
Current Assets to Working Capital 38	2.6	•	1.5	1.1	1.6	1.9	2.3	2.0	2.2	2.0	2.2	4.1	3.1
Current Liabilities to Working Capital 39	1.6	•	0.5	0.1	0.6	0.9	1.3	1.0	1.2	1.0	1.2	3.1	2.1
Working Capital to Net Sales 40	0.3	•	0.3	0.3	0.2	0.3	0.2	0.3	0.3	0.3	0.3	0.1	0.5
Inventory to Working Capital 41	0.6	•	0.7	0.3	0.6	0.8	0.9	0.6	0.5	0.5	0.6	1.2	0.4
Total Receipts to Cash Flow 42	10.3	•	3.4	11.5	8.6	15.8	19.3	18.1	13.7	10.7	7.8	9.3	9.2
Cost of Goods to Cash Flow 43	6.8	•	1.5	7.3	5.2	10.7	13.8	13.0	9.6	7.0	5.3	6.2	5.9
Cash Flow to Total Debt 44	0.1	•	1.0	0.3	0.4	0.1	0.1	0.1	0.1	0.2	0.2	0.1	0.1

Selected Financial Factors (in Percentages)

Debt Ratio 45	52.7	•	61.1	73.2	48.7	66.5	55.6	71.9	56.3	47.2	66.7	67.1	44.6
Return on Total Assets 46	2.6	•	12.1	13.8	15.1	1.5	•	•	3.0	2.0	8.4	6.6	0.7
Return on Equity Before Income Taxes 47	2.7	•	26.3	40.0	25.9	0.7	•	•	2.6	1.5	18.4	13.9	•
Return on Equity After Income Taxes 48	1.3	•	26.3	38.5	25.0	•	•	•	0.1	0.3	12.2	10.1	•
Profit Margin (Before Income Tax) 49	2.0	•	5.1	4.1	7.1	0.2	•	•	1.3	1.0	6.5	5.7	•
Profit Margin (After Income Tax) 50	1.0	•	5.1	4.0	6.9	•	•	•	0.1	0.2	4.3	4.1	•

Table II

Corporations with Net Income

INDUSTRIAL MACHINERY

MONEY AMOUNTS AND SIZE OF ASSETS IN THOUSANDS OF DOLLARS

Item Description for Accounting Period 7/09 Through 6/10	Total	Zero Assets	Under 500	500 to 1,000	1,000 to 5,000	5,000 to 10,000	10,000 to 25,000	25,000 to 50,000	50,000 to 100,000	100,000 to 250,000	250,000 to 500,000	500,000 to 2,500,000	2,500,000 and over
Number of Enterprises 1	1666	•	497	311	597	112	61	30	21	17	9	•	•
Revenues ($ in Thousands)													
Net Sales 2	25574105	•	314144	500170	3271272	1638635	1403753	1391420	1261049	2242720	3269396	•	•
Interest 3	77630	•	0	118	637	152	2687	2391	3603	8183	8709	•	•
Rents 4	74740	•	0	0	301	163	2563	2620	602	8068	48109	•	•
Royalties 5	92434	•	0	0	0	0	0	523	0	87	37601	•	•
Other Portfolio Income 6	408219	•	0	140	451	9112	2043	7521	1978	4336	59659	•	•
Other Receipts 7	381475	•	0	5201	35974	26373	4537	8808	17672	12373	47033	•	•
Total Receipts 8	26775603	•	314144	505629	3308635	1674435	1415583	1413283	1284904	2275767	3470507	•	•
Average Total Receipts 9	16072	•	632	1626	5542	14950	23206	47109	61186	133869	385612	•	•
Operating Costs/Operating Income (%)													
Cost of Operations 10	64.0	•	37.0	59.8	59.5	67.8	69.0	71.8	67.9	60.6	64.4	•	•
Salaries and Wages 11	10.4	•	0.3	5.3	12.5	8.1	10.1	6.8	8.1	11.9	9.8	•	•
Taxes Paid 12	1.7	•	0.4	1.4	2.4	1.8	1.2	1.0	1.8	1.4	1.1	•	•
Interest Paid 13	2.1	•	1.2	1.2	0.7	0.4	0.7	0.8	1.0	0.9	2.2	•	•
Depreciation 14	2.1	•	0.8	3.7	1.4	1.1	2.2	1.6	2.3	2.3	2.6	•	•
Amortization and Depletion 15	1.1	•	•	0.1	0.1	0.1	0.1	0.2	0.5	0.9	1.5	•	•
Pensions and Other Deferred Comp. 16	1.1	•	1.2	0.4	0.7	0.5	0.7	0.4	1.1	0.4	1.3	•	•
Employee Benefits 17	2.0	•	0.5	2.8	2.7	1.8	1.7	1.5	1.5	2.6	2.6	•	•
Advertising 18	0.5	•	0.0	2.7	0.3	0.2	0.4	0.7	0.5	0.4	0.4	•	•
Other Expenses 19	10.3	•	32.7	6.6	6.5	7.7	8.1	7.6	7.7	10.5	11.1	•	•
Officers' Compensation 20	2.0	•	6.9	9.0	4.5	4.8	2.8	2.4	1.6	1.2	0.6	•	•
Operating Margin 21	2.8	•	19.1	7.1	8.7	5.8	3.1	5.2	6.0	6.9	2.4	•	•
Operating Margin Before Officers' Comp. 22	4.8	•	26.0	16.1	13.3	10.6	5.9	7.6	7.6	8.1	3.0	•	•

Selected Average Balance Sheet ($ in Thousands)

Net Receivables 23	3973	11	232	875	1465	2410	7436	12610	21902	93897
Inventories 24	2861	133	182	524	3495	4768	7670	15037	22833	49192
Net Property, Plant and Equipment 25	1979	31	58	552	930	3099	5060	13343	23118	46575
Total Assets 26	23125	370	644	2716	7539	14369	34824	65854	143808	357107
Notes and Loans Payable 27	5394	151	319	519	1699	3619	4312	8035	28891	103022
All Other Liabilities 28	5723	80	41	633	1718	5369	11046	19049	37944	156037
Net Worth 29	12009	139	285	1565	4122	5380	19466	38770	76973	98048

Selected Financial Ratios (Times to 1)

Current Ratio 30	1.6	4.0	13.9	3.1	1.7	1.4	2.3	2.0	2.1	1.4
Quick Ratio 31	1.1	0.1	9.5	1.9	0.8	0.8	1.6	1.3	1.2	0.9
Net Sales to Working Capital 32	4.9	2.5	3.0	4.1	8.3	8.4	3.3	3.0	3.3	7.0
Coverage Ratio 33	4.8	16.9	7.6	15.7	22.6	6.7	9.3	9.3	9.9	5.8
Total Asset Turnover 34	0.7	1.7	2.5	2.0	1.9	1.6	1.3	0.9	0.9	1.0
Inventory Turnover 35	3.5	1.8	5.3	6.2	2.8	3.3	4.3	2.7	3.5	4.8
Receivables Turnover 36	3.1	120.2	6.6	7.2	6.6	5.4	5.7	3.2	4.0	•
Total Liabilities to Net Worth 37	0.9	1.7	1.3	0.7	0.8	1.7	0.8	0.7	0.9	2.6
Current Assets to Working Capital 38	2.6	1.3	1.1	1.5	2.4	3.6	1.8	2.0	1.9	3.4
Current Liabilities to Working Capital 39	1.6	0.3	0.1	0.5	1.4	2.6	0.8	1.0	0.9	2.4
Working Capital to Net Sales 40	0.2	0.4	0.3	0.2	0.1	0.1	0.3	0.3	0.3	0.1
Inventory to Working Capital 41	0.6	0.5	0.3	0.5	0.9	1.5	0.4	0.6	0.4	1.0
Total Receipts to Cash Flow 42	6.8	2.0	8.4	7.4	7.6	9.6	7.8	7.1	6.3	5.8
Cost of Goods to Cash Flow 43	4.3	0.7	5.0	4.4	5.2	6.6	5.6	4.8	3.8	3.7
Cash Flow to Total Debt 44	0.2	1.4	0.5	0.6	0.6	0.3	0.4	0.3	0.3	0.2

Selected Financial Factors (in Percentages)

Debt Ratio 45	48.1	62.5	55.8	42.4	45.3	62.6	44.1	41.1	46.5	72.5
Return on Total Assets 46	6.8	34.6	23.6	21.3	16.3	7.4	10.2	8.1	8.5	12.7
Return on Equity Before Income Taxes 47	10.4	87.0	46.4	34.6	28.4	16.7	16.3	12.3	14.3	38.2
Return on Equity After Income Taxes 48	8.3	87.0	45.5	33.7	25.4	15.1	13.6	9.0	11.9	27.4
Profit Margin (Before Income Tax) 49	8.1	19.1	8.2	9.9	8.0	3.9	6.9	7.9	8.3	10.3
Profit Margin (After Income Tax) 50	6.5	19.1	8.0	9.6	7.1	3.5	5.7	5.8	6.9	7.4

Table I

Corporations with and without Net Income

COMMERCIAL AND SERVICE INDUSTRY MACHINERY

MONEY AMOUNTS AND SIZE OF ASSETS IN THOUSANDS OF DOLLARS

Item Description for Accounting Period 7/09 Through 6/10	Total	Zero Assets	Under 500	500 to 1,000	1,000 to 5,000	5,000 to 10,000	10,000 to 25,000	25,000 to 50,000	50,000 to 100,000	100,000 to 250,000	250,000 to 500,000	500,000 to 2,500,000	2,500,000 and over
Number of Enterprises **1**	2719	439	1319	247	486	101	63	22	11	13	6	8	3
Revenues ($ in Thousands)													
Net Sales **2**	30880632	109436	398790	250202	2365467	1009266	1300268	836983	868175	2121929	1940380	3574381	16105355
Interest **3**	498012	425	33	0	1081	1533	2566	1260	2086	8272	5034	10062	465660
Rents **4**	83299	0	1050	0	1018	165	5	1180	1349	2917	973	18076	56566
Royalties **5**	1069330	0	0	0	1721	0	181	379	1845	523	15049	28754	1020877
Other Portfolio Income **6**	337816	0	232	0	623	416	137	4228	3243	27567	7531	110343	183497
Other Receipts **7**	1622034	-1	3346	0	22961	10145	9680	43955	26386	38371	7537	48399	1411254
Total Receipts **8**	34491123	109860	403451	250202	2392871	1021525	1312837	887985	903084	2199579	1976504	3790015	19243209
Average Total Receipts **9**	12685	250	306	1013	4924	10114	20839	40363	82099	169198	329417	473752	6414403
Operating Costs/Operating Income (%)													
Cost of Operations **10**	58.5	40.6	64.7	48.1	64.2	66.3	70.1	69.5	56.5	68.6	65.2	50.1	55.5
Salaries and Wages **11**	14.6	4.5	6.3	1.4	12.8	8.5	8.2	12.8	13.3	12.9	11.6	20.3	15.8
Taxes Paid **12**	2.5	41.9	2.1	0.4	2.1	1.6	1.8	1.7	1.6	2.3	1.1	2.8	2.7
Interest Paid **13**	4.0	0.2	0.5	0.1	1.3	1.4	1.3	1.6	1.3	2.0	1.9	3.5	5.8
Depreciation **14**	5.8	1.5	0.7	0.0	1.0	1.7	1.6	2.4	2.5	3.5	2.3	4.0	8.8
Amortization and Depletion **15**	1.1	•	•	•	0.1	1.0	0.5	0.5	1.0	0.5	2.4	1.8	1.1
Pensions and Other Deferred Comp. **16**	1.4	0.0	1.1	0.0	0.5	0.4	0.3	0.3	1.4	0.4	1.1	0.4	2.1
Employee Benefits **17**	2.7	1.1	4.5	0.0	2.7	2.5	1.9	2.6	3.8	2.6	1.2	2.2	3.1
Advertising **18**	1.5	0.5	0.4	0.2	1.3	1.4	0.4	0.9	1.4	0.7	0.7	0.6	2.1
Other Expenses **19**	18.2	6.8	15.0	6.2	11.6	13.3	7.8	16.1	16.6	12.0	12.2	21.0	21.9
Officers' Compensation **20**	1.1	•	7.1	1.6	2.9	2.2	2.4	1.8	1.9	1.3	0.7	1.1	0.4
Operating Margin **21**	•	2.8	•	41.9	•	•	3.8	•	•	•	•	•	•
Operating Margin Before Officers' Comp. **22**	•	2.8	4.4	43.6	2.5	1.8	6.2	•	0.4	•	0.3	•	•

Selected Average Balance Sheet ($ in Thousands)

Net Receivables 23	3512	0	11	243	595	1130	2674	8994	13831	40199	62233	99140	2287881
Inventories 24	1443	0	24	234	743	1853	5369	11165	19622	27068	54760	93217	353307
Net Property, Plant and Equipment 25	1740	0	14	0	268	1190	2373	5970	10031	25786	42050	80128	947297
Total Assets 26	19566	0	104	729	2663	7061	16472	37570	77195	157222	373074	787417	12527329
Notes and Loans Payable 27	8098	0	43	0	1061	2136	4003	10460	16961	30285	126600	338858	5565528
All Other Liabilities 28	7330	0	7	402	817	2858	4891	11444	22784	70451	93809	280434	4867366
Net Worth 29	4139	0	53	327	785	2068	7578	15666	37450	56486	152664	168125	2094435

Selected Financial Ratios (Times to 1)

Current Ratio 30	1.7	•	2.8	1.5	1.7	1.5	1.9	1.5	2.0	1.3	1.9	1.1	1.8
Quick Ratio 31	1.1	•	1.6	1.1	0.9	0.7	0.9	1.0	1.0	0.8	1.1	0.7	1.3
Net Sales to Working Capital 32	3.5	•	6.4	4.9	5.3	8.5	3.9	4.6	3.4	7.8	4.9	14.3	2.5
Coverage Ratio 33	1.3	17.1	•	640.9	1.5	1.6	5.8	•	2.9	•	1.8	0.7	1.3
Total Asset Turnover 34	0.6	•	2.9	1.4	1.8	1.4	1.3	1.0	1.0	1.0	0.9	0.6	0.4
Inventory Turnover 35	4.6	•	8.1	2.1	4.2	3.6	2.7	2.4	2.3	4.1	3.8	2.4	8.4
Receivables Turnover 36	3.0	•	20.7	5.0	10.5	7.0	7.4	4.2	6.2	4.3	4.2	4.1	2.1
Total Liabilities to Net Worth 37	3.7	•	1.0	1.2	2.4	2.4	1.2	1.4	1.1	1.8	1.4	3.7	5.0
Current Assets to Working Capital 38	2.5	•	1.6	3.0	2.4	3.1	2.1	3.1	2.0	4.3	2.1	8.2	2.3
Current Liabilities to Working Capital 39	1.5	•	0.6	2.0	1.4	2.1	1.1	2.1	1.0	3.3	1.1	7.2	1.3
Working Capital to Net Sales 40	0.3	•	0.2	0.2	0.2	0.1	0.3	0.2	0.3	0.1	0.2	0.1	0.4
Inventory to Working Capital 41	0.4	•	0.6	0.7	1.0	1.4	1.0	0.9	0.7	1.3	0.7	2.0	0.1
Total Receipts to Cash Flow 42	6.9	15.0	8.5	2.1	11.1	8.2	8.9	10.8	6.0	15.1	8.4	7.7	5.8
Cost of Goods to Cash Flow 43	4.0	6.1	5.5	1.0	7.1	5.4	6.3	7.5	3.4	10.4	5.4	3.9	3.2
Cash Flow to Total Debt 44	0.1	0.7	0.7	1.2	0.2	0.2	0.3	0.2	0.3	0.1	0.2	0.1	0.1

Selected Financial Factors (in Percentages)

Debt Ratio 45	78.8	•	48.7	55.1	70.5	70.7	54.0	58.3	51.5	64.1	59.1	78.6	83.3
Return on Total Assets 46	3.1	•	•	58.3	3.5	3.1	9.1	•	3.9	•	2.9	1.3	3.3
Return on Equity Before Income Taxes 47	3.8	•	•	129.8	4.2	4.0	16.3	•	5.3	•	3.1	•	4.9
Return on Equity After Income Taxes 48	1.0	•	•	129.8	2.4	0.2	12.6	•	4.4	•	2.1	•	1.1
Profit Margin (Before Income Tax) 49	1.4	3.2	•	41.9	0.7	0.8	6.0	•	2.5	•	1.5	•	1.9
Profit Margin (After Income Tax) 50	0.4	2.1	•	41.9	0.4	0.1	4.6	•	2.1	•	1.0	•	0.4

Table II
Corporations with Net Income

COMMERCIAL AND SERVICE INDUSTRY MACHINERY

Money Amounts and Size of Assets in Thousands of Dollars

Item Description for Accounting Period 7/09 Through 6/10	Total	Zero Assets	Under 500	500 to 1,000	1,000 to 5,000	5,000 to 10,000	10,000 to 25,000	25,000 to 50,000	50,000 to 100,000	100,000 to 250,000	250,000 to 500,000	500,000 to 2,500,000	2,500,000 and over
Number of Enterprises **1**	1282	8	657	247	238	60	46	3	6	•	•	8	0
Revenues ($ in Thousands)													
Net Sales **2**	20609386	109436	244775	250202	1528829	740161	993478	140649	543215	•	•	13752678	0
Interest **3**	477940	425	0	0	412	1210	2210	179	429	•	•	465701	0
Rents **4**	8768	0	0	0	0	165	5	0	1291	•	•	5656	0
Royalties **5**	425783	0	0	0	1721	0	128	0	0	•	•	408730	0
Other Portfolio Income **6**	184871	0	0	0	466	256	122	1	3225	•	•	155676	0
Other Receipts **7**	1166694	-1	0	0	17155	1708	6676	407	3954	•	•	1118651	0
Total Receipts **8**	22873442	109860	244775	250202	1548583	743500	1002619	141236	552114	•	•	15907092	0
Average Total Receipts **9**	17842	13732	373	1013	6507	12392	21796	47079	92019	•	•	1988386	•
Operating Costs/Operating Income (%)													
Cost of Operations **10**	51.1	40.6	65.2	48.1	64.4	63.5	67.6	59.4	54.9	•	•	45.0	•
Salaries and Wages **11**	15.4	4.5	6.8	1.4	10.1	7.6	8.2	10.4	9.8	•	•	18.2	•
Taxes Paid **12**	2.8	41.9	0.6	0.4	1.7	1.5	1.9	1.0	1.4	•	•	3.1	•
Interest Paid **13**	4.5	0.2	•	0.1	0.4	1.0	0.8	0.1	0.3	•	•	6.3	•
Depreciation **14**	6.9	1.5	0.5	0.0	0.8	0.4	1.5	1.2	2.5	•	•	9.6	•
Amortization and Depletion **15**	1.1	•	•	•	0.0	0.7	0.5	0.1	0.1	•	•	1.4	•
Pensions and Other Deferred Comp. **16**	1.0	0.0	•	0.0	0.6	0.4	0.4	0.8	2.2	•	•	1.1	•
Employee Benefits **17**	2.7	1.1	•	0.0	2.2	2.7	1.8	1.4	4.0	•	•	3.0	•
Advertising **18**	0.7	0.5	0.6	0.2	0.4	1.1	0.4	0.2	2.1	•	•	0.8	•
Other Expenses **19**	17.9	6.8	11.2	6.2	8.5	10.3	7.4	8.2	12.4	•	•	22.0	•
Officers' Compensation **20**	1.0	•	6.2	1.6	2.5	1.7	2.4	4.7	2.9	•	•	0.5	•
Operating Margin **21**	•	2.8	9.0	41.9	8.2	9.1	7.2	12.4	7.4	•	•	•	•
Operating Margin Before Officers' Comp. **22**	•	2.8	15.2	43.6	10.7	10.8	9.6	17.1	10.3	•	•	•	•

Selected Average Balance Sheet ($ in Thousands)

	•	•	•	•	•	•	•	•	•	•	•
Net Receivables 23	6512	0	0	243	826	1270	2839	10978	10916	•	890214
Inventories 24	1794	0	19	234	998	2210	5573	37554	25365	•	101384
Net Property, Plant and Equipment 25	2348	0	5	0	213	648	1986	1714	13044	•	301454
Total Assets 26	30168	0	62	729	3337	7162	16770	41408	80443	•	4176334
Notes and Loans Payable 27	13667	0	3	0	607	1219	2299	276	7739	•	2087738
All Other Liabilities 28	9377	0	-3	402	820	3918	5255	11054	18032	•	1269940
Net Worth 29	7125	0	62	327	1910	2025	9215	30077	54672	•	818656

Selected Financial Ratios (Times to 1)

	•	•	•	•	•	•	•	•	•	•	•
Current Ratio 30	2.2	•	15.0	1.5	2.7	1.3	2.1	2.9	3.4	•	2.3
Quick Ratio 31	1.8	•	13.6	1.1	1.7	0.6	1.0	2.7	1.8	•	2.0
Net Sales to Working Capital 32	2.4	•	7.1	4.9	3.6	15.3	3.6	2.2	2.5	•	2.0
Coverage Ratio 33	2.5	17.1	•	640.9	22.2	10.5	13.5	105.4	27.4	•	2.0
Total Asset Turnover 34	0.5	•	6.0	1.4	1.9	1.7	1.3	1.1	1.1	•	0.4
Inventory Turnover 35	4.6	•	13.1	2.1	4.1	3.5	2.6	0.7	2.0	•	7.6
Receivables Turnover 36	2.3	•	34.4	5.0	9.2	7.1	7.3	1.7	6.8	•	•
Total Liabilities to Net Worth 37	3.2	•	•	1.2	0.7	2.5	0.8	0.4	0.5	•	4.1
Current Assets to Working Capital 38	1.8	•	1.1	3.0	1.6	4.8	1.9	1.5	1.4	•	1.8
Current Liabilities to Working Capital 39	0.8	•	0.1	2.0	0.6	3.8	0.9	0.5	0.4	•	0.8
Working Capital to Net Sales 40	0.4	•	0.1	0.2	0.3	0.1	0.3	0.4	0.4	•	0.5
Inventory to Working Capital 41	0.2	•	0.1	0.7	0.6	2.3	0.9	0.1	0.1	•	0.1
Total Receipts to Cash Flow 42	5.1	15.0	5.0	2.1	6.4	5.4	7.1	5.0	5.2	•	4.7
Cost of Goods to Cash Flow 43	2.6	6.1	3.2	1.0	4.2	3.4	4.8	3.0	2.8	•	2.1
Cash Flow to Total Debt 44	0.1	•	1.2	0.7	0.4	0.4	0.8	0.7	•	•	0.1

Selected Financial Factors (in Percentages)

	•	•	•	•	•	•	•	•	•	•	•
Debt Ratio 45	76.4	•	55.1	42.8	71.7	45.0	27.4	32.0	•	•	80.4
Return on Total Assets 46	6.0	•	54.3	58.3	19.2	18.2	13.5	14.7	10.4	•	5.1
Return on Equity Before Income Taxes 47	15.5	•	54.2	129.8	32.0	58.2	22.7	20.0	14.8	•	12.8
Return on Equity After Income Taxes 48	12.0	•	54.1	129.8	30.4	51.7	18.4	19.9	13.7	•	8.8
Profit Margin (Before Income Tax) 49	6.9	3.2	9.0	41.9	9.5	9.5	9.7	12.8	8.9	•	6.1
Profit Margin (After Income Tax) 50	5.3	2.1	9.0	41.9	9.0	8.5	7.9	12.8	8.3	•	4.2

Table I
Corporations with and without Net Income

VENTILATION, HEATING, A.C. & COMMERCIAL REFRIGERATION EQUIP.

MONEY AMOUNTS AND SIZE OF ASSETS IN THOUSANDS OF DOLLARS

Item Description for Accounting Period 7/09 Through 6/10	Total	Zero Assets	Under 500	500 to 1,000	1,000 to 5,000	5,000 to 10,000	10,000 to 25,000	25,000 to 50,000	50,000 to 100,000	100,000 to 250,000	250,000 to 500,000	500,000 to 2,500,000	2,500,000 and over
Number of Enterprises **1**	1185	5	658	62	179	117	63	41	26	15	6	8	3
Revenues ($ in Thousands)													
Net Sales **2**	31081391	1475191	364406	136759	721464	1570492	1653858	2146794	2262102	2577614	1631106	7100662	9440944
Interest **3**	94481	190	258	13	478	289	1529	1346	2500	2801	6230	45119	33728
Rents **4**	18530	26	108	0	21	428	219	404	377	2139	746	14056	6
Royalties **5**	247284	39	0	0	0	0	1786	5322	3162	2374	1159	222084	11358
Other Portfolio Income **6**	126657	47110	11464	0	194	376	1910	8713	25635	5397	938	20647	4273
Other Receipts **7**	324857	14617	1257	57	2902	3512	21029	80516	6956	24596	12429	120672	36314
Total Receipts **8**	31893200	1537173	377493	136829	725059	1575097	1680331	2243095	2300732	2614921	1652608	7523240	9526623
Average Total Receipts **9**	26914	307435	574	2207	4051	13462	26672	54710	88490	174328	275435	940405	3175541
Operating Costs/Operating Income (%)													
Cost of Operations **10**	70.7	69.2	44.6	62.3	71.7	76.8	72.9	64.8	67.7	67.5	70.3	69.9	74.1
Salaries and Wages **11**	8.1	8.4	7.6	4.3	10.5	5.6	8.9	10.9	8.9	7.2	8.8	10.4	5.7
Taxes Paid **12**	1.1	0.2	1.2	1.8	2.7	0.7	1.4	1.4	1.7	1.6	1.1	1.6	0.4
Interest Paid **13**	3.9	12.9	0.0	0.1	1.3	0.6	0.7	0.9	1.3	1.7	2.2	2.0	7.7
Depreciation **14**	2.1	1.0	0.4	0.2	2.1	1.0	1.8	2.2	2.6	3.2	3.4	2.1	1.9
Amortization and Depletion **15**	1.2	1.4	0.1	•	1.0	0.2	0.4	0.2	0.4	0.9	0.9	0.7	2.3
Pensions and Other Deferred Comp. **16**	0.5	0.3	0.1	0.6	0.4	0.4	0.6	0.5	0.5	1.1	0.3	0.9	0.0
Employee Benefits **17**	2.0	1.0	0.1	3.4	0.8	0.5	1.4	2.7	2.3	2.4	1.0	1.9	2.6
Advertising **18**	0.8	0.4	0.4	0.2	0.7	0.2	0.9	0.7	0.7	0.7	0.7	1.3	0.7
Other Expenses **19**	11.2	13.1	29.4	4.3	19.0	7.8	7.9	14.9	9.7	8.7	13.8	13.5	8.7
Officers' Compensation **20**	1.1	0.5	1.6	8.8	6.0	2.7	1.5	1.4	2.7	0.6	1.1	0.9	0.3
Operating Margin **21**	•	•	14.6	14.1	•	3.4	1.6	•	1.6	4.3	•	•	•
Operating Margin Before Officers' Comp. **22**	•	•	16.2	22.9	•	6.1	3.1	0.8	4.2	5.0	•	•	•

Selected Average Balance Sheet ($ in Thousands)

Net Receivables **23**	4714	0	64	255	594	1688	4337	8236	13507	24984	66296	155369	748836
Inventories **24**	3081	0	3	347	438	1725	3824	5946	10999	29951	29787	128947	305591
Net Property, Plant and Equipment **25**	3638	0	52	36	267	1353	2891	8447	13737	29972	54357	175691	333924
Total Assets **26**	33323	0	157	778	2173	6613	16047	35737	68553	153866	385400	1327861	6223853
Notes and Loans Payable **27**	7277	0	8	34	962	1924	4156	8842	19250	51207	85469	211051	1374872
All Other Liabilities **28**	17945	0	15	243	1006	4948	9593	18627	56521	119934		590821	4475664
Net Worth **29**	8100	0	133	502	205	3412	6943	17301	30676	46138	179996	525989	373317

Selected Financial Ratios (Times to 1)

Current Ratio **30**	1.2	•	6.4	2.8	1.8	3.3	1.7	1.9	2.1	1.6	1.4	1.7	0.7
Quick Ratio **31**	0.8	•	6.1	1.7	1.2	2.0	1.0	1.3	1.2	0.8	0.9	1.0	0.5
Net Sales to Working Capital **32**	12.6	•	6.7	4.7	5.0	4.3	5.8	5.2	4.4	7.0	7.2	4.9	•
Coverage Ratio **33**	1.1	0.7	11041.0	105.2	•	7.4	5.5	5.4	3.5	4.6	0.1	1.7	0.6
Total Asset Turnover **34**	0.8	•	3.5	2.8	1.9	2.0	1.6	1.5	1.3	1.1	0.7	0.7	0.5
Inventory Turnover **35**	6.0	•	84.1	4.0	6.6	6.0	5.0	5.7	5.4	3.9	6.4	4.8	7.6
Receivables Turnover **36**	5.6	•	15.7	3.4	7.6	6.8	5.8	5.4	6.6	5.4	4.0	6.1	4.5
Total Liabilities to Net Worth **37**	3.1	•	0.2	0.6	9.6	0.9	1.3	1.1	1.2	2.3	1.1	1.5	15.7
Current Assets to Working Capital **38**	5.1	•	1.2	1.6	2.3	1.4	2.4	2.1	1.9	2.8	3.7	2.4	•
Current Liabilities to Working Capital **39**	4.1	•	0.2	0.6	1.3	0.4	1.4	1.1	0.9	1.8	2.7	1.4	•
Working Capital to Net Sales **40**	0.1	•	0.1	0.2	0.2	0.2	0.2	0.2	0.2	0.1	0.1	0.2	•
Inventory to Working Capital **41**	1.4	•	0.0	0.6	0.5	0.5	0.2	0.6	0.5	1.0	1.0	0.7	•
Total Receipts to Cash Flow **42**	10.5	14.4	2.5	6.1	•	9.9	10.3	5.7	9.6	8.0	10.9	8.3	22.5
Cost of Goods to Cash Flow **43**	7.5	10.0	1.1	3.8	•	7.6	7.5	3.7	6.5	5.4	7.6	5.8	16.6
Cash Flow to Total Debt **44**	0.1	•	9.4	1.3	•	0.4	0.3	0.5	0.2	0.2	0.1	0.1	0.0

Selected Financial Factors (in Percentages)

Debt Ratio **45**	75.7	•	15.1	35.5	90.6	48.4	56.7	51.6	55.3	70.0	53.3	60.4	94.0
Return on Total Assets **46**	3.3	•	64.2	40.5	•	8.8	6.2	7.1	5.7	8.6	0.2	2.3	2.2
Return on Equity Before Income Taxes **47**	0.9	•	75.6	62.3	•	14.7	11.8	11.9	9.2	22.3	•	2.3	•
Return on Equity After Income Taxes **48**	•	•	68.4	41.8	•	12.9	9.3	8.8	6.6	16.8	•	0.6	•
Profit Margin (Before Income Tax) **49**	0.3	•	18.2	14.2	•	3.7	3.1	3.9	3.2	6.0	•	1.4	•
Profit Margin (After Income Tax) **50**	•	•	16.4	9.5	•	3.3	2.5	2.9	2.3	4.5	•	0.4	•

VENTILATION, HEATING, A.C. & COMMERCIAL REFRIGERATION EQUIP.

Table II
Corporations with Net Income

MONEY AMOUNTS AND SIZE OF ASSETS IN THOUSANDS OF DOLLARS

Item Description for Accounting Period 7/09 Through 6/10	Total	Zero Assets	Under 500	500 to 1,000	1,000 to 5,000	5,000 to 10,000	10,000 to 25,000	25,000 to 50,000	50,000 to 100,000	100,000 to 250,000	250,000 to 500,000	500,000 to 2,500,000	2,500,000 and over
Number of Enterprises 1	674	•	287	•	108	109	44	28	16	•	3	4	0
Revenues ($ in Thousands)													
Net Sales 2	17980612	•	362800	•	610795	1569509	1263607	1615345	1690250	•	772933	7548131	0
Interest 3	22507	•	126	•	414	236	857	994	907	•	594	15543	0
Rents 4	12405	•	108	•	0	381	219	404	21	•	72	9084	0
Royalties 5	117739	•	0	•	0	0	1786	5322	3162	•	285	104810	0
Other Portfolio Income 6	76748	•	11464	•	187	376	1894	8417	13758	•	69	20197	0
Other Receipts 7	163253	•	1238	•	238	3507	17234	5317	2946	•	2301	107551	0
Total Receipts 8	18373264	•	375736	•	611634	1574009	1285597	1635799	1711044	•	776254	7805316	0
Average Total Receipts 9	27260	•	1309	•	5663	14440	29218	58421	106940	•	258751	1951329	•
Operating Costs/Operating Income (%)													
Cost of Operations 10	68.2	•	44.2	•	68.6	76.8	70.9	59.4	65.6	•	67.4	69.9	•
Salaries and Wages 11	8.1	•	7.6	•	8.0	5.5	8.1	13.1	8.5	•	5.8	8.0	•
Taxes Paid 12	1.3	•	1.2	•	2.0	0.7	1.2	1.5	1.6	•	1.1	1.2	•
Interest Paid 13	1.6	•	•	•	0.3	0.5	0.6	0.5	1.0	•	3.0	2.4	•
Depreciation 14	1.8	•	0.2	•	1.6	0.9	1.3	1.9	2.2	•	3.6	1.6	•
Amortization and Depletion 15	0.7	•	0.1	•	0.0	0.2	0.4	0.1	0.2	•	0.4	1.2	•
Pensions and Other Deferred Comp. 16	0.7	•	0.1	•	0.3	0.4	0.7	0.6	0.4	•	•	0.7	•
Employee Benefits 17	1.6	•	0.1	•	0.1	0.5	1.3	3.0	2.2	•	0.9	1.4	•
Advertising 18	0.8	•	0.3	•	0.5	0.2	0.4	0.7	0.7	•	0.9	1.1	•
Other Expenses 19	9.8	•	29.1	•	9.5	7.5	5.7	10.2	8.1	•	11.1	11.2	•
Officers' Compensation 20	1.6	•	1.6	•	5.8	2.5	1.6	1.5	3.1	•	0.9	0.9	•
Operating Margin 21	3.8	•	15.4	•	3.2	4.3	7.8	7.5	6.3	•	5.0	0.2	•
Operating Margin Before Officers' Comp. 22	5.4	•	17.0	•	6.8	6.8	9.4	9.0	9.5	•	5.9	1.1	•

Selected Average Balance Sheet ($ in Thousands)

Net Receivables 23	3119	138	561	1812	3965	9070	14958	48630	165338
Inventories 24	3168	7	281	1639	3579	6450	11091	27056	194248
Net Property, Plant and Equipment 25	3217	81	281	1379	2678	7949	13667	54661	218892
Total Assets 26	21377	307	2265	6617	15757	33894	65409	307894	1935748
Notes and Loans Payable 27	6491	0	540	1809	3652	6185	17278	73382	665230
All Other Liabilities 28	6669	35	527	1368	4155	10596	17366	129099	594322
Net Worth 29	8217	273	1198	3440	7951	17113	30765	105413	676197

Selected Financial Ratios (Times to 1)

Current Ratio 30	2.0	6.2	2.9	3.3	1.9	2.1	2.2	1.9	1.8
Quick Ratio 31	1.1	5.9	2.1	2.0	1.1	1.5	1.3	1.3	0.9
Net Sales to Working Capital 32	5.9	7.0	4.6	4.3	5.8	5.5	5.0	4.0	7.3
Coverage Ratio 33	4.9	•	11.0	10.8	16.4	17.1	8.2	3.2	2.7
Total Asset Turnover 34	1.2	4.1	2.5	2.2	1.8	1.7	1.6	0.8	1.0
Inventory Turnover 35	5.7	75.8	13.8	6.7	5.7	5.3	6.2	6.4	6.8
Receivables Turnover 36	7.3	•	15.6	7.0	7.3	4.6	7.9	10.6	1.9
Total Liabilities to Net Worth 37	1.6	0.1	0.9	0.9	1.0	1.0	1.1	1.9	1.9
Current Assets to Working Capital 38	2.1	1.2	1.5	1.4	2.1	1.9	1.8	2.1	2.3
Current Liabilities to Working Capital 39	1.1	0.2	0.5	0.4	1.1	0.9	0.8	1.1	1.3
Working Capital to Net Sales 40	0.2	0.1	0.2	0.2	0.2	0.2	0.2	0.2	0.1
Inventory to Working Capital 41	0.6	0.0	0.3	0.5	0.7	0.5	0.5	0.4	0.7
Total Receipts to Cash Flow 42	7.3	2.4	10.6	9.3	7.1	5.6	7.4	7.5	7.8
Cost of Goods to Cash Flow 43	5.0	1.1	7.3	7.2	5.0	3.3	4.9	5.0	5.5
Cash Flow to Total Debt 44	0.3	14.9	0.5	0.5	0.5	0.6	0.4	0.2	0.2

Selected Financial Factors (in Percentages)

Debt Ratio 45	61.6	11.3	47.1	48.0	49.5	49.5	53.0	65.8	65.1
Return on Total Assets 46	9.9	78.0	9.1	10.9	18.4	15.9	13.8	7.9	6.4
Return on Equity Before Income Taxes 47	20.5	88.0	15.6	19.0	34.3	29.6	25.8	15.9	11.6
Return on Equity After Income Taxes 48	15.9	79.8	10.7	17.1	31.2	25.0	21.5	10.4	7.5
Profit Margin (Before Income Tax) 49	6.3	19.0	3.3	4.5	9.5	8.8	7.5	6.5	4.1
Profit Margin (After Income Tax) 50	4.9	17.2	2.3	4.1	8.6	7.4	6.3	4.2	2.7

Table I

Corporations with and without Net Income

METALWORKING MACHINERY

MONEY AMOUNTS AND SIZE OF ASSETS IN THOUSANDS OF DOLLARS

Item Description for Accounting Period 7/09 Through 6/10	Total	Zero Assets	Under 500	500 to 1,000	1,000 to 5,000	5,000 to 10,000	10,000 to 25,000	25,000 to 50,000	50,000 to 100,000	100,000 to 250,000	250,000 to 500,000	500,000 to 2,500,000	2,500,000 and over
Number of Enterprises 1	6564	982	3348	857	1028	152	106	54	17	14	0	5	0
Revenues ($ in Thousands)													
Net Sales 2	18904548	64662	1256084	1036959	2877972	1582140	1562036	1819928	941034	2502418	0	5261315	0
Interest 3	44898	0	764	575	8678	388	852	1442	3084	4004	0	25110	0
Rents 4	16504	0	746	3777	3083	3051	159	600	0	4763	0	325	0
Royalties 5	7502	0	0	0	0	0	274	1	30	5932	0	1266	0
Other Portfolio Income 6	138091	12373	15269	2558	68719	170	5608	4442	2582	18438	0	7930	0
Other Receipts 7	265091	3213	11754	7330	91630	3009	34865	45751	2281	28356	0	36904	0
Total Receipts 8	19376634	80248	1284617	1051199	3050082	1588758	1603794	1872164	949011	2563911	0	5332850	0
Average Total Receipts 9	2952	82	384	1227	2967	10452	15130	34670	55824	183136	•	1066570	•
Operating Costs/Operating Income (%)													
Cost of Operations 10	63.5	72.1	30.6	46.3	62.7	69.7	69.5	66.6	70.5	67.3	•	67.4	•
Salaries and Wages 11	9.1	22.1	22.1	12.8	7.2	4.9	6.7	7.7	7.4	10.1	•	8.5	•
Taxes Paid 12	2.0	2.2	4.1	4.2	2.7	1.8	2.4	1.9	1.8	1.6	•	1.0	•
Interest Paid 13	2.3	0.5	1.9	2.2	0.9	0.9	1.2	1.1	2.0	2.4	•	4.3	•
Depreciation 14	3.9	1.0	1.5	5.8	5.0	4.4	4.9	4.2	5.0	3.2	•	3.1	•
Amortization and Depletion 15	0.6	•	0.0	0.0	0.2	0.0	0.1	0.2	0.5	0.8	•	1.5	•
Pensions and Other Deferred Comp. 16	0.5	0.0	0.0	0.1	0.3	0.9	0.3	0.8	0.4	0.5	•	0.6	•
Employee Benefits 17	2.9	2.9	2.6	4.9	1.8	1.1	3.4	3.1	2.6	2.9	•	3.6	•
Advertising 18	0.4	0.1	0.0	0.1	0.4	0.2	0.4	0.5	0.3	0.3	•	0.6	•
Other Expenses 19	11.8	31.2	29.5	20.5	11.3	5.4	8.9	11.9	7.8	9.3	•	10.7	•
Officers' Compensation 20	3.3	0.5	11.1	7.3	5.5	6.6	3.0	2.1	1.6	0.8	•	0.6	•
Operating Margin 21	•	•	•	•	2.1	4.0	•	•	0.1	0.8	•	•	•
Operating Margin Before Officers' Comp. 22	2.9	•	7.5	3.1	7.5	10.6	2.1	2.1	1.7	1.6	•	•	•

Selected Average Balance Sheet ($ in Thousands)

Net Receivables 23	459	0	40	184	466	1397	3053	6418	9000	30688	•	155355
Inventories 24	520	0	10	72	565	1335	3488	8288	15376	31756	•	170845
Net Property, Plant and Equipment 25	607	0	24	321	576	2068	3901	8833	15516	34560	•	217003
Total Assets 26	3261	0	125	682	2271	6329	14478	35442	66877	193441	•	1963011
Notes and Loans Payable 27	1128	0	189	475	515	1487	3598	7253	15416	68267	•	723788
All Other Liabilities 28	813	0	36	104	404	1608	3563	9609	11939	35538	•	574105
Net Worth 29	1320	0	-100	102	1352	3233	7318	18580	39522	89636	•	665117

Selected Financial Ratios (Times to 1)

Current Ratio 30	1.4	•	1.0	1.5	2.5	1.8	1.8	1.9	2.9	2.3	•	0.7
Quick Ratio 31	0.8	•	0.7	1.1	1.4	1.1	1.0	0.9	1.4	1.4	•	0.4
Net Sales to Working Capital 32	7.3	•	•	10.6	3.2	6.4	3.7	3.5	2.3	3.4	•	•
Coverage Ratio 33	2.1	•	0.3	•	9.8	5.7	2.5	3.6	1.5	3.2	•	1.0
Total Asset Turnover 34	0.9	•	3.0	1.8	1.2	1.6	1.0	1.0	0.8	0.9	•	0.5
Inventory Turnover 35	3.5	•	11.9	7.8	3.1	5.4	2.9	2.7	2.5	3.8	•	4.1
Receivables Turnover 36	5.7	•	9.2	7.9	5.1	6.3	4.0	6.3	4.8	5.7	•	6.4
Total Liabilities to Net Worth 37	1.5	•	•	5.7	0.7	1.0	1.0	0.9	0.7	1.2	•	2.0
Current Assets to Working Capital 38	3.3	•	•	2.8	1.7	2.2	2.3	2.1	1.5	1.8	•	•
Current Liabilities to Working Capital 39	2.3	•	•	1.8	0.7	1.2	1.3	1.1	0.5	0.8	•	•
Working Capital to Net Sales 40	0.1	•	•	0.1	0.3	0.2	0.3	0.3	0.4	0.3	•	•
Inventory to Working Capital 41	1.2	•	0.7	•	0.6	0.7	0.7	0.9	0.5	0.6	•	•
Total Receipts to Cash Flow 42	9.3	4.8	4.8	8.9	6.9	13.2	11.1	9.6	15.9	8.9	•	12.4
Cost of Goods to Cash Flow 43	5.9	3.4	1.5	4.1	4.3	9.2	7.7	6.4	11.2	6.0	•	8.4
Cash Flow to Total Debt 44	0.2	•	0.3	0.2	0.4	0.3	0.2	0.2	0.1	0.2	•	0.1

Selected Financial Factors (in Percentages)

Debt Ratio 45	59.5	•	180.0	85.1	40.5	48.9	49.5	47.6	40.9	53.7	•	66.1
Return on Total Assets 46	4.2	•	1.7	•	11.0	8.7	3.1	3.7	2.4	7.1	•	2.2
Return on Equity Before Income Taxes 47	5.3	•	5.0	•	16.5	14.1	3.7	5.2	1.3	10.4	•	•
Return on Equity After Income Taxes 48	4.2	•	5.2	•	15.9	13.3	3.5	4.1	0.3	8.8	•	•
Profit Margin (Before Income Tax) 49	2.4	•	•	•	8.0	4.4	1.8	2.8	1.0	5.2	•	•
Profit Margin (After Income Tax) 50	1.9	•	•	•	7.7	4.1	1.7	2.3	0.2	4.4	•	•

131

Table II
Corporations with Net Income

METALWORKING MACHINERY

MONEY AMOUNTS AND SIZE OF ASSETS IN THOUSANDS OF DOLLARS

Item Description for Accounting Period 7/09 Through 6/10		Total	Zero Assets	Under 500	500 to 1,000	1,000 to 5,000	5,000 to 10,000	10,000 to 25,000	25,000 to 50,000	50,000 to 100,000	100,000 to 250,000	250,000 to 500,000	500,000 to 2,500,000	2,500,000 and over
Number of Enterprises	1	3221	276	•	397	742	77	63	28	11	7	0	•	0
Revenues ($ in Thousands)														
Net Sales	2	12411363	38100	•	629327	2395198	937405	878770	1076876	647663	1453544	0	•	0
Interest	3	25989	0	•	0	2994	313	547	638	2957	2750	0	•	0
Rents	4	9520	0	•	0	3024	2809	81	137	0	3466	0	•	0
Royalties	5	7329	0	•	0	0	0	274	0	30	5827	0	•	0
Other Portfolio Income	6	101578	0	•	2100	67897	120	37	2582	1354	6784	0	•	0
Other Receipts	7	233045	51	•	5708	86434	1775	28933	40560	1983	27810	0	•	0
Total Receipts	8	12788824	38151	•	637135	2555547	942422	908642	1120793	653987	1500181	0	•	0
Average Total Receipts	9	3970	138	•	1605	3444	12239	14423	40028	59453	214312	•	•	•
Operating Costs/Operating Income (%)														
Cost of Operations	10	61.6	31.7	•	33.1	61.2	63.3	65.3	62.4	67.2	61.6	•	•	•
Salaries and Wages	11	8.0	23.6	•	15.1	7.1	4.8	5.8	7.6	8.1	9.2	•	•	•
Taxes Paid	12	1.9	1.8	•	4.9	2.6	2.1	2.2	2.1	2.0	1.5	•	•	•
Interest Paid	13	2.4	•	•	2.3	0.7	0.6	0.9	0.8	0.9	3.3	•	•	•
Depreciation	14	3.7	0.1	•	6.1	5.0	3.5	5.1	3.8	4.8	3.2	•	•	•
Amortization and Depletion	15	0.7	•	•	0.0	0.0	0.0	0.1	0.2	0.2	1.1	•	•	•
Pensions and Other Deferred Comp.	16	0.6	•	•	0.1	0.3	1.2	0.3	1.1	0.5	0.5	•	•	•
Employee Benefits	17	2.9	0.5	•	3.4	1.6	1.5	2.6	3.2	2.6	3.0	•	•	•
Advertising	18	0.3	0.1	•	0.1	0.4	0.1	0.3	0.4	0.3	0.2	•	•	•
Other Expenses	19	10.6	27.9	•	26.5	10.1	5.9	9.4	11.0	7.6	8.3	•	•	•
Officers' Compensation	20	2.7	•	•	7.5	4.3	7.0	2.8	1.9	1.4	0.7	•	•	•
Operating Margin	21	4.6	14.3	•	0.8	6.9	10.0	5.3	5.5	4.5	7.5	•	•	•
Operating Margin Before Officers' Comp.	22	7.3	14.3	•	8.3	11.1	17.0	8.1	7.4	5.9	8.3	•	•	•

Selected Average Balance Sheet ($ in Thousands)

Net Receivables 23	595	0	•	155	572	1454	3149	7239	9683	22747
Inventories 24	698	0	•	38	622	1559	3556	7872	17055	23654
Net Property, Plant and Equipment 25	748	0	•	511	581	1795	3382	8363	15592	34204
Total Assets 26	4535	0	•	709	2191	6235	14865	35607	70378	203698
Notes and Loans Payable 27	1387	0	•	583	426	1096	3209	5225	8577	104970
All Other Liabilities 28	1242	0	•	114	433	1866	3789	10363	15246	38085
Net Worth 29	1906	0	•	13	1333	3274	7867	20020	46555	60643

Selected Financial Ratios (Times to 1)

Current Ratio 30	1.4	•	•	0.8	2.2	2.1	1.8	2.0	3.3	2.9
Quick Ratio 31	0.8	•	•	0.8	1.2	1.3	1.1	1.1	1.6	1.9
Net Sales to Working Capital 32	8.2	•	•	•	4.4	5.7	3.2	3.6	2.0	3.6
Coverage Ratio 33	4.4	•	•	1.9	20.9	19.5	10.6	13.5	7.4	5.2
Total Asset Turnover 34	0.8	•	•	2.2	1.5	2.0	0.9	1.1	0.8	1.0
Inventory Turnover 35	3.4	•	•	13.7	3.2	4.9	2.6	3.0	2.3	5.4
Receivables Turnover 36	5.4	•	•	10.1	5.2	6.7	3.2	6.4	4.2	•
Total Liabilities to Net Worth 37	1.4	•	•	55.5	0.6	0.9	0.9	0.8	0.5	2.4
Current Assets to Working Capital 38	3.4	•	•	•	1.9	1.9	2.2	2.0	1.4	1.5
Current Liabilities to Working Capital 39	2.4	•	•	•	0.9	0.9	1.2	1.0	0.4	0.5
Working Capital to Net Sales 40	0.1	•	•	•	0.2	0.2	0.3	0.3	0.5	0.3
Inventory to Working Capital 41	1.1	•	•	•	0.7	0.7	0.6	0.7	0.4	0.4
Total Receipts to Cash Flow 42	6.7	2.5	•	4.8	5.4	7.3	6.1	6.7	9.6	5.7
Cost of Goods to Cash Flow 43	4.1	0.8	•	1.6	3.3	4.6	4.0	4.2	6.4	3.5
Cash Flow to Total Debt 44	0.2	•	•	0.5	0.7	0.6	0.3	0.4	0.3	0.3

Selected Financial Factors (in Percentages)

Debt Ratio 45	58.0	•	•	98.2	39.2	47.5	47.1	43.8	33.9	70.2
Return on Total Assets 46	8.9	•	•	9.7	20.9	21.6	9.0	11.2	5.3	17.4
Return on Equity Before Income Taxes 47	16.4	•	•	256.2	32.7	39.1	15.4	18.4	7.0	47.3
Return on Equity After Income Taxes 48	14.9	•	•	255.1	31.9	37.6	15.1	16.6	5.6	42.5
Profit Margin (Before Income Tax) 49	8.1	14.5	•	2.0	13.5	10.5	8.7	9.6	5.5	13.8
Profit Margin (After Income Tax) 50	7.3	14.1	•	2.0	13.2	10.1	8.5	8.6	4.4	12.4

Table I

Corporations with and without Net Income

ENGINE, TURBINE AND POWER TRANSMISSION EQUIPMENT

MONEY AMOUNTS AND SIZE OF ASSETS IN THOUSANDS OF DOLLARS

Item Description for Accounting Period 7/09 Through 6/10	Total	Zero Assets	Under 500	500 to 1,000	1,000 to 5,000	5,000 to 10,000	10,000 to 25,000	25,000 to 50,000	50,000 to 100,000	100,000 to 250,000	250,000 to 500,000	500,000 to 2,500,000	2,500,000 and over
Number of Enterprises **1**	584	•	•	•	43	35	34	6	10	10	7	8	4
Revenues ($ in Thousands)													
Net Sales **2**	26430680	•	•	•	197677	284150	538546	229063	306574	1489421	2537426	7544788	13187304
Interest **3**	164083	•	•	•	22	211	272	0	208	13294	3721	26011	119966
Rents **4**	5730	•	•	•	0	0	0	0	351	660	71	1232	3416
Royalties **5**	255745	•	•	•	0	0	0	0	0	204	8038	27351	220151
Other Portfolio Income **6**	475758	•	•	•	5	40	350	0	23589	896	4813	157982	263895
Other Receipts **7**	539811	•	•	•	57	382	985	1475	5092	16147	63365	51065	395898
Total Receipts **8**	27871807	•	•	•	197761	284783	540153	230538	335814	1520622	2617434	7808429	14190630
Average Total Receipts **9**	47726	•	•	•	4599	8137	15887	38423	33581	152062	373919	976054	3547658
Operating Costs/Operating Income (%)													
Cost of Operations **10**	71.2	•	•	•	59.7	68.4	57.0	75.6	75.8	75.5	73.1	74.4	69.5
Salaries and Wages **11**	9.2	•	•	•	17.2	4.1	7.0	7.3	15.7	8.0	8.6	8.9	9.4
Taxes Paid **12**	1.5	•	•	•	1.7	2.9	6.0	2.5	1.9	1.3	1.4	1.3	1.5
Interest Paid **13**	2.6	•	•	•	1.9	1.5	1.6	0.7	3.6	1.5	1.8	2.5	3.0
Depreciation **14**	3.2	•	•	•	2.5	3.8	3.0	2.2	5.3	4.8	1.6	2.8	3.5
Amortization and Depletion **15**	1.0	•	•	•	0.0	0.0	0.5	0.0	1.4	1.0	0.3	1.5	1.0
Pensions and Other Deferred Comp. **16**	1.4	•	•	•	0.4	0.3	0.3	1.6	0.2	0.5	0.9	1.3	1.7
Employee Benefits **17**	3.3	•	•	•	1.6	2.9	3.0	2.4	2.9	2.5	1.2	1.0	5.2
Advertising **18**	0.5	•	•	•	2.0	0.1	0.2	0.1	0.1	0.3	0.2	0.4	0.6
Other Expenses **19**	12.2	•	•	•	23.2	4.8	16.5	5.6	15.9	12.5	6.7	6.6	16.0
Officers' Compensation **20**	0.7	•	•	•	2.0	2.6	2.4	0.5	2.8	1.3	1.2	0.3	0.6
Operating Margin **21**	•	•	•	•	•	8.5	2.7	1.5	•	•	3.0	•	•
Operating Margin Before Officers' Comp. **22**	•	•	•	•	•	11.1	5.0	2.0	•	•	4.2	•	•

Selected Average Balance Sheet ($ in Thousands)

Net Receivables 23	8600	•	462	1102	2462	5589	13659	23920	83164	289583	392919
Inventories 24	6943	•	684	1689	4419	14720	11888	33115	31949	168612	425902
Net Property, Plant and Equipment 25	8369	•	763	2822	3707	5475	10137	47309	59629	139512	620854
Total Assets 26	56064	•	2709	7153	15623	26308	70142	163602	386823	1467663	3714235
Notes and Loans Payable 27	16119	•	1356	2443	4777	5524	13704	35913	116867	437948	1062214
All Other Liabilities 28	23252	•	893	913	3849	11636	18261	54396	249501	602719	1501786
Net Worth 29	16694	•	459	3797	6998	9148	38177	73293	20455	426996	1150236

Selected Financial Ratios (Times to 1)

Current Ratio 30	1.4	•	0.9	3.0	1.6	1.4	3.0	1.7	1.1	1.4	1.3
Quick Ratio 31	0.8	•	0.4	1.3	0.7	0.5	2.0	1.0	0.6	0.8	0.7
Net Sales to Working Capital 32	7.7	•	•	3.1	5.2	6.3	1.0	4.9	20.4	5.2	13.0
Coverage Ratio 33	1.0	•	•	6.8	3.3	4.0	•	•	4.8	2.7	0.0
Total Asset Turnover 34	0.8	•	1.7	1.1	1.0	1.5	0.4	0.9	0.9	0.6	0.9
Inventory Turnover 35	4.6	•	4.0	3.3	2.0	2.0	2.0	3.4	8.3	4.2	5.4
Receivables Turnover 36	5.5	•	10.5	7.2	5.6	6.1	2.9	5.1	4.1	4.1	7.4
Total Liabilities to Net Worth 37	2.4	•	4.9	0.9	1.2	1.9	0.8	1.2	17.9	2.4	2.2
Current Assets to Working Capital 38	3.8	•	•	1.5	2.7	3.4	2.5	1.5	12.7	3.3	4.7
Current Liabilities to Working Capital 39	2.8	•	•	0.5	1.7	2.4	1.5	0.5	11.7	2.3	3.7
Working Capital to Net Sales 40	0.1	•	•	0.3	0.2	0.2	1.0	0.2	0.0	0.2	0.1
Inventory to Working Capital 41	1.1	•	•	0.8	1.3	2.1	0.5	0.9	2.0	1.0	1.5
Total Receipts to Cash Flow 42	11.7	•	20.1	7.9	10.8	14.6	•	29.8	9.2	12.6	10.8
Cost of Goods to Cash Flow 43	8.3	•	12.0	5.4	6.2	11.0	•	22.5	6.7	9.4	7.5
Cash Flow to Total Debt 44	0.1	•	0.1	0.3	0.2	0.2	0.1	0.1	0.1	0.1	0.1

Selected Financial Factors (in Percentages)

Debt Ratio 45	70.2	•	83.0	46.9	55.2	65.2	45.6	55.2	94.7	70.9	69.0
Return on Total Assets 46	2.1	•	•	11.6	5.3	4.2	•	•	8.2	4.4	0.1
Return on Equity Before Income Taxes 47	•	•	•	18.6	8.1	9.1	•	•	122.6	9.4	•
Return on Equity After Income Taxes 48	•	•	•	11.5	5.7	8.8	•	•	75.7	4.8	•
Profit Margin (Before Income Tax) 49	•	•	•	8.7	3.6	2.2	•	•	6.9	4.3	•
Profit Margin (After Income Tax) 50	•	•	•	5.4	2.5	2.1	•	•	4.3	2.2	•

Table II

Corporations with Net Income

ENGINE, TURBINE AND POWER TRANSMISSION EQUIPMENT

MONEY AMOUNTS AND SIZE OF ASSETS IN THOUSANDS OF DOLLARS

Item Description for Accounting Period 7/09 Through 6/10	Total	Zero Assets	Under 500	500 to 1,000	1,000 to 5,000	5,000 to 10,000	10,000 to 25,000	25,000 to 50,000	50,000 to 100,000	100,000 to 250,000	250,000 to 500,000	500,000 to 2,500,000	2,500,000 and over
Number of Enterprises **1**	409	8	286	•	5	30	21	6	4	5	•	8	0
Revenues ($ in Thousands)													
Net Sales **2**	18976032	15522	37827	•	63279	239107	469704	229063	196971	808388	•	14695035	0
Interest **3**	118729	0	71	•	0	211	185	0	71	1771	•	112658	0
Rents **4**	4181	0	0	•	0	0	0	0	351	0	•	3759	0
Royalties **5**	215439	0	0	•	0	0	0	0	0	204	•	207232	0
Other Portfolio Income **6**	446163	0	24186	•	0	0	2	0	0	820	•	416308	0
Other Receipts **7**	299492	0	5339	•	54	79	503	1475	25	3811	•	225897	0
Total Receipts **8**	20060036	15522	67423	•	63333	239397	470394	230538	197452	814994	•	15660889	0
Average Total Receipts **9**	49047	1940	236	•	12667	7980	22400	38423	49363	162999	•	1957611	•
Operating Costs/Operating Income (%)													
Cost of Operations **10**	71.1	66.4	5.2	•	57.7	67.6	52.9	75.6	64.3	73.3	•	71.6	•
Salaries and Wages **11**	7.1	7.0	35.7	•	2.9	3.8	6.1	7.3	7.4	6.1	•	6.9	•
Taxes Paid **12**	1.4	1.0	3.9	•	0.5	2.9	6.5	2.5	1.4	0.9	•	1.2	•
Interest Paid **13**	2.4	•	1.1	•	0.0	0.9	1.5	0.7	3.6	0.8	•	2.8	•
Depreciation **14**	3.0	1.1	0.2	•	0.1	3.0	2.8	2.2	1.5	4.6	•	3.2	•
Amortization and Depletion **15**	0.8	•	•	•	0.0	0.0	0.0	0.0	0.2	0.2	•	0.9	•
Pensions and Other Deferred Comp. **16**	1.4	•	0.2	•	1.0	0.2	0.3	1.6	0.2	0.6	•	1.6	•
Employee Benefits **17**	2.2	•	1.3	•	2.0	2.0	3.3	2.4	1.4	2.5	•	2.3	•
Advertising **18**	0.2	1.1	0.2	•	2.8	0.1	0.2	0.1	0.0	0.4	•	0.2	•
Other Expenses **19**	11.5	21.4	35.3	•	5.1	5.1	15.4	5.6	6.3	7.1	•	12.5	•
Officers' Compensation **20**	0.8	•	4.9	•	2.4	2.7	2.3	0.5	2.4	1.3	•	0.5	•
Operating Margin **21**	•	2.0	12.0	•	27.4	11.6	8.7	1.5	11.1	2.3	•	•	•
Operating Margin Before Officers' Comp. **22**	•	2.0	17.0	•	29.8	14.4	11.0	2.0	13.5	3.6	•	•	•

Selected Average Balance Sheet ($ in Thousands)

Net Receivables 23	8273	0	0	•	154	996	3453	5589	12412	29683	•	350024
Inventories 24	6543	0	0	•	2916	1791	5613	12851	15119	50190	•	244323
Net Property, Plant and Equipment 25	6838	0	6	•	199	2257	4714	5475	4054	39494	•	281626
Total Assets 26	52008	0	13	•	4162	6525	17269	26308	62151	171386	•	2231205
Notes and Loans Payable 27	16004	0	7	•	0	1818	5234	5524	18559	31458	•	730769
All Other Liabilities 28	17755	0	10	•	200	831	4051	11636	13151	64561	•	758876
Net Worth 29	18250	0	-4	•	3962	3876	7984	9148	30442	75367	•	741560

Selected Financial Ratios (Times to 1)

Current Ratio 30	1.6	•	0.4	•	19.7	3.2	1.6	1.4	2.3	2.0	•	1.5
Quick Ratio 31	0.9	•	0.4	•	4.8	1.3	0.7	0.5	1.3	1.2	•	0.9
Net Sales to Working Capital 32	5.8	•	•	•	3.4	2.9	5.2	6.3	2.3	3.5	•	6.8
Coverage Ratio 33	3.4	•	85.9	•	916.8	14.4	6.8	4.0	4.1	5.1	•	2.7
Total Asset Turnover 34	0.9	•	10.3	•	3.0	1.2	1.3	1.5	0.8	0.9	•	0.8
Inventory Turnover 35	5.0	•	•	•	2.5	3.0	2.1	2.2	2.1	2.4	•	5.4
Receivables Turnover 36	6.2	•	•	•	48.8	6.8	6.0	•	4.0	3.8	•	•
Total Liabilities to Net Worth 37	1.8	•	•	•	0.1	0.7	1.2	1.9	1.0	1.3	•	2.0
Current Assets to Working Capital 38	2.6	•	•	•	1.1	1.5	2.6	3.4	1.8	2.0	•	3.0
Current Liabilities to Working Capital 39	1.6	•	•	•	0.1	0.5	1.6	2.4	0.8	1.0	•	2.0
Working Capital to Net Sales 40	0.2	•	•	•	0.3	0.3	0.2	0.2	0.4	0.3	•	0.1
Inventory to Working Capital 41	0.8	•	•	•	0.7	0.8	1.2	2.1	0.7	0.7	•	0.9
Total Receipts to Cash Flow 42	7.5	4.5	1.7	•	3.2	6.3	7.2	14.6	6.3	10.5	•	7.4
Cost of Goods to Cash Flow 43	5.3	3.0	0.1	•	1.8	4.3	3.8	11.0	4.1	7.7	•	5.3
Cash Flow to Total Debt 44	0.2	•	4.4	•	19.8	0.5	0.3	0.2	0.2	0.2	•	0.2

Selected Financial Factors (in Percentages)

Debt Ratio 45	64.9	•	133.7	•	4.8	40.6	53.8	65.2	51.0	56.0	•	66.8
Return on Total Assets 46	7.3	•	941.8	•	83.7	15.4	13.5	4.2	11.9	3.8	•	6.3
Return on Equity Before Income Taxes 47	14.5	•	•	•	87.8	24.1	24.9	9.1	18.3	7.0	•	12.1
Return on Equity After Income Taxes 48	10.1	•	•	•	87.8	15.9	21.4	8.8	13.9	5.0	•	8.1
Profit Margin (Before Income Tax) 49	5.7	2.0	90.3	•	27.5	11.7	8.9	2.2	11.3	3.2	•	4.9
Profit Margin (After Income Tax) 50	4.0	1.6	90.3	•	27.5	7.7	7.6	2.1	8.6	2.3	•	3.3

Table I
Corporations with and without Net Income

OTHER GENERAL PURPOSE MACHINERY

MONEY AMOUNTS AND SIZE OF ASSETS IN THOUSANDS OF DOLLARS

Item Description for Accounting Period 7/09 Through 6/10	Total	Zero Assets	Under 500	500 to 1,000	1,000 to 5,000	5,000 to 10,000	10,000 to 25,000	25,000 to 50,000	50,000 to 100,000	100,000 to 250,000	250,000 to 500,000	500,000 to 2,500,000	2,500,000 and over
Number of Enterprises **1**	5239	732	2765	321	840	258	187	54	23	27	10	15	7
Revenues ($ in Thousands)													
Net Sales **2**	56422281	173293	1257193	403518	3230187	2639301	3980297	2073395	2015390	4141099	3949356	13369709	19189543
Interest **3**	431002	491	307	2024	1166	640	4600	916	2010	14635	9785	155806	238623
Rents **4**	14333	0	0	0	661	2372	6786	528	910	499	590	842	1145
Royalties **5**	573073	145	0	0	0	0	0	1330	1037	12106	15701	143340	399414
Other Portfolio Income **6**	472689	4593	7	7900	2102	771	2779	3578	11636	26406	2955	310480	99480
Other Receipts **7**	725835	12565	1011	793	16698	14976	55120	10357	24019	25934	3823	115173	445369
Total Receipts **8**	58639213	191087	1258518	414235	3250814	2658060	4049582	2090104	2055002	4220679	3982210	14095350	20373574
Average Total Receipts **9**	11193	261	455	1290	3870	10303	21656	38706	89348	156321	398221	939690	2910511
Operating Costs/Operating Income (%)													
Cost of Operations **10**	67.8	65.9	34.0	59.0	62.3	60.9	70.0	71.6	67.9	68.7	64.2	65.3	73.6
Salaries and Wages **11**	9.5	8.7	15.9	6.8	8.8	12.2	9.2	8.2	10.4	9.3	9.9	9.2	9.1
Taxes Paid **12**	1.6	2.1	2.9	1.8	2.5	2.6	1.7	1.6	1.7	1.7	1.3	1.9	1.1
Interest Paid **13**	2.6	2.7	1.8	0.6	0.6	0.8	1.0	1.9	1.0	1.8	1.6	3.2	3.7
Depreciation **14**	2.7	5.0	2.6	1.3	2.2	2.1	2.4	2.6	2.3	2.6	3.4	3.0	2.6
Amortization and Depletion **15**	0.9	1.4	0.1	0.3	0.2	0.4	0.3	0.5	0.7	0.8	0.8	1.0	1.3
Pensions and Other Deferred Comp. **16**	1.8	0.2	0.2	4.2	0.5	0.5	0.4	0.7	0.8	1.1	1.1	1.2	3.4
Employee Benefits **17**	2.7	2.5	2.0	2.0	2.9	2.4	2.0	2.0	2.5	1.7	2.6	3.7	2.4
Advertising **18**	0.6	0.1	0.4	1.8	0.5	0.9	0.4	0.3	0.9	0.4	0.5	0.5	0.8
Other Expenses **19**	10.4	20.6	21.8	15.4	11.0	12.3	10.4	8.5	8.6	9.8	10.9	10.2	9.7
Officers' Compensation **20**	1.5	1.1	5.2	9.0	5.1	3.2	2.5	1.1	1.5	1.1	1.0	0.8	0.8
Operating Margin **21**	•	•	13.2	•	3.2	1.7	•	1.0	1.5	0.9	2.7	•	•
Operating Margin Before Officers' Comp. **22**	•	•	18.4	6.7	8.4	4.9	2.1	2.1	3.0	2.1	3.8	0.7	•

Selected Average Balance Sheet ($ in Thousands)

Line	Item													
23	Net Receivables	1691	0	25	117	401	1404	2874	7922	16300	29790	61562	122455	493822
24	Inventories	1649	0	29	169	554	2532	4109	8216	18884	25595	46503	126118	384280
25	Net Property, Plant and Equipment	1771	0	55	57	534	1113	3062	7096	12182	21416	52402	123678	596930
26	Total Assets	15653	0	135	665	2016	7078	14788	35320	72296	155512	344583	884091	7236911
27	Notes and Loans Payable	4817	0	94	657	582	1626	5140	10274	16690	35776	75246	302369	2242912
28	All Other Liabilities	4918	0	25	196	436	1902	3385	7925	22402	46927	49945	316904	2382980
29	Net Worth	5918		16	-188	999	3550	6263	17121	33204	72809	219392	264819	2611019

Selected Financial Ratios (Times to 1)

Line	Item													
30	Current Ratio	1.3	•	1.9	1.3	2.3	2.3	2.0	2.3	1.8	2.0	1.9	1.6	1.0
31	Quick Ratio	0.6	•	1.1	0.8	1.4	1.2	1.1	1.2	1.0	1.0	1.0	0.8	0.3
32	Net Sales to Working Capital	8.4	•	15.7	14.6	5.0	3.6	4.7	3.1	4.3	3.9	5.3	6.6	•
33	Coverage Ratio	2.1	1.0	8.4	1.6	7.1	3.9	2.3	1.9	4.7	2.7	3.3	3.1	0.8
34	Total Asset Turnover	0.7	•	3.4	1.9	1.9	1.4	1.4	1.1	1.2	1.0	1.1	1.0	0.4
35	Inventory Turnover	4.4	•	5.3	4.4	4.3	2.5	3.6	3.3	3.1	4.1	5.4	4.6	5.2
36	Receivables Turnover	5.4	•	18.0	12.1	8.7	6.8	5.7	4.9	4.9	4.9	8.4	6.2	4.3
37	Total Liabilities to Net Worth	1.6	•	7.6	•	1.0	1.0	1.4	1.1	1.2	1.1	0.6	2.3	1.8
38	Current Assets to Working Capital	4.5	•	2.1	4.2	1.8	1.8	2.0	1.7	2.2	2.0	2.2	2.7	•
39	Current Liabilities to Working Capital	3.5	•	1.1	3.2	0.8	0.8	1.0	0.7	1.2	1.0	1.2	1.7	•
40	Working Capital to Net Sales	0.1	•	0.1	0.1	0.2	0.3	0.2	0.3	0.2	0.3	0.2	0.2	•
41	Inventory to Working Capital	1.2	•	0.8	1.6	0.7	0.7	0.8	0.6	0.8	0.5	0.7	0.8	•
42	Total Receipts to Cash Flow	9.9	5.6	3.6	8.7	8.0	9.3	10.5	11.8	10.2	9.2	8.1	7.4	17.6
43	Cost of Goods to Cash Flow	6.7	3.7	1.2	5.1	5.0	5.6	7.3	8.5	6.9	6.3	5.2	4.9	13.0
44	Cash Flow to Total Debt	0.1	•	1.1	0.2	0.5	0.3	0.2	0.2	0.2	0.2	0.4	0.2	0.0

Selected Financial Factors (in Percentages)

Line	Item													
45	Debt Ratio	62.2	•	88.4	128.2	50.5	49.9	57.6	51.5	54.1	53.2	36.3	70.0	63.9
46	Return on Total Assets	3.7	•	51.0	1.9	8.6	4.7	3.5	3.8	5.7	4.8	6.0	10.1	1.1
47	Return on Equity Before Income Taxes	5.1	•	385.9	•	14.9	7.0	4.7	3.7	9.8	6.5	6.6	23.0	•
48	Return on Equity After Income Taxes	2.8	•	384.8	•	13.5	4.4	3.0	3.0	5.8	3.8	3.1	14.6	•
49	Profit Margin (Before Income Tax)	2.8	•	13.3	0.4	3.9	2.4	1.4	1.6	3.7	3.1	3.7	6.8	•
50	Profit Margin (After Income Tax)	1.5	•	13.3	0.1	3.5	1.5	0.9	1.3	2.2	1.8	1.7	4.4	•

135

Table II

Corporations with Net Income

OTHER GENERAL PURPOSE MACHINERY

MONEY AMOUNTS AND SIZE OF ASSETS IN THOUSANDS OF DOLLARS

Item Description for Accounting Period 7/09 Through 6/10		Total	Zero Assets	Under 500	500 to 1,000	1,000 to 5,000	5,000 to 10,000	10,000 to 25,000	25,000 to 50,000	50,000 to 100,000	100,000 to 250,000	250,000 to 500,000	500,000 to 2,500,000	2,500,000 and over
Number of Enterprises	1	3622	277	2215	233	527	183	107	28	14	17	6	•	•
Revenues ($ in Thousands)														
Net Sales	2	34619235	61309	1211521	316165	2490773	2095290	2479016	1325078	1112722	2740321	2595364	•	•
Interest	3	96794	306	0	2024	813	505	3373	549	1719	10442	4855	•	•
Rents	4	6380	0	0	0	661	426	2966	0	905	428	387	•	•
Royalties	5	222762	145	0	0	0	0	0	543	20	4225	15669	•	•
Other Portfolio Income	6	370520	4593	0	7900	879	771	2224	3234	11563	25336	2955	•	•
Other Receipts	7	328400	29304	678	18	7842	9761	44471	1647	23019	9855	2015	•	•
Total Receipts	8	35644091	95657	1212199	326107	2500968	2106753	2532050	1331051	1149948	2790607	2621245	•	•
Average Total Receipts	9	9841	345	547	1400	4746	11512	23664	47538	82139	164153	436874	•	•
Operating Costs/Operating Income (%)														
Cost of Operations	10	63.8	41.7	32.8	59.7	60.4	60.8	67.2	69.5	63.1	64.4	56.8	•	•
Salaries and Wages	11	9.4	21.3	16.5	6.7	8.0	10.5	8.3	7.2	11.1	9.1	10.3	•	•
Taxes Paid	12	1.8	2.1	2.9	1.8	2.6	2.3	1.9	1.7	1.9	2.0	1.5	•	•
Interest Paid	13	1.5	1.6	1.6	0.1	0.5	0.5	0.5	1.0	0.9	1.2	1.0	•	•
Depreciation	14	2.5	4.1	2.6	0.9	2.3	1.5	2.1	2.4	2.6	3.2	2.9	•	•
Amortization and Depletion	15	0.7	1.1	0.1	0.4	0.1	0.1	0.1	0.5	0.5	0.7	0.6	•	•
Pensions and Other Deferred Comp.	16	1.0	0.6	0.2	5.3	0.6	0.6	0.5	0.9	1.1	1.4	1.3	•	•
Employee Benefits	17	2.6	3.4	2.0	1.6	2.8	2.1	1.3	2.1	2.1	1.8	3.0	•	•
Advertising	18	0.7	0.2	0.4	1.6	0.4	0.8	0.5	0.2	0.5	0.5	0.4	•	•
Other Expenses	19	9.8	25.9	21.0	13.7	9.6	10.8	7.4	7.7	8.9	9.8	13.0	•	•
Officers' Compensation	20	1.7	0.7	5.3	9.0	5.0	3.0	2.3	1.0	1.8	1.2	1.3	•	•
Operating Margin	21	4.5	14.5	•	•	7.9	7.0	8.0	5.9	5.4	4.9	7.9	•	•
Operating Margin Before Officers' Comp.	22	6.2	•	•	8.2	12.9	10.0	10.3	6.8	7.2	6.2	9.2	•	•

Selected Average Balance Sheet ($ in Thousands)

		•	•	•	•	•	•	•	•	•	•	•
Net Receivables	23	1511	0	30	135	406	1599	3117	9153	16197	24603	75122
Inventories	24	1742	0	32	174	559	2556	4059	9487	22352	32824	30904
Net Property, Plant and Equipment	25	1211	0	68	55	503	1126	3005	7852	11736	25146	55051
Total Assets	26	10471	0	153	678	2041	7004	15082	36763	71849	169165	351888
Notes and Loans Payable	27	3247	0	100	154	383	1257	3689	6732	15424	33702	27038
All Other Liabilities	28	3115	0	20	224	441	1931	3186	8112	23626	42346	32932
Net Worth	29	4109	0	33	300	1217	3816	8206	21919	32799	93116	291918

Selected Financial Ratios (Times to 1)

		•	•	•	•	•	•	•	•	•	•	•
Current Ratio	30	1.6	•	3.0	1.6	2.8	2.5	2.8	2.5	1.8	2.1	1.7
Quick Ratio	31	0.9	•	1.8	1.1	1.8	1.5	1.7	1.4	1.0	1.0	1.3
Net Sales to Working Capital	32	5.1	•	11.3	8.8	5.2	3.6	3.5	3.2	4.1	3.5	6.9
Coverage Ratio	33	6.8	35.3	9.9	20.9	18.7	17.6	20.3	7.4	10.7	7.0	10.1
Total Asset Turnover	34	0.9	•	3.6	2.0	2.3	1.6	1.5	1.3	1.1	1.0	1.2
Inventory Turnover	35	3.5	•	5.6	4.7	5.1	2.7	3.8	3.5	2.2	3.2	8.0
Receivables Turnover	36	4.4	•	18.7	13.2	8.8	6.9	5.1	4.9	3.7	4.6	•
Total Liabilities to Net Worth	37	1.5	•	3.6	1.3	0.7	0.8	0.8	0.7	1.2	0.8	0.2
Current Assets to Working Capital	38	2.6	•	1.5	2.6	1.6	1.7	1.6	1.7	2.3	1.9	2.3
Current Liabilities to Working Capital	39	1.6	•	0.5	1.6	0.6	0.7	0.6	0.7	1.3	0.9	1.3
Working Capital to Net Sales	40	0.2	•	0.1	0.1	0.2	0.3	0.3	0.3	0.2	0.3	0.1
Inventory to Working Capital	41	0.7	•	0.6	0.8	0.5	0.6	0.5	0.5	0.8	0.5	0.5
Total Receipts to Cash Flow	42	6.6	•	3.4	8.6	6.4	6.1	6.3	8.2	6.4	6.9	5.2
Cost of Goods to Cash Flow	43	4.2	1.3	1.1	5.1	3.9	3.7	4.2	5.7	4.1	4.4	2.9
Cash Flow to Total Debt	44	0.2	0.6	1.3	0.4	0.9	0.6	0.5	0.4	0.3	0.3	1.4

Selected Financial Factors (in Percentages)

		•	•	•	•	•	•	•	•	•	•	•
Debt Ratio	45	60.8	•	78.2	55.8	40.3	45.5	45.6	40.4	54.4	45.0	17.0
Return on Total Assets	46	9.1	•	57.9	5.0	20.3	13.0	16.3	9.1	11.0	7.9	12.4
Return on Equity Before Income Taxes	47	19.8	•	238.5	10.9	32.3	22.5	28.5	13.2	21.8	12.3	13.4
Return on Equity After Income Taxes	48	15.0	•	237.8	9.0	30.4	19.1	26.3	12.2	15.1	8.9	9.0
Profit Margin (Before Income Tax)	49	8.5	53.3	14.5	2.4	8.3	7.5	10.1	6.1	9.0	7.1	9.1
Profit Margin (After Income Tax)	50	6.5	53.3	14.5	2.0	7.8	6.4	9.3	5.6	6.2	5.1	6.1

Table I

Corporations with and without Net Income

COMPUTER AND PERIPHERAL EQUIPMENT

MONEY AMOUNTS AND SIZE OF ASSETS IN THOUSANDS OF DOLLARS

Item Description for Accounting Period 7/09 Through 6/10	Total	Zero Assets	Under 500	500 to 1,000	1,000 to 5,000	5,000 to 10,000	10,000 to 25,000	25,000 to 50,000	50,000 to 100,000	100,000 to 250,000	250,000 to 500,000	500,000 to 2,500,000	2,500,000 and over
Number of Enterprises **1**	2775	732	1207	165	362	83	112	39	22	16	11	15	11
Revenues ($ in Thousands)													
Net Sales **2**	178888461	358408	677992	204618	919947	543259	2599621	1775808	5628246	2476425	3205141	10108038	150390958
Interest **3**	2255902	1499	2038	70	2724	1009	3801	2444	8354	7405	27601	26511	2172445
Rents **4**	1299381	0	0	0	0	0	0	254	167	226	100	16696	1281937
Royalties **5**	27964188	21997	0	0	0	0	4375	8154	88378	7883	75957	187304	27570140
Other Portfolio Income **6**	1334757	15526	4296	0	46	2923	12144	2990	14123	14439	32440	383537	852293
Other Receipts **7**	2196327	5621	9761	328	4211	2126	9283	17360	30970	17695	69737	614451	1414786
Total Receipts **8**	213939016	403051	694087	205016	926928	549317	2629224	1807010	5770238	2524073	3410976	11336537	183682559
Average Total Receipts **9**	77095	551	575	1243	2561	6618	23475	46334	262284	157755	310089	755769	16698414
Operating Costs/Operating Income (%)													
Cost of Operations **10**	63.1	30.4	56.0	78.8	54.7	60.8	62.2	61.5	62.3	58.7	59.3	67.5	63.2
Salaries and Wages **11**	17.6	30.3	12.0	28.6	27.7	19.9	17.3	18.4	25.8	18.1	16.7	18.8	17.1
Taxes Paid **12**	2.0	2.6	2.9	3.6	3.6	2.6	1.6	1.8	2.0	1.5	1.8	1.9	2.0
Interest Paid **13**	1.9	0.1	2.0	1.3	1.1	2.7	1.1	0.9	0.8	1.3	1.3	0.9	2.1
Depreciation **14**	3.4	3.2	3.0	0.7	3.2	4.2	2.1	2.0	2.9	2.3	2.7	3.1	3.5
Amortization and Depletion **15**	1.5	12.4	0.0	0.4	0.6	0.6	1.0	1.3	0.3	0.1	1.4	1.5	1.6
Pensions and Other Deferred Comp. **16**	0.6	0.0	0.3	0.1	0.5	0.0	0.1	0.1	1.4	0.2	0.2	0.1	0.7
Employee Benefits **17**	2.0	1.8	2.8	0.8	2.1	2.5	2.0	1.6	2.3	2.7	1.0	2.9	1.9
Advertising **18**	1.7	0.6	0.7	0.8	0.9	1.6	1.1	1.5	0.3	1.8	0.8	5.2	1.5
Other Expenses **19**	18.9	22.9	29.6	19.9	18.5	22.1	13.0	16.2	•	14.4	15.4	7.9	20.6
Officers' Compensation **20**	0.6	9.9	7.6	3.1	9.5	7.2	3.2	2.5	0.5	1.2	1.3	1.2	0.4
Operating Margin **21**	•	•	•	•	•	•	•	•	3.5	•	•	•	•
Operating Margin Before Officers' Comp. **22**	•	•	•	•	•	•	•	•	4.0	•	•	•	•

Selected Average Balance Sheet ($ in Thousands)

Net Receivables 23	16323	0	58	311	396	1336	3582	8647	16174	29803	62409	142413	3684247
Inventories 24	3108	0	41	57	436	1465	2558	5188	10365	18366	27207	61123	550900
Net Property, Plant and Equipment 25	8012	0	8	152	201	1645	1575	2465	4162	14541	17847	78165	1820300
Total Assets 26	128060	0	254	868	2180	7244	15260	34380	69866	166245	364559	1000982	29750429
Notes and Loans Payable 27	28044	0	176	435	883	1814	3484	3511	28426	34131	49760	153098	6593113
All Other Liabilities 28	42025	0	237	384	477	1390	4621	10904	38928	63958	109820	328005	9730254
Net Worth 29	57991	0	-158	49	821	4040	7155	19965	2511	68156	204979	519878	13427062

Selected Financial Ratios (Times to 1)

Current Ratio 30	1.1	•	0.7	1.2	2.5	2.9	2.1	1.9	1.5	1.4	2.0	1.6	1.1
Quick Ratio 31	0.6	•	0.4	1.2	1.5	2.1	1.5	1.2	0.8	0.9	1.2	1.0	0.6
Net Sales to Working Capital 32	13.8	•	19.8	2.5	2.5	2.4	4.0	3.8	16.1	7.3	2.7	4.4	21.0
Coverage Ratio 33	7.3	•	•	•	•	•	•	•	8.4	0.9	4.5	19.6	7.4
Total Asset Turnover 34	0.5	•	2.2	1.4	1.2	0.9	1.5	1.3	3.7	0.9	0.8	0.7	0.5
Inventory Turnover 35	13.1	•	7.7	17.1	3.2	2.7	5.6	5.4	15.4	4.9	6.4	7.4	15.7
Receivables Turnover 36	3.7	•	13.8	5.4	4.2	3.8	6.7	5.5	15.2	4.5	5.6	4.0	3.5
Total Liabilities to Net Worth 37	1.2	•	•	16.7	1.7	0.8	1.1	0.7	26.8	1.4	0.8	0.9	1.2
Current Assets to Working Capital 38	8.9	•	•	7.1	1.7	1.5	1.9	2.1	3.2	3.5	2.0	2.6	14.1
Current Liabilities to Working Capital 39	7.9	•	•	6.1	0.7	0.5	0.9	1.1	2.2	2.5	1.0	1.6	13.1
Working Capital to Net Sales 40	0.1	•	•	0.1	0.4	0.4	0.3	0.3	0.1	0.1	0.4	0.2	0.0
Inventory to Working Capital 41	0.6	•	•	0.0	0.4	0.3	0.5	0.4	0.6	0.7	0.3	0.3	0.8
Total Receipts to Cash Flow 42	4.4	7.3	14.8	•	•	•	15.3	12.3	89.5	9.2	5.6	39.4	3.8
Cost of Goods to Cash Flow 43	2.8	2.2	8.3	•	•	•	9.5	7.6	55.7	5.4	3.3	26.6	2.4
Cash Flow to Total Debt 44	0.2	0.1	•	•	•	•	0.2	0.3	0.0	0.2	0.3	0.0	0.2

Selected Financial Factors (in Percentages)

Debt Ratio 45	54.7	•	162.3	94.4	62.4	44.2	53.1	41.9	96.4	59.0	43.8	48.1	54.9
Return on Total Assets 46	6.9	•	•	•	•	•	•	•	25.1	1.1	4.7	11.9	7.0
Return on Equity Before Income Taxes 47	13.2	•	51.0	•	•	•	•	•	614.6	•	6.5	21.8	13.4
Return on Equity After Income Taxes 48	8.7	•	51.0	•	•	•	•	•	555.5	•	4.7	18.8	8.8
Profit Margin (Before Income Tax) 49	11.9	•	•	•	•	•	•	•	6.0	•	4.6	16.8	13.2
Profit Margin (After Income Tax) 50	7.9	•	•	•	•	•	•	•	5.5	•	3.3	14.5	8.6

Table II
Corporations with Net Income

COMPUTER AND PERIPHERAL EQUIPMENT

MONEY AMOUNTS AND SIZE OF ASSETS IN THOUSANDS OF DOLLARS

Item Description for Accounting Period 7/09 Through 6/10	Total	Zero Assets	Under 500	500 to 1,000	1,000 to 5,000	5,000 to 10,000	10,000 to 25,000	25,000 to 50,000	50,000 to 100,000	100,000 to 250,000	250,000 to 500,000	500,000 to 2,500,000	2,500,000 and over
Number of Enterprises **1**	962	304	376	0	146	29	46	16	13	8	8	9	7
Revenues ($ in Thousands)													
Net Sales **2**	152995138	327954	206152	0	619319	302120	1079695	825628	5091526	1486794	2262387	6833547	133960017
Interest **3**	2173955	1457	2038	0	1185	883	1367	887	7213	4307	18611	16560	2119447
Rents **4**	1284763	0	0	0	0	0	0	254	167	226	41	14696	1269378
Royalties **5**	27701407	21997	0	0	0	0	4375	86	74070	7529	5686	167639	27420024
Other Portfolio Income **6**	1254616	15521	4296	0	0	21	281	2872	407	3415	357	376845	850601
Other Receipts **7**	1368432	1624	0	0	2215	40	1054	676	21092	9440	76370	469355	786567
Total Receipts **8**	186778311	368553	212486	0	622719	303064	1086772	830403	5194475	1511711	2363452	7878642	166406034
Average Total Receipts **9**	194156	1212	565	•	4265	10450	23625	51900	399575	188964	295432	875405	23772291
Operating Costs/Operating Income (%)													
Cost of Operations **10**	61.1	29.3	41.9	•	55.9	55.5	55.9	55.5	61.2	58.6	56.0	66.2	61.2
Salaries and Wages **11**	17.8	27.8	18.6	•	14.7	16.3	12.2	16.6	26.5	16.4	17.5	18.7	17.5
Taxes Paid **12**	2.1	2.4	4.7	•	2.2	1.6	1.5	2.0	2.0	1.2	1.7	2.2	2.1
Interest Paid **13**	2.0	0.0	4.6	•	0.0	0.4	0.6	0.5	0.7	1.3	0.5	1.0	2.2
Depreciation **14**	3.5	3.2	0.5	•	0.7	1.8	1.5	2.5	3.1	1.8	2.0	3.4	3.6
Amortization and Depletion **15**	1.6	0.0	•	•	0.0	•	0.5	0.2	0.1	0.5	0.5	1.2	1.7
Pensions and Other Deferred Comp. **16**	0.7	0.0	1.1	•	0.7	0.0	0.1	0.1	1.5	0.3	0.1	0.1	0.7
Employee Benefits **17**	2.1	1.8	8.7	•	1.1	1.5	2.0	1.7	2.2	1.6	1.2	3.5	2.0
Advertising **18**	1.7	0.6	0.3	•	0.4	1.3	1.0	1.5	0.2	2.4	1.1	4.8	1.7
Other Expenses **19**	20.1	20.5	11.4	•	9.6	10.9	10.0	10.0	•	10.9	15.2	3.6	22.3
Officers' Compensation **20**	0.5	10.4	10.5	•	8.7	7.0	2.7	3.3	0.4	1.4	1.5	1.0	0.4
Operating Margin **21**	•	3.9	•	•	6.1	3.8	11.9	6.1	7.3	3.6	2.6	•	•
Operating Margin Before Officers' Comp. **22**	•	14.3	8.3	•	14.7	10.8	14.6	9.4	7.8	5.0	4.1	•	•

Selected Average Balance Sheet ($ in Thousands)

Net Receivables 23	42285	0	88	677	1867	3870	9243	16925	34846	65341	190546	5347128
Inventories 24	7371	0	20	691	2980	3332	5002	12785	16568	29171	58372	800788
Net Property, Plant and Equipment 25	19748	0	7	119	420	1049	4237	4951	15470	19394	99955	2515153
Total Assets 26	339516	0	190	2069	6808	15911	35705	70397	166814	360621	1117721	44220838
Notes and Loans Payable 27	76221	0	394	383	1194	2313	1879	5836	38984	9745	141491	10172955
All Other Liabilities 28	106257	0	205	449	1128	3422	13131	31305	66484	100315	347997	13828952
Net Worth 29	157038	0	-409	1237	4487	10176	20696	33257	61347	250561	628233	20218931

Selected Financial Ratios (Times to 1)

Current Ratio 30	1.1	0.6	•	5.1	5.2	3.6	2.2	1.8	1.5	2.2	1.4	1.1
Quick Ratio 31	0.6	0.6	•	3.6	3.8	2.4	1.3	1.0	1.1	1.2	1.0	0.5
Net Sales to Working Capital 32	14.7	•	•	2.7	2.1	2.5	3.6	15.9	6.7	2.2	5.9	20.0
Coverage Ratio 33	8.7	350.3	1.2	641.7	12.4	22.5	15.8	15.0	5.1	14.4	32.5	8.0
Total Asset Turnover 34	0.5	•	2.9	2.1	1.5	1.5	1.4	5.6	1.1	0.8	0.7	0.4
Inventory Turnover 35	13.2	•	11.5	3.4	1.9	3.9	5.7	18.7	6.6	5.4	8.6	14.6
Receivables Turnover 36	3.5	•	9.3	3.9	3.4	5.6	5.8	21.0	5.1	5.2	3.8	3.4
Total Liabilities to Net Worth 37	1.2	•	•	0.7	0.5	0.6	0.7	1.1	1.7	0.4	0.8	1.2
Current Assets to Working Capital 38	9.8	•	•	1.2	1.2	1.4	1.9	2.2	3.0	1.8	3.3	14.0
Current Liabilities to Working Capital 39	8.8	•	•	0.2	0.2	0.4	0.9	1.2	2.0	0.8	2.3	13.0
Working Capital to Net Sales 40	0.1	•	•	0.4	0.5	0.4	0.3	0.1	0.1	0.5	0.2	0.0
Inventory to Working Capital 41	0.6	•	•	0.3	0.3	0.4	0.4	0.4	0.6	0.2	0.4	0.8
Total Receipts to Cash Flow 42	3.8	3.4	16.7	7.5	8.9	5.0	6.6	49.4	6.9	4.9	19.7	3.5
Cost of Goods to Cash Flow 43	2.3	1.0	7.0	4.2	4.9	2.8	3.7	30.2	4.0	2.7	13.0	2.1
Cash Flow to Total Debt 44	0.2	0.1	•	0.7	0.5	0.8	0.5	0.2	0.3	0.5	0.1	0.2

Selected Financial Factors (in Percentages)

Debt Ratio 45	53.7	•	315.4	40.2	34.1	36.0	42.0	52.8	63.2	30.5	43.8	54.3
Return on Total Assets 46	8.1	15.5	•	13.6	6.8	19.4	10.6	56.0	7.6	6.2	22.8	7.5
Return on Equity Before Income Taxes 47	15.5	•	•	22.7	9.5	29.0	17.2	110.7	16.7	8.3	39.3	14.3
Return on Equity After Income Taxes 48	10.7	•	•	18.0	8.4	26.4	13.9	103.1	13.4	6.3	35.2	9.4
Profit Margin (Before Income Tax) 49	15.3	16.1	0.8	6.6	4.1	12.6	6.9	9.4	5.5	7.4	32.5	15.1
Profit Margin (After Income Tax) 50	10.6	15.0	0.8	5.2	3.6	11.4	5.6	8.8	4.4	5.6	29.2	9.9

Table I

Corporations with and without Net Income

COMMUNICATIONS EQUIPMENT

MONEY AMOUNTS AND SIZE OF ASSETS IN THOUSANDS OF DOLLARS

Item Description for Accounting Period 7/09 Through 6/10	Total	Zero Assets	Under 500	500 to 1,000	1,000 to 5,000	5,000 to 10,000	10,000 to 25,000	25,000 to 50,000	50,000 to 100,000	100,000 to 250,000	250,000 to 500,000	500,000 to 2,500,000	2,500,000 and over
Number of Enterprises **1**	1311	19	751	31	301	38	56	42	17	21	9	16	10
Revenues ($ in Thousands)													
Net Sales **2**	11294783	16424	81963	51459	1527523	363223	1741771	1482253	1218226	3368507	2293531	19966695	80813208
Interest **3**	676770	2	2	54	1223	202	1253	4245	974	10470	24288	83489	550567
Rents **4**	198326	0	0	0	67	734	126	42	130	9	6854	3325	187039
Royalties **5**	1059339	0	0	0	0	0	2416	0	704	12287	482	40209	1003240
Other Portfolio Income **6**	1467043	2260	0	0	59	56	289	2607	1281	3708	698	207238	1248845
Other Receipts **7**	856248	-1176	29	0	3295	451	5003	47612	1152	11146	68333	254994	465413
Total Receipts **8**	117182509	17510	81994	51513	1532167	364666	1750858	1536759	1222467	3406127	2394186	20555950	84268312
Average Total Receipts **9**	89384	922	109	1662	5090	9596	31265	36590	71910	162197	266021	1284747	8426831
Operating Costs/Operating Income (%)													
Cost of Operations **10**	64.9	104.6	51.2	79.8	41.4	62.6	68.1	55.1	60.4	62.1	59.0	78.9	62.4
Salaries and Wages **11**	14.9	66.6	4.1	23.6	25.2	20.5	10.7	19.4	16.7	13.3	18.9	6.4	16.7
Taxes Paid **12**	1.6	6.8	3.6	1.3	5.1	3.1	1.6	2.1	1.8	1.2	1.8	0.8	1.6
Interest Paid **13**	2.0	21.7	0.3	12.7	0.7	1.6	1.1	0.6	1.2	1.7	3.6	1.6	2.1
Depreciation **14**	2.6	1.2	10.2	1.0	0.8	1.7	1.5	2.2	2.1	2.0	4.2	1.4	3.0
Amortization and Depletion **15**	1.6	•	•	•	0.6	2.3	0.9	3.0	1.1	0.9	1.7	1.2	1.8
Pensions and Other Deferred Comp. **16**	0.7	•	0.0	•	0.4	0.2	0.4	0.1	0.3	0.3	0.1	0.3	0.9
Employee Benefits **17**	1.8	•	1.7	3.9	1.2	3.9	1.7	2.6	2.2	2.1	2.2	1.5	1.9
Advertising **18**	1.0	•	0.3	0.3	0.8	0.7	0.3	0.6	0.6	0.4	0.6	0.5	1.2
Other Expenses **19**	4.5	64.8	21.5	10.9	19.8	12.0	9.2	18.4	12.5	12.9	14.8	8.1	2.1
Officers' Compensation **20**	0.5	•	12.7	•	8.0	5.0	2.1	1.9	1.3	1.3	0.9	0.4	0.2
Operating Margin **21**	3.8	•	•	•	•	•	2.5	•	•	1.8	•	•	6.0
Operating Margin Before Officers' Comp. **22**	4.3	•	7.2	•	4.1	•	4.6	•	1.1	3.1	•	•	6.3

Selected Average Balance Sheet ($ in Thousands)

Net Receivables 23	19109	0	1	248	530	1947	4832	8121	13650	30241	77545	140101	2039186
Inventories 24	6274	0	29	742	588	2538	3606	6904	12398	15869	30775	90028	515413
Net Property, Plant and Equipment 25	8787	0	11	100	270	630	1525	3730	5501	8597	22241	104982	900723
Total Assets 26	111216	0	74	837	2612	7465	18077	35824	73894	150535	361269	1225214	11486357
Notes and Loans Payable 27	30909	0	21	2416	1667	1842	4573	10731	9395	34843	107007	301221	3247804
All Other Liabilities 28	50931	0	12	601	820	3663	8129	10566	22187	41522	101810	367599	5741004
Net Worth 29	29377	0	41	-2180	125	1960	5375	14528	42312	74170	152451	556394	2497549

Selected Financial Ratios (Times to 1)

Current Ratio 30	1.4	•	3.0	1.3	1.5	2.0	1.7	1.7	2.3	2.4	2.1	1.8	1.3
Quick Ratio 31	0.9	•	1.7	0.6	0.9	1.2	1.2	1.1	1.5	1.6	1.5	1.0	0.9
Net Sales to Working Capital 32	6.7	•	3.5	10.9	7.3	3.4	5.6	4.2	2.7	3.0	3.1	4.7	8.8
Coverage Ratio 33	5.9	•	•	•	•	•	3.7	•	1.1	2.8	0.1	2.3	7.2
Total Asset Turnover 34	0.8	•	1.5	2.0	1.9	1.3	1.7	1.0	1.0	1.1	0.7	1.0	0.7
Inventory Turnover 35	8.9	•	1.9	1.8	3.6	2.4	5.9	2.8	3.5	6.3	4.9	10.9	9.8
Receivables Turnover 36	4.1	•	20.6	11.6	12.8	3.9	5.5	3.4	4.1	5.9	3.6	8.8	3.6
Total Liabilities to Net Worth 37	2.8	•	0.8	•	20.0	2.8	2.4	1.5	0.7	1.0	1.4	1.2	3.6
Current Assets to Working Capital 38	3.6	•	1.5	4.9	2.9	2.0	2.4	2.5	1.7	1.7	1.9	2.2	4.9
Current Liabilities to Working Capital 39	2.6	•	0.5	3.9	1.9	1.0	1.4	1.5	0.7	0.7	0.9	1.2	3.9
Working Capital to Net Sales 40	0.1	•	0.3	0.1	0.1	0.3	0.2	0.2	0.4	0.3	0.3	0.2	0.1
Inventory to Working Capital 41	0.4	•	0.7	2.0	1.1	0.6	0.5	0.6	0.4	0.3	0.2	0.4	0.5
Total Receipts to Cash Flow 42	9.9	•	8.5	9.6	•	•	9.8	7.5	9.2	7.7	12.0	12.6	9.5
Cost of Goods to Cash Flow 43	6.4	•	4.4	4.0	•	•	6.7	4.1	5.6	4.8	7.1	10.0	5.9
Cash Flow to Total Debt 44	0.1	•	0.4	0.2	•	•	0.2	0.2	0.1	0.3	0.1	0.1	0.1

Selected Financial Factors (in Percentages)

Debt Ratio 45	73.6	•	45.4	360.3	95.2	73.7	70.3	59.4	42.7	50.7	57.8	54.6	78.3
Return on Total Assets 46	9.0	•	•	•	•	•	7.1	•	1.3	5.0	0.2	3.6	10.7
Return on Equity Before Income Taxes 47	28.1	•	•	25.4	•	•	17.4	•	0.3	6.6	•	4.4	42.2
Return on Equity After Income Taxes 48	19.7	•	•	25.4	•	•	13.8	•	•	2.6	•	3.7	29.8
Profit Margin (Before Income Tax) 49	9.6	•	•	3.0	•	•	3.0	0.1	0.1	3.0	•	2.0	13.1
Profit Margin (After Income Tax) 50	6.7	•	•	•	•	•	2.4	•	•	1.2	•	1.6	9.2

Table II

Corporations with Net Income

COMMUNICATIONS EQUIPMENT

MONEY AMOUNTS AND SIZE OF ASSETS IN THOUSANDS OF DOLLARS

Item Description for Accounting Period 7/09 Through 6/10	Total	Zero Assets	Under 500	500 to 1,000	1,000 to 5,000	5,000 to 10,000	10,000 to 25,000	25,000 to 50,000	50,000 to 100,000	100,000 to 250,000	250,000 to 500,000	500,000 to 2,500,000	2,500,000 and over
Number of Enterprises **1**	716	0	422	0	188	15	36	17	7	12	4	9	6
Revenues ($ in Thousands)													
Net Sales **2**	91259346	0	36841	0	1294013	128481	1314945	885835	569570	2599925	1115573	15525344	67788817
Interest **3**	373739	0	0	0	333	46	975	295	286	6048	5233	27874	332649
Rents **4**	184563	0	0	0	67	0	126	0	0	9	0	161	184200
Royalties **5**	812482	0	0	0	0	0	2416	0	0	8948	482	32182	768453
Other Portfolio Income **6**	1386508	0	0	0	0	15	148	2	8	2843	400	177662	1205431
Other Receipts **7**	546170	0	0	0	830	201	2884	44183	261	7450	7822	180068	302474
Total Receipts **8**	94562808	0	36841	0	1295243	128743	1321494	930315	570125	2625223	1129510	15943291	70582024
Average Total Receipts **9**	132071	•	87	•	6890	8583	36708	54724	81446	218769	282378	1771477	11763671
Operating Costs/Operating Income (%)													
Cost of Operations **10**	66.6	•	12.5	•	40.9	31.2	66.4	62.0	47.4	65.1	62.0	85.2	63.3
Salaries and Wages **11**	13.8	•	•	•	23.7	20.4	6.5	14.9	19.4	9.4	12.1	4.2	16.1
Taxes Paid **12**	1.4	•	5.0	•	5.4	2.7	1.4	2.0	1.8	1.0	1.3	0.5	1.6
Interest Paid **13**	1.4	•	0.7	•	0.6	1.8	0.8	0.6	0.9	1.5	5.3	0.2	1.6
Depreciation **14**	2.6	•	21.3	•	0.7	1.1	1.2	1.9	2.6	1.6	4.6	0.8	3.1
Amortization and Depletion **15**	0.8	•	•	•	0.0	•	0.1	0.9	0.2	0.5	1.0	0.3	1.0
Pensions and Other Deferred Comp. **16**	0.8	•	•	•	0.4	0.5	0.4	0.2	0.4	0.3	0.1	0.2	1.0
Employee Benefits **17**	1.2	•	•	•	0.6	2.2	1.5	1.8	2.8	1.7	1.3	0.9	1.3
Advertising **18**	1.1	•	•	•	0.7	0.7	0.2	0.5	0.9	0.2	0.5	0.5	1.4
Other Expenses **19**	2.4	•	33.2	•	17.0	13.6	5.2	10.4	12.2	10.5	8.9	5.8	0.6
Officers' Compensation **20**	0.4	•	22.9	•	6.6	7.0	1.8	1.2	1.2	1.0	0.7	0.3	0.2
Operating Margin **21**	7.4	•	4.4	•	3.3	18.9	14.5	3.6	10.3	7.1	2.1	1.0	8.8
Operating Margin Before Officers' Comp. **22**	7.8	•	27.3	•	9.9	25.8	16.3	4.8	11.5	8.2	2.8	1.3	9.1

Selected Average Balance Sheet ($ in Thousands)

Net Receivables 23	20658	•	697	1858	5121	8705	8873	38904	65395	152756	2022406
Inventories 24	7481	•	665	3090	2930	9283	12875	19122	24272	119226	564172
Net Property, Plant and Equipment 25	10819	•	408	512	1859	3911	7987	10452	21316	68339	1106594
Total Assets 26	136465	•	3213	5900	18820	34872	75613	160097	388949	1131710	13588878
Notes and Loans Payable 27	32744	•	2217	2072	5046	3846	9341	34896	144188	108305	3449882
All Other Liabilities 28	68823	•	947	1421	7748	11388	26400	45292	111801	483299	7179048
Net Worth 29	34898	•	50	2407	6026	19638	39872	79908	132961	540107	2955947

Selected Financial Ratios (Times to 1)

Current Ratio 30	1.2	•	1.9	3.8	2.2	2.0	2.0	2.6	2.6	1.7	1.1
Quick Ratio 31	0.8	•	1.1	2.6	1.6	1.3	1.3	1.8	1.5	0.8	0.8
Net Sales to Working Capital 32	12.0	•	5.6	2.3	4.6	4.4	3.5	3.2	3.0	6.2	22.7
Coverage Ratio 33	10.9	7.2	6.8	11.8	20.7	15.6	12.8	6.5	1.7	22.6	11.2
Total Asset Turnover 34	0.9	1.7	2.1	1.5	1.9	1.5	1.1	1.4	0.7	1.5	0.8
Inventory Turnover 35	11.4	4.0	4.2	0.9	8.3	3.5	3.0	7.4	7.1	12.3	12.7
Receivables Turnover 36	6.1	20.3	16.1	2.3	7.5	3.5	5.0	6.8	•	•	5.6
Total Liabilities to Net Worth 37	2.9	36.7	63.9	1.5	2.1	0.8	0.9	1.0	1.9	1.1	3.6
Current Assets to Working Capital 38	5.4	•	2.2	1.4	1.9	2.0	2.0	1.6	1.6	2.5	10.4
Current Liabilities to Working Capital 39	4.4	•	1.2	0.4	0.9	1.0	1.0	0.6	0.6	1.5	9.4
Working Capital to Net Sales 40	0.1	•	0.2	0.4	0.2	0.2	0.3	0.3	0.3	0.2	0.0
Inventory to Working Capital 41	0.7	•	0.8	0.4	0.4	0.5	0.4	0.3	0.3	0.4	1.2
Total Receipts to Cash Flow 42	8.6	3.0	6.8	3.3	5.3	6.1	4.7	6.3	9.1	12.6	8.4
Cost of Goods to Cash Flow 43	5.7	0.4	2.8	1.0	3.5	3.8	2.2	4.1	5.7	10.7	5.3
Cash Flow to Total Debt 44	0.1	0.6	0.3	0.7	0.5	0.6	0.5	0.4	0.1	0.2	0.1

Selected Financial Factors (in Percentages)

Debt Ratio 45	74.4	97.3	98.5	59.2	68.0	43.7	47.3	50.1	65.8	52.3	78.2
Return on Total Assets 46	13.8	8.9	8.6	30.2	30.5	14.1	12.3	13.1	6.5	6.3	14.8
Return on Equity Before Income Taxes 47	49.0	287.9	473.8	67.8	90.7	23.4	21.5	22.2	7.7	12.6	61.8
Return on Equity After Income Taxes 48	36.0	287.9	437.3	65.7	85.8	19.7	19.8	15.7	6.6	11.3	44.4
Profit Margin (Before Income Tax) 49	13.4	4.4	3.4	19.1	15.0	8.8	10.5	8.2	3.7	3.9	16.2
Profit Margin (After Income Tax) 50	9.9	4.4	3.1	18.5	14.1	7.4	9.7	5.8	3.2	3.5	11.6

140

Table I

Corporations with and without Net Income

AUDIO AND VIDEO EQUIP., REPRODUCING MAGNETIC & OPTICAL MEDIA

MONEY AMOUNTS AND SIZE OF ASSETS IN THOUSANDS OF DOLLARS

Item Description for Accounting Period 7/09 Through 6/10	Total	Zero Assets	Under 500	500 to 1,000	1,000 to 5,000	5,000 to 10,000	10,000 to 25,000	25,000 to 50,000	50,000 to 100,000	100,000 to 250,000	250,000 to 500,000	500,000 to 2,500,000	2,500,000 and over
Number of Enterprises 1	1405	16	1054	0	219	18	41	21	15	7	5	5	3
Revenues ($ in Thousands)													
Net Sales 2	27641699	79399	281901	0	725890	251398	727439	950330	1239874	810589	2320815	5617663	14636398
Interest 3	49550	530	4	0	1269	258	832	281	800	6108	2155	16971	20342
Rents 4	10563	0	0	0	0	0	420	0	0	0	2783	296	7063
Royalties 5	544530	0	0	0	0	0	0	0	0	5164	2509	300278	236578
Other Portfolio Income 6	119473	0	10435	0	1	1074	70	9390	2140	17156	7996	59314	11898
Other Receipts 7	622263	18	5844	0	499	176	52550	11856	-280	22300	15920	21929	491455
Total Receipts 8	28988078	79947	298184	0	727659	252906	781311	971857	1242534	861317	2352178	6016451	15403734
Average Total Receipts 9	20632	4997	283	•	3323	14050	19056	46279	82836	123045	470436	1203290	5134578
Operating Costs/Operating Income (%)													
Cost of Operations 10	66.3	93.3	13.7	•	56.6	59.0	54.8	67.7	51.3	62.5	78.3	54.9	72.2
Salaries and Wages 11	12.7	•	24.8	•	16.5	12.0	17.3	10.9	15.4	14.6	9.4	19.7	9.7
Taxes Paid 12	1.2	•	3.5	•	2.8	1.7	2.5	1.6	2.2	1.9	1.0	1.9	0.6
Interest Paid 13	0.8	0.2	0.0	•	1.5	1.1	1.9	3.7	3.6	2.1	0.2	1.2	0.3
Depreciation 14	2.4	•	1.4	•	0.9	1.0	2.3	2.0	2.7	4.3	2.3	2.8	2.2
Amortization and Depletion 15	1.5	•	0.5	•	1.1	•	1.0	0.6	1.6	0.5	0.3	2.0	1.7
Pensions and Other Deferred Comp. 16	0.4	•	0.5	•	0.6	0.2	0.5	0.1	0.1	0.8	0.3	0.5	0.4
Employee Benefits 17	2.1	•	0.5	•	2.1	0.3	2.2	1.7	3.0	1.8	1.0	3.1	1.8
Advertising 18	1.7	•	4.0	•	1.8	9.1	0.9	0.4	2.1	1.2	1.0	2.5	1.6
Other Expenses 19	17.6	11.8	27.4	•	16.2	16.4	18.1	21.1	15.7	13.2	5.0	15.3	20.6
Officers' Compensation 20	0.8	•	10.8	•	3.8	5.5	3.2	1.4	1.9	1.3	0.7	0.5	0.3
Operating Margin 21	•	13.2	•	•	•	•	•	•	0.4	•	0.6	•	•
Operating Margin Before Officers' Comp. 22	•	24.0	•	•	•	•	•	•	2.4	1.2	•	•	•

Selected Average Balance Sheet ($ in Thousands)

Net Receivables 23	3045	0	8	•	331	1785	4477	7324	16715	18195	69132	211200	682862
Inventories 24	2568	0	8	•	617	2080	1804	9303	14793	20731	75986	126342	593148
Net Property, Plant and Equipment 25	1829	0	0	•	99	595	1161	4316	6855	18663	44426	109236	465965
Total Assets 26	31166	0	72	•	1976	7102	14822	33097	65946	147337	344738	1204238	10694670
Notes and Loans Payable 27	11255	0	34	•	628	477	51673	22160	25259	18349	99004	81111	3879663
All Other Liabilities 28	9022	0	7	•	751	5267	12632	11582	20088	44360	101701	517586	2646352
Net Worth 29	10889	0	30	•	596	1358	-49484	-645	20600	84628	144033	605541	4168655

Selected Financial Ratios (Times to 1)

Current Ratio 30	1.4	•	8.7	•	2.3	1.2	0.9	1.8	2.3	2.5	1.5	1.5	1.2
Quick Ratio 31	0.8	•	7.2	•	1.5	0.7	0.7	0.9	1.4	1.5	0.8	1.0	0.5
Net Sales to Working Capital 32	8.0	•	5.0	•	3.5	12.5	•	4.8	3.4	2.2	7.5	5.4	15.9
Coverage Ratio 33	•	•	3344.2	•	•	•	2.5	•	1.2	2.5	16.7	3.8	•
Total Asset Turnover 34	0.6	•	3.7	•	1.7	2.0	1.2	1.4	1.3	0.8	1.3	0.9	0.5
Inventory Turnover 35	5.1	•	4.6	•	3.0	4.0	5.4	3.3	2.9	3.5	4.8	4.9	5.9
Receivables Turnover 36	6.1	•	30.8	•	7.9	6.9	4.8	6.3	4.8	4.5	7.2	4.8	6.7
Total Liabilities to Net Worth 37	1.9	•	1.4	•	2.3	4.2	•	•	2.2	0.7	1.4	1.0	1.6
Current Assets to Working Capital 38	3.5	•	1.1	•	1.8	5.8	•	2.2	1.8	1.7	2.9	3.0	5.8
Current Liabilities to Working Capital 39	2.5	•	0.1	•	0.8	4.8	•	1.2	0.8	0.7	1.9	2.0	4.8
Working Capital to Net Sales 40	0.1	•	0.2	•	0.3	0.1	•	0.2	0.3	0.5	0.1	0.2	0.1
Inventory to Working Capital 41	0.9	•	0.2	•	0.5	2.1	•	0.9	0.5	0.3	1.1	0.5	1.8
Total Receipts to Cash Flow 42	8.0	13.8	2.3	•	13.1	11.0	5.7	9.6	6.9	7.8	19.3	7.2	8.0
Cost of Goods to Cash Flow 43	5.3	12.8	0.3	•	7.4	6.5	3.1	6.5	3.5	4.9	15.1	4.0	5.8
Cash Flow to Total Debt 44	0.1	•	2.8	•	0.2	0.2	0.0	0.1	0.3	0.2	0.1	0.3	0.1

Selected Financial Factors (in Percentages)

Debt Ratio 45	65.1	•	57.8	•	69.8	80.9	433.9	101.9	68.8	42.6	58.2	49.7	61.0
Return on Total Assets 46	•	•	70.9	•	•	•	5.6	•	5.6	4.1	4.0	4.3	•
Return on Equity Before Income Taxes 47	•	•	167.9	•	•	•	•	628.5	3.3	4.3	9.1	6.4	•
Return on Equity After Income Taxes 48	•	•	165.8	•	•	•	•	642.4	•	0.8	5.3	3.7	•
Profit Margin (Before Income Tax) 49	•	•	19.0	•	•	•	2.8	•	0.8	3.1	2.8	3.4	•
Profit Margin (After Income Tax) 50	•	•	18.7	•	•	•	0.8	•	•	0.6	1.7	2.0	•

Table II
Corporations with Net Income

AUDIO AND VIDEO EQUIP., REPRODUCING MAGNETIC & OPTICAL MEDIA

MONEY AMOUNTS AND SIZE OF ASSETS IN THOUSANDS OF DOLLARS

Item Description for Accounting Period 7/09 Through 6/10	Total	Zero Assets	Under 500	500 to 1,000	1,000 to 5,000	5,000 to 10,000	10,000 to 25,000	25,000 to 50,000	50,000 to 100,000	100,000 to 250,000	250,000 to 500,000	500,000 to 2,500,000	2,500,000 and over
Number of Enterprises 1	1287	0	•	•	178	11	24	10	9	3	•	5	0
Revenues ($ in Thousands)													
Net Sales 2	11685892	0	•	0	665755	169791	503707	492919	824494	383877	•	6533416	0
Interest 3	14155	0	•	0	419	0	778	114	111	2242	•	8484	0
Rents 4	588	0	•	0	0	0	420	0	0	0	•	5	0
Royalties 5	324181	0	•	0	0	0	0	0	0	5164	•	316507	0
Other Portfolio Income 6	111336	0	•	0	0	0	70	9288	1804	17142	•	66314	0
Other Receipts 7	222099	0	•	0	462	68	52262	1927	-775	24092	•	124664	0
Total Receipts 8	12358251	0	•	0	666636	169859	557237	504248	825634	432517	•	7049390	0
Average Total Receipts 9	9602	•	•	•	3745	15442	23218	50425	91737	144172	•	1409878	•
Operating Costs/Operating Income (%)													
Cost of Operations 10	59.8	•	•	•	58.1	55.3	53.2	64.9	51.7	52.5	•	57.4	•
Salaries and Wages 11	15.7	•	•	•	10.1	6.9	15.0	7.5	10.9	19.3	•	19.2	•
Taxes Paid 12	1.7	•	•	•	2.4	1.9	2.4	0.9	1.9	2.4	•	1.7	•
Interest Paid 13	0.5	•	•	•	0.1	0.7	0.3	0.4	3.9	0.1	•	0.3	•
Depreciation 14	2.1	•	•	•	0.4	0.7	1.7	1.0	2.5	3.3	•	2.4	•
Amortization and Depletion 15	0.8	•	•	•	0.1	•	0.7	0.0	0.5	0.2	•	1.2	•
Pensions and Other Deferred Comp. 16	0.6	•	•	•	0.6	0.2	0.6	0.1	0.2	1.6	•	0.6	•
Employee Benefits 17	2.2	•	•	•	1.8	0.4	1.7	2.4	3.2	2.3	•	2.5	•
Advertising 18	2.2	•	•	•	1.9	13.3	0.7	0.5	2.6	1.3	•	2.7	•
Other Expenses 19	12.6	•	•	•	12.8	14.9	16.3	11.9	12.3	13.6	•	15.2	•
Officers' Compensation 20	1.2	•	•	•	3.1	4.3	4.0	1.7	1.7	1.7	•	0.4	•
Operating Margin 21	0.6	•	•	•	8.6	1.5	3.3	8.4	8.6	1.8	•	•	•
Operating Margin Before Officers' Comp. 22	1.9	•	•	•	11.7	5.8	7.3	10.2	10.3	3.4	•	•	•

Selected Average Balance Sheet ($ in Thousands)

Net Receivables 23	1524	350	1753	3372	8675	15406	25752	249035
Inventories 24	1689	697	2266	1534	13358	14125	17473	138061
Net Property, Plant and Equipment 25	703	64	485	967	2239	9088	21086	105507
Total Assets 26	9028	1832	6506	13599	31897	64667	176012	1677515
Notes and Loans Payable 27	1118	216	517	1630	4106	29230	330	194919
All Other Liabilities 28	2928	251	4766	3231	8297	19366	45631	560580
Net Worth 29	4982	1365	1224	8738	19494	16071	130051	922016

Selected Financial Ratios (Times to 1)

Current Ratio 30	2.4	5.5	1.3	2.4	2.5	2.4	3.0	2.5
Quick Ratio 31	1.4	3.5	0.6	1.9	1.2	1.3	2.3	1.3
Net Sales to Working Capital 32	2.9	2.7	12.1	4.3	3.2	4.0	1.5	2.4
Coverage Ratio 33	14.7	168.8	3.4	46.2	25.4	3.2	143.4	19.9
Total Asset Turnover 34	1.0	2.0	2.4	1.5	1.5	1.4	0.7	0.8
Inventory Turnover 35	3.2	3.1	3.8	7.3	2.4	3.4	3.8	5.4
Receivables Turnover 36	4.7	10.1	7.2	5.6	5.1	5.5	5.9	•
Total Liabilities to Net Worth 37	0.8	0.3	4.3	0.6	0.6	3.0	0.4	0.8
Current Assets to Working Capital 38	1.7	1.2	4.7	1.7	1.7	1.7	1.5	1.7
Current Liabilities to Working Capital 39	0.7	0.2	3.7	0.7	0.7	0.7	0.5	0.7
Working Capital to Net Sales 40	0.3	0.4	0.1	0.2	0.3	0.3	0.7	0.4
Inventory to Working Capital 41	0.4	0.4	2.5	0.2	0.7	0.6	0.2	0.3
Total Receipts to Cash Flow 42	6.2	5.9	6.5	3.6	4.7	5.1	4.0	6.1
Cost of Goods to Cash Flow 43	3.7	3.4	3.6	1.9	3.1	2.6	2.1	3.5
Cash Flow to Total Debt 44	0.4	1.4	0.4	1.2	0.8	0.4	0.7	0.3

Selected Financial Factors (in Percentages)

Debt Ratio 45	44.8	25.5	81.2	35.7	38.9	75.1	26.1	45.0
Return on Total Assets 46	7.4	18.0	5.3	22.0	17.2	18.0	12.2	4.1
Return on Equity Before Income Taxes 47	12.5	24.0	20.0	33.5	27.1	50.0	16.4	7.1
Return on Equity After Income Taxes 48	9.9	18.1	19.8	26.3	26.1	41.9	11.2	5.4
Profit Margin (Before Income Tax) 49	6.9	8.7	1.6	14.0	10.7	8.8	16.7	5.0
Profit Margin (After Income Tax) 50	5.4	6.6	1.6	11.0	10.3	7.3	11.3	3.8

Table I

Corporations with and without Net Income

SEMICONDUCTOR AND OTHER ELECTRONIC COMPONENT

MONEY AMOUNTS AND SIZE OF ASSETS IN THOUSANDS OF DOLLARS

Item Description for Accounting Period 7/09 Through 6/10	Total	Zero Assets	Under 500	500 to 1,000	1,000 to 5,000	5,000 to 10,000	10,000 to 25,000	25,000 to 50,000	50,000 to 100,000	100,000 to 250,000	250,000 to 500,000	500,000 to 2,500,000	2,500,000 and over
Number of Enterprises 1	4500	584	1370	483	1222	360	184	65	64	55	38	55	19
Revenues ($ in Thousands)													
Net Sales 2	161585765	392353	339534	455101	4852782	3940531	3774123	2262647	4145569	8984857	8442257	32249486	91746524
Interest 3	1075344	1159	1106	345	1522	3758	6826	5276	15976	32926	43779	256405	706266
Rents 4	52815	4	0	0	111	940	1535	63	4385	9419	9399	8321	18637
Royalties 5	5942418	3876	0	0	0	1	1425	8713	57779	81019	122953	792661	4873991
Other Portfolio Income 6	3099658	698	0	127	7546	30280	1872	2618	52342	49314	329888	759799	1865174
Other Receipts 7	5229968	9616	457	3749	-4491	38549	50817	27460	169587	431310	252954	750918	3499045
Total Receipts 8	176985968	407706	341097	459322	4857470	4014059	3836598	2306777	4445638	9588845	9201230	34817590	102709637
Average Total Receipts 9	39330	698	249	951	3975	11150	20851	35489	69463	174343	242138	633047	5405770
Operating Costs/Operating Income (%)													
Cost of Operations 10	66.1	61.7	40.0	46.1	59.6	62.0	66.4	64.2	69.2	74.7	62.4	68.5	65.3
Salaries and Wages 11	12.8	17.3	6.2	20.5	13.0	11.1	14.5	12.1	13.7	11.7	19.6	15.7	11.3
Taxes Paid 12	1.5	2.8	3.8	3.0	2.5	1.9	1.9	2.2	2.1	1.5	2.2	1.5	1.3
Interest Paid 13	2.4	2.1	1.4	0.9	1.2	0.9	2.2	1.2	1.2	0.8	1.4	2.8	2.7
Depreciation 14	6.2	2.8	0.9	4.4	2.6	2.0	2.9	3.7	3.9	3.7	4.0	6.8	7.2
Amortization and Depletion 15	1.9	2.7	0.8	1.6	0.9	0.3	0.5	0.3	1.9	0.9	4.2	1.7	2.1
Pensions and Other Deferred Comp. 16	0.6	2.9	0.2	0.2	0.9	0.5	0.4	1.4	0.6	0.3	0.3	0.5	0.6
Employee Benefits 17	2.3	2.2	2.6	3.0	1.9	1.5	2.0	2.1	1.7	1.6	2.5	2.6	2.3
Advertising 18	1.2	0.4	0.1	0.4	0.5	1.0	0.4	0.3	0.4	0.3	0.8	0.3	1.8
Other Expenses 19	11.5	22.6	43.6	40.9	13.9	11.1	11.8	11.8	15.5	13.5	11.4	8.5	11.8
Officers' Compensation 20	0.9	6.1	10.8	6.3	6.6	3.2	3.3	3.0	1.7	1.1	1.2	1.1	0.2
Operating Margin 21	•	•	•	•	•	4.4	•	•	•	•	•	•	•
Operating Margin Before Officers' Comp. 22	•	0.2	0.2	3.0	7.6	3.0	0.7	•	•	•	•	•	•

Selected Average Balance Sheet ($ in Thousands)

Net Receivables **23**	13304	0	14	171	450	1443	3050	5973	12810	29600	56136	160517	2333610
Inventories **24**	3556	0	16	153	586	1366	3596	6774	9715	20679	32497	63283	374728
Net Property, Plant and Equipment **25**	8549	0	11	48	618	1123	2530	5648	11856	26713	39886	158513	1261976
Total Assets **26**	65205	0	131	594	2538	6420	14878	33400	72255	167404	343969	1094044	10292583
Notes and Loans Payable **27**	10282	0	108	337	885	1775	5528	7902	13043	21656	55890	276387	1229346
All Other Liabilities **28**	23234	0	53	111	442	1395	3996	7808	22963	45359	77194	302995	4135666
Net Worth **29**	31689	0	-30	146	1211	3250	5354	17691	36249	100390	210885	514661	4927572

Selected Financial Ratios (Times to 1)

Current Ratio **30**	1.5	•	1.6	3.8	1.8	3.0	1.8	2.4	1.9	2.3	2.1	1.9	1.3
Quick Ratio **31**	1.1	•	1.1	2.8	1.0	1.7	1.1	1.4	1.3	1.4	1.3	1.3	1.0
Net Sales to Working Capital **32**	3.8	•	7.9	3.3	7.1	3.5	5.5	3.0	3.4	3.1	2.5	2.4	5.1
Coverage Ratio **33**	2.4	•	•	•	•	7.7	•	0.7	•	•	0.4	1.0	3.5
Total Asset Turnover **34**	0.6	•	1.9	1.6	1.6	1.7	1.4	1.0	0.9	1.0	0.6	0.5	0.5
Inventory Turnover **35**	6.7	•	6.2	2.8	4.0	5.0	3.8	3.3	4.6	5.9	4.3	6.4	8.4
Receivables Turnover **36**	2.9	•	8.0	5.1	7.0	8.2	6.1	5.1	5.3	5.3	3.9	3.5	2.3
Total Liabilities to Net Worth **37**	1.1	•	•	3.1	1.1	1.0	1.8	0.9	1.0	0.7	0.6	1.1	1.1
Current Assets to Working Capital **38**	3.0	•	2.8	1.4	2.3	1.5	2.3	1.7	2.1	1.8	1.9	2.1	4.4
Current Liabilities to Working Capital **39**	2.0	•	1.8	0.4	1.3	0.5	1.3	0.7	1.1	0.8	0.9	1.1	3.4
Working Capital to Net Sales **40**	0.3	•	0.1	0.3	0.1	0.3	0.2	0.3	0.3	0.3	0.4	0.4	0.2
Inventory to Working Capital **41**	0.3	•	0.4	0.3	0.9	0.5	0.8	0.6	0.5	0.4	0.3	0.2	0.3
Total Receipts to Cash Flow **42**	9.5	•	8.2	23.7	16.0	7.4	24.1	11.6	13.7	13.2	26.2	29.8	6.9
Cost of Goods to Cash Flow **43**	6.3	•	3.3	11.0	9.5	4.6	16.0	7.5	9.5	9.8	16.3	20.5	4.5
Cash Flow to Total Debt **44**	0.1	•	0.2	0.1	0.2	0.5	0.1	0.2	0.1	0.2	0.1	0.0	0.1

Selected Financial Factors (in Percentages)

Debt Ratio **45**	51.4	•	122.7	75.5	52.3	49.4	64.0	47.0	49.8	40.0	38.7	53.0	52.1
Return on Total Assets **46**	3.1	•	•	•	•	12.2	•	0.9	•	•	0.4	1.4	4.5
Return on Equity Before Income Taxes **47**	3.8	•	84.6	•	21.0	•	•	•	•	•	•	•	6.7
Return on Equity After Income Taxes **48**	1.1	•	88.1	•	19.3	•	•	•	•	•	•	•	3.6
Profit Margin (Before Income Tax) **49**	3.3	•	•	•	6.2	•	•	•	•	•	•	•	6.8
Profit Margin (After Income Tax) **50**	1.0	•	•	•	5.7	•	•	•	•	•	•	•	3.7

Table II
Corporations with Net Income

SEMICONDUCTOR AND OTHER ELECTRONIC COMPONENT

MONEY AMOUNTS AND SIZE OF ASSETS IN THOUSANDS OF DOLLARS

Item Description for Accounting Period 7/09 Through 6/10		Total	Zero Assets	Under 500	500 to 1,000	1,000 to 5,000	5,000 to 10,000	10,000 to 25,000	25,000 to 50,000	50,000 to 100,000	100,000 to 250,000	250,000 to 500,000	500,000 to 2,500,000	2,500,000 and over
Number of Enterprises	1	2322	276	849	59	608	293	87	42	22	28	20	25	12
Revenues ($ in Thousands)														
Net Sales	2	106411957	65316	256873	129602	3325740	3608065	2286002	1805743	1708746	5879034	5138875	14310225	67897736
Interest	3	716170	42	1060	7	550	820	750	2339	3701	19371	12460	73529	601542
Rents	4	41649	0	0	0	111	772	862	63	0	7042	9118	6483	17198
Royalties	5	5389050	0	0	0	0	0	0	6346	52269	78812	104251	476041	4671330
Other Portfolio Income	6	2131354	0	0	0	4	21200	156	152	39400	24421	258466	609912	1177647
Other Receipts	7	3626382	331	1	0	-12656	9126	25995	25507	33867	67979	184697	392911	2898622
Total Receipts	8	118316562	65689	257934	129609	3313749	3639983	2313765	1840150	1837983	6076659	5707867	15869101	77264075
Average Total Receipts	9	50955	238	304	2197	5450	12423	26595	43813	83545	217024	285393	634764	6438673
Operating Costs/Operating Income (%)														
Cost of Operations	10	58.8	50.3	26.5	17.3	55.7	60.5	66.3	61.1	68.8	75.7	60.8	55.3	57.6
Salaries and Wages	11	12.0	3.9	•	32.3	9.7	9.9	10.7	8.8	8.4	6.7	20.7	17.5	11.1
Taxes Paid	12	1.6	6.2	3.5	3.6	2.3	1.8	1.5	2.0	2.5	1.1	2.0	1.9	1.5
Interest Paid	13	1.9	•	0.3	•	0.9	0.5	0.7	0.6	1.0	0.4	0.4	3.1	2.2
Depreciation	14	6.6	0.7	0.2	0.1	2.2	1.7	1.9	2.8	1.9	2.1	2.8	4.6	8.7
Amortization and Depletion	15	1.6	0.0	•	0.2	0.6	0.1	0.3	0.1	1.0	0.6	1.2	1.8	1.8
Pensions and Other Deferred Comp.	16	0.7	0.1	•	•	0.4	0.6	0.6	1.7	0.3	0.2	0.3	0.8	0.7
Employee Benefits	17	2.6	0.6	1.2	•	2.2	1.4	1.5	1.9	1.4	1.0	2.3	3.0	2.8
Advertising	18	1.4	0.1	•	•	0.3	1.0	0.3	0.3	0.4	0.2	1.1	0.3	2.0
Other Expenses	19	11.2	29.8	17.1	40.9	11.3	7.3	7.0	9.8	9.7	8.2	8.2	9.2	12.5
Officers' Compensation	20	0.8	0.9	12.3	5.5	6.7	3.0	3.3	2.7	1.5	0.7	1.2	1.2	0.2
Operating Margin	21	0.7	7.6	39.0	0.2	7.8	12.1	5.9	8.1	3.0	3.0	1.2	1.4	•
Operating Margin Before Officers' Comp.	22	1.5	8.5	51.3	5.6	14.4	15.2	9.2	10.8	4.5	3.7	0.3	2.5	•

Selected Average Balance Sheet ($ in Thousands)

Net Receivables 23	9599	0	20	448	529	1462	3784	6643	11048	30982	49956	143055	1266811
Inventories 24	4296	0	10	839	876	1352	5394	6510	13977	24110	36221	70813	397387
Net Property, Plant and Equipment 25	11295	0	1	1	726	945	2461	5464	6893	22013	36121	118809	1716920
Total Assets 26	76164	0	128	545	2723	6142	15146	34338	69441	170485	352802	1204195	10586138
Notes and Loans Payable 27	9979	0	0	100	870	1319	3339	6284	11854	15590	15620	249699	1203549
All Other Liabilities 28	25331	0	31	0	404	1111	4709	8431	21025	45790	70009	305175	3890199
Net Worth 29	40854	0	97	445	1448	3712	7098	19623	36562	109105	267172	649320	5492390

Selected Financial Ratios (Times to 1)

Current Ratio 30	1.7	•	3.5	•	2.5	3.6	2.1	2.5	2.0	2.3	2.2	2.4	1.4
Quick Ratio 31	1.1	•	3.3	•	1.2	2.1	1.2	1.4	1.2	1.4	1.4	1.5	1.0
Net Sales to Working Capital 32	3.9	•	5.3	4.1	5.7	3.6	5.0	3.5	3.8	3.8	2.8	1.8	5.3
Coverage Ratio 33	7.9	•	133.6	•	9.4	24.9	11.9	16.6	11.5	16.6	29.3	6.2	7.5
Total Asset Turnover 34	0.6	•	2.4	4.0	2.0	2.0	1.7	1.3	1.1	1.2	0.7	0.5	0.5
Inventory Turnover 35	6.3	•	7.7	0.5	3.5	5.5	3.2	4.0	3.8	6.6	4.3	4.5	8.2
Receivables Turnover 36	3.6	•	9.9	2.6	6.5	8.9	5.9	6.2	5.3	6.6	4.7	3.4	3.2
Total Liabilities to Net Worth 37	0.9	•	0.3	0.2	0.9	0.7	1.1	0.7	0.9	0.6	0.3	0.9	0.9
Current Assets to Working Capital 38	2.5	•	1.4	1.0	1.7	1.4	1.9	1.7	2.0	1.8	1.8	1.7	3.3
Current Liabilities to Working Capital 39	1.5	•	0.4	•	0.7	0.4	0.9	0.7	1.0	0.8	0.8	0.7	2.3
Working Capital to Net Sales 40	0.3	•	0.2	0.2	0.2	0.3	0.2	0.3	0.3	0.3	0.4	0.5	0.2
Inventory to Working Capital 41	0.3	•	0.0	•	0.8	0.5	0.7	0.6	0.5	0.4	0.4	0.2	0.3
Total Receipts to Cash Flow 42	4.8	4.8	2.0	2.9	6.9	5.9	8.4	5.6	5.8	7.5	7.8	5.4	4.3
Cost of Goods to Cash Flow 43	2.8	2.4	0.5	0.5	3.8	3.6	5.6	3.4	4.0	5.7	4.8	3.0	2.5
Cash Flow to Total Debt 44	0.3	•	4.7	7.7	0.6	0.9	0.4	0.5	0.4	0.5	0.4	0.2	0.3

Selected Financial Factors (in Percentages)

Debt Ratio 45	46.4	24.5	18.4	•	46.8	39.6	53.1	42.9	47.3	36.0	24.3	46.1	48.1
Return on Total Assets 46	9.2	93.5	0.8	•	16.7	27.1	13.5	13.3	13.0	8.6	7.7	9.2	8.8
Return on Equity Before Income Taxes 47	15.0	122.9	0.9	•	28.0	43.1	26.3	21.8	22.6	12.6	9.9	14.3	14.7
Return on Equity After Income Taxes 48	11.1	121.2	0.8	•	26.1	41.3	23.4	19.8	18.8	10.2	8.4	10.5	10.3
Profit Margin (Before Income Tax) 49	13.4	39.4	0.2	•	7.4	13.0	7.1	10.0	10.6	6.5	10.2	16.2	14.2
Profit Margin (After Income Tax) 50	9.9	38.8	0.2	•	6.9	12.5	6.3	9.1	8.8	5.3	8.7	11.9	10.0

Table I

Corporations with and without Net Income

NAVIGATIONAL, MEASURING, ELECTROMEDICAL, AND CONTROL

MONEY AMOUNTS AND SIZE OF ASSETS IN THOUSANDS OF DOLLARS

Item Description for Accounting Period 7/09 Through 6/10	Total	Zero Assets	Under 500	500 to 1,000	1,000 to 5,000	5,000 to 10,000	10,000 to 25,000	25,000 to 50,000	50,000 to 100,000	100,000 to 250,000	250,000 to 500,000	500,000 to 2,500,000	2,500,000 and over
Number of Enterprises **1**	3291	39	1899	170	558	268	157	66	37	31	21	27	17
Revenues ($ in Thousands)													
Net Sales **2**	92978530	860752	708545	98363	2982894	2142952	3332394	2815841	2816797	4820067	4361683	15342178	52696065
Interest **3**	1383091	2449	166	463	1580	2923	4865	2925	6118	16327	49540	43213	1252523
Rents **4**	80028	15434	0	558	577	4003	300	1852	7591	1433	1070	15157	32054
Royalties **5**	636641	1732	0	0	0	0	451	93	7948	10553	7636	133289	474939
Other Portfolio Income **6**	639758	1097	709	0	1036	325	13423	10350	26791	6247	20969	115031	443779
Other Receipts **7**	1863745	28576	847	2852	5847	20391	23118	23664	35918	79951	73338	437500	1131742
Total Receipts **8**	97581793	910040	710267	102236	2991934	2170594	3374551	2854725	2901163	4934578	4514236	16086368	56031102
Average Total Receipts **9**	29651	23334	374	601	5362	8099	21494	43253	78410	159180	214964	595791	3295947
Operating Costs/Operating Income (%)													
Cost of Operations **10**	60.1	47.9	29.5	38.8	60.8	58.0	57.6	56.4	60.3	61.6	56.9	60.0	61.3
Salaries and Wages **11**	13.6	19.3	24.1	29.7	14.1	17.2	15.2	15.7	14.6	12.8	16.7	14.5	12.5
Taxes Paid **12**	1.8	1.8	3.4	5.3	2.7	3.0	2.0	2.0	1.7	1.6	2.1	1.7	1.7
Interest Paid **13**	3.6	5.4	1.0	1.9	0.8	0.9	1.1	1.4	0.9	1.3	3.3	2.5	4.8
Depreciation **14**	2.3	5.7	1.6	1.8	1.4	2.1	2.5	1.8	2.5	2.5	2.9	2.8	2.1
Amortization and Depletion **15**	1.4	7.1	0.0	2.8	0.2	0.7	0.5	0.8	1.1	0.9	2.0	2.2	1.3
Pensions and Other Deferred Comp. **16**	1.7	0.3	0.4	•	0.3	0.8	0.8	0.5	0.5	0.4	0.5	1.9	2.3
Employee Benefits **17**	1.9	0.8	1.4	3.0	2.1	3.8	2.4	2.5	2.7	2.7	2.8	2.3	1.4
Advertising **18**	0.6	0.6	2.1	1.3	1.2	0.8	0.7	1.3	1.4	0.6	1.3	0.6	0.4
Other Expenses **19**	12.3	23.4	36.3	23.1	15.0	13.2	11.7	12.4	13.1	13.4	11.1	12.0	11.7
Officers' Compensation **20**	1.2	2.8	12.6	11.0	4.9	4.0	4.4	2.4	2.0	1.4	1.1	0.9	0.4
Operating Margin **21**	•	•	•	•	•	•	1.2	2.9	•	0.6	•	•	0.0
Operating Margin Before Officers' Comp. **22**	0.6	0.3	0.3	1.4	1.4	•	5.5	5.3	1.1	2.0	0.3	•	0.4

Selected Average Balance Sheet ($ in Thousands)

Net Receivables 23	795214	152550	51236	30472	14485	7054	3371	1373	956	78	43	0	6741
Inventories 24	305185	75172	23362	26569	13012	6945	3880	1192	518	174	47	0	3284
Net Property, Plant and Equipment 25	341305	86495	25134	18672	7762	4543	2397	1315	229	85	9	0	3257
Total Assets 26	8476440	1139025	341599	153128	75561	34392	16007	7012	2582	774	197	0	60218
Notes and Loans Payable 27	1626224	291854	85325	19478	10431	6447	3681	1521	876	419	253	0	12385
All Other Liabilities 28	2574322	339749	72645	43983	19028	9783	3481	1158	1433	90	41	0	17905
Net Worth 29	4275894	507421	183629	89666	46101	18162	8845	4332	273	265	-98	0	29928

Selected Financial Ratios (Times to 1)

Current Ratio 30	1.0	1.3	2.0	2.1	2.2	2.0	2.4	3.5	1.2	2.2	1.1	•	1.2
Quick Ratio 31	0.7	0.8	1.3	1.3	1.4	1.1	1.4	2.0	0.8	1.2	0.7	•	0.8
Net Sales to Working Capital 32	88.2	7.7	3.1	3.7	3.1	4.1	3.3	2.7	15.4	2.8	35.7	•	10.4
Coverage Ratio 33	2.5	3.2	2.0	3.4	3.5	4.2	3.3	•	•	•	•	•	2.5
Total Asset Turnover 34	0.4	0.5	0.6	1.0	1.0	1.2	1.3	1.1	2.1	0.7	1.9	•	0.5
Inventory Turnover 35	6.2	4.5	5.1	3.6	3.5	3.5	3.2	3.9	6.3	1.3	2.3	•	5.2
Receivables Turnover 36	4.0	4.1	4.7	4.6	4.8	5.7	5.6	6.9	5.3	6.1	11.2	•	4.3
Total Liabilities to Net Worth 37	1.0	1.2	0.9	0.7	0.6	0.9	0.8	0.6	8.5	1.9	•	•	1.0
Current Assets to Working Capital 38	46.2	4.8	2.0	1.9	1.8	2.0	1.7	1.4	6.0	1.8	14.8	•	5.6
Current Liabilities to Working Capital 39	45.2	3.8	1.0	0.9	0.8	1.0	0.7	0.4	5.0	0.8	13.8	•	4.6
Working Capital to Net Sales 40	0.0	0.1	0.3	0.3	0.3	0.2	0.3	0.4	0.1	0.4	0.0	•	0.1
Inventory to Working Capital 41	8.1	1.1	0.4	0.5	0.5	0.6	0.6	0.4	1.5	0.8	4.9	•	1.2
Total Receipts to Cash Flow 42	6.3	7.4	9.0	7.1	7.8	6.7	8.6	13.6	12.9	19.2	6.5	9.0	7.0
Cost of Goods to Cash Flow 43	3.9	4.4	5.1	4.4	4.7	3.8	5.0	7.9	7.8	7.4	1.9	4.3	4.2
Cash Flow to Total Debt 44	0.1	0.1	0.1	0.3	0.3	0.4	0.3	0.2	0.2	0.1	0.2	•	0.1

Selected Financial Factors (in Percentages)

Debt Ratio 45	49.6	55.5	46.2	41.4	39.0	47.2	44.7	38.2	89.4	65.8	149.6	•	50.3
Return on Total Assets 46	4.4	4.1	4.1	4.5	3.3	7.0	4.7	•	•	•	•	•	4.2
Return on Equity Before Income Taxes 47	5.2	6.4	3.8	5.4	3.8	10.1	5.9	•	•	•	46.2	•	5.0
Return on Equity After Income Taxes 48	3.4	3.6	1.4	2.9	2.0	8.7	4.0	•	•	•	47.5	•	3.0
Profit Margin (Before Income Tax) 49	7.2	5.7	3.3	3.1	2.3	4.3	2.5	•	•	•	•	•	5.3
Profit Margin (After Income Tax) 50	4.8	3.2	1.2	1.7	1.2	3.7	1.7	•	•	•	•	•	3.2

Table II
Corporations with Net Income

NAVIGATIONAL, MEASURING, ELECTROMEDICAL, AND CONTROL

MONEY AMOUNTS AND SIZE OF ASSETS IN THOUSANDS OF DOLLARS

Item Description for Accounting Period 7/09 Through 6/10	Total	Zero Assets	Under 500	500 to 1,000	1,000 to 5,000	5,000 to 10,000	10,000 to 25,000	25,000 to 50,000	50,000 to 100,000	100,000 to 250,000	250,000 to 500,000	500,000 to 2,500,000	2,500,000 and over
Number of Enterprises **1**	1241	12	•	59	286	92	109	48	25	18	•	19	14
Revenues ($ in Thousands)													
Net Sales **2**	78216827	290258	•	50943	1688218	1166550	2690083	2341123	2103560	3058014	•	11747037	49601194
Interest **3**	1169176	272	•	0	307	193	2533	1467	4525	4661	•	25915	1085885
Rents **4**	56846	55	•	558	577	0	131	1142	7453	809	•	15157	30574
Royalties **5**	551158	0	•	0	0	0	0	19	5852	653	•	78928	459454
Other Portfolio Income **6**	588846	1082	•	0	272	120	11014	10162	25940	4793	•	102803	418477
Other Receipts **7**	1622679	883	•	2852	1574	2885	19993	12845	34683	60023	•	332700	1119575
Total Receipts **8**	82205532	292550	•	54353	1690948	1169748	2723754	2366758	2182013	3128953	•	12302540	52715159
Average Total Receipts **9**	66241	24379	•	921	5912	12715	24989	49307	87281	173831	•	647502	3765368
Operating Costs/Operating Income (%)													
Cost of Operations **10**	60.1	59.5	•	68.2	50.8	55.0	56.5	55.9	59.2	58.7	•	60.0	61.2
Salaries and Wages **11**	13.0	7.1	•	1.8	16.6	11.3	13.6	14.7	12.1	12.9	•	13.3	12.7
Taxes Paid **12**	1.8	1.8	•	2.9	2.5	2.1	1.9	1.8	1.7	1.7	•	1.9	1.7
Interest Paid **13**	3.4	0.9	•	3.7	0.5	0.4	0.5	0.9	1.0	1.1	•	1.5	4.5
Depreciation **14**	2.1	5.0	•	1.3	1.5	0.9	2.1	1.6	2.1	2.2	•	2.6	2.0
Amortization and Depletion **15**	1.2	0.1	•	0.1	0.0	0.0	0.2	0.5	1.0	0.9	•	1.7	1.2
Pensions and Other Deferred Comp. **16**	1.8	0.0	•	•	0.0	0.7	0.9	0.4	0.6	0.4	•	1.5	2.3
Employee Benefits **17**	1.8	1.7	•	0.3	1.2	2.6	2.2	2.4	2.7	2.2	•	2.4	1.5
Advertising **18**	0.6	0.2	•	1.3	1.5	0.5	0.5	1.2	1.6	0.5	•	0.7	0.4
Other Expenses **19**	11.0	8.9	•	8.6	15.0	11.4	9.2	9.7	11.1	12.5	•	10.9	11.3
Officers' Compensation **20**	0.9	1.7	•	6.3	4.2	3.0	4.6	2.3	2.0	1.4	•	0.9	0.4
Operating Margin **21**	2.3	13.0	•	5.4	5.8	12.0	7.9	8.6	5.0	5.6	•	2.7	0.7
Operating Margin Before Officers' Comp. **22**	3.3	14.7	•	11.7	10.0	15.1	12.5	10.9	7.0	7.0	•	3.6	1.1

Selected Average Balance Sheet ($ in Thousands)

Net Receivables 23	14871	0	•	97	937	2011	3941	8424	14587	33250	141755	919299
Inventories 24	7070	0	•	287	513	1851	3936	7657	14115	31057	84386	342420
Net Property, Plant and Equipment 25	6862	0	•	219	255	1200	2404	5063	8249	16954	82924	383401
Total Assets 26	128096	0	•	615	2645	6793	16242	34501	76088	148070	1135984	8831739
Notes and Loans Payable 27	26890	0	•	445	555	860	2711	5857	10105	12918	240999	1879016
All Other Liabilities 28	35400	0	•	137	839	1676	3423	10359	17229	47361	369059	2385662
Net Worth 29	65806	0	•	32	1251	4257	10108	18285	48753	87791	525925	4567061

Selected Financial Ratios (Times to 1)

Current Ratio 30	1.2	•	0.9	2.2	3.3	2.7	2.1	2.5	2.0	1.2	1.1
Quick Ratio 31	0.8	•	0.2	1.5	2.4	1.6	1.2	1.5	1.2	0.7	0.7
Net Sales to Working Capital 32	10.9	•	•	5.1	3.4	3.3	4.2	3.0	4.3	12.5	25.8
Coverage Ratio 33	3.5	16.1	4.3	13.4	32.8	19.1	11.6	10.2	8.7	7.8	2.8
Total Asset Turnover 34	0.5	•	1.4	2.2	1.9	1.5	1.4	1.1	1.1	0.5	0.4
Inventory Turnover 35	5.4	•	2.1	5.8	3.8	3.5	3.6	3.5	3.2	4.4	6.3
Receivables Turnover 36	4.4	•	17.7	6.4	5.9	6.0	6.1	5.2	4.0	4.3	4.1
Total Liabilities to Net Worth 37	0.9	•	18.0	1.1	0.6	0.6	0.9	0.6	0.7	1.2	0.9
Current Assets to Working Capital 38	5.7	•	•	1.8	1.4	1.6	1.9	1.7	2.0	7.1	13.6
Current Liabilities to Working Capital 39	4.7	•	•	0.8	0.4	0.4	0.6	0.9	0.7	1.0	12.6
Working Capital to Net Sales 40	0.1	•	•	0.2	0.3	0.3	0.2	0.3	0.2	0.1	0.0
Inventory to Working Capital 41	1.2	•	•	0.5	0.4	0.5	0.6	0.5	0.6	1.8	2.4
Total Receipts to Cash Flow 42	6.1	4.7	4.8	6.1	4.5	6.1	5.6	5.7	5.4	6.1	6.2
Cost of Goods to Cash Flow 43	3.7	2.8	3.3	3.1	2.5	3.5	3.1	3.4	3.2	3.6	3.8
Cash Flow to Total Debt 44	0.2	•	0.3	0.7	1.1	0.7	0.5	0.5	0.5	0.2	0.1

Selected Financial Factors (in Percentages)

Debt Ratio 45	48.6	•	94.7	52.7	37.3	37.8	47.0	35.9	40.7	53.7	48.3
Return on Total Assets 46	5.8	•	22.3	14.3	23.7	14.8	15.0	11.0	10.5	6.4	5.0
Return on Equity Before Income Taxes 47	8.1	•	324.3	27.9	36.7	22.5	25.9	15.5	15.7	12.1	6.1
Return on Equity After Income Taxes 48	5.7	13.8	324.3	26.6	35.0	20.0	24.1	12.9	11.4	8.2	4.1
Profit Margin (Before Income Tax) 49	8.5	13.8	12.1	5.9	12.3	9.2	9.7	9.0	8.1	10.3	7.9
Profit Margin (After Income Tax) 50	6.0	10.4	12.1	5.6	11.7	8.2	9.0	7.5	5.9	7.0	5.3

146

Table I

Corporations with and without Net Income

ELECTRICAL LIGHTING EQUIPMENT AND HOUSEHOLD APPLIANCE

Money Amounts and Size of Assets in Thousands of Dollars

Item Description for Accounting Period 7/09 Through 6/10		Total	Zero Assets	Under 500	500 to 1,000	1,000 to 5,000	5,000 to 10,000	10,000 to 25,000	25,000 to 50,000	50,000 to 100,000	100,000 to 250,000	250,000 to 500,000	500,000 to 2,500,000	2,500,000 and over
Number of Enterprises	1	926	10	388	169	125	86	87	12	15	18	7	3	6
Revenues ($ in Thousands)														
Net Sales	2	128310864	521532	5417	601491	377880	1239994	2416207	520036	1173210	3340988	3247742	6731964	108134403
Interest	3	56925093	4	0	36	7	1428	457	146	17042	5175	664	7670	56892461
Rents	4	11390921	0	0	0	0	0	1695	1746	114	596	0	244	11386526
Royalties	5	2109514	179	0	0	0	0	858	0	11	1357	944	18544	2087621
Other Portfolio Income	6	3786639	0	0	0	0	477	3764	256	4571	1892	652	342	3774682
Other Receipts	7	29076843	189	1	1	36792	24718	19404	441	5011	31833	4111	45372	28908977
Total Receipts	8	231599874	521904	5418	601528	414679	1266617	2442385	522625	1199959	3381841	3254113	6804136	211184670
Average Total Receipts	9	250108	52190	14	3559	3317	14728	28073	43552	79997	187880	464873	2268045	35197445
Operating Costs/Operating Income (%)														
Cost of Operations	10	68.1	102.7	23.2	48.7	64.1	65.7	66.9	75.5	63.3	63.2	67.5	74.7	67.9
Salaries and Wages	11	11.2	15.1	1.1	24.2	9.7	11.0	12.0	6.8	8.8	9.6	5.3	4.4	11.8
Taxes Paid	12	0.8	0.2	1.2	5.7	3.8	1.6	1.7	1.0	1.7	1.8	1.4	1.0	0.6
Interest Paid	13	44.8	3.4	0.2	0.0	0.6	0.5	0.8	1.2	4.5	2.1	2.0	1.4	52.9
Depreciation	14	7.5	2.4	0.1	0.0	2.5	1.1	1.6	1.8	1.9	2.9	3.4	1.6	8.5
Amortization and Depletion	15	4.3	•	•	•	0.8	0.1	0.1	0.4	1.3	0.6	0.5	0.2	5.0
Pensions and Other Deferred Comp.	16	0.6	•	•	0.0	0.0	0.1	0.3	0.1	0.5	0.8	0.5	2.7	0.5
Employee Benefits	17	2.5	•	•	•	2.0	2.0	1.9	0.6	1.8	2.4	1.5	0.8	2.7
Advertising	18	1.7	0.3	3.5	1.8	0.1	0.6	0.8	0.7	1.3	2.9	3.8	3.0	1.6
Other Expenses	19	37.0	•	66.7	13.6	18.7	16.1	11.5	9.7	13.6	10.5	10.6	10.5	41.9
Officers' Compensation	20	0.5	0.6	3.1	2.2	1.1	2.1	1.8	2.1	2.0	1.5	0.8	0.3	0.4
Operating Margin	21	•	•	1.0	3.7	•	•	0.5	•	•	1.8	2.7	•	•
Operating Margin Before Officers' Comp.	22	•	•	4.1	6.0	•	1.3	2.3	2.1	1.5	3.2	3.5	•	•

Selected Average Balance Sheet ($ in Thousands)

	1	2	3	4	5	6	7	8	9	10	11	12	13
Net Receivables 23	193650	0	0	229	318	1611	3770	3428	10463	32844	53494	350506	29430814
Inventories 24	12889	0	1	222	1095	2280	14091	6029	11578	34693	79283	205240	1483580
Net Property, Plant and Equipment 25	50473	0	0	4	667	623	2322	2565	9752	31421	72217	184153	7429866
Total Assets 26	948884	0	1	808	2557	6892	32749	15579	69858	156899	360225	1639369	144092937
Notes and Loans Payable 27	641315	0	10	91	899	1314	4983	3561	23807	38884	119045	151752	98482976
All Other Liabilities 28	164445	0	-30	129	1084	2375	6277	4549	26650	45272	90774	628193	24620040
Net Worth 29	143125	0	21	589	574	3204	21489	7469	19401	72743	150406	859423	20989920

Selected Financial Ratios (Times to 1)

	1	2	3	4	5	6	7	8	9	10	11	12	13
Current Ratio 30	0.8	•	4.0	5.9	1.2	2.3	2.4	3.6	1.4	2.1	2.1	1.0	0.8
Quick Ratio 31	0.7	•	2.4	2.3	0.4	1.2	1.2	1.5	0.8	1.1	0.9	0.7	0.7
Net Sales to Working Capital 32	•	•	31.1	5.6	12.4	4.4	4.3	2.9	7.1	4.2	5.8	93.2	•
Coverage Ratio 33	1.1	•	7.1	364.2	12.1	3.8	2.9	1.4	1.4	2.5	1.4	1.4	1.1
Total Asset Turnover 34	0.1	•	23.0	4.4	1.2	2.1	1.8	1.3	1.1	1.2	1.3	1.4	0.1
Inventory Turnover 35	7.3	•	3.8	7.8	1.8	4.2	3.1	2.3	4.3	3.4	4.0	8.2	8.2
Receivables Turnover 36	0.7	•	17.4	30.8	5.3	12.6	6.0	7.1	8.3	5.3	8.6	6.2	0.6
Total Liabilities to Net Worth 37	5.6	•	0.4	0.4	3.5	1.2	1.1	0.5	2.6	1.2	0.9	0.9	5.9
Current Assets to Working Capital 38	•	•	1.3	1.2	5.7	1.8	1.7	1.4	3.4	1.9	1.9	23.4	•
Current Liabilities to Working Capital 39	•	•	0.3	0.2	4.7	0.8	0.7	0.4	2.4	0.9	0.9	22.4	•
Working Capital to Net Sales 40	•	•	0.0	0.2	0.1	0.2	0.2	0.3	0.1	0.2	0.2	0.0	•
Inventory to Working Capital 41	•	•	0.4	0.6	3.7	0.8	0.7	0.7	1.1	0.6	0.9	6.1	•
Total Receipts to Cash Flow 42	2.8	•	3.0	7.0	4.3	7.4	9.3	12.3	7.7	8.9	8.6	9.9	2.5
Cost of Goods to Cash Flow 43	1.9	•	0.7	3.4	2.7	4.9	6.2	9.3	4.9	5.6	5.8	7.4	1.7
Cash Flow to Total Debt 44	0.1	•	•	2.3	0.4	0.5	0.4	0.3	0.2	0.2	0.3	0.3	0.1

Selected Financial Factors (in Percentages)

	1	2	3	4	5	6	7	8	9	10	11	12	13
Debt Ratio 45	84.9	•	•	27.2	77.6	53.5	52.1	34.4	72.2	53.6	58.2	47.6	85.4
Return on Total Assets 46	7.5	•	27.1	16.5	8.2	3.9	4.3	2.2	6.9	6.3	6.3	2.7	7.6
Return on Equity Before Income Taxes 47	6.4	•	0.7	22.6	33.6	6.2	5.8	0.9	6.7	8.1	9.0	1.5	6.5
Return on Equity After Income Taxes 48	4.1	•	0.7	22.6	33.5	4.5	4.5	0.7	2.0	5.6	8.9	0.1	4.1
Profit Margin (Before Income Tax) 49	6.6	•	1.0	3.7	6.4	1.4	1.6	0.4	1.7	3.2	2.9	0.6	7.6
Profit Margin (After Income Tax) 50	4.2	•	1.0	3.7	6.4	1.0	1.2	0.4	0.5	2.2	2.9	0.0	4.8

Table II
Corporations with Net Income

ELECTRICAL LIGHTING EQUIPMENT AND HOUSEHOLD APPLIANCE

MONEY AMOUNTS AND SIZE OF ASSETS IN THOUSANDS OF DOLLARS

Item Description for Accounting Period 7/09 Through 6/10	Total	Zero Assets	Under 500	500 to 1,000	1,000 to 5,000	5,000 to 10,000	10,000 to 25,000	25,000 to 50,000	50,000 to 100,000	100,000 to 250,000	250,000 to 500,000	500,000 to 2,500,000	2,500,000 and over
Number of Enterprises 1	761	0	•	109	120	50	56	8	8	12	•	•	•
Revenues ($ in Thousands)													
Net Sales 2	109940005	0	•	596211	372888	926924	1686507	452716	794519	2477807	•	•	•
Interest 3	56883545	0	•	0	0	156	71	142	90	4893	•	•	•
Rents 4	11374632	0	•	0	0	0	658	1746	114	386	•	•	•
Royalties 5	1645890	0	•	0	0	0	0	0	11	1357	•	•	•
Other Portfolio Income 6	3768586	0	•	0	0	477	3491	256	817	1490	•	•	•
Other Receipts 7	28915903	0	•	0	36792	21082	12766	436	3788	27529	•	•	•
Total Receipts 8	212528561	0	•	596211	409680	948639	1703493	455296	799339	2513462	•	•	•
Average Total Receipts 9	279275	•	•	5470	3414	18973	30420	56912	99917	209455	•	•	•
Operating Costs/Operating Income (%)													
Cost of Operations 10	66.5	•	•	48.5	63.5	69.5	65.3	77.2	58.9	61.7	•	•	•
Salaries and Wages 11	12.5	•	•	24.2	9.1	9.4	11.1	5.7	9.6	9.1	•	•	•
Taxes Paid 12	0.7	•	•	5.8	3.7	1.5	1.7	0.8	1.8	1.7	•	•	•
Interest Paid 13	51.9	•	•	0.0	0.5	0.5	0.4	0.2	0.6	0.9	•	•	•
Depreciation 14	8.3	•	•	0.0	2.6	1.0	1.3	1.7	1.5	2.2	•	•	•
Amortization and Depletion 15	5.0	•	•	0.7	0.7	0.0	0.0	0.0	0.1	0.3	•	•	•
Pensions and Other Deferred Comp. 16	0.5	•	•	•	•	0.1	0.3	0.1	0.7	0.9	•	•	•
Employee Benefits 17	2.2	•	•	•	1.8	1.3	1.6	0.4	2.2	2.6	•	•	•
Advertising 18	1.6	•	•	1.8	0.1	0.5	0.9	0.6	1.2	1.4	•	•	•
Other Expenses 19	40.8	•	•	13.2	16.1	10.2	9.8	7.3	12.5	10.2	•	•	•
Officers' Compensation 20	0.5	•	•	1.8	0.9	2.1	1.6	1.9	2.2	1.6	•	•	•
Operating Margin 21	•	•	•	4.7	1.0	4.0	6.1	4.0	8.8	7.4	•	•	•
Operating Margin Before Officers' Comp. 22	•	•	•	6.6	1.9	6.2	7.7	5.8	11.0	8.9	•	•	•

Selected Average Balance Sheet ($ in Thousands)

Net Receivables 23	217066	353	313	2129	3693	4757	12164	38170
Inventories 24	13580	567	790	2963	7318	15289	15018	32683
Net Property, Plant and Equipment 25	58452	7	688	742	2014	2906	10675	25677
Total Assets 26	1094903	970	2545	6684	15251	32149	67340	157896
Notes and Loans Payable 27	767910	139	926	1488	1900	2708	13249	24384
All Other Liabilities 28	178701	196	1107	1969	3839	5048	14325	49080
Net Worth 29	148292	636	511	3227	9512	24392	39767	84431

Selected Financial Ratios (Times to 1)

Current Ratio 30	0.8	4.9	1.1	2.0	3.2	3.3	4.4	2.0
Quick Ratio 31	0.7	2.0	0.3	1.0	1.7	1.2	2.7	1.2
Net Sales to Working Capital 32		7.1	18.0	6.7	3.7	3.4	2.6	4.8
Coverage Ratio 33	1.2	534.0	21.0	15.0	18.7	19.8	16.6	10.5
Total Asset Turnover 34	0.1	5.6	1.2	2.8	2.0	1.8	1.5	1.3
Inventory Turnover 35	7.1	4.7	2.5	4.3	2.7	2.9	3.9	3.9
Receivables Turnover 36	0.6	31.0	6.2	11.8	5.4	10.2	8.1	5.4
Total Liabilities to Net Worth 37	6.4	0.5	4.0	1.1	0.6	0.3	0.7	0.9
Current Assets to Working Capital 38		1.3	7.7	2.0	1.5	1.4	1.3	2.0
Current Liabilities to Working Capital 39		0.3	6.7	1.0	0.5	0.4	0.3	1.0
Working Capital to Net Sales 40		0.1	0.1	0.1	0.3	0.3	0.4	0.2
Inventory to Working Capital 41		0.7	5.2	0.9	0.6	0.9	0.4	0.6
Total Receipts to Cash Flow 42	2.4	6.7	3.9	8.0	7.0	10.0	4.9	5.8
Cost of Goods to Cash Flow 43	1.6	3.2	2.5	5.5	4.6	7.7	2.9	3.6
Cash Flow to Total Debt 44	0.1	2.4	0.4	0.7	0.8	0.7	0.7	0.5

Selected Financial Factors (in Percentages)

Debt Ratio 45	86.5	34.5	79.9	51.7	37.6	24.1	40.9	46.5
Return on Total Assets 46	8.0	26.8	14.0	18.9	14.9	8.4	14.7	13.0
Return on Equity Before Income Taxes 47	8.6	40.8	66.2	36.5	22.6	10.5	23.3	22.0
Return on Equity After Income Taxes 48	5.8	40.8	66.1	33.7	21.0	10.3	19.0	18.8
Profit Margin (Before Income Tax) 49	8.8	4.7	10.9	6.4	7.1	4.5	9.3	9.0
Profit Margin (After Income Tax) 50	6.0	4.7	10.9	5.9	6.6	4.4	7.6	7.7

Table I

Corporations with and without Net Income

ELECTRICAL EQUIPMENT

MONEY AMOUNTS AND SIZE OF ASSETS IN THOUSANDS OF DOLLARS

Item Description for Accounting Period 7/09 Through 6/10	Total	Zero Assets	Under 500	500 to 1,000	1,000 to 5,000	5,000 to 10,000	10,000 to 25,000	25,000 to 50,000	50,000 to 100,000	100,000 to 250,000	250,000 to 500,000	500,000 to 2,500,000	2,500,000 and over
Number of Enterprises **1**	651	8	6	174	268	74	53	26	11	12	8	6	4
Revenues ($ in Thousands)													
Net Sales **2**	39567995	0	11473	374809	1263500	856401	1195347	1063112	932334	2042967	2997326	4389676	24441050
Interest **3**	445543	0	2	0	160	27	544	1326	2895	7608	18578	6133	408268
Rents **4**	67566	0	0	0	418	0	178	456	135	292	0	150	65937
Royalties **5**	464454	0	0	0	0	0	9	888	2872	2073	2992	18056	437564
Other Portfolio Income **6**	589805	0	251	0	50	0	336	10803	1987	16952	5390	25036	529001
Other Receipts **7**	445594	26	202	90	4592	7916	3312	2922	1948	1301	12964	25670	384653
Total Receipts **8**	41580957	26	11928	374899	1268720	864344	1199726	1079507	942171	2071193	3037250	4464721	26266473
Average Total Receipts **9**	63872	3	1988	2155	4734	11680	22636	41520	85652	172599	379656	744120	6566618
Operating Costs/Operating Income (%)													
Cost of Operations **10**	68.5	•	122.1	52.2	65.3	55.6	58.7	68.7	66.3	63.0	67.9	70.5	70.1
Salaries and Wages **11**	7.8	•	28.1	7.3	8.5	7.5	9.3	8.5	8.9	12.6	7.3	7.1	7.5
Taxes Paid **12**	1.4	•	3.8	2.3	2.2	2.1	1.8	1.6	1.3	1.9	2.2	1.1	1.3
Interest Paid **13**	3.0	•	6.6	0.1	1.6	1.0	0.8	1.3	0.8	2.2	1.4	3.1	3.7
Depreciation **14**	2.3	•	1.8	0.8	1.5	1.3	2.3	2.4	1.8	3.0	3.4	3.0	2.0
Amortization and Depletion **15**	1.4	•	1.0	•	0.3	0.0	0.4	1.1	0.4	1.0	1.6	5.1	1.0
Pensions and Other Deferred Comp. **16**	1.9	•	•	•	0.3	0.2	1.1	0.3	0.7	0.7	1.4	1.4	2.4
Employee Benefits **17**	2.1	•	3.4	1.6	1.3	1.3	3.1	3.0	1.2	2.5	1.5	3.1	2.0
Advertising **18**	0.5	•	0.1	0.6	0.3	0.2	0.5	0.4	0.7	0.7	0.2	1.0	0.5
Other Expenses **19**	10.7	•	145.2	18.1	12.7	14.5	13.2	8.1	9.3	11.1	9.7	7.3	11.0
Officers' Compensation **20**	1.4	•	4.1	14.1	6.5	8.3	3.4	2.3	1.7	1.6	0.8	0.8	0.7
Operating Margin **21**	•	•	•	2.9	•	7.9	5.4	2.2	6.9	•	2.6	•	•
Operating Margin Before Officers' Comp. **22**	0.4	•	•	16.9	6.1	16.2	8.8	4.5	8.6	1.3	3.4	•	•

Selected Average Balance Sheet ($ in Thousands)

Net Receivables 23	14698	0	20	196	460	1292	3136	7084	14011	33208	54032	132306	1796557
Inventories 24	6815	0	27	261	1037	1486	3838	6633	15136	24687	55179	105999	521743
Net Property, Plant and Equipment 25	8556	0	134	154	250	734	2786	4341	7976	34764	105338	111780	785549
Total Assets 26	87964	0	386	800	2288	7005	13973	35039	73354	181506	351882	1185172	10357288
Notes and Loans Payable 27	21602	0	3856	154	1142	2189	2985	6655	8956	51468	125903	479122	2153832
All Other Liabilities 28	16205	0	625	167	571	1591	3570	8458	20443	48147	93406	300074	1621556
Net Worth 29	50158	0	-4095	479	574	3225	7418	19926	43955	81891	132574	405976	6581900

Selected Financial Ratios (Times to 1)

Current Ratio 30	1.3	•	0.3	2.9	2.6	1.7	3.0	2.0	2.7	1.8	1.5	1.9	1.0
Quick Ratio 31	0.8	•	0.2	1.5	1.1	1.1	1.6	1.2	1.5	1.0	0.8	1.1	0.7
Net Sales to Working Capital 32	10.7	•	•	5.8	4.5	5.8	3.7	4.8	3.6	4.3	5.7	4.6	55.5
Coverage Ratio 33	2.7	0.9	•	35.3	1.0	10.1	8.0	4.0	12.1	1.6	3.9	0.6	2.9
Total Asset Turnover 34	0.7	•	5.0	2.7	2.1	1.7	1.6	1.2	1.2	0.9	1.1	0.6	0.6
Inventory Turnover 35	6.1	•	86.7	4.3	3.0	4.3	3.5	4.2	3.7	4.3	4.6	4.9	8.2
Receivables Turnover 36	3.7	•	111.4	11.6	8.7	10.3	6.1	5.6	5.4	4.9	4.6	5.6	3.1
Total Liabilities to Net Worth 37	0.8	•	•	0.7	3.0	1.2	0.9	0.8	0.7	1.2	1.7	1.9	0.6
Current Assets to Working Capital 38	4.7	•	•	1.5	1.6	2.5	1.5	2.0	1.6	2.3	2.9	2.1	23.4
Current Liabilities to Working Capital 39	3.7	•	•	0.5	0.6	1.5	0.5	1.0	0.6	1.3	1.9	1.1	22.4
Working Capital to Net Sales 40	0.1	•	•	0.2	0.2	0.2	0.3	0.2	0.3	0.2	0.2	0.2	0.0
Inventory to Working Capital 41	1.1	•	•	0.7	0.9	0.7	0.6	0.7	0.6	0.6	0.8	0.6	4.1
Total Receipts to Cash Flow 42	7.8	•	•	6.1	9.5	5.0	6.0	9.7	6.6	9.7	8.8	25.0	6.9
Cost of Goods to Cash Flow 43	5.4	•	•	6.2	2.8	3.5	6.6	4.4	6.1	6.0	•	17.6	4.9
Cash Flow to Total Debt 44	0.2	•	•	1.1	0.3	0.6	0.6	0.3	0.4	0.2	0.2	0.0	0.2

Selected Financial Factors (in Percentages)

Debt Ratio 45	43.0	•	1160.8	40.2	74.9	54.0	46.9	43.1	40.1	54.9	62.3	65.7	36.5
Return on Total Assets 46	5.6	•	•	8.0	3.3	16.2	10.6	6.2	10.6	3.2	5.7	1.1	6.2
Return on Equity Before Income Taxes 47	6.2	•	99.1	12.9	31.7	17.5	8.1	16.2	2.7	11.3	•	•	6.4
Return on Equity After Income Taxes 48	4.2	•	99.1	10.6	31.5	17.1	5.8	14.9	0.9	6.7	•	•	4.4
Profit Margin (Before Income Tax) 49	5.1	•	•	2.9	8.8	5.7	3.9	8.4	1.3	4.0	•	•	6.9
Profit Margin (After Income Tax) 50	3.5	•	•	2.3	8.8	5.6	2.8	7.7	0.4	2.4	•	•	4.7

Table II
Corporations with Net Income

ELECTRICAL EQUIPMENT

MONEY AMOUNTS AND SIZE OF ASSETS IN THOUSANDS OF DOLLARS

Item Description for Accounting Period 7/09 Through 6/10	Total	Zero Assets	Under 500	500 to 1,000	1,000 to 5,000	5,000 to 10,000	10,000 to 25,000	25,000 to 50,000	50,000 to 100,000	100,000 to 250,000	250,000 to 500,000	500,000 to 2,500,000	2,500,000 and over
Number of Enterprises 1	508	0	•	174	180	64	41	20	•	•	•	0	•
Revenues ($ in Thousands)													
Net Sales 2	28317036	0	•	374809	968855	688064	977989	783674	•	•	•	0	•
Interest 3	402695	0	•	0	105	18	341	132	•	•	•	0	•
Rents 4	58434	0	•	0	418	0	85	0	•	•	•	0	•
Royalties 5	164227	0	•	0	0	0	0	888	•	•	•	0	•
Other Portfolio Income 6	564375	0	•	0	0	0	184	4344	•	•	•	0	•
Other Receipts 7	201401	0	•	90	3798	5374	3028	2919	•	•	•	0	•
Total Receipts 8	29708168	0	•	374899	973176	693456	981627	791957	•	•	•	0	•
Average Total Receipts 9	58481	•	•	2155	5407	10835	23942	39598	•	•	•	•	•
Operating Costs/Operating Income (%)													
Cost of Operations 10	66.7	•	•	52.2	62.9	48.7	55.1	65.2	•	•	•	•	•
Salaries and Wages 11	7.5	•	•	7.3	7.2	7.6	7.9	8.2	•	•	•	•	•
Taxes Paid 12	1.3	•	•	2.3	2.4	2.4	1.7	1.8	•	•	•	•	•
Interest Paid 13	3.0	•	•	0.1	1.7	0.6	0.5	0.6	•	•	•	•	•
Depreciation 14	2.3	•	•	0.8	1.5	1.3	1.5	1.7	•	•	•	•	•
Amortization and Depletion 15	1.2	•	•	•	0.0	0.0	0.1	0.8	•	•	•	•	•
Pensions and Other Deferred Comp. 16	1.5	•	•	•	0.1	0.2	1.0	0.3	•	•	•	•	•
Employee Benefits 17	1.8	•	•	1.6	1.2	1.4	2.9	3.2	•	•	•	•	•
Advertising 18	0.4	•	•	0.6	0.4	0.2	0.6	0.4	•	•	•	•	•
Other Expenses 19	10.1	•	•	18.1	11.4	15.0	12.4	7.6	•	•	•	•	•
Officers' Compensation 20	1.5	•	•	14.1	6.6	9.9	3.5	2.7	•	•	•	•	•
Operating Margin 21	2.7	•	•	2.9	4.5	12.6	12.8	7.4	•	•	•	•	•
Operating Margin Before Officers' Comp. 22	4.2	•	•	16.9	11.1	22.5	16.3	10.1	•	•	•	•	•

Selected Average Balance Sheet ($ in Thousands)

Net Receivables 23	14529	196	442	1220	3064	7271
Inventories 24	7039	250	1257	1245	4117	6954
Net Property, Plant and Equipment 25	7499	154	248	510	2541	3584
Total Assets 26	78604	800	2561	6981	13532	33666
Notes and Loans Payable 27	14488	154	1460	1645	2659	3752
All Other Liabilities 28	7789	167	446	1349	2838	9077
Net Worth 29	56327	479	656	3987	8034	20836

Selected Financial Ratios (Times to 1)

Current Ratio 30	1.4	2.9	3.4	2.1	3.1	2.0
Quick Ratio 31	0.9	1.5	1.3	1.5	1.6	1.3
Net Sales to Working Capital 32	8.0	5.8	4.1	4.0	3.9	4.7
Coverage Ratio 33	4.0	35.3	4.0	22.8	25.5	14.0
Total Asset Turnover 34	0.7	2.7	2.1	1.5	1.8	1.2
Inventory Turnover 35	5.3	4.5	2.7	4.2	3.2	3.7
Receivables Turnover 36	3.2	12.1	9.8	•	6.3	4.8
Total Liabilities to Net Worth 37	0.4	0.7	2.9	0.8	0.7	0.6
Current Assets to Working Capital 38	3.6	1.5	1.4	1.9	1.5	2.0
Current Liabilities to Working Capital 39	2.6	0.5	0.4	0.9	0.5	1.0
Working Capital to Net Sales 40	0.1	0.2	0.2	0.2	0.3	0.2
Inventory to Working Capital 41	0.8	0.7	0.8	0.5	0.7	0.6
Total Receipts to Cash Flow 42	6.3	6.1	7.0	4.0	4.2	6.9
Cost of Goods to Cash Flow 43	4.2	3.2	4.4	1.9	2.3	4.5
Cash Flow to Total Debt 44	0.4	1.1	0.4	0.9	1.0	0.4

Selected Financial Factors (in Percentages)

Debt Ratio 45	28.3	40.2	74.4	42.9	40.6	38.1
Return on Total Assets 46	8.5	8.0	14.0	21.5	24.2	10.5
Return on Equity Before Income Taxes 47	8.9	12.9	40.9	36.1	39.1	15.8
Return on Equity After Income Taxes 48	6.6	10.6	39.6	35.9	38.7	13.0
Profit Margin (Before Income Tax) 49	9.0	2.9	5.0	13.4	13.2	8.4
Profit Margin (After Income Tax) 50	6.7	2.3	4.8	13.3	13.0	6.9

Table I
Corporations with and without Net Income

OTHER ELECTRICAL EQUIPMENT AND COMPONENT

MONEY AMOUNTS AND SIZE OF ASSETS IN THOUSANDS OF DOLLARS

Item Description for Accounting Period 7/09 Through 6/10	Total	Zero Assets	Under 500	500 to 1,000	1,000 to 5,000	5,000 to 10,000	10,000 to 25,000	25,000 to 50,000	50,000 to 100,000	100,000 to 250,000	250,000 to 500,000	500,000 to 2,500,000	2,500,000 and over
Number of Enterprises 1	4047	895	1242	700	571	223	215	72	52	43	18	11	4
Revenues ($ in Thousands)													
Net Sales 2	56352676	618775	538218	1399324	2615782	2398070	5114155	3546741	3619704	6715828	4866651	7101462	17817966
Interest 3	358728	759	2	39	1386	1125	4096	4642	7734	9968	47153	33410	248415
Rents 4	21043	449	0	142	98	696	2073	25	1362	102	1095	1057	13944
Royalties 5	235351	376	1224	0	0	222	761	110	8694	34532	21392	8995	159043
Other Portfolio Income 6	486582	26775	0	0	3680	46742	1238	11478	14514	67336	24178	11428	279216
Other Receipts 7	383946	4156	18	14885	26842	1393	25713	47699	22021	67919	37275	4863	131159
Total Receipts 8	57838326	651290	539462	1414390	2647788	2448248	5148036	3610695	3674029	6895685	4997744	7161215	18649743
Average Total Receipts 9	14292	728	434	2021	4637	10979	23944	50149	70654	160365	277652	651020	4662436
Operating Costs/Operating Income (%)													
Cost of Operations 10	68.8	65.6	41.9	66.8	54.3	65.4	69.9	69.2	69.0	70.9	63.9	67.5	73.2
Salaries and Wages 11	9.0	20.1	10.0	8.4	13.2	10.8	8.5	10.3	9.2	10.2	9.1	9.3	7.1
Taxes Paid 12	1.6	7.5	2.9	1.9	2.0	2.1	1.9	1.5	1.9	1.4	1.6	1.4	1.2
Interest Paid 13	3.1	1.8	0.6	0.3	0.5	1.6	0.8	1.1	1.9	2.1	4.2	3.6	5.2
Depreciation 14	2.3	2.7	0.6	1.3	2.3	1.0	1.8	2.4	2.8	3.8	3.0	4.6	1.1
Amortization and Depletion 15	1.4	1.1	0.1	0.2	0.1	1.3	0.2	0.3	1.2	1.2	3.0	1.4	2.0
Pensions and Other Deferred Comp. 16	0.5	0.4	•	0.1	0.2	0.2	0.5	0.3	0.5	0.3	0.5	1.0	0.7
Employee Benefits 17	1.9	2.1	0.3	1.0	2.0	2.2	1.6	1.4	2.0	2.1	2.0	2.6	1.7
Advertising 18	1.3	0.1	0.1	0.3	0.5	0.9	0.6	0.4	0.6	0.6	0.9	0.9	2.6
Other Expenses 19	9.7	22.6	51.3	9.7	16.6	6.9	8.1	9.5	9.2	9.2	12.7	10.8	7.0
Officers' Compensation 20	1.7	9.4	7.4	7.0	5.5	3.0	3.1	1.6	1.9	1.9	0.7	1.0	0.2
Operating Margin 21	•	•	•	3.0	2.5	4.5	3.1	2.0	•	•	•	•	•
Operating Margin Before Officers' Comp. 22	0.2	•	•	10.0	8.1	7.5	6.2	3.6	1.5	•	•	•	•

Selected Average Balance Sheet ($ in Thousands)

Net Receivables 23	3736	0	45	261	449	1245	3888	9894	13371	30458	43643	110066	2199718
Inventories 24	1914	0	41	222	492	2810	3871	9146	14111	23800	36466	118427	355804
Net Property, Plant and Equipment 25	1894	0	20	22	725	882	2205	6379	11889	32556	37571	178537	355359
Total Assets 26	23768	0	163	698	2738	6458	15573	35821	70744	162630	330730	1178113	14246237
Notes and Loans Payable 27	4677	0	490	107	390	2226	3114	8039	16612	49131	133126	335772	1803072
All Other Liabilities 28	8031	0	328	133	745	1380	4757	9645	16519	35024	106472	369233	5301598
Net Worth 29	11061	0	-654	458	2853	1602	7702	18136	37614	78475	91132	473108	7141566

Selected Financial Ratios (Times to 1)

Current Ratio 30	1.5	•	0.3	3.8	2.2	2.0	2.1	2.0	2.1	2.0	2.3	1.2
Quick Ratio 31	1.0	•	0.2	2.3	1.4	1.1	1.2	1.2	1.2	1.1	1.2	0.8
Net Sales to Working Capital 32	5.3	•	•	4.1	5.2	4.3	4.2	3.6	3.9	4.5	4.2	8.5
Coverage Ratio 33	1.6	•	•	13.7	8.0	5.9	4.6	1.7	0.8	1.3	0.1	1.9
Total Asset Turnover 34	0.6	•	2.7	2.9	1.7	1.5	1.4	1.0	1.0	0.8	0.5	0.3
Inventory Turnover 35	5.0	•	4.4	6.0	5.1	4.3	3.7	3.4	4.7	4.7	3.7	9.2
Receivables Turnover 36	4.6	•	10.2	6.4	10.3	6.6	4.8	4.9	5.6	5.3	4.1	3.4
Total Liabilities to Net Worth 37	1.1	•	•	0.5	0.7	1.0	1.0	0.9	1.1	2.6	1.5	1.0
Current Assets to Working Capital 38	2.8	•	•	1.4	1.9	2.0	1.9	2.0	1.9	2.0	1.8	6.3
Current Liabilities to Working Capital 39	1.8	•	•	0.4	0.9	1.0	0.9	1.0	0.9	1.0	0.8	5.3
Working Capital to Net Sales 40	0.2	•	•	0.2	0.2	0.2	0.2	0.3	0.3	0.2	0.2	0.1
Inventory to Working Capital 41	0.7	•	•	0.5	0.5	0.7	0.7	0.7	0.6	0.5	0.6	0.7
Total Receipts to Cash Flow 42	11.3	•	3.8	8.4	5.7	9.8	8.6	11.5	16.9	8.2	19.5	12.5
Cost of Goods to Cash Flow 43	7.8	•	1.6	5.6	3.1	6.9	5.9	7.9	12.0	5.2	13.2	9.1
Cash Flow to Total Debt 44	0.1	•	0.1	1.0	0.7	0.3	0.3	0.2	0.1	0.2	0.0	0.1

Selected Financial Factors (in Percentages)

Debt Ratio 45	53.5	•	501.0	34.4	41.5	50.5	49.4	46.8	51.7	72.4	59.8	49.9
Return on Total Assets 46	2.9	•	•	12.7	7.2	7.0	6.7	3.2	1.5	4.5	0.3	3.0
Return on Equity Before Income Taxes 47	2.4	•	9.9	18.0	10.7	11.7	10.4	2.6	•	3.8	•	2.8
Return on Equity After Income Taxes 48	1.2	•	9.9	17.3	7.7	9.3	8.6	1.2	•	•	•	2.1
Profit Margin (Before Income Tax) 49	1.9	•	•	4.1	3.8	3.8	3.8	1.4	1.3	•	•	4.5
Profit Margin (After Income Tax) 50	1.0	•	•	4.0	2.7	3.0	3.2	0.7	•	•	•	3.4

151

Table II

Corporations with Net Income

OTHER ELECTRICAL EQUIPMENT AND COMPONENT

MONEY AMOUNTS AND SIZE OF ASSETS IN THOUSANDS OF DOLLARS

Item Description for Accounting Period 7/09 Through 6/10		Total	Zero Assets	Under 500	500 to 1000	1,000 to 5,000	5,000 to 10,000	10,000 to 25,000	25,000 to 50,000	50,000 to 100,000	100,000 to 250,000	250,000 to 500,000	500,000 to 2,500,000	2,500,000 and over
Number of Enterprises	1	2810	459	892	646	340	187	174	47	•	•	7	4	•
Revenues ($ in Thousands)														
Net Sales	2	39921936	194354	182884	1211259	1872946	2140941	4397415	2323053	•	•	1697027	3328722	•
Interest	3	218464	600	0	39	1332	910	2307	2433	•	•	14607	1608	•
Rents	4	19048	66	0	142	0	18	2073	25	•	•	270	1057	•
Royalties	5	153815	376	0	0	0	0	761	110	•	•	780	2293	•
Other Portfolio Income	6	308542	17269	0	0	2324	25539	923	8957	•	•	10856	1456	•
Other Receipts	7	290578	2210	0	14869	25702	1242	14203	21516	•	•	24615	-1691	•
Total Receipts	8	40912383	214875	182884	1226309	1902304	2168650	4417682	2356094	•	•	1748155	3333445	•
Average Total Receipts	9	14560	468	205	1898	5595	11597	25389	50130	•	•	249736	833361	•
Operating Costs/Operating Income (%)														
Cost of Operations	10	68.1	74.3	36.9	65.6	46.7	64.8	68.4	65.3	•	•	49.9	67.0	•
Salaries and Wages	11	8.2	4.5	8.5	8.8	13.3	9.8	7.6	9.3	•	•	8.5	7.6	•
Taxes Paid	12	1.5	1.0	3.3	1.7	2.1	2.1	1.9	1.4	•	•	2.1	1.1	•
Interest Paid	13	2.6	3.0	0.2	0.4	0.5	1.5	0.7	0.9	•	•	2.5	3.7	•
Depreciation	14	1.6	2.2	0.5	0.6	2.2	0.7	1.5	2.4	•	•	2.6	3.2	•
Amortization and Depletion	15	1.1	•	•	0.2	0.1	0.5	0.1	0.2	•	•	1.0	1.9	•
Pensions and Other Deferred Comp.	16	0.6	0.3	•	0.1	0.2	0.2	0.5	0.4	•	•	0.6	1.0	•
Employee Benefits	17	1.8	0.5	0.0	1.0	2.0	2.0	1.5	1.5	•	•	1.3	3.3	•
Advertising	18	1.3	0.0	•	0.3	0.6	0.9	0.7	0.4	•	•	1.3	0.9	•
Other Expenses	19	7.7	10.7	33.9	10.3	17.8	5.6	7.5	8.6	•	•	13.2	7.3	•
Officers' Compensation	20	1.6	3.8	7.0	7.6	5.5	2.8	3.1	1.6	•	•	0.9	1.0	•
Operating Margin	21	3.7	•	9.7	3.5	8.9	9.0	6.6	7.9	•	•	16.1	2.1	•
Operating Margin Before Officers' Comp.	22	5.3	3.4	16.7	11.1	14.5	11.8	9.7	9.5	•	•	16.9	3.0	•

Selected Average Balance Sheet ($ in Thousands)

Net Receivables 23	4466	0	14	251	551	1288	3856	9720	•	52882	146125
Inventories 24	1996	0	9	168	579	2290	4160	9446	•	52185	204577
Net Property, Plant and Equipment 25	1393	0	0	24	556	856	1971	6168	•	32883	140272
Total Assets 26	26369	0	79	672	2445	6390	15069	36317	•	309965	1543774
Notes and Loans Payable 27	3766	0	16	104	291	2168	3192	6821	•	79437	414124
All Other Liabilities 28	9435	0	48	115	680	1151	4581	7902	•	96848	624036
Net Worth 29	13168	0	15	453	1474	3072	7296	21594	•	133681	505614

Selected Financial Ratios (Times to 1)

Current Ratio 30	1.5	•	0.2	4.0	2.3	2.3	2.1	2.4	•	2.0	2.4
Quick Ratio 31	1.0	•	0.2	2.5	1.6	1.0	1.2	1.4	•	1.0	1.5
Net Sales to Working Capital 32	5.0	•	•	3.9	5.6	4.4	4.4	3.7	•	3.4	4.0
Coverage Ratio 33	3.7	5.0	56.4	14.6	23.7	7.7	11.6	11.2	•	8.8	1.6
Total Asset Turnover 34	0.5	•	2.6	2.8	2.3	1.8	1.7	1.4	•	0.8	0.5
Inventory Turnover 35	4.8	•	8.1	7.3	4.4	3.2	4.2	3.4	•	2.3	2.7
Receivables Turnover 36	4.1	•	18.2	7.0	9.8	7.6	6.7	5.2	•	3.0	4.1
Total Liabilities to Net Worth 37	1.0	•	4.1	0.5	0.7	1.1	1.1	0.7	•	1.3	2.1
Current Assets to Working Capital 38	2.9	•	•	1.3	1.7	1.8	2.0	1.7	•	2.0	1.7
Current Liabilities to Working Capital 39	1.9	•	•	0.3	0.7	0.8	1.0	0.7	•	1.0	0.7
Working Capital to Net Sales 40	0.2	•	•	0.3	0.2	0.2	0.2	0.3	•	0.3	0.2
Inventory to Working Capital 41	0.6	•	•	0.5	0.5	1.0	0.7	0.6	•	0.4	0.6
Total Receipts to Cash Flow 42	8.3	5.5	3.6	7.6	4.0	7.8	7.8	6.1	•	3.3	12.9
Cost of Goods to Cash Flow 43	5.6	4.1	1.3	5.0	1.9	5.0	5.3	4.0	•	1.6	8.7
Cash Flow to Total Debt 44	0.1	•	0.9	1.1	1.4	0.4	0.4	0.5	•	0.4	0.1

Selected Financial Factors (in Percentages)

Debt Ratio 45	50.1	•	80.5	32.7	39.7	51.9	51.6	40.5	•	56.9	67.2
Return on Total Assets 46	5.2	•	25.5	14.2	24.7	21.2	12.9	14.0	•	17.2	3.2
Return on Equity Before Income Taxes 47	7.6	•	128.3	19.7	39.2	38.4	24.4	21.5	•	35.3	3.7
Return on Equity After Income Taxes 48	6.2	•	127.5	19.0	33.6	36.6	21.2	19.2	•	23.4	2.9
Profit Margin (Before Income Tax) 49	7.0	12.1	9.7	4.8	10.5	10.3	7.0	9.4	•	19.5	2.2
Profit Margin (After Income Tax) 50	5.7	10.6	9.6	4.6	9.0	9.8	6.1	8.4	•	12.9	1.8

Table I

Corporations with and without Net Income

MOTOR VEHICLES AND PARTS

MONEY AMOUNTS AND SIZE OF ASSETS IN THOUSANDS OF DOLLARS

Item Description for Accounting Period 7/09 Through 6/10	Total	Zero Assets	Under 500	500 to 1,000	1,000 to 5,000	5,000 to 10,000	10,000 to 25,000	25,000 to 50,000	50,000 to 100,000	100,000 to 250,000	250,000 to 500,000	500,000 to 2,500,000	2,500,000 and over
Number of Enterprises **1**	5525	348	3163	246	756	310	228	157	118	86	44	45	24
Revenues ($ in Thousands)													
Net Sales **2**	376153316	935234	1509050	340034	3058418	3034604	5580652	7102188	11620409	18401023	23617996	42906836	258046873
Interest **3**	15424675	9209	189	27	1430	906	34998	5299	7184	23910	140029	544347	14657148
Rents **4**	5523523	14282	0	0	2957	714	1321	5075	2835	8688	10908	83659	5393083
Royalties **5**	5780904	761	0	0	0	41	3245	6365	3024	4948	135375	361531	5265614
Other Portfolio Income **6**	9053859	13497	192	901	6054	21857	17132	40733	17752	22353	73224	596599	7582564
Other Receipts **7**	13592019	73163	22113	-3932	19246	52539	69398	69022	111750	210326	439942	442777	12085675
Total Receipts **8**	425528296	1046146	1531544	337030	3088105	3110661	5706746	7228682	11762954	18671248	25078474	44935749	303030957
Average Total Receipts **9**	77019	3006	484	1370	4085	10034	25030	46043	99686	217108	569965	998572	12626290
Operating Costs/Operating Income (%)													
Cost of Operations **10**	82.3	82.7	67.2	68.2	67.2	72.4	78.1	80.0	81.7	85.2	85.1	80.4	82.7
Salaries and Wages **11**	4.8	5.9	8.7	6.3	8.1	11.1	6.2	6.0	4.1	4.2	9.9	5.6	4.0
Taxes Paid **12**	0.9	2.7	1.9	2.7	2.3	2.1	1.5	1.7	1.1	1.1	1.2	1.1	0.8
Interest Paid **13**	6.6	5.9	0.4	2.2	2.2	2.0	1.3	1.4	1.5	1.2	2.9	3.6	8.4
Depreciation **14**	7.3	13.4	1.4	2.0	2.4	3.4	3.7	4.5	4.1	4.5	4.2	5.3	8.5
Amortization and Depletion **15**	1.7	3.4	0.0	0.1	0.1	0.2	•	0.3	0.5	0.4	3.0	1.2	1.9
Pensions and Other Deferred Comp. **16**	2.0	0.1	0.0	0.3	0.1	0.5	0.2	0.3	0.2	0.4	0.3	1.7	2.5
Employee Benefits **17**	5.1	2.7	0.8	1.7	1.4	1.9	2.6	2.0	2.0	1.5	3.6	2.5	6.3
Advertising **18**	1.5	0.3	1.6	0.1	1.1	0.4	0.6	0.5	0.4	0.2	0.1	0.4	2.0
Other Expenses **19**	16.1	51.3	17.1	25.4	11.0	13.1	17.1	8.5	7.3	5.7	26.7	7.9	17.8
Officers' Compensation **20**	0.3	0.7	1.8	2.9	4.6	1.3	1.6	1.1	0.7	0.4	0.5	0.3	0.1
Operating Margin **21**	•	•	•	•	•	•	•	•	•	•	•	•	•
Operating Margin Before Officers' Comp. **22**	•	0.9	•	4.0	•	•	•	•	•	•	•	•	•

Selected Average Balance Sheet ($ in Thousands)

Net Receivables 23	41933	0	38	200	332	1199	3115	7119	14814	29313	66108	179671	8908186
Inventories 24	6523	0	47	337	913	2881	4871	8214	11135	26322	59305	105750	870030
Net Property, Plant and Equipment 25	22326	0	22	191	544	1322	4999	10782	24424	50993	96055	215962	4098622
Total Assets 26	153458	0	146	761	2286	7161	16291	34791	71921	150911	351405	1042675	31259744
Notes and Loans Payable 27	53040	0	57	499	1612	5165	6304	14134	24220	41975	112690	375112	10748299
All Other Liabilities 28	93504	0	72	191	745	2787	4449	12272	26045	49433	140369	398625	20022032
Net Worth 29	6914	0	16	71	-71	-791	5539	8385	21656	59504	98347	268937	489414

Selected Financial Ratios (Times to 1)

Current Ratio 30	1.0	•	1.3	1.8	1.6	1.5	1.1	1.3	1.3	1.4		1.2	1.0
Quick Ratio 31	0.7	•	0.7	0.7	0.7	0.7	0.6	0.8	0.7	0.8		0.7	0.7
Net Sales to Working Capital 32	24.7	•	17.6	5.8	7.0	7.4	19.0	11.0	12.6	12.7		13.6	48.2
Coverage Ratio 33	•	•	2.5	•	1.2	•	•	•	•	•	•	•	•
Total Asset Turnover 34	0.4	•	3.3	1.8	1.4	1.5	1.3	1.4	1.4	1.5		0.9	0.3
Inventory Turnover 35	8.6	•	6.9	2.8	3.0	3.9	4.4	7.2	6.9	7.7		7.2	10.2
Receivables Turnover 36	1.6	•	14.5	8.0	9.2	7.6	6.3	7.5	7.7	8.0		5.0	1.2
Total Liabilities to Net Worth 37	21.2	•	7.9	9.8	•	1.9	3.1	2.3	1.5	2.6		2.9	62.9
Current Assets to Working Capital 38	26.0	•	4.1	2.3	2.5	2.9	8.2	4.0	4.5	3.8		6.5	65.1
Current Liabilities to Working Capital 39	25.0	•	3.1	1.3	1.5	1.9	7.2	3.0	3.5	2.8		5.5	64.1
Working Capital to Net Sales 40	0.0	•	0.1	0.2	0.1	0.1	0.1	0.1	0.1	0.1		0.1	0.0
Inventory to Working Capital 41	2.3	•	1.7	1.3	1.6	1.5	3.2	1.2	1.5	1.2		1.5	3.8
Total Receipts to Cash Flow 42	•	•	8.1	23.9	13.5	43.8	67.0	41.2	91.6	157.3		•	•
Cost of Goods to Cash Flow 43	•	•	5.5	16.3	9.0	31.7	53.6	33.7	78.1	126.5		•	•
Cash Flow to Total Debt 44	0.5	•	0.1	0.1	0.1	0.0	0.0	0.0	0.0	0.0		0.0	0.0

Selected Financial Factors (in Percentages)

Debt Ratio 45	95.5	•	88.8	90.7	103.1	111.0	66.0	75.9	69.9	60.6	72.0	74.2	98.4
Return on Total Assets 46	3.4	•	•	•	•	4.6	•	•	•	•	•	•	•
Return on Equity Before Income Taxes 47	18.4	•	•	•	•	73.1	•	•	•	•	•	•	•
Return on Equity After Income Taxes 48	16.2	•	•	•	•	73.6	•	•	•	•	•	•	•
Profit Margin (Before Income Tax) 49	0.6	•	•	•	•	0.4	•	•	•	•	•	•	•
Profit Margin (After Income Tax) 50	0.6	•	•	•	•	0.2	•	•	•	•	•	•	•

Table II
Corporations with Net Income

MOTOR VEHICLES AND PARTS

MONEY AMOUNTS AND SIZE OF ASSETS IN THOUSANDS OF DOLLARS

Item Description for Accounting Period 7/09 Through 6/10		Total	Zero Assets	Under 500	500 to 1,000	1,000 to 5,000	5,000 to 10,000	10,000 to 25,000	25,000 to 50,000	50,000 to 100,000	100,000 to 250,000	250,000 to 500,000	500,000 to 2,500,000	2,500,000 and over
Number of Enterprises	1	2612	30	1620	187	387	102	96	65	50	41	16	14	5
Revenues ($ in Thousands)														
Net Sales	2	126843253	310458	958640	275941	1967903	1870567	2917385	3179648	5824237	10023474	7572369	13142840	78799791
Interest	3	1506499	115	0	26	284	219	172	922	2170	10639	12329	22211	1457412
Rents	4	76018	0	0	0	2705	0	0	954	1016	2670	2531	657	65486
Royalties	5	691858	0	0	0	0	0	0	6121	2875	4195	1287	33059	644322
Other Portfolio Income	6	1081724	0	0	901	2197	10749	1004	27769	3384	19997	15414	380483	619823
Other Receipts	7	2885243	25272	16907	518	6953	25988	8508	19704	29114	102884	44435	112379	2492583
Total Receipts	8	133084595	335845	975547	277386	1980042	1907523	2927069	3235118	5862796	10163859	7648365	13691629	84079417
Average Total Receipts	9	50951	11195	602	1483	5116	18701	30490	49771	117256	247899	478023	977974	16815883
Operating Costs/Operating Income (%)														
Cost of Operations	10	75.7	87.4	72.6	52.9	62.4	64.9	72.4	71.5	77.2	83.2	80.3	77.4	74.8
Salaries and Wages	11	3.2	1.5	4.2	6.7	8.2	11.1	5.8	6.4	4.3	4.0	3.6	4.8	2.1
Taxes Paid	12	0.8	0.6	0.9	2.4	2.1	2.0	1.4	2.1	1.2	1.0	1.3	1.2	0.5
Interest Paid	13	2.1	0.3	0.1	1.4	2.3	0.4	0.7	0.7	1.1	0.9	0.8	2.2	2.7
Depreciation	14	7.8	3.0	0.5	1.6	2.4	3.0	2.2	3.1	2.9	3.4	4.4	4.1	10.5
Amortization and Depletion	15	0.3	0.3	0.0	0.1	0.0	0.2	0.0	0.1	0.3	0.2	0.4	0.6	0.2
Pensions and Other Deferred Comp.	16	0.5	0.0	0.0	0.1	0.0	0.0	0.3	0.3	0.3	0.4	0.3	0.5	0.5
Employee Benefits	17	1.3	0.5	0.1	0.6	0.9	1.8	1.7	1.6	1.8	1.4	2.1	1.9	1.0
Advertising	18	1.4	0.0	1.9	0.1	1.0	0.2	0.8	0.9	0.5	0.2	0.0	0.2	2.1
Other Expenses	19	8.4	2.5	12.0	22.3	11.1	7.8	7.2	7.4	5.8	3.4	4.8	5.2	10.0
Officers' Compensation	20	0.3	0.2	0.4	3.6	2.5	0.7	1.8	1.5	0.7	0.3	0.5	0.3	0.1
Operating Margin	21	•	3.7	7.3	8.2	6.9	7.8	5.6	4.5	4.0	1.4	1.6	1.5	•
Operating Margin Before Officers' Comp.	22	•	3.9	7.7	11.8	9.4	8.5	7.4	5.9	4.7	1.7	2.1	1.9	•

Selected Average Balance Sheet ($ in Thousands)

Net Receivables 23	21302	0	51	220	399	2634	3559	7366	15398	33017	67127	172176	9733210
Inventories 24	4069	0	55	313	932	2016	6560	8367	11650	27674	69968	105350	1069853
Net Property, Plant and Equipment 25	16220	0	17	197	672	1618	3849	8645	20220	41154	104666	209877	6726966
Total Assets 26	57793	0	136	794	2348	8430	15205	34138	71378	147927	328612	1028166	23170546
Notes and Loans Payable 27	24458	0	23	306	1926	1988	4530	8482	16420	26046	67930	267138	11028238
All Other Liabilities 28	18926	0	42	58	637	3541	3913	9448	24394	55819	102838	359473	7514548
Net Worth 29	14408	0	71	430	-214	2901	6763	16209	30564	66062	157845	401555	4627760

Selected Financial Ratios (Times to 1)

Current Ratio 30	1.6	•	2.9	8.7	1.8	1.5	2.0	1.6	1.5	1.5	1.6	2.0	1.6
Quick Ratio 31	1.3	•	1.9	3.9	0.6	1.0	0.9	0.9	0.9	0.8	0.9	1.2	1.3
Net Sales to Working Capital 32	4.2	•	7.4	2.9	7.4	9.6	6.2	6.5	8.5	9.5	7.0	4.0	3.5
Coverage Ratio 33	2.6	34.9	77.8	7.1	4.2	24.4	9.1	10.6	5.4	4.1	4.5	4.4	1.8
Total Asset Turnover 34	0.8	•	4.3	1.9	2.2	2.2	2.0	1.4	1.6	1.7	1.4	0.9	0.7
Inventory Turnover 35	9.0	•	7.8	2.5	3.4	5.9	3.4	4.2	7.7	7.4	5.4	6.9	11.0
Receivables Turnover 36	3.3	•	14.6	8.3	10.1	6.5	7.8	6.5	•	•	7.1	4.8	•
Total Liabilities to Net Worth 37	3.0	•	0.9	0.8	•	1.9	1.2	1.1	1.3	1.2	1.1	1.6	4.0
Current Assets to Working Capital 38	2.7	•	1.5	1.1	2.2	3.1	2.1	2.7	2.9	3.2	2.6	2.0	2.8
Current Liabilities to Working Capital 39	1.7	•	0.5	0.1	1.2	2.1	1.1	1.7	1.9	2.2	1.6	1.0	1.8
Working Capital to Net Sales 40	0.2	•	0.1	0.3	0.1	0.1	0.2	0.2	0.1	0.1	0.1	0.3	0.3
Inventory to Working Capital 41	0.4	•	0.5	0.6	1.4	0.8	1.0	1.1	0.9	1.1	0.9	0.5	0.2
Total Receipts to Cash Flow 42	9.3	7.3	5.8	4.5	6.7	7.1	8.4	9.2	11.0	19.9	16.1	10.1	8.5
Cost of Goods to Cash Flow 43	7.1	6.3	4.2	2.4	4.2	4.6	6.1	6.6	8.5	16.5	12.9	7.8	6.4
Cash Flow to Total Debt 44	0.1	•	1.6	0.9	0.3	0.5	0.4	0.3	0.3	0.2	0.2	0.1	0.1

Selected Financial Factors (in Percentages)

Debt Ratio 45	75.1	•	47.9	45.8	109.1	65.6	55.5	52.5	57.2	55.3	52.0	60.9	80.0
Return on Total Assets 46	4.6	•	39.7	18.9	21.3	22.1	13.5	9.9	9.3	6.2	5.2	8.6	3.3
Return on Equity Before Income Taxes 47	11.3	•	75.1	30.0	•	61.6	26.9	18.9	17.7	10.5	8.4	17.0	7.2
Return on Equity After Income Taxes 48	8.9	•	74.1	29.1	•	61.2	24.3	15.8	14.1	8.4	7.1	11.9	5.5
Profit Margin (Before Income Tax) 49	3.3	11.8	9.0	8.8	7.5	9.7	6.0	6.3	4.7	2.8	2.8	7.3	2.1
Profit Margin (After Income Tax) 50	2.6	10.6	8.9	8.5	7.2	9.7	5.4	5.2	3.7	2.3	2.4	5.1	1.6

Table I

Corporations with and without Net Income

AEROSPACE PRODUCT AND PARTS

MONEY AMOUNTS AND SIZE OF ASSETS IN THOUSANDS OF DOLLARS

Item Description for Accounting Period 7/09 Through 6/10		Total	Zero Assets	Under 500	500 to 1,000	1,000 to 5,000	5,000 to 10,000	10,000 to 25,000	25,000 to 50,000	50,000 to 100,000	100,000 to 250,000	250,000 to 500,000	500,000 to 2,500,000	2,500,000 and over
Number of Enterprises	1	1275	25	•	70	335	88	87	30	24	19	5	16	•
Revenues ($ in Thousands)														
Net Sales	2	288711277	85028	•	53763	1253423	607622	2136245	1239752	1746594	2702674	1530666	18818372	•
Interest	3	1049855	6		0	519	500	462	1145	1323	3684	14796	56003	
Rents	4	915824	0		0	0	0	23	402	741	3622	368	11289	
Royalties	5	1556561	0		0	0	0	0	0	0	3064	0	4392	
Other Portfolio Income	6	2478897	0		0	203	96	538	2268	1639	296	8791	161030	
Other Receipts	7	3634604	0		12	2760	1150	7475	6634	17235	8443	3629	38023	
Total Receipts	8	298347018	85034		53775	1256905	609368	2144743	1250201	1767532	2721783	1558250	19089109	
Average Total Receipts	9	233998	3401		768	3752	6925	24652	41673	73647	143252	311650	1193069	
Operating Costs/Operating Income (%)														
Cost of Operations	10	72.5	48.8	•	74.9	62.0	68.1	70.7	63.2	68.9	67.3	71.0	68.3	•
Salaries and Wages	11	4.1	17.2	•	19.3	8.8	8.1	5.2	8.0	10.5	8.4	5.3	6.7	•
Taxes Paid	12	1.7	3.0	•	2.5	1.7	3.7	2.2	2.2	1.9	2.1	2.3	3.6	•
Interest Paid	13	1.6	15.2	•	0.2	0.9	2.3	1.8	1.6	1.8	4.0	5.4	2.9	•
Depreciation	14	2.7	1.2	•	3.1	2.6	2.9	2.6	3.5	3.4	3.4	4.3	2.7	•
Amortization and Depletion	15	0.8	•	•	5.0	0.2	0.1	0.2	0.3	1.1	0.6	2.7	1.4	•
Pensions and Other Deferred Comp.	16	3.6	0.9	•	•	0.4	0.9	0.4	0.3	0.4	0.5	0.2	0.7	•
Employee Benefits	17	2.6	2.0	•	•	0.9	3.4	2.4	2.6	2.1	2.1	2.9	2.9	•
Advertising	18	0.3	0.0	•	0.9	0.3	0.1	0.1	0.2	0.4	0.1	0.1	0.1	•
Other Expenses	19	8.9	24.4	•	22.2	9.7	14.3	8.8	9.2	9.4	7.9	8.2	4.6	•
Officers' Compensation	20	0.3	7.4	•	6.4	6.3	1.5	2.5	5.3	3.1	1.0	1.8	0.7	•
Operating Margin	21	1.0	•	•	•	6.2	•	3.1	3.6	•	2.6	•	5.4	•
Operating Margin Before Officers' Comp.	22	1.3	•	•	•	12.5	•	5.6	8.8	•	3.6	•	6.1	•

Selected Average Balance Sheet ($ in Thousands)

Net Receivables 23	30271	0	•	109	485	1257	3176	4880	9788	23686	40545	184150
Inventories 24	37936	0	•	131	585	2942	5869	10598	14655	43908	213999	274463
Net Property, Plant and Equipment 25	32501	0	•	39	303	883	3124	9178	16342	34125	75449	208720
Total Assets 26	280033	0	•	641	1920	6395	17716	35988	72194	158140	364705	1551139
Notes and Loans Payable 27	66333	0	•	527	762	3408	5993	10219	17812	61435	176470	450774
All Other Liabilities 28	131003	0	•	58	317	1249	3550	5560	24082	63980	79320	475269
Net Worth 29	82697	0	•	56	841	1738	7573	20209	30300	32725	108915	625096

Selected Financial Ratios (Times to 1)

Current Ratio 30	1.3	•	2.6	2.9	1.9	2.6	1.5	1.5	2.6	1.5	
Quick Ratio 31	0.7	•	1.2	1.6	0.9	0.8	1.3	0.7	0.6	0.9	0.7
Net Sales to Working Capital 32	10.6	•	4.4	4.0	2.0	4.9	3.4	5.3	5.7	2.9	5.4
Coverage Ratio 33	4.0	•	•	8.2	•	2.9	3.8	•	1.8	0.6	3.4
Total Asset Turnover 34	0.8	•	1.2	1.9	1.1	1.4	1.1	1.0	0.9	0.8	0.8
Inventory Turnover 35	4.3	•	4.4	4.0	1.6	3.0	2.5	3.4	2.2	1.0	2.9
Receivables Turnover 36	7.4	•	9.9	7.5	6.7	6.5	6.3	8.3	6.1	4.6	5.8
Total Liabilities to Net Worth 37	2.4	•	10.4	1.3	2.7	1.3	0.8	1.4	3.8	2.3	1.5
Current Assets to Working Capital 38	4.5	•	1.6	1.5	1.5	2.2	1.6	2.9	3.0	1.6	2.9
Current Liabilities to Working Capital 39	3.5	•	0.6	0.5	0.5	1.2	0.6	1.9	2.0	0.6	1.9
Working Capital to Net Sales 40	0.1	•	0.2	0.3	0.5	0.2	0.3	0.2	0.2	0.3	0.2
Inventory to Working Capital 41	1.8	•	0.9	0.5	1.1	1.1	0.7	1.2	1.5	0.9	1.3
Total Receipts to Cash Flow 42	9.2	•	8.1	45.5	10.2	8.8	18.3	11.3	26.1	10.4	
Cost of Goods to Cash Flow 43	6.7	•	5.0	31.0	7.2	5.5	12.6	7.6	18.5	7.1	
Cash Flow to Total Debt 44	0.1	•	0.4	0.0	0.3	0.3	0.1	0.1	0.0	0.1	

Selected Financial Factors (in Percentages)

Debt Ratio 45	70.5	•	91.2	72.8	55.8	43.8	58.0	79.3	70.1	59.7
Return on Total Assets 46	5.1	•	14.3	7.7	6.9	6.5	2.6	7.4
Return on Equity Before Income Taxes 47	13.1	•	28.7	11.4	9.0	14.3	13.0
Return on Equity After Income Taxes 48	8.5	•	23.9	10.3	6.8	10.5	10.3
Profit Margin (Before Income Tax) 49	4.8	•	6.5	3.5	4.4	3.3	3.3	6.9
Profit Margin (After Income Tax) 50	3.1	•	5.4	3.2	3.3	2.4	5.5

Table II

Corporations with Net Income

AEROSPACE PRODUCT AND PARTS

MONEY AMOUNTS AND SIZE OF ASSETS IN THOUSANDS OF DOLLARS

Item Description for Accounting Period 7/09 Through 6/10	Total	Zero Assets	Under 500	500 to 1,000	1,000 to 5,000	5,000 to 10,000	10,000 to 25,000	25,000 to 50,000	50,000 to 100,000	100,000 to 250,000	250,000 to 500,000	500,000 to 2,500,000	2,500,000 and over
Number of Enterprises 1	679	•	230	5	271	27	52	24	15	14	0	•	•

Revenues ($ in Thousands)

Item	Total	Zero Assets	Under 500	500 to 1,000	1,000 to 5,000	5,000 to 10,000	10,000 to 25,000	25,000 to 50,000	50,000 to 100,000	100,000 to 250,000	250,000 to 500,000	500,000 to 2,500,000	2,500,000 and over
Net Sales 2	257181362	•	3063	24013	1216463	325746	1524330	1000652	1068635	2414228	0	•	•
Interest 3	917300	•	233	0	513	450	161	676	860	2421	0	•	•
Rents 4	849606	•	0	0	0	0	0	402	240	408	0	•	•
Royalties 5	902701	•	0	0	0	0	0	0	0	2895	0	•	•
Other Portfolio Income 6	2449113	•	28	0	199	0	117	2151	1257	226	0	•	•
Other Receipts 7	2929470	•	0	0	2752	444	2762	2077	15982	8185	0	•	•
Total Receipts 8	265229552	•	3324	24013	1219927	326640	1527370	1005958	1086974	2428363	0	•	•
Average Total Receipts 9	390618	•	14	4803	4502	12098	29372	41915	72465	173454	•	•	•

Operating Costs/Operating Income (%)

Item	Total	Zero Assets	Under 500	500 to 1,000	1,000 to 5,000	5,000 to 10,000	10,000 to 25,000	25,000 to 50,000	50,000 to 100,000	100,000 to 250,000	250,000 to 500,000	500,000 to 2,500,000	2,500,000 and over
Cost of Operations 10	72.3	•	•	8.1	62.6	60.2	68.8	62.9	69.3	64.4	•	•	•
Salaries and Wages 11	3.9	•	•	17.2	8.4	3.1	4.6	7.9	6.2	7.8	•	•	•
Taxes Paid 12	1.8	•	4.2	1.7	1.6	2.1	2.3	2.3	1.3	2.2	•	•	•
Interest Paid 13	1.4	•	•	•	0.7	0.8	0.6	1.3	1.5	2.5	•	•	•
Depreciation 14	2.7	•	•	0.1	2.6	0.8	2.3	3.9	2.5	3.0	•	•	•
Amortization and Depletion 15	0.7	•	•	•	0.0	0.3	0.2	0.1	0.4	0.7	•	•	•
Pensions and Other Deferred Comp. 16	3.5	•	•	•	0.4	1.6	0.4	0.2	0.2	0.4	•	•	•
Employee Benefits 17	2.5	•	47.5	•	0.9	1.0	2.6	2.0	0.9	2.7	•	•	•
Advertising 18	0.3	•	•	•	0.2	0.1	0.1	0.2	0.3	0.1	•	•	•
Other Expenses 19	8.4	•	13.3	6.9	8.5	8.5	8.0	6.9	7.1	7.9	•	•	•
Officers' Compensation 20	0.3	•	•	3.6	6.2	1.3	2.8	3.0	3.1	1.3	•	•	•
Operating Margin 21	2.3	•	34.9	62.4	7.8	20.1	7.3	9.2	7.1	6.9	•	•	•
Operating Margin Before Officers' Comp. 22	2.6	•	34.9	66.0	14.0	21.5	10.1	12.3	10.2	8.1	•	•	•

Selected Average Balance Sheet ($ in Thousands)

Net Receivables 23	48853	•	0	783	592	1756	3994	4940	11197	26927
Inventories 24	52772	•	0		449	3779	6762	9688	12149	43747
Net Property, Plant and Equipment 25	53613	•	0	10	367	737	3210	10613	10772	34908
Total Assets 26	412218	•		1072	1977	7651	17099	35470	70026	172057
Notes and Loans Payable 27	91130	•	0		644	1663	3858	8889	14742	45104
All Other Liabilities 28	218739	•	0	4	388	309	3877	4453	15720	69525
Net Worth 29	102349	•	0	1068	946	5679	9363	22128	39564	57429

Selected Financial Ratios (Times to 1)

Current Ratio 30	1.3	•	241.3	3.3	7.1	2.1	3.8	2.4	1.4
Quick Ratio 31	0.7	•	241.3	2.0	3.1	1.0	2.1	1.4	0.6
Net Sales to Working Capital 32	10.2	•	4.5	4.0	2.2	4.7	3.0	3.0	7.5
Coverage Ratio 33	5.1	•	•	11.9	25.8	13.4	8.4	6.7	3.9
Total Asset Turnover 34	0.9	•	4.5	2.3	1.6	1.7	1.2	1.0	1.0
Inventory Turnover 35	5.2	•	•	6.3	1.9	3.0	2.7	4.1	2.5
Receivables Turnover 36	7.7	•	7.7	8.4	6.7	5.6	6.2	7.2	6.8
Total Liabilities to Net Worth 37	3.0	•	0.0	1.1	0.3	0.8	0.6	0.8	2.0
Current Assets to Working Capital 38	4.3	•	1.0	1.4	1.2	1.9	1.4	1.7	3.5
Current Liabilities to Working Capital 39	3.3	•	0.0	0.4	0.2	0.9	0.4	0.7	2.5
Working Capital to Net Sales 40	0.1	•	0.2	0.2	0.5	0.2	0.3	0.3	0.1
Inventory to Working Capital 41	1.7	•	•	0.4	0.6	0.9	0.5	0.5	1.7
Total Receipts to Cash Flow 42	8.8	1.9	1.5	7.7	3.7	7.6	6.8	6.9	7.6
Cost of Goods to Cash Flow 43	6.4	•	0.1	4.8	2.2	5.2	4.3	4.8	4.9
Cash Flow to Total Debt 44	0.1	•	754.8	0.6	1.7	0.5	0.5	0.3	0.2

Selected Financial Factors (in Percentages)

Debt Ratio 45	75.2	•	0.4	52.2	25.8	45.2	37.6	43.5	66.6
Return on Total Assets 46	6.6	•	279.6	20.1	33.5	13.8	13.0	10.6	10.0
Return on Equity Before Income Taxes 47	21.3	•	280.7	38.5	43.4	23.4	18.4	16.0	22.4
Return on Equity After Income Taxes 48	14.4	•	280.7	33.2	43.0	21.8	15.9	13.3	18.9
Profit Margin (Before Income Tax) 49	5.8	43.5	62.4	8.1	20.4	7.5	9.7	8.9	7.4
Profit Margin (After Income Tax) 50	3.9	43.5	62.4	7.0	20.2	7.0	8.4	7.4	6.3

Table I

Corporations with and without Net Income

SHIP AND BOAT BUILDING

MONEY AMOUNTS AND SIZE OF ASSETS IN THOUSANDS OF DOLLARS

Item Description for Accounting Period 7/09 Through 6/10	Total	Zero Assets	Under 500	500 to 1,000	1,000 to 5,000	5,000 to 10,000	10,000 to 25,000	25,000 to 50,000	50,000 to 100,000	100,000 to 250,000	250,000 to 500,000	500,000 to 2,500,000	2,500,000 and over
Number of Enterprises **1**	1472	425	•	0	243	63	63	23	13	11	•	•	•
Revenues ($ in Thousands)													
Net Sales **2**	32907903	0	•	0	728410	757862	1532964	778410	1112163	1908880	•	•	•
Interest **3**	26872	0	•	0	666	221	826	1197	951	4617	•	•	•
Rents **4**	30744	0	•	0	0	0	0	1189	386	1174	•	•	•
Royalties **5**	1368	0	•	0	0	24	0	0	309	0	•	•	•
Other Portfolio Income **6**	177428	0	•	0	261	75	262	3366	1674	299	•	•	•
Other Receipts **7**	82343	0	•	0	4661	-3133	14255	19041	6483	24180	•	•	•
Total Receipts **8**	33226658	0	•	0	733998	755049	1548307	803203	1121966	1939150	•	•	•
Average Total Receipts **9**	22572	0	•	•	3021	11985	24576	34922	86305	176286	•	•	•
Operating Costs/Operating Income (%)													
Cost of Operations **10**	74.0	•	•	•	83.3	64.9	85.8	73.5	81.9	79.6	•	•	•
Salaries and Wages **11**	2.3	•	•	•	5.0	5.5	2.5	5.7	3.7	3.9	•	•	•
Taxes Paid **12**	1.5	•	•	•	1.5	1.7	1.0	2.0	1.5	2.5	•	•	•
Interest Paid **13**	1.0	•	•	•	2.0	1.0	1.2	3.7	3.1	0.4	•	•	•
Depreciation **14**	2.7	•	•	•	3.5	2.7	2.9	3.3	3.9	4.3	•	•	•
Amortization and Depletion **15**	1.5	•	•	•	0.1	0.1	0.1	1.1	0.2	0.0	•	•	•
Pensions and Other Deferred Comp. **16**	1.2	•	•	•	0.3	0.7	0.2	0.9	0.7	0.7	•	•	•
Employee Benefits **17**	1.7	•	•	•	1.5	2.0	1.0	2.7	1.0	2.5	•	•	•
Advertising **18**	0.9	•	•	•	0.3	0.8	0.6	0.6	0.8	0.6	•	•	•
Other Expenses **19**	6.4	•	•	•	11.2	12.6	5.4	13.0	5.4	4.9	•	•	•
Officers' Compensation **20**	1.1	•	•	•	5.8	3.9	1.8	2.6	1.3	1.1	•	•	•
Operating Margin **21**	5.7	•	•	•	•	4.0	•	•	•	•	•	•	•
Operating Margin Before Officers' Comp. **22**	6.8	•	•	•	•	7.9	•	•	•	0.5	•	•	•

Selected Average Balance Sheet ($ in Thousands)

Net Receivables 23	1944	0	166	1577	2679	2764	9281	21217
Inventories 24	3721	0	900	5266	2674	7739	13484	17411
Net Property, Plant and Equipment 25	3255	0	826	1656	6158	13887	26857	47384
Total Assets 26	23117	0	1920	7342	16385	38624	71406	153384
Notes and Loans Payable 27	5149	0	1018	1949	6485	18914	30794	49194
All Other Liabilities 28	8137	0	241	2273	6531	11374	26231	55486
Net Worth 29	9831	0	661	3120	3370	8337	14381	48704

Selected Financial Ratios (Times to 1)

Current Ratio 30	1.4	•	1.2	2.2	1.0	1.3	1.1	1.3
Quick Ratio 31	0.5		0.3	1.1	0.5	0.5	0.5	0.6
Net Sales to Working Capital 32	10.1		20.1	4.8	75.7	7.6	48.8	10.3
Coverage Ratio 33	7.8		•	4.7	•	•	0.1	3.3
Total Asset Turnover 34	1.0		1.6	1.6	1.5	0.9	1.2	1.1
Inventory Turnover 35	4.4		2.8	1.5	7.8	3.2	5.2	7.9
Receivables Turnover 36	11.0		11.1	9.2	7.5	6.8	8.9	10.2
Total Liabilities to Net Worth 37	1.4		1.9	1.4	3.9	3.6	4.0	2.1
Current Assets to Working Capital 38	3.8		6.6	1.8	26.6	4.0	17.1	4.9
Current Liabilities to Working Capital 39	2.8		5.6	0.8	25.6	3.0	16.1	3.9
Working Capital to Net Sales 40	0.1		0.0	0.2	0.0	0.1	0.0	0.1
Inventory to Working Capital 41	1.4		4.3	0.8	7.3	1.4	5.3	1.2
Total Receipts to Cash Flow 42	9.2		•	8.3	45.6	22.7	123.9	22.4
Cost of Goods to Cash Flow 43	6.8		•	5.4	39.1	16.7	101.5	17.8
Cash Flow to Total Debt 44	0.2		•	0.3	0.0	0.0	0.0	0.1

Selected Financial Factors (in Percentages)

Debt Ratio 45	57.5	•	65.6	57.5	79.4	78.4	79.9	68.2
Return on Total Assets 46	7.7		•	7.6	•	•	0.4	1.5
Return on Equity Before Income Taxes 47	15.8		•	14.1	•	•	•	3.4
Return on Equity After Income Taxes 48	9.4		•	12.5	•	•	•	•
Profit Margin (Before Income Tax) 49	6.9		•	3.7	•	•	•	0.9
Profit Margin (After Income Tax) 50	4.1		•	3.2	•	•	•	•

Table II

Corporations with Net Income

SHIP AND BOAT BUILDING

MONEY AMOUNTS AND SIZE OF ASSETS IN THOUSANDS OF DOLLARS

Item Description for Accounting Period 7/09 Through 6/10	Total	Zero Assets	Under 500	500 to 1,000	1,000 to 5,000	5,000 to 10,000	10,000 to 25,000	25,000 to 50,000	50,000 to 100,000	100,000 to 250,000	250,000 to 500,000	500,000 to 2,500,000	2,500,000 and over
Number of Enterprises 1	129	0	0	0	•	39	26	4	6	6	•	•	•
Revenues ($ in Thousands)													
Net Sales 2	29158073	0	0	0	•	569905	787250	346977	669138	1291092	•	•	•
Interest 3	23562	0	0	0	•	135	248	703	280	3585	•	•	•
Rents 4	30271	0	0	0	•	0	0	1189	46	1040	•	•	•
Royalties 5	1035	0	0	0	•	0	0	0	0	0	•	•	•
Other Portfolio Income 6	171914	0	0	0	•	0	65	231	103	256	•	•	•
Other Receipts 7	38386	0	0	0	•	2061	5248	1689	4864	5414	•	•	•
Total Receipts 8	29423241	0	0	0	•	572101	792811	350789	674431	1301387	•	•	•
Average Total Receipts 9	228087	•	•	•	•	14669	30493	87697	112405	216898	•	•	•
Operating Costs/Operating Income (%)													
Cost of Operations 10	72.9	•	•	•	•	59.3	75.9	64.7	78.8	73.7	•	•	•
Salaries and Wages 11	2.0	•	•	•	•	5.8	2.7	5.8	2.8	4.6	•	•	•
Taxes Paid 12	1.4	•	•	•	•	1.7	1.2	1.6	1.3	2.7	•	•	•
Interest Paid 13	0.8	•	•	•	•	0.4	0.4	0.4	0.5	0.2	•	•	•
Depreciation 14	2.3	•	•	•	•	2.8	3.3	1.7	3.6	2.6	•	•	•
Amortization and Depletion 15	1.7	•	•	•	•	0.1	0.0	0.2	0.0	0.0	•	•	•
Pensions and Other Deferred Comp. 16	1.3	•	•	•	•	0.6	0.4	1.1	1.0	0.9	•	•	•
Employee Benefits 17	1.6	•	•	•	•	2.6	1.4	1.2	1.5	2.6	•	•	•
Advertising 18	0.8	•	•	•	•	0.8	0.4	0.0	0.3	0.0	•	•	•
Other Expenses 19	5.6	•	•	•	•	9.0	5.7	14.3	1.4	4.4	•	•	•
Officers' Compensation 20	0.8	•	•	•	•	3.9	2.3	0.7	1.3	1.1	•	•	•
Operating Margin 21	8.7	•	•	•	•	12.9	6.2	8.2	7.3	7.2	•	•	•
Operating Margin Before Officers' Comp. 22	9.5	•	•	•	•	16.9	8.5	8.9	8.6	8.3	•	•	•

Selected Average Balance Sheet ($ in Thousands)

Net Receivables 23	18852	2343	3190	8790	11891	21936
Inventories 24	34412	1055	2615	6328	14177	2335
Net Property, Plant and Equipment 25	26163	2351	5543	8921	26053	45837
Total Assets 26	235742	7154	14969	39618	69858	164106
Notes and Loans Payable 27	44595	1050	2881	13052	13122	19978
All Other Liabilities 28	85032	1369	4603	11632	29959	74270
Net Worth 29	106115	4735	7486	14934	26777	69857

Selected Financial Ratios (Times to 1)

Current Ratio 30	1.4	3.6	1.9	1.2	1.2	1.3
Quick Ratio 31	0.5	2.8	1.0	0.5	0.6	0.8
Net Sales to Working Capital 32	9.6	4.3	7.0	22.8	17.8	10.6
Coverage Ratio 33	13.3	35.6	17.4	23.1	16.1	40.1
Total Asset Turnover 34	1.0	2.0	2.0	2.2	1.6	1.3
Inventory Turnover 35	4.8	8.2	8.8	8.9	6.2	67.9
Receivables Turnover 36	12.2	7.6	7.2	4.4	7.8	•
Total Liabilities to Net Worth 37	1.2	0.5	1.0	1.7	1.6	1.3
Current Assets to Working Capital 38	3.5	1.4	2.1	6.3	6.1	4.2
Current Liabilities to Working Capital 39	2.5	0.4	1.1	5.3	5.1	3.2
Working Capital to Net Sales 40	0.1	0.2	0.1	0.0	0.1	0.1
Inventory to Working Capital 41	1.2	0.3	0.2	0.1	1.5	0.1
Total Receipts to Cash Flow 42	7.5	5.3	9.3	4.9	12.4	8.9
Cost of Goods to Cash Flow 43	5.5	3.2	7.0	3.2	9.7	6.6
Cash Flow to Total Debt 44	0.2	1.1	0.4	0.7	0.2	0.3

Selected Financial Factors (in Percentages)

Debt Ratio 45	55.0	33.8	50.0	62.3	61.7	57.4
Return on Total Assets 46	10.3	28.0	14.9	21.3	13.7	10.8
Return on Equity Before Income Taxes 47	21.2	41.1	28.0	54.0	33.6	24.7
Return on Equity After Income Taxes 48	14.5	39.4	27.4	41.8	31.8	17.0
Profit Margin (Before Income Tax) 49	10.0	13.3	6.9	9.3	8.1	8.0
Profit Margin (After Income Tax) 50	6.8	12.8	6.8	7.2	7.6	5.5

158

Table I

Corporations with and without Net Income

OTHER TRANSPORTATION EQUIPMENT AND RAILROAD ROLLING STOCK

MONEY AMOUNTS AND SIZE OF ASSETS IN THOUSANDS OF DOLLARS

Item Description for Accounting Period 7/09 Through 6/10		Total	Zero Assets	Under 500	500 to 1,000	1,000 to 5,000	5,000 to 10,000	10,000 to 25,000	25,000 to 50,000	50,000 to 100,000	100,000 to 250,000	250,000 to 500,000	500,000 to 2,500,000	2,500,000 and over
Number of Enterprises	1	1595	7	•	48	316	72	42	10	16	8	•	•	•
Revenues ($ in Thousands)														
Net Sales	2	23558653	184113	•	31858	997582	1322568	1097413	383921	1222377	917051	•	•	•
Interest	3	743588	12	•	176	243	965	359	295	2375	383	•	•	•
Rents	4	64363	0	•	0	3682	0	0	0	1385	0	•	•	•
Royalties	5	58435	243	•	0	0	0	0	696	183	5921			•
Other Portfolio Income	6	176685	0	•	13440	0	423	1569	348	3872	794	•	•	•
Other Receipts	7	149568	6364	•	1118	2064	851	13000	1237	8054	3168	•	•	•
Total Receipts	8	24781292	190732	•	46592	1003571	1324807	1112341	386497	1238246	927317	•	•	•
Average Total Receipts	9	15537	27247	•	971	3176	18400	26484	38650	77390	115915			
Operating Costs/Operating Income (%)														
Cost of Operations	10	70.4	70.3	•	160.7	83.3	78.2	74.0	70.3	73.4	70.7	•	•	•
Salaries and Wages	11	7.3	4.6	•	23.5	4.1	10.1	8.7	5.7	7.3	6.6	•	•	•
Taxes Paid	12	1.4	0.6	•	4.0	2.1	1.3	1.5	1.7	1.7	1.4	•	•	•
Interest Paid	13	3.7	0.7	•	0.4	1.2	0.4	0.9	1.3	1.3	2.2	•	•	•
Depreciation	14	4.6	0.5	•	8.6	2.2	1.0	2.3	3.2	2.5	3.8	•	•	•
Amortization and Depletion	15	0.9	1.3	•	0.2	0.5	0.2	0.1	1.7	0.9	1.0	•	•	•
Pensions and Other Deferred Comp.	16	1.4	0.2	•	•	0.1	0.1	0.1	0.1	0.6	0.3	•	•	•
Employee Benefits	17	1.9	0.9	•	2.0	0.9	1.7	0.5	1.4	2.4	1.6	•	•	•
Advertising	18	0.8	0.7	•	3.2	0.7	0.2	1.1	1.1	0.4	0.5	•	•	•
Other Expenses	19	10.3	20.2	•	36.8	7.2	5.5	13.7	5.7	6.2	5.3	•	•	•
Officers' Compensation	20	0.8	•	•	•	3.1	0.8	2.8	0.7	2.0	1.3	•	•	•
Operating Margin	21	•	0.1	•	•	•	0.4	•	7.0	1.2	5.4	•	•	•
Operating Margin Before Officers' Comp.	22	•	0.1	•	•	•	1.3	•	7.7	3.2	6.7	•	•	•

Selected Average Balance Sheet ($ in Thousands)

Net Receivables 23	4765	0	19	375	1771	2964	8672	8712	19393
Inventories 24	2410	0	458	585	4388	4902	11494	11551	34972
Net Property, Plant and Equipment 25	4239	0	223	204	1133	4613	6825	1145	22279
Total Assets 26	17464	0	917	1603	8103	16719	33464	68985	154225
Notes and Loans Payable 27	7978	0	2302	762	3393	5025	9123	24180	39673
All Other Liabilities 28	4459	0	296	316	2095	3403	11472	15745	63164
Net Worth 29	5027	0	-1682	525	2615	8291	12869	29060	51388

Selected Financial Ratios (Times to 1)

Current Ratio 30	1.5		2.4	1.8	3.3	2.3	1.9	1.5	1.2
Quick Ratio 31	1.0		0.9	0.9	1.0	1.2	1.1	0.7	0.6
Net Sales to Working Capital 32	4.0		1.6	6.1	3.8	4.8	3.8	6.3	9.9
Coverage Ratio 33	1.4	6.4			2.4		6.8	2.9	4.0
Total Asset Turnover 34	0.8		0.7	2.0	2.3	1.6	1.1	1.1	0.7
Inventory Turnover 35	4.3		2.3	4.5	3.3	3.9	2.3	4.9	2.3
Receivables Turnover 36	3.1		2.8	6.9	11.4	7.0	3.8	9.4	4.8
Total Liabilities to Net Worth 37	2.5		2.1	2.1	1.0	1.6		1.4	2.0
Current Assets to Working Capital 38	2.8		1.7	2.3	1.4	1.8	2.1	2.9	6.3
Current Liabilities to Working Capital 39	1.8		0.7	1.3	0.4	0.8	1.1	1.9	5.3
Working Capital to Net Sales 40	0.2		0.6	0.2	0.3	0.2	0.3	0.2	0.1
Inventory to Working Capital 41	0.6		1.0	1.1	1.0	0.7	0.7	1.1	2.2
Total Receipts to Cash Flow 42	10.6	4.6		458.4	22.7	17.0	9.1	15.5	9.3
Cost of Goods to Cash Flow 43	7.5	3.2		382.1	17.8	12.6	6.4	11.4	6.6
Cash Flow to Total Debt 44	0.1		0.0	0.1	0.2	0.2	0.2	0.1	0.1

Selected Financial Factors (in Percentages)

Debt Ratio 45	71.2		283.4	67.3	67.7	50.4	61.5	57.9	66.7
Return on Total Assets 46	4.5				2.4		10.3	4.2	6.4
Return on Equity Before Income Taxes 47	4.7		36.7		4.3		22.9	6.5	14.5
Return on Equity After Income Taxes 48	1.8		36.7		1.5		17.7	4.0	10.5
Profit Margin (Before Income Tax) 49	1.6	3.7			0.6		7.7	2.5	6.5
Profit Margin (After Income Tax) 50	0.6	2.2			0.2		5.9	1.5	4.7

Table II
Corporations with Net Income

OTHER TRANSPORTATION EQUIPMENT AND RAILROAD ROLLING STOCK

MONEY AMOUNTS AND SIZE OF ASSETS IN THOUSANDS OF DOLLARS

Item Description for Accounting Period 7/09 Through 6/10	Total	Zero Assets	Under 500	500 to 1,000	1,000 to 5,000	5,000 to 10,000	10,000 to 25,000	25,000 to 50,000	50,000 to 100,000	100,000 to 250,000	250,000 to 500,000	500,000 to 2,500,000	2,500,000 and over
Number of Enterprises **1**	414	•	60	0	•	65	18	5	10	5	•	•	0
Revenues ($ in Thousands)													
Net Sales **2**	15829852	•	69199	0	•	1252165	380578	204984	653535	671181	•	•	0
Interest **3**	714885	•	1	0	•	8	77	129	1649	153	•	•	0
Rents **4**	2076	•	0	0	•	0	0	0	1292	0	•	•	0
Royalties **5**	50291	•	0	0	•	0	0	0	163	0	•	•	0
Other Portfolio Income **6**	38028	•	71	0	•	208	1525	43	3499	794	•	•	0
Other Receipts **7**	81976	•	0	0	•	191	3218	663	5189	3571	•	•	0
Total Receipts **8**	16717108	•	69271	0	•	1252572	385398	205819	665327	675699	•	•	0
Average Total Receipts **9**	40379	•	1155	•	•	19270	21411	41164	66533	135140	•	•	•
Operating Costs/Operating Income (%)													
Cost of Operations **10**	71.3	•	39.8	•	•	77.2	77.7	66.3	68.9	71.2	•	•	•
Salaries and Wages **11**	6.2	•	8.4	•	•	9.7	3.5	4.2	7.7	3.7	•	•	•
Taxes Paid **12**	1.2	•	1.5	•	•	1.3	0.7	1.6	1.8	1.3	•	•	•
Interest Paid **13**	3.2	•	2.5	•	•	0.4	1.1	0.6	1.4	1.2	•	•	•
Depreciation **14**	2.8	•	2.5	•	•	0.9	1.6	1.8	3.1	4.5	•	•	•
Amortization and Depletion **15**	0.8	•	•	•	•	0.0	0.2	0.1	1.0	0.2	•	•	•
Pensions and Other Deferred Comp. **16**	1.9	•	•	•	•	0.1	0.1	0.2	0.8	0.1	•	•	•
Employee Benefits **17**	2.0	•	0.1	•	•	1.7	0.9	0.6	2.0	1.7	•	•	•
Advertising **18**	0.9	•	0.8	•	•	0.2	0.5	0.2	0.4	0.0	•	•	•
Other Expenses **19**	8.8	•	10.8	•	•	5.2	8.3	5.3	1.8	4.3	•	•	•
Officers' Compensation **20**	0.8	•	6.0	•	•	0.7	4.5	0.7	2.4	0.8	•	•	•
Operating Margin **21**	0.1	•	27.5	•	•	2.6	0.8	18.3	8.8	11.1	•	•	•
Operating Margin Before Officers' Comp. **22**	0.9	•	33.5	•	•	3.3	5.4	19.0	11.2	11.9	•	•	•

Selected Average Balance Sheet ($ in Thousands)

Net Receivables 23	15949	60	1831	2872	3088	7712	20278
Inventories 24	5377	233	4604	6557	17472	9417	28464
Net Property, Plant and Equipment 25	5044	31	1050	2401	6967	13418	30697
Total Assets 26	41103	450	8181	13760	30190	61458	157637
Notes and Loans Payable 27	17985	221	2167	5156	4961	19598	49167
All Other Liabilities 28	10402	97	1921	3020	4210	13711	49851
Net Worth 29	12716	132	4094	5585	21019	28149	58619

Selected Financial Ratios (Times to 1)

Current Ratio 30	1.5	2.9	3.8	1.7	4.3	2.2	1.2
Quick Ratio 31	1.0	0.9	1.2	0.9	2.1	1.2	0.7
Net Sales to Working Capital 32	3.7	6.3	3.6	6.5	2.7	4.4	10.1
Coverage Ratio 33	2.8	11.9	7.8	3.0	29.9	8.5	10.8
Total Asset Turnover 34	0.9	2.6	2.4	1.5	1.4	1.1	0.9
Inventory Turnover 35	5.1	2.0	3.2	2.5	1.6	4.8	3.4
Receivables Turnover 36	2.4	21.0	11.3	3.9	3.6		6.9
Total Liabilities to Net Worth 37	2.2	2.4	1.0	1.5	0.4	1.2	1.7
Current Assets to Working Capital 38	3.0	1.5	1.4	2.5	1.3	1.8	5.5
Current Liabilities to Working Capital 39	2.0	0.5	0.4	1.5	0.3	0.8	4.5
Working Capital to Net Sales 40	0.3	0.2	0.3	0.2	0.4	0.2	0.1
Inventory to Working Capital 41	0.5	1.1	0.9	1.1	0.6	0.6	1.6
Total Receipts to Cash Flow 42	7.7	2.8	16.6	18.9	4.7	9.4	6.6
Cost of Goods to Cash Flow 43	5.5	1.1	12.8	14.7	3.1	6.5	4.7
Cash Flow to Total Debt 44	0.2	1.3	0.3	0.1	0.9	0.2	0.2

Selected Financial Factors (in Percentages)

Debt Ratio 45	69.1	70.7	50.0	59.4	30.4	54.2	62.8
Return on Total Assets 46	8.4	77.3	7.1	4.9	26.3	12.8	11.0
Return on Equity Before Income Taxes 47	17.3	241.5	12.4	8.0	36.5	24.7	26.9
Return on Equity After Income Taxes 48	12.9	194.7	10.5	6.5	30.2	20.5	21.2
Profit Margin (Before Income Tax) 49	5.8	27.6	2.6	2.1	18.7	10.6	11.8
Profit Margin (After Income Tax) 50	4.3	22.3	2.2	1.7	15.5	8.8	9.3

Table I

Corporations with and without Net Income

FURNITURE AND RELATED PRODUCT MANUFACTURING

MONEY AMOUNTS AND SIZE OF ASSETS IN THOUSANDS OF DOLLARS

Item Description for Accounting Period 7/09 Through 6/10	Total	Zero Assets	Under 500	500 to 1,000	1,000 to 5,000	5,000 to 10,000	10,000 to 25,000	25,000 to 50,000	50,000 to 100,000	100,000 to 250,000	250,000 to 500,000	500,000 to 2,500,000	2,500,000 and over
Number of Enterprises **1**	13149	1764	9138	754	1028	173	162	59	29	23	6	13	0
Revenues ($ in Thousands)													
Net Sales **2**	49397689	125431	4619296	1299470	6111173	2128266	4045390	3764131	3264373	4801572	2168726	17069861	0
Interest **3**	41540	25	659	228	2662	525	853	2085	2035	4373	11244	16852	0
Rents **4**	29608	0	178	0	308	63	419	2893	1328	8509	1908	14002	0
Royalties **5**	48177	345	0	0	0	0	0	0	1718	3440	350	42324	0
Other Portfolio Income **6**	192604	16806	4953	3795	371	449	5778	1263	5341	9770	124145	19931	0
Other Receipts **7**	434487	3103	10386	19007	13582	21943	650	14823	15015	25622	11934	298422	0
Total Receipts **8**	50144105	145710	4635472	1322500	6128096	2151246	4053090	3785195	3289810	4853286	2318307	17461392	0
Average Total Receipts **9**	3814	83	507	1754	5961	12435	25019	64156	113442	211012	386384	1343184	•
Operating Costs/Operating Income (%)													
Cost of Operations **10**	66.9	57.4	56.0	63.1	71.0	71.7	70.6	70.6	70.7	70.5	63.4	65.2	•
Salaries and Wages **11**	9.8	19.2	15.4	6.2	10.2	9.0	7.9	8.7	7.4	8.4	10.5	9.8	•
Taxes Paid **12**	2.1	3.6	3.1	2.3	2.2	2.4	1.6	1.9	1.5	1.8	2.1	2.0	•
Interest Paid **13**	1.3	6.7	0.6	0.7	0.7	2.7	1.1	1.4	1.5	1.2	1.0	1.7	•
Depreciation **14**	2.2	0.8	2.3	1.2	1.5	3.8	2.0	1.5	2.0	2.8	3.5	2.3	•
Amortization and Depletion **15**	0.5	9.5	0.3	0.1	0.0	0.0	0.2	0.1	1.0	0.5	0.2	1.0	•
Pensions and Other Deferred Comp. **16**	0.6	0.1	0.6	0.7	0.1	0.2	0.4	0.2	0.2	0.8	0.2	1.0	•
Employee Benefits **17**	2.1	1.4	1.2	3.5	1.7	2.3	2.1	1.7	2.1	2.9	2.3	2.2	•
Advertising **18**	1.8	3.9	0.5	0.6	1.0	1.1	1.5	0.9	1.6	1.1	4.1	2.9	•
Other Expenses **19**	11.8	35.4	13.9	14.7	9.3	10.8	10.3	9.6	9.9	10.1	14.7	13.1	•
Officers' Compensation **20**	2.0	0.2	9.2	6.7	2.5	2.2	2.0	1.2	1.1	0.8	0.7	0.5	•
Operating Margin **21**	•	•	•	0.2	•	•	0.3	2.0	0.9	0.8	•	•	•
Operating Margin Before Officers' Comp. **22**	0.8	•	6.1	6.8	2.4	•	2.2	3.2	2.0	•	•	•	•

Selected Average Balance Sheet ($ in Thousands)

	C1	C2	C3	C4	C5	C6	C7	C8	C9	C10	C11	
Net Receivables 23	392	0	214	609	1003	2411	7732	16864	25707	31370	145013	•
Inventories 24	399	0	112	597	1304	3257	9115	15623	26946	43106	128473	•
Net Property, Plant and Equipment 25	554	0	111	794	3413	3616	9038	14615	38741	68889	203713	•
Total Assets 26	2391	0	654	2358	7102	13829	32630	70349	140908	267642	1164132	•
Notes and Loans Payable 27	775	0	237	1299	4377	3310	11954	26070	37790	32445	323735	•
All Other Liabilities 28	760	0	143	1047	1352	3067	7614	17826	33627	66398	419087	•
Net Worth 29	857	-3	275	13	1373	7451	13062	26453	69490	168799	421309	•

Selected Financial Ratios (Times to 1)

	C1	C2	C3	C4	C5	C6	C7	C8	C9	C10	C11	C12	
Current Ratio 30	1.6	1.0	2.1	1.4	1.8	2.3	1.9	2.0	2.2	2.2	1.3		•
Quick Ratio 31	0.8	0.5	1.5	0.8	0.9	1.2	0.9	1.1	1.2	1.1	0.6		•
Net Sales to Working Capital 32	9.4	357.7	6.8	13.7	7.9	5.6	6.9	6.0	5.6	6.1	13.3		•
Coverage Ratio 33	1.2	•	3.9	1.3	•	1.4	2.8	2.2	1.2	5.2	1.3		•
Total Asset Turnover 34	1.6	4.2	2.6	2.5	1.7	1.8	2.0	1.6	1.5	1.4	1.1		•
Inventory Turnover 35	6.3	10.3	9.7	7.1	6.8	5.4	4.9	5.1	5.5	5.3	6.7		•
Receivables Turnover 36	8.7	23.7	7.7	9.1	8.5	8.5	7.2	6.8	8.5	7.6	8.3		•
Total Liabilities to Net Worth 37	1.8	•	1.4	185.5	4.2	0.9	1.5	1.7	1.0	0.6	1.8		•
Current Assets to Working Capital 38	2.8	50.3	1.9	3.4	2.2	1.8	2.2	2.0	1.8	1.8	4.5		•
Current Liabilities to Working Capital 39	1.8	49.3	0.9	2.4	1.2	0.8	1.2	1.0	0.8	0.8	3.5		•
Working Capital to Net Sales 40	0.1	0.0	0.1	0.1	0.1	0.2	0.1	0.2	0.2	0.2	0.1		•
Inventory to Working Capital 41	0.9	22.5	0.4	1.2	0.9	0.6	0.9	0.7	0.7	0.7	1.1		•
Total Receipts to Cash Flow 42	11.4	19.6	14.0	10.0	17.2	35.9	11.8	9.7	10.5	14.0	11.7	9.0	•
Cost of Goods to Cash Flow 43	7.6	11.2	7.9	6.3	12.2	25.8	8.3	6.9	7.5	9.9	7.4	5.9	•
Cash Flow to Total Debt 44	0.2	0.3	0.5	0.1	0.2	0.3	0.3	0.2	0.2	0.3	0.2		•

Selected Financial Factors (in Percentages)

	C1	C2	C3	C4	C5	C6	C7	C8	C9	C10	C11	
Debt Ratio 45	64.2	102.3	57.9	99.5	80.7	46.1	60.0	62.4	50.7	36.9	63.8	•
Return on Total Assets 46	2.6	•	6.8	2.1	•	2.9	7.8	5.3	2.1	6.9	2.6	•
Return on Equity Before Income Taxes 47	1.3	496.8	12.1	81.7	•	1.6	12.5	7.5	0.7	8.8	1.9	•
Return on Equity After Income Taxes 48	0.1	496.9	10.9	67.8	•	0.5	12.2	6.5	•	5.2	1.0	•
Profit Margin (Before Income Tax) 49	0.3	•	1.9	0.2	•	0.5	2.6	1.8	0.2	4.1	0.6	•
Profit Margin (After Income Tax) 50	0.0	•	1.7	0.1	•	0.2	2.5	1.5	•	2.4	0.3	•

Table II
Corporations with Net Income

FURNITURE AND RELATED PRODUCT MANUFACTURING

MONEY AMOUNTS AND SIZE OF ASSETS IN THOUSANDS OF DOLLARS

Item Description for Accounting Period 7/09 Through 6/10	Total	Zero Assets	Under 500	500 to 1,000	1,000 to 5,000	5,000 to 10,000	10,000 to 25,000	25,000 to 50,000	50,000 to 100,000	100,000 to 250,000	250,000 to 500,000	500,000 to 2,500,000	2,500,000 and over
Number of Enterprises **1**	5136	790	3047	600	489	49	89	35	16	10	3	8	0
Revenues ($ in Thousands)													
Net Sales **2**	28850823	21469	1837020	1040240	3329202	987915	2458637	2602723	1943070	2678360	738517	11213670	0
Interest **3**	17187	0	0	95	815	317	315	1466	631	1022	7657	4869	0
Rents **4**	6383	0	0	0	45	0	5	2389	1310	60	227	2347	0
Royalties **5**	35260	0	0	0	0	0	0	0	1718	26	350	33165	0
Other Portfolio Income **6**	150332	0	2093	3600	240	139	658	816	5323	4345	123856	9261	0
Other Receipts **7**	359917	0	710	15244	5284	12616	6806	9790	8800	16201	9329	275139	0
Total Receipts **8**	29419902	21469	1839823	1059179	3335586	1000987	2466421	2617184	1960852	2700014	879936	11538451	0
Average Total Receipts **9**	5728	27	604	1765	6821	20428	27713	74777	122553	270001	293312	1442306	•
Operating Costs/Operating Income (%)													
Cost of Operations **10**	65.4	35.8	56.4	58.6	72.7	65.9	69.2	68.5	69.1	69.4	75.5	61.6	•
Salaries and Wages **11**	8.6	•	14.6	7.0	7.5	7.0	7.3	8.7	7.8	9.2	6.2	8.6	•
Taxes Paid **12**	1.8	•	3.0	1.9	1.5	1.8	1.5	1.7	1.6	1.6	2.6	1.9	•
Interest Paid **13**	1.3	3.3	0.2	0.5	0.3	1.9	0.6	1.0	1.0	1.0	1.0	2.1	•
Depreciation **14**	1.7	1.4	0.8	0.8	0.9	1.6	1.5	1.5	1.6	2.3	2.9	2.0	•
Amortization and Depletion **15**	0.6	•	0.3	0.1	0.0	0.0	0.1	0.0	0.4	0.2	0.1	1.3	•
Pensions and Other Deferred Comp. **16**	0.5	•	0.3	0.7	0.1	0.2	0.2	0.3	0.3	0.8	0.4	0.8	•
Employee Benefits **17**	1.8	•	0.8	3.6	0.7	1.9	1.8	1.8	1.6	2.9	2.9	1.7	•
Advertising **18**	1.9	1.8	0.8	0.7	0.9	1.6	1.6	0.6	2.0	0.6	0.3	3.3	•
Other Expenses **19**	11.0	32.8	11.4	14.5	8.1	11.3	8.5	8.8	7.5	5.2	9.1	14.7	•
Officers' Compensation **20**	1.8	•	7.6	7.2	2.6	2.5	2.2	1.2	1.1	0.8	1.1	0.4	•
Operating Margin **21**	3.6	25.0	3.8	4.3	4.6	4.2	5.6	6.0	5.8	5.9	•	1.6	•
Operating Margin Before Officers' Comp. **22**	5.4	25.0	11.4	11.6	7.2	6.7	7.9	7.2	7.0	6.7	•	2.0	•

Selected Average Balance Sheet ($ in Thousands)

Net Receivables 23	605	0	41	224	757	1854	2554	8748	15714	29262	28736	152789	•
Inventories 24	509	0	26	52	680	1922	3467	7509	12433	28500	39576	113082	•
Net Property, Plant and Equipment 25	669	0	23	104	508	1056	3105	10149	12887	33852	55145	207822	•
Total Assets 26	3440	0	118	650	2251	6743	13370	33557	66999	144363	262921	1227177	•
Notes and Loans Payable 27	1141	0	77	190	444	1113	2883	10800	14844	34053	48359	485348	•
All Other Liabilities 28	991	0	48	123	647	2534	2675	8854	16320	39727	68614	377306	•
Net Worth 29	1308	0	-7	337	1160	3096	7813	13903	35834	70583	145949	364524	•

Selected Financial Ratios (Times to 1)

Current Ratio 30	1.6	•	0.9	2.5	2.5	2.7	2.8	1.6	2.4	2.0	2.2	1.2	•
Quick Ratio 31	0.9	•	0.7	1.9	1.7	1.7	1.5	0.9	1.5	1.0	1.1	0.6	•
Net Sales to Working Capital 32	9.4	•	6.0	6.7	5.8	5.2	9.5	5.8	7.5	4.8	17.0		•
Coverage Ratio 33	5.4	8.6	13.7	16.7	3.9	11.8	7.8	8.1	7.9	17.5	3.1		•
Total Asset Turnover 34	1.6	5.1	2.7	3.0	3.0	2.1	2.2	1.8	1.9	0.9	1.1		•
Inventory Turnover 35	7.2	13.0	19.5	7.3	6.9	5.5	6.8	6.8	6.5	4.7	7.6		•
Receivables Turnover 36	8.1	14.9	8.3	8.5	6.1	8.4	7.7	8.4	9.4	4.7	7.8		•
Total Liabilities to Net Worth 37	1.6	•	0.9	0.9	1.2	0.7	1.4	0.9	1.0	0.8	2.4		•
Current Assets to Working Capital 38	2.8	•	1.7	1.7	1.6	1.6	2.6	1.7	2.1	1.8	5.9		•
Current Liabilities to Working Capital 39	1.8	•	0.7	0.7	0.6	0.6	1.6	0.7	1.1	0.8	4.9		•
Working Capital to Net Sales 40	0.1	•	0.2	0.1	0.2	0.2	0.1	0.2	0.1	0.2	0.1		•
Inventory to Working Capital 41	0.8	•	0.3	0.5	0.5	0.6	0.9	0.6	0.8	0.7	1.3		•
Total Receipts to Cash Flow 42	7.3	1.8	7.3	10.3	7.3	8.1	7.4	8.0	9.8	16.0	6.0		•
Cost of Goods to Cash Flow 43	4.8	0.6	4.3	7.5	4.8	5.6	5.1	5.5	6.8	12.1	3.7		•
Cash Flow to Total Debt 44	0.4	•	0.8	0.6	0.8	0.6	0.5	0.5	0.4	0.1	0.3		•

Selected Financial Factors (in Percentages)

Debt Ratio 45	62.0	105.7	48.2	48.5	54.1	41.6	58.6	46.5	51.1	44.5	70.3		•
Return on Total Assets 46	11.2	21.5	17.7	15.3	22.3	13.4	16.5	14.0	14.2	16.8	7.5		•
Return on Equity Before Income Taxes 47	24.0	•	31.6	28.0	36.1	21.0	34.8	23.0	25.4	28.6	17.2		•
Return on Equity After Income Taxes 48	21.9	•	30.4	27.7	35.9	19.2	34.3	21.6	21.2	20.1	15.6		•
Profit Margin (Before Income Tax) 49	5.6	25.0	6.1	4.8	5.5	5.9	6.5	6.8	6.7	17.0	4.5		•
Profit Margin (After Income Tax) 50	5.1	25.0	5.9	4.7	5.5	5.4	6.4	6.4	5.6	11.9	4.1		•

Table I

Corporations with and without Net Income

MEDICAL EQUIPMENT AND SUPPLIES

MONEY AMOUNTS AND SIZE OF ASSETS IN THOUSANDS OF DOLLARS

Item Description for Accounting Period 7/09 Through 6/10		Total	Zero Assets	Under 500	500 to 1,000	1,000 to 5,000	5,000 to 10,000	10,000 to 25,000	25,000 to 50,000	50,000 to 100,000	100,000 to 250,000	250,000 to 500,000	500,000 to 2,500,000	2,500,000 and over
Number of Enterprises	1	8265	420	5909	414	945	150	140	100	59	41	29	40	16
Revenues ($ in Thousands)														
Net Sales	2	151205981	389875	2228435	811336	5409239	1298740	2707649	4895781	4804303	5211223	7231799	33726920	82490680
Interest	3	2163092	2689	3638	637	11049	2452	4539	8435	10366	17191	126787	117240	1858069
Rents	4	809102	9	0	1	0	393	433	342	758	2682	1156	29645	773683
Royalties	5	342204	3813	0	0	0	1636	3219	35380	10900	16730	124143	146845	3085538
Other Portfolio Income	6	2227422	5738	2103	6	29763	34	9992	57576	19583	8184	93974	529412	1471058
Other Receipts	7	3227420	37871	1707	2038	37906	15629	63256	33596	33336	93209	319748	166925	2422199
Total Receipts	8	16306121	439995	2235883	814018	5487957	1318884	2789088	5031110	4879246	5349219	7897607	34716987	92101227
Average Total Receipts	9	19729	1048	378	1966	5807	8793	19922	50311	82699	130469	272331	867925	5756327
Operating Costs/Operating Income (%)														
Cost of Operations	10	55.7	50.5	35.0	38.0	60.0	52.4	52.3	57.6	56.4	46.2	51.4	50.8	59.1
Salaries and Wages	11	16.1	27.8	13.8	16.6	10.4	20.1	18.2	15.4	14.1	18.1	14.5	13.9	17.3
Taxes Paid	12	1.5	3.0	3.7	4.0	2.3	3.0	2.6	2.0	1.6	1.9	1.7	1.5	1.3
Interest Paid	13	3.8	3.1	0.5	2.0	0.9	1.4	1.1	1.8	1.4	2.7	4.2	2.5	5.1
Depreciation	14	3.4	3.9	2.6	0.7	1.0	2.9	2.3	2.6	2.6	4.3	3.7	3.1	3.8
Amortization and Depletion	15	1.3	2.4	0.1	0.1	0.4	0.8	0.6	0.9	1.0	2.0	1.9	1.8	1.2
Pensions and Other Deferred Comp.	16	0.8	0.2	0.3	0.2	0.5	0.4	0.4	0.3	0.5	0.3	0.5	0.6	1.1
Employee Benefits	17	2.9	3.6	1.7	4.1	1.4	2.1	2.2	1.8	2.2	2.7	2.2	2.5	3.4
Advertising	18	0.9	1.2	0.7	0.4	1.3	1.5	1.9	2.0	1.1	1.5	1.0	0.9	0.7
Other Expenses	19	13.3	68.1	21.9	18.9	17.2	27.4	22.2	16.1	14.6	17.8	18.6	14.0	10.7
Officers' Compensation	20	1.3	11.2	17.6	9.2	4.8	6.2	4.3	2.4	1.6	1.9	1.2	1.0	0.4
Operating Margin	21	•	•	2.0	5.9	•	•	•	•	2.9	0.7	•	7.5	•
Operating Margin Before Officers' Comp.	22	0.3	•	19.6	15.1	4.6	•	•	•	4.5	2.6	0.4	8.4	•

Selected Average Balance Sheet ($ in Thousands)

Net Receivables 23	3511	0	10	488	739	1485	3268	7542	12970	23186	54279	169775	1033904
Inventories 24	2466	0	11	88	507	1420	3390	6049	10528	17177	31457	104116	756770
Net Property, Plant and Equipment 25	2945	0	25	90	228	758	2027	6447	9762	27557	37592	153791	871943
Total Assets 26	29913	0	87	740	2134	7276	16302	36751	72089	169227	362297	1147563	10608809
Notes and Loans Payable 27	9405	0	48	463	761	1285	3952	11473	12890	40775	63116	320881	3596828
All Other Liabilities 28	9108	0	19	322	884	2025	5109	8737	19419	37935	125240	300754	3371327
Net Worth 29	11399	0	20	-45	489	3966	7241	16541	39780	90516	173941	525927	3640654

Selected Financial Ratios (Times to 1)

Current Ratio 30	1.8	•	1.2	1.0	1.5	2.3	2.4	2.3	2.0	2.4	3.7	2.1	1.6
Quick Ratio 31	1.0	•	0.7	0.8	1.4	1.6	1.5	1.3	1.3	2.2	1.3	0.8	
Net Sales to Working Capital 32	4.2	•	66.2	•	11.0	2.8	2.7	4.0	3.6	3.7	2.0	3.7	4.7
Coverage Ratio 33	3.2	•	5.5	4.1	2.3	•	0.9	4.3	2.3	3.2	5.6	2.9	
Total Asset Turnover 34	0.6	•	4.3	2.6	2.7	1.2	1.2	1.3	1.1	0.8	0.7	0.7	0.5
Inventory Turnover 35	4.1	•	12.6	8.5	6.8	3.2	3.0	4.7	4.4	3.4	4.1	4.1	4.0
Receivables Turnover 36	5.2	•	36.2	4.7	7.9	6.4	5.9	6.5	6.1	5.9	4.6	5.3	4.8
Total Liabilities to Net Worth 37	1.6	•	3.3	•	3.4	0.8	1.3	1.2	0.8	0.9	1.1	1.2	1.9
Current Assets to Working Capital 38	2.2	•	6.7	•	3.2	1.8	1.7	1.8	1.7	2.0	1.4	1.9	2.6
Current Liabilities to Working Capital 39	1.2	•	5.7	•	2.2	0.8	0.7	0.8	0.7	1.0	0.4	0.9	1.6
Working Capital to Net Sales 40	0.2	•	0.0	•	0.1	0.4	0.4	0.2	0.3	0.3	0.5	0.3	0.2
Inventory to Working Capital 41	0.6	•	1.9	•	1.0	0.5	0.5	0.5	0.5	0.5	0.2	0.5	0.7
Total Receipts to Cash Flow 42	5.7	•	5.5	4.5	7.5	14.8	7.3	7.9	5.9	5.3	4.0	4.5	6.3
Cost of Goods to Cash Flow 43	3.2	•	1.9	1.7	4.5	7.8	3.8	4.6	3.3	2.5	2.1	2.3	3.7
Cash Flow to Total Debt 44	0.2	•	1.0	0.6	0.5	0.2	0.3	0.3	0.4	0.3	0.3	0.3	0.1

Selected Financial Factors (in Percentages)

Debt Ratio 45	61.9	•	76.9	106.1	77.1	45.5	55.6	55.0	44.8	46.5	52.0	54.2	65.7
Return on Total Assets 46	7.4	•	12.4	21.7	5.8	•	2.2	6.7	4.5	9.1	10.2	7.2	
Return on Equity Before Income Taxes 47	13.2	•	43.9	•	14.5	•	9.4	12.9	18.3	13.7			
Return on Equity After Income Taxes 48	8.7	•	43.7	•	10.2	•	7.0	8.7	13.8	8.9			
Profit Margin (Before Income Tax) 49	8.2	•	2.3	6.2	1.2	1.2	1.7	4.6	3.4	4.6	9.0	11.4	
Profit Margin (After Income Tax) 50	5.4	•	2.3	6.0	0.9	•	3.4	6.1	8.6	6.3			

Table II

Corporations with Net Income

MEDICAL EQUIPMENT AND SUPPLIES

MONEY AMOUNTS AND SIZE OF ASSETS IN THOUSANDS OF DOLLARS

Item Description for Accounting Period 7/09 Through 6/10		Total	Zero Assets	Under 500	500 to 1,000	1,000 to 5,000	5,000 to 10,000	10,000 to 25,000	25,000 to 50,000	50,000 to 100,000	100,000 to 250,000	250,000 to 500,000	500,000 to 2,500,000	2,500,000 and over
Number of Enterprises	1	5733	8	4237	372	798	56	67	60	42	24	22	34	13
Revenues ($ in Thousands)														
Net Sales	2	132071115	216552	1684341	791869	5119983	681516	1651309	3932942	3812528	3694436	5492976	30689897	74302765
Interest	3	1962754	2445	496	586	2312	82	1152	5020	5058	12938	122772	104066	1705826
Rents	4	797448	9	0	1	0	0	215	0	381	1848	1013	20297	773683
Royalties	5	2914684	3813	0	0	0	0	1245	235	6917	11654	121393	116826	2652600
Other Portfolio Income	6	2146697	4316	2028	6	26286	0	9820	45517	19119	5549	93974	529403	1410678
Other Receipts	7	2587693	37397	1086	621	32949	6759	44375	14923	32227	15097	317445	165174	1919643
Total Receipts	8	142480391	264532	1687951	793083	5181530	688357	1708116	3998637	3876230	3741522	6149573	31625663	82765195
Average Total Receipts	9	24853	33066	398	2132	6493	12292	25494	66644	92291	155897	279526	930167	6366553
Operating Costs/Operating Income (%)														
Cost of Operations	10	56.0	54.4	35.5	38.8	59.6	47.1	47.6	57.5	54.7	44.8	50.9	50.8	59.8
Salaries and Wages	11	15.3	9.9	13.0	14.3	8.9	10.1	13.7	12.3	13.1	15.5	14.3	13.4	17.0
Taxes Paid	12	1.5	2.5	3.6	3.8	2.2	1.7	2.4	1.7	1.5	1.9	1.9	1.6	1.2
Interest Paid	13	3.6	3.2	0.3	0.3	0.8	0.4	0.4	1.0	1.1	2.1	4.6	2.2	4.8
Depreciation	14	3.4	2.2	2.2	0.5	0.7	1.9	2.3	2.3	2.2	4.2	3.1	3.1	3.9
Amortization and Depletion	15	0.9	1.3	0.0	•	0.0	0.0	0.2	0.6	0.9	1.6	1.8	1.2	0.8
Pensions and Other Deferred Comp.	16	0.9	0.4	0.2	0.2	0.5	0.7	0.6	0.4	0.5	0.3	0.6	0.7	1.1
Employee Benefits	17	2.9	1.1	0.7	4.1	1.2	0.9	2.0	1.3	1.8	2.6	1.8	2.5	3.5
Advertising	18	0.8	0.5	0.6	0.2	1.3	1.4	1.7	2.0	1.3	1.2	0.9	0.9	0.7
Other Expenses	19	11.3	21.3	17.7	16.4	14.4	14.5	13.6	12.9	13.8	14.1	18.3	14.0	8.8
Officers' Compensation	20	1.2	3.7	15.8	7.8	4.6	4.6	4.2	2.1	1.7	1.7	1.3	1.0	0.4
Operating Margin	21	2.3	•	10.3	13.6	5.9	16.6	11.3	5.8	7.5	9.8	0.5	8.8	•
Operating Margin Before Officers' Comp.	22	3.4	3.3	26.1	21.4	10.5	21.2	15.5	7.9	9.1	11.5	1.8	9.8	•

Selected Average Balance Sheet ($ in Thousands)

Net Receivables 23	4285	6	538	789	1956	4281	9612	14583	25442	59776	173171	1100824
Inventories 24	2893	6	55	394	1518	3915	6063	10879	19301	28208	100262	812736
Net Property, Plant and Equipment 25	3582	21	89	221	754	2471	7243	8965	33216	32731	158143	947871
Total Assets 26	33656	73	751	2042	7619	16654	37704	73436	168051	355074	1169243	10172425
Notes and Loans Payable 27	10978	26	138	545	669	1895	10755	11718	33007	73643	295097	3737760
All Other Liabilities 28	1115	16	215	588	1872	3665	9196	20438	37353	130677	290666	3668708
Net Worth 29	11563	31	397	909	5078	11094	17753	41280	97692	150754	583480	2765957

Selected Financial Ratios (Times to 1)

Current Ratio 30	1.7	•	1.6	2.2	2.6	3.0	2.1	2.6	1.8	3.3	2.1	1.5
Quick Ratio 31	1.0	•	1.0	1.9	1.7	2.0	1.4	1.4	1.1	2.1	1.3	0.8
Net Sales to Working Capital 32	4.9	34.0	6.0	7.3	3.9	2.8	5.5	3.6	5.1	2.3	3.8	5.9
Coverage Ratio 33	4.3	7.8	33.1	51.6	42.1	33.8	8.5	9.4	6.2	3.9	7.0	3.5
Total Asset Turnover 34	0.7	•	2.8	3.1	1.6	1.5	1.7	1.2	0.9	0.7	0.8	0.6
Inventory Turnover 35	4.5	•	24.7	15.1	9.7	3.0	6.2	4.6	3.6	4.5	4.6	4.2
Receivables Turnover 36	6.0	•	63.8	9.6	6.9	5.6	7.1	6.7	6.2	4.8	5.8	5.8
Total Liabilities to Net Worth 37	1.9	•	1.3	0.9	0.5	0.5	1.1	0.8	0.7	1.4	1.0	2.7
Current Assets to Working Capital 38	2.4	•	2.7	1.9	1.6	1.5	1.9	1.6	2.3	1.4	1.9	3.0
Current Liabilities to Working Capital 39	1.4	•	1.7	0.9	0.6	0.5	0.9	0.6	1.3	0.4	0.9	2.0
Working Capital to Net Sales 40	0.2	•	0.0	0.2	0.3	0.4	0.2	0.3	0.2	0.4	0.3	0.2
Inventory to Working Capital 41	0.6	•	0.6	0.2	0.5	0.4	0.5	0.5	0.6	0.3	0.4	0.9
Total Receipts to Cash Flow 42	5.3	2.5	4.3	3.7	5.9	3.9	5.9	4.7	4.3	3.5	4.2	6.4
Cost of Goods to Cash Flow 43	3.0	1.3	1.5	1.4	1.6	1.9	3.4	2.6	1.9	1.8	2.1	3.8
Cash Flow to Total Debt 44	0.2	•	2.2	1.6	1.4	1.1	0.6	0.6	0.5	0.3	0.4	0.1

Selected Financial Factors (in Percentages)

Debt Ratio 45	65.6	•	57.1	47.1	55.5	33.4	52.9	43.8	41.9	57.5	50.1	72.8
Return on Total Assets 46	10.5	•	58.5	39.8	24.7	22.5	14.8	12.9	12.1	12.7	11.7	9.3
Return on Equity Before Income Taxes 47	23.4	•	132.3	73.7	50.2	32.7	27.7	20.5	17.5	22.2	20.1	24.2
Return on Equity After Income Taxes 48	17.0	•	132.2	72.5	47.4	30.5	24.1	17.2	12.8	15.8	15.3	16.3
Profit Margin (Before Income Tax) 49	11.8	21.7	10.5	13.8	7.1	14.7	7.5	9.3	11.1	13.4	13.0	11.7
Profit Margin (After Income Tax) 50	8.5	15.5	10.5	13.5	6.7	13.8	6.5	7.8	8.1	9.5	9.9	7.9

Table I

Corporations with and without Net Income

OTHER MISCELLANEOUS MANUFACTURING

MONEY AMOUNTS AND SIZE OF ASSETS IN THOUSANDS OF DOLLARS

Item Description for Accounting Period 7/09 Through 6/10		Total	Zero Assets	Under 500	500 to 1,000	1,000 to 5,000	5,000 to 10,000	10,000 to 25,000	25,000 to 50,000	50,000 to 100,000	100,000 to 250,000	250,000 to 500,000	500,000 to 2,500,000	2,500,000 and over
Number of Enterprises	1	22638	2520	16012	1422	1807	313	298	108	69	49	21	16	4
Revenues ($ in Thousands)														
Net Sales	2	78288618	401917	4977128	1413949	10279932	3046431	6436426	5452732	5182517	7821431	6138829	17244829	9892498
Interest	3	651961	942	441	313	5420	656	3006	3320	15688	20113	38815	169386	393861
Rents	4	21903	0	0	2461	964	575	1618	1220	576	5854	6493	1472	670
Royalties	5	975684	650	100	0	2	0	2197	9689	6025	44503	43860	99468	769189
Other Portfolio Income	6	364990	30553	24416	1218	1950	306	11192	2229	19857	33233	30097	166535	43404
Other Receipts	7	1132668	-12923	53091	1514	25784	4385	69238	39514	66856	74436	161351	48084	601338
Total Receipts	8	81435824	421139	5055176	1419455	10314052	3052353	6523677	5508704	5291519	7999570	6419445	17729774	11700960
Average Total Receipts	9	3597	167	316	998	5708	9752	21892	51007	76689	163257	305688	1108111	2925240
Operating Costs/Operating Income (%)														
Cost of Operations	10	62.2	64.1	48.8	45.9	62.2	64.3	67.7	65.1	61.9	65.5	60.7	69.7	50.9
Salaries and Wages	11	10.3	8.5	15.3	11.8	9.6	11.9	8.7	10.0	10.3	9.7	12.7	7.1	13.3
Taxes Paid	12	1.9	1.2	3.1	3.0	2.2	1.9	1.9	1.8	2.1	1.8	1.9	1.2	1.8
Interest Paid	13	3.0	5.5	1.4	1.5	0.9	1.8	1.1	1.3	1.8	2.8	3.7	3.6	7.8
Depreciation	14	2.6	2.9	1.3	1.2	1.6	2.4	2.4	2.1	3.1	2.9	2.8	2.6	4.1
Amortization and Depletion	15	1.0	4.9	0.5	0.5	0.2	0.4	0.5	0.6	0.9	1.0	1.5	1.1	2.6
Pensions and Other Deferred Comp.	16	0.6	0.3	0.3	0.1	0.4	0.3	0.4	0.3	0.7	0.3	0.8	0.7	1.5
Employee Benefits	17	1.8	0.7	2.0	2.0	1.3	2.4	2.0	1.5	1.9	1.7	2.5	2.0	1.6
Advertising	18	1.9	6.1	2.3	2.6	1.0	0.8	0.9	2.3	2.7	3.0	1.0	1.1	3.7
Other Expenses	19	13.7	39.1	20.0	15.3	14.4	12.8	10.4	10.8	12.2	11.2	13.4	10.5	20.9
Officers' Compensation	20	2.5	1.8	10.5	8.7	5.3	2.5	2.5	1.8	2.5	1.1	0.8	0.7	0.1
Operating Margin	21	•	•	•	7.4	0.9	•	1.4	2.4	•	•	•	•	•
Operating Margin Before Officers' Comp.	22	1.1	•	5.1	16.1	6.2	1.0	3.8	4.2	2.3	0.2	0.6	•	•

Selected Average Balance Sheet ($ in Thousands)

Net Receivables 23	479	0	21	101	672	1532	3519	6605	12404	22200	53279	119908	481029
Inventories 24	536	0	25	226	818	2901	4805	8199	13704	31662	51525	101609	373864
Net Property, Plant and Equipment 25	463	0	18	93	412	1361	2625	7234	11920	27892	59538	141364	402982
Total Assets 26	3066	0	100	647	2553	7100	15714	34986	67480	163194	348930	1044997	3722692
Notes and Loans Payable 27	1212	0	79	263	1111	2811	4472	9338	21756	54232	147610	418533	1656925
All Other Liabilities 28	958	0	45	99	988	1648	3861	12308	21093	38634	92229	379533	1169196
Net Worth 29	896	0	-24	285	454	2641	7381	13340	24631	70328	109091	246931	896570

Selected Financial Ratios (Times to 1)

Current Ratio 30	1.6	•	1.1	2.8	1.6	1.8	1.9	1.7	1.9	1.7	2.1	1.4	1.5
Quick Ratio 31	0.8	•	0.6	1.3	0.9	0.8	0.9	0.8	1.1	0.8	1.1	0.8	0.8
Net Sales to Working Capital 32	6.4	•	69.3	4.4	8.0	4.0	4.5	5.8	4.3	5.4	3.7	12.2	5.7
Coverage Ratio 33	2.0	•	•	6.3	2.3	0.2	3.5	3.6	2.1	1.6	1.9	1.8	2.4
Total Asset Turnover 34	1.1	•	3.1	1.5	2.2	1.4	1.4	1.4	1.1	1.0	0.8	1.0	0.7
Inventory Turnover 35	4.0	•	6.0	2.0	4.3	2.2	3.0	4.0	3.4	3.3	3.4	7.4	3.4
Receivables Turnover 36	6.8	•	14.5	6.8	8.5	5.5	5.6	6.1	5.8	5.9	5.1	8.1	6.1
Total Liabilities to Net Worth 37	2.4	•	•	1.3	4.6	1.7	1.1	1.6	1.7	1.3	2.2	3.2	3.2
Current Assets to Working Capital 38	2.6	•	14.3	1.6	2.7	2.2	2.1	2.5	2.1	2.5	1.9	3.6	3.0
Current Liabilities to Working Capital 39	1.6	•	13.3	0.6	1.7	1.2	1.1	1.5	1.1	1.5	0.9	2.6	2.0
Working Capital to Net Sales 40	0.2	•	0.0	0.2	0.1	0.2	0.2	0.2	0.2	0.2	0.3	0.1	0.2
Inventory to Working Capital 41	0.9	•	5.4	0.8	1.1	1.2	0.9	0.9	0.7	0.9	0.6	1.0	1.1
Total Receipts to Cash Flow 42	7.7	•	10.1	5.8	8.9	12.7	9.7	8.2	8.5	10.1	7.1	8.8	3.9
Cost of Goods to Cash Flow 43	4.8	•	4.9	2.6	5.5	8.2	6.6	5.3	5.3	6.6	4.3	6.1	2.0
Cash Flow to Total Debt 44	0.2	•	0.2	0.5	0.3	0.2	0.3	0.3	0.2	0.2	0.2	0.2	0.2

Selected Financial Factors (in Percentages)

Debt Ratio 45	70.8	•	123.4	55.9	82.2	62.8	53.0	61.9	63.5	56.9	68.7	76.4	75.9
Return on Total Assets 46	6.6	•	•	14.2	4.8	0.6	5.3	6.9	4.3	4.3	5.8	6.8	12.4
Return on Equity Before Income Taxes 47	11.2	•	51.0	27.1	15.4	•	8.1	13.0	6.3	3.6	8.8	13.1	30.1
Return on Equity After Income Taxes 48	7.1	•	51.7	26.4	13.7	•	6.7	11.7	3.2	2.5	7.2	6.7	19.7
Profit Margin (Before Income Tax) 49	2.9	•	•	7.8	1.2	•	2.8	3.4	2.1	1.6	3.3	3.0	10.9
Profit Margin (After Income Tax) 50	1.8	•	•	7.6	1.1	•	2.3	3.1	1.0	1.1	2.7	1.5	7.1

Table II
Corporations with Net Income

OTHER MISCELLANEOUS MANUFACTURING

MONEY AMOUNTS AND SIZE OF ASSETS IN THOUSANDS OF DOLLARS

Item Description for Accounting Period 7/09 Through 6/10	Total	Zero Assets	Under 500	500 to 1,000	1,000 to 5,000	5,000 to 10,000	10,000 to 25,000	25,000 to 50,000	50,000 to 100,000	100,000 to 250,000	250,000 to 500,000	500,000 to 2,500,000	2,500,000 and over
Number of Enterprises 1	10371	379	7190	1230	1052	165	182	76	42	29	12	11	4
Revenues ($ in Thousands)													
Net Sales 2	53128033	181455	3415121	1164108	7051827	2097889	4445362	4032020	3824442	5112755	4176757	7733800	9892498
Interest 3	485463	423	125	312	1879	570	2000	1398	10433	3996	29246	41220	393861
Rents 4	17241	0	0	2461	959	547	919	729	194	2883	6406	1472	670
Royalties 5	909021	650	100	0	2	0	1548	9530	2083	28372	25328	72217	769189
Other Portfolio Income 6	309023	15648	20825	228	1858	110	10372	2061	12436	17975	19225	164879	43404
Other Receipts 7	990205	457	40179	1514	26506	1873	60786	27536	48663	60814	90934	29609	601338
Total Receipts 8	55838986	198633	3476350	1168623	7083031	2100989	4520987	4073274	3898251	5226795	4347896	8043197	11700960
Average Total Receipts 9	5384	524	483	950	6733	12733	24841	53596	92816	180234	362325	731200	2925240
Operating Costs/Operating Income (%)													
Cost of Operations 10	56.5	61.0	48.6	44.1	62.0	57.0	67.4	63.4	59.5	64.7	54.4	48.3	50.9
Salaries and Wages 11	11.0	8.0	13.5	10.7	8.9	12.2	7.9	9.2	9.3	8.9	14.1	11.7	13.3
Taxes Paid 12	2.0	1.4	2.4	3.0	2.2	1.8	1.7	1.8	2.2	2.0	1.8	2.1	1.8
Interest Paid 13	2.9	1.0	0.8	1.4	0.6	1.0	0.9	0.7	1.0	1.5	3.3	4.2	7.8
Depreciation 14	2.8	2.7	1.1	1.0	1.5	2.8	2.1	1.9	2.9	2.9	3.0	4.1	4.1
Amortization and Depletion 15	1.0	1.7	0.4	0.4	0.1	0.1	0.3	0.2	0.3	0.5	1.0	1.7	2.6
Pensions and Other Deferred Comp. 16	0.8	0.6	0.4	0.2	0.4	0.4	0.3	0.3	0.7	0.4	0.9	1.3	1.5
Employee Benefits 17	1.9	0.7	1.9	1.6	1.3	2.6	1.5	1.4	2.0	1.6	2.8	3.1	1.6
Advertising 18	1.9	1.4	1.9	2.8	1.1	0.8	1.0	1.9	2.8	2.4	1.2	1.0	3.7
Other Expenses 19	13.5	12.6	13.5	14.5	10.2	10.5	9.5	10.3	10.2	9.6	14.5	15.6	20.9
Officers' Compensation 20	2.6	3.3	9.9	9.2	5.5	2.7	2.2	2.1	2.7	1.0	0.7	1.3	0.1
Operating Margin 21	3.1	5.6	5.7	11.2	6.3	8.1	5.2	6.8	6.3	4.4	2.5	5.5	•
Operating Margin Before Officers' Comp. 22	5.7	8.9	15.6	20.3	11.9	10.8	7.4	8.8	9.1	5.4	3.3	6.8	•

Selected Average Balance Sheet ($ in Thousands)

Net Receivables 23	747	0	37	100	663	2140	3764	6745	13479	23949	59235	110350	481029
Inventories 24	785	0	29	174	885	2675	4816	7523	14764	35680	57584	94656	458082
Net Property, Plant and Equipment 25	743	0	28	92	422	1937	2541	6669	13174	33564	73557	148467	402982
Total Assets 26	4831	0	136	636	2693	7549	15804	34827	67632	171894	369686	1053562	3722692
Notes and Loans Payable 27	1726	0	61	247	983	1972	3934	6501	14414	45893	126265	410012	1656925
All Other Liabilities 28	1370	0	46	62	787	1776	3762	11228	18449	38016	103532	304801	1169196
Net Worth 29	1734	0	29	327	923	3801	8109	17098	34768	87985	139889	338748	896570

Selected Financial Ratios (Times to 1)

Current Ratio 30	1.9	•	1.9	4.0	2.2	1.6	2.0	2.0	2.3	2.0	2.6	1.8	1.5
Quick Ratio 31	1.0	•	1.2	1.9	1.2	0.9	1.0	0.9	1.3	1.0	1.2	1.1	0.8
Net Sales to Working Capital 32	5.0	•	11.3	3.6	5.9	6.8	4.6	4.7	4.2	4.4	3.4	4.9	5.7
Coverage Ratio 33	4.0	16.1	9.9	9.4	12.6	9.3	8.4	11.7	9.1	5.5	3.2	3.4	2.4
Total Asset Turnover 34	1.1	•	3.5	1.5	2.5	1.7	1.5	1.5	1.3	1.0	0.9	0.7	0.7
Inventory Turnover 35	3.7	•	8.0	2.4	4.7	2.7	3.4	4.5	3.7	3.2	3.3	3.6	2.8
Receivables Turnover 36	6.5	•	14.1	6.9	8.8	5.3	6.1	•	6.9	6.1	5.1	5.2	•
Total Liabilities to Net Worth 37	1.8	•	3.7	0.9	1.9	1.0	0.9	1.0	0.9	1.0	1.6	2.1	3.2
Current Assets to Working Capital 38	2.1	•	2.1	1.3	1.8	2.8	2.0	2.0	1.8	2.0	1.6	2.2	3.0
Current Liabilities to Working Capital 39	1.1	•	1.1	0.3	0.8	1.8	1.0	1.0	0.8	1.0	0.6	1.2	2.0
Working Capital to Net Sales 40	0.2	•	0.1	0.3	0.2	0.1	0.2	0.2	0.2	0.2	0.3	0.2	0.2
Inventory to Working Capital 41	0.7	•	0.8	0.6	0.7	1.1	0.8	0.7	0.6	0.7	0.5	0.5	1.1
Total Receipts to Cash Flow 42	5.4	3.9	6.0	4.8	7.1	6.6	7.4	6.2	6.2	7.2	5.3	4.6	3.9
Cost of Goods to Cash Flow 43	3.1	2.4	2.9	2.1	4.4	3.8	5.0	3.9	3.7	4.6	2.9	2.2	2.0
Cash Flow to Total Debt 44	0.3	•	0.7	0.6	0.5	0.5	0.4	0.5	0.4	0.3	0.2	0.2	0.2

Selected Financial Factors (in Percentages)

Debt Ratio 45	64.1	•	78.9	48.5	65.7	49.7	48.7	50.9	48.6	48.8	62.2	67.8	75.9
Return on Total Assets 46	12.1	•	29.1	19.2	18.3	15.6	12.2	13.0	12.5	8.6	9.9	9.6	12.4
Return on Equity Before Income Taxes 47	25.2	•	124.0	33.4	49.2	27.7	21.0	24.2	21.7	13.8	17.9	21.2	30.1
Return on Equity After Income Taxes 48	20.6	•	122.7	32.7	47.8	26.4	18.9	22.7	18.1	12.3	15.6	14.4	19.7
Profit Margin (Before Income Tax) 49	8.5	15.1	7.5	11.6	6.8	8.3	7.0	7.8	8.3	6.9	7.2	10.2	10.9
Profit Margin (After Income Tax) 50	7.0	14.2	7.4	11.3	6.6	7.9	6.3	7.3	6.9	6.1	6.3	7.0	7.1

Table I
Corporations with and without Net Income

MOTOR VEHICLE AND MOTOR VEHICLE PARTS AND SUPPLIES

MONEY AMOUNTS AND SIZE OF ASSETS IN THOUSANDS OF DOLLARS

Item Description for Accounting Period 7/09 Through 6/10	Total	Zero Assets	Under 500	500 to 1,000	1,000 to 5,000	5,000 to 10,000	10,000 to 25,000	25,000 to 50,000	50,000 to 100,000	100,000 to 250,000	250,000 to 500,000	500,000 to 2,500,000	2,500,000 and over
Number of Enterprises 1	17153	1015	10615	2093	2513	388	301	122	41	26	15	17	7
Revenues ($ in Thousands)													
Net Sales 2	226050426	745796	7327043	5473646	15034300	5281257	10692996	8712910	5628639	5926157	13741971	37460847	110024865
Interest 3	2103640	30	176	1255	11839	4963	9501	2573	4825	10133	14733	203721	1839891
Rents 4	729047	0	489	2380	2536	1381	1155	6243	1339	4373	4662	47806	656684
Royalties 5	54269	0	0	0	1201	0	0	73	45	3	6017	12080	34850
Other Portfolio Income 6	1694758	45	2251	1031	20101	6800	33197	18052	49976	36015	18472	264563	1244254
Other Receipts 7	2155783	2	19757	24407	64059	22562	116915	63316	49550	112318	271127	120332	1291439
Total Receipts 8	232787923	745873	7349716	5502719	15134036	5316963	10853764	8803167	5734374	6088999	14056982	38109349	115091983
Average Total Receipts 9	13571	735	692	2629	6022	13704	36059	72157	139863	234192	937132	2241726	16441712
Operating Costs/Operating Income (%)													
Cost of Operations 10	82.4	96.8	80.9	83.3	79.5	76.0	80.1	77.9	78.0	77.9	87.0	88.3	81.5
Salaries and Wages 11	4.4	2.3	5.9	5.2	6.0	7.5	7.5	7.4	7.5	7.7	3.5	4.0	3.2
Taxes Paid 12	0.7	0.3	1.2	1.0	1.2	1.4	1.2	1.2	1.2	1.4	0.5	0.7	0.4
Interest Paid 13	1.4	0.3	0.6	0.4	0.5	0.9	0.7	1.0	1.1	1.1	1.0	1.0	1.9
Depreciation 14	4.7	0.4	0.3	0.6	0.4	0.6	1.1	1.2	1.5	1.9	1.0	2.5	8.2
Amortization and Depletion 15	0.1	0.4	0.1	0.1	0.0	0.0	0.1	0.2	0.3	0.4	0.2	0.2	0.1
Pensions and Other Deferred Comp. 16	0.3	0.0	0.1	0.0	0.1	0.3	0.1	0.2	0.1	0.3	0.1	0.1	0.4
Employee Benefits 17	0.5	0.1	0.4	0.5	0.7	0.7	0.9	0.9	0.7	1.0	0.6	0.5	0.5
Advertising 18	2.7	0.1	0.2	0.3	0.5	0.6	0.4	0.5	0.4	0.8	1.7	2.1	4.4
Other Expenses 19	6.2	8.3	8.9	6.4	7.9	7.2	6.5	7.0	8.9	7.6	4.5	5.6	5.9
Officers' Compensation 20	0.6	0.0	3.1	2.2	2.3	2.1	1.2	1.4	1.0	0.7	0.5	0.2	0.1
Operating Margin 21	•	•	•	•	0.9	2.6	0.3	1.3	•	•	•	•	•
Operating Margin Before Officers' Comp. 22	•	•	1.4	2.2	3.2	4.8	1.5	2.7	0.2	0.1	0.5	•	•

Selected Average Balance Sheet ($ in Thousands)

Net Receivables 23	3043	0	31	86	605	1399	3835	8077	11651	32070	67166	294627	5736409
Inventories 24	1737	0	49	304	751	3641	6841	15106	27499	51351	101978	387426	1530798
Net Property, Plant and Equipment 25	2297	0	8	125	164	1090	1767	3557	11193	22239	51164	151449	4697242
Total Assets 26	9690	0	132	705	2086	6992	15206	34525	71674	158030	371443	1242809	16119787
Notes and Loans Payable 27	3381	0	74	258	474	2123	5146	12015	24884	52883	114547	417951	5775243
All Other Liabilities 28	4041	0	37	170	644	2226	4863	11452	21058	45848	145661	608221	6949988
Net Worth 29	2267	0	21	278	967	2644	5197	11059	25732	59299	111234	216637	3394556

Selected Financial Ratios (Times to 1)

Current Ratio 30	1.6	•	2.4	2.7	2.1	1.9	1.8	1.6	1.6	1.5	1.6	1.3	1.7
Quick Ratio 31	1.1	•	1.3	1.2	1.1	0.8	0.8	0.6	0.6	0.7	0.7	0.6	1.2
Net Sales to Working Capital 32	5.5	•	11.3	7.9	6.7	5.3	6.9	6.9	7.2	7.3	9.9	11.0	4.0
Coverage Ratio 33	0.2	•	•	2.2	4.5	4.7	3.7	3.4	2.0	2.8	2.7	•	•
Total Asset Turnover 34	1.4	•	5.2	3.7	2.9	1.9	2.3	2.1	1.9	1.4	2.5	1.8	1.0
Inventory Turnover 35	6.2	•	11.4	7.2	6.3	2.8	4.2	3.7	3.9	3.5	7.8	5.0	8.4
Receivables Turnover 36	4.5	•	24.6	21.8	•	7.8	8.7	8.5	9.3	7.9	16.1	7.8	2.9
Total Liabilities to Net Worth 37	3.3	•	5.4	1.5	1.2	1.6	1.9	2.1	1.8	1.7	2.3	4.7	3.7
Current Assets to Working Capital 38	2.6	•	1.7	1.6	1.9	2.1	2.3	2.6	2.6	3.1	2.6	4.1	2.5
Current Liabilities to Working Capital 39	1.6	•	0.7	0.6	0.9	1.1	1.3	1.6	1.6	2.1	1.6	3.1	1.5
Working Capital to Net Sales 40	0.2	•	0.1	0.1	0.2	0.2	0.1	0.1	0.1	0.1	0.1	0.1	0.3
Inventory to Working Capital 41	0.6	•	0.7	0.9	0.8	1.1	1.2	1.5	1.4	1.5	1.2	1.8	0.3
Total Receipts to Cash Flow 42	25.8	•	20.3	19.5	14.9	12.1	15.7	13.6	13.6	13.5	19.3	168.6	30.8
Cost of Goods to Cash Flow 43	21.3	•	16.4	16.3	11.9	9.2	12.6	10.6	10.6	10.5	16.8	148.9	25.1
Cash Flow to Total Debt 44	0.1	•	0.3	0.3	0.4	0.3	0.2	0.2	0.2	0.2	0.2	0.0	0.0

Selected Financial Factors (in Percentages)

Debt Ratio 45	76.6	•	84.3	60.6	53.6	62.2	65.8	68.0	64.1	62.5	70.1	82.6	78.9
Return on Total Assets 46	0.4	•	•	3.5	6.0	8.1	5.8	6.7	4.1	4.6	6.8	•	•
Return on Equity Before Income Taxes 47	•	•	•	4.7	10.1	17.0	12.4	14.6	5.6	7.9	14.5	•	•
Return on Equity After Income Taxes 48	•	•	•	4.4	8.5	15.4	10.4	12.9	4.2	5.9	12.3	•	•
Profit Margin (Before Income Tax) 49	•	•	•	0.5	1.6	3.3	1.8	2.3	1.0	2.1	1.8	•	•
Profit Margin (After Income Tax) 50	•	•	•	0.5	1.4	3.0	1.5	2.0	0.8	1.5	1.5	•	•

MOTOR VEHICLE AND MOTOR VEHICLE PARTS AND SUPPLIES

Table II
Corporations with Net Income

MONEY AMOUNTS AND SIZE OF ASSETS IN THOUSANDS OF DOLLARS

Item Description for Accounting Period 7/09 Through 6/10	Total	Zero Assets	Under 500	500 to 1,000	1,000 to 5,000	5,000 to 10,000	10,000 to 25,000	25,000 to 50,000	50,000 to 100,000	100,000 to 250,000	250,000 to 500,000	500,000 to 2,500,000	2,500,000 and over
Number of Enterprises 1	9579	259	5543	1247	1780	356	229	100	30	17	9	7	3
Revenues ($ in Thousands)													
Net Sales 2	96862001	118454	3267024	4038986	12195479	4991931	8504006	7533398	4210079	4160102	11101270	17613692	19127579
Interest 3	537150	18	126	957	8458	4791	6960	1723	2540	9285	5309	27834	469149
Rents 4	399935	0	0	0	1616	1381	1138	1543	1339	4166	4260	25206	359287
Royalties 5	43070	0	0	0	0	0	0	73	0	3	6001	3095	33899
Other Portfolio Income 6	169871	45	93	284	16863	6688	19865	7687	3609	30251	5954	19488	59045
Other Receipts 7	1237663	0	17223	1232	57152	22115	69130	53540	27190	102955	239073	121815	526236
Total Receipts 8	99249690	118517	3284466	4041459	12279568	5026906	8601099	7597964	4244757	4306762	11361867	17811130	20575195
Average Total Receipts 9	10361	458	593	3241	6899	14121	37559	75980	141492	253339	1262430	2544447	6858398
Operating Costs/Operating Income (%)													
Cost of Operations 10	81.0	75.4	77.4	85.3	80.6	75.5	79.4	77.5	77.2	76.0	88.2	89.6	74.4
Salaries and Wages 11	6.4	6.7	5.9	4.1	5.1	7.6	7.2	7.5	7.6	8.5	3.1	2.8	11.3
Taxes Paid 12	1.0	1.0	1.1	0.6	1.1	1.3	1.1	1.2	1.1	1.6	0.5	0.6	1.1
Interest Paid 13	0.9	0.2	0.3	0.4	0.4	0.8	0.6	0.8	0.7	0.6	0.3	0.7	2.4
Depreciation 14	1.0	0.8	0.3	0.5	0.4	0.6	0.9	1.1	1.1	0.8	0.8	0.6	2.3
Amortization and Depletion 15	0.2	0.1	0.1	0.0	0.0	0.0	0.0	0.1	0.2	0.4	0.1	0.2	0.4
Pensions and Other Deferred Comp. 16	0.2	•	0.1	0.0	0.1	0.3	0.1	0.2	0.1	0.3	0.1	0.1	0.6
Employee Benefits 17	0.6	0.0	0.3	0.1	0.4	0.7	0.9	0.9	0.6	0.7	0.5	0.3	1.1
Advertising 18	0.9	0.6	0.1	0.2	0.5	0.6	0.3	0.4	0.4	1.0	1.7	2.2	0.6
Other Expenses 19	5.8	9.6	8.9	4.9	6.6	6.9	5.8	6.7	7.8	7.6	3.6	2.3	7.9
Officers' Compensation 20	1.0	•	3.2	1.7	2.0	2.2	1.2	1.4	1.1	0.9	0.5	0.2	0.3
Operating Margin 21	1.0	5.6	2.3	2.0	2.7	3.5	2.4	2.2	2.2	1.6	0.7	0.6	•
Operating Margin Before Officers' Comp. 22	2.0	5.6	5.5	3.8	4.6	5.7	3.7	3.6	3.3	2.5	1.2	0.8	•

Selected Average Balance Sheet ($ in Thousands)

Net Receivables 23	1593	0	28	57	649	1378	4175	8029	12300	26837	76742	349932	2553374
Inventories 24	1570	0	52	335	760	3188	6869	13223	26027	52107	129065	711294	683566
Net Property, Plant and Equipment 25	666	0	7	164	153	1138	1503	3509	9440	14254	58752	114313	968855
Total Assets 26	5301	0	102	715	2191	6926	15281	33851	69935	150933	389680	1139498	6640365
Notes and Loans Payable 27	1759	0	34	316	378	2039	4775	10716	15472	37930	80971	357007	2789780
All Other Liabilities 28	1753	0	32	112	628	2100	4600	10942	22275	34894	153427	522625	2052778
Net Worth 29	1789	0	36	287	1185	2788	5906	12193	32187	78109	155281	259867	1797807

Selected Financial Ratios (Times to 1)

Current Ratio 30	1.5	•	2.1	4.7	2.3	2.1	1.9	1.7	1.7	2.0	1.9	1.3	1.1
Quick Ratio 31	0.8	•	1.2	2.4	1.3	0.9	0.9	0.7	0.7	0.8	0.9	0.7	0.8
Net Sales to Working Capital 32	8.9	•	13.5	8.4	6.5	5.1	6.1	7.2	7.1	4.7	9.6	12.7	22.6
Coverage Ratio 33	4.7	30.5	9.1	5.7	8.8	6.3	6.9	4.9	5.2	9.9	10.0	3.5	3.1
Total Asset Turnover 34	1.9	•	5.8	4.5	3.1	2.0	2.4	2.2	2.0	1.6	3.2	2.2	1.0
Inventory Turnover 35	5.2	•	8.7	8.2	7.3	3.3	4.3	4.4	4.2	3.6	8.4	3.2	6.9
Receivables Turnover 36	7.7	•	22.2	22.5	•	8.5	8.5	9.8	9.7	9.7	19.4	5.0	5.0
Total Liabilities to Net Worth 37	2.0	•	1.8	1.5	0.8	1.5	1.6	1.8	1.2	0.9	1.5	3.4	2.7
Current Assets to Working Capital 38	3.2	•	1.9	1.3	1.7	1.9	2.1	2.5	2.5	2.0	2.1	4.1	13.7
Current Liabilities to Working Capital 39	2.2	•	0.9	0.3	0.7	0.9	1.1	1.5	1.5	1.0	1.1	3.1	12.7
Working Capital to Net Sales 40	0.1	•	0.1	0.1	0.2	0.2	0.2	0.1	0.1	0.2	0.1	0.1	0.0
Inventory to Working Capital 41	1.2	•	0.8	0.6	0.7	1.0	1.1	1.4	1.3	1.0	1.0	1.6	2.4
Total Receipts to Cash Flow 42	13.2	7.7	11.5	18.5	12.5	11.2	13.2	12.8	11.7	9.4	17.7	30.7	8.8
Cost of Goods to Cash Flow 43	10.7	5.8	8.9	15.7	10.1	8.5	10.5	9.9	9.0	7.2	15.6	27.5	6.6
Cash Flow to Total Debt 44	0.2	•	0.8	0.4	0.5	0.3	0.3	0.3	0.3	0.4	0.3	0.1	0.1

Selected Financial Factors (in Percentages)

Debt Ratio 45	66.3	•	64.7	59.9	45.9	59.8	61.3	64.0	54.0	48.2	60.2	77.2	72.9
Return on Total Assets 46	8.3	•	18.1	11.5	12.2	10.2	10.1	8.6	7.6	9.1	10.8	5.2	7.3
Return on Equity Before Income Taxes 47	19.4	•	45.7	23.7	20.0	21.4	22.5	19.1	13.3	15.8	24.4	16.4	18.4
Return on Equity After Income Taxes 48	15.9	•	43.7	23.1	18.1	19.7	20.1	17.2	11.7	13.5	21.8	11.3	12.5
Profit Margin (Before Income Tax) 49	3.4	5.7	2.8	2.1	3.5	4.2	3.6	3.1	3.0	5.0	3.1	1.7	5.2
Profit Margin (After Income Tax) 50	2.8	4.2	2.7	2.0	3.1	3.9	3.2	2.8	2.7	4.3	2.7	1.2	3.5

Table I

Corporations with and without Net Income

LUMBER AND OTHER CONSTRUCTION MATERIALS

MONEY AMOUNTS AND SIZE OF ASSETS IN THOUSANDS OF DOLLARS

Item Description for Accounting Period 7/09 Through 6/10	Total	Zero Assets	Under 500	500 to 1,000	1,000 to 5,000	5,000 to 10,000	10,000 to 25,000	25,000 to 50,000	50,000 to 100,000	100,000 to 250,000	250,000 to 500,000	500,000 to 2,500,000	2,500,000 and over
Number of Enterprises **1**	17440	2660	8134	1193	4028	902	368	95	37	12	6	6	0
Revenues ($ in Thousands)													
Net Sales **2**	91710683	251187	5443483	2993645	27103840	15028757	13109255	7998849	5146437	3906576	2818469	7910184	0
Interest **3**	69427	611	1250	5421	15855	5486	13841	5034	5722	2777	8828	4602	0
Rents **4**	20806	545	12	1682	5955	3781	1928	2271	353	1103	1150	2028	0
Royalties **5**	1894	0	0	0	5	22	0	66	0	0	0	1801	0
Other Portfolio Income **6**	398455	1420	8020	1141	21923	11492	66919	5241	1592	1461	257486	21760	0
Other Receipts **7**	388445	37731	-78465	1796	154067	72916	93852	19865	32368	23658	19376	11280	0
Total Receipts **8**	92589710	291494	5374300	3003685	27301645	15122454	13285795	8031326	5186472	3935575	3105309	7951655	0
Average Total Receipts **9**	5309	110	661	2518	6778	16765	36103	84540	140175	327965	517552	1325276	•
Operating Costs/Operating Income (%)													
Cost of Operations **10**	77.6	72.2	65.7	70.8	75.6	82.1	79.5	81.1	79.2	81.6	68.8	80.5	•
Salaries and Wages **11**	7.7	7.9	4.9	5.7	8.3	6.4	8.5	6.6	8.3	6.9	12.7	8.5	•
Taxes Paid **12**	1.4	2.1	1.1	2.5	1.5	1.0	1.4	1.0	1.4	1.0	2.3	1.3	•
Interest Paid **13**	0.8	5.4	0.5	0.7	0.6	0.9	0.5	0.8	0.6	0.9	1.7	1.6	•
Depreciation **14**	1.2	0.6	0.6	1.1	0.9	0.9	1.4	1.0	1.1	1.1	1.1	3.3	•
Amortization and Depletion **15**	0.1	0.0	0.1	0.0	0.0	0.0	0.1	0.1	0.1	0.3	0.7	0.5	•
Pensions and Other Deferred Comp. **16**	0.3	0.1	0.6	0.2	0.3	0.2	0.2	0.1	0.1	0.2	0.3	0.5	•
Employee Benefits **17**	0.7	1.0	0.4	0.5	0.6	0.6	0.9	0.7	1.0	0.7	1.4	1.2	•
Advertising **18**	0.3	0.5	1.5	0.7	0.2	0.2	0.3	0.2	0.2	0.2	0.3	0.1	•
Other Expenses **19**	8.6	27.8	14.5	14.1	9.6	6.4	7.1	7.1	7.5	8.2	14.5	6.0	•
Officers' Compensation **20**	1.9	3.1	4.6	5.2	2.4	1.5	1.3	0.9	0.8	0.5	1.5	1.3	•
Operating Margin **21**	•	•	5.6	•	•	•	•	0.4	•	•	•	•	•
Operating Margin Before Officers' Comp. **22**	1.2	•	10.2	3.7	2.3	1.1	1.3	1.3	0.4	•	•	•	•

Selected Average Balance Sheet ($ in Thousands)

Net Receivables 23	571	0	27	155	779	1715	3679	8187	16320	31129	82932	212213	•
Inventories 24	651	0	35	149	700	2927	5014	11867	21732	53533	33118	133889	•
Net Property, Plant and Equipment 25	408	0	11	139	375	1074	2804	5556	10384	24580	76485	279256	•
Total Assets 26	2200	0	136	722	2383	7007	15234	34935	67896	124135	335365	923069	•
Notes and Loans Payable 27	682	0	62	290	775	2486	4178	13344	13638	42289	81438	229614	•
All Other Liabilities 28	610	0	65	185	718	1772	3173	8669	16701	40490	102481	281478	•
Net Worth 29	908	0	9	248	890	2749	7883	12922	37558	41356	151447	411977	•

Selected Financial Ratios (Times to 1)

Current Ratio 30	1.9	•	1.5	2.1	1.9	1.7	2.2	1.7	2.4	1.3	1.7	2.4	•
Quick Ratio 31	1.0	•	0.8	1.3	1.1	0.8	1.2	0.7	1.1	0.6	1.1	1.4	•
Net Sales to Working Capital 32	7.4	•	16.8	10.2	7.7	7.3	6.1	8.5	4.9	20.4	7.6	5.4	•
Coverage Ratio 33	1.3	0.1	8.9	•	1.9	1.2	1.0	1.9	1.6	•	4.0	•	•
Total Asset Turnover 34	2.4	•	4.9	3.5	2.8	2.4	2.3	2.4	2.0	2.6	1.4	1.4	•
Inventory Turnover 35	6.3	•	12.4	11.9	7.3	4.7	5.6	5.8	5.1	5.0	9.8	7.9	•
Receivables Turnover 36	8.3	•	24.1	13.2	8.9	8.0	7.7	10.1	6.7	6.5	7.7	5.6	•
Total Liabilities to Net Worth 37	1.4	•	13.5	1.9	1.7	1.5	0.9	1.7	0.8	2.0	1.2	1.2	•
Current Assets to Working Capital 38	2.1	•	2.9	1.9	2.1	2.3	1.8	2.4	1.7	4.5	2.4	1.7	•
Current Liabilities to Working Capital 39	1.1	•	1.9	0.9	1.1	1.3	0.8	1.4	0.7	3.5	1.4	0.7	•
Working Capital to Net Sales 40	0.1	•	0.1	0.1	0.1	0.1	0.2	0.1	0.2	0.0	0.1	0.2	•
Inventory to Working Capital 41	0.8	•	1.0	0.6	0.8	1.1	0.7	1.1	0.7	2.2	0.7	0.5	•
Total Receipts to Cash Flow 42	16.1	5.1	6.6	10.7	14.4	20.9	22.5	17.8	19.4	20.4	6.4	2360.5	•
Cost of Goods to Cash Flow 43	12.5	3.7	4.4	7.5	10.9	17.2	17.8	14.4	15.3	16.6	4.4	1899.1	•
Cash Flow to Total Debt 44	0.3	0.8	0.5	0.3	0.3	0.2	0.2	0.2	0.2	0.2	0.4	0.0	•

Selected Financial Factors (in Percentages)

Debt Ratio 45	58.7	•	93.1	65.7	62.7	60.8	48.3	63.0	44.7	66.7	54.8	55.4	•
Return on Total Assets 46	2.6	•	24.1	•	3.4	2.6	1.2	3.9	1.9	•	9.4	•	•
Return on Equity Before Income Taxes 47	1.6	•	310.1	•	4.4	1.3	•	5.1	1.2	•	15.7	•	•
Return on Equity After Income Taxes 48	0.3	•	307.1	•	3.9	0.6	•	2.0	1.1	•	9.2	•	•
Profit Margin (Before Income Tax) 49	0.3	•	4.3	•	0.6	0.2	•	0.8	0.3	•	5.1	•	•
Profit Margin (After Income Tax) 50	0.1	•	4.3	•	0.5	0.1	•	0.3	0.3	•	3.0	•	•

Table II

Corporations with Net Income

LUMBER AND OTHER CONSTRUCTION MATERIALS

Money Amounts and Size of Assets in Thousands of Dollars

Item Description for Accounting Period 7/09 Through 6/10		Total	Zero Assets	Under 500	500 to 1,000	1,000 to 5,000	5,000 to 10,000	10,000 to 25,000	25,000 to 50,000	50,000 to 100,000	100,000 to 250,000	250,000 to 500,000	500,000 to 2,500,000	2,500,000 and over
Number of Enterprises	1	9202	809	4475	846	2140	644	203	59	•	4	•	0	0
Revenues ($ in Thousands)														
Net Sales	2	57660265	147126	3366247	1736272	17964870	12036312	7972695	5748760	•	1067166	•	0	0
Interest	3	27261	64	730	2096	12403	3741	4340	727	•	296	•	0	0
Rents	4	11131	0	1	1682	3463	3510	1366	76	•	0	•	0	0
Royalties	5	0	0	0	0	0	0	0	0	•	0	•	0	0
Other Portfolio Income	6	353818	1400	7755	118	15245	8568	58432	3837	•	105	•	0	0
Other Receipts	7	148974	27361	-82018	1224	55885	59442	37378	27471	•	1668	•	0	0
Total Receipts	8	58201449	175951	3292715	1741392	18051866	12111573	8074211	5780871	•	1069235	•	0	0
Average Total Receipts	9	6325	217	736	2058	8435	18807	39774	97981	•	267309	•	•	•
Operating Costs/Operating Income (%)														
Cost of Operations	10	76.8	64.6	54.5	62.5	75.0	82.8	80.8	81.8	•	74.9	•	•	•
Salaries and Wages	11	6.8	6.8	4.6	8.6	7.4	5.7	7.0	5.9	•	7.8	•	•	•
Taxes Paid	12	1.2	2.2	1.1	3.9	1.2	0.8	1.0	0.9	•	1.2	•	•	•
Interest Paid	13	0.6	1.1	0.4	0.8	0.4	0.7	0.4	0.6	•	0.6	•	•	•
Depreciation	14	0.8	0.5	0.5	1.6	0.8	0.6	1.1	0.7	•	0.7	•	•	•
Amortization and Depletion	15	0.1	0.1	0.0	0.0	0.0	0.0	0.1	0.1	•	0.7	•	•	•
Pensions and Other Deferred Comp.	16	0.3	•	0.7	0.3	0.3	0.2	0.2	0.1	•	0.4	•	•	•
Employee Benefits	17	0.6	0.4	0.5	0.7	0.4	0.5	0.7	0.6	•	0.5	•	•	•
Advertising	18	0.3	0.0	1.8	1.1	0.2	0.2	0.2	0.2	•	0.3	•	•	•
Other Expenses	19	7.2	15.9	16.7	10.7	7.6	4.9	5.5	5.7	•	9.7	•	•	•
Officers' Compensation	20	1.9	3.9	5.3	7.9	2.2	1.5	1.2	1.0	•	0.8	•	•	•
Operating Margin	21	3.4	4.6	14.0	1.9	4.4	2.2	1.8	2.4	•	2.4	•	•	•
Operating Margin Before Officers' Comp.	22	5.3	8.5	19.3	9.8	6.6	3.6	3.0	3.4	•	3.3	•	•	•

Selected Average Balance Sheet ($ in Thousands)

Net Receivables 23	638	0	14	168	824	1872	3887	8942	33539
Inventories 24	757	0	15	113	821	2938	5924	12009	65847
Net Property, Plant and Equipment 25	314	0	15	175	323	860	2174	3986	9556
Total Assets 26	2168	0	109	731	2388	7220	14610	34921	113343
Notes and Loans Payable 27	614	0	47	237	604	2502	3533	11592	22551
All Other Liabilities 28	523	0	28	178	690	1378	2801	7256	28081
Net Worth 29	1030	0	34	315	1094	3340	8275	16072	62711

Selected Financial Ratios (Times to 1)

Current Ratio 30	2.2	•	2.2	2.3	2.1	2.0	2.5	1.9	1.8
Quick Ratio 31	1.2	•	1.6	1.5	1.4	0.9	1.4	0.7	1.0
Net Sales to Working Capital 32	7.0	•	15.5	7.3	8.2	6.5	5.9	7.7	8.6
Coverage Ratio 33	8.6	23.3	30.6	3.7	12.7	4.9	9.3	5.7	5.7
Total Asset Turnover 34	2.9	•	6.9	2.8	3.5	2.6	2.7	2.8	2.4
Inventory Turnover 35	6.4	•	27.8	11.3	7.7	5.3	5.4	6.6	3.0
Receivables Turnover 36	8.1	•	66.9	11.5	9.0	8.6	7.3	•	3.2
Total Liabilities to Net Worth 37	1.1	•	2.2	1.3	1.2	1.2	0.8	1.2	0.8
Current Assets to Working Capital 38	1.8	•	1.8	1.8	1.9	2.0	1.7	2.1	2.2
Current Liabilities to Working Capital 39	0.8	•	0.8	0.8	0.9	1.0	0.7	1.1	1.2
Working Capital to Net Sales 40	0.1	•	0.1	0.1	0.1	0.2	0.2	0.1	0.1
Inventory to Working Capital 41	0.7	•	0.4	0.5	0.6	0.9	0.6	1.0	1.0
Total Receipts to Cash Flow 42	10.7	2.6	4.2	10.3	9.9	16.1	15.5	14.9	12.0
Cost of Goods to Cash Flow 43	8.2	1.7	2.3	6.4	7.4	13.3	12.5	12.2	9.0
Cash Flow to Total Debt 44	0.5	•	2.4	0.5	0.7	0.3	0.4	0.3	0.4

Selected Financial Factors (in Percentages)

Debt Ratio 45	52.5	•	69.1	56.9	54.2	53.7	43.4	54.0	44.7
Return on Total Assets 46	14.2	•	84.4	8.5	18.7	9.0	9.3	10.3	7.5
Return on Equity Before Income Taxes 47	26.4	•	264.5	14.4	37.6	15.5	14.7	18.4	11.2
Return on Equity After Income Taxes 48	24.4	•	262.9	13.0	36.9	14.6	13.6	14.4	10.7
Profit Margin (Before Income Tax) 49	4.3	24.1	11.8	2.2	4.9	2.8	3.1	3.0	2.6
Profit Margin (After Income Tax) 50	4.0	23.7	11.7	2.0	4.8	2.6	2.9	2.4	2.5

Table I

Corporations with and without Net Income

PROFESSIONAL AND COMMERCIAL EQUIPMENT AND SUPPLIES

MONEY AMOUNTS AND SIZE OF ASSETS IN THOUSANDS OF DOLLARS

Item Description for Accounting Period 7/09 Through 6/10	Total	Zero Assets	Under 500	500 to 1,000	1,000 to 5,000	5,000 to 10,000	10,000 to 25,000	25,000 to 50,000	50,000 to 100,000	100,000 to 250,000	250,000 to 500,000	500,000 to 2,500,000	2,500,000 and over
Number of Enterprises 1	35634	5890	21404	2984	4128	501	384	158	65	59	27	24	10
Revenues ($ in Thousands)													
Net Sales 2	213514226	8931760	10381926	5793062	25822967	9798175	14374379	13173888	9563358	18033228	15969294	35987821	45684367
Interest 3	381153	188	3320	2332	5723	6665	4893	15852	8831	16346	25158	122186	169660
Rents 4	269471	0	33	411	2777	5310	548	402	17370	1855	64323	78540	97902
Royalties 5	450929	7	0	0	214	0	14016	363	0	14671	87311	130435	203912
Other Portfolio Income 6	298088	1468	5086	2035	22072	10762	5023	3589	19762	11802	42236	61009	113241
Other Receipts 7	1940047	71335	47436	68789	125556	61426	92063	67205	55843	133044	457506	451046	308801
Total Receipts 8	216853914	9004758	10437801	5866629	25979309	9882338	14490922	13261299	9665164	18210946	16645828	36831037	46577883
Average Total Receipts 9	6086	1529	488	1966	6293	19725	37737	83932	148695	308660	616512	1534627	4657788
Operating Costs/Operating Income (%)													
Cost of Operations 10	74.2	90.8	56.6	58.2	70.4	70.1	75.4	75.2	75.3	78.9	77.8	76.9	74.0
Salaries and Wages 11	9.4	3.0	10.4	13.0	10.5	11.5	9.2	9.6	8.8	7.8	10.1	9.3	9.4
Taxes Paid 12	1.2	0.3	2.0	2.0	1.5	1.3	1.1	1.1	1.1	0.8	1.1	1.0	1.1
Interest Paid 13	0.7	0.2	0.5	0.5	0.6	0.3	0.6	0.4	0.6	0.9	0.4	1.1	1.0
Depreciation 14	1.5	0.1	0.5	0.5	0.8	0.8	0.9	1.1	1.5	1.1	1.3	1.4	3.2
Amortization and Depletion 15	0.4	0.2	0.1	0.1	0.1	0.1	0.2	0.3	0.4	0.5	0.4	0.8	0.4
Pensions and Other Deferred Comp. 16	0.2	0.0	0.4	0.3	0.3	0.2	0.3	0.2	0.2	0.2	0.3	0.3	0.2
Employee Benefits 17	0.9	0.2	0.8	0.9	0.9	1.1	0.7	0.9	0.8	0.8	1.1	1.2	1.1
Advertising 18	0.8	0.1	1.0	1.2	0.7	0.6	0.9	0.6	0.6	0.8	1.3	0.9	0.8
Other Expenses 19	8.5	5.2	16.7	14.7	10.6	10.0	8.4	7.8	9.0	6.3	8.9	6.3	7.4
Officers' Compensation 20	1.5	0.5	7.8	4.8	3.2	3.0	1.6	1.4	0.7	0.6	0.6	0.3	0.3
Operating Margin 21	0.7	•	3.1	3.7	0.4	1.1	0.8	1.3	0.9	1.4	•	0.5	1.1
Operating Margin Before Officers' Comp. 22	2.2	•	10.9	8.5	3.5	4.1	2.4	2.7	1.7	2.0	•	0.9	1.4

Selected Average Balance Sheet ($ in Thousands)

Net Receivables 23	842	0	20	215	627	2473	5196	11920	23131	45557	96651	246688	851102
Inventories 24	508	0	23	174	539	1703	3857	6814	15528	28391	46361	142229	410039
Net Property, Plant and Equipment 25	259	0	13	55	311	582	1561	2866	6236	11801	26561	73556	258265
Total Assets 26	3472	0	108	694	2023	6824	14886	34812	72567	151118	357002	1159219	4523376
Notes and Loans Payable 27	877	0	57	249	773	1439	4244	6710	15287	36566	51800	315725	1055879
All Other Liabilities 28	1250	0	49	236	895	2920	7151	15083	26383	62066	144393	443220	1260975
Net Worth 29	1344	0	3	209	355	2465	3491	13019	30897	52486	160809	400274	2206521

Selected Financial Ratios (Times to 1)

Current Ratio 30	1.5	•	1.7	1.9	1.5	1.7	1.5	1.6	1.6	1.4	1.4	1.9	1.3
Quick Ratio 31	0.9	•	1.1	1.1	0.9	1.2	0.9	1.0	1.0	0.9	0.9	1.1	0.8
Net Sales to Working Capital 32	9.1	•	15.0	7.6	12.2	8.8	9.4	8.4	8.1	10.8	9.0	5.0	11.4
Coverage Ratio 33	4.2	2.6	8.4	10.9	2.6	8.0	3.7	5.5	4.5	3.9	3.4	3.9	4.1
Total Asset Turnover 34	1.7	•	4.5	2.8	3.1	2.9	2.5	2.4	2.0	2.0	1.7	1.3	1.0
Inventory Turnover 35	8.8	•	11.9	6.5	8.2	8.1	7.3	9.2	7.1	8.5	9.9	8.1	8.2
Receivables Turnover 36	7.3	•	23.6	9.8	10.0	7.1	7.3	7.0	6.5	6.4	7.8	6.4	5.4
Total Liabilities to Net Worth 37	1.6	•	36.1	2.3	4.7	1.8	3.3	1.7	1.3	1.9	1.2	1.9	1.1
Current Assets to Working Capital 38	2.9	•	2.5	2.2	3.0	2.5	2.9	2.6	2.7	3.4	3.3	2.1	4.5
Current Liabilities to Working Capital 39	1.9	•	1.5	1.2	2.0	1.5	1.9	1.6	1.7	2.4	2.3	1.1	3.5
Working Capital to Net Sales 40	0.1	•	0.1	0.1	0.1	0.1	0.1	0.1	0.1	0.1	0.1	0.2	0.1
Inventory to Working Capital 41	0.7	•	0.7	0.7	1.0	0.7	0.9	0.7	0.9	0.9	0.8	0.5	1.0
Total Receipts to Cash Flow 42	11.0	22.3	6.1	5.8	10.4	10.3	12.1	11.5	10.4	13.1	12.4	12.8	11.2
Cost of Goods to Cash Flow 43	8.2	20.2	3.5	3.4	7.3	7.2	9.2	8.7	7.8	10.3	9.6	9.9	8.3
Cash Flow to Total Debt 44	0.3	•	0.7	0.7	0.4	0.4	0.3	0.3	0.3	0.2	0.2	0.2	0.2

Selected Financial Factors (in Percentages)

Debt Ratio 45	61.3	•	97.3	69.8	82.4	63.9	76.5	62.6	57.4	65.3	55.0	65.5	51.2
Return on Total Assets 46	5.2	•	18.5	15.4	4.7	6.3	5.4	5.9	5.2	6.6	2.2	5.3	4.2
Return on Equity Before Income Taxes 47	10.3	•	604.8	46.4	16.4	15.1	17.0	12.8	9.5	14.2	3.4	11.5	6.5
Return on Equity After Income Taxes 48	7.4	•	592.9	45.5	14.0	13.0	12.8	10.2	7.1	11.0	1.1	7.6	3.9
Profit Margin (Before Income Tax) 49	2.3	0.2	3.6	5.0	0.9	1.9	1.6	2.0	2.0	2.4	0.9	3.1	3.2
Profit Margin (After Income Tax) 50	1.7	0.2	3.6	4.9	0.8	1.6	1.2	1.6	1.5	1.9	0.3	2.0	1.9

Table II
Corporations with Net Income

PROFESSIONAL AND COMMERCIAL EQUIPMENT AND SUPPLIES

MONEY AMOUNTS AND SIZE OF ASSETS IN THOUSANDS OF DOLLARS

Item Description for Accounting Period 7/09 Through 6/10		Total	Zero Assets	Under 500	500 to 1,000	1,000 to 5,000	5,000 to 10,000	10,000 to 25,000	25,000 to 50,000	50,000 to 100,000	100,000 to 250,000	250,000 to 500,000	500,000 to 2,500,000	2,500,000 and over
Number of Enterprises	1	23752	4169	13691	2112	2874	389	267	117	46	43	18	20	6
Revenues ($ in Thousands)														
Net Sales	2	159327511	8414752	7644652	4521129	17759926	8404017	11351256	11045972	7368233	14018339	9563219	32691147	26544869
Interest	3	223962	43	2938	906	3867	5603	3135	7805	4151	13871	19783	105534	56326
Rents	4	137091	0	33	0	1523	0	504	342	15876	1847	64206	49914	2845
Royalties	5	346920	0	0	0	214	0	14016	318	0	9765	19044	109553	194010
Other Portfolio Income	6	204259	1324	2911	1228	1615	2790	3911	3208	16136	9609	31912	33887	95727
Other Receipts	7	1350319	78040	41734	70386	97602	40722	52608	47746	42662	103709	195792	401200	178121
Total Receipts	8	161590062	8494159	7692268	4593649	17864747	8453132	11425430	11105391	7447058	14157140	9893956	33391235	27071898
Average Total Receipts	9	6803	2037	562	2175	6216	21730	42792	94918	161893	329236	549664	1669562	4511983
Operating Costs/Operating Income (%)														
Cost of Operations	10	75.1	92.9	57.6	55.8	65.3	69.9	76.7	76.2	76.5	78.3	77.8	78.5	77.8
Salaries and Wages	11	8.4	1.4	8.3	12.3	10.6	10.9	8.0	9.0	7.6	7.6	8.1	8.4	8.2
Taxes Paid	12	1.1	0.2	1.7	1.9	1.6	1.2	1.0	1.1	1.0	0.8	1.1	0.9	0.9
Interest Paid	13	0.6	0.1	0.2	0.3	0.6	0.1	0.5	0.4	0.5	0.6	0.4	0.9	0.8
Depreciation	14	1.1	0.4	0.4	0.4	0.7	0.7	0.8	0.7	1.4	1.1	1.3	1.3	1.9
Amortization and Depletion	15	0.3	0.1	0.0	0.2	0.2	0.0	0.1	0.2	0.4	0.3	0.4	0.5	0.3
Pensions and Other Deferred Comp.	16	0.3	0.0	0.4	0.3	0.4	0.2	0.3	0.2	0.2	0.2	0.3	0.3	0.2
Employee Benefits	17	0.8	0.1	0.7	0.7	0.9	1.0	0.6	0.8	0.7	0.8	0.9	0.9	0.7
Advertising	18	0.7	0.0	0.8	0.8	0.8	0.6	0.6	0.5	0.5	0.9	1.5	0.9	0.2
Other Expenses	19	7.2	3.3	13.3	15.2	11.4	9.2	6.6	6.5	7.4	6.0	8.0	5.5	4.6
Officers' Compensation	20	1.6	0.4	8.3	4.6	3.8	2.8	1.4	1.4	0.8	0.5	0.6	0.3	0.4
Operating Margin	21	3.1	1.2	8.2	7.4	3.6	3.3	3.5	3.1	3.1	2.8	•	1.6	4.1
Operating Margin Before Officers' Comp.	22	4.6	1.6	16.5	12.0	7.4	6.1	4.9	4.4	3.8	3.3	0.2	1.9	4.5

Selected Average Balance Sheet ($ in Thousands)

Net Receivables 23	939	0	13	213	670	2631	5883	12774	21143	48831	103265	227114	1029865
Inventories 24	535	0	21	184	488	1740	4073	7434	15137	32132	53216	137971	367266
Net Property, Plant and Equipment 25	261	0	9	57	316	474	1326	3135	6285	12267	28574	72682	226681
Total Assets 26	3578	0	103	711	2061	6800	14761	34421	70710	147977	345872	1153904	4434980
Notes and Loans Payable 27	676	0	27	143	574	966	3898	5724	14504	31245	54661	282356	502619
All Other Liabilities 28	1387	0	36	185	772	2773	6041	14451	24352	63407	157067	485146	1512517
Net Worth 29	1515	0	41	383	716	3062	4822	14245	31854	53325	134144	386402	2419844

Selected Financial Ratios (Times to 1)

Current Ratio 30	1.6	•	2.2	2.8	1.7	1.8	1.7	1.8	1.6	1.4	1.4	1.6	1.4
Quick Ratio 31	1.0	•	1.5	1.6	1.1	1.2	1.1	1.1	1.0	0.9	0.9	0.9	1.0
Net Sales to Working Capital 32	8.9	•	13.3	5.8	9.5	8.3	8.3	8.2	9.1	11.2	7.8	7.2	8.3
Coverage Ratio 33	8.9	19.7	37.7	30.8	8.0	28.7	9.9	10.3	9.4	7.4	8.8	5.2	9.3
Total Asset Turnover 34	1.9	•	5.4	3.0	3.0	3.2	2.9	2.7	2.3	2.2	1.5	1.4	1.0
Inventory Turnover 35	9.4	•	15.6	6.5	8.3	8.7	8.0	9.7	8.1	7.9	7.8	9.3	9.4
Receivables Turnover 36	7.5	•	34.0	11.1	9.0	7.7	7.6	7.4	7.9	6.3	6.0	7.4	4.9
Total Liabilities to Net Worth 37	1.4	•	1.5	0.9	1.9	1.2	2.1	1.4	1.2	1.8	1.6	2.0	0.8
Current Assets to Working Capital 38	2.8	•	1.9	1.6	2.4	2.2	2.4	2.3	2.6	3.4	3.3	2.6	3.8
Current Liabilities to Working Capital 39	1.8	•	0.9	0.6	1.4	1.2	1.4	1.3	1.6	2.4	2.3	1.6	2.8
Working Capital to Net Sales 40	0.1	•	0.1	0.2	0.1	0.1	0.1	0.1	0.1	0.1	0.1	0.1	0.1
Inventory to Working Capital 41	0.7	•	0.4	0.5	0.7	0.6	0.7	0.7	0.9	1.0	0.9	0.6	0.7
Total Receipts to Cash Flow 42	9.8	20.6	5.4	4.6	7.4	9.0	10.9	11.1	9.6	11.4	10.3	12.5	10.8
Cost of Goods to Cash Flow 43	7.4	19.1	3.1	2.6	4.9	6.3	8.4	8.5	7.4	8.9	8.0	9.8	8.4
Cash Flow to Total Debt 44	0.3	•	1.7	1.4	0.6	0.6	0.4	0.4	0.4	0.3	0.2	0.2	0.2

Selected Financial Factors (in Percentages)

Debt Ratio 45	57.7	•	60.5	46.1	65.3	55.0	67.3	58.6	55.0	64.0	61.2	66.5	45.4
Return on Total Assets 46	9.6	•	49.1	28.1	14.5	12.7	13.1	11.0	10.4	9.7	5.6	6.8	6.9
Return on Equity Before Income Taxes 47	20.2	•	121.0	50.4	36.5	27.2	36.2	23.9	20.7	23.4	12.8	16.3	11.4
Return on Equity After Income Taxes 48	16.3	•	119.6	49.7	34.8	25.0	31.9	20.7	17.4	19.1	8.7	11.5	7.4
Profit Margin (Before Income Tax) 49	4.6	2.2	8.8	9.0	4.2	3.9	4.1	3.6	4.1	3.8	3.2	3.9	6.2
Profit Margin (After Income Tax) 50	3.7	2.2	8.7	8.9	4.0	3.5	3.6	3.1	3.5	3.1	2.2	2.7	4.0

Table I

Corporations with and without Net Income

METAL AND MINERAL (EXCEPT PETROLEUM)

MONEY AMOUNTS AND SIZE OF ASSETS IN THOUSANDS OF DOLLARS

Item Description for Accounting Period 7/09 Through 6/10		Total	Zero Assets	Under 500	500 to 1,000	1,000 to 5,000	5,000 to 10,000	10,000 to 25,000	25,000 to 50,000	50,000 to 100,000	100,000 to 250,000	250,000 to 500,000	500,000 to 2,500,000	2,500,000 and over
Number of Enterprises	1	5314	644	2462	598	719	400	287	82	53	41	14	14	0
Revenues ($ in Thousands)														
Net Sales	2	86105000	50990	1639136	950378	4615938	10213745	15038083	5690825	6863139	12444727	6267326	22330713	0
Interest	3	101252	0	0	1011	2339	2177	5162	5850	4999	23940	8692	47081	0
Rents	4	31356	0	0	0	0	230	863	1144	398	910	11875	15937	0
Royalties	5	251	0	0	0	0	0	251	0	0	0	0	0	0
Other Portfolio Income	6	227282	0	1105	1693	1936	16014	3623	1422	1924	72691	25693	101182	0
Other Receipts	7	551107	2	32	1571	-69182	48898	51264	25687	21765	366199	49372	55497	0
Total Receipts	8	87016248	50992	1640273	954653	4551031	10281064	15099246	5724928	6892225	12908467	6362958	22550410	0
Average Total Receipts	9	16375	79	666	1596	6330	25703	52611	69816	130042	314841	454497	1610744	•
Operating Costs/Operating Income (%)														
Cost of Operations	10	87.7	73.0	63.5	70.1	81.6	89.2	90.4	85.5	89.8	91.8	88.8	86.2	•
Salaries and Wages	11	4.0	9.6	5.8	8.0	4.5	3.6	2.7	4.5	3.1	3.0	5.0	5.0	•
Taxes Paid	12	0.8	1.6	1.8	1.3	0.9	0.6	0.5	0.8	0.7	0.7	1.2	0.8	•
Interest Paid	13	0.9	6.6	0.3	0.3	0.4	0.4	0.4	0.9	0.6	0.6	1.7	1.9	•
Depreciation	14	0.9	2.1	0.3	0.8	0.3	0.3	0.8	1.3	0.9	0.6	1.7	1.2	•
Amortization and Depletion	15	0.3	1.0	0.1	•	0.0	0.0	0.0	0.1	0.1	0.1	0.5	0.7	•
Pensions and Other Deferred Comp.	16	0.2	0.1	0.4	0.5	0.3	0.1	0.1	0.1	0.2	0.3	0.3	0.3	•
Employee Benefits	17	0.8	0.4	0.3	1.2	0.6	0.4	0.4	0.6	0.4	0.6	0.9	1.4	•
Advertising	18	0.1	0.1	0.2	0.2	0.1	0.1	0.1	0.1	0.0	0.0	0.1	0.0	•
Other Expenses	19	4.5	13.4	9.9	9.1	6.1	3.7	2.9	4.5	2.4	4.9	9.2	3.9	•
Officers' Compensation	20	1.3	2.1	14.9	7.7	4.1	1.2	1.0	1.2	0.8	0.4	0.7	0.5	•
Operating Margin	21	•	•	2.7	0.9	1.0	0.3	0.6	0.4	1.1	•	•	•	•
Operating Margin Before Officers' Comp.	22	0.0	•	17.6	8.6	5.1	1.5	1.6	1.6	1.9	•	•	•	•

Selected Average Balance Sheet ($ in Thousands)

	•	•	•	•	•	•	•	•	•	•	•	•
Net Receivables 23	1697	0	56	201	652	1697	4392	7684	13978	39057	75822	165688
Inventories 24	3117	0	50	142	906	2484	5648	16087	34189	64017	128772	295427
Net Property, Plant and Equipment 25	1175	0	13	45	89	427	1902	4501	6490	12424	63658	235022
Total Assets 26	8116	0	169	684	2577	6531	16367	35117	69374	159454	373874	1057876
Notes and Loans Payable 27	2248	0	162	97	409	1851	3426	12341	21058	36095	119233	299725
All Other Liabilities 28	2528	0	22	225	783	2160	4662	9905	16271	55384	93162	373499
Net Worth 29	3340	0	-15	362	1386	2520	8280	12871	32045	67974	161479	384652

Selected Financial Ratios (Times to 1)

	•	•	•	•	•	•	•	•	•	•	•	•
Current Ratio 30	1.9	•	3.2	2.4	2.2	1.8	2.2	1.6	2.1	2.0	2.2	1.7
Quick Ratio 31	0.9	•	2.1	1.8	1.3	0.9	1.2	0.7	0.8	0.9	1.0	0.7
Net Sales to Working Capital 32	6.2	•	7.1	4.7	5.4	9.9	7.3	6.3	4.2	5.2	3.8	7.6
Coverage Ratio 33	0.8	•	9.8	4.8	•	3.3	3.9	2.0	3.6	2.6	•	0.5
Total Asset Turnover 34	2.0	•	3.9	2.3	2.5	3.9	3.2	2.0	1.9	1.9	1.2	1.5
Inventory Turnover 35	4.6	•	8.5	7.9	5.8	9.2	8.4	3.7	3.4	4.4	3.1	4.7
Receivables Turnover 36	6.8	•	11.4	10.2	7.7	14.7	11.4	7.0	6.9	7.0	4.8	7.4
Total Liabilities to Net Worth 37	1.4	•	•	0.9	0.9	1.6	1.0	1.7	1.2	1.3	1.3	1.8
Current Assets to Working Capital 38	2.1	•	1.4	1.7	1.8	2.2	1.8	2.6	1.9	2.0	1.8	2.4
Current Liabilities to Working Capital 39	1.1	•	0.4	0.7	0.8	1.2	0.8	1.6	0.9	1.0	0.8	1.4
Working Capital to Net Sales 40	0.2	•	0.1	0.2	0.2	0.1	0.1	0.2	0.2	0.2	0.3	0.1
Inventory to Working Capital 41	0.9	•	0.4	0.4	0.7	1.0	0.8	1.3	1.0	0.9	0.8	1.1
Total Receipts to Cash Flow 42	33.4	46.7	8.6	14.5	23.4	27.5	31.8	25.6	30.5	21.3	•	62.8
Cost of Goods to Cash Flow 43	29.2	34.1	5.5	10.2	19.1	24.6	28.7	21.9	27.4	19.6	•	54.2
Cash Flow to Total Debt 44	0.1	•	0.4	0.3	0.2	0.2	0.2	0.1	0.1	0.2	•	0.0

Selected Financial Factors (in Percentages)

	•	•	•	•	•	•	•	•	•	•	•	•
Debt Ratio 45	58.9	•	108.9	47.1	46.2	61.4	49.4	63.3	53.8	57.4	56.8	63.6
Return on Total Assets 46	1.5	•	12.0	3.5	•	5.4	4.5	3.8	3.9	2.8	•	1.4
Return on Equity Before Income Taxes 47	•	•	•	5.2	•	9.7	6.7	5.3	6.2	4.0	•	•
Return on Equity After Income Taxes 48	•	•	•	4.8	•	8.4	5.5	4.0	4.6	0.9	•	•
Profit Margin (Before Income Tax) 49	•	2.7	1.2	•	•	1.0	1.1	1.0	1.5	0.9	•	•
Profit Margin (After Income Tax) 50	•	2.6	1.1	•	•	0.8	0.7	0.9	1.1	0.2	•	•

Table II
Corporations with Net Income

METAL AND MINERAL (EXCEPT PETROLEUM)

MONEY AMOUNTS AND SIZE OF ASSETS IN THOUSANDS OF DOLLARS

Item Description for Accounting Period 7/09 Through 6/10	Total	Zero Assets	Under 500	500 to 1,000	1,000 to 5,000	5,000 to 10,000	10,000 to 25,000	25,000 to 50,000	50,000 to 100,000	100,000 to 250,000	250,000 to 500,000	500,000 to 2,500,000	2,500,000 and over
Number of Enterprises **1**	3279	•	1861	•	437	204	179	•	34	22	4	•	0
Revenues ($ in Thousands)													
Net Sales **2**	46444052	•	1458318	•	3535706	6502625	11625333	•	5362293	6536242	1404287	•	0
Interest **3**	56263	•	0	•	1326	1957	2230	•	4835	11564	2515	•	0
Rents **4**	17323	•	0	•	0	230	420	•	325	125	1881	•	0
Royalties **5**	0	•	0	•	0	0	0	•	0	0	0	•	0
Other Portfolio Income **6**	136774	•	1105	•	1534	11378	1116	•	1737	66445	7495	•	0
Other Receipts **7**	475557	•	24	•	7852	15055	36457	•	799	355590	15247	•	0
Total Receipts **8**	47129969	•	1459447	•	3546418	6531245	11665556	•	5369989	6969966	1431425	•	0
Average Total Receipts **9**	14373	•	784	•	8115	32016	65171	•	157941	316817	357856	•	•
Operating Costs/Operating Income (%)													
Cost of Operations **10**	87.0	•	60.5	•	81.4	90.6	89.0	•	89.6	89.7	71.6	•	•
Salaries and Wages **11**	3.1	•	6.4	•	3.7	2.6	2.5	•	2.5	3.3	5.5	•	•
Taxes Paid **12**	0.7	•	1.9	•	0.9	0.4	0.5	•	0.5	0.7	1.6	•	•
Interest Paid **13**	0.3	•	0.3	•	0.3	0.2	0.2	•	0.4	0.4	1.0	•	•
Depreciation **14**	0.6	•	0.3	•	0.2	0.1	0.5	•	0.6	0.6	2.3	•	•
Amortization and Depletion **15**	0.1	•	0.1	•	0.0	0.0	0.0	•	0.1	0.0	0.8	•	•
Pensions and Other Deferred Comp. **16**	0.2	•	0.4	•	0.4	0.1	0.1	•	0.2	0.2	0.1	•	•
Employee Benefits **17**	0.5	•	0.3	•	0.7	0.3	0.4	•	0.3	0.7	0.3	•	•
Advertising **18**	0.1	•	0.1	•	0.1	0.0	0.1	•	0.0	0.0	0.1	•	•
Other Expenses **19**	3.8	•	9.8	•	5.0	2.1	2.7	•	1.6	5.8	12.4	•	•
Officers' Compensation **20**	1.7	•	16.6	•	4.9	1.1	1.0	•	0.7	0.4	0.7	•	•
Operating Margin **21**	2.0	•	3.4	•	2.6	2.4	2.9	•	3.5	•	3.5	•	•
Operating Margin Before Officers' Comp. **22**	3.7	•	20.0	•	7.5	3.5	3.9	•	4.2	•	4.2	•	•

Selected Average Balance Sheet ($ in Thousands)

Net Receivables 23	1517	60	718	1529	4446	15807	39748	81338
Inventories 24	3297	55	1134	2909	6211	36673	95960	219849
Net Property, Plant and Equipment 25	551	17	100	294	1750	5768	9811	91007
Total Assets 26	5665	194	2941	6298	15988	71710	152290	325046
Notes and Loans Payable 27	954	59	212	784	2343	18230	32398	27690
All Other Liabilities 28	1535	19	884	1585	4495	14843	57305	77389
Net Worth 29	3175	116	1845	3928	9150	38637	62588	219967

Selected Financial Ratios (Times to 1)

Current Ratio 30	2.3	3.6	2.4	3.2	2.5	2.3	1.9	3.2
Quick Ratio 31	1.2	2.3	1.3	1.9	1.4	1.0	0.8	2.2
Net Sales to Working Capital 32	5.5	7.3	5.6	8.5	8.3	4.6	5.4	2.8
Coverage Ratio 33	11.3	13.5	11.8	15.5	16.0	9.4	12.8	6.6
Total Asset Turnover 34	2.5	4.0	2.8	5.1	4.1	2.2	2.0	1.1
Inventory Turnover 35	3.7	8.6	5.8	9.9	9.3	3.9	2.8	1.1
Receivables Turnover 36	5.4	12.3	7.9	18.6	11.8	6.9	5.1	1.9
Total Liabilities to Net Worth 37	0.8	0.7	0.6	0.6	0.7	0.9	1.4	0.5
Current Assets to Working Capital 38	1.7	1.4	1.7	1.4	1.7	1.8	2.2	1.4
Current Liabilities to Working Capital 39	0.7	0.4	0.7	0.4	0.7	0.8	1.2	0.4
Working Capital to Net Sales 40	0.2	0.1	0.2	0.1	0.1	0.2	0.2	0.4
Inventory to Working Capital 41	0.7	0.4	0.7	0.6	0.7	0.8	1.1	0.3
Total Receipts to Cash Flow 42	16.1	8.2	15.3	23.3	19.4	20.6	10.7	7.1
Cost of Goods to Cash Flow 43	14.0	5.0	12.4	21.2	17.2	18.4	9.6	5.1
Cash Flow to Total Debt 44	0.4	1.2	0.5	0.6	0.5	0.2	0.3	0.5

Selected Financial Factors (in Percentages)

Debt Ratio 45	44.0	40.1	37.3	37.6	42.8	46.1	58.9	32.3
Return on Total Assets 46	9.5	15.0	8.7	15.6	14.1	8.9	10.1	7.1
Return on Equity Before Income Taxes 47	15.4	23.2	12.7	23.4	23.0	14.7	22.7	8.9
Return on Equity After Income Taxes 48	13.2	22.4	12.3	21.8	21.3	12.7	16.4	7.5
Profit Margin (Before Income Tax) 49	3.5	3.4	2.9	2.9	3.2	3.6	4.8	5.6
Profit Margin (After Income Tax) 50	3.0	3.3	2.8	2.7	3.0	3.1	3.4	4.7

ELECTRICAL GOODS

Table I

Corporations with and without Net Income

MONEY AMOUNTS AND SIZE OF ASSETS IN THOUSANDS OF DOLLARS

Item Description for Accounting Period 7/09 Through 6/10		Total	Zero Assets	Under 500	500 to 1,000	1,000 to 5,000	5,000 to 10,000	10,000 to 25,000	25,000 to 50,000	50,000 to 100,000	100,000 to 250,000	250,000 to 500,000	500,000 to 2,500,000	2,500,000 and over
Number of Enterprises	1	28235	3795	16172	3133	3588	697	430	197	100	62	19	31	11
Revenues ($ in Thousands)														
Net Sales	2	298153268	2166865	10783331	7390348	21658280	11743292	17941940	15095345	15341896	22840585	12443148	63360915	97387324
Interest	3	479189	2433	1592	5283	7480	3988	11715	14543	13920	13753	10357	157156	236969
Rents	4	146209	0	0	278	6371	4117	2077	324	3114	14775	1840	23704	89609
Royalties	5	1578800	0	0	0	0	0	1516	0	5803	3774	6622	52847	1508237
Other Portfolio Income	6	789300	5935	440	2587	4162	2639	20490	13394	4803	25255	4684	109708	595201
Other Receipts	7	3312266	76410	94048	71423	103972	110755	78499	109183	73721	269056	50787	351708	1922706
Total Receipts	8	304459032	2251643	10879411	7469919	21780265	11864791	18056237	15232789	15443257	23167198	12517438	64056038	101740046
Average Total Receipts	9	10783	593	673	2384	6070	17023	41991	77324	154433	373664	658813	2066324	9249095
Operating Costs/Operating Income (%)														
Cost of Operations	10	82.3	78.9	63.8	72.2	73.2	76.7	83.2	79.9	82.6	82.7	90.2	87.6	83.3
Salaries and Wages	11	6.4	10.5	11.0	7.6	9.0	8.8	6.7	8.6	6.9	6.7	4.6	4.9	5.5
Taxes Paid	12	0.8	1.4	2.0	1.5	1.4	1.1	0.8	0.9	0.9	0.8	0.4	0.5	0.7
Interest Paid	13	0.6	0.3	1.5	0.5	0.4	0.5	0.3	0.6	0.5	0.5	0.1	0.6	0.7
Depreciation	14	0.9	0.6	0.4	0.4	0.5	0.8	0.4	0.5	0.7	0.7	0.5	0.7	1.4
Amortization and Depletion	15	1.2	0.1	0.1	0.1	0.0	0.1	0.1	0.3	0.2	0.2	0.1	0.3	3.3
Pensions and Other Deferred Comp.	16	0.2	0.1	0.2	0.7	0.2	0.2	0.2	0.3	0.5	0.2	0.1	0.2	0.3
Employee Benefits	17	0.7	1.2	1.1	0.7	0.9	0.7	0.6	0.8	0.7	0.8	0.4	0.6	0.7
Advertising	18	0.7	0.4	0.6	0.4	0.9	0.5	0.3	0.4	0.5	1.0	0.2	0.5	0.9
Other Expenses	19	6.1	14.3	13.5	9.1	9.5	8.5	5.1	6.3	5.1	5.8	3.4	3.6	6.2
Officers' Compensation	20	1.0	1.1	5.3	6.5	3.1	2.3	1.4	0.9	0.7	0.5	0.3	0.2	0.1
Operating Margin	21	•	•	0.6	0.4	0.9	•	0.9	0.6	0.7	0.1	•	0.2	•
Operating Margin Before Officers' Comp.	22	0.2	•	5.9	6.9	4.0	2.3	2.3	1.6	1.4	0.6	0.1	0.4	•

Selected Average Balance Sheet ($ in Thousands)

Net Receivables 23	1655	0	31	168	694	2405	5320	11828	23998	59367	104812	341669	1657874
Inventories 24	960	0	24	234	797	2303	4478	9687	18888	40946	62988	171881	613885
Net Property, Plant and Equipment 25	409	0	17	114	167	622	1052	1717	6303	10261	15390	70128	487489
Total Assets 26	5980	0	120	730	2286	7612	15594	35053	67414	165913	338951	1058591	7384282
Notes and Loans Payable 27	1270	0	143	312	615	1947	3259	6257	18439	27075	10906	134195	1680506
All Other Liabilities 28	2506	0	70	207	916	2973	6805	14677	25379	71571	167964	443533	3081349
Net Worth 29	2204	0	-93	211	756	2692	5530	14118	23596	67267	160080	480863	2622427

Selected Financial Ratios (Times to 1)

Current Ratio 30	1.4	•	1.2	2.1	1.9	1.8	1.7	1.8	1.8	1.8	1.4	1.4	1.1
Quick Ratio 31	0.8	•	0.8	1.2	1.0	1.1	1.0	1.1	1.1	1.1	0.9	1.0	0.6
Net Sales to Working Capital 32	10.5	•	54.5	8.0	6.6	6.0	8.1	6.0	6.4	6.6	11.1	9.7	26.0
Coverage Ratio 33	3.4	•	2.0	4.1	4.8	3.2	5.8	3.8	4.3	4.3	7.1	3.6	3.0
Total Asset Turnover 34	1.8	•	5.6	3.2	2.6	2.2	2.7	2.2	2.3	2.2	1.9	1.9	1.2
Inventory Turnover 35	9.0	•	18.1	7.3	5.5	5.6	7.8	6.3	6.7	7.4	9.4	10.4	12.0
Receivables Turnover 36	6.4	•	22.9	13.4	8.3	7.2	7.8	6.6	6.3	5.9	5.1	6.4	5.4
Total Liabilities to Net Worth 37	1.7	•	•	2.5	2.0	1.8	1.8	1.5	1.9	1.5	1.1	1.2	1.8
Current Assets to Working Capital 38	3.7	•	6.8	1.9	2.2	2.2	2.5	2.2	2.2	2.3	3.7	3.2	10.6
Current Liabilities to Working Capital 39	2.7	•	5.8	0.9	1.2	1.2	1.5	1.2	1.2	1.3	2.7	2.2	9.6
Working Capital to Net Sales 40	0.1	•	0.0	0.1	0.2	0.2	0.1	0.2	0.2	0.2	0.1	0.1	0.0
Inventory to Working Capital 41	0.9	•	1.7	0.8	0.8	0.8	0.9	0.7	0.7	0.7	1.0	0.8	1.7
Total Receipts to Cash Flow 42	16.6	16.1	9.0	13.1	11.3	12.3	18.7	15.7	19.5	16.0	31.0	23.7	16.4
Cost of Goods to Cash Flow 43	13.7	12.7	5.7	9.5	8.3	9.4	15.6	12.6	16.1	13.2	27.9	20.8	13.6
Cash Flow to Total Debt 44	0.2	•	0.3	0.3	0.3	0.3	0.2	0.2	0.2	0.2	0.1	0.1	0.1

Selected Financial Factors (in Percentages)

Debt Ratio 45	63.2	•	178.0	71.1	67.0	64.6	64.5	59.7	65.0	59.5	52.8	54.6	64.5
Return on Total Assets 46	3.5	•	16.3	6.2	4.7	3.3	5.1	4.6	4.4	4.7	0.9	4.2	2.6
Return on Equity Before Income Taxes 47	6.7	•	•	16.1	11.3	6.4	12.0	8.4	9.7	9.0	1.6	6.7	4.9
Return on Equity After Income Taxes 48	5.4	•	•	13.9	9.8	4.5	10.3	6.8	8.2	6.1	1.0	4.8	4.2
Profit Margin (Before Income Tax) 49	1.4	•	1.5	1.4	1.4	1.0	1.6	1.6	1.5	1.6	0.4	1.6	1.5
Profit Margin (After Income Tax) 50	1.1	•	1.4	1.2	1.2	0.7	1.4	1.3	1.3	1.1	0.3	1.1	1.3

Table II

Corporations with Net Income

ELECTRICAL GOODS

MONEY AMOUNTS AND SIZE OF ASSETS IN THOUSANDS OF DOLLARS

Item Description for Accounting Period 7/09 Through 6/10		Total	Zero Assets	Under 500	500 to 1,000	1,000 to 5,000	5,000 to 10,000	10,000 to 25,000	25,000 to 50,000	50,000 to 100,000	100,000 to 250,000	250,000 to 500,000	500,000 to 2,500,000	2,500,000 and over
Number of Enterprises	1	15205	1521	8021	•	2473	462	299	136	72	44	11	23	•
Revenues ($ in Thousands)														
Net Sales	2	254274821	1210045	7655146	•	18025137	9282723	13895363	11436852	12564002	18199323	10871664	53583328	•
Interest	3	414411	835	1085	•	6510	3381	10573	7364	11721	6277	6196	149139	•
Rents	4	127148	0	0	•	5932	1704	253	212	948	14372	0	19792	•
Royalties	5	1194072	0	0	•	0	0	0	0	5786	2044	19	41381	•
Other Portfolio Income	6	652481	5888	440	•	2467	1802	17992	5027	4538	23557	1642	89478	•
Other Receipts	7	1910284	26790	57275	•	100830	103132	37892	74337	49019	221304	34480	267498	•
Total Receipts	8	258573217	1243558	7713946	•	18140876	9392742	13962073	11523792	12636014	18466877	10914001	54150616	•
Average Total Receipts	9	17006	818	962	•	7336	20331	46696	84734	175500	419702	992182	2354375	•
Operating Costs/Operating Income (%)														
Cost of Operations	10	83.0	71.2	64.9	•	73.6	75.3	83.8	78.4	83.3	85.1	91.2	89.0	•
Salaries and Wages	11	5.6	10.7	10.2	•	8.5	8.2	5.6	8.8	6.3	5.4	3.8	4.3	•
Taxes Paid	12	0.7	1.7	1.5	•	1.2	1.2	0.7	0.9	0.8	0.6	0.3	0.4	•
Interest Paid	13	0.4	0.2	0.5	•	0.3	0.3	0.2	0.3	0.4	0.2	0.1	0.6	•
Depreciation	14	0.8	0.3	0.3	•	0.5	0.9	0.3	0.4	0.5	0.5	0.3	0.6	•
Amortization and Depletion	15	1.3	0.0	0.0	•	0.0	0.1	0.1	0.2	0.1	0.1	0.0	0.1	•
Pensions and Other Deferred Comp.	16	0.2	0.2	0.2	•	0.2	0.2	0.2	0.2	0.5	0.2	0.1	0.2	•
Employee Benefits	17	0.6	1.1	0.9	•	0.8	0.7	0.5	0.8	0.6	0.6	0.3	0.5	•
Advertising	18	0.6	0.6	0.6	•	1.0	0.5	0.3	0.3	0.4	1.0	0.1	0.4	•
Other Expenses	19	5.1	8.3	10.3	•	8.0	8.4	4.1	5.6	4.6	4.2	2.3	2.8	•
Officers' Compensation	20	0.9	1.7	4.6	•	2.8	2.4	1.3	0.9	0.7	0.5	0.2	0.2	•
Operating Margin	21	0.7	4.0	6.1	•	3.0	1.8	2.7	3.1	1.8	1.6	1.3	0.9	•
Operating Margin Before Officers' Comp.	22	1.6	5.7	10.7	•	5.8	4.2	4.1	4.0	2.5	2.1	1.5	1.1	•

Selected Average Balance Sheet ($ in Thousands)

Net Receivables 23	2503	0	808	2306	5514	12060	25953	62053	141818	360461
Inventories 24	1316	0	789	2334	4505	10950	19440	40284	85983	184310
Net Property, Plant and Equipment 25	613	0	160	777	856	1771	6003	9320	19129	70084
Total Assets 26	8412	0	2370	7883	15438	35336	67023	163446	342488	1071167
Notes and Loans Payable 27	1567	0	447	1626	2366	4731	14697	18604	8447	112100
All Other Liabilities 28	3719	0	940	3336	6438	13312	25104	70499	214249	460359
Net Worth 29	3126	0	983	2920	6634	17293	27222	74342	119792	498708

Selected Financial Ratios (Times to 1)

Current Ratio 30	1.4	•	1.3	1.9	1.7	1.8	2.1	1.8	1.9	1.3	1.6
Quick Ratio 31	0.8	•	1.0	1.1	1.0	1.1	1.2	1.1	1.2	0.9	1.1
Net Sales to Working Capital 32	11.0	•	40.4	7.3	7.5	8.1	5.4	7.3	6.6	14.4	8.5
Coverage Ratio 33	6.8	28.6	14.9	11.6	10.0	15.3	13.0	7.6	14.6	34.4	4.8
Total Asset Turnover 34	2.0	•	7.5	3.1	2.5	3.0	2.4	2.6	2.5	2.9	2.2
Inventory Turnover 35	10.6	•	23.4	6.8	6.5	8.6	6.0	7.5	8.7	10.5	11.2
Receivables Turnover 36	7.2	•	28.0	8.9	8.5	8.1	6.8	6.5	6.3	5.4	7.0
Total Liabilities to Net Worth 37	1.7	•	4.2	1.4	1.7	1.3	1.0	1.5	1.2	1.9	1.1
Current Assets to Working Capital 38	3.7	•	4.1	2.1	2.4	2.3	1.9	2.2	2.1	4.0	2.8
Current Liabilities to Working Capital 39	2.7	•	3.1	1.1	1.4	1.3	0.9	1.2	1.1	3.0	1.8
Working Capital to Net Sales 40	0.1	•	0.0	0.1	0.1	0.1	0.2	0.1	0.2	0.1	0.1
Inventory to Working Capital 41	0.9	•	0.7	0.8	0.9	0.7	0.7	0.7	0.6	1.2	0.7
Total Receipts to Cash Flow 42	15.9	7.5	7.1	10.2	9.8	16.0	12.4	17.3	15.5	28.6	24.0
Cost of Goods to Cash Flow 43	13.2	5.3	4.6	7.5	7.4	13.4	9.7	14.4	13.2	26.1	21.3
Cash Flow to Total Debt 44	0.2	•	1.3	0.5	0.4	0.3	0.4	0.3	0.2	0.2	0.2

Selected Financial Factors (in Percentages)

Debt Ratio 45	62.8	•	80.9	58.5	63.0	57.0	51.1	59.4	54.5	65.0	53.4
Return on Total Assets 46	5.9	•	55.6	12.3	8.5	10.4	9.9	7.8	8.5	5.1	5.9
Return on Equity Before Income Taxes 47	13.4	•	271.9	27.0	20.7	22.6	18.7	16.6	17.3	14.1	10.1
Return on Equity After Income Taxes 48	11.7	•	267.8	25.4	18.2	20.6	16.9	14.8	13.8	12.9	7.6
Profit Margin (Before Income Tax) 49	2.5	6.8	6.9	3.6	3.0	3.2	3.9	2.6	3.1	1.7	2.2
Profit Margin (After Income Tax) 50	2.2	6.2	6.8	3.4	2.6	2.9	3.5	2.3	2.5	1.6	1.6

Table I

Corporations with and without Net Income

HARDWARE, PLUMBING, HEATING EQUIPMENT, AND SUPPLIES

MONEY AMOUNTS AND SIZE OF ASSETS IN THOUSANDS OF DOLLARS

Item Description for Accounting Period 7/09 Through 6/10		Total	Zero Assets	Under 500	500 to 1,000	1,000 to 5,000	5,000 to 10,000	10,000 to 25,000	25,000 to 50,000	50,000 to 100,000	100,000 to 250,000	250,000 to 500,000	500,000 to 2,500,000	2,500,000 and over
Number of Enterprises	1	15862	1974	7789	2023	2975	622	314	89	46	15	6	7	0
Revenues ($ in Thousands)														
Net Sales	2	82163416	286742	2943902	4306708	15143572	10789865	11566086	7264962	5972099	3531337	3620398	16737746	0
Interest	3	148851	241	237	1419	13074	5404	4094	3935	2488	2497	6958	108305	0
Rents	4	10090	0	330	0	3207	1267	2141	1390	498	1128	18	111	0
Royalties	5	3292	0	0	0	0	0	0	0	381	0	0	2911	0
Other Portfolio Income	6	94402	247	5574	288	11666	2116	28860	13382	12550	16739	749	2228	0
Other Receipts	7	1898910	6211	16646	5485	247517	139546	77829	39591	31608	36922	66216	1231339	0
Total Receipts	8	84318761	293441	2966689	4313900	15419036	10938198	11679010	7323260	6019624	3588623	3694339	18082640	0
Average Total Receipts	9	5316	149	381	2132	5183	17586	37194	82284	130861	239242	615723	2583234	•
Operating Costs/Operating Income (%)														
Cost of Operations	10	71.4	54.9	57.2	67.8	72.0	71.0	74.7	75.5	73.2	77.6	73.1	68.4	•
Salaries and Wages	11	10.5	6.2	10.1	10.2	10.0	10.8	9.4	9.8	10.2	9.2	11.2	12.2	•
Taxes Paid	12	1.5	1.7	2.3	1.7	1.4	1.6	1.2	1.2	1.4	1.5	1.5	1.6	•
Interest Paid	13	0.7	0.2	0.9	0.3	0.5	0.7	0.5	0.6	0.7	0.9	1.1	1.1	•
Depreciation	14	0.9	0.7	1.5	0.5	0.5	1.0	0.5	0.6	1.0	1.1	1.0	1.3	•
Amortization and Depletion	15	0.2	0.1	0.3	0.0	0.1	0.0	0.1	0.1	0.2	0.1	0.5	0.7	•
Pensions and Other Deferred Comp.	16	0.4	0.1	0.5	0.2	0.4	0.4	0.3	0.5	0.3	0.2	0.3	0.4	•
Employee Benefits	17	1.1	0.4	1.5	0.7	1.0	1.2	0.9	0.9	1.1	0.8	1.8	1.4	•
Advertising	18	0.5	0.5	2.0	0.3	0.4	0.7	0.4	0.6	0.5	0.6	0.1	0.2	•
Other Expenses	19	12.2	28.7	17.2	9.4	9.3	9.3	8.8	6.5	7.7	7.8	8.9	24.5	•
Officers' Compensation	20	2.4	14.1	6.6	5.8	4.9	2.8	2.1	1.2	1.0	0.7	1.0	0.2	•
Operating Margin	21	•	•	3.0	•	•	0.6	1.1	2.4	2.8	•	•	•	•
Operating Margin Before Officers' Comp.	22	0.6	6.6	6.5	8.8	4.3	3.4	3.2	3.7	3.8	0.3	0.4	•	•

Selected Average Balance Sheet ($ in Thousands)

Net Receivables 23	609	0	15	226	572	2026	4373	9503	18815	32875	64584	309247
Inventories 24	810	0	11	242	829	2785	6626	13632	27044	58041	85953	307572
Net Property, Plant and Equipment 25	258	0	15	49	163	720	1310	3742	10855	21264	37134	165774
Total Assets 26	2456	0	72	762	2170	6964	15763	34026	71914	152587	329460	1502176
Notes and Loans Payable 27	643	0	62	171	464	1789	3868	8364	15015	30367	76556	472163
All Other Liabilities 28	684	0	35	228	783	1996	3702	8601	19072	48913	111269	333635
Net Worth 29	1129	0	-25	363	923	3179	8193	17062	37827	73307	141635	696378

Selected Financial Ratios (Times to 1)

Current Ratio 30	2.3	•	1.3	2.4	2.2	2.4	2.2	2.3	2.3	2.1	2.1	2.4
Quick Ratio 31	1.2	•	0.9	1.4	1.1	1.1	1.1	1.2	1.1	1.0	0.8	1.4
Net Sales to Working Capital 32	5.5	•	37.7	5.8	5.2	5.0	5.3	5.4	4.4	4.4	6.3	6.0
Coverage Ratio 33	2.2	•	1.8	10.6	3.7	4.0	5.3	6.0	6.1	2.5	2.3	•
Total Asset Turnover 34	2.1	•	5.2	2.8	2.3	2.5	2.3	2.4	1.8	1.5	1.8	1.6
Inventory Turnover 35	4.6	•	19.7	6.0	4.4	4.4	4.2	4.5	3.5	3.1	5.1	5.3
Receivables Turnover 36	6.9	•	19.0	10.6	8.0	9.2	7.4	8.0	6.3	6.4	10.6	4.2
Total Liabilities to Net Worth 37	1.2	•	•	1.1	1.4	1.2	0.9	1.0	0.9	1.1	1.3	1.2
Current Assets to Working Capital 38	1.8	•	4.5	1.7	1.8	1.7	1.9	1.7	1.8	1.9	1.9	1.7
Current Liabilities to Working Capital 39	0.8	•	3.5	0.7	0.8	0.7	0.9	0.7	0.8	0.9	0.9	0.7
Working Capital to Net Sales 40	0.2	•	0.0	0.2	0.2	0.2	0.2	0.2	0.2	0.2	0.2	0.2
Inventory to Working Capital 41	0.8	•	1.0	0.7	0.8	0.8	0.9	0.8	0.8	0.9	1.0	0.6
Total Receipts to Cash Flow 42	11.4	7.6	7.0	9.7	12.7	12.1	12.1	14.0	11.5	14.7	13.0	9.9
Cost of Goods to Cash Flow 43	8.2	4.2	4.0	6.6	9.2	8.6	9.1	10.6	8.4	11.4	9.5	6.7
Cash Flow to Total Debt 44	0.3	0.6	0.5	0.3	0.4	0.4	0.3	0.3	0.3	0.2	0.2	0.3

Selected Financial Factors (in Percentages)

Debt Ratio 45	54.0	•	135.1	52.4	57.5	54.4	48.0	49.9	47.4	52.0	57.0	53.6
Return on Total Assets 46	3.3	•	7.9	9.8	4.0	6.7	6.0	9.4	7.7	3.3	4.5	•
Return on Equity Before Income Taxes 47	3.9	•	•	18.6	6.8	11.0	9.4	15.6	12.2	4.1	5.9	•
Return on Equity After Income Taxes 48	2.1	•	•	16.7	5.0	9.6	8.1	13.9	10.7	2.8	3.5	•
Profit Margin (Before Income Tax) 49	0.8	•	0.7	3.2	1.2	2.0	2.1	3.3	3.6	1.3	1.4	•
Profit Margin (After Income Tax) 50	0.5	•	0.6	2.8	0.9	1.8	1.8	2.9	3.1	0.9	0.8	•

Table II
Corporations with Net Income

HARDWARE, PLUMBING, HEATING EQUIPMENT, AND SUPPLIES

MONEY AMOUNTS AND SIZE OF ASSETS IN THOUSANDS OF DOLLARS

Item Description for Accounting Period 7/09 Through 6/10	Total	Zero Assets	Under 500	500 to 1,000	1,000 to 5,000	5,000 to 10,000	10,000 to 25,000	25,000 to 50,000	50,000 to 100,000	100,000 to 250,000	250,000 to 500,000	500,000 to 2,500,000	2,500,000 and over
Number of Enterprises 1	9337	•	4149	1258	2087	424	234	75	34	11	•	•	0
Revenues ($ in Thousands)													
Net Sales 2	55095927	•	1787412	2679153	11896439	7184795	8922893	6378269	4678169	2961840	•	•	0
Interest 3	30727	•	205	1020	8834	3941	2769	2123	1874	2488	•	•	0
Rents 4	5870	•	330	0	1020	630	2141	1176	454	9	•	•	0
Royalties 5	3292	•	0	0	0	0	0	0	381	0	•	•	0
Other Portfolio Income 6	85873	•	5082	3	8369	369	27750	13283	12002	16739	•	•	0
Other Receipts 7	652012	•	4729	3431	232238	78289	60527	44580	31686	34750	•	•	0
Total Receipts 8	55873701	•	1797758	2683607	12146900	7268024	9016080	6439431	4724566	3015826	•	•	0
Average Total Receipts 9	5984	•	433	2133	5820	17142	38530	85859	138958	274166	•	•	•
Operating Costs/Operating Income (%)													
Cost of Operations 10	70.4	•	46.3	66.7	71.4	68.6	73.6	75.4	72.7	76.1	•	•	•
Salaries and Wages 11	10.2	•	11.3	8.4	10.1	11.2	9.4	9.8	10.0	10.0	•	•	•
Taxes Paid 12	1.5	•	2.5	1.6	1.4	1.5	1.2	1.2	1.4	1.4	•	•	•
Interest Paid 13	0.5	•	1.0	0.1	0.4	0.3	0.3	0.6	0.4	0.5	•	•	•
Depreciation 14	0.8	•	1.8	0.6	0.5	1.2	0.4	0.5	0.9	1.1	•	•	•
Amortization and Depletion 15	0.1	•	0.1	0.0	0.1	0.0	0.0	0.0	0.2	0.2	•	•	•
Pensions and Other Deferred Comp. 16	0.4	•	0.7	0.2	0.5	0.5	0.3	0.5	0.3	0.2	•	•	•
Employee Benefits 17	1.0	•	1.5	0.5	1.2	1.1	0.8	0.8	1.0	0.7	•	•	•
Advertising 18	0.5	•	3.1	0.2	0.4	0.8	0.4	0.6	0.5	0.6	•	•	•
Other Expenses 19	8.6	•	18.4	8.9	8.3	8.3	8.4	5.7	7.1	7.7	•	•	•
Officers' Compensation 20	2.8	•	7.2	6.1	5.0	3.3	2.4	1.3	1.0	0.7	•	•	•
Operating Margin 21	3.2	•	5.9	6.8	1.0	3.1	2.7	3.5	4.6	0.9	•	•	•
Operating Margin Before Officers' Comp. 22	5.9	•	13.1	12.8	6.0	6.4	5.1	4.8	5.5	1.6	•	•	•

Selected Average Balance Sheet ($ in Thousands)

	1	2	3	4	5	6	7	8	9
Net Receivables 23	665	10	227	589	2065	4404	9942	19519	30652
Inventories 24	1083	7	258	893	3295	7307	13207	26875	62243
Net Property, Plant and Equipment 25	259	17	39	154	761	1013	3206	10262	23704
Total Assets 26	2657	56	840	2057	6867	15291	33738	71968	152628
Notes and Loans Payable 27	490	75	25	441	1102	3046	7959	9573	25121
All Other Liabilities 28	675	19	217	623	1963	3245	8575	20251	44765
Net Worth 29	1492	-38	599	993	3801	9000	17203	42144	82742

Selected Financial Ratios (Times to 1)

	1	2	3	4	5	6	7	8	9
Current Ratio 30	2.5	2.4	3.6	2.4	2.5	2.6	2.5	2.3	1.9
Quick Ratio 31	1.3	1.9	2.1	1.3	1.1	1.3	1.2	1.2	0.9
Net Sales to Working Capital 32	5.0	23.1	4.4	5.5	4.8	4.9	5.1	4.5	5.3
Coverage Ratio 33	10.6	7.3	55.3	9.4	13.6	11.9	9.1	13.9	6.3
Total Asset Turnover 34	2.2	7.7	2.5	2.8	2.5	2.5	2.5	1.9	1.8
Inventory Turnover 35	3.8	27.2	5.5	4.6	3.5	3.8	4.9	3.7	3.3
Receivables Turnover 36	5.8	34.9	9.8	8.1	7.9	6.7	•	6.5	6.8
Total Liabilities to Net Worth 37	0.8	•	0.4	1.1	0.8	0.7	1.0	0.7	0.8
Current Assets to Working Capital 38	1.7	1.7	1.4	1.7	1.7	1.6	1.7	1.8	2.1
Current Liabilities to Working Capital 39	0.7	0.7	0.4	0.7	0.7	0.6	0.7	0.8	1.1
Working Capital to Net Sales 40	0.2	0.0	0.2	0.2	0.2	0.2	0.2	0.2	0.2
Inventory to Working Capital 41	0.8	0.3	0.6	0.7	0.9	0.7	0.8	0.8	1.0
Total Receipts to Cash Flow 42	9.4	4.7	7.4	11.0	9.8	10.4	12.7	9.8	12.4
Cost of Goods to Cash Flow 43	6.6	2.2	4.9	7.9	6.7	7.6	9.6	7.2	9.5
Cash Flow to Total Debt 44	0.5	1.0	1.2	0.5	0.6	0.6	0.4	0.5	0.3

Selected Financial Factors (in Percentages)

	1	2	3	4	5	6	7	8	9
Debt Ratio 45	43.9	168.1	28.8	51.7	44.6	41.1	49.0	41.4	45.8
Return on Total Assets 46	11.3	57.6	17.9	9.6	11.5	10.1	12.8	11.4	5.7
Return on Equity Before Income Taxes 47	18.2	•	24.6	17.7	19.2	15.8	22.4	18.1	8.9
Return on Equity After Income Taxes 48	15.8	•	22.7	15.3	17.5	14.1	20.4	16.2	7.2
Profit Margin (Before Income Tax) 49	4.6	6.4	6.9	3.1	4.3	3.7	4.5	5.5	2.7
Profit Margin (After Income Tax) 50	4.0	6.4	6.4	2.7	3.9	3.3	4.1	5.0	2.2

Table I

Corporations with and without Net Income

MACHINERY, EQUIPMENT, AND SUPPLIES

MONEY AMOUNTS AND SIZE OF ASSETS IN THOUSANDS OF DOLLARS

Item Description for Accounting Period 7/09 Through 6/10	Total	Zero Assets	Under 500	500 to 1,000	1,000 to 5,000	5,000 to 10,000	10,000 to 25,000	25,000 to 50,000	50,000 to 100,000	100,000 to 250,000	250,000 to 500,000	500,000 to 2,500,000	2,500,000 and over
Number of Enterprises **1**	47406	3945	27632	4843	7861	1526	988	327	133	93	33	19	6
Revenues ($ in Thousands)													
Net Sales **2**	223492385	5930207	13718100	7103871	41255631	21935414	29337027	18749647	13138375	17269606	11604229	16311944	27138333
Interest **3**	280878	2832	4283	8234	21863	11479	16875	21790	11667	22916	20990	43267	94681
Rents **4**	129576	24	0	631	12846	15500	16244	19908	3395	25463	17977	12822	4765
Royalties **5**	40221	0	12774	0	238	7	10649	707	772	210	1362	10785	2716
Other Portfolio Income **6**	1247628	23032	41333	10975	111895	94054	134918	113849	188923	226029	165592	130582	6446
Other Receipts **7**	2074313	33085	156799	76522	300662	215658	254501	166169	234781	208612	174428	134930	118169
Total Receipts **8**	227265001	5989180	13933289	7200233	41703135	22272112	29770214	19072070	13577913	17752836	11984578	16644330	27365110
Average Total Receipts **9**	4794	1518	504	1487	5305	14595	30132	58324	102090	190891	363169	876017	4560852
Operating Costs/Operating Income (%)													
Cost of Operations **10**	74.8	93.8	61.9	66.9	71.3	76.7	76.4	77.2	76.0	73.7	70.3	68.0	85.8
Salaries and Wages **11**	8.0	1.3	6.8	8.7	9.7	8.4	8.6	7.7	8.5	8.4	9.9	9.8	4.6
Taxes Paid **12**	1.3	0.2	1.5	1.9	1.5	1.4	1.2	1.2	1.2	1.4	1.2	1.5	0.8
Interest Paid **13**	0.9	0.4	0.4	0.8	0.6	0.8	0.7	0.8	1.0	1.5	1.8	1.6	0.8
Depreciation **14**	1.9	0.5	0.6	1.0	1.0	1.2	1.6	2.4	3.2	3.7	5.3	3.9	0.9
Amortization and Depletion **15**	0.2	0.0	0.0	0.0	0.1	0.1	0.1	0.1	0.2	0.3	0.6	1.0	0.4
Pensions and Other Deferred Comp. **16**	0.4	0.0	1.5	0.3	0.4	0.2	0.2	0.3	0.3	0.4	0.3	0.7	0.5
Employee Benefits **17**	1.1	0.1	0.6	1.1	0.8	0.9	0.9	1.0	1.1	1.6	2.0	1.9	0.9
Advertising **18**	0.4	0.1	0.6	0.5	0.5	0.4	0.4	0.5	0.3	0.5	0.4	0.4	0.5
Other Expenses **19**	8.1	3.1	14.4	12.2	9.6	7.9	7.1	7.7	7.4	8.7	10.0	7.5	3.6
Officers' Compensation **20**	2.2	1.0	8.8	6.6	3.6	2.4	1.8	1.0	0.9	0.9	0.5	0.7	0.3
Operating Margin **21**	0.6	•	3.0	•	0.9	•	1.0	•	•	•	•	3.0	1.0
Operating Margin Before Officers' Comp. **22**	2.8	0.4	11.7	6.6	4.5	2.0	2.8	0.9	0.7	0.0	•	•	1.3

Selected Average Balance Sheet ($ in Thousands)

Net Receivables 23	591	0	26	195	556	1425	3374	6910	12612	28102	57143	151072	866919
Inventories 24	921	0	32	241	849	3273	6436	14847	25407	50558	106097	227406	471204
Net Property, Plant and Equipment 25	406	0	16	68	248	692	2140	5434	12370	26709	73402	177103	280601
Total Assets 26	2796	0	120	713	2226	6943	14980	33736	68269	155833	344493	919753	3241352
Notes and Loans Payable 27	832	0	54	314	612	2197	4365	9056	20920	51166	118918	259405	767808
All Other Liabilities 28	920	0	29	174	779	2093	5099	11196	19657	43941	95412	271793	1489677
Net Worth 29	1044	0	37	224	835	2653	5516	13484	27692	60726	130163	388555	983867

Selected Financial Ratios (Times to 1)

Current Ratio 30	1.8	•	2.6	2.6	1.7	1.9	1.6	1.7	1.6	1.8	1.8	1.8	2.1
Quick Ratio 31	0.8	•	1.5	1.4	0.8	0.7	0.7	0.6	0.6	0.7	0.7	0.9	1.1
Net Sales to Working Capital 32	5.6	•	9.1	4.0	6.9	5.3	6.7	5.7	5.5	4.3	4.3	4.1	4.8
Coverage Ratio 33	3.6	2.0	12.9	2.5	4.2	2.5	4.7	3.0	4.3	2.4	1.6	4.2	3.3
Total Asset Turnover 34	1.7	•	4.1	2.1	2.4	2.1	2.0	1.7	1.4	1.2	1.0	0.9	1.4
Inventory Turnover 35	3.8	•	9.7	4.1	4.4	3.4	3.5	3.0	3.0	2.7	2.3	2.6	8.2
Receivables Turnover 36	7.4	•	18.2	7.8	9.2	9.8	7.9	7.8	6.7	6.4	5.9	5.1	4.8
Total Liabilities to Net Worth 37	1.7	•	2.2	2.2	1.7	1.6	1.7	1.5	1.5	1.6	1.6	1.4	2.3
Current Assets to Working Capital 38	2.2	•	1.6	1.6	2.4	2.1	2.6	2.5	2.6	2.2	2.3	2.3	1.9
Current Liabilities to Working Capital 39	1.2	•	0.6	0.6	1.4	1.1	1.6	1.5	1.6	1.2	1.3	1.3	0.9
Working Capital to Net Sales 40	0.2	•	0.1	0.3	0.1	0.2	0.2	0.2	0.2	0.2	0.2	0.2	0.2
Inventory to Working Capital 41	1.0	•	0.6	0.6	1.1	1.3	1.3	1.4	1.3	1.1	1.3	0.9	0.4
Total Receipts to Cash Flow 42	12.0	31.8	6.3	10.4	10.8	13.9	12.7	12.9	11.7	12.1	12.7	9.5	21.5
Cost of Goods to Cash Flow 43	9.0	29.8	3.9	6.9	7.7	10.7	9.7	10.0	8.9	8.9	8.9	6.5	18.4
Cash Flow to Total Debt 44	0.2	•	1.0	0.3	0.3	0.2	0.2	0.2	0.2	0.2	0.1	0.2	0.1

Selected Financial Factors (in Percentages)

Debt Ratio 45	62.7	•	69.0	68.5	62.5	61.8	63.2	60.0	59.4	61.0	62.2	57.8	69.6
Return on Total Assets 46	5.3	•	20.4	4.3	6.1	4.0	6.2	4.2	6.3	4.1	2.9	6.2	3.7
Return on Equity Before Income Taxes 47	10.2	•	60.7	8.4	12.5	6.3	13.3	6.9	11.8	6.1	2.8	11.1	8.5
Return on Equity After Income Taxes 48	7.6	•	59.3	6.6	10.8	4.2	11.6	4.9	9.1	4.3	0.8	6.7	3.9
Profit Margin (Before Income Tax) 49	2.3	0.4	4.5	1.3	2.0	1.2	2.5	1.6	3.3	2.0	1.0	5.0	1.8
Profit Margin (After Income Tax) 50	1.7	0.2	4.4	1.0	1.7	0.8	2.1	1.1	2.6	1.4	0.3	3.0	0.8

Table II

Corporations with Net Income

MACHINERY, EQUIPMENT, AND SUPPLIES

MONEY AMOUNTS AND SIZE OF ASSETS IN THOUSANDS OF DOLLARS

Item Description for Accounting Period 7/09 Through 6/10	Total	Zero Assets	Under 500	500 to 1,000	1,000 to 5,000	5,000 to 10,000	10,000 to 25,000	25,000 to 50,000	50,000 to 100,000	100,000 to 250,000	250,000 to 500,000	500,000 to 2,500,000	2,500,000 and over
Number of Enterprises 1	29049	2296	16217	2852	5507	1056	746	211	•	51	19	11	•
Revenues ($ in Thousands)													
Net Sales 2	162026485	5510492	10433155	5002048	31893319	17827913	23783568	13891536	•	10352362	7064652	12110209	•
Interest 3	209823	2495	3104	6185	16999	7570	11575	16371	•	13933	12348	23267	•
Rents 4	83366	24	0	0	9128	13127	13824	17515	•	5505	16774	1108	•
Royalties 5	26812	0	12774	0	238	7	10489	583	•	7	1290	269	•
Other Portfolio Income 6	802686	18820	39446	3779	92660	63445	110037	53575	•	151756	46488	60860	•
Other Receipts 7	1502618	32348	149625	41236	220473	137649	225221	133889	•	159660	134560	43648	•
Total Receipts 8	164651790	5564179	10638104	5053248	32232817	18049711	24154714	14113469	•	10683223	7276112	12239361	•
Average Total Receipts 9	5668	2423	656	1772	5853	17093	32379	66888	•	209475	382953	1112669	•
Operating Costs/Operating Income (%)													
Cost of Operations 10	73.5	95.2	60.6	65.8	70.7	77.7	76.0	78.2	•	72.8	70.1	68.3	•
Salaries and Wages 11	7.9	0.5	6.0	7.6	9.2	7.3	8.3	6.7	•	7.8	9.6	9.6	•
Taxes Paid 12	1.3	0.1	1.5	1.8	1.4	1.2	1.1	1.1	•	1.3	1.1	1.5	•
Interest Paid 13	0.7	0.2	0.3	0.7	0.6	0.5	0.5	0.7	•	1.2	1.5	1.1	•
Depreciation 14	1.4	0.1	0.4	0.9	0.9	0.8	1.4	1.5	•	2.9	3.7	2.0	•
Amortization and Depletion 15	0.1	0.0	0.0	0.1	0.0	0.1	0.1	0.1	•	0.3	0.8	0.8	•
Pensions and Other Deferred Comp. 16	0.5	0.0	2.0	0.3	0.4	0.2	0.2	0.3	•	0.5	0.3	0.8	•
Employee Benefits 17	1.0	0.1	0.7	0.8	0.7	0.8	0.9	0.8	•	1.5	2.1	1.0	•
Advertising 18	0.5	0.1	0.5	0.5	0.5	0.4	0.4	0.5	•	0.5	0.3	0.4	•
Other Expenses 19	7.3	1.7	13.0	10.1	8.7	6.9	6.6	6.4	•	7.4	8.5	5.5	•
Officers' Compensation 20	2.3	0.8	8.7	6.9	3.6	2.2	1.8	0.9	•	0.9	0.5	0.7	•
Operating Margin 21	3.4	1.2	6.1	4.5	3.3	1.8	2.6	3.0	•	2.8	1.4	7.3	•
Operating Margin Before Officers' Comp. 22	5.8	2.0	14.8	11.4	6.9	4.1	4.4	3.8	•	3.8	1.9	8.0	•

Selected Average Balance Sheet ($ in Thousands)

Net Receivables 23	676	0	30	235	588	1544	3295	6934	•	27341	61277	143411
Inventories 24	1086	0	30	215	913	3610	6692	15845	•	59893	113697	240767
Net Property, Plant and Equipment 25	365	0	16	75	236	560	1914	4292	•	22830	51730	145028
Total Assets 26	3003	0	136	722	2260	6968	15015	33799	•	158140	326329	1037006
Notes and Loans Payable 27	830	0	50	227	579	1825	3912	7959	•	42598	93251	276850
All Other Liabilities 28	891	0	33	172	675	2220	4952	11353	•	44211	100241	332442
Net Worth 29	1282	0	53	323	1006	2923	6151	14488	•	71331	132836	427714

Selected Financial Ratios (Times to 1)

Current Ratio 30	1.9	•	2.9	2.8	2.1	1.9	1.7	1.8	•	1.8	2.1	1.5
Quick Ratio 31	0.9	•	1.8	1.7	1.0	0.7	0.7	0.7	•	0.7	0.8	0.6
Net Sales to Working Capital 32	5.7	•	9.4	4.6	5.8	5.9	6.5	5.7	•	4.7	3.8	5.8
Coverage Ratio 33	8.0	13.1	24.2	9.2	8.7	7.2	9.0	8.0	•	6.2	4.1	8.3
Total Asset Turnover 34	1.9	•	4.7	2.4	2.6	2.4	2.1	1.9	•	1.3	1.1	1.1
Inventory Turnover 35	3.8	•	13.2	5.4	4.5	3.6	3.6	3.2	•	2.5	2.3	3.1
Receivables Turnover 36	7.3	•	20.7	7.6	9.3	10.1	8.1	8.1	•	6.1	5.3	•
Total Liabilities to Net Worth 37	1.3	•	1.6	1.2	1.2	1.4	1.4	1.3	•	1.2	1.5	1.4
Current Assets to Working Capital 38	2.1	•	1.5	1.5	1.9	2.1	2.4	2.3	•	2.2	1.9	3.0
Current Liabilities to Working Capital 39	1.1	•	0.5	0.5	0.9	1.1	1.4	1.3	•	1.2	0.9	2.0
Working Capital to Net Sales 40	0.2	•	0.1	0.2	0.2	0.2	0.2	0.2	•	0.2	0.3	0.2
Inventory to Working Capital 41	1.0	•	0.5	0.4	0.9	1.2	1.2	1.3	•	1.1	1.0	1.3
Total Receipts to Cash Flow 42	9.5	27.1	5.4	8.1	9.2	12.0	10.9	10.4	•	8.9	9.9	8.2
Cost of Goods to Cash Flow 43	7.0	25.8	3.3	5.3	6.5	9.3	8.2	8.1	•	6.5	6.9	5.6
Cash Flow to Total Debt 44	0.3	•	1.4	0.5	0.5	0.3	0.3	0.3	•	0.3	0.2	0.2

Selected Financial Factors (in Percentages)

Debt Ratio 45	57.3	•	61.1	55.2	55.5	58.1	59.0	57.1	•	54.9	59.3	58.8
Return on Total Assets 46	10.8	•	39.8	15.1	12.6	8.7	10.0	10.2	•	9.3	6.9	10.1
Return on Equity Before Income Taxes 47	22.1	•	98.1	30.2	24.9	17.8	21.7	20.7	•	17.3	12.8	21.5
Return on Equity After Income Taxes 48	18.6	•	96.4	28.1	23.0	15.2	19.7	17.7	•	14.6	9.3	14.7
Profit Margin (Before Income Tax) 49	5.1	2.2	8.1	5.6	4.3	3.1	4.2	4.6	•	6.1	4.6	8.4
Profit Margin (After Income Tax) 50	4.3	2.0	7.9	5.2	4.0	2.6	3.8	3.9	•	5.1	3.3	5.7

Table I

Corporations with and without Net Income

FURNITURE, SPORTS, TOYS, JEWELRY, OTHER DURABLE GOODS

MONEY AMOUNTS AND SIZE OF ASSETS IN THOUSANDS OF DOLLARS

Item Description for Accounting Period 7/09 Through 6/10	Total	Zero Assets	Under 500	500 to 1,000	1,000 to 5,000	5,000 to 10,000	10,000 to 25,000	25,000 to 50,000	50,000 to 100,000	100,000 to 250,000	250,000 to 500,000	500,000 to 2,500,000	2,500,000 and over
Number of Enterprises **1**	71785	12967	41886	6147	8321	1221	816	221	118	54	18	11	4
Revenues ($ in Thousands)													
Net Sales **2**	225274926	2332932	16917850	11869070	45425615	18259156	27752551	25233436	14007585	19715837	7352118	11517441	2489136
Interest **3**	233816	4568	1579	12757	18224	6941	16428	11100	10791	29879	12966	7451	101134
Rents **4**	79812	1123	6018	2038	8157	3371	4531	3287	6788	3391	204	33196	7709
Royalties **5**	287992	109	0	30469	1599	2670	11843	1034	39839	60282	72495	113	67540
Other Portfolio Income **6**	406568	31207	4566	3519	20828	35507	23665	10002	38480	67843	35997	76595	58357
Other Receipts **7**	1417368	106656	107286	18698	126249	132583	184316	144683	154671	125087	148493	28792	139852
Total Receipts **8**	227700482	2476595	17037299	11936551	45600672	18440228	27993334	25403542	14258154	20002319	7622273	11663588	25265928
Average Total Receipts **9**	3172	191	407	1942	5480	15103	34306	114948	120832	370413	423460	1060326	6316482
Operating Costs/Operating Income (%)													
Cost of Operations **10**	78.7	82.1	65.1	74.6	75.7	73.3	79.5	86.1	76.9	85.3	73.4	80.5	87.4
Salaries and Wages **11**	5.7	2.6	6.5	6.2	6.7	7.9	6.3	3.9	6.5	4.3	9.1	5.3	3.3
Taxes Paid **12**	1.0	1.0	1.4	1.4	1.1	1.3	1.1	0.6	1.1	0.6	1.3	0.9	0.7
Interest Paid **13**	0.7	1.0	0.5	0.5	0.5	0.8	0.6	0.5	1.2	0.9	1.1	1.3	0.5
Depreciation **14**	0.7	0.3	0.5	0.7	0.6	0.7	0.7	0.6	1.1	0.7	2.0	1.3	0.6
Amortization and Depletion **15**	0.3	0.2	0.2	0.2	0.1	0.1	0.1	0.1	0.4	0.5	0.7	0.6	0.7
Pensions and Other Deferred Comp. **16**	0.2	0.3	0.5	0.1	0.2	0.2	0.2	0.1	0.2	0.1	0.2	0.2	0.2
Employee Benefits **17**	0.5	0.6	0.5	0.5	0.4	0.4	0.5	0.3	0.7	0.7	1.4	0.7	0.1
Advertising **18**	1.2	1.1	1.0	1.2	0.6	1.0	1.0	0.9	1.8	1.6	3.5	1.6	2.1
Other Expenses **19**	8.1	20.1	15.3	11.7	10.3	8.9	7.4	5.0	8.4	5.8	9.8	5.3	2.1
Officers' Compensation **20**	2.2	1.6	7.0	3.6	3.0	3.9	1.9	0.8	1.0	0.5	1.1	0.6	0.3
Operating Margin **21**	0.6	•	1.5	•	0.7	1.6	0.7	1.1	0.7	•	•	1.9	1.9
Operating Margin Before Officers' Comp. **22**	2.8	•	8.5	3.0	3.7	5.5	2.6	1.9	1.6	•	•	2.4	2.2

Selected Average Balance Sheet ($ in Thousands)

Net Receivables 23	344	0	14	193	520	2019	4401	10063	17603	42238	100004	116515	724571
Inventories 24	441	0	46	252	830	2758	5733	12992	21272	39994	69017	139196	733650
Net Property, Plant and Equipment 25	127	0	10	94	179	563	1423	4087	7221	12553	33946	91821	181007
Total Assets 26	1454	0	112	694	2181	7138	15077	37197	67781	153561	317505	865807	4129705
Notes and Loans Payable 27	441	0	91	223	700	2127	4362	11318	23221	32966	76050	272218	788796
All Other Liabilities 28	527	0	33	323	765	2703	5338	12956	22111	48394	135540	252118	1789859
Net Worth 29	486	0	-11	149	717	2308	5377	12922	22450	72202	105915	341471	1551050

Selected Financial Ratios (Times to 1)

Current Ratio 30	1.7	•	2.2	1.7	1.9	1.7	1.7	1.7	1.6	1.9	1.4	2.1	1.3
Quick Ratio 31	0.8	•	0.9	0.8	0.9	0.9	0.8	0.8	0.8	1.1	0.9	0.9	0.5
Net Sales to Working Capital 32	7.3	•	8.3	8.6	6.2	6.2	6.7	9.8	6.2	7.5	6.1	5.7	10.3
Coverage Ratio 33	3.5	•	5.4	0.9	3.1	4.2	3.7	4.3	3.1	1.6	1.7	3.6	8.5
Total Asset Turnover 34	2.2	•	3.6	2.8	2.5	2.1	2.3	3.1	1.8	2.4	1.3	1.2	1.5
Inventory Turnover 35	5.6	•	5.7	5.7	5.0	4.0	4.7	7.6	4.3	7.8	4.3	6.1	7.4
Receivables Turnover 36	8.9	•	27.9	11.7	10.4	7.5	7.5	10.2	6.4	8.7	3.5	9.4	8.7
Total Liabilities to Net Worth 37	2.0	•	•	3.7	2.0	2.1	1.8	1.9	2.0	1.1	2.0	1.5	1.7
Current Assets to Working Capital 38	2.4	•	1.8	2.5	2.1	2.4	2.4	2.5	2.5	2.1	3.3	1.9	4.1
Current Liabilities to Working Capital 39	1.4	•	0.8	1.5	1.1	1.4	1.4	1.5	1.5	1.1	2.3	0.9	3.1
Working Capital to Net Sales 40	0.1	•	0.1	0.1	0.2	0.2	0.1	0.1	0.2	0.1	0.2	0.2	0.1
Inventory to Working Capital 41	1.0	•	1.0	1.1	0.9	1.0	1.1	1.0	1.0	0.8	0.9	0.7	1.2
Total Receipts to Cash Flow 42	13.5	10.0	7.7	12.4	12.3	11.3	14.3	17.9	11.2	20.3	15.0	15.6	21.8
Cost of Goods to Cash Flow 43	10.6	8.2	5.0	9.3	9.3	8.3	11.4	15.4	8.6	17.3	11.1	12.5	19.1
Cash Flow to Total Debt 44	0.2	•	0.4	0.3	0.3	0.3	0.2	0.3	0.2	0.2	0.1	0.1	0.1

Selected Financial Factors (in Percentages)

Debt Ratio 45	66.6	•	110.2	78.6	67.1	67.7	64.3	65.3	66.9	53.0	66.6	60.6	62.4
Return on Total Assets 46	5.2	•	10.0	1.3	4.1	7.0	5.1	7.1	6.4	3.5	2.5	5.5	6.1
Return on Equity Before Income Taxes 47	11.3	•	•	•	8.5	16.4	10.5	15.6	13.2	2.7	3.1	10.2	14.3
Return on Equity After Income Taxes 48	8.7	•	•	•	7.5	14.8	9.1	13.9	10.8	0.7	•	6.1	10.4
Profit Margin (Before Income Tax) 49	1.7	•	2.3	•	1.1	2.5	1.7	1.8	2.5	0.5	0.8	3.3	3.6
Profit Margin (After Income Tax) 50	1.4	•	2.2	•	1.0	2.3	1.4	1.6	2.0	0.1	•	2.0	2.6

Table II
Corporations with Net Income

FURNITURE, SPORTS, TOYS, JEWELRY, OTHER DURABLE GOODS

MONEY AMOUNTS AND SIZE OF ASSETS IN THOUSANDS OF DOLLARS

Item Description for Accounting Period 7/09 Through 6/10	Total	Zero Assets	Under 500	500 to 1,000	1,000 to 5,000	5,000 to 10,000	10,000 to 25,000	25,000 to 50,000	50,000 to 100,000	100,000 to 250,000	250,000 to 500,000	500,000 to 2,500,000	2,500,000 and over
Number of Enterprises 1	39317	5094	23251	3668	5566	819	625	158	81	33	12	5	4
Revenues ($ in Thousands)													
Net Sales 2	175299482	1577694	11238925	7994125	35016754	13640932	22752791	22323735	10643662	10184078	5630687	9404763	24491336
Interest 3	181730	4542	1343	10480	11553	3693	12132	2724	5063	13840	9866	5359	101134
Rents 4	35102	0	0	0	5285	3035	3627	1968	5157	2196	201	5924	7709
Royalties 5	199934	0	0	0	347	2659	9995	719	38791	46945	32827	113	67540
Other Portfolio Income 6	251215	31152	4228	3069	10133	33031	6049	3397	36151	4207	5905	55535	58357
Other Receipts 7	1091772	103512	123915	13064	133577	71725	133067	90632	133412	29684	117763	1569	139852
Total Receipts 8	177059235	1716900	11368411	8020738	35177649	13755075	22917661	22423175	10862236	10280950	5799249	9473263	25265928
Average Total Receipts 9	4503	337	489	2187	6320	16795	36668	141919	134102	311544	483104	1894653	6316482
Operating Costs/Operating Income (%)													
Cost of Operations 10	79.4	81.6	63.1	75.5	77.9	72.2	79.6	87.3	76.9	80.3	75.8	81.5	87.4
Salaries and Wages 11	5.1	2.3	6.1	5.1	5.1	7.3	5.7	3.5	6.2	4.9	7.7	5.4	3.3
Taxes Paid 12	0.9	0.9	1.2	1.1	0.9	1.3	1.1	0.5	1.0	0.7	1.2	1.0	0.7
Interest Paid 13	0.5	0.6	0.3	0.3	0.4	0.4	0.5	0.3	0.8	0.7	0.7	0.9	0.5
Depreciation 14	0.6	0.2	0.4	0.6	0.4	0.6	0.6	0.4	0.9	0.7	1.5	1.0	0.6
Amortization and Depletion 15	0.2	0.1	0.1	0.0	0.0	0.0	0.1	0.1	0.2	0.2	0.5	0.3	0.7
Pensions and Other Deferred Comp. 16	0.2	0.5	0.7	0.1	0.3	0.2	0.1	0.1	0.3	0.1	0.2	0.2	0.2
Employee Benefits 17	0.4	0.2	0.4	0.4	0.3	0.4	0.4	0.2	0.7	0.8	1.2	0.7	0.1
Advertising 18	1.1	1.0	0.6	1.5	0.4	0.7	0.9	0.8	1.5	2.1	2.1	0.8	2.1
Other Expenses 19	6.4	11.1	13.9	9.4	7.9	7.1	6.0	3.8	7.9	6.1	7.0	4.4	2.1
Officers' Compensation 20	2.0	1.8	6.0	2.6	2.9	4.6	1.9	0.7	1.0	0.6	1.0	0.3	0.3
Operating Margin 21	3.2	•	7.2	3.2	3.5	5.0	3.1	2.3	2.7	2.8	1.0	3.7	1.9
Operating Margin Before Officers' Comp. 22	5.2	1.5	13.2	5.9	6.4	9.6	5.0	3.0	3.7	3.4	2.0	3.9	2.2

Selected Average Balance Sheet ($ in Thousands)

Net Receivables 23	459	0	13	179	551	1972	4450	10530	19111	50636	72196	194160	724571
Inventories 24	576	0	35	267	894	2891	5517	13129	20781	45069	70253	250756	702621
Net Property, Plant and Equipment 25	151	0	10	80	183	421	1304	3800	7073	10457	36758	111283	181007
Total Assets 26	1899	0	112	681	2244	7210	14856	37456	66679	152745	314749	1046007	4129705
Notes and Loans Payable 27	491	0	56	218	675	1245	3828	10638	18229	31097	78192	351851	788796
All Other Liabilities 28	666	0	24	310	689	2570	5016	12525	21820	52830	98386	315177	1789859
Net Worth 29	743	0	33	154	879	3394	6011	14293	26630	68819	138171	378980	1551050

Selected Financial Ratios (Times to 1)

Current Ratio 30	1.8	•	2.9	1.7	2.2	2.1	1.9	1.7	1.8	2.0	1.9	2.0	1.3
Quick Ratio 31	0.9	•	1.5	0.8	1.1	1.1	0.9	0.9	0.9	1.1	0.9	0.9	0.5
Net Sales to Working Capital 32	7.2	•	8.6	9.6	6.1	5.3	6.4	11.5	6.1	5.5	4.8	8.5	10.3
Coverage Ratio 33	9.8	15.3	29.5	11.8	10.0	14.9	9.1	9.5	7.3	6.8	7.7	6.2	8.5
Total Asset Turnover 34	2.3	•	4.3	3.2	2.8	2.3	2.5	3.8	2.0	2.0	1.5	1.8	1.5
Inventory Turnover 35	6.1	•	8.8	6.2	5.5	4.2	5.3	9.4	4.9	5.5	5.1	6.1	7.7
Receivables Turnover 36	9.4	•	32.0	12.8	10.6	7.8	8.1	12.8	6.6	6.1	•	9.5	•
Total Liabilities to Net Worth 37	1.6	•	2.4	3.4	1.6	1.1	1.5	1.6	1.5	1.2	1.3	1.8	1.7
Current Assets to Working Capital 38	2.2	•	1.5	2.5	1.8	1.9	2.2	2.4	2.3	2.0	2.1	2.0	4.1
Current Liabilities to Working Capital 39	1.2	•	0.5	1.5	0.8	0.9	1.2	1.4	1.3	1.0	1.1	1.0	3.1
Working Capital to Net Sales 40	0.1	•	0.1	0.1	0.2	0.2	0.2	0.1	0.2	0.2	0.2	0.1	0.1
Inventory to Working Capital 41	0.9	•	0.7	1.2	0.8	0.8	1.0	1.0	0.9	0.7	0.7	1.0	1.2
Total Receipts to Cash Flow 42	11.4	6.3	5.4	10.0	10.3	9.5	12.3	17.6	9.2	11.9	12.2	14.5	21.8
Cost of Goods to Cash Flow 43	9.1	5.1	3.4	7.5	8.0	6.9	9.8	15.4	7.1	9.6	9.3	11.8	19.1
Cash Flow to Total Debt 44	0.3	•	1.1	0.4	0.4	0.5	0.3	0.3	0.4	0.3	0.2	0.2	0.1

Selected Financial Factors (in Percentages)

Debt Ratio 45	60.9	•	71.0	77.4	60.8	52.9	59.5	61.8	60.1	54.9	56.1	63.8	62.4
Return on Total Assets 46	11.2	•	37.2	12.4	12.3	14.5	10.7	11.7	10.8	9.2	8.2	9.9	6.1
Return on Equity Before Income Taxes 47	25.8	•	123.7	50.3	28.1	28.8	23.4	27.4	23.4	17.4	16.3	22.8	14.3
Return on Equity After Income Taxes 48	22.8	•	122.6	47.8	26.9	27.1	21.8	25.2	20.5	13.9	10.7	14.8	10.4
Profit Margin (Before Income Tax) 49	4.3	8.5	8.3	3.6	3.9	3.9	3.9	2.8	4.7	3.9	4.8	4.6	3.6
Profit Margin (After Income Tax) 50	3.8	8.1	8.2	3.4	3.8	3.6	3.6	2.6	4.1	3.1	3.0	3.0	2.6

Table I

Corporations with and without Net Income

PAPER AND PAPER PRODUCT

MONEY AMOUNTS AND SIZE OF ASSETS IN THOUSANDS OF DOLLARS

Item Description for Accounting Period 7/09 Through 6/10		Total	Zero Assets	Under 500	500 to 1,000	1,000 to 5,000	5,000 to 10,000	10,000 to 25,000	25,000 to 50,000	50,000 to 100,000	100,000 to 250,000	250,000 to 500,000	500,000 to 2,500,000	2,500,000 and over
Number of Enterprises	1	10394	2291	6372	698	731	92	110	62	17	13	3	5	0
Revenues ($ in Thousands)														
Net Sales	2	49115597	327846	2432907	2121437	6833545	1822922	5777531	6547564	3889083	6760784	2174120	10427859	0
Interest	3	16014	0	1521	537	1338	4128	759	1032	756	659	1627	3656	0
Rents	4	11218	0	0	0	3967	0	415	1273	1226	1103	687	2546	0
Royalties	5	8611	0	0	0	2120	0	0	1	0	0	0	6489	0
Other Portfolio Income	6	12360	0	7370	630	1629	448	395	247	1406	22	210	2	0
Other Receipts	7	229519	230	8921	268	29617	14170	5525	39098	38461	73557	1370	18304	0
Total Receipts	8	49393319	328076	2450719	2122872	6872216	1841668	5784625	6589215	3930932	6836125	2178014	10458856	0
Average Total Receipts	9	4752	143	385	3041	9401	20018	52588	106278	231231	525856	726005	2091771	•
Operating Costs/Operating Income (%)														
Cost of Operations	10	81.4	51.8	60.0	68.9	73.7	76.7	80.6	83.3	87.2	88.1	93.5	86.1	•
Salaries and Wages	11	6.1	8.7	6.1	7.7	9.9	9.0	6.4	6.3	4.6	4.7	2.3	4.6	•
Taxes Paid	12	0.9	1.7	1.8	1.0	1.3	1.4	0.8	0.8	0.6	0.5	0.2	0.7	•
Interest Paid	13	0.6	1.3	0.4	0.0	0.4	0.6	0.2	0.7	0.4	0.7	1.0	0.9	•
Depreciation	14	0.8	3.8	0.7	0.8	0.5	0.6	0.7	0.8	1.3	0.5	2.5	0.7	•
Amortization and Depletion	15	0.2	0.0	0.1	•	0.1	0.1	0.1	0.1	0.1	0.1	0.1	0.5	•
Pensions and Other Deferred Comp.	16	0.2	0.0	0.1	0.8	0.2	0.1	0.3	0.2	0.2	0.1	0.0	0.3	•
Employee Benefits	17	0.5	3.3	0.1	0.7	0.8	0.5	0.5	0.7	0.3	0.4	0.3	0.4	•
Advertising	18	0.2	1.2	0.9	0.2	0.2	0.2	0.8	0.1	0.1	0.0	0.0	0.1	•
Other Expenses	19	5.9	21.2	17.1	7.7	7.4	6.9	5.6	5.2	4.2	4.9	2.9	3.6	•
Officers' Compensation	20	1.4	6.0	6.6	3.6	2.4	2.2	1.6	1.0	0.8	0.3	0.2	0.2	•
Operating Margin	21	1.8	0.9	6.1	8.5	3.3	1.8	2.4	0.9	0.3	•	•	1.8	•
Operating Margin Before Officers' Comp.	22	3.2	6.8	12.7	12.1	5.7	4.0	4.0	1.9	1.2	0.0	0.2	1.9	•

Selected Average Balance Sheet ($ in Thousands)

Net Receivables 23	575	0	34	176	1101	2385	5685	13275	28026	87537	121472	236617	•
Inventories 24	332	0	20	124	548	1820	3695	8975	27414	32397	41320	139590	•
Net Property, Plant and Equipment 25	175	0	15	76	189	837	1476	4015	11205	15227	105093	69295	•
Total Assets 26	1510	0	123	768	2360	7245	15989	34531	76628	157214	307102	764569	•
Notes and Loans Payable 27	444	0	79	3	545	2127	2598	10829	25211	49903	111591	230042	•
All Other Liabilities 28	625	0	48	190	817	1596	6407	13966	28432	67656	137188	392934	•
Net Worth 29	441		-4	576	998	3522	6983	9737	22984	39656	58323	141593	•

Selected Financial Ratios (Times to 1)

Current Ratio 30	1.5	•	2.0	3.2	1.8	2.5	1.8	1.5	1.5	1.9	1.3	0.9	•
Quick Ratio 31	0.9	•	1.1	2.5	1.2	1.5	1.1	0.9	0.8	1.4	0.8	0.6	•
Net Sales to Working Capital 32	13.2	•	8.8	7.4	11.0	5.7	9.6	12.7	11.7	8.2	17.9	•	•
Coverage Ratio 33	5.0	1.7	17.3	267.3	11.8	5.7	11.2	3.4	4.5	2.2	•	3.2	•
Total Asset Turnover 34	3.1	•	3.1	4.0	4.0	2.7	3.3	3.1	3.0	3.3	2.4	2.7	•
Inventory Turnover 35	11.6	•	11.4	16.9	12.6	8.3	11.4	9.8	7.3	14.1	16.4	12.9	•
Receivables Turnover 36	8.3	•	15.1	14.6	10.5	5.0	9.1	8.3	7.9	5.7	7.4	8.6	•
Total Liabilities to Net Worth 37	2.4	•	•	0.3	1.4	1.1	1.3	2.5	2.3	3.0	4.3	4.4	•
Current Assets to Working Capital 38	3.0	•	2.0	1.5	2.3	1.7	2.3	3.1	3.1	2.1	4.9	•	•
Current Liabilities to Working Capital 39	2.0	•	1.0	0.5	1.3	0.7	1.3	2.1	2.1	1.1	3.9	•	•
Working Capital to Net Sales 40	0.1	•	0.1	0.1	0.1	0.2	0.1	0.1	0.1	0.1	0.1	•	•
Inventory to Working Capital 41	0.9	•	0.6	0.3	0.7	0.4	0.7	1.1	1.2	0.5	1.0	•	•
Total Receipts to Cash Flow 42	15.5	7.5	5.5	7.0	11.8	12.8	14.8	18.6	22.4	23.4	•	22.8	•
Cost of Goods to Cash Flow 43	12.6	3.9	3.3	4.8	8.7	9.8	11.9	15.5	19.5	20.6	•	19.6	•
Cash Flow to Total Debt 44	0.3	0.6	2.3	0.6	0.4	0.4	0.2	0.2	0.2	0.2	•	0.1	•

Selected Financial Factors (in Percentages)

Debt Ratio 45	70.8	•	103.6	25.1	57.7	51.4	56.3	71.8	70.0	74.8	81.0	81.5	•
Return on Total Assets 46	9.3	•	22.7	34.0	16.7	9.3	9.1	6.7	5.3	5.1	•	8.2	•
Return on Equity Before Income Taxes 47	25.6	•	•	45.2	36.1	15.8	19.0	16.8	13.7	10.9	•	30.4	•
Return on Equity After Income Taxes 48	22.9	•	•	45.1	34.4	14.7	17.4	13.9	13.0	9.6	•	21.6	•
Profit Margin (Before Income Tax) 49	2.4	0.9	6.9	8.6	3.9	2.8	2.5	1.6	1.4	0.8	•	2.1	•
Profit Margin (After Income Tax) 50	2.1	0.9	6.8	8.5	3.7	2.6	2.3	1.3	1.3	0.7	•	1.5	•

Table II

Corporations with Net Income

PAPER AND PAPER PRODUCT

MONEY AMOUNTS AND SIZE OF ASSETS IN THOUSANDS OF DOLLARS

Item Description for Accounting Period 7/09 Through 6/10		Total	Zero Assets	Under 500	500 to 1,000	1,000 to 5,000	5,000 to 10,000	10,000 to 25,000	25,000 to 50,000	50,000 to 100,000	100,000 to 250,000	250,000 to 500,000	500,000 to 2,500,000	2,500,000 and over
Number of Enterprises	1	6980	2281	3260	586	608	80	85	51	14	0	0	•	0
Revenues ($ in Thousands)														
Net Sales	2	38850960	303935	1419811	1953539	6254523	1560385	4684131	5463955	2907754	0	0	•	0
Interest	3	10441	0	1516	1	1136	3485	665	859	553	0	0	•	0
Rents	4	7504	0	0	0	3967	0	415	106	1226	0	0	•	0
Royalties	5	0	0	0	0	0	0	0	0	0	0	0	•	0
Other Portfolio Income	6	11097	0	7034	630	1040	368	298	90	1406	0	0	•	0
Other Receipts	7	192348	15	206	104	25125	9258	14358	33600	24074	0	0	•	0
Total Receipts	8	39072350	303950	1428567	1954274	6285791	1573496	4699867	5498610	2935013	0	0	•	0
Average Total Receipts	9	5598	133	438	3335	10338	19669	55293	107816	209644	•	•	•	•
Operating Costs/Operating Income (%)														
Cost of Operations	10	80.7	50.4	52.9	68.5	73.5	78.5	80.5	83.3	84.5	•	•	•	•
Salaries and Wages	11	6.2	9.1	6.0	7.9	10.0	6.7	6.3	6.2	5.5	•	•	•	•
Taxes Paid	12	0.9	1.8	1.9	0.9	1.2	1.3	0.8	0.8	0.7	•	•	•	•
Interest Paid	13	0.4	0.9	0.3	0.0	0.4	0.4	0.1	0.5	0.4	•	•	•	•
Depreciation	14	0.6	3.6	0.8	0.9	0.5	0.4	0.4	0.6	0.8	•	•	•	•
Amortization and Depletion	15	0.1	•	0.0	•	0.1	0.2	0.1	0.1	0.1	•	•	•	•
Pensions and Other Deferred Comp.	16	0.2	•	0.2	0.5	0.2	0.1	0.3	0.2	0.2	•	•	•	•
Employee Benefits	17	0.5	3.3	0.1	0.7	0.7	0.5	0.4	0.6	0.3	•	•	•	•
Advertising	18	0.2	1.2	1.5	0.2	0.2	0.2	0.6	0.1	0.1	•	•	•	•
Other Expenses	19	5.5	21.0	15.5	7.4	7.0	6.5	5.2	4.8	5.1	•	•	•	•
Officers' Compensation	20	1.5	6.3	7.2	3.4	2.3	2.5	1.7	0.9	0.9	•	•	•	•
Operating Margin	21	3.1	2.5	13.5	9.6	4.0	2.7	3.6	1.9	1.3	•	•	•	•
Operating Margin Before Officers' Comp.	22	4.6	8.8	20.7	13.0	6.4	5.2	5.4	2.9	2.2	•	•	•	•

Selected Average Balance Sheet ($ in Thousands)

Net Receivables 23	656	0	35	186	1163	2311	5406	13921	22667
Inventories 24	377	0	12	102	507	1843	4145	9005	30018
Net Property, Plant and Equipment 25	156	0	10	84	209	666	1310	2528	8824
Total Assets 26	1655	0	118	794	2440	6975	15420	34219	72460
Notes and Loans Payable 27	359	0	37	3	571	1683	2434	9461	19798
All Other Liabilities 28	717	0	25	215	859	1716	5811	13520	25634
Net Worth 29	579	0	55	576	1010	3576	7174	11238	27028

Selected Financial Ratios (Times to 1)

Current Ratio 30	1.5	•	3.6	2.8	1.7	2.3	2.0	1.6	1.6
Quick Ratio 31	1.0	•	2.5	2.3	1.2	1.4	1.2	0.9	0.8
Net Sales to Working Capital 32	13.4	•	7.1	8.6	12.3	6.1	8.8	10.7	9.2
Coverage Ratio 33	9.4	3.6	46.8	276.1	13.8	8.9	28.7	6.5	6.3
Total Asset Turnover 34	3.4	•	3.7	4.2	4.2	2.8	3.6	3.1	2.9
Inventory Turnover 35	11.9	•	18.8	22.4	14.9	8.3	10.7	9.9	5.8
Receivables Turnover 36	8.5	•	15.1	17.2	12.0	4.7	8.9	8.5	7.4
Total Liabilities to Net Worth 37	1.9	•	1.2	0.4	1.4	1.0	1.1	2.0	1.7
Current Assets to Working Capital 38	3.0	•	1.4	1.6	2.4	1.8	2.0	2.8	2.6
Current Liabilities to Working Capital 39	2.0	•	0.4	0.6	1.4	0.8	1.0	1.8	1.6
Working Capital to Net Sales 40	0.1	•	0.1	0.1	0.1	0.2	0.1	0.1	0.1
Inventory to Working Capital 41	0.9	•	0.3	0.3	0.7	0.4	0.6	1.0	1.2
Total Receipts to Cash Flow 42	13.3	7.2	3.9	6.5	11.4	12.1	12.6	16.6	17.1
Cost of Goods to Cash Flow 43	10.7	3.6	2.1	4.5	8.4	9.5	10.2	13.8	14.4
Cash Flow to Total Debt 44	0.4	•	1.8	2.4	0.6	0.5	0.5	0.3	0.3

Selected Financial Factors (in Percentages)

Debt Ratio 45	65.0	•	53.5	27.4	58.6	48.7	53.5	67.2	62.7
Return on Total Assets 46	13.9	•	53.6	40.5	20.5	11.2	14.7	9.5	7.6
Return on Equity Before Income Taxes 47	35.6	•	112.9	55.6	46.0	19.3	30.5	24.4	17.1
Return on Equity After Income Taxes 48	32.6	•	112.5	55.5	44.0	18.1	28.5	21.3	16.3
Profit Margin (Before Income Tax) 49	3.7	2.5	14.2	9.6	4.5	3.5	4.0	2.6	2.2
Profit Margin (After Income Tax) 50	3.4	2.5	14.1	9.6	4.3	3.3	3.7	2.2	2.1

Table I

Corporations with and without Net Income

DRUGS AND DRUGGISTS' SUNDRIES

MONEY AMOUNTS AND SIZE OF ASSETS IN THOUSANDS OF DOLLARS

Item Description for Accounting Period 7/09 Through 6/10	Total	Zero Assets	Under 500	500 to 1,000	1,000 to 5,000	5,000 to 10,000	10,000 to 25,000	25,000 to 50,000	50,000 to 100,000	100,000 to 250,000	250,000 to 500,000	500,000 to 2,500,000	2,500,000 and over
Number of Enterprises 1	7224	776	4535	476	941	185	137	55	34	41	12	17	15
Revenues ($ in Thousands)													
Net Sales 2	386285002	739975	1380358	672856	5294142	3400315	4666197	5398724	3950507	9470435	12609542	19170081	319531869
Interest 3	414107	220	180	772	1769	2731	1883	3487	4038	8572	9241	209309	171907
Rents 4	117248	0	0	738	706	13	741	528	78	984	626	6522	106312
Royalties 5	2862668	4010	0	0	35450	59	0	1979	42802	43043	36523	73512	2625291
Other Portfolio Income 6	752936	54137	4733	526	145053	10432	3360	2969	80783	15435	15141	90903	329464
Other Receipts 7	3742196	20656	73453	1290	22464	41916	55069	40395	33318	79969	41316	312499	3019849
Total Receipts 8	394174157	818998	1458724	676182	5499584	3455466	4727250	5448082	4111526	9618438	12712389	19862826	325784692
Average Total Receipts 9	54565	1055	322	1421	5844	18678	34505	99056	120927	234596	1059366	1168402	21718979
Operating Costs/Operating Income (%)													
Cost of Operations 10	85.1	57.4	46.3	67.0	50.2	76.6	66.8	80.3	69.2	69.7	90.1	49.7	88.9
Salaries and Wages 11	3.7	12.5	13.0	6.0	7.1	7.8	10.4	5.8	9.6	8.3	2.7	11.2	2.8
Taxes Paid 12	0.5	1.6	1.7	1.3	1.3	1.1	1.4	0.7	1.0	1.0	0.5	1.3	0.3
Interest Paid 13	0.5	4.7	0.8	1.1	1.3	0.6	0.6	0.4	1.3	1.4	0.5	2.1	0.4
Depreciation 14	0.5	0.8	0.6	0.9	0.5	0.3	0.7	0.6	1.0	0.9	0.4	1.3	0.4
Amortization and Depletion 15	0.3	1.3	0.2	0.0	0.1	0.1	0.4	0.4	0.7	0.8	0.2	1.3	0.3
Pensions and Other Deferred Comp. 16	0.2	0.1	•	1.0	0.1	0.1	0.1	0.1	0.2	0.8	0.3	0.4	0.1
Employee Benefits 17	0.4	2.0	0.5	0.5	0.5	0.5	0.6	0.6	0.9	0.6	0.2	1.6	0.4
Advertising 18	0.8	1.1	3.3	0.6	1.2	1.5	0.9	1.6	3.5	1.8	0.4	2.8	0.6
Other Expenses 19	6.2	19.8	34.8	15.0	33.3	8.5	13.0	6.1	14.0	12.6	3.3	21.1	4.4
Officers' Compensation 20	0.4	5.2	2.9	6.6	5.5	1.7	2.3	1.1	1.2	0.8	0.2	0.5	0.2
Operating Margin 21	1.4	•	•	0.2	•	1.4	2.7	2.2	•	1.3	1.1	6.7	1.2
Operating Margin Before Officers' Comp. 22	1.8	•	•	6.7	4.4	3.1	5.0	3.3	•	2.1	1.3	7.2	1.4

Selected Average Balance Sheet ($ in Thousands)

Net Receivables 23	4356	0	3	121	509	2228	4724	11615	13579	28745	108471	144034	1588769
Inventories 24	4260	0	32	135	669	2629	5521	8596	14850	23049	99490	110675	1579503
Net Property, Plant and Equipment 25	1599	0	6	108	153	450	1289	1943	6417	17153	37537	59666	571478
Total Assets 26	25519	0	63	716	2352	8439	17102	37015	71316	152667	376763	1145770	9525686
Notes and Loans Payable 27	4170	0	169	148	1052	1525	3453	6020	15932	60255	89084	156327	1364875
All Other Liabilities 28	11170	0	18	154	1050	3099	5697	15983	27872	43849	170007	307862	4486164
Net Worth 29	10179	0	-125	413	250	3815	7951	15012	27512	48563	117673	681582	3674647

Selected Financial Ratios (Times to 1)

Current Ratio 30	1.2	•	2.1	1.7	1.6	1.5	1.8	1.6	1.7	1.5	1.5	1.9	1.1
Quick Ratio 31	0.7	•	0.7	1.2	0.8	0.7	1.0	0.9	1.0	0.8	0.9	1.0	0.7
Net Sales to Working Capital 32	22.4	•	12.6	11.0	8.2	9.1	5.7	10.5	5.9	8.3	11.7	4.7	41.2
Coverage Ratio 33	7.6	1.9	2.9	1.6	3.1	5.9	7.4	9.2	2.2	3.1	4.5	6.2	9.5
Total Asset Turnover 34	2.1	•	4.8	2.0	2.4	2.2	2.0	2.7	1.6	1.5	2.8	1.0	2.2
Inventory Turnover 35	10.7	•	4.4	7.0	4.2	5.4	4.1	9.2	5.4	7.0	9.5	5.1	12.0
Receivables Turnover 36	12.1	•	69.8	11.4	10.3	8.9	7.3	9.5	7.4	9.9	9.2	7.2	13.2
Total Liabilities to Net Worth 37	1.5	•	•	0.7	8.4	1.2	1.2	1.5	1.6	2.1	2.2	0.7	1.6
Current Assets to Working Capital 38	5.3	•	1.9	2.4	2.8	3.1	2.2	2.8	2.4	3.1	2.8	2.1	8.7
Current Liabilities to Working Capital 39	4.3	•	0.9	1.4	1.8	2.1	1.2	1.8	1.4	2.1	1.8	1.1	7.7
Working Capital to Net Sales 40	0.0	•	0.1	0.1	0.1	0.1	0.2	0.1	0.2	0.1	0.1	0.2	0.0
Inventory to Working Capital 41	1.8	•	1.2	0.7	0.9	1.4	0.8	0.9	0.7	0.9	1.0	0.4	3.1
Total Receipts to Cash Flow 42	11.1	6.7	4.0	8.0	3.0	9.9	6.6	12.1	8.0	6.9	20.7	3.4	14.0
Cost of Goods to Cash Flow 43	9.4	3.8	1.8	5.4	1.5	7.6	4.4	9.7	5.5	4.8	18.7	1.7	12.5
Cash Flow to Total Debt 44	0.3	•	0.4	0.6	0.9	0.4	0.6	0.4	0.3	0.3	0.2	0.7	0.3

Selected Financial Factors (in Percentages)

Debt Ratio 45	60.1	•	298.7	42.2	89.4	54.8	53.5	59.4	61.4	68.2	68.8	40.5	61.4
Return on Total Assets 46	8.7	•	11.4	3.5	9.6	8.0	9.1	9.2	4.8	6.4	6.9	12.7	8.3
Return on Equity Before Income Taxes 47	19.0	•	•	2.2	61.3	14.7	16.8	20.2	6.9	13.7	17.3	18.0	19.3
Return on Equity After Income Taxes 48	13.2	•	•	0.1	58.4	12.6	15.2	17.6	2.4	10.4	10.3	11.9	13.3
Profit Margin (Before Income Tax) 49	3.6	4.2	1.5	0.7	2.7	3.0	3.9	3.1	1.6	2.9	1.9	10.9	3.3
Profit Margin (After Income Tax) 50	2.5	2.6	1.5	0.0	2.6	2.6	3.6	2.7	0.6	2.2	1.2	7.2	2.3

Table II

Corporations with Net Income

DRUGS AND DRUGGISTS' SUNDRIES

MONEY AMOUNTS AND SIZE OF ASSETS IN THOUSANDS OF DOLLARS

Item Description for Accounting Period 7/09 Through 6/10	Total	Zero Assets	Under 500	500 to 1,000	1,000 to 5,000	5,000 to 10,000	10,000 to 25,000	25,000 to 50,000	50,000 to 100,000	100,000 to 250,000	250,000 to 500,000	500,000 to 2,500,000	2,500,000 and over
Number of Enterprises 1	3547	270	1948	305	639	129	118	46	22	29	•	•	15
Revenues ($ in Thousands)													
Net Sales 2	379830195	459330	771299	332906	4709029	2797059	4489925	5147666	3304155	8361243	•	•	319531869
Interest 3	257288	147	0	265	1522	523	1776	2682	1952	5896	•	•	171907
Rents 4	116452	0	0	0	706	0	741	484	78	984	•	•	106312
Royalties 5	2817532	60	0	0	35341	0	0	1979	27579	43043	•	•	2625291
Other Portfolio Income 6	696698	48444	4733	526	144898	287	591	2964	66418	4771	•	•	329464
Other Receipts 7	3690743	12711	73389	688	19181	31611	53275	39414	20993	81338	•	•	3019849
Total Receipts 8	387408908	520692	849421	334385	4910677	2829480	4546308	5195189	3421175	8497275	•	•	325784692
Average Total Receipts 9	109222	1928	436	1096	7685	21934	38528	112939	155508	293009	•	•	21718979
Operating Costs/Operating Income (%)													
Cost of Operations 10	85.5	65.2	55.8	60.9	48.8	76.1	67.9	82.7	71.3	72.7	•	•	88.9
Salaries and Wages 11	3.5	7.2	4.1	3.8	6.6	6.7	9.2	5.2	8.0	8.0	•	•	2.8
Taxes Paid 12	0.4	2.1	1.1	1.2	1.1	1.1	1.3	0.7	0.9	0.9	•	•	0.3
Interest Paid 13	0.4	0.2	0.1	1.0	1.2	0.4	0.6	0.3	1.2	0.5	•	•	0.4
Depreciation 14	0.4	0.2	0.6	0.4	0.4	0.3	0.6	0.4	0.7	0.6	•	•	0.4
Amortization and Depletion 15	0.3	0.4	0.1	0.0	0.1	0.0	0.4	0.2	0.4	0.6	•	•	0.3
Pensions and Other Deferred Comp. 16	0.2	0.0	•	1.8	0.1	0.1	0.1	0.1	0.2	0.9	•	•	0.1
Employee Benefits 17	0.4	2.2	0.0	0.4	0.4	0.4	0.5	0.6	0.9	0.5	•	•	0.4
Advertising 18	0.7	0.9	4.6	1.1	1.1	0.7	0.9	1.0	3.0	1.2	•	•	0.6
Other Expenses 19	5.9	9.4	22.7	15.1	32.1	6.9	11.3	5.3	10.5	9.9	•	•	4.4
Officers' Compensation 20	0.4	5.7	3.2	7.2	4.6	1.8	2.2	1.0	1.0	0.8	•	•	0.2
Operating Margin 21	1.8	6.4	7.8	7.0	3.5	5.5	5.1	2.5	1.9	3.5	•	•	1.2
Operating Margin Before Officers' Comp. 22	2.2	12.1	11.1	14.2	8.1	7.3	7.3	3.5	2.9	4.2	•	•	1.4

Selected Average Balance Sheet ($ in Thousands)

Net Receivables 23	8634	0	1	106	679	2539	5308	13179	16635	34494	•	1588769
Inventories 24	8286	0	38	90	796	3452	4834	9868	18761	24099	•	1580315
Net Property, Plant and Equipment 25	3091	0	9	39	164	471	832	2216	4763	19785	•	571478
Total Assets 26	49925	0	82	760	2571	8995	16993	36625	69993	151953	•	9525686
Notes and Loans Payable 27	7367	0	29	12	1186	1031	3227	4474	16462	47735	•	1364875
All Other Liabilities 28	22230	0	11	85	1125	2720	6147	18077	29617	54257	•	4486164
Net Worth 29	20329	0	42	662	259	5244	7619	14075	23914	49961	•	3674647

Selected Financial Ratios (Times to 1)

Current Ratio 30	1.2	•	4.6	3.5	1.5	2.0	1.8	1.6	1.7	1.5	•	1.1
Quick Ratio 31	0.7	•	0.9	2.5	0.8	1.0	1.0	0.9	0.9	0.8	•	0.7
Net Sales to Working Capital 32	23.5	•	7.9	5.1	10.4	5.9	6.0	10.7	7.3	8.6	•	41.2
Coverage Ratio 33	10.0	89.4	248.1	8.5	7.7	16.9	12.2	13.5	5.8	11.0	•	9.5
Total Asset Turnover 34	2.1	•	4.8	1.4	2.9	2.4	2.2	3.1	2.1	1.9	•	2.2
Inventory Turnover 35	11.0	•	5.9	7.4	4.5	4.8	5.3	9.4	5.7	8.7	•	12.0
Receivables Turnover 36	12.3	•	866.6	•	10.3	8.6	8.8	9.4	8.0	10.2	•	•
Total Liabilities to Net Worth 37	1.5	•	0.9	0.1	8.9	0.7	1.2	1.6	1.9	2.0	•	1.6
Current Assets to Working Capital 38	5.4	•	1.3	1.4	2.9	2.0	2.3	2.7	2.5	3.0	•	8.7
Current Liabilities to Working Capital 39	4.4	•	0.3	0.4	1.9	1.0	1.3	1.7	1.5	2.0	•	7.7
Working Capital to Net Sales 40	0.0	•	0.1	0.2	0.1	0.2	0.2	0.1	0.1	0.1	•	0.0
Inventory to Working Capital 41	1.8	•	1.0	0.4	1.1	1.0	0.9	1.0	0.9	0.9	•	3.1
Total Receipts to Cash Flow 42	11.1	5.9	3.1	5.3	2.6	8.3	6.2	12.8	7.7	7.0	•	14.0
Cost of Goods to Cash Flow 43	9.5	3.8	1.7	3.3	1.3	6.3	4.2	10.6	5.5	5.1	•	12.5
Cash Flow to Total Debt 44	0.3	•	3.2	2.1	1.2	0.7	0.7	0.4	0.4	0.4	•	0.3

Selected Financial Factors (in Percentages)

Debt Ratio 45	59.3	•	48.6	12.9	89.9	41.7	55.2	61.6	65.8	67.1	•	61.4
Return on Total Assets 46	9.5	•	86.7	12.2	25.6	17.1	15.5	11.3	15.0	10.6	•	8.3
Return on Equity Before Income Taxes 47	20.9	•	168.0	12.3	221.5	27.6	31.7	27.1	36.4	29.4	•	19.3
Return on Equity After Income Taxes 48	14.9	•	167.7	10.3	217.4	25.5	29.8	23.9	28.4	25.0	•	13.3
Profit Margin (Before Income Tax) 49	4.0	19.8	18.0	7.5	7.8	6.7	6.3	3.4	5.8	5.1	•	3.3
Profit Margin (After Income Tax) 50	2.8	17.1	17.9	6.2	7.6	6.2	6.0	3.0	4.5	4.3	•	2.3

Table I

Corporations with and without Net Income

APPAREL, PIECE GOODS, AND NOTIONS

MONEY AMOUNTS AND SIZE OF ASSETS IN THOUSANDS OF DOLLARS

Item Description for Accounting Period 7/09 Through 6/10		Total	Zero Assets	Under 500	500 to 1,000	1,000 to 5,000	5,000 to 10,000	10,000 to 25,000	25,000 to 50,000	50,000 to 100,000	100,000 to 250,000	250,000 to 500,000	500,000 to 2,500,000	2,500,000 and over
Number of Enterprises	1	17846	2324	11449	1587	1810	279	220	80	43	23	18	11	3
Revenues ($ in Thousands)														
Net Sales	2	82336643	570577	5055968	3159999	9404026	6196368	8319667	5871535	5368356	5124389	7010264	12793458	13462037
Interest	3	69250	181	629	58	3701	773	2089	1027	6999	10463	9134	12223	21973
Rents	4	38701	0	0	0	3184	261	173	1158	2375	5586	6162	17609	2193
Royalties	5	1158680	0	0	0	0	0	647	27468	30664	24120	79518	339701	656563
Other Portfolio Income	6	694232	0	2385	0	4152	163	396	604	247	10182	10882	175066	490157
Other Receipts	7	782447	602	29867	15235	18272	4662	87375	94583	66851	51335	52754	56940	303967
Total Receipts	8	85079953	571360	5088849	3175292	9433335	6202227	8410347	5996375	5475492	5226075	7168714	13394997	14936890
Average Total Receipts	9	4767	246	444	2001	5212	22230	38229	74955	127337	227221	398262	1217727	4978963
Operating Costs/Operating Income (%)														
Cost of Operations	10	66.0	66.6	67.2	68.5	72.5	78.2	74.4	73.4	72.2	66.3	66.2	56.9	52.4
Salaries and Wages	11	9.6	4.6	4.7	7.1	5.2	6.3	7.7	7.1	8.0	8.0	11.4	12.9	16.4
Taxes Paid	12	2.5	1.4	1.9	3.5	2.1	2.3	2.4	2.6	2.2	3.2	1.7	2.9	2.6
Interest Paid	13	0.9	0.4	0.4	0.6	0.8	0.6	0.6	0.6	1.0	2.2	1.7	1.3	0.5
Depreciation	14	1.2	0.2	0.4	0.4	0.4	0.4	0.4	0.7	0.8	1.5	1.8·	2.5	2.2
Amortization and Depletion	15	0.4	0.0	0.1	0.0	0.2	0.0	0.2	0.2	0.3	0.4	1.1	0.5	0.4
Pensions and Other Deferred Comp.	16	0.2	0.0	0.3	0.5	0.2	0.1	0.1	0.2	0.2	0.3	0.3	0.3	0.3
Employee Benefits	17	0.7	1.1	0.2	0.2	0.2	0.6	0.5	0.4	0.8	0.8	1.2	1.0	0.6
Advertising	18	2.2	0.3	0.6	1.2	0.7	0.8	0.6	1.1	1.5	3.0	1.9	3.5	5.5
Other Expenses	19	14.0	28.2	16.4	15.1	12.0	7.2	9.6	9.4	11.3	12.9	13.3	18.3	19.2
Officers' Compensation	20	2.1	3.2	6.6	2.9	3.6	1.8	2.4	3.1	1.8	1.1	0.7	0.8	0.9
Operating Margin	21	0.1	•	1.2	0.1	1.8	1.6	1.0	1.3	•	0.4	•	•	•
Operating Margin Before Officers' Comp.	22	2.2	•	7.7	3.0	5.4	3.4	3.5	4.5	1.6	1.6	0.7	•	•

Selected Average Balance Sheet ($ in Thousands)

Net Receivables 23	546	0	22	153	581	2519	3852	9068	19144	37624	46632	148299	585149
Inventories 24	687	0	24	365	620	3501	5945	13123	20924	47823	76730	151557	634669
Net Property, Plant and Equipment 25	328	0	6	14	110	1057	794	3247	5737	17578	33747	148554	649773
Total Assets 26	3895	0	93	669	2168	6977	15600	33409	71987	163445	335994	1073730	10231418
Notes and Loans Payable 27	768	0	40	354	681	3287	3761	8487	21449	68462	105833	195808	825541
All Other Liabilities 28	861	0	35	229	806	2718	5870	12543	18868	31752	86287	277288	1316769
Net Worth 29	2266	0	19	87	681	971	5968	12379	31670	63231	143874	600634	8089108

Selected Financial Ratios (Times to 1)

Current Ratio 30	1.8	•	1.8	2.3	1.7	1.3	1.7	1.8	1.9	2.5	2.0	1.9	1.7
Quick Ratio 31	1.0	•	1.2	0.8	0.9	0.7	0.8	0.8	0.9	1.2	0.8	1.0	1.1
Net Sales to Working Capital 32	5.9	•	14.6	5.6	7.5	16.2	7.1	6.0	5.1	3.5	4.7	5.2	5.0
Coverage Ratio 33	6.2	•	6.0	2.0	3.8	3.7	4.5	6.4	2.9	2.1	1.8	4.0	34.5
Total Asset Turnover 34	1.2	•	4.7	3.0	2.4	3.2	2.4	2.2	1.7	1.4	1.2	1.1	0.4
Inventory Turnover 35	4.4	•	12.6	3.7	6.1	5.0	4.7	4.1	4.3	3.1	3.4	4.4	3.7
Receivables Turnover 36	7.6	•	19.7	12.5	7.7	8.1	9.5	8.1	6.6	5.5	8.1	5.7	7.3
Total Liabilities to Net Worth 37	0.7	•	4.0	6.7	2.2	6.2	1.6	1.7	1.3	1.6	1.3	0.8	0.3
Current Assets to Working Capital 38	2.2	•	2.3	1.8	2.5	4.1	2.4	2.3	2.1	1.7	2.0	2.1	2.5
Current Liabilities to Working Capital 39	1.2	•	1.3	0.8	1.5	3.1	1.4	1.3	1.1	0.7	1.0	1.1	1.5
Working Capital to Net Sales 40	0.2	•	0.1	0.2	0.1	0.1	0.1	0.2	0.2	0.3	0.2	0.2	0.2
Inventory to Working Capital 41	0.8	•	0.7	1.0	0.9	1.7	1.2	0.9	0.8	0.6	0.8	0.7	0.6
Total Receipts to Cash Flow 42	7.3	6.0	7.8	9.4	8.9	13.4	10.7	9.2	9.5	8.4	11.3	6.2	4.0
Cost of Goods to Cash Flow 43	4.8	4.0	5.3	6.5	6.5	10.5	7.9	6.7	6.8	5.6	7.5	3.5	2.1
Cash Flow to Total Debt 44	0.4	•	0.8	0.4	0.4	0.3	0.4	0.4	0.3	0.3	0.2	0.4	0.5

Selected Financial Factors (in Percentages)

Debt Ratio 45	41.8	•	80.1	87.0	68.6	86.1	61.7	62.9	56.0	61.3	57.2	44.1	20.9
Return on Total Assets 46	6.8	•	10.3	3.5	7.0	7.4	6.6	9.0	5.0	6.3	3.5	5.8	7.8
Return on Equity Before Income Taxes 47	9.7	•	43.0	13.4	16.5	38.6	13.3	20.6	7.4	8.6	3.6	7.8	9.6
Return on Equity After Income Taxes 48	6.4	•	42.0	11.0	15.9	35.4	12.5	18.2	6.2	4.8	0.9	2.6	6.3
Profit Margin (Before Income Tax) 49	4.8	•	1.8	0.6	2.2	1.7	2.1	3.5	1.9	2.5	1.3	4.1	17.4
Profit Margin (After Income Tax) 50	3.1	•	1.8	0.5	2.1	1.5	2.0	3.1	1.6	1.4	0.3	1.3	11.3

Table II

Corporations with Net Income

APPAREL, PIECE GOODS, AND NOTIONS

MONEY AMOUNTS AND SIZE OF ASSETS IN THOUSANDS OF DOLLARS

Item Description for Accounting Period 7/09 Through 6/10	Total	Zero Assets	Under 500	500 to 1,000	1,000 to 5,000	5,000 to 10,000	10,000 to 25,000	25,000 to 50,000	50,000 to 100,000	100,000 to 250,000	250,000 to 500,000	500,000 to 2,500,000	2,500,000 and over
Number of Enterprises 1	11010	1062	7040	1026	1358	249	151	57	31	17	9	8	3
Revenues ($ in Thousands)													
Net Sales 2	64510035	335551	3883402	2306551	7428496	5614985	6723336	4444116	4110694	3834727	4051582	8314558	13462037
Interest 3	57946	0	325	32	3274	712	258	670	5186	9230	6097	10190	21973
Rents 4	15465	0	0	0	3076	149	0	43	1183	4276	2747	1797	2193
Royalties 5	923346	0	0	0	0	0	163	72	17584	22261	16541	210163	656563
Other Portfolio Income 6	683656	0	5	0	2214	163	197	557	242	9885	5170	175066	490157
Other Receipts 7	567828	240	21057	14421	7014	4864	55106	52538	59242	37656	-8177	19899	303967
Total Receipts 8	66758276	335791	3904789	2321004	7444074	5620873	6779060	4497996	4194131	3918035	4073960	8731673	14936890
Average Total Receipts 9	6063	316	555	2262	5482	22574	44894	78912	135295	230473	452662	1091459	4978963
Operating Costs/Operating Income (%)													
Cost of Operations 10	64.9	48.4	66.7	69.4	71.9	78.9	73.6	72.7	72.2	65.1	61.4	54.6	52.4
Salaries and Wages 11	9.5	3.5	4.2	6.4	5.0	5.9	7.1	7.0	7.7	7.8	11.2	12.9	16.4
Taxes Paid 12	2.4	2.1	1.9	3.2	2.1	1.8	2.7	2.3	1.8	3.8	1.8	2.3	2.6
Interest Paid 13	0.7	0.1	0.3	0.5	0.8	0.6	0.4	0.5	0.8	1.7	0.7	0.8	0.5
Depreciation 14	1.2	0.2	0.5	0.4	0.4	0.4	0.3	0.6	0.6	1.4	1.7	2.5	2.2
Amortization and Depletion 15	0.2	•	0.1	0.0	0.1	0.0	0.1	0.1	0.2	0.4	0.3	0.4	0.4
Pensions and Other Deferred Comp. 16	0.2	•	0.2	0.1	0.3	0.1	0.1	0.2	0.2	0.3	0.2	0.3	0.3
Employee Benefits 17	0.6	1.7	0.2	0.0	0.6	0.6	0.4	0.3	0.7	0.6	1.2	0.9	0.6
Advertising 18	2.2	0.1	0.8	1.4	0.6	0.3	0.6	0.7	1.5	3.0	1.9	3.1	5.5
Other Expenses 19	12.6	31.2	13.4	14.8	11.4	6.2	7.9	7.2	9.7	12.4	13.0	13.9	19.2
Officers' Compensation 20	2.1	5.5	6.0	2.1	2.7	1.9	2.7	3.5	1.9	1.3	0.7	1.2	0.9
Operating Margin 21	3.4	7.3	5.8	1.5	4.1	3.3	4.1	4.9	2.9	2.2	5.9	7.3	•
Operating Margin Before Officers' Comp. 22	5.4	12.8	11.8	3.6	6.8	5.2	6.7	8.4	4.8	3.5	6.6	8.4	•

Selected Average Balance Sheet ($ in Thousands)

Net Receivables 23	664	0	24	130	606	2609	3918	9289	21929	41233	37486	116930	585149
Inventories 24	789	0	21	325	626	2088	6501	14838	19750	45290	99735	134213	531092
Net Property, Plant and Equipment 25	422	0	6	14	112	1082	771	3465	3904	16575	41548	140560	649773
Total Assets 26	5132	0	100	672	2132	7076	16045	34072	71675	161196	339002	922727	10231418
Notes and Loans Payable 27	738	0	29	280	646	3222	2737	7822	18101	52324	29695	112021	825541
All Other Liabilities 28	1031	0	36	220	793	2352	5968	10617	18217	29898	87956	235790	1316769
Net Worth 29	3364	0	35	172	693	1502	7340	15633	35357	78973	221351	574916	8089108

Selected Financial Ratios (Times to 1)

Current Ratio 30	2.0	•	2.0	2.7	1.8	1.5	1.9	2.0	2.1	3.0	2.0	2.4	1.7
Quick Ratio 31	1.1	•	1.4	1.0	0.9	0.8	1.0	1.0	1.0	1.5	0.9	1.4	1.1
Net Sales to Working Capital 32	5.4	•	16.1	5.7	6.8	11.6	6.6	5.5	4.7	3.2	4.9	3.7	5.0
Coverage Ratio 33	13.8	120.4	24.3	4.8	6.3	6.9	12.3	12.1	7.3	3.6	11.7	17.5	34.5
Total Asset Turnover 34	1.1	•	5.5	3.3	2.6	3.2	2.8	2.3	1.9	1.4	1.3	1.1	0.4
Inventory Turnover 35	4.8	•	17.9	4.8	6.3	8.5	5.0	3.8	4.8	3.2	2.8	4.2	4.4
Receivables Turnover 36	8.0	•	23.7	•	7.5	10.4	10.8	7.9	6.9	5.1	8.5	•	15.3
Total Liabilities to Net Worth 37	0.5	•	1.9	2.9	2.1	3.7	1.2	1.2	1.0	1.0	0.5	0.6	0.3
Current Assets to Working Capital 38	2.0	•	2.1	1.6	2.2	2.9	2.1	2.0	1.9	1.5	2.0	1.7	2.5
Current Liabilities to Working Capital 39	1.0	•	1.1	0.6	1.2	1.9	1.1	1.0	0.9	0.5	1.0	0.7	1.5
Working Capital to Net Sales 40	0.2	•	0.1	0.2	0.1	0.1	0.2	0.2	0.2	0.3	0.2	0.3	0.2
Inventory to Working Capital 41	0.7	•	0.6	0.8	0.8	1.2	1.1	0.9	0.8	0.6	0.8	0.5	0.6
Total Receipts to Cash Flow 42	6.2	3.1	6.5	7.9	7.9	11.7	9.1	8.3	7.9	7.1	7.4	4.9	4.0
Cost of Goods to Cash Flow 43	4.0	1.5	4.4	5.5	5.7	9.3	6.7	6.0	5.7	4.6	4.6	2.7	2.1
Cash Flow to Total Debt 44	0.5	•	1.3	0.6	0.5	0.3	0.6	0.5	0.5	0.4	0.5	0.6	0.5

Selected Financial Factors (in Percentages)

Debt Ratio 45	34.5	•	65.0	74.4	67.5	78.8	54.3	54.1	50.7	51.0	34.7	37.7	20.9
Return on Total Assets 46	10.5	•	36.6	8.9	13.1	12.8	14.8	15.2	10.6	8.5	10.4	15.0	7.8
Return on Equity Before Income Taxes 47	14.8	•	100.3	27.5	33.9	51.6	29.7	30.4	18.6	12.5	14.6	22.7	9.6
Return on Equity After Income Taxes 48	11.1	•	99.5	25.6	33.2	49.3	28.7	27.8	17.1	8.4	11.0	15.2	6.3
Profit Margin (Before Income Tax) 49	8.5	7.4	6.4	2.1	4.3	3.4	4.9	6.1	5.0	4.4	7.2	12.6	17.4
Profit Margin (After Income Tax) 50	6.4	7.3	6.3	2.0	4.2	3.3	4.7	5.6	4.6	2.9	5.4	8.4	11.3

Table I

Corporations with and without Net Income

GROCERY AND RELATED PRODUCT

MONEY AMOUNTS AND SIZE OF ASSETS IN THOUSANDS OF DOLLARS

Item Description for Accounting Period 7/09 Through 6/10	Total	Zero Assets	Under 500	500 to 1,000	1,000 to 5,000	5,000 to 10,000	10,000 to 25,000	25,000 to 50,000	50,000 to 100,000	100,000 to 250,000	250,000 to 500,000	500,000 to 2,500,000	2,500,000 and over
Number of Enterprises 1	33754	3921	19796	2951	5198	874	596	210	117	53	13	20	5
Revenues ($ in Thousands)													
Net Sales 2	535096629	2537048	16128430	10042548	60851719	30581707	40314232	27832159	28457976	24679144	23311403	72059456	198300807
Interest 3	5367464	761	6814	1233	16461	15512	7935	10656	9053	8805	2204	58059	5229970
Rents 4	932638	0	1122	2804	19436	5688	10460	4748	3161	7662	1308	59583	816665
Royalties 5	456152	63	0	0	0	0	663	0	593	289	5558	4929	444057
Other Portfolio Income 6	3438948	29660	6919	2581	43709	1771	11688	10438	3105	20834	10335	14869	3283033
Other Receipts 7	2612701	6411	22108	72055	436132	158087	190570	158773	288154	299986	60173	761960	158301
Total Receipts 8	547904532	2573943	16165393	10121221	61367457	30762765	40535548	28016774	28762042	25016720	23390981	72958856	208232833
Average Total Receipts 9	16232	656	817	3430	11806	35198	68013	133413	245829	472014	1799306	3647943	41646567
Operating Costs/Operating Income (%)													
Cost of Operations 10	80.5	84.0	77.0	79.1	85.5	88.3	86.6	86.2	85.0	85.8	88.0	84.9	72.4
Salaries and Wages 11	5.9	3.2	4.0	6.5	3.9	3.1	4.2	4.1	5.1	4.0	3.3	5.2	8.7
Taxes Paid 12	1.1	0.7	1.0	1.3	1.0	0.6	0.8	0.7	0.7	1.7	0.5	0.8	1.4
Interest Paid 13	1.1	0.6	0.2	0.6	0.3	0.3	0.3	0.3	0.5	0.6	0.3	0.6	2.4
Depreciation 14	1.5	0.5	0.6	0.6	0.6	0.3	0.5	0.6	0.8	0.9	1.0	0.8	3.0
Amortization and Depletion 15	0.3	0.5	0.0	0.1	0.1	0.0	0.0	0.0	0.1	0.2	0.1	0.2	0.5
Pensions and Other Deferred Comp. 16	0.4	0.2	0.2	0.1	0.1	0.1	0.2	0.1	0.2	0.2	0.2	0.2	0.8
Employee Benefits 17	0.8	0.3	0.2	0.6	0.4	0.3	0.4	0.5	0.5	0.6	0.5	0.7	1.2
Advertising 18	0.6	0.4	0.3	0.2	0.1	0.1	0.3	0.3	0.7	1.1	0.5	0.6	1.0
Other Expenses 19	6.9	8.0	10.6	8.3	5.7	4.8	4.2	4.6	4.7	4.2	4.2	5.4	9.7
Officers' Compensation 20	0.8	2.5	4.5	2.5	1.6	0.9	1.2	0.8	0.8	0.6	0.2	0.2	0.3
Operating Margin 21	0.1	•	1.3	0.1	0.7	1.0	1.3	1.7	1.0	0.3	1.3	0.6	•
Operating Margin Before Officers' Comp. 22	0.8	1.6	5.9	2.7	2.4	1.9	2.5	2.5	1.8	0.8	1.5	0.7	•

Selected Average Balance Sheet ($ in Thousands)

Net Receivables 23	1240	0	25	232	755	2684	5454	10394	18899	33664	98480	157930	4108141
Inventories 24	936	0	18	129	461	1726	3811	9542	18217	43511	102476	208502	2544826
Net Property, Plant and Equipment 25	1825	0	20	142	301	623	2153	4992	11499	22955	101445	220515	9611473
Total Assets 26	15302	0	119	707	2082	7111	15653	33669	67732	140940	391260	1040443	87468164
Notes and Loans Payable 27	2774	0	67	451	561	2516	4174	8208	21542	49941	65346	323907	13831537
All Other Liabilities 28	4248	0	33	254	731	2342	5484	13187	22546	39555	179562	351588	23198988
Net Worth 29	8280	0	19	2	790	2253	5996	12275	23644	51445	146352	364948	50437639

Selected Financial Ratios (Times to 1)

Current Ratio 30	1.2	•	2.2	1.7	1.9	1.7	1.6	1.6	1.5	1.6	1.7	1.5	1.1
Quick Ratio 31	0.8	•	1.4	1.2	1.3	1.0	1.0	0.8	0.8	0.8	0.8	0.6	0.7
Net Sales to Working Capital 32	19.9	•	21.0	17.1	15.6	16.0	15.1	13.9	16.0	13.3	18.6	22.5	28.6
Coverage Ratio 33	3.2	1.9	8.7	2.6	6.6	7.0	8.0	8.1	5.2	3.5	7.0	4.2	2.6
Total Asset Turnover 34	1.0	•	6.8	4.8	5.6	4.9	4.3	3.9	3.6	3.3	4.6	3.5	0.5
Inventory Turnover 35	13.6	•	34.3	20.8	21.7	17.9	15.4	12.0	11.3	9.2	15.4	14.7	11.3
Receivables Turnover 36	13.0	•	32.1	18.2	15.0	12.6	12.3	12.1	13.4	14.0	18.6	23.4	10.1
Total Liabilities to Net Worth 37	0.8	•	5.2	377.9	1.6	2.2	1.6	1.7	1.9	1.7	1.7	1.9	0.7
Current Assets to Working Capital 38	5.2	•	1.8	2.4	2.2	2.5	2.6	2.6	2.9	2.6	2.4	3.0	12.7
Current Liabilities to Working Capital 39	4.2	•	0.8	1.4	1.2	1.5	1.6	1.6	1.9	1.6	1.4	2.0	11.7
Working Capital to Net Sales 40	0.1	•	0.0	0.1	0.1	0.1	0.1	0.1	0.1	0.1	0.1	0.0	0.0
Inventory to Working Capital 41	1.1	•	0.5	0.6	0.6	0.8	0.8	1.0	1.1	1.2	1.1	1.2	1.7
Total Receipts to Cash Flow 42	12.6	17.0	10.0	13.0	17.6	18.1	20.6	18.0	17.3	20.9	21.3	17.4	8.5
Cost of Goods to Cash Flow 43	10.1	14.3	7.7	10.3	15.1	16.0	17.8	15.5	14.7	17.9	18.8	14.7	6.2
Cash Flow to Total Debt 44	0.2	•	0.8	0.4	0.5	0.4	0.3	0.3	0.3	0.2	0.3	0.3	0.1

Selected Financial Factors (in Percentages)

Debt Ratio 45	45.9	•	83.9	99.7	62.1	68.3	61.7	63.5	65.1	63.5	62.6	64.9	42.3
Return on Total Assets 46	3.8	•	12.0	7.1	10.6	9.1	9.2	10.7	9.1	7.4	8.8	8.3	2.8
Return on Equity Before Income Taxes 47	4.8	•	66.2	1674.9	23.7	24.6	21.0	25.7	21.1	14.6	20.2	17.9	3.0
Return on Equity After Income Taxes 48	3.5	•	65.3	1672.1	22.2	23.1	19.1	23.1	19.3	11.6	17.0	12.1	1.9
Profit Margin (Before Income Tax) 49	2.5	0.5	1.6	0.9	1.6	1.6	1.9	2.4	2.1	1.6	1.7	1.8	3.8
Profit Margin (After Income Tax) 50	1.8	•	1.5	0.9	1.5	1.5	1.7	2.1	1.9	1.3	1.4	1.2	2.4

Table II

Corporations with Net Income

GROCERY AND RELATED PRODUCT

MONEY AMOUNTS AND SIZE OF ASSETS IN THOUSANDS OF DOLLARS

Item Description for Accounting Period 7/09 Through 6/10		Total	Zero Assets	Under 500	500 to 1,000	1,000 to 5,000	5,000 to 10,000	10,000 to 25,000	25,000 to 50,000	50,000 to 100,000	100,000 to 250,000	250,000 to 500,000	500,000 to 2,500,000	2,500,000 and over
Number of Enterprises	1	20086	1841	11174	1631	3910	675	500	181	100	43	•	17	•
Revenues ($ in Thousands)														
Net Sales	2	456687169	1583138	10980482	4473861	47056284	26354227	36378609	23899642	24912817	21846961	•	6018987	•
Interest	3	5326263	406	6652	720	13932	14966	6251	8683	8014	6507	•	35087	•
Rents	4	882316	0	1122	837	922	4531	8815	3913	2746	4317	•	39453	•
Royalties	5	449123	63	0	0	0	0	663	0	593	289	•	4006	•
Other Portfolio Income	6	3390985	29563	4518	2099	16993	1593	10714	9318	3002	10649	•	10583	•
Other Receipts	7	2236432	25315	10507	25486	329754	170853	177054	137305	254795	289682	•	738612	•
Total Receipts	8	468972288	1638485	11003281	4503003	47417885	26546170	36582106	24058861	25181967	22158405	•	61014728	•
Average Total Receipts	9	23348	890	985	2761	12127	39328	73164	132922	251820	515312	•	3589102	•
Operating Costs/Operating Income (%)														
Cost of Operations	10	79.7	85.1	73.5	72.6	84.9	87.8	86.8	86.2	84.5	86.7	•	84.6	•
Salaries and Wages	11	6.0	2.2	4.4	7.1	3.7	3.2	4.1	4.0	5.3	3.5	•	5.0	•
Taxes Paid	12	1.1	0.5	1.1	1.6	1.0	0.6	0.8	0.7	0.7	1.7	•	0.8	•
Interest Paid	13	1.2	0.7	0.2	0.5	0.3	0.2	0.2	0.3	0.5	0.5	•	0.5	•
Depreciation	14	1.7	0.5	0.6	0.6	0.6	0.3	0.4	0.6	0.8	0.8	•	0.8	•
Amortization and Depletion	15	0.3	0.4	0.0	0.2	0.1	0.0	0.0	0.0	0.1	0.2	•	0.2	•
Pensions and Other Deferred Comp.	16	0.4	0.3	0.3	0.1	0.1	0.1	0.1	0.1	0.2	0.2	•	0.2	•
Employee Benefits	17	0.8	0.3	0.3	0.4	0.4	0.3	0.4	0.5	0.5	0.5	•	0.7	•
Advertising	18	0.7	0.2	0.2	0.1	0.1	0.1	0.3	0.3	0.7	1.0	•	0.6	•
Other Expenses	19	7.1	5.1	10.3	10.7	5.3	4.9	3.8	4.1	4.4	3.8	•	5.5	•
Officers' Compensation	20	0.7	1.4	4.7	2.0	1.6	1.0	1.2	0.8	0.7	0.6	•	0.2	•
Operating Margin	21	0.5	3.3	4.5	4.1	1.9	1.5	1.8	2.5	1.5	0.6	•	1.0	•
Operating Margin Before Officers' Comp.	22	1.2	4.7	9.2	6.1	3.5	2.5	3.1	3.2	2.2	1.1	•	1.1	•

Selected Average Balance Sheet ($ in Thousands)

Net Receivables 23	1823	0	20	255	789	2850	5816	10446	18677	35580	141501
Inventories 24	1320	0	15	137	461	1857	3972	9874	17859	40683	168927
Net Property, Plant and Equipment 25	2861	0	22	115	291	512	1769	4897	11430	24326	216985
Total Assets 26	24447	0	118	672	2049	7296	15739	33394	67147	140272	970295
Notes and Loans Payable 27	4073	0	55	292	515	2251	3627	7645	20717	47982	288080
All Other Liabilities 28	6752	0	24	270	700	2337	5802	12247	21327	40476	350116
Net Worth 29	13623	0	39	110	835	2707	6310	13502	25104	51815	332098

Selected Financial Ratios (Times to 1)

Current Ratio 30	1.2	•	2.9	1.8	2.0	1.8	1.7	1.7	1.6	1.6	1.5
Quick Ratio 31	0.8	•	2.0	1.4	1.4	1.1	1.0	0.9	0.8	0.8	0.6
Net Sales to Working Capital 32	20.0	•	22.4	13.7	14.4	15.5	15.0	13.3	15.4	13.9	22.4
Coverage Ratio 33	3.8	11.1	32.2	10.1	10.7	11.4	10.9	11.0	6.5	4.7	5.8
Total Asset Turnover 34	0.9	•	8.3	4.1	5.9	5.4	4.6	4.0	3.7	3.6	3.6
Inventory Turnover 35	13.7	•	48.0	14.6	22.2	18.5	15.9	11.5	11.8	10.8	17.7
Receivables Turnover 36	12.9	•	43.4	12.3	14.9	12.6	12.5	11.9	14.6	15.6	27.9
Total Liabilities to Net Worth 37	0.8	•	2.0	5.1	1.5	1.7	1.5	1.5	1.7	1.7	1.9
Current Assets to Working Capital 38	5.6	•	1.5	2.3	2.0	2.3	2.5	2.5	2.8	2.6	3.0
Current Liabilities to Working Capital 39	4.6	•	0.5	1.3	1.0	1.3	1.5	1.5	1.8	1.6	2.0
Working Capital to Net Sales 40	0.0	•	0.0	0.1	0.1	0.1	0.1	0.1	0.1	0.1	0.0
Inventory to Working Capital 41	1.1	•	0.4	0.4	0.5	0.7	0.8	1.0	1.1	1.1	1.2
Total Receipts to Cash Flow 42	11.4	10.4	7.8	7.7	15.3	16.0	19.9	16.7	16.4	20.7	15.6
Cost of Goods to Cash Flow 43	9.1	8.8	5.7	5.6	13.0	14.0	17.2	14.4	13.9	18.0	13.2
Cash Flow to Total Debt 44	0.2	•	1.6	0.6	0.6	0.5	0.4	0.4	0.4	0.3	0.4

Selected Financial Factors (in Percentages)

Debt Ratio 45	44.3	•	66.8	83.6	59.3	62.9	59.9	59.6	62.6	63.1	65.8
Return on Total Assets 46	4.1	•	40.6	21.6	17.4	13.1	12.1	13.5	11.2	9.2	10.4
Return on Equity Before Income Taxes 47	5.4	•	118.7	118.6	38.6	32.2	27.4	30.4	25.4	19.6	25.1
Return on Equity After Income Taxes 48	4.1	•	117.9	118.5	36.8	30.6	25.3	27.7	23.4	16.0	17.6
Profit Margin (Before Income Tax) 49	3.3	6.8	4.7	4.8	2.7	2.2	2.4	3.1	2.6	2.0	2.4
Profit Margin (After Income Tax) 50	2.4	5.7	4.7	4.8	2.6	2.1	2.2	2.8	2.4	1.6	1.7

Table I

Corporations with and without Net Income

FARM PRODUCT RAW MATERIAL

MONEY AMOUNTS AND SIZE OF ASSETS IN THOUSANDS OF DOLLARS

Item Description for Accounting Period 7/09 Through 6/10	Total	Zero Assets	Under 500	500 to 1,000	1,000 to 5,000	5,000 to 10,000	10,000 to 25,000	25,000 to 50,000	50,000 to 100,000	100,000 to 250,000	250,000 to 500,000	500,000 to 2,500,000	2,500,000 and over
Number of Enterprises **1**	4629	20	2153	879	1102	240	121	68	16	13	7	6	3
Revenues ($ in Thousands)													
Net Sales **2**	143423567	703	1868681	3272364	9602873	5882897	7186531	7999324	3322307	4947080	13650127	14849107	70841571
Interest **3**	358484	21	71	3649	9566	8569	4746	3608	1703	2597	4745	34922	284287
Rents **4**	56276	4	5	890	4048	1922	1729	2850	1208	2866	735	1303	38717
Royalties **5**	63974	0	0	0	0	570	0	0	1024	124	0	220	62036
Other Portfolio Income **6**	1250888	0	3076	6242	3175	33106	10824	1318	2041	4480	2224	86151	1098250
Other Receipts **7**	2299860	1227	77332	114516	108535	50016	85467	83778	27669	59606	54772	149183	1487759
Total Receipts **8**	147453049	1955	1949165	3397661	9728197	5977080	7289297	8090878	3355952	5016753	13712603	15120886	73812620
Average Total Receipts **9**	31854	98	905	3865	8828	24904	60242	118984	209747	385904	1958943	2520148	24604207
Operating Costs/Operating Income (%)													
Cost of Operations **10**	91.9	16.4	80.3	85.5	88.3	76.5	93.4	91.9	92.0	93.6	95.6	94.4	92.8
Salaries and Wages **11**	2.3	42.4	2.5	3.3	2.7	12.0	2.0	2.8	1.7	1.9	1.0	1.4	1.9
Taxes Paid **12**	0.4	12.2	0.7	0.7	0.5	1.2	0.3	0.4	0.4	0.5	0.1	0.3	0.4
Interest Paid **13**	1.0	•	0.9	0.3	0.4	0.6	0.4	0.5	0.4	0.5	0.3	0.6	1.5
Depreciation **14**	1.0	2.4	1.2	1.0	1.0	0.7	0.7	0.7	1.1	0.7	0.4	0.7	1.2
Amortization and Depletion **15**	0.0	0.1	0.0	0.0	0.0	0.0	•	0.0	0.0	0.1	0.1	0.1	0.0
Pensions and Other Deferred Comp. **16**	0.2	•	0.1	0.1	0.1	0.7	0.1	0.1	0.1	0.1	0.1	0.2	0.3
Employee Benefits **17**	0.5	3.7	0.2	0.1	0.3	0.8	0.2	0.2	0.1	0.1	0.1	0.2	0.7
Advertising **18**	0.1	•	0.3	0.1	0.1	0.1	0.0	0.0	0.1	0.1	0.2	0.0	0.1
Other Expenses **19**	2.7	1743.1	11.7	5.3	5.4	4.1	3.1	2.5	2.7	1.8	1.2	2.0	2.4
Officers' Compensation **20**	0.7	19.1	2.4	1.8	1.4	4.5	0.6	0.5	0.4	0.4	0.3	0.2	0.4
Operating Margin **21**	•	•	•	1.6	•	•	•	0.5	1.1	0.1	0.6	0.0	•
Operating Margin Before Officers' Comp. **22**	•	•	2.2	3.4	1.1	3.3	•	0.9	1.5	0.5	0.9	0.2	•

Selected Average Balance Sheet ($ in Thousands)

Net Receivables 23	2555	0	12	113	540	1282	3593	8801	23290	29072	78383	339790	2141987
Inventories 24	2607	0	4	62	474	1311	5761	12366	23716	51523	96622	209472	2215974
Net Property, Plant and Equipment 25	1848	0	24	227	545	755	3150	4506	13539	19577	44374	131333	1754831
Total Assets 26	17074	0	157	693	2536	7238	14737	34621	69805	144704	369791	1050910	19175519
Notes and Loans Payable 27	6405	0	264	177	744	2616	5320	11662	15117	44609	114833	394072	7349848
All Other Liabilities 28	4095	0	64	135	933	2610	5705	13314	24707	49465	114191	334506	3868305
Net Worth 29	6574	0	-170	381	859	2012	3712	9645	29982	50630	140767	322332	7957366

Selected Financial Ratios (Times to 1)

Current Ratio 30	1.6	•	1.4	2.9	1.6	1.7	1.6	1.4	1.7	1.3	1.5	1.4	1.7
Quick Ratio 31	0.7	•	1.2	2.1	0.8	0.7	0.8	0.6	1.0	0.4	0.6	0.8	0.7
Net Sales to Working Capital 32	10.5	•	27.4	15.0	12.9	11.9	15.1	16.0	10.6	16.8	21.6	12.1	8.2
Coverage Ratio 33	3.5	•	5.5	18.4	3.7	1.7	2.3	4.4	6.2	4.1	4.7	5.1	3.1
Total Asset Turnover 34	1.8	•	5.5	5.4	3.4	3.4	4.0	3.4	3.0	2.6	5.3	2.4	1.2
Inventory Turnover 35	10.9	•	173.4	51.2	16.2	14.3	9.6	8.7	8.1	6.9	19.3	11.1	9.9
Receivables Turnover 36	10.9	•	43.0	32.3	18.1	20.1	15.6	12.0	9.8	9.9	31.2	6.4	9.5
Total Liabilities to Net Worth 37	1.6	•	•	0.8	2.0	2.6	3.0	2.6	1.3	1.9	1.6	2.3	1.4
Current Assets to Working Capital 38	2.6	•	3.8	1.5	2.7	2.5	2.7	3.6	2.5	4.4	3.0	3.6	2.4
Current Liabilities to Working Capital 39	1.6	•	2.8	0.5	1.7	1.5	1.7	2.6	1.5	3.4	2.0	2.6	1.4
Working Capital to Net Sales 40	0.1	•	0.0	0.1	0.1	0.1	0.1	0.1	0.1	0.1	0.0	0.1	0.1
Inventory to Working Capital 41	0.9	•	0.2	0.2	0.8	0.7	1.2	1.7	0.9	2.4	1.2	1.3	0.8
Total Receipts to Cash Flow 42	26.7	•	7.1	10.4	20.1	30.6	35.7	30.3	24.5	35.2	51.2	34.8	26.3
Cost of Goods to Cash Flow 43	24.5	0.6	5.7	8.9	17.7	23.4	33.3	27.9	22.5	33.0	49.0	32.9	24.4
Cash Flow to Total Debt 44	0.1	0.1	0.4	1.2	0.3	0.2	0.2	0.2	0.2	0.1	0.2	0.1	0.1

Selected Financial Factors (in Percentages)

Debt Ratio 45	61.5	•	208.3	45.0	66.1	72.2	74.8	72.1	57.0	65.0	61.9	69.3	58.5
Return on Total Assets 46	6.1	•	27.4	30.9	4.9	3.4	3.7	7.1	7.6	5.3	7.3	7.0	5.7
Return on Equity Before Income Taxes 47	11.2	•	•	53.2	10.6	5.2	8.5	19.7	14.8	11.4	15.1	18.4	9.3
Return on Equity After Income Taxes 48	8.8	•	•	52.0	9.9	3.3	6.4	18.1	12.5	9.4	8.7	12.1	7.3
Profit Margin (Before Income Tax) 49	2.4	•	4.1	5.4	1.0	0.4	0.5	1.6	2.1	1.5	1.1	2.4	3.1
Profit Margin (After Income Tax) 50	1.9	•	4.0	5.3	1.0	0.3	0.4	1.5	1.8	1.2	0.6	1.6	2.4

Table II

Corporations with Net Income

FARM PRODUCT RAW MATERIAL

MONEY AMOUNTS AND SIZE OF ASSETS IN THOUSANDS OF DOLLARS

Item Description for Accounting Period 7/09 Through 6/10	Total	Zero Assets	Under 500	500 to 1,000	1,000 to 5,000	5,000 to 10,000	10,000 to 25,000	25,000 to 50,000	50,000 to 100,000	100,000 to 250,000	250,000 to 500,000	500,000 to 2,500,000	2,500,000 and over
Number of Enterprises **1**	3258	9	1265	685	895	204	101	62	13	10	•	6	•
Revenues ($ in Thousands)													
Net Sales **2**	137984636	703	1847736	2697035	8824809	4830433	5895506	7259144	3140263	4642378	•	14849107	•
Interest **3**	348468	21	65	2055	3819	7887	3715	3564	1074	2315	•	34922	•
Rents **4**	53062	4	5	890	4043	337	1243	2850	404	2532	•	1303	•
Royalties **5**	62380	0	0	0	0	0	0	0	0	124	•	220	•
Other Portfolio Income **6**	1212039	0	3071	6231	2521	5724	2234	1258	1938	2438	•	86151	•
Other Receipts **7**	2195305	1227	77183	114516	74273	40510	58001	81459	15868	57086	•	149183	•
Total Receipts **8**	141855890	1955	1928060	2820727	8909465	4884891	5960699	7348275	3159547	4706873	•	15120886	•
Average Total Receipts **9**	43541	217	1524	4118	9955	23946	59017	118521	243042	470687	•	2520148	•
Operating Costs/Operating Income (%)													
Cost of Operations **10**	91.9	16.4	80.6	84.1	88.7	72.4	92.5	92.5	91.8	94.1	•	94.4	•
Salaries and Wages **11**	2.2	42.4	2.3	3.9	1.9	13.9	1.8	2.1	1.6	1.7	•	1.4	•
Taxes Paid **12**	0.4	12.2	0.6	0.7	0.5	1.3	0.3	0.3	0.3	0.5	•	0.3	•
Interest Paid **13**	0.9	•	0.7	0.2	0.3	0.4	0.3	0.4	0.3	0.4	•	0.6	•
Depreciation **14**	0.9	2.4	0.7	1.0	0.5	0.7	0.8	0.7	1.0	0.5	•	0.7	•
Amortization and Depletion **15**	0.0	0.1	0.0	•	0.0	0.0	0.0	0.0	0.0	0.0	•	0.1	•
Pensions and Other Deferred Comp. **16**	0.2	•	0.1	0.2	0.1	0.9	0.1	0.1	0.1	0.1	•	0.2	•
Employee Benefits **17**	0.5	3.7	0.1	0.1	0.2	1.0	0.2	0.2	0.1	0.1	•	0.2	•
Advertising **18**	0.1	•	0.3	0.2	0.1	0.1	0.0	0.0	0.1	0.0	•	0.0	•
Other Expenses **19**	2.6	21.6	9.4	5.1	5.2	3.0	3.0	2.5	2.5	1.4	•	2.0	•
Officers' Compensation **20**	0.7	19.1	2.4	1.8	1.3	5.3	0.6	0.4	0.3	0.4	•	0.2	•
Operating Margin **21**	•	•	2.7	2.8	1.3	1.1	0.3	0.7	1.9	0.7	•	0.0	•
Operating Margin Before Officers' Comp. **22**	0.2	1.3	5.1	4.6	2.6	6.4	0.9	1.1	2.2	1.0	•	0.2	•

Selected Average Balance Sheet ($ in Thousands)

Net Receivables 23	3492	0	20	118	607	1053	3927	8466	25804	29252	339790
Inventories 24	2861	0	6	63	533	1044	6438	11945	21137	63162	255815
Net Property, Plant and Equipment 25	2450	0	28	225	379	781	3126	4642	11568	18118	131333
Total Assets 26	23493	0	226	720	2476	7148	15082	33514	69404	150596	1050910
Notes and Loans Payable 27	8590	0	145	180	526	2113	4292	9978	15351	47951	394072
All Other Liabilities 28	5623	0	105	102	1021	2301	6213	13475	25475	53665	334506
Net Worth 29	9280	0	-24	438	929	2734	4577	10061	28579	48980	322332

Selected Financial Ratios (Times to 1)

Current Ratio 30	1.6	•	1.3	3.4	1.7	2.1	1.5	1.4	1.6	1.3	1.4
Quick Ratio 31	0.7	•	1.2	2.6	1.0	0.9	0.7	0.7	1.0	0.4	0.8
Net Sales to Working Capital 32	10.4	•	31.6	13.1	11.8	9.1	14.6	14.9	11.8	21.1	12.1
Coverage Ratio 33	3.9	•	10.5	34.6	9.3	6.7	5.2	5.7	8.8	5.7	5.1
Total Asset Turnover 34	1.8	•	6.5	5.5	4.0	3.3	3.9	3.5	3.5	3.1	2.4
Inventory Turnover 35	13.6	•	210.3	52.4	16.4	16.4	8.4	9.1	10.5	6.9	9.0
Receivables Turnover 36	14.7	•	78.7	33.0	20.1	22.9	15.0	12.1	10.3	•	•
Total Liabilities to Net Worth 37	1.5	•	•	0.6	1.7	1.6	2.3	2.3	1.4	2.1	2.3
Current Assets to Working Capital 38	2.6	•	4.2	1.4	2.4	1.9	2.9	3.3	2.6	4.8	3.6
Current Liabilities to Working Capital 39	1.6	•	3.2	0.4	1.4	0.9	1.9	2.3	1.6	3.8	2.6
Working Capital to Net Sales 40	0.1	•	0.0	0.1	0.1	0.1	0.1	0.1	0.1	0.0	0.1
Inventory to Working Capital 41	0.9	•	0.2	0.2	0.7	0.4	1.3	1.5	0.9	2.9	1.3
Total Receipts to Cash Flow 42	25.0	0.6	6.7	8.7	16.8	22.4	26.7	26.3	22.9	33.0	34.8
Cost of Goods to Cash Flow 43	23.0	0.1	5.4	7.3	14.9	16.2	24.7	24.3	21.1	31.1	32.9
Cash Flow to Total Debt 44	0.1	•	0.9	1.6	0.4	0.2	0.2	0.2	0.3	0.1	0.1

Selected Financial Factors (in Percentages)

Debt Ratio 45	60.5	•	110.7	39.2	62.5	61.8	69.7	70.0	58.8	67.5	69.3
Return on Total Assets 46	6.7	•	50.3	41.4	10.0	8.7	6.7	8.2	9.8	7.7	7.0
Return on Equity Before Income Taxes 47	12.5	•	•	66.1	23.9	19.2	17.8	22.6	21.0	19.5	18.4
Return on Equity After Income Taxes 48	10.1	•	•	64.7	23.0	17.6	15.8	20.9	18.0	16.8	12.1
Profit Margin (Before Income Tax) 49	2.7	160.3	7.0	7.4	2.2	2.2	1.4	1.9	2.5	2.1	2.4
Profit Margin (After Income Tax) 50	2.2	116.4	7.0	7.2	2.2	2.0	1.2	1.8	2.1	1.8	1.6

192

Table I
Corporations with and without Net Income

CHEMICAL AND ALLIED PRODUCTS

MONEY AMOUNTS AND SIZE OF ASSETS IN THOUSANDS OF DOLLARS

Item Description for Accounting Period 7/09 Through 6/10		Total	Zero Assets	Under 500	500 to 1,000	1,000 to 5,000	5,000 to 10,000	10,000 to 25,000	25,000 to 50,000	50,000 to 100,000	100,000 to 250,000	250,000 to 500,000	500,000 to 2,500,000	2,500,000 and over
Number of Enterprises	1	7438	901	4113	435	1338	316	203	65	33	21	3	7	3
Revenues ($ in Thousands)														
Net Sales	2	65776373	146636	2708019	414284	8693093	7122769	7026935	5997360	5239609	5395423	1049242	10340540	11642464
Interest	3	122517	39	7504	306	1469	1558	5808	2925	1757	6196	1008	24890	69058
Rents	4	12713	0	0	0	184	658	652	241	1276	6493	7	1098	2104
Royalties	5	9602	0	0	0	0	0	44	142	0	1072	0	8321	22
Other Portfolio Income	6	127064	18834	0	19	18805	1568	5083	1863	4882	3135	0	46149	26722
Other Receipts	7	686592	14623	12054	-675	-38802	35614	26644	-237	105216	-1075	-12562	197880	347914
Total Receipts	8	66734861	180132	2727577	413934	8674749	7162167	7065166	6002294	5352740	5411244	1037695	10618878	12088284
Average Total Receipts	9	8972	200	663	952	6483	22665	34804	92343	162204	257678	345898	1516983	4029428
Operating Costs/Operating Income (%)														
Cost of Operations	10	76.9	96.7	59.4	57.3	61.4	80.2	77.2	82.2	83.4	86.8	74.0	83.7	74.8
Salaries and Wages	11	6.8	1.6	12.1	8.0	11.8	5.5	6.8	5.6	4.6	2.8	4.7	4.2	8.4
Taxes Paid	12	1.0	1.0	1.5	1.4	1.4	0.7	1.1	1.3	0.8	0.5	0.6	1.1	0.7
Interest Paid	13	1.0	0.1	0.5	0.1	0.6	0.3	0.5	0.3	0.9	0.5	1.1	1.4	2.3
Depreciation	14	1.7	0.1	1.2	0.2	0.9	0.4	1.2	1.0	0.7	0.7	2.9	0.8	5.3
Amortization and Depletion	15	0.4	0.0	0.0	0.0	0.1	0.0	0.1	0.2	0.2	0.2	0.3	0.6	1.4
Pensions and Other Deferred Comp.	16	0.5	0.0	1.3	0.1	0.4	0.5	0.3	0.7	0.2	0.2	0.2	0.3	0.7
Employee Benefits	17	1.0	0.5	1.0	0.8	0.8	0.3	0.6	0.7	0.6	0.5	1.2	0.6	2.9
Advertising	18	0.2	0.1	0.5	0.1	0.2	0.1	0.3	0.2	0.1	0.1	2.8	0.1	0.1
Other Expenses	19	6.9	6.9	15.0	21.0	11.9	6.0	6.8	4.4	4.7	3.6	3.8	5.6	6.7
Officers' Compensation	20	1.6	0.3	5.6	3.8	3.3	2.8	1.4	0.9	1.1	1.0	0.6	0.5	0.5
Operating Margin	21	2.1	•	1.9	7.3	7.2	3.3	3.6	2.4	2.8	2.9	7.8	1.2	•
Operating Margin Before Officers' Comp.	22	3.7	•	7.5	11.1	10.5	6.1	5.1	3.4	3.9	3.9	8.4	1.7	•

Selected Average Balance Sheet ($ in Thousands)

Net Receivables 23	1214	0	33	228	676	2399	5330	10490	21123	34435	71968	175567	833271
Inventories 24	900	0	23	59	430	1619	4606	9382	21472	30114	132275	143354	401330
Net Property, Plant and Equipment 25	962	0	8	21	326	632	2312	5092	8654	18309	90125	88839	1371155
Total Assets 26	5659	0	122	752	2256	6436	15568	34544	73764	152642	332695	1076726	5542963
Notes and Loans Payable 27	1553	0	84	123	596	1236	3973	7781	20239	34446	47404	396123	1447090
All Other Liabilities 28	1898	0	55	222	758	2567	4977	10237	22907	55896	66254	347541	1909071
Net Worth 29	2208	0	-18	406	902	2632	6619	16526	30618	62300	219036	333063	2186802

Selected Financial Ratios (Times to 1)

Current Ratio 30	1.6	•	1.5	3.6	1.7	1.6	1.7	1.6	1.5	1.3	2.6	1.3	1.6
Quick Ratio 31	0.9	•	1.1	3.5	1.1	1.1	1.0	1.0	0.9	0.6	1.3	0.7	0.7
Net Sales to Working Capital 32	8.4	•	18.1	1.9	10.3	10.6	7.0	9.8	9.5	12.8	3.5	17.5	4.7
Coverage Ratio 33	4.7	153.0	6.4	79.3	13.0	15.4	9.2	9.2	6.7	7.6	7.2	3.9	1.0
Total Asset Turnover 34	1.6	•	5.4	1.3	2.9	3.5	2.2	2.7	2.2	1.7	1.1	1.4	0.7
Inventory Turnover 35	7.6	•	17.3	9.2	9.3	11.2	5.8	8.1	6.2	7.4	2.0	8.6	7.2
Receivables Turnover 36	7.5	•	28.6	3.5	9.5	9.6	6.1	8.0	6.4	7.9	2.2	8.3	6.6
Total Liabilities to Net Worth 37	1.6	•	•	0.9	1.5	1.4	1.4	1.1	1.4	1.5	0.5	2.2	1.5
Current Assets to Working Capital 38	2.7	•	2.9	1.4	2.4	2.6	2.3	2.5	2.8	4.3	1.6	4.8	2.5
Current Liabilities to Working Capital 39	1.7	•	1.9	0.4	1.4	1.6	1.3	1.5	1.8	3.3	0.6	3.8	1.5
Working Capital to Net Sales 40	0.1	•	0.1	0.5	0.1	0.1	0.1	0.1	0.1	0.1	0.3	0.1	0.2
Inventory to Working Capital 41	0.8	•	0.6	0.0	0.7	0.9	0.8	0.9	0.9	1.7	0.5	1.5	0.4
Total Receipts to Cash Flow 42	11.4	•	6.5	3.6	6.1	11.4	10.2	17.7	11.9	16.2	10.6	11.7	32.6
Cost of Goods to Cash Flow 43	8.8	4.5	3.9	2.1	3.7	9.1	7.9	14.6	9.9	14.1	7.8	9.8	24.4
Cash Flow to Total Debt 44	0.2	4.4	0.7	0.8	0.8	0.5	0.4	0.3	0.3	0.2	0.3	0.2	0.0

Selected Financial Factors (in Percentages)

Debt Ratio 45	61.0	•	114.9	46.0	60.0	59.1	57.5	52.2	58.5	59.2	34.2	69.1	60.5
Return on Total Assets 46	7.2	•	16.9	9.3	21.8	14.4	10.4	7.5	12.6	6.4	8.4	7.4	1.7
Return on Equity Before Income Taxes 47	14.5	•	•	16.9	50.3	32.9	21.9	14.1	25.9	13.5	11.0	17.9	0.2
Return on Equity After Income Taxes 48	12.5	•	•	14.1	48.0	31.0	18.6	11.7	21.7	10.5	9.6	13.4	•
Profit Margin (Before Income Tax) 49	3.6	15.6	2.6	7.2	7.0	3.8	4.2	2.5	5.0	3.3	6.9	4.0	0.1
Profit Margin (After Income Tax) 50	3.1	15.5	2.4	6.0	6.7	3.6	3.6	2.1	4.2	2.5	6.0	3.0	•

Table II

Corporations with Net Income

CHEMICAL AND ALLIED PRODUCTS

MONEY AMOUNTS AND SIZE OF ASSETS IN THOUSANDS OF DOLLARS

Item Description for Accounting Period 7/09 Through 6/10	Total	Zero Assets	Under 500	500 to 1,000	1,000 to 5,000	5,000 to 10,000	10,000 to 25,000	25,000 to 50,000	50,000 to 100,000	100,000 to 250,000	250,000 to 500,000	500,000 to 2,500,000	2,500,000 and over
Number of Enterprises 1	4189	12	2264	251	1108	292	153	54	27	17	3	7	0
Revenues ($ in Thousands)													
Net Sales 2	56970107	140782	1357121	414283	7841436	6621349	6060624	5643547	4706677	5173350	1049242	17961694	0
Interest 3	86779	39	7503	303	735	1096	3565	2095	1636	5814	1008	62984	0
Rents 4	12595	0	0	0	171	658	652	241	1257	6407	7	3202	0
Royalties 5	1277	0	0	0	0	0	42	142	0	1071	0	22	0
Other Portfolio Income 6	107198	18834	0	5	16451	1568	5079	1863	4693	3114	0	55591	0
Other Receipts 7	380340	14624	12053	-684	-55976	34500	20169	38345	110869	4331	-12562	214673	0
Total Receipts 8	57558296	174279	1376677	413907	7802817	6659171	6090131	5686233	4825132	5194087	1037695	18298166	0
Average Total Receipts 9	13740	14523	608	1649	7042	22805	39805	105301	178709	305535	345898	2614024	•
Operating Costs/Operating Income (%)													
Cost of Operations 10	76.3	96.0	41.2	57.3	61.7	79.9	77.4	82.4	83.8	87.0	74.0	77.1	•
Salaries and Wages 11	7.1	1.4	19.7	8.0	11.6	5.5	6.6	5.3	4.0	2.6	4.7	7.7	•
Taxes Paid 12	1.0	0.9	2.3	1.3	1.2	0.7	1.1	1.3	0.7	0.5	0.6	1.0	•
Interest Paid 13	0.9	0.1	0.8	0.1	0.5	0.2	0.4	0.3	0.4	0.5	1.1	1.9	•
Depreciation 14	1.3	0.1	0.7	0.1	0.8	0.4	0.7	0.9	0.5	0.7	2.9	2.4	•
Amortization and Depletion 15	0.3	0.0	•	0.0	0.1	0.0	0.1	0.1	0.1	0.2	0.3	0.7	•
Pensions and Other Deferred Comp. 16	0.4	0.0	2.3	0.1	0.4	0.5	0.3	0.7	0.2	0.2	0.2	0.3	•
Employee Benefits 17	0.8	0.5	1.4	0.8	0.8	0.3	0.6	0.7	0.6	0.4	1.2	1.3	•
Advertising 18	0.2	0.1	0.7	0.1	0.2	0.1	0.3	0.2	0.1	0.1	2.8	0.1	•
Other Expenses 19	6.3	6.0	15.8	20.9	11.3	5.8	6.1	4.0	4.2	3.0	3.8	5.6	•
Officers' Compensation 20	1.5	0.2	7.7	3.8	2.8	2.8	1.4	1.0	1.1	1.0	0.6	0.4	•
Operating Margin 21	4.0	•	7.5	7.4	8.7	3.8	5.1	3.2	4.1	3.8	7.8	1.4	•
Operating Margin Before Officers' Comp. 22	5.5	•	15.2	11.3	11.6	6.7	6.5	4.1	5.2	4.8	8.4	1.8	•

Selected Average Balance Sheet ($ in Thousands)

Net Receivables 23	1684	0	44	395	693	2393	6019	11422	22814	40311	71968	333523 •
Inventories 24	1290	0	35	101	440	1630	5090	10010	21651	40374	66793	177479 •
Net Property, Plant and Equipment 25	1203	0	6	37	308	669	1641	5457	8062	15756	90125	453878 •
Total Assets 26	6868	0	183	745	2210	6401	15388	34156	75942	147173	332695	2014395 •
Notes and Loans Payable 27	1717	0	123	36	542	1192	3426	7277	13396	40542	47404	549418 •
All Other Liabilities 28	2823	0	58	385	680	2481	5503	10962	24704	50070	66254	995223 •
Net Worth 29	2329	0	2	324	988	2728	6459	15917	37842	56561	219036	469754 •

Selected Financial Ratios (Times to 1)

Current Ratio 30	1.7	•	2.3	2.0	1.9	1.7	1.8	1.8	1.6	1.4	2.6	1.6
Quick Ratio 31	1.0	•	1.6	1.9	1.3	1.1	1.1	1.1	1.0	0.7	1.3	1.0
Net Sales to Working Capital 32	9.2	•	6.5	4.9	9.5	10.0	7.2	9.1	9.5	10.2	3.5	10.9
Coverage Ratio 33	6.7	206.8	12.7	80.7	19.1	19.8	14.5	14.8	17.9	9.4	7.2	2.7
Total Asset Turnover 34	2.0	•	3.3	2.2	3.2	3.5	2.6	3.1	2.3	2.1	1.1	1.3
Inventory Turnover 35	8.0	•	7.0	9.3	9.9	11.1	6.0	8.6	6.8	6.6	3.9	11.1
Receivables Turnover 36	8.0	•	21.7	5.5	9.9	9.7	6.1	8.3	6.6	•	4.8	•
Total Liabilities to Net Worth 37	1.9	•	75.5	1.3	1.2	1.3	1.4	1.1	1.0	1.6	0.5	3.3
Current Assets to Working Capital 38	2.5	•	1.8	2.0	2.1	2.5	2.3	2.3	2.8	3.4	1.6	2.7
Current Liabilities to Working Capital 39	1.5	•	0.8	1.0	1.1	1.5	1.3	1.3	1.8	2.4	0.6	1.7
Working Capital to Net Sales 40	0.1	•	0.2	0.2	0.1	0.1	0.1	0.1	0.1	0.1	0.3	0.1
Inventory to Working Capital 41	0.8	•	0.5	0.1	0.5	0.8	0.8	0.8	0.8	1.3	0.5	0.8
Total Receipts to Cash Flow 42	10.3	4.1	4.6	3.6	5.7	10.8	9.4	14.9	10.3	15.3	10.6	14.8
Cost of Goods to Cash Flow 43	7.8	3.9	1.9	2.1	3.5	8.6	7.2	12.3	8.6	13.3	7.8	11.4
Cash Flow to Total Debt 44	0.3	0.7	0.7	1.1	1.0	0.6	0.5	0.4	0.4	0.2	0.3	0.1

Selected Financial Factors (in Percentages)

Debt Ratio 45	66.1	•	98.7	56.5	55.3	57.4	58.0	53.4	50.2	61.6	34.2	76.7
Return on Total Assets 46	11.8	•	31.7	16.5	27.8	16.5	15.4	12.9	16.1	9.9	8.4	6.8
Return on Equity Before Income Taxes 47	29.6	•	2232.1	37.4	58.9	36.7	34.2	25.8	30.6	23.0	11.0	18.6
Return on Equity After Income Taxes 48	26.2	•	2132.1	31.3	56.4	34.7	29.6	22.8	26.4	18.9	9.6	14.9
Profit Margin (Before Income Tax) 49	5.1	18.6	8.9	7.3	8.2	4.4	5.6	3.9	6.6	4.3	6.9	3.4
Profit Margin (After Income Tax) 50	4.5	18.5	8.5	6.2	7.9	4.2	4.8	3.5	5.7		6.0	2.7

Table I
Corporations with and without Net Income

PETROLEUM AND PETROLEUM PRODUCTS

MONEY AMOUNTS AND SIZE OF ASSETS IN THOUSANDS OF DOLLARS

Item Description for Accounting Period 7/09 Through 6/10	Total	Zero Assets	Under 500	500 to 1,000	1,000 to 5,000	5,000 to 10,000	10,000 to 25,000	25,000 to 50,000	50,000 to 100,000	100,000 to 250,000	250,000 to 500,000	500,000 to 2,500,000	2,500,000 and over
Number of Enterprises 1	7967	406	2858	1025	2428	628	360	132	62	24	20	18	6
Revenues ($ in Thousands)													
Net Sales 2	414892590	29284411	2915938	3263788	46575360	35777891	38756067	28443088	24733931	23290519	47778537	60989806	73083256
Interest 3	313091	3899	2386	2588	11549	11891	11006	6913	3777	1646	10506	19463	227466
Rents 4	372743	0	0	308	16751	22968	46437	10210	10521	10447	20964	99925	134211
Royalties 5	42941	0	0	0	0	26	19	347	375	3	568	826	40777
Other Portfolio Income 6	595600	38648	15861	3607	74776	23108	14860	5374	12474	3369	12480	24994	366049
Other Receipts 7	1797333	15322	2293	10243	221959	102442	143409	69930	76346	35842	48162	162821	908564
Total Receipts 8	418014298	29342280	2936478	3280534	46900395	35938326	38971798	28535862	24837424	23341826	47871217	61297835	74760323
Average Total Receipts 9	52468	72272	1027	3201	19316	57227	108255	216181	400604	972576	2393561	3405435	12460054
Operating Costs/Operating Income (%)													
Cost of Operations 10	92.2	97.4	71.9	84.6	92.0	91.8	92.1	93.3	94.0	95.5	96.5	96.2	83.6
Salaries and Wages 11	1.6	0.3	10.1	2.9	2.3	1.8	2.4	1.9	1.5	0.8	0.7	0.8	2.1
Taxes Paid 12	0.7	0.2	1.6	1.5	0.5	2.6	0.7	0.4	0.4	0.7	0.3	0.2	0.9
Interest Paid 13	0.6	0.3	0.6	0.1	0.2	0.2	0.2	0.2	0.2	0.2	0.1	0.3	2.4
Depreciation 14	1.1	0.1	1.3	0.6	0.5	0.4	0.7	0.8	0.7	0.4	0.2	0.5	3.8
Amortization and Depletion 15	0.4	0.0	0.2	0.0	0.0	0.0	0.1	0.0	0.1	0.1	0.0	0.1	2.0
Pensions and Other Deferred Comp. 16	0.1	0.0	0.0	0.2	0.1	0.0	0.1	0.0	0.0	0.0	0.0	0.1	0.3
Employee Benefits 17	0.1	0.0	0.3	0.5	0.1	0.1	0.1	0.1	0.1	0.1	0.2	0.1	0.2
Advertising 18	0.0	0.0	0.1	0.1	0.1	0.0	0.1	0.0	0.1	0.0	0.0	0.0	0.0
Other Expenses 19	2.8	0.7	9.8	3.8	3.6	2.3	3.1	2.6	2.3	1.4	1.0	1.2	6.3
Officers' Compensation 20	0.4	0.0	3.2	4.1	0.8	0.5	0.4	0.4	0.2	0.2	0.1	0.3	0.1
Operating Margin 21	•	0.9	0.8	1.6	•	0.3	0.1	0.1	0.4	0.5	0.7	0.2	•
Operating Margin Before Officers' Comp. 22	0.3	0.9	4.0	5.7	0.7	0.8	0.5	0.5	0.6	0.7	0.8	0.6	•

Selected Average Balance Sheet ($ in Thousands)

Net Receivables 23	2654	0	52	220	733	2329	4231	9922	21056	56262	128745	210100	947319
Inventories 24	1543	0	27	70	361	726	2219	3711	8284	44006	58591	168429	624217
Net Property, Plant and Equipment 25	8956	0	23	76	615	1396	5329	11007	15661	27385	38401	141692	10086458
Total Assets 26	18777	0	171	677	2452	7059	16402	34839	65975	151528	350407	1072531	15580447
Notes and Loans Payable 27	6140	0	94	54	618	1989	4554	10959	15641	39853	103033	236892	5751258
All Other Liabilities 28	6452	0	51	174	859	2606	5579	11931	29260	67004	186811	462594	4714734
Net Worth 29	6185	0	26	449	975	2464	6268	11949	21075	44671	60562	373046	5114456

Selected Financial Ratios (Times to 1)

Current Ratio 30	1.3	•	2.1	2.5	1.6	1.5	1.3	1.4	1.4	1.4	1.2	1.3	1.2
Quick Ratio 31	0.8	•	1.9	1.9	1.2	1.2	0.9	1.0	0.9	0.8	0.6	0.8	0.7
Net Sales to Working Capital 32	35.0	•	15.8	10.7	31.0	35.6	48.1	46.2	35.6	30.6	61.4	27.3	24.6
Coverage Ratio 33	2.4	4.6	3.8	16.5	4.7	5.2	3.9	2.9	4.7	5.7	8.3	3.5	1.5
Total Asset Turnover 34	2.8	•	6.0	4.7	7.8	8.1	6.6	6.2	6.0	6.4	6.8	3.2	0.8
Inventory Turnover 35	31.1	•	26.9	38.5	48.9	72.0	44.7	54.2	45.3	21.1	39.4	19.3	16.3
Receivables Turnover 36	20.5	•	22.9	17.3	28.8	24.2	23.4	22.5	19.1	14.9	25.1	17.1	13.2
Total Liabilities to Net Worth 37	2.0	•	5.6	0.5	1.5	1.9	1.6	1.9	2.1	2.4	4.8	1.9	2.0
Current Assets to Working Capital 38	4.3	•	1.9	1.7	2.6	2.9	4.0	3.8	3.6	3.4	7.1	4.6	5.5
Current Liabilities to Working Capital 39	3.3	•	0.9	0.7	1.6	1.9	3.0	2.8	2.6	2.4	6.1	3.6	4.5
Working Capital to Net Sales 40	0.0	•	0.1	0.1	0.0	0.0	0.0	0.0	0.0	0.0	0.0	0.0	0.0
Inventory to Working Capital 41	1.2	•	0.2	0.3	0.6	0.4	1.0	0.8	0.9	1.2	2.3	1.6	1.6
Total Receipts to Cash Flow 42	34.7	60.8	12.1	19.4	31.3	44.0	34.9	40.9	43.9	64.8	67.8	69.0	16.4
Cost of Goods to Cash Flow 43	32.0	59.2	8.7	16.4	28.8	40.4	32.2	38.1	41.3	61.9	65.4	66.4	13.7
Cash Flow to Total Debt 44	0.1	•	0.6	0.7	0.4	0.3	0.3	0.2	0.2	0.1	0.1	0.1	0.1

Selected Financial Factors (in Percentages)

Debt Ratio 45	67.1	•	84.9	33.8	60.2	65.1	61.8	65.7	68.1	70.5	82.7	65.2	67.2
Return on Total Assets 46	3.9	•	12.4	10.7	5.6	7.0	5.9	4.4	6.0	5.5	7.0	3.4	2.7
Return on Equity Before Income Taxes 47	6.9	•	60.1	15.2	11.1	16.1	11.4	8.3	14.7	15.5	35.5	6.9	2.7
Return on Equity After Income Taxes 48	5.2	•	57.3	14.9	10.3	15.4	10.3	7.7	12.4	13.2	32.7	4.2	1.2
Profit Margin (Before Income Tax) 49	0.8	1.1	1.5	2.1	0.6	0.7	0.7	0.5	0.8	0.7	0.9	0.8	1.1
Profit Margin (After Income Tax) 50	0.6	1.0	1.5	2.1	0.5	0.7	0.6	0.4	0.7	0.6	0.8	0.5	0.5

Table II
Corporations with Net Income

PETROLEUM AND PETROLEUM PRODUCTS

MONEY AMOUNTS AND SIZE OF ASSETS IN THOUSANDS OF DOLLARS

Item Description for Accounting Period 7/09 Through 6/10	Total	Zero Assets	Under 500	500 to 1,000	1,000 to 5,000	5,000 to 10,000	10,000 to 25,000	25,000 to 50,000	50,000 to 100,000	100,000 to 250,000	250,000 to 500,000	500,000 to 2,500,000	2,500,000 and over
Number of Enterprises **1**	5506	389	1783	829	1555	502	280	75	43	18	17	12	3
Revenues ($ in Thousands)													
Net Sales **2**	32310105	29031523	1938771	2807916	34011272	31653301	30058939	16365823	17527965	20692463	43761379	47575582	47676170
Interest **3**	137843	3899	2185	2419	7909	5446	7380	4098	2953	1119	9194	9172	82068
Rents **4**	116177	0	0	308	8070	13901	34671	5915	9946	10230	16867	16028	242
Royalties **5**	628	0	0	0	0	26	19	0	375	3	69	135	0
Other Portfolio Income **6**	326386	38648	2633	3109	61720	16876	11729	3737	11277	2386	11676	21489	141106
Other Receipts **7**	1075809	15278	2177	9006	197486	84737	109189	55406	64627	30849	62122	276950	167985
Total Receipts **8**	324757948	29089348	1945766	2822758	34286457	31774287	30221927	16434979	17617143	20737050	43861307	47899356	48067571
Average Total Receipts **9**	58983	74780	1091	3405	22049	63295	107935	219133	409701	1152058	2580077	3991613	16022524
Operating Costs/Operating Income (%)													
Cost of Operations **10**	93.0	97.5	63.6	83.8	91.6	91.9	91.5	92.6	93.5	95.5	96.4	96.2	87.0
Salaries and Wages **11**	1.3	0.3	13.1	3.1	2.0	1.5	2.5	1.9	1.5	0.8	0.7	0.8	1.0
Taxes Paid **12**	0.7	0.0	1.9	1.3	0.5	2.8	0.8	0.4	0.4	0.8	0.4	0.2	0.5
Interest Paid **13**	0.4	0.3	0.3	0.1	0.1	0.1	0.2	0.2	0.2	0.1	0.1	0.2	1.5
Depreciation **14**	0.7	0.1	1.6	0.6	0.5	0.3	0.7	0.7	0.7	0.4	0.2	0.4	2.2
Amortization and Depletion **15**	0.3	0.0	0.2	0.0	0.0	0.0	0.0	0.0	0.0	0.0	0.0	0.1	1.5
Pensions and Other Deferred Comp. **16**	0.0	0.0	0.1	0.2	0.0	0.0	0.0	0.1	0.1	0.0	0.0	0.0	0.1
Employee Benefits **17**	0.1	0.0	0.3	0.4	0.1	0.1	0.1	0.2	0.1	0.1	0.2	0.0	0.1
Advertising **18**	0.0	•	0.1	0.1	0.1	0.0	0.1	0.0	0.1	0.0	0.0	0.0	0.0
Other Expenses **19**	2.3	0.7	11.9	3.8	4.0	2.0	3.2	2.5	2.3	1.3	1.0	0.8	4.2
Officers' Compensation **20**	0.4	0.0	3.5	4.3	0.8	0.5	0.3	0.6	0.3	0.2	0.1	0.4	0.0
Operating Margin **21**	0.9	1.0	3.5	2.2	0.4	0.5	0.5	0.8	0.9	0.7	0.8	0.9	1.9
Operating Margin Before Officers' Comp. **22**	1.3	1.0	7.1	6.5	1.2	1.0	0.9	1.3	1.2	1.0	0.9	1.3	1.9

Selected Average Balance Sheet ($ in Thousands)

Net Receivables 23	2619	0	69	205	854	2612	4611	11813	21717	58119	129426	247327	721383
Inventories 24	1655	0	39	105	413	720	2374	4646	8919	44736	46239	197895	923830
Net Property, Plant and Equipment 25	4722	0	23	77	634	1161	5009	8867	15139	31409	42983	160337	6129655
Total Assets 26	12893	0	206	688	2650	7091	16306	34812	66861	153942	345213	1080799	10237388
Notes and Loans Payable 27	4607	0	55	44	465	1812	4231	8792	13864	37611	114073	281547	5055195
All Other Liabilities 28	4471	0	56	188	851	2665	5744	12260	28723	66268	162621	445930	2876502
Net Worth 29	3815	0	96	456	1334	2614	6332	13760	24275	50064	68518	353322	2305692

Selected Financial Ratios (Times to 1)

Current Ratio 30	1.3	•	2.4	2.6	2.0	1.6	1.4	1.4	1.6	1.4	1.2	1.4	0.9
Quick Ratio 31	0.8	•	2.2	2.0	1.5	1.3	0.9	1.0	1.0	0.8	0.7	0.6	0.4
Net Sales to Working Capital 32	44.9	•	11.4	10.8	23.3	33.7	40.5	32.5	25.2	35.0	53.8	25.0	•
Coverage Ratio 33	5.0	4.8	14.3	21.4	13.7	7.8	6.2	7.0	10.3	9.4	8.9	7.9	2.9
Total Asset Turnover 34	4.6	•	5.3	4.9	8.3	8.9	6.6	6.3	6.1	7.5	7.5	3.7	1.6
Inventory Turnover 35	33.0	•	17.7	27.1	48.5	80.5	41.4	43.5	42.8	24.6	53.6	19.3	15.0
Receivables Turnover 36	22.2	•	17.2	•	26.2	24.6	21.5	18.3	18.3	17.3	30.8	21.4	•
Total Liabilities to Net Worth 37	2.4	•	1.2	0.5	1.0	1.7	1.6	1.5	1.8	2.1	4.0	2.1	3.4
Current Assets to Working Capital 38	4.4	•	1.7	1.6	2.0	2.7	3.6	3.2	2.8	3.4	5.6	3.8	•
Current Liabilities to Working Capital 39	3.4	•	0.7	0.6	1.0	1.7	2.6	2.2	1.8	2.4	4.6	2.8	•
Working Capital to Net Sales 40	0.0	•	0.1	0.1	0.0	0.0	0.0	0.0	0.0	0.0	0.0	0.0	•
Inventory to Working Capital 41	1.5	•	0.1	0.3	0.5	0.4	0.9	0.7	0.7	1.1	1.7	1.7	•
Total Receipts to Cash Flow 42	31.2	57.7	8.2	17.0	23.2	43.2	29.5	32.7	34.3	59.6	60.5	48.9	15.1
Cost of Goods to Cash Flow 43	29.0	56.3	5.2	14.3	21.2	39.7	27.0	30.2	32.1	56.9	58.3	47.0	13.1
Cash Flow to Total Debt 44	0.2	•	1.2	0.9	0.7	0.3	0.4	0.3	0.3	0.2	0.2	0.1	0.1

Selected Financial Factors (in Percentages)

Debt Ratio 45	70.4	•	53.6	33.7	49.7	63.1	61.2	60.5	63.7	67.5	80.2	67.3	77.5
Return on Total Assets 46	8.3	•	22.1	14.2	10.9	9.4	8.5	8.7	9.7	7.9	8.6	6.8	6.5
Return on Equity Before Income Taxes 47	22.4	•	44.2	20.4	20.2	22.1	18.3	19.0	24.1	21.8	38.4	18.1	18.9
Return on Equity After Income Taxes 48	18.4	•	43.0	20.1	19.2	21.2	16.9	17.9	21.3	19.1	35.6	13.8	12.3
Profit Margin (Before Income Tax) 49	1.5	1.2	3.9	2.8	1.2	0.9	1.1	1.2	1.4	1.0	1.0	1.6	2.7
Profit Margin (After Income Tax) 50	1.2	1.1	3.8	2.7	1.2	0.9	1.0	1.1	1.3	0.8	0.9	1.2	1.8

Table I

Corporations with and without Net Income

BEER, WINE, AND DISTILLED ALCOHOLIC BEVERAGE

MONEY AMOUNTS AND SIZE OF ASSETS IN THOUSANDS OF DOLLARS

Item Description for Accounting Period 7/09 Through 6/10	Total	Zero Assets	Under 500	500 to 1,000	1,000 to 5,000	5,000 to 10,000	10,000 to 25,000	25,000 to 50,000	50,000 to 100,000	100,000 to 250,000	250,000 to 500,000	500,000 to 2,500,000	2,500,000 and over
Number of Enterprises 1	3103	949	280	145	861	412	264	73	66	29	11	10	3
Revenues ($ in Thousands)													
Net Sales 2	79295119	625256	273231	473425	10068625	8165069	11460972	5765102	9013751	8593234	6365948	8876991	9613516
Interest 3	106683	1871	330	44	2126	2244	267	820	4056	1523	719	15255	77428
Rents 4	57024	39	0	350	737	156	0	99	616	13649	13477	23774	4127
Royalties 5	44572	0	0	0	0	0	0	0	35829	277	2240	5155	1070
Other Portfolio Income 6	662386	35013	16322	22817	35343	24765	12332	3212	6880	77802	7881	9974	410045
Other Receipts 7	951532	23502	48	1391	72777	80461	80086	72305	139954	297851	80967	151815	-49622
Total Receipts 8	81117316	685681	289931	498027	10179608	8272695	11553657	5841538	9201086	8984336	6471232	9082964	10056564
Average Total Receipts 9	26142	723	1035	3435	11823	20079	43764	80021	139410	309805	588294	908296	3352188
Operating Costs/Operating Income (%)													
Cost of Operations 10	75.1	73.6	45.1	58.5	75.1	74.3	74.5	75.3	75.4	76.1	78.3	72.8	77.2
Salaries and Wages 11	8.3	14.1	3.8	17.3	9.1	8.7	8.1	7.8	7.7	8.4	6.6	7.9	9.2
Taxes Paid 12	2.8	4.2	1.7	2.1	2.8	2.4	2.9	3.4	2.8	2.3	1.8	6.3	0.8
Interest Paid 13	1.3	1.7	1.9	0.5	0.2	0.4	0.6	0.5	0.7	0.5	0.9	1.4	5.9
Depreciation 14	0.7	0.4	0.6	0.4	0.6	1.1	0.7	0.6	1.1	0.6	0.4	1.0	0.4
Amortization and Depletion 15	1.4	0.8	0.1	0.2	0.1	0.3	0.6	0.8	0.9	0.5	1.7	1.3	6.2
Pensions and Other Deferred Comp. 16	0.4	1.0	0.0	•	0.1	0.9	0.4	0.2	0.2	0.3	0.5	0.5	0.5
Employee Benefits 17	0.9	0.2	0.1	0.9	1.1	0.9	0.9	0.9	0.8	0.8	0.6	0.5	1.0
Advertising 18	1.5	0.2	0.5	3.7	0.6	0.6	0.7	1.6	1.5	3.4	3.7	1.0	1.5
Other Expenses 19	5.5	9.4	10.7	21.3	5.9	5.2	5.5	5.1	5.9	5.6	4.5	5.8	4.7
Officers' Compensation 20	1.1	0.7	9.9	1.2	2.0	2.0	1.5	1.2	0.8	1.2	0.5	0.5	0.2
Operating Margin 21	0.9	•	25.6	•	2.4	3.1	3.6	2.6	2.2	0.4	0.6	1.1	•
Operating Margin Before Officers' Comp. 22	2.0	•	35.5	•	4.4	5.1	5.1	3.8	2.9	1.6	1.1	1.5	•

Selected Average Balance Sheet ($ in Thousands)

	1	2	3	4	5	6	7	8	9	10	11	12	13
Net Receivables 23	1844	0	0	176	393	910	1784	4809	9851	25255	55873	94929	405435
Inventories 24	2530	0	37	372	764	1802	2879	7703	11027	37662	53222	196450	461270
Net Property, Plant and Equipment 25	1391	0	77	23	360	1291	2341	3656	9090	17131	27272	91205	84957
Total Assets 26	16371	0	268	840	2188	6912	15277	32466	68857	148785	322528	765291	6469442
Notes and Loans Payable 27	6033	0	104	419	411	1291	5167	9241	22671	38916	122490	245145	3094691
All Other Liabilities 28	3020	0	14	206	724	1595	2705	5846	13412	45894	82419	210610	562521
Net Worth 29	7317	0	150	215	1053	4025	7405	17378	32774	63975	117619	309535	2812229

Selected Financial Ratios (Times to 1)

	1	2	3	4	5	6	7	8	9	10	11	12	13
Current Ratio 30	1.2	•	8.7	2.6	2.0	1.9	2.4	1.8	1.6	1.7	1.2	1.6	0.5
Quick Ratio 31	0.6	•	5.7	1.5	1.1	0.9	1.2	0.8	0.9	0.8	0.6	0.8	0.2
Net Sales to Working Capital 32	24.7	•	8.7	9.2	14.4	11.0	10.8	10.6	12.6	8.4	24.2	7.9	•
Coverage Ratio 33	3.5	3.0	17.5	•	15.2	11.7	8.4	9.5	6.8	11.1	3.6	3.5	0.5
Total Asset Turnover 34	1.6	•	3.6	3.9	5.3	2.9	2.8	2.4	2.0	2.0	1.8	1.2	0.5
Inventory Turnover 35	7.6	•	12.0	5.1	11.5	8.2	11.2	7.7	9.3	6.0	8.5	3.3	5.4
Receivables Turnover 36	13.9	•	26.8	20.1	25.3	22.8	25.5	14.5	13.6	10.1	13.5	5.9	15.8
Total Liabilities to Net Worth 37	1.2	•	0.8	2.9	1.1	0.7	1.1	0.9	1.1	1.3	1.7	1.5	1.3
Current Assets to Working Capital 38	5.7	•	1.1	1.6	2.0	2.1	1.7	2.3	2.6	2.4	5.6	2.6	•
Current Liabilities to Working Capital 39	4.7	•	0.1	0.6	1.0	1.1	0.7	1.3	1.6	1.4	4.6	1.6	•
Working Capital to Net Sales 40	0.0	•	0.1	0.1	0.1	0.1	0.1	0.1	0.1	0.1	0.0	0.1	•
Inventory to Working Capital 41	2.4	•	0.4	0.6	0.9	1.0	0.8	0.9	0.9	1.1	2.4	1.1	•
Total Receipts to Cash Flow 42	15.0	9.8	2.9	7.5	13.7	12.4	12.0	13.2	11.4	11.2	16.7	12.8	•
Cost of Goods to Cash Flow 43	11.3	7.2	1.3	4.4	10.3	9.2	9.0	9.9	8.6	8.5	13.1	9.3	•
Cash Flow to Total Debt 44	0.2	•	2.9	0.7	0.8	0.6	0.5	0.4	0.3	0.3	0.2	0.2	•

Selected Financial Factors (in Percentages)

	1	2	3	4	5	6	7	8	9	10	11	12	13
Debt Ratio 45	55.3	•	44.1	74.4	51.9	41.8	51.5	46.5	52.4	57.0	63.5	59.6	56.5
Return on Total Assets 46	7.0	•	122.4	•	20.0	13.7	14.2	10.6	9.9	10.8	5.7	5.6	1.5
Return on Equity Before Income Taxes 47	11.1	•	206.2	•	38.7	21.5	25.8	17.8	17.7	22.9	11.2	9.8	•
Return on Equity After Income Taxes 48	10.1	•	205.3	•	37.0	20.3	25.6	16.5	16.7	20.9	9.2	7.3	•
Profit Margin (Before Income Tax) 49	3.2	3.3	31.7	•	3.5	4.4	4.4	3.9	4.3	4.9	2.3	3.4	•
Profit Margin (After Income Tax) 50	2.9	3.1	31.5	•	3.3	4.1	4.4	3.6	4.0	4.5	1.9	2.6	•

Table II

Corporations with Net Income

BEER, WINE, AND DISTILLED ALCOHOLIC BEVERAGE

MONEY AMOUNTS AND SIZE OF ASSETS IN THOUSANDS OF DOLLARS

Item Description for Accounting Period 7/09 Through 6/10	Total	Zero Assets	Under 500	500 to 1,000	1,000 to 5,000	5,000 to 10,000	10,000 to 25,000	25,000 to 50,000	50,000 to 100,000	100,000 to 250,000	250,000 to 500,000	500,000 to 2,500,000	2,500,000 and over
Number of Enterprises **1**	2160	430	159	113	706	334	246	70	59	26	8	10	0
Revenues ($ in Thousands)													
Net Sales **2**	71604030	381480	216507	392096	8474693	6574430	10990122	5638927	8270754	8066960	5238374	17359687	0
Interest **3**	26701	716	330	25	2056	1558	264	820	3713	1458	507	15255	0
Rents **4**	37984	0	0	350	737	156	0	99	595	12274	0	23774	0
Royalties **5**	41262	0	0	0	0	0	0	0	35829	277	0	5155	0
Other Portfolio Income **6**	224031	35013	0	22817	35302	24406	12283	2121	3623	77784	709	9972	0
Other Receipts **7**	1024637	4715	200	1390	72074	78431	79356	72032	140597	277804	79831	218206	0
Total Receipts **8**	72958645	421924	217037	416678	8584862	6678981	11082025	5713999	8455111	8436557	5319421	17632049	0
Average Total Receipts **9**	33777	981	1365	3687	12160	19997	45049	81629	143307	324483	664928	1763205	•
Operating Costs/Operating Income (%)													
Cost of Operations **10**	75.5	70.6	33.4	53.8	72.9	74.1	74.4	75.4	75.7	75.8	80.3	77.3	•
Salaries and Wages **11**	8.3	9.7	3.4	18.1	9.8	8.6	8.0	7.7	7.5	8.2	6.8	8.4	•
Taxes Paid **12**	2.9	4.0	1.9	2.2	2.9	2.5	2.9	3.4	2.8	2.3	1.1	3.6	•
Interest Paid **13**	0.6	0.7	0.2	0.4	0.2	0.4	0.5	0.5	0.7	0.4	0.6	1.1	•
Depreciation **14**	0.6	0.6	0.7	0.4	0.5	0.6	0.7	0.6	0.8	0.6	0.4	0.6	•
Amortization and Depletion **15**	0.6	0.9	0.1	0.2	0.1	0.3	0.6	0.5	0.9	0.5	0.9	0.9	•
Pensions and Other Deferred Comp. **16**	0.3	1.4	0.0	•	0.1	0.5	0.4	0.2	0.9	0.3	0.3	0.4	•
Employee Benefits **17**	0.9	0.3	0.0	0.9	1.3	1.1	0.9	0.9	0.8	0.8	0.7	0.8	•
Advertising **18**	1.3	0.3	0.6	3.1	0.7	0.4	0.7	1.5	1.6	3.5	2.5	0.6	•
Other Expenses **19**	5.3	9.2	7.1	20.5	6.3	5.4	5.3	5.1	5.5	5.4	4.5	4.4	•
Officers' Compensation **20**	1.1	1.0	12.5	0.3	2.2	2.1	1.5	1.0	0.7	1.2	0.4	0.3	•
Operating Margin **21**	2.6	1.2	40.1	0.2	3.0	4.1	3.9	3.0	2.8	0.9	1.5	1.5	•
Operating Margin Before Officers' Comp. **22**	3.7	2.2	52.5	0.5	5.2	6.2	5.5	4.0	3.5	2.1	1.9	1.8	•

Selected Average Balance Sheet ($ in Thousands)

	1	2	3	4	5	6	7	8	9	10	11	12
Net Receivables 23	2370	0	0	114	361	980	1844	4618	10014	25762	67005	195034
Inventories 24	3239	0	37	373	835	1967	2675	6803	10601	35861	60585	252509
Net Property, Plant and Equipment 25	1474	0	135	27	372	842	2456	3621	7663	17247	35112	57595
Total Assets 26	14093	0	295	869	2262	6728	15348	32159	69136	149762	316491	992130
Notes and Loans Payable 27	4266	0	28	200	354	1240	4960	9534	21866	35765	128798	338613
All Other Liabilities 28	3590	0	24	111	650	1397	2762	5702	13840	46168	91481	298389
Net Worth 29	6238	0	242	558	1257	4091	7626	16922	33430	67830	96213	355128

Selected Financial Ratios (Times to 1)

	1	2	3	4	5	6	7	8	9	10	11	12
Current Ratio 30	2.0	•	6.0	2.3	1.8	2.4	1.8	1.6	1.7	1.5		2.3
Quick Ratio 31	0.9	•	5.2	2.0	1.2	0.8	1.2	0.8	0.9	0.9	0.7	1.0
Net Sales to Working Capital 32	9.3	•	11.1	8.4	12.9	11.5	10.9	10.9	12.5	8.5	12.7	6.0
Coverage Ratio 33	8.2	17.1	238.3	18.6	19.8	14.9	9.7	10.2	8.1	13.3	6.3	3.9
Total Asset Turnover 34	2.4	•	4.6	4.0	5.3	2.9	2.9	2.5	2.0	2.1	2.1	1.7
Inventory Turnover 35	7.7	•	12.3	5.0	10.5	7.4	12.4	8.9	10.0	6.6	8.7	5.3
Receivables Turnover 36	14.3	•	14433.8	25.9	26.6	21.2	28.1	15.7	14.1	10.6	13.6	9.2
Total Liabilities to Net Worth 37	1.3	•	0.2	0.6	0.8	0.6	1.0	0.9	1.1	1.2	2.3	1.8
Current Assets to Working Capital 38	2.0	•	1.2	1.3	1.8	2.2	1.7	2.3	2.5	2.4	3.1	1.8
Current Liabilities to Working Capital 39	1.0	•	0.2	0.3	0.8	1.2	0.7	1.3	1.5	1.4	2.1	0.8
Working Capital to Net Sales 40	0.1	•	0.1	0.1	0.1	0.1	0.1	0.1	0.1	0.1	0.1	0.2
Inventory to Working Capital 41	0.9	•	0.2	0.6	0.8	1.1	0.7	0.9	0.9	1.0	1.4	0.9
Total Receipts to Cash Flow 42	12.2	5.6	2.2	5.3	12.1	10.6	11.7	12.5	10.9	10.8	14.7	16.3
Cost of Goods to Cash Flow 43	9.2	4.0	0.7	2.9	8.8	7.9	8.7	9.4	8.2	8.2	11.8	12.6
Cash Flow to Total Debt 44	0.3	•	11.9	2.1	1.0	0.7	0.5	0.4	0.4	0.3	0.2	0.2

Selected Financial Factors (in Percentages)

	1	2	3	4	5	6	7	8	9	10	11	12
Debt Ratio 45	55.7	•	17.7	35.8	44.4	39.2	50.3	47.4	51.6	54.7	69.6	64.2
Return on Total Assets 46	12.0	•	187.2	27.3	24.0	17.9	15.4	12.0	11.6	12.1	7.5	7.3
Return on Equity Before Income Taxes 47	23.9	•	226.6	40.3	41.0	27.4	27.8	20.6	21.1	24.8	20.7	15.2
Return on Equity After Income Taxes 48	22.2	•	225.6	28.1	39.3	26.0	27.6	19.3	19.9	22.7	17.2	13.1
Profit Margin (Before Income Tax) 49	4.5	11.8	40.3	6.5	4.3	5.7	4.7	4.3	5.0	5.4	3.0	3.1
Profit Margin (After Income Tax) 50	4.2	11.5	40.2	4.5	4.1	5.4	4.7	4.1	4.8	5.0	2.5	2.7

Table I

Corporations with and without Net Income

MISCELLANEOUS NONDURABLE GOODS

MONEY AMOUNTS AND SIZE OF ASSETS IN THOUSANDS OF DOLLARS

Item Description for Accounting Period 7/09 Through 6/10	Total	Zero Assets	Under 500	500 to 1,000	1,000 to 5,000	5,000 to 10,000	10,000 to 25,000	25,000 to 50,000	50,000 to 100,000	100,000 to 250,000	250,000 to 500,000	500,000 to 2,500,000	2,500,000 and over
Number of Enterprises 1	29720	5054	17226	3271	3119	•	364	137	•	37	14	8	3
Revenues ($ in Thousands)													
Net Sales 2	15306028	596120	10549224	8943166	29840871	•	18925724	12119299	•	11239288	7192747	17667737	12443987
Interest 3	235518	87	3282	3273	9209	•	8830	5071	•	12499	7798	7899	157924
Rents 4	65453	30	0	328	7330	•	2621	5178	•	1837	297	1625	45036
Royalties 5	371437	0	0	3531	0	•	828	1939	•	13025	1443	4283	343212
Other Portfolio Income 6	592246	0	21663	24566	25676	•	2769	12006	•	28441	5061	17392	445656
Other Receipts 7	1662288	6713	67807	213097	158997	•	312781	84818	•	125700	204229	126224	196651
Total Receipts 8	156032970	602950	10641976	9187961	30042083	•	19253553	12228311	•	11420790	7411575	17825160	13612466
Average Total Receipts 9	5250	119	618	2809	9632	•	52894	89258	•	308670	529398	2228145	4537489
Operating Costs/Operating Income (%)													
Cost of Operations 10	82.0	69.0	82.8	78.2	85.8	•	79.8	82.7	•	78.4	70.3	85.0	75.3
Salaries and Wages 11	5.1	6.1	3.7	6.7	3.7	•	6.2	4.9	•	6.2	9.0	3.9	6.5
Taxes Paid 12	1.3	4.1	0.9	2.1	0.8	•	3.6	0.8	•	1.3	1.1	0.6	1.0
Interest Paid 13	0.8	0.8	0.3	0.5	0.3	•	0.4	0.6	•	1.0	0.6	1.2	3.1
Depreciation 14	0.9	0.5	0.6	0.8	0.4	•	0.7	0.7	•	1.3	1.3	1.5	1.8
Amortization and Depletion 15	0.3	0.2	0.1	0.0	0.0	•	0.3	0.5	•	0.4	0.8	0.7	0.3
Pensions and Other Deferred Comp. 16	0.2	0.0	0.2	0.1	0.2	•	0.1	0.2	•	0.2	0.3	0.1	0.4
Employee Benefits 17	0.5	0.2	0.3	0.6	0.3	•	0.5	0.5	•	0.7	0.6	0.8	0.8
Advertising 18	0.8	0.2	0.5	0.5	0.2	•	0.3	0.9	•	1.0	3.7	0.3	2.8
Other Expenses 19	6.6	19.1	9.2	9.2	5.4	•	6.3	5.7	•	7.0	9.1	4.5	10.9
Officers' Compensation 20	1.2	5.8	3.6	3.2	1.4	•	1.2	1.0	•	0.6	0.7	0.2	0.2
Operating Margin 21	0.5	•	•	•	1.4	•	0.4	1.5	•	1.8	2.4	1.1	•
Operating Margin Before Officers' Comp. 22	1.7	•	1.4	1.3	2.9	•	1.6	2.5	•	2.4	3.1	1.4	•

Selected Average Balance Sheet ($ in Thousands)

Net Receivables 23	509	0	17	200	770	4939	9421	•	27924	72067	152783	1073133
Inventories 24	479	0	32	239	669	4421	11591	•	33618	63947	268346	817689
Net Property, Plant and Equipment 25	264	0	13	83	269	1725	4662	•	25177	37308	187806	501283
Total Assets 26	2334	0	102	757	2353	15178	33245	•	141629	342885	1042988	7309557
Notes and Loans Payable 27	952	0	57	379	579	5194	8942	•	52258	86692	354834	4336995
All Other Liabilities 28	755	0	36	225	1259	5541	12734	•	44818	115139	350229	1540670
Net Worth 29	627	0	9	153	514	4443	11568	•	44553	141054	337925	1431892

Selected Financial Ratios (Times to 1)

Current Ratio 30	1.4	•	1.6	2.0	1.3	1.3	1.5	•	1.7	1.3	1.5	1.3
Quick Ratio 31	0.8	•	0.8	1.0	0.8	0.7	0.7	•	0.8	0.6	0.8	1.0
Net Sales to Working Capital 32	11.9	•	24.6	9.5	22.2	17.0	11.4	•	8.8	10.2	14.6	4.8
Coverage Ratio 33	4.2	•	•	3.2	7.7	6.0	4.7	•	4.5	10.5	2.7	3.1
Total Asset Turnover 34	2.2	•	6.0	3.6	4.1	3.4	2.7	•	2.1	1.5	2.1	0.6
Inventory Turnover 35	8.8	•	15.7	8.9	12.3	9.4	6.3	•	7.1	5.7	7.0	3.8
Receivables Turnover 36	10.7	•	34.0	11.8	12.9	11.0	9.0	•	8.8	8.5	9.4	7.7
Total Liabilities to Net Worth 37	2.7	•	9.9	3.9	3.6	2.4	1.9	•	2.2	1.4	2.1	4.1
Current Assets to Working Capital 38	3.4	•	2.8	2.0	4.3	3.9	3.1	•	2.5	4.0	2.9	4.6
Current Liabilities to Working Capital 39	2.4	•	1.8	1.0	3.3	2.9	2.1	•	1.5	3.0	1.9	3.6
Working Capital to Net Sales 40	0.1	•	0.0	0.1	0.0	0.1	0.1	•	0.1	0.1	0.1	0.2
Inventory to Working Capital 41	1.1	•	1.2	0.9	1.5	1.5	1.3	•	1.1	1.3	1.1	1.0
Total Receipts to Cash Flow 42	13.7	17.8	18.1	13.2	15.8	13.9	15.2	•	11.2	7.9	19.6	6.8
Cost of Goods to Cash Flow 43	11.2	12.3	15.0	10.3	13.5	11.1	12.6	•	8.8	5.6	16.6	5.2
Cash Flow to Total Debt 44	0.2	0.4	0.3	0.3	0.3	0.3	0.3	•	0.3	0.3	0.2	0.1

Selected Financial Factors (in Percentages)

Debt Ratio 45	73.1	•	90.8	79.8	78.1	70.7	65.2	•	68.5	58.9	67.6	80.4
Return on Total Assets 46	7.0	•	5.3	9.9	8.6	8.2		•	9.5	10.0	6.9	5.4
Return on Equity Before Income Taxes 47	19.9	•	17.9	39.4	24.6	18.5		•	23.7	22.1	13.4	18.8
Return on Equity After Income Taxes 48	16.8	•	15.3	37.6	21.7	16.2		•	18.2	20.5	8.8	15.0
Profit Margin (Before Income Tax) 49	2.4	•	1.0	2.1	2.1	2.4		•	3.5	6.1	2.1	6.5
Profit Margin (After Income Tax) 50	2.0	•	0.9	2.0	1.9	2.1		•	2.7	5.6	1.3	5.2

Table II

Corporations with Net Income

MISCELLANEOUS NONDURABLE GOODS

MONEY AMOUNTS AND SIZE OF ASSETS IN THOUSANDS OF DOLLARS

Item Description for Accounting Period 7/09 Through 6/10		Total	Zero Assets	Under 500	500 to 1,000	1,000 to 5,000	5,000 to 10,000	10,000 to 25,000	25,000 to 50,000	50,000 to 100,000	100,000 to 250,000	250,000 to 500,000	500,000 to 2,500,000	2,500,000 and over
Number of Enterprises	1	12188	1641	5888	1635	2179	352	289	102	52	•	•	•	3
Revenues ($ in Thousands)														
Net Sales	2	126572417	373610	7706110	6358060	22391270	11071285	16082967	9522716	10314029	•	•	•	12423987
Interest	3	216343	76	707	2858	8027	8118	7402	4331	5721	•	•	•	157924
Rents	4	55717	30	0	328	5422	129	608	1770	466	•	•	•	45036
Royalties	5	364478	0	0	0	0	0	46	450	2019	•	•	•	343212
Other Portfolio Income	6	567901	0	12923	14709	25529	799	794	11829	5965	•	•	•	445656
Other Receipts	7	1268994	6841	46650	191896	73761	14947	157981	77080	126053	•	•	•	196651
Total Receipts	8	129045850	380557	7766390	6567851	22504009	11095278	16249798	9618176	10454253	•	•	•	13612466
Average Total Receipts	9	10588	232	1319	4017	10328	31521	56228	94296	201043	•	•	•	4537489
Operating Costs/Operating Income (%)														
Cost of Operations	10	81.9	63.6	89.5	80.6	84.4	86.1	79.1	81.1	86.1	•	•	•	75.3
Salaries and Wages	11	4.9	4.8	2.7	5.9	3.8	4.1	5.9	5.0	4.5	•	•	•	6.5
Taxes Paid	12	1.2	5.4	0.5	2.1	0.8	0.6	3.5	0.8	1.0	•	•	•	1.0
Interest Paid	13	0.7	0.3	0.1	0.3	0.2	0.3	0.3	0.6	0.4	•	•	•	3.1
Depreciation	14	0.8	0.3	0.1	0.3	0.5	0.3	0.6	0.7	0.7	•	•	•	1.8
Amortization and Depletion	15	0.3	0.2	0.0	0.0	0.0	0.0	0.3	0.7	0.2	•	•	•	0.3
Pensions and Other Deferred Comp.	16	0.2	0.0	0.0	0.1	0.2	0.1	0.1	0.2	0.2	•	•	•	0.4
Employee Benefits	17	0.5	0.3	0.2	0.2	0.3	0.2	0.5	0.5	0.4	•	•	•	0.8
Advertising	18	0.9	0.3	0.3	0.3	0.2	0.1	0.3	1.1	0.8	•	•	•	2.8
Other Expenses	19	5.6	11.4	3.9	6.7	4.6	4.4	5.9	5.5	3.4	•	•	•	10.9
Officers' Compensation	20	1.1	8.2	1.7	3.0	1.6	1.2	1.3	1.1	0.7	•	•	•	0.2
Operating Margin	21	1.9	5.2	1.0	0.4	3.4	2.5	2.3	3.0	1.6	•	•	•	•
Operating Margin Before Officers' Comp.	22	3.0	13.4	2.7	3.4	5.0	3.7	3.6	4.1	2.4	•	•	•	•

Selected Average Balance Sheet ($ in Thousands)

Net Receivables 23	1008	0	24	241	779	2415	4956	9952	20560	•	1073133
Inventories 24	915	0	47	248	721	1966	4485	9394	19732	•	817689
Net Property, Plant and Equipment 25	503	0	9	48	240	513	1533	4764	7438	•	501283
Total Assets 26	4699	0	122	756	2484	7454	14945	33878	67721	•	7309557
Notes and Loans Payable 27	1813	0	51	273	377	1679	4307	8121	14502	•	4336995
All Other Liabilities 28	1443	0	39	273	1316	2407	4856	12414	24685	•	1540670
Net Worth 29	1443	0	32	210	791	3368	5782	13343	28534	•	1431892

Selected Financial Ratios (Times to 1)

Current Ratio 30	1.5	•	2.0	1.9	1.4	2.0	1.6	1.5	1.6	•	1.3
Quick Ratio 31	0.9	•	1.1	1.2	0.8	1.1	0.9	0.8	0.9	•	1.0
Net Sales to Working Capital 32	11.0	•	26.8	12.9	18.4	9.6	12.7	10.8	11.0	•	4.8
Coverage Ratio 33	6.7	25.0	15.1	14.8	19.6	10.1	11.4	7.8	9.5	•	3.1
Total Asset Turnover 34	2.2	•	10.7	5.1	4.1	4.2	3.7	2.8	2.9	•	0.6
Inventory Turnover 35	9.3	•	24.7	12.6	12.0	13.8	9.8	8.1	8.6	•	3.8
Receivables Turnover 36	11.1	•	50.1	13.3	13.6	13.4	•	•	10.6	•	7.7
Total Liabilities to Net Worth 37	2.3	•	2.8	2.6	2.1	1.2	1.6	1.5	1.4	•	4.1
Current Assets to Working Capital 38	3.1	•	2.0	2.1	3.6	2.0	2.7	2.9	2.7	•	4.6
Current Liabilities to Working Capital 39	2.1	•	1.0	1.1	2.6	1.0	1.7	1.9	1.7	•	3.6
Working Capital to Net Sales 40	0.1	•	0.0	0.1	0.1	0.1	0.1	0.1	0.1	•	0.2
Inventory to Working Capital 41	1.0	•	0.7	0.8	1.3	0.6	1.0	1.1	1.0	•	1.0
Total Receipts to Cash Flow 42	12.5	6.2	24.0	11.4	13.7	17.3	12.4	12.5	17.7	•	6.8
Cost of Goods to Cash Flow 43	10.3	3.9	21.5	9.2	11.6	14.9	9.8	10.1	15.2	•	5.2
Cash Flow to Total Debt 44	0.3	•	0.6	0.6	0.4	0.4	0.5	0.4	0.3	•	0.1

Selected Financial Factors (in Percentages)

Debt Ratio 45	69.3	•	73.7	72.2	68.1	54.8	61.3	60.6	57.9	•	80.4
Return on Total Assets 46	10.1	•	20.1	21.3	17.1	12.6	13.5	12.6	9.8	•	5.4
Return on Equity Before Income Taxes 47	28.0	•	71.3	71.2	51.0	25.1	31.8	28.0	20.9	•	18.8
Return on Equity After Income Taxes 48	24.7	•	70.3	67.4	49.3	24.2	29.0	25.3	19.0	•	15.0
Profit Margin (Before Income Tax) 49	3.9	7.1	1.7	3.9	3.9	2.7	3.3	4.0	3.0	•	6.5
Profit Margin (After Income Tax) 50	3.4	6.5	1.7	3.6	3.8	2.6	3.0	3.6	2.7	•	5.2

Table I

Corporations with and without Net Income

WHOLESALE ELECTRONIC MARKETS AND AGENTS AND BROKERS

MONEY AMOUNTS AND SIZE OF ASSETS IN THOUSANDS OF DOLLARS

Item Description for Accounting Period 7/09 Through 6/10		Total	Zero Assets	Under 500	500 to 1,000	1,000 to 5,000	5,000 to 10,000	10,000 to 25,000	25,000 to 50,000	50,000 to 100,000	100,000 to 250,000	250,000 to 500,000	500,000 to 2,500,000	2,500,000 and over
Number of Enterprises	1	15018	4278	10455	194	69	•	0	7	•	0	0	0	0
Revenues ($ in Thousands)														
Net Sales	2	5505650	285901	4437535	129299	161435	•	0	28311	•	0	0	0	0
Interest	3	3618	285	253	995	906	•	0	167	•	0	0	0	0
Rents	4	3119	0	0	0	0	•	0	280	•	0	0	0	0
Royalties	5	330	0	0	0	0	•	0	0	•	0	0	0	0
Other Portfolio Income	6	5145	0	0	0	731	•	0	4368	•	0	0	0	0
Other Receipts	7	-1237	3781	1075	0	-15049	•	0	1165	•	0	0	0	0
Total Receipts	8	5516625	289967	4438863	130294	148023	•	0	34291	•	0	0	0	0
Average Total Receipts	9	367	68	425	672	2145	•	•	4899	•	•	•	•	•
Operating Costs/Operating Income (%)														
Cost of Operations	10	0.3	•	•	•	•	•	•	•	•	•	•	•	•
Salaries and Wages	11	34.1	12.8	33.6	38.9	29.6	•	•	17.7	•	•	•	•	•
Taxes Paid	12	3.5	2.9	3.2	4.9	4.0	•	•	3.1	•	•	•	•	•
Interest Paid	13	0.6	0.8	0.2	2.0	3.4	•	•	6.1	•	•	•	•	•
Depreciation	14	0.8	1.4	0.7	0.2	1.8	•	•	0.7	•	•	•	•	•
Amortization and Depletion	15	0.2	0.0	0.1	0.6	•	•	•	3.7	•	•	•	•	•
Pensions and Other Deferred Comp.	16	0.9	0.0	0.8	•	0.1	•	•	0.0	•	•	•	•	•
Employee Benefits	17	2.3	0.8	2.1	5.7	1.3	•	•	0.4	•	•	•	•	•
Advertising	18	0.3	0.6	0.2	0.0	2.5	•	•	0.0	•	•	•	•	•
Other Expenses	19	35.4	46.5	35.4	47.0	53.7	•	•	13.9	•	•	•	•	•
Officers' Compensation	20	19.9	25.6	21.5	29.5	6.9	•	•	52.1	•	•	•	•	•
Operating Margin	21	1.7	7.5	2.3	0.0	•	•	•	2.1	•	•	•	•	•
Operating Margin Before Officers' Comp.	22	21.6	33.2	23.7	0.6	3.6	•	•	54.3	•	•	•	•	•

Selected Average Balance Sheet ($ in Thousands)

Net Receivables 23	11	0	0	18	707	1769
Inventories 24	0	0	0	0	0	104
Net Property, Plant and Equipment 25	12	0	10	2	181	1129
Total Assets 26	108	0	61	672	2450	27182
Notes and Loans Payable 27	53	0	32	778	586	3168
All Other Liabilities 28	32	0	21	148	207	13324
Net Worth 29	22	0	9	-255	1656	10690

Selected Financial Ratios (Times to 1)

Current Ratio 30	1.4	•	•	1.0	5.4	6.1	1.1
Quick Ratio 31	1.1	•	•	0.9	4.4	3.4	0.6
Net Sales to Working Capital 32	22.5	•	•	1.9	2.2	•	2.0
Coverage Ratio 33	4.5	11.7	11.5	6.9	•	•	4.8
Total Asset Turnover 34	3.4	•	•	6.9	1.0	1.0	0.1
Inventory Turnover 35	23.4	•	•	•	•	•	•
Receivables Turnover 36	29.6	•	•	299.9	73.4	2.0	•
Total Liabilities to Net Worth 37	3.8	•	•	5.7	1.2	0.5	1.5
Current Assets to Working Capital 38	3.5	•	•	1.2	0.2	1.2	7.7
Current Liabilities to Working Capital 39	2.5	•	•	0.2	0.2	0.2	6.7
Working Capital to Net Sales 40	0.0	•	•	0.5	0.5	0.5	0.5
Inventory to Working Capital 41	0.0	•	•	0.1	•	•	0.1
Total Receipts to Cash Flow 42	3.1	1.8	3.0	7.1	3.0	3.1	2.9
Cost of Goods to Cash Flow 43	0.0	•	•	•	•	•	•
Cash Flow to Total Debt 44	1.4	2.7	•	0.1	1.0	•	0.1

Selected Financial Factors (in Percentages)

Debt Ratio 45	79.2	•	85.0	137.9	32.4	60.7
Return on Total Assets 46	8.5	•	17.3	•	•	4.4
Return on Equity Before Income Taxes 47	31.5	•	105.5	73.7	•	8.8
Return on Equity After Income Taxes 48	27.7	•	100.3	73.9	•	7.5
Profit Margin (Before Income Tax) 49	1.9	8.9	2.3	2.3	•	23.3
Profit Margin (After Income Tax) 50	1.7	8.9	2.2	•	•	19.9

Table II

Corporations with Net Income

WHOLESALE ELECTRONIC MARKETS AND AGENTS AND BROKERS

MONEY AMOUNTS AND SIZE OF ASSETS IN THOUSANDS OF DOLLARS

Item Description for Accounting Period 7/09 Through 6/10	Total	Zero Assets	Under 500	500 to 1000	1,000 to 5,000	5,000 to 10,000	10,000 to 25,000	25,000 to 50,000	50,000 to 100,000	100,000 to 250,000	250,000 to 500,000	500,000 to 2,500,000	2,500,000 and over
Number of Enterprises **1**	9154	2345	6701	56	33	10	0	•	•	0	0	0	0
Revenues ($ in Thousands)													
Net Sales **2**	2623175	214848	1761018	1350	155774	7290	0	•	•	0	0	0	0
Interest **3**	1855	0	0	612	64	429	0	•	•	0	0	0	0
Rents **4**	3119	0	0	0	0	0	0	•	•	0	0	0	0
Royalties **5**	330	0	0	0	0	0	0	•	•	0	0	0	0
Other Portfolio Income **6**	4415	0	0	0	0	0	0	•	•	0	0	0	0
Other Receipts **7**	9396	20	6	1	423	320	0	•	•	0	0	0	0
Total Receipts **8**	2642290	214868	1761024	1963	156261	8039	0	•	•	0	0	0	0
Average Total Receipts **9**	289	92	263	35	4735	804	•	•	•	•	•	•	•
Operating Costs/Operating Income (%)													
Cost of Operations **10**	0.6	•	•	•	•	•	•	•	•	•	•	•	•
Salaries and Wages **11**	22.5	13.9	14.9	•	26.9	47.6	•	•	•	•	•	•	•
Taxes Paid **12**	3.1	3.0	2.3	4.8	3.8	3.0	•	•	•	•	•	•	•
Interest Paid **13**	0.9	0.4	0.5	•	3.5	1.3	•	•	•	•	•	•	•
Depreciation **14**	1.0	1.4	0.8	•	1.7	0.4	•	•	•	•	•	•	•
Amortization and Depletion **15**	0.3	0.0	0.1	•	•	0.1	•	•	•	•	•	•	•
Pensions and Other Deferred Comp. **16**	1.4	1.3	1.4	•	•	•	•	•	•	•	•	•	•
Employee Benefits **17**	2.8	•	2.8	•	0.7	•	•	•	•	•	•	•	•
Advertising **18**	0.4	•	0.3	•	2.6	0.2	•	•	•	•	•	•	•
Other Expenses **19**	39.4	21.4	45.8	21.0	51.7	33.8	•	•	•	•	•	•	•
Officers' Compensation **20**	14.3	30.4	15.8	74.2	6.4	17.7	•	•	•	•	•	•	•
Operating Margin **21**	13.3	28.3	15.2	•	2.9	•	•	•	•	•	•	•	•
Operating Margin Before Officers' Comp. **22**	27.6	58.7	31.0	74.2	9.3	13.6	•	•	•	•	•	•	•

Selected Average Balance Sheet ($ in Thousands)

Net Receivables 23	16	0	-1	0	1479	601
Inventories 24	0	0	0	0	0	0
Net Property, Plant and Equipment 25	11	5	5	0	363	50
Total Assets 26	120	50	50	505	3137	9222
Notes and Loans Payable 27	60	37	37	29	1173	245
All Other Liabilities 28	31	5	5	446	32	8526
Net Worth 29	29	8	8	30	1932	451

Selected Financial Ratios (Times to 1)

Current Ratio 30	1.7	•	1.0	138.5	59.1	25.5
Quick Ratio 31	1.2	•	0.9	138.5	32.8	25.2
Net Sales to Working Capital 32	10.5	•	386.6	0.0	1.8	0.1
Coverage Ratio 33	15.8	65.1	33.5	•	1.9	5.9
Total Asset Turnover 34	2.4	•	5.2	0.0	1.5	0.1
Inventory Turnover 35	57.1	•	•	•	•	•
Receivables Turnover 36	18.6	•	5426.9	•	2.7	2.4
Total Liabilities to Net Worth 37	3.1	•	5.3	15.9	0.6	19.4
Current Assets to Working Capital 38	2.5	•	38.0	1.0	1.0	1.0
Current Liabilities to Working Capital 39	1.5	•	37.0	0.0	0.0	0.0
Working Capital to Net Sales 40	0.1	•	0.0	20.8	0.6	8.5
Inventory to Working Capital 41	0.0	•	•	•	•	•
Total Receipts to Cash Flow 42	2.1	2.0	1.9	1.5	2.2	3.1
Cost of Goods to Cash Flow 43	0.0	•	•	•	•	•
Cash Flow to Total Debt 44	1.5	•	3.4	0.0	1.8	0.0

Selected Financial Factors (in Percentages)

Debt Ratio 45	75.5	•	84.1	94.1	38.4	95.1
Return on Total Assets 46	35.8	•	81.9	2.2	10.1	0.6
Return on Equity Before Income Taxes 47	137.0	•	500.0	36.6	7.8	10.0
Return on Equity After Income Taxes 48	132.2	•	490.8	31.2	5.2	9.8
Profit Margin (Before Income Tax) 49	14.1	28.3	15.2	45.3	3.2	6.2
Profit Margin (After Income Tax) 50	13.6	28.3	14.9	38.7	2.1	6.1

Table I

Corporations with and without Net Income

NEW AND USED CAR DEALERS

MONEY AMOUNTS AND SIZE OF ASSETS IN THOUSANDS OF DOLLARS

Item Description for Accounting Period 7/09 Through 6/10	Total	Zero Assets	Under 500	500 to 1,000	1,000 to 5,000	5,000 to 10,000	10,000 to 25,000	25,000 to 50,000	50,000 to 100,000	100,000 to 250,000	250,000 to 500,000	500,000 to 2,500,000	2,500,000 and over
Number of Enterprises 1	44509	4784	20225	3350	9018	4202	2271	478	121	42	8	9	0
Revenues ($ in Thousands)													
Net Sales 2	476088475	2956701	16399244	9736669	83748340	113549016	119041121	49038868	22274143	13930521	4318522	41095331	0
Interest 3	598946	325	14698	15565	115511	83216	95990	35266	29506	29635	39125	140110	0
Rents 4	282693	0	4644	870	9033	14228	17061	20522	12342	28039	5476	170478	0
Royalties 5	3578	0	0	0	0	0	793	22	0	2470	0	292	0
Other Portfolio Income 6	499624	27129	109010	1387	59619	37882	74275	54389	87139	28545	5844	14405	0
Other Receipts 7	9260791	150483	171978	75476	1479095	2078792	2530972	1003106	432335	347812	66612	924128	0
Total Receipts 8	486734107	3134638	16699574	9829967	85411598	115763134	121760212	50152173	22835465	14367022	4435579	42344744	0
Average Total Receipts 9	10936	655	826	2934	9471	27550	53615	104921	188723	342072	554447	4704972	•
Operating Costs/Operating Income (%)													
Cost of Operations 10	86.3	87.3	81.0	88.2	86.0	87.5	86.9	86.7	85.8	83.7	84.2	84.5	•
Salaries and Wages 11	5.6	5.1	3.1	3.8	5.7	5.2	5.6	5.5	6.0	6.3	7.0	7.0	•
Taxes Paid 12	1.0	1.9	2.2	1.3	1.1	0.9	0.9	0.9	1.0	0.9	1.0	1.3	•
Interest Paid 13	0.6	0.4	0.7	0.5	0.7	0.4	0.5	0.5	0.6	0.8	1.0	1.3	•
Depreciation 14	0.5	0.3	0.3	0.3	0.3	0.3	0.4	0.8	1.2	1.0	1.2	1.1	•
Amortization and Depletion 15	0.2	0.0	0.2	0.1	0.0	0.1	0.1	0.1	0.1	0.2	0.2	0.8	•
Pensions and Other Deferred Comp. 16	0.1	0.0	0.1	0.1	0.1	0.0	0.1	0.1	0.1	0.0	0.1	0.1	•
Employee Benefits 17	0.5	0.4	0.3	0.2	0.6	0.5	0.5	0.5	0.5	0.6	0.6	0.6	•
Advertising 18	1.0	1.1	0.8	0.8	1.2	1.0	1.1	1.0	1.0	1.0	0.9	0.8	•
Other Expenses 19	5.1	12.7	10.2	5.8	5.4	4.6	4.5	4.3	5.1	6.4	5.0	5.0	•
Officers' Compensation 20	0.8	2.0	2.5	2.0	1.0	0.8	0.7	0.6	0.5	0.6	0.6	0.1	•
Operating Margin 21	•	•	•	•	•	•	•	•	•	•	•	•	•
Operating Margin Before Officers' Comp. 22	•	•	1.1	•	•	•	•	•	•	•	•	•	•

Selected Average Balance Sheet ($ in Thousands)

	•	•	•	•	•	•	•	•	•	•	•	•
Net Receivables 23	395	0	28	107	382	1060	1729	3435	8290	17208	29971	135461
Inventories 24	1773	0	79	386	1479	4481	9876	19037	30865	57812	80023	612884
Net Property, Plant and Equipment 25	466	0	16	74	210	609	1895	6004	13416	28794	92899	550194
Total Assets 26	3229	0	170	698	2607	7029	14792	33112	66710	139916	274800	2147576
Notes and Loans Payable 27	1957	0	119	438	1619	4543	9655	20252	38982	79892	142564	967321
All Other Liabilities 28	404	0	30	83	415	677	1532	3486	8806	14569	38722	377118
Net Worth 29	868	0	22	177	573	1810	3604	9374	18922	45455	93514	803137

Selected Financial Ratios (Times to 1)

	•	•	•	•	•	•	•	•	•	•	•	•
Current Ratio 30	1.4	•	2.5	2.7	1.6	1.4	1.3	1.4	1.2	1.3	1.1	1.2
Quick Ratio 31	0.4	•	0.9	1.0	0.5	0.4	0.4	0.5	0.5	0.5	0.4	0.3
Net Sales to Working Capital 32	16.3	•	9.7	8.1	11.7	16.1	19.8	16.7	22.2	15.2	38.4	35.2
Coverage Ratio 33	1.9	•	1.6	•	1.0	2.2	3.2	3.3	2.2	3.1	1.8	1.5
Total Asset Turnover 34	3.3	•	4.8	4.2	3.6	3.8	3.5	3.1	2.8	2.4	2.0	2.1
Inventory Turnover 35	5.2	•	8.3	6.6	5.4	5.3	4.6	4.7	5.1	4.8	5.7	6.3
Receivables Turnover 36	27.4	•	31.9	23.8	26.4	30.3	27.5	26.2	21.0	17.1	18.0	33.4
Total Liabilities to Net Worth 37	2.7	•	6.8	2.9	3.6	2.9	3.1	2.5	2.5	2.1	1.9	1.7
Current Assets to Working Capital 38	3.5	•	1.7	1.6	2.8	3.5	4.3	3.8	5.2	3.9	8.6	6.3
Current Liabilities to Working Capital 39	2.5	•	0.7	0.6	1.8	2.5	3.3	2.8	4.2	2.9	7.6	5.3
Working Capital to Net Sales 40	0.1	•	0.1	0.1	0.1	0.1	0.1	0.1	0.0	0.1	0.0	0.0
Inventory to Working Capital 41	2.3	•	1.0	0.9	1.9	2.3	2.8	2.3	3.0	2.1	4.7	4.4
Total Receipts to Cash Flow 42	25.6	52.2	14.2	70.7	27.0	28.0	25.1	23.6	23.9	21.9	21.1	27.8
Cost of Goods to Cash Flow 43	22.1	45.5	11.5	62.3	23.2	24.5	21.8	20.5	20.6	18.4	17.8	23.4
Cash Flow to Total Debt 44	0.2	•	0.4	0.1	0.2	0.2	0.2	0.2	0.2	0.2	0.1	0.1

Selected Financial Factors (in Percentages)

	•	•	•	•	•	•	•	•	•	•	•	•
Debt Ratio 45	73.1	•	87.2	74.6	78.0	74.3	75.6	71.7	71.6	67.5	66.0	62.6
Return on Total Assets 46	3.9	•	5.1	•	2.5	3.6	5.2	5.7	3.4	5.7	3.6	4.0
Return on Equity Before Income Taxes 47	7.1	•	14.6	•	•	7.6	14.7	14.1	6.7	11.9	4.9	3.4
Return on Equity After Income Taxes 48	6.1	•	13.9	•	•	7.3	14.0	13.5	5.7	11.0	3.3	1.1
Profit Margin (Before Income Tax) 49	0.6	•	0.4	•	•	0.5	1.0	1.3	0.7	1.6	0.8	0.6
Profit Margin (After Income Tax) 50	0.5	•	0.4	•	•	0.5	1.0	1.2	0.6	1.5	0.6	0.2

Table II

Corporations with Net Income

NEW AND USED CAR DEALERS

MONEY AMOUNTS AND SIZE OF ASSETS IN THOUSANDS OF DOLLARS

Item Description for Accounting Period 7/09 Through 6/10	Total	Zero Assets	Under 500	500 to 1,000	1,000 to 5,000	5,000 to 10,000	10,000 to 25,000	25,000 to 50,000	50,000 to 100,000	100,000 to 250,000	250,000 to 500,000	500,000 to 2,500,000	2,500,000 and over
Number of Enterprises 1	25123	2050	11470	1475	5114	2860	1654	375	83	32	•	•	0
Revenues ($ in Thousands)													
Net Sales 2	330314129	1416125	9874198	6202515	50293392	82478685	88580048	39860982	16990183	11222300	•	•	0
Interest 3	360955	0	4894	8107	84755	52828	70837	25622	23866	27776	•	•	0
Rents 4	99415	0	0	870	5209	9845	9708	17597	10258	26012	•	•	0
Royalties 5	3286	0	0	0	0	0	793	22	0	2470	•	•	0
Other Portfolio Income 6	295693	19986	19746	1315	31590	31488	56880	36966	57920	24367	•	•	0
Other Receipts 7	6252598	138611	85068	12724	733189	1535866	1900333	805436	315669	293264	•	•	0
Total Receipts 8	337326076	1574722	9983906	6225531	51148135	84108712	90618599	40746625	17397896	11596189	•	•	0
Average Total Receipts 9	13427	768	870	4221	10002	29409	54788	108658	209613	362381	•	•	•
Operating Costs/Operating Income (%)													
Cost of Operations 10	86.3	82.2	78.2	90.4	84.9	88.0	86.6	86.7	86.0	83.2	•	•	•
Salaries and Wages 11	5.3	4.1	2.4	1.6	5.5	4.8	5.6	5.4	5.8	6.3	•	•	•
Taxes Paid 12	1.0	1.9	2.5	1.0	1.0	0.9	0.9	0.9	0.9	0.9	•	•	•
Interest Paid 13	0.5	0.3	0.4	0.2	0.7	0.3	0.4	0.4	0.5	0.8	•	•	•
Depreciation 14	0.4	0.5	0.3	0.2	0.3	0.3	0.4	0.6	1.0	1.0	•	•	•
Amortization and Depletion 15	0.1	•	0.1	0.0	0.0	0.1	0.1	0.1	0.1	0.1	•	•	•
Pensions and Other Deferred Comp. 16	0.1	0.0	0.1	0.2	0.1	0.0	0.0	0.1	0.1	0.0	•	•	•
Employee Benefits 17	0.5	0.6	0.1	0.1	0.5	0.5	0.5	0.5	0.5	0.6	•	•	•
Advertising 18	0.9	1.0	0.6	0.4	1.1	0.9	1.0	1.0	0.9	1.0	•	•	•
Other Expenses 19	4.4	7.1	8.7	3.0	4.7	4.1	4.3	4.1	4.3	6.8	•	•	•
Officers' Compensation 20	0.8	1.3	2.7	1.6	1.1	0.8	0.7	0.6	0.5	0.6	•	•	•
Operating Margin 21	•	1.3	3.9	1.4	0.2	•	•	•	•	•	•	•	•
Operating Margin Before Officers' Comp. 22	0.6	2.6	6.6	3.0	1.3	0.3	0.1	0.2	•	•	•	•	•

Selected Average Balance Sheet ($ in Thousands)

Net Receivables 23	497	0	30	73	440	1193	1849	3561	8314	17623
Inventories 24	1749	0	83	345	1311	3378	8103	15860	28125	47178
Net Property, Plant and Equipment 25	524	0	14	33	181	588	1809	5530	12571	25881
Total Assets 26	3767	0	180	711	2749	7046	14919	33160	67001	136779
Notes and Loans Payable 27	2136	0	84	264	1585	4146	9413	19485	39876	73243
All Other Liabilities 28	419	0	32	45	414	582	1511	3528	7837	12726
Net Worth 29	1211	0	64	402	750	2318	3995	10148	19289	50810

Selected Financial Ratios (Times to 1)

Current Ratio 30	1.5	•	2.9	5.5	1.7	1.5	1.3	1.4	1.3	1.4
Quick Ratio 31	0.5	•	1.1	2.3	0.5	0.5	0.4	0.5	0.5	0.6
Net Sales to Working Capital 32	14.5	•	8.8	8.6	10.2	13.9	17.8	15.4	21.1	14.7
Coverage Ratio 33	5.2	47.1	14.9	11.2	3.7	5.4	5.3	5.2	4.4	3.9
Total Asset Turnover 34	3.5	•	4.8	5.9	3.6	4.1	3.6	3.2	3.1	2.6
Inventory Turnover 35	6.5	•	8.2	11.0	6.4	7.5	5.7	5.8	6.3	6.2
Receivables Turnover 36	31.3	•	31.4	39.3	26.4	34.3	32.5	31.3	27.6	23.8
Total Liabilities to Net Worth 37	2.1	•	1.8	0.8	2.7	2.0	2.7	2.3	2.5	1.7
Current Assets to Working Capital 38	3.1	•	1.5	1.2	2.5	2.9	3.9	3.5	4.7	3.5
Current Liabilities to Working Capital 39	2.1	•	0.5	0.2	1.5	1.9	2.9	2.5	3.7	2.5
Working Capital to Net Sales 40	0.1	•	0.1	0.1	0.1	0.1	0.1	0.1	0.0	0.1
Inventory to Working Capital 41	2.0	•	0.9	0.7	1.6	1.8	2.5	2.1	2.8	1.9
Total Receipts to Cash Flow 42	20.8	5.7	9.3	28.3	19.4	23.3	21.9	21.5	21.2	19.5
Cost of Goods to Cash Flow 43	17.9	4.7	7.3	25.6	16.5	20.5	19.0	18.7	18.2	16.2
Cash Flow to Total Debt 44	0.2	•	0.8	0.5	0.3	0.3	0.2	0.2	0.2	0.2

Selected Financial Factors (in Percentages)

Debt Ratio 45	67.8	•	64.6	43.5	72.7	67.1	73.2	69.4	71.2	62.9
Return on Total Assets 46	8.3	•	25.8	11.5	9.2	7.5	7.7	7.4	6.9	7.7
Return on Equity Before Income Taxes 47	20.8	•	67.9	18.5	24.8	18.5	23.5	19.4	18.4	15.5
Return on Equity After Income Taxes 48	19.6	•	67.5	18.1	24.1	18.2	22.7	18.8	17.0	14.4
Profit Margin (Before Income Tax) 49	1.9	12.5	5.0	1.8	1.9	1.5	1.7	1.9	1.7	2.2
Profit Margin (After Income Tax) 50	1.8	12.2	5.0	1.7	1.8	1.5	1.7	1.8	1.6	2.1

Table I

Corporations with and without Net Income

OTHER MOTOR VEHICLE AND PARTS DEALERS

MONEY AMOUNTS AND SIZE OF ASSETS IN THOUSANDS OF DOLLARS

Item Description for Accounting Period 7/09 Through 6/10	Total	Zero Assets	Under 500	500 to 1,000	1,000 to 5,000	5,000 to 10,000	10,000 to 25,000	25,000 to 50,000	50,000 to 100,000	100,000 to 250,000	250,000 to 500,000	500,000 to 2,500,000	2,500,000 and over
Number of Enterprises 1	40681	4320	23157	5432	6449	866	305	84	37	18	5	5	3
Revenues ($ in Thousands)													
Net Sales 2	11887896	726970	12729471	9420516	32204807	11414285	9617956	5822942	5355530	4335797	1907705	7073241	18269676
Interest 3	75212	951	5719	4285	17109	6435	6153	8321	8552	695	8774	1460	6757
Rents 4	58285	1445	1154	1108	21069	3045	4610	1348	20903	235	0	2361	1007
Royalties 5	11615	0	0	0	271	1139	1217	0	656	0	0	477	7855
Other Portfolio Income 6	226612	663	12300	9122	64251	36106	20796	19181	18974	20286	10385	12331	2215
Other Receipts 7	1331153	8962	22197	123484	434243	106860	104640	89458	84509	26421	58916	230305	41161
Total Receipts 8	120581773	738991	12770841	9558515	32741750	11567870	9755372	5941250	5489124	4383434	1985780	7320175	18328671
Average Total Receipts 9	2964	171	551	1760	5077	13358	31985	70729	148355	243524	397156	1464035	6109557
Operating Costs/Operating Income (%)													
Cost of Operations 10	69.2	80.9	64.9	70.9	74.6	76.9	78.3	75.6	75.1	68.3	67.1	56.3	53.3
Salaries and Wages 11	10.9	6.7	9.6	9.3	9.3	8.4	8.6	10.2	8.7	10.9	13.9	17.6	16.7
Taxes Paid 12	2.1	1.9	2.8	2.2	1.8	1.4	1.3	1.4	1.6	1.8	2.0	2.6	3.0
Interest Paid 13	1.2	2.8	0.8	1.2	1.3	1.5	1.3	1.0	1.0	0.9	1.2	1.9	0.9
Depreciation 14	1.6	2.0	0.9	0.9	0.8	1.6	1.4	1.7	2.4	4.0	5.4	2.1	2.8
Amortization and Depletion 15	0.2	0.7	0.1	0.1	0.1	0.2	0.1	0.1	0.2	0.1	0.9	0.7	0.2
Pensions and Other Deferred Comp. 16	0.1	0.0	0.0	0.0	0.1	0.1	0.1	0.1	0.3	0.4	0.4	0.2	0.1
Employee Benefits 17	0.9	0.7	0.3	0.8	0.8	0.6	0.7	1.0	1.1	1.2	2.6	1.0	1.3
Advertising 18	1.2	0.6	1.4	1.0	1.3	1.1	1.2	0.7	1.3	0.6	1.3	1.8	1.2
Other Expenses 19	10.8	9.9	14.3	11.9	9.6	8.1	7.2	9.2	9.2	9.0	12.5	15.6	12.9
Officers' Compensation 20	1.7	1.6	4.7	3.6	2.1	1.3	0.9	1.0	0.7	0.7	0.4	0.3	0.1
Operating Margin 21	0.0	•	•	•	•	•	•	•	•	2.2	•	•	7.5
Operating Margin Before Officers' Comp. 22	1.8	4.7	4.7	1.7	0.3	0.2	•	•	0.7	2.9	•	•	7.7

Selected Average Balance Sheet ($ in Thousands)

Net Receivables 23	146	0	12	69	192	478	1666	4240	8951	24560	45323	245583	181152
Inventories 24	813	0	68	356	1629	4855	9602	21658	33393	49232	116323	379741	1830112
Net Property, Plant and Equipment 25	301	0	20	107	298	1113	3298	7531	17839	37526	88163	223156	1260715
Total Assets 26	1506	0	130	703	2250	6819	15947	33907	71426	146430	314463	1180686	4517062
Notes and Loans Payable 27	626	0	62	431	937	3432	9010	17333	32899	56900	110206	384334	1257464
All Other Liabilities 28	462	0	34	157	718	1713	3258	7831	18097	39129	57252	395211	1908301
Net Worth 29	418	0	34	116	594	1673	3678	8742	20429	50401	147005	401141	1351297

Selected Financial Ratios (Times to 1)

Current Ratio 30	1.6	•	2.3	1.8	1.7	1.4	1.5	1.4	1.3	1.5	1.7	2.1	1.3
Quick Ratio 31	0.4	•	0.7	0.5	0.3	0.3	0.4	0.4	0.4	0.6	0.7	1.0	0.1
Net Sales to Working Capital 32	8.3	•	9.8	7.6	6.9	9.6	8.4	9.9	16.5	7.7	4.9	4.7	12.9
Coverage Ratio 33	2.2	•	1.4	0.7	1.0	1.1	1.1	1.0	2.0	4.5	•	2.6	10.0
Total Asset Turnover 34	1.9	•	4.2	2.5	2.2	1.9	2.0	2.0	2.0	1.6	1.2	1.2	1.3
Inventory Turnover 35	2.5	•	5.2	3.4	2.3	2.1	2.6	2.4	3.3	3.3	2.2	2.1	1.8
Receivables Turnover 36	18.7	•	41.9	25.7	23.7	24.7	19.0	13.5	13.3	9.7	7.1	5.8	31.4
Total Liabilities to Net Worth 37	2.6	•	2.8	5.1	2.8	3.1	3.3	2.9	2.5	1.9	1.1	1.9	2.3
Current Assets to Working Capital 38	2.8	•	1.8	2.3	2.5	3.6	3.0	3.3	4.7	3.0	2.5	1.9	4.7
Current Liabilities to Working Capital 39	1.8	•	0.8	1.3	1.5	2.6	2.0	2.3	3.7	2.0	1.5	0.9	3.7
Working Capital to Net Sales 40	0.1	•	0.1	0.1	0.1	0.1	0.1	0.1	0.1	0.1	0.2	0.2	0.1
Inventory to Working Capital 41	2.0	•	1.2	1.6	2.0	2.6	2.1	2.1	3.0	1.7	1.5	0.8	4.0
Total Receipts to Cash Flow 42	11.6	1817.4	10.1	13.9	14.8	18.1	21.0	15.5	14.4	10.3	20.3	7.4	6.5
Cost of Goods to Cash Flow 43	8.1	1469.5	6.6	9.8	11.1	13.9	16.4	11.7	10.8	7.1	13.6	4.2	3.5
Cash Flow to Total Debt 44	0.2	•	0.6	0.2	0.2	0.1	0.1	0.2	0.2	0.2	0.1	0.2	0.3

Selected Financial Factors (in Percentages)

Debt Ratio 45	72.2	•	74.0	83.6	73.6	75.5	76.9	74.2	71.4	65.6	53.3	66.0	70.1
Return on Total Assets 46	5.2	•	4.9	2.0	2.7	3.4	2.8	2.0	4.1	6.9	•	6.1	11.8
Return on Equity Before Income Taxes 47	10.3	•	5.1	•	•	1.5	1.3	0.1	7.1	15.6	•	11.1	35.4
Return on Equity After Income Taxes 48	6.7	•	4.1	•	•	0.9	0.2	•	6.1	14.5	•	8.5	23.4
Profit Margin (Before Income Tax) 49	1.5	•	0.3	•	•	0.2	0.1	0.0	1.0	3.3	•	3.1	7.8
Profit Margin (After Income Tax) 50	1.0	•	0.3	•	•	0.1	0.0	•	0.9	3.0	•	2.4	5.2

Table II
Corporations with Net Income

OTHER MOTOR VEHICLE AND PARTS DEALERS

MONEY AMOUNTS AND SIZE OF ASSETS IN THOUSANDS OF DOLLARS

Item Description for Accounting Period 7/09 Through 6/10		Total	Zero Assets	Under 500	500 to 1,000	1,000 to 5,000	5,000 to 10,000	10,000 to 25,000	25,000 to 50,000	50,000 to 100,000	100,000 to 250,000	250,000 to 500,000	500,000 to 2,500,000	2,500,000 and over
Number of Enterprises	1	18622	875	10390	3165	3513	385	193	54	21	15	•	•	3
Revenues ($ in Thousands)														
Net Sales	2	82330509	180231	7525454	6118670	18867877	5414354	7301998	3806223	3512879	3935776	•	•	18269676
Interest	3	47137	0	5111	2757	13938	1805	4911	2318	7636	443	•	•	6757
Rents	4	42437	0	567	212	14227	87	4314	36	19581	179	•	•	1007
Royalties	5	10466	0	0	0	271	0	1217	0	653	0	•	•	7855
Other Portfolio Income	6	160891	0	9808	2045	44736	31898	11674	18478	7544	19981	•	•	2215
Other Receipts	7	796632	19727	2393	22817	242006	54507	50667	39241	37754	26022	•	•	41161
Total Receipts	8	83388072	199958	7543333	6146501	19183055	5502651	7374781	3886296	3586047	3982401	•	•	18328671
Average Total Receipts	9	4478	229	726	1942	5461	14293	38211	71598	170764	265493	•	•	6109557
Operating Costs/Operating Income (%)														
Cost of Operations	10	66.4	65.8	65.6	68.4	73.0	74.3	77.0	74.5	75.5	68.3	•	•	53.3
Salaries and Wages	11	11.3	3.1	8.6	8.3	8.7	8.0	8.3	10.4	7.6	10.9	•	•	16.7
Taxes Paid	12	2.1	3.2	2.5	2.4	1.8	1.4	1.3	1.3	1.5	1.7	•	•	3.0
Interest Paid	13	0.9	0.9	0.4	0.8	0.8	1.2	0.9	0.8	0.8	0.9	•	•	0.9
Depreciation	14	1.7	0.1	0.8	0.8	0.7	2.5	1.1	1.5	2.3	3.7	•	•	2.8
Amortization and Depletion	15	0.1	0.0	0.1	0.1	0.0	0.0	0.1	0.1	0.1	0.1	•	•	0.2
Pensions and Other Deferred Comp.	16	0.2	•	0.0	0.1	0.2	0.2	0.1	0.2	0.2	0.4	•	•	0.1
Employee Benefits	17	0.9	0.5	0.3	0.7	0.7	0.5	0.7	1.2	0.9	1.0	•	•	1.3
Advertising	18	1.1	0.2	1.5	0.9	0.9	0.9	1.2	0.6	1.1	0.6	•	•	1.2
Other Expenses	19	10.9	11.0	13.2	10.7	9.9	7.1	6.5	8.8	8.7	8.9	•	•	12.9
Officers' Compensation	20	1.5	5.3	3.9	3.8	2.2	1.8	0.9	0.6	0.7	0.6	•	•	0.1
Operating Margin	21	2.8	9.9	3.0	3.0	0.9	2.1	1.7	0.1	0.6	2.8	•	•	7.5
Operating Margin Before Officers' Comp.	22	4.4	15.2	7.0	6.8	3.2	3.9	2.6	0.7	1.4	3.5	•	•	7.7

Selected Average Balance Sheet ($ in Thousands)

Net Receivables 23	224	0	16	78	250	554	1979	3917	11311	27043	181152
Inventories 24	1099	0	71	322	1618	4791	8487	22609	34111	47041	1830112
Net Property, Plant and Equipment 25	487	0	21	119	281	1660	2675	5339	18018	34495	1260715
Total Assets 26	2241	0	147	695	2178	7200	15628	33382	75744	147123	4517062
Notes and Loans Payable 27	800	0	54	437	797	2708	8115	16356	26550	59996	1257464
All Other Liabilities 28	690	0	44	150	549	1485	3121	7880	20762	38649	1908301
Net Worth 29	750	0	48	109	832	3006	4392	9146	28432	48478	1351297

Selected Financial Ratios (Times to 1)

Current Ratio 30	1.6	•	2.3	1.6	1.9	1.7	1.6	1.5	1.5	1.5	1.3
Quick Ratio 31	0.4	•	0.9	0.4	0.5	0.7	0.5	0.4	0.5	0.6	0.1
Net Sales to Working Capital 32	8.2	23.1	11.5	10.3	6.4	7.4	8.8	9.2	10.0	7.6	12.9
Coverage Ratio 33	5.8	•	9.4	5.5	4.1	4.2	3.8	3.2	4.4	5.5	10.0
Total Asset Turnover 34	2.0	•	4.9	2.8	2.5	2.0	2.4	2.1	2.2	1.8	1.3
Inventory Turnover 35	2.7	•	6.7	4.1	2.4	2.2	3.4	2.3	3.7	3.8	1.8
Receivables Turnover 36	18.5	•	43.6	26.0	18.3	21.6	18.6	14.1	13.7	10.7	31.4
Total Liabilities to Net Worth 37	2.0	•	2.0	5.4	1.6	1.4	2.6	2.6	1.7	2.0	2.3
Current Assets to Working Capital 38	2.6	•	1.8	2.8	2.2	2.4	2.7	3.2	2.9	2.9	4.7
Current Liabilities to Working Capital 39	1.6	•	0.8	1.8	1.2	1.4	1.7	2.2	1.9	1.9	3.7
Working Capital to Net Sales 40	0.1	•	0.1	0.1	0.2	0.1	0.1	0.1	0.1	0.1	0.1
Inventory to Working Capital 41	1.8	•	1.1	1.9	1.5	1.4	1.8	1.9	1.8	1.6	4.0
Total Receipts to Cash Flow 42	8.9	3.5	8.3	9.4	10.2	12.1	14.8	12.8	11.5	9.7	6.5
Cost of Goods to Cash Flow 43	5.9	2.3	5.4	6.4	7.4	9.0	11.4	9.5	8.7	6.6	3.5
Cash Flow to Total Debt 44	0.3	•	0.9	0.4	0.4	0.3	0.2	0.2	0.3	0.3	0.3

Selected Financial Factors (in Percentages)

Debt Ratio 45	66.5	•	67.0	84.4	61.8	58.2	71.9	72.6	62.5	67.0	70.1
Return on Total Assets 46	9.8	•	18.1	11.8	8.5	9.4	8.7	5.2	7.5	8.7	11.8
Return on Equity Before Income Taxes 47	24.3	•	49.1	62.0	16.8	17.2	22.9	13.1	15.4	21.6	35.4
Return on Equity After Income Taxes 48	19.9	•	47.6	60.9	15.8	16.5	21.4	12.6	14.1	20.2	23.4
Profit Margin (Before Income Tax) 49	4.1	20.8	3.3	3.5	2.6	3.7	2.7	1.7	2.6	4.0	7.8
Profit Margin (After Income Tax) 50	3.4	20.8	3.2	3.4	2.4	3.5	2.5	1.6	2.4	3.7	5.2

Table I
Corporations with and without Net Income

FURNITURE AND HOME FURNISHINGS STORES

MONEY AMOUNTS AND SIZE OF ASSETS IN THOUSANDS OF DOLLARS

Item Description for Accounting Period 7/09 Through 6/10	Total	Zero Assets	Under 500	500 to 1,000	1,000 to 5,000	5,000 to 10,000	10,000 to 25,000	25,000 to 50,000	50,000 to 100,000	100,000 to 250,000	250,000 to 500,000	500,000 to 2,500,000	2,500,000 and over
Number of Enterprises 1	37218	5033	24426	4191	3057	283	150	30	20	11	10	7	0
Revenues ($ in Thousands)													
Net Sales 2	75329916	880867	12028193	7110730	13805592	4629401	4981360	2172980	2683726	2599844	5350091	19087133	0
Interest 3	246313	7	3443	15811	37722	12460	4410	666	362	27894	133182	10355	0
Rents 4	30822	126	3811	1182	4689	2049	6887	2199	0	3363	2347	4169	0
Royalties 5	3997	0	0	0	0	0	0	0	267	0	2520	1210	0
Other Portfolio Income 6	99533	9032	14514	1691	14751	7447	31217	21	924	3410	1858	14668	0
Other Receipts 7	652213	44463	21615	36201	122024	57688	91828	33229	76561	43988	92800	31817	0
Total Receipts 8	76362794	934495	12071576	7165615	13984778	4709045	5115702	2209095	2761840	2678499	5582798	19149352	0
Average Total Receipts 9	2052	186	494	1710	4575	16640	34105	73636	138092	243500	558280	2735622	•
Operating Costs/Operating Income (%)													
Cost of Operations 10	58.1	71.6	60.3	62.5	61.5	56.3	60.6	60.3	54.8	53.9	53.8	53.7	•
Salaries and Wages 11	12.8	5.2	9.8	11.0	12.9	11.1	15.5	16.0	14.7	15.6	16.4	13.4	•
Taxes Paid 12	2.5	1.7	2.3	3.0	2.4	1.8	2.4	2.1	2.6	3.0	2.2	2.7	•
Interest Paid 13	0.8	0.4	0.8	0.8	0.9	0.9	0.5	0.8	0.6	1.1	1.4	0.8	•
Depreciation 14	1.5	1.5	0.8	0.8	0.8	1.3	0.9	1.2	2.9	1.9	1.9	2.6	•
Amortization and Depletion 15	0.2	0.3	0.1	0.2	0.2	0.0	0.0	0.2	0.2	0.2	0.2	0.2	•
Pensions and Other Deferred Comp. 16	0.1	0.0	0.2	0.1	0.1	0.1	0.1	0.2	0.2	0.1	0.1	0.1	•
Employee Benefits 17	1.0	0.6	0.7	0.9	0.5	0.9	0.9	1.9	1.1	1.3	1.2	1.3	•
Advertising 18	4.0	1.1	3.0	3.0	3.1	7.3	4.2	2.3	4.3	6.0	5.5	4.4	•
Other Expenses 19	17.2	31.6	18.3	15.1	17.1	19.3	14.2	18.8	18.7	20.0	21.1	15.1	•
Officers' Compensation 20	2.7	1.6	5.9	5.0	4.1	2.0	1.2	1.6	1.2	0.4	0.6	0.5	•
Operating Margin 21	•	•	•	•	•	•	•	•	•	•	•	5.2	•
Operating Margin Before Officers' Comp. 22	1.9	•	3.8	2.7	0.6	1.1	0.6	•	•	•	•	5.7	•

Selected Average Balance Sheet ($ in Thousands)

Net Receivables 23	215	0	17	121	321	960	2975	7732	6351	24131	85610	560172	•
Inventories 24	347	0	61	260	853	3410	6248	8437	27432	36236	97310	521137	•
Net Property, Plant and Equipment 25	278	0	27	139	405	2029	2106	7309	19337	55084	79984	709030	•
Total Assets 26	1070	0	140	664	2033	7032	14991	35198	73185	146550	355124	2209513	•
Notes and Loans Payable 27	399	0	100	366	773	2616	5030	9191	21526	45013	99742	689942	•
All Other Liabilities 28	336	0	44	157	753	2085	7491	13266	22006	45985	111096	615429	•
Net Worth 29	335	0	-3	141	508	2331	2469	12742	29653	55553	144286	904142	•

Selected Financial Ratios (Times to 1)

Current Ratio 30	1.7	•	2.0	2.4	1.7	1.5	1.2	1.2	1.7	1.7	2.0	1.8
Quick Ratio 31	0.8	•	0.8	1.0	0.6	0.5	0.4	0.6	0.6	0.9	0.9	1.0
Net Sales to Working Capital 32	6.8	•	9.5	6.5	7.7	10.8	21.4	17.1	8.2	7.5	5.2	4.3
Coverage Ratio 33	1.7	•	•	•	•	1.9	5.2	•	4.0	0.5	1.0	8.1
Total Asset Turnover 34	1.9	•	3.5	2.6	2.2	2.3	2.2	2.1	1.8	1.6	1.5	1.2
Inventory Turnover 35	3.4	•	4.8	4.1	3.3	2.7	3.2	5.2	2.7	3.5	3.0	2.8
Receivables Turnover 36	11.0	•	26.6	11.7	14.8	14.8	10.4	9.2	23.0	9.2	6.2	7.5
Total Liabilities to Net Worth 37	2.2	•	3.7	3.7	3.0	2.0	5.1	1.8	1.5	1.6	1.5	1.4
Current Assets to Working Capital 38	2.4	2.0	2.0	1.7	2.5	2.9	7.6	5.4	2.4	2.4	2.0	2.3
Current Liabilities to Working Capital 39	1.4	1.0	1.0	0.7	1.5	1.9	6.6	4.4	1.4	1.4	1.0	1.3
Working Capital to Net Sales 40	0.1	0.1	0.1	0.2	0.1	0.1	0.0	0.1	0.1	0.1	0.2	0.2
Inventory to Working Capital 41	1.1	1.1	1.1	1.0	1.4	1.8	3.7	2.0	1.5	1.0	1.0	0.7
Total Receipts to Cash Flow 42	9.3	7.8	10.8	11.9	11.9	8.1	10.8	13.2	7.8	8.4	8.3	7.4
Cost of Goods to Cash Flow 43	5.4	5.6	6.5	7.4	7.3	4.5	6.5	8.0	4.3	4.5	4.5	4.0
Cash Flow to Total Debt 44	0.3	•	0.3	0.3	0.2	0.4	0.2	0.2	0.4	0.3	0.3	0.3

Selected Financial Factors (in Percentages)

Debt Ratio 45	68.7	•	102.3	78.8	75.0	66.9	83.5	63.8	59.5	62.1	59.4	59.1
Return on Total Assets 46	2.7	•	•	•	•	4.0	5.8	•	4.6	0.9	2.1	7.8
Return on Equity Before Income Taxes 47	3.6	•	270.4	•	•	5.9	28.2	•	8.5	•	•	16.7
Return on Equity After Income Taxes 48	•	•	274.3	•	•	5.2	25.9	•	6.5	•	•	10.5
Profit Margin (Before Income Tax) 49	0.6	•	•	•	0.8	0.8	2.1	•	1.9	•	•	5.5
Profit Margin (After Income Tax) 50	•	•	•	•	0.7	0.7	1.9	•	1.4	•	•	3.5

Table II
Corporations with Net Income

FURNITURE AND HOME FURNISHINGS STORES

MONEY AMOUNTS AND SIZE OF ASSETS IN THOUSANDS OF DOLLARS

Item Description for Accounting Period 7/09 Through 6/10	Total	Zero Assets	Under 500	500 to 1,000	1,000 to 5,000	5,000 to 10,000	10,000 to 25,000	25,000 to 50,000	50,000 to 100,000	100,000 to 250,000	250,000 to 500,000	500,000 to 2,500,000	2,500,000 and over
Number of Enterprises 1	17162	•	12083	1822	1341	163	102	•	13	5	6	•	0
Revenues ($ in Thousands)													
Net Sales 2	47960418	•	6894020	3884928	5685609	3115028	3722172	•	1862711	901009	3182032	•	0
Interest 3	157948	•	825	1094	19405	10965	3654	•	326	11019	100538	•	0
Rents 4	14898	•	3064	2	120	766	3153	•	0	3176	2155	•	0
Royalties 5	1210	•	0	0	0	0	0	•	0	0	0	•	0
Other Portfolio Income 6	82946	•	10712	1559	13216	6688	30961	•	95	3028	1829	•	0
Other Receipts 7	336819	•	8458	4385	31831	36043	71915	•	42860	18416	76437	•	0
Total Receipts 8	48554239	•	6917079	3891968	5750181	3169490	3831855	•	1905992	936648	3362991	•	0
Average Total Receipts 9	2829	•	572	2136	4288	19445	37567	•	146615	187330	560498	•	•
Operating Costs/Operating Income (%)													
Cost of Operations 10	56.9	•	60.4	64.4	56.0	57.0	59.5	•	55.7	54.8	52.4	•	•
Salaries and Wages 11	11.8	•	8.5	8.5	10.6	10.0	14.8	•	13.6	14.7	16.4	•	•
Taxes Paid 12	2.3	•	2.1	2.3	2.2	1.4	2.3	•	2.2	3.1	2.8	•	•
Interest Paid 13	0.7	•	0.8	0.4	1.0	0.7	0.3	•	0.6	0.5	0.5	•	•
Depreciation 14	1.6	•	0.7	0.8	0.5	0.7	0.6	•	3.5	1.9	1.8	•	•
Amortization and Depletion 15	0.1	•	0.1	0.1	0.0	0.0	0.0	•	0.1	0.1	0.1	•	•
Pensions and Other Deferred Comp. 16	0.1	•	0.1	0.1	0.2	0.1	0.1	•	0.2	0.1	0.2	•	•
Employee Benefits 17	0.9	•	0.6	0.5	0.3	0.7	1.0	•	1.1	1.0	1.6	•	•
Advertising 18	3.9	•	2.6	2.1	4.3	4.1	4.7	•	3.1	5.7	5.4	•	•
Other Expenses 19	15.6	•	14.6	13.4	16.2	20.9	13.6	•	17.1	15.5	20.7	•	•
Officers' Compensation 20	2.3	•	5.6	4.6	4.8	1.5	1.2	•	0.7	0.7	0.8	•	•
Operating Margin 21	3.8	•	4.0	2.8	3.8	2.7	1.7	•	2.0	1.9	•	•	•
Operating Margin Before Officers' Comp. 22	6.1	•	9.6	7.4	8.6	4.3	2.9	•	2.7	2.6	•	•	•

Selected Average Balance Sheet ($ in Thousands)

							•			
Net Receivables 23	313	17	116	248	1024	3085	•	8644	28156	100830
Inventories 24	452	55	256	923	3805	5796	•	19235	18794	102064
Net Property, Plant and Equipment 25	414	28	98	459	1610	2212	•	16151	51511	81309
Total Assets 26	1513	149	636	1971	6891	15633	•	71164	148371	328696
Notes and Loans Payable 27	490	71	153	628	2634	4812	•	19865	32631	66612
All Other Liabilities 28	389	41	119	381	1986	8339	•	22472	24084	85057
Net Worth 29	635	37	364	961	2271	2482	•	28826	91655	177028

Selected Financial Ratios (Times to 1)

							•			
Current Ratio 30	1.9	2.1	3.2	3.0	1.7	1.0	•	1.8	2.6	2.3
Quick Ratio 31	0.9	1.1	1.3	1.3	0.6	0.4	•	0.6	1.7	1.2
Net Sales to Working Capital 32	5.7	9.7	6.5	4.8	8.9	123.7	•	8.1	3.6	4.0
Coverage Ratio 33	8.2	6.1	8.1	6.1	7.5	15.5	•	8.1	12.0	7.5
Total Asset Turnover 34	1.8	3.8	3.4	2.2	2.8	2.3	•	2.0	1.2	1.6
Inventory Turnover 35	3.5	6.2	5.4	2.6	2.9	3.7	•	4.1	5.3	2.7
Receivables Turnover 36	11.0	26.5	15.2	10.9	17.3	10.0	•	21.1	6.1	5.4
Total Liabilities to Net Worth 37	1.4	3.0	0.7	1.0	2.0	5.3	•	1.5	0.6	0.9
Current Assets to Working Capital 38	2.1	1.9	1.5	1.5	2.4	41.5	•	2.2	1.6	1.8
Current Liabilities to Working Capital 39	1.1	0.9	0.5	0.5	1.4	40.5	•	1.2	0.6	0.8
Working Capital to Net Sales 40	0.2	0.1	0.2	0.2	0.1	0.0	•	0.1	0.3	0.2
Inventory to Working Capital 41	0.9	0.9	0.8	0.8	1.5	18.5	•	1.3	0.4	0.8
Total Receipts to Cash Flow 42	7.1	7.6	8.8	6.4	5.7	8.6	•	6.9	5.6	6.6
Cost of Goods to Cash Flow 43	4.0	4.6	5.7	3.6	3.3	5.1	•	3.8	3.1	3.5
Cash Flow to Total Debt 44	0.5	0.7	0.9	0.7	0.7	0.3	•	0.5	0.6	0.5

Selected Financial Factors (in Percentages)

							•			
Debt Ratio 45	58.1	75.0	42.8	51.2	67.0	84.1	•	59.5	38.2	46.1
Return on Total Assets 46	10.6	19.6	11.3	12.6	14.4	11.5	•	10.5	7.4	5.9
Return on Equity Before Income Taxes 47	22.2	65.5	17.3	21.6	37.8	68.0	•	22.7	10.9	9.5
Return on Equity After Income Taxes 48	17.9	64.8	16.2	20.9	36.5	64.6	•	19.5	7.5	7.7
Profit Margin (Before Income Tax) 49	5.0	4.3	3.0	4.9	4.5	4.6	•	4.6	5.6	3.2
Profit Margin (After Income Tax) 50	4.1	4.2	2.8	4.7	4.3	4.4	•	3.9	3.8	2.6

Table I

Corporations with and without Net Income

ELECTRONICS AND APPLIANCE STORES

MONEY AMOUNTS AND SIZE OF ASSETS IN THOUSANDS OF DOLLARS

Item Description for Accounting Period 7/09 Through 6/10	Total	Zero Assets	Under 500	500 to 1,000	1,000 to 5,000	5,000 to 10,000	10,000 to 25,000	25,000 to 50,000	50,000 to 100,000	100,000 to 250,000	250,000 to 500,000	500,000 to 2,500,000	2,500,000 and over
Number of Enterprises 1	28031	7087	17228	1703	1696	189	58	21	24	10	5	7	3
Revenues ($ in Thousands)													
Net Sales 2	96122910	1563202	8255626	3347059	8033444	3355889	1623144	2247283	3732841	4139741	3119139	8780116	47925426
Interest 3	204744	984	3164	1445	3886	2220	815	1617	3189	32	7239	172042	8111
Rents 4	15769	155	1846	1576	167	100	0	0	517	0	1088	8177	2142
Royalties 5	60358	7082	0	0	0	0	5333	0	2243	0	0	1837	43863
Other Portfolio Income 6	163184	11030	192	5936	12958	1721	2479	1703	8839	1839	7285	1316	107886
Other Receipts 7	1113168	10215	26059	13534	55698	21291	13373	1129	39168	58302	-2013	80083	796331
Total Receipts 8	97680133	1592668	8286887	3369550	8106153	3381221	1645144	2251732	3786797	4199914	3132738	9043571	48883759
Average Total Receipts 9	3485	225	481	1979	4780	17890	28365	107225	157783	419991	626548	1291939	16294586
Operating Costs/Operating Income (%)													
Cost of Operations 10	70.5	55.2	52.4	51.7	68.7	61.6	63.0	75.7	69.7	80.0	64.6	81.2	74.1
Salaries and Wages 11	10.2	11.5	15.7	21.3	10.7	14.9	15.9	10.3	11.9	9.4	9.0	8.8	8.0
Taxes Paid 12	1.6	2.3	2.6	2.6	1.8	2.0	1.7	1.2	1.3	1.2	1.1	1.3	1.5
Interest Paid 13	0.6	0.7	0.6	0.5	0.7	0.3	0.5	0.7	0.2	0.1	1.8	1.0	0.5
Depreciation 14	1.0	0.6	1.0	0.8	0.6	0.7	1.8	2.2	1.5	0.9	1.0	0.9	1.0
Amortization and Depletion 15	0.2	0.4	0.1	0.1	0.1	0.3	0.3	0.1	0.1	0.0	0.8	0.3	0.1
Pensions and Other Deferred Comp. 16	0.1	0.3	0.2	0.1	0.3	0.3	0.1	0.1	0.1	0.1	0.0	0.1	0.1
Employee Benefits 17	0.7	0.5	0.8	1.4	1.1	1.2	0.9	0.2	0.5	0.5	0.8	0.6	0.7
Advertising 18	1.8	0.7	1.6	1.0	1.3	2.4	1.5	1.3	1.3	1.0	4.2	1.3	2.1
Other Expenses 19	10.8	26.8	18.6	15.7	11.1	11.1	9.0	17.4	6.9	5.3	17.5	10.1	8.6
Officers' Compensation 20	1.5	5.8	6.5	4.9	4.0	1.8	2.2	0.8	4.5	0.5	0.6	0.3	0.0
Operating Margin 21	1.0	•	0.0	•	•	3.4	3.0	•	2.0	0.9	•	•	3.2
Operating Margin Before Officers' Comp. 22	2.5	1.0	6.5	4.8	5.2	5.2	5.2	•	6.5	1.5	•	•	3.3

Selected Average Balance Sheet ($ in Thousands)

Net Receivables 23	318	0	12	119	447	1116	3312	12037	14062	40951	71588	199787	1530204
Inventories 24	339	0	43	177	609	1058	3431	8059	12400	36014	57263	457365	1813026
Net Property, Plant and Equipment 25	213	0	19	170	216	584	1040	3967	7269	16465	26835	86856	1213340
Total Assets 26	1574	0	113	700	1739	6900	14659	36205	70552	158452	368084	898233	7901057
Notes and Loans Payable 27	266	0	59	240	440	837	2879	9792	9787	9647	99475	231563	765612
All Other Liabilities 28	828	0	60	310	742	2637	6920	22641	23215	70800	229295	527265	4301539
Net Worth 29	480	0	-6	149	558	3427	4860	3772	37551	78005	39314	139405	2833906

Selected Financial Ratios (Times to 1)

Current Ratio 30	1.2	•	1.2	1.5	1.6	1.7	1.6	1.2	1.9	1.4	0.8	1.1	1.1
Quick Ratio 31	0.7	•	0.5	0.8	0.9	1.1	0.9	0.7	1.2	0.8	0.5	0.7	0.6
Net Sales to Working Capital 32	21.1	•	48.2	13.9	9.3	9.2	7.5	26.5	7.2	15.2	•	24.4	28.5
Coverage Ratio 33	5.8	•	1.6	2.2	1.7	14.4	10.3	•	16.2	18.7	0.4	•	13.0
Total Asset Turnover 34	2.2	•	4.2	2.8	2.7	2.6	1.9	3.0	2.2	2.6	1.7	1.4	2.0
Inventory Turnover 35	7.1	•	5.9	5.7	5.3	10.3	5.1	10.1	8.7	9.2	7.0	2.2	6.5
Receivables Turnover 36	11.7	•	30.2	19.4	9.7	13.5	8.0	6.6	10.8	10.4	6.4	3.4	20.9
Total Liabilities to Net Worth 37	2.3	•	•	3.7	2.1	1.0	2.0	8.6	0.9	1.0	8.4	5.4	1.8
Current Assets to Working Capital 38	5.8	•	7.5	3.1	2.6	2.4	2.7	6.4	2.2	3.7	•	10.2	8.1
Current Liabilities to Working Capital 39	4.8	•	6.5	2.1	1.6	1.4	1.7	5.4	1.2	2.7	•	9.2	7.1
Working Capital to Net Sales 40	0.0	•	0.0	0.1	0.1	0.1	0.1	0.0	0.1	0.1	•	0.0	0.0
Inventory to Working Capital 41	2.0	•	3.8	1.0	1.0	0.7	0.7	1.7	0.6	1.3	•	2.0	3.2
Total Receipts to Cash Flow 42	10.5	6.8	8.1	7.7	12.0	8.3	8.8	•	11.7	15.8	6.9	37.5	9.6
Cost of Goods to Cash Flow 43	7.4	3.8	4.3	4.0	8.2	5.1	5.6	•	8.2	12.6	4.5	30.4	7.1
Cash Flow to Total Debt 44	0.3	0.5	0.5	0.5	0.3	0.6	0.3	0.4	0.4	0.3	0.3	0.0	0.3

Selected Financial Factors (in Percentages)

Debt Ratio 45	69.5	•	105.7	78.7	67.9	50.3	66.8	89.6	46.8	50.8	89.3	84.5	64.1
Return on Total Assets 46	7.2	•	4.2	3.2	3.1	11.5	10.6	•	8.1	6.6	1.3	•	12.2
Return on Equity Before Income Taxes 47	19.7	•	•	8.3	4.1	21.5	29.0	•	14.2	12.8	•	•	31.3
Return on Equity After Income Taxes 48	11.9	•	•	6.9	2.7	21.0	28.1	•	11.6	12.8	•	•	20.4
Profit Margin (Before Income Tax) 49	2.8	•	0.4	0.6	0.5	4.2	5.0	•	3.4	2.4	•	•	5.6
Profit Margin (After Income Tax) 50	1.7	•	0.3	0.5	0.3	4.1	4.9	•	2.8	2.4	•	•	3.6

Table II

Corporations with Net Income

ELECTRONICS AND APPLIANCE STORES

MONEY AMOUNTS AND SIZE OF ASSETS IN THOUSANDS OF DOLLARS

Item Description for Accounting Period 7/09 Through 6/10	Total	Zero Assets	Under 500	500 to 1,000	1,000 to 5,000	5,000 to 10,000	10,000 to 25,000	25,000 to 50,000	50,000 to 100,000	100,000 to 250,000	250,000 to 500,000	500,000 to 2,500,000	2,500,000 and over
Number of Enterprises 1	14265	3739	7972	1196	1117	138	46	17	19	•	•	•	3
Revenues ($ in Thousands)													
Net Sales 2	84518014	871062	5547686	2106324	5970451	2361519	1399990	1697961	3287639	•	•	•	47925426
Interest 3	194151	971	3022	540	2532	1922	332	1402	3108	•	•	•	8111
Rents 4	13988	0	1384	1576	0	47	0	0	517	•	•	•	2142
Royalties 5	60358	7082	0	0	0	0	5333	0	2243	•	•	•	43863
Other Portfolio Income 6	153951	10708	192	1237	12282	1721	1768	280	8286	•	•	•	107886
Other Receipts 7	1116400	5328	7737	11414	36806	18108	12345	912	36433	•	•	•	796331
Total Receipts 8	86056862	895151	5560021	2121091	6022071	2383317	1419768	1700555	3338226	•	•	•	48883759
Average Total Receipts 9	6033	239	697	1773	5391	17270	30865	100033	175696	•	•	•	16294586
Operating Costs/Operating Income (%)													
Cost of Operations 10	71.3	49.9	51.1	63.0	65.8	62.0	60.9	77.0	68.8	•	•	•	74.1
Salaries and Wages 11	9.5	6.7	15.6	14.0	10.9	13.3	16.4	8.3	12.3	•	•	•	8.0
Taxes Paid 12	1.5	1.8	2.2	1.8	2.0	1.8	1.6	1.0	1.3	•	•	•	1.5
Interest Paid 13	0.6	0.5	0.5	0.5	0.6	0.2	0.6	0.6	0.3	•	•	•	0.5
Depreciation 14	1.0	0.4	0.8	0.6	0.6	0.4	2.0	2.3	1.6	•	•	•	1.0
Amortization and Depletion 15	0.2	0.7	0.0	0.0	0.0	0.4	0.3	0.1	0.1	•	•	•	0.1
Pensions and Other Deferred Comp. 16	0.2	0.5	0.2	0.1	0.0	0.3	0.3	0.1	0.1	•	•	•	0.1
Employee Benefits 17	0.7	0.0	0.8	1.0	1.1	1.2	0.7	0.2	0.5	•	•	•	0.7
Advertising 18	1.7	0.7	1.3	1.4	1.5	2.1	1.4	1.2	0.9	•	•	•	2.1
Other Expenses 19	9.3	24.6	17.7	11.1	11.1	8.1	9.1	7.2	6.5	•	•	•	8.6
Officers' Compensation 20	1.2	4.4	5.8	3.6	4.4	1.9	2.2	0.9	4.9	•	•	•	0.0
Operating Margin 21	2.8	9.9	4.0	3.0	1.6	8.2	4.5	1.1	2.8	•	•	•	3.2
Operating Margin Before Officers' Comp. 22	4.1	14.3	9.8	6.5	6.0	10.1	6.7	2.1	7.7	•	•	•	3.3

Selected Average Balance Sheet ($ in Thousands)

Net Receivables 23	547	0	14	136	537	866	2942	12369	13002	1530204
Inventories 24	570	0	54	156	627	676	2847	7946	14537	1813026
Net Property, Plant and Equipment 25	374	0	18	204	198	416	800	4097	7477	1213340
Total Assets 26	2694	0	146	719	1849	6891	15129	35759	69434	7901057
Notes and Loans Payable 27	373	0	53	198	426	670	3219	9541	8275	765612
All Other Liabilities 28	1336	0	56	352	780	1820	7560	18161	22719	4301539
Net Worth 29	985	0	38	168	643	4402	4350	8057	38440	2833906

Selected Financial Ratios (Times to 1)

Current Ratio 30	1.3	•	1.6	1.3	1.8	2.1	1.3	1.3	1.9	1.1
Quick Ratio 31	0.7	•	0.7	0.7	1.0	1.5	0.7	0.8	1.2	0.6
Net Sales to Working Capital 32	16.3	•	17.9	15.1	8.6	7.3	12.0	15.4	7.8	28.5
Coverage Ratio 33	9.6	25.4	10.3	9.0	5.1	49.4	12.1	3.0	18.0	13.0
Total Asset Turnover 34	2.2	•	4.8	2.5	2.9	2.5	2.0	2.8	2.5	2.0
Inventory Turnover 35	7.4	•	6.6	7.1	5.6	15.7	6.5	9.7	8.2	6.5
Receivables Turnover 36	12.1	•	32.7	16.7	8.9	27.3	9.8	5.9	11.1	20.9
Total Liabilities to Net Worth 37	1.7	•	2.9	3.3	1.9	0.6	2.5	3.4	0.8	1.8
Current Assets to Working Capital 38	4.4	•	2.6	4.0	2.3	1.9	3.9	3.9	2.1	8.1
Current Liabilities to Working Capital 39	3.4	•	1.6	3.0	1.3	0.9	2.9	2.9	1.1	7.1
Working Capital to Net Sales 40	0.1	•	0.1	0.1	0.1	0.1	0.1	0.1	0.1	0.0
Inventory to Working Capital 41	1.6	•	1.4	1.4	0.9	0.4	1.0	1.3	0.7	3.2
Total Receipts to Cash Flow 42	9.4	3.0	6.7	7.9	9.3	6.8	7.5	15.4	11.0	9.6
Cost of Goods to Cash Flow 43	6.7	1.5	3.4	5.0	6.1	4.2	4.6	11.9	7.6	7.1
Cash Flow to Total Debt 44	0.4	1.0	0.4	0.5	1.0	0.4	0.2	0.5		0.3

Selected Financial Factors (in Percentages)

Debt Ratio 45	63.4	•	74.3	76.6	65.2	36.1	71.2	77.5	44.6	64.1
Return on Total Assets 46	11.9	•	22.5	10.1	8.6	22.9	14.7	5.4	11.4	12.2
Return on Equity Before Income Taxes 47	29.1	•	79.0	38.4	19.9	35.2	46.9	15.9	19.4	31.3
Return on Equity After Income Taxes 48	21.7	•	78.1	36.7	18.1	34.6	45.7	15.3	16.1	20.4
Profit Margin (Before Income Tax) 49	4.8	12.7	4.3	3.7	2.4	9.1	6.7	1.3	4.3	5.6
Profit Margin (After Income Tax) 50	3.6	12.5	4.2	3.5	2.2	8.9	6.5	1.2	3.6	3.6

Table I

Corporations with and without Net Income

HOMES CENTERS; PAINT AND WALLPAPER STORES

MONEY AMOUNTS AND SIZE OF ASSETS IN THOUSANDS OF DOLLARS

Item Description for Accounting Period 7/09 Through 6/10		Total	Zero Assets	Under 500	500 to 1,000	1,000 to 5,000	5,000 to 10,000	10,000 to 25,000	25,000 to 50,000	50,000 to 100,000	100,000 to 250,000	250,000 to 500,000	500,000 to 2,500,000	2,500,000 and over
Number of Enterprises	1	3043	394	1693	409	449	38	44	7	5	0	0	0	3
Revenues ($ in Thousands)														
Net Sales	2	123236839	18427	2077601	397280	2283054	555985	1132621	675523	783322	0	0	0	115313027
Interest	3	28899	0	401	395	3192	1603	898	262	452	0	0	0	21696
Rents	4	364003	0	0	0	1219	3529	0	0	0	0	0	0	359255
Royalties	5	213464	0	0	0	0	0	0	0	0	0	0	0	213464
Other Portfolio Income	6	1083775	0	0	0	6810	774	580	377	1199	0	0	0	1074032
Other Receipts	7	1666353	430	1229	900	9233	2917	7954	2697	8459	0	0	0	1632536
Total Receipts	8	126593333	18857	2079231	398575	2303508	564808	1142053	678859	793432	0	0	0	118614010
Average Total Receipts	9	41601	48	1228	975	5130	14863	25956	96980	158686	•	•	•	39538003
Operating Costs/Operating Income (%)														
Cost of Operations	10	66.0	66.0	60.5	64.6	67.4	69.0	66.7	71.5	71.7	•	•	•	65.9
Salaries and Wages	11	13.5	68.0	11.1	6.2	13.5	12.1	15.1	13.1	10.9	•	•	•	13.5
Taxes Paid	12	2.4	9.3	6.2	1.7	2.5	2.3	2.0	1.7	1.8	•	•	•	2.3
Interest Paid	13	1.1	11.5	0.2	3.0	0.5	0.9	0.5	0.9	0.8	•	•	•	1.1
Depreciation	14	2.6	0.2	0.3	2.3	0.6	0.9	1.5	1.9	2.1	•	•	•	2.7
Amortization and Depletion	15	0.0	•	0.0	0.0	0.1	0.0	0.2	0.1	0.0	•	•	•	0.0
Pensions and Other Deferred Comp.	16	0.3	•	•	0.1	0.3	0.8	0.3	0.1	1.1	•	•	•	0.3
Employee Benefits	17	1.3	0.5	0.4	1.2	1.1	2.4	1.0	1.2	1.6	•	•	•	1.3
Advertising	18	1.5	9.1	1.0	1.2	0.5	1.0	1.0	0.6	1.6	•	•	•	1.6
Other Expenses	19	7.0	90.7	14.3	12.4	10.2	6.9	12.1	8.1	8.3	•	•	•	6.7
Officers' Compensation	20	0.3	•	4.5	9.5	3.2	3.2	1.3	1.9	0.7	•	•	•	0.1
Operating Margin	21	4.1	•	1.6	•	0.0	0.5	•	•	•	•	•	•	4.4
Operating Margin Before Officers' Comp.	22	4.4	•	6.1	7.4	3.2	3.7	0.9	•	0.0	•	•	•	4.5

Selected Average Balance Sheet ($ in Thousands)

Net Receivables 23	804	0	58	113	426	1349	2595	7835	10327	•	•	613137
Inventories 24	6533	0	120	186	709	2943	4583	14111	36482	•	•	6229215
Net Property, Plant and Equipment 25	13348	0	24	394	186	1778	3355	10912	30551	•	•	13295698
Total Assets 26	36972	0	213	745	2171	7422	12959	38426	89892	•	•	36431833
Notes and Loans Payable 27	13644	0	34	550	537	2297	4267	11818	21160	•	•	13511042
All Other Liabilities 28	11302	0	85	120	270	1325	2284	9555	19669	•	•	11254341
Net Worth 29	12025	0	94	74	1363	3800	6408	17053	49063	•	•	11666450

Selected Financial Ratios (Times to 1)

Current Ratio 30	1.2	•	2.0	1.8	5.3	2.2	1.8	2.1	3.4	•	•	1.1
Quick Ratio 31	0.1	•	0.8	0.9	3.1	1.1	0.8	0.9	1.0	•	•	0.1
Net Sales to Working Capital 32	22.9	•	13.1	7.6	3.5	5.7	6.8	7.7	4.4	•	•	29.0
Coverage Ratio 33	7.9	•	10.0	0.4	2.7	3.4	•	0.4	1.8	•	•	8.2
Total Asset Turnover 34	1.1	•	5.8	1.3	2.3	2.0	2.0	2.5	1.7	•	•	1.1
Inventory Turnover 35	4.1	•	6.2	3.4	4.8	3.4	3.7	4.9	3.1	•	•	4.1
Receivables Turnover 36	41.6	•	23.8	10.2	10.3	9.1	8.6	11.0	13.4	•	•	50.1
Total Liabilities to Net Worth 37	2.1	•	1.3	9.0	0.6	1.0	1.0	1.3	0.8	•	•	2.1
Current Assets to Working Capital 38	7.0	•	2.0	2.3	1.2	1.8	2.3	1.9	1.4	•	•	8.9
Current Liabilities to Working Capital 39	6.0	•	1.0	1.3	0.2	0.8	1.3	0.9	0.4	•	•	7.9
Working Capital to Net Sales 40	0.0	•	0.1	0.1	0.3	0.2	0.1	0.1	0.2	•	•	0.0
Inventory to Working Capital 41	3.6	•	1.2	1.2	0.5	0.8	1.2	1.0	1.0	•	•	4.6
Total Receipts to Cash Flow 42	8.9	•	8.9	14.1	12.3	14.3	15.5	21.3	17.6	•	•	8.7
Cost of Goods to Cash Flow 43	5.9	•	5.4	9.1	8.3	9.9	10.3	15.2	12.6	•	•	5.8
Cash Flow to Total Debt 44	0.2	•	1.2	0.1	0.5	0.3	0.3	0.2	0.2	•	•	0.2

Selected Financial Factors (in Percentages)

Debt Ratio 45	67.5	•	55.7	90.0	37.2	48.8	50.6	55.6	45.4	•	•	68.0
Return on Total Assets 46	9.2	•	11.0	1.6	3.3	5.7	•	0.9	2.6	•	•	9.4
Return on Equity Before Income Taxes 47	24.8	•	22.4	•	3.3	7.9	•	•	2.1	•	•	25.9
Return on Equity After Income Taxes 48	16.9	•	22.3	•	3.0	4.3	•	•	1.6	•	•	17.6
Profit Margin (Before Income Tax) 49	7.4	•	1.7	•	0.9	2.0	•	•	0.6	•	•	7.9
Profit Margin (After Income Tax) 50	5.0	•	1.7	•	0.8	1.1	•	•	0.5	•	•	5.3

Table II

Corporations with Net Income

HOMES CENTERS; PAINT AND WALLPAPER STORES

MONEY AMOUNTS AND SIZE OF ASSETS IN THOUSANDS OF DOLLARS

Item Description for Accounting Period 7/09 Through 6/10	Total	Zero Assets	Under 500	500 to 1,000	1,000 to 5,000	5,000 to 10,000	10,000 to 25,000	25,000 to 50,000	50,000 to 100,000	100,000 to 250,000	250,000 to 500,000	500,000 to 2,500,000	2,500,000 and over
Number of Enterprises 1	2156	0	1496	240	351	29	29	•	0	0	0	0	3
Revenues ($ in Thousands)													
Net Sales 2	121387376	0	1916743	261503	1903071	446433	566444	•	0	0	0	0	115313027
Interest 3	26351	0	29	0	2391	1423	98	•	0	0	0	0	21696
Rents 4	363014	0	0	0	272	3488	0	•	0	0	0	0	359255
Royalties 5	213464	0	0	0	0	0	0	•	0	0	0	0	213464
Other Portfolio Income 6	1078040	0	0	0	2553	522	532	•	0	0	0	0	1074032
Other Receipts 7	1652869	0	123	416	6473	41	4573	•	0	0	0	0	1632536
Total Receipts 8	124721114	0	1916895	261919	1914760	451907	571647	•	0	0	0	0	118614010
Average Total Receipts 9	57848	•	1281	1091	5455	15583	19712	•	•	•	•	•	39538003
Operating Costs/Operating Income (%)													
Cost of Operations 10	65.9	•	60.6	63.6	67.1	69.6	67.1	•	•	•	•	•	65.9
Salaries and Wages 11	13.5	•	11.0	5.2	13.1	10.6	12.7	•	•	•	•	•	13.5
Taxes Paid 12	2.4	•	6.5	1.4	2.1	2.2	1.8	•	•	•	•	•	2.3
Interest Paid 13	1.1	•	0.1	2.6	0.4	0.7	0.7	•	•	•	•	•	1.1
Depreciation 14	2.6	•	0.2	1.8	0.5	0.8	1.3	•	•	•	•	•	2.7
Amortization and Depletion 15	0.0	•	•	0.0	0.0	0.0	0.1	•	•	•	•	•	0.0
Pensions and Other Deferred Comp. 16	0.3	•	•	•	0.3	0.9	0.5	•	•	•	•	•	0.3
Employee Benefits 17	1.3	•	0.1	0.3	1.0	2.3	1.1	•	•	•	•	•	1.3
Advertising 18	1.5	•	0.9	0.9	0.5	0.9	1.2	•	•	•	•	•	1.6
Other Expenses 19	6.9	•	13.7	13.9	9.1	6.3	8.6	•	•	•	•	•	6.7
Officers' Compensation 20	0.2	•	4.4	9.9	3.4	3.6	1.1	•	•	•	•	•	0.1
Operating Margin 21	4.3	•	2.4	0.4	2.5	2.2	3.9	•	•	•	•	•	4.4
Operating Margin Before Officers' Comp. 22	4.5	•	6.8	10.3	5.9	5.8	4.9	•	•	•	•	•	4.5

Selected Average Balance Sheet ($ in Thousands)

Net Receivables 23	1054	59	117	480	858	1744	•	•	•	•	•	613137
Inventories 24	9002	78	129	588	3367	3997	•	•	•	•	•	6229215
Net Property, Plant and Equipment 25	18737	22	425	149	1803	3672	•	•	•	•	•	13295698
Total Assets 26	51738	192	771	2081	7047	12747	•	•	•	•	•	36431833
Notes and Loans Payable 27	19059	13	594	346	1448	3526	•	•	•	•	•	13511042
All Other Liabilities 28	15853	82	156	241	1399	1827	•	•	•	•	•	11254341
Net Worth 29	16826	98	22	1494	4201	7394	•	•	•	•	•	11666450

Selected Financial Ratios (Times to 1)

Current Ratio 30	1.2	1.9	1.6	6.4	2.0	1.9	•	•	•	•	•	1.1
Quick Ratio 31	0.1	0.9	0.9	4.4	0.8	0.8	•	•	•	•	•	0.1
Net Sales to Working Capital 32	24.2	16.1	9.9	3.7	7.4	5.0	•	•	•	•	•	29.0
Coverage Ratio 33	8.1	30.6	1.2	8.0	6.1	8.2	•	•	•	•	•	8.2
Total Asset Turnover 34	1.1	6.7	1.4	2.6	2.2	1.5	•	•	•	•	•	1.1
Inventory Turnover 35	4.1	9.9	5.4	6.2	3.2	3.3	•	•	•	•	•	4.1
Receivables Turnover 36	43.9	25.8	14.5	9.6	10.3	11.1	•	•	•	•	•	50.1
Total Liabilities to Net Worth 37	2.1	1.0	34.9	0.4	0.7	0.7	•	•	•	•	•	2.1
Current Assets to Working Capital 38	7.4	2.1	2.6	1.2	2.0	2.1	•	•	•	•	•	8.9
Current Liabilities to Working Capital 39	6.4	1.1	1.6	0.2	1.0	1.1	•	•	•	•	•	7.9
Working Capital to Net Sales 40	0.0	0.1	0.1	0.3	0.1	0.2	•	•	•	•	•	0.0
Inventory to Working Capital 41	3.8	1.1	1.1	0.3	1.1	1.1	•	•	•	•	•	4.6
Total Receipts to Cash Flow 42	8.8	8.8	10.1	10.2	13.2	9.6	•	•	•	•	•	8.7
Cost of Goods to Cash Flow 43	5.8	5.3	6.4	6.9	9.2	6.4	•	•	•	•	•	5.8
Cash Flow to Total Debt 44	0.2	1.5	0.1	0.9	0.4	0.4	•	•	•	•	•	0.2

Selected Financial Factors (in Percentages)

Debt Ratio 45	67.5	49.1	97.2	28.2	40.4	42.0	•	•	•	•	•	68.0
Return on Total Assets 46	9.4	16.7	4.5	9.2	8.7	8.2	•	•	•	•	•	9.4
Return on Equity Before Income Taxes 47	25.4	31.7	28.8	11.2	12.3	12.4	•	•	•	•	•	25.9
Return on Equity After Income Taxes 48	17.4	31.5	25.6	10.9	8.1	11.7	•	•	•	•	•	17.6
Profit Margin (Before Income Tax) 49	7.6	2.4	0.6	3.1	3.4	4.7	•	•	•	•	•	7.9
Profit Margin (After Income Tax) 50	5.2	2.4	0.5	3.0	2.2	4.4	•	•	•	•	•	5.3

Table I

Corporations with and without Net Income

HARDWARE STORES

MONEY AMOUNTS AND SIZE OF ASSETS IN THOUSANDS OF DOLLARS

Item Description for Accounting Period 7/09 Through 6/10	Total	Zero Assets	Under 500	500 to 1,000	1,000 to 5,000	5,000 to 10,000	10,000 to 25,000	25,000 to 50,000	50,000 to 100,000	100,000 to 250,000	250,000 to 500,000	500,000 to 2,500,000	2,500,000 and over
Number of Enterprises 1	7622	0	3015	2563	1923	•	33	11	•	•	0	•	0

Revenues ($ in Thousands)

Net Sales 2	16432330	0	1917753	4133497	6864023	•	1007393	716935	•	•	0	•	0
Interest 3	12750	0	823	2581	7813	•	403	155	•	•	0	•	0
Rents 4	11531	0	753	6577	2477	•	12	922	•	•	0	•	0
Royalties 5	14	0	0	14	0	•	0	0	•	•	0	•	0
Other Portfolio Income 6	10125	0	638	1930	6856	•	499	73	•	•	0	•	0
Other Receipts 7	169030	0	23623	34824	87406	•	9119	2991	•	•	0	•	0
Total Receipts 8	16635780	0	1943590	4179423	6968575	•	1017426	721076	•	•	0	•	0
Average Total Receipts 9	2183	•	645	1631	3624	•	30831	65552	•	•	•	•	•

Operating Costs/Operating Income (%)

Cost of Operations 10	62.6	•	58.3	63.5	63.3	•	69.1	63.1	•	•	•	•	•
Salaries and Wages 11	13.1	•	12.3	11.2	13.6	•	14.0	14.9	•	•	•	•	•
Taxes Paid 12	2.6	•	2.5	2.3	2.7	•	1.9	3.3	•	•	•	•	•
Interest Paid 13	0.9	•	0.8	0.8	0.9	•	0.6	1.4	•	•	•	•	•
Depreciation 14	1.3	•	1.5	0.9	1.4	•	1.1	1.8	•	•	•	•	•
Amortization and Depletion 15	0.1	•	0.0	0.0	0.1	•	0.1	0.5	•	•	•	•	•
Pensions and Other Deferred Comp. 16	0.2	•	0.0	0.2	0.2	•	0.2	0.2	•	•	•	•	•
Employee Benefits 17	1.1	•	1.5	0.9	1.1	•	1.3	1.3	•	•	•	•	•
Advertising 18	1.6	•	1.3	1.9	1.5	•	0.7	1.4	•	•	•	•	•
Other Expenses 19	12.6	•	16.8	13.7	11.7	•	9.9	11.1	•	•	•	•	•
Officers' Compensation 20	3.9	•	8.9	4.5	3.3	•	1.3	1.3	•	•	•	•	•
Operating Margin 21	0.1	•	•	0.1	0.2	•	•	•	•	•	•	•	•
Operating Margin Before Officers' Comp. 22	4.0	•	5.0	4.6	3.5	•	1.2	1.1	•	•	•	•	•

Selected Average Balance Sheet ($ in Thousands)

Net Receivables 23	92	•	22	60	174	•	2147	1815
Inventories 24	510	•	155	394	859	•	5661	14000
Net Property, Plant and Equipment 25	229	•	37	79	315	•	4793	11763
Total Assets 26	1106	•	294	717	1831	•	15069	33433
Notes and Loans Payable 27	412	•	150	294	575	•	5046	15035
All Other Liabilities 28	189	•	82	94	267	•	2012	6325
Net Worth 29	505	•	61	329	988	•	8010	12073

Selected Financial Ratios (Times to 1)

Current Ratio 30	2.8	•	2.0	4.1	3.3	•	2.1	1.8
Quick Ratio 31	0.8	•	0.4	1.0	1.1	•	0.6	0.3
Net Sales to Working Capital 32	4.6	•	6.1	4.0	4.0	•	6.4	8.7
Coverage Ratio 33	2.4	•	•	2.5	2.9	•	2.4	1.3
Total Asset Turnover 34	1.9	•	2.2	2.2	1.9	•	2.0	1.9
Inventory Turnover 35	2.6	•	2.4	2.6	2.6	•	3.7	2.9
Receivables Turnover 36	21.0	•	25.1	27.2	17.9	•	•	27.5
Total Liabilities to Net Worth 37	1.2	•	3.8	1.2	0.9	•	0.9	1.8
Current Assets to Working Capital 38	1.6	•	2.0	1.3	1.4	•	1.9	2.3
Current Liabilities to Working Capital 39	0.6	•	1.0	0.3	0.4	•	0.9	1.3
Working Capital to Net Sales 40	0.2	•	0.2	0.3	0.3	•	0.2	0.1
Inventory to Working Capital 41	1.1	•	1.5	1.0	0.9	•	1.2	1.7
Total Receipts to Cash Flow 42	11.5	•	13.0	11.9	11.1	•	13.4	14.4
Cost of Goods to Cash Flow 43	7.2	•	7.5	7.6	7.0	•	9.2	9.1
Cash Flow to Total Debt 44	0.3	•	0.2	0.3	0.4	•	0.3	0.2

Selected Financial Factors (in Percentages)

Debt Ratio 45	54.3	•	79.1	54.1	46.0	•	46.8	63.9
Return on Total Assets 46	4.5	•	•	4.5	5.2	•	2.9	3.4
Return on Equity Before Income Taxes 47	5.8	•	•	6.0	6.3	•	3.2	2.0
Return on Equity After Income Taxes 48	4.5	•	•	5.6	5.5	•	3.1	1.2
Profit Margin (Before Income Tax) 49	1.3	•	•	1.2	1.7	•	0.8	0.4
Profit Margin (After Income Tax) 50	1.1	•	•	1.1	1.5	•	0.8	0.2

213

Table II

Corporations with Net Income

HARDWARE STORES

MONEY AMOUNTS AND SIZE OF ASSETS IN THOUSANDS OF DOLLARS

Item Description for Accounting Period 7/09 Through 6/10	Total	Zero Assets	Under 500	500 to 1,000	1,000 to 5,000	5,000 to 10,000	10,000 to 25,000	25,000 to 50,000	50,000 to 100,000	100,000 to 250,000	250,000 to 500,000	500,000 to 2,500,000	2,500,000 and over
Number of Enterprises **1**	4292	0	1152	1646	1410	•	15	6	•	•	0	•	0
Revenues ($ in Thousands)													
Net Sales **2**	11183982	0	739985	3145550	4949544	•	278032	452358	•	•	•	•	0
Interest **3**	5971	0	409	822	3919	•	0	20	•	•	0	•	0
Rents **4**	10446	0	751	6577	1604	•	0	724	•	•	0	•	0
Royalties **5**	14	0	0	14	0	•	0	0	•	•	0	•	0
Other Portfolio Income **6**	7677	0	573	789	5911	•	352	53	•	•	0	•	0
Other Receipts **7**	135262	0	15525	32471	71817	•	4684	2669	•	•	0	•	0
Total Receipts **8**	11343352	0	757243	3186223	5032795	•	283068	455824	•	•	0	•	0
Average Total Receipts **9**	2643	•	657	1936	3569	•	18871	75971	•	•	•	•	•
Operating Costs/Operating Income (%)													
Cost of Operations **10**	61.3	•	59.6	64.4	60.6	•	56.3	63.7	•	•	•	•	•
Salaries and Wages **11**	13.3	•	11.3	10.5	14.8	•	16.2	14.1	•	•	•	•	•
Taxes Paid **12**	2.6	•	2.5	2.1	2.9	•	2.5	3.3	•	•	•	•	•
Interest Paid **13**	0.9	•	0.4	0.8	0.8	•	0.9	1.1	•	•	•	•	•
Depreciation **14**	1.2	•	0.8	0.8	1.2	•	2.0	2.0	•	•	•	•	•
Amortization and Depletion **15**	0.1	•	0.0	0.0	0.1	•	0.1	0.0	•	•	•	•	•
Pensions and Other Deferred Comp. **16**	0.2	•	0.1	0.3	0.2	•	0.6	0.3	•	•	•	•	•
Employee Benefits **17**	1.0	•	1.0	1.0	1.0	•	0.5	1.1	•	•	•	•	•
Advertising **18**	1.6	•	0.9	1.9	1.4	•	2.0	1.7	•	•	•	•	•
Other Expenses **19**	12.2	•	13.5	12.9	12.1	•	10.1	10.8	•	•	•	•	•
Officers' Compensation **20**	3.5	•	10.1	3.7	3.3	•	2.0	1.3	•	•	•	•	•
Operating Margin **21**	2.1	•	•	1.6	1.6	•	6.9	0.7	•	•	•	•	•
Operating Margin Before Officers' Comp. **22**	5.7	•	9.9	5.3	5.0	•	8.8	2.0	•	•	•	•	•

Selected Average Balance Sheet ($ in Thousands)

Net Receivables 23	86	20	62	128	492	1767
Inventories 24	621	222	458	771	3392	12980
Net Property, Plant and Equipment 25	291	14	78	331	5465	11210
Total Assets 26	1335	277	728	1874	12034	30346
Notes and Loans Payable 27	425	39	325	461	2963	14682
All Other Liabilities 28	195	18	100	226	1468	5072
Net Worth 29	715	220	303	1187	7603	10592

Selected Financial Ratios (Times to 1)

Current Ratio 30	3.2	10.6	3.6	3.9	2.6	1.5
Quick Ratio 31	0.9	2.0	0.8	1.4	0.7	0.3
Net Sales to Working Capital 32	4.5	3.5	4.9	3.7	5.7	12.7
Coverage Ratio 33	5.0	7.1	4.6	5.1	10.3	2.3
Total Asset Turnover 34	2.0	2.3	2.6	1.9	1.5	2.5
Inventory Turnover 35	2.6	1.7	2.7	2.8	3.1	3.7
Receivables Turnover 36	23.4	21.0	30.7	21.2		25.2
Total Liabilities to Net Worth 37	0.9	0.3	1.4	0.6	0.6	1.9
Current Assets to Working Capital 38	1.4	1.1	1.4	1.3	1.6	2.9
Current Liabilities to Working Capital 39	0.4	0.1	0.4	0.3	0.6	1.9
Working Capital to Net Sales 40	0.2	0.3	0.2	0.3	0.2	0.1
Inventory to Working Capital 41	1.0	0.9	1.1	0.8	1.0	2.3
Total Receipts to Cash Flow 42	9.5	10.7	9.9	9.2	6.1	12.9
Cost of Goods to Cash Flow 43	5.8	6.4	6.4	5.6	3.4	8.2
Cash Flow to Total Debt 44	0.4	1.0	0.5	0.6	0.7	0.3

Selected Financial Factors (in Percentages)

Debt Ratio 45	46.4	20.6	58.4	36.6	36.8	65.1
Return on Total Assets 46	8.7	5.8	9.6	7.7	14.7	6.4
Return on Equity Before Income Taxes 47	13.0	6.3	18.0	9.8	21.0	10.4
Return on Equity After Income Taxes 48	11.4	6.1	17.4	8.9	20.8	8.8
Profit Margin (Before Income Tax) 49	3.6	2.2	2.9	3.3	8.6	1.5
Profit Margin (After Income Tax) 50	3.1	2.1	2.8	3.0	8.5	1.2

Table I

Corporations with and without Net Income

OTHER BUILDING MATERIAL DEALERS

MONEY AMOUNTS AND SIZE OF ASSETS IN THOUSANDS OF DOLLARS

Item Description for Accounting Period 7/09 Through 6/10		Total	Zero Assets	Under 500	500 to 1,000	1,000 to 5,000	5,000 to 10,000	10,000 to 25,000	25,000 to 50,000	50,000 to 100,000	100,000 to 250,000	250,000 to 500,000	500,000 to 2,500,000	2,500,000 and over
Number of Enterprises	1	20529	2330	11746	2734	2997	•	174	39	13	•	•	•	0
Revenues ($ in Thousands)														
Net Sales	2	47851321	756506	5718336	5614778	13787281	•	4555884	2144946	1539143	•	•	•	0
Interest	3	392875	1123	668	4930	19030	•	7207	3158	1835	•	•	•	0
Rents	4	34009	7137	3367	1520	6981	•	7292	3301	209	•	•	•	0
Royalties	5	25310	0	1213	0	0	•	111	0	0	•	•	•	0
Other Portfolio Income	6	135619	5633	6750	22799	28226	•	6408	12028	5155	•	•	•	0
Other Receipts	7	445572	5065	11613	58668	70673	•	49677	28213	11781	•	•	•	0
Total Receipts	8	48884706	775464	5741947	5702695	13912191	•	4626579	2191646	1558123	•	•	•	0
Average Total Receipts	9	2381	333	489	2086	4642	•	26590	56196	119856	•	•	•	•
Operating Costs/Operating Income (%)														
Cost of Operations	10	72.1	78.7	61.9	71.5	71.7	•	73.6	73.1	73.7	•	•	•	•
Salaries and Wages	11	10.5	2.0	8.9	7.6	10.2	•	11.9	12.9	12.5	•	•	•	•
Taxes Paid	12	2.0	2.1	2.9	2.5	2.0	•	1.9	2.1	1.8	•	•	•	•
Interest Paid	13	1.8	2.7	0.7	0.5	0.6	•	0.8	0.7	1.1	•	•	•	•
Depreciation	14	1.3	2.8	1.2	0.5	1.1	•	1.4	1.6	1.5	•	•	•	•
Amortization and Depletion	15	0.4	1.1	0.1	0.0	0.0	•	0.2	0.1	0.2	•	•	•	•
Pensions and Other Deferred Comp.	16	0.2	0.0	0.1	0.3	0.3	•	0.4	0.2	0.5	•	•	•	•
Employee Benefits	17	1.2	0.9	1.0	1.0	1.1	•	1.3	1.0	1.5	•	•	•	•
Advertising	18	0.9	0.5	1.4	1.8	0.7	•	0.9	0.5	0.5	•	•	•	•
Other Expenses	19	11.2	16.7	18.6	9.6	10.4	•	9.8	9.7	7.6	•	•	•	•
Officers' Compensation	20	2.6	1.9	5.3	4.0	3.1	•	1.6	1.3	0.8	•	•	•	•
Operating Margin	21	•	•	•	0.7	•		•	•	•	•	•	•	•
Operating Margin Before Officers' Comp.	22	•	•	3.2	4.8	1.8		•	•	•	•	•	•	•

Selected Average Balance Sheet ($ in Thousands)

Net Receivables 23	216	0	26	136	405	•	3214	5560	12473
Inventories 24	384	0	49	317	866	•	5069	9294	19733
Net Property, Plant and Equipment 25	240	0	26	56	327	•	3124	7616	20473
Total Assets 26	1504	0	147	723	2088	•	15182	36603	69699
Notes and Loans Payable 27	724	0	100	268	629	•	4086	6731	16757
All Other Liabilities 28	299	0	64	144	429	•	3211	5390	13736
Net Worth 29	481	0	-17	311	1030	•	7885	24482	39206

Selected Financial Ratios (Times to 1)

Current Ratio 30	2.3	•	1.3	3.0	2.9	•	2.2	3.7	2.2
Quick Ratio 31	1.1	•	0.5	1.3	1.3	•	1.1	1.7	1.2
Net Sales to Working Capital 32	4.8	•	18.6	5.0	4.4	•	4.8	3.2	6.3
Coverage Ratio 33	•	•	•	5.8	0.3	•	•	•	0.4
Total Asset Turnover 34	1.6	•	3.3	2.8	2.2	•	1.7	1.5	1.7
Inventory Turnover 35	4.4	•	6.2	4.6	3.8	•	3.8	4.3	4.4
Receivables Turnover 36	9.5	•	22.0	11.7	10.6	•	7.0	8.7	6.5
Total Liabilities to Net Worth 37	2.1	•	•	1.3	1.0	•	0.9	0.5	0.8
Current Assets to Working Capital 38	1.7	•	4.1	1.5	1.5	•	1.8	1.4	1.8
Current Liabilities to Working Capital 39	0.7	•	3.1	0.5	0.5	•	0.8	0.4	0.8
Working Capital to Net Sales 40	0.2	•	0.1	0.2	0.2	•	0.2	0.3	0.2
Inventory to Working Capital 41	0.7	•	2.0	0.7	0.8	•	0.8	0.5	0.7
Total Receipts to Cash Flow 42	18.4	31.6	8.9	10.9	15.6	•	23.9	18.3	27.8
Cost of Goods to Cash Flow 43	13.3	24.8	5.5	7.8	11.2	•	17.6	13.3	20.5
Cash Flow to Total Debt 44	0.1	•	0.3	0.5	0.3	•	0.2	0.2	0.1

Selected Financial Factors (in Percentages)

Debt Ratio 45	68.0	•	111.3	56.9	50.7	•	48.1	33.1	43.7
Return on Total Assets 46	•	•	•	7.9	0.4	•	•	•	0.7
Return on Equity Before Income Taxes 47	•	•	49.1	15.2	•	•	•	•	•
Return on Equity After Income Taxes 48	•	•	49.8	14.9	•	•	•	•	•
Profit Margin (Before Income Tax) 49	•	•	•	2.3	•	•	•	•	•
Profit Margin (After Income Tax) 50	•	•	•	2.3	•	•	•	•	•

Table II

Corporations with Net Income

OTHER BUILDING MATERIAL DEALERS

MONEY AMOUNTS AND SIZE OF ASSETS IN THOUSANDS OF DOLLARS

Item Description for Accounting Period 7/09 Through 6/10		Total	Zero Assets	Under 500	500 to 1,000	1,000 to 5,000	5,000 to 10,000	10,000 to 25,000	25,000 to 50,000	50,000 to 100,000	100,000 to 250,000	250,000 to 500,000	500,000 to 2,500,000	2,500,000 and over
Number of Enterprises	1	9341	400	5371	1720	1569	176	78	•	5	•	0	0	0
Revenues ($ in Thousands)														
Net Sales	2	23348346	11934	2801195	4278177	7815630	2927515	2277637	•	632188	•	0	0	0
Interest	3	26032	0	399	4582	12254	133	1592	•	26	•	0	0	0
Rents	4	11414	0	3367	247	2738	0	772	•	0	•	0	0	0
Royalties	5	1325	0	1213	0	0	0	111	•	0	•	0	0	0
Other Portfolio Income	6	54606	0	2769	1594	1525	68	2506	•	426	•	0	0	0
Other Receipts	7	166172	0	7484	42201	34446	18449	18101	•	5227	•	0	0	0
Total Receipts	8	23607895	11934	2816427	4326801	7866593	2946165	2300719	•	637867	•	0	0	0
Average Total Receipts	9	2527	30	524	2516	5014	16740	29496	•	127573	•	•	•	•
Operating Costs/Operating Income (%)														
Cost of Operations	10	70.1	25.8	54.9	71.4	69.8	80.9	72.7	•	70.8	•	•	•	•
Salaries and Wages	11	8.6	•	8.3	5.5	9.4	8.4	9.0	•	11.8	•	•	•	•
Taxes Paid	12	1.9	0.2	2.7	2.6	1.7	1.1	1.7	•	1.5	•	•	•	•
Interest Paid	13	0.5	2.7	0.5	0.3	0.4	0.8	0.5	•	0.3	•	•	•	•
Depreciation	14	1.0	•	1.6	0.3	1.0	0.4	1.2	•	1.7	•	•	•	•
Amortization and Depletion	15	0.0	•	•	0.0	0.0	•	0.0	•	0.0	•	•	•	•
Pensions and Other Deferred Comp.	16	0.3	•	0.1	0.4	0.4	0.0	0.5	•	0.6	•	•	•	•
Employee Benefits	17	0.9	•	1.1	0.9	0.8	0.7	1.1	•	1.0	•	•	•	•
Advertising	18	1.1	6.8	1.4	2.2	0.5	0.2	1.1	•	0.7	•	•	•	•
Other Expenses	19	9.0	37.6	18.1	8.1	8.3	5.4	8.9	•	4.8	•	•	•	•
Officers' Compensation	20	2.8	•	6.0	4.1	2.8	0.7	1.5	•	0.9	•	•	•	•
Operating Margin	21	3.8	27.0	5.4	4.1	4.8	1.4	1.7	•	5.8	•	•	•	•
Operating Margin Before Officers' Comp.	22	6.6	27.0	11.3	8.2	7.6	2.1	3.2	•	6.7	•	•	•	•

Selected Average Balance Sheet ($ in Thousands)

Net Receivables 23	184	0	27	166	354	1281	3177	14604
Inventories 24	427	0	50	267	989	2150	5609	21066
Net Property, Plant and Equipment 25	181	0	35	61	298	1200	2965	15224
Total Assets 26	1060	0	183	692	2109	6856	15150	75183
Notes and Loans Payable 27	263	0	97	186	441	2459	2963	9467
All Other Liabilities 28	205	0	43	134	397	947	3498	10167
Net Worth 29	593	0	43	373	1271	3450	8689	55549

Selected Financial Ratios (Times to 1)

Current Ratio 30	3.2	•	3.0	3.8	3.4	3.2	2.6	4.0
Quick Ratio 31	1.5	•	1.0	1.9	1.5	2.0	1.2	2.5
Net Sales to Working Capital 32	4.5	•	5.5	5.7	4.3	4.3	4.1	3.5
Coverage Ratio 33	11.6	11.0	13.9	16.4	13.8	3.5	6.3	22.2
Total Asset Turnover 34	2.4	•	2.8	3.6	2.4	2.4	1.9	1.7
Inventory Turnover 35	4.1	•	5.7	6.7	3.5	6.3	3.8	4.3
Receivables Turnover 36	9.6	•	19.9	12.3	11.4	8.3	•	6.2
Total Liabilities to Net Worth 37	0.8	•	3.3	0.9	0.7	1.0	0.7	0.4
Current Assets to Working Capital 38	1.5	•	1.5	1.4	1.4	1.4	1.6	1.3
Current Liabilities to Working Capital 39	0.5	•	0.5	0.4	0.4	0.4	0.6	0.3
Working Capital to Net Sales 40	0.2	•	0.2	0.2	0.2	0.2	0.2	0.3
Inventory to Working Capital 41	0.7	•	0.8	0.6	0.8	0.4	0.8	0.5
Total Receipts to Cash Flow 42	9.1	1.7	5.7	9.1	9.3	16.5	11.9	9.9
Cost of Goods to Cash Flow 43	6.4	0.4	3.1	6.5	6.5	13.3	8.7	7.0
Cash Flow to Total Debt 44	0.6	•	0.7	0.9	0.6	0.3	0.4	0.7

Selected Financial Factors (in Percentages)

Debt Ratio 45	44.1	•	76.7	46.2	39.7	49.7	42.6	26.1
Return on Total Assets 46	12.7	•	18.1	20.0	13.9	6.9	6.2	11.8
Return on Equity Before Income Taxes 47	20.8	•	72.1	34.9	21.4	9.8	9.1	15.2
Return on Equity After Income Taxes 48	19.7	•	71.6	34.4	20.7	9.8	7.5	14.1
Profit Margin (Before Income Tax) 49	4.9	27.0	5.9	5.2	5.4	2.0	2.7	6.7
Profit Margin (After Income Tax) 50	4.7	27.0	5.9	5.3	5.2	2.0	2.2	6.2

Table I

Corporations with and without Net Income

LAWN AND GARDEN EQUIPMENT AND SUPPLIES STORES

MONEY AMOUNTS AND SIZE OF ASSETS IN THOUSANDS OF DOLLARS

Item Description for Accounting Period 7/09 Through 6/10		Total	Zero Assets	Under 500	500 to 1,000	1,000 to 5,000	5,000 to 10,000	10,000 to 25,000	25,000 to 50,000	50,000 to 100,000	100,000 to 250,000	250,000 to 500,000	500,000 to 2,500,000	2,500,000 and over
Number of Enterprises	1	7007	259	4064	1368	1172	•	30	24	•	0	0	0	0
Revenues ($ in Thousands)														
Net Sales	2	15154540	42874	2096061	2599856	5782897	•	813003	1390134	•	0	0	0	0
Interest	3	15337	538	620	690	9966	•	0	1487	•	0	0	0	0
Rents	4	4095	32	121	0	3904	•	0	37	•	0	0	0	0
Royalties	5	0	0	0	0	0	•	0	0	•	0	0	0	0
Other Portfolio Income	6	20358	465	404	86	4491	•	1056	13456	•	0	0	0	0
Other Receipts	7	129162	594	1949	1963	38896	•	15951	53090	•	0	0	0	0
Total Receipts	8	15323492	44503	2099155	2602595	5840154	•	830010	1458204	•	0	0	0	0
Average Total Receipts	9	2187	172	517	1902	4983	•	27667	60758	•	•	•	•	•
Operating Costs/Operating Income (%)														
Cost of Operations	10	70.4	84.3	75.2	63.5	74.7	•	69.8	70.3	•	•	•	•	•
Salaries and Wages	11	10.2	5.0	8.4	12.1	9.2	•	8.5	11.8	•	•	•	•	•
Taxes Paid	12	2.1	1.4	2.2	3.3	1.5	•	1.5	1.8	•	•	•	•	•
Interest Paid	13	0.8	2.3	0.9	0.5	0.9	•	0.6	0.8	•	•	•	•	•
Depreciation	14	1.4	4.2	1.5	1.2	1.4	•	1.3	2.6	•	•	•	•	•
Amortization and Depletion	15	0.0	0.0	0.0	0.0	0.0	•	0.0	0.1	•	•	•	•	•
Pensions and Other Deferred Comp.	16	0.1	0.2	•	0.1	0.2	•	0.4	0.1	•	•	•	•	•
Employee Benefits	17	0.7	1.5	0.5	0.9	0.9	•	0.6	0.4	•	•	•	•	•
Advertising	18	1.1	0.5	1.0	0.9	1.3	•	1.1	0.7	•	•	•	•	•
Other Expenses	19	12.4	10.1	11.2	11.8	8.9	•	13.9	10.4	•	•	•	•	•
Officers' Compensation	20	2.5	2.9	5.4	3.6	2.3	•	0.7	1.2	•	•	•	•	•
Operating Margin	21	•	•	•	2.1	•	•	1.5	•	•	•	•	•	•
Operating Margin Before Officers' Comp.	22	0.8	•	•	5.7	1.0	•	2.2	0.8	•	•	•	•	•

Selected Average Balance Sheet ($ in Thousands)

Net Receivables	23	109	0	21	46	237	•	1396	8036
Inventories	24	478	0	112	321	1069	•	7149	10484
Net Property, Plant and Equipment	25	220	0	46	217	555	•	1823	7272
Total Assets	26	1004	0	249	727	2243	•	13831	32942
Notes and Loans Payable	27	485	0	124	192	1072	•	6419	12763
All Other Liabilities	28	260	0	109	86	491	•	2977	7067
Net Worth	29	259	0	16	449	680	•	4434	13112

Selected Financial Ratios (Times to 1)

Current Ratio	30	1.5	•	1.6	5.0	1.7	•	1.4	1.7
Quick Ratio	31	0.4	•	0.4	2.3	0.4	•	0.2	0.7
Net Sales to Working Capital	32	10.1	•	8.1	4.7	7.8	•	10.9	6.5
Coverage Ratio	33	0.2	•	•	5.1	0.6	•	6.7	6.3
Total Asset Turnover	34	2.2	•	2.1	2.6	2.2	•	2.0	1.8
Inventory Turnover	35	3.2	•	3.5	3.8	3.4	•	2.6	3.9
Receivables Turnover	36	17.5	•	21.1	31.8	23.5	•	•	8.3
Total Liabilities to Net Worth	37	2.9	•	14.5	0.6	2.3	•	2.1	1.5
Current Assets to Working Capital	38	3.2	•	2.5	1.2	2.5	•	3.6	2.5
Current Liabilities to Working Capital	39	2.2	•	1.5	0.2	1.5	•	2.6	1.5
Working Capital to Net Sales	40	0.1	•	0.1	0.2	0.1	•	0.1	0.2
Inventory to Working Capital	41	2.1	•	1.9	0.7	1.7	•	2.9	1.4
Total Receipts to Cash Flow	42	11.2	•	85.1	9.6	17.0	•	6.6	8.2
Cost of Goods to Cash Flow	43	7.9	•	63.9	6.1	12.7	•	4.6	5.8
Cash Flow to Total Debt	44	0.3	•	0.0	0.7	0.2	•	0.4	0.4

Selected Financial Factors (in Percentages)

Debt Ratio	45	74.2	•	93.5	38.1	69.7	•	67.9	60.2
Return on Total Assets	46	0.4	•	•	7.1	1.3	•	8.3	9.4
Return on Equity Before Income Taxes	47	•	•	•	9.2	•	•	22.2	19.9
Return on Equity After Income Taxes	48	•	•	•	8.9	•	•	22.2	19.0
Profit Margin (Before Income Tax)	49	•	•	•	2.2	•	•	3.6	4.5
Profit Margin (After Income Tax)	50	•	•	•	2.1	•	•	3.6	4.3

Table II
Corporations with Net Income

LAWN AND GARDEN EQUIPMENT AND SUPPLIES STORES

MONEY AMOUNTS AND SIZE OF ASSETS IN THOUSANDS OF DOLLARS

Item Description for Accounting Period 7/09 Through 6/10	Total	Zero Assets	Under 500	500 to 1,000	1,000 to 5,000	5,000 to 10,000	10,000 to 25,000	25,000 to 50,000	50,000 to 100,000	100,000 to 250,000	250,000 to 500,000	500,000 to 2,500,000	2,500,000 and over
Number of Enterprises **1**	2583	•	949	850	700	•	30	20	•	0	0	0	0
Revenues ($ in Thousands)													
Net Sales **2**	8763608	•	548609	1885066	3408072	•	813003	1221681	•	0	0	0	0
Interest **3**	10195	•	614	690	7154	•	0	361	•	0	0	0	0
Rents **4**	1449	•	121	0	1258	•	0	37	•	0	0	0	0
Royalties **5**	0	•	0	0	0	•	0	0	•	0	0	0	0
Other Portfolio Income **6**	13945	•	34	86	3565	•	1056	8410	•	0	0	0	0
Other Receipts **7**	99829	•	1638	1139	19832	•	15951	52940	•	0	0	0	0
Total Receipts **8**	8889026	•	551016	1886981	3439881	•	830010	1283429	•	0	0	0	0
Average Total Receipts **9**	3441	•	581	2220	4914	•	27667	64171	•	•	•	•	•
Operating Costs/Operating Income (%)													
Cost of Operations **10**	71.8	•	66.8	62.1	75.6	•	69.8	70.8	•	•	•	•	•
Salaries and Wages **11**	9.4	•	7.7	12.2	8.5	•	8.5	11.7	•	•	•	•	•
Taxes Paid **12**	1.8	•	2.1	3.0	1.3	•	1.5	1.9	•	•	•	•	•
Interest Paid **13**	0.7	•	0.6	0.3	0.9	•	0.6	0.8	•	•	•	•	•
Depreciation **14**	1.3	•	1.3	1.5	1.2	•	1.3	1.8	•	•	•	•	•
Amortization and Depletion **15**	0.0	•	0.1	0.0	0.0	•	0.0	0.1	•	•	•	•	•
Pensions and Other Deferred Comp. **16**	0.1	•	•	0.1	0.2	•	0.4	0.2	•	•	•	•	•
Employee Benefits **17**	0.7	•	0.2	0.6	0.8	•	0.6	0.4	•	•	•	•	•
Advertising **18**	0.9	•	0.9	0.7	1.2	•	1.1	0.8	•	•	•	•	•
Other Expenses **19**	9.3	•	10.3	12.0	7.3	•	13.9	10.0	•	•	•	•	•
Officers' Compensation **20**	2.3	•	6.2	3.0	2.4	•	0.7	1.2	•	•	•	•	•
Operating Margin **21**	1.7	•	3.7	4.5	0.7	•	1.5	0.3	•	•	•	•	•
Operating Margin Before Officers' Comp. **22**	4.0	•	10.0	7.4	3.1	•	2.2	1.5	•	•	•	•	•

Selected Average Balance Sheet ($ in Thousands)

Net Receivables 23	210	22	65	255	1396	8760
Inventories 24	857	169	250	1317	9718	10769
Net Property, Plant and Equipment 25	232	34	223	255	1823	5756
Total Assets 26	1508	248	750	2183	13831	32319
Notes and Loans Payable 27	568	135	121	984	6419	13216
All Other Liabilities 28	414	52	109	623	2977	7347
Net Worth 29	526	61	520	575	4434	11756

Selected Financial Ratios (Times to 1)

Current Ratio 30	1.8	3.1	3.9	1.7	1.4	1.7
Quick Ratio 31	0.5	0.8	2.1	0.4	0.2	0.7
Net Sales to Working Capital 32	6.5	4.3	5.7	6.1	10.9	6.5
Coverage Ratio 33	5.2	8.3	14.5	2.8	6.7	7.8
Total Asset Turnover 34	2.3	2.3	3.0	2.2	2.0	1.9
Inventory Turnover 35	2.8	2.3	5.5	2.8	1.9	4.0
Receivables Turnover 36	15.3	15.6	29.3	20.7	17.4	8.3
Total Liabilities to Net Worth 37	1.9	3.1	0.4	2.8	2.1	1.7
Current Assets to Working Capital 38	2.3	1.5	1.3	2.3	3.6	2.5
Current Liabilities to Working Capital 39	1.3	0.5	0.3	1.3	2.6	1.5
Working Capital to Net Sales 40	0.2	0.2	0.2	0.2	0.1	0.2
Inventory to Working Capital 41	1.5	1.1	0.6	1.7	2.9	1.4
Total Receipts to Cash Flow 42	10.2	9.0	7.4	15.7	6.6	7.8
Cost of Goods to Cash Flow 43	7.3	6.0	4.6	11.9	4.6	5.5
Cash Flow to Total Debt 44	0.3	0.3	1.3	0.2	0.4	0.4

Selected Financial Factors (in Percentages)

Debt Ratio 45	65.1	75.3	30.6	73.6	67.9	63.6
Return on Total Assets 46	8.7	11.1	14.5	5.6	8.3	11.6
Return on Equity Before Income Taxes 47	20.1	39.5	19.4	13.6	22.2	27.9
Return on Equity After Income Taxes 48	18.9	38.7	18.9	11.1	22.2	26.6
Profit Margin (Before Income Tax) 49	3.1	4.2	4.6	1.6	3.6	5.4
Profit Margin (After Income Tax) 50	2.9	4.1	4.4	1.3	3.6	5.1

Table I

Corporations with and without Net Income

FOOD AND BEVERAGE STORES

MONEY AMOUNTS AND SIZE OF ASSETS IN THOUSANDS OF DOLLARS

Item Description for Accounting Period 7/09 Through 6/10	Total	Zero Assets	Under 500	500 to 1,000	1,000 to 5,000	5,000 to 10,000	10,000 to 25,000	25,000 to 50,000	50,000 to 100,000	100,000 to 250,000	250,000 to 500,000	500,000 to 2,500,000	2,500,000 and over
Number of Enterprises 1	79207	8592	60276	4832	4372	693	245	64	47	40	10	25	10
Revenues ($ in Thousands)													
Net Sales 2	485494327	2955739	43183403	16488946	34275923	15980180	18468347	10637519	12539079	23105551	10830884	89422654	207606102
Interest 3	564908	3135	3375	3112	8671	4588	1675	2718	8930	1953	5433	67265	454053
Rents 4	576235	354	31	7120	18203	19025	18957	10836	4098	16589	13182	140421	327419
Royalties 5	1637555	0	0	44	401	0	2791	327	16688	3202	0	59127	1554974
Other Portfolio Income 6	321384	73541	13430	8202	31281	80400	12284	880	9671	11487	3597	26371	50234
Other Receipts 7	4928758	12450	658359	126631	374058	412057	182061	102278	155971	202538	105068	1382320	1214974
Total Receipts 8	493523167	3045219	43858598	16634055	34708537	16496250	18686115	10754558	12734437	23341320	10958164	91098158	211207756
Average Total Receipts 9	6231	354	728	3442	7939	23804	76270	168040	270945	583533	1095816	3643926	21120776
Operating Costs/Operating Income (%)													
Cost of Operations 10	73.5	71.4	71.1	76.6	74.6	74.4	75.9	77.9	73.1	72.5	74.5	73.9	73.0
Salaries and Wages 11	9.6	9.8	7.4	7.6	8.6	10.1	9.0	8.0	10.9	11.6	11.0	10.5	9.7
Taxes Paid 12	1.6	2.3	2.3	1.3	1.4	1.6	1.4	1.3	1.6	1.8	1.3	1.4	1.6
Interest Paid 13	0.6	0.2	0.4	0.4	0.4	0.5	0.3	0.4	0.5	0.4	0.4	0.6	0.9
Depreciation 14	2.0	0.9	0.9	0.6	1.2	1.2	1.2	1.5	1.7	2.0	1.7	2.3	2.5
Amortization and Depletion 15	0.1	0.5	0.2	0.1	0.1	0.1	0.1	0.1	0.1	0.1	0.1	0.2	0.0
Pensions and Other Deferred Comp. 16	0.4	0.0	0.0	0.0	0.1	0.1	0.1	0.2	0.4	0.3	0.4	0.5	0.6
Employee Benefits 17	1.2	0.3	0.2	0.3	0.4	0.9	1.0	0.9	1.7	1.3	1.4	1.6	1.4
Advertising 18	0.7	0.3	0.6	0.7	1.0	1.1	0.7	0.9	0.8	0.8	0.8	0.8	0.6
Other Expenses 19	9.5	14.9	13.9	10.0	10.9	9.8	9.4	8.1	8.9	9.0	8.0	8.9	8.7
Officers' Compensation 20	0.6	1.2	3.2	1.5	0.9	1.3	0.5	0.5	0.5	0.3	0.3	0.2	0.0
Operating Margin 21	0.2	•	•	1.1	0.4	•	0.4	0.2	•	•	0.0	•	0.8
Operating Margin Before Officers' Comp. 22	0.7	•	2.9	2.5	1.3	0.1	0.9	0.7	0.2	0.0	0.4	0.8	0.8

Selected Average Balance Sheet ($ in Thousands)

Net Receivables 23	157	0	2	63	228	595	1639	2509	4990	8295	22147	54813	787826
Inventories 24	319	0	32	155	411	1136	3248	8230	12194	26797	57997	189778	1171540
Net Property, Plant and Equipment 25	965	0	40	185	635	2758	5172	16046	28252	71659	158978	621346	4487235
Total Assets 26	2164	0	127	705	1883	6381	16216	36831	72029	152705	379740	1258719	9662100
Notes and Loans Payable 27	633	0	84	296	775	2574	4638	12150	22348	38537	103444	329861	2470368
All Other Liabilities 28	917	0	18	143	470	1440	6758	11032	22880	52270	127148	435487	5011870
Net Worth 29	614	0	25	266	639	2367	4820	13649	26801	61898	149148	493371	2179862

Selected Financial Ratios (Times to 1)

Current Ratio 30	1.0	•	2.6	2.5	1.7	1.7	1.5	1.4	1.2	1.2	1.0	1.4	0.7
Quick Ratio 31	0.5	•	0.8	1.2	0.9	0.9	0.7	0.5	0.6	0.5	0.4	0.6	0.3
Net Sales to Working Capital 32	875.5	•	19.9	14.9	20.3	20.4	29.7	35.4	53.8	72.3	1469.2	31.3	•
Coverage Ratio 33	3.9	8.9	4.3	6.3	5.4	4.7	5.8	4.7	3.6	2.7	3.7	2.6	3.9
Total Asset Turnover 34	2.8	•	5.6	4.8	4.2	3.6	4.6	4.5	3.7	3.8	2.9	2.8	2.1
Inventory Turnover 35	14.1	•	15.9	16.9	14.2	15.1	17.6	15.7	16.0	15.6	13.9	13.9	12.9
Receivables Turnover 36	40.0	•	238.9	69.5	34.7	47.8	51.8	66.9	49.9	70.8	47.9	70.6	26.6
Total Liabilities to Net Worth 37	2.5	•	4.2	1.7	1.9	1.7	2.4	1.7	1.7	1.5	1.5	1.6	3.4
Current Assets to Working Capital 38	103.5	•	1.6	1.7	2.4	2.4	3.2	3.6	5.4	6.5	157.3	3.8	•
Current Liabilities to Working Capital 39	102.5	•	0.6	0.7	1.4	1.4	2.2	2.6	4.4	5.5	156.3	2.8	•
Working Capital to Net Sales 40	0.0	•	0.1	0.1	0.0	0.0	0.0	0.0	0.0	0.0	0.0	0.0	•
Inventory to Working Capital 41	45.7	•	1.0	0.7	1.0	1.1	1.3	1.9	2.3	3.2	77.9	1.7	•
Total Receipts to Cash Flow 42	12.5	14.2	10.9	12.0	11.4	10.8	13.2	15.8	14.4	15.5	16.1	14.2	11.9
Cost of Goods to Cash Flow 43	9.2	10.1	7.8	9.2	8.5	8.0	10.0	12.3	10.5	11.3	12.0	10.5	8.7
Cash Flow to Total Debt 44	0.3	•	0.6	0.6	0.6	0.5	0.5	0.5	0.4	0.4	0.3	0.3	0.2

Selected Financial Factors (in Percentages)

Debt Ratio 45	71.6	•	80.6	62.3	66.1	62.9	70.3	62.9	62.8	59.5	60.7	60.8	77.4
Return on Total Assets 46	6.9	•	9.3	11.1	8.3	9.2	8.9	7.6	6.8	4.5	4.7	4.2	7.3
Return on Equity Before Income Taxes 47	18.0	•	36.8	24.8	19.9	19.6	24.7	16.1	13.2	7.1	8.7	6.6	24.1
Return on Equity After Income Taxes 48	13.2	•	35.7	24.6	19.0	17.0	22.9	13.5	12.0	5.1	5.8	4.4	15.8
Profit Margin (Before Income Tax) 49	1.8	1.2	1.3	1.9	1.6	2.0	1.6	1.3	1.3	0.8	1.2	0.9	2.5
Profit Margin (After Income Tax) 50	1.3	1.1	1.2	1.9	1.5	1.7	1.5	1.1	1.2	0.5	0.8	0.6	1.7

Table II

Corporations with Net Income

FOOD AND BEVERAGE STORES

MONEY AMOUNTS AND SIZE OF ASSETS IN THOUSANDS OF DOLLARS

Item Description for Accounting Period 7/09 Through 6/10	Total	Zero Assets	Under 500	500 to 1,000	1,000 to 5,000	5,000 to 10,000	10,000 to 25,000	25,000 to 50,000	50,000 to 100,000	100,000 to 250,000	250,000 to 500,000	500,000 to 2,500,000	2,500,000 and over
Number of Enterprises 1	46835	3802	35546	3528	3020	591	•	•	37	27	•	18	•
Revenues ($ in Thousands)													
Net Sales 2	416485945	1911787	30752236	14819163	27772627	14641676	•	•	10529711	16223929	•	69382668	•
Interest 3	548458	114	785	1618	7156	4351	•	•	3536	1786	•	65846	•
Rents 4	477593	49	22	6748	13081	8889	•	•	2815	12126	•	127004	•
Royalties 5	1623665	0	0	0	242	0	•	•	4928	1274	•	59127	•
Other Portfolio Income 6	286889	73536	154	6708	27506	79911	•	•	8756	10591	•	18115	•
Other Receipts 7	4310754	9356	467898	117039	325015	407218	•	•	122877	137528	•	1235159	•
Total Receipts 8	423733304	1994842	31221095	14951276	28145627	15142045	•	•	10672623	16387234	•	70887919	•
Average Total Receipts 9	9047	525	878	4238	9320	25621	•	•	288449	606935	•	3938218	•
Operating Costs/Operating Income (%)													
Cost of Operations 10	73.5	69.4	71.6	77.8	74.6	74.2	•	•	73.9	72.3	•	73.0	•
Salaries and Wages 11	9.5	11.3	6.4	7.2	8.5	10.1	•	•	10.6	11.5	•	10.9	•
Taxes Paid 12	1.6	2.9	2.3	1.2	1.5	1.6	•	•	1.6	1.8	•	1.5	•
Interest Paid 13	0.6	0.2	0.4	0.3	0.3	0.5	•	•	0.3	0.3	•	0.5	•
Depreciation 14	2.0	0.5	0.8	0.5	0.8	1.0	•	•	1.7	1.9	•	2.3	•
Amortization and Depletion 15	0.1	0.3	0.2	0.1	0.1	0.1	•	•	0.1	0.1	•	0.2	•
Pensions and Other Deferred Comp. 16	0.4	0.0	0.0	0.0	0.1	0.1	•	•	0.3	0.3	•	0.6	•
Employee Benefits 17	1.3	0.3	0.2	0.2	0.4	1.0	•	•	1.6	1.2	•	1.9	•
Advertising 18	0.7	0.4	0.5	0.5	1.0	1.1	•	•	0.6	0.8	•	0.7	•
Other Expenses 19	9.0	11.3	12.6	9.0	10.0	9.4	•	•	8.3	8.4	•	8.4	•
Officers' Compensation 20	0.5	1.1	3.2	1.5	1.0	1.3	•	•	0.5	0.3	•	0.2	•
Operating Margin 21	0.9	2.4	1.8	1.8	1.8	•	•	•	0.5	1.1	•	•	•
Operating Margin Before Officers' Comp. 22	1.4	3.5	5.0	3.2	2.7	0.9	•	•	1.0	1.4	•	0.2	•

Selected Average Balance Sheet ($ in Thousands)

	•	•	•	•	•	•	•	•	•	•	•
Net Receivables 23	240	0	2	78	213	652	•	5069	8744	•	62213
Inventories 24	436	0	37	161	439	1123	•	11444	27547	•	178682
Net Property, Plant and Equipment 25	1424	0	37	195	580	2627	•	29178	72722	•	660434
Total Assets 26	3204	0	143	712	1873	6405	•	72954	153431	•	1346237
Notes and Loans Payable 27	829	0	70	294	521	2118	•	18561	33921	•	326248
All Other Liabilities 28	1383	0	20	143	448	1319	•	22831	48259	•	442201
Net Worth 29	992	0	53	274	905	2969	•	31562	71251	•	577788

Selected Financial Ratios (Times to 1)

	•	•	•	•	•	•	•	•	•	•	•
Current Ratio 30	1.0	•	3.3	2.4	2.1	2.0	•	1.2	1.2	•	1.5
Quick Ratio 31	0.5	•	1.2	1.3	1.1	1.0	•	0.6	0.5	•	0.8
Net Sales to Working Capital 32	•	•	16.8	17.8	16.7	17.4	•	54.1	53.5	•	24.7
Coverage Ratio 33	5.4	44.5	9.7	8.6	11.0	7.1	•	6.5	8.2	•	4.5
Total Asset Turnover 34	2.8	•	6.0	5.9	4.9	3.9	•	3.9	3.9	•	2.9
Inventory Turnover 35	15.0	•	16.6	20.3	15.6	16.4	•	18.4	15.8	•	15.7
Receivables Turnover 36	39.4	•	203.8	93.6	44.7	48.6	•	•	74.6	•	70.9
Total Liabilities to Net Worth 37	2.2	•	1.7	1.6	1.1	1.2	•	1.3	1.2	•	1.3
Current Assets to Working Capital 38	•	•	1.4	1.7	1.9	2.0	•	5.2	5.1	•	3.2
Current Liabilities to Working Capital 39	•	•	0.4	0.7	0.9	1.0	•	4.2	4.1	•	2.2
Working Capital to Net Sales 40	•	•	0.1	0.1	0.1	0.1	•	0.0	0.0	•	0.0
Inventory to Working Capital 41	•	•	0.8	0.7	0.8	0.9	•	2.2	2.5	•	1.3
Total Receipts to Cash Flow 42	11.7	9.6	9.7	11.6	10.5	9.9	•	14.2	13.9	•	12.8
Cost of Goods to Cash Flow 43	8.6	6.7	6.9	9.0	7.9	7.3	•	10.5	10.0	•	9.4
Cash Flow to Total Debt 44	0.3	•	1.0	0.8	0.9	0.7	•	0.5	0.5	•	0.4

Selected Financial Factors (in Percentages)

	•	•	•	•	•	•	•	•	•	•	•
Debt Ratio 45	69.0	•	63.2	61.4	51.7	53.7	•	56.7	53.6	•	57.1
Return on Total Assets 46	8.9	•	22.6	17.6	16.7	13.4	•	8.6	9.3	•	7.1
Return on Equity Before Income Taxes 47	23.5	•	55.1	40.4	31.5	24.9	•	16.9	17.5	•	12.9
Return on Equity After Income Taxes 48	18.5	•	54.3	40.2	30.6	22.5	•	15.5	15.0	•	10.3
Profit Margin (Before Income Tax) 49	2.6	6.8	3.4	2.6	3.1	3.0	•	1.9	2.1	•	1.9
Profit Margin (After Income Tax) 50	2.1	6.5	3.3	2.6	3.0	2.7	•	1.7	1.8	•	1.5

Table I

Corporations with and without Net Income

BEER, WINE, AND LIQUOR STORES

MONEY AMOUNTS AND SIZE OF ASSETS IN THOUSANDS OF DOLLARS

Item Description for Accounting Period 7/09 Through 6/10	Total	Zero Assets	Under 500	500 to 1,000	1,000 to 5,000	5,000 to 10,000	10,000 to 25,000	25,000 to 50,000	50,000 to 100,000	100,000 to 250,000	250,000 to 500,000	500,000 to 2,500,000	2,500,000 and over
Number of Enterprises 1	20607	1608	15212	2784	883	95	4	13	4	3	0	0	0
Revenues ($ in Thousands)													
Net Sales 2	27305488	73316	13292592	4742892	4366552	1351104	99832	1231785	644597	1502818	0	0	0
Interest 3	6685	0	1919	306	2543	1521	2	0	0	394	0	0	0
Rents 4	1382	0	323	0	160	1	52	0	0	845	0	0	0
Royalties 5	592	0	0	0	0	592	0	0	0	0	0	0	0
Other Portfolio Income 6	11698	750	10240	0	2	0	0	18	3	684	0	0	0
Other Receipts 7	439598	-1	314817	65050	12391	34496	0	3725	948	8173	0	0	0
Total Receipts 8	27765443	74065	13619891	4808248	4381648	1387714	99886	1235528	645548	1512914	0	0	0
Average Total Receipts 9	1347	46	895	1727	4962	14608	24972	95041	161387	504305	•	•	•
Operating Costs/Operating Income (%)													
Cost of Operations 10	78.7	90.6	78.4	79.1	79.1	82.8	71.5	78.4	76.2	77.6	•	•	•
Salaries and Wages 11	5.3	•	4.9	5.1	5.1	5.0	8.2	6.9	9.5	7.4	•	•	•
Taxes Paid 12	2.0	9.2	2.9	1.4	1.0	0.6	1.3	1.6	0.8	1.2	•	•	•
Interest Paid 13	0.7	2.3	0.6	0.7	0.7	0.1	0.7	0.9	0.7	1.3	•	•	•
Depreciation 14	0.7	2.1	0.7	0.9	0.4	0.7	1.4	0.7	1.0	1.4	•	•	•
Amortization and Depletion 15	0.3	1.0	0.4	0.6	0.2	0.1	0.1	0.2	0.4	0.2	•	•	•
Pensions and Other Deferred Comp. 16	0.1	•	0.0	0.1	0.1	0.1	0.6	0.0	0.5	0.1	•	•	•
Employee Benefits 17	0.2	0.2	0.2	0.1	0.3	0.0	0.7	0.2	0.3	0.9	•	•	•
Advertising 18	0.5	•	0.3	0.7	0.5	0.8	1.0	0.5	1.0	1.1	•	•	•
Other Expenses 19	9.4	25.3	9.8	10.3	8.2	7.9	9.9	8.5	7.4	8.3	•	•	•
Officers' Compensation 20	2.7	•	3.7	2.2	2.2	0.9	4.5	1.1	0.8	0.3	•	•	•
Operating Margin 21	•	•	•	•	2.0	1.0	0.1	1.0	1.4	0.4	•	•	•
Operating Margin Before Officers' Comp. 22	2.0	1.9	•	1.0	4.3	1.8	4.6	2.1	2.2	0.8	•	•	•

Selected Average Balance Sheet ($ in Thousands)

Net Receivables 23	13	1	0	5	27	1416	409	3670	728	6593
Inventories 24	182	96	0	266	905	1952	8134	18125	26335	64603
Net Property, Plant and Equipment 25	65	35	0	80	202	580	1728	6636	7687	76056
Total Assets 26	417	213	0	694	1557	6949	9525	35490	70096	206964
Notes and Loans Payable 27	219	127	0	407	785	1727	4026	14428	33485	81857
All Other Liabilities 28	70	29	0	89	257	1330	2526	10207	16033	63978
Net Worth 29	129	57	0	198	515	3891	2973	10856	20578	61129

Selected Financial Ratios (Times to 1)

Current Ratio 30	2.8	3.9	•	4.1	2.4	2.4	1.5	1.6	1.9	1.4
Quick Ratio 31	0.7	1.0	•	1.1	0.5	1.3	0.1	0.3	0.2	0.2
Net Sales to Working Capital 32	7.6	8.8	•	5.6	7.7	3.9	10.1	9.0	7.3	23.1
Coverage Ratio 33	2.4	2.1	•	1.2	4.2	57.1	1.3	2.4	3.1	1.9
Total Asset Turnover 34	3.2	4.1	•	2.5	3.2	2.0	2.6	2.7	2.3	2.4
Inventory Turnover 35	5.7	7.1	•	5.1	4.3	6.0	2.2	4.1	4.7	6.0
Receivables Turnover 36	96.3	735.5	•	244.5	131.7	10.2	3.8	40.1	189.8	76.9
Total Liabilities to Net Worth 37	2.2	2.8	•	2.5	2.0	0.8	2.2	2.3	2.4	2.4
Current Assets to Working Capital 38	1.5	1.3	•	1.3	1.7	1.7	3.0	2.6	2.1	3.7
Current Liabilities to Working Capital 39	0.5	0.3	•	0.3	0.7	0.7	2.0	1.6	1.1	2.7
Working Capital to Net Sales 40	0.1	0.1	•	0.2	0.1	0.3	0.1	0.1	0.1	0.0
Inventory to Working Capital 41	1.1	1.0	•	0.9	1.2	0.7	2.7	1.8	1.4	3.1
Total Receipts to Cash Flow 42	15.5	15.5	•	16.3	13.2	11.1	15.7	18.2	22.0	20.6
Cost of Goods to Cash Flow 43	12.2	12.2	•	12.9	10.4	9.2	11.3	14.3	16.8	16.0
Cash Flow to Total Debt 44	0.3	0.4	•	0.2	0.4	0.4	0.2	0.2	0.1	0.2

Selected Financial Factors (in Percentages)

Debt Ratio 45	69.1	73.4	•	71.4	67.0	44.0	68.8	69.4	70.6	70.5
Return on Total Assets 46	5.4	5.4	•	2.3	10.0	7.6	2.2	5.9	5.3	5.7
Return on Equity Before Income Taxes 47	10.3	10.6	•	1.6	23.0	13.4	1.6	11.3	12.1	9.1
Return on Equity After Income Taxes 48	9.6	10.1	•	1.3	20.7	13.1	1.3	11.3	12.1	7.0
Profit Margin (Before Income Tax) 49	1.0	0.7	•	0.2	2.4	3.7	0.2	1.3	1.5	1.1
Profit Margin (After Income Tax) 50	0.9	0.7	•	0.2	2.2	3.6	0.2	1.3	1.5	0.9

Table II

Corporations with Net Income

BEER, WINE, AND LIQUOR STORES

MONEY AMOUNTS AND SIZE OF ASSETS IN THOUSANDS OF DOLLARS

Item Description for Accounting Period 7/09 Through 6/10	Total	Zero Assets	Under 500	500 to 1,000	1,000 to 5,000	5,000 to 10,000	10,000 to 25,000	25,000 to 50,000	50,000 to 100,000	100,000 to 250,000	250,000 to 500,000	500,000 to 2,500,000	2,500,000 and over
Number of Enterprises **1**	11982	392	9446	1347	683	95	•	•	0	3	0	0	0
Revenues ($ in Thousands)													
Net Sales **2**	20752093	1468	9362483	2936012	3906049	1351104	•	•	0	1502818	0	0	0
Interest **3**	5909	0	1147	303	2543	1521	•	•	0	394	0	0	0
Rents **4**	1059	0	0	0	160	1	•	•	0	845	0	0	0
Royalties **5**	592	0	0	0	0	592	•	•	0	0	0	0	0
Other Portfolio Income **6**	9584	0	8879	0	2	0	•	•	0	684	0	0	0
Other Receipts **7**	351992	0	242548	53045	9380	34496	•	•	0	8173	0	0	0
Total Receipts **8**	21121229	1468	9615057	2989360	3918134	1387714	•	•	0	1512914	0	0	0
Average Total Receipts **9**	1763	4	1018	2219	5737	14608	•	•	•	504305	•	•	•
Operating Costs/Operating Income (%)													
Cost of Operations **10**	78.3	•	77.4	78.8	79.1	82.8	•	•	•	77.6	•	•	•
Salaries and Wages **11**	5.2	•	4.5	4.9	5.4	5.0	•	•	•	7.4	•	•	•
Taxes Paid **12**	1.8	8.3	2.6	1.5	1.0	0.6	•	•	•	1.2	•	•	•
Interest Paid **13**	0.4	•	0.3	0.4	0.5	0.1	•	•	•	1.3	•	•	•
Depreciation **14**	0.6	•	0.7	0.4	0.2	0.7	•	•	•	1.4	•	•	•
Amortization and Depletion **15**	0.3	•	0.5	0.1	0.2	0.1	•	•	•	0.2	•	•	•
Pensions and Other Deferred Comp. **16**	0.1	•	0.1	0.1	0.2	0.1	•	•	•	0.1	•	•	•
Employee Benefits **17**	0.2	•	0.2	0.1	0.3	0.0	•	•	•	0.9	•	•	•
Advertising **18**	0.6	•	0.4	0.9	0.6	0.8	•	•	•	1.1	•	•	•
Other Expenses **19**	8.9	80.3	9.6	9.7	7.6	7.9	•	•	•	8.3	•	•	•
Officers' Compensation **20**	2.6	•	3.6	2.5	2.1	0.9	•	•	•	0.3	•	•	•
Operating Margin **21**	0.9	11.4	0.1	0.7	2.9	1.0	•	•	•	0.4	•	•	•
Operating Margin Before Officers' Comp. **22**	3.5	11.4	3.8	3.1	5.0	1.8	•	•	•	0.8	•	•	•

Selected Average Balance Sheet ($ in Thousands)

Net Receivables 23	17	0	108	328	34	1416	6593
Inventories 24	235	0	328	1003	1952		67081
Net Property, Plant and Equipment 25	69	0	30	50	168	580	76056
Total Assets 26	519	0	236	730	1671	6949	206964
Notes and Loans Payable 27	209	0	96	305	764	1727	81857
All Other Liabilities 28	96	0	31	124	286	1330	63978
Net Worth 29	214	0	109	301	621	3891	61129

Selected Financial Ratios (Times to 1)

Current Ratio 30	2.7		4.8	3.5	2.3	2.4	1.4
Quick Ratio 31	0.8		1.4	1.2	0.5	1.3	0.2
Net Sales to Working Capital 32	7.5		8.0	6.0	7.7	3.9	23.1
Coverage Ratio 33	7.1		10.0	7.6	7.7	57.1	1.9
Total Asset Turnover 34	3.3		4.2	3.0	3.4	2.0	2.4
Inventory Turnover 35	5.8		7.1	5.2	4.5	6.0	5.8
Receivables Turnover 36	98.1		1050.6	353.9	176.5	10.2	152.0
Total Liabilities to Net Worth 37	1.4		1.2	1.4	1.7	0.8	2.4
Current Assets to Working Capital 38	1.6		1.3	1.4	1.8	1.7	3.7
Current Liabilities to Working Capital 39	0.6		0.3	0.4	0.8	0.7	2.7
Working Capital to Net Sales 40	0.1		0.1	0.2	0.1	0.3	0.0
Inventory to Working Capital 41	1.0		0.9	0.9	1.3	0.7	3.1
Total Receipts to Cash Flow 42	12.9	1.1	12.2	12.4	12.3	11.1	20.6
Cost of Goods to Cash Flow 43	10.1		9.5	9.7	9.7	9.2	16.0
Cash Flow to Total Debt 44	0.4		0.6	0.4	0.4	0.4	0.2

Selected Financial Factors (in Percentages)

Debt Ratio 45	58.8		53.9	58.8	62.8	44.0	70.5
Return on Total Assets 46	10.6		13.2	8.6	12.7	7.6	5.7
Return on Equity Before Income Taxes 47	22.1		25.8	18.1	29.8	13.4	9.1
Return on Equity After Income Taxes 48	21.3		25.5	17.7	27.4	13.1	7.0
Profit Margin (Before Income Tax) 49	2.7	11.4	2.8	2.5	3.2	3.7	1.1
Profit Margin (After Income Tax) 50	2.6	11.4	2.8	2.4	3.0	3.6	0.9

Table I

Corporations with and without Net Income

HEALTH AND PERSONAL CARE STORES

MONEY AMOUNTS AND SIZE OF ASSETS IN THOUSANDS OF DOLLARS

Item Description for Accounting Period 7/09 Through 6/10	Total	Zero Assets	Under 500	500 to 1,000	1,000 to 5,000	5,000 to 10,000	10,000 to 25,000	25,000 to 50,000	50,000 to 100,000	100,000 to 250,000	250,000 to 500,000	500,000 to 2,500,000	2,500,000 and over
Number of Enterprises 1	42782	3259	31000	4854	3320	175	105	22	16	14	8	4	6
Revenues ($ in Thousands)													
Net Sales 2	320840628	270369	25166285	16578319	21440052	4192944	3811725	1444425	2924262	4291001	5279943	4914925	230526378
Interest 3	189099	0	1560	3403	5347	2916	1810	112	277	2475	14155	3039	154003
Rents 4	149890	0	9	1809	1379	865	17983	1400	0	8063	6238	113	112032
Royalties 5	76774	0	0	5	0	0	1249	0	2575	2045	0	39773	31128
Other Portfolio Income 6	220881	29304	27105	20985	2631	961	15759	817	403	31817	3668	0	87428
Other Receipts 7	5512417	-15266	12400	36136	75023	41725	72896	61956	36641	60784	43114	21659	5065352
Total Receipts 8	326989689	284407	25207359	16640657	21524432	4239411	3921422	1508710	2964158	4396185	5347118	4979509	235976321
Average Total Receipts 9	7643	87	813	3428	6483	24225	37347	68578	185260	314013	668390	1244877	39329387
Operating Costs/Operating Income (%)													
Cost of Operations 10	72.8	43.7	70.8	72.0	71.2	74.3	68.0	54.6	72.4	68.7	64.8	56.4	74.0
Salaries and Wages 11	9.4	3.9	6.9	8.4	10.6	10.6	15.1	19.6	11.6	14.1	11.4	15.1	9.2
Taxes Paid 12	1.2	2.8	1.5	1.6	1.7	1.0	1.3	3.2	1.2	1.7	2.0	2.1	1.0
Interest Paid 13	0.7	0.3	0.2	0.2	0.6	0.4	0.7	1.7	0.7	1.9	1.5	1.7	0.8
Depreciation 14	1.2	0.4	0.3	0.4	0.7	1.3	1.7	1.6	1.4	1.3	1.8	2.5	1.3
Amortization and Depletion 15	0.3	•	0.1	0.1	0.2	0.2	0.4	0.2	0.4	0.5	0.5	1.8	0.3
Pensions and Other Deferred Comp. 16	0.2	•	0.2	0.5	0.3	0.2	0.3	0.3	0.1	0.1	0.1	0.2	0.2
Employee Benefits 17	0.6	0.1	0.3	0.5	0.4	1.1	1.3	0.6	0.8	2.0	0.9	1.1	0.6
Advertising 18	0.8	1.4	1.0	0.7	0.7	0.8	0.8	1.2	1.0	1.6	0.9	1.7	0.7
Other Expenses 19	10.1	42.2	10.7	7.9	8.2	10.9	9.2	17.5	11.3	10.1	12.0	14.6	10.1
Officers' Compensation 20	1.0	10.9	5.2	5.7	2.6	1.7	1.6	0.8	0.6	0.5	0.5	0.4	0.0
Operating Margin 21	1.7	•	2.8	2.1	2.7	•	•	•	•	•	3.5	2.3	1.7
Operating Margin Before Officers' Comp. 22	2.7	5.2	8.0	7.8	5.4	•	1.1	•	•	•	4.1	2.8	1.7

Selected Average Balance Sheet ($ in Thousands)

Net Receivables 23	614	0	12	91	373	2175	3725	4731	18150	16844	41250	88189	3688280
Inventories 24	666	0	60	252	467	1309	2416	6918	9109	29806	59306	166787	3590756
Net Property, Plant and Equipment 25	534	0	16	59	265	1019	1773	5825	12360	22705	63884	135641	3183230
Total Assets 26	3696	0	136	704	1791	6587	13800	32167	74856	143711	344960	1023244	21867044
Notes and Loans Payable 27	947	0	56	188	691	1339	3715	10994	21803	78214	110504	380892	5143618
All Other Liabilities 28	1147	0	46	172	462	4295	13250	15264	32177	51063	82267	231320	6662214
Net Worth 29	1603	0	34	343	638	953	-3164	5909	20876	14433	152189	411031	10061211

Selected Financial Ratios (Times to 1)

Current Ratio 30	1.4	•	2.2	2.8	2.0	1.0	0.7	1.2	1.1	1.3	2.0	3.0	1.4
Quick Ratio 31	0.7	•	0.9	1.3	1.0	0.7	0.5	0.6	0.7	0.6	0.9	1.2	0.7
Net Sales to Working Capital 32	15.2	•	14.4	10.3	10.7	118.6	•	31.1	50.9	20.0	8.9	5.3	16.2
Coverage Ratio 33	5.8	•	13.2	11.3	6.6	•	4.5	2.9	0.9	0.9	4.2	3.1	6.0
Total Asset Turnover 34	2.0	•	6.0	4.9	3.6	3.6	2.6	2.0	2.4	2.1	1.9	1.2	1.8
Inventory Turnover 35	8.2	•	9.6	9.8	9.8	13.6	10.2	5.2	14.5	7.1	7.2	4.2	7.9
Receivables Turnover 36	13.6	•	53.7	39.8	16.5	12.5	10.6	14.9	11.6	14.6	16.4	16.7	11.8
Total Liabilities to Net Worth 37	1.3	•	3.0	1.1	1.8	5.9	•	4.4	2.6	9.0	1.3	1.5	1.2
Current Assets to Working Capital 38	3.2	•	1.8	1.6	2.0	23.1	•	7.3	10.5	4.1	2.0	1.5	3.7
Current Liabilities to Working Capital 39	2.2	•	0.8	0.6	1.0	22.1	•	6.3	9.5	3.1	1.0	0.5	2.7
Working Capital to Net Sales 40	0.1	•	0.1	0.1	0.1	0.0	•	0.0	0.0	0.0	0.1	0.2	0.1
Inventory to Working Capital 41	1.4	•	1.1	0.8	0.8	7.2	•	3.4	3.1	1.6	1.0	0.7	1.5
Total Receipts to Cash Flow 42	9.4	3.5	10.9	13.5	10.5	13.0	11.2	6.8	12.8	16.3	8.6	8.4	9.0
Cost of Goods to Cash Flow 43	6.9	1.5	7.7	9.7	7.5	9.6	7.6	3.7	9.3	11.2	5.6	4.7	6.6
Cash Flow to Total Debt 44	0.4	•	0.7	0.7	0.5	0.3	0.2	0.4	0.3	0.1	0.4	0.2	0.4

Selected Financial Factors (in Percentages)

Debt Ratio 45	56.6	•	75.0	51.3	64.4	85.5	122.9	81.6	72.1	90.0	55.9	59.8	54.0
Return on Total Assets 46	8.9	•	19.5	13.1	13.3	•	7.9	9.9	1.6	3.9	11.9	6.5	8.5
Return on Equity Before Income Taxes 47	17.0	•	72.0	24.4	31.8	•	•	35.3	•	•	20.6	10.9	15.4
Return on Equity After Income Taxes 48	11.8	•	70.9	23.8	30.3	•	•	31.3	•	•	14.8	7.9	9.9
Profit Margin (Before Income Tax) 49	3.6	•	3.0	2.5	3.1	•	2.3	3.2	•	•	4.7	3.7	4.0
Profit Margin (After Income Tax) 50	2.5	•	3.0	2.4	3.0	•	2.3	2.8	•	•	3.4	2.6	2.6

Table II

Corporations with Net Income

HEALTH AND PERSONAL CARE STORES

MONEY AMOUNTS AND SIZE OF ASSETS IN THOUSANDS OF DOLLARS

Item Description for Accounting Period 7/09 Through 6/10	Total	Zero Assets	Under 500	500 to 1,000	1,000 to 5,000	5,000 to 10,000	10,000 to 25,000	25,000 to 50,000	50,000 to 100,000	100,000 to 250,000	250,000 to 500,000	500,000 to 2,500,000	2,500,000 and over
Number of Enterprises **1**	27088	690	19988	3497	2724	85	61	•	8	9	•	4	•
Revenues ($ in Thousands)													
Net Sales **2**	277455635	58740	21581192	13358404	18227123	1425193	2437142	•	1736681	3372336	•	4914925	•
Interest **3**	166465	0	448	2242	3462	617	423	•	204	1662	•	3039	•
Rents **4**	92097	0	0	1336	1221	738	1620	•	0	8063	•	113	•
Royalties **5**	75525	0	0	5	0	0	0	•	2575	2045	•	39773	•
Other Portfolio Income **6**	180611	14546	26879	11277	2608	961	516	•	362	31618	•	0	•
Other Receipts **7**	4756676	15	8562	19337	67671	28605	61704	•	12774	28112	•	21659	•
Total Receipts **8**	282727009	73301	21617081	13392601	18302085	1456114	2501405	•	1752596	3443836	•	4979509	•
Average Total Receipts **9**	10437	106	1082	3830	6719	17131	41007	•	219074	382648	•	1244877	•
Operating Costs/Operating Income (%)													
Cost of Operations **10**	72.6	10.0	72.1	71.2	70.4	57.8	66.6	•	73.3	66.9	•	56.4	•
Salaries and Wages **11**	9.0	0.8	6.2	8.2	10.5	15.2	15.1	•	9.8	15.0	•	15.1	•
Taxes Paid **12**	1.1	3.0	1.4	1.4	1.4	1.5	1.3	•	1.0	1.7	•	2.1	•
Interest Paid **13**	0.6	0.0	0.2	0.2	0.6	0.4	0.3	•	0.5	0.2	•	1.7	•
Depreciation **14**	1.2	•	0.3	0.3	0.7	1.4	1.7	•	1.2	1.4	•	2.5	•
Amortization and Depletion **15**	0.3	•	0.1	0.1	0.2	0.3	0.3	•	0.5	0.1	•	1.8	•
Pensions and Other Deferred Comp. **16**	0.2	•	0.1	0.5	0.3	0.3	0.4	•	0.1	0.1	•	0.2	•
Employee Benefits **17**	0.5	0.1	0.3	0.5	0.5	1.3	1.3	•	0.4	2.3	•	1.1	•
Advertising **18**	0.7	0.2	0.8	0.7	0.7	2.0	0.3	•	1.2	1.8	•	1.7	•
Other Expenses **19**	10.2	14.3	9.0	7.7	8.2	13.6	7.6	•	10.2	10.2	•	14.6	•
Officers' Compensation **20**	0.9	13.2	4.8	5.8	2.5	1.8	1.7	•	0.6	0.5	•	0.4	•
Operating Margin **21**	2.7	58.4	4.8	3.3	4.1	4.3	3.4	•	1.1	•	•	2.3	•
Operating Margin Before Officers' Comp. **22**	3.6	71.6	9.6	9.1	6.5	6.1	5.1	•	1.7	0.3	•	2.8	•

Selected Average Balance Sheet ($ in Thousands)

Net Receivables 23	894	0	14	106	376	1885	4894	19544	11112	88189
Inventories 24	869	0	69	261	472	1867	2488	11651	40052	171024
Net Property, Plant and Equipment 25	729	0	19	49	291	534	1520	15210	28431	135641
Total Assets 26	5328	0	165	713	1836	6389	14218	75055	146225	1023244
Notes and Loans Payable 27	1149	0	56	176	642	1386	2752	19564	32727	380892
All Other Liabilities 28	1554	0	47	189	458	2271	4004	35063	44376	231320
Net Worth 29	2624	0	63	347	736	2732	7462	20428	69123	411031

Selected Financial Ratios (Times to 1)

Current Ratio 30	1.5		2.6	2.6	2.2	2.0	2.6	1.2	1.8	3.0
Quick Ratio 31	0.8		1.1	1.3	1.2	1.1	1.7	0.8	0.7	1.2
Net Sales to Working Capital 32	14.5		14.2	11.7	9.4	7.1	5.8	32.1	11.8	5.3
Coverage Ratio 33	8.8	3490.8	25.7	16.5	8.9	18.9	24.5	4.9	10.0	3.1
Total Asset Turnover 34	1.9		6.5	5.4	3.6	2.6	2.8	2.9	2.6	1.2
Inventory Turnover 35	8.6		11.3	10.4	10.0	5.2	10.7	13.7	6.3	4.1
Receivables Turnover 36	12.8		59.2	43.8	17.1	9.7	9.3		20.6	27.9
Total Liabilities to Net Worth 37	1.0		1.6	1.1	1.5	1.3	0.9	2.7	1.1	1.5
Current Assets to Working Capital 38	3.1		1.6	1.6	1.8	2.0	1.6	6.3	2.2	1.5
Current Liabilities to Working Capital 39	2.1		0.6	0.6	0.8	1.0	0.6	5.3	1.2	0.5
Working Capital to Net Sales 40	0.1		0.1	0.1	0.1	0.1	0.2	0.0	0.1	0.2
Inventory to Working Capital 41	1.3		0.9	0.8	0.8	0.9	0.3	1.7	1.0	0.7
Total Receipts to Cash Flow 42	8.3	1.4	9.6	11.3	9.3	5.6	8.3	11.6	13.0	8.4
Cost of Goods to Cash Flow 43	6.1	0.1	6.9	8.0	6.5	3.2	5.5	8.5	8.7	4.7
Cash Flow to Total Debt 44	0.5		1.1	0.9	0.7	0.8	0.7	0.3	0.4	0.2

Selected Financial Factors (in Percentages)

Debt Ratio 45	50.7		62.2	51.3	59.9	57.2	47.5	72.8	52.7	59.8
Return on Total Assets 46	10.0		34.1	20.5	18.4	17.9	17.7	7.4	5.4	6.5
Return on Equity Before Income Taxes 47	18.0		86.5	39.6	40.8	39.7	32.3	21.5	10.4	10.9
Return on Equity After Income Taxes 48	13.1		85.5	38.7	39.1	34.4	31.6	21.3	10.1	7.9
Profit Margin (Before Income Tax) 49	4.6	83.2	5.0	3.6	4.5	6.5	6.0	2.0	1.9	3.7
Profit Margin (After Income Tax) 50	3.3	76.3	5.0	3.5	4.3	5.6	5.9	2.0	1.9	2.6

224

Table I

Corporations with and without Net Income

GASOLINE STATIONS

MONEY AMOUNTS AND SIZE OF ASSETS IN THOUSANDS OF DOLLARS

Item Description for Accounting Period 7/09 Through 6/10	Total	Zero Assets	Under 500	500 to 1,000	1,000 to 5,000	5,000 to 10,000	10,000 to 25,000	25,000 to 50,000	50,000 to 100,000	100,000 to 250,000	250,000 to 500,000	500,000 to 2,500,000	2,500,000 and over
Number of Enterprises **1**	40306	2847	26283	6341	4188	338	173	69	31	20	3	13	0

Revenues ($ in Thousands)

	Total	Zero Assets	Under 500	500 to 1,000	1,000 to 5,000	5,000 to 10,000	10,000 to 25,000	25,000 to 50,000	50,000 to 100,000	100,000 to 250,000	250,000 to 500,000	500,000 to 2,500,000	2,500,000 and over
Net Sales **2**	253312956	1109912	46024809	25387898	45403500	6326661	14456737	14879837	9551485	12139874	6757887	71274356	0
Interest **3**	55430	900	1776	1267	4934	902	1478	5022	1760	366	3249	33775	0
Rents **4**	111196	42	49	7713	4224	6316	14911	7343	6500	3014	3105	57978	0
Royalties **5**	50631	0	54	0	0	0	0	1	0	0	0	50576	0
Other Portfolio Income **6**	329550	80265	13843	2561	90471	484	7116	4228	12478	1957	3248	112900	0
Other Receipts **7**	1722010	24338	355414	136543	202544	35751	149286	75858	41360	286251	13941	400724	0
Total Receipts **8**	255581773	1215457	46395945	25535982	45705673	6370114	14629528	14972289	9613583	12431462	6781430	71930309	0
Average Total Receipts **9**	6341	427	1765	4027	10913	18846	84564	216990	310116	621573	2260477	5533101	•

Operating Costs/Operating Income (%)

	Total	Zero Assets	Under 500	500 to 1,000	1,000 to 5,000	5,000 to 10,000	10,000 to 25,000	25,000 to 50,000	50,000 to 100,000	100,000 to 250,000	250,000 to 500,000	500,000 to 2,500,000	2,500,000 and over
Cost of Operations **10**	88.9	86.3	87.9	88.2	90.0	87.6	85.7	91.1	90.6	88.3	93.2	88.8	•
Salaries and Wages **11**	3.4	2.1	2.8	3.0	3.3	3.8	5.6	3.3	3.1	4.2	2.3	3.6	•
Taxes Paid **12**	0.9	1.2	0.8	1.5	1.2	1.0	1.1	0.6	0.6	0.8	0.3	0.6	•
Interest Paid **13**	0.4	0.6	0.2	0.6	0.6	1.1	0.4	0.3	0.4	0.4	0.1	0.5	•
Depreciation **14**	1.2	0.7	0.5	1.0	0.7	1.2	1.3	1.2	1.1	1.5	1.0	2.0	•
Amortization and Depletion **15**	0.1	0.2	0.1	0.2	0.1	0.2	0.0	0.0	0.1	0.1	0.0	0.1	•
Pensions and Other Deferred Comp. **16**	0.0	0.1	0.0	0.0	0.0	0.0	0.0	0.0	0.0	0.1	0.0	0.1	•
Employee Benefits **17**	0.2	0.0	0.1	0.1	0.1	0.2	0.2	0.1	0.2	0.3	0.4	0.3	•
Advertising **18**	0.1	0.0	0.1	0.0	0.1	0.1	0.2	0.1	0.1	0.2	0.0	0.2	•
Other Expenses **19**	5.0	11.7	6.9	5.3	4.4	5.3	5.9	3.7	4.0	3.9	1.6	4.8	•
Officers' Compensation **20**	0.5	2.6	1.1	0.7	0.5	0.5	0.4	0.2	0.2	0.2	0.1	0.1	•
Operating Margin **21**	•	•	•	•	•	•	•	•	•	0.1	0.9	•	•
Operating Margin Before Officers' Comp. **22**	•	0.5	0.2	0.2	•	•	•	•	•	0.3	1.0	•	•

Selected Average Balance Sheet ($ in Thousands)

	1	2	3	4	5	6	7	8	9	10	11	12	13
Net Receivables 23	88	0	8	32	74	466	1109	3198	4937	9452	50587	135103	•
Inventories 24	130	0	47	84	206	599	1863	3508	6022	14383	29880	75387	•
Net Property, Plant and Equipment 25	632	0	60	364	1195	3912	8043	18944	32215	82583	153110	728548	•
Total Assets 26	1200	0	186	720	1861	7083	16054	35108	62669	153303	350614	1342595	•
Notes and Loans Payable 27	550	0	111	449	1443	4907	6089	13046	23921	50561	35372	374594	•
All Other Liabilities 28	326	0	40	129	258	1045	4696	10880	19347	41984	137473	494578	•
Net Worth 29	324	0	35	142	160	1131	5269	11182	19401	60758	177769	473422	•

Selected Financial Ratios (Times to 1)

	1	2	3	4	5	6	7	8	9	10	11	12	13
Current Ratio 30	1.3	•	2.0	1.7	1.5	1.5	1.1	1.1	1.1	1.1	1.1	0.9	1.1
Quick Ratio 31	0.7	•	0.9	0.8	0.7	0.8	0.6	0.6	0.6	0.6	0.6	0.6	0.7
Net Sales to Working Capital 32	71.4	•	38.9	37.9	68.3	32.9	177.6	153.7	190.0	159.3	•	129.5	•
Coverage Ratio 33	1.4	8.0	2.0	1.1	0.4	0.8	2.1	0.9	1.6	7.0	16.4	1.2	•
Total Asset Turnover 34	5.2	•	9.4	5.6	5.8	2.6	5.2	6.1	4.9	4.0	6.4	4.1	•
Inventory Turnover 35	43.0	•	32.9	41.9	47.4	27.4	38.4	56.0	46.3	37.3	70.3	64.6	•
Receivables Turnover 36	76.1	•	192.0	135.5	142.0	38.1	69.3	77.4	55.4	58.2	43.2	58.9	•
Total Liabilities to Net Worth 37	2.7	•	4.3	4.1	10.7	5.3	2.0	2.1	2.2	1.5	1.0	1.8	•
Current Assets to Working Capital 38	4.2	•	2.0	2.4	2.8	2.9	10.6	8.9	12.5	10.9	•	9.3	•
Current Liabilities to Working Capital 39	3.2	•	1.0	1.4	1.8	1.9	9.6	7.9	11.5	9.9	•	8.3	•
Working Capital to Net Sales 40	0.0	•	0.0	0.0	0.0	0.0	0.0	0.0	0.0	0.0	0.0	0.0	•
Inventory to Working Capital 41	1.5	•	1.0	1.0	1.3	0.9	3.7	2.8	3.6	4.1	2.4	•	•
Total Receipts to Cash Flow 42	29.8	8.9	24.1	29.7	38.9	29.4	22.8	37.2	36.4	20.1	42.0	32.9	•
Cost of Goods to Cash Flow 43	26.5	7.7	21.2	26.2	35.0	25.7	19.6	33.9	33.0	17.7	39.2	29.2	•
Cash Flow to Total Debt 44	0.2	0.5	0.2	0.2	0.1	0.3	0.2	0.2	0.0	0.3	0.3	0.2	•

Selected Financial Factors (in Percentages)

	1	2	3	4	5	6	7	8	9	10	11	12	13
Debt Ratio 45	73.0	•	81.3	80.3	91.4	84.0	67.2	68.2	69.0	60.4	49.3	64.7	•
Return on Total Assets 46	3.4	•	4.2	3.4	1.6	2.1	3.9	1.7	3.0	11.6	8.3	2.2	•
Return on Equity Before Income Taxes 47	3.8	•	11.1	1.1	•	•	6.3	•	3.5	25.1	15.4	0.9	•
Return on Equity After Income Taxes 48	2.7	•	10.6	0.9	•	•	5.5	•	3.0	24.1	11.2	•	•
Profit Margin (Before Income Tax) 49	0.2	4.0	0.2	0.0	•	•	0.4	•	0.2	2.5	1.2	•	•
Profit Margin (After Income Tax) 50	0.1	4.0	0.2	0.0	•	•	0.3	•	0.2	2.4	0.9	0.1	•

Table II

Corporations with Net Income

GASOLINE STATIONS

MONEY AMOUNTS AND SIZE OF ASSETS IN THOUSANDS OF DOLLARS

Item Description for Accounting Period 7/09 Through 6/10	Total	Zero Assets	Under 500	500 to 1,000	1,000 to 5,000	5,000 to 10,000	10,000 to 25,000	25,000 to 50,000	50,000 to 100,000	100,000 to 250,000	250,000 to 500,000	500,000 to 2,500,000	2,500,000 and over
Number of Enterprises 1	20310	1516	13089	3108	2265	134	113	39	18	17	3	8	0
Revenues ($ in Thousands)													
Net Sales 2	166259252	464165	27294215	14619905	32291284	3102841	10867823	8080186	6424436	11019181	6757887	45337329	0
Interest 3	45660	877	1278	240	4363	661	1131	2783	1101	366	3249	29611	0
Rents 4	51693	42	49	28	3538	6080	11488	6410	1866	3014	3105	16072	0
Royalties 5	39829	0	0	0	0	0	0	1	0	0	0	39828	0
Other Portfolio Income 6	202836	77322	13743	1989	83580	385	5934	3498	4578	1682	3248	6880	0
Other Receipts 7	1254635	15658	223036	44029	163742	16967	134559	54527	30393	285519	13941	272262	0
Total Receipts 8	167853905	558064	27532321	14666191	32546507	3126934	11020935	8147405	6462374	11309762	6781430	45701982	0
Average Total Receipts 9	8265	368	2103	4719	14369	23335	97530	208908	359021	665280	2260477	5712748	•
Operating Costs/Operating Income (%)													
Cost of Operations 10	88.5	83.0	87.6	87.9	91.1	86.3	84.7	90.6	91.6	87.7	93.2	87.3	•
Salaries and Wages 11	3.5	1.7	2.7	3.1	2.8	4.7	6.3	3.3	2.6	4.6	2.3	4.0	•
Taxes Paid 12	0.8	1.2	0.7	1.0	1.0	1.0	1.1	0.7	0.6	0.8	0.3	0.6	•
Interest Paid 13	0.4	1.4	0.1	0.5	0.4	0.5	0.3	0.2	0.2	0.4	0.1	0.5	•
Depreciation 14	1.0	1.3	0.2	0.8	0.5	0.6	1.2	1.0	0.8	1.5	1.0	1.9	•
Amortization and Depletion 15	0.1	0.0	0.2	0.1	0.0	0.2	0.0	0.0	0.0	0.1	0.0	0.1	•
Pensions and Other Deferred Comp. 16	0.0	•	0.0	0.0	0.0	0.0	0.0	0.0	0.0	0.1	0.2	0.1	•
Employee Benefits 17	0.2	•	0.1	0.1	0.1	0.3	0.2	0.1	0.1	0.3	0.4	0.3	•
Advertising 18	0.1	0.0	0.1	0.1	0.1	0.1	0.2	0.1	0.1	0.2	0.0	0.2	•
Other Expenses 19	4.5	10.5	6.1	4.6	3.5	5.5	6.0	4.1	3.3	3.9	1.6	4.6	•
Officers' Compensation 20	0.5	4.3	1.3	0.7	0.5	0.5	0.4	0.2	0.2	0.2	0.1	0.1	•
Operating Margin 21	0.3	•	0.9	1.1	•	0.5	•	•	0.3	0.3	0.9	0.2	•
Operating Margin Before Officers' Comp. 22	0.8	0.9	2.2	1.8	0.4	1.0	•	•	0.5	0.5	1.0	0.3	•

Selected Average Balance Sheet ($ in Thousands)

	•	•	•	•	•	•	•	•	•	•	•	•
Net Receivables 23	107	0	5	49	73	266	1152	4033	5113	9892	50587	131109
Inventories 24	160	0	51	87	206	1151	1982	3700	6876	17604	29880	108002
Net Property, Plant and Equipment 25	691	0	47	348	1152	2318	7521	16838	28852	81355	153110	693155
Total Assets 26	1371	0	189	732	1896	6317	16378	35223	60587	158769	350614	1236458
Notes and Loans Payable 27	480	0	70	351	1058	2756	5160	9257	19714	46172	35372	347582
All Other Liabilities 28	414	0	37	162	267	1250	5608	11839	17113	45896	137473	506695
Net Worth 29	477	0	82	220	571	2312	5611	14128	23760	66702	177769	382180

Selected Financial Ratios (Times to 1)

Current Ratio 30	1.3	•	2.7	1.8	1.7	1.7	1.1	1.3	1.2	1.1	0.9	1.0
Quick Ratio 31	0.7	•	1.4	0.8	0.9	0.7	0.6	0.7	0.6	0.6	0.6	0.6
Net Sales to Working Capital 32	74.4	•	32.4	34.8	66.2	22.4	209.8	64.9	80.0	153.9	•	1216.9
Coverage Ratio 33	4.5	13.3	18.8	3.6	2.7	3.6	3.8	3.6	5.6	9.2	16.4	3.1
Total Asset Turnover 34	6.0	•	11.0	6.4	7.5	3.7	5.9	5.9	5.9	4.1	6.4	4.6
Inventory Turnover 35	45.4	•	35.7	47.5	62.9	17.4	41.1	50.7	47.5	32.3	70.3	45.8
Receivables Turnover 36	77.3	•	253.3	115.2	164.0	32.2	87.0	59.1	53.3	•	43.2	•
Total Liabilities to Net Worth 37	1.9	•	1.3	2.3	2.3	1.7	1.9	1.5	1.6	1.4	1.0	2.2
Current Assets to Working Capital 38	4.0	•	1.6	2.3	2.3	2.4	12.3	4.4	5.1	10.8	•	69.9
Current Liabilities to Working Capital 39	3.0	•	0.6	1.3	1.3	1.4	11.3	3.4	4.1	9.8	•	68.9
Working Capital to Net Sales 40	0.0	•	0.0	0.0	0.0	0.0	0.0	0.0	0.0	0.0	•	0.0
Inventory to Working Capital 41	1.5	•	0.7	0.7	1.1	0.9	4.6	1.3	1.4	4.2	•	23.2
Total Receipts to Cash Flow 42	23.9	3.9	18.8	22.6	34.0	19.9	20.1	27.7	31.0	18.7	42.0	24.6
Cost of Goods to Cash Flow 43	21.2	3.3	16.5	19.9	31.0	17.1	17.0	25.1	28.4	16.4	39.2	21.5
Cash Flow to Total Debt 44	0.4	1.0	0.4	0.4	0.3	0.3	0.4	0.4	0.3	0.4	0.3	0.3

Selected Financial Factors (in Percentages)

Debt Ratio 45	65.2	•	56.8	70.0	69.9	63.4	65.7	59.9	60.8	58.0	49.3	69.1
Return on Total Assets 46	9.8	•	21.0	12.5	8.7	6.4	6.9	5.0	6.7	13.3	8.3	6.9
Return on Equity Before Income Taxes 47	21.8	•	45.9	30.2	18.0	12.6	14.8	9.0	14.1	28.3	15.4	15.1
Return on Equity After Income Taxes 48	20.4	•	45.5	29.8	17.6	11.3	13.7	8.2	13.4	27.3	11.2	12.8
Profit Margin (Before Income Tax) 49	1.3	16.8	1.8	1.4	0.7	1.3	0.9	0.6	0.9	2.9	1.2	1.0
Profit Margin (After Income Tax) 50	1.2	16.7	1.8	1.4	0.7	1.1	0.8	0.6	0.9	2.8	0.9	0.9

Table I
Corporations with and without Net Income

CLOTHING AND CLOTHING ACCESSORIES STORES

MONEY AMOUNTS AND SIZE OF ASSETS IN THOUSANDS OF DOLLARS

Item Description for Accounting Period 7/09 Through 6/10	Total	Zero Assets	Under 500	500 to 1,000	1,000 to 5,000	5,000 to 10,000	10,000 to 25,000	25,000 to 50,000	50,000 to 100,000	100,000 to 250,000	250,000 to 500,000	500,000 to 2,500,000	2,500,000 and over
Number of Enterprises 1	53722	10894	36103	3819	2349	261	135	46	29	27	17	36	7
Revenues ($ in Thousands)													
Net Sales 2	173729565	1549412	11852376	4515754	8138220	2970931	3164699	3419108	3999508	8652961	12439947	55445769	57580879
Interest 3	575645	884	1566	2235	5350	4503	16638	1908	7986	6368	21550	203177	303481
Rents 4	116492	0	1085	161	6630	4049	957	4050	35	3066	16174	42269	38019
Royalties 5	866687	74	0	0	173	0	0	6076	10523	50482	10664	593379	195317
Other Portfolio Income 6	546457	27029	4661	2177	14796	1549	322	2071	7288	1634	6108	339537	139286
Other Receipts 7	2691784	91630	158534	52887	37010	16918	71189	20196	108560	208171	100584	1142796	683303
Total Receipts 8	178526630	1669029	12018222	4573214	8202179	2997950	3253805	3453409	4133900	8922682	12595027	57766927	58940285
Average Total Receipts 9	3323	153	333	1197	3492	11486	24102	75074	142548	330470	740884	1604637	8420041
Operating Costs/Operating Income (%)													
Cost of Operations 10	53.4	63.7	51.1	59.2	61.6	62.1	56.4	58.4	54.6	50.2	54.9	50.9	53.6
Salaries and Wages 11	14.5	11.4	12.0	11.7	11.5	12.5	14.8	15.0	15.3	16.2	15.3	15.6	14.2
Taxes Paid 12	2.4	2.6	2.6	2.2	2.0	1.9	2.7	3.5	2.3	2.4	2.0	2.5	2.2
Interest Paid 13	1.0	0.9	0.5	0.6	1.1	0.6	0.7	0.7	2.1	1.7	0.2	1.0	1.0
Depreciation 14	2.8	2.6	0.7	0.6	1.0	0.9	1.5	2.1	1.9	3.1	2.6	3.9	2.8
Amortization and Depletion 15	0.3	0.4	0.2	0.0	0.1	0.0	0.2	0.1	0.4	0.3	0.1	0.4	0.4
Pensions and Other Deferred Comp. 16	0.3	0.1	0.1	0.3	0.2	0.6	0.2	0.2	0.1	0.0	0.1	0.4	0.4
Employee Benefits 17	1.2	1.1	0.4	0.7	0.6	0.5	0.8	0.7	1.6	1.4	1.0	1.4	1.4
Advertising 18	2.2	2.0	2.1	3.5	2.8	2.9	2.4	3.2	2.4	1.8	1.5	2.9	1.5
Other Expenses 19	20.2	40.9	26.1	15.1	17.3	18.6	22.6	18.1	22.7	25.0	20.3	23.0	15.6
Officers' Compensation 20	1.3	5.1	6.7	5.5	4.5	1.3	1.7	1.2	0.7	0.8	0.5	0.6	0.4
Operating Margin 21	0.4	•	•	0.4	•	•	•	•	•	•	1.8	•	•
Operating Margin Before Officers' Comp. 22	1.7	•	4.1	5.9	1.8	•	•	•	•	•	2.2	6.3	6.7

Selected Average Balance Sheet ($ in Thousands)

	1	2	3	4	5	6	7	8	9	10	11	12	13
Net Receivables 23	142	0	4	31	72	174	1218	4144	2966	8367	6923	95072	420664
Inventories 24	575	0	75	427	1108	3475	6800	14071	29269	51553	110747	263323	1128650
Net Property, Plant and Equipment 25	478	0	10	56	285	844	3146	7374	13806	43400	121226	288022	1350922
Total Assets 26	2048	0	125	679	1951	6222	15293	35958	70261	171860	372339	1139135	5568255
Notes and Loans Payable 27	452	0	65	240	823	2015	5169	8365	17294	47532	12857	181403	1273883
All Other Liabilities 28	761	0	52	139	542	1739	5421	18970	48388	71234	120283	460191	1887937
Net Worth 29	836	0	8	300	586	2468	4703	8622	4579	53094	239199	497541	2406434

Selected Financial Ratios (Times to 1)

	1	2	3	4	5	6	7	8	9	10	11	12	13
Current Ratio 30	1.9	•	1.8	3.6	1.9	1.9	1.7	1.2	1.2	1.8	2.3	2.0	1.8
Quick Ratio 31	0.8	•	0.5	0.7	0.4	0.2	0.5	0.4	0.3	0.6	0.9	0.8	1.0
Net Sales to Working Capital 32	6.0	•	7.2	2.8	5.1	4.9	5.4	15.8	16.9	7.7	5.9	5.2	6.9
Coverage Ratio 33	4.5	•	•	3.6	•	•	•	•	0.7	1.2	17.5	3.0	9.4
Total Asset Turnover 34	1.6	•	2.6	1.7	1.8	1.8	1.5	2.1	2.0	1.9	2.0	1.4	1.5
Inventory Turnover 35	3.0	•	2.2	1.6	1.9	2.0	1.9	3.1	2.6	3.1	3.6	3.0	3.9
Receivables Turnover 36	22.8	•	74.6	36.7	40.4	29.8	14.0	22.9	27.7	36.4	93.7	21.0	16.4
Total Liabilities to Net Worth 37	1.5	•	14.0	1.3	2.3	1.5	2.3	3.2	14.3	2.2	0.6	1.3	1.3
Current Assets to Working Capital 38	2.1	•	2.3	1.4	2.2	2.1	2.4	5.3	5.3	2.3	1.8	2.0	2.2
Current Liabilities to Working Capital 39	1.1	•	1.3	0.4	1.2	1.1	1.4	4.3	4.3	1.3	0.8	1.0	1.2
Working Capital to Net Sales 40	0.2	•	0.1	0.4	0.2	0.2	0.2	0.1	0.1	0.1	0.2	0.2	0.1
Inventory to Working Capital 41	1.0	•	1.6	1.0	1.7	1.2	1.5	2.8	3.3	1.2	0.8	0.9	0.8
Total Receipts to Cash Flow 42	7.4	•	7.5	10.0	13.0	11.7	9.9	15.8	8.4	8.0	9.2	8.0	5.7
Cost of Goods to Cash Flow 43	4.0	•	3.8	5.9	8.0	7.3	5.6	9.2	4.6	4.0	5.1	4.1	3.1
Cash Flow to Total Debt 44	0.4	•	0.4	0.3	0.2	0.3	0.2	0.2	0.2	0.3	0.6	0.3	0.5

Selected Financial Factors (in Percentages)

	1	2	3	4	5	6	7	8	9	10	11	12	13
Debt Ratio 45	59.2	•	93.4	55.8	70.0	60.3	69.2	76.0	93.5	69.1	35.8	56.3	56.8
Return on Total Assets 46	6.8	•	•	3.9	•	•	•	•	2.7	3.6	6.2	4.2	14.5
Return on Equity Before Income Taxes 47	13.0	•	•	6.4	•	•	•	•	1.7	1.7	9.0	6.3	30.0
Return on Equity After Income Taxes 48	6.7	•	•	6.1	•	•	•	•	•	•	5.7	1.7	19.8
Profit Margin (Before Income Tax) 49	3.3	•	1.6	1.6	•	•	•	•	0.3	0.3	3.0	2.0	8.8
Profit Margin (After Income Tax) 50	1.7	•	1.5	1.5	•	•	•	•	•	•	1.9	0.5	5.8

Table II
Corporations with Net Income

CLOTHING AND CLOTHING ACCESSORIES STORES

MONEY AMOUNTS AND SIZE OF ASSETS IN THOUSANDS OF DOLLARS

Item Description for Accounting Period 7/09 Through 6/10	Total	Zero Assets	Under 500	500 to 1,000	1,000 to 5,000	5,000 to 10,000	10,000 to 25,000	25,000 to 50,000	50,000 to 100,000	100,000 to 250,000	250,000 to 500,000	500,000 to 2,500,000	2,500,000 and over
Number of Enterprises 1	26375	4007	17928	2602	1474	207	72	19	15	11	11	22	7
Revenues ($ in Thousands)													
Net Sales 2	126935633	485557	7214106	3446692	4745306	2208583	1995302	1944455	2330262	4338180	8435026	32211285	57580879
Interest 3	469408	0	1023	1980	1366	383	14539	1287	156	765	9914	134513	303481
Rents 4	74747	0	0	161	4926	0	957	3340	35	0	0	27310	38019
Royalties 5	648588	0	0	0	0	0	0	0	1359	15898	0	195317	436014
Other Portfolio Income 6	426100	2256	1523	1371	10429	1448	322	1383	7160	56	6108	254759	139286
Other Receipts 7	1626308	44361	74480	58890	23319	6190	51231	8667	14321	72407	29056	560081	683303
Total Receipts 8	130180784	532174	7291132	3509094	4785346	2216604	2062351	1959132	2353293	4427306	8480104	33623962	58940285
Average Total Receipts 9	4936	133	407	1349	3247	10708	28644	103112	156886	402482	770919	1528362	8420041
Operating Costs/Operating Income (%)													
Cost of Operations 10	52.8	39.5	47.4	57.3	62.7	62.1	55.6	53.6	56.1	47.6	55.4	49.8	53.6
Salaries and Wages 11	14.1	5.0	10.8	12.4	10.5	11.7	13.8	16.0	13.2	16.4	15.2	15.2	14.2
Taxes Paid 12	2.2	4.1	2.2	2.3	1.7	1.9	2.9	4.4	2.1	2.2	1.9	2.3	2.2
Interest Paid 13	0.8	0.2	0.4	0.6	1.0	0.3	0.6	0.5	0.6	0.3	0.1	0.8	1.0
Depreciation 14	2.6	0.1	0.4	0.4	0.8	0.7	1.1	1.5	1.2	3.2	2.5	3.7	2.8
Amortization and Depletion 15	0.3	0.3	0.1	0.0	0.0	0.0	0.2	0.1	0.1	0.4	0.0	0.3	0.4
Pensions and Other Deferred Comp. 16	0.3	•	0.2	0.2	0.2	0.7	0.2	0.0	0.1	0.1	0.0	0.2	0.4
Employee Benefits 17	1.2	0.6	0.4	0.4	0.6	0.3	0.6	0.6	1.0	1.1	0.7	1.4	1.4
Advertising 18	2.1	1.3	2.1	3.8	2.8	2.2	2.4	3.8	2.4	1.4	1.3	3.1	1.5
Other Expenses 19	17.7	34.8	26.1	14.1	13.9	15.9	18.5	16.8	18.0	21.7	17.1	19.8	15.6
Officers' Compensation 20	1.1	11.8	5.4	5.6	3.7	1.4	1.9	1.0	0.9	0.7	0.5	0.5	0.4
Operating Margin 21	4.7	2.4	4.5	2.9	2.0	2.7	2.2	1.7	4.3	4.9	5.2	2.9	6.3
Operating Margin Before Officers' Comp. 22	5.8	14.2	9.9	8.5	5.6	4.1	4.1	2.7	5.2	5.6	5.7	3.4	6.7

Selected Average Balance Sheet ($ in Thousands)

Net Receivables 23	198	0	6	33	58	147	1359	3106	2209	9958	7278	72019	420664
Inventories 24	801	0	82	443	1131	3373	7133	18086	26101	44368	101260	248564	938526
Net Property, Plant and Equipment 25	720	0	10	42	252	739	3474	8234	11556	56630	117682	282711	1350922
Total Assets 26	3041	0	146	700	1816	6007	16154	37080	65940	189707	372048	1082930	5568255
Notes and Loans Payable 27	600	0	48	199	647	1067	3748	5430	10387	26472	9645	156111	1273883
All Other Liabilities 28	1011	0	43	138	439	1391	4475	22695	28164	69431	119899	369416	1887937
Net Worth 29	1430	0	55	364	730	3549	7930	8955	27389	93805	242503	557403	2406434

Selected Financial Ratios (Times to 1)

Current Ratio 30	2.0	•	2.3	3.9	2.5	2.4	2.4	1.3	1.8	2.1	2.4	2.1	1.8
Quick Ratio 31	0.9	•	0.7	0.8	0.5	0.2	0.8	0.4	0.6	0.8	1.0	0.9	1.0
Net Sales to Working Capital 32	5.7	•	5.9	2.9	3.8	3.9	4.5	17.5	8.4	7.3	5.7	4.8	6.9
Coverage Ratio 33	10.3	64.9	14.0	9.3	3.7	11.8	10.4	6.2	10.2	25.7	87.8	10.7	9.4
Total Asset Turnover 34	1.6	•	2.8	1.9	1.8	1.8	1.7	2.8	2.4	2.1	2.1	1.4	1.5
Inventory Turnover 35	3.2	•	2.3	1.7	1.8	2.0	2.2	3.0	3.3	4.2	4.2	2.9	4.7
Receivables Turnover 36	22.6	•	57.6	36.0	39.4	70.8	19.4	30.0	•	61.7	111.2	23.9	•
Total Liabilities to Net Worth 37	1.1	•	1.6	0.9	1.5	0.7	1.0	3.1	1.4	1.0	0.5	0.9	1.3
Current Assets to Working Capital 38	2.0	•	1.8	1.3	1.7	1.7	1.7	4.8	2.3	1.9	1.7	1.9	2.2
Current Liabilities to Working Capital 39	1.0	•	0.8	0.3	0.7	0.7	0.7	3.8	1.3	0.9	0.7	0.9	1.2
Working Capital to Net Sales 40	0.2	•	0.2	0.3	0.3	0.3	0.2	0.1	0.1	0.1	0.2	0.2	0.1
Inventory to Working Capital 41	0.9	•	1.2	1.0	1.3	0.9	1.0	3.0	1.4	1.0	0.8	0.8	0.8
Total Receipts to Cash Flow 42	6.1	4.0	4.9	7.8	8.5	8.9	6.5	10.2	6.4	5.8	8.1	6.2	5.7
Cost of Goods to Cash Flow 43	3.2	1.6	2.3	4.5	5.3	5.5	3.6	5.5	3.6	2.8	4.5	3.1	3.1
Cash Flow to Total Debt 44	0.5	•	0.9	0.5	0.4	0.5	0.5	0.4	0.6	0.7	0.7	0.5	0.5

Selected Financial Factors (in Percentages)

Debt Ratio 45	53.0	•	62.2	48.0	59.8	40.9	50.9	75.8	58.5	50.6	34.8	48.5	56.8
Return on Total Assets 46	13.0	•	16.4	10.0	6.8	6.0	10.6	7.8	13.9	15.0	11.8	11.6	14.5
Return on Equity Before Income Taxes 47	25.0	•	40.4	17.1	12.5	9.2	19.6	27.2	30.3	29.2	17.9	20.4	30.0
Return on Equity After Income Taxes 48	17.6	•	40.0	16.7	10.7	8.4	17.6	24.7	28.5	23.4	12.8	13.6	19.8
Profit Margin (Before Income Tax) 49	7.4	12.0	5.5	4.7	2.8	3.1	5.6	2.4	5.3	6.9	5.7	7.8	8.8
Profit Margin (After Income Tax) 50	5.2	12.0	5.5	4.6	2.4	2.8	5.0	2.2	5.0	5.6	4.1	5.2	5.8

Table I
Corporations with and without Net Income

SPORTING GOODS, HOBBY, BOOK, AND MUSIC STORES

MONEY AMOUNTS AND SIZE OF ASSETS IN THOUSANDS OF DOLLARS

Item Description for Accounting Period 7/09 Through 6/10	Total	Zero Assets	Under 500	500 to 1,000	1,000 to 5,000	5,000 to 10,000	10,000 to 25,000	25,000 to 50,000	50,000 to 100,000	100,000 to 250,000	250,000 to 500,000	500,000 to 2,500,000	2,500,000 and over
Number of Enterprises 1	29559	5167	19679	2567	1785	252	48	15	8	13	7	17	0
Revenues ($ in Thousands)													
Net Sales 2	80429498	625015	6236555	3585293	6836235	3379328	1651478	650542	1191879	4386221	4210926	47676026	0
Interest 3	323663	26	2804	2253	5379	4115	228	926	76	345	442	307069	0
Rents 4	118250	0	0	133	3170	341	0	6552	0	2322	19	105713	0
Royalties 5	136850	0	0	24	0	0	0	0	0	219	10091	126517	0
Other Portfolio Income 6	37824	0	2134	379	6807	4840	767	12	235	1963	571	20113	0
Other Receipts 7	1590642	4216	97946	245823	24637	23491	17290	31596	16627	68794	42304	1017921	0
Total Receipts 8	82636727	629257	6339439	3833905	6876228	3412115	1669763	689628	1208817	4459864	4264353	49253359	0
Average Total Receipts 9	2796	122	322	1494	3852	13540	34787	45975	151102	343066	609193	2897256	•
Operating Costs/Operating Income (%)													
Cost of Operations 10	61.1	63.5	58.9	61.9	58.9	71.2	73.3	66.0	57.2	60.5	61.8	60.5	•
Salaries and Wages 11	12.6	7.3	9.8	16.7	13.5	9.9	9.4	10.9	14.8	13.0	13.8	12.7	•
Taxes Paid 12	2.2	2.3	2.6	2.2	2.4	2.7	1.4	1.5	2.7	1.7	2.0	2.2	•
Interest Paid 13	2.0	0.7	0.9	0.9	0.7	1.0	0.4	1.4	2.1	1.1	0.8	2.8	•
Depreciation 14	2.1	1.5	1.3	0.9	1.2	0.6	1.1	1.1	1.8	2.0	2.3	2.6	•
Amortization and Depletion 15	0.3	0.7	0.1	0.2	0.1	0.1	0.2	1.0	0.4	0.7	0.4	0.3	•
Pensions and Other Deferred Comp. 16	0.2	0.0	0.0	0.1	0.1	0.1	0.1	0.1	0.1	0.6	0.1	0.2	•
Employee Benefits 17	0.7	0.2	0.8	1.5	0.6	0.6	0.7	1.1	1.4	1.0	0.5	0.7	•
Advertising 18	2.5	1.8	1.6	1.8	1.9	2.2	2.7	5.3	2.0	3.3	3.0	2.6	•
Other Expenses 19	16.4	20.8	20.7	16.4	15.3	11.7	12.1	17.6	18.7	18.4	16.2	16.2	•
Officers' Compensation 20	1.5	2.8	5.5	5.9	4.1	1.4	1.1	1.5	0.5	0.8	0.4	0.4	•
Operating Margin 21	•	•	•	•	0.9	•	•	•	•	•	•	•	•
Operating Margin Before Officers' Comp. 22	•	1.3	3.3	5.0	•	•	•	•	•	•	•	•	•

Selected Average Balance Sheet ($ in Thousands)

Net Receivables 23	83	0	4	38	121	300	2282	1729	15499	20715	18062	78618
Inventories 24	621	0	73	449	959	2445	8179	10075	32875	75561	198574	603536
Net Property, Plant and Equipment 25	386	0	15	87	395	587	2235	4324	12181	29565	78021	519156
Total Assets 26	1605	0	123	764	2011	6348	14185	31753	72489	152698	316546	1879479
Notes and Loans Payable 27	613	0	79	318	515	2004	4449	8649	38449	50559	71009	735912
All Other Liabilities 28	722	0	38	183	635	1981	8511	9207	34224	73851	125103	932014
Net Worth 29	270	0	6	263	860	2363	1224	13897	-184	28288	120433	211553

Selected Financial Ratios (Times to 1)

Current Ratio 30	1.5	•	2.1	3.1	2.4	1.5	1.4	2.1	1.5	1.6	1.7	1.3
Quick Ratio 31	0.4	•	0.5	0.8	0.7	0.2	0.5	0.7	0.5	0.4	0.3	0.3
Net Sales to Working Capital 32	8.7	•	6.2	3.4	4.6	9.1	11.4	3.8	7.9	8.7	7.3	12.9
Coverage Ratio 33	1.6	•	0.5	•	3.0	0.5	•	•	0.8	•	1.1	1.9
Total Asset Turnover 34	1.7	•	2.6	1.8	1.9	2.1	2.4	1.4	2.1	2.2	1.9	1.5
Inventory Turnover 35	2.7	•	2.5	1.9	2.4	3.9	3.1	2.8	2.6	2.7	1.9	2.8
Receivables Turnover 36	32.0	•	74.3	35.0	33.3	44.8	16.0	15.0	14.9	16.5	15.5	37.2
Total Liabilities to Net Worth 37	4.9	•	20.9	1.9	1.3	1.7	10.6	1.3	•	4.4	1.6	7.9
Current Assets to Working Capital 38	3.0	•	1.9	1.5	1.7	2.9	3.5	1.9	3.1	2.7	2.5	4.4
Current Liabilities to Working Capital 39	2.0	•	0.9	0.5	0.7	1.9	2.5	0.9	2.1	1.7	1.5	3.4
Working Capital to Net Sales 40	0.1	•	0.2	0.3	0.2	0.1	0.1	0.3	0.1	0.1	0.1	0.1
Inventory to Working Capital 41	2.0	•	1.5	1.1	1.1	2.4	1.9	1.0	1.9	2.0	1.8	2.7
Total Receipts to Cash Flow 42	10.4	9.1	9.4	12.7	9.5	18.2	17.1	8.5	11.9	14.8	11.2	9.8
Cost of Goods to Cash Flow 43	6.3	5.8	5.5	7.9	5.6	13.0	12.6	5.6	6.8	8.9	6.9	5.9
Cash Flow to Total Debt 44	0.2	•	0.3	0.2	0.4	0.2	0.3	0.3	0.2	0.2	0.3	0.2

Selected Financial Factors (in Percentages)

Debt Ratio 45	83.2	•	95.4	65.6	57.2	62.8	91.4	56.2	100.3	81.5	62.0	88.7
Return on Total Assets 46	5.6	•	1.1	•	4.3	1.1	•	•	3.6	•	1.7	7.7
Return on Equity Before Income Taxes 47	12.9	•	6.6	•	6.6	•	•	•	290.5	•	0.3	31.6
Return on Equity After Income Taxes 48	8.0	•	•	•	5.8	•	•	•	314.4	•	•	22.8
Profit Margin (Before Income Tax) 49	1.3	•	1.5	•	1.5	•	•	•	•	•	0.1	2.4
Profit Margin (After Income Tax) 50	0.8	•	1.3	•	1.3	•	•	•	•	•	•	1.7

229

Table II
Corporations with Net Income

SPORTING GOODS, HOBBY, BOOK, AND MUSIC STORES

MONEY AMOUNTS AND SIZE OF ASSETS IN THOUSANDS OF DOLLARS

Item Description for Accounting Period 7/09 Through 6/10	Total	Zero Assets	Under 500	500 to 1,000	1,000 to 5,000	5,000 to 10,000	10,000 to 25,000	25,000 to 50,000	50,000 to 100,000	100,000 to 250,000	250,000 to 500,000	500,000 to 2,500,000	2,500,000 and over
Number of Enterprises **1**	15441	3029	9443	1328	1394	180	32	10	4	6	4	12	0

Revenues ($ in Thousands)

	Total	Zero Assets	Under 500	500 to 1,000	1,000 to 5,000	5,000 to 10,000	10,000 to 25,000	25,000 to 50,000	50,000 to 100,000	100,000 to 250,000	250,000 to 500,000	500,000 to 2,500,000	2,500,000 and over
Net Sales **2**	59997487	416919	3681070	2094569	5546966	2030173	1219244	329607	556581	2530321	2618345	38973691	0
Interest **3**	313938	0	1112	1233	4093	3912	217	879	61	235	28	302169	0
Rents **4**	101950	0	0	0	3170	341	0	6552	0	0	19	91868	0
Royalties **5**	118832	0	0	24	0	0	0	0	0	0	1616	117192	0
Other Portfolio Income **6**	33384	0	535	299	6807	4828	767	9	0	14	363	19760	0
Other Receipts **7**	1323463	308	44744	248028	23183	21045	9125	7800	1428	24116	34713	908974	0
Total Receipts **8**	61889054	417227	3727461	2344153	5584219	2060299	1229353	344847	558070	2554686	2655084	40413654	0
Average Total Receipts **9**	4008	138	395	1765	4006	11446	38417	34485	139518	425781	663771	3367804	•

Operating Costs/Operating Income (%)

	Total	Zero Assets	Under 500	500 to 1,000	1,000 to 5,000	5,000 to 10,000	10,000 to 25,000	25,000 to 50,000	50,000 to 100,000	100,000 to 250,000	250,000 to 500,000	500,000 to 2,500,000	2,500,000 and over
Cost of Operations **10**	61.0	62.1	59.1	63.6	58.1	74.7	74.8	58.7	57.4	56.0	63.8	60.5	•
Salaries and Wages **11**	12.3	5.1	8.0	17.2	13.3	7.4	7.6	8.4	14.6	13.2	12.7	12.8	•
Taxes Paid **12**	2.2	2.6	2.2	2.1	2.1	3.0	1.0	2.1	2.4	2.0	1.5	2.2	•
Interest Paid **13**	2.0	0.1	0.8	0.4	0.8	1.0	0.2	1.7	0.7	0.4	1.2	2.7	•
Depreciation **14**	2.1	0.8	0.8	1.1	1.1	0.4	1.2	1.2	1.8	1.8	2.2	2.6	•
Amortization and Depletion **15**	0.2	1.0	0.2	0.0	0.1	0.1	0.1	1.3	0.0	0.4	0.4	0.2	•
Pensions and Other Deferred Comp. **16**	0.2	0.0	0.0	0.2	0.5	0.1	0.2	0.1	•	1.0	0.1	0.2	•
Employee Benefits **17**	0.7	0.0	0.4	2.2	0.7	0.5	0.3	0.5	1.3	1.0	0.1	0.7	•
Advertising **18**	2.5	0.6	1.5	2.1	1.9	1.3	1.6	0.9	1.5	4.2	2.9	2.6	•
Other Expenses **19**	15.0	19.0	19.1	11.7	14.1	8.3	8.9	24.1	17.7	16.7	12.1	15.4	•
Officers' Compensation **20**	1.3	3.3	4.3	6.8	4.0	1.7	0.6	1.1	0.5	0.6	0.3	0.4	•
Operating Margin **21**	0.5	5.5	3.6	•	3.4	1.6	3.5	•	2.1	2.7	2.6	•	•
Operating Margin Before Officers' Comp. **22**	1.8	8.8	7.9	•	7.4	3.2	4.1	1.0	2.6	3.3	2.9	0.1	•

Selected Average Balance Sheet ($ in Thousands)

Net Receivables 23	119	0	6	18	107	361	2080	2129	8306	16934	26352	101357
Inventories 24	816	0	68	377	983	1859	7095	11291	35724	89404	212390	654306
Net Property, Plant and Equipment 25	603	0	11	80	401	456	2300	4186	11462	37446	87292	643803
Total Assets 26	2238	0	121	786	2007	6114	14509	32503	63584	170382	316808	2094212
Notes and Loans Payable 27	861	0	63	173	509	1804	2822	9298	9250	37050	100828	881695
All Other Liabilities 28	976	0	30	203	574	1309	4405	10462	30221	94728	134574	1000959
Net Worth 29	401	0	28	409	924	3000	7282	12743	24114	38604	81405	211557

Selected Financial Ratios (Times to 1)

Current Ratio 30	1.5	•	2.1	2.8	2.9	2.2	1.7	2.1	1.7	2.0	1.6	1.3
Quick Ratio 31	0.4	•	0.6	1.0	0.9	0.5	0.7	0.6	0.4	0.4	0.3	0.3
Net Sales to Working Capital 32	9.2	•	7.3	3.8	4.3	5.2	8.5	2.8	6.8	6.9	9.1	13.9
Coverage Ratio 33	2.9	55.2	7.0	13.4	6.3	4.0	21.9	3.7	4.4	9.3	4.4	2.3
Total Asset Turnover 34	1.7	•	3.2	2.0	2.0	1.8	2.6	1.0	2.2	2.5	2.1	1.6
Inventory Turnover 35	2.9	•	3.4	2.7	2.3	4.5	4.0	1.7	2.2	2.6	2.0	3.0
Receivables Turnover 36	31.6	•	80.3	72.9	33.7	40.7	18.3	17.5	•	•	12.7	33.4
Total Liabilities to Net Worth 37	4.6	•	3.4	0.9	1.2	1.0	1.0	1.6	1.6	3.4	2.9	8.9
Current Assets to Working Capital 38	3.1	•	1.9	1.6	1.5	1.8	2.4	1.9	2.5	2.0	2.8	4.8
Current Liabilities to Working Capital 39	2.1	•	0.9	0.6	0.5	0.8	1.4	0.9	1.5	1.0	1.8	3.8
Working Capital to Net Sales 40	0.1	•	0.1	0.3	0.2	0.2	0.1	0.4	0.1	0.1	0.1	0.1
Inventory to Working Capital 41	1.9	•	1.3	1.0	1.0	1.4	1.3	1.1	1.8	1.5	2.2	2.7
Total Receipts to Cash Flow 42	8.4	5.9	6.4	8.0	7.7	12.2	10.1	4.3	8.9	7.7	7.9	8.8
Cost of Goods to Cash Flow 43	5.1	3.7	3.8	5.1	4.5	9.1	7.6	2.5	5.1	4.3	5.0	5.3
Cash Flow to Total Debt 44	0.3	•	0.6	0.5	0.5	0.3	0.5	0.4	0.4	0.4	0.4	0.2

Selected Financial Factors (in Percentages)

Debt Ratio 45	82.1	•	77.3	47.9	54.0	50.9	49.8	60.8	62.1	77.3	74.3	89.9
Return on Total Assets 46	9.9	•	18.3	9.9	9.6	7.6	11.9	6.3	6.8	10.1	10.7	9.5
Return on Equity Before Income Taxes 47	35.9	•	69.0	17.7	17.5	11.5	22.6	11.8	13.8	39.8	32.3	53.3
Return on Equity After Income Taxes 48	29.5	•	68.5	17.2	16.6	11.0	21.6	7.9	13.4	33.5	22.1	40.8
Profit Margin (Before Income Tax) 49	3.7	5.5	4.9	4.6	4.1	3.1	4.3	4.5	2.4	3.6	4.0	3.5
Profit Margin (After Income Tax) 50	3.0	5.5	4.8	4.5	3.8	2.9	4.1	3.0	2.3	3.1	2.7	2.7

Table I

Corporations with and without Net Income

GENERAL MERCHANDISE STORES

MONEY AMOUNTS AND SIZE OF ASSETS IN THOUSANDS OF DOLLARS

Item Description for Accounting Period 7/09 Through 6/10	Total	Zero Assets	Under 500	500 to 1,000	1,000 to 5,000	5,000 to 10,000	10,000 to 25,000	25,000 to 50,000	50,000 to 100,000	100,000 to 250,000	250,000 to 500,000	500,000 to 2,500,000	2,500,000 and over
Number of Enterprises 1	9453	1352	7106	551	293	70	19	16	7	9	6	10	13
Revenues ($ in Thousands)													
Net Sales 2	614028670	55036	1972619	552865	1583431	2019967	405939	1568428	1009173	3520044	3562429	33904182	56384556
Interest 3	2918383	4	1030	741	1319	1795	4	648	10721	180	5969	6190	2889781
Rents 4	871603	0	0	0	0	0	501	493	7150	4378	645	43176	815261
Royalties 5	1821823	0	0	0	92	0	0	0	183	0	396	91867	1729286
Other Portfolio Income 6	427099	1355	13019	146	376	327	1418	92	14813	5809	985	10281	378476
Other Receipts 7	13902987	4687	5688	10744	10952	7243	1459	5167	37377	30679	21281	543565	13224148
Total Receipts 8	633970565	61082	1992356	564496	1596170	2029332	409321	1574828	1079417	3561090	3591705	34599261	582911508
Average Total Receipts 9	67066	45	280	1024	5448	28990	21543	98427	154202	395677	598618	3459926	44839347
Operating Costs/Operating Income (%)													
Cost of Operations 10	73.0	97.3	59.8	73.7	61.0	62.3	43.8	74.1	60.3	66.5	70.0	71.1	73.3
Salaries and Wages 11	11.0	7.2	6.0	8.2	10.5	15.4	21.6	10.2	15.4	11.2	12.2	10.6	11.0
Taxes Paid 12	1.9	4.8	2.4	1.5	1.5	1.4	3.5	1.3	2.9	1.6	1.5	2.3	1.8
Interest Paid 13	1.0	13.7	0.5	1.1	1.1	0.0	0.8	0.4	0.3	0.6	0.7	0.5	1.1
Depreciation 14	2.1	0.5	1.2	0.5	0.7	0.4	1.0	1.1	1.6	2.3	1.8	1.9	2.1
Amortization and Depletion 15	0.0	•	0.1	0.3	0.1	0.0	•	0.2	0.0	0.0	0.1	0.1	0.0
Pensions and Other Deferred Comp. 16	0.5	•	•	0.2	0.9	0.2	0.2	0.1	0.4	0.1	0.1	0.2	0.5
Employee Benefits 17	1.0	0.0	0.1	0.8	0.7	1.7	1.1	0.9	1.3	1.5	1.8	1.1	0.9
Advertising 18	1.3	3.2	0.7	0.2	1.3	2.1	0.6	0.9	1.9	1.5	1.1	1.0	1.3
Other Expenses 19	7.4	27.8	23.1	11.6	17.2	16.9	21.0	12.2	20.3	11.5	8.6	9.4	7.1
Officers' Compensation 20	0.1	3.6	7.8	2.7	3.1	0.2	0.9	0.4	0.2	1.4	0.6	0.3	0.0
Operating Margin 21	0.7	•	•	•	1.8	•	5.6	•	•	1.9	1.4	1.5	0.7
Operating Margin Before Officers' Comp. 22	0.8	•	6.2	1.9	4.9	•	6.4	•	•	3.3	2.0	1.8	0.8

Selected Average Balance Sheet ($ in Thousands)

Net Receivables **23**	1610	0	0	66	141	810	550	925	10389	13469	28349	27056	1109509
Inventories **24**	7280	0	55	186	1087	2200	3640	16213	23971	65461	107194	493954	4706636
Net Property, Plant and Equipment **25**	11090	0	26	50	390	798	2775	4597	10874	47241	56351	433365	7627306
Total Assets **26**	36271	108	620	1789	5421	12791	34912	67896	168950	319762	1377687	24797267	
Notes and Loans Payable **27**	9184	57	322	564	300	1965	8910	12150	34704	53347	234637	6369129	
All Other Liabilities **28**	12443	24	52	427	2158	6493	62961	27922	53911	88664	467091	8472090	
Net Worth **29**	14644	26	245	799	2963	4332	-36959	27824	80335	177751	675960	9956049	

Selected Financial Ratios (Times to 1)

Current Ratio **30**	1.1	2.2	3.0	3.0	1.0	2.4	1.2	0.4	2.1	1.6	1.4	1.8	1.0
Quick Ratio **31**	0.3	0.5	1.1	1.0	0.7	0.7	0.1	•	1.0	0.4	0.4	0.4	0.3
Net Sales to Working Capital **32**	106.6	6.7	4.2	6.6	12.3	19.5	•	5.2	11.7	13.9	10.1	412.4	
Coverage Ratio **33**	5.2	•	2.2	3.4	•	8.4	•	9.1	6.5	4.3	7.9	5.1	
Total Asset Turnover **34**	1.8	2.6	1.6	3.0	3.0	5.3	1.7	2.8	2.1	2.3	1.9	2.5	1.7
Inventory Turnover **35**	6.5	3.0	4.0	3.0	8.2	2.6	4.5	3.6	4.0	3.9	4.9	6.8	
Receivables Turnover **36**	44.4	771.5	12.2	34.6	55.3	26.1	114.1	14.5	28.5	20.2	114.7	43.3	
Total Liabilities to Net Worth **37**	1.5	3.1	1.5	1.2	0.8	2.0	•	1.4	1.1	0.8	1.0	1.5	
Current Assets to Working Capital **38**	19.3	1.8	1.5	1.5	1.7	6.4	•	1.9	2.8	3.3	2.2	73.2	
Current Liabilities to Working Capital **39**	18.3	0.8	0.5	0.5	0.7	5.4	•	0.9	1.8	2.3	1.2	72.2	
Working Capital to Net Sales **40**	0.0	0.1	0.2	0.2	0.1	0.1	•	0.2	0.1	0.1	0.1	0.0	
Inventory to Working Capital **41**	11.7	1.3	0.7	1.0	1.2	1.9	•	0.7	2.0	2.2	1.5	43.9	
Total Receipts to Cash Flow **42**	11.2	9.6	11.7	7.1	8.7	4.9	25.3	7.5	9.8	12.6	11.6	11.2	
Cost of Goods to Cash Flow **43**	8.2	5.8	8.6	4.3	5.4	2.2	18.7	4.5	6.5	8.8	8.3	8.2	
Cash Flow to Total Debt **44**	0.3	0.4	0.2	0.8	1.4	0.5	0.1	0.5	0.5	0.3	0.4	0.3	

Selected Financial Factors (in Percentages)

Debt Ratio **45**	59.6	75.6	60.5	55.4	45.3	66.1	205.9	59.0	52.5	44.4	50.9	59.9	
Return on Total Assets **46**	9.7	•	4.0	11.2	•	11.8	•	6.0	8.5	5.5	10.0	9.8	
Return on Equity Before Income Taxes **47**	19.4	•	5.5	17.7	•	30.6	3.8	12.9	15.0	7.5	17.9	19.7	
Return on Equity After Income Taxes **48**	12.5	•	5.0	16.7	•	30.6	4.1	6.4	13.3	6.4	11.1	12.7	
Profit Margin (Before Income Tax) **49**	4.4	•	1.3	2.6	2.6	6.2	•	2.5	3.1	2.3	3.6	4.5	
Profit Margin (After Income Tax) **50**	2.8	•	1.2	2.5	2.5	6.2	•	1.2	2.7	1.9	2.2	2.9	

Table II

Corporations with Net Income

GENERAL MERCHANDISE STORES

MONEY AMOUNTS AND SIZE OF ASSETS IN THOUSANDS OF DOLLARS

Item Description for Accounting Period 7/09 Through 6/10		Total	Zero Assets	Under 500	500 to 1,000	1,000 to 5,000	5,000 to 10,000	10,000 to 25,000	25,000 to 50,000	50,000 to 100,000	100,000 to 250,000	250,000 to 500,000	500,000 to 2,500,000	2,500,000 and over
Number of Enterprises	1	4140	211	3213	452	154	53	10	•	3	•	•	•	•
Revenues ($ in Thousands)														
Net Sales	2	563221194	19160	996645	321059	1251878	1704940	385686	•	723908	•	•	•	•
Interest	3	2901799	0	104	579	774	643	0	•	21	•	•	•	•
Rents	4	789780	0	0	0	0	0	0	•	0	•	•	•	•
Royalties	5	1796134	0	0	0	92	0	0	•	183	•	•	•	•
Other Portfolio Income	6	356463	1032	0	140	90	321	1	•	1	•	•	•	•
Other Receipts	7	12889146	4686	1091	10587	9165	1287	482	•	26693	•	•	•	•
Total Receipts	8	581954516	24878	997840	332365	1261999	1707191	386169	•	750806	•	•	•	•
Average Total Receipts	9	140569	118	311	735	8195	32211	38617	•	250269	•	•	•	•
Operating Costs/Operating Income (%)														
Cost of Operations	10	73.4	54.7	57.4	63.7	63.1	59.7	42.7	•	58.2	•	•	•	•
Salaries and Wages	11	10.8	11.4	3.9	10.3	9.1	16.7	21.5	•	15.9	•	•	•	•
Taxes Paid	12	1.8	10.3	2.2	1.8	1.2	1.3	3.4	•	3.3	•	•	•	•
Interest Paid	13	1.1	•	0.2	1.8	0.6	0.1	0.0	•	0.1	•	•	•	•
Depreciation	14	2.1	0.8	1.1	0.8	0.4	0.4	0.4	•	1.5	•	•	•	•
Amortization and Depletion	15	0.0	•	0.0	0.5	0.0	0.0	•	•	0.0	•	•	•	•
Pensions and Other Deferred Comp.	16	0.5	•	•	0.3	1.0	0.0	0.1	•	0.2	•	•	•	•
Employee Benefits	17	1.0	•	0.0	1.2	0.6	1.7	1.0	•	0.9	•	•	•	•
Advertising	18	1.1	•	1.0	0.3	1.2	2.2	0.4	•	1.9	•	•	•	•
Other Expenses	19	7.0	20.2	16.9	15.8	17.4	16.9	19.3	•	15.3	•	•	•	•
Officers' Compensation	20	0.1	2.4	7.5	4.2	2.5	0.1	0.8	•	0.1	•	•	•	•
Operating Margin	21	1.2	0.2	9.8	•	2.9	1.0	10.4	•	2.7	•	•	•	•
Operating Margin Before Officers' Comp.	22	1.3	2.6	17.3	3.5	5.4	1.0	11.3	•	2.7	•	•	•	•

Selected Average Balance Sheet ($ in Thousands)

	C1	C2	C3	C4	C5	C6	C7	C8
Net Receivables 23	3516	0	0	59	253	1042	997	15456
Inventories 24	13879	0	48	160	1468	1823	5248	34997
Net Property, Plant and Equipment 25	23087	0	35	61	140	684	1060	11725
Total Assets 26	74495	0	108	620	1952	5446	12617	78688
Notes and Loans Payable 27	18135	0	27	292	405	396	0	506
All Other Liabilities 28	24779	0	11	31	557	1460	1988	26901
Net Worth 29	31582	0	70	297	991	3590	10629	51281

Selected Financial Ratios (Times to 1)

	C1	C2	C3	C4	C5	C6	C7	C8
Current Ratio 30	1.1	•	4.1	3.0	3.2	2.9	6.5	2.5
Quick Ratio 31	0.3	•	1.4	1.2	1.2	0.8	4.5	0.9
Net Sales to Working Capital 32	77.9	•	5.7	3.4	7.2	10.8	4.0	6.3
Coverage Ratio 33	5.7	•	45.5	2.5	7.3	21.6	222.6	44.3
Total Asset Turnover 34	1.8	•	2.9	1.1	4.2	5.9	3.1	3.1
Inventory Turnover 35	7.2	•	3.7	2.8	3.5	10.5	3.1	4.0
Receivables Turnover 36	43.2	•	3384.2	16.8	28.3	59.1	26.3	•
Total Liabilities to Net Worth 37	1.4	•	0.5	1.1	1.0	0.5	0.2	0.5
Current Assets to Working Capital 38	13.5	•	1.3	1.5	1.4	1.5	1.2	1.7
Current Liabilities to Working Capital 39	12.5	•	0.3	0.5	0.4	0.5	0.2	0.7
Working Capital to Net Sales 40	0.0	•	0.2	0.3	0.1	0.1	0.3	0.2
Inventory to Working Capital 41	8.0	•	0.9	0.7	0.9	1.1	0.3	0.9
Total Receipts to Cash Flow 42	11.0	2.7	5.4	8.3	6.3	7.3	4.2	7.1
Cost of Goods to Cash Flow 43	8.0	1.5	3.1	5.3	4.0	4.3	1.8	4.2
Cash Flow to Total Debt 44	0.3	•	1.5	0.3	1.3	2.4	4.6	1.2

Selected Financial Factors (in Percentages)

	C1	C2	C3	C4	C5	C6	C7	C8
Debt Ratio 45	57.6	•	35.0	52.2	49.2	34.1	15.8	34.8
Return on Total Assets 46	10.9	•	29.2	5.3	17.8	6.7	32.5	20.0
Return on Equity Before Income Taxes 47	21.2	•	43.9	6.8	30.3	9.7	38.4	30.0
Return on Equity After Income Taxes 48	13.9	•	42.2	6.3	28.7	9.3	38.4	21.8
Profit Margin (Before Income Tax) 49	4.9	30.1	10.0	2.8	3.7	1.1	10.6	6.4
Profit Margin (After Income Tax) 50	3.2	30.1	9.6	2.6	3.5	1.0	10.6	4.6

Table I

Corporations with and without Net Income

MISCELLANEOUS STORE RETAILERS

MONEY AMOUNTS AND SIZE OF ASSETS IN THOUSANDS OF DOLLARS

Item Description for Accounting Period 7/09 Through 6/10	Total	Zero Assets	Under 500	500 to 1,000	1,000 to 5,000	5,000 to 10,000	10,000 to 25,000	25,000 to 50,000	50,000 to 100,000	100,000 to 250,000	250,000 to 500,000	500,000 to 2,500,000	2,500,000 and over
Number of Enterprises **1**	80542	12246	60584	3810	3248	368	179	50	23	16	9	6	3
Revenues ($ in Thousands)													
Net Sales **2**	107675079	1947989	24290791	5768308	11342819	3428966	5669979	3245258	2903511	3657691	4046671	10435136	30937961
Interest **3**	238867	218	6180	1339	25007	4191	2707	1019	1201	3827	4715	13932	174531
Rents **4**	41420	0	693	3986	7198	1160	7597	851	74	2825	3727	1881	11428
Royalties **5**	166916	0	1	0	1820	19762	412	7961	33999	0	1234	32173	69554
Other Portfolio Income **6**	483207	11153	13074	3208	11415	5767	4614	5698	5779	5336	0	4765	412398
Other Receipts **7**	1084633	79150	100180	48203	157417	29045	59815	77708	79972	20356	50578	264193	118014
Total Receipts **8**	109690122	2038510	24410919	5825044	11545676	3488891	5745124	3338495	3024536	3690035	4106925	10752080	31723886
Average Total Receipts **9**	1362	166	403	1529	3555	9481	32096	66770	131502	230627	456325	1792013	10574629
Operating Costs/Operating Income (%)													
Cost of Operations **10**	62.3	61.0	56.1	65.0	65.5	67.2	72.1	67.2	63.7	54.0	58.5	49.8	68.4
Salaries and Wages **11**	11.7	10.7	11.3	12.3	11.6	11.3	10.0	10.7	10.8	14.3	12.2	17.5	10.1
Taxes Paid **12**	2.1	1.9	2.6	2.1	2.3	2.2	1.5	1.9	1.5	2.4	1.8	3.1	1.4
Interest Paid **13**	1.4	2.3	0.7	1.2	1.0	1.6	0.8	1.2	1.4	3.5	2.5	2.3	1.3
Depreciation **14**	1.6	4.2	1.1	1.1	1.0	1.3	1.3	1.4	2.6	2.1	1.8	3.1	1.6
Amortization and Depletion **15**	0.2	0.2	0.2	0.1	0.2	0.4	0.1	0.2	0.2	0.3	0.3	0.4	0.3
Pensions and Other Deferred Comp. **16**	0.1	0.2	0.1	0.0	0.2	0.4	0.2	0.2	0.3	0.1	0.1	0.1	0.0
Employee Benefits **17**	1.0	0.8	0.7	0.7	0.7	0.8	0.5	0.9	1.2	1.8	1.2	1.5	1.2
Advertising **18**	1.8	3.6	1.3	1.3	0.8	0.7	0.8	1.2	3.4	2.6	3.3	2.0	2.3
Other Expenses **19**	15.7	14.6	21.0	14.8	13.8	14.6	9.9	14.0	17.0	15.4	15.4	18.2	12.9
Officers' Compensation **20**	2.2	1.8	5.3	3.4	4.1	2.8	1.9	1.2	1.0	0.9	0.5	0.3	0.0
Operating Margin **21**	•	•	•	•	•	•	1.0	•	•	2.5	2.4	1.5	0.4
Operating Margin Before Officers' Comp. **22**	2.1	0.4	4.9	1.3	2.8	•	2.9	1.0	•	3.4	2.9	1.8	0.4

Selected Average Balance Sheet ($ in Thousands)

Net Receivables 23	94	0	9	93	282	1053	2615	5598	14497	16092	33832	106182	1032308
Inventories 24	206	0	42	319	792	3566	6514	11818	22381	44525	89317	264069	1191131
Net Property, Plant and Equipment 25	126	0	20	127	352	1135	2215	6474	13780	38864	34958	360110	920138
Total Assets 26	733	0	105	703	2116	7067	15123	35280	68711	162084	345997	1522308	6532347
Notes and Loans Payable 27	290	0	72	375	651	2657	5448	13717	27288	106760	150551	564228	1894269
All Other Liabilities 28	226	0	30	171	510	2111	4371	8558	27999	54881	108349	421010	2359004
Net Worth 29	217	0	3	157	955	2299	5304	13005	13423	442	87097	537069	2279074

Selected Financial Ratios (Times to 1)

Current Ratio 30	1.9	•	1.8	1.9	2.1	2.2	1.9	1.7	1.4	1.4	2.1	1.5	2.3
Quick Ratio 31	0.8	•	0.7	0.7	0.8	0.6	0.8	0.7	0.6	0.5	0.8	0.7	1.1
Net Sales to Working Capital 32	6.9	•	13.0	6.5	4.6	3.1	6.0	7.5	10.1	10.2	4.0	11.3	5.7
Coverage Ratio 33	2.5	2.4	1.1	0.0	1.5	0.0	3.8	3.3	1.7	2.0	2.6	3.0	3.7
Total Asset Turnover 34	1.8	•	3.8	2.2	1.7	1.3	2.1	1.8	1.8	1.4	1.3	1.1	1.6
Inventory Turnover 35	4.0	•	5.4	3.1	2.9	1.8	3.5	3.7	3.6	2.8	2.9	3.3	5.9
Receivables Turnover 36	15.4	•	41.5	15.8	11.3	8.1	12.3	10.2	9.5	13.8	20.0	13.4	13.6
Total Liabilities to Net Worth 37	2.4	•	29.9	3.5	1.2	2.1	1.9	1.7	4.1	365.7	3.0	1.8	1.9
Current Assets to Working Capital 38	2.1	•	2.2	2.2	1.9	1.8	2.1	2.5	3.6	3.7	1.9	3.2	1.8
Current Liabilities to Working Capital 39	1.1	•	1.2	1.2	0.9	0.8	1.1	1.5	2.6	2.7	0.9	2.2	0.8
Working Capital to Net Sales 40	0.1	•	0.1	0.2	0.2	0.3	0.2	0.1	0.1	0.1	0.3	0.1	0.2
Inventory to Working Capital 41	1.0	•	1.3	1.3	1.0	1.2	1.1	1.2	1.7	1.9	1.0	1.4	0.6
Total Receipts to Cash Flow 42	9.0	10.6	8.0	13.3	9.7	11.7	12.6	8.9	7.2	8.6	8.6	7.6	9.2
Cost of Goods to Cash Flow 43	5.6	6.5	4.5	8.7	6.4	7.9	9.1	6.0	4.6	4.7	5.1	3.8	6.3
Cash Flow to Total Debt 44	0.3	•	0.5	0.2	0.3	0.2	0.3	0.3	0.3	0.2	0.2	0.2	0.3

Selected Financial Factors (in Percentages)

Debt Ratio 45	70.3	•	96.8	77.6	54.9	67.5	64.9	63.1	80.5	99.7	74.8	64.7	65.1
Return on Total Assets 46	6.2	•	2.9	0.1	2.6	0.0	6.5	7.2	4.6	9.8	8.2	8.1	7.8
Return on Equity Before Income Taxes 47	12.4	•	8.4	•	1.8	•	13.7	13.5	10.1	1752.7	19.9	15.5	16.4
Return on Equity After Income Taxes 48	7.9	•	4.8	•	1.2	•	12.5	11.4	6.9	1191.8	16.7	9.9	9.8
Profit Margin (Before Income Tax) 49	2.0	3.2	0.1	•	0.5	•	2.3	2.7	1.1	3.4	3.9	4.8	3.6
Profit Margin (After Income Tax) 50	1.3	2.6	0.0	•	0.3	•	2.1	2.3	0.7	2.3	3.2	3.1	2.2

Table II
Corporations with Net Income

MISCELLANEOUS STORE RETAILERS

Money Amounts and Size of Assets in Thousands of Dollars

Item Description for Accounting Period 7/09 Through 6/10	Total	Zero Assets	Under 500	500 to 1,000	1,000 to 5,000	5,000 to 10,000	10,000 to 25,000	25,000 to 50,000	50,000 to 100,000	100,000 to 250,000	250,000 to 500,000	500,000 to 2,500,000	2,500,000 and over
Number of Enterprises 1	36138	3890	27891	1914	2076	175	121	•	16	11	5	•	0
Revenues ($ in Thousands)													
Net Sales 2	71472519	1284803	15388692	3286646	8245391	1964235	4709442	•	2200653	3152710	2422511	•	0
Interest 3	46383	54	2704	677	21396	440	2634	•	638	1674	3382	•	0
Rents 4	23163	0	693	1267	2648	0	7303	•	73	335	0	•	0
Royalties 5	129455	0	0	0	1820	0	197	•	33999	0	0	•	0
Other Portfolio Income 6	421207	3	12687	659	6874	1784	2177	•	5752	3720	0	•	0
Other Receipts 7	656705	62367	76799	26905	108079	23845	50979	•	39372	16665	41982	•	0
Total Receipts 8	72749432	1347227	15481575	3316154	8386208	1990304	4772732	•	2280487	3175104	2467875	•	0
Average Total Receipts 9	2013	346	555	1733	4040	11373	39444	•	142530	288646	493575	•	•
Operating Costs/Operating Income (%)													
Cost of Operations 10	59.2	50.8	53.3	65.6	62.9	69.6	70.5	•	58.4	53.4	56.3	•	•
Salaries and Wages 11	12.2	12.3	11.1	11.5	12.0	8.6	10.8	•	11.2	14.7	12.4	•	•
Taxes Paid 12	2.1	2.0	2.6	1.8	2.3	1.4	1.6	•	1.6	2.1	2.0	•	•
Interest Paid 13	1.2	2.3	0.7	1.1	0.7	1.0	0.5	•	0.9	3.3	2.3	•	•
Depreciation 14	1.7	5.7	0.9	1.0	0.9	0.9	1.2	•	3.1	1.8	1.4	•	•
Amortization and Depletion 15	0.2	0.0	0.2	0.0	0.2	0.0	0.0	•	0.2	0.2	0.1	•	•
Pensions and Other Deferred Comp. 16	0.1	0.3	0.1	0.0	0.3	0.2	0.2	•	0.3	0.2	0.2	•	•
Employee Benefits 17	1.0	1.0	0.7	0.7	0.7	0.3	0.5	•	1.4	1.6	1.3	•	•
Advertising 18	1.6	4.7	1.1	0.9	0.7	0.5	0.8	•	4.1	2.8	2.0	•	•
Other Expenses 19	14.7	8.9	19.2	10.8	12.8	12.6	8.8	•	17.8	15.3	14.7	•	•
Officers' Compensation 20	2.2	1.0	5.4	3.9	4.2	2.6	2.0	•	0.7	0.9	0.7	•	•
Operating Margin 21	3.9	11.0	4.8	2.6	2.4	2.2	2.9	•	0.3	3.6	6.7	•	•
Operating Margin Before Officers' Comp. 22	6.1	12.0	10.1	6.5	6.6	4.8	4.9	•	1.0	4.6	7.4	•	•

Selected Average Balance Sheet ($ in Thousands)

Net Receivables 23	110	0	11	141	350	1351	2775	•	10961	14232	45505
Inventories 24	269	0	47	239	765	4934	6268	•	18449	50611	144510
Net Property, Plant and Equipment 25	165	0	24	163	235	510	2112	•	16928	35560	33949
Total Assets 26	938	0	127	731	2068	6992	15083	•	69788	156494	372866
Notes and Loans Payable 27	331	0	52	337	543	2476	4215	•	19506	117717	132159
All Other Liabilities 28	206	0	30	191	431	2535	4544	•	29355	48610	130685
Net Worth 29	401	0	45	203	1093	1981	6324	•	20927	-9833	110022

Selected Financial Ratios (Times to 1)

Current Ratio 30	2.1	•	2.2	1.8	2.2	2.2	1.8	•	1.2	1.6	1.8
Quick Ratio 31	0.8	•	0.9	0.9	1.0	0.5	0.9	•	0.5	0.6	0.5
Net Sales to Working Capital 32	7.3	•	12.1	8.0	5.1	3.3	7.7	•	20.9	8.2	4.4
Coverage Ratio 33	5.8	8.0	9.1	4.1	6.7	4.6	9.0	•	5.4	2.3	4.8
Total Asset Turnover 34	2.1	•	4.3	2.3	1.9	1.6	2.6	•	2.0	1.8	1.3
Inventory Turnover 35	4.3	•	6.2	4.7	3.3	1.6	4.4	•	4.4	3.0	1.9
Receivables Turnover 36	19.1	•	43.9	13.7	10.3	6.7	13.1	•	14.0	19.0	•
Total Liabilities to Net Worth 37	1.3	•	1.9	2.6	0.9	2.5	1.4	•	2.3	•	2.4
Current Assets to Working Capital 38	1.9	•	1.8	2.2	1.8	1.9	2.2	•	6.2	2.7	2.2
Current Liabilities to Working Capital 39	0.9	•	0.8	1.2	0.8	0.9	1.2	•	5.2	1.7	1.2
Working Capital to Net Sales 40	0.1	•	0.1	0.1	0.2	0.3	0.1	•	0.0	0.1	0.2
Inventory to Working Capital 41	0.9	•	1.0	1.1	0.9	1.3	1.0	•	3.4	1.3	1.3
Total Receipts to Cash Flow 42	6.8	5.9	5.7	9.6	7.7	8.8	11.3	•	5.8	7.8	6.0
Cost of Goods to Cash Flow 43	4.0	3.0	3.0	6.3	4.8	6.1	8.0	•	3.4	4.2	3.4
Cash Flow to Total Debt 44	0.5	•	1.2	0.3	0.5	0.3	0.4	•	0.5	0.2	0.3

Selected Financial Factors (in Percentages)

Debt Ratio 45	57.2	•	64.9	72.3	47.1	71.7	58.1	•	70.0	106.3	70.5
Return on Total Assets 46	15.1	•	26.2	10.9	9.3	7.3	12.5	•	9.4	14.0	14.1
Return on Equity Before Income Taxes 47	29.2	•	66.3	29.7	15.0	20.1	26.4	•	25.6	•	37.7
Return on Equity After Income Taxes 48	23.9	•	65.7	28.4	14.1	19.4	24.9	•	22.7	•	33.1
Profit Margin (Before Income Tax) 49	5.9	15.8	5.4	3.5	4.1	3.6	4.3	•	3.9	4.3	8.6
Profit Margin (After Income Tax) 50	4.8	14.9	5.3	3.3	3.9	3.4	4.1	•	3.5	3.1	7.5

Table I

Corporations with and without Net Income

NONSTORE RETAILERS

MONEY AMOUNTS AND SIZE OF ASSETS IN THOUSANDS OF DOLLARS

Item Description for Accounting Period 7/09 Through 6/10		Total	Zero Assets	Under 500	500 to 1,000	1,000 to 5,000	5,000 to 10,000	10,000 to 25,000	25,000 to 50,000	50,000 to 100,000	100,000 to 250,000	250,000 to 500,000	500,000 to 2,500,000	2,500,000 and over
Number of Enterprises	1	51893	14714	32305	2113	2107	284	173	69	51	34	12	15	14
Revenues ($ in Thousands)														
Net Sales	2	162886189	2707573	15150049	6964578	17035277	5111910	7609760	5333759	8062619	11212459	8647939	13643671	61406594
Interest	3	1315981	564	2078	6122	4736	3604	2838	5002	8512	23642	132028	121476	1005378
Rents	4	86415	0	0	10107	926	2837	1696	1693	8945	3515	183	3574	52939
Royalties	5	1268872	603	0	18407	0	361	0	0	5715	680	0	84297	1158810
Other Portfolio Income	6	1221416	29978	68069	15572	39979	3773	18150	8151	22073	1669	69	98537	915392
Other Receipts	7	3048046	41719	44099	21580	165561	72314	46316	25811	161151	157783	93835	352955	1864928
Total Receipts	8	169826919	2780437	15526295	7036366	17246479	5194799	7678760	5374416	8269015	11399748	8874054	14304510	66404041
Average Total Receipts	9	3273	189	473	3330	8185	18292	44386	77890	162138	335287	739504	953634	4743146
Operating Costs/Operating Income (%)														
Cost of Operations	10	68.0	52.5	68.8	70.8	71.5	62.6	62.9	66.8	65.3	68.9	76.8	64.5	68.1
Salaries and Wages	11	8.4	13.4	5.1	7.6	8.3	11.1	9.6	7.9	7.6	8.7	6.2	10.7	8.6
Taxes Paid	12	1.1	2.4	1.3	1.9	1.2	1.3	1.2	1.0	1.2	1.0	0.7	1.2	0.9
Interest Paid	13	1.8	0.6	0.6	0.3	0.7	0.7	0.4	0.5	0.9	0.8	1.6	2.1	3.3
Depreciation	14	1.3	1.3	1.0	0.8	1.1	2.0	1.4	1.4	1.5	1.1	1.0	1.7	1.4
Amortization and Depletion	15	0.5	0.6	0.2	0.0	0.2	0.3	0.2	0.4	0.6	0.5	0.6	0.7	0.7
Pensions and Other Deferred Comp.	16	0.2	0.0	0.1	0.5	0.1	0.1	0.2	0.1	0.2	0.2	0.1	1.1	0.1
Employee Benefits	17	0.8	1.1	0.5	0.8	0.4	1.0	0.8	1.2	0.8	0.7	0.5	1.3	0.9
Advertising	18	2.8	4.6	1.9	1.1	2.5	4.5	4.5	3.6	3.5	3.4	3.5	4.0	2.1
Other Expenses	19	14.7	25.1	15.0	10.2	11.2	12.2	15.5	15.5	16.2	13.2	8.8	17.9	15.8
Officers' Compensation	20	1.5	2.7	5.3	4.3	1.8	2.3	1.2	1.0	1.0	1.0	0.5	0.4	0.6
Operating Margin	21	•	•	0.2	1.8	1.0	2.0	2.1	0.7	1.1	0.4	•	•	•
Operating Margin Before Officers' Comp.	22	0.4	5.5	5.5	6.1	2.7	4.3	3.3	1.7	2.2	1.3	0.3	•	•

Selected Average Balance Sheet ($ in Thousands)

Net Receivables 23	1386	0	10	195	724	1610	2693	7491	12499	28061	78932	153951	4526842
Inventories 24	502	0	23	155	415	1435	2471	7927	11943	33505	64468	72864	1364148
Net Property, Plant and Equipment 25	228	0	14	84	424	1577	2660	3539	9725	13496	22826	71500	487331
Total Assets 26	8256	0	76	720	2250	6758	15097	33681	70060	144732	371230	966323	27529819
Notes and Loans Payable 27	2150	0	47	113	900	2741	3777	6208	17654	33352	110685	290821	7023150
All Other Liabilities 28	2801	0	28	230	916	3326	6254	14478	23510	51032	107468	313560	9291718
Net Worth 29	3305	0	1	377	434	691	5066	12995	28895	60347	153077	361942	11214951

Selected Financial Ratios (Times to 1)

Current Ratio 30	1.7	•	1.7	1.9	1.3	1.1	1.5	1.4	1.8	1.5	2.0	1.3	1.7
Quick Ratio 31	1.0	•	0.9	1.5	0.9	0.6	0.9	0.8	1.1	0.8	1.2	0.9	1.1
Net Sales to Working Capital 32	1.9	•	20.9	13.8	20.0	71.8	14.6	10.8	8.4	10.8	7.4	9.8	0.8
Coverage Ratio 33	3.0	•	2.7	10.3	4.2	6.2	8.2	4.3	5.2	3.7	2.6	0.9	2.9
Total Asset Turnover 34	0.4	•	6.2	4.6	3.6	2.7	2.9	2.3	2.3	2.3	1.9	0.9	0.2
Inventory Turnover 35	4.3	•	14.0	15.0	13.9	7.8	11.2	6.5	8.6	6.8	8.6	8.1	2.2
Receivables Turnover 36	3.7	•	58.6	16.9	11.9	9.2	17.0	9.5	12.6	11.4	7.7	6.7	1.7
Total Liabilities to Net Worth 37	1.5	•	67.3	0.9	4.2	8.8	2.0	1.6	1.4	1.4	1.4	1.7	1.5
Current Assets to Working Capital 38	2.5	•	2.5	2.1	3.9	17.4	3.1	3.3	2.2	2.9	2.0	4.0	2.4
Current Liabilities to Working Capital 39	1.5	•	1.5	1.1	2.9	16.4	2.1	2.3	1.2	1.9	1.0	3.0	1.4
Working Capital to Net Sales 40	0.5	•	0.0	0.1	0.0	0.0	0.1	0.1	0.1	0.1	0.1	0.1	1.3
Inventory to Working Capital 41	0.5	•	1.0	0.4	1.0	5.5	0.7	0.9	0.6	1.1	0.6	0.8	0.5
Total Receipts to Cash Flow 42	6.2	5.2	7.4	8.9	8.9	7.2	6.1	6.4	5.5	7.3	9.7	6.7	5.0
Cost of Goods to Cash Flow 43	4.2	2.7	5.1	6.3	6.3	4.5	3.8	4.3	3.6	5.0	7.5	4.3	3.4
Cash Flow to Total Debt 44	0.1	•	0.8	1.1	0.5	0.4	0.7	0.6	0.7	0.5	0.3	0.2	0.1

Selected Financial Factors (in Percentages)

Debt Ratio 45	60.0	•	98.5	47.7	80.7	89.8	66.4	61.4	58.8	58.3	58.8	62.5	59.3
Return on Total Assets 46	2.1	•	9.3	14.4	10.3	11.4	10.1	4.6	10.3	7.2	7.8	1.8	1.6
Return on Equity Before Income Taxes 47	3.4	•	400.3	24.8	40.8	93.3	26.5	9.1	20.3	12.6	11.5	•	2.5
Return on Equity After Income Taxes 48	2.5	•	388.1	23.6	37.6	90.4	23.5	7.8	15.0	8.7	8.2	•	1.8
Profit Margin (Before Income Tax) 49	3.6	•	1.0	2.8	2.2	3.6	3.0	1.5	3.7	2.3	2.4	•	6.4
Profit Margin (After Income Tax) 50	2.6	•	0.9	2.7	2.0	3.5	2.7	1.3	2.7	1.6	1.7	•	4.5

Table II
Corporations with Net Income

NONSTORE RETAILERS

MONEY AMOUNTS AND SIZE OF ASSETS IN THOUSANDS OF DOLLARS

Item Description for Accounting Period 7/09 Through 6/10	Total	Zero Assets	Under 500	500 to 1,000	1,000 to 5,000	5,000 to 10,000	10,000 to 25,000	25,000 to 50,000	50,000 to 100,000	100,000 to 250,000	250,000 to 500,000	500,000 to 2,500,000	2,500,000 and over
Number of Enterprises **1**	22035	3998	14500	1488	1553	241	123	•	38	25	9	11	•
Revenues ($ in Thousands)													
Net Sales **2**	137162207	1769525	9395118	6112722	13976861	4685531	5823924	•	7018140	9122230	6603691	12177786	•
Interest **3**	1271797	381	1867	1848	3428	2695	2389	•	7777	21786	128845	113725	•
Rents **4**	82328	0	0	9162	859	2837	1598	•	8762	3411	58	3573	•
Royalties **5**	1232072	603	0	0	0	0	0	•	5715	680	0	66264	•
Other Portfolio Income **6**	1146599	27150	28155	12922	23538	3662	17745	•	19696	1260	37	95594	•
Other Receipts **7**	2809927	8575	29964	16553	126613	64741	37592	•	145225	88694	105350	301737	•
Total Receipts **8**	143704930	1806234	9455104	6153207	14131299	4759466	5883248	•	7205315	9238061	6837981	12758679	•
Average Total Receipts **9**	6522	452	652	4135	9099	19749	47831	•	189614	369522	759776	1159880	•
Operating Costs/Operating Income (%)													
Cost of Operations **10**	67.9	52.2	68.0	72.1	73.6	63.4	60.8	•	66.2	72.1	77.3	68.0	•
Salaries and Wages **11**	8.2	8.5	4.6	6.8	7.1	9.7	10.0	•	6.7	7.2	5.8	9.8	•
Taxes Paid **12**	1.0	1.9	1.0	1.6	1.0	1.2	1.2	•	1.1	0.8	0.7	1.0	•
Interest Paid **13**	1.9	0.4	0.3	0.3	0.5	0.7	0.3	•	0.6	0.7	1.1	1.4	•
Depreciation **14**	1.2	0.9	0.5	0.7	0.6	1.9	1.4	•	1.1	0.9	1.0	1.3	•
Amortization and Depletion **15**	0.5	0.2	0.3	0.0	0.1	0.3	0.1	•	0.3	0.2	0.5	0.6	•
Pensions and Other Deferred Comp. **16**	0.3	•	0.2	0.4	0.1	0.1	0.2	•	0.2	0.2	0.1	1.2	•
Employee Benefits **17**	0.8	0.5	0.3	0.6	0.4	1.0	0.7	•	0.7	0.6	0.5	1.2	•
Advertising **18**	2.6	4.5	1.5	1.0	2.5	4.8	4.3	•	3.1	3.1	4.2	3.6	•
Other Expenses **19**	13.9	21.4	12.1	8.7	8.6	11.1	15.3	•	16.3	10.6	8.3	13.5	•
Officers' Compensation **20**	1.3	2.0	5.3	3.3	1.7	2.3	1.3	•	1.0	0.9	0.5	0.3	•
Operating Margin **21**	0.5	7.4	5.8	4.4	3.8	3.6	4.2	•	2.7	2.6	0.2	•	•
Operating Margin Before Officers' Comp. **22**	1.8	9.3	11.1	7.8	5.6	5.9	5.4	•	3.7	3.6	0.5	0.6	•

Selected Average Balance Sheet ($ in Thousands)

Net Receivables 23	3158	0	15	203	843	1819	2928	•	14040	29803	74196	196321
Inventories 24	1082	0	33	166	402	1242	2047	•	9881	37151	73380	78955
Net Property, Plant and Equipment 25	462	0	12	77	335	1663	2760	•	9554	13399	19197	72955
Total Assets 26	18542	0	102	717	2310	6783	15336	•	72475	143503	369843	994021
Notes and Loans Payable 27	4792	0	26	95	650	3045	3026	•	12695	32611	65549	251612
All Other Liabilities 28	6337	0	26	222	981	2146	6592	•	25688	50655	108588	391089
Net Worth 29	7414	0	50	399	679	1591	5718	•	34091	60237	195705	351320

Selected Financial Ratios (Times to 1)

Current Ratio 30	1.7	•	2.8	2.2	1.5	1.4	1.5	•	1.9	1.7	2.2	1.2
Quick Ratio 31	1.1	•	1.6	1.7	1.1	0.8	0.9	•	1.2	0.8	1.4	0.8
Net Sales to Working Capital 32	1.6	•	12.2	15.4	14.9	16.7	14.8	•	8.2	9.7	6.9	16.7
Coverage Ratio 33	4.1	24.0	23.7	21.1	11.6	8.4	16.7	•	10.1	6.9	4.3	3.4
Total Asset Turnover 34	0.3	•	6.3	5.7	3.9	2.9	3.1	•	2.5	2.5	2.0	1.1
Inventory Turnover 35	3.9	•	13.3	17.8	16.5	9.9	14.1	•	12.4	7.1	7.7	9.5
Receivables Turnover 36	3.3	•	52.5	21.1	11.7	10.2	19.2	•	13.6		8.3	6.6
Total Liabilities to Net Worth 37	1.5	•	1.0	0.8	2.4	3.3	1.7	•	1.1	1.4	0.9	1.8
Current Assets to Working Capital 38	2.4	•	1.5	1.9	2.9	3.7	3.0	•	2.1	2.5	1.9	6.1
Current Liabilities to Working Capital 39	1.4	•	0.5	0.9	1.9	2.7	2.0	•	1.1	1.5	0.9	5.1
Working Capital to Net Sales 40	0.6	•	0.1	0.1	0.1	0.1	0.1	•	0.1	0.1	0.1	0.1
Inventory to Working Capital 41	0.5	•	0.6	0.3	0.7	1.3	0.7	•	0.6	1.0	0.6	1.4
Total Receipts to Cash Flow 42	5.7	3.7	6.1	8.2	8.2	6.8	5.5	•	5.0	7.7	9.0	6.9
Cost of Goods to Cash Flow 43	3.9	1.9	4.1	5.9	6.0	4.3	3.3	•	3.3	5.5	7.0	4.7
Cash Flow to Total Debt 44	0.1	•	2.0	1.6	0.7	0.5	0.9	•	1.0	0.6	0.5	0.2

Selected Financial Factors (in Percentages)

Debt Ratio 45	60.0	•	51.1	44.3	70.6	76.5	62.7	•	53.0	58.0	47.1	64.7
Return on Total Assets 46	2.6	•	42.8	30.7	21.1	16.8	17.1	•	15.2	12.5	9.6	5.3
Return on Equity Before Income Taxes 47	4.8	•	83.8	52.4	65.5	62.9	43.1	•	29.1	25.5	13.9	10.5
Return on Equity After Income Taxes 48	3.9	•	83.2	50.9	62.7	61.4	39.3	•	23.1	20.2	10.5	8.9
Profit Margin (Before Income Tax) 49	5.8	9.4	6.5	5.1	4.9	5.2	5.2	•	5.4	4.2	3.7	3.3
Profit Margin (After Income Tax) 50	4.6	9.0	6.4	5.0	4.7	5.0	4.7	•	4.3	3.3	3.7	2.8

Table I

Corporations with and without Net Income

AIR TRANSPORTATION

MONEY AMOUNTS AND SIZE OF ASSETS IN THOUSANDS OF DOLLARS

Item Description for Accounting Period 7/09 Through 6/10	Total	Zero Assets	Under 500	500 to 1,000	1,000 to 5,000	5,000 to 10,000	10,000 to 25,000	25,000 to 50,000	50,000 to 100,000	100,000 to 250,000	250,000 to 500,000	500,000 to 2,500,000	2,500,000 and over
Number of Enterprises 1	7084	1197	3784	1048	647	161	126	54	25	9	8	14	10
Revenues ($ in Thousands)													
Net Sales 2	135314205	1834043	365247	824391	1375775	1082377	2581739	1394659	2687487	791276	3787168	11447011	107143032
Interest 3	228752	1087	2	153	1591	396	1453	847	776	341	3892	30155	188059
Rents 4	274027	9	0	1022	0	0	0	2958	44	70	820	20321	248784
Royalties 5	12	0	0	0	1	0	0	0	0	0	0	0	11
Other Portfolio Income 6	701816	58160	1404	5486	25647	19686	10375	73631	1388	3241	427	60474	441896
Other Receipts 7	1715651	8295	77	6116	4212	18072	33825	-3464	-13438	-66737	39275	141829	1547589
Total Receipts 8	138234463	1901594	366730	837168	1407226	1120531	2627392	1468631	2676257	728191	3831582	11699790	109569371
Average Total Receipts 9	19514	1589	97	799	2175	6960	20852	27197	107050	80910	478948	835699	10956937
Operating Costs/Operating Income (%)													
Cost of Operations 10	17.3	15.3	45.7	71.5	60.8	62.0	58.3	40.2	42.1	23.2	25.3	20.9	13.2
Salaries and Wages 11	19.2	12.3	5.1	7.0	12.8	11.1	6.6	8.7	14.1	20.1	17.0	17.2	20.4
Taxes Paid 12	2.3	1.0	1.8	1.8	1.8	1.6	1.6	1.4	2.5	2.8	1.7	2.6	2.4
Interest Paid 13	2.9	2.4	0.0	1.5	3.4	1.9	2.2	2.4	1.0	3.4	3.7	4.2	2.8
Depreciation 14	6.4	5.8	7.3	16.0	9.3	13.7	8.0	5.9	3.4	9.9	6.6	9.4	5.9
Amortization and Depletion 15	0.7	0.4	•	0.0	0.1	0.0	0.2	0.0	0.2	0.3	1.1	0.8	0.7
Pensions and Other Deferred Comp. 16	2.1	0.1	0.7	0.4	0.2	0.1	0.2	0.0	0.2	0.1	0.5	1.6	2.4
Employee Benefits 17	2.8	0.9	•	0.1	1.5	1.2	0.4	0.5	1.4	5.2	2.2	2.0	3.1
Advertising 18	0.7	0.4	0.1	0.4	0.2	0.0	0.2	0.5	0.1	0.1	1.8	0.5	0.8
Other Expenses 19	52.0	63.1	26.3	19.1	24.4	22.4	27.0	41.8	35.6	36.0	44.3	46.0	55.0
Officers' Compensation 20	0.4	2.6	14.2	7.3	1.3	1.6	1.9	1.0	0.3	1.8	0.3	0.6	0.1
Operating Margin 21	•	•	•	•	•	•	•	•	•	•	•	•	•
Operating Margin Before Officers' Comp. 22	•	•	13.0	•	•	•	•	•	•	•	•	•	•

Selected Average Balance Sheet ($ in Thousands)

Net Receivables 23	1001	0	13	83	473	1170	3187	2893	18519	18749	26875	63507	416629
Inventories 24	424	0	20	17	41	20	318	1163	3542	9332	11953	29844	208977
Net Property, Plant and Equipment 25	13275	0	44	508	1726	2709	8459	12791	21272	63256	162598	539706	8007588
Total Assets 26	24208	0	88	727	3037	7397	15208	33472	71118	150686	363582	1074198	14243228
Notes and Loans Payable 27	10776	0	141	617	2272	3522	8544	14446	30008	55010	190907	484471	6170481
All Other Liabilities 28	11999	0	9	136	712	988	5641	4770	23380	61621	127394	304753	7681428
Net Worth 29	1433	0	-62	-26	53	2887	1022	14255	17731	34055	45280	284974	391318

Selected Financial Ratios (Times to 1)

Current Ratio 30	1.0	•	5.2	2.6	1.7	3.3	1.1	2.0	1.0	1.3	1.4	1.5	1.0
Quick Ratio 31	0.7	•	2.8	1.9	1.2	2.9	0.8	1.4	0.8	0.9	0.9	1.1	0.7
Net Sales to Working Capital 32	69.2	•	2.7	7.4	4.7	2.4	66.2	5.7	207.3	7.5	10.2	7.7	•
Coverage Ratio 33	•	0.7	•	•	•	•	•	2.2	•	•	0.1	0.2	•
Total Asset Turnover 34	0.8	•	1.1	1.1	0.7	0.9	1.3	0.8	1.5	0.6	1.3	0.8	0.8
Inventory Turnover 35	7.8	•	2.2	33.1	31.2	209.1	37.6	8.9	12.8	2.2	10.0	5.7	6.8
Receivables Turnover 36	15.0	•	5.3	10.7	7.4	7.4	5.9	9.1	6.6	4.7	20.3	9.9	17.8
Total Liabilities to Net Worth 37	15.9	•	•	•	56.0	1.6	13.9	1.3	3.0	3.4	7.0	2.8	35.4
Current Assets to Working Capital 38	23.5	•	1.2	1.6	2.5	1.4	17.8	2.0	61.3	4.2	3.2	2.9	•
Current Liabilities to Working Capital 39	22.5	•	0.2	0.6	1.5	0.4	16.8	1.0	60.3	3.2	2.2	1.9	•
Working Capital to Net Sales 40	0.0	•	0.4	0.1	0.2	0.4	0.0	0.2	0.0	0.1	0.1	0.1	•
Inventory to Working Capital 41	1.5	•	0.6	0.3	0.2	0.0	1.0	0.2	4.3	0.8	0.2	0.3	•
Total Receipts to Cash Flow 42	3.1	2.1	5.6	•	26.1	143.3	7.1	5.7	4.2	6.5	4.4	4.5	2.8
Cost of Goods to Cash Flow 43	0.5	0.3	2.6	•	15.9	88.9	4.2	2.3	1.8	1.5	1.1	0.9	0.4
Cash Flow to Total Debt 44	0.3	•	0.1	•	0.0	0.0	0.2	0.2	0.5	0.1	0.3	0.2	0.3

Selected Financial Factors (in Percentages)

Debt Ratio 45	94.1	•	169.6	103.6	98.2	61.0	93.3	57.4	75.1	77.4	87.5	73.5	97.3
Return on Total Assets 46	•	•	•	•	•	•	•	4.1	•	•	0.5	0.6	•
Return on Equity Before Income Taxes 47	•	•	1.1	698.7	•	•	•	5.3	•	•	•	•	•
Return on Equity After Income Taxes 48	•	•	1.2	698.7	•	•	•	4.7	•	•	•	•	•
Profit Margin (Before Income Tax) 49	•	•	•	•	•	•	•	2.9	•	•	•	•	•
Profit Margin (After Income Tax) 50	•	•	•	•	•	•	•	2.6	•	•	•	•	•

Table II
Corporations with Net Income

AIR TRANSPORTATION

MONEY AMOUNTS AND SIZE OF ASSETS IN THOUSANDS OF DOLLARS

Item Description for Accounting Period 7/09 Through 6/10	Total	Zero Assets	Under 500	500 to 1,000	1,000 to 5,000	5,000 to 10,000	10,000 to 25,000	25,000 to 50,000	50,000 to 100,000	100,000 to 250,000	250,000 to 500,000	500,000 to 2,500,000	2,500,000 and over
Number of Enterprises **1**	1803	•	1504	0	•	63	41	18	11	4	3	•	0
Revenues ($ in Thousands)													
Net Sales **2**	16436390	•	273513	0	•	666352	1249737	826923	1686153	634079	1936750	•	0
Interest **3**	23157	•	1	0	•	0	483	203	406	154	2820	•	0
Rents **4**	30922	•	0	0	•	0	0	565	44	70	0	•	0
Royalties **5**	0	•	0	0	•	0	0	0	0	0	0	•	0
Other Portfolio Income **6**	182112	•	1404	0	•	19113	5360	63848	665	1088	225	•	0
Other Receipts **7**	93225	•	76	0	•	1929	9308	-5433	7073	5673	19348	•	0
Total Receipts **8**	16765806	•	274994	0	•	687394	1264888	886106	1694341	641064	1959143	•	0
Average Total Receipts **9**	9299	•	183	•	•	10911	30851	49228	154031	160266	653048	•	•
Operating Costs/Operating Income (%)													
Cost of Operations **10**	31.1	•	61.0	•	•	68.3	58.4	26.7	25.7	28.9	36.7	•	•
Salaries and Wages **11**	13.1	•	•	•	•	11.6	7.3	9.0	13.7	19.4	10.1	•	•
Taxes Paid **12**	2.6	•	2.4	•	•	1.4	1.6	1.0	2.7	3.0	1.1	•	•
Interest Paid **13**	2.6	•	0.0	•	•	0.4	1.0	1.3	0.7	2.1	2.9	•	•
Depreciation **14**	6.7	•	7.0	•	•	3.3	3.8	3.4	1.5	6.7	5.5	•	•
Amortization and Depletion **15**	0.1	•	•	•	•	0.0	0.0	0.0	0.2	0.4	0.0	•	•
Pensions and Other Deferred Comp. **16**	1.3	•	0.9	•	•	0.1	0.1	0.0	0.2	0.1	0.2	•	•
Employee Benefits **17**	1.8	•	•	•	•	1.6	0.5	0.2	1.4	6.1	2.3	•	•
Advertising **18**	0.6	•	0.1	•	•	0.0	0.2	0.2	0.2	0.2	0.6	•	•
Other Expenses **19**	35.8	•	19.2	•	•	7.9	17.9	54.0	46.1	24.1	33.0	•	•
Officers' Compensation **20**	0.7	•	1.7	•	•	1.5	2.8	0.7	0.3	2.3	0.2	•	•
Operating Margin **21**	3.7	•	7.7	•	•	3.9	6.3	3.5	7.4	6.8	7.4	•	•
Operating Margin Before Officers' Comp. **22**	4.4	•	9.5	•	•	5.4	9.1	4.3	7.7	9.0	7.6	•	•

Selected Average Balance Sheet ($ in Thousands)

Net Receivables	23	632	23	909	4518	4991	21027	20308	33620
Inventories	24	501	50	0	110	979	2943	20608	98
Net Property, Plant and Equipment	25	4363	64	514	5149	9744	13714	67671	137988
Total Assets	26	8756	165	6423	12562	33065	71936	159630	426871
Notes and Loans Payable	27	3641	64	1043	5759	13852	22104	63063	132289
All Other Liabilities	28	2569	18	857	3197	6482	32679	43247	156190
Net Worth	29	2546	83	4523	3606	12731	17153	53320	138391

Selected Financial Ratios (Times to 1)

Current Ratio	30	1.5	5.5	4.8	1.7	2.9	1.0		1.7
Quick Ratio	31	1.2	2.7	4.8	1.5	1.9	0.8	0.5	1.1
Net Sales to Working Capital	32	8.4	2.2	2.3	11.8	5.4	130.4	185.2	7.0
Coverage Ratio	33	3.2	378.7	20.3	8.2	9.4	11.7	4.7	4.0
Total Asset Turnover	34	1.0	1.1	1.6	2.4	1.4	2.1	1.0	1.5
Inventory Turnover	35	5.7	2.2	•	162.3	12.5	13.4	2.2	2417.5
Receivables Turnover	36	8.9	8.9	•	5.2	10.3	8.1	9.6	38.4
Total Liabilities to Net Worth	37	2.4	1.0	0.4	2.5	1.6	3.2	2.0	2.1
Current Assets to Working Capital	38	2.8	1.2	1.3	2.5	1.5	35.3	70.0	2.4
Current Liabilities to Working Capital	39	1.8	0.2	0.3	1.5	0.5	34.3	69.0	1.4
Working Capital to Net Sales	40	0.1	0.5	0.4	0.1	0.2	0.0	0.0	0.1
Inventory to Working Capital	41	0.2	0.6	•	0.0	0.1	1.8	24.7	0.0
Total Receipts to Cash Flow	42	3.5	4.6	8.8	6.1	4.2	2.5	4.2	3.3
Cost of Goods to Cash Flow	43	1.1	2.8	6.0	3.6	1.1	0.6	1.2	1.2
Cash Flow to Total Debt	44	0.4	0.5	0.6	0.6	0.5	1.1	0.4	0.7

Selected Financial Factors (in Percentages)

Debt Ratio	45	70.9	49.7	29.6	71.3	61.5	76.2	66.6	67.6
Return on Total Assets	46	8.6	9.1	12.2	20.6	16.6	18.5	9.9	17.3
Return on Equity Before Income Taxes	47	20.4	18.1	16.4	63.1	38.5	70.9	23.5	39.8
Return on Equity After Income Taxes	48	18.4	18.1	16.3	61.9	36.8	68.8	15.8	31.0
Profit Margin (Before Income Tax)	49	5.7	8.3	7.0	7.5	10.7	7.9	7.9	8.5
Profit Margin (After Income Tax)	50	5.1	8.3	7.0	7.3	10.2	7.7	5.3	6.6

Table I

Corporations with and without Net Income

RAIL TRANSPORTATION

MONEY AMOUNTS AND SIZE OF ASSETS IN THOUSANDS OF DOLLARS

Item Description for Accounting Period 7/09 Through 6/10	Total	Zero Assets	Under 500	500 to 1,000	1,000 to 5,000	5,000 to 10,000	10,000 to 25,000	25,000 to 50,000	50,000 to 100,000	100,000 to 250,000	250,000 to 500,000	500,000 to 2,500,000	2,500,000 and over
Number of Enterprises **1**	514	290	102	0	49	4	22	15	9	7	4	4	8
Revenues ($ in Thousands)													
Net Sales **2**	56987789	1850413	0	0	284836	24624	236476	965531	197190	366893	670645	1109502	51281679
Interest **3**	292424	2299	676	0	207	22	197	638	863	1391	350	32261	253519
Rents **4**	470698	12424	41	0	433	0	6	3830	2593	3064	3036	22003	423268
Royalties **5**	32386	0	0	0	197	0	0	0	11	256	0	0	31922
Other Portfolio Income **6**	458143	49345	0	0	795	139	1015	3619	956	3112	33189	64112	301858
Other Receipts **7**	996717	-6609	0	0	21805	0	135	8472	5288	2499	4341	133311	827479
Total Receipts **8**	59238157	1907872	717	0	308273	24785	237829	982090	206901	377215	711561	1361189	53119725
Average Total Receipts **9**	115249	6579	7	•	6291	6196	10810	65473	22989	53888	177890	340297	6639966
Operating Costs/Operating Income (%)													
Cost of Operations **10**	20.2	34.2	•	•	•	12.8	11.5	81.3	4.0	31.6	24.7	2.9	18.9
Salaries and Wages **11**	20.3	20.6	•	•	3.0	26.1	14.9	3.7	19.5	19.8	12.9	23.6	20.7
Taxes Paid **12**	5.6	5.1	•	•	1.1	4.5	5.2	1.1	6.6	3.8	4.3	6.3	5.7
Interest Paid **13**	5.7	4.5	•	•	0.5	8.0	0.8	0.7	5.0	2.7	1.5	14.4	5.8
Depreciation **14**	13.8	8.3	•	•	7.3	5.1	4.5	3.4	26.9	11.4	9.7	18.0	14.2
Amortization and Depletion **15**	0.3	0.7	•	•	0.0	0.1	0.0	0.0	0.0	0.1	0.1	1.0	0.3
Pensions and Other Deferred Comp. **16**	1.3	0.5	•	•	0.4	•	0.0	0.1	0.5	1.9	0.1	0.3	1.4
Employee Benefits **17**	5.2	3.6	•	•	0.0	8.8	2.3	0.2	4.2	5.1	1.8	7.3	5.4
Advertising **18**	0.2	0.1	•	•	0.0	0.4	0.2	0.1	0.3	0.0	0.0	0.0	0.2
Other Expenses **19**	26.0	19.5	•	•	95.4	30.5	36.9	7.5	36.4	26.5	30.8	47.9	25.5
Officers' Compensation **20**	0.4	0.2	•	•	0.1	•	1.1	1.2	1.3	1.5	0.8	1.5	0.4
Operating Margin **21**	1.2	2.8	•	•	•	3.6	22.5	0.6	•	•	13.3	•	1.5
Operating Margin Before Officers' Comp. **22**	1.6	3.0	•	•	•	3.6	23.6	1.8	•	•	14.1	•	1.9

Selected Average Balance Sheet ($ in Thousands)

Net Receivables 23	11039	0	1	•	448	1689	1763	8194	3108	6658	36658	148094	583734
Inventories 24	2423	0	0	•	4	228	96	744	1240	544	11202	770	146003
Net Property, Plant and Equipment 25	278837	0	101	•	1206	2399	5784	17330	47042	106635	227499	709394	17248745
Total Assets 26	347416	0	315	•	3257	5274	16380	31492	73358	138067	364812	1534732	21037704
Notes and Loans Payable 27	83447	0	0	•	916	1205	1515	8496	20461	28192	117862	445684	5005705
All Other Liabilities 28	138467	0	0	•	743	8509	2508	8637	20105	53322	114080	313006	8581805
Net Worth 29	125502	0	314	•	1597	-4440	12357	14359	32792	56553	132870	776042	7450194

Selected Financial Ratios (Times to 1)

Current Ratio 30	0.9	•	908.2	1.4	1.2	1.8	1.1	2.9	1.3	1.0	2.0	0.9
Quick Ratio 31	0.7	•	908.2	1.3	1.0	1.7	0.9	2.2	0.9	0.8	1.8	0.7
Net Sales to Working Capital 32	•	•	•	17.4	12.9	6.5	56.2	2.3	11.2	61.8	2.3	•
Coverage Ratio 33	1.9	2.3	•	2.1	1.5	28.3	4.4	1.1	0.4	13.9	1.0	1.9
Total Asset Turnover 34	0.3	•	•	1.8	1.2	0.7	2.0	0.3	0.4	0.5	0.2	0.3
Inventory Turnover 35	9.2	•	•	•	3.5	12.9	70.3	0.7	30.5	3.7	10.4	8.3
Receivables Turnover 36	10.5	•	•	13.5	3.2	8.2	10.9	7.3	7.5	4.6	1.9	11.5
Total Liabilities to Net Worth 37	1.8	0.0	•	1.0	0.3	1.2	1.2	1.4	1.7	1.0	1.8	
Current Assets to Working Capital 38	•	•	1.0	3.2	5.6	2.2	11.1	1.5	4.7	26.5	2.0	•
Current Liabilities to Working Capital 39	•	•	0.0	2.2	4.6	1.2	10.1	0.5	3.7	25.5	1.0	•
Working Capital to Net Sales 40	•	•	•	0.1	0.1	0.2	0.0	0.4	0.1	0.0	0.4	•
Inventory to Working Capital 41	•	•	•	•	0.8	0.1	0.7	0.1	0.1	4.6	0.0	•
Total Receipts to Cash Flow 42	4.3	10.3	•	2.0	3.2	2.3	12.3	3.8	6.9	2.4	3.2	4.3
Cost of Goods to Cash Flow 43	0.9	3.5	•	•	0.4	0.3	10.0	0.1	2.2	0.6	0.1	0.8
Cash Flow to Total Debt 44	0.1	•	24.2	1.7	0.2	1.1	0.3	0.1	0.1	0.3	0.1	0.1

Selected Financial Factors (in Percentages)

Debt Ratio 45	63.9	•	0.1	50.9	184.2	24.6	54.4	55.3	59.0	63.6	49.4	64.6
Return on Total Assets 46	3.5	•	•	1.7	14.3	15.7	6.2	1.6	0.4	9.6	2.5	3.3
Return on Equity Before Income Taxes 47	4.6	•	•	1.8	•	20.1	10.6	0.2	•	24.5	•	4.4
Return on Equity After Income Taxes 48	2.6	•	•	0.8	•	18.2	8.5	•	•	21.0	•	2.5
Profit Margin (Before Income Tax) 49	5.2	6.0	•	0.5	4.3	23.1	2.4	0.3	•	19.4	•	5.1
Profit Margin (After Income Tax) 50	3.0	3.7	•	0.2	2.8	21.0	1.9	0.1	•	16.7	•	2.9

Table II
Corporations with Net Income

RAIL TRANSPORTATION

MONEY AMOUNTS AND SIZE OF ASSETS IN THOUSANDS OF DOLLARS

Item Description for Accounting Period 7/09 Through 6/10	Total	Zero Assets	Under 500	500 to 1,000	1,000 to 5,000	5,000 to 10,000	10,000 to 25,000	25,000 to 50,000	50,000 to 100,000	100,000 to 250,000	250,000 to 500,000	500,000 to 2,500,000	2,500,000 and over
Number of Enterprises **1**	93	•	0	0	•	4	18	12	4	4	4	•	4
Revenues ($ in Thousands)													
Net Sales **2**	50347577	•	0	0	•	24624	236476	910564	79917	202126	670645	•	45165469
Interest **3**	221189	•	0	0	•	22	197	638	702	508	350	•	184195
Rents **4**	310823	•	0	0	•	0	6	3830	1422	1244	3036	•	268525
Royalties **5**	31945	•	0	0	•	0	0	0	0	256	0	•	31492
Other Portfolio Income **6**	331158	•	0	0	•	139	1015	2508	18	2047	33189	•	226275
Other Receipts **7**	315838	•	0	0	•	0	135	8221	1554	1986	4341	•	103384
Total Receipts **8**	51558530	•	0	0	•	24785	237829	925761	83613	208167	711561	•	45979340
Average Total Receipts **9**	554393	•	•	•	•	6196	13213	77147	20903	52042	177890	•	11494835
Operating Costs/Operating Income (%)													
Cost of Operations **10**	22.3	•	•	•	•	12.8	11.5	84.9	6.5	8.5	24.7	•	21.2
Salaries and Wages **11**	18.8	•	•	•	•	26.1	14.9	2.8	10.1	23.4	12.9	•	19.2
Taxes Paid **12**	5.2	•	•	•	•	4.5	5.2	1.0	5.3	4.2	4.3	•	5.3
Interest Paid **13**	5.2	•	•	•	•	8.0	0.8	0.6	1.7	2.5	1.5	•	5.3
Depreciation **14**	13.6	•	•	•	•	5.1	4.5	2.4	22.4	12.5	9.7	•	14.3
Amortization and Depletion **15**	0.3	•	•	•	•	0.1	0.0	0.0	0.0	0.1	0.1	•	0.3
Pensions and Other Deferred Comp. **16**	1.3	•	•	•	•	•	•	0.1	1.1	2.2	0.1	•	1.5
Employee Benefits **17**	5.4	•	•	•	•	8.8	2.3	0.2	2.2	3.3	1.8	•	5.6
Advertising **18**	0.0	•	•	•	•	0.4	0.2	0.1	0.1	0.0	0.0	•	0.0
Other Expenses **19**	22.4	•	•	•	•	30.5	36.2	5.3	16.4	37.9	30.8	•	21.7
Officers' Compensation **20**	0.4	•	•	•	•	•	1.1	1.2	0.3	2.2	0.8	•	0.4
Operating Margin **21**	4.9	•	•	•	•	3.6	23.2	1.3	33.9	3.2	13.3	•	5.3
Operating Margin Before Officers' Comp. **22**	5.4	•	•	•	•	3.6	24.4	2.6	34.2	5.4	14.1	•	5.7

Selected Average Balance Sheet ($ in Thousands)

Net Receivables 23	55655	1689	2155	9646	2634	4583	36658	1062452
Inventories 24	12413	228	117	511	888	204	12556	209492
Net Property, Plant and Equipment 25	1270839	2399	7070	16686	34266	107280	227499	28571554
Total Assets 26	1587979	5274	17176	33387	63226	137888	364812	34815979
Notes and Loans Payable 27	403813	1205	1852	10462	15472	31474	117862	8876451
All Other Liabilities 28	616084	8509	2301	6362	11739	62550	114080	13786862
Net Worth 29	568082	-4440	13023	16563	36015	43864	132870	12152666

Selected Financial Ratios (Times to 1)

Current Ratio 30	1.0	1.2	1.8	1.4	8.0	1.5	1.0	0.9
Quick Ratio 31	0.7	1.0	1.7	1.2	7.2	1.0	0.8	0.7
Net Sales to Working Capital 32	•	12.9	6.5	19.1	1.1	6.6	61.8	•
Coverage Ratio 33	2.4	1.5	30.9	5.7	23.2	3.5	13.9	2.3
Total Asset Turnover 34	0.3	1.2	0.8	2.3	0.3	0.4	0.5	0.3
Inventory Turnover 35	9.7	3.5	12.9	126.1	1.5	21.0	3.3	11.4
Receivables Turnover 36	10.2	3.2	8.2	13.7	10.1	11.1	•	•
Total Liabilities to Net Worth 37	1.8	•	0.3	1.0	0.8	2.1	1.7	1.9
Current Assets to Working Capital 38	•	5.6	2.2	3.7	1.1	2.9	26.5	•
Current Liabilities to Working Capital 39	•	4.6	1.2	2.7	0.1	1.9	25.5	•
Working Capital to Net Sales 40	•	0.1	0.2	0.1	0.9	0.2	0.0	•
Inventory to Working Capital 41	•	0.8	0.1	0.2	0.1	0.0	4.6	•
Total Receipts to Cash Flow 42	4.5	3.2	2.3	12.5	2.1	3.3	2.4	4.5
Cost of Goods to Cash Flow 43	1.0	0.4	0.3	10.6	0.1	0.3	0.6	1.0
Cash Flow to Total Debt 44	0.1	0.2	1.4	0.4	0.4	0.2	0.3	0.1

Selected Financial Factors (in Percentages)

Debt Ratio 45	64.2	184.2	24.2	50.4	43.0	68.2	63.6	65.1
Return on Total Assets 46	4.3	14.3	18.8	8.3	12.7	3.2	9.6	4.0
Return on Equity Before Income Taxes 47	7.0	•	24.0	13.8	21.4	7.1	24.5	6.6
Return on Equity After Income Taxes 48	4.7	•	21.9	11.5	14.4	6.6	21.0	4.3
Profit Margin (Before Income Tax) 49	7.4	4.3	23.8	3.0	38.5	6.2	19.4	7.1
Profit Margin (After Income Tax) 50	4.9	2.8	21.7	2.5	25.9	5.7	16.7	4.7

Table I

Corporations with and without Net Income

WATER TRANSPORTATION

MONEY AMOUNTS AND SIZE OF ASSETS IN THOUSANDS OF DOLLARS

Item Description for Accounting Period 7/09 Through 6/10		Total	Zero Assets	Under 500	500 to 1,000	1,000 to 5,000	5,000 to 10,000	10,000 to 25,000	25,000 to 50,000	50,000 to 100,000	100,000 to 250,000	250,000 to 500,000	500,000 to 2,500,000	2,500,000 and over
Number of Enterprises	1	4382	523	2539	312	637	181	98	25	21	22	10	15	0
Revenues ($ in Thousands)														
Net Sales	2	28056599	1387774	2048434	450217	1990989	1134915	1419854	393191	865620	1901973	1155879	15307752	0
Interest	3	87499	416	2	391	387	424	2671	794	2835	2088	6820	70671	0
Rents	4	123175	528	0	0	0	0	460	924	878	21	11503	108862	0
Royalties	5	473	465	0	0	0	0	0	0	0	6	1	0	0
Other Portfolio Income	6	830699	369963	0	8	75830	59139	2261	3037	3189	23844	18535	274893	0
Other Receipts	7	536723	71670	135755	3078	5893	167702	25400	26937	-38681	12016	447014	-320059	0
Total Receipts	8	29635168	1830816	2184191	453694	2073099	1362180	1450646	424883	833841	1939948	1639752	15442119	0
Average Total Receipts	9	6763	3501	860	1454	3254	7526	14803	16995	39707	88179	163975	1029475	•
Operating Costs/Operating Income (%)														
Cost of Operations	10	39.8	28.8	57.4	0.4	34.9	30.0	37.4	38.9	44.8	33.0	46.9	41.2	•
Salaries and Wages	11	11.5	9.5	7.3	21.2	18.4	19.2	14.4	19.1	10.4	11.2	8.3	10.3	•
Taxes Paid	12	1.9	0.7	1.3	2.6	1.2	1.8	2.9	2.9	2.5	2.7	1.5	1.9	•
Interest Paid	13	3.1	12.0	0.2	1.1	2.8	2.3	2.3	5.4	3.5	4.1	8.5	2.3	•
Depreciation	14	10.3	8.3	0.3	5.0	8.4	4.8	9.3	11.6	10.5	14.7	28.7	10.8	•
Amortization and Depletion	15	0.6	1.2	0.0	•	0.0	1.8	0.0	0.3	0.5	0.3	0.3	0.8	•
Pensions and Other Deferred Comp.	16	0.7	0.1	0.3	0.0	0.1	0.2	0.6	1.0	1.6	0.6	1.0	0.9	•
Employee Benefits	17	2.4	0.9	0.2	2.5	0.9	1.0	2.5	3.1	1.2	3.4	1.9	3.1	•
Advertising	18	0.3	2.2	0.1	0.4	0.3	0.1	0.6	0.2	0.5	0.1	0.1	0.2	•
Other Expenses	19	33.7	52.9	32.3	63.7	32.0	54.0	33.6	22.9	17.1	34.0	59.0	29.3	•
Officers' Compensation	20	1.6	0.1	6.0	8.7	0.4	4.9	1.1	2.3	1.5	0.8	1.8	1.0	•
Operating Margin	21	•	•	•	0.7	0.7	•	•	•	5.9	•	•	•	•
Operating Margin Before Officers' Comp.	22	•	•	0.7	3.1	1.1	•	•	•	7.4	•	•	•	•

Selected Average Balance Sheet ($ in Thousands)

Net Receivables 23	954	0	4	8	285	2132	2949	2638	5353	12348	47861	158830
Inventories 24	101	0	6	0	18	0	76	352	193	538	1225	25565
Net Property, Plant and Equipment 25	4835		41	360	1234	3652	8314	18046	47779	105984	271029	814037
Total Assets 26	8623		155	777	2415	7484	15179	33272	77318	162037	345744	1552908
Notes and Loans Payable 27	3538		124	576	1683	2282	8016	16494	28012	75281	315763	461444
All Other Liabilities 28	2022		28	201	263	934	4006	7162	15765	19195	101338	403470
Net Worth 29	3063		2	0	469	4268	3157	9616	33541	67561	-71357	687994

Selected Financial Ratios (Times to 1)

Current Ratio 30	1.2	•	1.2	0.9	2.1	3.6	1.1	1.1	1.1	1.5	1.2	1.1
Quick Ratio 31	0.9	•	0.9	0.8	1.5	3.4	0.8	0.8	0.6	1.1	1.0	0.7
Net Sales to Working Capital 32	18.6	•	148.8	•	9.2	2.7	36.9	23.4	21.1	9.3	7.3	38.4
Coverage Ratio 33	0.9	2.3	8.5	•	2.7	1.0	•	1.1	1.6	0.2	•	0.7
Total Asset Turnover 34	0.7	•	5.2	1.9	1.3	0.8	1.0	0.5	0.5	0.5	0.3	0.7
Inventory Turnover 35	25.3	•	71.9	•	60.5	•	71.0	17.4	95.8	53.0	44.2	16.5
Receivables Turnover 36	7.2	•	455.8	329.7	18.9	4.9	4.1	6.8	6.5	6.8	2.3	6.8
Total Liabilities to Net Worth 37	1.8	•	69.1	10540.0	4.2	0.8	3.8	2.5	1.3	1.4	•	1.3
Current Assets to Working Capital 38	5.7	•	6.6	•	1.9	1.4	12.9	10.2	9.1	3.0	5.6	12.2
Current Liabilities to Working Capital 39	4.7	•	5.6	•	0.9	0.4	11.9	9.2	8.1	2.0	4.6	11.2
Working Capital to Net Sales 40	0.1	•	0.0	•	0.1	0.4	0.0	0.0	0.0	0.1	0.1	0.0
Inventory to Working Capital 41	0.3	•	1.2	•	0.1	•	0.2	0.3	0.1	0.1	0.1	0.9
Total Receipts to Cash Flow 42	4.1	1.5	3.5	3.1	3.8	7.3	6.0	6.9	6.8	4.2	2.6	4.7
Cost of Goods to Cash Flow 43	1.6	0.4	2.0	0.0	1.3	2.2	2.2	2.7	3.0	1.4	1.2	1.9
Cash Flow to Total Debt 44	0.3	•	1.5	0.6	0.4	0.3	0.2	0.1	0.1	0.2	0.1	0.2

Selected Financial Factors (in Percentages)

Debt Ratio 45	64.5	•	98.6	100.0	80.6	43.0	79.2	71.1	56.6	58.3	120.6	55.7
Return on Total Assets 46	2.2	•	7.8	•	9.8	1.9	•	2.7	3.1	0.5	•	1.1
Return on Equity Before Income Taxes 47	•	•	480.0	•	32.1	•	•	0.6	2.7	•	•	25.5
Return on Equity After Income Taxes 48	•	•	480.0	•	31.9	•	•	•	2.1	•	•	27.0
Profit Margin (Before Income Tax) 49	•	15.2	1.3	•	4.8	•	•	0.4	2.2	•	•	•
Profit Margin (After Income Tax) 50	•	13.8	1.3	•	4.8	•	•	•	1.7	•	•	•

Table II

Corporations with Net Income

WATER TRANSPORTATION

MONEY AMOUNTS AND SIZE OF ASSETS IN THOUSANDS OF DOLLARS

Item Description for Accounting Period 7/09 Through 6/10	Total	Zero Assets	Under 500	500 to 1,000	1,000 to 5,000	5,000 to 10,000	10,000 to 25,000	25,000 to 50,000	50,000 to 100,000	100,000 to 250,000	250,000 to 500,000	500,000 to 2,500,000	2,500,000 and over
Number of Enterprises 1	1529	8	798	178	297	175	28	9	11	11	4	9	0
Revenues ($ in Thousands)													
Net Sales 2	16343414	1278493	307879	193144	1190106	1131486	475352	153510	623755	1019635	354587	9615466	0
Interest 3	54634	207	0	8	271	231	2058	522	2831	1612	1305	45588	0
Rents 4	109343	528	0	0	0	0	460	839	878	0	0	106638	0
Royalties 5	472	465	0	0	0	0	0	0	0	6	0	0	0
Other Portfolio Income 6	703816	369955	0	0	75830	59097	1015	3019	2328	11478	6260	174835	0
Other Receipts 7	132369	-6597	135337	579	5665	3494	14019	2521	-39446	17938	330180	-331318	0
Total Receipts 8	17344048	1643051	443216	193731	1271872	1194308	492904	160411	590346	1050669	692332	9611209	0
Average Total Receipts 9	11343	205381	555	1088	4282	6825	17604	17823	53668	95515	173083	1067912	•
Operating Costs/Operating Income (%)													
Cost of Operations 10	31.1	25.8	•	•	5.0	30.1	40.3	45.6	44.3	28.8	27.3	35.6	•
Salaries and Wages 11	11.7	8.5	0.7	35.6	29.2	19.1	16.3	7.8	10.6	12.9	8.4	8.8	•
Taxes Paid 12	1.9	0.6	2.1	4.2	1.8	1.7	2.7	3.1	2.4	4.1	1.7	1.7	•
Interest Paid 13	2.8	12.8	0.0	0.4	1.0	1.4	0.9	3.0	2.1	3.3	2.7	2.1	•
Depreciation 14	7.7	8.5	0.0	3.0	4.9	3.9	4.7	11.5	6.2	10.9	21.8	8.1	•
Amortization and Depletion 15	0.4	0.9	•	•	0.0	0.2	0.0	0.1	0.1	0.3	0.0	0.5	•
Pensions and Other Deferred Comp. 16	0.7	0.2	1.7	•	0.1	0.2	0.4	0.3	1.9	0.8	1.0	0.9	•
Employee Benefits 17	2.4	0.7	•	0.1	1.4	1.0	2.4	2.1	1.2	5.2	2.1	2.8	•
Advertising 18	0.3	2.3	0.2	0.5	0.3	0.1	0.2	0.4	0.7	0.1	0.0	0.1	•
Other Expenses 19	38.5	49.2	97.6	33.2	46.3	35.5	29.5	17.8	17.8	31.4	117.8	34.6	•
Officers' Compensation 20	1.9	0.1	17.4	20.4	0.5	4.9	1.7	2.9	1.2	0.8	1.6	1.2	•
Operating Margin 21	0.6	•	•	2.7	9.6	1.9	0.9	5.5	11.5	1.5	•	3.6	•
Operating Margin Before Officers' Comp. 22	2.5	•	•	23.0	10.1	6.8	2.5	8.5	12.7	2.3	•	4.8	•

Selected Average Balance Sheet ($ in Thousands)

Net Receivables 23	1743	0	0	0	7	2202	4230	3783	8158	13797	91644	168629
Inventories 24	223	0	0	0	15	0	177	588	251	663	492	34973
Net Property, Plant and Equipment 25	7073	0	0	356	763	3504	4423	16666	48215	107942	137971	818576
Total Assets 26	14445	0	80	699	2294	7427	13452	34239	78050	173055	327014	1684597
Notes and Loans Payable 27	3920	0	3	124	896	1894	4567	7121	25023	71769	40851	439135
All Other Liabilities 28	3489	0	1	67	273	944	4529	11181	12328	19871	63912	470845
Net Worth 29	7036	0	76	508	1125	4589	4355	15936	40699	81415	222252	774617

Selected Financial Ratios (Times to 1)

Current Ratio 30	1.4	•	20.6	3.4	1.4	3.7	1.8	1.4	1.1	2.3	2.2	1.2
Quick Ratio 31	1.1	•	20.6	2.9	0.6	3.5	1.4	1.2	0.8	1.7	2.0	0.8
Net Sales to Working Capital 32	10.4	•	15.7	6.8	24.4	2.6	4.6	5.6	27.2	4.4	1.3	24.6
Coverage Ratio 33	3.4	2.5	846.0	8.9	18.2	6.4	5.8	4.4	4.0	2.3	5.1	2.7
Total Asset Turnover 34	0.7	•	4.8	1.6	1.7	0.9	1.3	0.5	0.7	0.5	0.3	0.6
Inventory Turnover 35	14.9	•	•	•	13.6	•	38.7	13.2	100.2	40.3	49.1	10.9
Receivables Turnover 36	6.2	•	•	2840.4	459.9	•	2.5	4.0	6.7	6.3	•	6.2
Total Liabilities to Net Worth 37	1.1	•	0.1	0.4	1.0	0.6	2.1	1.1	0.9	1.1	0.5	1.2
Current Assets to Working Capital 38	3.3	•	1.1	1.4	3.7	1.4	2.2	3.3	8.5	1.8	1.8	7.6
Current Liabilities to Working Capital 39	2.3	•	0.1	0.4	2.7	0.4	1.2	2.3	7.5	0.8	0.8	6.6
Working Capital to Net Sales 40	0.1	•	0.1	0.0	0.0	0.4	0.2	0.2	0.0	0.2	0.7	0.0
Inventory to Working Capital 41	0.2	•	•	0.1	0.1	•	0.0	0.1	0.1	0.1	0.0	0.6
Total Receipts to Cash Flow 42	2.8	1.5	0.8	4.3	2.0	5.2	6.3	6.5	5.1	3.4	0.8	3.3
Cost of Goods to Cash Flow 43	0.9	0.4	•	•	0.1	1.6	2.5	3.0	2.3	1.0	0.2	1.2
Cash Flow to Total Debt 44	0.5	•	113.2	1.3	1.7	0.4	0.3	0.1	0.3	0.3	1.0	0.4

Selected Financial Factors (in Percentages)

Debt Ratio 45	51.3	•	5.1	27.3	50.9	38.2	67.6	53.5	47.9	53.0	32.0	54.0
Return on Total Assets 46	7.1	•	116.6	5.2	30.4	7.7	7.0	6.5	6.0	4.2	3.7	3.7
Return on Equity Before Income Taxes 47	10.3	•	122.7	6.3	58.6	10.5	17.8	10.7	8.6	5.0	4.3	5.1
Return on Equity After Income Taxes 48	8.8	•	122.7	6.0	58.5	10.1	12.4	7.5	7.5	4.7	3.1	3.5
Profit Margin (Before Income Tax) 49	6.8	18.8	24.2	3.0	16.5	7.4	4.6	10.0	6.2	4.4	10.9	3.7
Profit Margin (After Income Tax) 50	5.8	17.3	24.2	2.8	16.4	7.2	3.2	7.0	5.4	4.1	7.9	2.5

Table I

Corporations with and without Net Income

TRUCK TRANSPORTATION

MONEY AMOUNTS AND SIZE OF ASSETS IN THOUSANDS OF DOLLARS

Item Description for Accounting Period 7/09 Through 6/10		Total	Zero Assets	Under 500	500 to 1,000	1,000 to 5,000	5,000 to 10,000	10,000 to 25,000	25,000 to 50,000	50,000 to 100,000	100,000 to 250,000	250,000 to 500,000	500,000 to 2,500,000	2,500,000 and over
Number of Enterprises	1	107748	26103	71122	3582	5452	833	387	121	67	37	23	18	3
Revenues ($ in Thousands)														
Net Sales	2	192069221	9950291	38574737	9156459	35300435	14294346	13467044	9257587	7370185	8745715	10500974	23072523	12378924
Interest	3	337464	9038	2422	3945	14124	4666	7597	4563	5297	11441	12903	59724	201744
Rents	4	255748	17712	380	5686	13122	3892	38902	17220	5755	33890	54081	41329	23779
Royalties	5	19108	932	0	0	47	0	6	4	1359	0	179	1506	15074
Other Portfolio Income	6	1461169	102513	265802	29758	147741	100222	167496	45349	51004	60543	76637	170971	243133
Other Receipts	7	4339841	394304	382199	39319	400936	202095	117617	45693	73804	134336	557729	1239548	752262
Total Receipts	8	198482551	10474790	39225540	9235167	35876405	14605221	13798662	9370416	7507404	8985925	11202503	24585601	13614916
Average Total Receipts	9	1842	401	552	2578	6580	17533	35655	77441	112051	242863	487065	1365867	4538305
Operating Costs/Operating Income (%)														
Cost of Operations	10	32.1	18.0	30.6	45.9	42.2	36.7	40.6	42.1	28.3	24.1	22.2	25.3	15.2
Salaries and Wages	11	17.6	5.9	13.1	13.1	13.2	17.8	15.9	15.2	22.5	21.7	24.1	25.0	34.9
Taxes Paid	12	3.6	1.5	3.1	3.4	3.3	3.1	3.5	3.5	4.6	3.5	4.5	4.7	5.9
Interest Paid	13	1.4	1.4	0.8	1.2	1.0	1.3	1.1	0.9	2.0	2.0	1.8	0.9	4.9
Depreciation	14	4.7	2.5	3.6	3.3	4.7	4.7	4.4	4.6	6.3	5.8	7.6	6.5	4.0
Amortization and Depletion	15	0.1	0.3	0.0	0.0	0.1	0.0	0.1	0.2	0.1	0.3	0.4	0.1	0.2
Pensions and Other Deferred Comp.	16	0.4	0.2	0.1	0.1	0.3	0.2	0.1	0.4	0.2	0.3	0.4	0.9	1.4
Employee Benefits	17	2.5	0.2	1.1	1.4	1.9	2.3	2.2	2.2	3.6	2.4	3.2	4.4	8.0
Advertising	18	0.2	0.0	0.5	0.3	0.3	0.2	0.2	0.1	0.1	0.1	0.1	0.2	0.1
Other Expenses	19	34.9	25.6	41.3	26.7	31.7	33.8	30.6	30.1	33.0	40.7	41.4	36.2	36.6
Officers' Compensation	20	4.3	48.3	4.4	2.7	2.2	1.3	1.4	0.9	1.0	0.6	0.6	0.3	0.2
Operating Margin	21	•	1.3	1.8									•	•
Operating Margin Before Officers' Comp.	22	2.4	44.3	5.8	4.5	1.4	•	1.2	0.6				•	•

Selected Average Balance Sheet ($ in Thousands)

Net Receivables 23	194	0	10	140	536	1933	3910	9332	11267	32798	53412	183023	1988318
Inventories 24	9	0	1	20	28	118	365	587	1310	1410	4088	8222	10006
Net Property, Plant and Equipment 25	343	0	32	321	840	2691	6365	15534	33513	77029	189963	471992	1488829
Total Assets 26	833	0	73	724	2019	6543	15170	34592	67207	153037	345589	935354	6852214
Notes and Loans Payable 27	337	0	62	426	1090	3143	6949	12402	32477	73446	112174	229766	2019264
All Other Liabilities 28	268	0	17	154	457	1801	3364	7771	17907	30235	90560	286469	3782058
Net Worth 29	228	0	-6	144	472	1599	4856	14419	16824	49356	142855	419119	1050893

Selected Financial Ratios (Times to 1)

Current Ratio 30	1.1	•	1.2	1.2	1.3	1.2	1.2	1.4	1.1	1.0	1.4	1.8	0.8
Quick Ratio 31	0.9	•	0.9	1.0	1.1	1.0	0.9	1.2	0.7	0.8	1.1	1.4	0.7
Net Sales to Working Capital 32	49.0	•	121.4	68.6	27.4	27.9	35.4	17.6	80.0	134.7	17.4	9.5	•
Coverage Ratio 33	2.1	2.0	4.8	3.2	1.9	1.6	3.1	2.0	1.1	1.6	1.3	3.5	0.7
Total Asset Turnover 34	2.1	•	7.5	3.5	3.2	2.6	2.3	2.2	1.6	1.5	1.3	1.4	0.6
Inventory Turnover 35	61.0	•	199.0	58.4	96.5	53.2	38.7	54.9	23.8	40.3	24.8	39.5	62.5
Receivables Turnover 36	10.1	•	57.9	15.0	12.3	9.2	8.8	8.5	8.5	7.5	8.0	6.6	3.2
Total Liabilities to Net Worth 37	2.7	•	4.0	3.3	3.1	3.1	2.1	1.4	3.0	2.1	1.4	1.2	5.5
Current Assets to Working Capital 38	8.8	•	7.2	6.7	4.1	5.4	6.7	3.5	17.0	29.8	3.6	2.3	•
Current Liabilities to Working Capital 39	7.8	•	6.2	5.7	3.1	4.4	5.7	2.5	16.0	28.8	2.6	1.3	•
Working Capital to Net Sales 40	0.0	•	0.0	0.0	0.0	0.0	0.0	0.1	0.0	0.0	0.1	0.1	•
Inventory to Working Capital 41	0.3	•	0.7	0.7	0.1	0.1	0.5	0.1	0.9	0.8	0.1	0.1	•
Total Receipts to Cash Flow 42	3.5	4.4	2.8	4.4	4.3	4.1	4.5	4.9	4.0	3.2	3.2	2.9	3.4
Cost of Goods to Cash Flow 43	1.1	0.8	0.9	2.0	1.8	1.5	1.8	2.1	1.1	0.8	0.7	0.7	0.5
Cash Flow to Total Debt 44	0.8	•	2.5	1.0	1.0	0.8	0.8	0.8	0.6	0.7	0.7	0.8	0.2

Selected Financial Factors (in Percentages)

Debt Ratio 45	72.7	•	108.3	80.2	76.6	75.6	68.0	58.3	75.0	67.7	58.7	55.2	84.7
Return on Total Assets 46	6.1	•	28.2	13.5	6.0	5.2	7.9	4.1	3.4	5.1	3.0	4.0	2.1
Return on Equity Before Income Taxes 47	11.5	•	•	46.6	12.3	7.7	16.7	4.9	0.9	6.0	1.5	6.4	•
Return on Equity After Income Taxes 48	9.7	•	•	45.8	10.6	6.8	15.2	4.1	0.0	4.6	0.1	3.7	•
Profit Margin (Before Income Tax) 49	1.5	1.3	3.0	2.6	0.9	0.7	2.3	0.9	0.1	1.3	0.5	2.1	•
Profit Margin (After Income Tax) 50	1.2	1.1	2.9	2.6	0.8	0.6	2.1	0.8	0.0	1.0	0.0	1.2	•

Table II
Corporations with Net Income

TRUCK TRANSPORTATION

MONEY AMOUNTS AND SIZE OF ASSETS IN THOUSANDS OF DOLLARS

Item Description for Accounting Period 7/09 Through 6/10	Total	Zero Assets	Under 500	500 to 1,000	1,000 to 5,000	5,000 to 10,000	10,000 to 25,000	25,000 to 50,000	50,000 to 100,000	100,000 to 250,000	250,000 to 500,000	500,000 to 2,500,000	2,500,000 and over
Number of Enterprises 1	63230	13027	44477	2037	2857	417	258	74	33	23	13	14	0
Revenues ($ in Thousands)													
Net Sales 2	109226657	2684465	25095945	5222483	19139305	7153015	9357275	5582562	4172696	5565722	5642049	19611141	0
Interest 3	99327	2607	1065	1726	8493	3910	5750	2849	4519	3482	8311	56615	0
Rents 4	175398	16739	1	4680	8290	2436	17809	10068	2991	18334	53297	40753	0
Royalties 5	1579	0	0	0	47	0	0	4	22	0	0	1506	0
Other Portfolio Income 6	879059	66066	198987	21732	91199	78345	155169	17896	12058	39276	50173	148160	0
Other Receipts 7	3277781	359363	344399	6244	172790	140688	98289	41266	46357	97847	529517	1441019	0
Total Receipts 8	113659801	3129240	25640397	5256865	19420124	7378394	9634292	5654645	4238643	5724661	6283347	21299194	0
Average Total Receipts 9	1798	240	576	2581	6797	17694	37342	76414	128444	248898	483334	1521371	•
Operating Costs/Operating Income (%)													
Cost of Operations 10	31.9	8.2	32.1	48.6	34.4	30.6	37.6	48.1	27.4	30.3	30.7	23.2	•
Salaries and Wages 11	16.5	12.3	11.2	9.9	15.4	16.9	15.9	11.1	21.2	18.1	19.8	25.7	•
Taxes Paid 12	3.5	3.6	3.0	2.7	3.3	3.0	3.5	3.1	3.9	3.5	3.6	4.8	•
Interest Paid 13	1.0	2.5	0.7	0.6	0.8	1.1	0.8	0.5	1.3	2.1	0.8	1.6	•
Depreciation 14	4.8	5.9	2.8	2.3	4.8	5.6	3.7	3.9	4.8	5.5	7.8	7.3	•
Amortization and Depletion 15	0.1	0.4	0.0	0.0	0.1	0.1	0.2	0.2	0.1	0.2	0.2	0.2	•
Pensions and Other Deferred Comp. 16	0.3	0.5	0.2	0.1	0.3	0.3	0.1	0.3	0.2	0.3	0.2	0.4	•
Employee Benefits 17	2.1	0.6	1.0	1.2	2.0	1.2	2.5	1.5	2.5	2.8	2.5	4.0	•
Advertising 18	0.3	0.0	0.5	0.4	0.5	0.1	0.2	0.1	0.1	0.1	0.1	0.1	•
Other Expenses 19	35.9	61.9	39.8	24.0	31.7	38.2	32.7	27.7	34.7	36.0	39.5	37.1	•
Officers' Compensation 20	2.1	3.9	3.9	3.3	2.8	2.0	1.3	0.9	0.9	0.6	0.7	0.3	•
Operating Margin 21	1.4	0.0	4.8	6.9	3.8	1.0	1.5	2.4	2.8	0.6	0.6	•	•
Operating Margin Before Officers' Comp. 22	3.5	3.9	8.8	10.3	6.6	3.0	2.8	3.3	3.7	1.2	•	•	•

Selected Average Balance Sheet ($ in Thousands)

Net Receivables 23	143	0	6	151	526	1762	3747	8271	13545	30907	52975	198742	•
Inventories 24	11	0	1	23	40	134	401	565	1959	1534	3185	5368	•
Net Property, Plant and Equipment 25	344	0	29	255	862	2760	6090	14476	28602	84798	195467	590166	•
Total Assets 26	735	0	72	733	2184	6742	15168	33836	67981	154803	346352	1141373	•
Notes and Loans Payable 27	280	0	53	240	978	2819	6092	8849	28245	75001	67571	367483	•
All Other Liabilities 28	179	0	13	146	361	1639	3362	6812	17121	30438	82283	355826	•
Net Worth 29	276	0	6	348	846	2283	5714	18175	22615	49364	196498	418064	•

Selected Financial Ratios (Times to 1)

Current Ratio 30	1.6	•	1.5	2.1	1.4	1.4	1.6	1.4	1.0	2.0	1.8		
Quick Ratio 31	1.3	•	1.3	1.7	1.0	1.0	1.3	1.0	0.8	1.5	1.5		
Net Sales to Working Capital 32	16.3	•	26.2	11.6	19.5	19.9	13.4	14.7	183.7	8.5	9.1		
Coverage Ratio 33	6.2	7.7	13.2	7.3	4.8	6.3	7.8	4.4	2.6	7.8	3.4		
Total Asset Turnover 34	2.4	•	7.8	3.5	3.1	2.5	2.4	2.2	1.9	1.6	1.3	1.2	
Inventory Turnover 35	51.6	•	54.2	57.2	39.1	34.0	64.3	17.7	47.9	41.9	60.5		
Receivables Turnover 36	10.6	•	11.4	12.6	7.8	9.6	9.5	•	8.4	7.4	•		
Total Liabilities to Net Worth 37	1.7	•	1.1	1.6	2.0	1.7	0.9	2.0	2.1	0.8	1.7		
Current Assets to Working Capital 38	2.7	•	3.0	1.9	3.8	3.7	2.7	3.5	38.1	2.0	2.2		
Current Liabilities to Working Capital 39	1.7	•	2.0	0.9	2.8	2.7	1.7	2.5	37.1	1.0	1.2		
Working Capital to Net Sales 40	0.1	•	0.0	0.1	0.1	0.1	0.1	0.1	0.0	0.1	0.1		
Inventory to Working Capital 41	0.1	•	0.3	0.1	0.0	0.3	0.1	0.2	1.5	0.1	0.0		
Total Receipts to Cash Flow 42	3.0	1.4	4.0	3.5	3.0	3.9	4.6	3.2	3.4	3.3	2.7		
Cost of Goods to Cash Flow 43	1.0	0.1	1.9	1.2	0.9	1.5	2.2	0.9	1.0	1.0	0.6		
Cash Flow to Total Debt 44	1.3	•	1.7	1.4	1.3	1.0	1.0	0.9	0.7	0.9	0.7		

Selected Financial Factors (in Percentages)

Debt Ratio 45	62.5	•	92.1	52.6	61.3	66.1	62.3	46.3	66.7	68.1	43.3	63.4	
Return on Total Assets 46	15.3	•	60.1	28.7	18.9	13.3	12.7	9.5	10.6	8.7	7.8	6.6	
Return on Equity Before Income Taxes 47	34.2	•	699.2	55.9	42.1	31.0	28.3	15.4	24.5	16.9	11.9	12.7	
Return on Equity After Income Taxes 48	31.7	•	691.4	55.3	40.4	29.7	26.5	14.5	23.2	14.6	10.1	9.2	
Profit Margin (Before Income Tax) 49	5.5	16.6	7.0	7.6	5.3	4.1	4.5	3.7	4.4	3.4	5.4	3.8	
Profit Margin (After Income Tax) 50	5.1	15.7	6.9	7.5	5.1	4.0	4.2	3.5	4.2	3.0	5.4	2.8	

Table I

Corporations with and without Net Income

TRANSIT AND GROUND PASSENGER TRANSPORTATION

MONEY AMOUNTS AND SIZE OF ASSETS IN THOUSANDS OF DOLLARS

Item Description for Accounting Period 7/09 Through 6/10	Total	Zero Assets	Under 500	500 to 1,000	1,000 to 5,000	5,000 to 10,000	10,000 to 25,000	25,000 to 50,000	50,000 to 100,000	100,000 to 250,000	250,000 to 500,000	500,000 to 2,500,000	2,500,000 and over
Number of Enterprises 1	29668	6348	19049	2635	1438	84	79	17	8	5	3	3	0
Revenues ($ in Thousands)													
Net Sales 2	22001880	1071855	3834430	924682	4769666	1349253	1554938	742280	486503	1038917	1002946	5226408	0
Interest 3	201073	942	185	0	1444	575	403	448	402	1344	2313	193017	0
Rents 4	42764	1055	30	0	0	1117	222	0	79	0	0	40261	0
Royalties 5	0	0	0	0	0	0	0	0	0	0	0	0	0
Other Portfolio Income 6	142434	36995	22111	0	11827	5742	40059	4330	193	1541	6386	13251	0
Other Receipts 7	220278	18967	56198	14561	35584	28079	13603	5447	-3026	7164	12933	30768	0
Total Receipts 8	22608429	1129814	3912954	939243	4818521	1384766	1609225	752505	484151	1048966	1024578	5503705	0
Average Total Receipts 9	762	178	205	356	3351	16485	20370	44265	60519	209793	341526	1834568	•
Operating Costs/Operating Income (%)													
Cost of Operations 10	28.9	51.8	7.9	26.3	45.2	55.0	35.2	32.8	60.9	25.2	17.6	15.8	•
Salaries and Wages 11	24.5	4.7	34.2	3.5	13.1	11.4	14.4	27.8	9.1	40.0	28.7	39.2	•
Taxes Paid 12	4.4	4.3	4.5	2.8	3.2	4.7	3.4	4.1	2.5	3.9	6.0	6.0	•
Interest Paid 13	3.8	3.4	2.4	7.2	1.6	0.3	1.9	2.6	2.2	2.9	5.2	8.1	•
Depreciation 14	6.0	3.1	4.3	4.2	6.9	2.4	13.4	12.4	7.2	1.0	9.2	5.5	•
Amortization and Depletion 15	0.7	0.0	0.3	3.7	0.3	0.0	0.1	0.1	0.4	0.2	1.5	1.3	•
Pensions and Other Deferred Comp. 16	0.4	0.8	0.1	•	0.3	0.4	1.1	0.1	0.3	0.1	0.3	0.4	•
Employee Benefits 17	2.2	5.4	0.4	0.1	1.1	1.1	2.9	1.7	2.5	3.4	4.6	3.5	•
Advertising 18	0.6	1.0	0.8	1.5	0.7	0.3	0.3	0.2	1.3	0.5	0.6	0.2	•
Other Expenses 19	27.2	24.4	39.3	43.8	22.7	19.6	24.6	17.4	14.7	21.9	31.5	25.5	•
Officers' Compensation 20	2.5	2.6	6.8	0.7	4.1	0.8	1.5	0.9	1.7	0.8	0.1	0.1	•
Operating Margin 21	•	•	•	6.1	0.7	3.9	1.1	•	•	0.0	0.1	•	•
Operating Margin Before Officers' Comp. 22	1.4	1.0	5.9	6.9	4.8	4.6	2.6	0.8	•	0.9	•	•	•

Selected Average Balance Sheet ($ in Thousands)

Net Receivables **23**	64	0	3	3	326	2623	1088	5823	12166	42797	26306	193557	•
Inventories **24**	4	0	0	0	8	28	111	173	2640	1859	2775	19555	•
Net Property, Plant and Equipment **25**	186	0	20	82	655	1896	8302	19211	22191	13628	157985	708276	•
Total Assets **26**	592	0	82	742	1792	6338	14446	36226	65462	150688	392242	2248911	•
Notes and Loans Payable **27**	343	0	50	589	1090	1794	6972	15065	43481	55011	224088	1279058	•
All Other Liabilities **28**	126	0	25	60	277	1849	1328	6233	6432	57621	77735	587132	•
Net Worth **29**	124	0	6	92	425	2695	6145	14928	15548	38057	90418	382721	•

Selected Financial Ratios (Times to 1)

Current Ratio **30**	1.1	•	1.7	0.7	1.6	1.4	1.4	1.1	1.8	1.5	1.2	0.7	
Quick Ratio **31**	0.8	•	0.7	0.4	1.3	1.1	1.0	0.9	1.4	1.0	1.0	0.5	
Net Sales to Working Capital **32**	41.4	•	22.6	•	14.7	14.5	16.0	33.2	4.8	8.7	18.7	•	
Coverage Ratio **33**	1.4	2.1	1.5	2.1	2.1	20.6	3.4	1.5	•	1.6	0.4	1.0	
Total Asset Turnover **34**	1.3	•	2.5	0.5	1.9	2.5	1.4	1.2	0.9	1.4	0.9	0.8	
Inventory Turnover **35**	51.8	•	94.8	419.7	187.6	311.0	62.6	82.7	14.0	28.2	21.2	14.1	
Receivables Turnover **36**	11.0	•	63.2	151.6	9.3	6.0	14.0	9.5	4.9	4.5	25.4	8.3	
Total Liabilities to Net Worth **37**	3.8	•	11.6	7.0	3.2	1.4	1.4	1.4	3.2	3.0	3.3	4.9	
Current Assets to Working Capital **38**	7.9	•	2.5	•	2.7	3.5	3.5	8.0	2.2	3.1	5.1	•	
Current Liabilities to Working Capital **39**	6.9	•	1.5	•	1.7	2.5	2.5	7.0	1.2	2.1	4.1	•	
Working Capital to Net Sales **40**	0.0	•	0.0	•	0.1	0.1	0.1	0.0	0.2	0.1	0.1	0.1	
Inventory to Working Capital **41**	0.2	•	0.0	•	0.0	0.0	0.1	0.2	0.3	0.1	0.2	•	
Total Receipts to Cash Flow **42**	4.8	5.6	3.1	2.2	6.3	7.8	4.2	7.5	16.2	5.9	5.8	5.2	
Cost of Goods to Cash Flow **43**	1.4	2.9	0.2	0.6	2.8	4.3	1.5	2.5	9.9	1.5	1.0	0.8	
Cash Flow to Total Debt **44**	0.3	•	0.9	0.2	0.4	0.6	0.6	0.3	0.1	0.3	0.2	0.2	

Selected Financial Factors (in Percentages)

Debt Ratio **45**	79.1	•	92.1	87.5	76.3	57.5	57.5	58.8	76.2	74.7	76.9	83.0	
Return on Total Assets **46**	6.9	•	8.8	7.1	6.2	17.3	8.8	4.8	•	6.3	1.7	6.0	
Return on Equity Before Income Taxes **47**	9.9	•	37.3	29.3	13.8	38.6	14.6	3.8	•	9.1	•	•	
Return on Equity After Income Taxes **48**	8.7	•	31.6	28.9	11.9	38.3	13.5	3.1	•	0.5	•	•	
Profit Margin (Before Income Tax) **49**	1.7	3.8	1.2	7.7	1.8	6.5	4.6	1.3	•	1.7	•	•	
Profit Margin (After Income Tax) **50**	1.4	3.5	1.0	7.6	1.5	6.4	4.2	1.1	•	0.1	•	•	

Table II
Corporations with Net Income

TRANSIT AND GROUND PASSENGER TRANSPORTATION

MONEY AMOUNTS AND SIZE OF ASSETS IN THOUSANDS OF DOLLARS

Item Description for Accounting Period 7/09 Through 6/10	Total	Zero Assets	Under 500	500 to 1,000	1,000 to 5,000	5,000 to 10,000	10,000 to 25,000	25,000 to 50,000	50,000 to 100,000	100,000 to 250,000	250,000 to 500,000	500,000 to 2,500,000	2,500,000 and over
Number of Enterprises **1**	16920	2424	12036	1449	870	72	49	•	5	•	0	0	0
Revenues ($ in Thousands)													
Net Sales **2**	15062751	551382	3148090	810531	2636849	1201683	1135653	•	401267	•	0	0	0
Interest **3**	195960	733	88	0	984	222	138	•	340	•	0	0	0
Rents **4**	6459	464	0	0	0	1088	222	•	79	•	0	0	0
Royalties **5**	0	0	0	0	0	0	0	•	0	•	0	0	0
Other Portfolio Income **6**	80922	36979	22070	0	7143	5359	1662	•	161	•	0	0	0
Other Receipts **7**	186790	18842	52905	13785	27877	24989	12881	•	1726	•	0	0	0
Total Receipts **8**	15532882	608400	3223153	824316	2672853	1233341	1150556	•	403573	•	0	0	0
Average Total Receipts **9**	918	251	268	569	3072	17130	23481	•	80715	•	•	•	•
Operating Costs/Operating Income (%)													
Cost of Operations **10**	22.7	44.6	3.3	29.6	36.8	56.4	27.0	•	66.6	•	•	•	•
Salaries and Wages **11**	28.8	6.3	37.6	3.6	17.6	9.1	16.9	•	4.1	•	•	•	•
Taxes Paid **12**	4.6	3.4	4.8	2.8	3.9	4.8	3.9	•	1.6	•	•	•	•
Interest Paid **13**	3.8	3.5	1.7	4.2	1.4	0.2	1.3	•	1.8	•	•	•	•
Depreciation **14**	4.9	3.8	3.8	2.1	6.8	2.1	7.9	•	7.3	•	•	•	•
Amortization and Depletion **15**	0.5	0.0	0.0	0.9	0.1	0.0	0.1	•	0.1	•	•	•	•
Pensions and Other Deferred Comp. **16**	0.4	0.4	0.1	•	0.5	0.4	1.4	•	0.3	•	•	•	•
Employee Benefits **17**	1.8	3.0	0.2	0.1	1.0	1.0	3.6	•	2.9	•	•	•	•
Advertising **18**	0.5	1.5	0.7	1.7	0.8	0.3	0.2	•	0.4	•	•	•	•
Other Expenses **19**	27.1	27.7	37.3	45.6	21.4	20.0	28.0	•	10.5	•	•	•	•
Officers' Compensation **20**	2.8	2.8	7.2	0.5	5.3	0.7	1.5	•	1.4	•	•	•	•
Operating Margin **21**	2.1	3.0	3.3	9.0	4.4	5.1	8.2	•	3.0	•	•	•	•
Operating Margin Before Officers' Comp. **22**	4.9	5.8	10.4	9.5	9.7	5.8	9.6	•	4.4	•	•	•	•

Selected Average Balance Sheet ($ in Thousands)

Net Receivables 23	68	0	2	6	336	2934	1067	•	15801
Inventories 24	3	0	0	0	2	11	94	•	5383
Net Property, Plant and Equipment 25	212	0	24	123	640	1626	6828	•	31839
Total Assets 26	668	0	87	737	1702	6205	14507	•	67050
Notes and Loans Payable 27	348	0	49	466	940	1577	4833	•	32973
All Other Liabilities 28	142	0	16	100	230	1929	1553	•	9226
Net Worth 29	178	0	23	171	533	2698	8121	•	24851

Selected Financial Ratios (Times to 1)

Current Ratio 30	1.2	2.7	•	1.0	2.0	1.4	1.8	•	1.7
Quick Ratio 31	0.8	1.0	•	0.6	1.8	1.1	1.3	•	1.2
Net Sales to Working Capital 32	40.1	15.3	•	109.7	9.4	15.1	11.0	•	6.5
Coverage Ratio 33	2.4	4.3	4.8	3.6	5.3	34.3	8.0	•	3.0
Total Asset Turnover 34	1.3	3.0	•	0.8	1.8	2.7	1.6	•	1.2
Inventory Turnover 35	59.8	74.6	•	413.4	586.7	821.1	66.8	•	9.9
Receivables Turnover 36	14.4	74.2	•	166.6	7.7	6.0	13.9	•	•
Total Liabilities to Net Worth 37	2.8	2.9	•	3.3	2.2	1.3	0.8	•	1.7
Current Assets to Working Capital 38	6.8	1.6	•	26.4	2.0	3.6	2.3	•	2.4
Current Liabilities to Working Capital 39	5.8	0.6	•	25.4	1.0	2.6	1.3	•	1.4
Working Capital to Net Sales 40	0.0	0.1	•	0.0	0.1	0.1	0.1	•	0.2
Inventory to Working Capital 41	0.2	•	•	0.1	0.0	0.0	0.0	•	0.4
Total Receipts to Cash Flow 42	4.0	2.8	3.6	2.0	5.7	7.5	3.2	•	10.9
Cost of Goods to Cash Flow 43	0.9	0.1	1.6	0.6	2.1	4.2	0.9	•	7.3
Cash Flow to Total Debt 44	0.5	1.4	•	0.5	0.5	0.6	1.1	•	0.2

Selected Financial Factors (in Percentages)

Debt Ratio 45	73.3	74.2	•	76.8	68.7	56.5	44.0	•	62.9
Return on Total Assets 46	12.0	22.1	•	11.3	12.7	21.4	17.2	•	6.5
Return on Equity Before Income Taxes 47	26.3	65.5	•	34.9	32.8	47.7	26.9	•	11.7
Return on Equity After Income Taxes 48	24.7	62.9	•	34.6	30.2	47.3	25.6	•	11.4
Profit Margin (Before Income Tax) 49	5.3	5.6	13.3	10.7	5.8	7.7	9.4	•	3.6
Profit Margin (After Income Tax) 50	4.9	5.4	12.8	10.6	5.3	7.7	9.0	•	3.5

Table I

Corporations with and without Net Income

PIPELINE TRANSPORTATION 486000

MONEY AMOUNTS AND SIZE OF ASSETS IN THOUSANDS OF DOLLARS

Item Description for Accounting Period 7/09 Through 6/10	Total	Zero Assets	Under 500	500 to 1,000	1,000 to 5,000	5,000 to 10,000	10,000 to 25,000	25,000 to 50,000	50,000 to 100,000	100,000 to 250,000	250,000 to 500,000	500,000 to 2,500,000	2,500,000 and over
Number of Enterprises **1**	248	0	0	0	144	60	18	7	5	4	0	7	4
Revenues ($ in Thousands)													
Net Sales **2**	10810058	0	0	0	329390	131365	340597	227124	456459	290636	0	1916324	7718163
Interest **3**	107758	0	0	0	177	4	161	194	75	242	0	1003	105902
Rents **4**	40823	0	0	0	0	0	1006	1540	256	8502	0	7103	22417
Royalties **5**	545	0	0	0	464	0	0	0	0	0	0	0	81
Other Portfolio Income **6**	318895	0	0	0	0	0	35016	0	151	0	0	17436	266293
Other Receipts **7**	1444663	0	0	0	32415	28084	7416	769	7125	55875	0	32385	1280593
Total Receipts **8**	12722742	0	0	0	362446	159453	384196	229627	464066	355255	0	1974251	8793449
Average Total Receipts **9**	51301	•	•	•	2517	2658	21344	32804	92813	88814	•	282036	2198362
Operating Costs/Operating Income (%)													
Cost of Operations **10**	45.7	•	•	•	36.5	38.4	62.8	30.3	20.1	46.1	•	12.4	56.5
Salaries and Wages **11**	6.3	•	•	•	25.6	9.1	2.3	2.8	18.8	4.5	•	4.8	5.4
Taxes Paid **12**	3.9	•	•	•	2.9	2.5	2.5	5.6	4.9	4.2	•	5.6	3.4
Interest Paid **13**	15.0	•	•	•	0.3	0.1	0.0	0.4	0.7	6.5	•	10.4	19.6
Depreciation **14**	11.8	•	•	•	0.4	11.4	2.1	9.2	11.6	11.6	•	17.1	11.5
Amortization and Depletion **15**	3.8	•	•	•	0.4	•	0.4	0.1	0.0	•	•	0.8	5.6
Pensions and Other Deferred Comp. **16**	0.5	•	•	•	•	0.0	0.0	0.0	1.3	0.1	•	2.0	0.1
Employee Benefits **17**	1.0	•	•	•	0.1	4.6	0.4	0.7	4.6	1.3	•	0.8	0.9
Advertising **18**	0.0	•	•	•	1.0	•	0.0	•	0.0	•	•	0.0	0.0
Other Expenses **19**	20.0	•	•	•	28.0	17.1	14.0	23.2	35.1	29.8	•	26.9	16.7
Officers' Compensation **20**	0.5	•	•	•	4.0	0.8	0.2	•	0.4	•	•	0.4	0.4
Operating Margin **21**	•	•	•	•	0.7	16.1	15.4	27.7	2.4	•	•	18.7	•
Operating Margin Before Officers' Comp. **22**	•	•	•	•	4.8	16.8	15.6	27.7	2.7	•	•	19.1	•

Selected Average Balance Sheet ($ in Thousands)

Net Receivables 23	14104	229	251	1744	3257	10909	105187	78309	593037
Inventories 24	2310	169	163	218	555	769	953	28590	160677
Net Property, Plant and Equipment 25	83982	48	985	5054	27551	57516	107792	605737	3879722
Total Assets 26	163590	1849	5894	14431	40556	81763	242516	1045637	7677118
Notes and Loans Payable 27	93823	248	2337	0	5593	27217	75878	490283	4795341
All Other Liabilities 28	35738	148	601	3761	18231	22692	138047	266377	1519976
Net Worth 29	34030	1453	2956	10670	16732	31854	28591	288978	1361801

Selected Financial Ratios (Times to 1)

Current Ratio 30	1.1	4.1	4.6	1.6	1.2	0.8	1.2	0.9	1.1
Quick Ratio 31	0.8	3.0	1.6	1.3	0.9	0.7	1.1	0.7	0.8
Net Sales to Working Capital 32	23.7	2.8	1.6	11.2	14.3	•	3.6	•	21.4
Coverage Ratio 33	1.6	34.4	524.7	1652.3	68.1	6.5	3.8	3.1	1.2
Total Asset Turnover 34	0.3	1.2	0.4	1.3	0.8	1.1	0.3	0.3	0.2
Inventory Turnover 35	8.6	4.9	5.2	54.4	17.7	23.9	35.1	1.2	6.3
Receivables Turnover 36	4.2	10.6	3.5	6.6	5.5	8.5	1.3	2.5	6.0
Total Liabilities to Net Worth 37	3.8	0.3	1.0	0.4	1.4	1.6	7.5	2.6	4.6
Current Assets to Working Capital 38	14.9	1.3	1.3	2.8	5.1	•	6.6	•	13.0
Current Liabilities to Working Capital 39	13.9	0.3	0.3	1.8	4.1	•	5.6	•	12.0
Working Capital to Net Sales 40	0.0	0.4	0.6	0.1	0.1	•	0.3	•	0.0
Inventory to Working Capital 41	1.9	0.2	0.1	0.1	0.2	•	0.1	•	1.9
Total Receipts to Cash Flow 42	3.9	3.4	2.0	2.7	2.0	3.0	2.2	2.3	5.7
Cost of Goods to Cash Flow 43	1.8	1.2	0.8	1.7	0.6	0.6	1.0	0.3	3.2
Cash Flow to Total Debt 44	0.1	1.7	0.4	1.9	0.7	0.6	0.2	0.2	0.0

Selected Financial Factors (in Percentages)

Debt Ratio 45	79.2	21.4	49.8	26.1	58.7	61.0	88.2	72.4	82.3
Return on Total Assets 46	6.5	13.7	13.9	36.9	23.4	5.3	7.4	8.4	5.4
Return on Equity Before Income Taxes 47	11.8	16.9	27.8	49.9	55.8	11.6	46.0	20.5	4.9
Return on Equity After Income Taxes 48	8.5	12.9	27.8	32.0	31.8	4.2	30.0	13.3	4.3
Profit Margin (Before Income Tax) 49	9.2	10.7	37.5	28.1	28.8	4.0	18.1	21.7	3.7
Profit Margin (After Income Tax) 50	6.7	8.2	37.5	18.1	16.4	1.5	11.8	14.1	3.3

Table II

Corporations with Net Income

PIPELINE TRANSPORTATION

MONEY AMOUNTS AND SIZE OF ASSETS IN THOUSANDS OF DOLLARS

Item Description for Accounting Period 7/09 Through 6/10	Total	Zero Assets	Under 500	500 to 1,000	1,000 to 5,000	5,000 to 10,000	10,000 to 25,000	25,000 to 50,000	50,000 to 100,000	100,000 to 250,000	250,000 to 500,000	500,000 to 2,500,000	2,500,000 and over
Number of Enterprises **1**	224	0	0	0	138	50	•	•	•	•	0	4	4
Revenues ($ in Thousands)													
Net Sales **2**	10032305	0	0	0	269862	75729	•	•	•	•	0	1516851	7118163
Interest **3**	107338	0	0	0	177	0	•	•	•	•	0	842	105902
Rents **4**	33762	0	0	0	0	0	•	•	•	•	0	42	22417
Royalties **5**	545	0	0	0	464	0	•	•	•	•	0	0	81
Other Portfolio Income **6**	318893	0	0	0	0	0	•	•	•	•	0	17436	266293
Other Receipts **7**	1444353	0	0	0	31633	27898	•	•	•	•	0	34073	1280593
Total Receipts **8**	11937196	0	0	0	302136	103627	•	•	•	•	0	1569244	8793449
Average Total Receipts **9**	53291	•	•	•	2189	2073	•	•	•	•	•	392311	2198362
Operating Costs/Operating Income (%)													
Cost of Operations **10**	43.8	•	•	•	28.2	25.0	•	•	•	•	•	0.8	56.5
Salaries and Wages **11**	6.6	•	•	•	30.5	0.5	•	•	•	•	•	5.5	5.4
Taxes Paid **12**	4.0	•	•	•	3.2	1.7	•	•	•	•	•	6.1	3.4
Interest Paid **13**	15.6	•	•	•	0.4	•	•	•	•	•	•	9.9	19.6
Depreciation **14**	11.5	•	•	•	0.4	12.9	•	•	•	•	•	16.4	11.5
Amortization and Depletion **15**	4.0	•	•	•	0.5	•	•	•	•	•	•	0.3	5.6
Pensions and Other Deferred Comp. **16**	0.5	•	•	•	•	0.0	•	•	•	•	•	2.5	0.1
Employee Benefits **17**	1.1	•	•	•	•	2.9	•	•	•	•	•	0.9	0.9
Advertising **18**	0.0	•	•	•	1.2	•	•	•	•	•	•	•	0.0
Other Expenses **19**	20.8	•	•	•	29.8	19.5	•	•	•	•	•	31.8	16.7
Officers' Compensation **20**	0.5	•	•	•	3.8	1.3	•	•	•	•	•	0.5	0.4
Operating Margin **21**	•	•	•	•	1.9	36.2	•	•	•	•	•	25.2	•
Operating Margin Before Officers' Comp. **22**	•	•	•	•	5.6	37.5	•	•	•	•	•	25.7	•

Selected Average Balance Sheet ($ in Thousands)

Net Receivables 23	11936	187	72	35779	593037
Inventories 24	1890	177	73	14683	160677
Net Property, Plant and Equipment 25	86011	49	588	706230	3879722
Total Assets 26	162862	1863	5998	965142	7677118
Notes and Loans Payable 27	98908	251	2804	597636	4795341
All Other Liabilities 28	32902	91	178	219798	1519976
Net Worth 29	31052	1521	3016	147707	1361801

Selected Financial Ratios (Times to 1)

Current Ratio 30	1.0	5.1	9.2	0.4	1.1
Quick Ratio 31	0.8	3.6	2.9	0.3	0.8
Net Sales to Working Capital 32	54.4	2.3	1.0	*	21.4
Coverage Ratio 33	1.7	38.8	*	3.9	1.2
Total Asset Turnover 34	0.3	1.0	0.3	0.4	0.2
Inventory Turnover 35	10.4	3.1	5.2	0.2	6.3
Receivables Turnover 36	5.3	9.8	13.2	3.0	6.0
Total Liabilities to Net Worth 37	4.2	0.2	1.0	5.5	4.6
Current Assets to Working Capital 38	28.2	1.2	1.1	*	13.0
Current Liabilities to Working Capital 39	27.2	0.2	0.1	*	12.0
Working Capital to Net Sales 40	0.0	0.4	1.0	*	0.0
Inventory to Working Capital 41	3.7	0.2	0.0	*	1.9
Total Receipts to Cash Flow 42	3.6	3.0	1.1	1.8	5.7
Cost of Goods to Cash Flow 43	1.6	0.9	0.3	0.0	3.2
Cash Flow to Total Debt 44	0.1	1.9	0.5	0.3	0.0

Selected Financial Factors (in Percentages)

Debt Ratio 45	80.9	18.3	49.7	84.7	82.3
Return on Total Assets 46	7.2	14.9	18.5	15.2	5.4
Return on Equity Before Income Taxes 47	15.3	17.8	36.7	73.5	4.9
Return on Equity After Income Taxes 48	11.3	13.8	36.7	48.8	4.3
Profit Margin (Before Income Tax) 49	10.6	13.8	73.1	28.6	3.7
Profit Margin (After Income Tax) 50	7.9	10.7	73.1	19.0	3.3

Table I

Corporations with and without Net Income

OTHER TRANSPORTATION AND SUPPORT ACTIVITIES

MONEY AMOUNTS AND SIZE OF ASSETS IN THOUSANDS OF DOLLARS

Item Description for Accounting Period 7/09 Through 6/10		Total	Zero Assets	Under 500	500 to 1,000	1,000 to 5,000	5,000 to 10,000	10,000 to 25,000	25,000 to 50,000	50,000 to 100,000	100,000 to 250,000	250,000 to 500,000	500,000 to 2,500,000	2,500,000 and over
Number of Enterprises	1	40499	7365	26428	3178	2750	355	191	98	53	42	14	21	4
Revenues ($ in Thousands)														
Net Sales	2	190534107	739968	14970516	6668479	18343465	7697689	5831455	6654234	5791601	6463536	4774636	14163000	98435529
Interest	3	977340	73	2648	2431	8218	2870	3616	3937	7426	4498	27635	115491	798497
Rents	4	213731	0	270	94	0	5261	3478	1164	8360	33308	8124	27369	126303
Royalties	5	1598179	0	0	40	4	0	0	3403	20	1423	0	4796	1588492
Other Portfolio Income	6	706333	4961	28890	30887	11077	2447	7608	21179	6570	31175	9621	350040	201874
Other Receipts	7	2804630	16814	51805	36185	69116	42211	48128	77811	292292	47031	52693	192542	1878007
Total Receipts	8	196834320	761816	15054129	6738116	18431880	7750478	5894285	6761728	6106269	6580971	4872709	14853238	103028702
Average Total Receipts	9	4860	103	570	2120	6703	21832	30860	68997	115213	156690	348051	707297	25757176
Operating Costs/Operating Income (%)														
Cost of Operations	10	37.4	21.1	50.1	52.9	58.2	61.3	65.3	69.2	61.4	57.1	37.0	46.0	21.0
Salaries and Wages	11	19.1	6.3	10.1	12.1	16.5	13.8	12.4	10.7	16.1	14.3	22.3	17.0	23.5
Taxes Paid	12	3.2	1.8	2.2	7.6	5.0	2.5	1.8	2.2	3.4	2.3	3.5	2.8	3.1
Interest Paid	13	1.4	1.8	0.6	0.6	0.7	0.4	0.6	1.1	1.4	1.3	1.4	4.7	1.4
Depreciation	14	3.6	5.2	1.5	2.9	1.6	1.0	1.9	2.7	2.4	4.0	4.2	2.8	4.8
Amortization and Depletion	15	0.3	0.5	0.1	0.1	0.2	0.3	0.2	0.3	0.6	1.1	0.8	0.6	0.3
Pensions and Other Deferred Comp.	16	1.8	0.0	0.1	0.1	0.4	0.5	0.4	0.1	0.3	0.4	0.6	0.6	3.1
Employee Benefits	17	4.1	0.7	0.7	1.2	1.2	1.4	1.3	1.5	2.1	2.4	3.2	4.1	6.2
Advertising	18	0.4	0.3	0.3	0.4	0.2	0.1	0.2	0.2	0.2	0.3	0.2	0.5	0.5
Other Expenses	19	28.7	56.8	27.6	17.3	11.8	15.1	13.4	11.6	19.8	17.7	26.9	22.5	37.8
Officers' Compensation	20	1.3	5.6	5.1	4.8	2.5	2.6	2.7	1.2	0.9	1.1	0.9	0.7	0.3
Operating Margin	21	•	•	1.6	•	1.6	1.0	•	•	•	•	•	•	•
Operating Margin Before Officers' Comp.	22	0.1	5.5	6.8	4.8	4.1	3.6	2.6	0.4	•	•	•	•	•

Selected Average Balance Sheet ($ in Thousands)

Net Receivables 23	531	14	187	697	3445	5528	7800	17541	31872	66212	145816	2326691
Inventories 24	40	2	12	72	151	229	534	3352	3861	1500	10532	148902
Net Property, Plant and Equipment 25	1042	34	189	655	1304	5253	9532	17127	40110	75569	184123	7245975
Total Assets 26	3161	92	681	2252	7396	15634	32754	69136	146506	363112	1145953	17361276
Notes and Loans Payable 27	836	48	301	1062	1845	4155	16434	22625	48205	116646	386340	3165272
All Other Liabilities 28	1402	32	243	675	2843	6207	13051	25567	46741	90004	377821	9330422
Net Worth 29	923	12	137	515	2708	5273	3269	20943	51560	156462	381791	4865582

Selected Financial Ratios (Times to 1)

Current Ratio 30	1.0	•	1.1	1.5	1.5	1.2	1.1	1.7	1.2	1.5	1.4	0.8
Quick Ratio 31	0.8	•	0.8	1.2	1.3	1.0	0.9	1.3	0.9	1.3	0.9	0.6
Net Sales to Working Capital 32	244.8	•	115.2	17.7	13.4	23.0	42.7	8.3	16.9	8.4	7.8	•
Coverage Ratio 33	2.6	2.6	2.6	4.2	5.5	2.5	1.7	•	1.1	1.7	1.7	3.0
Total Asset Turnover 34	1.5	•	3.1	3.0	2.9	2.0	2.1	1.6	1.1	0.9	0.6	1.4
Inventory Turnover 35	43.8	•	94.2	54.0	88.2	87.0	88.0	20.0	22.8	84.2	29.4	34.7
Receivables Turnover 36	7.8	•	12.9	9.1	8.1	4.7	8.7	5.8	5.0	6.9	4.6	7.9
Total Liabilities to Net Worth 37	2.4	•	4.0	3.4	1.7	2.0	9.0	2.3	1.8	1.3	2.0	2.6
Current Assets to Working Capital 38	50.1	•	20.6	3.2	3.2	6.6	9.8	2.5	6.5	2.9	3.7	•
Current Liabilities to Working Capital 39	49.1	•	19.6	2.2	2.2	5.6	8.8	1.5	5.5	1.9	2.7	•
Working Capital to Net Sales 40	0.0	•	0.0	0.1	0.1	0.0	0.0	0.1	0.1	0.1	0.1	•
Inventory to Working Capital 41	2.1	0.1	0.7	0.2	0.0	0.2	0.3	0.2	0.4	0.0	0.2	•
Total Receipts to Cash Flow 42	4.0	•	7.4	8.8	7.2	9.8	11.6	8.5	9.2	4.8	5.1	2.9
Cost of Goods to Cash Flow 43	1.5	0.4	3.9	5.2	4.4	6.4	8.0	5.2	5.2	1.8	2.3	0.6
Cash Flow to Total Debt 44	0.5	•	0.5	0.4	0.6	0.3	0.2	0.3	0.2	0.3	0.2	0.7

Selected Financial Factors (in Percentages)

Debt Ratio 45	70.8	87.3	79.8	77.1	63.4	66.3	90.0	69.7	64.8	56.9	66.7	72.0
Return on Total Assets 46	5.4	17.1	4.9	8.2	6.0	3.1	3.9	•	1.4	2.2	4.7	6.0
Return on Equity Before Income Taxes 47	11.2	106.4	14.8	27.2	13.5	5.6	16.6	•	0.4	2.1	5.9	14.4
Return on Equity After Income Taxes 48	6.6	101.2	11.0	25.3	12.5	4.1	7.2	•	•	•	1.4	8.9
Profit Margin (Before Income Tax) 49	2.2	2.8	2.2	2.1	1.0	1.0	0.8	•	0.1	•	3.3	2.8
Profit Margin (After Income Tax) 50	1.3	1.6	2.1	2.0	0.7	0.7	0.3	•	•	•	0.8	1.8

Table II
Corporations with Net Income

OTHER TRANSPORTATION AND SUPPORT ACTIVITIES

MONEY AMOUNTS AND SIZE OF ASSETS IN THOUSANDS OF DOLLARS

Item Description for Accounting Period 7/09 Through 6/10	Total	Zero Assets	Under 500	500 to 1,000	1,000 to 5,000	5,000 to 10,000	10,000 to 25,000	25,000 to 50,000	50,000 to 100,000	100,000 to 250,000	250,000 to 500,000	500,000 to 2,500,000	2,500,000 and over
Number of Enterprises 1	20360	3809	12791	1574	1721	224	109	60	34	21	6	10	0
Revenues ($ in Thousands)													
Net Sales 2	147249555	279264	9668865	4100781	14459628	5056529	3975673	5069945	4174337	3929321	2032458	94502755	0
Interest 3	774601	10	369	916	7013	1715	3352	1927	4524	3392	6002	745380	0
Rents 4	167024	0	264	94	0	5200	1403	216	3669	23588	2294	130295	0
Royalties 5	1590044	0	0	40	4	0	0	64	20	1423	0	1588492	0
Other Portfolio Income 6	618999	4934	10964	27712	11077	2223	3717	20143	6387	28320	8792	494727	0
Other Receipts 7	646067	16813	44175	33180	46058	28514	49700	60646	151803	36838	23111	155233	0
Total Receipts 8	151046290	301021	9724637	4162723	14523780	5094181	4033845	5152941	4340740	4022882	2072657	97616882	0
Average Total Receipts 9	7419	79	760	2645	8439	22742	37008	85882	127669	191566	345443	9761688	•
Operating Costs/Operating Income (%)													
Cost of Operations 10	34.0	10.4	55.6	43.8	59.8	55.7	64.1	71.5	61.9	57.4	36.6	20.8	•
Salaries and Wages 11	19.7	0.2	8.0	12.7	15.0	15.4	12.1	9.0	15.7	13.8	18.7	23.6	•
Taxes Paid 12	3.4	2.5	1.9	10.9	5.3	3.0	1.7	2.3	2.4	2.1	4.4	3.1	•
Interest Paid 13	1.0	1.1	0.5	0.6	0.5	0.2	0.4	0.7	0.9	0.9	1.0	1.2	•
Depreciation 14	3.8	4.3	1.2	3.3	1.3	0.7	1.2	2.6	1.9	3.8	3.9	4.9	•
Amortization and Depletion 15	0.3	•	0.0	0.0	0.2	0.0	0.1	0.1	0.4	0.8	1.3	0.3	•
Pensions and Other Deferred Comp. 16	2.2	•	0.1	0.2	0.2	0.7	0.2	0.1	0.2	0.3	0.5	3.3	•
Employee Benefits 17	4.4	1.1	0.6	0.9	0.7	0.9	1.3	1.0	2.0	2.1	2.0	6.2	•
Advertising 18	0.4	0.3	0.2	0.6	0.2	0.1	0.1	0.1	0.1	0.2	0.3	0.5	•
Other Expenses 19	27.7	53.7	21.3	16.2	10.2	15.8	13.1	8.8	12.9	15.2	24.9	34.9	•
Officers' Compensation 20	1.2	11.6	4.5	6.1	2.4	3.1	3.1	1.2	0.9	1.2	0.9	0.3	•
Operating Margin 21	2.0	14.9	6.1	4.7	4.1	4.3	2.7	2.5	0.5	2.2	5.4	0.9	•
Operating Margin Before Officers' Comp. 22	3.2	26.4	10.7	10.8	6.5	7.4	5.8	3.7	1.4	3.4	6.3	1.2	•

Selected Average Balance Sheet ($ in Thousands)

Net Receivables 23	792	0	15	170	683	3891	7350	9855	21023	35981	76992	1029080
Inventories 24	52	0	4	19	45	178	270	582	3374	4828	1809	46499
Net Property, Plant and Equipment 25	1712	0	38	177	619	1195	3556	9142	15541	41621	61492	3006163
Total Assets 26	4109	0	102	716	2301	7807	15822	32536	69847	147992	342712	6430674
Notes and Loans Payable 27	946	0	46	293	924	1385	3534	11693	17102	47453	54047	1331911
All Other Liabilities 28	1573	0	39	143	669	3060	8382	11916	21172	40948	91580	2569945
Net Worth 29	1590	0	16	280	708	3361	3906	8927	31573	59591	197086	2528817

Selected Financial Ratios (Times to 1)

Current Ratio 30	1.0	•	1.2	1.9	1.5	1.7	1.1	1.2	1.7	1.3	1.8	0.9
Quick Ratio 31	0.9	•	1.0	1.6	1.3	1.6	1.0	1.0	1.4	1.0	1.5	0.7
Net Sales to Working Capital 32	168.5	22.3	110.5	13.3	19.2	9.3	48.5	27.0	8.3	14.1	6.0	•
Coverage Ratio 33	5.8	•	15.4	10.8	10.7	24.4	11.0	7.0	6.1	6.6	8.7	4.6
Total Asset Turnover 34	1.8	•	7.4	3.6	3.7	2.9	2.3	2.6	1.8	1.3	1.0	1.5
Inventory Turnover 35	47.0	•	117.6	61.0	111.3	70.9	86.8	103.8	22.5	22.3	68.5	42.3
Receivables Turnover 36	8.1	•	47.9	15.2	12.2	7.8	3.8	8.2	5.7	•	•	•
Total Liabilities to Net Worth 37	1.6	•	5.2	1.6	2.2	1.3	3.1	2.6	1.2	1.5	0.7	1.5
Current Assets to Working Capital 38	32.1	•	6.4	2.1	2.8	2.4	14.4	5.6	2.4	4.7	2.2	•
Current Liabilities to Working Capital 39	31.1	•	5.4	1.1	1.8	1.4	13.4	4.6	1.4	3.7	1.2	•
Working Capital to Net Sales 40	0.0	•	0.0	0.1	0.1	0.0	0.0	0.0	0.1	0.1	0.2	•
Inventory to Working Capital 41	1.0	•	0.4	0.1	0.0	0.4	0.0	0.1	0.2	0.4	0.0	•
Total Receipts to Cash Flow 42	3.8	1.6	4.8	5.8	8.0	5.3	7.5	9.3	8.2	8.3	4.1	3.1
Cost of Goods to Cash Flow 43	1.3	0.2	2.7	2.6	4.8	3.0	4.8	6.7	5.1	4.8	1.5	0.6
Cash Flow to Total Debt 44	0.8	•	1.8	1.0	0.7	1.0	0.4	0.4	0.4	0.3	0.6	0.8

Selected Financial Factors (in Percentages)

Debt Ratio 45	61.3	•	83.9	60.9	69.2	56.9	75.3	72.6	54.8	59.7	42.5	60.7
Return on Total Assets 46	10.1	•	53.5	25.0	18.5	15.3	10.5	12.5	9.5	7.1	8.4	8.3
Return on Equity Before Income Taxes 47	21.5	•	311.8	58.0	54.3	34.1	38.8	39.0	17.5	15.1	13.0	16.5
Return on Equity After Income Taxes 48	16.3	•	304.2	54.2	52.2	32.8	35.1	33.3	13.9	11.3	8.5	10.9
Profit Margin (Before Income Tax) 49	4.7	22.7	6.7	6.2	4.6	5.1	4.2	4.1	4.5	4.8	7.6	4.4
Profit Margin (After Income Tax) 50	3.6	19.8	6.6	5.8	4.9	4.9	3.8	3.5	3.6	4.9	4.8	2.9

Table I

Corporations with and without Net Income

WAREHOUSING AND STORAGE

MONEY AMOUNTS AND SIZE OF ASSETS IN THOUSANDS OF DOLLARS

Item Description for Accounting Period 7/09 Through 6/10		Total	Zero Assets	Under 500	500 to 1,000	1,000 to 5,000	5,000 to 10,000	10,000 to 25,000	25,000 to 50,000	50,000 to 100,000	100,000 to 250,000	250,000 to 500,000	500,000 to 2,500,000	2,500,000 and over
Number of Enterprises	1	5452	14	3112	1063	814	170	201	35	17	14	3	10	0
Revenues ($ in Thousands)														
Net Sales	2	20199130	72692	707438	1053386	3138259	1662450	3280030	584991	1140454	1968757	368434	6222239	0
Interest	3	49477	0	0	2304	1225	955	4397	594	3566	1893	4631	29911	0
Rents	4	26391	0	0	656	2039	4366	1835	749	4261	4264	2010	6211	0
Royalties	5	33917	0	40	0	0	938	0	0	0	1520	71	31349	0
Other Portfolio Income	6	89518	0	38	630	49740	1904	5779	2937	11617	2736	9256	4880	0
Other Receipts	7	481632	18427	29345	3384	60516	24551	101471	10046	17630	104299	30359	81603	0
Total Receipts	8	20880065	91119	736863	1060360	3251779	1695164	3393512	599317	1177528	2083469	414761	6376193	0
Average Total Receipts	9	3830	6508	237	998	3995	9972	16883	17123	69266	148819	138254	637619	•
Operating Costs/Operating Income (%)														
Cost of Operations	10	32.0	27.0	9.0	15.6	66.4	35.3	42.3	11.6	41.1	18.2	1.5	20.3	•
Salaries and Wages	11	19.3	40.4	15.3	22.0	8.7	11.9	19.5	23.8	14.7	34.6	23.7	21.7	•
Taxes Paid	12	3.8	2.1	1.8	4.1	2.3	2.9	3.8	5.3	3.9	4.7	5.7	4.2	•
Interest Paid	13	3.4	0.2	1.0	1.9	1.5	1.8	1.5	4.0	1.7	1.6	7.4	6.8	•
Depreciation	14	5.6	1.0	2.6	2.8	2.4	4.7	4.5	12.0	3.9	4.0	11.5	8.7	•
Amortization and Depletion	15	0.9	•	0.5	0.0	0.1	0.1	0.2	0.7	0.6	0.3	0.1	2.3	•
Pensions and Other Deferred Comp.	16	0.4	•	0.0	0.5	0.3	0.5	0.4	0.5	0.9	0.6	2.4	0.3	•
Employee Benefits	17	2.3	1.5	0.0	2.1	1.6	2.0	1.7	2.0	3.8	4.3	3.3	2.5	•
Advertising	18	0.3	0.2	0.8	1.3	0.2	0.3	0.1	0.3	0.1	0.1	0.0	0.3	•
Other Expenses	19	29.9	23.0	67.7	46.3	12.9	33.3	22.9	37.7	26.8	31.9	56.9	31.8	•
Officers' Compensation	20	1.6	•	0.1	4.2	2.5	4.0	2.3	1.4	1.6	0.7	0.4	0.3	•
Operating Margin	21	0.5	4.6	1.3	•	1.1	3.1	0.9	0.6	0.8	•	•	0.6	•
Operating Margin Before Officers' Comp.	22	2.1	4.6	1.4	3.4	3.6	7.1	3.2	2.0	2.4	•	•	0.9	•

Selected Average Balance Sheet ($ in Thousands)

Net Receivables 23	519	0	18	119	315	818	1715	2761	10878	32683	8357	114274
Inventories 24	100	0	0	8	203	208	543	279	1319	11571	121	3035
Net Property, Plant and Equipment 25	1939	0	60	360	1245	3325	6862	23180	31287	54762	169285	442616
Total Assets 26	5614	0	115	679	2254	6839	15119	36568	66058	143823	332845	1807906
Notes and Loans Payable 27	2259	0	86	591	1068	2606	5579	19260	15340	43125	65347	725244
All Other Liabilities 28	1071	0	33	138	543	1367	2300	5620	19859	22152	152296	315068
Net Worth 29	2284	0	-4	-49	643	2865	7240	11689	30859	78545	115202	767593

Selected Financial Ratios (Times to 1)

Current Ratio 30	1.3	•	1.7	1.6	0.9	1.4	1.9	1.6	1.0	1.9	0.6	1.2
Quick Ratio 31	1.1	•	1.3	1.4	0.6	1.1	1.2	1.4	0.7	1.4	0.4	1.1
Net Sales to Working Capital 32	13.4	•	13.2	9.8	•	12.2	6.6	6.5	•	5.5	•	17.6
Coverage Ratio 33	2.2	155.3	6.6	0.9	4.2	3.8	3.9	1.8	3.3	4.0	1.1	1.5
Total Asset Turnover 34	0.7	•	2.0	1.5	1.7	1.4	1.1	0.5	1.0	1.0	0.4	0.3
Inventory Turnover 35	11.9	•	27.7	19.4	12.6	16.6	12.7	7.0	20.9	2.2	15.3	41.6
Receivables Turnover 36	7.1	•	25.1	8.5	13.9	10.9	9.1	6.6	6.6	4.3	7.4	5.3
Total Liabilities to Net Worth 37	1.5	•	•	•	2.5	1.4	1.1	2.1	1.1	0.8	1.9	1.4
Current Assets to Working Capital 38	4.0	•	2.4	2.6	•	3.3	2.1	2.7	•	2.2	•	5.5
Current Liabilities to Working Capital 39	3.0	•	1.4	1.6	•	2.3	1.1	1.7	•	1.2	•	4.5
Working Capital to Net Sales 40	0.1	•	0.1	0.1	•	0.1	0.2	0.2	•	0.2	•	0.1
Inventory to Working Capital 41	0.4	•	0.0	0.1	•	0.2	0.3	0.1	•	0.5	•	0.1
Total Receipts to Cash Flow 42	4.5	2.2	5.0	3.8	7.6	5.1	5.7	3.6	4.5	3.7	1.9	4.0
Cost of Goods to Cash Flow 43	1.4	0.6	0.4	0.6	5.1	1.8	2.4	0.4	1.8	0.7	0.0	0.8
Cash Flow to Total Debt 44	0.2	•	0.4	0.4	0.3	0.5	0.4	0.2	0.4	0.6	0.3	0.2

Selected Financial Factors (in Percentages)

Debt Ratio 45	59.3	•	103.6	107.3	71.5	58.1	52.1	68.0	53.3	45.4	65.4	57.5
Return on Total Assets 46	4.8	•	12.8	2.6	10.7	9.8	6.2	3.2	5.8	6.2	3.1	3.4
Return on Equity Before Income Taxes 47	6.3	•	•	2.6	28.5	17.4	9.7	4.4	8.7	8.5	1.0	2.5
Return on Equity After Income Taxes 48	4.5	•	•	3.6	25.3	16.7	8.2	2.1	7.1	5.8	•	1.0
Profit Margin (Before Income Tax) 49	3.9	29.9	5.5	•	4.8	5.1	4.3	3.1	4.0	4.8	0.9	3.1
Profit Margin (After Income Tax) 50	2.8	28.1	5.1	•	4.2	4.9	3.6	1.4	3.2	0.3	•	1.3

Table II

Corporations with Net Income

WAREHOUSING AND STORAGE

MONEY AMOUNTS AND SIZE OF ASSETS IN THOUSANDS OF DOLLARS

Item Description for Accounting Period 7/09 Through 6/10	Total	Zero Assets	Under 500	500 to 1000	1,000 to 5,000	5,000 to 10,000	10,000 to 25,000	25,000 to 50,000	50,000 to 100,000	100,000 to 250,000	250,000 to 500,000	500,000 to 2,500,000	2,500,000 and over
Number of Enterprises **1**	3285	14	1684	748	527	123	•	16	•	•	0	4	0
Revenues ($ in Thousands)													
Net Sales **2**	14249283	72692	444877	803856	2003631	1415420	•	302629	•	•	•	3635357	0
Interest **3**	16239	0	1	266	1187	955	•	581	•	•	•	2791	0
Rents **4**	22594	0	0	0	2034	4366	•	749	•	•	•	4029	0
Royalties **5**	33807	0	0	0	0	938	•	0	•	•	•	31349	0
Other Portfolio Income **6**	79322	0	0	10	49606	1272	•	1833	•	•	•	4392	0
Other Receipts **7**	367195	18427	29031	1982	54116	14575	•	9986	•	•	•	33813	0
Total Receipts **8**	14768440	91119	473909	806114	2110574	1437526	•	315778	•	•	•	3711731	0
Average Total Receipts **9**	4496	6508	281	1078	4005	11687	•	19736	•	•	•	927933	•
Operating Costs/Operating Income (%)													
Cost of Operations **10**	25.5	27.0	0.1	2.0	60.4	37.8	•	10.9	•	•	•	3.4	•
Salaries and Wages **11**	22.0	40.4	5.3	25.8	9.0	11.9	•	21.6	•	•	•	28.8	•
Taxes Paid **12**	3.9	2.1	1.1	4.1	2.6	2.3	•	5.3	•	•	•	4.9	•
Interest Paid **13**	2.9	0.2	0.5	1.5	1.1	1.1	•	3.0	•	•	•	7.1	•
Depreciation **14**	4.9	1.0	0.7	2.6	2.7	3.2	•	8.5	•	•	•	7.9	•
Amortization and Depletion **15**	0.8	•	0.7	•	0.0	0.1	•	0.8	•	•	•	2.5	•
Pensions and Other Deferred Comp. **16**	0.4	•	0.0	0.3	0.4	0.5	•	0.8	•	•	•	0.3	•
Employee Benefits **17**	2.5	1.5	0.0	0.7	2.0	1.4	•	2.5	•	•	•	3.1	•
Advertising **18**	0.3	0.2	0.0	1.7	0.2	0.2	•	0.4	•	•	•	0.5	•
Other Expenses **19**	29.4	23.0	76.8	53.6	13.4	30.2	•	34.4	•	•	•	33.3	•
Officers' Compensation **20**	1.8	•	0.1	3.1	3.2	4.5	•	1.7	•	•	•	0.3	•
Operating Margin **21**	5.5	4.6	14.7	4.6	5.0	6.9	•	10.1	•	•	•	8.0	•
Operating Margin Before Officers' Comp. **22**	7.4	4.6	14.8	8.2	11.3	11.8	•	11.8	•	•	•	8.3	•

Selected Average Balance Sheet ($ in Thousands)

Net Receivables 23	649	0	21	146	329	923	3440	• 207924	•
Inventories 24	107	0	0	5	82	202	432	• 3454	•
Net Property, Plant and Equipment 25	2078	0	85	361	1153	2978	14228	• 631720	•
Total Assets 26	5386	0	154	705	2114	7245	33880	• 2256313	•
Notes and Loans Payable 27	1996	0	89	440	695	2412	8735	• 942852	•
All Other Liabilities 28	1058	0	33	67	241	818	9375	• 479823	•
Net Worth 29	2332	0	32	197	1178	4015	15770	• 833637	•

Selected Financial Ratios (Times to 1)

Current Ratio 30	1.8	•	1.3	3.8	2.6	3.6	1.8	• 1.4	•
Quick Ratio 31	1.5	•	0.9	3.6	2.2	2.9	1.7	• 1.3	•
Net Sales to Working Capital 32	6.7	•	20.9	4.8	7.6	4.8	4.1	• 8.1	•
Coverage Ratio 33	4.2	155.3	47.8	4.2	10.2	8.9	5.9	• 2.4	•
Total Asset Turnover 34	0.8	•	1.7	1.5	1.8	1.6	0.6	• 0.4	•
Inventory Turnover 35	10.4	•	•	4.4	27.9	21.6	4.8	• 9.1	•
Receivables Turnover 36	6.5	•	24.2	8.0	13.4	11.4	4.9	• 4.0	•
Total Liabilities to Net Worth 37	1.3	•	3.9	2.6	0.8	0.8	1.1	• 1.7	•
Current Assets to Working Capital 38	2.2	•	3.9	1.4	1.6	1.4	2.2	• 3.4	•
Current Liabilities to Working Capital 39	1.2	•	2.9	0.4	0.6	0.4	1.2	• 2.4	•
Working Capital to Net Sales 40	0.1	•	0.0	0.2	0.1	0.2	0.2	• 0.1	•
Inventory to Working Capital 41	0.2	•	•	0.0	0.2	0.1	0.0	• 0.0	•
Total Receipts to Cash Flow 42	3.8	2.2	3.5	2.8	5.4	5.0	3.1	• 3.1	•
Cost of Goods to Cash Flow 43	1.0	0.6	0.0	0.1	3.3	1.9	0.3	• 0.1	•
Cash Flow to Total Debt 44	0.4	•	0.6	0.8	0.7	0.7	0.3	• 0.2	•

Selected Financial Factors (in Percentages)

Debt Ratio 45	56.7	•	79.4	72.0	44.3	44.6	53.5	• 63.1	•
Return on Total Assets 46	9.8	•	37.3	9.7	20.6	15.1	9.7	• 6.9	•
Return on Equity Before Income Taxes 47	17.1	•	177.1	26.4	33.4	24.1	17.3	• 11.1	•
Return on Equity After Income Taxes 48	14.2	•	172.3	26.0	30.6	23.8	13.5	• 7.6	•
Profit Margin (Before Income Tax) 49	9.2	29.9	21.2	4.9	10.3	8.4	14.4	• 10.1	•
Profit Margin (After Income Tax) 50	7.6	28.1	20.7	4.8	9.5	8.3	11.3	• 6.9	•

Table I

Corporations with and without Net Income

NEWSPAPER PUBLISHERS

MONEY AMOUNTS AND SIZE OF ASSETS IN THOUSANDS OF DOLLARS

Item Description for Accounting Period 7/09 Through 6/10	Total	Zero Assets	Under 500	500 to 1,000	1,000 to 5,000	5,000 to 10,000	10,000 to 25,000	25,000 to 50,000	50,000 to 100,000	100,000 to 250,000	250,000 to 500,000	500,000 to 2,500,000	2,500,000 and over
Number of Enterprises **1**	5429	286	3821	709	397	26	86	41	27	12	11	9	5
Revenues ($ in Thousands)													
Net Sales **2**	28723326	42187	1798312	584972	2302832	160925	1145717	1388061	1195186	1631575	2835605	4231964	11405992
Interest **3**	78430	0	294	514	637	849	5571	7087	3587	2832	29205	19979	7876
Rents **4**	65307	0	1105	0	0	212	1451	4647	4665	8548	11581	11808	21289
Royalties **5**	31511	0	0	0	0	0	1	1315	0	20	1607	265	28303
Other Portfolio Income **6**	291252	0	899	25	12908	151	2711	1413	6188	85535	16540	91609	73272
Other Receipts **7**	1092024	-4186	39470	1029	66595	4355	18546	4131	47468	5298	47757	69582	791979
Total Receipts **8**	30281850	38001	1840080	586540	2382972	166492	1173997	1406654	1257094	1733808	2942295	4425207	12328711
Average Total Receipts **9**	5578	133	482	827	6002	6404	13651	34309	46559	144484	267481	491690	2465742
Operating Costs/Operating Income (%)													
Cost of Operations **10**	29.3	1.9	35.1	49.8	48.6	27.5	34.4	19.8	31.2	19.4	24.2	24.7	28.3
Salaries and Wages **11**	25.9	8.5	18.8	11.9	22.8	29.2	26.4	28.5	29.0	29.7	28.0	25.2	27.0
Taxes Paid **12**	3.4	2.2	2.7	2.2	2.6	3.0	4.0	3.4	4.0	4.1	3.9	3.4	3.4
Interest Paid **13**	6.2	3.7	2.4	0.9	1.2	2.2	1.3	2.7	3.2	2.4	4.5	9.2	9.3
Depreciation **14**	4.3	0.2	1.2	1.1	1.2	1.6	5.2	3.4	5.6	5.7	6.3	4.7	4.8
Amortization and Depletion **15**	5.2	0.1	0.1	2.6	0.1	2.7	0.8	2.4	2.5	4.2	5.6	11.9	5.8
Pensions and Other Deferred Comp. **16**	1.3	0.4	0.1	0.2	0.3	0.3	0.6	0.7	1.6	2.0	1.4	0.8	2.0
Employee Benefits **17**	3.6	0.8	1.2	5.3	1.7	1.5	3.9	3.5	5.4	4.3	3.3	4.1	3.8
Advertising **18**	1.5	•	3.2	0.9	0.4	4.6	0.7	1.2	1.4	1.2	1.2	1.4	1.8
Other Expenses **19**	25.9	115.4	35.7	26.7	21.4	20.5	22.8	33.9	25.2	34.3	29.7	32.9	19.5
Officers' Compensation **20**	1.7	•	5.0	5.3	2.3	1.1	3.0	1.7	4.3	1.9	1.3	0.8	0.8
Operating Margin **21**	•	•	•	•	•	5.9	•	•	•	•	•	•	•
Operating Margin Before Officers' Comp. **22**	•	•	•	•	•	7.0	0.0	0.5	•	•	•	•	•

Selected Average Balance Sheet ($ in Thousands)

Net Receivables 23	959	0	30	136	779	851	1724	6054	5058	16075	45689	165858	388618
Inventories 24	91	0	2	5	64	120	233	552	795	2410	4008	9778	46084
Net Property, Plant and Equipment 25	1897	0	18	70	1044	979	4361	9433	22301	58595	101269	177958	992122
Total Assets 26	9305	0	83	570	2963	6863	15621	33390	64104	184278	384086	1155864	5431823
Notes and Loans Payable 27	3443	0	44	641	1217	2929	4042	15767	29803	58004	127436	761761	1351498
All Other Liabilities 28	5139	0	50	733	873	1776	2091	12409	14431	53551	90870	436913	4029008
Net Worth 29	723	0	-11	-804	874	2159	9487	5213	19870	72723	165780	-42810	51317

Selected Financial Ratios (Times to 1)

Current Ratio 30	1.2	•	1.7	0.3	1.2	4.1	3.1	0.9	1.5	2.1	1.4	0.7	1.9
Quick Ratio 31	1.0	•	1.6	0.3	0.9	2.1	2.3	0.8	0.9	1.8	1.1	0.6	1.5
Net Sales to Working Capital 32	16.7	•	20.5	•	28.6	2.9	3.1	•	8.0	4.8	11.7	•	6.5
Coverage Ratio 33	0.5	•	•	•	1.7	5.2	0.5	1.0	•	•	•	•	1.2
Total Asset Turnover 34	0.6	•	5.7	1.4	2.0	0.9	0.9	1.0	0.7	0.7	0.7	0.4	0.4
Inventory Turnover 35	17.0	•	80.5	82.3	44.2	14.2	19.6	12.1	17.4	10.9	15.6	11.9	14.0
Receivables Turnover 36	4.0	•	12.0	6.1	9.1	6.5	7.6	7.9	7.1	7.8	6.2	3.5	2.7
Total Liabilities to Net Worth 37	11.9	•	•	•	2.4	2.2	0.6	5.4	2.2	1.5	1.3	•	104.8
Current Assets to Working Capital 38	5.6	•	2.5	•	5.7	1.3	1.5	•	2.9	1.9	3.7	•	2.1
Current Liabilities to Working Capital 39	4.6	•	1.5	•	4.7	0.3	0.5	•	1.9	0.9	2.7	•	1.1
Working Capital to Net Sales 40	0.1	•	0.0	•	0.0	0.3	0.3	•	0.1	0.2	0.1	•	0.2
Inventory to Working Capital 41	0.2	•	0.1	•	0.5	0.0	0.0	•	0.1	0.1	0.1	•	0.1
Total Receipts to Cash Flow 42	5.4	•	3.8	•	5.0	3.6	5.1	•	7.8	4.8	5.1	8.6	5.6
Cost of Goods to Cash Flow 43	1.6	1.5	1.3	7.0	2.4	1.0	1.8	3.2	2.4	0.9	1.2	2.1	1.6
Cash Flow to Total Debt 44	0.1	0.0	1.3	3.5	0.6	0.4	0.4	0.6	0.1	0.3	0.2	0.0	0.1

Selected Financial Factors (in Percentages)

Debt Ratio 45	92.2	•	112.8	241.1	70.5	68.5	39.3	84.4	69.0	60.5	56.8	103.7	99.1
Return on Total Assets 46	1.9	•	•	•	4.1	10.5	0.6	2.9	•	•	•	•	4.5
Return on Equity Before Income Taxes 47	•	•	133.5	•	5.5	26.8	•	0.8	•	•	•	160.1	68.5
Return on Equity After Income Taxes 48	•	•	136.8	•	4.8	24.1	•	•	•	•	•	161.2	19.9
Profit Margin (Before Income Tax) 49	•	•	•	•	0.8	9.4	•	0.1	•	•	•	•	1.5
Profit Margin (After Income Tax) 50	•	•	•	•	0.7	8.4	•	•	•	•	•	•	0.4

Table II

Corporations with Net Income

NEWSPAPER PUBLISHERS

MONEY AMOUNTS AND SIZE OF ASSETS IN THOUSANDS OF DOLLARS

Item Description for Accounting Period 7/09 Through 6/10	Total	Zero Assets	Under 500	500 to 1,000	1,000 to 5,000	5,000 to 10,000	10,000 to 25,000	25,000 to 50,000	50,000 to 100,000	100,000 to 250,000	250,000 to 500,000	500,000 to 2,500,000	2,500,000 and over
Number of Enterprises **1**	2763	8	2102	312	228	16	46	23	13	•	6	0	•
Revenues ($ in Thousands)													
Net Sales **2**	13299011	14546	696231	475824	1438767	112424	827623	909892	510259	•	1487823	0	•
Interest **3**	32842	0	284	507	570	573	2512	1433	1286	•	18480	0	•
Rents **4**	24008	0	1	0	0	164	771	570	1543	•	9329	0	•
Royalties **5**	1383	0	0	0	0	0	0	14	0	•	362	0	•
Other Portfolio Income **6**	124629	0	889	0	12895	151	1783	721	4015	•	14875	0	•
Other Receipts **7**	511702	0	17537	0	59687	4345	6170	4204	38777	•	28544	0	•
Total Receipts **8**	13993575	14546	714942	476331	1511919	117657	838859	916834	555880	•	1559413	0	•
Average Total Receipts **9**	5065	1818	340	1527	6631	7354	18236	39862	42760	•	259902	•	•
Operating Costs/Operating Income (%)													
Cost of Operations **10**	32.9	•	44.3	57.8	66.9	25.8	37.3	15.9	31.2	•	32.1	•	•
Salaries and Wages **11**	23.4	•	14.0	8.8	10.1	28.0	22.0	29.5	24.3	•	22.7	•	•
Taxes Paid **12**	3.3	0.2	2.5	1.8	1.7	2.9	3.7	3.1	3.6	•	3.8	•	•
Interest Paid **13**	3.2	•	0.2	0.4	0.5	0.8	0.7	1.1	2.6	•	3.4	•	•
Depreciation **14**	3.3	0.4	1.1	0.9	0.6	1.9	3.2	2.4	4.5	•	4.7	•	•
Amortization and Depletion **15**	3.0	•	•	1.9	0.0	0.5	0.3	1.5	1.6	•	6.2	•	•
Pensions and Other Deferred Comp. **16**	0.8	1.1	0.0	0.2	0.4	0.4	0.5	0.3	1.2	•	0.4	•	•
Employee Benefits **17**	3.7	•	1.3	5.5	0.7	1.8	3.1	3.5	4.3	•	2.5	•	•
Advertising **18**	1.4	•	0.7	0.2	0.7	5.6	0.7	1.3	0.8	•	1.2	•	•
Other Expenses **19**	20.6	90.7	22.4	14.6	14.8	17.1	20.5	37.0	22.1	•	20.4	•	•
Officers' Compensation **20**	2.1	•	12.0	5.5	3.1	1.5	2.9	1.4	4.0	•	1.9	•	•
Operating Margin **21**	2.4	7.5	1.4	2.5	0.5	13.6	5.3	3.1	•	•	0.6	•	•
Operating Margin Before Officers' Comp. **22**	4.5	7.5	13.4	8.0	3.6	15.2	8.2	4.4	3.8	•	2.6	•	•

Selected Average Balance Sheet ($ in Thousands)

Net Receivables 23	746	0	32	141	954	809	1933	7782	5069	•	32103
Inventories 24	118	0	0	11	65	178	227	1278	635	•	3584
Net Property, Plant and Equipment 25	1605	0	14	73	738	1509	4363	7862	18255	•	98927
Total Assets 26	9554	0	71	537	2527	7321	16995	32207	64414	•	442623
Notes and Loans Payable 27	2977	0	2	124	870	1750	3976	7722	16059	•	203858
All Other Liabilities 28	2213	0	46	46	826	2266	2054	15156	11078	•	100002
Net Worth 29	4364	0	23	368	831	3305	10965	9328	37276	•	138763

Selected Financial Ratios (Times to 1)

Current Ratio 30	1.6	•	3.8	5.5	1.3	6.3	3.2	0.9	2.1	•	0.8
Quick Ratio 31	1.2	•	3.8	5.2	1.1	2.8	2.3	0.8	1.2	•	0.5
Net Sales to Working Capital 32	9.6	•	9.5	7.4	25.9	2.1	3.1	•	3.9	•	2.6
Coverage Ratio 33	3.4	•	25.6	8.3	11.2	24.7	10.9	4.4	4.4	•	2.6
Total Asset Turnover 34	0.5	•	4.7	2.8	2.5	1.0	1.1	1.2	0.6	•	0.6
Inventory Turnover 35	13.4	•	1033.8	77.8	65.1	10.2	29.6	4.9	19.3	•	22.2
Receivables Turnover 36	3.7	•	7.4	12.4	10.0	6.8	9.6	•	8.2	•	7.7
Total Liabilities to Net Worth 37	1.2	•	2.1	0.5	2.0	1.2	0.5	2.5	0.7	•	2.2
Current Assets to Working Capital 38	2.7	•	1.4	1.2	4.9	1.2	1.5	•	1.9	•	•
Current Liabilities to Working Capital 39	1.7	•	0.4	0.2	3.9	0.2	0.5	•	0.9	•	•
Working Capital to Net Sales 40	0.1	•	0.1	0.1	0.0	0.5	0.3	•	0.3	•	•
Inventory to Working Capital 41	0.2	•	0.0	0.0	0.5	0.0	0.0	•	0.1	•	•
Total Receipts to Cash Flow 42	4.0	1.0	4.1	7.1	5.3	2.9	4.1	2.6	3.6	•	4.6
Cost of Goods to Cash Flow 43	1.3	•	1.8	4.1	3.6	0.8	1.5	0.4	1.1	•	1.5
Cash Flow to Total Debt 44	0.2	•	1.7	1.3	0.7	0.6	0.7	0.7	0.4	•	0.2

Selected Financial Factors (in Percentages)

Debt Ratio 45	54.3	•	67.7	31.5	67.1	54.9	35.5	71.0	42.1	•	68.6
Return on Total Assets 46	5.4	•	19.8	8.3	15.4	18.3	7.6	6.1	6.9	•	4.9
Return on Equity Before Income Taxes 47	8.4	•	58.9	10.7	42.7	38.8	10.7	16.3	9.2	•	9.8
Return on Equity After Income Taxes 48	6.8	•	56.2	10.7	41.2	35.9	9.9	12.2	7.7	•	6.8
Profit Margin (Before Income Tax) 49	7.6	7.5	4.1	2.6	5.6	18.3	6.5	3.8	3.8	•	5.5
Profit Margin (After Income Tax) 50	6.1	5.5	3.9	2.6	5.4	16.9	6.0	2.9	7.3	•	3.8

Table I

Corporations with and without Net Income

PERIODICAL PUBLISHERS

MONEY AMOUNTS AND SIZE OF ASSETS IN THOUSANDS OF DOLLARS

Item Description for Accounting Period 7/09 Through 6/10		Total	Zero Assets	Under 500	500 to 1,000	1,000 to 5,000	5,000 to 10,000	10,000 to 25,000	25,000 to 50,000	50,000 to 100,000	100,000 to 250,000	250,000 to 500,000	500,000 to 2,500,000	2,500,000 and over
Number of Enterprises	1	7478	777	5741	195	573	53	57	27	17	18	7	10	3
Revenues ($ in Thousands)														
Net Sales	2	27262908	90310	1553452	154357	3134497	747783	1303391	1086980	1189919	1990524	1302250	4930355	9779091
Interest	3	113521	2026	78	0	1960	2590	417	1085	1531	3271	1533	10851	88180
Rents	4	124218	7	18	0	0	743	56	349	39	1386	5240	7563	108817
Royalties	5	808652	0	0	0	0	1815	0	3506	13089	55342	52695	490526	191679
Other Portfolio Income	6	833868	66694	10118	0	691	3074	11944	740	2150	21807	16264	61624	638759
Other Receipts	7	1206847	13379	953	2458	93056	4148	-1309	9151	20085	158991	20542	83972	801421
Total Receipts	8	30350014	172416	1564619	156815	3230204	760153	1314499	1101811	1226813	2231321	1398524	5584891	11607947
Average Total Receipts	9	4059	222	273	804	5637	14343	23061	40808	72165	123962	199789	558489	3869316
Operating Costs/Operating Income (%)														
Cost of Operations	10	34.4	8.5	17.9	0.8	66.3	34.3	56.0	43.5	25.3	38.4	28.8	35.6	24.2
Salaries and Wages	11	22.2	28.2	20.0	27.0	5.8	26.7	14.2	23.3	22.0	17.9	30.5	17.3	30.7
Taxes Paid	12	2.6	2.3	2.9	2.0	2.5	3.0	1.8	2.8	1.7	2.0	3.2	1.7	3.2
Interest Paid	13	6.1	20.8	0.6	1.2	1.2	0.5	1.0	2.6	4.1	5.5	4.1	7.3	10.2
Depreciation	14	2.5	1.0	1.8	0.1	0.7	0.9	2.1	3.6	1.8	2.9	3.7	1.6	3.6
Amortization and Depletion	15	4.5	14.0	0.1	7.1	0.4	0.8	0.6	1.7	3.4	6.2	4.8	8.5	5.3
Pensions and Other Deferred Comp.	16	1.0	•	•	2.0	0.5	2.0	0.7	0.5	0.5	0.5	0.9	0.8	1.5
Employee Benefits	17	2.4	•	4.6	0.0	1.1	3.2	2.1	2.2	3.2	2.3	4.4	1.6	2.5
Advertising	18	1.7	4.6	2.4	0.2	2.0	2.3	1.7	1.1	2.1	2.8	2.9	2.0	1.0
Other Expenses	19	31.6	142.8	43.3	46.9	17.6	24.4	20.1	21.3	32.4	35.8	24.3	33.6	35.3
Officers' Compensation	20	2.6	1.2	13.8	10.3	2.7	2.9	2.1	1.6	1.2	1.9	2.8	1.6	1.5
Operating Margin	21	•	•	•	2.3	•	•	•	•	2.3	•	•	•	•
Operating Margin Before Officers' Comp.	22	•	•	6.4	12.6	2.0	1.9	•	•	3.5	•	•	•	•

Selected Average Balance Sheet ($ in Thousands)

Net Receivables **23**	531	0	16	56	675	1339	2977	4681	10835	20732	30568	61978	573243
Inventories **24**	82	0	5	10	37	597	1638	1394	1684	2572	5866	9761	60663
Net Property, Plant and Equipment **25**	474	0	22	8	139	740	4711	9484	5688	13065	35868	33157	621491
Total Assets **26**	6957	83	758	1789	7479	16591	34207	67102	160703	361755	878955	10919214	
Notes and Loans Payable **27**	3239	163	0	308	1536	4469	12748	25230	89376	111575	495593	4884746	
All Other Liabilities **28**	2583	52	143	1474	4272	10416	15255	33010	53163	158866	236079	3973604	
Net Worth **29**	1136	-132	0	615	7	1671	1707	6204	8862	18165	91314	147283	2060864

Selected Financial Ratios (Times to 1)

Current Ratio **30**	1.0	•	0.9	0.5	1.8	1.1	1.2	1.3	1.1	0.7	1.5	0.8	1.0
Quick Ratio **31**	0.7	•	0.6	0.5	1.4	0.9	0.7	1.0	0.6	0.5	1.3	0.6	0.6
Net Sales to Working Capital **32**	14889.6	•	•	•	9.2	26.6	15.2	11.5	39.6	•	4.9	•	•
Coverage Ratio **33**	1.0	•	•	4.2	3.0	2.1	•	•	2.3	0.3	0.0	1.3	1.0
Total Asset Turnover **34**	0.5	•	3.3	1.0	3.1	1.9	1.4	1.2	1.0	0.7	0.5	0.6	0.3
Inventory Turnover **35**	15.4	•	9.5	0.7	98.2	8.1	7.8	12.5	10.5	16.5	9.1	18.0	13.0
Receivables Turnover **36**	6.7	•	12.9	3.6	10.1	5.1	7.4	6.9	5.7	6.2	4.2	8.0	5.9
Total Liabilities to Net Worth **37**	5.1	•	•	0.2	252.8	3.5	8.7	4.5	6.6	7.8	3.0	5.0	4.3
Current Assets to Working Capital **38**	5128.3	•	•	•	2.3	10.4	5.1	4.0	15.6	•	3.0	•	•
Current Liabilities to Working Capital **39**	5127.3	•	•	•	1.3	9.4	4.1	3.0	14.6	•	2.0	•	•
Working Capital to Net Sales **40**	0.0	•	•	•	0.1	0.0	0.1	0.1	0.0	•	0.2	•	•
Inventory to Working Capital **41**	330.2	•	•	•	0.1	0.9	1.0	0.3	0.8	•	0.2	•	•
Total Receipts to Cash Flow **42**	3.9	•	3.1	2.2	6.0	4.7	6.2	6.9	2.9	4.0	6.0	3.2	3.7
Cost of Goods to Cash Flow **43**	1.4	•	0.6	0.0	4.0	1.6	3.5	3.0	0.7	1.5	1.7	1.1	0.9
Cash Flow to Total Debt **44**	0.2	•	0.4	2.5	0.5	0.5	0.2	0.2	0.4	0.2	0.1	0.2	0.1

Selected Financial Factors (in Percentages)

Debt Ratio **45**	83.7	•	259.1	18.9	99.6	77.7	89.7	81.9	86.8	88.7	74.8	83.2	81.1
Return on Total Assets **46**	3.1	•	•	5.3	11.0	2.0	•	•	9.8	1.0	0.1	5.2	3.1
Return on Equity Before Income Taxes **47**	•	•	13.7	5.0	1871.9	4.6	•	•	41.6	•	•	6.9	0.4
Return on Equity After Income Taxes **48**	•	•	13.7	5.0	1869.0	0.9	•	•	30.1	•	•	2.3	•
Profit Margin (Before Income Tax) **49**	•	•	•	3.8	2.4	0.5	•	•	5.3	•	•	2.1	0.3
Profit Margin (After Income Tax) **50**	•	•	•	3.8	2.4	0.1	•	•	3.8	•	•	0.7	•

Table II
Corporations with Net Income

PERIODICAL PUBLISHERS

MONEY AMOUNTS AND SIZE OF ASSETS IN THOUSANDS OF DOLLARS

Item Description for Accounting Period 7/09 Through 6/10	Total	Zero Assets	Under 500	500 to 1,000	1,000 to 5,000	5,000 to 10,000	10,000 to 25,000	25,000 to 50,000	50,000 to 100,000	100,000 to 250,000	250,000 to 500,000	500,000 to 2,500,000	2,500,000 and over
1 Number of Enterprises	2675	102	1912	195	375	30	31	6	10	7	0	7	0
Revenues ($ in Thousands)													
2 Net Sales	15245900	1004	393167	154357	2741394	388043	978207	327437	789945	1094247	0	8378100	0
3 Interest	103754	1981	0	0	29	2086	249	252	1398	1965	0	95793	0
4 Rents	90097	7	0	0	0	0	56	0	39	3431	0	86563	0
5 Royalties	600839	0	0	0	0	0	0	3506	13089	346	0	583898	0
6 Other Portfolio Income	786212	66694	10118	0	289	266	9655	395	643	24862	0	673290	0
7 Other Receipts	988579	6353	1	2458	79975	873	1289	5250	13581	8510	0	870290	0
8 Total Receipts	17815381	76039	403286	156815	2821687	391268	989456	336840	818695	1133361	0	10687934	0
9 Average Total Receipts	6660	745	211	804	7524	13042	31918	56140	81870	161909	•	1526848	•
Operating Costs/Operating Income (%)													
10 Cost of Operations	37.6	1.1	4.8	0.8	70.1	39.9	61.7	43.4	21.0	23.2	•	29.5	•
11 Salaries and Wages	19.9	0.7	4.6	27.0	3.8	23.4	10.5	20.5	22.1	23.7	•	25.9	•
12 Taxes Paid	2.7	12.7	1.3	2.0	2.4	3.2	1.3	3.1	2.0	3.1	•	3.0	•
13 Interest Paid	1.9	34.5	•	1.2	1.3	0.1	0.5	0.8	1.4	1.0	•	2.7	•
14 Depreciation	1.9	•	0.3	0.1	0.5	1.0	2.2	2.5	2.1	1.5	•	2.5	•
15 Amortization and Depletion	3.7	•	•	7.1	0.3	0.2	0.4	1.7	2.0	3.4	•	5.7	•
16 Pensions and Other Deferred Comp.	0.9	•	•	2.0	0.6	3.2	0.2	0.3	0.7	1.3	•	1.1	•
17 Employee Benefits	1.9	•	•	0.0	1.0	1.8	2.3	2.4	4.1	3.2	•	1.8	•
18 Advertising	1.4	•	0.4	0.2	1.2	2.1	0.8	0.3	2.1	2.9	•	1.4	•
19 Other Expenses	32.6	80.4	63.2	46.9	12.9	11.2	12.6	14.5	29.3	24.2	•	42.7	•
20 Officers' Compensation	2.5	6.1	3.5	10.3	2.5	3.1	2.2	2.0	1.2	1.5	•	2.6	•
21 Operating Margin	•	•	21.8	2.3	3.5	10.8	5.4	8.5	12.1	10.9	•	•	•
22 Operating Margin Before Officers' Comp.	•	•	25.3	12.6	6.0	13.9	7.5	10.5	13.2	12.5	•	•	•

Selected Average Balance Sheet ($ in Thousands)

Net Receivables 23	762	0	0	56	804	886	4161	7308	12021	29675	171184
Inventories 24	118	0	0	8	14	906	1768	2568	1797	4530	19806
Net Property, Plant and Equipment 25	880	6	21	8	86	1018	4997	7910	8127	26318	254589
Total Assets 26	11685	0	39	758	1876	7652	17457	42493	64304	199239	3895575
Notes and Loans Payable 27	1204	0	29	0	334	176	2862	5588	13627	26339	370210
All Other Liabilities 28	4816	0	2	143	1782	1960	11900	20316	35357	133366	1478061
Net Worth 29	5665	0	8	615	-239	5516	2695	16589	15320	39533	2047304

Selected Financial Ratios (Times to 1)

Current Ratio 30	1.4		10.9	0.5	2.1	3.1	1.6	1.5	1.0	0.9	1.5
Quick Ratio 31	0.9		7.2	0.5	1.8	2.6	0.9	1.0	0.6	0.7	0.9
Net Sales to Working Capital 32	9.6		13.3		9.3	3.0	9.2	6.7	53.5		8.1
Coverage Ratio 33	6.4	216.8		4.2	6.1	115.2	13.8	14.8	12.6	16.1	4.6
Total Asset Turnover 34	0.5		5.3	1.0	3.9	1.7	1.8	1.3	1.2	0.8	0.3
Inventory Turnover 35	18.2		1.7	0.8	376.7	5.7	11.0	9.2	9.2	8.0	17.8
Receivables Turnover 36	7.1		10.4	4.0	11.3	10.3	10.3	4.7	6.4	6.8	6.8
Total Liabilities to Net Worth 37	1.1		3.8	0.2		0.4	5.5	1.6	3.2	4.0	0.9
Current Assets to Working Capital 38	3.3		1.1		1.9	1.5	2.7	2.9	21.9		3.0
Current Liabilities to Working Capital 39	2.3		0.1		0.9	0.5	1.7	1.9	20.9		2.0
Working Capital to Net Sales 40	0.1		0.1		0.1	0.3	0.1	0.1	0.0		0.1
Inventory to Working Capital 41	0.2		0.4		0.0	0.2	0.7	0.3	1.1		0.1
Total Receipts to Cash Flow 42	2.7	0.1	1.2	2.2	6.1	4.8	5.7	4.5	2.4	2.9	2.3
Cost of Goods to Cash Flow 43	1.0	0.0	0.1	0.0	4.2	1.9	3.5	1.9	0.5	0.7	0.7
Cash Flow to Total Debt 44	0.3		5.6	2.5	0.6	1.3	0.4	0.5	0.7	0.3	0.3

Selected Financial Factors (in Percentages)

Debt Ratio 45	51.5		79.3	18.9	112.8	27.9	84.6	61.0	76.2	80.2	47.4
Return on Total Assets 46	6.0		128.8	5.3	29.9	19.8	12.7	15.5	20.9	12.2	3.8
Return on Equity Before Income Taxes 47	10.5	623.2		5.0		27.2	76.2	37.0	80.8	57.9	5.6
Return on Equity After Income Taxes 48	9.0	623.2		5.0		25.2	76.0	31.9	69.5	46.4	4.6
Profit Margin (Before Income Tax) 49	10.4	7438.1	24.4	3.8	6.4	11.6	6.5	11.2	15.7	14.6	9.7
Profit Margin (After Income Tax) 50	8.9	5077.4	24.4	3.8	6.4	10.7	6.5	9.7	13.5	11.7	7.9

Table I

Corporations with and without Net Income

BOOK PUBLISHERS

MONEY AMOUNTS AND SIZE OF ASSETS IN THOUSANDS OF DOLLARS

Item Description for Accounting Period 7/09 Through 6/10		Total	Zero Assets	Under 500	500 to 1,000	1,000 to 5,000	5,000 to 10,000	10,000 to 25,000	25,000 to 50,000	50,000 to 100,000	100,000 to 250,000	250,000 to 500,000	500,000 to 2,500,000	2,500,000 and over
Number of Enterprises	1	4828	548	3395	510	221	54	46	21	10	11	0	5	7
Revenues ($ in Thousands)														
Net Sales	2	27962568	17255	124138	693152	1297082	375100	852731	561400	639153	1479849	0	3866053	18056655
Interest	3	276792	0	221	2101	1322	0	1221	1038	625	5426	0	21558	243280
Rents	4	23163	0	0	0	109	0	0	1532	1196	0	0	5139	15188
Royalties	5	276427	0	0	0	2513	0	14	4465	8145	3791	0	39117	218382
Other Portfolio Income	6	234621	0	0	0	195	656	821	724	614	788	0	8391	222430
Other Receipts	7	543595	10	45	6336	488	5110	9983	14931	4196	128955	0	172153	201390
Total Receipts	8	29317166	17265	124404	701589	1301709	380866	864770	584090	653929	1618809	0	4112411	18957325
Average Total Receipts	9	6072	32	37	1376	5890	7053	18799	27814	65393	147164	•	822482	2708189
Operating Costs/Operating Income (%)														
Cost of Operations	10	32.4	2.1	16.7	44.4	20.9	41.4	42.6	46.5	39.1	40.0	•	44.6	28.3
Salaries and Wages	11	21.6	49.8	50.5	7.0	20.8	13.6	19.1	19.2	21.4	17.9	•	21.8	22.6
Taxes Paid	12	2.5	4.1	4.4	1.5	2.1	1.8	2.4	2.2	2.1	2.1	•	2.8	2.5
Interest Paid	13	6.8	•	0.5	2.1	0.3	1.7	3.2	0.4	1.4	7.6	•	3.9	8.8
Depreciation	14	5.0	0.0	1.0	0.9	0.3	0.3	1.9	1.3	2.2	1.1	•	3.3	6.7
Amortization and Depletion	15	5.7	•	1.1	0.0	0.0	0.4	0.3	2.2	1.5	5.5	•	3.1	7.5
Pensions and Other Deferred Comp.	16	1.3	0.5	•	6.6	1.9	0.3	0.7	0.8	0.5	0.5	•	1.1	1.2
Employee Benefits	17	2.5	13.8	1.3	0.4	2.2	2.2	2.6	3.4	1.9	1.8	•	2.6	2.7
Advertising	18	1.7	1.2	10.2	0.0	1.9	2.1	2.5	3.5	3.4	3.3	•	3.1	1.0
Other Expenses	19	19.0	19.8	25.6	25.3	31.9	28.0	22.3	19.4	22.8	31.5	•	14.6	17.2
Officers' Compensation	20	1.7	•	9.6	12.1	11.8	1.7	4.8	3.4	2.6	2.3	•	0.9	0.4
Operating Margin	21	•	8.7	•	•	6.0	6.5	•	•	1.1	•	•	•	1.1
Operating Margin Before Officers' Comp.	22	1.6	8.7	•	11.6	17.8	8.1	2.3	1.2	3.6	•	•	•	1.5

Selected Average Balance Sheet ($ in Thousands)

	Total	1	2	3	4	5	6	7	8	9	10	11
Net Receivables 23	1089	6	83	552	1274	3588	3265	13052	28291	•	220262	460822
Inventories 24	720	23	212	768	1363	2429	7458	10751	19979	•	84723	289613
Net Property, Plant and Equipment 25	448	10	211	99	206	1797	2080	7168	9840	•	85169	179406
Total Assets 26	12428	66	627	3004	6814	15639	32484	66815	212135	•	1526783	6627507
Notes and Loans Payable 27	6397	42	1140	90	1373	5559	1604	44903	115247	•	542241	3621519
All Other Liabilities 28	4109	11	266	1341	2899	7629	11301	26623	63596	•	643717	2062651
Net Worth 29	1923	13	-779	1573	2541	2452	19579	-4712	33291	•	340824	943336

Selected Financial Ratios (Times to 1)

	Total	1	2	3	4	5	6	7	8	9	10	11
Current Ratio 30	0.9	1.7	1.0	1.6	1.5	1.2	2.7	1.7	1.4	•	1.0	0.8
Quick Ratio 31	0.4	0.7	0.3	0.9	0.7	0.9	0.8	0.7	0.7	•	0.7	0.3
Net Sales to Working Capital 32	•	2.1	1.3	7.0	5.4	13.7	2.4	3.9	6.2	•	60.1	•
Coverage Ratio 33	1.7	•	2.2	22.7	5.6	0.7	5.9	3.4	0.4	•	2.1	1.7
Total Asset Turnover 34	0.5	0.6	2.2	2.0	1.0	1.2	0.8	1.0	0.6	•	0.5	0.4
Inventory Turnover 35	2.6	0.3	2.9	1.6	2.1	3.3	1.7	2.3	2.7	•	4.1	2.5
Receivables Turnover 36	4.9	8.8	12.1	11.1	6.8	5.7	6.9	5.7	4.6	•	4.1	4.6
Total Liabilities to Net Worth 37	5.5	4.1	4.1	0.9	1.7	5.4	0.7	5.4	5.4	•	3.5	6.0
Current Assets to Working Capital 38	•	2.5	2.5	2.6	2.9	6.3	1.6	2.5	3.7	•	35.3	•
Current Liabilities to Working Capital 39	•	1.5	1.5	1.6	1.9	5.3	0.6	1.5	2.7	•	34.3	•
Working Capital to Net Sales 40	•	0.5	0.1	0.1	0.2	0.1	0.4	0.3	0.2	•	0.0	•
Inventory to Working Capital 41	•	1.3	1.0	1.0	1.2	1.2	0.7	0.6	0.9	•	6.3	•
Total Receipts to Cash Flow 42	5.0	26.4	6.0	2.9	3.0	5.3	5.7	4.4	4.2	•	6.8	5.1
Cost of Goods to Cash Flow 43	1.6	4.4	2.7	0.6	1.2	2.3	2.7	1.7	1.7	•	3.0	1.4
Cash Flow to Total Debt 44	0.1	0.1	0.0	0.2	0.5	0.3	0.4	0.2	0.2	•	0.1	0.1

Selected Financial Factors (in Percentages)

	Total	1	2	3	4	5	6	7	8	9	10	11
Debt Ratio 45	84.5	80.3	224.3	47.6	62.7	84.3	39.7	107.1	84.3	•	77.7	85.8
Return on Total Assets 46	5.5	•	6.2	13.0	9.8	2.5	1.8	4.5	2.1	•	4.3	5.9
Return on Equity Before Income Taxes 47	15.0	•	•	23.7	21.5	2.5	•	•	•	•	10.2	17.6
Return on Equity After Income Taxes 48	10.0	•	•	23.6	20.5	0.9	•	•	•	•	7.3	11.8
Profit Margin (Before Income Tax) 49	5.0	8.8	0.7	6.4	7.8	1.8	3.4	•	•	•	4.5	6.5
Profit Margin (After Income Tax) 50	3.3	7.4	0.7	6.3	7.5	0.7	2.3	•	3.2	•	3.2	4.3

Table II
Corporations with Net Income

BOOK PUBLISHERS

MONEY AMOUNTS AND SIZE OF ASSETS IN THOUSANDS OF DOLLARS

Item Description for Accounting Period 7/09 Through 6/10	Total	Zero Assets	Under 500	500 to 1,000	1,000 to 5,000	5,000 to 10,000	10,000 to 25,000	25,000 to 50,000	50,000 to 100,000	100,000 to 250,000	250,000 to 500,000	500,000 to 2,500,000	2,500,000 and over
Number of Enterprises 1	2122	548	957	317	221	25	26	7	7	5	0	•	•

Revenues ($ in Thousands)

Item	Total	Zero Assets	Under 500	500 to 1,000	1,000 to 5,000	5,000 to 10,000	10,000 to 25,000	25,000 to 50,000	50,000 to 100,000	100,000 to 250,000	250,000 to 500,000	500,000 to 2,500,000	2,500,000 and over
Net Sales 2	23845205	17255	65000	673717	1297082	193963	647858	269374	485993	483078		•	•
Interest 3	263699	0	0	2101	1322	0	111	447	592	5083	0	•	•
Rents 4	22508	0	0	0	109	0	0	876	1196	0	0	•	•
Royalties 5	245190	0	0	0	2513	0	0	3907	4352	0	0	•	•
Other Portfolio Income 6	230689	0	0	0	195	0	124	0	275	441	0	•	•
Other Receipts 7	400865	10	0	6336	488	508	2737	9668	2763	70104	0	•	•
Total Receipts 8	25008156	17265	65000	682154	1301709	194471	650830	284272	495171	558706	0	•	•
Average Total Receipts 9	11785	32	68	2152	5890	7779	25032	40610	70739	111741	•	•	•

Operating Costs/Operating Income (%)

Item	Total	Zero Assets	Under 500	500 to 1,000	1,000 to 5,000	5,000 to 10,000	10,000 to 25,000	25,000 to 50,000	50,000 to 100,000	100,000 to 250,000	250,000 to 500,000	500,000 to 2,500,000	2,500,000 and over
Cost of Operations 10	31.7	2.1	11.7	43.6	20.9	36.5	40.8	36.3	39.2	54.9		•	•
Salaries and Wages 11	21.9	49.8	49.8	6.3	20.8	15.7	19.1	20.1	20.6	16.4		•	•
Taxes Paid 12	2.5	4.1	2.1	1.5	2.1	1.2	2.3	3.0	2.2	1.9		•	•
Interest Paid 13	6.2	•	•	0.2	0.3	0.8	0.6	0.1	0.7	1.5		•	•
Depreciation 14	5.5	0.0	0.3	0.9	0.3	0.4	1.9	1.3	2.5	1.2		•	•
Amortization and Depletion 15	3.0	•	•	0.0	0.0	•	0.3	3.3	0.6	2.1		•	•
Pensions and Other Deferred Comp. 16	1.4	0.5	•	6.8	1.9	0.5	0.9	0.8	0.7	0.7		•	•
Employee Benefits 17	2.6	13.8	•	0.5	2.2	1.5	2.6	2.8	1.7	1.7		•	•
Advertising 18	1.6	1.2	9.6	0.0	1.9	2.2	1.0	2.9	4.0	4.6		•	•
Other Expenses 19	18.2	19.8	10.9	23.0	31.9	16.9	15.4	15.1	22.4	16.9		•	•
Officers' Compensation 20	1.8	•	•	12.5	11.8	2.3	5.7	5.6	2.5	4.1		•	•
Operating Margin 21	3.7	8.7	15.5	4.7	6.0	22.1	9.5	8.6	2.9	•		•	•
Operating Margin Before Officers' Comp. 22	5.5	8.7	15.5	17.2	17.8	24.4	15.2	14.2	5.4	•		•	•

Selected Average Balance Sheet ($ in Thousands)

Net Receivables **23**	1994	0	6	124	552	1719	3752	3231	13343	21788
Inventories **24**	1160	0	51	1	767	1646	2624	10706	8883	16581
Net Property, Plant and Equipment **25**	845	0	0	340	99	412	2364	1033	8875	3543
Total Assets **26**	21669	0	59	622	3004	6569	18373	36873	67474	147118
Notes and Loans Payable **27**	7830	0	5	215	90	1105	5448	447	7624	4471
All Other Liabilities **28**	7575	0	2	151	1341	1383	4899	11679	25244	53440
Net Worth **29**	6263	0	53	256	1573	4081	8026	24448	34606	89208

Selected Financial Ratios (Times to 1)

Current Ratio **30**	1.0	•	34.6	0.7	1.6	3.0	1.2	2.6	2.3	2.0
Quick Ratio **31**	0.4	•	4.5	0.7	0.9	1.5	0.9	0.9	1.0	1.0
Net Sales to Working Capital **32**	•	•	1.2	•	7.0	2.4	16.8	2.8	2.8	3.2
Coverage Ratio **33**	2.4	•	•	25.4	22.7	30.0	18.9	105.5	7.4	7.4
Total Asset Turnover **34**	0.5	•	1.2	3.4	2.0	1.2	1.4	1.1	1.0	0.7
Inventory Turnover **35**	3.1	•	0.2	741.2	1.6	1.7	3.9	1.3	3.1	3.2
Receivables Turnover **36**	5.1	•	20.9	16.9	11.2	5.6	7.1	•	•	4.3
Total Liabilities to Net Worth **37**	2.5	•	0.1	1.4	0.9	0.6	1.3	0.5	0.9	0.6
Current Assets to Working Capital **38**	•	•	1.0	2.6	1.6	1.5	6.3	1.6	1.8	2.0
Current Liabilities to Working Capital **39**	•	•	0.0	•	1.6	0.5	5.3	0.6	0.8	1.0
Working Capital to Net Sales **40**	•	•	0.8	•	0.1	0.4	0.1	0.4	0.4	0.3
Inventory to Working Capital **41**	•	•	0.9	•	1.0	0.7	1.1	0.8	0.4	0.5
Total Receipts to Cash Flow **42**	4.4	3.7	3.8	5.1	2.9	2.7	4.3	4.0	4.2	4.3
Cost of Goods to Cash Flow **43**	1.4	0.1	0.4	2.2	0.6	1.0	1.8	1.4	1.6	2.4
Cash Flow to Total Debt **44**	0.2	•	2.9	1.1	1.4	1.2	0.6	0.8	0.5	0.4

Selected Financial Factors (in Percentages)

Debt Ratio **45**	71.1	•	10.6	58.9	47.6	37.9	56.3	33.2	48.7	39.4
Return on Total Assets **46**	7.8	•	17.9	21.3	13.0	27.3	14.3	15.0	5.7	7.3
Return on Equity Before Income Taxes **47**	15.9	•	20.0	49.8	23.7	42.5	30.9	22.2	9.6	10.5
Return on Equity After Income Taxes **48**	12.4	•	20.0	49.8	23.6	41.2	30.6	18.4	6.8	7.8
Profit Margin (Before Income Tax) **49**	8.9	8.8	15.5	6.0	6.4	22.4	10.0	14.1	4.8	9.7
Profit Margin (After Income Tax) **50**	6.9	7.4	15.5	6.0	6.3	21.7	9.8	11.7	3.4	7.2

Table I

Corporations with and without Net Income

DATABASE, DIRECTORY, AND OTHER PUBLISHERS

MONEY AMOUNTS AND SIZE OF ASSETS IN THOUSANDS OF DOLLARS

Item Description for Accounting Period 7/09 Through 6/10	Total	Zero Assets	Under 500	500 to 1,000	1,000 to 5,000	5,000 to 10,000	10,000 to 25,000	25,000 to 50,000	50,000 to 100,000	100,000 to 250,000	250,000 to 500,000	500,000 to 2,500,000	2,500,000 and over
Number of Enterprises **1**	4305	1559	2156	303	185	31	33	6	12	7	3	5	5
Revenues ($ in Thousands)													
Net Sales **2**	19794838	140293	1010544	375207	1448611	144177	559500	201878	1008525	851379	217399	3156931	10680392
Interest **3**	254571	373	113	557	16	913	298	377	1199	1615	1205	4755	243149
Rents **4**	64090	0	0	0	0	0	0	1312	597	279	52	1220	60630
Royalties **5**	91732	0	0	0	2086	0	0	1261	21	2292	706	36657	48708
Other Portfolio Income **6**	331972	5198	230	0	434	27	205	2309	2418	96071	0	203450	21631
Other Receipts **7**	501822	885	5298	311	1693	841	8382	29032	9082	54300	2214	225998	163786
Total Receipts **8**	21039025	146749	1016185	376075	1452840	145958	568385	236169	1021842	1005936	221576	3629011	11218296
Average Total Receipts **9**	4887	94	471	1241	7853	4708	17224	39362	85154	143705	73859	725802	2243659
Operating Costs/Operating Income (%)													
Cost of Operations **10**	29.2	32.9	68.8	24.7	28.3	59.5	51.4	26.6	32.4	30.9	23.1	29.9	23.7
Salaries and Wages **11**	18.5	18.1	9.9	18.8	29.5	21.2	12.1	26.5	19.5	14.5	23.2	31.5	14.2
Taxes Paid **12**	2.7	4.0	0.8	2.7	2.9	1.5	2.2	3.8	2.0	1.7	1.7	2.9	2.9
Interest Paid **13**	10.3	1.1	0.4	0.5	0.1	2.9	3.1	1.0	2.1	5.3	9.2	8.1	15.6
Depreciation **14**	2.4	7.8	0.0	14.8	1.1	0.9	1.8	0.8	2.9	1.7	3.8	4.0	1.9
Amortization and Depletion **15**	6.8	1.7	•	0.0	0.1	2.6	1.9	1.0	1.6	4.7	12.5	7.0	9.6
Pensions and Other Deferred Comp. **16**	0.5	5.4	•	1.9	0.3	•	0.5	0.2	0.8	0.2	0.0	0.7	0.5
Employee Benefits **17**	2.2	0.8	•	2.5	1.3	1.2	1.5	2.9	2.8	1.5	2.6	4.2	2.0
Advertising **18**	3.2	0.1	2.7	0.1	0.8	0.7	5.1	6.2	3.9	5.5	0.6	0.9	4.0
Other Expenses **19**	30.1	27.9	14.2	22.0	11.9	20.3	13.3	37.1	24.3	46.4	27.6	22.5	36.7
Officers' Compensation **20**	2.3	8.2	1.5	11.4	18.4	1.8	1.5	4.2	1.5	0.9	1.3	0.7	0.5
Operating Margin **21**	•	•	1.6	0.7	5.4	•	5.6	•	6.1	•	•	•	•
Operating Margin Before Officers' Comp. **22**	•	0.2	3.1	12.0	23.8	•	7.1	•	7.6	•	•	•	•

Selected Average Balance Sheet ($ in Thousands)

Net Receivables	23	1223	0	12	23	1954	1454	2034	9496	13415	26799	11359	306546	556602
Inventories	24	255	0	53	0	14	159	504	198	1128	2489	4674	33237	149567
Net Property, Plant and Equipment	25	410	0	0	242	247	91	948	2010	12970	8033	4045	90759	184686
Total Assets	26	7944	0	84	861	3128	7128	14976	34022	73652	158416	309318	1257948	4610025
Notes and Loans Payable	27	4377	0	26	669	103	2148	6222	9392	23393	87668	146671	701309	2678958
All Other Liabilities	28	4328	0	53	122	1659	2966	2971	16928	21994	71494	39775	382856	3016663
Net Worth	29	-760	0	4	71	1366	2015	5784	7701	28264	-746	122872	173783	-1085595

Selected Financial Ratios (Times to 1)

Current Ratio	30	0.9	•	2.0	4.0	1.7	1.3	2.2	1.4	1.2	0.9	0.5	1.0	0.8
Quick Ratio	31	0.6	•	0.7	3.4	1.4	0.8	1.8	1.1	1.1	0.6	0.3	0.8	0.5
Net Sales to Working Capital	32	•	•	11.3	3.4	6.8	5.1	4.3	5.9	10.9	•	•	•	•
Coverage Ratio	33	0.9	•	6.0	3.0	75.1	•	3.3	8.0	4.5	2.2	0.6	1.5	0.6
Total Asset Turnover	34	0.6	•	5.6	1.4	2.5	0.7	1.1	1.0	1.1	0.8	0.2	0.5	0.5
Inventory Turnover	35	5.3	•	6.1	•	160.2	17.4	17.3	45.3	24.1	15.1	3.6	5.7	3.4
Receivables Turnover	36	3.9	•	36.8	7.9	4.8	0.9	5.5	3.5	7.2	4.1	3.5	1.9	4.4
Total Liabilities to Net Worth	37	•	•	17.9	11.2	1.3	2.5	1.6	3.4	1.6	•	1.5	6.2	•
Current Assets to Working Capital	38	•	•	2.0	1.3	2.5	3.9	1.8	3.3	5.0	•	•	•	•
Current Liabilities to Working Capital	39	•	•	1.0	0.3	1.5	2.9	0.8	2.3	4.0	•	•	•	•
Working Capital to Net Sales	40	•	•	0.1	0.3	0.1	0.2	0.2	0.2	0.1	•	•	•	•
Inventory to Working Capital	41	•	•	1.1	•	0.0	0.2	0.0	•	0.2	•	•	•	•
Total Receipts to Cash Flow	42	4.6	4.4	8.0	6.7	6.6	15.3	5.7	2.6	3.5	2.0	5.0	6.2	4.4
Cost of Goods to Cash Flow	43	1.3	1.4	5.5	1.7	1.9	9.1	2.9	0.7	1.1	0.6	1.2	1.8	1.0
Cash Flow to Total Debt	44	0.1	•	0.7	0.2	0.7	0.1	0.3	0.5	0.5	0.4	0.1	0.1	0.1

Selected Financial Factors (in Percentages)

Debt Ratio	45	109.6	•	94.7	91.8	56.3	71.7	61.4	77.4	61.6	100.5	60.3	86.2	123.5
Return on Total Assets	46	5.1	•	14.1	2.0	14.4	•	11.6	8.0	10.8	9.0	1.3	5.9	4.3
Return on Equity Before Income Taxes	47	9.3	•	222.4	15.8	32.6	•	21.0	31.0	21.9	•	•	13.3	12.6
Return on Equity After Income Taxes	48	17.1	•	222.1	15.8	29.7	•	14.7	26.5	18.7	•	•	1.6	14.8
Profit Margin (Before Income Tax)	49	•	•	2.1	0.9	5.7	•	7.2	7.1	7.4	6.4	•	3.7	•
Profit Margin (After Income Tax)	50	•	•	2.1	0.9	5.2	•	5.0	6.1	6.3	6.3	•	0.4	•

Table II

Corporations with Net Income

DATABASE, DIRECTORY, AND OTHER PUBLISHERS

MONEY AMOUNTS AND SIZE OF ASSETS IN THOUSANDS OF DOLLARS

Item Description for Accounting Period 7/09 Through 6/10	Total	Zero Assets	Under 500	500 to 1,000	1,000 to 5,000	5,000 to 10,000	10,000 to 25,000	25,000 to 50,000	50,000 to 100,000	100,000 to 250,000	250,000 to 500,000	500,000 to 2,500,000	2,500,000 and over
Number of Enterprises **1**	2100	667	980	244	162	5	19	6	7	•	0	•	•
Revenues ($ in Thousands)													
Net Sales **2**	14998288	48754	997404	293438	1424793	43169	277904	201878	539943	•	•	•	•
Interest **3**	28704	0	59	0	16	813	290	377	233	•	0	0	•
Rents **4**	63051	0	0	0	0	0	0	1312	0	•	0	0	•
Royalties **5**	67228	0	0	0	0	0	0	1261	0	•	0	0	•
Other Portfolio Income **6**	330316	5198	230	0	0	0	0	2309	1622	•	0	0	•
Other Receipts **7**	303595	570	0	49	60	679	6427	29032	-10187	•	0	0	•
Total Receipts **8**	15791182	54522	997693	293487	1424869	44661	284621	236169	531611	•	0	0	•
Average Total Receipts **9**	7520	82	1018	1203	8795	8932	14980	39362	75944	•	•	•	•
Operating Costs/Operating Income (%)													
Cost of Operations **10**	31.7	37.0	69.4	12.6	28.1	31.8	28.3	26.6	14.9	•	•	•	•
Salaries and Wages **11**	20.2	9.6	9.0	22.6	29.0	11.8	17.8	26.5	20.3	•	•	•	•
Taxes Paid **12**	3.1	3.1	0.8	2.6	2.8	0.5	2.4	3.8	2.2	•	•	•	•
Interest Paid **13**	4.1	3.0	•	0.6	0.1	0.2	2.7	1.0	0.9	•	•	•	•
Depreciation **14**	2.4	2.7	•	18.9	1.0	0.8	1.5	0.8	3.2	•	•	•	•
Amortization and Depletion **15**	2.1	2.7	•	•	0.0	•	0.9	1.0	0.8	•	•	•	•
Pensions and Other Deferred Comp. **16**	0.6	•	•	2.4	0.3	•	0.7	0.2	0.6	•	•	•	•
Employee Benefits **17**	2.3	2.4	•	2.8	1.2	•	1.5	2.9	2.5	•	•	•	•
Advertising **18**	3.6	0.2	2.7	0.2	0.8	0.0	10.3	6.2	5.9	•	•	•	•
Other Expenses **19**	25.3	17.7	11.2	21.9	11.3	8.8	14.8	37.1	25.4	•	•	•	•
Officers' Compensation **20**	2.7	1.5	1.6	13.2	18.6	1.1	2.3	4.2	1.3	•	•	•	•
Operating Margin **21**	2.0	20.2	5.4	2.3	6.9	44.9	16.9	•	22.0	•	•	•	•
Operating Margin Before Officers' Comp. **22**	4.6	21.7	7.0	15.5	25.5	46.0	19.2	•	23.3	•	•	•	•

Selected Average Balance Sheet ($ in Thousands)

Net Receivables 23	1850	0	27	0	2218	6155	1380	9496	5718
Inventories 24	494	0	116	0	7	0	210	198	1261
Net Property, Plant and Equipment 25	624	0	0	301	214	134	785	2010	10000
Total Assets 26	8732	0	148	883	3193	8310	13340	34022	70734
Notes and Loans Payable 27	3187	0	4	830	106	1331	4996	9392	9596
All Other Liabilities 28	3032	0	60	96	1828	1667	2879	16928	15634
Net Worth 29	2513	0	84	-44	1259	5311	5465	7701	45504

Selected Financial Ratios (Times to 1)

Current Ratio 30	1.1	•	2.5	6.0	1.6	3.5	2.0	1.4	4.6
Quick Ratio 31	0.8	•	0.5	5.1	1.5	3.3	1.8	1.1	4.0
Net Sales to Working Capital 32	18.3	•	11.4	2.5	8.0	1.5	4.8	5.9	2.3
Coverage Ratio 33	2.9	11.6	•	5.0	98.0	249.6	8.2	8.0	22.6
Total Asset Turnover 34	0.8	•	6.9	1.4	2.8	1.0	1.1	1.0	1.1
Inventory Turnover 35	4.6	•	6.1	•	354.0	•	19.7	45.3	9.1
Receivables Turnover 36	4.0	•	36.6	•	5.0	0.3	6.4	3.5	7.9
Total Liabilities to Net Worth 37	2.5	•	0.8	•	1.5	0.6	1.4	3.4	0.6
Current Assets to Working Capital 38	8.6	•	1.7	1.2	2.7	1.4	2.0	3.3	1.3
Current Liabilities to Working Capital 39	7.6	•	0.7	0.2	1.7	0.4	1.0	2.3	0.3
Working Capital to Net Sales 40	0.1	•	0.1	0.4	0.1	0.7	0.2	0.2	0.4
Inventory to Working Capital 41	1.1	•	1.1	•	•	•	0.0	•	0.1
Total Receipts to Cash Flow 42	4.0	2.1	7.3	6.8	6.3	1.8	3.1	2.6	2.3
Cost of Goods to Cash Flow 43	1.3	0.8	5.1	0.9	1.8	0.6	0.9	0.7	0.3
Cash Flow to Total Debt 44	0.3	•	2.2	0.2	0.7	1.6	0.6	0.5	1.3

Selected Financial Factors (in Percentages)

Debt Ratio 45	71.2	•	43.3	105.0	60.6	36.1	59.0	77.4	35.7
Return on Total Assets 46	9.6	•	37.4	4.0	19.1	50.5	24.1	8.0	23.1
Return on Equity Before Income Taxes 47	21.8	•	66.1	•	47.9	78.6	51.8	31.0	34.3
Return on Equity After Income Taxes 48	16.9	•	66.0	•	44.3	78.6	40.2	26.5	31.0
Profit Margin (Before Income Tax) 49	7.7	32.1	5.4	2.3	6.9	48.4	19.3	7.1	20.2
Profit Margin (After Income Tax) 50	6.0	31.9	5.4	2.3	6.3	48.3	15.0	6.1	18.3

Table I

Corporations with and without Net Income

SOFTWARE PUBLISHERS

MONEY AMOUNTS AND SIZE OF ASSETS IN THOUSANDS OF DOLLARS

Item Description for Accounting Period 7/09 Through 6/10		Total	Zero Assets	Under 500	500 to 1,000	1,000 to 5,000	5,000 to 10,000	10,000 to 25,000	25,000 to 50,000	50,000 to 100,000	100,000 to 250,000	250,000 to 500,000	500,000 to 2,500,000	2,500,000 and over
Number of Enterprises	1	8225	950	5681	237	768	171	181	66	45	43	23	45	15
Revenues ($ in Thousands)														
Net Sales	2	116314261	1877555	1786559	478330	2864715	1146913	3441301	2199296	2116621	4196563	4251321	21174560	70780527
Interest	3	899919	2315	174	1321	3081	1295	13828	6337	12755	24510	13492	120179	700632
Rents	4	125652	145	0	0	0	579	419	0	474	891	8247	21325	93571
Royalties	5	8580285	1399	0	2131	49517	0	4238	12906	91199	64830	82077	1835325	6436662
Other Portfolio Income	6	1893134	36590	170	19425	270	168	528	3885	1077	15302	64093	421026	1330602
Other Receipts	7	20013982	73350	286	9976	32468	66961	24308	66607	184104	39059	85116	520572	1891175
Total Receipts	8	147827233	1991354	1787189	511183	2950051	1215916	3484622	2289031	2406230	4341155	4504346	24092987	98253169
Average Total Receipts	9	17973	2096	315	2157	3841	7111	19252	34682	53472	100957	195841	535400	6550211
Operating Costs/Operating Income (%)														
Cost of Operations	10	29.3	39.5	8.3	50.9	17.6	9.5	27.8	27.8	29.8	19.6	19.0	29.5	31.5
Salaries and Wages	11	32.2	23.4	38.3	28.7	43.1	45.4	34.3	31.3	35.6	32.6	33.1	33.2	31.1
Taxes Paid	12	3.2	3.9	6.8	3.0	4.4	4.4	3.7	3.4	3.4	3.7	3.9	2.4	3.1
Interest Paid	13	2.7	1.8	1.2	3.5	1.0	1.6	1.5	0.7	1.7	1.2	2.3	3.7	2.8
Depreciation	14	3.4	1.1	0.6	1.1	1.7	2.4	2.5	2.7	3.0	3.0	3.0	3.1	3.8
Amortization and Depletion	15	1.9	1.6	0.7	4.9	1.0	1.5	1.1	1.0	3.3	3.3	3.3	2.4	1.6
Pensions and Other Deferred Comp.	16	0.4	0.0	•	0.3	0.9	0.5	0.7	0.2	1.0	0.3	0.4	0.9	0.2
Employee Benefits	17	3.5	1.5	2.0	1.0	3.3	3.9	3.9	2.7	3.4	3.1	3.6	3.5	3.6
Advertising	18	4.8	1.3	1.9	1.7	1.4	3.0	2.4	3.5	1.8	3.7	1.2	3.1	6.2
Other Expenses	19	29.5	36.3	37.1	30.1	29.3	30.8	26.1	37.8	24.1	24.9	29.4	26.2	30.4
Officers' Compensation	20	1.7	3.0	14.9	7.0	6.4	6.1	3.0	2.4	3.8	2.7	2.2	1.5	0.8
Operating Margin	21	•	•	•	•	•	•	•	•	•	2.0	•	•	•
Operating Margin Before Officers' Comp.	22	•	•	3.1	•	•	•	•	•	•	4.7	2.0	0.9	•

Selected Average Balance Sheet ($ in Thousands)

	1	2	3	4	5	6	7	8	9	10	11	12
Net Receivables 23	3579	9	344	597	1212	3845	10013	10112	25803	61956	127097	1237953
Inventories 24	238	0	5	73	88	315	197	684	806	2742	13845	70656
Net Property, Plant and Equipment 25	1863	4	34	284	548	993	2945	3288	7149	20729	56748	741643
Total Assets 26	31851	54	682	2202	7589	15807	34817	69635	155837	357105	1037887	12573294
Notes and Loans Payable 27	4874	55	877	1508	907	3889	9200	8682	23552	63415	212776	1633998
All Other Liabilities 28	13676	137	1332	2575	4800	10146	21142	27198	46833	125867	350904	5562469
Net Worth 29	13300	-138	-1527	-1881	1882	1773	4476	33755	85452	167823	474208	5376827

Selected Financial Ratios (Times to 1)

	1	2	3	4	5	6	7	8	9	10	11	12
Current Ratio 30	0.7	•	0.4	0.5	1.0	1.2	1.1	1.2	1.7	1.5	1.3	0.6
Quick Ratio 31	0.6	•	0.4	0.4	0.8	1.0	0.9	0.9	1.3	1.3	1.0	0.4
Net Sales to Working Capital 32	•	•	•	•	44.9	13.5	14.3	9.4	3.1	3.4	6.3	•
Coverage Ratio 33	7.2	•	•	•	•	•	•	2.7	5.6	3.1	2.3	10.7
Total Asset Turnover 34	0.4	5.8	3.0	1.7	0.9	1.2	1.0	0.7	0.6	0.5	0.5	0.4
Inventory Turnover 35	17.5	361.6	203.1	9.1	7.2	16.8	47.0	20.5	23.7	12.8	10.0	21.0
Receivables Turnover 36	4.3	40.0	9.3	6.0	4.7	5.1	3.9	4.1	3.2	3.4	3.7	4.3
Total Liabilities to Net Worth 37	1.4	•	•	•	3.0	7.9	6.8	1.1	0.8	1.1	1.2	1.3
Current Assets to Working Capital 38	•	•	•	•	29.3	6.9	9.5	6.2	2.5	2.9	4.5	•
Current Liabilities to Working Capital 39	•	•	•	•	28.3	5.9	8.5	5.2	1.5	1.9	3.5	•
Working Capital to Net Sales 40	•	•	•	•	0.0	0.1	0.1	0.1	0.3	0.3	0.2	•
Inventory to Working Capital 41	•	•	•	0.4	0.1	0.1	0.1	0.0	0.1	0.1	•	•
Total Receipts to Cash Flow 42	2.5	4.0	4.4	5.8	4.4	6.2	4.7	4.2	3.7	3.3	3.9	2.0
Cost of Goods to Cash Flow 43	0.7	1.6	0.4	1.0	0.4	1.7	1.3	1.3	0.7	0.6	1.2	0.6
Cash Flow to Total Debt 44	0.3	•	0.4	0.2	0.3	0.2	0.2	0.3	0.4	0.3	0.2	0.3

Selected Financial Factors (in Percentages)

	1	2	3	4	5	6	7	8	9	10	11	12
Debt Ratio 45	58.2	353.3	324.1	185.4	75.2	88.8	87.1	51.5	45.2	53.0	54.3	57.2
Return on Total Assets 46	8.6	•	•	•	•	•	•	3.1	4.2	3.7	3.8	11.1
Return on Equity Before Income Taxes 47	17.7	•	26.9	33.6	14.2	•	•	4.1	6.3	5.3	4.6	23.5
Return on Equity After Income Taxes 48	11.2	•	26.9	34.6	15.1	•	•	2.8	4.0	2.1	2.8	15.5
Profit Margin (Before Income Tax) 49	16.6	•	•	•	•	•	•	2.9	5.6	4.8	4.7	26.8
Profit Margin (After Income Tax) 50	10.5	•	•	•	•	•	•	2.0	3.5	1.9	2.9	17.7

Table II

Corporations with Net Income

SOFTWARE PUBLISHERS

MONEY AMOUNTS AND SIZE OF ASSETS IN THOUSANDS OF DOLLARS

Item Description for Accounting Period 7/09 Through 6/10	Total	Zero Assets	Under 500	500 to 1,000	1,000 to 5,000	5,000 to 10,000	10,000 to 25,000	25,000 to 50,000	50,000 to 100,000	100,000 to 250,000	250,000 to 500,000	500,000 to 2,500,000	2,500,000 and over
Number of Enterprises 1	2797	10	1907	155	369	125	82	36	25	•	13	•	31
Revenues ($ in Thousands)													
Net Sales 2	98254799	1103924	621215	358260	2254155	950828	2145170	1457096	1372515	•	2291041	•	13959697
Interest 3	837613	431	63	1113	1666	980	8839	2651	8524	•	5960	•	104543
Rents 4	108310	0	0	0	0	579	21	0	474	•	8247	•	4526
Royalties 5	7754468	0	0	2131	0	168	0	0	24475	•	77195	•	1211810
Other Portfolio Income 6	1819949	8730	0	19425	270	168	429	1989	1061	•	39018	•	416838
Other Receipts 7	20026013	744	0	8875	43608	66118	20020	49399	168481	•	34420	•	414431
Total Receipts 8	128801152	1113829	621278	389804	2299699	1018673	2174479	1511135	1575530	•	2455881	•	16111845
Average Total Receipts 9	46050	111383	326	2515	6232	8149	26518	41976	63021	•	188914	•	519737
Operating Costs/Operating Income (%)													
Cost of Operations 10	26.8	54.6	1.0	58.3	17.8	10.8	26.9	25.0	26.1	•	16.1	•	11.7
Salaries and Wages 11	32.2	11.0	25.5	14.3	33.0	35.7	30.2	28.2	32.7	•	30.6	•	38.4
Taxes Paid 12	3.2	4.4	4.9	1.9	3.6	3.7	3.8	3.5	3.5	•	3.9	•	3.0
Interest Paid 13	2.7	0.4	1.3	0.0	0.4	1.1	1.2	0.7	0.9	•	2.8	•	3.4
Depreciation 14	3.5	0.5	0.4	0.6	1.2	2.2	2.2	2.6	2.7	•	2.5	•	3.4
Amortization and Depletion 15	1.7	0.5	0.0	0.8	0.9	1.2	0.4	0.6	2.3	•	2.8	•	2.6
Pensions and Other Deferred Comp. 16	0.4	0.0	•	0.4	0.9	0.6	0.7	0.3	1.4	•	0.6	•	1.3
Employee Benefits 17	3.6	1.0	2.7	0.3	2.8	3.5	3.6	2.3	3.5	•	3.8	•	4.3
Advertising 18	4.8	0.4	0.3	0.3	0.9	3.0	2.5	1.4	1.5	•	1.3	•	2.1
Other Expenses 19	29.0	19.8	32.4	11.7	21.3	24.0	20.7	25.9	17.4	•	21.0	•	28.1
Officers' Compensation 20	1.4	0.4	21.9	7.1	4.3	5.6	2.4	2.2	3.5	•	2.7	•	1.7
Operating Margin 21	•	6.9	9.6	4.2	12.9	8.6	5.5	7.5	4.5	•	11.9	•	0.0
Operating Margin Before Officers' Comp. 22	•	7.3	31.5	11.4	14.2	17.2	7.9	9.6	8.0	•	14.5	•	1.7

Selected Average Balance Sheet ($ in Thousands)

	•	•	•	•	•	•	•	•	•	•	•
Net Receivables 23	8927	4	0	390	882	1346	4615	9331	10823	71217	119161
Inventories 24	420	0	0	8	101	44	146	289	827	253	3101
Net Property, Plant and Equipment 25	4942	4	0	16	209	604	1271	4371	3909	24232	63581
Total Assets 26	84474	36	0	669	2506	7921	15695	34274	68466	360780	1133085
Notes and Loans Payable 27	11819	47	0	0	1998	600	3387	6115	8841	82897	170803
All Other Liabilities 28	36175	41	0	1062	3800	5076	11334	20088	30565	129614	362664
Net Worth 29	36481	-52	0	-393	-3292	2244	974	8072	29060	148269	599618

Selected Financial Ratios (Times to 1)

	•	•	•	•	•	•	•	•	•	•	•
Current Ratio 30	0.7	•	0.4	0.8	0.4	0.9	1.1	1.2	1.3	1.5	1.5
Quick Ratio 31	0.5	•	0.4	0.6	0.3	0.7	1.0	1.0	0.9	1.3	1.3
Net Sales to Working Capital 32	•	21.1	•	•	•	•	17.7	15.4	7.9	3.6	4.1
Coverage Ratio 33	10.0	•	8.5	278.5	39.5	14.7	6.6	17.6	23.0	7.8	5.7
Total Asset Turnover 34	0.4	9.1	•	3.5	2.4	1.0	1.7	1.2	0.8	0.5	0.4
Inventory Turnover 35	22.4	•	•	174.1	10.7	18.7	48.3	35.0	17.3	112.1	17.1
Receivables Turnover 36	4.3	77.7	•	10.5	6.7	7.0	6.1	5.2	•	•	3.5
Total Liabilities to Net Worth 37	1.3	•	•	•	•	•	2.5	15.1	3.2	1.4	0.9
Current Assets to Working Capital 38	•	•	•	•	•	•	7.8	7.4	4.7	2.9	3.1
Current Liabilities to Working Capital 39	•	•	•	•	•	•	6.8	6.4	3.7	1.9	2.1
Working Capital to Net Sales 40	•	•	•	•	•	•	0.1	0.1	0.1	0.3	0.2
Inventory to Working Capital 41	•	•	•	•	•	•	0.2	0.1	0.1	0.0	0.0
Total Receipts to Cash Flow 42	2.2	3.8	•	2.5	5.5	3.1	2.8	4.2	3.0	2.7	2.6
Cost of Goods to Cash Flow 43	0.6	2.1	0.0	3.2	0.6	0.3	1.1	0.8	•	0.4	0.3
Cash Flow to Total Debt 44	0.3	•	1.5	0.4	0.3	0.5	0.4	0.5	•	0.3	0.3

Selected Financial Factors (in Percentages)

	•	•	•	•	•	•	•	•	•	•	•
Debt Ratio 45	56.8	•	245.1	158.8	231.4	71.7	93.8	76.4	57.6	58.9	47.1
Return on Total Assets 46	11.1	•	98.7	45.1	37.2	16.2	13.5	14.0	16.3	10.7	7.7
Return on Equity Before Income Taxes 47	23.1	•	•	•	•	53.2	184.2	56.0	36.7	22.8	12.0
Return on Equity After Income Taxes 48	16.1	•	•	•	•	47.7	169.6	51.7	33.9	16.4	9.9
Profit Margin (Before Income Tax) 49	24.0	8.1	9.6	13.0	14.9	15.7	6.9	11.2	19.4	19.2	16.0
Profit Margin (After Income Tax) 50	16.8	5.6	9.6	12.0	14.4	14.1	6.3	10.3	18.0	13.8	13.2

Table I

Corporations with and without Net Income

MOTION PICTURE AND VIDEO INDUSTRIES (EXCEPT VIDEO RENTAL)

MONEY AMOUNTS AND SIZE OF ASSETS IN THOUSANDS OF DOLLARS

Item Description for Accounting Period 7/09 Through 6/10	Total	Zero Assets	Under 500	500 to 1,000	1,000 to 5,000	5,000 to 10,000	10,000 to 25,000	25,000 to 50,000	50,000 to 100,000	100,000 to 250,000	250,000 to 500,000	500,000 to 2,500,000	2,500,000 and over
Number of Enterprises 1	26853	5408	19622	505	936	191	102	26	23	13	8	11	7
Revenues ($ in Thousands)													
Net Sales 2	69650327	544841	5004083	540665	3268647	1210362	2240663	622553	1116871	1071240	1806194	5063217	47160990
Interest 3	703486	2534	2720	468	3871	944	558	749	1029	3740	10988	78832	597053
Rents 4	161162	0	0	0	494	293	233	848	195	174	3898	28877	126151
Royalties 5	1350542	275887	9522	0	0	0	1371	200	3	4735	0	777854	280970
Other Portfolio Income 6	1364703	11	13528	0	5824	725	1662	22	1681	6996	12076	12410	1309765
Other Receipts 7	3243796	100224	170740	46356	67167	63969	41738	13369	219765	40891	65915	723976	1689687
Total Receipts 8	76474016	923497	5200593	587489	3346003	1276293	2286225	637741	1339544	1127776	1899071	6685166	51164616
Average Total Receipts 9	2848	171	265	1163	3575	6682	22414	24528	58241	86752	237384	607742	7309231
Operating Costs/Operating Income (%)													
Cost of Operations 10	26.8	6.3	29.9	40.8	13.7	27.5	48.5	54.7	39.1	36.4	34.0	35.2	24.3
Salaries and Wages 11	10.1	0.6	5.6	12.0	13.9	15.9	7.3	12.2	10.9	7.0	7.9	14.1	10.0
Taxes Paid 12	2.7	1.7	1.7	4.6	2.0	2.9	2.6	2.8	2.2	1.3	2.6	2.8	2.9
Interest Paid 13	5.2	0.9	0.6	1.3	1.9	1.8	1.5	2.6	2.9	4.1	3.5	14.7	5.4
Depreciation 14	9.3	27.3	1.7	1.5	2.0	6.5	5.8	7.5	6.2	4.6	10.8	13.3	10.4
Amortization and Depletion 15	11.8	0.0	2.1	2.7	0.5	5.4	0.2	7.7	4.7	25.8	2.3	15.5	14.4
Pensions and Other Deferred Comp. 16	0.8	2.9	2.7	1.4	0.5	0.0	0.1	0.3	0.2	0.0	0.1	0.3	0.8
Employee Benefits 17	1.1	0.6	1.5	0.6	0.8	1.5	0.6	1.4	0.7	0.5	0.9	1.2	1.2
Advertising 18	4.7	4.0	0.4	1.5	1.2	1.0	0.7	2.7	1.1	0.5	0.1	5.1	6.1
Other Expenses 19	28.7	126.6	30.0	32.6	55.8	22.1	26.0	33.0	46.0	21.2	26.9	25.6	25.9
Officers' Compensation 20	3.4	16.1	23.2	13.8	8.0	13.3	5.0	3.6	7.8	1.8	7.8	2.4	0.2
Operating Margin 21	•	0.6	•	•	•	2.2	1.6	•	•	3.3	•	•	•
Operating Margin Before Officers' Comp. 22	•	•	23.9	0.9	7.7	15.5	6.7	•	•	11.0	•	•	•

Selected Average Balance Sheet ($ in Thousands)

Net Receivables 23	356	0	4	57	43	550	3557	4155	8388	16584	25745	99185	1016858
Inventories 24	170	0	0	123	37	30	780	407	3529	9315	2589	9213	575991
Net Property, Plant and Equipment 25	547	0	9	327	644	2096	4290	7048	15547	23755	91904	138753	1402092
Total Assets 26	4885	47	47	700	1999	6873	15323	33722	65507	149582	331550	1251408	14916169
Notes and Loans Payable 27	1639		159	833	1615	2063	7387	19139	27260	45911	169200	519535	4147832
All Other Liabilities 28	1578		39	224	537	1193	4927	12251	24334	50677	91515	634514	4430524
Net Worth 29	1668		-150	-357	-152	3617	3010	2332	13914	52994	70834	97358	6337813

Selected Financial Ratios (Times to 1)

Current Ratio 30	1.4	•	0.8	0.8	1.1	2.9	1.5	0.9	1.3	1.5	1.5	0.7	1.6
Quick Ratio 31	0.8	•	0.8	0.5	0.7	2.5	1.1	0.7	0.7	1.0	0.6	0.4	0.9
Net Sales to Working Capital 32	7.2	•	•	55.5	•	3.1	8.4	•	7.8	5.7	5.1	•	4.8
Coverage Ratio 33	2.1	•	8.4	•	2.1	5.3	3.4	•	0.3	1.5	3.4	1.1	2.3
Total Asset Turnover 34	0.5	•	5.4	1.5	1.7	0.9	1.4	0.7	0.3	0.7	0.6	0.4	0.5
Inventory Turnover 35	4.1	•	84.3	3.5	12.9	58.4	13.7	32.2	5.4	3.2	29.6	17.6	2.8
Receivables Turnover 36	6.1	•	58.9	13.3	41.6	15.8	5.5	5.7	5.0	4.2	3.7	4.4	5.6
Total Liabilities to Net Worth 37	1.9	•	•	13.5	•	0.9	4.1	13.5	3.7	1.8	3.7	11.9	1.4
Current Assets to Working Capital 38	3.6	•	•	13.5	•	1.5	3.0	4.3	2.9	3.1	•	•	2.6
Current Liabilities to Working Capital 39	2.6	•	•	12.5	•	0.5	2.0	3.3	1.9	2.1	•	•	1.6
Working Capital to Net Sales 40	0.1	•	•	0.0	•	0.3	0.1	0.1	0.2	0.2	•	•	0.2
Inventory to Working Capital 41	0.4	•	•	0.2	•	0.0	0.3	0.8	0.5	0.1	•	•	0.4
Total Receipts to Cash Flow 42	4.5	1.1	3.4	5.1	3.6	3.8	50.3	5.0	2.7	8.0	3.6	4.7	5.0
Cost of Goods to Cash Flow 43	1.2	0.1	1.0	2.1	0.5	1.0	27.5	0.5	2.4	2.9	1.2	1.7	1.2
Cash Flow to Total Debt 44	0.2	0.1	0.4	0.2	0.5	0.4	0.0	•	0.4	0.1	0.2	0.1	0.2

Selected Financial Factors (in Percentages)

Debt Ratio 45	65.9	•	418.8	151.0	107.6	47.4	80.4	93.1	78.8	64.6	78.6	92.2	57.5
Return on Total Assets 46	5.7	•	27.9	•	7.0	8.7	7.4	•	0.7	3.4	8.0	6.0	5.7
Return on Equity Before Income Taxes 47	8.5	•	•	12.6	•	13.3	26.6	•	3.1	3.1	26.4	7.4	7.7
Return on Equity After Income Taxes 48	5.2	•	•	12.6	•	13.2	24.6	•	0.1	0.1	23.3	7.4	4.9
Profit Margin (Before Income Tax) 49	5.5	4.5	•	2.1	•	7.6	3.6	•	0.8	2.0	8.3	1.6	7.2
Profit Margin (After Income Tax) 50	3.3	4.3	•	1.9	•	7.5	3.4	•	0.1	0.1	7.3	•	4.6

Table II

Corporations with Net Income

MOTION PICTURE AND VIDEO INDUSTRIES (EXCEPT VIDEO RENTAL)

MONEY AMOUNTS AND SIZE OF ASSETS IN THOUSANDS OF DOLLARS

Item Description for Accounting Period 7/09 Through 6/10		Total	Zero Assets	Under 500	500 to 1,000	1,000 to 5,000	5,000 to 10,000	10,000 to 25,000	25,000 to 50,000	50,000 to 100,000	100,000 to 250,000	250,000 to 500,000	500,000 to 2,500,000	2,500,000 and over
Number of Enterprises	1	13037	3845	8593	67	305	127	65	7	11	•	3	•	•
Revenues ($ in Thousands)														
Net Sales	2	57150024	343147	3550628	111271	1145453	1021789	1912986	127139	558734	•	1276800	•	•
Interest	3	492749	540	1242	27	1074	21	531	81	500	•	421	•	•
Rents	4	136892	0	0	0	494	260	0	0	195	•	1125	•	•
Royalties	5	293392	0	9522	0	0	0	0	25	0	•	0	•	•
Other Portfolio Income	6	1333080	11	0	0	5703	518	1285	18	7	•	11808	•	•
Other Receipts	7	2835962	5158	174670	37985	54816	63966	39526	8111	174730	•	32101	•	•
Total Receipts	8	62242099	348856	3736062	149283	1207540	1086554	1954328	135374	734166	•	1322255	•	•
Average Total Receipts	9	4774	91	435	2228	3959	8556	30067	19339	66742	•	440752	•	•
Operating Costs/Operating Income (%)														
Cost of Operations	10	28.1	9.0	37.8	18.7	12.4	26.3	48.0	33.6	33.4	•	41.5	•	•
Salaries and Wages	11	9.7	0.0	5.4	7.4	5.4	16.5	6.5	13.1	11.0	•	8.4	•	•
Taxes Paid	12	2.7	2.4	1.0	4.2	2.2	2.4	2.5	1.7	2.6	•	2.2	•	•
Interest Paid	13	4.3	0.6	0.7	0.0	0.7	0.9	0.9	1.2	1.1	•	1.0	•	•
Depreciation	14	9.0	1.9	1.2	1.1	1.3	5.0	2.6	1.0	3.4	•	2.8	•	•
Amortization and Depletion	15	12.7	•	2.9	•	0.0	0.0	0.0	1.3	0.5	•	1.1	•	•
Pensions and Other Deferred Comp.	16	0.9	4.5	3.0	0.5	0.8	0.0	0.1	0.2	0.1	•	0.1	•	•
Employee Benefits	17	1.1	0.6	0.8	•	0.4	1.0	0.5	0.2	0.7	•	0.9	•	•
Advertising	18	5.2	0.4	0.3	0.0	0.2	1.1	0.7	4.9	1.4	•	0.0	•	•
Other Expenses	19	21.8	36.8	21.4	12.2	44.9	22.5	27.3	23.8	47.9	•	18.5	•	•
Officers' Compensation	20	2.5	25.4	13.5	22.6	19.1	14.3	4.6	7.3	13.6	•	10.4	•	•
Operating Margin	21	2.0	18.2	11.9	33.0	12.5	9.9	6.2	11.9	•	•	13.0	•	•
Operating Margin Before Officers' Comp.	22	4.5	43.6	25.4	55.7	31.6	24.2	10.8	19.2	•	•	23.4	•	•

Selected Average Balance Sheet ($ in Thousands)

Net Receivables 23	593	0	6	156	71	651	4015	963	10296	9892
Inventories 24	321	0	1	5	31	1	308	59	297	5646
Net Property, Plant and Equipment 25	732	0	11	27	373	2288	4822	645	15756	136204
Total Assets 26	8098	0	64	809	1992	6658	15899	32980	64201	367377
Notes and Loans Payable 27	2243	0	80	0	413	2406	5335	10131	16796	149319
All Other Liabilities 28	2533	0	20	1229	277	861	5661	14603	18009	85080
Net Worth 29	3323	0	-37	-421	1302	3391	4903	8246	29396	132978

Selected Financial Ratios (Times to 1)

Current Ratio 30	1.6	•	2.3	1.5	4.1	4.7	1.4	0.6	1.3	1.1
Quick Ratio 31	0.9	•	2.1	1.4	2.9	4.3	1.2	0.5	0.8	0.3
Net Sales to Working Capital 32	5.8	•	16.4	11.5	3.1	2.4	11.7	•	8.8	43.9
Coverage Ratio 33	3.6	31.6	24.3	2267.2	28.1	18.2	9.9	17.4	15.1	16.7
Total Asset Turnover 34	0.5	•	6.5	2.1	1.9	1.2	1.9	0.6	0.8	1.2
Inventory Turnover 35	3.8	•	143.8	68.8	14.9	2774.2	45.8	102.6	57.1	31.3
Receivables Turnover 36	6.6	•	66.7	17.4	36.3	•	6.2	•	5.7	
Total Liabilities to Net Worth 37	1.4	•	•	0.5	1.0	2.2	3.0	1.2	1.8	
Current Assets to Working Capital 38	2.7	•	1.8	2.8	1.3	1.3	3.4	•	3.9	12.6
Current Liabilities to Working Capital 39	1.7	•	0.8	1.8	0.3	0.3	2.4	•	2.9	11.6
Working Capital to Net Sales 40	0.2	•	0.1	0.1	0.3	0.4	0.1	•	0.1	0.0
Inventory to Working Capital 41	0.4	•	0.1	0.0	0.0	0.0	0.2	•	0.1	1.1
Total Receipts to Cash Flow 42	4.2	2.0	2.9	1.3	2.0	2.8	4.0	2.5	1.8	3.7
Cost of Goods to Cash Flow 43	1.2	0.2	1.1	0.2	0.2	0.7	1.9	0.8	0.6	1.5
Cash Flow to Total Debt 44	0.2	•	1.4	1.0	2.8	0.9	0.7	0.3	0.8	0.5

Selected Financial Factors (in Percentages)

Debt Ratio 45	59.0	•	157.5	152.1	34.7	49.1	69.2	75.0	54.2	63.8
Return on Total Assets 46	8.3	•	115.2	138.1	35.1	20.7	17.3	11.1	13.2	20.2
Return on Equity Before Income Taxes 47	14.6	•	•	•	51.8	38.4	50.3	41.7	26.9	52.4
Return on Equity After Income Taxes 48	11.1	•	•	•	50.2	38.2	48.4	38.4	25.5	48.0
Profit Margin (Before Income Tax) 49	11.1	19.8	17.1	67.2	18.0	16.2	8.4	18.9	15.6	16.4
Profit Margin (After Income Tax) 50	8.4	19.7	16.7	67.2	17.4	16.1	8.1	17.4	14.8	15.0

Table I

Corporations with and without Net Income

SOUND RECORDING INDUSTRIES

MONEY AMOUNTS AND SIZE OF ASSETS IN THOUSANDS OF DOLLARS

Item Description for Accounting Period 7/09 Through 6/10	Total	Zero Assets	Under 500	500 to 1,000	1,000 to 5,000	5,000 to 10,000	10,000 to 25,000	25,000 to 50,000	50,000 to 100,000	100,000 to 250,000	250,000 to 500,000	500,000 to 2,500,000	2,500,000 and over
Number of Enterprises 1	5624	1123	4023	33	358	53	8	15	3	4	0	3	0
Revenues ($ in Thousands)													
Net Sales 2	6031740	71367	453894	207669	592485	140659	24023	215243	143564	289281	0	3893556	0
Interest 3	19145	20	18	0	675	0	268	2111	667	923	0	14464	0
Rents 4	272	0	0	0	0	0	0	254	0	0	0	18	0
Royalties 5	2834053	3235	0	0	14254	0	0	84882	529	2054	0	2729099	0
Other Portfolio Income 6	57277	0	351	1	0	0	0	4004	566	0	0	52354	0
Other Receipts 7	497319	13856	167	0	17318	0	22	157461	380	8505	0	299609	0
Total Receipts 8	9439806	88478	454430	207670	624732	140659	24313	463955	145706	300763	0	6989100	0
Average Total Receipts 9	1678	79	113	6293	1745	2654	3039	30930	48569	75191	•	2329700	•
Operating Costs/Operating Income (%)													
Cost of Operations 10	34.9	3.0	26.4	0.0	22.8	35.7	14.6	62.3	51.2	58.7	•	36.4	•
Salaries and Wages 11	15.9	11.9	3.0	6.9	21.8	18.9	27.2	27.0	9.9	8.7	•	17.1	•
Taxes Paid 12	3.0	7.8	2.0	0.6	2.8	2.9	3.7	3.3	3.2	1.2	•	3.4	•
Interest Paid 13	8.4	1.8	0.2	•	1.2	0.6	1.0	1.4	3.7	6.0	•	12.1	•
Depreciation 14	6.6	2.9	0.7	3.0	4.2	1.3	3.5	1.8	0.9	1.2	•	9.0	•
Amortization and Depletion 15	6.1	6.3	•	•	0.0	0.0	21.2	8.5	1.9	18.0	•	7.3	•
Pensions and Other Deferred Comp. 16	0.2	0.1	1.0	•	0.7	0.5	•	0.9	0.3	0.3	•	0.0	•
Employee Benefits 17	1.3	4.6	1.7	0.5	0.2	1.3	1.4	3.0	1.0	0.9	•	1.3	•
Advertising 18	2.3	2.3	1.3	0.2	0.8	0.4	•	3.5	0.3	5.9	•	2.6	•
Other Expenses 19	75.2	94.5	31.1	60.2	27.9	21.2	85.8	97.1	13.1	9.0	•	95.9	•
Officers' Compensation 20	3.1	12.1	21.0	5.8	3.2	0.4	12.0	6.1	1.9	3.6	•	0.5	•
Operating Margin 21	•	•	11.6	22.7	14.4	16.8	•	•	12.6	•	•	•	•
Operating Margin Before Officers' Comp. 22	•	•	32.6	28.6	17.6	17.2	•	•	14.5	•	•	•	•

Selected Average Balance Sheet ($ in Thousands)

Net Receivables **23**	698	0	2	0	179	773	10	1657	3184	9958	•	1244936	•
Inventories **24**	87	0	0	15	114	834	0	1760	134	5485	•	118474	•
Net Property, Plant and Equipment **25**	102	0	5	43	319	1814	145	2874	1510	3814	•	93462	•
Total Assets **26**	4337	0	36	629	1571	6083	16547	34331	73657	175842	•	7256839	•
Notes and Loans Payable **27**	779	0	11	3504	513	1243	0	10342	46400	53002	•	1155146	•
All Other Liabilities **28**	1180	0	6	0	471	924	5059	15168	19984	73272	•	1924396	•
Net Worth **29**	2379	0	20	-2875	588	3916	11488	8820	7273	49569	•	4177298	•

Selected Financial Ratios (Times to 1)

Current Ratio **30**	0.9	•	5.2	0.2	1.4	4.2	1.5	1.2	2.5	0.9	•	0.9	•
Quick Ratio **31**	0.7	•	5.2	0.0	1.0	1.5	1.4	0.6	1.4	0.5	•	0.7	•
Net Sales to Working Capital **32**	•	•	4.5	•	7.1	0.9	1.2	4.3	1.5	•	•	•	•
Coverage Ratio **33**	1.2	•	58.6	•	17.5	30.8	•	3.5	4.8	0.8	•	•	•
Total Asset Turnover **34**	0.2	•	3.1	10.0	1.1	0.4	0.2	0.4	0.6	0.4	•	0.2	•
Inventory Turnover **35**	4.3	•	•	0.1	3.3	1.1	•	5.1	182.5	7.7	•	4.0	•
Receivables Turnover **36**	1.6	•	53.7	•	9.4	2.9	64.6	3.9	30.1	11.6	•	1.1	•
Total Liabilities to Net Worth **37**	0.8	•	0.8	•	1.7	0.6	0.4	2.9	9.1	2.5	•	0.7	•
Current Assets to Working Capital **38**	•	•	1.2	•	3.2	1.3	3.0	5.7	1.7	•	•	•	•
Current Liabilities to Working Capital **39**	•	•	0.2	•	2.2	0.3	2.0	4.7	0.7	•	•	•	•
Working Capital to Net Sales **40**	•	•	0.2	•	0.1	1.1	0.9	0.2	0.7	•	•	•	•
Inventory to Working Capital **41**	•	•	•	•	0.9	0.3	0.0	0.0	•	•	•	•	•
Total Receipts to Cash Flow **42**	1.4	3.0	3.0	1.2	2.6	2.9	7.4	1.1	3.9	•	•	1.1	•
Cost of Goods to Cash Flow **43**	0.5	0.1	0.8	0.0	0.6	1.0	1.1	0.7	2.0	•	•	0.4	•
Cash Flow to Total Debt **44**	0.4	•	2.3	1.5	0.6	0.4	0.1	0.5	0.2	•	•	0.4	•

Selected Financial Factors (in Percentages)

Debt Ratio **45**	45.2	•	45.1	557.2	62.6	35.6	30.6	74.3	90.1	71.8	•	42.4	•
Return on Total Assets **46**	2.5	•	37.3	227.3	22.1	7.6	•	2.1	11.6	•	•	1.6	•
Return on Equity Before Income Taxes **47**	0.7	•	66.8	•	55.8	11.4	•	5.9	92.8	•	•	•	•
Return on Equity After Income Taxes **48**	0.6	•	66.8	•	54.8	11.4	•	1.0	45.5	•	•	•	•
Profit Margin (Before Income Tax) **49**	1.6	•	11.7	22.7	19.8	16.8	•	3.6	14.1	•	•	•	•
Profit Margin (After Income Tax) **50**	1.3	•	11.7	22.6	19.5	16.8	•	0.6	6.9	•	•	•	•

Table II

Corporations with Net Income

SOUND RECORDING INDUSTRIES

MONEY AMOUNTS AND SIZE OF ASSETS IN THOUSANDS OF DOLLARS

Item Description for Accounting Period 7/09 Through 6/10	Total	Zero Assets	Under 500	500 to 1,000	1,000 to 5,000	5,000 to 10,000	10,000 to 25,000	25,000 to 50,000	50,000 to 100,000	100,000 to 250,000	250,000 to 500,000	500,000 to 2,500,000	2,500,000 and over
Number of Enterprises 1	2940	243	2249	•	348	53	0	9	0	•	0	•	•
Revenues ($ in Thousands)													
Net Sales 2	4069613	62360	421440	•	561477	140659	0	251860	0	0	0	•	•
Interest 3	16834	20	0	•	0	0	0	1857	0	0	0	•	•
Rents 4	272	0	0	•	0	0	0	254	0	0	0	•	•
Royalties 5	811516	1215	0	•	14254	0	0	44316	0	0	0	•	•
Other Portfolio Income 6	53639	0	351	•	0	0	0	933	0	0	0	•	•
Other Receipts 7	361451	317	363	•	17190	0	0	6935	0	0	0	•	•
Total Receipts 8	5313325	63912	422154	•	592921	140659	0	306155	0	0	0	•	•
Average Total Receipts 9	1807	263	188	•	1704	2654	•	34017	•	•	•	•	•
Operating Costs/Operating Income (%)													
Cost of Operations 10	29.6	3.4	28.5	•	18.3	35.7	•	51.1	•	•	•	•	•
Salaries and Wages 11	13.8	0.4	3.2	•	23.0	18.9	•	12.1	•	•	•	•	•
Taxes Paid 12	3.6	8.4	1.5	•	2.9	2.9	•	2.6	•	•	•	•	•
Interest Paid 13	6.9	1.5	0.0	•	1.3	0.6	•	2.7	•	•	•	•	•
Depreciation 14	9.3	3.3	0.4	•	4.5	1.3	•	0.8	•	•	•	•	•
Amortization and Depletion 15	4.4	0.2	•	•	•	0.0	•	4.1	•	•	•	•	•
Pensions and Other Deferred Comp. 16	0.3	0.0	1.1	•	0.8	0.5	•	0.4	•	•	•	•	•
Employee Benefits 17	0.7	5.1	1.8	•	0.2	1.3	•	1.2	•	•	•	•	•
Advertising 18	2.3	0.3	1.3	•	0.8	0.4	•	2.5	•	•	•	•	•
Other Expenses 19	47.9	61.3	19.4	•	28.7	21.2	•	21.3	•	•	•	•	•
Officers' Compensation 20	4.1	13.9	21.3	•	3.4	0.4	•	4.5	•	•	•	•	•
Operating Margin 21	•	2.1	21.4	•	16.1	16.8	•	•	•	•	•	•	•
Operating Margin Before Officers' Comp. 22	•	16.0	42.8	•	19.5	17.2	•	1.4	•	•	•	•	•

Selected Average Balance Sheet ($ in Thousands)

Net Receivables 23	1213	0	4	•	•	133	773	•	2137
Inventories 24	112	0	0	•	•	117	828	•	108
Net Property, Plant and Equipment 25	155	0	1	•	•	328	1814	•	4026
Total Assets 26	3225	0	42	•	•	1520	6083	•	42279
Notes and Loans Payable 27	1380	0	3	•	•	499	1243	•	19656
All Other Liabilities 28	1767	0	10	•	•	469	924	•	11345
Net Worth 29	78	0	29	•	•	552	3916	•	11278

Selected Financial Ratios (Times to 1)

Current Ratio 30	1.0	•	4.0	•	•	1.3	4.2	•	1.5
Quick Ratio 31	0.8	•	4.0	•	•	0.9	1.5	•	0.9
Net Sales to Working Capital 32	374.8	•	6.2	4.0	•	9.6	0.9	•	3.6
Coverage Ratio 33	2.3	4.0	488.2	•	•	18.2	30.8	•	8.8
Total Asset Turnover 34	0.4	•	4.5	•	•	1.1	0.4	•	0.7
Inventory Turnover 35	3.7	•	•	•	•	2.5	1.1	•	132.6
Receivables Turnover 36	2.0	•	49.9	•	•	10.4	•	•	•
Total Liabilities to Net Worth 37	40.4	•	0.5	•	•	1.8	0.6	•	2.7
Current Assets to Working Capital 38	480.9	•	1.3	•	•	4.1	1.3	•	3.1
Current Liabilities to Working Capital 39	479.9	•	0.3	•	•	3.1	0.3	•	2.1
Working Capital to Net Sales 40	0.0	•	0.2	•	•	0.1	1.1	•	0.3
Inventory to Working Capital 41	17.0	•	•	•	•	1.3	0.3	•	0.0
Total Receipts to Cash Flow 42	2.0	3.6	3.0	•	•	2.5	2.9	•	2.6
Cost of Goods to Cash Flow 43	0.6	0.1	0.9	•	•	0.5	1.0	•	1.3
Cash Flow to Total Debt 44	0.2	•	4.8	•	•	0.7	0.4	•	0.3

Selected Financial Factors (in Percentages)

Debt Ratio 45	97.6	•	31.4	•	•	63.7	35.6	•	73.3
Return on Total Assets 46	6.9	•	97.2	•	•	24.4	7.6	•	15.6
Return on Equity Before Income Taxes 47	161.8	•	141.2	•	•	63.5	11.4	•	51.8
Return on Equity After Income Taxes 48	153.3	•	141.2	•	•	62.5	11.4	•	35.3
Profit Margin (Before Income Tax) 49	9.1	4.6	21.6	•	•	21.7	16.8	•	20.9
Profit Margin (After Income Tax) 50	8.6	4.4	21.6	•	•	21.4	16.8	•	14.2

Table I
Corporations with and without Net Income

BROADCASTING (EXCEPT INTERNET)

MONEY AMOUNTS AND SIZE OF ASSETS IN THOUSANDS OF DOLLARS

Item Description for Accounting Period 7/09 Through 6/10	Total	Zero Assets	Under 500	500 to 1,000	1,000 to 5,000	5,000 to 10,000	10,000 to 25,000	25,000 to 50,000	50,000 to 100,000	100,000 to 250,000	250,000 to 500,000	500,000 to 2,500,000	2,500,000 and over
Number of Enterprises **1**	6748	931	4293	461	654	144	117	36	38	20	18	25	11
Revenues ($ in Thousands)													
Net Sales **2**	88908660	65500	826336	753969	1316831	1042980	1499292	633636	1511435	1223685	5236421	7033941	67764633
Interest **3**	2081303	20	40	208	1560	2755	4637	490	1960	12019	7040	123393	1927180
Rents **4**	330110	0	0	0	6876	531	813	3008	1123	9902	13167	15988	278701
Royalties **5**	487696	0	0	0	52869	4455	0	1	3415	192	32530	146245	4647990
Other Portfolio Income **6**	889115	0	0	0	110001	41656	2504	21736	29420	8816	13930	60344	600706
Other Receipts **7**	5068450	4021	39870	8308	6711	15276	29251	6174	39619	39454	183928	210093	4485749
Total Receipts **8**	102165334	69541	866246	762485	1494848	1107653	1536497	665045	1586972	1294068	5487016	7590004	79704959
Average Total Receipts **9**	15140	75	202	1654	2286	7692	13132	18473	41762	64703	304834	303600	7245905
Operating Costs/Operating Income (%)													
Cost of Operations **10**	12.9	13.6	•	21.1	24.0	25.5	34.4	12.9	21.7	9.2	49.0	5.7	9.9
Salaries and Wages **11**	17.0	11.5	22.5	37.6	23.5	24.9	22.8	18.3	21.5	19.4	15.3	27.4	15.3
Taxes Paid **12**	2.5	1.3	21.2	4.5	5.6	2.9	3.4	3.0	3.0	4.3	2.9	4.9	1.8
Interest Paid **13**	8.7	2.0	0.2	2.1	3.2	2.2	2.5	8.1	11.5	10.1	7.8	12.9	8.8
Depreciation **14**	5.0	1.1	3.1	0.8	5.4	6.2	3.6	12.0	4.7	6.4	6.5	7.9	4.6
Amortization and Depletion **15**	9.8	1.5	0.6	0.6	5.6	2.2	6.3	10.0	10.3	10.4	6.9	15.9	9.8
Pensions and Other Deferred Comp. **16**	0.9	•	1.3	0.0	0.3	0.2	0.7	1.1	0.3	0.4	0.5	1.7	0.9
Employee Benefits **17**	2.6	1.4	3.6	1.8	1.8	2.2	1.1	1.0	1.4	1.4	1.7	2.3	2.7
Advertising **18**	3.4	0.0	0.4	1.0	1.8	0.9	1.4	1.5	2.1	3.3	0.9	1.5	4.1
Other Expenses **19**	49.4	101.8	28.1	22.4	50.0	30.2	32.2	41.6	43.8	41.9	19.3	52.7	52.9
Officers' Compensation **20**	1.5	•	19.6	9.1	6.0	5.2	5.0	2.5	2.7	2.7	0.9	1.3	1.0
Operating Margin **21**	•	•	•	•	•	•	•	•	•	•	•	•	•
Operating Margin Before Officers' Comp. **22**	•	•	18.9	8.1	2.6	•	•	•	•	•	•	•	•

Selected Average Balance Sheet ($ in Thousands)

	1	2	3	4	5	6	7	8	9	10	11	12	13
Net Receivables 23	2621	0	11	256	498	792	1710	2690	7958	24387	37977	66760	1240099
Inventories 24	228	0	0	2	22	18	68	125	301	5440	1216	1317	120950
Net Property, Plant and Equipment 25	4649	0	15	105	576	1501	2588	7204	10003	27160	75343	116579	2264520
Total Assets 26	36475	0	69	743	2303	7346	15549	41339	74164	165791	337819	1062370	18259021
Notes and Loans Payable 27	14842	0	139	494	3644	2646	5955	22228	50790	79541	282044	550342	6610305
All Other Liabilities 28	11405	0	39	242	-270	1313	3337	9050	23372	52954	131339	279180	5878568
Net Worth 29	10227	0	-109	7	-1070	3387	6256	10062	2	33297	-75564	232848	5770148

Selected Financial Ratios (Times to 1)

	1	2	3	4	5	6	7	8	9	10	11	12	13
Current Ratio 30	0.9	•	0.7	1.9	0.6	1.5	2.3	1.5	1.4	1.8	0.7	1.6	0.8
Quick Ratio 31	0.6	•	0.7	1.8	0.4	1.1	1.9	0.7	1.0	1.3	0.5	1.2	0.5
Net Sales to Working Capital 32	•	•	•	7.7	•	10.6	3.5	5.9	7.0	2.7	•	4.8	•
Coverage Ratio 33	1.1	•	26.2	1.1	•	2.6	0.3	0.3	•	0.6	0.1	•	1.7
Total Asset Turnover 34	0.4	•	2.8	2.2	0.9	1.0	0.8	0.4	0.5	0.4	0.9	0.3	0.3
Inventory Turnover 35	7.5	•	169.9	21.8	102.9	64.7	18.1	28.7	•	1.0	117.2	12.2	5.1
Receivables Turnover 36	4.4	30.4	6.5	4.8	8.5	6.9	6.2	5.3	2.4	•	8.4	3.4	4.3
Total Liabilities to Net Worth 37	2.6	•	105.3	•	•	1.2	1.5	3.1	32769.1	4.0	•	3.6	2.2
Current Assets to Working Capital 38	•	•	•	2.1	•	3.0	1.8	3.2	3.8	2.2	•	2.6	•
Current Liabilities to Working Capital 39	•	•	1.1	1.1	•	2.0	0.8	2.2	2.8	1.2	•	1.6	•
Working Capital to Net Sales 40	•	•	0.1	0.1	•	0.1	0.3	0.2	0.1	0.4	•	0.2	•
Inventory to Working Capital 41	•	•	0.0	0.0	•	0.0	0.0	0.0	0.0	0.2	•	0.0	•
Total Receipts to Cash Flow 42	2.2	2.0	3.6	6.8	3.3	4.0	10.9	3.2	5.1	3.0	10.6	4.6	1.8
Cost of Goods to Cash Flow 43	0.3	0.3	1.4	0.8	1.0	3.7	0.4	1.1	•	0.3	5.2	0.3	0.2
Cash Flow to Total Debt 44	0.2	•	0.3	0.3	0.2	0.5	0.2	0.1	0.1	0.3	0.1	0.3	0.3

Selected Financial Factors (in Percentages)

	1	2	3	4	5	6	7	8	9	10	11	12	13
Debt Ratio 45	72.0	•	259.4	99.1	146.5	53.9	59.8	75.7	100.0	79.9	122.4	78.1	68.4
Return on Total Assets 46	3.6	•	12.0	4.9	•	5.8	•	1.1	•	2.3	0.7	•	4.9
Return on Equity Before Income Taxes 47	1.5	•	•	36.9	25.9	7.7	•	•	•	•	26.6	•	6.2
Return on Equity After Income Taxes 48	•	•	•	34.9	26.5	5.0	•	•	•	•	26.9	•	3.0
Profit Margin (Before Income Tax) 49	1.2	4.1	0.2	0.2	3.6	•	•	•	•	•	•	•	5.8
Profit Margin (After Income Tax) 50	•	4.1	0.1	0.1	2.3	•	•	•	•	•	•	•	2.8

Table II
Corporations with Net Income

BROADCASTING (EXCEPT INTERNET)

MONEY AMOUNTS AND SIZE OF ASSETS IN THOUSANDS OF DOLLARS

Item Description for Accounting Period 7/09 Through 6/10	Total	Zero Assets	Under 500	500 to 1,000	1,000 to 5,000	5,000 to 10,000	10,000 to 25,000	25,000 to 50,000	50,000 to 100,000	100,000 to 250,000	250,000 to 500,000	500,000 to 2,500,000	2,500,000 and over
Number of Enterprises 1	2974	407	1860	211	274	113	54	13	15	9	5	9	5
Revenues ($ in Thousands)													
Net Sales 2	65399579	38392	708445	414190	526299	920364	784388	367279	877981	611754	1259933	1782727	57107826
Interest 3	1801190	20	40	177	287	907	2091	452	1350	4533	1219	84526	1705588
Rents 4	273122	0	0	0	3459	318	805	1857	148	7683	11144	3034	244674
Royalties 5	4647877	0	0	0	50882	0	0	0	3415	132	0	94	4593354
Other Portfolio Income 6	762639	0	0	0	103533	40627	1202	20116	22247	1216	20	40463	533212
Other Receipts 7	4342946	4020	34558	8307	3462	13915	24621	767	26310	30206	48686	61179	4086917
Total Receipts 8	77227353	42432	743043	422674	687922	976131	813107	390471	931451	655524	1321002	1972023	68271571
Average Total Receipts 9	25968	104	399	2003	2511	8638	15058	30036	62097	72836	264200	219114	13654314
Operating Costs/Operating Income (%)													
Cost of Operations 10	9.6	11.2	•	0.1	14.5	24.8	20.8	19.2	35.0	7.4	20.9	14.1	8.6
Salaries and Wages 11	15.1	13.0	19.0	46.6	20.3	23.9	25.3	16.1	15.2	15.8	17.4	16.2	14.4
Taxes Paid 12	1.9	1.6	23.4	4.6	9.4	2.9	3.5	2.4	2.2	2.6	2.4	2.8	1.5
Interest Paid 13	6.3	2.3	0.2	1.8	1.8	2.0	1.1	2.5	2.3	4.6	6.9	11.3	6.6
Depreciation 14	4.4	1.5	1.4	0.3	3.4	5.9	2.1	13.9	2.5	5.4	13.3	9.6	4.1
Amortization and Depletion 15	8.7	2.5	0.2	0.0	9.2	2.4	1.1	4.3	6.6	3.2	1.9	3.8	9.5
Pensions and Other Deferred Comp. 16	1.0	•	1.5	0.1	0.7	0.2	0.8	1.1	0.5	0.6	1.5	0.4	1.1
Employee Benefits 17	2.8	0.8	3.2	1.9	1.8	2.1	1.2	1.1	1.0	0.8	3.9	1.7	2.9
Advertising 18	4.1	•	0.3	1.0	0.8	0.9	1.0	1.6	2.3	5.2	0.7	0.7	4.5
Other Expenses 19	51.7	53.4	26.3	16.8	45.2	26.2	24.4	29.9	26.1	46.6	30.6	35.0	54.6
Officers' Compensation 20	1.7	•	19.7	15.7	7.7	5.4	8.6	2.9	2.0	2.8	1.0	1.2	1.1
Operating Margin 21	•	13.7	4.8	11.0	•	3.4	10.0	4.9	4.3	4.8	•	2.9	•
Operating Margin Before Officers' Comp. 22	•	13.7	24.5	26.7	8.9	•	18.6	7.8	6.3	7.6	0.6	4.1	•

Selected Average Balance Sheet ($ in Thousands)

Net Receivables 23	4724	0	19	263	935	661	2628	4758	11318	21881	28225	64283	2467638
Inventories 24	470	0	0	2	17	22	59	28	215	12080	3982	1819	247849
Net Property, Plant and Equipment 25	6979	0	14	113	194	1621	1960	11559	6340	22444	116361	90081	3704838
Total Assets 26	57314	0	62	830	1771	7314	16393	40661	72729	165791	384016	1073033	30655100
Notes and Loans Payable 27	14711	0	93	279	2409	2571	1372	14377	22312	46348	326139	343388	7367012
All Other Liabilities 28	17240	0	79	198	1018	1418	2429	6595	30243	63520	150521	381794	9042564
Net Worth 29	25363	0	-110	353	-1655	3326	12592	19688	20174	55924	-92645	347851	14245523

Selected Financial Ratios (Times to 1)

Current Ratio 30	1.2	•	0.6	7.8	1.3	1.7	8.7	2.6	1.4	2.9	1.0	1.3	1.1
Quick Ratio 31	0.7	•	0.6	7.6	1.2	1.2	7.5	1.2	1.0	1.5	0.8	0.9	0.6
Net Sales to Working Capital 32	12.6	•	•	3.3	6.4	10.0	1.7	2.7	7.4	1.7	116.5	4.3	16.4
Coverage Ratio 33	2.7	11.4	52.1	8.1	9.7	5.8	13.8	6.3	5.6	3.6	1.6	2.1	2.6
Total Asset Turnover 34	0.4	•	6.1	2.4	1.1	1.1	0.9	0.7	0.8	0.4	0.7	0.2	0.4
Inventory Turnover 35	4.5	•	•	0.6	16.5	90.1	51.3	191.5	95.4	0.4	13.2	15.4	4.0
Receivables Turnover 36	4.1	•	40.4	5.2	2.8	14.1	4.9	7.2	5.1	3.2	6.9	2.1	4.1
Total Liabilities to Net Worth 37	1.3	•	•	1.3	•	1.2	0.3	1.1	2.6	2.0	•	2.1	1.2
Current Assets to Working Capital 38	6.1	•	•	1.1	4.3	2.5	1.1	1.6	3.7	1.5	42.0	3.9	7.9
Current Liabilities to Working Capital 39	5.1	•	•	0.1	3.3	1.5	0.1	0.6	2.7	0.5	41.0	2.9	6.9
Working Capital to Net Sales 40	0.1	•	•	0.3	0.2	0.1	0.6	0.4	0.1	0.6	0.0	0.2	0.1
Inventory to Working Capital 41	0.3	•	•	•	0.1	0.0	0.0	0.0	0.0	0.3	3.3	0.0	0.4
Total Receipts to Cash Flow 42	1.7	1.5	3.1	3.5	1.8	3.8	3.0	2.6	3.2	1.8	3.2	2.2	1.6
Cost of Goods to Cash Flow 43	0.2	0.2	•	0.0	0.3	0.9	0.6	0.5	1.1	0.1	0.7	0.3	0.1
Cash Flow to Total Debt 44	0.4	•	0.7	1.2	0.3	0.5	1.3	0.5	0.3	0.3	0.2	0.1	0.4

Selected Financial Factors (in Percentages)

Debt Ratio 45	55.7	•	277.1	57.4	193.5	54.5	23.2	51.6	72.3	66.3	124.1	67.6	53.5
Return on Total Assets 46	6.5	•	60.6	35.3	19.2	12.8	12.9	11.0	10.2	6.8	7.5	4.4	6.4
Return on Equity Before Income Taxes 47	9.3	•	•	72.6	•	23.3	15.6	19.1	30.2	14.5	•	7.0	8.6
Return on Equity After Income Taxes 48	6.5	•	•	72.5	•	19.7	13.5	17.6	27.2	9.6	•	5.9	5.7
Profit Margin (Before Income Tax) 49	10.7	24.2	9.7	13.1	15.8	9.5	13.5	13.3	10.4	11.9	4.4	12.3	10.7
Profit Margin (After Income Tax) 50	7.4	20.8	9.7	13.0	15.1	8.1	11.7	12.3	9.4	7.9	4.1	10.3	7.1

268

Table I

Corporations with and without Net Income

TELECOMMUNICATIONS (WIRED, WIRELESS, SATELLITE, INTERNET PROVIDERS)

MONEY AMOUNTS AND SIZE OF ASSETS IN THOUSANDS OF DOLLARS

Item Description for Accounting Period 7/09 Through 6/10		Total	Zero Assets	Under 500	500 to 1,000	1,000 to 5,000	5,000 to 10,000	10,000 to 25,000	25,000 to 50,000	50,000 to 100,000	100,000 to 250,000	250,000 to 500,000	500,000 to 2,500,000	2,500,000 and over
Number of Enterprises	1	17348	2592	11340	773	1390	411	340	172	122	89	38	50	31
Revenues ($ in Thousands)														
Net Sales	2	455878368	982296	12950087	1314433	7725803	5238195	5159390	4486022	5048613	9125617	10575723	26103034	367169157
Interest	3	11990473	1519	5393	607	9040	17078	19483	13616	33581	78685	36335	165887	11609250
Rents	4	9476156	2606	3902	0	2325	3018	22499	7258	9962	17897	10907	52005	9343778
Royalties	5	6654809	0	0	0	0	0	408	216	4817	184475	5777	30981	6428136
Other Portfolio Income	6	3359580	710	460	0	67307	14092	156872	63222	90499	87310	33646	156850	2688611
Other Receipts	7	22497175	22504	67856	7831	90944	137313	167339	540751	200928	-116953	178377	914450	20285832
Total Receipts	8	509856561	1009635	13027698	1322871	7895419	5409696	5525991	5111085	5388400	9377031	10840765	27423207	417524764
Average Total Receipts	9	29390	390	1149	1711	5680	13162	16253	29716	44167	105360	285283	548464	13468541
Operating Costs/Operating Income (%)														
Cost of Operations	10	22.5	40.2	62.7	58.7	67.9	71.1	46.1	45.0	40.7	41.7	49.4	41.9	15.8
Salaries and Wages	11	13.7	11.9	9.3	11.6	13.5	9.6	12.1	14.1	11.4	11.9	13.6	15.1	13.9
Taxes Paid	12	3.1	1.9	1.7	3.0	1.5	1.4	2.1	2.1	2.2	2.5	2.0	2.5	3.4
Interest Paid	13	7.3	3.1	0.2	2.2	0.7	1.0	2.1	2.8	2.8	3.0	4.3	5.6	8.3
Depreciation	14	12.2	10.6	0.4	2.9	1.8	4.0	8.6	8.6	13.3	10.6	8.3	13.2	13.1
Amortization and Depletion	15	2.7	5.7	0.2	0.3	0.2	0.3	0.7	1.2	1.6	2.0	1.5	2.7	3.0
Pensions and Other Deferred Comp.	16	0.7	1.8	0.4	0.1	0.2	0.1	0.3	0.2	0.2	0.2	0.3	0.7	0.8
Employee Benefits	17	2.7	2.3	0.5	0.9	1.0	0.7	1.3	1.3	1.4	1.5	1.8	1.9	3.1
Advertising	18	2.3	1.3	0.8	0.6	0.8	0.7	1.4	3.7	1.2	0.9	2.5	1.4	2.5
Other Expenses	19	40.3	45.2	18.3	16.1	13.5	15.7	35.4	33.8	32.1	27.7	16.2	18.7	44.9
Officers' Compensation	20	0.6	3.7	3.8	4.0	3.1	1.7	2.1	1.5	1.4	1.0	0.9	0.9	0.3
Operating Margin	21	•	•	1.6									•	•
Operating Margin Before Officers' Comp.	22	5.4	•	•	3.7							0.2	•	•

Selected Average Balance Sheet ($ in Thousands)

Net Receivables 23	7796	0	18	95	585	982	2176	3835	6447	20172	60096	94178	3960579
Inventories 24	720	0	9	63	154	113	380	1027	1659	4042	4603	11927	336719
Net Property, Plant and Equipment 25	16666	0	15	169	441	1922	5650	12372	27592	53379	84899	312813	8270828
Total Assets 26	81078	0	106	716	2153	7337	15964	35888	68690	155290	335697	1033741	41952516
Notes and Loans Payable 27	27781	0	57	1073	827	2750	3462	10089	31020	44700	129923	417708	14248164
All Other Liabilities 28	26482	0	66	391	1092	3620	2345	9279	19200	60376	99100	284126	13783004
Net Worth 29	26815	0	-17	-748	233	967	10157	16520	18470	50214	106675	331908	13921348

Selected Financial Ratios (Times to 1)

Current Ratio 30	0.8	•	0.9	0.6	1.1	1.2	1.5	1.5	0.8	1.7	1.6	1.5	0.8
Quick Ratio 31	0.7	•	0.6	0.5	0.9	0.8	1.2	1.0	0.6	1.2	1.2	1.2	0.6
Net Sales to Working Capital 32	•	•	•	•	44.3	20.5	7.2	6.6	•	4.7	5.3	6.2	•
Coverage Ratio 33	1.5	•	11.0	1.2	•	1.7	•	1.1	0.5	0.9	1.5	1.1	1.6
Total Asset Turnover 34	0.3	•	10.8	2.4	2.6	1.7	1.0	0.7	0.6	0.7	0.8	0.5	0.3
Inventory Turnover 35	8.2	•	81.7	15.7	24.5	79.9	18.4	11.4	10.1	10.6	29.9	18.4	5.6
Receivables Turnover 36	3.5	•	61.4	14.7	9.2	12.4	6.5	6.5	5.9	5.6	5.7	5.4	3.2
Total Liabilities to Net Worth 37	2.0	•	•	•	8.2	6.6	0.6	1.2	2.7	2.1	2.1	2.1	2.0
Current Assets to Working Capital 38	•	•	•	•	10.3	6.6	3.0	3.2	•	2.4	2.7	3.0	•
Current Liabilities to Working Capital 39	•	•	•	•	9.3	5.6	2.0	2.2	•	1.4	1.7	2.0	•
Working Capital to Net Sales 40	•	•	•	•	0.0	0.0	0.1	0.2	•	0.2	0.2	0.2	•
Inventory to Working Capital 41	•	•	•	•	1.2	0.2	0.2	0.3	0.2	0.1	0.1	0.1	•
Total Receipts to Cash Flow 42	2.6	62.8	5.6	7.0	11.6	9.3	4.3	3.7	4.3	4.5	6.7	6.8	2.2
Cost of Goods to Cash Flow 43	0.6	25.2	3.5	4.1	7.9	6.6	2.0	1.7	1.7	1.9	3.3	2.8	0.4
Cash Flow to Total Debt 44	0.2	1.7	•	0.2	0.2	0.2	0.6	0.4	0.2	0.2	0.2	0.1	0.2

Selected Financial Factors (in Percentages)

Debt Ratio 45	66.9	•	116.0	204.4	89.2	86.8	36.4	54.0	73.1	67.7	68.2	67.9	66.8
Return on Total Assets 46	3.6	•	26.4	6.0	•	•	•	2.2	0.8	1.8	5.2	3.0	3.7
Return on Equity Before Income Taxes 47	3.7	•	•	•	•	•	•	0.4	•	•	5.4	0.7	4.1
Return on Equity After Income Taxes 48	2.0	•	•	•	•	•	•	•	•	•	3.0	•	2.4
Profit Margin (Before Income Tax) 49	3.8	•	2.2	0.4	•	0.2	0.2	•	•	•	2.1	0.4	4.8
Profit Margin (After Income Tax) 50	2.1	•	2.1	0.0	•	•	•	•	•	•	1.1	•	2.9

Table II

Corporations with Net Income

TELECOMMUNICATIONS (WIRED, WIRELESS, SATELLITE, INTERNET PROVIDERS)

MONEY AMOUNTS AND SIZE OF ASSETS IN THOUSANDS OF DOLLARS

Item Description for Accounting Period 7/09 Through 6/10	Total	Zero Assets	Under 500	500 to 1,000	1,000 to 5,000	5,000 to 10,000	10,000 to 25,000	25,000 to 50,000	50,000 to 100,000	100,000 to 250,000	250,000 to 500,000	500,000 to 2,500,000	2,500,000 and over
Number of Enterprises **1**	8679	446	6438	349	703	254	197	95	67	62	25	23	20
Revenues ($ in Thousands)													
Net Sales **2**	330374252	421212	4936482	1209606	5082952	4355672	3337021	2941538	3214402	6684449	5901526	15230387	277059006
Interest **3**	6876711	1052	2408	321	7041	6708	16139	10033	17171	54547	19430	83400	6658462
Rents **4**	5988310	2424	3902	0	1828	2513	21129	4809	6996	17719	8291	15230	5903470
Royalties **5**	6437445	0	0	0	0	0	0	216	4817	0	5777	0	6426635
Other Portfolio Income **6**	2542593	469	460	0	60874	12103	48717	61722	81500	74605	32402	91715	2078028
Other Receipts **7**	15646841	17830	66618	7169	40783	90402	137914	500729	130396	336739	72694	723016	13522548
Total Receipts **8**	367866152	442987	5009870	1217096	5193478	4467398	3560920	3519047	3455282	7168059	6040120	16143748	311648149
Average Total Receipts **9**	42386	993	778	3487	7388	17588	18076	37043	51571	115614	241605	701902	15582407
Operating Costs/Operating Income (%)													
Cost of Operations **10**	22.2	20.9	33.1	59.3	71.8	77.7	53.6	49.7	39.5	38.8	51.3	36.2	17.4
Salaries and Wages **11**	12.4	17.4	12.0	10.3	8.3	6.1	5.9	11.9	10.0	11.4	10.2	14.1	12.6
Taxes Paid **12**	3.2	2.1	2.2	1.8	0.9	0.9	1.8	2.0	2.0	2.7	1.8	2.8	3.4
Interest Paid **13**	7.1	2.4	0.3	1.9	0.3	0.4	0.8	2.0	1.9	2.5	2.3	5.3	8.0
Depreciation **14**	10.7	13.7	0.7	1.3	1.4	2.5	7.1	6.5	10.7	10.7	7.6	12.7	11.3
Amortization and Depletion **15**	3.3	0.2	0.2	0.3	0.1	0.1	0.3	0.9	1.0	1.0	1.5	2.7	3.6
Pensions and Other Deferred Comp. **16**	0.6	3.5	0.6	0.1	0.1	0.1	0.5	0.1	0.3	0.3	0.2	0.8	0.6
Employee Benefits **17**	2.4	2.3	0.7	0.7	0.7	0.2	0.8	0.8	1.2	1.4	1.7	1.6	2.6
Advertising **18**	2.0	1.8	1.9	0.5	0.4	0.6	1.5	0.8	1.2	0.8	0.3	1.6	2.2
Other Expenses **19**	38.1	25.6	32.5	11.7	9.6	9.1	22.0	31.0	28.0	26.6	17.8	17.7	41.5
Officers' Compensation **20**	0.5	1.2	5.0	4.0	2.5	1.0	1.5	1.0	1.5	1.0	1.1	0.7	0.3
Operating Margin **21**	•	8.9	10.7	7.9	3.8	1.3	4.3	•	2.7	3.0	4.2	3.8	•
Operating Margin Before Officers' Comp. **22**	•	10.1	15.6	11.9	6.3	2.3	5.8	•	4.2	5.4	3.9	4.5	•

Selected Average Balance Sheet ($ in Thousands)

Net Receivables 23	13122	0	28	171	607	791	2435	4297	6233	18372	59588	109767	5328073
Inventories 24	1202	0	7	31	165	122	335	1230	1942	4057	5021	15141	459525
Net Property, Plant and Equipment 25	22367	0	22	170	406	1840	5776	12558	28352	57986	83665	350315	8759854
Total Assets 26	117892	0	115	746	2202	7664	16110	36138	67056	157276	335905	1150672	48148764
Notes and Loans Payable 27	41207	0	71	2040	300	948	2426	8884	37499	45952	86220	589383	16680900
All Other Liabilities 28	34932	0	89	720	742	3052	4245	7922	16593	34948	100549	261712	14382528
Net Worth 29	41753	0	-45	-2013	1159	3664	9439	19333	12964	76376	149136	299577	17085336

Selected Financial Ratios (Times to 1)

Current Ratio 30	0.9	•	0.8	0.6	2.0	1.4	1.7	2.0	0.6	1.7	1.6	1.6	0.8
Quick Ratio 31	0.7	•	0.7	0.5	1.5	0.9	1.4	1.3	0.5	1.2	1.3	1.3	0.7
Net Sales to Working Capital 32	•	•	•	•	10.3	14.8	6.1	4.8	•	5.7	4.5	5.8	•
Coverage Ratio 33	2.3	6.9	5.4	5.4	20.2	10.6	15.1	8.0	6.4	5.1	4.0	2.9	2.1
Total Asset Turnover 34	0.3	•	6.6	4.6	3.3	2.2	1.1	0.9	0.7	0.7	0.7	0.6	0.3
Inventory Turnover 35	7.0	•	37.3	66.9	31.4	109.6	27.1	12.5	9.7	10.3	24.1	15.8	5.2
Receivables Turnover 36	2.9	•	33.5	26.3	11.6	18.0	7.8	7.1	6.4	6.2	5.6	6.1	2.6
Total Liabilities to Net Worth 37	1.8	•	•	0.9	0.9	1.1	0.7	0.9	4.2	1.1	1.3	2.8	1.8
Current Assets to Working Capital 38	•	•	•	•	2.0	3.7	2.4	2.0	•	2.4	2.6	2.8	•
Current Liabilities to Working Capital 39	•	•	•	•	1.0	2.7	1.4	1.0	•	1.4	1.6	1.8	•
Working Capital to Net Sales 40	•	•	•	•	0.1	0.1	0.2	0.2	•	0.2	0.2	0.2	•
Inventory to Working Capital 41	•	•	•	0.3	0.3	0.1	0.1	0.2	•	0.2	0.1	0.1	•
Total Receipts to Cash Flow 42	2.3	3.2	2.4	5.4	7.9	8.5	3.5	2.6	3.3	3.1	4.7	4.3	2.2
Cost of Goods to Cash Flow 43	0.5	0.7	0.8	3.2	5.7	6.6	1.9	1.3	1.3	1.2	2.4	1.6	0.4
Cash Flow to Total Debt 44	0.2	•	2.0	0.2	0.9	0.5	0.7	0.7	0.3	0.4	0.3	0.2	0.2

Selected Financial Factors (in Percentages)

Debt Ratio 45	64.6	•	139.0	370.0	47.3	52.2	41.4	46.5	80.7	51.4	55.6	74.0	64.5
Return on Total Assets 46	5.2	•	82.7	48.4	20.7	9.6	12.4	13.5	8.7	8.7	6.5	8.7	4.9
Return on Equity Before Income Taxes 47	8.2	•	•	•	37.4	18.2	19.8	22.0	38.1	14.4	10.9	21.8	7.2
Return on Equity After Income Taxes 48	6.0	•	•	•	33.6	15.0	15.9	17.8	30.7	10.6	8.3	17.4	5.2
Profit Margin (Before Income Tax) 49	9.0	14.1	12.1	8.5	6.0	3.9	11.0	13.7	10.3	10.2	6.9	9.9	8.9
Profit Margin (After Income Tax) 50	6.6	11.0	11.9	8.1	5.4	3.2	8.9	11.1	8.3	7.5	5.2		6.4

Table I

Corporations with and without Net Income

DATA PROCESSING, HOSTING AND RELATED SERVICES

MONEY AMOUNTS AND SIZE OF ASSETS IN THOUSANDS OF DOLLARS

Item Description for Accounting Period 7/09 Through 6/10	Total	Zero Assets	Under 500	500 to 1,000	1,000 to 5,000	5,000 to 10,000	10,000 to 25,000	25,000 to 50,000	50,000 to 100,000	100,000 to 250,000	250,000 to 500,000	500,000 to 2,500,000	2,500,000 and over
Number of Enterprises 1	8212	2306	5104	63	498	84	67	30	19	20	6	14	0
Revenues ($ in Thousands)													
Net Sales 2	2690369	679476	2411747	162487	3564859	692221	934538	1051541	1267164	1752887	1493610	12889840	0
Interest 3	112753	213	71	191	1799	1661	966	4728	1063	2091	4574	95396	0
Rents 4	62473	0	4546	0	0	125	4597	0	805	0	0	52400	0
Royalties 5	210371	0	0	0	0	0	282	0	52	12022	0	198015	0
Other Portfolio Income 6	89034	2846	2284	13694	1408	465	16676	555	6331	4659	13367	26748	0
Other Receipts 7	1638459	1090057	1649	2907	51981	25273	9675	6479	17413	106777	4644	321605	0
Total Receipts 8	29013459	1772592	2420297	179279	3620047	719745	966734	1063303	1292828	1878436	1516195	13584004	0
Average Total Receipts 9	3533	769	474	2846	7269	8568	14429	35443	68044	93922	252699	970286	•
Operating Costs/Operating Income (%)													
Cost of Operations 10	26.8	44.4	31.1	4.2	25.8	61.8	34.8	46.4	26.6	20.7	31.3	22.0	•
Salaries and Wages 11	24.5	49.7	14.3	43.4	27.3	20.7	26.8	22.9	24.6	32.5	21.7	23.4	•
Taxes Paid 12	2.6	5.0	3.2	4.7	1.7	1.6	3.3	2.2	3.2	3.3	2.4	2.5	•
Interest Paid 13	5.6	15.0	0.4	3.3	1.1	2.5	4.4	1.7	4.0	6.8	1.1	8.4	•
Depreciation 14	7.4	7.8	0.8	1.5	2.8	2.7	3.9	3.4	5.5	7.9	3.5	11.3	•
Amortization and Depletion 15	2.7	7.0	0.0	0.1	0.3	3.3	3.1	3.7	1.4	5.0	2.0	3.4	•
Pensions and Other Deferred Comp. 16	0.5	3.4	0.0	•	0.4	0.1	0.8	0.9	0.4	0.4	0.3	0.5	•
Employee Benefits 17	2.1	6.3	0.9	2.2	1.5	1.0	2.6	2.2	1.8	3.2	2.2	2.2	•
Advertising 18	1.3	1.1	0.3	1.1	1.1	2.3	2.3	0.6	1.9	1.2	5.4	0.9	•
Other Expenses 19	30.6	82.2	46.8	35.2	31.2	26.0	25.8	19.9	29.1	27.4	18.6	28.0	•
Officers' Compensation 20	3.5	20.8	7.7	13.7	10.1	2.9	4.2	3.6	2.3	1.6	1.3	0.5	•
Operating Margin 21	•	•	•	•	•	•	•	•	•	•	10.2	•	•
Operating Margin Before Officers' Comp. 22	•	•	2.1	4.2	6.8	•	•	•	•	1.3	11.5	•	•

Selected Average Balance Sheet ($ in Thousands)

Net Receivables 23	486	0	16	246	340	1076	1782	9220	10470	17115	55927	168738
Inventories 24	18	0	0	156	46	150	196	213	218	345	40	3270
Net Property, Plant and Equipment 25	1067	0	10	122	534	345	1589	4721	14755	21374	26956	520966
Total Assets 26	5762	103	747	2178	7138	14455	34947	73988	139714	375903		2613564
Notes and Loans Payable 27	2311	0	118	1577	846	2571	1240	14065	29432	62035	43509	1076515
All Other Liabilities 28	1583	0	71	531	1118	2462	7382	6056	18047	36678	204474	633088
Net Worth 29	1868	0	-87	-1361	215	2104	5833	14825	26509	41001	127920	903961

Selected Financial Ratios (Times to 1)

Current Ratio 30	1.2	•	0.8	0.9	1.0	1.2	1.2	1.3	1.6	1.0	1.2	1.2
Quick Ratio 31	1.0	•	0.5	0.7	0.8	1.0	1.1	1.1	1.3	0.8	0.8	1.1
Net Sales to Working Capital 32	15.1	•	•	•	•	15.4	9.7	7.3	6.7	251.5	9.1	10.4
Coverage Ratio 33	1.1	2.2	1.3	•	•	•	•	•	1.3	0.6	12.5	1.3
Total Asset Turnover 34	0.6	•	4.6	3.5	3.3	1.2	1.0	1.0	0.9	0.6	0.7	0.4
Inventory Turnover 35	48.1	•	477.2	0.7	39.8	34.1	24.8	76.4	81.2	52.5	1966.8	62.0
Receivables Turnover 36	5.6	•	31.2	7.3	18.9	5.5	8.0	3.7	8.8	4.7	4.6	8.1
Total Liabilities to Net Worth 37	2.1	•	•	•	9.2	2.4	1.5	1.4	1.8	2.4	1.9	1.9
Current Assets to Working Capital 38	6.2	•	•	•	•	5.9	5.2	4.2	2.7	103.2	6.5	5.3
Current Liabilities to Working Capital 39	5.2	•	•	•	•	4.9	4.2	3.2	1.7	102.2	5.5	4.3
Working Capital to Net Sales 40	0.1	•	•	•	0.1	0.1	0.1	0.1	0.1	0.0	0.1	0.1
Inventory to Working Capital 41	0.1	•	•	•	•	0.3	0.2	0.0	0.0	0.0	0.0	0.0
Total Receipts to Cash Flow 42	3.9	1.2	2.7	4.3	•	3.9	8.4	9.7	4.4	5.7	3.5	4.1
Cost of Goods to Cash Flow 43	1.1	0.5	0.8	0.2	•	1.0	2.9	4.5	1.2	1.2	1.1	0.9
Cash Flow to Total Debt 44	0.2	•	0.9	0.3	0.9	0.2	0.2	•	0.3	0.3	0.2	0.1

Selected Financial Factors (in Percentages)

Debt Ratio 45	67.6	•	184.5	282.1	90.1	70.5	59.6	57.6	64.2	70.7	66.0	65.4
Return on Total Assets 46	3.5	•	•	14.2	•	•	•	•	4.7	2.5	8.7	3.9
Return on Equity Before Income Taxes 47	1.0	•	28.7	•	•	•	•	•	3.0	•	23.6	2.8
Return on Equity After Income Taxes 48	•	•	28.8	•	•	•	•	•	1.3	•	18.2	0.6
Profit Margin (Before Income Tax) 49	0.6	18.3	•	0.8	•	•	•	•	1.2	•	12.1	2.7
Profit Margin (After Income Tax) 50	•	9.2	•	0.7	•	•	•	•	0.5	•	9.4	0.5

271

Table II

Corporations with Net Income

DATA PROCESSING, HOSTING AND RELATED SERVICES

MONEY AMOUNTS AND SIZE OF ASSETS IN THOUSANDS OF DOLLARS

Item Description for Accounting Period 7/09 Through 6/10	Total	Zero Assets	Under 500	500 to 1,000	1,000 to 5,000	5,000 to 10,000	10,000 to 25,000	25,000 to 50,000	50,000 to 100,000	100,000 to 250,000	250,000 to 500,000	500,000 to 2,500,000	2,500,000 and over
Number of Enterprises **1**	3786	1382	2061	35	198	31	32	12	9	10	6	11	0
Revenues ($ in Thousands)													
Net Sales **2**	17349629	321795	1133120	139522	2321155	454910	530886	705508	701781	1065865	1493610	8481477	0
Interest **3**	58671	203	10	123	775	214	388	3670	303	990	4574	47422	0
Rents **4**	57866	0	4546	0	0	0	4547	0	805	0	0	47968	0
Royalties **5**	199769	0	0	0	0	0	282	0	0	3627	0	195860	0
Other Portfolio Income **6**	85200	2846	2284	13575	0	459	16676	207	5187	3902	13367	26696	0
Other Receipts **7**	1500480	1090057	86	2907	50863	23735	11033	2958	14976	-1260	4644	300482	0
Total Receipts **8**	19251615	1414901	1140046	156127	2372793	479318	563812	712343	723052	1073124	1516195	9099905	0
Average Total Receipts **9**	5085	1024	553	4461	11984	15462	17619	59362	80339	107312	252699	827264	•
Operating Costs/Operating Income (%)													
Cost of Operations **10**	20.2	34.3	14.0	2.0	18.4	74.9	35.0	53.8	14.8	22.5	31.3	12.7	•
Salaries and Wages **11**	27.2	96.9	10.4	32.5	34.6	10.9	21.2	14.8	26.5	26.1	21.7	28.2	•
Taxes Paid **12**	2.3	9.6	2.6	3.8	1.7	0.8	3.3	1.8	3.6	3.0	2.4	1.9	•
Interest Paid **13**	3.9	28.0	0.2	1.5	0.3	2.0	0.4	1.0	5.3	5.5	1.1	5.3	•
Depreciation **14**	4.6	12.7	0.4	1.3	2.8	0.7	2.3	2.3	6.3	5.1	3.5	5.9	•
Amortization and Depletion **15**	2.7	12.3	0.0	0.1	0.0	0.2	2.7	0.6	2.2	2.7	2.0	3.9	•
Pensions and Other Deferred Comp. **16**	0.7	6.5	•	•	0.5	0.2	1.3	1.3	0.4	0.6	0.3	0.6	•
Employee Benefits **17**	2.2	9.2	0.0	0.1	1.4	0.2	3.3	1.9	1.2	1.8	2.2	2.7	•
Advertising **18**	1.5	2.2	0.2	1.3	1.3	1.3	1.7	0.4	2.2	1.0	5.4	1.0	•
Other Expenses **19**	31.6	129.5	58.0	29.2	28.5	6.1	20.6	15.2	29.8	21.2	18.6	32.4	•
Officers' Compensation **20**	3.2	33.3	10.6	10.8	6.5	2.6	3.6	3.2	2.2	1.7	1.3	0.7	•
Operating Margin **21**	•	•	3.5	17.4	4.0	0.2	4.7	3.7	5.5	8.9	10.2	4.6	•
Operating Margin Before Officers' Comp. **22**	3.2	•	14.1	28.2	10.5	2.8	8.3	6.9	7.7	10.5	11.5	5.2	•

Selected Average Balance Sheet ($ in Thousands)

Net Receivables 23	788	0	10	265	412	1964	1952	12353	8084	20072	55927	181054
Inventories 24	23	0	0	281	2	219	334	173	230	267	26	2189
Net Property, Plant and Equipment 25	580	0	6	208	863	169	1060	3602	14451	19036	26956	131066
Total Assets 26	8627	0	107	705	2381	6839	15110	34589	79836	131904	375903	2412806
Notes and Loans Payable 27	2608	0	32	2204	691	2001	958	26603	38663	57445	43509	727331
All Other Liabilities 28	2444	0	95	382	1114	1937	6525	-6898	23222	35154	204474	622788
Net Worth 29	3574	-20	-1881	576	2901	7627	14884	17950	127920	1062688		

Selected Financial Ratios (Times to 1)

Current Ratio 30	1.3	•	0.9	0.7	0.6	1.2	1.4	0.9	1.3	0.9	1.2	1.4
Quick Ratio 31	1.1	•	0.5	0.5	0.5	1.1	1.2	0.7	1.1	0.7	0.8	1.3
Net Sales to Working Capital 32	10.4	•	•	•	25.9	6.9	•	14.7	•	•	9.1	5.4
Coverage Ratio 33	3.9	3.3	19.8	21.2	21.5	3.7	28.4	5.8	2.7	2.8	12.5	3.4
Total Asset Turnover 34	0.5	•	5.2	5.7	4.9	2.1	1.1	1.7	1.0	0.8	0.7	0.3
Inventory Turnover 35	40.9	•	823.8	0.3	913.7	50.2	17.4	182.6	49.9	89.8	3039.7	44.9
Receivables Turnover 36	5.0	•	35.6	7.3	32.4	9.2	8.0	4.6	9.9	6.1	•	7.3
Total Liabilities to Net Worth 37	1.4	•	•	3.1	3.1	1.4	1.0	1.3	3.4	2.4	1.9	1.3
Current Assets to Working Capital 38	4.7	•	•	•	5.7	3.6	•	4.2	•	•	6.5	3.3
Current Liabilities to Working Capital 39	3.7	•	•	•	4.7	2.6	•	3.2	•	•	5.5	2.3
Working Capital to Net Sales 40	0.1	•	•	•	0.0	0.1	•	0.1	•	•	0.1	0.2
Inventory to Working Capital 41	0.0	•	•	•	0.5	0.2	•	0.0	•	•	0.0	0.0
Total Receipts to Cash Flow 42	2.6	0.6	1.7	2.3	3.2	4.1	9.5	5.6	3.0	3.7	3.5	2.5
Cost of Goods to Cash Flow 43	0.5	0.2	0.2	0.0	0.6	1.4	7.1	3.0	0.4	0.8	1.1	0.3
Cash Flow to Total Debt 44	0.3	•	2.6	0.7	2.0	0.5	0.4	0.5	0.4	0.3	0.3	0.2

Selected Financial Factors (in Percentages)

Debt Ratio 45	58.6	•	118.7	366.9	75.8	57.6	49.5	57.0	77.5	70.2	66.0	56.0
Return on Total Assets 46	8.1	•	22.3	173.8	32.3	16.4	12.4	9.5	13.7	12.1	8.7	5.7
Return on Equity Before Income Taxes 47	14.6	•	•	•	127.1	28.4	23.7	18.4	37.9	25.9	23.6	9.1
Return on Equity After Income Taxes 48	11.3	•	•	•	120.4	21.8	22.1	14.0	32.9	20.7	18.2	6.7
Profit Margin (Before Income Tax) 49	11.4	65.5	4.1	29.3	6.2	5.6	10.9	4.6	8.7	9.6	12.1	12.6
Profit Margin (After Income Tax) 50	8.8	46.3	4.1	29.1	5.9	4.3	10.2	3.5	7.6	7.6	9.4	9.2

Table I
Corporations with and without Net Income

OTHER INFORMATION SERVICES, INTERNET PUBLISHING, WEB PORTALS

MONEY AMOUNTS AND SIZE OF ASSETS IN THOUSANDS OF DOLLARS

Item Description for Accounting Period 7/09 Through 6/10		Total	Zero Assets	Under 500	500 to 1,000	1,000 to 5,000	5,000 to 10,000	10,000 to 25,000	25,000 to 50,000	50,000 to 100,000	100,000 to 250,000	250,000 to 500,000	500,000 to 2,500,000	2,500,000 and over
Number of Enterprises	1	21465	5084	14630	641	664	278	72	32	20	17	10	13	5
Revenues ($ in Thousands)														
Net Sales	2	56800905	395091	4730440	726907	3036476	6141274	1055015	1193042	1512111	1392637	2302212	6257101	28058598
Interest	3	218425	1665	971	709	4766	2765	2055	2686	1779	4667	8843	14802	172717
Rents	4	88457	14	4444	0	198	103	606	696	270	338	4514	7521	69752
Royalties	5	1174190	470	41	0	42	0	0	177	3081	10041	3696	636139	520503
Other Portfolio Income	6	449237	10105	0	5	1032	63670	19603	2	194	1596	13651	259258	80122
Other Receipts	7	2537875	188629	33664	199	22032	15159	6385	56678	1364	6205	-6571	206235	2007898
Total Receipts	8	61269089	595974	4769560	727820	3064546	6222971	1083664	1253281	1518799	1415484	2326345	7381056	30909590
Average Total Receipts	9	2854	117	326	1135	4615	22385	15051	39165	75940	83264	232634	567774	6181918
Operating Costs/Operating Income (%)														
Cost of Operations	10	29.5	18.1	42.3	42.0	45.9	61.4	28.9	32.6	29.6	13.4	11.0	39.9	18.4
Salaries and Wages	11	20.9	37.4	9.9	20.4	27.1	11.4	34.6	24.5	20.4	22.7	27.9	25.5	21.7
Taxes Paid	12	2.8	3.7	1.6	3.4	3.1	1.9	4.7	2.8	2.7	3.2	3.1	2.9	3.0
Interest Paid	13	2.9	1.7	0.8	2.0	0.7	0.8	1.8	2.7	1.7	1.1	1.0	5.6	3.7
Depreciation	14	3.8	2.0	1.9	1.4	1.4	1.6	3.9	5.1	2.9	3.5	4.1	3.4	5.1
Amortization and Depletion	15	1.7	5.2	0.5	0.5	1.3	0.8	3.7	2.1	2.1	2.0	2.8	4.5	1.2
Pensions and Other Deferred Comp.	16	0.6	3.3	0.5	0.2	0.1	0.5	0.1	0.1	0.5	1.0	0.8	0.7	0.6
Employee Benefits	17	1.8	5.5	0.7	2.1	1.3	1.5	2.7	1.7	3.6	2.3	2.6	2.5	1.7
Advertising	18	2.5	1.5	3.2	0.5	3.0	6.0	3.8	2.2	1.1	14.6	2.3	2.2	1.1
Other Expenses	19	31.0	103.9	22.5	39.9	28.4	14.2	28.6	30.2	31.0	23.6	37.4	20.7	37.3
Officers' Compensation	20	2.5	18.6	11.4	9.4	6.1	2.4	3.5	2.7	1.7	2.2	1.2	1.8	0.5
Operating Margin	21	0.1	•	4.5	•	•	•	•	•	2.6	10.3	5.7	•	•
Operating Margin Before Officers' Comp.	22	2.5	15.9	•	•	•	•	•	•	4.4	12.4	6.9	5.8	6.3

Selected Average Balance Sheet ($ in Thousands)

Net Receivables 23	562	0	7	50	330	1509	2610	4908	9520	11037	46091	76927	1822413
Inventories 24	33	0	1	11	8	3	76	156	2369	15	2154	29431	46076
Net Property, Plant and Equipment 25	426	0	10	61	251	897	1071	3171	9247	9565	21189	59453	1407603
Total Assets 26	4916	0	51	705	2161	6872	15070	34601	70603	158483	351519	1097113	15379906
Notes and Loans Payable 27	778	0	87	360	610	1962	4033	6858	9886	10186	100704	314633	1653348
All Other Liabilities 28	1191	0	35	321	855	1803	9604	15801	32523	37256	104828	356045	3125189
Net Worth 29	2947	0	-71	24	697	3107	1433	11942	28194	111041	145987	426436	10601369

Selected Financial Ratios (Times to 1)

Current Ratio 30	2.0	•	0.7	0.9	1.3	2.7	1.1	1.6	1.2	2.1	1.3	0.9	2.7
Quick Ratio 31	1.0	•	0.6	0.8	1.2	2.2	1.0	1.3	0.9	1.7	1.1	0.4	1.2
Net Sales to Working Capital 32	2.8	•	•	•	15.9	7.3	15.3	5.8	16.7	2.3	5.8	•	1.5
Coverage Ratio 33	3.9	7.4	•	•	•	•	1.0	0.4	2.8	11.8	7.8	2.8	5.5
Total Asset Turnover 34	0.5	•	6.4	1.6	2.1	3.2	1.0	1.1	1.1	0.5	0.7	0.4	0.4
Inventory Turnover 35	23.5	•	237.6	45.2	249.3	4798.4	55.6	77.8	9.5	724.0	11.8	6.5	22.4
Receivables Turnover 36	5.5	•	43.2	22.2	13.7	16.6	5.9	5.5	8.5	6.8	5.0	6.7	3.8
Total Liabilities to Net Worth 37	0.7	•	•	28.8	2.1	1.2	9.5	1.9	1.5	0.4	1.4	1.6	0.5
Current Assets to Working Capital 38	2.0	•	•	•	4.3	1.6	10.3	2.5	6.9	1.9	4.5	•	1.6
Current Liabilities to Working Capital 39	1.0	•	•	•	3.3	0.6	9.3	1.5	5.9	0.9	3.5	•	0.6
Working Capital to Net Sales 40	0.4	•	•	•	0.1	0.1	0.1	0.2	0.1	0.4	0.2	•	0.7
Inventory to Working Capital 41	0.0	•	•	•	0.0	0.0	0.1	0.0	0.2	0.0	0.0	•	0.0
Total Receipts to Cash Flow 42	2.8	3.2	4.0	7.1	13.5	10.7	9.2	3.9	3.6	3.2	2.5	4.1	2.0
Cost of Goods to Cash Flow 43	0.8	0.6	1.7	3.0	6.2	6.6	2.7	1.3	1.1	0.4	0.3	1.6	0.4
Cash Flow to Total Debt 44	0.5	0.7	•	0.2	0.2	0.5	0.1	0.4	0.5	0.5	0.5	0.2	0.6

Selected Financial Factors (in Percentages)

Debt Ratio 45	40.1	•	239.9	96.6	67.8	54.8	90.5	65.5	60.1	29.9	58.5	61.1	31.1
Return on Total Assets 46	6.1	•	39.4	•	•	•	•	1.3	5.1	6.7	5.3	6.9	7.4
Return on Equity Before Income Taxes 47	7.5	•	•	•	•	•	•	•	8.2	8.8	11.1	11.3	8.7
Return on Equity After Income Taxes 48	4.4	•	•	•	•	•	•	•	•	4.8	4.3	8.5	5.8
Profit Margin (Before Income Tax) 49	8.4	•	5.3	•	•	•	•	•	3.1	11.9	7.1	10.0	16.5
Profit Margin (After Income Tax) 50	4.9	•	5.3	•	•	•	•	•	•	6.5	2.7	7.6	10.9

Table II
Corporations with Net Income

OTHER INFORMATION SERVICES, INTERNET PUBLISHING, WEB PORTALS

MONEY AMOUNTS AND SIZE OF ASSETS IN THOUSANDS OF DOLLARS

Item Description for Accounting Period 7/09 Through 6/10	Total	Zero Assets	Under 500	500 to 1,000	1,000 to 5,000	5,000 to 10,000	10,000 to 25,000	25,000 to 50,000	50,000 to 100,000	100,000 to 250,000	250,000 to 500,000	500,000 to 2,500,000	2,500,000 and over
Number of Enterprises **1**	13261	2483	10030	•	150	159	28	16	9	9	6	10	•
Revenues ($ in Thousands)													
Net Sales **2**	48798322	199926	4438393	•	1094648	5265329	453819	812080	1078130	1010870	1717993	4545951	•
Interest **3**	198732	2	264	•	1687	1461	852	1130	754	3476	4067	12840	•
Rents **4**	82002	0	4444	•	0	0	0	0	0	338	0	7342	•
Royalties **5**	1167143	0	0	•	0	0	0	177	0	10041	286	636139	•
Other Portfolio Income **6**	414180	0	0	•	0	63658	7775	2	39	358	10002	252224	•
Other Receipts **7**	2364669	665	33269	•	11669	7594	1549	49870	-680	1265	1890	182783	•
Total Receipts **8**	53025048	200593	4476370	•	1108004	5338042	463995	863635	1078243	1026348	1734238	5637279	•
Average Total Receipts **9**	3999	81	446	•	7387	33573	16571	53977	119805	114039	289040	563728	•
Operating Costs/Operating Income (%)													
Cost of Operations **10**	29.0	14.5	43.9	•	74.8	66.1	30.2	41.0	25.3	13.4	6.5	34.4	•
Salaries and Wages **11**	19.2	13.4	9.0	•	5.7	7.8	22.4	17.8	18.3	16.5	24.1	29.2	•
Taxes Paid **12**	2.6	2.0	1.5	•	0.7	1.7	2.8	2.3	2.1	3.2	2.8	3.4	•
Interest Paid **13**	2.6	1.0	0.2	•	0.1	0.2	1.5	1.5	0.7	0.1	0.4	4.3	•
Depreciation **14**	3.8	0.9	1.7	•	0.4	1.3	2.7	1.7	2.2	2.3	3.1	3.9	•
Amortization and Depletion **15**	1.3	•	0.0	•	0.1	0.0	0.8	0.6	1.7	1.6	2.7	4.2	•
Pensions and Other Deferred Comp. **16**	0.6	4.4	0.6	•	0.2	0.6	•	0.1	0.7	0.2	1.1	0.9	•
Employee Benefits **17**	1.6	3.4	0.7	•	0.5	1.1	0.9	0.9	3.5	1.3	2.6	2.7	•
Advertising **18**	2.3	•	1.1	•	0.0	6.4	3.7	1.9	0.6	19.6	2.8	2.8	•
Other Expenses **19**	29.4	28.7	18.2	•	11.0	9.9	24.0	26.0	29.1	16.7	36.8	22.7	•
Officers' Compensation **20**	2.0	19.3	11.3	•	2.1	1.9	2.3	2.0	1.0	1.4	1.2	2.2	•
Operating Margin **21**	5.4	12.5	11.8	•	4.3	3.0	8.7	4.1	14.9	23.7	16.0	•	•
Operating Margin Before Officers' Comp. **22**	7.5	31.8	23.1	•	6.5	4.8	11.0	6.1	15.9	25.0	17.2	•	•

Selected Average Balance Sheet ($ in Thousands)

Net Receivables 23	581	0	9	•	375	1967	1952	5824	13803	14176	70908	79330
Inventories 24	38	0	0	•	31	3	23	117	509	26	451	25213
Net Property, Plant and Equipment 25	577	0	9	•	53	887	659	1705	9094	5547	25124	57952
Total Assets 26	6128	0	52	•	2628	7036	15035	36589	81782	162361	383156	1066114
Notes and Loans Payable 27	863	0	44	•	782	440	3132	4449	11301	3593	27915	203440
All Other Liabilities 28	1429	0	21	•	564	1680	8060	17364	50091	33850	58314	377835
Net Worth 29	3835	0	-13	•	1283	4916	3844	14776	20389	124918	296927	484840

Selected Financial Ratios (Times to 1)

Current Ratio 30	2.4	•	1.2	•	2.9	3.4	1.5	1.1	1.0	2.4	2.0	1.0
Quick Ratio 31	1.0	•	1.0	•	2.7	2.7	1.4	1.0	0.8	2.2	1.9	0.4
Net Sales to Working Capital 32	2.5	•	83.1	•	7.0	8.3	5.2	37.1	68.4	2.5	3.2	2518.5
Coverage Ratio 33	6.5	14.4	72.0	•	65.8	21.4	8.2	7.8	23.5	232.1	47.1	4.6
Total Asset Turnover 34	0.6	•	8.5	•	2.8	4.7	1.1	1.4	1.5	0.7	0.7	0.4
Inventory Turnover 35	27.8	•	•	•	177.4	6811.0	212.5	177.7	59.5	578.5	41.0	6.2
Receivables Turnover 36	6.3	•	56.3	•	10.8	19.6	9.4	11.0	9.1	6.5	•	6.0
Total Liabilities to Net Worth 37	0.6	•	•	•	1.0	0.4	2.9	1.5	3.0	0.3	0.3	1.2
Current Assets to Working Capital 38	1.7	•	7.0	•	1.5	1.4	2.8	9.6	22.5	1.7	2.0	1890.3
Current Liabilities to Working Capital 39	0.7	•	6.0	•	0.5	0.4	1.8	8.6	21.5	0.7	1.0	1889.3
Working Capital to Net Sales 40	0.4	•	0.0	•	0.1	0.1	0.2	0.0	0.0	0.4	0.3	0.0
Inventory to Working Capital 41	0.0	•	•	•	0.0	0.0	•	0.1	0.5	•	0.0	138.3
Total Receipts to Cash Flow 42	2.5	3.0	3.4	•	6.9	8.8	3.0	2.9	2.5	2.6	2.0	3.3
Cost of Goods to Cash Flow 43	0.7	0.4	1.5	•	5.2	5.8	0.9	1.2	0.6	0.3	0.1	1.1
Cash Flow to Total Debt 44	0.7	•	2.0	•	0.8	1.8	0.5	0.8	0.8	1.2	1.7	0.2

Selected Financial Factors (in Percentages)

Debt Ratio 45	37.4	•	124.6	•	51.2	30.1	74.4	59.6	75.1	23.1	22.5	54.5
Return on Total Assets 46	10.4	•	108.9	•	15.7	21.5	13.5	16.7	22.8	17.5	13.3	8.5
Return on Equity Before Income Taxes 47	14.0	•	•	•	31.6	29.4	46.2	35.9	87.5	22.7	16.8	14.6
Return on Equity After Income Taxes 48	10.2	•	•	•	29.2	29.2	44.0	33.5	58.5	16.0	11.2	11.4
Profit Margin (Before Income Tax) 49	14.6	12.8	12.7	•	5.6	4.4	11.0	10.5	14.9	25.2	17.4	15.6
Profit Margin (After Income Tax) 50	10.6	12.8	12.6	•	5.1	4.3	10.4	9.7	10.0	17.8	11.6	12.2

Table I

Corporations with and without Net Income

CREDIT INTERMEDIATION

MONEY AMOUNTS AND SIZE OF ASSETS IN THOUSANDS OF DOLLARS

Item Description for Accounting Period 7/09 Through 6/10	Total	Zero Assets	Under 500	500 to 1,000	1,000 to 5,000	5,000 to 10,000	10,000 to 25,000	25,000 to 50,000	50,000 to 100,000	100,000 to 250,000	250,000 to 500,000	500,000 to 2,500,000	2,500,000 and over
Number of Enterprises **1**	47542	11151	24279	3850	3596	850	793	526	713	879	394	385	126
Revenues ($ in Thousands)													
Net Sales **2**	507596109	54303885	6348016	1471680	3935903	2121465	4783133	3918283	6432018	13292574	12838773	37132881	361017498
Interest **3**	298343542	33291290	57638	49452	239295	153777	321120	784179	1827184	5181919	5194490	18338621	232904574
Rents **4**	1075531	289773	534	134	4700	1900	5134	6917	5376	17249	31077	174565	538173
Royalties **5**	663522	23864	0	39	0	0	3	663	9033	182	4	8260	621474
Other Portfolio Income **6**	12314011	1754975	1140	371	19105	9957	36758	38104	183453	404695	287884	1782296	7795270
Other Receipts **7**	195199503	18943983	6288704	1421684	3672803	1955831	4420118	3088420	4406972	7688529	7325318	16829139	119158007
Total Receipts **8**	507596109	54303885	6348016	1471680	3935903	2121465	4783133	3918283	6432018	13292574	12838773	37132881	361017498
Average Total Receipts **9**	10677	4870	261	382	1095	2496	6032	7449	9021	15122	32586	96449	2865218
Operating Costs/Operating Income (%)													
Cost of Operations **10**	0.6	0.3	•	•	0.1	4.5	3.4	•	0.2	0.2	5.1	1.3	0.4
Salaries and Wages **11**	7.6	6.8	29.6	34.1	27.6	24.5	27.3	25.9	21.4	18.1	21.9	14.7	4.6
Taxes Paid **12**	1.3	2.7	4.0	4.7	3.6	3.7	3.8	3.0	2.6	2.6	2.6	1.9	0.8
Interest Paid **13**	42.1	31.1	1.5	3.1	7.5	10.7	9.4	19.0	16.0	20.9	20.7	23.7	49.8
Depreciation **14**	2.6	0.9	1.3	1.1	1.3	1.9	1.4	1.4	2.6	3.1	2.5	2.6	2.9
Amortization and Depletion **15**	0.6	0.3	0.2	1.1	0.4	0.3	0.6	0.3	1.0	0.6	1.4	1.6	0.5
Pensions and Other Deferred Comp. **16**	0.4	0.4	0.4	0.1	0.4	0.5	0.4	0.4	0.6	0.8	0.9	1.0	0.4
Employee Benefits **17**	0.8	0.7	1.1	0.9	1.3	1.3	1.2	1.5	2.0	2.1	1.9	1.9	0.6
Advertising **18**	1.0	0.1	3.2	4.0	2.2	2.2	1.5	1.8	1.1	1.3	1.6	1.4	1.0
Other Expenses **19**	45.1	54.0	44.8	46.9	49.2	59.8	43.1	132.6	50.3	45.7	43.1	57.0	41.5
Officers' Compensation **20**	1.0	1.1	11.2	6.9	6.2	4.9	5.0	6.2	4.7	4.5	2.8	1.7	0.2
Operating Margin **21**	•	1.8	2.7	0.2	0.2	•	3.0	•	•	0.1	•	•	•
Operating Margin Before Officers' Comp. **22**	•	2.9	13.9	4.0	6.4	•	8.0	•	2.3	4.6	•	•	•

Selected Average Balance Sheet ($ in Thousands)

Net Receivables 23	15866	0	16	161	985	2392	6894	15144	30829	67031	103093	233398	4150178
Inventories 24	•	•	•	•	•	•	•	•	•	•	•	•	•
Net Property, Plant and Equipment 25	1330	0	17	88	117	365	649	713	1678	3440	6517	16329	379220
Total Assets 26	91960	0	93	731	2358	6657	16087	36647	72462	160567	350577	989883	28640210
Notes and Loans Payable 27	52297	0	68	352	1193	4541	8853	11275	10840	19886	56898	191421	18578555
All Other Liabilities 28	33848	0	41	108	1858	2857	5284	21230	57825	122973	261224	678767	8490154
Net Worth 29	5814	0	-16	272	-692	-741	1950	4143	3797	17707	32455	119694	1571500

Selected Financial Ratios (Times to 1)

Current Ratio 30	0.7	•	2.0	3.2	0.8	1.4	1.3	1.0	0.9	0.8	0.6	0.6	0.6
Quick Ratio 31	0.6	•	1.6	2.3	0.8	1.2	1.1	0.9	0.8	0.8	0.5	0.5	0.5
Net Sales to Working Capital 32	•	•	9.6	1.2	•	2.2	2.5	•	•	•	•	•	•
Coverage Ratio 33	0.9	1.0	2.7	0.1	1.0	1.3	•	0.8	1.0	0.7	0.6	0.6	0.9
Total Asset Turnover 34	0.1	•	2.8	0.5	0.5	0.4	0.4	0.2	0.1	0.1	0.1	0.1	0.1
Inventory Turnover 35	•	•	•	•	•	•	•	•	•	•	•	•	•
Receivables Turnover 36	•	•	•	•	•	•	•	•	•	•	•	•	•
Total Liabilities to Net Worth 37	14.8	•	•	1.7	•	•	7.2	7.8	18.1	8.1	9.8	7.3	17.2
Current Assets to Working Capital 38	•	•	2.0	1.5	2.0	3.5	4.2	•	•	•	•	•	•
Current Liabilities to Working Capital 39	•	•	1.0	0.5	1.0	2.5	3.2	•	•	•	•	•	•
Working Capital to Net Sales 40	•	•	0.1	0.8	0.8	0.4	0.4	•	•	•	•	•	•
Inventory to Working Capital 41	•	•	•	•	•	•	•	•	•	•	•	•	•
Total Receipts to Cash Flow 42	3.0	2.0	2.6	2.8	2.3	2.7	2.5	2.8	3.1	3.1	2.9	2.9	3.2
Cost of Goods to Cash Flow 43	0.0	0.0	•	•	0.0	0.1	0.1	•	0.0	0.0	0.2	0.0	0.0
Cash Flow to Total Debt 44	0.0	•	0.9	0.3	0.2	0.1	0.2	•	0.0	0.0	0.0	0.0	0.0

Selected Financial Factors (in Percentages)

Debt Ratio 45	93.7	•	116.7	62.8	129.4	111.1	87.9	88.7	94.8	89.0	90.7	87.9	94.5
Return on Total Assets 46	4.5	11.8	0.1	3.6	•	4.6	1.6	1.9	1.4	1.4	•	•	4.7
Return on Equity Before Income Taxes 47	•	•	•	•	48.9	9.1	•	•	•	•	•	•	•
Return on Equity After Income Taxes 48	•	•	•	0.9	50.6	3.2	•	•	•	•	•	•	•
Profit Margin (Before Income Tax) 49	•	2.6	•	0.2	2.6	2.9	•	•	•	•	•	•	•
Profit Margin (After Income Tax) 50	•	2.5	•	•	0.5	1.0	•	•	•	•	•	•	•

Table II

Corporations with Net Income

CREDIT INTERMEDIATION

MONEY AMOUNTS AND SIZE OF ASSETS IN THOUSANDS OF DOLLARS

Item Description for Accounting Period 7/09 Through 6/10	Total	Zero Assets	Under 500	500 to 1,000	1,000 to 5,000	5,000 to 10,000	10,000 to 25,000	25,000 to 50,000	50,000 to 100,000	100,000 to 250,000	250,000 to 500,000	500,000 to 2,500,000	2,500,000 and over
Number of Enterprises 1	25320	4252	14007	1647	2423	555	479	360	447	534	277	260	80
Revenues ($ in Thousands)													
Net Sales 2	200802635	28558170	4861708	861431	3012929	1459591	3489164	3071008	4307240	9459169	10727977	24323205	106671043
Interest 3	69152879	17734886	40100	43048	145632	66809	134911	257809	1008963	3170289	3497033	11238832	32414567
Rents 4	504356	188376	534	134	3592	1051	4081	3678	3018	10143	17719	17051	154979
Royalties 5	612513	15	0	0	0	0	0	663	8821	18	4	8259	594733
Other Portfolio Income 6	5777884	925548	84	34	6699	7291	6975	27426	113706	314991	230245	1442884	2702002
Other Receipts 7	124755003	10309345	4820990	818215	2857006	1384440	3343197	2781432	3172732	5963728	6982976	11516179	70804762
Total Receipts 8	200802635	28558170	4861708	861431	3012929	1459591	3489164	3071008	4307240	9459169	10727977	24323205	106671043
Average Total Receipts 9	7931	6716	347	523	1243	2630	7284	8531	9636	17714	38729	93551	1333388
Operating Costs/Operating Income (%)													
Cost of Operations 10	0.8	0.1	•	•	0.2	5.8	3.0	•	0.0	0.1	5.9	1.4	0.3
Salaries and Wages 11	12.6	5.8	28.6	15.4	23.5	27.6	28.7	27.7	22.8	18.8	21.2	15.8	9.7
Taxes Paid 12	2.4	3.6	4.1	2.5	3.6	4.2	4.2	3.2	2.8	2.7	2.5	2.2	1.9
Interest Paid 13	17.6	27.8	1.1	2.2	4.0	5.8	6.9	8.9	13.4	16.7	15.7	20.1	16.8
Depreciation 14	3.4	0.5	1.1	1.1	1.2	1.9	1.1	1.1	2.1	2.1	2.3	2.2	5.1
Amortization and Depletion 15	0.8	0.2	0.1	0.0	0.4	0.0	0.3	0.2	0.5	0.6	1.4	1.8	0.7
Pensions and Other Deferred Comp. 16	0.7	0.2	0.5	0.1	0.3	0.4	0.4	0.3	0.6	0.8	0.8	1.2	0.8
Employee Benefits 17	1.2	0.7	0.8	0.1	1.0	1.4	1.2	1.5	1.8	1.9	1.8	2.1	1.1
Advertising 18	2.2	0.1	2.3	4.4	2.4	2.7	1.6	1.9	1.2	1.5	1.7	1.7	3.0
Other Expenses 19	40.2	35.2	39.8	45.6	37.9	27.2	29.7	32.4	29.8	32.8	30.4	32.3	46.2
Officers' Compensation 20	1.6	0.7	8.5	6.2	6.5	5.9	5.5	6.2	4.6	4.3	2.6	1.9	0.4
Operating Margin 21	16.4	25.0	13.2	22.4	18.9	17.0	17.4	16.6	20.2	17.9	13.7	17.4	13.9
Operating Margin Before Officers' Comp. 22	18.0	25.7	21.7	28.5	25.4	22.9	22.9	22.8	24.8	22.2	16.4	19.3	14.3

Selected Average Balance Sheet ($ in Thousands)

Net Receivables 23	17406	0	15	203	1089	2548	7392	16133	30070	65947	96335	226950	3655391
Inventories 24	•	•	•	•	•	•	•	•	•	•	•	•	•
Net Property, Plant and Equipment 25	1412	0	14	39	63	351	584	586	1422	3211	6764	17148	324753
Total Assets 26	59041	0	84	740	2243	6271	15704	36289	72063	162312	352590	979770	12396495
Notes and Loans Payable 27	15684	0	37	254	1006	4360	7764	11712	11426	20667	39219	165713	3916295
All Other Liabilities 28	33898	0	15	94	405	766	4486	17733	50877	119043	265812	653975	6475311
Net Worth 29	9459	0	32	392	833	1144	3454	6845	9760	22602	47559	160082	2004889

Selected Financial Ratios (Times to 1)

Current Ratio 30	0.8	•	1.9	3.5	2.7	1.5	1.4	1.1	0.9	0.8	0.6	0.6	0.9
Quick Ratio 31	0.7	•	1.5	2.5	2.4	1.2	1.2	1.0	0.9	0.8	0.5	0.5	0.8
Net Sales to Working Capital 32	•	•	15.2	1.1	1.2	2.0	2.4	5.1	•	•	•	•	•
Coverage Ratio 33	1.9	1.9	12.7	11.3	5.7	3.9	3.5	2.8	2.4	2.1	1.8	1.9	1.8
Total Asset Turnover 34	0.1	•	4.1	0.7	0.6	0.4	0.5	0.2	0.1	0.1	0.1	0.1	0.1
Inventory Turnover 35	•	•	•	•	•	•	•	•	•	•	•	•	•
Receivables Turnover 36	•	•	•	•	•	•	•	•	•	•	•	•	•
Total Liabilities to Net Worth 37	5.2	•	1.6	0.9	1.7	4.5	3.5	4.3	6.4	6.2	6.4	5.1	5.2
Current Assets to Working Capital 38	•	•	2.1	1.4	1.6	3.0	3.5	14.9	•	•	•	•	•
Current Liabilities to Working Capital 39	•	•	1.1	0.4	0.6	2.0	2.5	13.9	•	•	•	•	•
Working Capital to Net Sales 40	•	•	0.1	0.9	0.8	0.5	0.4	0.2	•	•	•	•	•
Inventory to Working Capital 41	•	•	•	•	0.0	•	0.0	0.0	•	•	•	•	•
Total Receipts to Cash Flow 42	1.9	1.9	2.2	1.7	1.9	2.6	2.3	2.2	2.2	2.1	2.5	2.2	1.7
Cost of Goods to Cash Flow 43	0.0	0.0	•	•	0.0	0.1	0.1	0.0	0.0	0.1	0.1	0.0	0.0
Cash Flow to Total Debt 44	0.1	•	3.1	0.9	0.5	0.2	0.3	0.1	0.1	0.1	0.1	0.1	0.1

Selected Financial Factors (in Percentages)

Debt Ratio 45	84.0	•	61.7	47.1	62.9	81.8	78.0	81.1	86.5	86.1	86.5	83.7	83.8
Return on Total Assets 46	4.5	•	58.9	17.3	12.7	9.6	11.2	6.0	4.4	3.7	3.1	3.6	3.3
Return on Equity Before Income Taxes 47	13.6	•	141.5	29.9	28.1	39.0	36.6	20.4	19.0	13.8	10.5	10.0	9.3
Return on Equity After Income Taxes 48	10.3	•	139.7	28.8	26.7	37.3	31.2	19.1	17.0	11.0	8.0	7.3	6.3
Profit Margin (Before Income Tax) 49	16.2	23.8	13.2	22.4	18.9	17.0	17.4	16.4	19.3	17.6	12.9	17.2	14.0
Profit Margin (After Income Tax) 50	12.2	20.2	13.0	21.5	17.9	16.3	14.8	15.3	17.2	14.1	9.8	12.5	9.4

Table I

Corporations with and without Net Income

COMMERCIAL BANKING

MONEY AMOUNTS AND SIZE OF ASSETS IN THOUSANDS OF DOLLARS

Item Description for Accounting Period 7/09 Through 6/10		Total	Zero Assets	Under 500	500 to 1,000	1,000 to 5,000	5,000 to 10,000	10,000 to 25,000	25,000 to 50,000	50,000 to 100,000	100,000 to 250,000	250,000 to 500,000	500,000 to 2,500,000	2,500,000 and over
Number of Enterprises	1	1615	232	3	0	13	14	93	172	389	485	132	67	14
Revenues ($ in Thousands)														
Net Sales	2	70312960	52555905	67707	0	179810	91070	188829	419188	1851705	4440422	2745278	4721883	3051164
Interest	3	42536034	32735851	8992	0	27840	21555	63339	197235	893604	2515375	1573998	2429632	2068612
Rents	4	241203	132503	0	0	0	0	56	423	1245	5303	12070	7284	82319
Royalties	5	23946	23853	0	0	0	0	0	0	37	16	4	0	35
Other Portfolio Income	6	2683111	1733125	0	0	895	1056	3334	15674	64839	161524	121245	264217	317202
Other Receipts	7	24828666	17930573	58715	0	151075	68459	122100	205856	891980	1758204	1037961	2020750	582996
Total Receipts	8	70312960	52555905	67707	0	179810	91070	188829	419188	1851705	4440422	2745278	4721883	3051164
Average Total Receipts	9	43537	226534	22569	•	13832	6505	2030	2437	4760	9156	20798	70476	217940
Operating Costs/Operating Income (%)														
Cost of Operations	10	0.0	•	•	•	•	•	•	•	•	•	0.9	•	•
Salaries and Wages	11	8.2	6.5	4.0	•	6.5	8.5	7.8	11.4	13.2	15.2	16.3	12.3	10.4
Taxes Paid	12	2.5	2.6	0.1	•	0.8	0.5	2.2	2.7	2.5	2.6	2.5	2.0	2.0
Interest Paid	13	30.1	31.4	7.1	•	10.5	20.1	13.0	23.9	23.1	28.7	27.1	27.2	26.4
Depreciation	14	1.4	0.9	0.5	•	0.7	0.8	2.3	2.8	2.4	2.7	2.4	2.0	5.9
Amortization and Depletion	15	0.4	0.3	0.1	•	0.0	0.1	0.1	0.8	0.4	1.0	0.6	0.6	1.0
Pensions and Other Deferred Comp.	16	0.5	0.4	•	•	0.0	0.0	0.4	0.8	0.6	0.7	0.6	0.9	0.7
Employee Benefits	17	1.0	0.7	0.6	•	0.3	0.7	2.2	3.2	2.5	2.4	2.0	1.7	1.8
Advertising	18	0.2	0.1	0.8	•	0.7	1.6	0.6	0.9	0.7	0.8	0.7	0.5	0.5
Other Expenses	19	53.4	54.2	119.9	•	144.1	189.6	77.0	54.4	57.5	42.0	39.5	60.3	43.3
Officers' Compensation	20	2.1	1.0	0.8	•	•	•	8.2	11.9	7.8	6.8	5.0	2.8	5.7
Operating Margin	21	0.1	2.0	•	•	•	•	•	•	•	•	2.3	•	2.3
Operating Margin Before Officers' Comp.	22	2.2	3.0	•	•	•	•	•	•	•	3.8	7.2	•	8.0

Selected Average Balance Sheet ($ in Thousands)

Net Receivables 23	92624	0	0	•	8638	21078	41864	95356	199869	522408	1517377
Inventories 24	•	•	•	•	•	•	•	•	•	•	•
Net Property, Plant and Equipment 25	2578	0	0	•	200	517	1347	2932	5480	12872	37471
Total Assets 26	180411	210	2658	7579	18101	38067	72534	156782	345422	1026070	4599556
Notes and Loans Payable 27	9636	0	6	28	166	364	1863	5679	15704	67963	384121
All Other Liabilities 28	152019	31215	32577	69026	16039	33996	63761	135527	296530	862773	3514734
Net Worth 29	18756	-31005	-29925	-61475	1896	3708	6910	15575	33188	95334	700701

Selected Financial Ratios (Times to 1)

Current Ratio 30	0.9	•	0.0	0.4	1.1	1.0	1.0	1.0	0.9	0.9	0.8
Quick Ratio 31	0.9	•	0.0	0.3	1.1	1.0	1.0	0.9	0.9	0.9	0.8
Net Sales to Working Capital 32	•	1.0	•	•	1.2	1.9	•	•	•	•	•
Coverage Ratio 33	1.0	•	•	•	•	0.3	0.4	0.8	1.0	0.5	1.0
Total Asset Turnover 34	0.2	•	107.5	5.2	0.9	0.1	0.1	0.1	0.1	0.1	0.0
Inventory Turnover 35	•	•	•	•	0.1	•	•	•	•	•	•
Receivables Turnover 36	•	•	•	•	•	•	•	•	•	•	•
Total Liabilities to Net Worth 37	8.6	•	•	•	8.5	9.3	9.5	9.1	9.4	9.8	5.6
Current Assets to Working Capital 38	•	•	•	•	9.5	26.5	•	•	•	•	•
Current Liabilities to Working Capital 39	•	•	•	•	8.5	25.5	•	•	•	•	•
Working Capital to Net Sales 40	•	•	•	•	0.8	0.5	•	•	•	•	•
Inventory to Working Capital 41	•	•	•	•	•	•	•	•	•	•	•
Total Receipts to Cash Flow 42	2.2	2.0	1.4	1.8	13.6	5.4	5.1	3.1	3.0	3.8	2.5
Cost of Goods to Cash Flow 43	0.0	•	•	•	0.0	0.0	0.0	0.0	0.0	0.0	0.0
Cash Flow to Total Debt 44	0.1	0.6	0.3	0.1	0.0	0.0	0.0	0.0	0.0	0.0	0.0

Selected Financial Factors (in Percentages)

Debt Ratio 45	89.6	•	1225.7	911.1	89.5	90.3	90.5	90.1	90.4	90.7	84.8
Return on Total Assets 46	6.9	•	14864.3	•	•	0.5	0.7	1.4	1.7	1.0	1.3
Return on Equity Before Income Taxes 47	•	•	24.7	29.5	12.9	•	•	•	•	0.2	0.2
Return on Equity After Income Taxes 48	•	24.7	24.7	29.5	12.9	•	•	•	•	•	•
Profit Margin (Before Income Tax) 49	•	0.6	•	•	•	•	•	•	•	•	0.4
Profit Margin (After Income Tax) 50	•	•	•	•	•	•	•	•	•	•	0.6

Table II
Corporations with Net Income

COMMERCIAL BANKING

MONEY AMOUNTS AND SIZE OF ASSETS IN THOUSANDS OF DOLLARS

Item Description for Accounting Period 7/09 Through 6/10		Total	Zero Assets	Under 500	500 to 1,000	1,000 to 5,000	5,000 to 10,000	10,000 to 25,000	25,000 to 50,000	50,000 to 100,000	100,000 to 250,000	250,000 to 500,000	500,000 to 2,500,000	2,500,000 and over
Number of Enterprises	1	914	116	0	0	0	0	54	115	228	268	84	40	10
Revenues ($ in Thousands)														
Net Sales	2	37469706	27465413	0	0	0	0	56525	240676	927405	2553132	1719560	2200774	2306222
Interest	3	22278015	16807593	0	0	0	0	35754	98976	433664	1287691	940058	1058579	1615701
Rents	4	54415	31184	0	0	0	0	42	91	682	3272	2798	4692	11655
Royalties	5	87	15	0	0	0	0	0	0	16	16	4	0	35
Other Portfolio Income	6	1622131	910662	0	0	0	0	2224	12518	46682	108096	97820	130436	313695
Other Receipts	7	13515058	9715959	0	0	0	0	18505	129091	446361	1154057	678880	1007067	365136
Total Receipts	8	37469706	27465413	0	0	0	0	56525	240676	927405	2553132	1719560	2200774	2306222
Average Total Receipts	9	40995	236771	•	•	•	•	1047	2093	4068	9527	20471	55019	230622
Operating Costs/Operating Income (%)														
Cost of Operations	10	•	•	•	•	•	•	•	•	•	•	•	•	•
Salaries and Wages	11	7.7	5.6	•	•	•	•	11.9	11.0	12.9	13.5	15.5	14.1	11.6
Taxes Paid	12	3.4	3.7	•	•	•	•	3.4	2.7	2.9	2.7	2.7	2.5	2.3
Interest Paid	13	27.4	28.0	•	•	•	•	23.7	23.7	25.5	26.0	24.8	24.8	27.4
Depreciation	14	1.1	0.5	•	•	•	•	2.7	1.6	2.2	2.3	2.4	2.1	4.2
Amortization and Depletion	15	0.3	0.2	•	•	•	•	0.0	0.2	0.3	1.3	0.5	0.2	1.0
Pensions and Other Deferred Comp.	16	0.4	0.2	•	•	•	•	0.6	1.1	0.8	0.8	0.6	1.1	0.5
Employee Benefits	17	1.1	0.7	•	•	•	•	4.9	3.5	3.0	2.5	2.3	2.1	1.5
Advertising	18	0.2	0.0	•	•	•	•	0.9	0.9	0.7	0.7	0.7	0.6	0.6
Other Expenses	19	32.5	35.2	•	•	•	•	23.1	23.4	24.4	26.9	24.6	24.7	25.3
Officers' Compensation	20	2.1	0.7	•	•	•	•	16.1	12.9	9.7	7.0	5.7	4.2	3.8
Operating Margin	21	23.8	25.2	•	•	•	•	12.8	19.0	17.6	16.3	20.0	23.5	21.7
Operating Margin Before Officers' Comp.	22	25.8	25.8	•	•	•	•	28.8	31.9	27.3	23.3	25.8	27.7	25.5

Selected Average Balance Sheet ($ in Thousands)

Net Receivables 23	102422	0	9796	20811	40783	95926	206694	492885	1860723
Inventories 24	•	•	•	•	•	•	•	•	•
Net Property, Plant and Equipment 25	2592	0	175	380	1156	2637	5390	10752	46272
Total Assets 26	193298	0	18217	37926	71796	159539	350088	975161	4378982
Notes and Loans Payable 27	9017	0	163	392	1922	5192	12784	56395	302853
All Other Liabilities 28	158965	0	15836	32318	60959	136446	297982	818974	3246686
Net Worth 29	25316	0	2217	5216	8915	17901	39323	99792	829443

Selected Financial Ratios (Times to 1)

Current Ratio 30	0.9	•	1.1	1.1	1.0	1.0	0.9	0.9	0.9
Quick Ratio 31	0.9	•	1.1	1.1	1.0	1.0	0.9	0.9	0.8
Net Sales to Working Capital 32	•	•	0.7	0.7	1.5	8.2	1.7	•	•
Coverage Ratio 33	1.8	1.9	1.4	1.6	1.6	1.5	1.7	1.8	1.7
Total Asset Turnover 34	0.2	•	0.1	0.1	0.1	0.1	0.1	0.1	0.1
Inventory Turnover 35	•	•	•	•	•	•	•	•	•
Receivables Turnover 36	•	•	•	•	•	•	•	•	•
Total Liabilities to Net Worth 37	6.6	•	7.2	6.3	7.1	7.9	7.9	8.8	4.3
Current Assets to Working Capital 38	•	•	11.1	12.4	23.2	118.8	•	•	•
Current Liabilities to Working Capital 39	•	•	10.1	11.4	22.2	117.8	•	•	•
Working Capital to Net Sales 40	•	•	1.5	1.4	0.7	0.1	•	•	•
Inventory to Working Capital 41	•	•	•	•	•	•	•	•	•
Total Receipts to Cash Flow 42	2.0	1.9	3.0	2.5	2.5	2.5	2.4	2.3	2.3
Cost of Goods to Cash Flow 43	•	•	•	•	•	•	•	•	•
Cash Flow to Total Debt 44	0.1	•	0.0	0.0	0.0	0.0	0.0	0.0	0.0

Selected Financial Factors (in Percentages)

Debt Ratio 45	86.9	•	87.8	86.2	87.6	88.8	88.8	89.8	81.1
Return on Total Assets 46	10.5	•	1.9	2.1	2.2	2.4	2.5	2.5	2.5
Return on Equity Before Income Taxes 47	35.8	•	4.6	6.0	6.5	7.3	9.2	11.2	5.4
Return on Equity After Income Taxes 48	29.9	•	4.1	5.1	5.6	6.1	7.3	8.8	3.9
Profit Margin (Before Income Tax) 49	22.1	23.9	9.7	14.9	14.2	13.7	17.6	20.4	19.5
Profit Margin (After Income Tax) 50	18.5	20.3	8.6	12.8	12.2	11.4	14.1	16.0	13.9

Table I

Corporations with and without Net Income

SAVINGS INSTITUTIONS AND OTHER DEPOSITORY CREDIT

MONEY AMOUNTS AND SIZE OF ASSETS IN THOUSANDS OF DOLLARS

Item Description for Accounting Period 7/09 Through 6/10	Total	Zero Assets	Under 500	500 to 1,000	1,000 to 5,000	5,000 to 10,000	10,000 to 25,000	25,000 to 50,000	50,000 to 100,000	100,000 to 250,000	250,000 to 500,000	500,000 to 2,500,000	2,500,000 and over
Number of Enterprises **1**	1486	39	366	0	32	3	35	105	155	262	204	233	53
Revenues ($ in Thousands)													
Net Sales **2**	82314244	196495	14923	0	182646	287170	64526	586376	883362	2761685	4017345	15787600	57552116
Interest **3**	45359843	85253	0	0	66075	54737	38921	497444	609916	2018351	3171852	10880314	27936978
Rents **4**	351332	12808	0	0	183	117	373	1185	1937	8688	10812	124891	190340
Royalties **5**	4710	0	0	0	0	0	0	14	0	0	1339		3356
Other Portfolio Income **6**	2401618	4375	0	0	8922	127	7281	6905	47385	86670	151958	851691	1236303
Other Receipts **7**	34196741	94059	14923	0	107466	232189	17951	80828	224124	647976	682723	3929365	28165139
Total Receipts **8**	82314244	196495	14923	0	182646	287170	64526	586376	883362	2761685	4017345	15787600	57552116
Average Total Receipts **9**	55393	5038	41	•	5708	95723	1844	5585	5699	10541	19693	67758	1085512
Operating Costs/Operating Income (%)													
Cost of Operations **10**	0.1	0.0	•	•	•	•	•	•	0.5	•	0.0	0.1	0.1
Salaries and Wages **11**	9.8	12.7	•	•	30.4	•	33.5	17.3	13.9	13.6	16.0	15.3	7.5
Taxes Paid **12**	1.6	3.9	0.7	•	4.4	0.1	4.1	1.3	2.7	2.7	2.8	2.2	1.3
Interest Paid **13**	28.4	27.5	103.6	•	39.3	12.6	46.0	70.2	30.3	32.0	34.5	31.6	26.5
Depreciation **14**	1.6	4.5	11.7	•	2.0	0.6	1.8	0.7	2.3	4.7	2.5	2.5	1.2
Amortization and Depletion **15**	0.9	0.7	10.3	•	0.1	0.0	0.1	0.1	0.9	0.2	0.3	0.5	1.1
Pensions and Other Deferred Comp. **16**	0.8	1.8	•	•	0.7	•	0.8	0.8	1.1	1.7	1.9	1.3	0.6
Employee Benefits **17**	1.4	1.2	•	•	3.5	0.3	2.2	1.3	2.5	2.4	2.7	2.1	1.0
Advertising **18**	0.8	1.4	•	•	0.4	0.3	1.7	1.1	0.9	0.9	1.4	1.0	0.7
Other Expenses **19**	65.1	59.1	71.3	•	79.4	126.3	73.8	643.0	71.9	50.4	30.9	60.4	63.1
Officers' Compensation **20**	1.1	0.7	•	•	0.7	•	3.7	6.5	4.6	4.0	1.9	0.5	
Operating Margin **21**	•	•	•	•	•	•	•	•	•	•	2.9	•	•
Operating Margin Before Officers' Comp. **22**	•	•	•	•	•	•	•	•	•	•	7.0	•	•

Selected Average Balance Sheet ($ in Thousands)

Net Receivables 23	69482	0	3	114	18	763	3590	5780	15517	35831	75899	1375201
Inventories 24	•	•	•	•	•	•	•	•	•	•	•	•
Net Property, Plant and Equipment 25	7828	0	13	37	0	329	548	1506	3392	6674	16925	96804
Total Assets 26	723246	0	112	1999	8188	15924	38012	76487	167234	357492	962328	13552910
Notes and Loans Payable 27	99923	0	20	1644	16670	1338	5599	3986	13956	31692	89904	2189702
All Other Liabilities 28	567056	0	658	138319	213166	12391	29947	73814	139200	286740	782693	10282773
Net Worth 29	56267	0	-567	-137965	-221648	2196	2466	-1313	14078	39059	89732	1060435

Selected Financial Ratios (Times to 1)

Current Ratio 30	0.3	•	1.4	0.0	0.4	0.3	0.3	0.3	0.3	0.3	0.3	0.4
Quick Ratio 31	0.3	•	1.4	0.0	0.1	0.2	0.3	0.3	0.3	0.3	0.3	0.3
Net Sales to Working Capital 32	•	•	2.5	•	•	•	•	•	•	•	•	•
Coverage Ratio 33	0.6	0.5	0.1	•	•	•	•	0.5	0.5	1.0	0.4	0.8
Total Asset Turnover 34	0.1	•	0.4	2.9	11.7	0.1	0.1	0.1	0.1	0.1	0.1	0.1
Inventory Turnover 35	•	•	•	•	•	•	•	•	•	•	•	•
Receivables Turnover 36	•	•	•	•	•	•	•	•	•	•	•	•
Total Liabilities to Net Worth 37	11.9	•	•	•	•	6.3	14.4	•	10.9	8.2	9.7	11.8
Current Assets to Working Capital 38	•	•	3.4	•	•	•	•	•	•	•	•	•
Current Liabilities to Working Capital 39	•	•	2.4	•	•	•	•	•	•	•	•	•
Working Capital to Net Sales 40	•	•	0.4	•	•	•	•	•	•	•	•	•
Inventory to Working Capital 41	•	•	•	•	•	•	•	•	•	•	•	•
Total Receipts to Cash Flow 42	6.1	2.6	•	7.7	1.5	•	36.4	3.7	4.2	3.3	4.6	5.4
Cost of Goods to Cash Flow 43	0.0	0.0	•	•	•	•	•	•	•	0.0	0.0	0.0
Cash Flow to Total Debt 44	0.0	0.0	•	0.0	0.3	•	•	•	0.0	0.0	0.0	0.0

Selected Financial Factors (in Percentages)

Debt Ratio 45	92.2	•	606.7	7003.3	2807.1	86.2	93.5	101.7	91.6	89.1	90.7	92.2
Return on Total Assets 46	1.2	•	2.2	•	•	•	•	•	1.1	2.0	0.8	1.8
Return on Equity Before Income Taxes 47	•	•	7.0	2.5	19.2	•	•	147.5	•	0.7	•	•
Return on Equity After Income Taxes 48	•	•	7.0	2.7	19.2	•	•	155.7	•	•	•	•
Profit Margin (Before Income Tax) 49	•	•	•	•	•	•	•	•	1.4	•	•	•
Profit Margin (After Income Tax) 50	•	•	•	•	•	•	•	•	•	•	•	•

Table II

Corporations with Net Income

SAVINGS INSTITUTIONS AND OTHER DEPOSITORY CREDIT

MONEY AMOUNTS AND SIZE OF ASSETS IN THOUSANDS OF DOLLARS

Item Description for Accounting Period 7/09 Through 6/10		Total	Zero Assets	Under 500	500 to 1,000	1,000 to 5,000	5,000 to 10,000	10,000 to 25,000	25,000 to 50,000	50,000 to 100,000	100,000 to 250,000	250,000 to 500,000	500,000 to 2,500,000	2,500,000 and over
Number of Enterprises	1	743	34	0	0	•	0	12	•	104	177	156	164	35
Revenues ($ in Thousands)														
Net Sales	2	34724094	111907	0	0	•	0	9776	•	431573	1655757	3072341	9339649	19886861
Interest	3	25016530	25470	0	0	•	0	9455	•	368043	1385675	2426902	7078680	13574710
Rents	4	184070	12766	0	0	•	0	0	•	905	3767	6799	81918	77434
Royalties	5	1352	0	0	0	•	0	0	•	0	0	0	1338	0
Other Portfolio Income	6	1378723	3556	0	0	•	0	10	•	13776	58343	121497	658263	518759
Other Receipts	7	8143419	70115	0	0	•	0	311	•	48849	207972	517143	1519450	5715958
Total Receipts	8	34724094	111907	0	0	•	0	9776	•	431573	1655757	3072341	9339649	19886861
Average Total Receipts	9	46735	3291	•	•	•	•	815	•	4150	9355	19694	56949	568196
Operating Costs/Operating Income (%)														
Cost of Operations	10	0.0	0.1	•	•	•	•	•	•	•	•	•	0.0	0.0
Salaries and Wages	11	13.0	13.6	•	•	•	•	13.8	•	12.5	13.3	15.4	17.1	10.7
Taxes Paid	12	2.4	4.7	•	•	•	•	2.8	•	3.0	3.0	2.8	2.8	2.1
Interest Paid	13	35.1	18.9	•	•	•	•	41.4	•	36.2	34.1	33.2	32.0	37.0
Depreciation	14	2.1	7.0	•	•	•	•	1.2	•	2.2	2.3	2.5	2.9	1.6
Amortization and Depletion	15	0.7	1.3	•	•	•	•	•	•	0.0	0.1	0.2	0.5	0.9
Pensions and Other Deferred Comp.	16	1.4	0.7	•	•	•	•	1.6	•	1.5	1.9	1.8	1.7	1.2
Employee Benefits	17	2.1	0.9	•	•	•	•	2.4	•	2.7	2.7	2.8	2.6	1.8
Advertising	18	1.0	2.1	•	•	•	•	0.2	•	0.9	1.0	1.5	1.2	0.8
Other Expenses	19	20.2	38.6	•	•	•	•	18.2	•	20.3	22.0	22.3	22.5	18.5
Officers' Compensation	20	1.9	0.5	•	•	•	•	9.3	•	7.3	5.8	4.2	2.5	0.7
Operating Margin	21	20.1	11.6	•	•	•	•	9.1	•	13.3	13.7	13.1	14.3	24.7
Operating Margin Before Officers' Comp.	22	22.0	12.1	•	•	•	•	18.4	•	20.6	19.5	17.3	16.7	25.4

Selected Average Balance Sheet ($ in Thousands)

Net Receivables 23	57254	•	65	•	5657	14774	29783	68490	666419
Inventories 24	•	•	•	•	•	•	•	•	•
Net Property, Plant and Equipment 25	9674	•	196	•	1341	3086	6445	17930	72268
Total Assets 26	825923	•	14243	•	76879	167738	357524	939644	10394214
Notes and Loans Payable 27	120916	•	1216	•	3945	12790	31904	83400	1953840
All Other Liabilities 28	608258	•	11364	•	61827	134196	285274	747654	7226425
Net Worth 29	96749	•	1663	•	11107	20752	40347	108589	1213949

Selected Financial Ratios (Times to 1)

Current Ratio 30	0.3	•	0.2	•	0.3	0.3	0.3	0.3	0.3
Quick Ratio 31	0.2	•	0.2	•	0.3	0.3	0.2	0.2	0.2
Net Sales to Working Capital 32	•	•	•	•	•	•	•	•	•
Coverage Ratio 33	1.6	•	1.2	•	1.3	1.3	1.3	1.4	1.7
Total Asset Turnover 34	0.1	•	0.1	•	0.1	0.1	0.1	0.1	0.1
Inventory Turnover 35	•	•	•	•	•	•	•	•	•
Receivables Turnover 36	•	•	•	•	•	•	•	•	•
Total Liabilities to Net Worth 37	7.5	•	7.6	•	5.9	7.1	7.9	7.7	7.6
Current Assets to Working Capital 38	•	•	•	•	•	•	•	•	•
Current Liabilities to Working Capital 39	•	•	•	•	•	•	•	•	•
Working Capital to Net Sales 40	•	•	•	•	•	•	•	•	•
Inventory to Working Capital 41	•	•	•	•	•	•	•	•	•
Total Receipts to Cash Flow 42	2.7	•	3.9	•	3.2	3.0	3.1	3.3	2.5
Cost of Goods to Cash Flow 43	0.0	•	0.0	•	0.0	0.0	0.0	0.0	0.0
Cash Flow to Total Debt 44	0.0	•	0.0	•	0.0	0.0	0.0	0.0	0.0

Selected Financial Factors (in Percentages)

Debt Ratio 45	88.3	•	88.3	•	85.6	87.6	88.7	88.4	88.3
Return on Total Assets 46	3.1	•	2.9	•	2.6	2.6	2.5	2.8	3.4
Return on Equity Before Income Taxes 47	9.4	•	4.5	•	4.5	5.4	5.7	7.0	11.4
Return on Equity After Income Taxes 48	6.5	•	3.5	•	3.1	3.8	3.9	4.8	7.9
Profit Margin (Before Income Tax) 49	19.4	11.6	9.1	•	12.1	11.9	11.6	13.4	24.3
Profit Margin (After Income Tax) 50	13.5	8.5	7.2	•	8.2	8.4	9.1	9.1	16.9

Table I
Corporations with and without Net Income

CREDIT CARD ISSUING AND OTHER CONSUMER CREDIT

MONEY AMOUNTS AND SIZE OF ASSETS IN THOUSANDS OF DOLLARS

Item Description for Accounting Period 7/09 Through 6/10		Total	Zero Assets	Under 500	500 to 1,000	1,000 to 5,000	5,000 to 10,000	10,000 to 25,000	25,000 to 50,000	50,000 to 100,000	100,000 to 250,000	250,000 to 500,000	500,000 to 2,500,000	2,500,000 and over
Number of Enterprises	1	7403	2104	2546	1060	1045	139	271	70	52	45	21	33	17
Revenues ($ in Thousands)														
Net Sales	2	91515713	536078	217829	202895	1050284	198487	1695385	840015	1093802	2463401	3792225	5768096	73365216
Interest	3	25167177	158387	11192	15341	56424	30568	96708	29289	182953	343838	235780	3218859	20787838
Rents	4	57536	35	0	3	33	369	1113	0	574	605	7229	2347	45228
Royalties	5	367508	0	0	0	0	0	0	0	8805	0	0	0	358703
Other Portfolio Income	6	2152315	6072	71	361	2686	34	1895	1415	1130	5004	6578	31625	2095444
Other Receipts	7	63771177	371584	206566	187190	991141	167516	1595669	809311	900340	2113954	3542638	2515265	50370003
Total Receipts	8	91515713	536078	217829	202895	1050284	198487	1695385	840015	1093802	2463401	3792225	5768096	73365216
Average Total Receipts	9	12362	255	86	191	1005	1428	6256	12000	21035	54742	180582	174791	4332777
Operating Costs/Operating Income (%)														
Cost of Operations	10	1.3	•	•	•	•	•	1.4	•	1.0	0.1	0.1	0.3	1.5
Salaries and Wages	11	9.4	20.0	53.1	16.5	16.0	17.0	18.2	19.9	24.3	17.5	30.4	11.4	7.0
Taxes Paid	12	1.4	11.9	4.1	5.8	2.6	3.5	2.3	2.7	2.3	2.3	2.6	1.5	1.1
Interest Paid	13	18.3	22.3	7.0	5.9	7.0	26.7	10.6	7.9	10.3	10.7	5.7	21.7	19.6
Depreciation	14	9.9	3.9	4.2	1.1	1.0	1.4	0.9	1.1	3.1	3.5	1.8	4.0	11.7
Amortization and Depletion	15	0.5	0.2	•	0.6	0.3	1.6	0.4	0.3	0.9	0.5	0.6	1.7	0.4
Pensions and Other Deferred Comp.	16	0.5	0.0	0.3	0.3	0.2	0.7	0.4	0.1	0.8	0.3	0.1	0.2	0.5
Employee Benefits	17	0.8	0.3	2.0	0.8	1.4	0.5	1.2	1.1	1.8	1.3	1.3	1.2	0.7
Advertising	18	2.4	0.8	1.1	4.2	1.2	1.1	1.4	2.4	1.3	2.5	1.2	0.8	2.6
Other Expenses	19	54.7	48.8	70.4	67.9	49.8	76.5	52.9	51.4	38.4	50.0	49.3	68.7	54.3
Officers' Compensation	20	0.6	1.9	5.0	6.2	8.3	5.6	5.7	2.9	2.7	3.0	0.7	1.2	0.1
Operating Margin	21	0.3	•	•	•	12.1	•	4.7	10.1	13.1	8.2	6.1	•	0.4
Operating Margin Before Officers' Comp.	22	0.8	•	•	•	20.4	•	10.4	13.1	15.8	11.2	6.9	•	0.6

Selected Average Balance Sheet ($ in Thousands)

Net Receivables 23	43449	0	64	326	1776	4104	11966	21726	47232	92173	196282	534356	16799447
Inventories 24	•	•	•	•	•	•	•	•	•	•	•	•	•
Net Property, Plant and Equipment 25	5138	0	13	27	31	78	316	495	2872	3124	9148	6591	2182914
Total Assets 26	94053	0	139	704	2484	6403	15818	34886	68551	162500	352856	1008717	37258032
Notes and Loans Payable 27	44213	0	264	287	1008	4356	9606	20621	42129	93988	190523	604719	17073395
All Other Liabilities 28	36008	0	26	134	406	398	2968	4351	12451	27796	68993	251321	14889837
Net Worth 29	13833	0	-152	282	1071	1649	3245	9914	13972	40716	93340	152677	5294800

Selected Financial Ratios (Times to 1)

Current Ratio 30	1.6	•	3.6	4.2	3.3	4.1	2.5	2.1	2.2	2.9	1.7	1.7	1.6
Quick Ratio 31	1.5	•	2.9	2.6	3.1	3.8	2.3	1.7	1.9	2.3	1.6	1.6	1.5
Net Sales to Working Capital 32	0.6	•	1.2	0.4	0.7	0.4	0.8	0.9	0.7	0.6	1.8	0.6	0.6
Coverage Ratio 33	1.0	0.5	•	•	2.7	•	1.4	2.3	2.3	1.8	2.1	0.4	1.0
Total Asset Turnover 34	0.1	•	0.6	0.3	0.4	0.2	0.4	0.3	0.3	0.3	0.5	0.2	0.1
Inventory Turnover 35	•	•	•	•	•	•	•	•	•	•	•	•	•
Receivables Turnover 36	•	•	•	•	•	•	•	•	•	•	•	•	•
Total Liabilities to Net Worth 37	5.8	•	•	1.5	1.3	2.9	3.9	2.5	3.9	3.0	2.8	5.6	6.0
Current Assets to Working Capital 38	2.6	•	1.4	1.3	1.4	1.3	1.7	1.9	1.8	1.5	2.4	2.4	2.7
Current Liabilities to Working Capital 39	1.6	•	0.4	0.3	0.4	0.3	0.7	0.9	0.8	0.5	1.4	1.4	1.7
Working Capital to Net Sales 40	1.7	•	0.8	2.5	1.5	2.5	1.3	1.2	1.5	1.5	0.5	1.6	1.8
Inventory to Working Capital 41	0.0	•	•	0.0	0.0	0.0	0.0	•	0.0	0.0	•	0.0	0.0
Total Receipts to Cash Flow 42	1.9	2.9	•	1.9	1.7	2.6	1.8	1.8	2.1	2.0	2.0	1.9	1.9
Cost of Goods to Cash Flow 43	0.0	•	•	•	•	•	0.0	•	0.0	0.0	0.0	0.0	0.0
Cash Flow to Total Debt 44	0.1	•	•	0.2	0.4	0.1	0.3	0.3	0.2	0.2	0.3	0.1	0.1

Selected Financial Factors (in Percentages)

Debt Ratio 45	85.3	•	209.4	59.9	74.2	56.9	79.5	71.6	79.6	74.9	73.5	84.9	85.8
Return on Total Assets 46	2.5	•	•	•	7.8	6.1	6.2	7.2	6.4	6.1	•	1.6	2.4
Return on Equity Before Income Taxes 47	0.4	•	26.6	26.6	11.4	11.4	9.1	12.2	19.7	11.0	11.9	•	0.6
Return on Equity After Income Taxes 48	•	•	26.6	26.6	10.6	10.6	6.7	11.8	16.7	7.8	5.7	•	•
Profit Margin (Before Income Tax) 49	0.5	•	•	•	12.1	12.1	4.7	10.1	13.1	8.2	6.2	•	0.7
Profit Margin (After Income Tax) 50	•	•	•	•	11.3	11.3	3.5	9.8	11.1	5.8	3.0	•	•

Table II
Corporations with Net Income

CREDIT CARD ISSUING AND OTHER CONSUMER CREDIT

MONEY AMOUNTS AND SIZE OF ASSETS IN THOUSANDS OF DOLLARS

Item Description for Accounting Period 7/09 Through 6/10	Total	Zero Assets	Under 500	500 to 1,000	1,000 to 5,000	5,000 to 10,000	10,000 to 25,000	25,000 to 50,000	50,000 to 100,000	100,000 to 250,000	250,000 to 500,000	500,000 to 2,500,000	2,500,000 and over
Number of Enterprises 1	3073	432	879	561	772	77	179	55	39	33	16	19	10
Revenues ($ in Thousands)													
Net Sales 2	71363442	227487	107520	190575	919486	120472	1172892	753056	939294	2165937	3561736	3272911	57932077
Interest 3	16548988	5193	11192	13196	32816	30257	15597	22474	150858	299897	83868	1617178	14266463
Rents 4	54614	0	0	0	0	369	864	0	71	605	7229	246	45228
Royalties 5	367508	0	0	0	0	0	0	0	8805	0	0	0	358703
Other Portfolio Income 6	445314	239	71	24	2502	1	346	1414	432	1338	6578	25138	407233
Other Receipts 7	53947018	222055	96257	177352	884168	89845	1156085	729168	779128	1864097	3464061	1630349	42854450
Total Receipts 8	71363442	227487	107520	190575	919486	120472	1172892	753056	939294	2165937	3561736	3272911	57932077
Average Total Receipts 9	23223	527	122	340	1191	1565	6552	13692	24084	65634	222608	172258	5793208
Operating Costs/Operating Income (%)													
Cost of Operations 10	0.5	•	•	•	•	•	0.9	•	•	0.1	0.1	•	0.6
Salaries and Wages 11	9.9	5.9	38.4	6.3	13.7	16.3	20.5	18.7	25.3	17.5	32.0	11.5	7.4
Taxes Paid 12	1.4	2.9	1.4	1.3	2.3	3.8	2.8	2.6	2.4	2.4	2.7	1.6	1.2
Interest Paid 13	12.5	8.9	8.7	4.4	3.8	11.8	7.7	7.5	7.6	7.4	3.2	15.4	13.6
Depreciation 14	6.6	0.9	1.0	0.2	0.9	0.7	1.0	0.9	3.0	2.3	1.7	1.7	7.7
Amortization and Depletion 15	0.5	0.1	•	•	0.3	0.0	0.4	0.3	0.2	0.5	0.6	2.3	0.5
Pensions and Other Deferred Comp. 16	0.4	0.0	•	0.1	0.2	0.3	0.4	0.1	0.9	0.4	0.1	0.3	0.5
Employee Benefits 17	0.8	0.3	0.0	0.1	1.1	0.5	1.3	0.9	1.8	1.1	1.3	1.2	0.7
Advertising 18	2.6	0.7	2.2	1.2	0.8	1.2	1.7	2.4	1.1	2.6	1.3	0.7	2.9
Other Expenses 19	55.0	49.1	38.5	64.0	50.2	37.8	39.0	46.9	32.5	45.4	44.0	42.4	57.7
Officers' Compensation 20	0.6	0.6	3.5	3.6	7.8	7.4	6.8	2.5	2.8	3.0	0.7	0.9	0.1
Operating Margin 21	9.1	30.6	6.3	18.8	19.0	20.2	17.5	17.1	22.4	17.4	12.1	21.5	7.1
Operating Margin Before Officers' Comp. 22	9.7	31.3	9.7	22.4	26.8	27.6	24.3	19.6	25.3	20.4	12.8	22.4	7.2

Selected Average Balance Sheet ($ in Thousands)

Net Receivables 23	73192	0	137	436	1804	3495	12713	23112	47544	101884	203931	633033	19883971
Inventories 24	•	•	•	•	•	•	•	•	•	•	•	•	•
Net Property, Plant and Equipment 25	6939	0	2	10	28	45	215	324	1963	3631	11950	7071	2071250
Total Assets 26	144178	0	195	727	2407	6531	15551	35265	67279	162090	365687	1022629	40214067
Notes and Loans Payable 27	57134	0	78	302	946	4212	9073	23439	38807	94124	170448	465537	15517578
All Other Liabilities 28	63262	0	21	163	236	422	2233	3013	13123	24495	84773	267391	18575744
Net Worth 29	23781	0	96	262	1225	1897	4245	8813	15349	43472	110466	289701	6120745

Selected Financial Ratios (Times to 1)

Current Ratio 30	1.9	•	6.7	2.7	5.1	3.1	2.8	2.1	2.6	3.4	1.9	2.4	1.8
Quick Ratio 31	1.8	•	6.5	1.9	5.0	3.0	2.7	1.8	2.4	2.9	1.7	2.2	1.7
Net Sales to Working Capital 32	0.6	•	1.0	0.8	0.7	0.6	0.7	1.0	0.7	0.7	1.9	0.4	0.5
Coverage Ratio 33	1.7	4.4	1.7	5.3	6.1	2.7	3.3	3.3	4.0	3.4	4.7	2.4	1.5
Total Asset Turnover 34	0.2	•	0.6	0.5	0.5	0.2	0.4	0.4	0.4	0.4	0.6	0.2	0.1
Inventory Turnover 35	•	•	•	•	•	•	•	•	•	•	•	•	•
Receivables Turnover 36	•	•	•	•	•	•	•	•	•	•	•	•	•
Total Liabilities to Net Worth 37	5.1	•	1.0	1.8	1.0	2.4	2.7	3.0	3.4	2.7	2.3	2.5	5.6
Current Assets to Working Capital 38	2.2	•	1.2	1.6	1.2	1.5	1.6	2.0	1.6	1.4	2.1	1.7	2.3
Current Liabilities to Working Capital 39	1.2	•	0.2	0.6	0.2	0.5	0.6	1.0	0.6	0.4	1.1	0.7	1.3
Working Capital to Net Sales 40	1.8	•	1.0	1.2	1.4	1.7	1.4	1.0	1.4	1.5	0.5	2.6	1.9
Inventory to Working Capital 41	0.0	•	•	•	•	0.0	0.0	•	•	0.0	•	0.0	0.0
Total Receipts to Cash Flow 42	1.6	1.3	2.3	1.3	1.5	1.8	1.9	1.7	2.0	1.7	2.0	1.6	1.6
Cost of Goods to Cash Flow 43	0.0	•	•	•	•	0.0	0.0	•	•	0.0	0.0	0.0	0.0
Cash Flow to Total Debt 44	0.1	•	0.5	0.6	0.7	0.2	0.3	0.3	0.2	0.3	0.4	0.1	0.1

Selected Financial Factors (in Percentages)

Debt Ratio 45	83.5	•	50.6	63.9	49.1	71.0	72.7	75.0	77.2	73.2	69.8	71.7	84.8
Return on Total Assets 46	3.5	•	9.4	10.8	11.3	7.7	10.6	9.6	10.7	10.0	9.3	6.2	3.0
Return on Equity Before Income Taxes 47	8.9	•	7.9	24.3	18.5	16.6	27.0	26.6	35.2	26.3	24.3	12.7	6.8
Return on Equity After Income Taxes 48	6.2	•	7.9	21.6	17.5	14.6	24.2	26.0	31.6	22.2	17.4	8.9	4.3
Profit Margin (Before Income Tax) 49	9.1	30.6	6.3	18.8	19.0	20.2	17.5	17.1	22.4	17.4	12.0	21.4	7.1
Profit Margin (After Income Tax) 50	6.3	27.0	6.2	16.7	18.0	17.7	15.7	16.7	20.1	14.7	8.7	14.9	4.5

Table I

Corporations with and without Net Income

REAL ESTATE CREDIT INCL. MORTGAGE BANKERS AND ORIGINATORS

MONEY AMOUNTS AND SIZE OF ASSETS IN THOUSANDS OF DOLLARS

Item Description for Accounting Period 7/09 Through 6/10	Total	Zero Assets	Under 500	500 to 1,000	1,000 to 5,000	5,000 to 10,000	10,000 to 25,000	25,000 to 50,000	50,000 to 100,000	100,000 to 250,000	250,000 to 500,000	500,000 to 2,500,000	2,500,000 and over
Number of Enterprises 1	9735	1472	6026	742	894	225	178	89	41	40	14	7	7
Revenues ($ in Thousands)													
Net Sales 2	14945614	231509	1518437	266790	939438	582648	1203013	1128834	893850	1458804	11350	1727474	4983468
Interest 3	2981331	55592	6967	2711	24746	44559	46508	9130	18751	113261	116629	154825	2387653
Rents 4	194311	140786	0	131	3679	929	399	4662	1417	1349	73	13205	27681
Royalties 5	164	0	0	0	0	0	0	0	0	164	0	0	0
Other Portfolio Income 6	551676	7	1069	0	1296	8633	19269	6012	62940	15602	4786	378664	53396
Other Receipts 7	11218132	35124	1510401	263948	909717	528527	1136837	1109030	810742	1328428	-110138	1180780	2514738
Total Receipts 8	14945614	231509	1518437	266790	939438	582648	1203013	1128834	893850	1458804	11350	1727474	4983468
Average Total Receipts 9	1535	157	252	360	1051	2590	6758	12684	21801	36470	811	246782	711924
Operating Costs/Operating Income (%)													
Cost of Operations 10	0.7	3.3	•	•	•	•	•	•	0.0	•	•	2.0	1.2
Salaries and Wages 11	27.3	12.6	27.4	41.5	38.9	36.7	41.6	37.8	36.2	33.6	1989.3	20.2	12.7
Taxes Paid 12	3.3	1.3	5.3	6.7	4.6	4.9	5.3	3.8	3.5	3.3	182.0	2.1	1.6
Interest Paid 13	16.1	1.4	0.6	4.6	7.2	7.4	7.8	8.6	7.6	14.2	1062.1	6.6	31.6
Depreciation 14	1.6	0.2	1.7	0.8	1.1	1.2	0.9	0.8	0.7	1.9	87.0	1.6	1.9
Amortization and Depletion 15	0.7	0.0	0.0	•	0.3	0.5	0.5	0.2	0.9	0.5	7.0	0.2	1.4
Pensions and Other Deferred Comp. 16	0.3	0.5	0.1	0.3	0.1	1.1	0.1	0.3	0.2	0.5	105.2	0.2	0.2
Employee Benefits 17	1.3	0.4	1.0	0.8	1.3	1.8	1.2	1.7	1.1	1.6	71.1	1.6	1.1
Advertising 18	2.0	0.2	5.4	1.3	3.3	2.0	2.5	1.3	1.6	1.6	43.3	4.4	0.1
Other Expenses 19	57.7	83.9	44.2	66.7	33.9	41.1	40.6	37.4	32.2	41.3	6132.8	31.5	79.9
Officers' Compensation 20	3.8	0.6	10.2	9.2	6.1	7.8	4.3	7.1	3.4	3.6	84.0	2.0	0.5
Operating Margin 21	•	•	4.1	•	3.2	•	•	1.0	12.6	•	•	27.4	•
Operating Margin Before Officers' Comp. 22	•	•	14.4	•	9.3	3.2	•	8.1	16.0	1.6	•	29.5	•

Selected Average Balance Sheet ($ in Thousands)

Net Receivables 23	1648	0	11	139	750	915	2916	11711	8078	15694	30633	225738	1496135
Inventories 24	•	•	•	•	•	•	•	•	•	•	•	•	•
Net Property, Plant and Equipment 25	190	0	11	167	247	325	990	1025	1518	8425	4245	20195	70354
Total Assets 26	8577	100	760	2769	6775	16139	34643	68872	159675	347737	725611		7603144
Notes and Loans Payable 27	4336	51	292	1583	2779	9846	23822	35535	93591	462174	310795		3132831
All Other Liabilities 28	3246	38	103	604	1485	4417	15867	58172	53986	88304	305178		2900913
Net Worth 29	995	11	366	582	2510	1877	-5047	-24835	12098	-202740	109638		1569399

Selected Financial Ratios (Times to 1)

Current Ratio 30	1.0	•	2.5	2.9	1.0	1.2	0.8	0.8	0.6	0.7	0.3	1.0	1.4
Quick Ratio 31	0.9	•	2.1	2.5	0.9	1.0	0.6	0.7	0.4	0.4	0.2	0.9	1.4
Net Sales to Working Capital 32	•	•	7.4	1.7	31.9	5.0	•	•	•	•	•	•	1.0
Coverage Ratio 33	0.1	•	7.7	1.4	0.3	0.3	0.4	1.1	2.6	0.9	0.0	5.2	0.0
Total Asset Turnover 34	0.2	•	2.5	0.5	0.4	0.4	0.4	0.4	0.3	0.2	0.0	0.3	0.1
Inventory Turnover 35	•	•	•	•	•	•	•	•	•	•	•	•	•
Receivables Turnover 36	•	•	•	•	•	•	•	•	•	•	•	•	•
Total Liabilities to Net Worth 37	7.6	•	7.8	1.1	3.8	1.7	7.6	•	12.2	•	•	5.6	3.8
Current Assets to Working Capital 38	•	•	1.7	1.5	36.4	6.7	1.5	•	•	•	•	•	3.3
Current Liabilities to Working Capital 39	•	•	0.7	0.5	35.4	5.7	0.5	•	•	•	•	•	2.3
Working Capital to Net Sales 40	•	•	0.1	0.6	0.0	0.2	0.6	•	•	•	•	•	1.0
Inventory to Working Capital 41	•	•	•	•	•	•	•	•	•	•	•	•	0.0
Total Receipts to Cash Flow 42	3.9	1.4	2.6	3.6	3.4	3.4	3.0	3.0	2.9	3.4	3.4	1.8	8.7
Cost of Goods to Cash Flow 43	0.0	0.0	•	•	•	•	•	0.0	0.0	•	•	0.0	0.1
Cash Flow to Total Debt 44	0.1	•	1.1	0.3	0.2	0.1	0.1	0.1	0.1	0.1	•	0.2	0.0

Selected Financial Factors (in Percentages)

Debt Ratio 45	88.4	•	88.7	51.9	79.0	62.9	88.4	114.6	136.1	92.4	158.3	84.9	79.4
Return on Total Assets 46	0.3	•	11.8	•	3.9	0.9	1.3	3.5	6.4	2.8	•	11.6	0.0
Return on Equity Before Income Taxes 47	•	•	90.4	5.7	•	•	•	•	•	•	38.6	61.8	•
Return on Equity After Income Taxes 48	•	•	89.8	4.0	•	•	•	•	•	•	38.8	60.7	•
Profit Margin (Before Income Tax) 49	•	•	4.1	3.2	•	•	1.0	12.5	•	•	•	27.4	•
Profit Margin (After Income Tax) 50	•	•	4.0	2.2	•	•	0.2	10.6	•	•	•	27.0	•

Table II
Corporations with Net Income

REAL ESTATE CREDIT INCL. MORTGAGE BANKERS AND ORIGINATORS

MONEY AMOUNTS AND SIZE OF ASSETS IN THOUSANDS OF DOLLARS

Item Description for Accounting Period 7/09 Through 6/10	Total	Zero Assets	Under 500	500 to 1,000	1,000 to 5,000	5,000 to 10,000	10,000 to 25,000	25,000 to 50,000	50,000 to 100,000	100,000 to 250,000	250,000 to 500,000	500,000 to 2,500,000	2,500,000 and over
Number of Enterprises **1**	5916	880	3977	127	590	121	100	62	25	20	5	4	4
Revenues ($ in Thousands)													
Net Sales **2**	10243868	283922	917805	104962	924990	415977	1089463	1062462	782510	1129835	411418	1609842	1510681
Interest **3**	1216911	55542	4924	240	14128	36026	23265	6337	10541	16852	17237	60280	971540
Rents **4**	163411	140786	0	131	3408	196	0	2642	1342	1252	0	4647	9005
Royalties **5**	0	0	0	0	0	0	0	0	0	0	0	0	0
Other Portfolio Income **6**	458018	7	13	0	0	7260	940	935	48446	12019	1030	378562	8806
Other Receipts **7**	8405528	87587	912868	104591	907454	372495	1065258	1052548	722181	1099712	393151	1166353	521330
Total Receipts **8**	10243868	283922	917805	104962	924990	415977	1089463	1062462	782510	1129835	411418	1609842	1510681
Average Total Receipts **9**	1732	323	231	826	1568	3438	10895	17136	31300	56492	82284	402460	377670
Operating Costs/Operating Income (%)													
Cost of Operations **10**	0.4	2.7	•	•	•	•	•	•	•	•	•	2.1	•
Salaries and Wages **11**	29.1	10.3	23.5	20.4	38.7	34.7	42.8	38.3	38.5	37.7	32.3	20.9	9.5
Taxes Paid **12**	3.4	1.0	6.5	2.5	4.5	4.3	5.3	3.6	3.8	3.5	2.2	2.0	1.5
Interest Paid **13**	8.3	1.2	0.4	2.1	5.0	6.9	5.2	6.5	4.8	6.6	5.9	4.0	29.2
Depreciation **14**	1.1	0.2	1.8	0.6	1.0	0.7	0.8	0.7	0.6	1.2	0.5	1.6	1.4
Amortization and Depletion **15**	0.1	0.0	0.0	•	0.2	•	0.1	0.2	0.0	0.0	0.0	0.2	0.0
Pensions and Other Deferred Comp. **16**	0.3	0.4	0.2	0.8	0.1	0.6	0.1	0.1	0.2	0.5	1.7	0.2	0.2
Employee Benefits **17**	1.3	0.3	1.3	0.3	1.3	1.6	1.2	1.5	1.0	1.4	1.2	1.7	1.2
Advertising **18**	2.3	0.2	4.0	0.1	3.4	2.1	2.5	1.4	1.8	1.8	0.4	4.7	0.1
Other Expenses **19**	30.3	64.1	33.6	60.5	26.9	27.5	29.4	27.3	25.2	20.2	26.6	30.8	36.2
Officers' Compensation **20**	4.2	0.5	11.3	9.7	6.0	8.2	4.0	6.3	3.1	4.0	1.3	1.9	0.9
Operating Margin **21**	19.1	19.3	17.4	3.0	12.9	13.5	8.6	14.1	21.0	23.1	27.9	29.8	19.8
Operating Margin Before Officers' Comp. **22**	23.3	19.7	28.7	12.8	18.9	21.6	12.6	20.4	24.1	27.0	29.2	31.7	20.7

Selected Average Balance Sheet ($ in Thousands)

Net Receivables 23	1727	0	1	8	720	676	2933	14352	12002	12431	3555	289295	1699919
Inventories 24	•	•	•	•	•	•	•	•	•	•	•	•	•
Net Property, Plant and Equipment 25	109	0	6	104	115	249	844	1089	900	7956	2005	21671	19937
Total Assets 26	6857	0	60	674	2810	6010	17020	36110	66883	146800	318608	788161	6140082
Notes and Loans Payable 27	2919	0	13	242	1432	2830	9963	25455	35077	85202	95747	261292	2330493
All Other Liabilities 28	1493	0	4	96	688	1023	4354	9921	16963	33450	190140	368828	926777
Net Worth 29	2444	0	44	336	689	2156	2703	734	14843	28149	32722	158041	2882812

Selected Financial Ratios (Times to 1)

Current Ratio 30	1.1	•	2.7	3.7	1.1	0.9	0.7	1.1	0.6	0.7	0.1	0.7	2.0
Quick Ratio 31	1.0	•	2.3	3.2	0.9	0.8	0.5	1.0	0.5	0.3	0.1	0.6	2.0
Net Sales to Working Capital 32	7.5	•	12.1	3.2	13.9	•	•	10.3	•	•	•	•	0.4
Coverage Ratio 33	3.3	17.7	48.1	2.4	3.6	2.9	2.7	3.2	5.4	4.5	5.7	8.4	1.7
Total Asset Turnover 34	0.3	•	3.8	1.2	0.6	0.6	0.6	0.5	0.5	0.4	0.3	0.5	0.1
Inventory Turnover 35	•	•	•	•	•	•	•	•	•	•	•	•	•
Receivables Turnover 36	•	•	•	•	•	•	•	•	•	•	•	•	•
Total Liabilities to Net Worth 37	1.8	•	0.4	1.0	3.1	1.8	5.3	48.2	3.5	4.2	8.7	4.0	1.1
Current Assets to Working Capital 38	10.9	•	1.6	1.4	10.9	•	•	13.0	•	•	•	•	2.0
Current Liabilities to Working Capital 39	9.9	•	0.6	0.4	9.9	•	•	12.0	•	•	•	•	1.0
Working Capital to Net Sales 40	0.1	•	0.1	0.3	0.1	•	•	0.1	•	•	•	•	2.7
Inventory to Working Capital 41	0.0	•	•	•	•	•	•	•	•	•	•	•	•
Total Receipts to Cash Flow 42	2.2	1.3	2.3	1.8	2.9	2.8	3.1	2.7	2.7	2.6	1.9	1.7	1.9
Cost of Goods to Cash Flow 43	0.0	0.0	•	•	•	•	•	•	•	•	•	•	•
Cash Flow to Total Debt 44	0.2	•	5.9	1.4	0.3	0.3	0.2	0.2	0.2	0.2	0.1	0.4	0.1

Selected Financial Factors (in Percentages)

Debt Ratio 45	64.4	•	27.9	50.1	75.5	64.1	84.1	98.0	77.8	80.8	89.7	79.9	53.0
Return on Total Assets 46	6.9	•	68.0	6.3	10.0	11.6	8.9	9.8	12.1	11.4	8.7	17.3	3.0
Return on Equity Before Income Taxes 47	13.5	•	92.4	7.4	29.3	21.4	34.7	329.4	44.2	46.2	70.0	75.8	2.5
Return on Equity After Income Taxes 48	12.1	•	92.1	7.2	27.2	21.0	31.6	309.1	39.8	42.9	67.4	74.6	1.6
Profit Margin (Before Income Tax) 49	19.0	19.3	17.4	3.0	12.9	13.4	8.6	14.1	21.0	23.0	27.8	29.8	19.3
Profit Margin (After Income Tax) 50	17.1	13.8	17.4	2.9	11.9	13.2	7.8	13.2	18.9	21.4	26.8	29.3	12.5

Table I

Corporations with and without Net Income

INTL. TRADE, SECONDARY FINANCING, OTHER NONDEPOSITORY CREDIT

MONEY AMOUNTS AND SIZE OF ASSETS IN THOUSANDS OF DOLLARS

Item Description for Accounting Period 7/09 Through 6/10		Total	Zero Assets	Under 500	500 to 1,000	1,000 to 5,000	5,000 to 10,000	10,000 to 25,000	25,000 to 50,000	50,000 to 100,000	100,000 to 250,000	250,000 to 500,000	500,000 to 2,500,000	2,500,000 and over
Number of Enterprises	1	5573	672	2987	667	728	256	100	42	32	26	11	26	26
Revenues ($ in Thousands)														
Net Sales	2	202230760	483642	1003264	266581	454702	496752	451464	280166	284817	482210	619556	2830793	194576813
Interest	3	181123150	253154	26629	29808	52925	471	24657	44676	93640	175349	85101	1297344	179039397
Rents	4	59220	3640	0	0	0	0	16	647	203	506	893	5960	47355
Royalties	5	7614	0	0	39	0	0	3	648	0	2	0	6921	0
Other Portfolio Income	6	2841775	2	0	0	5298	0	3318	8041	4694	2068	2994	143206	2672152
Other Receipts	7	18199001	226846	976635	236734	396479	496281	423470	226154	186280	304285	530568	1377362	12817909
Total Receipts	8	202230760	483642	1003264	266581	454702	496752	451464	280166	284817	482210	619556	2830793	194576813
Average Total Receipts	9	36288	720	336	400	625	1940	4515	6671	8901	18547	56323	108877	7483724
Operating Costs/Operating Income (%)														
Cost of Operations	10	0.3	30.3	•	•	1.3	•	10.4	•	•	•	•	9.4	•
Salaries and Wages	11	1.5	2.6	14.2	20.3	20.7	31.0	27.2	19.9	13.8	13.4	22.3	11.5	1.0
Taxes Paid	12	0.2	2.0	6.3	4.4	3.8	3.9	3.4	3.1	1.8	1.6	0.9	1.7	0.1
Interest Paid	13	72.6	45.1	0.8	4.2	10.0	3.5	11.2	12.6	32.7	20.9	19.6	25.9	74.7
Depreciation	14	0.2	0.2	0.9	1.1	1.1	4.7	1.9	4.1	1.5	0.8	2.2	3.0	0.1
Amortization and Depletion	15	0.2	0.0	0.1	0.1	1.1	0.1	0.7	0.3	0.7	0.6	0.8	2.0	0.2
Pensions and Other Deferred Comp.	16	0.1	0.0	0.8	•	0.3	0.4	0.5	0.6	0.1	0.6	0.1	0.2	0.1
Employee Benefits	17	0.2	0.0	0.2	1.0	2.1	1.7	0.9	1.5	1.8	1.1	1.0	0.6	0.2
Advertising	18	0.1	0.2	1.2	10.8	1.6	3.9	1.3	0.7	0.3	0.7	0.4	1.7	0.0
Other Expenses	19	29.3	7.1	64.2	45.3	55.7	31.8	37.8	32.7	44.8	47.5	36.9	43.9	28.8
Officers' Compensation	20	0.2	3.6	7.8	12.7	9.9	3.9	4.8	6.0	3.4	2.1	0.9	1.1	0.1
Operating Margin	21	•	9.0	3.3	0.0	•	15.1	•	18.4	•	10.7	1.5	•	•
Operating Margin Before Officers' Comp.	22	•	12.6	11.1	12.8	2.4	19.0	4.7	24.4	2.5	12.8	2.4	0.1	•

Selected Average Balance Sheet ($ in Thousands)

Net Receivables 23	27128	·	32	207	1140	3219	4879	21506	38941	110448	162099	541572	4919986
Inventories 24	·	·	·	·	·	·	·	·	·	·	·	·	·
Net Property, Plant and Equipment 25	459	0	15	17	109	590	1079	1110	1414	1090	5931	11181	64845
Total Assets 26	372755	0	112	725	1765	6200	15481	33233	69928	159839	324170	1236630	78023882
Notes and Loans Payable 27	339836	0	44	601	1136	4608	13663	15112	34480	94443	208404	778605	71664169
All Other Liabilities 28	30920	0	16	40	260	964	2254	3961	16208	29168	83475	159277	6349103
Net Worth 29	2000	0	51	84	369	628	-435	14159	19240	36229	32290	298748	10611

Selected Financial Ratios (Times to 1)

Current Ratio 30	0.5	·	8.9	2.9	2.1	2.6	1.1	2.2	1.7	1.6	0.8	1.5	0.5
Quick Ratio 31	0.4	·	5.0	2.0	1.9	2.0	0.7	2.0	1.4	1.3	0.7	1.2	0.4
Net Sales to Working Capital 32	·	·	4.1	1.1	0.7	0.7	4.0	0.4	0.4	0.4	·	0.4	·
Coverage Ratio 33	0.9	1.2	5.0	1.0	0.2	5.3	1.0	2.6	1.0	1.5	1.1	1.1	0.9
Total Asset Turnover 34	0.1	·	3.0	0.6	0.4	0.3	0.3	0.2	0.1	0.1	0.2	0.1	0.1
Inventory Turnover 35	·	·	·	·	·	·	·	·	·	·	·	·	·
Receivables Turnover 36	·	·	·	·	·	·	·	·	·	·	·	·	·
Total Liabilities to Net Worth 37	185.4	·	1.2	7.6	3.8	8.9	1.3	1.8	2.6	3.4	9.0	3.1	7352.2
Current Assets to Working Capital 38	1.1	·	1.1	1.5	1.9	1.6	0.9	2.4	2.7	2.9	·	·	·
Current Liabilities to Working Capital 39	0.1	·	0.1	0.5	0.9	0.6	0.8	1.4	1.7	1.9	·	·	·
Working Capital to Net Sales 40	0.2	·	0.2	0.9	1.3	1.5	0.2	2.3	2.5	2.7	2.4	·	·
Inventory to Working Capital 41	·	·	0.0	0.0	0.0	0.2	0.2	0.0	0.0	0.0	0.0	·	·
Total Receipts to Cash Flow 42	4.2	6.5	1.6	2.8	2.6	2.5	3.2	2.2	2.4	1.8	3.2	2.6	4.3
Cost of Goods to Cash Flow 43	0.0	2.0	·	0.0	0.0	0.0	0.3	·	·	·	0.7	0.2	·
Cash Flow to Total Debt 44	0.0	·	3.4	0.2	0.2	0.1	0.1	0.2	0.0	0.1	·	0.1	0.0

Selected Financial Factors (in Percentages)

Debt Ratio 45	99.5	·	53.9	88.4	79.1	89.9	102.8	57.4	72.5	77.3	90.0	75.8	100.0
Return on Total Assets 46	6.5	·	12.4	2.4	0.9	5.8	3.2	6.5	4.0	3.7	3.7	2.5	6.6
Return on Equity Before Income Taxes 47	·	·	21.6	0.2	·	46.6	0.8	9.4	·	5.5	2.6	1.0	·
Return on Equity After Income Taxes 48	·	·	17.6	·	·	43.8	16.6	8.0	·	3.7	·	3.7	·
Profit Margin (Before Income Tax) 49	9.0	·	3.3	0.0	·	15.1	·	19.9	10.7	·	1.5	2.6	·
Profit Margin (After Income Tax) 50	6.3	·	2.7	·	·	14.2	·	17.0	7.1	·	·	·	·

Table II

Corporations with Net Income

INTL. TRADE, SECONDARY FINANCING, OTHER NONDEPOSITORY CREDIT

Money Amounts and Size of Assets in Thousands of Dollars

Item Description for Accounting Period 7/09 Through 6/10	Total	Zero Assets	Under 500	500 to 1,000	1,000 to 5,000	5,000 to 10,000	10,000 to 25,000	25,000 to 50,000	50,000 to 100,000	100,000 to 250,000	250,000 to 500,000	500,000 to 2,500,000	2,500,000 and over
Number of Enterprises 1	3713	647	1735	365	555	230	58	•	21	21	7	19	•
Revenues ($ in Thousands)													
Net Sales 2	9596902	347716	971054	244864	366042	488116	255916	•	129462	414437	458150	2420459	•
Interest 3	3054230	241063	22899	28537	29075	15	10037	•	29705	166250	20838	1088500	•
Rents 4	13430	3640	0	0	0	0	0	•	19	448	893	5834	•
Royalties 5	7571	0	0	0	0	0	0	•	0	2	0	6921	•
Other Portfolio Income 6	248854	2	0	0	4187	0	3314	•	2328	2068	2994	137599	•
Other Receipts 7	6272817	103011	948155	216327	332780	488101	246565	•	97410	245669	433425	1181605	•
Total Receipts 8	9596902	347716	971054	244864	366042	488116	255916	•	129462	414437	458150	2420459	•
Average Total Receipts 9	2585	537	560	671	660	2122	4481	•	6165	19735	65450	127393	•
Operating Costs/Operating Income (%)													
Cost of Operations 10	4.5	6.6	•	•	1.6	•	•	•	•	•	30.2	11.0	•
Salaries and Wages 11	11.1	3.4	10.1	21.3	18.4	29.4	23.0	•	10.8	14.1	13.3	12.1	•
Taxes Paid 12	2.5	2.7	6.1	4.0	3.9	3.6	2.9	•	1.8	1.6	0.9	1.8	•
Interest Paid 13	19.7	59.3	0.7	0.6	5.5	3.4	10.1	•	27.5	20.2	6.0	19.8	•
Depreciation 14	1.4	0.1	0.7	0.9	0.6	4.6	1.6	•	1.1	0.7	2.6	1.6	•
Amortization and Depletion 15	1.0	•	0.1	0.1	1.3	0.1	0.2	•	0.3	0.5	1.0	2.4	•
Pensions and Other Deferred Comp. 16	0.4	0.0	0.8	•	0.1	0.4	0.1	•	0.3	0.6	0.1	0.2	•
Employee Benefits 17	0.6	0.0	0.0	0.0	0.6	1.7	1.0	•	1.6	1.2	0.6	0.5	•
Advertising 18	1.5	0.2	0.9	11.8	1.5	3.6	1.7	•	0.5	0.8	0.5	2.0	•
Other Expenses 19	33.4	8.0	61.6	39.0	41.5	25.7	26.4	•	25.3	40.1	28.6	29.2	•
Officers' Compensation 20	2.7	5.0	7.8	9.6	7.2	3.7	7.1	•	4.2	2.2	1.0	1.1	•
Operating Margin 21	21.2	14.6	11.0	12.7	17.9	23.7	25.9	•	26.5	18.0	15.1	18.3	•
Operating Margin Before Officers' Comp. 22	23.9	19.6	18.9	22.3	25.0	27.4	32.9	•	30.8	20.2	16.2	19.4	•

Selected Average Balance Sheet ($ in Thousands)

Net Receivables 23	16313	0	46	161	1245	3418	4640	•	43846	113900	154800	625343	•
Inventories 24	•	•	•	•	•	•	•	•	•	•	•	•	•
Net Property, Plant and Equipment 25	198	0	13	23	42	645	1355	•	1729	1232	7531	9420	•
Total Assets 26	34284	0	151	765	1683	6157	14167	•	71067	163030	308329	1304871	•
Notes and Loans Payable 27	22125	0	36	237	830	5127	9129	•	38251	92088	166553	653856	•
All Other Liabilities 28	6610	0	10	48	295	523	1146	•	12451	28915	47781	173651	•
Net Worth 29	5549	0	105	480	557	506	3892	•	20366	42027	93995	477363	•

Selected Financial Ratios (Times to 1)

Current Ratio 30	1.8	•	10.0	5.3	2.9	3.2	1.6	•	1.9	1.7	1.0	2.1	•
Quick Ratio 31	1.6	•	5.8	3.3	2.5	2.4	1.0	•	1.5	1.4	0.9	1.8	•
Net Sales to Working Capital 32	0.2	•	4.7	1.2	0.6	0.6	1.3	•	0.2	0.4	•	0.3	•
Coverage Ratio 33	2.1	1.2	16.5	22.4	4.2	7.9	3.6	•	2.0	1.9	3.5	2.1	•
Total Asset Turnover 34	0.1	•	3.7	0.9	0.4	0.3	0.3	•	0.1	0.1	0.2	0.1	•
Inventory Turnover 35	•	•	•	•	•	•	•	•	•	•	•	•	•
Receivables Turnover 36	•	•	•	•	•	•	•	•	•	•	•	•	•
Total Liabilities to Net Worth 37	5.2	•	0.4	0.6	2.0	11.2	2.6	•	2.5	2.9	2.3	1.7	•
Current Assets to Working Capital 38	2.3	•	1.1	1.2	1.5	1.5	2.8	•	2.1	2.5	1.9	1.9	•
Current Liabilities to Working Capital 39	1.3	•	0.1	0.2	0.5	0.5	1.8	•	1.1	1.5	0.9	0.9	•
Working Capital to Net Sales 40	4.1	•	0.2	0.8	1.5	1.6	0.7	•	4.5	2.7	3.4	3.4	•
Inventory to Working Capital 41	0.0	•	•	0.0	0.0	•	•	•	0.0	0.0	•	0.0	•
Total Receipts to Cash Flow 42	2.0	4.6	1.5	2.3	2.0	2.0	2.2	•	2.0	1.8	2.8	2.4	•
Cost of Goods to Cash Flow 43	0.1	0.3	•	•	0.0	0.0	•	•	0.1	0.8	0.3	•	•
Cash Flow to Total Debt 44	0.0	•	8.2	1.0	0.3	0.2	0.2	•	0.1	0.1	0.1	0.1	•

Selected Financial Factors (in Percentages)

Debt Ratio 45	83.8	•	30.3	37.2	66.9	91.8	72.5	•	71.3	74.2	69.5	63.4	•
Return on Total Assets 46	3.1	•	43.5	11.7	9.2	9.4	11.4	•	4.7	4.6	4.5	4.1	•
Return on Equity Before Income Taxes 47	10.0	•	58.7	17.8	21.2	99.5	29.8	•	8.0	8.4	10.5	6.0	•
Return on Equity After Income Taxes 48	8.0	•	55.3	16.0	20.8	95.7	26.7	•	7.0	6.5	7.4	4.2	•
Profit Margin (Before Income Tax) 49	21.5	14.6	11.0	12.7	17.9	23.7	25.9	•	26.3	18.0	15.1	22.6	•
Profit Margin (After Income Tax) 50	17.2	10.9	10.4	11.5	17.5	22.8	23.2	•	23.1	13.9	10.6	15.6	•

Table I

Corporations with and without Net Income

ACTIVITIES RELATED TO CREDIT INTERMEDIATION

MONEY AMOUNTS AND SIZE OF ASSETS IN THOUSANDS OF DOLLARS

Item Description for Accounting Period 7/09 Through 6/10		Total	Zero Assets	Under 500	500 to 1,000	1,000 to 5,000	5,000 to 10,000	10,000 to 25,000	25,000 to 50,000	50,000 to 100,000	100,000 to 250,000	250,000 to 500,000	500,000 to 2,500,000	2,500,000 and over
Number of Enterprises	1	21731	6632	12351	1381	884	214	116	48	43	21	12	19	9
Revenues ($ in Thousands)														
Net Sales	2	46276818	300256	3525856	735415	1129023	465338	1179916	663704	1424482	1686052	1653019	6297034	27216722
Interest	3	1176007	3052	3858	1592	11284	1887	50988	6407	28320	15746	11129	357647	684097
Rents	4	171928	0	534	0	805	485	3175	0	0	799	0	20879	145250
Royalties	5	259582	11	0	0	0	0	0	0	191	0	0	0	259380
Other Portfolio Income	6	1683516	11395	0	10	8	106	1661	57	2461	133825	327	112893	1420773
Other Receipts	7	42985785	285798	3521464	733813	1116926	462860	1124092	657240	1393510	1535682	1641563	5805615	24707222
Total Receipts	8	46276818	300256	3525856	735415	1129023	465338	1179916	663704	1424482	1686052	1653019	6297034	27216722
Average Total Receipts	9	2130	45	285	533	1277	2174	10172	13827	33127	80288	137752	331423	3024080
Operating Costs/Operating Income (%)														
Cost of Operations	10	2.3	2.1	•	•	•	20.7	7.9	•	0.1	0.4	29.9	2.6	0.8
Salaries and Wages	11	19.6	22.3	34.0	41.3	34.8	21.3	28.6	32.3	26.4	22.2	16.0	17.6	15.9
Taxes Paid	12	2.8	3.6	3.0	3.8	3.8	5.2	5.0	3.6	2.6	2.4	1.4	1.5	3.0
Interest Paid	13	7.4	1.8	1.3	1.5	1.5	12.6	6.0	5.1	4.5	2.5	4.1	6.8	9.5
Depreciation	14	2.5	1.1	1.1	1.3	2.0	1.0	2.2	1.4	4.1	2.5	3.4	2.0	2.9
Amortization and Depletion	15	2.3	•	0.2	2.0	0.3	0.0	0.9	0.2	1.9	0.7	7.6	5.1	1.9
Pensions and Other Deferred Comp.	16	1.2	0.0	0.4	0.0	0.7	0.3	0.6	0.3	0.4	0.6	0.1	1.5	1.5
Employee Benefits	17	1.9	2.0	1.3	0.8	0.7	1.2	0.9	1.0	1.8	2.3	1.1	2.7	1.9
Advertising	18	3.9	1.7	3.0	2.3	2.8	2.4	0.8	3.4	1.3	1.5	4.5	2.4	4.9
Other Expenses	19	43.2	71.6	36.4	34.6	38.7	39.3	26.6	37.9	49.0	44.9	25.2	48.5	44.5
Officers' Compensation	20	2.0	0.8	13.3	4.2	4.9	6.0	4.5	7.3	2.0	1.8	1.2	1.0	0.4
Operating Margin	21	10.9	•	6.1	8.2	9.7	•	16.1	7.4	6.0	18.2	5.4	8.3	12.8
Operating Margin Before Officers' Comp.	22	12.9	•	19.4	12.4	14.6	•	20.6	14.8	8.0	20.0	6.6	9.3	13.2

Selected Average Balance Sheet ($ in Thousands)

Net Receivables 23	580	5	24	206	2021	3341	10357	17834	45729	49359	204078	534476
Inventories 24	•	•	•	•	•	•	•	•	•	•	•	•
Net Property, Plant and Equipment 25	230	21	126	96	353	993	1169	4235	9857	13842	43752	315392
Total Assets 26	6843	75	739	2290	7132	15591	37846	69019	163258	313256	927177	12422106
Notes and Loans Payable 27	2708	43	313	1065	6536	10658	22533	38038	30497	92990	306377	4891131
All Other Liabilities 28	2327	26	123	766	870	3871	6085	33335	82099	140154	346376	4117324
Net Worth 29	1808	7	304	459	-275	1062	9227	-2354	50662	80113	274424	3413651

Selected Financial Ratios (Times to 1)

Current Ratio 30	1.3	1.1	2.7	1.9	0.6	1.1	0.8	1.0	1.7	1.0	1.4	1.4
Quick Ratio 31	0.8	1.0	2.1	1.7	0.6	0.8	0.6	0.9	1.4	0.9	1.3	0.6
Net Sales to Working Capital 32	3.9	72.0	2.4	2.1	•	19.4	2.5	2.1	•	•	3.3	3.1
Coverage Ratio 33	2.6	5.8	6.7	7.3	0.2	3.7	2.5	2.3	9.8	2.3	2.2	2.5
Total Asset Turnover 34	0.3	3.8	0.7	0.6	0.3	0.7	0.4	0.5	0.5	0.4	0.4	0.2
Inventory Turnover 35	•	•	•	•	•	•	•	•	•	•	•	•
Receivables Turnover 36	•	•	•	•	•	•	•	•	•	•	•	•
Total Liabilities to Net Worth 37	2.8	9.7	1.4	4.0	•	13.7	3.1	2.2	2.9	•	2.4	2.6
Current Assets to Working Capital 38	4.0	9.2	1.6	2.1	•	12.4	2.5	•	•	•	3.2	3.6
Current Liabilities to Working Capital 39	3.0	8.2	0.6	1.1	•	11.4	1.5	•	•	•	2.2	2.6
Working Capital to Net Sales 40	0.3	0.0	0.4	0.5	•	0.1	0.5	•	•	•	0.3	0.3
Inventory to Working Capital 41	0.0	•	•	•	•	0.1	0.0	•	•	•	0.0	0.0
Total Receipts to Cash Flow 42	2.1	2.8	3.0	2.4	4.3	2.6	2.3	2.0	1.8	3.7	2.1	1.9
Cost of Goods to Cash Flow 43	0.0	0.0	•	0.9	0.2	•	0.0	0.0	•	1.1	0.1	0.0
Cash Flow to Total Debt 44	0.2	1.5	0.4	0.3	0.1	0.3	•	0.2	•	0.4	0.2	0.2

Selected Financial Factors (in Percentages)

Debt Ratio 45	73.6	90.6	58.9	80.0	103.9	93.2	75.6	103.4	69.0	74.4	70.4	72.5
Return on Total Assets 46	6.0	27.8	7.0	6.3	0.8	14.4	4.6	5.0	12.2	4.2	5.4	5.8
Return on Equity Before Income Taxes 47	14.1	245.3	14.4	27.0	78.7	154.7	11.1	•	35.2	9.3	10.1	12.7
Return on Equity After Income Taxes 48	9.0	243.4	14.4	26.0	82.3	111.2	10.2	24.1	•	7.5	5.3	7.7
Profit Margin (Before Income Tax) 49	12.0	6.1	8.2	9.7	•	16.1	7.4	6.0	22.2	5.4	8.4	14.3
Profit Margin (After Income Tax) 50	7.6	6.0	8.2	9.3	•	11.6	6.8	5.1	15.2	4.4	4.4	8.7

Table II

Corporations with Net Income

ACTIVITIES RELATED TO CREDIT INTERMEDIATION

MONEY AMOUNTS AND SIZE OF ASSETS IN THOUSANDS OF DOLLARS

Item Description for Accounting Period 7/09 Through 6/10		Total	Zero Assets	Under 500	500 to 1,000	1,000 to 5,000	5,000 to 10,000	10,000 to 25,000	25,000 to 50,000	50,000 to 100,000	100,000 to 250,000	250,000 to 500,000	500,000 to 2,500,000	2,500,000 and over
Number of Enterprises	1	10963	2143	7416	594	•	127	74	29	29	15	9	14	•
Revenues ($ in Thousands)														
Net Sales	2	37404623	121726	2865329	321030	•	435025	900591	596229	1096997	1540072	1504772	5479570	•
Interest	3	1038205	25	1086	1075	•	511	40804	5600	16152	13923	8131	335616	•
Rents	4	34415	0	534	0	•	485	3175	0	0	799	0	19713	•
Royalties	5	235996	0	0	0	•	0	0	0	0	0	0	0	•
Other Portfolio Income	6	1624843	11083	0	10	•	30	140	1	2041	133127	327	112885	•
Other Receipts	7	34471164	110618	2863709	319945	•	433999	856472	590628	1078804	1392223	1496314	5011356	•
Total Receipts	8	37404623	121726	2865329	321030	•	435025	900591	596229	1096997	1540072	1504772	5479570	•
Average Total Receipts	9	3412	57	386	540	•	3425	12170	20560	37827	102671	167197	391398	•
Operating Costs/Operating Income (%)														
Cost of Operations	10	1.9	5.1	•	•	•	19.4	10.4	•	0.1	0.4	32.9	0.1	•
Salaries and Wages	11	18.2	25.2	36.1	14.7	•	21.8	25.1	31.8	23.4	22.4	13.3	16.8	•
Taxes Paid	12	3.1	2.5	2.7	2.0	•	4.7	5.2	3.3	2.4	2.4	1.3	1.4	•
Interest Paid	13	3.3	0.1	1.2	2.1	•	5.9	5.5	3.4	3.7	2.2	4.2	5.5	•
Depreciation	14	2.3	0.8	1.0	2.0	•	0.5	1.5	0.4	2.5	2.2	3.6	2.0	•
Amortization and Depletion	15	1.9	•	0.2	•	•	•	0.5	0.1	1.7	0.6	7.4	4.7	•
Pensions and Other Deferred Comp.	16	1.3	0.0	0.4	0.0	•	0.3	0.8	0.3	0.2	0.3	0.1	1.7	•
Employee Benefits	17	1.5	0.8	0.9	0.1	•	1.3	0.8	0.9	1.1	1.5	0.9	2.8	•
Advertising	18	4.5	0.8	2.1	2.1	•	2.6	0.5	3.7	1.6	1.5	4.9	2.6	•
Other Expenses	19	42.8	30.6	34.5	34.9	•	25.9	19.4	29.9	39.4	43.4	22.8	47.7	•
Officers' Compensation	20	1.6	1.9	8.0	3.9	•	5.8	4.6	7.4	2.1	1.2	1.3	1.0	•
Operating Margin	21	17.7	32.2	12.9	38.2	•	11.9	25.7	18.7	21.7	21.7	7.3	13.6	•
Operating Margin Before Officers' Comp.	22	19.3	34.1	20.8	42.1	•	17.7	30.3	26.2	23.8	22.9	8.6	14.6	•

Selected Average Balance Sheet ($ in Thousands)

Net Receivables 23	808	•	0	1	50	•	2182	2334	9017	16528	59345	34667	213783
Inventories 24	•	•	•	•	•	•	•	•	•	•	•	•
Net Property, Plant and Equipment 25	320	0	•	20	63	•	101	896	701	3353	10453	17933	49139
Total Assets 26	8544	0	•	69	752	6570	14327	37370	71000	167993	320422	1018370
Notes and Loans Payable 27	2194	0	•	45	224	4520	7371	21071	36737	42472	49009	345599
All Other Liabilities 28	3037	0	•	22	58	1171	3457	5108	41931	77601	161695	343144
Net Worth 29	3313	0	•	2	471	880	3499	11192	-7669	47921	109718	329627

Selected Financial Ratios (Times to 1)

Current Ratio 30	1.5	•	0.7	4.0	•	0.6	0.9	0.7	1.1	1.8	1.0	1.4
Quick Ratio 31	0.9	•	0.6	3.0	•	0.6	0.6	0.9	1.5	0.9	1.4
Net Sales to Working Capital 32	2.9	•	•	1.1	•	•	19.7	2.1	3.7
Coverage Ratio 33	6.7	389.6	11.5	19.3	3.0	5.7	6.5	6.8	12.9	2.7	3.5
Total Asset Turnover 34	0.4	5.6	0.7	0.5	0.8	0.6	0.5	0.6	0.5	0.4
Inventory Turnover 35	•	•	•	•	•	•	•	•	•	•	•
Receivables Turnover 36	•	•	•	•	•	•	•	•	•	•	•
Total Liabilities to Net Worth 37	1.6	37.6	0.6	6.5	3.1	2.3	2.5	1.9	2.1
Current Assets to Working Capital 38	3.0	•	•	1.3	•	18.2	2.3	3.2
Current Liabilities to Working Capital 39	2.0	•	•	0.3	•	17.2	1.3	2.2
Working Capital to Net Sales 40	0.3	•	•	0.9	•	0.1	0.5	0.3
Inventory to Working Capital 41	0.0	•	•	0.0	•	0.0	0.0	0.0
Total Receipts to Cash Flow 42	1.8	2.1	2.5	1.7	3.0	2.4	2.2	1.7	1.7	3.7	1.8
Cost of Goods to Cash Flow 43	0.0	0.1	•	0.6	0.2	•	0.0	0.0	1.2	0.0
Cash Flow to Total Debt 44	0.4	•	2.3	1.1	0.2	0.5	0.4	0.3	0.5	0.2	0.3

Selected Financial Factors (in Percentages)

Debt Ratio 45	61.2	•	97.4	37.4	86.6	75.6	70.1	110.8	71.5	65.8	67.6
Return on Total Assets 46	8.8	•	79.1	28.9	9.2	26.6	12.2	13.6	17.3	6.0	7.4
Return on Equity Before Income Taxes 47	19.4	•	2787.3	43.8	46.2	89.9	34.4	•	56.0	11.2	16.3
Return on Equity After Income Taxes 48	13.9	•	2774.7	43.8	44.3	69.9	33.1	•	39.6	9.5	10.8
Profit Margin (Before Income Tax) 49	18.8	32.2	12.9	38.2	11.9	25.8	18.7	21.7	26.1	7.3	13.7
Profit Margin (After Income Tax) 50	13.5	31.8	12.8	38.1	11.4	20.1	18.0	20.6	18.5	6.2	9.1

Table I

Corporations with and without Net Income

INVESTMENT BANKING AND SECURITIES DEALING

MONEY AMOUNTS AND SIZE OF ASSETS IN THOUSANDS OF DOLLARS

Item Description for Accounting Period 7/09 Through 6/10		Total	Zero Assets	Under 500	500 to 1,000	1,000 to 5,000	5,000 to 10,000	10,000 to 25,000	25,000 to 50,000	50,000 to 100,000	100,000 to 250,000	250,000 to 500,000	500,000 to 2,500,000	2,500,000 and over
Number of Enterprises	1	2882	927	1016	352	435	20	38	26	20	13	6	15	16
Revenues ($ in Thousands)														
Net Sales	2	122787114	97388	178492	-8121	963121	84765	137675	306018	584330	397706	368378	2337020	117340342
Interest	3	42983771	21133	30	256	8063	4290	2199	1859	21566	17759	52195	471384	42383037
Rents	4	101073	552	0	0	8187	24	0	0	0	27	11	1054	91218
Royalties	5	55778	0	0	0	13	0	0	14	0	13	10177	1093	44468
Other Portfolio Income	6	2386945	17151	1963	128	2309	264	1396	18581	10455	15710	15540	125697	2177748
Other Receipts	7	77259547	58552	176499	-8505	944549	80187	134080	285564	552309	364197	290455	1737792	72643871
Total Receipts	8	122787114	97388	178492	-8121	963121	84765	137675	306018	584330	397706	368378	2337020	117340342
Average Total Receipts	9	42605	105	176	-23	2214	4238	3623	11770	29216	30593	61396	155801	7333771
Operating Costs/Operating Income (%)														
Cost of Operations	10	6.6	•	•	•	•	•	•	•	•	•	•	•	6.9
Salaries and Wages	11	15.3	11.4	•	•	3.6	16.2	29.5	40.1	42.9	39.5	17.5	25.2	14.9
Taxes Paid	12	1.2	4.4	2.1	•	1.0	3.6	3.8	2.7	2.3	4.0	2.7	2.3	1.2
Interest Paid	13	27.1	2.7	•	•	0.2	2.8	0.8	2.2	4.9	3.5	9.7	10.6	28.1
Depreciation	14	1.1	2.1	0.6	•	0.1	1.2	5.7	1.3	1.0	1.9	0.6	0.9	1.1
Amortization and Depletion	15	0.5	•	•	•	•	0.0	0.2	0.2	2.0	0.3	0.2	1.3	0.5
Pensions and Other Deferred Comp.	16	0.7	•	2.4	•	0.1	0.0	0.1	0.9	1.4	0.4	0.3	0.1	0.7
Employee Benefits	17	0.5	•	0.7	•	0.7	2.8	1.4	2.0	0.9	2.7	0.6	0.8	0.5
Advertising	18	0.1	2.6	0.2	•	0.1	0.5	0.0	1.8	0.1	1.6	9.2	0.0	0.1
Other Expenses	19	27.9	53.9	8.5	•	17.9	40.9	32.7	36.1	35.7	59.8	33.3	43.8	27.5
Officers' Compensation	20	0.7	•	28.7	•	3.1	59.4	26.2	5.8	8.1	5.3	3.2	2.9	0.4
Operating Margin	21	18.2	22.9	56.8	490.7	73.2	•	•	6.7	0.7	•	22.9	12.1	18.1
Operating Margin Before Officers' Comp.	22	18.9	22.9	85.5	423.0	76.3	31.8	25.8	12.6	8.8	•	26.0	15.0	18.5

Selected Average Balance Sheet ($ in Thousands)

Net Receivables 23	317078	0	6	16	472	1215	5653	7893	19405	109223	161799	56882071
Inventories 24	•	•	•	•	•	•	•	•	•	•	•	•
Net Property, Plant and Equipment 25	3286	0	1	71	225	454	2532	1789	4968	1230	14557	564098
Total Assets 26	1425255	93	666	2900	6250	14643	35063	71701	156801	364394	860054	255365143
Notes and Loans Payable 27	225722	16	384	951	1307	297	2034	16949	17135	85799	91772	4046896
All Other Liabilities 28	1079121	22	15	57	1403	3346	12738	14954	55537	175188	395105	193843108
Net Worth 29	120412	54	267	1893	3541	11000	20292	39798	84129	103406	373177	21058140

Selected Financial Ratios (Times to 1)

Current Ratio 30	1.1	3.5	27.5	10.0	1.6	4.0	1.8	1.5	1.6	1.9	1.6	1.1
Quick Ratio 31	0.5	2.3	8.2	1.9	1.5	2.7	1.3	0.8	1.1	1.1	1.2	0.5
Net Sales to Working Capital 32	0.9	3.1	•	4.3	5.0	0.5	2.2	2.6	0.6	0.8	0.8	0.8
Coverage Ratio 33	1.7	9.5	•	406.1	•	3.4	0.9	3.3	•	2.1	1.7	•
Total Asset Turnover 34	0.0	1.9	•	0.8	0.7	0.2	0.3	0.4	0.2	0.2	0.2	0.0
Inventory Turnover 35	•	•	•	•	•	•	•	•	•	•	•	•
Receivables Turnover 36	•	•	•	•	•	•	•	•	•	•	•	•
Total Liabilities to Net Worth 37	10.8	0.7	1.5	0.5	0.8	0.3	0.7	0.8	0.9	2.5	1.3	11.1
Current Assets to Working Capital 38	17.6	1.4	1.0	1.1	2.6	1.3	2.3	2.9	2.5	2.1	2.5	18.1
Current Liabilities to Working Capital 39	16.6	0.4	0.0	0.1	1.6	0.3	1.3	1.9	1.5	1.1	1.5	17.1
Working Capital to Net Sales 40	1.2	0.3	0.0	0.2	0.2	0.5	0.5	0.4	1.3	1.7	1.3	1.2
Inventory to Working Capital 41	0.0	•	•	•	•	•	•	•	•	•	•	0.0
Total Receipts to Cash Flow 42	2.3	1.4	0.4	1.1	9.5	3.9	3.1	3.4	4.3	2.0	2.2	2.4
Cost of Goods to Cash Flow 43	0.2	•	•	•	•	•	•	•	•	•	•	0.2
Cash Flow to Total Debt 44	0.0	2.8	1.9	0.2	0.3	0.3	0.3	0.1	0.1	0.1	0.1	0.0

Selected Financial Factors (in Percentages)

Debt Ratio 45	91.6	41.4	59.9	34.7	24.9	42.1	44.5	46.3	•	•	71.6	91.8
Return on Total Assets 46	1.4	•	•	•	•	2.6	1.9	•	•	5.5	4.1	1.4
Return on Equity Before Income Taxes 47	7.0	107.3	183.0	85.6	•	3.2	•	•	•	13.5	5.0	6.9
Return on Equity After Income Taxes 48	5.6	•	182.2	85.5	•	1.9	•	•	•	10.3	3.7	5.5
Profit Margin (Before Income Tax) 49	19.8	22.9	56.6	490.7	73.2	5.4	•	•	•	22.7	12.0	19.8
Profit Margin (After Income Tax) 50	15.9	17.4	56.4	490.7	73.1	3.3	•	•	•	17.4	8.8	15.8

Table II

Corporations with Net Income

INVESTMENT BANKING AND SECURITIES DEALING

MONEY AMOUNTS AND SIZE OF ASSETS IN THOUSANDS OF DOLLARS

Item Description for Accounting Period 7/09 Through 6/10		Total	Zero Assets	Under 500	500 to 1,000	1,000 to 5,000	5,000 to 10,000	10,000 to 25,000	25,000 to 50,000	50,000 to 100,000	100,000 to 250,000	250,000 to 500,000	500,000 to 2,500,000	2,500,000 and over
Number of Enterprises	1	985	245	248	107	312	5	12	18	11	•	•	11	10
Revenues ($ in Thousands)														
Net Sales	2	121928026	95924	174499	9859	778095	33217	91056	215152	278297	•	•	2064067	117786758
Interest	3	42012848	21067	30	101	326	3466	1766	1859	19457	•	•	355095	41554991
Rents	4	100464	0	0	0	8187	0	0	0	0	•	•	1054	91218
Royalties	5	54600	0	0	0	13	0	0	14	0	•	•	0	44402
Other Portfolio Income	6	2206040	17140	1963	128	2154	0	0	17818	8403	•	•	26627	2111361
Other Receipts	7	77554074	57717	172506	9630	767415	29751	89290	195461	250437	•	•	1681291	73984786
Total Receipts	8	121928026	95924	174499	9859	778095	33217	91056	215152	278297	•	•	2064067	117786758
Average Total Receipts	9	123785	392	704	92	2494	6643	7588	11953	25300	•	•	187642	11778676
Operating Costs/Operating Income (%)														
Cost of Operations	10	6.7	•	•	•	•	•	•	•	•	•	•	•	6.9
Salaries and Wages	11	14.9	11.6	•	•	0.5	4.7	4.5	33.2	33.1	•	•	22.3	14.8
Taxes Paid	12	1.2	3.2	1.9	4.7	0.3	2.5	1.6	2.8	2.4	•	•	2.3	1.2
Interest Paid	13	26.6	2.7	•	•	0.2	7.1	0.6	3.0	9.0	•	•	7.7	27.3
Depreciation	14	1.1	2.2	•	•	0.0	0.2	0.1	0.4	0.2	•	•	0.8	1.1
Amortization and Depletion	15	0.5	•	•	•	•	0.0	0.1	0.3	0.4	•	•	1.5	0.5
Pensions and Other Deferred Comp.	16	0.7	•	2.5	6.5	•	0.1	0.1	0.6	0.3	•	•	0.1	0.7
Employee Benefits	17	0.5	•	0.7	•	0.0	1.1	1.4	0.7	0.3	•	•	0.9	0.5
Advertising	18	0.1	2.7	•	•	0.1	•	0.0	2.5	0.0	•	•	0.0	0.1
Other Expenses	19	26.6	47.5	6.5	39.1	1.3	6.7	9.0	26.9	19.1	•	•	44.5	26.5
Officers' Compensation	20	0.6	•	29.3	43.3	0.6	16.4	35.2	6.7	13.8	•	•	3.2	0.4
Operating Margin	21	20.6	30.2	59.0	6.3	96.8	61.3	47.3	22.7	21.4	•	•	16.8	20.0
Operating Margin Before Officers' Comp.	22	21.2	30.2	88.4	49.7	97.4	77.6	82.5	29.4	35.1	•	•	20.0	20.4

Selected Average Balance Sheet ($ in Thousands)

Net Receivables **23**	880756	•	0	20	6	90	3519	7720	693	•	181373	86481306
Inventories **24**	•	•	•	•	•	•	•	•	•	•	•	•
Net Property, Plant and Equipment **25**	9419	•	0	0	91	31	134	1526	535	•	16305	901788
Total Assets **26**	4072804	•	303	834	3230	6808	14760	31296	70905	•	925853	399968200
Notes and Loans Payable **27**	646946	•	0	218	652	5227	89	2589	13447	•	90623	63557354
All Other Liabilities **28**	3076562	•	92	49	27	846	6433	8236	17291	•	486818	302366018
Net Worth **29**	349296	•	212	568	2551	735	8238	20470	40166	•	348412	33764827

Selected Financial Ratios (Times to 1)

Current Ratio **30**	1.1	•	3.3	9.4	4.6	1.2	4.0	3.3	1.2	•	1.6	1.1
Quick Ratio **31**	0.5	•	2.1	7.3	3.6	0.9	3.7	2.5	0.5	•	1.2	0.5
Net Sales to Working Capital **32**	0.9	•	3.3	0.2	25.7	37.6	0.9	1.1	4.5	•	0.8	0.9
Coverage Ratio **33**	1.8	12.3	•	•	597.1	9.6	74.2	8.0	3.2	•	3.1	1.8
Total Asset Turnover **34**	0.0	•	2.3	0.1	0.8	1.0	0.5	0.4	0.4	•	0.2	0.0
Inventory Turnover **35**	•	•	•	•	•	•	•	•	•	•	•	•
Receivables Turnover **36**	•	•	•	•	•	•	•	•	•	•	•	•
Total Liabilities to Net Worth **37**	10.7	•	0.4	0.5	0.3	0.8	0.8	0.5	0.8	•	1.7	10.8
Current Assets to Working Capital **38**	18.9	•	1.4	1.1	1.3	5.8	1.3	1.4	5.0	•	2.7	19.3
Current Liabilities to Working Capital **39**	17.9	•	0.4	0.1	0.3	4.8	0.3	0.4	4.0	•	1.7	18.3
Working Capital to Net Sales **40**	1.1	•	0.3	4.4	0.0	0.0	1.2	0.9	0.2	•	1.2	1.1
Inventory to Working Capital **41**	0.0	•	•	•	•	•	•	•	•	•	•	0.0
Total Receipts to Cash Flow **42**	2.3	1.4	1.6	2.4	1.0	1.5	1.8	2.2	2.7	•	1.7	2.3
Cost of Goods to Cash Flow **43**	0.2	•	•	•	•	•	•	•	•	•	•	0.2
Cash Flow to Total Debt **44**	0.0	•	4.8	0.1	3.6	0.7	0.6	0.5	0.3	•	0.2	0.0

Selected Financial Factors (in Percentages)

Debt Ratio **45**	91.4	•	30.2	31.9	21.0	89.2	44.2	34.6	43.4	•	62.4	91.6
Return on Total Assets **46**	1.5	•	136.5	0.7	74.8	66.7	24.7	9.3	10.3	•	4.9	1.4
Return on Equity Before Income Taxes **47**	7.9	•	195.6	1.0	94.6	553.8	43.6	12.4	12.6	•	8.8	7.6
Return on Equity After Income Taxes **48**	6.5	•	194.7	1.0	94.5	553.8	42.5	10.6	12.6	•	6.8	6.2
Profit Margin (Before Income Tax) **49**	22.2	30.2	58.8	6.3	96.8	61.3	47.3	21.2	20.0	•	16.3	21.7
Profit Margin (After Income Tax) **50**	18.3	24.7	58.6	6.3	96.7	61.3	46.2	18.2	19.9	•	12.7	17.8

Table I

Corporations with and without Net Income

SECURITIES BROKERAGE

Money Amounts and Size of Assets in Thousands of Dollars

Item Description for Accounting Period 7/09 Through 6/10	Total	Zero Assets	Under 500	500 to 1,000	1,000 to 5,000	5,000 to 10,000	10,000 to 25,000	25,000 to 50,000	50,000 to 100,000	100,000 to 250,000	250,000 to 500,000	500,000 to 2,500,000	2,500,000 and over
Number of Enterprises **1**	7338	887	4848	663	614	100	91	43	26	20	3	18	26
Revenues ($ in Thousands)													
Net Sales **2**	93388313	336861	1602502	1036500	2535730	675500	2232274	1128820	1291485	1994586	690433	5007000	74856620
Interest **3**	36629179	4690	13538	737	2434	3208	10968	3726	18302	31456	1556	209707	36328858
Rents **4**	203170	0	0	0	1603	0	8714	0	5642	1285	0	2320	183605
Royalties **5**	36579	0	0	22	0	0	5774	0	0	1	0	1511	29272
Other Portfolio Income **6**	1095401	24073	1928	0	13383	9310	44206	37496	58138	11645	16717	35374	843134
Other Receipts **7**	55423984	308098	1587036	1035741	2518310	662982	2162612	1087598	1209403	1950199	672160	4758088	37471751
Total Receipts **8**	93388313	336861	1602502	1036500	2535730	675500	2232274	1128820	1291485	1994586	690433	5007000	74856620
Average Total Receipts **9**	12727	380	331	1563	4130	6755	24530	26252	49672	99729	230144	278167	2879101
Operating Costs/Operating Income (%)													
Cost of Operations **10**	0.2	•	•	•	•	27.5	•	0.4	•	0.3	•	0.1	0.0
Salaries and Wages **11**	22.8	2.2	16.1	37.2	40.9	28.8	24.5	46.3	43.0	42.0	57.1	45.8	19.0
Taxes Paid **12**	2.2	0.6	3.8	2.8	3.1	2.4	2.5	4.1	3.5	3.1	9.3	3.5	1.9
Interest Paid **13**	23.7	2.6	1.9	0.2	0.3	0.2	1.1	0.6	1.5	1.3	1.6	4.5	29.1
Depreciation **14**	1.1	0.1	1.0	0.2	0.2	0.3	0.8	0.7	0.9	1.3	2.8	1.8	1.1
Amortization and Depletion **15**	0.7	0.0	0.1	•	0.0	0.1	0.2	0.8	1.2	0.9	0.5	0.9	0.7
Pensions and Other Deferred Comp. **16**	0.7	0.0	0.2	1.4	0.2	0.7	0.2	0.6	0.2	0.5	1.3	0.4	0.8
Employee Benefits **17**	1.2	0.1	1.3	2.4	1.6	1.5	1.5	1.4	1.4	2.0	2.1	1.4	1.1
Advertising **18**	0.8	0.3	1.2	0.0	0.5	0.0	0.2	0.3	0.9	0.6	0.8	0.9	0.8
Other Expenses **19**	31.7	77.2	42.1	33.5	38.8	23.3	66.2	25.7	37.1	44.9	22.0	28.5	29.9
Officers' Compensation **20**	4.5	2.2	19.8	16.2	12.3	9.1	3.8	11.0	6.4	1.3	0.5	1.3	4.0
Operating Margin **21**	10.5	14.6	12.6	6.1	2.0	6.2	•	8.1	3.9	1.9	2.1	11.0	11.7
Operating Margin Before Officers' Comp. **22**	15.1	16.8	32.4	22.3	14.3	15.4	2.8	19.1	10.3	3.1	2.6	12.3	15.7

Selected Average Balance Sheet ($ in Thousands)

Net Receivables 23	45169	0	158	3	176	686	1795	1367	10547	30031	67787	409877	12402741
Inventories 24	•	•	•	•	•	•	•	•	•	•	•	•	•
Net Property, Plant and Equipment 25	570	0	13	12	64	106	996	892	1426	4792	23782	15506	133024
Total Assets 26	213540	0	695	98	2292	8213	16597	35500	67912	163735	367330	1266865	58915617
Notes and Loans Payable 27	33035	0	37	55	153	250	3277	2251	11115	23379	8706	73283	9211667
All Other Liabilities 28	167902	0	154	13	730	2786	6471	13563	25074	69247	169690	824759	46638729
Net Worth 29	12603	0	504	30	1409	5176	6849	19686	31723	71109	188934	368823	3065221

Selected Financial Ratios (Times to 1)

Current Ratio 30	1.1	•	4.8	1.6	3.3	5.6	2.0	2.0	1.6	1.4	2.0	1.1	1.1
Quick Ratio 31	0.5	•	4.5	1.4	2.1	5.0	1.4	1.3	1.0	1.1	1.8	0.9	0.5
Net Sales to Working Capital 32	0.9	•	3.5	24.9	3.8	1.5	4.2	2.6	3.6	3.3	1.7	6.4	0.8
Coverage Ratio 33	1.4	6.7	27.8	7.8	6.7	35.3	•	13.4	3.3	2.1	2.3	3.4	1.4
Total Asset Turnover 34	0.1	•	2.2	3.4	1.8	0.8	1.5	0.7	0.7	0.6	0.6	0.2	0.0
Inventory Turnover 35	•	•	•	•	•	•	•	•	•	•	•	•	•
Receivables Turnover 36	•	•	•	•	•	•	•	•	•	•	•	•	•
Total Liabilities to Net Worth 37	15.9	•	0.4	2.3	0.6	0.6	1.4	0.8	1.1	1.3	0.9	2.4	18.2
Current Assets to Working Capital 38	11.2	•	1.3	2.7	1.4	1.2	2.0	2.0	2.8	3.3	2.0	18.7	11.5
Current Liabilities to Working Capital 39	10.2	•	0.3	1.7	0.4	0.2	1.0	1.0	1.8	2.3	1.0	17.7	10.5
Working Capital to Net Sales 40	1.1	•	0.3	0.0	0.3	0.7	0.2	0.4	0.3	0.3	0.6	0.2	1.3
Inventory to Working Capital 41	0.0	•	•	•	•	•	•	0.0	0.0	0.0	•	0.0	0.0
Total Receipts to Cash Flow 42	2.6	1.2	3.0	2.4	2.7	3.7	1.7	3.6	2.6	2.4	5.4	2.8	2.7
Cost of Goods to Cash Flow 43	0.0	•	•	•	1.0	•	0.0	•	•	0.0	0.0	0.0	0.0
Cash Flow to Total Debt 44	0.0	•	2.8	2.0	1.7	0.6	1.5	0.5	0.5	0.5	0.2	0.1	0.0

Selected Financial Factors (in Percentages)

Debt Ratio 45	94.1	•	27.6	69.5	38.5	37.0	58.7	44.5	53.3	56.6	48.6	70.9	94.8
Return on Total Assets 46	2.0	•	14.2	48.7	4.1	4.5	•	6.4	3.6	1.6	2.3	3.4	2.0
Return on Equity Before Income Taxes 47	10.7	•	18.9	139.2	5.7	7.0	•	10.7	5.3	2.0	2.5	8.2	11.0
Return on Equity After Income Taxes 48	8.6	•	18.9	139.0	5.4	4.8	•	8.0	3.2	0.6	•	5.4	9.0
Profit Margin (Before Income Tax) 49	10.6	14.6	6.1	12.6	1.9	5.3	•	8.0	3.4	1.4	2.0	10.9	11.7
Profit Margin (After Income Tax) 50	8.6	11.8	6.1	12.6	1.8	3.6	•	6.0	2.1	0.4	•	7.1	9.6

Table II
Corporations with Net Income

SECURITIES BROKERAGE

MONEY AMOUNTS AND SIZE OF ASSETS IN THOUSANDS OF DOLLARS

Item Description for Accounting Period 7/09 Through 6/10	Total	Zero Assets	Under 500	500 to 1,000	1,000 to 5,000	5,000 to 10,000	10,000 to 25,000	25,000 to 50,000	50,000 to 100,000	100,000 to 250,000	250,000 to 500,000	500,000 to 2,500,000	2,500,000 and over
Number of Enterprises **1**	4520	399	3088	427	404	68	46	30	12	10	0	15	21
Revenues ($ in Thousands)													
Net Sales **2**	75807677	334022	987062	860808	1518629	356368	976292	936192	737400	1275965	0	3703585	64121354
Interest **3**	31763947	4690	105	2	2249	1680	6937	2681	13753	15590	0	166792	31549468
Rents **4**	142201	0	0	0	0	0	6454	0	5642	21	0	2320	127764
Royalties **5**	36394	0	0	0	0	0	5774	0	0	0	0	1349	29271
Other Portfolio Income **6**	791797	24073	0	0	787	9179	43626	27193	56972	10282	0	29636	590047
Other Receipts **7**	43073338	305259	986957	860806	1515593	345509	913501	906318	661033	1250072	0	3503488	31824804
Total Receipts **8**	75807677	334022	987062	860808	1518629	356368	976292	936192	737400	1275965	0	3703585	64121354
Average Total Receipts **9**	16772	837	320	2016	3759	5241	21224	31206	61450	127596	•	246906	3053398
Operating Costs/Operating Income (%)													
Cost of Operations **10**	0.0	•		•	•	•	•	0.5	•	•	•	0.1	0.0
Salaries and Wages **11**	18.9	1.9	14.4	38.2	24.2	42.8	15.7	44.2	46.5	40.3	•	39.1	16.3
Taxes Paid **12**	2.0	0.5	4.0	2.5	2.3	3.6	2.1	4.2	4.0	6.8	•	3.6	1.7
Interest Paid **13**	24.8	2.6	1.1	0.3	0.2	0.2	1.1	0.6	1.0	1.0	•	5.0	28.9
Depreciation **14**	1.0	0.0	0.3	0.2	0.1	0.4	0.7	0.6	1.1	2.0	•	1.7	1.0
Amortization and Depletion **15**	0.6	0.0	0.0	•	•	0.2	0.0	0.9	0.2	0.2	•	0.8	0.6
Pensions and Other Deferred Comp. **16**	0.5	0.0	0.3	0.1	0.3	0.2	0.0	0.5	0.2	0.6	•	0.6	0.6
Employee Benefits **17**	1.1	0.1	1.7	2.2	0.6	1.1	0.4	1.2	0.1	1.7	•	1.5	1.1
Advertising **18**	0.9	0.3	0.8	0.0	0.1	0.1	0.3	0.2	0.7	0.7	•	1.0	1.0
Other Expenses **19**	29.8	76.8	31.7	22.6	43.5	10.7	65.5	19.1	24.4	26.8	•	28.9	29.2
Officers' Compensation **20**	4.8	2.2	22.0	15.7	16.6	14.8	4.3	11.9	4.7	1.4	•	1.5	4.3
Operating Margin **21**	15.5	15.5	23.7	18.3	12.1	24.3	8.9	16.2	15.7	18.5	•	16.3	15.4
Operating Margin Before Officers' Comp. **22**	20.4	17.7	45.7	34.0	28.7	39.1	13.2	28.1	20.4	20.0	•	17.8	19.7

Selected Average Balance Sheet ($ in Thousands)

Net Receivables 23	62326	0	1	224	243	334	791	1145	14255	41677	398570	13088493
Inventories 24	•	•	•	•	•	•	•	•	•	•	•	•
Net Property, Plant and Equipment 25	629	0	8	13	68	48	1230	1079	1607	8964	10128	115801
Total Assets 26	300669	0	96	724	2228	8456	16659	35200	66198	199541	1245436	63507238
Notes and Loans Payable 27	49304	0	23	0	155	84	2346	2276	12168	39996	69606	10521498
All Other Liabilities 28	235494	0	9	149	755	3588	6004	11569	27131	65040	826562	49990174
Net Worth 29	15871	0	64	574	1317	4784	8309	21355	26899	94506	349268	2995565

Selected Financial Ratios (Times to 1)

Current Ratio 30	1.2	•	1.3	4.2	3.6	7.4	2.2	2.0	1.4	1.7	•	1.0	1.2
Quick Ratio 31	0.5	•	1.1	4.0	2.5	6.7	1.3	1.1	0.9	1.4	•	0.9	0.5
Net Sales to Working Capital 32	0.5	•	44.5	4.2	3.2	1.2	3.5	2.8	5.8	2.5	•	6.6	0.4
Coverage Ratio 33	1.6	6.9	22.8	68.0	59.6	151.1	8.2	30.0	15.8	19.5	•	4.2	1.5
Total Asset Turnover 34	0.1	•	3.3	2.8	1.7	0.6	1.3	0.9	0.9	0.6	•	0.2	0.0
Inventory Turnover 35	•	•	•	•	•	•	•	•	•	•	•	•	•
Receivables Turnover 36	•	•	•	•	•	•	•	•	•	•	•	•	•
Total Liabilities to Net Worth 37	17.9	•	0.5	0.3	0.7	0.8	1.0	0.6	1.5	1.1	•	2.6	20.2
Current Assets to Working Capital 38	6.5	•	4.2	1.3	1.4	1.2	1.9	2.0	3.6	2.5	•	22.3	6.6
Current Liabilities to Working Capital 39	5.5	•	3.2	0.3	0.4	0.2	0.9	1.0	2.6	1.5	•	21.3	5.6
Working Capital to Net Sales 40	2.1	•	0.0	0.2	0.3	0.8	0.3	0.4	0.2	0.4	•	0.2	2.4
Inventory to Working Capital 41	0.0	•	•	•	•	•	•	0.0	0.0	•	•	0.0	0.0
Total Receipts to Cash Flow 42	2.4	1.2	2.3	2.6	1.9	3.2	1.5	3.3	2.7	2.4	•	2.4	2.4
Cost of Goods to Cash Flow 43	0.0	•	•	•	•	•	•	0.0	•	•	•	0.0	0.0
Cash Flow to Total Debt 44	0.0	•	4.3	5.1	2.2	0.5	1.7	0.7	0.6	0.5	•	0.1	0.0

Selected Financial Factors (in Percentages)

Debt Ratio 45	94.7	•	33.1	20.7	40.9	43.4	50.1	39.3	59.4	52.6	•	72.0	95.3
Return on Total Assets 46	2.3	•	82.6	51.9	20.8	14.1	12.0	14.8	14.7	12.0	•	4.2	2.1
Return on Equity Before Income Taxes 47	16.5	•	117.9	64.4	34.5	24.8	21.2	23.5	33.9	24.1	•	11.5	15.8
Return on Equity After Income Taxes 48	13.9	•	117.8	64.4	34.1	21.3	16.5	20.1	28.5	20.2	•	7.9	13.3
Profit Margin (Before Income Tax) 49	15.6	15.5	23.7	18.3	12.1	22.7	8.3	16.1	14.8	17.9	•	16.2	15.5
Profit Margin (After Income Tax) 50	13.1	12.6	23.7	18.3	11.9	19.4	6.5	13.7	12.5	15.0	•	11.2	13.1

Table I

Corporations with and without Net Income

COMMODITY CONTRACTS DEALING AND BROKERAGE

MONEY AMOUNTS AND SIZE OF ASSETS IN THOUSANDS OF DOLLARS

Item Description for Accounting Period 7/09 Through 6/10		Total	Zero Assets	Under 500	500 to 1,000	1,000 to 5,000	5,000 to 10,000	10,000 to 25,000	25,000 to 50,000	50,000 to 100,000	100,000 to 250,000	250,000 to 500,000	500,000 to 2,500,000	2,500,000 and over
Number of Enterprises	1	2109	389	1112	284	204	26	40	17	10	9	5	7	6
Revenues ($ in Thousands)														
Net Sales	2	4755842	232253	89044	47722	33319	116212	189125	136385	79145	302519	369012	355184	2803923
Interest	3	662134	605	0	200	388	143	535	2607	987	8496	6726	45832	595615
Rents	4	33907	3840	0	0	0	0	0	0	184	9762	38	111	19972
Royalties	5	240	0	0	0	0	0	0	0	0	0	168	0	71
Other Portfolio Income	6	116859	21	0	0	232	71	2916	12275	49188	589	448	8901	42220
Other Receipts	7	3940702	227787	89044	47522	32699	115998	185674	121503	28786	283672	361632	300340	2146045
Total Receipts	8	4755842	232253	89044	47722	33319	116212	189125	136385	79145	302519	369012	355184	2803923
Average Total Receipts	9	2254	597	80	168	163	4470	4728	8023	7914	33613	73802	50741	467320
Operating Costs/Operating Income (%)														
Cost of Operations	10	6.5	48.4	•	•	•	•	•	•	•	•	43.1	7.0	0.5
Salaries and Wages	11	24.4	12.2	16.1	3.8	28.7	14.1	28.7	59.2	29.4	17.6	18.7	30.0	25.1
Taxes Paid	12	2.0	0.8	2.1	2.6	6.2	1.8	6.1	5.3	4.2	3.2	1.8	3.6	1.3
Interest Paid	13	11.4	5.1	1.3	1.5	38.1	1.6	1.4	5.3	3.2	5.3	2.5	13.9	15.3
Depreciation	14	3.1	0.5	13.5	0.4	5.3	0.7	1.6	2.1	0.6	1.1	3.6	2.9	3.5
Amortization and Depletion	15	2.3	0.0	•	•	19.3	0.6	0.1	0.0	0.4	1.0	3.2	1.1	2.9
Pensions and Other Deferred Comp.	16	0.4	1.8	•	•	•	1.3	0.4	0.4	0.3	0.6	0.6	1.6	0.1
Employee Benefits	17	1.9	0.4	6.6	0.8	•	0.7	2.2	3.5	3.0	1.0	2.4	1.7	2.0
Advertising	18	0.5	0.1	3.5	•	1.8	4.8	1.6	0.1	0.0	0.0	0.1	0.7	0.3
Other Expenses	19	52.3	22.3	65.7	48.8	94.4	10.7	38.3	56.7	62.5	25.2	14.6	125.3	54.7
Officers' Compensation	20	4.1	3.6	23.6	17.5	24.1	4.9	4.7	7.3	5.2	9.1	2.9	3.8	2.4
Operating Margin	21	•	4.9	•	24.5	•	58.8	14.9	•	•	35.8	6.5	•	•
Operating Margin Before Officers' Comp.	22	•	8.4	•	42.0	•	63.7	19.6	•	•	44.9	9.5	•	•

Selected Average Balance Sheet ($ in Thousands)

Net Receivables 23	8268	0	0	87	382	3409	2814	2324	16120	36611	53140	352016	2310868
Inventories 24	•	•	•	•	•	•	•	•	•	•	•	•	•
Net Property, Plant and Equipment 25	218	65	3	12	351	377	1234	296	6269	1830	13630		29188
Total Assets 26	54344	121	702	2075	7915	15597	33970	71172	166549	343611	948821		16979360
Notes and Loans Payable 27	3620	97	0	638	1439	1732	7062	9978	30024	94246	126506		907014
All Other Liabilities 28	48174	21	10	496	3189	12256	11582	27851	72929	154033	844095		1551746
Net Worth 29	2550	3	692	941	3287	1609	15326	33343	63596	95332	-21780		557600

Selected Financial Ratios (Times to 1)

Current Ratio 30	1.3	0.5	21.8	3.4	1.9	1.5	1.6	1.6	1.0	1.0	0.8	1.0	1.3
Quick Ratio 31	0.6	0.4	21.3	1.5	1.6	0.8	0.8	0.9	0.6	0.7	0.7		0.6
Net Sales to Working Capital 32	0.2	•	0.8	0.1	1.6	1.4	1.6	0.4	13.9	•	28.5		0.1
Coverage Ratio 33	0.2	2.0	17.1	•	37.5	11.7	•	•	7.7	3.6	•		0.5
Total Asset Turnover 34	0.0	0.7	0.2	0.1	0.6	0.3	0.2	0.1	0.1	0.2	0.2	0.1	0.0
Inventory Turnover 35	•	•	•	•	•	•	•	•	•	•	•	•	•
Receivables Turnover 36	•	•	•	•	•	•	•	•	•	•	•	•	•
Total Liabilities to Net Worth 37	20.3	40.6	0.0	1.2	1.4	8.7	1.2	2.7	1.1	1.6	2.6	385.9	29.5
Current Assets to Working Capital 38	4.6	•	1.0	1.4	2.1	2.9	2.7	2.8	42.5	•	4.3		
Current Liabilities to Working Capital 39	3.6	•	0.0	0.4	1.1	1.9	1.7	1.8	41.5	384.9	3.3		
Working Capital to Net Sales 40	4.4	•	1.2	7.3	0.6	0.7	0.6	2.5	0.1	0.0	7.2		
Inventory to Working Capital 41	0.0	•	•	•	•	•	•	•	•	0.0	0.0		
Total Receipts to Cash Flow 42	2.6	3.8	4.0	1.4	1.5	2.6	154.6	2.2	1.7	5.7	3.6	2.3	
Cost of Goods to Cash Flow 43	0.2	1.8	•	•	•	•	•	•	•	2.5	0.3	0.0	
Cash Flow to Total Debt 44	0.0	0.2	11.7	0.2	0.7	0.1	0.0	0.1	0.2	0.1	0.0	0.0	

Selected Financial Factors (in Percentages)

Debt Ratio 45	95.3	97.6	1.4	54.7	58.5	89.7	54.9	53.2	61.8	72.3	102.3	96.7	
Return on Total Assets 46	0.1	•	6.2	•	34.1	5.1	•	•	8.3	1.9	•	0.2	
Return on Equity Before Income Taxes 47	•	•	5.9	•	79.9	45.4	•	•	19.0	5.1	213.0	•	
Return on Equity After Income Taxes 48	•	•	5.6	•	79.9	43.7	•	•	15.2	1.9	215.5	•	
Profit Margin (Before Income Tax) 49	•	4.9	24.5	•	58.8	15.4	•	•	35.9	6.5	•	•	
Profit Margin (After Income Tax) 50	•	3.4	22.9	•	58.8	14.9	•	•	28.8	2.5	•	•	

Table II

Corporations with Net Income

COMMODITY CONTRACTS DEALING AND BROKERAGE

MONEY AMOUNTS AND SIZE OF ASSETS IN THOUSANDS OF DOLLARS

Item Description for Accounting Period 7/09 Through 6/10	Total	Zero Assets	Under 500	500 to 1,000	1,000 to 5,000	5,000 to 10,000	10,000 to 25,000	25,000 to 50,000	50,000 to 100,000	100,000 to 250,000	250,000 to 500,000	500,000 to 2,500,000	2,500,000 and over
1 Number of Enterprises	771	382	0	284	32	22	21	10	5	•	•	3	0
Revenues ($ in Thousands)													
2 Net Sales	1920548	174224	0	47722	18636	115321	119131	157380	78311	•	•	609421	0
3 Interest	92270	1	0	200	219	106	20	63	987	•	•	76907	0
4 Rents	19847	3826	0	0	0	0	0	0	184	•	•	6041	0
5 Royalties	240	0	0	0	0	0	0	0	0	•	•	71	0
6 Other Portfolio Income	65374	0	0	0	48	71	2916	12270	49188	•	•	138	0
7 Other Receipts	1742817	170397	0	47522	18369	115144	116195	145047	27952	•	•	526264	0
8 Total Receipts	1920548	174224	0	47722	18636	115321	119131	157380	78311	•	•	609421	0
9 Average Total Receipts	2491	456	•	168	582	5242	5673	15738	15662	•	•	203140	•
Operating Costs/Operating Income (%)													
10 Cost of Operations	14.8	63.6	•	•	•	•	•	•	•	•	•	2.2	•
11 Salaries and Wages	18.9	1.2	•	3.8	•	14.2	15.9	32.2	7.8	•	•	30.1	•
12 Taxes Paid	1.9	0.6	•	2.6	0.2	1.9	4.4	3.2	2.9	•	•	1.0	•
13 Interest Paid	7.6	1.8	•	1.5	38.6	1.6	1.0	3.5	0.9	•	•	16.8	•
14 Depreciation	1.5	0.3	•	0.4	•	0.7	1.0	1.7	0.3	•	•	1.3	•
15 Amortization and Depletion	0.7	•	•	•	34.4	0.6	0.2	0.0	0.4	•	•	0.6	•
16 Pensions and Other Deferred Comp.	0.3	•	•	•	•	1.3	0.6	0.3	0.3	•	•	•	•
17 Employee Benefits	1.0	0.0	•	0.8	•	0.7	0.6	2.7	0.3	•	•	1.1	•
18 Advertising	0.3	•	•	•	•	4.8	0.0	0.1	0.0	•	•	0.1	•
19 Other Expenses	24.0	5.5	•	48.8	11.7	9.9	12.5	35.2	9.7	•	•	41.3	•
20 Officers' Compensation	3.6	0.5	•	17.5	•	5.0	3.8	5.3	2.8	•	•	1.4	•
21 Operating Margin	25.4	26.5	•	24.5	15.1	59.3	59.6	15.8	74.7	•	•	4.1	•
22 Operating Margin Before Officers' Comp.	29.0	27.0	•	42.0	15.1	64.3	63.4	21.2	77.5	•	•	5.5	•

Selected Average Balance Sheet ($ in Thousands)

Net Receivables 23	1909	•	87	591	3325	5176	3878	26744	194174
Inventories 24	•	0	•	•	•	•	•	•	•
Net Property, Plant and Equipment 25	209	0	3	0	415	108	1928	324	23013
Total Assets 26	26296	0	702	1913	7740	14339	31141	67404	5411812
Notes and Loans Payable 27	1425	0	0	1553	1697	688	11973	16171	96633
All Other Liabilities 28	22614	0	10	514	2714	9821	14344	17670	5235596
Net Worth 29	2258	0	692	-154	3329	3830	4824	33562	79582

Selected Financial Ratios (Times to 1)

Current Ratio 30	1.4	•	21.8	1.4	2.2	0.9	2.0	1.9	1.7
Quick Ratio 31	0.7	•	21.3	1.4	2.2	0.6	1.0	1.1	0.6
Net Sales to Working Capital 32	1.1	•	0.8	2.9	1.6	•	1.8	0.6	0.4
Coverage Ratio 33	4.4	15.9	17.1	1.4	37.6	62.3	5.5	83.0	1.2
Total Asset Turnover 34	0.1	•	0.2	0.3	0.7	0.4	0.5	0.2	0.0
Inventory Turnover 35	•	•	•	•	•	•	•	•	•
Receivables Turnover 36	•	•	•	•	•	•	•	•	•
Total Liabilities to Net Worth 37	10.6	•	0.0	•	1.3	2.7	5.5	1.0	67.0
Current Assets to Working Capital 38	3.4	•	1.0	3.5	1.8	•	2.0	2.1	2.5
Current Liabilities to Working Capital 39	2.4	•	0.0	2.5	0.8	•	1.0	1.1	1.5
Working Capital to Net Sales 40	0.9	•	1.2	0.4	0.6	•	0.5	1.7	2.5
Inventory to Working Capital 41	0.2	•	•	•	•	•	•	•	0.2
Total Receipts to Cash Flow 42	2.2	3.2	1.4	3.7	1.5	1.4	2.6	1.2	2.3
Cost of Goods to Cash Flow 43	0.3	2.0	•	•	•	•	•	•	0.1
Cash Flow to Total Debt 44	0.0	•	11.7	0.1	0.8	0.4	0.2	0.4	0.0

Selected Financial Factors (in Percentages)

Debt Ratio 45	91.4	•	1.4	108.0	57.0	73.3	84.5	50.2	98.5
Return on Total Assets 46	3.1	•	6.2	16.3	41.3	24.3	9.8	17.6	0.8
Return on Equity Before Income Taxes 47	28.1	•	5.9	•	93.4	89.5	51.6	34.8	10.4
Return on Equity After Income Taxes 48	24.9	•	5.6	•	93.4	88.2	48.7	32.4	6.9
Profit Margin (Before Income Tax) 49	25.5	26.5	24.5	14.8	59.3	60.4	15.8	74.7	4.1
Profit Margin (After Income Tax) 50	22.6	24.6	22.9	14.8	59.3	59.5	14.9	69.4	2.7

294

SECURITIES & COMMODITY EXCHANGES, OTHER FINANCIAL INVESTMENT

Table I

Corporations with and without Net Income

MONEY AMOUNTS AND SIZE OF ASSETS IN THOUSANDS OF DOLLARS

Item Description for Accounting Period 7/09 Through 6/10		Total	Zero Assets	Under 500	500 to 1,000	1,000 to 5,000	5,000 to 10,000	10,000 to 25,000	25,000 to 50,000	50,000 to 100,000	100,000 to 250,000	250,000 to 500,000	500,000 to 2,500,000	2,500,000 and over
Number of Enterprises	1	43285	7050	30009	1841	2500	701	534	248	162	97	49	57	36
Revenues ($ in Thousands)														
Net Sales	2	115390055	3215956	7186801	1480091	4275508	5075745	3545067	3349880	3909916	5720837	2264752	14404787	60960715
Interest	3	9832531	1012288	3219	5111	18799	18666	69985	62405	82920	202623	295707	510165	7550643
Rents	4	443314	136	5381	0	251718	191	11463	1543	16154	3132	7204	27429	118962
Royalties	5	83585	15	5689	86	2803	196	5150	0	2277	6537	2443	50	58339
Other Portfolio Income	6	3081039	86888	19527	13944	49569	26821	187378	428816	115436	89196	236945	321425	1505092
Other Receipts	7	101949586	2116629	7152985	1460950	3952619	5029871	3271091	2857116	3693129	5419349	1722453	13545718	51727679
Total Receipts	8	115390055	3215956	7186801	1480091	4275508	5075745	3545067	3349880	3909916	5720837	2264752	14404787	60960715
Average Total Receipts	9	2666	456	239	804	1710	7241	6639	13508	24135	58978	46219	252716	1693353
Operating Costs/Operating Income (%)														
Cost of Operations	10	1.8	2.0	•	•	0.1	1.1	0.1	0.3	0.9	0.2	0.0	0.5	3.0
Salaries and Wages	11	25.2	6.6	18.8	28.4	20.6	45.5	28.3	31.8	23.4	24.1	22.1	25.2	25.2
Taxes Paid	12	2.7	1.7	3.1	4.1	2.1	3.3	2.9	3.0	2.7	2.1	3.0	2.7	2.7
Interest Paid	13	9.5	4.7	0.4	0.4	1.3	1.8	2.3	3.2	3.3	4.8	13.0	6.4	14.5
Depreciation	14	2.0	1.0	0.9	1.2	1.0	2.7	1.6	2.5	2.5	1.9	2.6	2.1	2.1
Amortization and Depletion	15	2.1	4.1	0.1	0.1	0.2	0.6	0.8	0.7	0.8	1.9	4.1	2.9	2.5
Pensions and Other Deferred Comp.	16	1.4	1.0	1.8	3.9	0.8	0.6	1.3	0.7	1.4	1.0	0.4	0.7	1.7
Employee Benefits	17	1.9	0.7	2.2	3.3	1.4	2.0	2.1	1.8	1.8	1.4	2.0	1.6	2.1
Advertising	18	1.1	0.2	1.2	1.6	0.2	0.2	0.4	0.3	1.3	0.6	0.1	0.8	1.4
Other Expenses	19	37.1	81.4	37.0	27.5	36.8	25.5	32.7	26.8	44.9	42.7	45.0	51.8	32.0
Officers' Compensation	20	7.3	4.4	26.5	24.4	14.7	20.4	13.8	15.9	11.4	10.4	1.9	5.8	2.4
Operating Margin	21	7.9	•	7.9	5.1	20.9	•	13.8	12.9	5.6	8.9	5.8	•	10.4
Operating Margin Before Officers' Comp.	22	15.3	•	34.4	29.5	35.6	16.7	27.6	28.7	17.0	19.3	7.8	5.2	12.8

Selected Average Balance Sheet ($ in Thousands)

Net Receivables 23	1080	0	3	85	286	541	1512	4302	5910	14621	54472	103028	906377
Inventories 24	•	•	•	•	•	•	•	•	•	•	•	•	•
Net Property, Plant and Equipment 25	417	0	12	72	154	891	998	2141	5356	8549	8393	33023	318785
Total Assets 26	14927	0	68	711	2351	7061	15488	35184	70677	158152	375231	1025011	14203484
Notes and Loans Payable 27	3235	0	26	170	923	2155	4978	8785	18243	40051	103054	293685	2823214
All Other Liabilities 28	6400	0	20	130	495	1493	2550	5475	12807	48215	84500	297290	6759314
Net Worth 29	5293	0	23	411	933	3413	7959	20924	39627	69887	187677	434036	4620956

Selected Financial Ratios (Times to 1)

Current Ratio 30	0.9	•	2.7	2.1	3.2	1.8	1.4	2.2	2.0	1.7	1.6	1.2	0.8
Quick Ratio 31	0.6	•	1.9	1.5	2.1	1.2	1.0	1.6	1.3	1.1	1.2	0.7	0.5
Net Sales to Working Capital 32	•	•	8.6	6.4	2.5	7.5	4.8	1.9	2.0	2.6	0.9	5.2	1.8
Coverage Ratio 33	1.9	•	18.7	12.5	17.4	•	6.9	5.0	2.7	2.8	1.4	0.9	1.8
Total Asset Turnover 34	0.2	•	3.5	1.1	0.7	1.0	0.4	0.4	0.3	0.4	0.1	0.2	0.1
Inventory Turnover 35	•	•	•	•	•	•	•	•	•	•	•	•	•
Receivables Turnover 36	•	•	•	•	•	•	•	•	•	•	•	•	•
Total Liabilities to Net Worth 37	1.8	•	2.0	0.7	1.5	1.1	0.9	0.7	0.8	1.3	1.0	1.4	2.1
Current Assets to Working Capital 38	•	•	1.6	1.9	1.5	2.3	3.5	1.8	2.0	2.5	2.7	7.3	•
Current Liabilities to Working Capital 39	•	•	0.6	0.9	0.5	1.3	2.5	0.8	1.0	1.5	1.7	6.3	•
Working Capital to Net Sales 40	•	•	0.1	0.2	0.4	0.1	0.2	0.5	0.5	0.4	1.1	0.2	•
Inventory to Working Capital 41	•	•	0.0	0.0	0.0	0.0	0.0	0.0	0.0	0.0	0.0	0.1	•
Total Receipts to Cash Flow 42	2.5	1.5	2.7	3.9	2.1	5.7	2.6	4.1	2.2	2.1	2.6	2.1	2.6
Cost of Goods to Cash Flow 43	0.0	0.0	•	0.0	0.0	0.1	0.0	0.0	0.0	0.0	0.0	0.0	0.1
Cash Flow to Total Debt 44	0.1	0.7	2.0	0.7	0.6	0.4	0.3	0.2	0.4	0.3	0.1	0.2	0.1

Selected Financial Factors (in Percentages)

Debt Ratio 45	64.5	•	66.9	42.2	60.3	51.7	48.6	40.5	43.9	55.8	50.0	57.7	67.5
Return on Total Assets 46	3.2	•	29.4	6.3	16.1	6.9	6.1	3.0	5.1	2.3	1.4	•	3.0
Return on Equity Before Income Taxes 47	4.1	•	84.1	10.0	38.4	11.4	8.2	3.3	7.4	•	•	1.4	4.0
Return on Equity After Income Taxes 48	2.5	•	83.1	8.7	36.7	8.8	4.5	•	5.9	6.3	•	0.2	2.6
Profit Margin (Before Income Tax) 49	8.2	•	7.9	5.1	20.9	13.7	12.8	5.5	8.8	5.7	•	5.7	11.0
Profit Margin (After Income Tax) 50	4.9	•	7.8	4.5	20.0	10.5	7.0	0.9	7.0	0.8	•	0.8	7.0

Table II
Corporations with Net Income

SECURITIES & COMMODITY EXCHANGES, OTHER FINANCIAL INVESTMENT

MONEY AMOUNTS AND SIZE OF ASSETS IN THOUSANDS OF DOLLARS

Item Description for Accounting Period 7/09 Through 6/10		Total	Zero Assets	Under 500	500 to 1,000	1,000 to 5,000	5,000 to 10,000	10,000 to 25,000	25,000 to 50,000	50,000 to 100,000	100,000 to 250,000	250,000 to 500,000	500,000 to 2,500,000	2,500,000 and over
Number of Enterprises	1	22877	2326	17085	1258	1418	250	237	109	65	51	26	29	22
Revenues ($ in Thousands)														
Net Sales	2	87939855	1877647	4678003	1442917	3323460	2496650	2753783	2859670	3569755	4432971	1601873	9315715	49587409
Interest	3	8523156	968298	565	3044	6176	2820	60477	28690	54040	73870	79693	238789	7006693
Rents	4	156936	18	3741	0	7	0	7188	572	15761	1334	1133	10925	116256
Royalties	5	47880	14	0	0	0	0	0	0	303	341	2435	0	44787
Other Portfolio Income	6	2345915	80564	18537	1819	41397	1678	148728	416652	95354	71033	107193	139135	1223822
Other Receipts	7	76865968	828753	4655160	1438054	3275880	2492152	2537390	2413756	3404297	4286393	1411419	8926866	41195851
Total Receipts	8	87939855	1877647	4678003	1442917	3323460	2496650	2753783	2859670	3569755	4432971	1601873	9315715	49587409
Average Total Receipts	9	3844	807	274	1147	2344	9987	11619	26236	54919	86921	61610	321232	2253973
Operating Costs/Operating Income (%)														
Cost of Operations	10	0.7	3.1	•	•	•	0.4	0.0	0.2	1.0	•	0.0	0.7	1.0
Salaries and Wages	11	23.8	5.8	14.2	25.3	20.0	40.7	23.0	27.6	18.5	20.6	24.2	23.6	25.2
Taxes Paid	12	2.7	2.0	2.8	3.9	1.9	2.4	2.8	2.7	2.2	1.9	3.0	2.9	2.8
Interest Paid	13	9.2	4.5	0.5	0.2	0.6	0.9	1.2	1.5	1.2	3.1	5.9	5.3	14.3
Depreciation	14	1.9	1.3	1.1	1.2	0.9	1.1	0.8	2.0	1.3	1.4	1.1	2.4	2.2
Amortization and Depletion	15	1.2	1.6	0.1	0.1	0.1	0.6	0.3	0.5	0.3	0.6	3.4	2.6	1.3
Pensions and Other Deferred Comp.	16	1.5	0.7	1.5	2.5	0.8	1.1	1.0	0.5	1.3	0.7	0.5	0.9	1.9
Employee Benefits	17	1.9	0.7	2.2	3.3	1.1	2.8	2.0	1.5	1.4	0.6	2.0	1.7	2.1
Advertising	18	1.1	0.1	0.9	1.7	0.3	0.2	0.3	0.3	1.3	0.6	0.1	0.6	1.6
Other Expenses	19	29.0	45.5	31.6	21.4	25.9	23.5	20.5	16.2	34.4	37.6	33.0	34.2	27.7
Officers' Compensation	20	6.0	3.5	23.0	24.9	10.4	8.3	14.8	16.2	10.6	12.0	2.0	4.2	2.0
Operating Margin	21	21.0	31.2	22.0	15.7	37.8	18.0	33.3	31.0	26.6	20.9	24.9	20.8	17.9
Operating Margin Before Officers' Comp.	22	27.0	34.7	45.0	40.6	48.3	26.3	48.1	47.2	37.2	32.9	26.9	25.0	19.9

Selected Average Balance Sheet ($ in Thousands)

Net Receivables 23	1588	•	3	80	227	828	1753	3970	7571	20595	52659	99545	1317995
Inventories 24	•	•	•	•	•	•	•	•	•	•	•	•	•
Net Property, Plant and Equipment 25	591	0	14	104	212	587	692	3527	4273	6708	3686	49965	453706
Total Assets 26	20221	0	78	714	2379	6316	15815	34537	70773	155134	377816	1143568	17835866
Notes and Loans Payable 27	4290	0	19	151	835	1738	3324	6055	13544	33748	77785	338813	3641016
All Other Liabilities 28	9707	0	19	129	592	1515	2883	7493	13009	57300	102423	235747	9345444
Net Worth 29	6224	0	41	433	952	3063	9608	20989	44220	64085	197608	569008	4849406

Selected Financial Ratios (Times to 1)

Current Ratio 30	0.9	•	3.0	1.8	3.9	2.7	2.1	2.0	2.0	1.9	1.4	1.4	0.8
Quick Ratio 31	0.5	•	2.4	1.5	2.4	2.0	1.5	1.7	1.4	1.2	0.9	0.9	0.4
Net Sales to Working Capital 32	•	•	8.3	11.6	2.7	4.9	3.8	3.3	4.0	2.3	1.9	3.1	•
Coverage Ratio 33	3.3	8.0	48.3	66.9	65.0	20.7	30.0	22.3	22.5	7.7	5.2	4.9	2.3
Total Asset Turnover 34	0.2	•	3.5	1.6	1.0	1.6	0.7	0.8	0.8	0.6	0.2	0.3	0.1
Inventory Turnover 35	•	•	•	•	•	•	•	•	•	•	•	•	•
Receivables Turnover 36	•	•	•	•	•	•	•	•	•	•	•	•	•
Total Liabilities to Net Worth 37	2.2	•	0.9	0.6	1.5	1.1	0.6	0.6	0.6	1.4	0.9	1.0	2.7
Current Assets to Working Capital 38	•	•	1.5	2.3	1.3	1.6	1.9	2.0	2.0	2.1	3.7	3.8	•
Current Liabilities to Working Capital 39	•	•	0.5	1.3	0.3	0.6	0.9	1.0	1.0	1.1	2.7	2.8	•
Working Capital to Net Sales 40	•	•	0.1	0.1	0.4	0.2	0.3	0.3	0.3	0.4	0.5	0.3	•
Inventory to Working Capital 41	•	•	•	•	•	•	•	•	•	•	•	•	•
Total Receipts to Cash Flow 42	2.2	1.4	2.1	3.1	1.7	2.6	2.1	3.2	1.8	1.8	2.0	1.9	2.3
Cost of Goods to Cash Flow 43	0.0	0.0	•	•	•	0.0	0.0	0.0	0.0	0.0	0.0	0.0	0.0
Cash Flow to Total Debt 44	0.1	3.5	1.3	1.0	1.0	1.2	0.9	0.6	1.2	0.5	0.2	0.3	0.1

Selected Financial Factors (in Percentages)

Debt Ratio 45	69.2	•	47.8	39.4	60.0	51.5	39.3	39.2	37.5	58.7	47.7	50.2	72.8
Return on Total Assets 46	5.8	•	78.6	25.6	37.9	30.0	25.4	24.6	21.6	13.4	5.0	7.3	4.2
Return on Equity Before Income Taxes 47	13.3	•	147.6	41.6	93.2	58.9	40.4	38.7	33.0	28.2	7.7	11.7	8.7
Return on Equity After Income Taxes 48	10.6	•	146.6	39.8	90.3	57.8	35.5	30.3	26.8	25.0	5.5	8.7	6.5
Profit Margin (Before Income Tax) 49	21.5	31.1	22.0	15.7	37.8	18.1	33.4	31.0	26.5	20.8	24.6	20.7	18.8
Profit Margin (After Income Tax) 50	17.1	23.3	21.9	15.0	36.7	17.7	29.3	24.2	21.6	18.5	17.7	15.5	13.9

Table I

Corporations with and without Net Income

LIFE INSURANCE

MONEY AMOUNTS AND SIZE OF ASSETS IN THOUSANDS OF DOLLARS

Item Description for Accounting Period 7/09 Through 6/10	Total	Zero Assets	Under 500	500 to 1,000	1,000 to 5,000	5,000 to 10,000	10,000 to 25,000	25,000 to 50,000	50,000 to 100,000	100,000 to 250,000	250,000 to 500,000	500,000 to 2,500,000	2,500,000 and over
Number of Enterprises **1**	866	36	185	77	120	58	76	55	33	32	39	66	90
Revenues ($ in Thousands)													
Net Sales **2**	1097834761	82375777	30912	23303	82306	94281	503629	692274	1171333	1542553	4640945	23806797	982870651
Interest **3**	166051936	155254	1774	943	8767	11711	32009	64296	82345	186808	507586	3345770	161654673
Rents **4**	8779668	1877	0	0	48	273	1731	3230	4899	7474	11007	26507	8722622
Royalties **5**	33089	0	0	0	0	0	1	0	0	821	10	12271	19986
Other Portfolio Income **6**	15244406	10661	134	209	1397	1809	4119	8341	13001	9683	44566	140866	15009616
Other Receipts **7**	907725662	82207985	29004	22151	72094	80488	465769	616407	1071088	1337767	4077776	20281383	797463754
Total Receipts **8**	1097834761	82375777	30912	23303	82306	94281	503629	692274	1171333	1542553	4640945	23806797	982870651
Average Total Receipts **9**	1267708	2288216	167	303	686	1626	6627	12587	35495	48205	118999	360709	10920785
Operating Costs/Operating Income (%)													
Cost of Operations **10**	47.6	0.9	30.7	36.5	41.8	26.1	45.5	45.0	35.4	47.2	41.7	48.8	51.6
Salaries and Wages **11**	1.8	*	*	*	*	*	*	0.4	1.4	0.5	1.6	0.5	2.0
Taxes Paid **12**	0.7	0.0	1.4	0.6	1.0	3.0	1.9	1.6	1.4	1.5	1.5	0.7	0.8
Interest Paid **13**	4.2	0.0	0.3	0.3	0.2	0.2	0.5	0.6	0.1	0.4	0.5	0.4	4.7
Depreciation **14**	0.7	0.0	0.0	0.1	0.0	0.4	0.2	0.6	0.7	0.3	0.3	0.2	0.7
Amortization and Depletion **15**	1.1	0.0	3.6	0.8	1.3	1.6	1.6	2.9	2.3	4.0	2.2	1.5	1.1
Pensions and Other Deferred Comp. **16**	0.5	0.0	*	0.0	0.1	0.8	0.5	0.6	1.1	0.6	0.6	0.5	0.5
Employee Benefits **17**	0.3	0.0	*	*	0.1	0.1	0.3	0.6	0.7	0.4	0.3	0.2	0.3
Advertising **18**	0.2	0.0	*	*	0.0	0.1	0.1	0.4	0.2	0.1	0.1	0.4	0.2
Other Expenses **19**	42.5	98.9	34.8	47.5	39.0	60.7	44.1	38.3	36.4	44.3	50.5	45.7	37.7
Officers' Compensation **20**	0.1	*	0.0	*	*	0.1	*	0.1	0.1	0.1	0.4	0.1	0.1
Operating Margin **21**	0.4	0.1	29.2	14.3	16.4	6.8	5.2	9.0	20.4	0.7	0.3	1.0	0.4
Operating Margin Before Officers' Comp. **22**	0.5	0.1	29.2	14.3	16.4	6.9	5.2	9.1	20.4	0.8	0.6	1.1	0.4

Selected Average Balance Sheet ($ in Thousands)

Net Receivables 23	125163	0	7	32	70	43	1519	1882	708	5114	4491	15622	1186267
Inventories 24	•												•
Net Property, Plant and Equipment 25	66914	0	0	0	2	59	64	157	1262	1262	1910	3171	639610
Total Assets 26	6952521	•	192	778	2320	6668	15956	35496	73860	159995	362893	1273262	65680138
Notes and Loans Payable 27	219850	0	0	0	0	0	61	138	97	1086	3060	5202	2109751
All Other Liabilities 28	5849959	0	135	396	1194	3916	9419	22140	61004	136212	290199	1073932	55279289
Net Worth 29	882712	0	57	382	1127	2751	6476	13217	12759	22697	69634	194129	8291098

Selected Financial Ratios (Times to 1)

Current Ratio 30	0.4	•	7.0	15.7	3.6	14.5	1.7	2.9	2.4	1.2	1.3	1.0	0.4
Quick Ratio 31	0.3	•	6.2	11.6	2.7	13.6	1.3	2.1	1.7	0.9	0.9	0.7	0.3
Net Sales to Working Capital 32	•	•	1.2	0.5	0.6	0.1	2.3	1.1	2.3	7.2	3.4	•	•
Coverage Ratio 33	1.5	61.8	113.3	46.2	97.0	43.7	11.9	14.6	205.6	3.4	1.1	3.2	1.5
Total Asset Turnover 34	0.2	•	0.9	0.4	0.3	0.2	0.4	0.4	0.5	0.3	0.3	0.3	0.2
Inventory Turnover 35	•	•	•	•	•	•	•	•	•	•	•	•	•
Receivables Turnover 36	•	•	•	•	•	•	•	•	•	•	•	•	•
Total Liabilities to Net Worth 37	6.9	•	2.4	1.0	1.1	1.4	1.5	1.7	4.8	6.0	4.2	5.6	6.9
Current Assets to Working Capital 38	•	•	1.2	1.1	1.4	1.1	2.4	1.5	1.7	7.0	6.0	•	•
Current Liabilities to Working Capital 39	0.2	•	0.5	0.6	0.1	0.4	0.1	0.5	0.7	6.0	3.4	•	•
Working Capital to Net Sales 40	0.8	•	1.8	1.5	8.9	0.4	0.4	0.9	0.4	0.1	0.3	•	•
Inventory to Working Capital 41	•	•	•	•	•	•	•	•	•	•	•	•	•
Total Receipts to Cash Flow 42	2.4	1.0	1.6	1.6	1.8	1.5	2.1	2.2	1.8	2.3	2.0	2.2	2.7
Cost of Goods to Cash Flow 43	1.1	0.0	0.5	0.6	0.8	0.4	0.9	1.0	0.6	1.1	0.8	1.1	1.4
Cash Flow to Total Debt 44	0.1	•	0.8	0.5	0.3	0.3	0.3	0.3	0.2	0.2	0.2	0.2	0.1

Selected Financial Factors (in Percentages)

Debt Ratio 45	87.3	•	70.4	50.9	51.4	58.7	59.4	62.8	82.7	85.8	80.8	84.8	87.4
Return on Total Assets 46	1.2	•	25.5	5.6	4.8	1.6	2.3	3.3	9.8	0.4	0.2	0.3	1.2
Return on Equity Before Income Taxes 47	3.3	•	85.6	11.1	9.9	3.9	5.3	8.3	56.5	1.8	0.1	1.6	3.3
Return on Equity After Income Taxes 48	2.2	•	75.0	9.9	8.6	2.4	4.0	5.7	35.3	•	•	•	2.2
Profit Margin (Before Income Tax) 49	2.3	0.1	29.1	14.0	16.2	6.6	5.1	8.7	20.3	0.9	0.0	0.9	2.5
Profit Margin (After Income Tax) 50	1.5	0.1	25.5	12.5	14.1	4.1	3.9	6.0	12.7	0.2	•	•	1.7

Table II
Corporations with Net Income

LIFE INSURANCE

MONEY AMOUNTS AND SIZE OF ASSETS IN THOUSANDS OF DOLLARS

Item Description for Accounting Period 7/09 Through 6/10		Total	Zero Assets	Under 500	500 to 1,000	1,000 to 5,000	5,000 to 10,000	10,000 to 25,000	25,000 to 50,000	50,000 to 100,000	100,000 to 250,000	250,000 to 500,000	500,000 to 2,500,000	2,500,000 and over
Number of Enterprises	1	628	18	134	53	92	43	58	45	21	21	30	47	65
Revenues ($ in Thousands)														
Net Sales	2	881099126	81186053	26519	11732	79489	85655	333298	638958	749924	1045775	4021012	14606279	778314430
Interest	3	140135574	140593	1732	629	8119	9661	25159	61235	56218	112447	441642	2568959	136709179
Rents	4	7994455	1877	0	0	48	204	1256	2831	2040	6250	11007	25774	7943170
Royalties	5	27514	0	0	0	0	0	1	0	0	3	10	12265	15235
Other Portfolio Income	6	11671140	10517	134	127	1116	1449	3248	9066	9548	7081	39965	90599	11498290
Other Receipts	7	721270443	81033066	24653	10976	70206	74341	303634	565826	682118	919994	3528388	11908682	622148556
Total Receipts	8	881099126	81186053	26519	11732	79489	85655	333298	638958	749924	1045775	4021012	14606279	778314430
Average Total Receipts	9	1403024	4510336	198	221	864	1992	5747	14199	35711	49799	134034	310772	11974068
Operating Costs/Operating Income (%)														
Cost of Operations	10	43.8	0.9	19.5	28.6	36.2	24.7	37.3	46.6	23.5	44.6	41.2	39.4	48.4
Salaries and Wages	11	2.0	•	•	•	•	•	•	0.4	2.2	0.6	1.8	0.6	2.2
Taxes Paid	12	0.8	0.0	1.5	0.7	1.0	2.3	1.7	1.3	1.1	1.2	1.6	1.0	0.8
Interest Paid	13	4.9	0.0	0.1	0.6	0.2	0.2	0.6	0.1	0.1	0.4	0.6	0.4	5.6
Depreciation	14	0.7	0.0	0.0	0.1	0.1	0.4	0.2	0.5	0.5	0.2	0.3	0.3	0.8
Amortization and Depletion	15	1.0	0.0	4.0	0.4	1.0	0.7	1.8	2.6	1.7	2.5	2.3	1.8	1.1
Pensions and Other Deferred Comp.	16	0.5	0.0	•	0.0	0.1	0.1	0.5	0.6	0.7	0.6	0.6	0.7	0.6
Employee Benefits	17	0.3	0.0	•	•	0.1	0.1	0.2	0.6	0.7	0.1	0.3	0.2	0.3
Advertising	18	0.2	0.0	•	•	0.0	0.2	0.1	0.4	0.1	0.1	0.2	0.7	0.2
Other Expenses	19	44.1	98.9	35.9	31.4	37.2	53.9	47.3	34.4	32.8	42.6	43.8	46.6	38.3
Officers' Compensation	20	0.1	•	•	•	•	0.1	•	0.1	0.1	0.1	0.5	0.2	0.1
Operating Margin	21	1.6	0.1	38.9	38.1	24.1	17.4	10.3	12.5	36.5	7.0	6.9	8.1	1.6
Operating Margin Before Officers' Comp.	22	1.7	0.1	38.9	38.1	24.1	17.5	10.3	12.6	36.6	7.1	7.3	8.3	1.6

Selected Average Balance Sheet ($ in Thousands)

	C1	C2	C3	C4	C5	C6	C7	C8	C9	C10	C11	C12	C13
Net Receivables 23	148961	0	7	47	92	49	1940	1376	718	6648	5238	16317	1419694
Inventories 24	•	•	•	•	•	•	•	•	•	•	•	•	•
Net Property, Plant and Equipment 25	83257	0	0	0	2	50	72	169	1222	1120	2430	3323	799891
Total Assets 26	7353328	212	772	2545	6696	16040	38149	74849	154130	370653	1300745		69809055
Notes and Loans Payable 27	270646	0	0	0	0	80	124	153	1156	3978	5464		2608491
All Other Liabilities 28	6095199	149	333	1435	3713	8666	23994	58710	128814	285049	1044134		57912455
Net Worth 29	987483	63	439	1110	2983	7294	14030	15986	24161	81626	251147		9288109

Selected Financial Ratios (Times to 1)

	C1	C2	C3	C4	C5	C6	C7	C8	C9	C10	C11	C12	C13
Current Ratio 30	0.4	•	8.1	22.8	4.0	3.3	2.7	2.0	1.0	2.5	1.0	1.6	1.1 / 0.4
Quick Ratio 31	0.3	•	7.1	17.1	3.2	2.4	2.1	1.3	0.8	2.1	0.8	1.1	0.8 / 0.3
Net Sales to Working Capital 32	•	•	1.3	0.4	0.8	1.3	1.7	2.2	23.5	2.3	6.4	•	
Coverage Ratio 33	1.8	74.0	429.3	67.7	138.4	102.2	19.3	174.8	305.8	19.6	12.0	20.6	1.8
Total Asset Turnover 34	0.2	•	0.9	0.3	0.3	0.3	0.4	0.4	0.5	0.3	0.4	0.2	0.2
Inventory Turnover 35	•	•	•	•	•	•	•	•	•	•	•	•	•
Receivables Turnover 36	•	•	•	•	•	•	•	•	•	•	•	•	•
Total Liabilities to Net Worth 37	6.4	•	2.4	0.8	1.3	1.2	1.7	3.7	5.4	3.5	4.2	6.5	
Current Assets to Working Capital 38	•	•	1.1	1.0	1.3	1.4	2.0	1.6	22.2	2.7	8.6	•	
Current Liabilities to Working Capital 39	•	•	0.1	0.0	0.3	0.4	1.0	0.6	21.2	1.7	7.6	•	
Working Capital to Net Sales 40	•	•	0.8	2.7	1.3	1.3	0.6	0.5	0.0	0.4	0.2	•	
Inventory to Working Capital 41	•	•	•	•	•	•	•	•	•	•	•	•	
Total Receipts to Cash Flow 42	2.2	1.0	1.3	1.5	1.7	1.4	1.8	2.2	2.1	2.0	1.8	2.6	
Cost of Goods to Cash Flow 43	1.0	0.0	0.3	0.4	0.6	0.3	0.7	1.0	0.9	0.8	0.7	1.2	
Cash Flow to Total Debt 44	0.1	•	1.0	0.5	0.4	0.4	0.4	0.3	0.2	0.2	0.2	0.1	

Selected Financial Factors (in Percentages)

	C1	C2	C3	C4	C5	C6	C7	C8	C9	C10	C11	C12	C13
Debt Ratio 45	86.6	•	70.3	43.2	56.4	55.4	54.5	63.2	78.6	84.3	78.0	80.7	86.7
Return on Total Assets 46	1.7	•	36.3	11.1	8.2	5.1	4.6	17.4	2.4	2.6	2.0	1.7	
Return on Equity Before Income Taxes 47	5.7	•	122.0	19.2	18.7	11.4	8.1	12.4	81.3	14.7	10.9	9.8	5.5
Return on Equity After Income Taxes 48	4.3	108.9	17.7	16.7	9.6	6.7	9.4	54.7	10.4	8.0	6.8	4.1	
Profit Margin (Before Income Tax) 49	4.0	0.1	38.8	38.1	24.0	17.1	10.2	12.3	36.4	7.2	6.6	8.0	4.3
Profit Margin (After Income Tax) 50	3.0	0.1	34.6	35.1	21.4	14.4	8.5	9.3	24.5	5.1	4.9	5.5	3.2

Table I

Corporations with and without Net Income

LIFE INSURANCE, STOCK COMPANIES (FORM 1120L)

MONEY AMOUNTS AND SIZE OF ASSETS IN THOUSANDS OF DOLLARS

Item Description for Accounting Period 7/09 Through 6/10	Total	Zero Assets	Under 500	500 to 1,000	1,000 to 5,000	5,000 to 10,000	10,000 to 25,000	25,000 to 50,000	50,000 to 100,000	100,000 to 250,000	250,000 to 500,000	500,000 to 2,500,000	2,500,000 and over
Number of Enterprises 1	812	33	180	75	112	58	73	52	30	28	34	56	81
Revenues ($ in Thousands)													
Net Sales 2	987729766	82375694	30846	23143	79846	94281	492463	655407	1130506	1426049	4038246	20838392	876544891
Interest 3	142846150	155253	1731	897	7895	11711	30929	59028	74870	158848	432835	2586048	139326104
Rents 4	8336248	1877	0	0	0	273	1731	3230	4464	7246	8275	23491	8285661
Royalties 5	11477	0	0	0	0	0	1	0	0	3	10	155	11308
Other Portfolio Income 6	14594293	10661	134	103	1105	1809	3915	8232	12564	8210	40983	134016	14372560
Other Receipts 7	821941598	82207903	28981	22143	70846	80488	455887	584917	1038608	1251742	3556143	18094682	714549258
Total Receipts 8	987729766	82375694	30846	23143	79846	94281	492463	655407	1130506	1426049	4038246	20838392	876544891
Average Total Receipts 9	1216416	2496233	171	309	713	1626	6746	12604	37684	50930	118772	372114	10821542
Operating Costs/Operating Income (%)													
Cost of Operations 10	47.3	0.9	30.7	36.7	38.6	26.1	46.3	43.6	34.5	47.0	43.0	48.9	51.7
Salaries and Wages 11	1.9	*	*	*	*	*	*	0.5	1.4	0.5	1.8	0.5	2.1
Taxes Paid 12	0.7	0.0	1.4	0.6	1.0	3.0	1.9	1.5	1.3	1.4	1.5	0.6	0.8
Interest Paid 13	4.6	0.0	0.3	0.0	0.2	0.2	0.5	0.7	0.1	0.4	0.6	0.3	5.2
Depreciation 14	0.7	0.0	0.0	0.1	0.0	0.4	0.2	0.5	0.7	0.3	0.3	0.2	0.8
Amortization and Depletion 15	1.0	0.0	3.6	0.8	1.3	1.6	1.6	3.0	2.2	4.0	2.1	1.3	1.1
Pensions and Other Deferred Comp. 16	0.5	0.0	*	0.0	0.1	0.8	0.6	0.5	0.7	0.6	0.6	0.4	0.5
Employee Benefits 17	0.3	0.0	*	*	0.0	0.1	0.3	0.7	0.7	0.3	0.2	0.2	0.3
Advertising 18	0.2	0.0	*	*	0.0	0.1	0.1	0.4	0.2	0.1	0.2	0.5	0.2
Other Expenses 19	42.3	98.9	34.7	47.7	40.8	60.7	43.6	39.6	36.3	44.4	49.1	46.4	36.9
Officers' Compensation 20	0.1	*	*	0.1	*	0.1	*	0.1	0.1	0.1	0.4	0.1	0.1
Operating Margin 21	0.4	0.1	29.4	14.2	18.1	6.8	5.0	9.0	21.9	0.9	0.1	0.6	0.4
Operating Margin Before Officers' Comp. 22	0.4	0.1	29.4	14.2	18.1	6.9	5.0	9.1	22.0	1.1	0.5	0.7	0.4

Selected Average Balance Sheet ($ in Thousands)

Net Receivables 23	130493	•	0	7	33	75	43	1581	1982	779	5820	4457	18155	1288546
Inventories 24	•	•	•	•	•	•	•	•	•	•	•	•	•	•
Net Property, Plant and Equipment 25	69273	•	0	0	0	2	59	66	160	1320	1344	2032	3017	690338
Total Assets 26	6628914	•	190	766	2305	6668	16147	35364	74292	161993	363404	1235288	6516395	
Notes and Loans Payable 27	233117	•	0	0	0	0	63	146	107	1241	3510	6006	2330679	
All Other Liabilities 28	5530383	•	131	400	1166	3916	9342	21785	59061	136603	286873	1032394	54509639	
Net Worth 29	865414	•	58	366	1139	2751	6743	13433	15124	24149	73021	196888	8476076	

Selected Financial Ratios (Times to 1)

Current Ratio 30	0.4	•	6.7	15.7	3.9	14.5	1.8	3.0	2.2	1.2	1.2	1.0	0.4
Quick Ratio 31	0.2	•	5.9	11.7	3.0	13.6	1.3	2.1	1.5	0.9	0.8	0.7	0.2
Net Sales to Working Capital 32	•	•	1.3	0.5	0.6	0.1	2.1	1.1	2.7	7.6	4.8	209.4	•
Coverage Ratio 33	1.5	61.8	113.8	458.9	104.0	43.7	11.2	13.9	214.0	3.8	0.9	2.3	1.5
Total Asset Turnover 34	0.2	•	0.9	0.4	0.3	0.2	0.4	0.4	0.5	0.3	0.3	0.3	0.2
Inventory Turnover 35	•	•	•	•	•	•	•	•	•	•	•	•	•
Receivables Turnover 36	•	•	•	•	•	•	•	•	•	•	•	•	•
Total Liabilities to Net Worth 37	6.7	•	2.2	1.1	1.0	1.4	1.4	1.6	3.9	5.7	4.0	5.3	6.7
Current Assets to Working Capital 38	•	•	1.2	1.1	1.3	1.1	2.2	1.5	1.9	7.0	6.2	221.7	•
Current Liabilities to Working Capital 39	•	•	0.2	0.1	0.3	0.1	1.2	0.5	0.9	6.0	5.2	220.7	•
Working Capital to Net Sales 40	•	•	0.8	1.8	1.6	8.9	0.5	0.9	0.4	0.1	0.2	0.0	•
Inventory to Working Capital 41	•	•	•	•	•	•	•	•	•	•	•	•	•
Total Receipts to Cash Flow 42	2.4	1.0	1.6	1.6	1.7	1.5	2.1	2.1	1.8	2.2	2.1	2.2	2.8
Cost of Goods to Cash Flow 43	1.1	0.0	0.5	0.6	0.7	0.4	1.0	0.9	0.6	1.1	0.9	1.1	1.4
Cash Flow to Total Debt 44	0.1	•	0.8	0.5	0.4	0.3	0.3	0.3	0.4	0.2	0.2	0.2	0.1

Selected Financial Factors (in Percentages)

Debt Ratio 45	86.9	•	69.2	52.2	50.6	58.7	58.2	62.0	79.6	85.1	79.9	84.1	87.0
Return on Total Assets 46	1.3	•	26.7	5.6	5.6	1.6	2.3	3.3	11.1	0.5	0.2	0.2	1.3
Return on Equity Before Income Taxes 47	3.5	•	86.0	11.7	11.2	3.9	4.9	8.2	54.5	2.3	•	0.7	3.5
Return on Equity After Income Taxes 48	2.4	•	75.4	10.4	9.8	2.4	3.7	5.5	34.7	•	•	•	2.4
Profit Margin (Before Income Tax) 49	2.5	0.1	29.3	13.8	17.9	6.6	4.9	8.7	21.9	1.1	0.4	0.4	2.8
Profit Margin (After Income Tax) 50	1.7	0.1	25.7	12.3	15.7	4.1	3.7	5.9	13.9	•	0.2	•	1.9

Table II

Corporations with Net Income

LIFE INSURANCE, STOCK COMPANIES (FORM 1120L)

MONEY AMOUNTS AND SIZE OF ASSETS IN THOUSANDS OF DOLLARS

Item Description for Accounting Period 7/09 Through 6/10	Total	Zero Assets	Under 500	500 to 1,000	1,000 to 5,000	5,000 to 10,000	10,000 to 25,000	25,000 to 50,000	50,000 to 100,000	100,000 to 250,000	250,000 to 500,000	500,000 to 2,500,000	2,500,000 and over
Number of Enterprises 1	595	18	•	•	50	88	43	58	•	21	21	•	•	•
Revenues ($ in Thousands)													
Net Sales 2	794850061	81186053	•	•	11572	68875	85655	333298	•	749924	1045775	•	•	•
Interest 3	121104200	140593	•	•	583	6831	9661	25159	•	56218	112447	•	•	•
Rents 4	7751315	1877	•	•	0	0	204	1256	•	2040	6250	•	•	•
Royalties 5	11029	0	•	•	0	0	0	1	•	0	3	•	•	•
Other Portfolio Income 6	11242260	10517	•	•	21	908	1449	3248	•	9548	7081	•	•	•
Other Receipts 7	654741257	81033066	•	•	10968	61136	74341	303634	•	682118	919994	•	•	•
Total Receipts 8	794850061	81186053	•	•	11572	68875	85655	333298	•	749924	1045775	•	•	•
Average Total Receipts 9	1335882	4510336	•	•	231	783	1992	5747	•	35711	49799	•	•	•
Operating Costs/Operating Income (%)													
Cost of Operations 10	43.7	0.9	•	•	29.0	40.6	24.7	37.3	•	23.5	44.6	•	•	•
Salaries and Wages 11	2.2	•	•	•	•	•	•	•	•	2.2	0.6	•	•	•
Taxes Paid 12	0.8	0.0	•	•	0.7	0.6	2.3	1.7	•	1.1	1.2	•	•	•
Interest Paid 13	5.4	0.0	•	•	0.0	0.2	0.2	0.6	•	0.1	0.4	•	•	•
Depreciation 14	0.8	0.0	•	•	0.1	0.1	0.4	0.2	•	0.5	0.2	•	•	•
Amortization and Depletion 15	0.9	0.0	•	•	0.4	0.9	0.7	1.8	•	1.7	2.5	•	•	•
Pensions and Other Deferred Comp. 16	0.5	0.0	•	•	0.0	0.1	0.1	0.5	•	0.7	0.6	•	•	•
Employee Benefits 17	0.3	0.0	•	•	0.0	0.1	0.1	0.2	•	0.7	0.1	•	•	•
Advertising 18	0.2	0.0	•	•	•	0.0	0.2	0.1	•	0.1	0.1	•	•	•
Other Expenses 19	43.5	98.9	•	•	31.6	32.7	53.9	47.3	•	32.8	42.6	•	•	•
Officers' Compensation 20	0.1	•	•	•	•	0.1	0.1	•	•	0.1	0.1	•	•	•
Operating Margin 21	1.6	0.1	•	•	38.2	24.9	17.4	10.3	•	36.5	7.0	•	•	•
Operating Margin Before Officers' Comp. 22	1.6	0.1	•	•	38.2	24.9	17.5	10.3	•	36.6	7.1	•	•	•

Selected Average Balance Sheet ($ in Thousands)

Net Receivables 23	153911	•	49	96	49	1940	718	6648
Inventories 24	•	•	•	•	•	•	•	•
Net Property, Plant and Equipment 25	85565	0	0	2	50	72	1222	1120
Total Assets 26	6956462	•	769	2298	6696	16040	74849	154130
Notes and Loans Payable 27	283820	0	0	0	0	80	153	1156
All Other Liabilities 28	5710132	0	343	1138	3713	8666	58710	128814
Net Worth 29	962511	0	425	1161	2983	7294	15986	24161

Selected Financial Ratios (Times to 1)

Current Ratio 30	0.4	•	22.9	5.3	3.3	2.7	2.5	1.0
Quick Ratio 31	0.3	•	17.3	4.3	2.4	2.1	2.1	0.8
Net Sales to Working Capital 32	•	74.0	0.4	0.7	0.8	1.3	2.2	23.5
Coverage Ratio 33	1.8	•	4418.0	123.9	102.2	19.3	305.8	19.6
Total Asset Turnover 34	0.2	•	0.3	0.3	0.3	0.4	0.5	0.3
Inventory Turnover 35	•	•	•	•	•	•	•	•
Receivables Turnover 36	•	•	•	•	•	•	•	•
Total Liabilities to Net Worth 37	6.2	•	0.8	1.0	1.2	1.2	3.7	5.4
Current Assets to Working Capital 38	•	•	1.0	1.2	1.4	1.6	1.6	22.2
Current Liabilities to Working Capital 39	•	•	0.0	0.2	0.4	0.6	0.6	21.2
Working Capital to Net Sales 40	•	•	2.7	1.5	1.3	0.8	0.5	0.0
Inventory to Working Capital 41	•	•	•	•	•	•	•	•
Total Receipts to Cash Flow 42	2.3	1.0	1.4	1.8	1.4	1.8	1.5	2.1
Cost of Goods to Cash Flow 43	1.0	0.0	0.4	0.7	0.3	0.7	0.3	0.9
Cash Flow to Total Debt 44	0.1	0.1	0.5	0.4	0.4	0.4	0.4	0.2

Selected Financial Factors (in Percentages)

Debt Ratio 45	86.2	•	44.6	49.5	55.4	54.5	78.6	84.3
Return on Total Assets 46	1.8	•	11.5	8.5	5.1	3.9	17.4	2.4
Return on Equity Before Income Taxes 47	5.8	•	20.8	16.7	11.4	8.1	81.3	14.7
Return on Equity After Income Taxes 48	4.4	•	19.1	15.0	9.6	6.7	54.7	10.4
Profit Margin (Before Income Tax) 49	4.2	0.1	38.2	24.8	17.1	10.2	36.4	7.2
Profit Margin (After Income Tax) 50	3.2	0.1	35.2	22.2	14.4	8.5	24.5	5.1

Table I

Corporations with and without Net Income

LIFE INSURANCE, MUTUAL COMPANIES (FORM 1120L)

MONEY AMOUNTS AND SIZE OF ASSETS IN THOUSANDS OF DOLLARS

Item Description for Accounting Period 7/09 Through 6/10		Total	Zero Assets	Under 500	500 to 1,000	1,000 to 5,000	5,000 to 10,000	10,000 to 25,000	25,000 to 50,000	50,000 to 100,000	100,000 to 250,000	250,000 to 500,000	500,000 to 2,500,000	2,500,000 and over
Number of Enterprises	1	55	3	5	3	8	0	3	3	3	3	5	10	9
Revenues ($ in Thousands)														
Net Sales	2	110104995	82	66	160	2461	0	11165	36867	40827	116504	602699	2968404	106325760
Interest	3	23205787	1	43	45	872	0	1080	5268	7475	27960	74751	759722	22328569
Rents	4	443420	0	0	0	48	0	0	0	435	228	2732	3016	436961
Royalties	5	21612	0	0	0	0	0	0	0	0	818	0	12116	8678
Other Portfolio Income	6	650112	0	0	106	292	0	203	109	438	1472	3583	6850	637057
Other Receipts	7	85784064	81	23	9	1249	0	9882	31490	32479	86026	521633	2186700	82914495
Total Receipts	8	110104995	82	66	160	2461	0	11165	36867	40827	116504	602699	2968404	106325760
Average Total Receipts	9	2001909	27	13	53	308	•	3722	12289	13609	38835	120540	296840	11813973
Operating Costs/Operating Income (%)														
Cost of Operations	10	50.3	128.0	36.4	5.0	148.3	•	12.6	68.2	60.5	50.6	33.0	48.0	50.4
Salaries and Wages	11	0.7	•	•	•	•	•	•	•	•	•	0.0	0.3	0.7
Taxes Paid	12	0.8	•	1.5	1.9	2.0	•	3.1	2.1	5.4	1.9	1.8	1.4	0.8
Interest Paid	13	0.8	•	•	41.2	•	•	•	•	0.0	0.0	0.1	0.8	0.8
Depreciation	14	0.4	•	•	•	0.2	•	0.4	2.6	0.5	0.2	0.4	0.4	0.4
Amortization and Depletion	15	1.6	•	•	•	2.3	•	2.2	1.0	4.0	3.3	2.8	2.9	1.5
Pensions and Other Deferred Comp.	16	0.8	•	•	•	1.7	•	0.0	3.3	11.5	1.4	0.4	1.0	0.8
Employee Benefits	17	0.1	•	•	•	2.0	•	•	•	0.7	1.7	0.5	0.2	0.1
Advertising	18	0.2	•	•	•	•	•	0.0	0.0	0.1	0.2	0.0	0.3	0.2
Other Expenses	19	43.9	11.0	118.2	20.0	•	•	66.9	13.9	39.6	42.5	59.9	40.5	43.9
Officers' Compensation	20	0.0	•	6.1	•	•	•	•	•	•	•	•	0.2	0.0
Operating Margin	21	0.5	•	•	31.9	•	•	14.8	8.9	•	•	1.0	4.1	0.4
Operating Margin Before Officers' Comp.	22	0.5	•	•	31.9	•	•	14.8	8.9	•	•	1.0	4.3	0.4

Selected Average Balance Sheet ($ in Thousands)

Net Receivables 23	44198	•	0	0	0	148	•	0	231	4721	1436	265757
Inventories 24	•	•	•	•	•	•	•	•	•	•	•	•
Net Property, Plant and Equipment 25	30879	•	0	2535	0	93	675	915	1080	4036	•	183057
Total Assets 26	11603723	271	822	11312	37775	69542	194678	359420	1485915	•	•	68953831
Notes and Loans Payable 27	19992	0	0	0	0	0	•	0	•	699	•	121393
All Other Liabilities 28	10461697	271	163	11312	28302	80436	177967	312817	1306541	•	•	62206141
Net Worth 29	1122035	0	658	0	9473	-10893	16711	46603	178675	•	•	6626296

Selected Financial Ratios (Times to 1)

Current Ratio 30	0.9	•	1.1	16.6	•	0.3	1.5	15.8	1.2	5.5	0.8	0.9
Quick Ratio 31	0.7	•	0.5	•	•	0.3	1.3	13.5	0.9	4.4	0.7	0.7
Net Sales to Working Capital 32	•	0.1	3.0	0.5	•	•	2.8	0.5	4.2	1.2	•	•
Coverage Ratio 33	1.9	•	•	1.8	•	•	•	•	7.5	5.9	1.7	•
Total Asset Turnover 34	0.2	0.0	0.1	0.1	•	0.3	0.3	0.2	0.2	0.3	0.2	0.2
Inventory Turnover 35	•	•	•	•	•	•	•	•	•	•	•	•
Receivables Turnover 36	•	•	•	•	•	•	•	•	•	•	•	•
Total Liabilities to Net Worth 37	9.3	•	1.7	0.2	•	3.0	•	10.6	6.7	7.3	9.4	
Current Assets to Working Capital 38	•	1.0	8.1	1.1	•	•	2.8	1.1	7.0	1.2	•	
Current Liabilities to Working Capital 39	•	•	7.1	0.1	•	•	1.8	0.1	6.0	0.2	•	
Working Capital to Net Sales 40	•	18.3	0.3	1.9	•	•	0.4	2.1	0.2	0.8	•	
Inventory to Working Capital 41	•	•	•	•	•	•	•	•	•	•	•	
Total Receipts to Cash Flow 42	2.3	1.7	•	1.7	•	1.3	4.4	6.9	2.6	1.7	2.3	
Cost of Goods to Cash Flow 43	1.1	0.6	•	0.6	•	0.2	3.0	4.2	1.3	0.6	1.1	
Cash Flow to Total Debt 44	0.1	0.0	•	0.0	•	0.3	0.1	0.0	0.1	0.2	0.1	

Selected Financial Factors (in Percentages)

Debt Ratio 45	90.3	100.0	62.4	19.9	•	100.0	74.9	115.7	91.4	87.0	88.0	90.4
Return on Total Assets 46	0.3	•	•	4.7	•	4.9	2.9	•	•	0.3	1.0	0.2
Return on Equity Before Income Taxes 47	1.2	•	•	2.6	•	•	11.5	28.0	•	2.2	6.7	1.0
Return on Equity After Income Taxes 48	0.2	•	•	2.6	•	•	10.8	28.0	•	1.1	4.4	0.1
Profit Margin (Before Income Tax) 49	0.7	•	•	31.9	•	•	8.9	•	•	0.8	4.1	0.6
Profit Margin (After Income Tax) 50	0.1	•	•	31.9	•	•	8.3	•	•	0.4	2.6	0.0

Table II

Corporations with Net Income

LIFE INSURANCE, MUTUAL COMPANIES (FORM 1120L)

MONEY AMOUNTS AND SIZE OF ASSETS IN THOUSANDS OF DOLLARS

Item Description for Accounting Period 7/09 Through 6/10	Total	Zero Assets	Under 500	500 to 1000	1,000 to 5,000	5,000 to 10,000	10,000 to 25,000	25,000 to 50,000	50,000 to 100,000	100,000 to 250,000	250,000 to 500,000	500,000 to 2,500,000	2,500,000 and over
Number of Enterprises **1**	33	0	•	3	5	0	0	•	0	0	•	•	•

Revenues ($ in Thousands)

	Total	Zero Assets	Under 500	500 to 1000	1,000 to 5,000	5,000 to 10,000	10,000 to 25,000	25,000 to 50,000	50,000 to 100,000	100,000 to 250,000	250,000 to 500,000	500,000 to 2,500,000	2,500,000 and over
Net Sales **2**	86249065	0	•	160	10615	0	0	•	0	0	•	•	•
Interest **3**	19031374	0	•	45	1288	0	0	•	0	0	•	•	•
Rents **4**	243141	0	•	0	48	0	0	•	0	0	•	•	•
Royalties **5**	16485	0	•	0	0	0	0	•	0	0	•	•	•
Other Portfolio Income **6**	428879	0	•	106	209	0	0	•	0	0	•	•	•
Other Receipts **7**	66529186	0	•	9	9070	0	0	•	0	0	•	•	•
Total Receipts **8**	86249065	0	•	160	10615	0	0	•	0	0	•	•	•
Average Total Receipts **9**	2613608	•	•	53	2123	•	•	•	•	•	•	•	•

Operating Costs/Operating Income (%)

	Total	Zero Assets	Under 500	500 to 1000	1,000 to 5,000	5,000 to 10,000	10,000 to 25,000	25,000 to 50,000	50,000 to 100,000	100,000 to 250,000	250,000 to 500,000	500,000 to 2,500,000	2,500,000 and over
Cost of Operations **10**	44.5	•	•	5.0	7.4	•	•	•	•	•	•	•	•
Salaries and Wages **11**	0.3	•	•	•	•	•	•	•	•	•	•	•	•
Taxes Paid **12**	0.8	•	•	1.9	3.6	•	•	•	•	•	•	•	•
Interest Paid **13**	0.9	•	•	41.2	•	•	•	•	•	•	•	•	•
Depreciation **14**	0.3	•	•	•	0.5	•	•	•	•	•	•	•	•
Amortization and Depletion **15**	1.5	•	•	•	2.1	•	•	•	•	•	•	•	•
Pensions and Other Deferred Comp. **16**	0.7	•	•	•	0.4	•	•	•	•	•	•	•	•
Employee Benefits **17**	0.1	•	•	•	0.5	•	•	•	•	•	•	•	•
Advertising **18**	0.2	•	•	•	•	•	•	•	•	•	•	•	•
Other Expenses **19**	48.9	•	•	20.0	66.5	•	•	•	•	•	•	•	•
Officers' Compensation **20**	0.0	•	•	•	•	•	•	•	•	•	•	•	•
Operating Margin **21**	1.9	•	•	31.9	19.0	•	•	•	•	•	•	•	•
Operating Margin Before Officers' Comp. **22**	1.9	•	•	31.9	19.0	•	•	•	•	•	•	•	•

Selected Average Balance Sheet ($ in Thousands)

Net Receivables 23	59712	0	0
Inventories 24			
Net Property, Plant and Equipment 25	41650	0	0
Total Assets 26	14508944	822	6384
Notes and Loans Payable 27	3116	0	0
All Other Liabilities 28	13038082	163	6384
Net Worth 29	1437746	658	0

Selected Financial Ratios (Times to 1)

Current Ratio 30	1.6	16.6	0.5
Quick Ratio 31	1.1		0.5
Net Sales to Working Capital 32	2.5	0.5	
Coverage Ratio 33	3.4	1.8	
Total Asset Turnover 34	0.2	0.1	0.3
Inventory Turnover 35			
Receivables Turnover 36			
Total Liabilities to Net Worth 37	9.1	0.2	
Current Assets to Working Capital 38	2.8	1.1	
Current Liabilities to Working Capital 39	1.8	0.1	
Working Capital to Net Sales 40	0.4	1.9	
Inventory to Working Capital 41	0.0		
Total Receipts to Cash Flow 42	2.0		1.2
Cost of Goods to Cash Flow 43	0.9		0.1
Cash Flow to Total Debt 44	0.1		0.3

Selected Financial Factors (in Percentages)

Debt Ratio 45	90.1	19.9	100.0
Return on Total Assets 46	0.5	4.7	6.3
Return on Equity Before Income Taxes 47	3.8	2.6	
Return on Equity After Income Taxes 48	2.5	2.6	
Profit Margin (Before Income Tax) 49	2.1	31.9	19.0
Profit Margin (After Income Tax) 50	1.4	31.9	16.2

302

Table I

Corporations with and without Net Income

MUTUAL PROPERTY AND CASUALTY COMPANIES (FORM 1120-PC)

MONEY AMOUNTS AND SIZE OF ASSETS IN THOUSANDS OF DOLLARS

Item Description for Accounting Period 7/09 Through 6/10	Total	Zero Assets	Under 500	500 to 1,000	1,000 to 5,000	5,000 to 10,000	10,000 to 25,000	25,000 to 50,000	50,000 to 100,000	100,000 to 250,000	250,000 to 500,000	500,000 to 2,500,000	2,500,000 and over
Number of Enterprises **1**	1473	22	104	21	515	163	215	120	85	73	60	67	26
Revenues ($ in Thousands)													
Net Sales **2**	237999942	373003	399	11954	447947	516277	1231254	1849529	2171213	5917876	9472178	50332403	165675909
Interest **3**	12249665	21624	225	0	35047	22354	69458	89802	147775	265313	461497	1767604	9368967
Rents **4**	457154	2531	52	0	1076	714	2253	1135	3127	7926	18940	58703	360694
Royalties **5**	563	0	0	0	0	0	1	0	0	16	4	348	194
Other Portfolio Income **6**	6330212	14413	117	0	7374	13355	32045	27764	57808	154235	264348	964266	4794489
Other Receipts **7**	218962348	334435	5	11954	404450	479854	1127497	1730828	1962503	5490386	8727389	47541482	151151565
Total Receipts **8**	237999942	373003	399	11954	447947	516277	1231254	1849529	2171213	5917876	9472178	50332403	165675909
Average Total Receipts **9**	161575	16955	4	569	870	3167	5727	15413	25544	81067	157870	751230	6372150
Operating Costs/Operating Income (%)													
Cost of Operations **10**	62.3	57.4	146.9	62.8	52.7	55.1	61.0	63.5	46.5	61.6	58.1	69.9	60.5
Salaries and Wages **11**	13.8	20.1	7.8	•	15.3	11.3	10.9	10.1	16.6	15.4	15.4	12.7	14.1
Taxes Paid **12**	2.3	1.6	0.3	6.0	3.0	2.4	2.6	2.0	3.4	2.5	2.5	2.1	2.3
Interest Paid **13**	0.5	0.0	•	•	0.1	0.0	0.1	0.1	0.4	0.2	0.2	0.3	0.6
Depreciation **14**	1.2	0.4	1.3	•	0.4	0.3	0.5	0.4	1.1	1.2	1.4	1.2	1.2
Amortization and Depletion **15**	0.2	•	•	•	0.0	•	1.4	0.0	0.0	0.0	0.2	0.1	0.2
Pensions and Other Deferred Comp. **16**	0.7	0.5	•	•	0.1	0.2	0.2	0.5	0.2	0.3	0.8	0.5	0.8
Employee Benefits **17**	1.5	1.8	•	•	1.5	0.5	0.9	0.9	1.5	2.5	2.1	1.5	1.5
Advertising **18**	0.7	0.2	•	0.3	0.4	0.3	0.2	0.3	0.4	0.5	0.3	0.3	0.8
Other Expenses **19**	12.6	10.3	162.2	28.7	26.8	28.0	26.2	19.7	23.4	14.1	14.0	8.8	13.3
Officers' Compensation **20**	0.3	0.4	•	•	2.4	1.3	1.0	1.1	1.3	0.6	0.8	0.3	0.2
Operating Margin **21**	3.9	7.3	•	2.3	•	0.6	•	1.2	4.9	1.1	4.1	2.3	4.5
Operating Margin Before Officers' Comp. **22**	4.1	7.8	•	2.3	•	1.9	•	2.3	6.3	1.7	4.9	2.6	4.7

Selected Average Balance Sheet ($ in Thousands)

Net Receivables 23	28294	4	48	84	225	1051	2066	5183	14356	34820	115602	1146082
Inventories 24	•	•	•	•	•	•	•	•	•	•	•	•
Net Property, Plant and Equipment 25	5650	9	0	62	101	135	292	1151	3428	5711	30730	210006
Total Assets 26	391032	192	813	2697	7437	15763	35140	70127	159384	340780	1207506	17184670
Notes and Loans Payable 27	6030	14	0	6	29	207	28	264	1314	1195	19947	280728
All Other Liabilities 28	223705	112	728	1035	3963	10316	25451	44490	96612	208340	700473	9722057
Net Worth 29	161297	66	85	1655	3446	5240	9661	25373	61458	131245	487086	7181885

Selected Financial Ratios (Times to 1)

Current Ratio 30	1.0	2.1	1.2	1.8	1.6	1.1	0.8	1.0	1.0	1.0	1.0	1.0
Quick Ratio 31	0.9	1.7	1.2	1.6	1.3	0.9	0.7	0.8	0.8	0.9	1.0	0.9
Net Sales to Working Capital 32	54.5	0.0	3.7	1.3	1.6	8.9	•	•	•	•	46.8	47.6
Coverage Ratio 33	5.2	•	530.5	•	•	3.7	3.7	10.1	•	12.1	5.5	5.1
Total Asset Turnover 34	0.4	0.0	0.7	0.3	0.4	0.4	0.4	0.4	0.5	0.5	0.6	0.4
Inventory Turnover 35	•	•	•	•	•	•	•	•	•	•	•	•
Receivables Turnover 36	•	•	•	•	•	•	•	•	•	•	•	•
Total Liabilities to Net Worth 37	1.4	1.9	8.6	0.6	1.2	2.0	2.6	1.8	1.6	1.6	1.5	1.4
Current Assets to Working Capital 38	60.3	1.9	5.2	2.3	2.7	16.0	•	•	•	•	40.5	55.3
Current Liabilities to Working Capital 39	59.3	0.9	4.2	1.3	1.7	15.0	•	•	•	39.5	•	54.3
Working Capital to Net Sales 40	0.0	20.7	0.3	0.8	0.6	0.1	•	•	•	0.0	0.0	0.0
Inventory to Working Capital 41	0.0	•	•	•	0.0	0.0	•	•	•	0.0	0.0	0.0
Total Receipts to Cash Flow 42	6.5	5.9	3.2	4.3	3.6	4.9	5.0	3.7	7.2	5.9	10.0	6.0
Cost of Goods to Cash Flow 43	4.0	3.4	2.0	2.3	2.0	3.0	3.2	1.7	4.4	3.4	7.0	3.6
Cash Flow to Total Debt 44	0.1	•	0.2	0.2	0.2	0.1	0.1	0.2	0.1	0.1	0.1	0.1

Selected Financial Factors (in Percentages)

Debt Ratio 45	58.8	65.6	89.5	38.6	53.7	66.8	72.5	63.8	61.4	61.5	59.7	58.2
Return on Total Assets 46	1.1	•	1.6	•	•	•	0.2	1.5	•	1.2	0.9	1.2
Return on Equity Before Income Taxes 47	2.1	•	15.4	•	•	•	0.6	3.8	•	3.0	1.7	2.3
Return on Equity After Income Taxes 48	0.9	•	13.1	•	•	•	1.6	1.6	•	1.1	0.1	1.2
Profit Margin (Before Income Tax) 49	2.1	4.4	2.3	•	•	•	0.4	3.8	•	2.5	1.1	2.6
Profit Margin (After Income Tax) 50	0.9	3.1	1.9	•	•	•	0.4	1.6	•	1.0	0.1	1.4

Table II

Corporations with Net Income

MUTUAL PROPERTY AND CASUALTY COMPANIES (FORM 1120-PC)

MONEY AMOUNTS AND SIZE OF ASSETS IN THOUSANDS OF DOLLARS

Item Description for Accounting Period 7/09 Through 6/10	Total	Zero Assets	Under 500	500 to 1,000	1,000 to 5,000	5,000 to 10,000	10,000 to 25,000	25,000 to 50,000	50,000 to 100,000	100,000 to 250,000	250,000 to 500,000	500,000 to 2,500,000	2,500,000 and over
Number of Enterprises **1**	902	22	42	10	344	90	106	78	60	48	40	45	18
Revenues ($ in Thousands)													
Net Sales **2**	10486987	373003	317	3759	224926	249113	592433	1149640	1459329	3925234	7185750	31902221	57801263
Interest **3**	4709146	21624	143	0	23992	12240	37048	58090	95238	177731	301762	1235502	2745776
Rents **4**	164416	2531	52	0	739	385	773	710	2082	4527	15770	29220	107627
Royalties **5**	441	0	0	0	0	0	0	0	0	0	4	348	88
Other Portfolio Income **6**	2752618	14413	117	0	4434	9354	14013	21764	46488	116569	186432	676555	1662478
Other Receipts **7**	97240366	334435	5	3759	195761	227134	540599	1069076	1315521	3626407	6681782	29960596	53285294
Total Receipts **8**	104866987	373003	317	3759	224926	249113	592433	1149640	1459329	3925234	7185750	31902221	57801263
Average Total Receipts **9**	116261	16955	8	376	654	2768	5589	14739	24322	81776	179644	708938	3211181
Operating Costs/Operating Income (%)													
Cost of Operations **10**	59.2	57.4	4.4	88.5	37.5	44.5	47.6	51.8	38.8	53.2	55.5	65.0	57.7
Salaries and Wages **11**	12.9	20.1	9.8	•	15.3	14.0	10.4	11.3	18.6	14.8	15.0	12.5	12.5
Taxes Paid **12**	2.4	1.6	•	1.5	2.9	2.3	2.7	1.7	3.4	2.5	2.6	2.3	2.5
Interest Paid **13**	0.3	0.0	•	•	0.0	0.0	0.1	0.1	0.4	0.2	0.2	0.4	0.3
Depreciation **14**	1.3	0.4	1.6	•	0.4	0.5	0.4	0.5	0.9	1.4	1.6	1.4	1.3
Amortization and Depletion **15**	0.1	•	•	•	0.0	0.0	0.0	0.0	0.0	0.1	0.2	0.1	0.2
Pensions and Other Deferred Comp. **16**	0.8	0.5	•	•	0.1	0.3	0.2	0.4	0.3	0.3	0.9	0.4	1.0
Employee Benefits **17**	1.9	1.8	•	•	2.0	0.7	0.7	0.8	1.3	3.0	2.2	1.7	2.0
Advertising **18**	0.7	0.2	•	•	0.5	0.3	0.2	0.5	0.4	0.7	0.3	0.3	1.0
Other Expenses **19**	11.3	10.3	47.6	2.8	22.3	22.4	23.8	20.0	21.6	15.0	13.2	9.6	11.1
Officers' Compensation **20**	0.4	0.4	•	•	2.6	1.9	1.1	1.2	1.8	0.6	0.8	0.3	0.2
Operating Margin **21**	8.7	7.3	36.3	7.3	16.4	13.0	12.7	11.7	12.5	8.3	7.5	5.9	10.1
Operating Margin Before Officers' Comp. **22**	9.0	7.8	36.3	7.3	19.0	14.9	13.8	12.9	14.3	8.9	8.3	6.2	10.4

Selected Average Balance Sheet ($ in Thousands)

Net Receivables 23	20930	•	11	0	60	165	1172	1524	5217	13813	31986	118331	612195
Inventories 24	•	•	•	•	•	•	•	•	•	•	•	•	•
Net Property, Plant and Equipment 25	4731	•	21	0	58	130	124	299	1135	3575	7271	27507	134994
Total Assets 26	260497	•	317	767	2741	7370	16216	35144	68713	161491	340865	1231535	8219589
Notes and Loans Payable 27	1928	•	0	0	2	16	35	14	127	1911	1721	22135	31560
All Other Liabilities 28	146182	•	132	663	814	3134	9534	22740	42876	89523	183920	717455	4554762
Net Worth 29	112386	•	185	104	1925	4220	6647	12391	25710	70057	155224	491945	3633267

Selected Financial Ratios (Times to 1)

Current Ratio 30	1.0	•	5.4	1.2	2.2	1.9	1.2	0.9	1.0	1.1	1.1	1.0	1.0
Quick Ratio 31	1.0	•	3.8	1.2	2.1	1.6	1.0	0.8	0.8	1.0	1.0	1.0	1.0
Net Sales to Working Capital 32	21.0	•	0.0	3.6	0.8	1.1	3.8	•	17.1	12.9	19.1	30.2	21.9
Coverage Ratio 33	23.9	530.5	•	•	466.9	1084.1	85.4	78.5	28.0	39.2	32.0	14.4	27.2
Total Asset Turnover 34	0.4	•	0.0	0.5	0.2	0.4	0.3	0.4	0.4	0.5	0.5	0.6	0.4
Inventory Turnover 35	•	•	•	•	•	•	•	•	•	•	•	•	•
Receivables Turnover 36	•	•	•	•	•	•	•	•	•	•	•	•	•
Total Liabilities to Net Worth 37	1.3	•	0.7	6.4	0.4	0.7	1.4	1.8	1.7	1.3	1.2	1.5	1.3
Current Assets to Working Capital 38	22.8	•	1.2	7.4	1.8	2.1	7.1	•	29.1	14.1	19.6	28.3	25.1
Current Liabilities to Working Capital 39	21.8	•	0.2	6.4	0.8	1.1	6.1	•	28.1	13.1	18.6	27.3	24.1
Working Capital to Net Sales 40	0.0	•	24.2	0.3	1.3	0.9	0.3	•	0.1	0.1	0.1	0.0	0.0
Inventory to Working Capital 41	0.0	•	•	•	•	•	•	•	•	•	•	0.0	0.0
Total Receipts to Cash Flow 42	5.4	5.9	1.4	9.9	2.9	2.6	2.8	3.2	3.1	4.6	5.2	7.1	5.0
Cost of Goods to Cash Flow 43	3.2	3.4	0.1	8.8	1.0	1.3	1.3	1.7	1.2	2.5	2.9	4.6	2.9
Cash Flow to Total Debt 44	0.1	•	0.0	0.1	0.3	0.3	0.2	0.2	0.2	0.2	0.2	0.1	0.1

Selected Financial Factors (in Percentages)

Debt Ratio 45	56.9	•	41.7	86.4	29.8	42.7	59.0	64.7	62.6	56.6	54.5	60.1	55.8
Return on Total Assets 46	3.3	•	0.9	3.6	3.7	4.1	4.0	4.5	4.1	3.5	3.2	2.9	3.4
Return on Equity Before Income Taxes 47	7.3	•	1.5	26.3	5.3	7.1	9.7	12.6	10.6	7.8	6.9	6.8	7.3
Return on Equity After Income Taxes 48	4.9	•	1.2	22.4	4.1	5.0	7.3	9.2	7.5	5.5	4.6	4.5	4.9
Profit Margin (Before Income Tax) 49	7.1	4.4	36.3	7.3	15.5	10.9	11.5	10.6	11.2	6.7	5.9	4.7	8.3
Profit Margin (After Income Tax) 50	4.8	3.1	29.0	6.2	12.0	7.7	8.6	7.7	7.9	4.7	4.0	3.1	5.6

Table I

Corporations with and without Net Income

STOCK PROPERTY AND CASUALTY COMPANIES (FORM 1120-PC)

MONEY AMOUNTS AND SIZE OF ASSETS IN THOUSANDS OF DOLLARS

Item Description for Accounting Period 7/09 Through 6/10		Total	Zero Assets	Under 500	500 to 1,000	1,000 to 5,000	5,000 to 10,000	10,000 to 25,000	25,000 to 50,000	50,000 to 100,000	100,000 to 250,000	250,000 to 500,000	500,000 to 2,500,000	2,500,000 and over
Number of Enterprises	1	6417	314	2371	804	1563	356	330	181	139	104	69	106	81
Revenues ($ in Thousands)														
Net Sales	2	700546141	1223087	93383	102099	414535	788709	3057872	3353935	7343021	13427077	15307170	70924625	584510628
Interest	3	38536596	116426	10480	10576	50285	42548	87801	110902	149691	307214	530778	2193236	34926658
Rents	4	1122527	156	0	0	4082	2785	1206	2024	2059	17508	15770	54554	1022382
Royalties	5	28829	0	0	0	0	206	2	1	2	0	6957	3205	18455
Other Portfolio Income	6	17254991	15463	1302	5355	14139	17659	28149	32509	57822	99550	181151	1085870	15716023
Other Receipts	7	64363198	1091042	81601	86168	346029	725511	2940714	3208499	7133447	13002805	14572514	67587760	532827110
Total Receipts	8	700546141	1223087	93383	102099	414535	788709	3057872	3353935	7343021	13427077	15307170	70924625	584510628
Average Total Receipts	9	109170	3895	39	127	265	2215	9266	18530	52827	129107	221843	669100	7216181
Operating Costs/Operating Income (%)														
Cost of Operations	10	63.3	70.2	103.3	51.2	74.8	56.5	66.6	65.5	64.6	61.9	59.6	69.6	62.5
Salaries and Wages	11	11.8	30.6	2.3	5.6	9.7	10.9	13.1	13.0	10.5	11.3	12.1	14.1	11.4
Taxes Paid	12	2.1	1.0	0.5	0.2	1.6	2.7	2.1	2.2	2.2	2.1	1.8	2.3	2.1
Interest Paid	13	1.7	1.1	0.3	0.1	0.5	0.3	0.2	0.3	0.2	0.5	0.4	0.7	1.9
Depreciation	14	0.8	0.5	•	•	0.4	0.4	0.4	0.6	0.7	0.7	0.7	0.9	0.8
Amortization and Depletion	15	0.3	0.2	0.2	•	0.1	0.0	0.1	0.0	0.2	0.5	0.2	0.3	0.3
Pensions and Other Deferred Comp.	16	0.3	0.1	•	•	0.0	0.1	0.1	0.1	0.1	0.1	0.2	0.4	0.3
Employee Benefits	17	1.1	0.7	0.1	•	0.2	0.9	0.5	0.7	3.6	0.7	1.0	1.6	1.0
Advertising	18	0.5	0.1	•	•	0.1	0.6	0.4	0.3	0.6	0.4	0.8	0.3	0.5
Other Expenses	19	13.1	21.1	11.7	16.6	25.4	13.7	15.4	14.2	15.2	19.9	18.4	10.2	13.1
Officers' Compensation	20	0.3	1.0	•	•	0.0	1.1	0.9	0.9	0.5	0.5	0.4	0.5	0.3
Operating Margin	21	4.8	•	•	26.3	•	12.8	0.3	2.1	1.6	1.3	4.4	•	5.7
Operating Margin Before Officers' Comp.	22	5.1	•	•	26.3	•	13.8	1.2	3.1	2.1	1.8	4.7	•	6.0

Selected Average Balance Sheet ($ in Thousands)

Net Receivables **23**	18529	•	0	4	6	125	282	1141	2193	6803	11040	28872	115830	1252493
Inventories **24**	•	•	•	•	•	•	•	•	•	•	•	•	•	•
Net Property, Plant and Equipment **25**	4160	•	0	0	14	73	101	314	563	2685	6748	16426	•	296217
Total Assets **26**	299418	•	224	720	2355	7027	15827	35974	69387	157035	339990	1110599	•	21421921
Notes and Loans Payable **27**	25395	•	1	11	19	118	369	432	1463	14163	11396	90338	•	1859597
All Other Liabilities **28**	170464	•	190	506	1346	8433	26130	10921	95136	101020	241406	665557	•	11958451
Net Worth **29**	103559	•	33	203	990	-1524	9475	4473	-27212	41853	87188	354704	•	7603872

Selected Financial Ratios (Times to 1)

Current Ratio **30**	0.7	•	0.9	0.9	1.2	1.1	0.9	1.1	0.5	1.0	0.9	0.9	•	0.7
Quick Ratio **31**	0.6	•	0.7	0.7	0.9	0.9	0.8	0.9	0.5	0.9	0.8	•	•	0.6
Net Sales to Working Capital **32**	•	•	•	1.4	5.3	9.8	•	•	304.6	•	•	•	•	3.4
Coverage Ratio **33**	3.3	•	203.8	37.9	•	0.6	6.9	6.4	2.8	10.5	•	•	•	3.4
Total Asset Turnover **34**	0.4	•	0.2	0.2	0.1	0.3	0.6	0.5	0.8	0.8	0.7	0.6	•	0.3
Inventory Turnover **35**	•	•	•	•	•	•	•	•	•	•	•	•	•	•
Receivables Turnover **36**	•	•	•	•	•	•	•	•	•	•	•	•	•	•
Total Liabilities to Net Worth **37**	1.9	5.7	2.5	•	1.4	2.5	2.8	2.8	2.8	2.9	2.1	1.8		
Current Assets to Working Capital **38**	•	•	•	7.3	9.8	8.8	•	9.8	206.8	10.9	•	•		
Current Liabilities to Working Capital **39**	•	•	•	6.3	8.8	9.9	•	8.8	205.8	9.9	•	•		
Working Capital to Net Sales **40**	•	•	0.7	•	0.2	0.1	•	0.1	0.0	•	•	•		
Inventory to Working Capital **41**	•	•	•	•	•	•	•	•	0.1	•	•	•		
Total Receipts to Cash Flow **42**	6.2	•	2.6	9.2	4.0	6.8	6.4	6.4	5.1	4.6	13.7	5.9		
Cost of Goods to Cash Flow **43**	3.9	•	1.3	6.9	2.2	4.5	4.2	4.1	3.2	2.8	9.5	3.7		
Cash Flow to Total Debt **44**	0.1	•	0.1	0.0	0.1	0.1	0.1	0.1	0.2	0.2	0.1	0.1		

Selected Financial Factors (in Percentages)

Debt Ratio **45**	65.4	85.1	71.8	58.0	121.7	71.7	73.7	139.2	73.3	74.4	68.1	64.5
Return on Total Assets **46**	2.0	•	4.6	•	3.7	0.1	•	0.9	1.2	1.2	2.7	2.2
Return on Equity Before Income Taxes **47**	3.9	•	16.3	•	•	•	•	2.9	2.8	9.5	4.3	
Return on Equity After Income Taxes **48**	1.9	•	14.2	•	•	•	•	0.5	5.1	2.5		
Profit Margin (Before Income Tax) **49**	3.7	•	26.0	11.5	•	1.5	1.3	0.9	3.7	4.6		
Profit Margin (After Income Tax) **50**	1.8	•	22.8	7.8	•	•	•	•	2.0	2.6		

Table II
Corporations with Net Income

STOCK PROPERTY AND CASUALTY COMPANIES (FORM 1120-PC)

MONEY AMOUNTS AND SIZE OF ASSETS IN THOUSANDS OF DOLLARS

Item Description for Accounting Period 7/09 Through 6/10	Total	Zero Assets	Under 500	500 to 1,000	1,000 to 5,000	5,000 to 10,000	10,000 to 25,000	25,000 to 50,000	50,000 to 100,000	100,000 to 250,000	250,000 to 500,000	500,000 to 2,500,000	2,500,000 and over
Number of Enterprises 1	4851	170	1734	700	1313	252	209	116	88	74	51	76	67
Revenues ($ in Thousands)													
Net Sales 2	645545305	377562	12759	98149	230239	485389	1536209	2216282	5573356	10530141	11795367	51831145	560858707
Interest 3	34774403	26305	7183	10128	45601	27837	56122	71803	101329	227748	410024	1517428	32272893
Rents 4	1075071	152	0	0	475	578	749	1758	1785	7328	10035	35281	1016928
Royalties 5	25644	0	0	0	0	206	2	2	2	0	6957	21	18455
Other Portfolio Income 6	15888752	10270	1253	5136	12658	15718	19260	21820	36502	77347	144455	793349	14750984
Other Receipts 7	593781435	340835	4323	82885	171505	441050	1460076	2120901	5433738	10217718	11223896	49485066	512799447
Total Receipts 8	645545305	377562	12759	98149	230239	485389	1536209	2216282	5573356	10530141	11795367	51831145	560858707
Average Total Receipts 9	133075	2221	7	140	175	1926	7350	19106	63334	142299	231282	681989	8371025
Operating Costs/Operating Income (%)													
Cost of Operations 10	61.4	32.2	13.0	51.3	34.3	46.5	53.5	56.0	64.5	58.6	57.3	63.4	61.4
Salaries and Wages 11	11.5	19.3	•	3.7	11.2	7.2	12.2	15.1	9.4	9.6	11.7	12.8	11.4
Taxes Paid 12	2.1	2.4	0.8	0.2	2.1	2.1	1.8	2.0	2.2	2.1	1.8	2.4	2.1
Interest Paid 13	1.4	0.6	•	0.1	0.2	0.5	0.2	0.2	0.2	0.4	0.3	0.5	1.5
Depreciation 14	0.8	0.5	•	•	0.3	0.2	0.2	0.6	0.7	0.6	0.7	0.8	0.8
Amortization and Depletion 15	0.3	0.5	•	•	0.0	0.0	0.1	0.0	0.2	0.1	0.2	0.2	0.3
Pensions and Other Deferred Comp. 16	0.3	0.3	•	•	•	0.1	0.1	0.1	0.1	0.1	0.2	0.4	0.3
Employee Benefits 17	1.0	1.5	•	•	0.2	0.7	0.5	0.7	0.9	0.7	0.9	1.8	1.0
Advertising 18	0.5	0.2	•	•	0.1	0.3	0.4	0.3	0.6	0.4	0.9	0.2	0.5
Other Expenses 19	12.8	31.0	19.4	16.4	17.3	13.0	16.3	14.0	14.1	20.4	15.9	9.4	12.9
Officers' Compensation 20	0.3	1.4	•	•	0.0	0.7	1.0	1.0	0.4	0.5	0.4	0.5	0.3
Operating Margin 21	7.4	10.1	66.7	28.3	34.4	28.8	13.8	9.9	6.8	6.5	9.7	7.4	7.3
Operating Margin Before Officers' Comp. 22	7.7	11.5	66.7	28.3	34.4	29.4	14.8	10.9	7.2	7.0	10.1	7.9	7.6

Selected Average Balance Sheet ($ in Thousands)

Net Receivables **23** — 19996	0	5	7	101	241	1062	2522	6594	12133	26924	118053	1260566
Inventories **24** — •	•	•	•	•	•	•	•	•	•	•	•	•
Net Property, Plant and Equipment **25** — 5205	•	0	0	10	13	63	335	476	1972	6716	16701	348970
Total Assets **26** — 353980	0	238	719	2321	6932	15761	35726	70186	153997	336507	1134739	23627354
Notes and Loans Payable **27** — 24516	0	0	1	10	84	208	262	1509	8136	8901	60471	1687025
All Other Liabilities **28** — 190765	0	181	522	1152	3947	9249	23334	44865	93323	205355	639568	12651366
Net Worth **29** — 138699	0	57	196	1159	2901	6305	12131	23812	52538	122250	434700	9288963

Selected Financial Ratios (Times to 1)

Current Ratio **30** — 0.7	•	0.8	0.8	1.2	1.0	1.2	1.1	1.2	1.1	1.1	1.0	0.7
Quick Ratio **31** — 0.6	•	0.7	0.7	1.0	0.9	1.1	0.9	1.1	1.0	1.0	0.9	0.6
Net Sales to Working Capital **32** — •	•	•	0.8	20.6	9.8	3.9	6.7	18.0	11.3	•	•	•
Coverage Ratio **33** — 5.6	14.2	•	210.8	144.3	59.9	71.3	60.1	41.9	14.8	34.4	13.7	5.1
Total Asset Turnover **34** — 0.4	•	0.2	0.0	0.2	0.3	0.5	0.5	0.9	0.9	0.7	0.6	0.4
Inventory Turnover **35** — •	•	•	•	•	•	•	•	•	•	•	•	•
Receivables Turnover **36** — •	•	•	•	•	•	•	•	•	•	•	•	•
Total Liabilities to Net Worth **37** — 1.6	•	3.2	2.7	1.0	1.4	1.5	1.9	1.9	1.9	1.8	1.6	1.5
Current Assets to Working Capital **38** — •	•	•	5.9	39.9	11.5	5.3	5.0	11.2	9.3	•	•	•
Current Liabilities to Working Capital **39** — •	•	•	4.9	38.9	10.5	4.3	4.0	10.2	8.3	•	•	•
Working Capital to Net Sales **40** — •	•	•	1.3	0.0	0.1	0.3	0.1	0.1	0.1	0.1	•	•
Inventory to Working Capital **41** — •	•	•	•	0.0	0.0	0.0	0.1	0.0	0.0	•	•	•
Total Receipts to Cash Flow **42** — 5.4	2.5	•	2.4	2.0	2.5	3.4	4.4	5.0	5.0	4.1	6.5	5.4
Cost of Goods to Cash Flow **43** — 3.3	0.8	•	1.2	0.7	1.1	1.8	2.4	3.2	2.3	2.3	4.2	3.3
Cash Flow to Total Debt **44** — 0.1	0.0	•	0.1	0.1	0.2	0.2	0.3	0.3	0.1	0.1	0.1	0.1

Selected Financial Factors (in Percentages)

Debt Ratio **45** — 60.8	76.1	•	72.8	50.1	58.2	60.0	66.0	66.1	65.9	63.7	61.7	60.7
Return on Total Assets **46** — 2.9	2.1	•	5.5	2.6	7.6	6.3	5.0	6.1	6.0	6.4	4.3	2.7
Return on Equity Before Income Taxes **47** — 6.1	8.6	•	20.1	5.1	17.9	15.4	14.5	17.4	16.4	17.1	10.4	5.6
Return on Equity After Income Taxes **48** — 4.1	7.4	•	17.7	3.9	13.9	11.1	10.1	12.1	11.3	12.9	6.9	3.7
Profit Margin (Before Income Tax) **49** — 6.3	8.0	66.7	28.0	33.8	26.9	13.2	9.2	6.6	6.1	9.0	6.6	6.2
Profit Margin (After Income Tax) **50** — 4.3	5.4	57.6	24.6	26.0	21.0	9.5	6.4	4.5	4.2	6.8	4.4	4.2

Table I

Corporations with and without Net Income

INSURANCE AGENCIES AND BROKERAGES

MONEY AMOUNTS AND SIZE OF ASSETS IN THOUSANDS OF DOLLARS

Item Description for Accounting Period 7/09 Through 6/10	Total	Zero Assets	Under 500	500 to 1,000	1,000 to 5,000	5,000 to 10,000	10,000 to 25,000	25,000 to 50,000	50,000 to 100,000	100,000 to 250,000	250,000 to 500,000	500,000 to 2,500,000	2,500,000 and over
Number of Enterprises **1**	92638	16967	65876	4690	4255	452	237	69	39	31	6	10	5
Revenues ($ in Thousands)													
Net Sales **2**	69843144	1619717	20282538	5067070	9812868	4015308	3853545	2251677	2012479	2402314	1082830	5128393	12314404
Interest **3**	407437	5208	14044	8831	16474	9546	10092	10628	20082	29346	11951	45910	225326
Rents **4**	54033	2059	4522	105	7832	10951	4386	7112	2272	2336	0	7545	4913
Royalties **5**	18949	0	0	0	3710	2	1936	256	40	0	0	0	13005
Other Portfolio Income **6**	683464	32387	18204	1156	55851	5410	6185	25371	10543	31464	8977	52901	435016
Other Receipts **7**	68679261	1580063	20245768	5056978	9729001	3989399	3830946	2208310	1979542	2339168	1061902	5022037	11636144
Total Receipts **8**	69843144	1619717	20282538	5067070	9812868	4015308	3853545	2251677	2012479	2402314	1082830	5128393	12314404
Average Total Receipts **9**	754	95	308	1080	2306	8883	16260	32633	51602	77494	180472	512839	2462881
Operating Costs/Operating Income (%)													
Cost of Operations **10**	2.0	3.8	0.3	•	4.6	0.5	2.2	0.9	13.4	15.1	2.9	•	0.0
Salaries and Wages **11**	32.8	19.7	24.7	29.5	35.6	43.8	31.8	28.4	31.6	30.9	18.2	30.7	47.1
Taxes Paid **12**	3.5	2.7	3.4	4.0	3.4	4.0	2.8	3.1	3.3	3.2	3.0	3.0	3.8
Interest Paid **13**	2.7	4.3	0.8	1.3	1.4	1.2	1.5	1.2	1.5	4.3	2.9	4.8	7.5
Depreciation **14**	1.3	1.9	0.9	1.1	0.8	1.8	1.1	1.3	1.5	1.4	0.9	1.5	2.0
Amortization and Depletion **15**	1.6	0.5	0.7	1.1	1.4	1.0	0.8	0.8	1.9	2.8	1.1	5.0	2.7
Pensions and Other Deferred Comp. **16**	1.8	0.5	1.2	1.2	1.4	0.6	1.2	1.0	2.0	0.8	0.3	0.8	4.9
Employee Benefits **17**	2.5	1.6	1.6	2.9	2.8	2.4	1.9	8.2	2.6	3.7	1.4	2.3	2.8
Advertising **18**	1.5	2.7	2.3	1.3	1.0	0.8	1.4	0.6	4.0	2.3	2.2	0.5	0.5
Other Expenses **19**	31.4	40.4	31.6	29.2	25.8	26.2	37.2	40.4	24.6	26.8	52.7	47.7	26.9
Officers' Compensation **20**	11.8	9.6	18.5	18.7	14.3	13.7	9.9	8.4	6.9	3.1	3.3	1.9	4.0
Operating Margin **21**	7.3	12.1	14.0	9.7	7.7	4.1	8.2	5.6	6.9	5.6	11.2	1.8	•
Operating Margin Before Officers' Comp. **22**	19.1	21.7	32.5	28.4	22.0	17.8	18.1	14.0	13.8	8.7	14.4	3.7	1.7

Selected Average Balance Sheet ($ in Thousands)

Net Receivables **23**	273	0	5	50	258	801	3360	9881	11744	22914	41739	160783	3747967
Inventories **24**	•	•	•	•	•	•	•	•	•	•	•	•	•
Net Property, Plant and Equipment **25**	45	14	85	97	95	995	801	1847	3302	4549	9708	31578	196904
Total Assets **26**	1254	0	85	660	1854	6434	14677	35341	64557	162303	306217	1297530	13673631
Notes and Loans Payable **27**	225	0	42	176	517	1865	3519	6782	13889	48625	73146	332566	1422421
All Other Liabilities **28**	535	0	23	186	909	2876	7744	19832	29285	78759	130075	453798	5990442
Net Worth **29**	493	0	20	298	428	1693	3414	8728	21383	34920	102997	511166	6260769

Selected Financial Ratios (Times to 1)

Current Ratio **30**	1.1	•	1.3	1.9	1.2	1.1	1.4	1.2	1.3	0.8	1.8	1.2	1.0
Quick Ratio **31**	1.0	•	1.2	1.6	1.1	1.0	1.1	1.1	1.0	0.6	1.5	0.8	0.9
Net Sales to Working Capital **32**	13.7	•	34.4	7.0	12.9	21.0	6.2	8.5	5.7	•	2.6	6.1	14.1
Coverage Ratio **33**	4.0	3.8	19.5	8.5	6.7	4.2	6.4	5.8	5.7	2.3	4.6	1.4	1.3
Total Asset Turnover **34**	0.6	•	3.6	1.6	1.2	1.4	1.1	0.9	0.8	0.5	0.6	0.4	0.2
Inventory Turnover **35**	•	•	•	•	•	•	•	•	•	•	•	•	•
Receivables Turnover **36**	•	•	•	•	•	•	•	•	•	•	•	•	•
Total Liabilities to Net Worth **37**	1.5	•	3.3	1.2	3.3	2.8	3.3	3.0	2.0	3.6	2.0	1.5	1.2
Current Assets to Working Capital **38**	9.3	•	4.2	2.1	5.9	7.8	3.8	5.6	4.5	•	2.3	5.2	28.3
Current Liabilities to Working Capital **39**	8.3	•	3.2	1.1	4.9	6.8	2.8	4.6	3.5	•	1.3	4.2	27.3
Working Capital to Net Sales **40**	0.1	•	0.0	0.1	0.1	0.0	0.2	0.1	0.2	•	0.4	0.2	0.1
Inventory to Working Capital **41**	0.0	•	•	•	•	0.0	0.0	0.0	0.0	•	•	•	•
Total Receipts to Cash Flow **42**	3.1	2.4	2.6	3.1	3.6	4.3	2.5	2.4	3.7	3.6	1.6	2.2	5.2
Cost of Goods to Cash Flow **43**	0.1	0.1	0.0	0.0	0.2	0.0	0.1	0.0	0.5	0.5	0.0	0.0	0.0
Cash Flow to Total Debt **44**	0.3	•	1.8	1.0	0.4	0.4	0.6	0.5	0.3	0.2	0.5	0.3	0.1

Selected Financial Factors (in Percentages)

Debt Ratio **45**	60.7	•	76.5	54.9	76.9	73.7	76.7	75.3	66.9	78.5	66.4	60.6	54.2
Return on Total Assets **46**	6.5	•	53.3	18.0	11.3	7.3	10.7	6.2	6.7	4.6	8.0	2.6	1.8
Return on Equity Before Income Taxes **47**	12.3	•	215.4	35.2	41.4	21.1	38.9	20.6	16.6	12.1	18.7	1.8	0.9
Return on Equity After Income Taxes **48**	10.9	•	213.7	34.8	39.6	18.2	36.5	15.7	14.4	9.6	9.6	12.0	•
Profit Margin (Before Income Tax) **49**	8.1	12.1	14.0	9.7	7.7	4.0	8.2	5.5	6.9	5.4	10.7	1.8	2.3
Profit Margin (After Income Tax) **50**	7.1	11.2	13.9	9.6	7.3	3.5	7.7	4.2	6.0	4.3	6.8	•	•

307

Table II

Corporations with Net Income

INSURANCE AGENCIES AND BROKERAGES

MONEY AMOUNTS AND SIZE OF ASSETS IN THOUSANDS OF DOLLARS

Item Description for Accounting Period 7/09 Through 6/10	Total	Zero Assets	Under 500	500 to 1,000	1,000 to 5,000	5,000 to 10,000	10,000 to 25,000	25,000 to 50,000	50,000 to 100,000	100,000 to 250,000	250,000 to 500,000	500,000 to 2,500,000	2,500,000 and over
Number of Enterprises 1	72779	12263	53029	3939	2900	343	184	55	30	22	•	•	0
Revenues ($ in Thousands)													
Net Sales 2	51536714	1022533	17229139	4312625	8071663	3063370	3326382	1733190	1702233	1750558	•	•	0
Interest 3	128155	590	12012	5078	13347	5633	3383	10010	6224	25198	•	•	0
Rents 4	41917	1311	3454	102	7068	10453	1374	7112	1164	2336	•	•	0
Royalties 5	4561	0	0	0	3710	2	0	256	40	0	•	•	0
Other Portfolio Income 6	514760	32387	17013	1151	43154	2009	5175	25151	3112	29306	•	•	0
Other Receipts 7	50847321	988245	17196660	4306294	8004384	3045273	3316450	1690661	1691693	1693718	•	•	0
Total Receipts 8	51536714	1022533	17229139	4312625	8071663	3063370	3326382	1733190	1702233	1750558	•	•	0
Average Total Receipts 9	708	83	325	1095	2783	8931	18078	31513	56741	79571	•	•	•
Operating Costs/Operating Income (%)													
Cost of Operations 10	2.2	2.3	0.4	•	5.6	•	1.6	1.2	15.6	12.6	•	•	•
Salaries and Wages 11	31.5	13.1	23.8	27.9	35.8	42.0	30.3	32.4	31.1	28.6	•	•	•
Taxes Paid 12	3.3	2.7	3.4	3.9	3.0	3.8	2.7	3.4	3.2	3.1	•	•	•
Interest Paid 13	1.8	0.6	0.7	1.3	1.1	1.5	0.9	1.5	1.0	2.0	•	•	•
Depreciation 14	1.1	1.0	0.8	1.1	0.7	2.0	0.8	1.6	1.4	1.3	•	•	•
Amortization and Depletion 15	1.4	0.5	0.6	1.1	1.2	1.3	0.8	0.9	1.6	1.7	•	•	•
Pensions and Other Deferred Comp. 16	1.2	0.0	1.3	0.7	1.3	0.6	1.3	1.3	1.4	1.0	•	•	•
Employee Benefits 17	2.3	1.1	1.4	2.9	2.5	2.5	1.6	10.1	2.6	4.2	•	•	•
Advertising 18	1.5	1.7	2.2	1.2	0.6	0.8	1.1	0.7	4.6	2.7	•	•	•
Other Expenses 19	28.0	33.5	28.8	30.1	22.7	24.9	36.8	27.7	21.6	27.1	•	•	•
Officers' Compensation 20	12.2	12.2	18.6	18.0	12.6	11.7	10.5	9.3	5.6	3.2	•	•	•
Operating Margin 21	13.5	31.2	18.1	11.8	12.8	8.9	11.5	10.0	10.3	12.4	•	•	•
Operating Margin Before Officers' Comp. 22	25.8	43.4	36.6	29.8	25.4	20.6	22.0	19.3	16.0	15.6	•	•	•

Selected Average Balance Sheet ($ in Thousands)

	1	2	3	4	5	6	7	8	9	10
Net Receivables 23	125	0	5	44	239	728	3482	9705	11463	21795
Inventories 24	•	•	•	•	•	•	•	•	•	•
Net Property, Plant and Equipment 25	37	0	12	87	112	1165	687	2167	3558	4777
Total Assets 26	698	•	85	640	1968	6435	14856	34782	64658	158746
Notes and Loans Payable 27	159	•	37	169	490	2249	2404	8161	13118	24015
All Other Liabilities 28	310	•	20	171	1013	2371	7524	18364	32387	92835
Net Worth 29	229	•	28	299	465	1815	4929	8257	19153	41897

Selected Financial Ratios (Times to 1)

	1	2	3	4	5	6	7	8	9	10
Current Ratio 30	1.2	•	1.5	2.0	1.2	1.3	1.5	1.2	1.3	0.9
Quick Ratio 31	1.1	•	1.3	1.8	1.1	1.2	1.3	1.1	1.1	0.7
Net Sales to Working Capital 32	11.3	•	26.8	7.2	12.8	11.7	5.5	7.8	5.9	•
Coverage Ratio 33	9.2	55.6	25.7	10.4	12.2	7.0	13.3	7.8	11.3	6.9
Total Asset Turnover 34	1.0	•	3.8	1.7	1.4	1.4	1.2	0.9	0.9	0.5
Inventory Turnover 35	•	•	•	•	•	•	•	•	•	•
Receivables Turnover 36	•	•	•	•	•	•	•	•	•	•
Total Liabilities to Net Worth 37	2.1	•	2.1	1.1	3.2	2.5	2.0	3.2	2.4	2.8
Current Assets to Working Capital 38	5.0	•	3.2	2.0	5.6	4.1	3.1	5.4	4.2	•
Current Liabilities to Working Capital 39	4.0	•	2.2	1.0	4.6	3.1	2.1	4.4	3.2	•
Working Capital to Net Sales 40	0.1	•	0.0	0.1	0.1	0.1	0.2	0.1	0.2	•
Inventory to Working Capital 41	0.0	•	•	•	•	•	0.0	0.0	•	•
Total Receipts to Cash Flow 42	2.8	1.8	2.5	2.8	3.3	3.8	2.3	3.0	3.6	2.8
Cost of Goods to Cash Flow 43	0.1	0.0	0.0	0.2	0.2	•	0.0	0.0	0.6	0.4
Cash Flow to Total Debt 44	0.5	2.3	1.1	0.6	0.5	0.8	0.4	0.4	0.2	•

Selected Financial Factors (in Percentages)

	1	2	3	4	5	6	7	8	9	10
Debt Ratio 45	67.2	•	67.2	53.2	76.4	71.8	66.8	76.3	70.4	73.6
Return on Total Assets 46	16.6	72.0	22.4	19.7	14.4	15.1	10.2	9.9	7.1	•
Return on Equity Before Income Taxes 47	45.2	211.0	43.4	76.6	43.7	42.0	37.6	30.5	23.1	•
Return on Equity After Income Taxes 48	41.3	209.5	42.8	74.1	40.2	39.9	31.6	27.3	20.2	•
Profit Margin (Before Income Tax) 49	14.6	31.2	18.1	11.8	12.8	8.9	11.5	9.8	10.3	12.2
Profit Margin (After Income Tax) 50	13.3	29.8	17.9	11.7	12.4	8.2	10.9	8.3	9.2	10.6

OTHER INSURANCE RELATED ACTIVITIES

Table I

Corporations with and without Net Income

MONEY AMOUNTS AND SIZE OF ASSETS IN THOUSANDS OF DOLLARS

Item Description for Accounting Period 7/09 Through 6/10	Total	Zero Assets	Under 500	500 to 1,000	1,000 to 5,000	5,000 to 10,000	10,000 to 25,000	25,000 to 50,000	50,000 to 100,000	100,000 to 250,000	250,000 to 500,000	500,000 to 2,500,000	2,500,000 and over
Number of Enterprises 1	12512	1487	8747	1050	792	156	129	46	36	33	15	16	4
Revenues ($ in Thousands)													
Net Sales 2	49381245	707933	218706	1117887	1943226	2085195	1602421	1648310	2430084	3570506	5654199	5793340	20709437
Interest 3	1136297	37707	1202	3135	8066	4464	15808	4170	22732	36646	84442	116007	801917
Rents 4	91159	0	0	0	1704	1282	151	2294	4349	2305	15052	1954	62068
Royalties 5	21104	0	0	0	5632	0	0	0	0	0	0	15391	82
Other Portfolio Income 6	376945	1459	10	9945	3734	1358	10928	18583	11062	41469	38455	20506	219434
Other Receipts 7	47755740	668767	2117494	1104807	1924090	2078091	1575534	1623263	2391941	3490086	5516250	5639482	19625936
Total Receipts 8	49381245	707933	218706	1117887	1943226	2085195	1602421	1648310	2430084	3570506	5654199	5793340	20709437
Average Total Receipts 9	3947	476	242	1065	2454	13367	12422	35833	67502	108197	376947	362084	5177359
Operating Costs/Operating Income (%)													
Cost of Operations 10	15.2	2.5	•	•	0.0	0.0	9.4	4.2	22.1	10.0	14.1	23.5	20.3
Salaries and Wages 11	17.8	30.3	13.4	10.8	34.6	18.9	35.4	30.2	24.4	26.5	17.4	21.5	10.9
Taxes Paid 12	2.3	0.9	2.7	1.3	3.4	2.0	3.5	3.5	4.4	3.5	3.1	2.5	1.3
Interest Paid 13	2.4	3.2	0.5	1.0	0.8	0.3	1.1	0.4	2.4	1.6	3.7	4.0	2.7
Depreciation 14	1.2	1.8	0.5	0.4	1.9	0.6	1.7	1.7	1.8	1.6	1.0	1.8	1.0
Amortization and Depletion 15	0.9	0.5	0.0	0.6	0.4	0.1	0.5	0.7	2.0	1.0	1.2	2.3	0.5
Pensions and Other Deferred Comp. 16	0.8	0.1	1.0	12.4	1.1	0.6	1.6	1.5	0.4	0.7	0.6	0.6	0.3
Employee Benefits 17	2.3	5.6	1.8	0.7	3.2	2.2	3.3	3.4	4.4	2.9	1.8	3.8	1.4
Advertising 18	0.7	0.2	0.7	0.2	2.2	0.2	0.5	2.6	0.3	0.3	0.2	2.2	0.3
Other Expenses 19	52.8	52.9	57.7	50.1	40.6	61.4	34.1	42.0	23.3	49.5	57.5	26.6	65.2
Officers' Compensation 20	2.3	2.5	12.5	8.7	5.3	7.0	2.3	3.4	7.3	1.4	0.8	2.1	0.1
Operating Margin 21	1.3	•	9.2	13.8	6.5	6.7	6.4	6.5	7.3	1.2	•	9.1	•
Operating Margin Before Officers' Comp. 22	3.6	2.0	21.7	22.5	11.8	13.6	8.7	9.9	14.7	2.5	•	11.2	•

Selected Average Balance Sheet ($ in Thousands)

Net Receivables **23**	687	0	5	242	544	1447	2230	8886	8584	19692	33819	170382	689295
Inventories **24**	•	•	•	•	•	•	•	•	•	•	•	•	•
Net Property, Plant and Equipment **25**	192	•	8	20	313	348	786	1868	5349	7734	14182	27769	179815
Total Assets **26**	6242	•	29	656	2369	6770	15275	36890	68986	155305	354616	895506	10824685
Notes and Loans Payable **27**	1207	•	40	211	578	1903	2637	3641	19586	15678	177633	198981	1550391
All Other Liabilities **28**	3012	•	3	212	1200	4593	5853	14310	31898	80728	108487	234932	6290065
Net Worth **29**	2023	•	-13	233	591	273	6785	18939	17502	58899	68496	461592	2984230

Selected Financial Ratios (Times to 1)

Current Ratio **30**	1.0	•	1.5	1.5	1.6	1.2	1.6	1.7	1.3	1.3	0.8	1.7	0.8
Quick Ratio **31**	0.9	•	1.5	1.4	1.4	1.0	1.4	1.3	1.0	0.9	0.6	1.4	0.7
Net Sales to Working Capital **32**	41.6	•	49.0	6.0	4.3	20.8	4.0	3.8	10.1	6.3	•	3.2	3.2
Coverage Ratio **33**	1.4	0.9	•	19.4	14.2	9.0	22.9	6.8	15.9	4.1	1.7	0.7	3.2
Total Asset Turnover **34**	0.6	•	8.3	1.6	1.0	2.0	0.8	1.0	1.0	0.7	1.1	0.4	0.5
Inventory Turnover **35**	•	•	•	•	•	•	•	•	•	•	•	•	•
Receivables Turnover **36**	•	•	•	•	•	•	•	•	•	•	•	•	•
Total Liabilities to Net Worth **37**	2.1	•	1.8	3.0	1.8	23.8	1.3	0.9	2.9	1.6	4.2	0.9	2.6
Current Assets to Working Capital **38**	23.6	•	2.9	2.8	2.9	7.0	2.7	2.3	4.9	4.2	1.6	2.5	•
Current Liabilities to Working Capital **39**	22.6	•	1.9	1.8	1.9	6.0	1.7	1.3	3.9	3.2	•	1.5	•
Working Capital to Net Sales **40**	0.0	•	0.0	0.2	0.2	0.0	0.3	0.3	0.1	0.2	0.3	0.2	•
Inventory to Working Capital **41**	0.1	•	0.0	0.2	0.0	0.0	0.0	0.0	0.0	0.0	0.0	0.0	•
Total Receipts to Cash Flow **42**	1.9	2.1	1.6	2.6	1.5	1.5	2.7	2.3	3.6	2.1	1.9	3.0	1.7
Cost of Goods to Cash Flow **43**	0.3	0.1	•	0.0	0.0	0.0	0.3	0.1	0.8	0.2	0.3	0.7	0.3
Cash Flow to Total Debt **44**	0.5	3.6	1.6	0.5	1.6	1.3	0.5	0.9	0.4	0.5	0.7	0.3	0.4

Selected Financial Factors (in Percentages)

Debt Ratio **45**	67.6	•	144.5	64.5	75.1	96.0	55.6	48.7	74.6	62.1	80.7	48.5	72.4
Return on Total Assets **46**	2.2	•	80.1	24.1	7.5	13.8	6.0	6.6	9.5	1.8	2.6	5.2	•
Return on Equity Before Income Taxes **47**	2.0	•	63.1	26.7	326.2	11.5	12.0	28.2	9.7	1.9	7.0	•	•
Return on Equity After Income Taxes **48**	•	•	62.1	24.4	282.1	10.2	9.7	22.3	6.3	1.0	4.2	•	•
Profit Margin (Before Income Tax) **49**	1.0	•	9.2	13.8	6.7	6.3	6.4	7.3	1.0	9.0	•	•	•
Profit Margin (After Income Tax) **50**	•	•	9.1	13.6	5.8	5.1	5.9	5.8	5.3	•	•	•	•

Table II
Corporations with Net Income

OTHER INSURANCE RELATED ACTIVITIES

MONEY AMOUNTS AND SIZE OF ASSETS IN THOUSANDS OF DOLLARS

Item Description for Accounting Period 7/09 Through 6/10	Total	Zero Assets	Under 500	500 to 1,000	1,000 to 5,000	5,000 to 10,000	10,000 to 25,000	25,000 to 50,000	50,000 to 100,000	100,000 to 250,000	250,000 to 500,000	500,000 to 2,500,000	2,500,000 and over
Number of Enterprises **1**	8466	763	•	916	480	124	75	•	27	18	•	•	10
Revenues ($ in Thousands)													
Net Sales **2**	42401690	334339	•	689509	1622159	1332493	1312214	•	1698351	1891276	•	•	4992482
Interest **3**	718757	35111	•	3135	4533	1859	5703	•	20183	23104	•	•	52297
Rents **4**	72445	0	•	0	1669	1282	151	•	2780	1902	•	•	0
Royalties **5**	19805	0	•	0	5632	0	0	•	0	0	•	•	14091
Other Portfolio Income **6**	185847	692	•	9945	2580	294	3246	•	11050	37060	•	•	12139
Other Receipts **7**	41404836	298536	•	676429	1607745	1329058	1303114	•	1664338	1829210	•	•	4913955
Total Receipts **8**	42401690	334339	•	689509	1622159	1332493	1312214	•	1698351	1891276	•	•	4992482
Average Total Receipts **9**	5008	438	•	753	3379	10746	17496	•	62902	105071	•	•	499248
Operating Costs/Operating Income (%)													
Cost of Operations **10**	11.2	5.3	•	•	0.0	•	11.1	•	4.8	15.3	•	•	25.4
Salaries and Wages **11**	16.9	9.8	•	14.8	33.3	28.6	36.4	•	28.1	31.6	•	•	21.0
Taxes Paid **12**	2.1	1.1	•	2.0	3.0	3.0	3.8	•	5.3	3.5	•	•	2.1
Interest Paid **13**	2.0	4.4	•	1.7	0.6	0.4	0.6	•	1.7	2.0	•	•	3.4
Depreciation **14**	1.1	0.3	•	0.5	1.0	1.0	2.0	•	1.8	1.9	•	•	1.7
Amortization and Depletion **15**	0.7	0.3	•	1.0	0.0	0.2	0.2	•	0.9	1.5	•	•	2.0
Pensions and Other Deferred Comp. **16**	0.9	0.2	•	20.1	1.2	0.9	1.9	•	0.5	1.0	•	•	0.6
Employee Benefits **17**	2.1	0.2	•	1.1	2.2	3.2	3.7	•	5.4	2.7	•	•	3.8
Advertising **18**	0.4	0.2	•	0.2	2.4	0.3	0.3	•	0.3	0.3	•	•	0.5
Other Expenses **19**	49.3	56.2	•	17.4	40.5	39.4	25.9	•	27.4	29.6	•	•	25.2
Officers' Compensation **20**	2.3	5.0	•	14.1	4.9	10.8	2.0	•	9.5	1.9	•	•	1.3
Operating Margin **21**	11.0	16.9	•	26.9	11.1	12.2	12.2	•	14.3	8.7	•	•	12.9
Operating Margin Before Officers' Comp. **22**	13.2	22.0	•	41.0	15.9	23.0	14.2	•	23.8	10.6	•	•	14.1

Selected Average Balance Sheet ($ in Thousands)

Net Receivables **23**		885	245	776	1804	3487	7544	18382	241472
Inventories **24**		0	•	•	•	•	•	•	•
Net Property, Plant and Equipment **25**		217	22	417	427	996	5385	7824	19918
Total Assets **26**		6403	641	2549	6536	15397	68897	151230	815359
Notes and Loans Payable **27**		1277	242	551	2295	2387	12903	12891	263687
All Other Liabilities **28**		2775	208	1641	2328	6886	36202	72368	256731
Net Worth **29**		2351	192	358	1912	6124	19792	65971	294941

Selected Financial Ratios (Times to 1)

Current Ratio **30**		1.1	1.4	1.3	2.3	1.7	1.2	1.3	1.8
Quick Ratio **31**		0.8	1.3	1.1	2.0	1.6	1.0	0.9	1.5
Net Sales to Working Capital **32**		38.5	5.8	8.6	4.0	4.4	10.4	7.8	3.2
Coverage Ratio **33**	4.9	6.5	16.9	19.9	29.2	22.2	9.2	5.3	4.7
Total Asset Turnover **34**		0.8	1.2	1.3	1.6	1.1	0.9	0.7	0.6
Inventory Turnover **35**		•	•	•	•	•	•	•	•
Receivables Turnover **36**		•	•	•	•	•	•	•	•
Total Liabilities to Net Worth **37**		1.7	2.3	6.1	2.4	1.5	2.5	1.3	1.8
Current Assets to Working Capital **38**		17.3	3.7	4.4	1.8	2.4	5.5	4.6	2.3
Current Liabilities to Working Capital **39**		16.3	2.7	3.4	0.8	1.4	4.5	3.6	1.3
Working Capital to Net Sales **40**		0.0	0.2	0.1	0.2	0.2	0.1	0.1	0.3
Inventory to Working Capital **41**		0.1	•	•	•	0.0	0.0	0.0	0.0
Total Receipts to Cash Flow **42**	1.4	1.7	2.4	2.3	2.1	2.9	2.5	3.0	2.8
Cost of Goods to Cash Flow **43**		0.2	0.1	0.0	0.0	0.3	0.1	0.5	0.7
Cash Flow to Total Debt **44**		0.7	0.7	0.7	1.1	0.7	0.5	0.4	0.3

Selected Financial Factors (in Percentages)

Debt Ratio **45**		63.3	70.1	86.0	70.7	60.2	71.3	56.4	63.8
Return on Total Assets **46**		10.2	33.6	15.3	20.8	14.3	14.6	7.3	9.9
Return on Equity Before Income Taxes **47**		23.5	105.4	103.3	68.7	34.4	45.3	13.6	21.6
Return on Equity After Income Taxes **48**		17.3	104.1	97.1	60.8	32.0	38.4	10.1	14.5
Profit Margin (Before Income Tax) **49**	17.4	11.0	26.9	10.9	12.2	12.1	14.3	8.6	12.8
Profit Margin (After Income Tax) **50**	15.6	8.1	26.6	10.3	10.8	11.2	12.1	6.3	8.6

Table I
Corporations with and without Net Income

OPEN-END INVESTMENT FUNDS (FORM 1120-RIC)

MONEY AMOUNTS AND SIZE OF ASSETS IN THOUSANDS OF DOLLARS

Item Description for Accounting Period 7/09 Through 6/10		Total	Zero Assets	Under 500	500 to 1,000	1,000 to 5,000	5,000 to 10,000	10,000 to 25,000	25,000 to 50,000	50,000 to 100,000	100,000 to 250,000	250,000 to 500,000	500,000 to 2,500,000	2,500,000 and over
Number of Enterprises	1	13043	1179	74	98	782	678	1029	1109	1213	2044	1524	2390	923
Revenues ($ in Thousands)														
Net Sales	2	330598377	3280467	5686	3766	111354	190848	401287	1049578	2605404	10388990	16683486	75936039	219941472
Interest	3	140627341	1843310	0	298	14564	45565	71213	322852	758496	3246060	5881980	27922090	100520914
Rents	4	0	0	0	0	0	0	0	0	0	0	0	0	0
Royalties	5	0	0	0	0	0	0	0	0	0	0	0	0	0
Other Portfolio Income	6	45199375	320355	5246	395	46865	55010	112871	250989	667486	2612638	3683633	13933491	23510396
Other Receipts	7	144771661	1116802	440	3073	49925	90273	217203	475737	1179422	4530292	7117873	34080458	95910162
Total Receipts	8	330598377	3280467	5686	3766	111354	190848	401287	1049578	2605404	10388990	16683486	75936039	219941472
Average Total Receipts	9	25347	2782	77	38	142	281	390	946	2148	5083	10947	31772	238290
Operating Costs/Operating Income (%)														
Cost of Operations	10	•	•	•	•	•	•	•	•	•	•	•	•	•
Salaries and Wages	11	0.1	0.1	0.6	•	0.0	0.0	0.2	0.2	0.1	0.1	0.1	0.1	0.0
Taxes Paid	12	0.3	0.4	0.1	0.9	0.2	0.3	0.4	0.4	0.5	0.4	0.5	0.4	0.2
Interest Paid	13	0.4	0.6	•	•	0.0	0.0	0.4	0.5	0.5	0.4	0.6	0.4	0.4
Depreciation	14	0.0	•	•	•	•	•	0.0	0.0	0.0	0.0	0.0	0.0	0.0
Amortization and Depletion	15	0.0	0.6	5.3	5.6	4.5	2.2	1.0	0.4	•	0.0	0.0	0.0	0.0
Pensions and Other Deferred Comp.	16	•	•	•	•	•	•	•	•	•	•	•	•	•
Employee Benefits	17	•	•	•	•	•	•	•	•	•	•	•	•	•
Advertising	18	0.0	0.0	•	•	•	0.0	0.0	0.0	•	0.0	0.0	0.0	0.0
Other Expenses	19	20.9	34.4	20.0	49.8	14.8	19.5	38.2	33.2	29.0	25.2	23.8	23.4	19.2
Officers' Compensation	20	0.0	0.0	•	•	0.0	0.0	0.2	0.1	0.1	0.0	0.0	0.0	0.0
Operating Margin	21	78.4	63.9	74.0	43.6	80.4	78.0	59.2	65.1	69.8	73.8	74.9	75.7	80.2
Operating Margin Before Officers' Comp.	22	78.4	63.9	74.0	43.6	80.4	78.0	59.7	65.4	69.8	73.8	74.9	75.7	80.2

Selected Average Balance Sheet ($ in Thousands)

	Total	1	2	3	4	5	6	7	8	9	10	11
Net Receivables 23	11382	1	16	11	51	289	402	1099	1955	4477	14479	109330
Inventories 24	•	•	•	•	•	•	•	•	•	•	•	•
Net Property, Plant and Equipment 25	1	0	0	0	0	0	0	0	0	0	3	1
Total Assets 26	1014814	269	810	2955	7366	16492	36640	73063	166235	359882	1109410	10338943
Notes and Loans Payable 27	1296	0	0	0	1	12	86	212	426	1216	3006	7183
All Other Liabilities 28	39201	36	43	74	246	636	1184	3255	8167	18055	58158	348798
Net Worth 29	974317	233	767	2880	7119	15844	35370	69596	157642	340612	1048246	9982962

Selected Financial Ratios (Times to 1)

	Total	1	2	3	4	5	6	7	8	9	10	11
Current Ratio 30	4.4	0.3	1.2	3.0	2.5	3.5	4.0	3.9	3.9	3.5	3.2	5.0
Quick Ratio 31	4.2	0.1	0.5	0.7	1.4	2.5	3.3	3.5	3.5	3.2	2.9	4.8
Net Sales to Working Capital 32	0.2	•	4.2	1.1	0.8	0.2	0.3	0.2	0.2	0.2	0.2	0.2
Coverage Ratio 33	175.1	93.7	•	9277.9	29209.8	119.3	102.4	96.2	123.5	92.1	140.4	208.1
Total Asset Turnover 34	0.0	0.3	0.0	0.0	0.0	0.0	0.0	0.0	0.0	0.0	0.0	0.0
Inventory Turnover 35	•	•	•	•	•	•	•	•	•	•	•	•
Receivables Turnover 36	•	•	•	•	•	•	•	•	•	•	•	•
Total Liabilities to Net Worth 37	0.0	0.2	0.1	0.0	0.0	0.0	0.0	0.0	0.1	0.1	0.1	0.0
Current Assets to Working Capital 38	1.3	•	5.7	1.5	1.7	1.3	1.3	1.3	1.3	1.4	1.4	1.2
Current Liabilities to Working Capital 39	0.3	•	4.7	0.5	0.7	0.3	0.3	0.3	0.3	0.4	0.4	0.2
Working Capital to Net Sales 40	5.3	•	0.2	0.9	1.3	4.1	3.8	4.3	4.5	4.2	4.1	5.9
Inventory to Working Capital 41	•	•	•	•	•	•	•	•	•	•	•	•
Total Receipts to Cash Flow 42	1.1	59.9	1.2	1.5	1.2	1.1	1.1	1.1	1.1	1.1	1.1	1.1
Cost of Goods to Cash Flow 43	•	•	•	•	•	•	•	•	•	•	•	•
Cash Flow to Total Debt 44	0.6	0.0	0.7	1.3	1.0	0.7	0.7	0.6	0.5	0.5	0.5	0.6

Selected Financial Factors (in Percentages)

	Total	1	2	3	4	5	6	7	8	9	10	11
Debt Ratio 45	4.0	13.5	5.3	2.5	3.4	3.9	3.5	4.7	5.2	5.4	5.5	3.4
Return on Total Assets 46	1.8	21.1	2.1	3.2	2.3	1.2	1.3	1.5	1.7	1.8	1.8	1.7
Return on Equity Before Income Taxes 47	1.8	24.4	2.2	3.3	2.4	1.2	1.3	1.5	1.8	1.9	1.9	1.8
Return on Equity After Income Taxes 48	1.8	24.4	2.2	3.3	2.4	1.2	1.3	1.5	1.8	1.9	1.9	1.8
Profit Margin (Before Income Tax) 49	69.9	58.9	74.0	43.7	66.6	61.2	49.2	49.6	54.8	58.8	62.1	74.6
Profit Margin (After Income Tax) 50	69.9	58.9	74.0	43.7	66.6	61.2	49.2	49.6	54.8	58.8	62.1	74.6

Table II

Corporations with Net Income

OPEN-END INVESTMENT FUNDS (FORM 1120-RIC)

MONEY AMOUNTS AND SIZE OF ASSETS IN THOUSANDS OF DOLLARS

Item Description for Accounting Period 7/09 Through 6/10		Total	Zero Assets	Under 500	500 to 1,000	1,000 to 5,000	5,000 to 10,000	10,000 to 25,000	25,000 to 50,000	50,000 to 100,000	100,000 to 250,000	250,000 to 500,000	500,000 to 2,500,000	2,500,000 and over
Number of Enterprises	1	10567	792	49	74	591	524	715	835	969	1724	1300	2117	877
Revenues ($ in Thousands)														
Net Sales	2	321987137	3175198	5552	3507	93704	158465	354244	967794	2400483	9683120	15586640	72379893	217178537
Interest	3	139229325	1830794	0	297	14379	45077	62952	273280	719212	3210425	5804609	27244310	100023990
Rents	4	0	0	0	0	0	0	0	0	0	0	0	0	0
Royalties	5	0	0	0	0	0	0	0	0	0	0	0	0	0
Other Portfolio Income	6	40549693	270699	5246	395	32512	27844	89840	189080	523930	2217732	3094635	11527641	22570138
Other Receipts	7	142208119	1073705	306	2815	46813	85544	201452	505434	1157341	4254963	6687396	33607942	94584409
Total Receipts	8	321987137	3175198	5552	3507	93704	158465	354244	967794	2400483	9683120	15586640	72379893	217178537
Average Total Receipts	9	30471	4009	113	47	159	302	495	1159	2477	5617	11990	34190	247638
Operating Costs/Operating Income (%)														
Cost of Operations	10	•	•	•	•	•	•	•	•	•	•	•	•	•
Salaries and Wages	11	0.0	0.1	0.0	•	0.0	0.0	0.1	0.1	0.1	0.1	0.1	0.0	0.0
Taxes Paid	12	0.3	0.4	0.1	1.0	0.2	0.3	0.2	0.3	0.4	0.4	0.5	0.4	0.2
Interest Paid	13	0.3	0.6	•	•	•	0.0	0.0	0.1	0.5	0.4	0.6	0.4	0.2
Depreciation	14	0.0	•	•	•	•	•	•	•	0.0	0.0	0.0	0.0	0.0
Amortization and Depletion	15	0.0	0.3	1.8	4.1	4.6	2.5	0.9	0.4	•	0.0	0.0	0.0	0.0
Pensions and Other Deferred Comp.	16	•	•	•	•	•	•	•	•	•	•	•	•	•
Employee Benefits	17	•	•	•	•	•	•	•	•	•	•	•	•	•
Advertising	18	0.0	0.0	•	•	•	•	•	•	•	0.0	0.0	0.0	0.0
Other Expenses	19	19.3	32.4	3.7	45.4	12.1	15.4	21.8	22.8	22.7	21.2	20.0	20.8	18.4
Officers' Compensation	20	0.0	•	•	•	•	0.0	0.0	•	0.1	0.0	0.0	0.0	0.0
Operating Margin	21	80.1	66.1	94.3	49.6	83.0	81.8	76.8	76.2	76.2	77.9	78.7	78.3	81.1
Operating Margin Before Officers' Comp.	22	80.1	66.1	94.3	49.6	83.0	81.8	76.8	76.2	76.3	77.9	78.7	78.3	81.1

Selected Average Balance Sheet ($ in Thousands)

Net Receivables 23	12989	1	19	10	45	290	340	1047	1928	4344	15001	108309
Inventories 24	•	•	•	•	•	•	•	•	•	•	•	•
Net Property, Plant and Equipment 25	0	0	0	0	0	0	0	0	0	0	1	1
Total Assets 26	1184675	290	798	2835	7288	16556	36712	73371	167281	361129	1113621	10585986
Notes and Loans Payable 27	1441	0	0	0	0	0	24	234	496	1373	3392	5881
All Other Liabilities 28	45515	50	26	63	158	629	1056	3315	8078	17938	58919	358394
Net Worth 29	1137719	240	772	2773	7130	15926	35632	69822	158706	341819	1051310	10221710

Selected Financial Ratios (Times to 1)

Current Ratio 30	4.4	•	0.3	2.4	4.6	3.8	4.0	3.7	3.8	3.5	3.1	5.0
Quick Ratio 31	4.1	•	0.0	1.0	1.8	2.8	3.3	3.2	3.4	3.1	2.8	4.8
Net Sales to Working Capital 32	0.2	•	1.3	0.9	0.7	0.3	0.4	0.3	0.3	0.3	0.3	0.2
Coverage Ratio 33	242.9	•	•	•	62376.5	1951.2	560.2	111.1	142.3	103.2	165.0	334.4
Total Asset Turnover 34	0.0	0.4	0.1	0.1	0.0	0.0	0.0	0.0	0.0	0.0	0.0	0.0
Inventory Turnover 35	•	•	•	•	•	•	•	•	•	•	•	•
Receivables Turnover 36	•	•	•	•	•	•	•	•	•	•	•	•
Total Liabilities to Net Worth 37	0.0	0.2	0.0	0.0	0.0	0.0	0.0	0.1	0.1	0.1	0.1	0.0
Current Assets to Working Capital 38	1.3	•	1.7	1.3	1.4	1.4	1.3	1.4	1.4	1.4	1.5	1.3
Current Liabilities to Working Capital 39	0.3	•	0.7	0.3	0.4	0.4	0.3	0.4	0.4	0.4	0.5	0.3
Working Capital to Net Sales 40	5.0	•	0.8	1.1	1.5	3.5	2.8	3.5	4.0	3.8	3.7	5.7
Inventory to Working Capital 41	•	•	•	•	•	•	•	•	•	•	•	•
Total Receipts to Cash Flow 42	1.1	27.9	1.2	1.6	1.2	1.3	1.1	1.1	1.1	1.1	1.1	1.1
Cost of Goods to Cash Flow 43	•	•	•	•	•	•	•	•	•	•	•	•
Cash Flow to Total Debt 44	0.6	0.1	1.5	1.6	1.6	0.6	1.0	0.6	0.6	0.6	0.5	0.6

Selected Financial Factors (in Percentages)

Debt Ratio 45	4.0	17.2	3.3	2.2	2.2	3.8	2.9	4.8	5.1	5.3	5.6	3.4
Return on Total Assets 46	1.9	36.8	2.9	4.6	3.3	2.1	2.1	2.1	2.1	2.2	2.1	1.8
Return on Equity Before Income Taxes 47	1.9	44.5	3.0	4.7	3.3	2.2	2.1	2.1	2.2	2.3	2.2	1.8
Return on Equity After Income Taxes 48	1.9	44.5	3.0	4.7	3.3	2.2	2.1	2.1	2.2	2.3	2.2	1.8
Profit Margin (Before Income Tax) 49	72.7	94.3	49.6	81.9	78.7	71.6	65.4	60.3	61.5	65.2	67.4	75.8
Profit Margin (After Income Tax) 50	72.7	94.3	49.6	81.9	78.7	71.6	65.4	60.3	61.5	65.2	67.4	75.8

Table I

Corporations with and without Net Income

OTHER FINANCIAL VEHICLES

MONEY AMOUNTS AND SIZE OF ASSETS IN THOUSANDS OF DOLLARS

Item Description for Accounting Period 7/09 Through 6/10	Total	Zero Assets	Under 500	500 to 1,000	1,000 to 5,000	5,000 to 10,000	10,000 to 25,000	25,000 to 50,000	50,000 to 100,000	100,000 to 250,000	250,000 to 500,000	500,000 to 2,500,000	2,500,000 and over
Number of Enterprises 1	9758	2986	4404	129	1091	257	245	96	120	105	88	149	87
Revenues ($ in Thousands)													
Net Sales 2	48897528	4172077	724532	2955	418819	299888	868602	274952	1154360	1511253	2656657	7852392	28961040
Interest 3	36313422	3138337	37585	1987	32016	125182	108993	99172	677298	985181	2001899	6094019	23011753
Rents 4	2888304	87278	711	0	868	9945	6511	22502	6662	91996	282764	647010	1712057
Royalties 5	19452	4889	0	0	203	7812	0	0	5793	323	97	0	334
Other Portfolio Income 6	1129466	37254	44529	926	51483	18069	27914	2579	29717	67096	71756	118049	660093
Other Receipts 7	8566884	904319	641707	42	334249	138880	725184	150699	434890	366657	300141	993314	3576803
Total Receipts 8	48897528	4172077	724532	2955	418819	299888	868602	274952	1154360	1511253	2656657	7852392	28961040
Average Total Receipts 9	5011	1397	165	23	384	1167	3545	2864	9620	14393	30189	52701	332886
Operating Costs/Operating Income (%)													
Cost of Operations 10	0.8	•	0.2	•	•	•	36.4	0.4	4.6	•	•	•	•
Salaries and Wages 11	1.1	0.0	1.4	•	3.7	8.0	10.7	6.3	1.3	1.0	0.5	0.4	1.1
Taxes Paid 12	0.8	0.2	0.4	3.7	1.7	2.6	0.8	3.7	0.7	1.1	0.5	1.4	0.6
Interest Paid 13	24.1	54.0	4.4	81.9	2.9	12.3	10.1	20.6	24.8	22.7	47.7	29.1	17.6
Depreciation 14	1.3	0.1	0.1	0.4	0.9	0.2	0.4	1.1	0.5	0.9	0.8	1.7	1.5
Amortization and Depletion 15	0.7	0.2	0.3	40.0	3.0	5.3	0.6	4.2	1.0	0.6	3.0	0.7	0.4
Pensions and Other Deferred Comp. 16	0.0	0.0	0.0	•	0.2	0.4	1.1	0.1	0.0	0.0	•	0.7	0.0
Employee Benefits 17	0.8	•	0.0	•	0.7	0.5	3.4	0.9	0.1	0.0	0.0	0.0	1.2
Advertising 18	0.1	•	0.2	•	0.0	0.0	0.1	1.0	0.1	0.1	0.0	0.0	0.1
Other Expenses 19	45.3	26.4	93.8	747.9	110.3	117.8	54.8	185.6	77.6	64.1	54.3	53.4	38.2
Officers' Compensation 20	0.3	0.2	0.2	•	2.2	2.5	1.0	2.9	0.1	0.2	0.2	0.2	0.2
Operating Margin 21	24.9	18.8	•	•	•	•	•	•	•	9.4	•	13.2	39.1
Operating Margin Before Officers' Comp. 22	25.1	19.0	•	•	•	•	•	•	•	9.6	•	13.4	39.3

Selected Average Balance Sheet ($ in Thousands)

	1	2	3	4	5	6	7	8	9	10	11	12	13
Net Receivables 23	4024	0	0	10	198	314	1189	476	4012	9293	21672	91586	248466
Inventories 24	•	•	•	•	•	•	•	•	•	•	•	•	•
Net Property, Plant and Equipment 25	2468	1	0	0	1	328	976	695	1812	3637	6876	50349	172242
Total Assets 26	92279	112	840	1851	6662	16212	36224	71360	165279	359364	1146026		7590581
Notes and Loans Payable 27	23602	28	0	578	1784	5088	9993	17307	37109	91573	366995		1818147
All Other Liabilities 28	13593	27	218	1300	1522	3649	7934	10050	20273	69519	213871		1008144
Net Worth 29	55084	56	622	-27	3356	7475	18297	44002	107896	198272	565160		4764290

Selected Financial Ratios (Times to 1)

	1	2	3	4	5	6	7	8	9	10	11	12	13
Current Ratio 30	0.8	•	3.3	24.8	2.7	1.0	1.6	2.1	1.1	1.5	1.1	0.8	0.8
Quick Ratio 31	0.6	•	2.6	4.8	2.7	0.9	1.0	1.0	0.9	1.0	1.0	0.6	0.6
Net Sales to Working Capital 32	•	•	7.7	0.1	0.9	•	1.9	0.7	8.8	1.6	4.2	•	•
Coverage Ratio 33	2.0	1.3	0.8	•	•	•	•	•	0.6	1.4	0.9	1.4	3.2
Total Asset Turnover 34	0.1	•	1.5	0.0	0.2	0.2	0.2	0.1	0.1	0.1	0.1	0.0	0.0
Inventory Turnover 35	•	•	•	•	•	•	•	•	•	•	•	•	•
Receivables Turnover 36	•	•	•	•	•	•	•	•	•	•	•	•	•
Total Liabilities to Net Worth 37	0.7	•	1.0	0.3	•	1.0	1.2	1.0	0.6	0.5	0.8	1.0	0.6
Current Assets to Working Capital 38	•	•	1.4	1.0	1.6	•	2.6	1.9	12.3	3.1	8.8	•	•
Current Liabilities to Working Capital 39	•	•	0.4	0.0	0.6	•	1.6	0.9	11.3	2.1	7.8	•	•
Working Capital to Net Sales 40	•	•	0.1	7.7	1.1	•	0.5	1.4	0.1	0.6	0.2	•	•
Inventory to Working Capital 41	•	•	•	•	0.0	•	0.0	0.0	0.0	•	•	•	•
Total Receipts to Cash Flow 42	1.5	2.3	1.3	•	1.6	1.7	3.6	1.8	1.6	1.5	2.2	1.5	1.3
Cost of Goods to Cash Flow 43	0.0	•	0.0	•	•	•	1.3	0.0	0.1	•	•	•	•
Cash Flow to Total Debt 44	0.1	•	2.4	0.1	0.1	0.2	0.1	0.2	0.2	0.6	0.1	0.1	0.1

Selected Financial Factors (in Percentages)

	1	2	3	4	5	6	7	8	9	10	11	12	13
Debt Ratio 45	40.3	•	49.7	25.9	101.5	49.6	53.9	49.5	38.3	34.7	44.8	50.7	37.2
Return on Total Assets 46	2.6	•	4.9	•	•	•	•	•	1.9	2.7	3.4	1.9	2.4
Return on Equity Before Income Taxes 47	2.2	•	•	•	359.5	•	•	•	•	•	•	1.2	2.7
Return on Equity After Income Taxes 48	2.0	•	•	•	415.6	•	•	•	•	•	0.9	1.0	2.5
Profit Margin (Before Income Tax) 49	24.3	18.8	•	•	•	•	•	•	•	•	8.6	13.0	38.2
Profit Margin (After Income Tax) 50	21.8	12.1	•	•	•	•	•	•	•	•	7.0	10.6	36.2

Table II

Corporations with Net Income

OTHER FINANCIAL VEHICLES

MONEY AMOUNTS AND SIZE OF ASSETS IN THOUSANDS OF DOLLARS

Item Description for Accounting Period 7/09 Through 6/10	Total	Zero Assets	Under 500	500 to 1,000	1,000 to 5,000	5,000 to 10,000	10,000 to 25,000	25,000 to 50,000	50,000 to 100,000	100,000 to 250,000	250,000 to 500,000	500,000 to 2,500,000	2,500,000 and over
Number of Enterprises **1**	3404	870	1447	0	522	78	105	39	59	63	50	103	67
Revenues ($ in Thousands)													
Net Sales **2**	3560996	3792267	235613	0	374688	170537	701274	176958	369437	1007866	1137412	5481705	2215241
Interest **3**	26748398	2899620	4404	0	10969	13168	65189	59313	225613	471638	775885	4272820	17949780
Rents **4**	1985224	7	706	0	868	0	5473	3211	0	32676	112140	428315	1401828
Royalties **5**	475	53	0	0	0	0	0	0	0	88	0	0	334
Other Portfolio Income **6**	979700	10510	44529	0	50677	17307	6958	250	23040	29924	24369	115045	657091
Other Receipts **7**	5887199	882077	185974	0	312174	140062	623654	114184	120784	473540	225018	665525	2144208
Total Receipts **8**	3560996	3792267	235613	0	374688	170537	701274	176958	369437	1007866	1137412	5481705	2215241
Average Total Receipts **9**	10459	4359	163	•	718	2186	6679	4537	6262	15998	22748	53220	330645
Operating Costs/Operating Income (%)													
Cost of Operations **10**	1.0	•	0.7	•	•	•	44.4	•	12.8	•	•	•	•
Salaries and Wages **11**	1.1	0.0	4.3	•	4.1	11.2	9.7	1.3	3.0	0.7	0.6	0.2	1.0
Taxes Paid **12**	0.8	0.2	1.2	•	1.5	4.4	0.6	4.1	1.3	1.2	0.5	1.2	0.7
Interest Paid **13**	19.1	53.8	0.3	•	1.9	3.0	5.5	11.6	9.9	8.2	11.0	19.3	15.3
Depreciation **14**	1.3	0.0	0.1	•	0.9	0.3	0.0	0.7	0.5	0.7	0.0	1.3	1.6
Amortization and Depletion **15**	0.5	0.0	0.6	•	0.1	0.8	0.1	3.3	1.2	0.4	4.8	0.8	0.3
Pensions and Other Deferred Comp. **16**	0.0	0.0	0.0	•	0.2	0.3	1.1	0.1	0.1	0.0	0.0	•	•
Employee Benefits **17**	0.1	•	0.0	•	0.2	0.9	3.5	0.4	0.2	0.0	0.0	0.0	•
Advertising **18**	0.1	•	0.6	•	0.0	0.0	0.0	1.4	0.3	0.0	0.0	0.0	0.1
Other Expenses **19**	17.2	3.2	67.6	•	20.0	13.2	11.5	15.1	13.9	36.6	21.8	20.6	17.4
Officers' Compensation **20**	0.2	0.0	0.7	•	0.4	4.3	0.8	0.0	0.2	0.2	0.4	0.1	0.2
Operating Margin **21**	58.6	42.7	23.9	•	70.6	61.5	22.7	62.1	56.6	52.0	60.8	56.4	63.3
Operating Margin Before Officers' Comp. **22**	58.8	42.7	24.6	•	71.0	65.8	23.5	62.2	56.7	52.2	61.2	56.5	63.6

Selected Average Balance Sheet ($ in Thousands)

Net Receivables 23	7740	0	0	268	88	2298	307	3748	9824	25211	72664	244227
Inventories 24	•	•	•	•	•	•	•	•	•	•	•	•
Net Property, Plant and Equipment 25	4756	0	2	0	30	15	1422	1259	2196	138	41547	173562
Total Assets 26	194386	0	156	1710	6581	17090	35270	71817	162391	356765	1149832	7554458
Notes and Loans Payable 27	34434	0	21	232	1671	4360	6514	8556	27793	46308	251062	1280430
All Other Liabilities 28	30324	0	13	2251	372	3367	4768	13152	20049	32692	144819	1236864
Net Worth 29	129628	0	123	-773	4537	9363	23988	50109	114549	277765	753951	5037163

Selected Financial Ratios (Times to 1)

Current Ratio 30	0.9	•	3.0	14.8	4.0	2.2	5.6	1.2	1.4	2.3	1.1	0.8
Quick Ratio 31	0.8	•	3.0	14.5	3.8	2.6	2.6	1.0	0.8	2.0	0.8	0.7
Net Sales to Working Capital 32	•	•	6.4	1.1	2.0	0.7	0.7	2.3	2.3	0.7	2.8	•
Coverage Ratio 33	4.0	1.8	88.6	38.4	21.4	5.1	6.4	6.7	7.3	6.5	3.9	5.1
Total Asset Turnover 34	0.1	•	1.0	0.4	0.3	0.4	0.1	0.1	0.1	0.1	0.0	0.0
Inventory Turnover 35	•	•	•	•	•	•	•	•	•	•	•	•
Receivables Turnover 36	•	•	•	•	•	•	•	•	•	•	•	•
Total Liabilities to Net Worth 37	0.5	•	0.3	•	0.5	0.8	0.5	0.4	0.4	0.3	0.5	0.5
Current Assets to Working Capital 38	•	•	1.5	1.1	1.3	1.9	1.2	5.8	3.6	1.8	10.6	•
Current Liabilities to Working Capital 39	•	•	0.5	0.1	0.3	0.9	0.2	4.8	2.6	0.8	9.6	•
Working Capital to Net Sales 40	•	•	0.2	0.9	0.5	0.5	1.5	0.4	0.4	1.4	0.4	•
Inventory to Working Capital 41	•	•	•	•	0.0	0.0	•	0.0	•	•	•	•
Total Receipts to Cash Flow 42	1.4	2.2	1.9	1.2	1.6	3.1	1.3	1.5	1.1	1.2	1.3	1.3
Cost of Goods to Cash Flow 43	0.0	•	0.0	•	1.4	•	0.2	0.2	•	•	•	•
Cash Flow to Total Debt 44	0.1	•	2.6	0.2	0.7	0.3	0.3	0.2	0.3	0.2	0.1	0.1

Selected Financial Factors (in Percentages)

Debt Ratio 45	33.3	•	21.3	145.2	31.1	45.2	32.0	30.2	29.5	22.1	34.4	33.3
Return on Total Assets 46	4.1	•	25.3	30.4	21.4	11.0	9.5	5.8	5.9	4.6	3.5	3.4
Return on Equity Before Income Taxes 47	4.7	•	31.7	•	29.6	16.2	11.8	7.1	7.3	5.0	4.0	4.1
Return on Equity After Income Taxes 48	4.4	•	31.4	•	25.1	12.8	10.0	6.6	6.9	4.8	3.7	3.9
Profit Margin (Before Income Tax) 49	57.9	42.8	23.9	70.5	61.5	22.7	62.1	56.5	52.0	60.8	56.1	62.2
Profit Margin (After Income Tax) 50	54.5	35.4	23.6	66.0	52.0	18.0	53.1	53.1	49.6	58.5	52.6	59.6

Table I

Corporations with and without Net Income

LESSORS OF BUILDINGS

MONEY AMOUNTS AND SIZE OF ASSETS IN THOUSANDS OF DOLLARS

Item Description for Accounting Period 7/09 Through 6/10	Total	Zero Assets	Under 500	500 to 1,000	1,000 to 5,000	5,000 to 10,000	10,000 to 25,000	25,000 to 50,000	50,000 to 100,000	100,000 to 250,000	250,000 to 500,000	500,000 to 2,500,000	2,500,000 and over
Number of Enterprises 1	220753	23529	111098	37888	40197	4586	2145	604	297	202	79	90	39
Revenues ($ in Thousands)													
Net Sales 2	63943898	2471568	2951910	2959155	5328809	2602790	2686241	2346974	3388244	3685530	4153828	8295620	23073230
Interest 3	2543812	40504	20136	28687	84907	45352	28814	56834	86119	148470	87294	593396	1323300
Rents 4	27894186	219299	30416	56770	143280	128103	259622	289068	476048	1876456	1835200	5108573	17471353
Royalties 5	30173	1651	31	1709	4744	2585	12	115	7351	825	0	11149	0
Other Portfolio Income 6	2536432	209934	94460	229862	274828	67615	71171	73718	44762	164341	41272	614953	649515
Other Receipts 7	30939295	2000180	2806867	2642127	4821050	2359135	2326622	1927239	2773964	1495438	2190062	1967549	3629062
Total Receipts 8	63943898	2471568	2951910	2959155	5328809	2602790	2686241	2346974	3388244	3685530	4153828	8295620	23073230
Average Total Receipts 9	290	105	27	78	133	568	1252	3886	11408	18245	52580	92174	591621
Operating Costs/Operating Income (%)													
Cost of Operations 10	4.7	8.4	4.8	12.4	6.5	3.8	10.3	9.0	9.1	5.4	13.9	1.0	0.7
Salaries and Wages 11	6.2	2.7	13.4	8.7	7.4	18.1	7.5	13.1	14.5	3.9	5.8	4.1	2.8
Taxes Paid 12	7.5	7.9	12.5	8.8	14.1	9.7	9.3	9.0	7.0	8.3	7.6	6.9	4.5
Interest Paid 13	13.1	18.3	6.3	6.2	14.9	13.5	15.2	12.8	12.8	19.1	13.8	16.4	11.4
Depreciation 14	14.2	11.3	7.5	6.3	13.0	11.4	12.8	10.6	9.3	14.1	11.4	12.7	19.3
Amortization and Depletion 15	1.1	1.1	0.1	0.3	0.6	0.4	0.9	1.0	0.7	1.4	1.8	1.4	1.2
Pensions and Other Deferred Comp. 16	0.2	0.0	0.3	0.4	0.7	0.9	0.4	0.5	0.3	0.4	0.0	0.1	0.0
Employee Benefits 17	0.5	0.1	0.4	1.0	1.1	1.6	0.7	1.1	1.9	0.3	0.5	0.2	0.0
Advertising 18	0.4	0.1	0.5	0.9	0.2	0.7	0.7	0.6	1.6	0.3	0.8	0.3	0.2
Other Expenses 19	37.9	66.2	44.0	35.4	36.6	33.1	40.8	41.7	42.3	49.1	41.1	45.4	28.9
Officers' Compensation 20	2.3	1.1	7.2	13.4	4.3	8.1	3.4	3.0	1.5	1.2	0.6	1.0	0.2
Operating Margin 21	11.9	•	3.0	6.3	0.6	•	•	•	•	•	2.7	10.4	30.6
Operating Margin Before Officers' Comp. 22	14.2	•	10.2	19.7	4.9	6.9	1.2	0.7	0.4	•	3.3	11.3	30.8

Selected Average Balance Sheet ($ in Thousands)

Net Receivables 23	65	0	3	24	40	282	490	730	2337	4061	8952	45451	60651
Inventories 24	•	•	•	•	•	•	•	•	•	•	•	•	•
Net Property, Plant and Equipment 25	1940	0	143	488	1482	4763	9795	20780	41463	89157	215519	557816	4651360
Total Assets 26	2933	0	190	707	2111	6919	14972	34433	69352	156129	360833	1080129	6470214
Notes and Loans Payable 27	1412	0	125	575	1464	4736	9870	19028	39192	78904	164707	482183	2021914
All Other Liabilities 28	236	0	5	57	162	478	1141	2983	6085	10192	35463	106546	515017
Net Worth 29	1285	0	60	74	485	1705	3960	12421	24075	67033	160663	491401	3933284

Selected Financial Ratios (Times to 1)

Current Ratio 30	1.4	•	3.1	0.8	1.9	1.8	1.9	3.1	1.6	2.2	1.6	1.9	0.8
Quick Ratio 31	0.9	•	2.4	0.6	1.2	1.3	1.2	2.0	1.1	1.5	1.1	1.4	0.5
Net Sales to Working Capital 32	3.7	•	1.5	•	0.9	1.5	1.3	1.0	3.4	1.7	3.6	1.9	•
Coverage Ratio 33	1.9	0.0	1.5	2.0	1.0	0.9	0.8	0.8	0.9	0.8	1.2	1.6	3.7
Total Asset Turnover 34	0.1	•	0.1	0.1	0.1	0.1	0.1	0.1	0.2	0.1	0.1	0.1	0.1
Inventory Turnover 35	•	•	•	•	•	•	•	•	•	•	•	•	•
Receivables Turnover 36	•	•	•	•	•	•	•	•	•	•	•	•	•
Total Liabilities to Net Worth 37	1.3	•	2.2	8.5	3.4	3.1	2.8	1.8	1.9	1.3	1.2	1.2	0.6
Current Assets to Working Capital 38	3.7	•	1.5	•	2.1	2.3	2.1	1.5	2.7	1.8	2.5	2.1	•
Current Liabilities to Working Capital 39	2.7	•	0.5	0.5	1.1	1.3	1.1	0.5	1.7	0.8	1.5	1.1	•
Working Capital to Net Sales 40	0.3	•	0.7	•	1.1	0.7	0.8	1.0	0.3	0.6	0.3	0.5	•
Inventory to Working Capital 41	0.0	•	•	•	0.0	0.0	0.0	0.0	0.0	0.0	0.0	0.0	•
Total Receipts to Cash Flow 42	2.7	4.6	3.0	4.3	4.0	4.2	3.5	3.3	3.6	3.8	3.9	2.4	2.0
Cost of Goods to Cash Flow 43	0.1	0.4	0.1	0.5	0.3	0.2	0.4	0.3	0.3	0.2	0.5	0.0	0.0
Cash Flow to Total Debt 44	0.1	•	0.1	0.0	0.0	0.0	0.0	0.1	0.1	0.1	0.1	0.1	0.1

Selected Financial Factors (in Percentages)

Debt Ratio 45	56.2	•	68.6	89.5	77.0	75.4	73.5	63.9	65.3	57.1	55.5	54.5	39.2
Return on Total Assets 46	2.5	•	1.3	1.4	1.0	1.0	1.1	1.2	1.9	1.8	2.4	2.3	3.8
Return on Income Before Income Taxes 47	2.7	•	1.3	6.5	0.1	•	•	•	•	•	0.9	1.9	4.6
Return on Equity After Income Taxes 48	2.5	•	0.7	5.5	•	•	•	•	•	•	0.8	1.9	4.6
Profit Margin (Before Income Tax) 49	11.8	•	3.0	6.2	0.3	•	•	•	•	•	2.7	10.3	30.6
Profit Margin (After Income Tax) 50	11.0	•	1.7	5.2	•	•	•	•	•	•	2.4	10.1	30.6

Table II

Corporations with Net Income

LESSORS OF BUILDINGS

MONEY AMOUNTS AND SIZE OF ASSETS IN THOUSANDS OF DOLLARS

Item Description for Accounting Period 7/09 Through 6/10	Total	Zero Assets	Under 500	500 to 1,000	1,000 to 5,000	5,000 to 10,000	10,000 to 25,000	25,000 to 50,000	50,000 to 100,000	100,000 to 250,000	250,000 to 500,000	500,000 to 2,500,000	2,500,000 and over
Number of Enterprises **1**	43136	5994	19399	7348	8125	1203	554	195	119	87	36	47	30
Revenues ($ in Thousands)													
Net Sales **2**	44949910	1750239	1686833	1685953	3181456	1557957	1395626	1398814	1689432	1756730	2440394	5689610	20716867
Interest **3**	2040062	34106	13573	21937	50385	16919	17281	20692	36516	77988	57680	471052	1221931
Rents **4**	22218292	79389	16202	55048	64310	11775	179690	138107	314168	665692	1193229	3705800	15794883
Royalties **5**	13777	1630	0	0	4560	201	12	23	7351	0	0	0	0
Other Portfolio Income **6**	2103622	165384	64995	200680	213439	46527	55429	60449	26728	142381	31473	466877	629260
Other Receipts **7**	18574157	1592063	1408288	2848762	1482535		1143214	1179543	1304669	870669	1158012	1045881	3070793
Total Receipts **8**	44949910	1750239	1686833	1685953	3181456	1557957	1395626	1398814	1689432	1756730	2440394	5689610	20716867
Average Total Receipts **9**	1042	292	87	229	392	1295	2519	7173	14197	20192	67789	121056	690562
Operating Costs/Operating Income (%)													
Cost of Operations **10**	3.4	9.0	0.3	9.9	6.2	1.7	4.6	6.4	9.1	4.0	21.5	0.2	0.3
Salaries and Wages **11**	4.6	3.0	7.5	4.1	5.0	22.6	4.5	17.3	10.4	4.4	3.2	2.3	2.6
Taxes Paid **12**	6.5	5.8	10.8	7.1	11.2	8.6	9.2	8.2	8.1	9.2	6.8	6.5	4.5
Interest Paid **13**	10.4	10.0	3.4	5.9	11.1	6.7	11.7	7.8	11.9	16.4	11.3	13.2	10.1
Depreciation **14**	13.9	6.3	5.1	5.8	8.5	7.1	10.3	7.4	8.0	13.4	9.8	11.5	19.5
Amortization and Depletion **15**	0.8	0.5	0.0	0.4	0.4	0.2	0.7	0.8	0.7	1.3	0.8	1.3	0.9
Pensions and Other Deferred Comp. **16**	0.1	0.1	0.0	0.4	0.3	0.5	0.2	0.6	0.3	0.2	0.0	0.0	•
Employee Benefits **17**	0.3	0.1	0.5	1.0	0.7	1.7	0.4	1.3	0.7	0.4	0.3	•	0.0
Advertising **18**	0.3	0.1	0.3	1.5	0.2	1.0	0.2	0.4	0.5	0.3	0.5	0.2	0.1
Other Expenses **19**	27.0	26.0	40.0	34.2	27.2	25.1	30.2	26.0	32.5	20.9	19.9	32.7	24.7
Officers' Compensation **20**	1.4	0.8	5.1	5.4	4.4	3.4	3.5	3.0	1.9	1.7	0.6	0.5	0.2
Operating Margin **21**	31.4	38.4	26.9	24.4	24.8	21.3	24.4	20.7	15.9	27.7	25.4	31.5	36.9
Operating Margin Before Officers' Comp. **22**	32.8	39.2	32.0	29.8	29.2	24.8	27.9	23.8	17.7	29.4	26.0	32.1	37.1

Selected Average Balance Sheet ($ in Thousands)

Net Receivables 23	127	0	8	30	69	357	346	802	3680	4117	4882	20428	61330
Inventories 24	•	•	•	•	•	•	•	•	•	•	•	•	•
Net Property, Plant and Equipment 25	5182	0	103	390	1445	4567	9659	20507	41762	99720	235585	603474	4719730
Total Assets 26	7923	0	178	708	2202	6869	15613	35325	70830	157205	388651	1170826	6676224
Notes and Loans Payable 27	2812	0	79	178	1173	3670	8516	14506	35498	73130	138429	381992	1944951
All Other Liabilities 28	531	0	12	63	194	531	1180	3787	7080	10316	30229	124637	331273
Net Worth 29	4580	0	88	-224	835	2668	5917	17033	28251	73760	219993	664197	4399999

Selected Financial Ratios (Times to 1)

Current Ratio 30	1.2	•	5.0	1.7	2.6	1.7	1.4	2.9	1.5	2.5	1.5	1.7	0.9
Quick Ratio 31	0.8	•	4.5	1.3	2.0	1.3	0.9	2.1	1.1	2.0	1.1	1.0	0.6
Net Sales to Working Capital 32	12.4	•	2.5	1.7	3.4	3.5	1.8	4.2	1.6	6.3	3.6	•	•
Coverage Ratio 33	4.0	4.8	8.8	5.1	3.2	4.2	3.0	3.6	2.3	2.7	3.2	3.4	4.6
Total Asset Turnover 34	0.1	•	0.5	0.3	0.2	0.2	0.2	0.2	0.2	0.1	0.2	0.1	0.1
Inventory Turnover 35	•	•	•	•	•	•	•	•	•	•	•	•	•
Receivables Turnover 36	•	•	•	•	•	•	•	•	•	•	•	•	•
Total Liabilities to Net Worth 37	0.7	•	1.0	1.6	2.5	1.6	1.1	1.5	1.1	1.7	0.8	0.8	0.5
Current Assets to Working Capital 38	6.9	•	1.3	1.6	2.5	3.4	1.5	3.1	1.7	2.9	2.4	•	•
Current Liabilities to Working Capital 39	5.9	•	0.3	0.6	1.5	2.4	0.5	2.1	0.7	1.9	1.4	•	•
Working Capital to Net Sales 40	0.1	•	0.4	0.6	0.3	0.3	0.6	0.2	0.6	0.2	0.3	•	•
Inventory to Working Capital 41	0.0	•	•	0.0	•	0.0	0.0	0.0	0.0	0.0	0.0	•	•
Total Receipts to Cash Flow 42	2.1	2.1	1.8	2.6	2.6	2.2	2.5	2.6	2.4	2.7	2.5	2.0	1.9
Cost of Goods to Cash Flow 43	0.1	0.2	0.0	0.3	0.0	0.1	0.2	0.2	0.2	0.1	0.5	0.0	0.0
Cash Flow to Total Debt 44	0.1	•	0.5	0.1	0.1	0.1	0.1	0.2	0.2	0.1	0.2	0.1	0.2

Selected Financial Factors (in Percentages)

Debt Ratio 45	42.2	•	50.9	131.7	62.2	61.2	62.1	51.8	60.1	53.1	43.4	43.3	34.1
Return on Total Assets 46	5.5	•	14.7	9.8	6.4	5.3	5.8	5.7	5.5	5.6	6.4	4.6	4.9
Return on Equity Before Income Taxes 47	7.1	•	26.6	•	11.6	10.3	10.2	8.6	7.9	7.5	7.8	5.7	5.8
Return on Equity After Income Taxes 48	6.9	•	24.3	•	10.0	8.9	8.5	7.2	6.6	6.4	7.7	5.7	5.8
Profit Margin (Before Income Tax) 49	31.3	38.4	26.8	24.4	24.7	21.3	24.0	20.4	15.7	27.5	25.3	31.5	36.9
Profit Margin (After Income Tax) 50	30.1	35.4	24.5	22.6	21.3	18.3	20.0	17.0	13.1	23.5	24.9	31.2	36.9

Table I

Corporations with and without Net Income

LESSORS OF MINIWAREHOUSES, SELF-STORAGE, OTHER REAL ESTATE

MONEY AMOUNTS AND SIZE OF ASSETS IN THOUSANDS OF DOLLARS

Item Description for Accounting Period 7/09 Through 6/10		Total	Zero Assets	Under 500	500 to 1,000	1,000 to 5,000	5,000 to 10,000	10,000 to 25,000	25,000 to 50,000	50,000 to 100,000	100,000 to 250,000	250,000 to 500,000	500,000 to 2,500,000	2,500,000 and over
Number of Enterprises	1	84810	11323	48116	10332	11675	1555	945	302	192	171	72	99	27
Revenues ($ in Thousands)														
Net Sales	2	37348433	984826	3965034	942834	2318965	886568	995006	845457	1278361	2850442	1543439	8727162	12010337
Interest	3	2644466	48253	13343	15315	68581	31347	45504	64215	58936	212451	127986	615797	1342738
Rents	4	15593142	120491	606	48725	7727	14431	257449	375725	579799	1347611	909192	5573239	6358147
Royalties	5	109054	27	6020	4	15261	13815	42662	5093	44	6424	23	19681	0
Other Portfolio Income	6	2434480	188632	43270	76288	131900	82509	113078	47202	75363	132785	116717	624334	802404
Other Receipts	7	16567291	627423	3901795	802502	2095496	744466	536313	353222	564219	1151171	389521	1894111	3507048
Total Receipts	8	37348433	984826	3965034	942834	2318965	886568	995006	845457	1278361	2850442	1543439	8727162	12010337
Average Total Receipts	9	440	87	82	91	199	570	1053	2800	6658	16669	21437	88153	444827
Operating Costs/Operating Income (%)														
Cost of Operations	10	0.7	0.6	0.2	0.2	1.0	0.2	0.7	0.1	0.8	0.5	1.5	0.9	0.9
Salaries and Wages	11	7.1	0.5	33.6	4.2	10.4	7.7	6.6	9.2	6.4	5.5	2.4	2.3	2.8
Taxes Paid	12	6.2	6.7	6.5	9.2	6.4	8.7	8.3	7.2	4.9	5.6	5.2	6.5	5.6
Interest Paid	13	16.9	27.4	2.7	8.8	13.0	21.9	19.5	23.9	15.0	18.6	20.3	20.0	18.3
Depreciation	14	11.0	8.2	3.1	7.2	12.8	11.8	9.8	9.0	9.3	10.6	10.3	13.4	12.6
Amortization and Depletion	15	1.3	0.7	0.4	0.1	0.2	0.8	1.2	1.2	0.8	1.3	1.4	1.2	2.2
Pensions and Other Deferred Comp.	16	0.2	0.0	0.6	1.3	0.3	0.4	0.2	0.4	0.7	0.2	0.0	0.0	0.0
Employee Benefits	17	0.5	0.0	3.1	0.2	0.6	0.8	2.3	0.6	0.6	0.4	0.1	0.1	0.0
Advertising	18	0.7	0.6	3.4	0.5	0.4	0.4	0.3	0.7	0.2	0.3	0.3	0.3	0.3
Other Expenses	19	47.9	106.3	46.7	74.6	56.7	62.0	79.8	81.7	88.6	81.5	86.9	43.7	19.3
Officers' Compensation	20	2.0	0.4	7.1	3.6	4.3	4.4	3.4	3.1	4.0	1.0	1.4	0.6	0.6
Operating Margin	21	5.4	•	•	•	•	•	•	•	•	•	•	11.0	37.4
Operating Margin Before Officers' Comp.	22	7.4	•	•	•	•	•	•	•	•	•	•	11.6	38.0

Selected Average Balance Sheet ($ in Thousands)

Net Receivables 23	90	•	6	66	219	652	743	2857	4816	6964	23663	•	43028
Inventories 24	•	•	•	•	•	•	•	•	•	•	•	•	•
Net Property, Plant and Equipment 25	2393	0	65	390	1156	3240	5413	12074	19999	55740	121618	519215	3515973
Total Assets 26	4781	0	136	670	2050	6932	15875	34903	70088	157425	362534	1079779	5866860
Notes and Loans Payable 27	1824	0	68	313	1225	3732	6973	13901	24170	55019	109154	342933	2274920
All Other Liabilities 28	350	0	25	68	256	732	2661	3132	7394	18311	16239	51582	346617
Net Worth 29	2607	0	43	288	569	2469	6241	17871	38524	84094	237141	685264	3245322

Selected Financial Ratios (Times to 1)

Current Ratio 30	1.9	•	1.3	2.0	2.5	2.2	2.3	2.5	2.4	1.7	2.2	1.7	1.9
Quick Ratio 31	1.3	•	1.0	1.2	1.3	1.0	1.2	1.3	1.5	1.3	1.4	1.2	1.8
Net Sales to Working Capital 32	2.1	•	12.1	1.6	0.8	0.7	0.5	0.7	1.0	2.5	2.0	2.6	3.6
Coverage Ratio 33	1.3	•	•	•	0.5	0.1	•	•	•	1.6	•	1.6	3.1
Total Asset Turnover 34	0.1	•	0.6	0.1	0.1	0.1	0.1	0.1	0.1	0.4	0.1	0.1	0.1
Inventory Turnover 35	•	•	•	•	•	•	•	•	•	•	•	•	•
Receivables Turnover 36	•	•	•	•	•	•	•	•	•	•	•	•	•
Total Liabilities to Net Worth 37	0.8	•	2.2	1.3	2.6	1.8	1.5	1.0	0.8	0.9	0.5	0.6	0.8
Current Assets to Working Capital 38	2.1	•	4.5	2.0	1.7	1.8	1.8	1.6	1.7	2.5	1.9	2.5	2.1
Current Liabilities to Working Capital 39	1.1	•	3.5	1.0	0.7	0.8	0.8	0.6	0.7	1.5	0.9	1.5	1.1
Working Capital to Net Sales 40	0.5	•	0.1	0.6	1.2	1.3	1.9	1.4	1.0	0.4	0.5	0.4	0.3
Inventory to Working Capital 41	0.0	•	•	0.0	0.0	0.0	0.0	0.0	0.0	0.0	0.0	0.0	0.0
Total Receipts to Cash Flow 42	2.7	7.2	4.6	2.4	2.4	5.6	3.3	3.0	2.8	2.5	3.8	2.6	2.2
Cost of Goods to Cash Flow 43	0.0	0.0	0.0	0.0	0.0	0.0	0.0	0.0	0.0	0.0	0.1	0.0	0.0
Cash Flow to Total Debt 44	0.1	•	0.2	0.1	0.1	0.0	0.0	0.1	0.1	0.0	0.0	0.1	0.1

Selected Financial Factors (in Percentages)

Debt Ratio 45	45.5	•	68.5	57.0	72.2	64.4	60.7	48.8	45.0	46.6	34.6	36.5	44.7
Return on Total Assets 46	2.1	•	•	•	0.7	0.2	•	•	•	•	•	2.5	4.2
Return on Equity Before Income Taxes 47	0.9	•	•	•	•	•	•	•	•	•	•	1.4	5.1
Return on Equity After Income Taxes 48	0.8	•	•	•	•	•	•	•	•	•	•	1.4	5.1
Profit Margin (Before Income Tax) 49	5.4	•	•	•	•	•	•	•	•	•	•	11.0	37.4
Profit Margin (After Income Tax) 50	4.5	•	•	•	•	•	•	•	•	•	•	10.6	37.4

Table II

Corporations with Net Income

LESSORS OF MINIWAREHOUSES, SELF-STORAGE, OTHER REAL ESTATE

MONEY AMOUNTS AND SIZE OF ASSETS IN THOUSANDS OF DOLLARS

Item Description for Accounting Period 7/09 Through 6/10		Total	Zero Assets	Under 500	500 to 1,000	1,000 to 5,000	5,000 to 10,000	10,000 to 25,000	25,000 to 50,000	50,000 to 100,000	100,000 to 250,000	250,000 to 500,000	500,000 to 2,500,000	2,500,000 and over
Number of Enterprises	1	23034	2741	14132	2272	2756	549	259	91	60	66	27	58	23
Revenues ($ in Thousands)														
Net Sales	2	27190158	537389	2942078	550935	1279419	559096	698420	445761	741186	1557118	766157	6263906	10848692
Interest	3	2106507	6065	8985	14211	27331	9916	31857	31248	28298	72380	61394	482321	1332500
Rents	4	11825686	51762	306	22712	3068	13107	109606	109886	193304	695799	432412	3984957	6208768
Royalties	5	88323	27	6020	4	15261	13815	41635	5093	43	6424	0	0	0
Other Portfolio Income	6	2145606	158879	26708	57793	116622	75664	102973	41300	65421	97702	35483	564655	802404
Other Receipts	7	11024036	320656	2900059	456215	1117137	446594	412349	258234	454120	684813	236868	1231973	2505020
Total Receipts	8	27190158	537389	2942078	550935	1279419	559096	698420	445761	741186	1557118	766157	6263906	10848692
Average Total Receipts	9	1180	196	208	242	464	1018	2697	4898	12353	23593	28376	107998	471682
Operating Costs/Operating Income (%)														
Cost of Operations	10	0.2	0.1	•	•	1.9	•	0.4	0.0	0.8	0.9	•	•	•
Salaries and Wages	11	5.2	0.6	18.9	4.1	9.2	5.8	3.9	8.9	8.1	6.6	1.7	2.0	2.9
Taxes Paid	12	5.8	5.8	5.0	7.9	6.7	6.8	6.9	6.5	4.0	6.2	3.2	6.3	5.5
Interest Paid	13	13.1	9.4	1.2	6.6	6.4	11.2	6.8	11.8	5.3	10.1	12.0	17.8	16.4
Depreciation	14	9.8	4.4	1.3	4.5	8.7	7.9	6.0	8.0	6.7	9.4	7.1	13.2	11.6
Amortization and Depletion	15	0.9	0.3	0.1	0.1	0.2	0.7	0.9	1.0	0.7	1.5	1.0	1.0	1.2
Pensions and Other Deferred Comp.	16	0.2	•	0.4	2.2	0.3	0.5	0.2	0.2	0.3	0.4	0.1	0.0	•
Employee Benefits	17	0.4	0.0	2.5	0.1	0.4	0.4	2.2	0.4	0.8	0.5	0.0	0.0	•
Advertising	18	0.7	1.1	4.4	0.6	0.4	0.2	0.2	0.3	0.1	0.2	0.3	0.1	0.3
Other Expenses	19	25.3	29.9	44.5	35.0	26.0	29.1	26.5	31.9	36.3	31.3	38.9	22.0	18.1
Officers' Compensation	20	1.7	0.1	5.0	5.8	4.8	4.1	3.1	1.8	5.6	1.4	0.8	0.8	0.5
Operating Margin	21	36.7	48.4	16.6	32.9	35.0	33.3	43.0	29.2	31.3	31.5	34.9	36.6	43.5
Operating Margin Before Officers' Comp.	22	38.5	48.5	21.6	38.7	39.8	37.4	46.1	31.0	36.8	33.0	35.7	37.4	44.0

Selected Average Balance Sheet ($ in Thousands)

Net Receivables 23	190	0	8	18	64	293	837	390	4543	5207	517	33661	46118
Inventories 24	•	•	•	•	•	•	•	•	•	•	•	•	•
Net Property, Plant and Equipment 25	5868	0	57	342	1063	3016	5887	11759	27198	75843	102602	635300	3484941
Total Assets 26	10983	0	140	649	2098	6580	16292	35158	72554	165577	377388	1171695	6055431
Notes and Loans Payable 27	3614	0	48	314	896	2432	5523	10592	19289	50831	96890	380800	2018885
All Other Liabilities 28	629	0	23	28	279	1063	2324	1028	6935	13254	11146	62077	297908
Net Worth 29	6740	0	69	308	923	3085	8445	23538	46330	101492	269352	728818	3738638

Selected Financial Ratios (Times to 1)

Current Ratio 30	2.0	•	2.4	4.5	1.7	2.8	2.6	4.1	4.7	1.4	1.8	1.8	1.9
Quick Ratio 31	1.6	•	1.8	3.7	1.2	1.7	2.0	2.3	3.3	1.1	1.3	1.4	1.8
Net Sales to Working Capital 32	2.8	•	7.6	1.9	2.9	1.2	1.2	0.9	1.1	4.3	8.7	2.2	3.6
Coverage Ratio 33	3.8	6.1	15.0	6.0	6.4	3.9	7.0	3.4	6.8	4.1	3.9	3.0	3.7
Total Asset Turnover 34	0.1	•	1.5	0.4	0.2	0.2	0.2	0.1	0.2	0.1	0.1	0.1	0.1
Inventory Turnover 35	•	•	•	•	•	•	•	•	•	•	•	•	•
Receivables Turnover 36	•	•	•	•	•	•	•	•	•	•	•	•	•
Total Liabilities to Net Worth 37	0.6	•	1.0	1.1	1.3	1.1	0.9	0.5	0.6	0.6	0.4	0.6	0.6
Current Assets to Working Capital 38	2.0	•	1.7	1.3	2.3	1.6	1.6	1.3	1.3	3.5	2.3	2.2	2.1
Current Liabilities to Working Capital 39	1.0	•	0.7	0.3	1.3	0.6	0.6	0.3	0.3	2.5	1.3	1.2	1.1
Working Capital to Net Sales 40	0.4	•	0.1	0.5	0.3	0.8	0.8	1.1	0.9	0.2	0.1	0.5	0.3
Inventory to Working Capital 41	0.0	•	0.0	0.0	0.0	0.0	0.0	•	0.0	0.0	0.0	•	•
Total Receipts to Cash Flow 42	2.1	2.3	2.4	2.1	2.0	2.6	1.8	2.0	1.8	2.0	2.3	2.2	2.0
Cost of Goods to Cash Flow 43	0.0	0.0	•	•	0.0	0.0	0.0	0.0	0.0	0.0	•	•	•
Cash Flow to Total Debt 44	0.1	•	1.2	0.3	0.2	0.1	0.2	0.2	0.3	0.2	0.1	0.1	0.1

Selected Financial Factors (in Percentages)

Debt Ratio 45	38.6	•	50.7	52.6	56.0	53.1	48.2	33.1	36.1	38.7	28.6	37.8	38.3
Return on Total Assets 46	5.3	•	26.4	14.7	9.1	6.8	7.9	5.6	6.2	6.0	3.5	5.0	4.7
Return on Equity Before Income Taxes 47	6.4	•	50.1	25.8	17.6	10.9	13.1	6.0	8.3	7.4	3.7	5.4	5.5
Return on Equity After Income Taxes 48	6.2	•	48.7	23.4	15.5	8.9	10.8	5.3	7.4	6.8	3.7	5.3	5.5
Profit Margin (Before Income Tax) 49	36.7	48.4	16.6	32.8	34.9	32.9	41.1	28.6	31.2	31.8	34.9	36.6	43.5
Profit Margin (After Income Tax) 50	35.5	42.5	16.1	29.7	30.8	27.0	33.7	25.6	27.7	29.1	34.9	36.1	43.5

Table I

Corporations with and without Net Income

OFFICES OF REAL ESTATE AGENTS AND BROKERS

MONEY AMOUNTS AND SIZE OF ASSETS IN THOUSANDS OF DOLLARS

Item Description for Accounting Period 7/09 Through 6/10	Total	Zero Assets	Under 500	500 to 1,000	1,000 to 5,000	5,000 to 10,000	10,000 to 25,000	25,000 to 50,000	50,000 to 100,000	100,000 to 250,000	250,000 to 500,000	500,000 to 2,500,000	2,500,000 and over
Number of Enterprises **1**	130556	28711	96272	2825	2256	314	115	17	17	12	6	10	0
Revenues ($ in Thousands)													
Net Sales **2**	39654417	3751446	17857444	3599365	2715110	458787	1687580	589555	471410	381700	1760496	6381523	0
Interest **3**	323420	25	19523	8027	15282	12433	1899	6965	3867	12030	31440	211928	0
Rents **4**	384394	14258	33995	9671	15518	34166	5584	299	13582	21654	28017	207650	0
Royalties **5**	513330	0	0	0	3	28	85	0	0	0	1535	511678	0
Other Portfolio Income **6**	251090	385	40188	1552	37184	6424	1576	4278	25612	14291	98110	21491	0
Other Receipts **7**	3818183	3736778	17763738	3580115	2647123	405736	1678436	578013	428349	333725	1601394	5428776	0
Total Receipts **8**	39654417	3751446	17857444	3599365	2715110	458787	1687580	589555	471410	381700	1760496	6381523	0
Average Total Receipts **9**	304	131	185	1274	1204	1461	14675	34680	27730	31808	293416	638152	•
Operating Costs/Operating Income (%)													
Cost of Operations **10**	0.7	0.5	0.0	•	0.6	0.0	•	32.9	0.0	1.1	•	0.7	•
Salaries and Wages **11**	39.6	52.9	32.9	46.8	41.9	24.9	59.4	20.6	46.2	37.1	9.1	51.5	•
Taxes Paid **12**	2.7	1.6	2.3	2.7	2.6	7.0	2.2	1.8	5.3	4.0	1.2	4.7	•
Interest Paid **13**	3.2	0.6	0.6	0.6	2.3	9.9	2.7	0.8	3.7	9.3	2.3	13.7	•
Depreciation **14**	1.5	0.6	1.0	1.3	2.3	3.3	1.8	1.7	5.3	4.1	1.1	2.8	•
Amortization and Depletion **15**	0.7	•	0.1	0.6	0.1	0.3	0.2	0.5	0.3	0.9	1.5	3.5	•
Pensions and Other Deferred Comp. **16**	0.7	1.4	0.7	1.5	0.3	0.4	0.1	0.0	0.5	0.4	0.1	0.2	•
Employee Benefits **17**	1.4	0.9	0.9	0.9	1.2	1.1	1.2	1.5	4.2	1.2	0.6	3.3	•
Advertising **18**	3.9	4.3	4.0	3.3	8.2	1.4	2.9	7.3	7.1	1.5	1.1	2.6	•
Other Expenses **19**	35.4	26.5	38.2	21.0	37.6	58.5	21.5	23.1	27.3	34.7	81.2	31.0	•
Officers' Compensation **20**	8.4	5.9	12.6	15.4	2.5	5.4	3.1	3.2	5.3	5.9	1.4	1.1	•
Operating Margin **21**	1.7	5.0	6.7	6.1	0.3	•	4.9	6.7	•	•	0.3	•	•
Operating Margin Before Officers' Comp. **22**	10.2	10.9	19.4	21.5	2.9	•	8.0	9.9	•	5.7	1.7	•	•

Selected Average Balance Sheet ($ in Thousands)

Net Receivables 23	22	0	231	340	1353	1749	2015	13560	40735	130222	
Inventories 24	•	•	•	•	•	•	•	•	•	•	•
Net Property, Plant and Equipment 25	69	0	17	215	537	1642	5243	8280	16247	50167	22800 · 325449
Total Assets 26	340	58	710	1899	6132	15988	33353	65469	140958	352504	2322090
Notes and Loans Payable 27	194	44	335	1150	4054	9518	12014	39638	67869	107056	1284053
All Other Liabilities 28	96	11	134	235	1699	3387	9252	7279	30828	85858	847682
Net Worth 29	50	3	240	513	379	3083	12087	18552	42261	159590	190356

Selected Financial Ratios (Times to 1)

Current Ratio 30	1.2	1.6	1.4	3.2	1.6	1.2	1.3	1.0	1.1	2.5	0.8
Quick Ratio 31	0.7	1.3	0.8	1.5	0.5	0.8	0.4	1.0	0.4	2.4	0.5
Net Sales to Working Capital 32	21.0	19.0	21.5	2.1	1.5	12.1	11.2	9.9	7.2	4.3	•
Coverage Ratio 33	1.5	12.7	11.2	1.1	2.8	9.9	1.0	1.0	1.1	•	•
Total Asset Turnover 34	0.9	3.2	1.8	0.6	0.2	0.9	1.0	0.4	0.2	0.8	0.3
Inventory Turnover 35	•	•	•	•	•	•	•	•	•	•	•
Receivables Turnover 36	•	•	•	•	•	•	•	•	•	•	11.2
Total Liabilities to Net Worth 37	5.8	17.1	2.0	2.7	4.2	15.2	1.8	2.5	2.3	1.2	•
Current Assets to Working Capital 38	7.2	2.8	3.7	1.5	6.0	2.6	4.2	15.2	1.6	•	•
Current Liabilities to Working Capital 39	6.2	1.8	2.7	0.5	5.0	1.6	3.2	14.2	0.6	•	•
Working Capital to Net Sales 40	0.0	0.1	0.0	0.5	0.1	0.7	0.1	0.1	0.2	•	•
Inventory to Working Capital 41	0.1	•	•	•	0.0	•	•	1.6	1.6	•	•
Total Receipts to Cash Flow 42	3.7	2.7	4.3	3.7	5.5	2.7	4.9	8.2	3.9	11.6	13.5
Cost of Goods to Cash Flow 43	0.0	0.0	0.0	0.0	1.6	0.0	0.0	0.1	0.1	•	•
Cash Flow to Total Debt 44	0.3	1.3	0.6	0.2	0.2	0.3	0.1	0.1	0.0	•	•

Selected Financial Factors (in Percentages)

Debt Ratio 45	85.3	94.5	66.2	73.0	93.8	80.7	63.8	71.7	70.0	54.7	91.8
Return on Total Assets 46	4.4	23.4	12.0	1.7	•	7.0	7.7	2.1	•	2.2	•
Return on Equity Before Income Taxes 47	10.6	389.8	32.3	0.8	•	23.3	19.2	•	•	0.6	•
Return on Equity After Income Taxes 48	9.8	384.9	32.1	0.5	•	22.6	17.5	•	•	0.5	•
Profit Margin (Before Income Tax) 49	1.7	5.0	6.7	6.1	0.3	4.9	6.7	•	0.3	0.5	•
Profit Margin (After Income Tax) 50	1.6	5.0	6.6	6.0	0.2	4.7	6.1	•	0.3	0.3	•

Table II

Corporations with Net Income

OFFICES OF REAL ESTATE AGENTS AND BROKERS

MONEY AMOUNTS AND SIZE OF ASSETS IN THOUSANDS OF DOLLARS

Item Description for Accounting Period 7/09 Through 6/10	Total	Zero Assets	Under 500	500 to 1,000	1,000 to 5,000	5,000 to 10,000	10,000 to 25,000	25,000 to 50,000	50,000 to 100,000	100,000 to 250,000	250,000 to 500,000	500,000 to 2,500,000	2,500,000 and over
Number of Enterprises **1**	69892	13722	53575	1480	943	90	47	•	6	•	6	0	0
Revenues ($ in Thousands)													
Net Sales **2**	24449495	1151478	12681354	3486870	1825256	398302	1266682	•	309096	•	2388537	0	0
Interest **3**	196152	5	11428	7636	6555	8263	866	•	6	•	147047	0	0
Rents **4**	269273	0	30201	274	5450	23696	2764	•	0	•	185234	0	0
Royalties **5**	1299	0	0	0	3	28	85	•	0	•	1182	0	0
Other Portfolio Income **6**	196315	385	7480	717	30361	4185	126	•	25600	•	113174	0	0
Other Receipts **7**	23786456	1151088	12632245	3478243	1782887	362130	1262841	•	283490	•	1941900	0	0
Total Receipts **8**	24449495	1151478	12681354	3486870	1825256	398302	1266682	•	309096	•	2388537	0	0
Average Total Receipts **9**	350	84	237	2356	1936	4426	26951	•	51516	•	398090	•	•
Operating Costs/Operating Income (%)													
Cost of Operations **10**	1.0	0.6	0.0	•	0.8	•	•	•	•	•	0.8	•	•
Salaries and Wages **11**	31.3	5.8	28.1	47.3	48.7	22.2	56.7	•	40.0	•	12.6	•	•
Taxes Paid **12**	2.3	2.7	2.1	2.5	1.9	6.2	2.0	•	3.2	•	3.1	•	•
Interest Paid **13**	1.1	0.9	0.4	0.4	1.1	3.5	1.9	•	1.7	•	4.3	•	•
Depreciation **14**	1.2	1.2	0.9	1.1	1.3	2.5	1.7	•	6.0	•	1.9	•	•
Amortization and Depletion **15**	0.2	•	0.1	0.5	0.0	0.1	0.1	•	0.1	•	1.1	•	•
Pensions and Other Deferred Comp. **16**	0.7	0.2	0.8	1.6	0.1	0.5	0.1	•	0.8	•	0.4	•	•
Employee Benefits **17**	0.8	1.2	0.5	0.9	0.8	0.4	1.0	•	4.4	•	1.2	•	•
Advertising **18**	3.5	2.7	3.8	3.2	5.7	1.2	2.4	•	9.2	•	0.9	•	•
Other Expenses **19**	33.7	34.3	34.8	18.7	27.5	45.6	20.9	•	15.4	•	64.5	•	•
Officers' Compensation **20**	10.0	12.7	12.3	15.4	3.0	4.7	2.7	•	6.5	•	1.3	•	•
Operating Margin **21**	14.1	37.8	16.2	8.5	9.1	13.2	10.4	•	12.8	•	7.8	•	•
Operating Margin Before Officers' Comp. **22**	24.0	50.5	28.5	23.9	12.1	17.9	13.1	•	19.3	•	9.1	•	•

Selected Average Balance Sheet ($ in Thousands)

Net Receivables 23	11	0	2	48	69	216	1911	1624	39902
Inventories 24	•	•	•	•	•	•	•	•	•
Net Property, Plant and Equipment 25	55	0	16	178	557	2167	3626	17383	180598
Total Assets 26	207	0	64	718	1824	6948	16157	66629	775926
Notes and Loans Payable 27	78	0	30	291	686	2207	6236	51355	215982
All Other Liabilities 28	50	0	8	97	228	2667	4500	13394	282451
Net Worth 29	79	0	26	329	910	2073	5421	1880	277492

Selected Financial Ratios (Times to 1)

Current Ratio 30	1.6	•	2.2	1.7	3.5	2.6	1.7	0.5	1.5
Quick Ratio 31	1.1	•	1.7	1.1	2.2	1.7	1.0	0.2	1.0
Net Sales to Working Capital 32	10.1	•	13.7	19.7	4.5	3.0	7.0	•	3.7
Coverage Ratio 33	13.3	41.7	38.0	24.6	9.7	4.8	6.3	8.8	2.8
Total Asset Turnover 34	1.7	•	3.7	3.3	1.1	0.6	1.7	0.8	0.5
Inventory Turnover 35	•	•	•	•	•	•	•	•	•
Receivables Turnover 36	•	•	•	•	•	•	•	•	•
Total Liabilities to Net Worth 37	1.6	•	1.5	1.2	1.0	2.4	2.0	34.4	1.8
Current Assets to Working Capital 38	2.6	•	1.9	2.4	1.4	1.6	2.4	•	3.1
Current Liabilities to Working Capital 39	1.6	•	0.9	1.4	0.4	0.6	1.4	•	2.1
Working Capital to Net Sales 40	0.1	•	0.1	0.1	0.2	0.3	0.1	•	0.3
Inventory to Working Capital 41	0.0	•	•	•	•	•	•	•	0.0
Total Receipts to Cash Flow 42	2.8	1.4	2.3	4.2	3.7	2.0	4.4	5.2	7.4
Cost of Goods to Cash Flow 43	0.0	•	0.0	0.0	0.0	0.0	0.0	•	0.1
Cash Flow to Total Debt 44	1.0	•	2.8	1.5	0.6	0.5	0.6	0.2	0.1

Selected Financial Factors (in Percentages)

Debt Ratio 45	61.9	•	59.5	54.1	50.1	70.2	66.4	97.2	64.2
Return on Total Assets 46	25.7	•	62.0	29.1	10.8	10.6	20.5	11.2	6.2
Return on Equity Before Income Taxes 47	62.3	•	149.2	60.8	19.5	28.1	51.6	351.5	11.2
Return on Equity After Income Taxes 48	61.3	•	148.1	60.5	19.0	26.5	50.5	348.0	10.2
Profit Margin (Before Income Tax) 49	14.1	37.8	16.2	8.5	9.1	13.2	10.4	12.8	7.8
Profit Margin (After Income Tax) 50	13.8	37.6	16.1	8.5	8.9	12.4	10.2	12.7	7.1

Table I
Corporations with and without Net Income

OTHER REAL ESTATE ACTIVITIES

MONEY AMOUNTS AND SIZE OF ASSETS IN THOUSANDS OF DOLLARS

Item Description for Accounting Period 7/09 Through 6/10		Total	Zero Assets	Under 500	500 to 1,000	1,000 to 5,000	5,000 to 10,000	10,000 to 25,000	25,000 to 50,000	50,000 to 100,000	100,000 to 250,000	250,000 to 500,000	500,000 to 2,500,000	2,500,000 and over
Number of Enterprises	1	165750	36634	108572	6802	10413	1725	1005	311	154	91	31	14	0
Revenues ($ in Thousands)														
Net Sales	2	47064730	2716459	17680625	2868353	7719121	2303173	1946635	1221836	1339777	1667342	2447656	5153752	0
Interest	3	1342224	18641	15971	6892	49793	24532	36039	35772	25529	165276	78922	884857	0
Rents	4	1950640	327936	223680	60144	122813	64214	215830	119611	171907	169715	288612	186179	0
Royalties	5	389768	645	3585	0	0	9814	9073	0	96	2033	35165	329355	0
Other Portfolio Income	6	1766017	100653	7965	20757	56937	16866	37228	36463	15855	67865	23955	1381474	0
Other Receipts	7	41616081	2268584	17429424	2780560	7489578	2187747	1648465	1029990	1126390	1262453	2021002	2371887	0
Total Receipts	8	47064730	2716459	17680625	2868353	7719121	2303173	1946635	1221836	1339777	1667342	2447656	5153752	0
Average Total Receipts	9	284	74	163	422	741	1335	1937	3929	8700	18322	78957	368125	•
Operating Costs/Operating Income (%)														
Cost of Operations	10	2.1	28.2	•	•	•	0.1	1.6	7.9	5.6	•	0.5	0.2	•
Salaries and Wages	11	30.6	15.4	23.5	49.5	49.9	34.5	28.0	29.2	14.4	40.9	35.0	21.5	•
Taxes Paid	12	4.2	3.5	3.4	5.2	5.7	6.4	6.5	5.5	5.2	6.1	3.1	2.5	•
Interest Paid	13	5.3	3.8	0.7	3.1	3.5	8.3	11.3	12.7	11.2	19.4	9.8	12.7	•
Depreciation	14	2.7	1.3	1.1	1.0	2.3	5.1	4.3	5.7	7.6	8.5	5.5	3.8	•
Amortization and Depletion	15	0.7	0.1	0.1	0.2	0.3	2.6	1.4	0.4	0.8	2.9	1.1	2.2	•
Pensions and Other Deferred Comp.	16	0.8	0.0	1.5	0.1	0.5	0.5	0.8	0.2	0.2	1.2	0.2	0.8	•
Employee Benefits	17	2.2	0.7	1.5	8.6	2.1	2.5	2.1	2.5	1.4	2.6	2.3	2.1	•
Advertising	18	1.2	0.4	1.6	0.2	0.4	2.6	0.4	1.4	0.7	1.0	1.3	1.5	•
Other Expenses	19	47.5	57.2	48.3	27.6	32.3	47.3	46.2	49.3	68.7	79.7	61.2	51.1	•
Officers' Compensation	20	9.3	7.0	16.1	9.8	7.9	4.1	7.3	5.3	3.0	3.1	0.7	1.1	•
Operating Margin	21	•	•	2.3	•	•	•	•	•	•	•	•	0.6	•
Operating Margin Before Officers' Comp.	22	2.6	•	18.4	4.5	3.0	•	•	•	•	•	•	1.7	•

Selected Average Balance Sheet ($ in Thousands)

	C1	C2	C3	C4	C5	C6	C7	C8	C9	C10	C11	C12	C13
Net Receivables 23	94	•	0	4	37	196	663	870	2141	3165	11247	50702	500125
Inventories 24	•	•	•	•	•	•	•	•	•	•	•	•	•
Net Property, Plant and Equipment 25	237	•	0	20	294	631	3060	4815	9437	27221	41391	109615	300483
Total Assets 26	828	•	0	73	695	2040	7637	14863	34864	69499	146896	341502	2121938
Notes and Loans Payable 27	450	•	0	56	461	1181	4103	8642	18186	31255	80528	184765	979111
All Other Liabilities 28	183	•	0	16	127	313	1342	2204	8008	11651	34572	84791	706506
Net Worth 29	195	•	0	0	106	545	2192	4017	8670	26592	31796	71946	436321

Selected Financial Ratios (Times to 1)

	C1	C2	C3	C4	C5	C6	C7	C8	C9	C10	C11	C12
Current Ratio 30	1.9	•	2.0	2.1	2.6	1.9	1.9	1.3	1.5	1.2	1.6	2.2
Quick Ratio 31	1.0	•	1.5	1.1	1.7	1.2	0.8	0.6	0.8	0.7	1.2	0.9
Net Sales to Working Capital 32	1.8	•	9.4	3.1	1.5	1.5	0.9	1.6	1.7	2.6	2.1	0.5
Coverage Ratio 33	•	•	4.5	•	•	•	0.1	•	•	•	•	1.1
Total Asset Turnover 34	0.3	•	2.2	0.6	0.4	0.2	0.1	0.1	0.1	0.1	0.2	0.2
Inventory Turnover 35	•	•	•	•	•	•	•	•	•	•	•	•
Receivables Turnover 36	•	•	•	•	•	•	•	•	•	•	•	•
Total Liabilities to Net Worth 37	3.2	•	152.2	5.5	2.7	2.5	2.7	3.0	1.6	3.6	3.7	3.9
Current Assets to Working Capital 38	2.1	•	2.0	1.9	1.6	2.2	2.2	4.0	2.9	5.1	2.6	1.8
Current Liabilities to Working Capital 39	1.1	•	1.0	0.9	0.6	1.2	1.2	3.0	1.9	4.1	1.6	0.8
Working Capital to Net Sales 40	0.5	•	0.1	0.3	0.7	0.7	1.2	0.6	0.6	0.4	0.5	2.0
Inventory to Working Capital 41	0.0	•	•	•	0.0	0.0	0.0	0.0	0.0	0.0	0.0	0.0
Total Receipts to Cash Flow 42	3.1	5.6	2.3	5.3	5.0	3.7	3.5	6.3	3.5	29.4	3.2	2.2
Cost of Goods to Cash Flow 43	0.1	1.6	•	•	•	0.0	0.1	0.5	0.2	•	0.0	0.0
Cash Flow to Total Debt 44	0.1	•	1.0	0.1	0.1	0.1	0.1	0.0	0.1	0.0	0.1	0.1

Selected Financial Factors (in Percentages)

	C1	C2	C3	C4	C5	C6	C7	C8	C9	C10	C11	C12
Debt Ratio 45	76.5	•	99.3	84.7	73.3	71.3	73.0	75.1	61.7	78.4	78.9	79.4
Return on Total Assets 46	•	•	6.7	•	•	•	0.2	•	•	•	•	2.4
Return on Equity Before Income Taxes 47	•	•	793.3	•	•	•	•	•	•	•	•	•
Return on Equity After Income Taxes 48	•	•	748.2	•	•	•	•	•	•	•	•	•
Profit Margin (Before Income Tax) 49	•	•	2.3	•	•	•	•	•	•	•	•	0.9
Profit Margin (After Income Tax) 50	•	•	2.2	•	•	•	•	•	•	•	•	0.9

Table II

Corporations with Net Income

OTHER REAL ESTATE ACTIVITIES

MONEY AMOUNTS AND SIZE OF ASSETS IN THOUSANDS OF DOLLARS

Item Description for Accounting Period 7/09 Through 6/10	Total	Zero Assets	Under 500	500 to 1,000	1,000 to 5,000	5,000 to 10,000	10,000 to 25,000	25,000 to 50,000	50,000 to 100,000	100,000 to 250,000	250,000 to 500,000	500,000 to 2,500,000	2,500,000 and over
Number of Enterprises **1**	70112	11710	52149	1834	3360	588	299	•	46	•	8	6	0
Revenues ($ in Thousands)													
Net Sales **2**	29131968	1429616	10979081	1282296	4606625	1818098	1244075	•	448170	•	1316297	3880124	0
Interest **3**	746343	15743	10139	3425	28717	16345	13838	•	12119	•	23077	558019	0
Rents **4**	899304	296820	63656	50784	55760	42104	162129	•	84433	•	0	32950	0
Royalties **5**	381433	0	3585	0	0	3291	9073	•	96	•	35165	329355	0
Other Portfolio Income **6**	1595418	92509	4247	19916	23943	14390	32281	•	13304	•	222	1306168	0
Other Receipts **7**	25509470	1024544	10897454	1208971	4498205	1741968	1026754	•	338218	•	1257833	1653632	0
Total Receipts **8**	29131968	1429616	10979081	1282296	4606625	1818098	1244075	•	448170	•	1316297	3880124	0
Average Total Receipts **9**	416	122	211	699	1371	3092	4161	•	9743	•	164537	646687	•
Operating Costs/Operating Income (%)													
Cost of Operations **10**	0.4	0.6	•	•	•	•	0.2	•	0.2	•	0.8	0.1	•
Salaries and Wages **11**	28.0	7.5	24.2	28.2	44.2	31.5	20.3	•	17.9	•	39.3	23.6	•
Taxes Paid **12**	3.3	2.7	2.9	3.2	4.5	5.6	5.3	•	6.4	•	1.3	1.9	•
Interest Paid **13**	2.6	3.6	0.2	1.1	1.6	2.5	4.3	•	9.3	•	2.2	7.8	•
Depreciation **14**	1.8	0.9	1.1	0.9	1.2	2.1	3.3	•	6.9	•	1.3	3.1	•
Amortization and Depletion **15**	0.5	0.0	0.1	0.3	0.1	0.4	0.2	•	0.5	•	0.9	2.1	•
Pensions and Other Deferred Comp. **16**	0.8	0.0	1.3	0.1	0.7	0.4	0.8	•	0.5	•	0.3	1.0	•
Employee Benefits **17**	1.6	0.4	0.9	4.1	1.9	2.5	2.0	•	1.8	•	1.7	1.9	•
Advertising **18**	1.0	0.5	1.2	0.4	0.5	0.5	0.4	•	0.4	•	0.7	1.8	•
Other Expenses **19**	34.8	44.1	36.3	39.3	22.1	34.9	29.5	•	32.3	•	41.3	43.7	•
Officers' Compensation **20**	8.6	6.3	15.8	12.9	5.6	3.5	4.6	•	4.2	•	0.0	0.9	•
Operating Margin **21**	16.7	33.5	15.9	9.6	17.5	16.2	29.0	•	19.5	•	10.3	12.1	•
Operating Margin Before Officers' Comp. **22**	25.2	39.8	31.8	22.5	23.1	19.7	33.6	•	23.8	•	10.3	13.0	•

Selected Average Balance Sheet ($ in Thousands)

Net Receivables 23	101	0	4	60	153	806	1040	3303	80024	672936
Inventories 24	•	•	0	•	•	•	•	•	•	•
Net Property, Plant and Equipment 25	139	0	13	151	566	2117	4406	24369	23164	229568
Total Assets 26	700	0	69	649	1891	6971	15080	70135	315080	2648039
Notes and Loans Payable 27	319	0	25	292	855	2394	6329	26743	167096	1408667
All Other Liabilities 28	125	0	10	179	264	1393	1818	11534	46643	486704
Net Worth 29	256	0	34	178	772	3184	6934	31858	101340	752667

Selected Financial Ratios (Times to 1)

Current Ratio 30	3.2	•	2.5	3.3	3.1	2.1	1.9	2.1	1.7	7.0
Quick Ratio 31	1.8	•	2.0	2.1	2.6	1.2	1.1	1.1	1.1	2.8
Net Sales to Working Capital 32	1.7	•	9.8	2.6	2.7	2.2	1.7	0.9	2.8	0.4
Coverage Ratio 33	7.5	10.3	66.0	9.7	11.9	7.5	7.7	3.0	5.8	2.6
Total Asset Turnover 34	0.6	•	3.0	1.1	0.7	0.4	0.3	0.1	0.5	0.2
Inventory Turnover 35	•	•	•	•	•	•	•	•	•	•
Receivables Turnover 36	•	•	•	•	•	•	•	•	•	•
Total Liabilities to Net Worth 37	1.7	•	1.0	2.6	1.4	1.2	1.2	1.2	2.1	2.5
Current Assets to Working Capital 38	1.4	•	1.7	1.4	1.5	1.9	2.2	1.9	2.4	1.2
Current Liabilities to Working Capital 39	0.4	•	0.7	0.4	0.5	0.9	1.2	0.9	1.4	0.2
Working Capital to Net Sales 40	0.6	•	0.1	0.4	0.4	0.5	0.6	1.1	0.4	2.6
Inventory to Working Capital 41	0.0	•	•	•	0.0	0.0	0.0	0.0	0.0	0.0
Total Receipts to Cash Flow 42	2.2	1.9	2.2	2.3	2.9	2.1	1.9	2.2	2.0	1.9
Cost of Goods to Cash Flow 43	0.0	0.0	•	•	•	•	•	•	0.0	0.0
Cash Flow to Total Debt 44	0.4	•	2.7	0.6	0.4	0.4	0.3	0.1	0.4	0.2

Selected Financial Factors (in Percentages)

Debt Ratio 45	63.4	•	50.4	72.6	59.1	54.3	54.0	54.6	67.8	71.6
Return on Total Assets 46	11.4	•	49.0	11.6	13.7	8.2	9.2	3.9	6.5	4.9
Return on Equity Before Income Taxes 47	27.0	•	97.3	37.9	30.8	15.6	17.4	5.8	16.7	10.6
Return on Equity After Income Taxes 48	25.0	•	96.0	34.7	30.0	14.7	16.3	4.7	11.2	8.0
Profit Margin (Before Income Tax) 49	16.7	33.5	15.9	9.6	17.4	16.1	28.9	18.9	10.3	12.3
Profit Margin (After Income Tax) 50	15.5	30.9	15.7	8.8	16.9	15.1	27.2	15.2	6.9	9.3

Table I

Corporations with and without Net Income

AUTOMOTIVE EQUIPMENT RENTAL AND LEASING

MONEY AMOUNTS AND SIZE OF ASSETS IN THOUSANDS OF DOLLARS

Item Description for Accounting Period 7/09 Through 6/10	Total	Zero Assets	Under 500	500 to 1,000	1,000 to 5,000	5,000 to 10,000	10,000 to 25,000	25,000 to 50,000	50,000 to 100,000	100,000 to 250,000	250,000 to 500,000	500,000 to 2,500,000	2,500,000 and over
Number of Enterprises **1**	7581	584	4995	824	668	263	139	51	33	15	0	3	7
Revenues ($ in Thousands)													
Net Sales **2**	47090221	28551	877468	296651	1328410	1223899	1417670	1286812	1231526	1391035	0	1894503	36113698
Interest **3**	957105	58	398	0	2777	496	500	1142	1469	4520	0	6046	939700
Rents **4**	137657	0	0	0	0	238	2329	25	1028	0	0	0	134037
Royalties **5**	244420	0	0	0	0	0	0	0	0	0	0	0	244420
Other Portfolio Income **6**	2666003	20390	12991	10153	84784	67884	102235	59953	156738	59407	0	62	2091403
Other Receipts **7**	43085036	8103	864079	286498	1240849	1155281	1312606	1225692	1072291	1327108	0	1888395	32704138
Total Receipts **8**	47090221	28551	877468	296651	1328410	1223899	1417670	1286812	1231526	1391035	0	1894503	36113698
Average Total Receipts **9**	6212	49	176	360	1989	4654	10199	25232	37319	92736	•	631501	5159100
Operating Costs/Operating Income (%)													
Cost of Operations **10**	16.1	•	40.1	13.7	4.9	43.8	37.6	49.7	31.6	22.2	•	0.9	13.1
Salaries and Wages **11**	11.9	0.2	6.7	8.5	9.4	6.8	7.3	5.9	6.4	6.5	•	4.8	13.5
Taxes Paid **12**	3.0	4.0	1.8	3.4	2.2	1.9	2.1	2.0	2.1	2.5	•	0.3	3.3
Interest Paid **13**	6.8	0.1	3.6	3.8	5.8	3.7	3.9	4.3	4.9	4.3	•	4.0	7.6
Depreciation **14**	33.7	17.3	10.5	29.6	30.5	20.4	27.1	25.8	38.8	32.4	•	93.0	32.2
Amortization and Depletion **15**	0.3	1.3	•	1.3	0.0	0.0	0.1	0.0	0.1	0.2	•	0.2	0.3
Pensions and Other Deferred Comp. **16**	0.6	0.8	0.1	•	0.0	0.2	0.1	0.1	0.3	0.2	•	0.1	0.7
Employee Benefits **17**	1.5	0.0	0.5	0.4	1.0	0.3	0.5	0.7	0.7	1.2	•	0.3	1.7
Advertising **18**	1.2	13.2	0.2	2.1	1.2	0.7	1.2	0.2	0.4	0.2	•	0.0	1.4
Other Expenses **19**	26.4	18.0	31.1	25.1	45.0	15.9	14.1	8.6	12.0	29.2	•	5.2	28.5
Officers' Compensation **20**	0.6	28.7	2.2	4.6	2.3	3.1	1.6	1.5	1.1	1.3	•	0.2	0.3
Operating Margin **21**	•	16.5	3.3	7.6	•	2.4	4.5	1.0	1.6	•	•	•	•
Operating Margin Before Officers' Comp. **22**	•	45.2	5.5	12.2	0.6	5.5	6.1	2.5	2.7	1.1	•	•	•

Selected Average Balance Sheet ($ in Thousands)

Net Receivables 23	971	0	18	16	120	1040	1556	6087	3618	8275	76631	843038
Inventories 24	•	•	•	•	•	•	•	•	•	•	•	•
Net Property, Plant and Equipment 25	5292	0	38	377	1530	3200	8723	17558	37258	109547	652471	4402761
Total Assets 26	9320	0	109	702	2109	6524	14918	33195	60218	147172	1272955	7804121
Notes and Loans Payable 27	5158	0	152	217	1721	3565	8813	22198	42036	80956	1236099	3916198
All Other Liabilities 28	2438	0	3	10	179	525	1812	5300	6745	28290	209894	2343203
Net Worth 29	1724	0	-46	474	208	2433	4292	5697	11436	37927	-173038	1544720

Selected Financial Ratios (Times to 1)

Current Ratio 30	0.8	•	2.2	14.6	1.2	3.9	0.8	1.3	1.0	0.6	0.2	0.8
Quick Ratio 31	0.6	•	1.4	9.0	0.6	1.9	0.6	0.9	0.5	0.4	0.1	0.7
Net Sales to Working Capital 32	•	•	7.2	1.6	24.5	2.0	•	7.8	•	•	•	•
Coverage Ratio 33	0.7	189.1	1.9	3.0	0.7	1.7	2.2	1.2	1.3	1.0	•	0.7
Total Asset Turnover 34	0.7	•	1.6	0.5	0.9	0.7	0.7	0.8	0.6	0.6	0.5	0.7
Inventory Turnover 35	•	•	•	•	•	•	•	•	•	•	•	•
Receivables Turnover 36	•	•	•	•	•	•	•	•	•	•	•	•
Total Liabilities to Net Worth 37	4.4	•	•	0.5	1.7	2.5	4.8	4.3	2.9	•	•	4.1
Current Assets to Working Capital 38	•	•	1.8	1.1	5.6	1.3	3.9	3.9	•	•	•	•
Current Liabilities to Working Capital 39	•	•	0.8	0.1	4.6	0.3	2.9	2.9	•	•	•	•
Working Capital to Net Sales 40	•	•	0.1	0.6	0.0	0.5	0.1	0.1	•	•	•	•
Inventory to Working Capital 41	•	•	0.1	•	0.1	0.2	0.4	•	•	•	•	•
Total Receipts to Cash Flow 42	6.5	4.0	5.9	8.1	10.7	6.5	17.1	12.1	5.6	•	•	5.9
Cost of Goods to Cash Flow 43	1.1	1.6	0.8	0.4	4.7	2.4	8.5	3.8	1.2	•	•	0.8
Cash Flow to Total Debt 44	0.1	0.3	0.3	0.1	0.1	0.1	0.1	0.2	0.1	•	•	0.1

Selected Financial Factors (in Percentages)

Debt Ratio 45	81.5	•	141.8	32.4	90.1	62.7	71.2	82.8	81.0	74.2	113.6	80.2
Return on Total Assets 46	3.2	•	11.1	5.8	3.9	4.4	5.7	4.1	4.0	2.6	•	3.3
Return on Equity Before Income Taxes 47	•	•	•	5.8	•	4.7	10.6	4.5	5.2	•	33.5	•
Return on Equity After Income Taxes 48	•	•	•	5.8	•	4.6	10.5	4.4	5.1	•	33.5	•
Profit Margin (Before Income Tax) 49	•	16.5	3.3	7.6	•	2.4	4.5	1.0	1.6	•	•	5.9
Profit Margin (After Income Tax) 50	•	12.2	3.3	7.6	•	2.4	4.4	1.0	1.6	•	•	•

Table II
Corporations with Net Income

AUTOMOTIVE EQUIPMENT RENTAL AND LEASING

MONEY AMOUNTS AND SIZE OF ASSETS IN THOUSANDS OF DOLLARS

Item Description for Accounting Period 7/09 Through 6/10	Total	Zero Assets	Under 500	500 to 1,000	1,000 to 5,000	5,000 to 10,000	10,000 to 25,000	25,000 to 50,000	50,000 to 100,000	100,000 to 250,000	250,000 to 500,000	500,000 to 2,500,000	2,500,000 and over
Number of Enterprises **1**	3530	97	2292	541	358	111	69	35	16	9	0	0	3
Revenues ($ in Thousands)													
Net Sales **2**	25458239	20813	706083	177504	776110	568143	657526	972831	521087	1270783	0	0	19787360
Interest **3**	912840	58	0	0	2777	470	325	632	764	6341	0	0	901474
Rents **4**	131009	0	0	0	0	238	2247	0	1028	0	0	0	127496
Royalties **5**	34589	0	0	0	0	0	0	0	0	0	0	0	34589
Other Portfolio Income **6**	2100767	20390	12191	2668	80604	33625	66866	41939	126197	43959	0	0	1672326
Other Receipts **7**	22279034	365	693892	174836	692729	533810	588088	930260	393098	1220483	0	0	17051475
Total Receipts **8**	25458239	20813	706083	177504	776110	568143	657526	972831	521087	1270783	0	0	19787360
Average Total Receipts **9**	7212	215	308	328	2168	5118	9529	27795	32568	141198	•	•	6595787
Operating Costs/Operating Income (%)													
Cost of Operations **10**	16.8	•	41.5	•	7.3	22.4	20.9	60.3	13.3	20.8	•	•	13.8
Salaries and Wages **11**	12.4	0.3	6.4	9.5	7.3	7.0	6.3	6.2	6.6	6.5	•	•	14.1
Taxes Paid **12**	2.9	5.3	1.8	3.3	1.7	2.9	2.1	1.7	1.7	2.4	•	•	3.1
Interest Paid **13**	6.9	0.1	2.6	5.7	4.1	4.2	4.1	2.8	5.2	4.9	•	•	7.7
Depreciation **14**	31.3	19.5	7.2	21.2	21.1	26.1	33.2	12.1	41.6	41.5	•	•	32.8
Amortization and Depletion **15**	0.1	•	0.1	•	0.0	0.0	0.0	0.1	0.1	0.4	•	•	0.1
Pensions and Other Deferred Comp. **16**	0.3	1.1	•	•	0.0	0.1	0.1	0.1	0.1	0.1	•	•	0.1
Employee Benefits **17**	1.1	0.0	0.3	•	0.5	1.1	0.3	0.8	0.4	1.2	•	•	1.2
Advertising **18**	0.6	•	0.1	2.1	0.4	0.5	0.5	0.2	0.6	0.1	•	•	0.7
Other Expenses **19**	21.9	5.3	32.9	29.9	49.3	19.9	15.3	7.1	13.3	16.8	•	•	21.9
Officers' Compensation **20**	0.7	35.9	•	7.5	2.2	4.4	1.9	1.1	1.1	0.9	•	•	0.3
Operating Margin **21**	5.2	32.6	7.3	20.7	6.0	11.3	15.4	7.7	15.4	4.6	•	•	4.0
Operating Margin Before Officers' Comp. **22**	5.8	68.5	7.3	28.1	8.1	15.7	17.3	8.7	16.5	5.5	•	•	4.4

Selected Average Balance Sheet ($ in Thousands)

Net Receivables 23	1254	0	16	146	•	1904	1770	5384	2799	12951	1212451
Inventories 24	•	•	20	•	•	•	•	•	•	•	•
Net Property, Plant and Equipment 25	5671	0	31	455	1221	3899	9425	16180	34246	79158	5451025
Total Assets 26	9744	0	112	736	1937	7176	15961	32629	60293	265503	8884614
Notes and Loans Payable 27	4605	0	157	287	1352	3154	7890	19382	38371	196699	3766767
All Other Liabilities 28	2690	0	7	10	122	659	2172	4038	7192	29951	2893766
Net Worth 29	2449	0	-51	439	463	3362	5900	9208	14730	38853	2224081

Selected Financial Ratios (Times to 1)

Current Ratio 30	0.7	•	3.2	26.6	2.8	4.6	0.9	1.5	1.1	0.2	0.7
Quick Ratio 31	0.6	•	1.9	20.1	1.9	4.2	0.7	0.9	0.6	0.1	0.6
Net Sales to Working Capital 32	•	•	6.7	1.3	6.3	2.3	•	6.7	24.3	•	•
Coverage Ratio 33	1.8	399.8	3.9	4.6	2.4	3.7	4.8	3.8	3.9	1.9	1.5
Total Asset Turnover 34	0.7	2.7	•	0.4	1.1	0.7	0.6	0.9	0.5	0.5	0.7
Inventory Turnover 35	•	•	•	•	•	•	•	•	•	•	•
Receivables Turnover 36	•	•	•	•	•	•	•	•	•	•	•
Total Liabilities to Net Worth 37	3.0	•	•	0.7	3.2	1.1	1.7	2.5	3.1	5.8	3.0
Current Assets to Working Capital 38	•	•	1.5	1.0	1.5	1.3	•	3.1	12.6	•	•
Current Liabilities to Working Capital 39	•	•	0.5	0.0	0.5	0.3	•	2.1	11.6	•	•
Working Capital to Net Sales 40	•	•	0.1	0.8	0.2	0.4	•	0.1	0.0	•	•
Inventory to Working Capital 41	•	•	•	•	0.0	0.1	•	0.5	1.3	•	•
Total Receipts to Cash Flow 42	5.0	93.3	3.1	3.4	5.9	5.6	3.6	8.7	4.4	9.2	4.9
Cost of Goods to Cash Flow 43	0.8	•	1.3	•	0.4	1.3	0.8	5.2	0.6	1.9	0.7
Cash Flow to Total Debt 44	0.2	•	0.6	0.3	0.2	0.2	0.3	0.1	0.2	0.1	0.2

Selected Financial Factors (in Percentages)

Debt Ratio 45	74.9	•	145.8	40.3	76.1	53.1	63.0	71.8	75.6	85.4	75.0
Return on Total Assets 46	8.9	•	27.1	11.8	11.3	11.0	11.6	8.9	11.2	5.0	8.7
Return on Equity Before Income Taxes 47	15.2	•	•	15.5	27.9	17.2	24.7	23.1	34.1	16.7	12.0
Return on Equity After Income Taxes 48	14.8	•	•	15.5	26.2	17.1	24.5	23.0	33.8	14.6	11.6
Profit Margin (Before Income Tax) 49	5.2	32.6	7.3	20.7	6.0	11.3	15.3	7.6	15.4	4.6	4.0
Profit Margin (After Income Tax) 50	5.0	26.7	7.3	20.7	5.6	11.3	15.2	7.6	15.3	4.0	3.9

Table I

Corporations with and without Net Income

OTHER CONSUMER GOODS AND GENERAL RENTAL CENTERS

MONEY AMOUNTS AND SIZE OF ASSETS IN THOUSANDS OF DOLLARS

Item Description for Accounting Period 7/09 Through 6/10		Total	Zero Assets	Under 500	500 to 1,000	1,000 to 5,000	5,000 to 10,000	10,000 to 25,000	25,000 to 50,000	50,000 to 100,000	100,000 to 250,000	250,000 to 500,000	500,000 to 2,500,000	2,500,000 and over
Number of Enterprises	1	9861	885	7551	715	543	99	39	19	0	6	0	5	0
Revenues ($ in Thousands)														
Net Sales	2	18899607	40027	2917850	876410	1064835	893450	849453	652914	0	950104	0	10654565	0
Interest	3	23129	0	21	313	740	0	34	4638	0	2691	0	14693	0
Rents	4	9511	0	0	0	1455	0	0	0	0	7974	0	83	0
Royalties	5	89924	0	0	0	0	0	0	0	0	0	0	89924	0
Other Portfolio Income	6	154683	0	5023	74881	4580	7449	15307	4695	0	2757	0	39992	0
Other Receipts	7	18622360	40027	2912806	801216	1058060	886001	834112	643581	0	936682	0	10509873	0
Total Receipts	8	18899607	40027	2917850	876410	1064835	893450	849453	652914	0	950104	0	10654565	0
Average Total Receipts	9	1917	45	386	1226	1961	9025	21781	34364	•	158351	•	2130913	•
Operating Costs/Operating Income (%)														
Cost of Operations	10	24.1	32.6	23.2	32.9	14.7	18.5	39.8	24.3	•	11.5	•	24.8	•
Salaries and Wages	11	19.9	15.4	21.0	15.7	23.5	19.5	16.6	17.0	•	20.4	•	20.0	•
Taxes Paid	12	3.8	5.6	4.5	4.0	4.7	4.4	2.3	3.0	•	5.8	•	3.5	•
Interest Paid	13	2.2	0.0	1.0	1.4	4.2	0.7	1.8	3.1	•	4.0	•	2.3	•
Depreciation	14	14.4	3.5	8.0	14.2	14.6	25.1	13.2	16.0	•	10.2	•	15.7	•
Amortization and Depletion	15	1.8	•	0.0	0.0	0.3	0.2	1.0	1.3	•	19.6	•	1.2	•
Pensions and Other Deferred Comp.	16	0.1	•	0.0	0.3	0.1	0.5	0.1	0.0	•	0.1	•	0.1	•
Employee Benefits	17	1.3	•	0.8	1.3	1.2	2.3	1.0	1.8	•	1.3	•	1.3	•
Advertising	18	3.0	1.1	1.7	1.9	2.3	2.4	1.4	3.9	•	1.2	•	3.8	•
Other Expenses	19	25.3	31.8	36.2	16.4	26.0	15.3	15.5	26.1	•	20.2	•	25.0	•
Officers' Compensation	20	2.0	3.7	5.0	4.6	4.4	3.5	1.4	1.8	•	1.5	•	0.7	•
Operating Margin	21	2.2	6.2	•	7.3	4.0	7.6	6.1	1.5	•	4.3	•	1.7	•
Operating Margin Before Officers' Comp.	22	4.2	9.9	3.5	12.0	8.3	11.2	7.5	3.3	•	5.8	•	2.4	•

Selected Average Balance Sheet ($ in Thousands)

	1	2	3	4	5	6	7	8	9
Net Receivables 23	61	•	52	246	164	3381	1319	2512	40358
Inventories 24	•	0	0	•	•	•	•	•	•
Net Property, Plant and Equipment 25	609	64	420	1061	3547	6198	22867	136227	559056
Total Assets 26	1353	124	727	1685	5790	15796	41758	209937	1545476
Notes and Loans Payable 27	679	75	695	1449	875	8529	19226	113842	674985
All Other Liabilities 28	421	17	78	214	697	6992	9342	30162	630412
Net Worth 29	253	32	-45	22	4217	275	13189	65932	240080

Selected Financial Ratios (Times to 1)

	1	2	3	4	5	6	7	8	9
Current Ratio 30	0.6	2.1	3.1	2.9	3.0	3.0	1.0	0.3	0.4
Quick Ratio 31	0.4	1.0	2.0	2.4	0.6	2.5	0.6	0.2	0.2
Net Sales to Working Capital 32	•	16.5	6.4	5.9	6.4	5.4	258.1	•	•
Coverage Ratio 33	2.0	494.4	6.3	1.9	12.7	4.5	1.5	2.1	1.7
Total Asset Turnover 34	1.4	3.1	1.7	1.2	1.6	1.4	0.8	0.8	1.4
Inventory Turnover 35	•	•	•	•	•	•	•	•	•
Receivables Turnover 36	•	•	•	•	•	•	•	•	•
Total Liabilities to Net Worth 37	4.3	2.9	•	75.0	0.4	56.4	2.2	2.2	5.4
Current Assets to Working Capital 38	•	1.9	1.5	1.5	1.5	57.3	2.2	•	•
Current Liabilities to Working Capital 39	•	0.9	0.5	0.5	0.5	56.3	0.5	•	•
Working Capital to Net Sales 40	0.1	0.7	0.2	0.2	0.2	0.2	0.2	•	0.0
Inventory to Working Capital 41	0.7	•	0.4	0.6	0.6	0.1	•	•	5.2
Total Receipts to Cash Flow 42	5.9	4.8	6.0	5.4	5.6	6.0	5.1	7.0	6.4
Cost of Goods to Cash Flow 43	1.4	1.3	2.0	0.8	1.0	2.4	1.2	0.8	1.6
Cash Flow to Total Debt 44	0.3	0.9	0.3	0.2	1.0	0.2	0.2	0.2	0.3

Selected Financial Factors (in Percentages)

	1	2	3	4	5	6	7	8	9
Debt Ratio 45	81.3	74.2	106.2	98.7	27.2	98.3	68.4	68.6	84.5
Return on Total Assets 46	6.2	14.7	9.5	12.9	10.8	•	3.8	6.2	5.5
Return on Equity Before Income Taxes 47	16.6	•	•	351.8	16.3	481.5	3.8	10.3	14.9
Return on Equity After Income Taxes 48	10.1	•	•	343.2	16.3	481.5	2.7	4.3	3.7
Profit Margin (Before Income Tax) 49	2.2	6.2	7.3	4.0	7.6	6.1	1.5	4.3	1.7
Profit Margin (After Income Tax) 50	1.3	5.4	7.3	3.9	7.6	6.1	1.1	1.8	0.4

Table II

Corporations with Net Income

OTHER CONSUMER GOODS AND GENERAL RENTAL CENTERS

MONEY AMOUNTS AND SIZE OF ASSETS IN THOUSANDS OF DOLLARS

Item Description for Accounting Period 7/09 Through 6/10	Total	Zero Assets	Under 500	500 to 1,000	1,000 to 5,000	5,000 to 10,000	10,000 to 25,000	25,000 to 50,000	50,000 to 100,000	100,000 to 250,000	250,000 to 500,000	500,000 to 2,500,000	2,500,000 and over
Number of Enterprises **1**	5082	631	3614	489	217	•	23	7	•	0	0	•	0
Revenues ($ in Thousands)													
Net Sales **2**	12004769	28095	2004618	826726	546120	•	613555	324544	•	0	0	•	0
Interest **3**	12762	0	0	313	267	•	0	114	•	0	0	•	0
Rents **4**	9511	0	0	0	1455	•	0	0	•	0	0	•	0
Royalties **5**	47010	0	0	0	0	•	0	0	•	0	0	•	0
Other Portfolio Income **6**	131483	0	295	74881	4580	•	15307	48	•	0	0	•	0
Other Receipts **7**	11804003	28095	2004323	751532	539818	•	598248	324382	•	0	0	•	0
Total Receipts **8**	12004769	28095	2004618	826726	546120	•	613555	324544	•	0	0	•	0
Average Total Receipts **9**	2362	45	555	1691	2517	•	26676	46363	•	•	•	•	•
Operating Costs/Operating Income (%)													
Cost of Operations **10**	20.0	18.2	19.1	29.3	25.7	•	22.4	27.6	•	•	•	•	•
Salaries and Wages **11**	19.8	22.0	21.5	16.6	19.5	•	20.8	11.2	•	•	•	•	•
Taxes Paid **12**	3.8	7.5	4.5	4.1	4.7	•	2.9	2.8	•	•	•	•	•
Interest Paid **13**	1.1	•	1.1	1.3	3.5	•	1.6	2.8	•	•	•	•	•
Depreciation **14**	17.8	2.3	7.1	13.8	10.6	•	18.1	14.3	•	•	•	•	•
Amortization and Depletion **15**	2.0	•	0.0	0.0	0.5	•	0.3	0.5	•	•	•	•	•
Pensions and Other Deferred Comp. **16**	0.1	•	0.0	0.3	0.1	•	0.1	0.0	•	•	•	•	•
Employee Benefits **17**	1.5	•	0.7	1.4	0.6	•	1.1	1.8	•	•	•	•	•
Advertising **18**	3.6	0.3	2.1	2.0	1.8	•	1.4	6.2	•	•	•	•	•
Other Expenses **19**	20.0	39.2	35.5	16.4	17.2	•	18.4	23.5	•	•	•	•	•
Officers' Compensation **20**	2.0	•	3.4	4.8	5.3	•	1.2	1.2	•	•	•	•	•
Operating Margin **21**	8.0	10.5	5.0	10.0	10.6	•	11.7	8.2	•	•	•	•	•
Operating Margin Before Officers' Comp. **22**	10.0	10.5	8.4	14.8	15.9	•	12.9	9.4	•	•	•	•	•

Selected Average Balance Sheet ($ in Thousands)

Net Receivables 23	74	0	5	76	268	4080	107
Inventories 24					916		26853
Net Property, Plant and Equipment 25	808	0	72	386	916	6854	26853
Total Assets 26	1846	0	139	778	1654	15588	36193
Notes and Loans Payable 27	663	0	95	600	955	8915	20405
All Other Liabilities 28	489	0	23	113	365	1825	6234
Net Worth 29	694	0	21	65	334	4849	9553

Selected Financial Ratios (Times to 1)

Current Ratio 30	0.7		1.5	2.7	2.7	3.8	0.8
Quick Ratio 31	0.5		1.0	1.9	2.0	3.7	0.5
Net Sales to Working Capital 32			33.6	7.6	6.7	5.3	
Coverage Ratio 33	8.4		5.8	8.9	4.1	8.4	3.9
Total Asset Turnover 34	1.3		4.0	2.2	1.5	1.7	1.3
Inventory Turnover 35							
Receivables Turnover 36							
Total Liabilities to Net Worth 37	1.7		5.6	11.0	4.0	2.2	2.8
Current Assets to Working Capital 38			2.9	1.6	1.6	1.4	
Current Liabilities to Working Capital 39			1.9	0.6	0.6	0.4	
Working Capital to Net Sales 40			0.0	0.1	0.1	0.2	
Inventory to Working Capital 41			0.9	0.3	0.3	0.0	
Total Receipts to Cash Flow 42	4.9	3.1	3.8	5.2	4.3	4.2	4.5
Cost of Goods to Cash Flow 43	1.0	0.6	0.7	1.5	1.1	0.9	1.2
Cash Flow to Total Debt 44	0.4		1.2	0.5	0.4	0.6	0.4

Selected Financial Factors (in Percentages)

Debt Ratio 45	62.4		84.8	91.7	79.8	68.9	73.6
Return on Total Assets 46	11.7		24.4	24.5	21.4	22.6	14.0
Return on Equity Before Income Taxes 47	27.4		132.6	262.3	80.2	63.9	39.7
Return on Equity After Income Taxes 48	22.8		132.5	261.7	78.8	63.9	38.2
Profit Margin (Before Income Tax) 49	8.0	10.5	5.0	10.0	10.6	11.6	8.2
Profit Margin (After Income Tax) 50	6.7	9.4	5.0	10.0	10.4	11.6	7.9

Table I

Corporations with and without Net Income

COMMERCIAL AND INDUSTRIAL MACHINERY AND EQUIPMENT RENTAL

MONEY AMOUNTS AND SIZE OF ASSETS IN THOUSANDS OF DOLLARS

Item Description for Accounting Period 7/09 Through 6/10		Total	Zero Assets	Under 500	500 to 1,000	1,000 to 5,000	5,000 to 10,000	10,000 to 25,000	25,000 to 50,000	50,000 to 100,000	100,000 to 250,000	250,000 to 500,000	500,000 to 2,500,000	2,500,000 and over
Number of Enterprises	1	25545	3763	14632	2396	3595	585	311	111	54	45	18	29	5
Revenues ($ in Thousands)														
Net Sales	2	41984994	313784	3912059	2349708	4712190	2847302	2780891	2155955	1722970	2933868	2573231	9219432	6463601
Interest	3	1065119	1081	3146	10469	8072	5959	7793	15411	26409	97784	39471	310006	539518
Rents	4	237626	0	19216	4930	67	0	365	2531	4026	99310	2144	105037	0
Royalties	5	3307	0	0	0	0	0	1228	0	0	1330	0	750	0
Other Portfolio Income	6	1838495	136999	114831	14052	100452	89727	82360	73102	56245	61572	102052	749407	257697
Other Receipts	7	38840447	175704	3774866	2320257	4603599	2751616	2689145	2064911	1636290	2673872	2429564	8054232	5566386
Total Receipts	8	41984994	313784	3912059	2349708	4712190	2847302	2780891	2155955	1722970	2933868	2573231	9219432	6463601
Average Total Receipts	9	1644	83	267	981	1311	4867	8942	19423	31907	65197	142957	317911	1292720
Operating Costs/Operating Income (%)														
Cost of Operations	10	27.6	3.5	32.8	49.8	24.1	45.5	34.4	34.2	32.6	27.4	36.9	19.3	14.1
Salaries and Wages	11	10.8	7.8	12.4	8.0	13.2	6.4	13.8	10.7	11.5	10.9	9.4	11.0	10.3
Taxes Paid	12	2.3	2.7	3.5	3.4	3.2	3.7	2.6	1.9	1.8	1.7	1.9	1.3	1.7
Interest Paid	13	8.0	5.1	2.8	1.9	3.4	2.8	3.8	5.2	6.7	8.3	9.1	12.6	15.5
Depreciation	14	26.5	28.0	10.3	8.1	20.6	18.7	21.6	24.1	29.3	27.3	24.4	37.5	37.5
Amortization and Depletion	15	1.0	0.1	0.1	0.1	0.7	0.2	0.1	1.5	0.7	1.1	2.3	1.0	2.2
Pensions and Other Deferred Comp.	16	0.4	0.0	0.3	0.6	1.7	0.4	0.2	0.3	0.3	0.3	0.3	0.2	0.3
Employee Benefits	17	1.3	1.1	0.9	2.4	1.0	1.0	1.6	1.4	1.1	1.2	1.4	1.9	0.9
Advertising	18	0.3	0.2	0.5	0.5	0.5	0.4	0.3	0.4	0.5	0.3	0.3	0.3	0.1
Other Expenses	19	21.9	12.6	24.4	23.9	26.5	16.7	23.2	24.2	18.8	23.6	15.6	18.6	25.1
Officers' Compensation	20	2.8	6.7	10.9	2.9	4.2	4.2	2.1	1.9	2.0	3.7	0.9	0.9	0.2
Operating Margin	21	•	32.2	1.1	•	1.0	0.1	•	•	•	•	•	•	•
Operating Margin Before Officers' Comp.	22	•	38.9	12.1	1.4	5.1	4.3	•	•	•	•	•	•	•

Selected Average Balance Sheet ($ in Thousands)

	1	2	3	4	5	6	7	8	9	10	11	12	13
Net Receivables **23**	795	•	7	111	208	951	1665	4614	9396	25847	57365	117127	2302891
Inventories **24**	•	•	•	•	•	•	•	•	•	•	•	•	•
Net Property, Plant and Equipment **25**	1705	•	58	319	1101	2985	6836	15157	32665	60464	162014	520233	1988471
Total Assets **26**	3828	0	133	734	1967	6919	15454	34686	68809	152415	348586	1074033	5262057
Notes and Loans Payable **27**	2344	0	150	331	1184	4290	5646	16999	34503	76978	191435	628598	3894804
All Other Liabilities **28**	792	0	19	142	260	710	2932	5800	10534	24869	94608	302514	911181
Net Worth **29**	692	0	-35	260	524	1919	6875	11887	23772	50568	62543	142920	456072

Selected Financial Ratios (Times to 1)

	1	2	3	4	5	6	7	8	9	10	11	12	13
Current Ratio **30**	1.5	•	1.3	1.6	1.4	1.5	1.4	1.6	1.8	1.7	1.5	1.0	2.3
Quick Ratio **31**	1.2	•	1.0	1.2	1.0	0.8	0.8	0.9	1.1	1.1	1.0	0.7	2.2
Net Sales to Working Capital **32**	3.7	•	21.8	9.9	8.2	4.4	6.0	4.8	3.3	3.4	4.0	•	0.9
Coverage Ratio **33**	0.6	7.3	1.4	0.2	1.3	1.0	0.1	•	0.2	0.3	0.7	0.6	0.5
Total Asset Turnover **34**	0.4	•	2.0	1.3	0.7	0.7	0.6	0.6	0.5	0.4	0.4	0.3	0.2
Inventory Turnover **35**	•	•	•	•	•	•	•	•	•	•	•	•	•
Receivables Turnover **36**	•	•	•	•	•	•	•	•	•	•	•	•	•
Total Liabilities to Net Worth **37**	4.5	•	1.8	2.8	2.8	2.6	1.9	1.9	1.9	2.0	4.6	6.5	10.5
Current Assets to Working Capital **38**	2.9	4.2	2.8	3.8	2.8	2.8	2.7	2.2	2.2	2.4	3.0	•	1.8
Current Liabilities to Working Capital **39**	1.9	3.2	1.8	2.8	1.8	2.4	1.7	1.2	1.2	1.4	2.0	•	0.8
Working Capital to Net Sales **40**	0.3	0.0	0.1	0.1	0.2	0.2	0.2	0.3	0.3	0.3	0.3	•	1.1
Inventory to Working Capital **41**	0.2	0.2	0.4	0.3	0.3	0.5	0.5	0.2	0.2	0.3	0.5	•	0.0
Total Receipts to Cash Flow **42**	11.3	2.8	6.1	8.4	6.3	11.7	11.6	9.2	13.7	18.1	16.2	19.6	20.8
Cost of Goods to Cash Flow **43**	3.1	0.1	2.0	4.2	1.5	5.3	3.1	4.5	5.0	6.0	3.8	•	2.9
Cash Flow to Total Debt **44**	0.0	•	0.3	0.2	0.1	0.1	0.1	0.1	0.1	0.0	0.0	0.0	0.0

Selected Financial Factors (in Percentages)

	1	2	3	4	5	6	7	8	9	10	11	12	13
Debt Ratio **45**	81.9	•	126.5	64.5	73.4	72.3	55.5	65.7	65.5	66.8	82.1	86.7	91.3
Return on Total Assets **46**	2.1	7.8	0.6	2.9	2.0	0.1	0.6	•	0.6	1.1	2.7	2.4	1.8
Return on Equity Before Income Taxes **47**	•	•	•	•	•	•	•	•	•	•	•	•	•
Return on Equity After Income Taxes **48**	•	•	•	1.6	•	•	•	•	•	•	•	•	•
Profit Margin (Before Income Tax) **49**	•	32.2	1.1	0.9	•	•	•	•	•	•	•	•	•
Profit Margin (After Income Tax) **50**	•	29.0	1.0	0.6	•	•	•	•	•	•	•	•	•

Table II

Corporations with Net Income

COMMERCIAL AND INDUSTRIAL MACHINERY AND EQUIPMENT RENTAL

MONEY AMOUNTS AND SIZE OF ASSETS IN THOUSANDS OF DOLLARS

Item Description for Accounting Period 7/09 Through 6/10		Total	Zero Assets	Under 500	500 to 1,000	1,000 to 5,000	5,000 to 10,000	10,000 to 25,000	25,000 to 50,000	50,000 to 100,000	100,000 to 250,000	250,000 to 500,000	500,000 to 2,500,000	2,500,000 and over
Number of Enterprises	1	10117	1119	6080	1102	1381	199	137	50	17	18	4	9	0
Revenues ($ in Thousands)														
Net Sales	2	14591094	269060	2911157	687014	1784324	928478	1210821	912485	742392	1531096	1004354	2609912	0
Interest	3	183076	995	2178	1121	1521	1668	4868	4829	11813	15893	17607	120583	0
Rents	4	23735	0	19006	0	19	0	9	0	4026	677	0	0	0
Royalties	5	2557	0	0	0	0	0	1228	0	0	1330	0	0	0
Other Portfolio Income	6	1039823	133926	104512	10620	51703	57647	25168	31176	31829	46137	30976	516129	0
Other Receipts	7	13341903	134139	2785461	675273	1731081	869163	1179548	876480	694724	1467059	955771	1973200	0
Total Receipts	8	14591094	269060	2911157	687014	1784324	928478	1210821	912485	742392	1531096	1004354	2609912	0
Average Total Receipts	9	1442	240	479	623	1292	4666	8838	18250	43670	85061	251088	289990	•
Operating Costs/Operating Income (%)														
Cost of Operations	10	23.7	1.3	31.2	11.9	13.8	31.9	29.6	29.7	41.3	28.1	36.3	7.5	•
Salaries and Wages	11	10.6	8.9	12.5	7.4	14.3	9.2	15.3	8.5	8.6	12.3	9.5	5.9	•
Taxes Paid	12	2.1	3.0	3.3	3.0	2.5	2.2	2.1	1.7	1.5	1.8	1.5	0.9	•
Interest Paid	13	3.9	3.0	1.3	2.2	2.0	1.5	3.2	4.5	3.8	4.0	5.6	8.8	•
Depreciation	14	17.3	17.7	6.5	14.9	19.2	14.8	18.1	24.4	18.1	19.3	17.7	25.4	•
Amortization and Depletion	15	0.3	0.0	0.0	•	0.2	0.1	0.0	0.2	0.2	0.3	0.7	0.6	•
Pensions and Other Deferred Comp.	16	0.3	0.0	0.4	0.0	0.1	0.8	0.1	0.4	0.3	0.2	0.2	0.3	•
Employee Benefits	17	1.0	1.3	0.9	1.2	0.6	0.7	1.0	1.7	0.8	1.5	1.8	0.9	•
Advertising	18	0.4	0.3	0.4	0.3	0.8	0.3	0.2	0.5	0.3	0.4	0.5	0.1	•
Other Expenses	19	20.0	8.0	22.7	22.4	19.4	16.2	16.7	15.1	13.8	17.1	16.8	27.4	•
Officers' Compensation	20	3.9	7.8	7.5	3.6	5.4	4.7	2.3	2.5	1.6	5.3	1.2	0.6	•
Operating Margin	21	16.4	48.6	13.4	33.0	21.7	17.7	11.3	10.7	9.6	9.6	8.2	21.6	•
Operating Margin Before Officers' Comp.	22	20.4	56.5	20.8	36.6	27.1	22.3	13.6	13.1	11.2	14.9	9.4	22.2	•

Selected Average Balance Sheet ($ in Thousands)

Net Receivables 23	319	•	0	66	126	1618	2094	6059	10279	26689	31370	136168	•
Inventories 24	•	•	•	•	•	•	•	•	•	•	•	•	•
Net Property, Plant and Equipment 25	798	0	66	340	980	3514	6482	11905	33008	61396	114490	181702	•
Total Assets 26	2180	0	166	802	1925	7370	15535	33488	67664	143592	321097	802190	•
Notes and Loans Payable 27	897	0	85	265	670	2822	4416	13450	30392	52950	79850	412492	•
All Other Liabilities 28	412	0	15	56	165	661	2385	5812	13808	16648	156248	208510	•
Net Worth 29	871	0	66	480	1089	3887	8734	14226	23465	73993	84998	181188	•

Selected Financial Ratios (Times to 1)

Current Ratio 30	2.0	•	1.4	3.5	2.2	3.3	2.0	1.8	2.3	2.6	1.9	1.6	•
Quick Ratio 31	1.3	•	1.2	2.5	1.4	2.4	1.3	1.0	1.2	1.5	0.6	1.3	•
Net Sales to Working Capital 32	3.8	•	24.7	3.4	4.1	2.1	3.2	2.9	2.6	2.5	4.7	3.3	•
Coverage Ratio 33	5.2	17.2	11.6	16.0	11.6	12.7	4.5	3.3	3.5	3.5	2.5	3.5	•
Total Asset Turnover 34	0.7	•	2.9	0.8	0.7	0.6	0.6	0.5	0.6	0.6	0.8	0.4	•
Inventory Turnover 35	•	•	•	•	•	•	•	•	•	•	•	•	•
Receivables Turnover 36	•	•	•	•	•	•	•	•	•	•	•	•	•
Total Liabilities to Net Worth 37	1.5	•	1.5	0.7	0.8	0.9	0.8	1.4	1.9	0.9	2.8	3.4	•
Current Assets to Working Capital 38	2.0	•	3.6	1.4	1.8	1.4	2.0	2.2	1.7	1.6	2.2	2.6	•
Current Liabilities to Working Capital 39	1.0	•	2.6	0.4	0.8	0.4	1.0	1.2	0.7	0.6	1.2	1.6	•
Working Capital to Net Sales 40	0.3	•	0.0	0.3	0.2	0.5	0.3	0.3	0.4	0.4	0.2	0.3	•
Inventory to Working Capital 41	0.3	•	0.0	0.1	0.0	0.2	0.1	0.4	0.3	0.3	1.3	0.3	•
Total Receipts to Cash Flow 42	3.6	2.1	3.7	2.1	3.1	3.8	4.5	4.6	5.6	5.5	5.6	2.8	•
Cost of Goods to Cash Flow 43	0.9	0.0	1.1	0.2	0.4	1.2	1.3	1.4	2.3	1.5	2.0	0.2	•
Cash Flow to Total Debt 44	0.3	•	1.3	0.9	0.5	0.4	0.3	0.2	0.2	0.2	0.2	0.2	•

Selected Financial Factors (in Percentages)

Debt Ratio 45	60.0	•	60.4	40.1	43.4	47.3	43.8	57.5	65.3	48.5	73.5	77.4	•
Return on Total Assets 46	13.4	•	42.2	27.3	15.9	12.1	8.3	8.3	8.7	8.2	10.8	11.0	•
Return on Equity Before Income Taxes 47	27.2	•	97.3	42.8	25.7	21.2	11.5	13.7	18.0	11.3	24.3	34.6	•
Return on Equity After Income Taxes 48	24.9	•	96.3	41.3	24.7	19.1	11.0	11.7	15.8	9.9	19.8	28.9	•
Profit Margin (Before Income Tax) 49	16.5	48.6	13.4	33.0	21.6	17.7	11.3	10.7	9.7	9.8	8.2	21.6	•
Profit Margin (After Income Tax) 50	15.0	45.0	13.2	31.8	20.8	15.9	10.9	9.1	8.5	8.6	6.7	18.1	•

Table I
Corporations with and without Net Income

LESSORS OF NONFINAN. INTANGIBLE ASSETS (EX. COPYRIGHTED WORKS)

MONEY AMOUNTS AND SIZE OF ASSETS IN THOUSANDS OF DOLLARS

Item Description for Accounting Period 7/09 Through 6/10	Total	Zero Assets	Under 500	500 to 1,000	1,000 to 5,000	5,000 to 10,000	10,000 to 25,000	25,000 to 50,000	50,000 to 100,000	100,000 to 250,000	250,000 to 500,000	500,000 to 2,500,000	2,500,000 and over
Number of Enterprises **1**	2181	8	1670	365	64	20	27	3	8	7	0	10	0
Revenues ($ in Thousands)													
Net Sales **2**	5678476	254073	464844	189424	142531	135851	195949	183338	270519	534879	0	3307068	0
Interest **3**	62372	1544	0	0	23	1438	472	26	2497	13219	0	43153	0
Rents **4**	5429	0	0	0	0	0	0	0	103	4492	0	834	0
Royalties **5**	2371706	0	55137	0	6640	79682	32275	0	33004	329472	0	1835496	0
Other Portfolio Income **6**	94035	0	0	0	18018	0	412	183	185	3233	0	72007	0
Other Receipts **7**	3144934	252529	409707	189424	117850	54731	162790	183129	234730	184463	0	1355578	0
Total Receipts **8**	5678476	254073	464844	189424	142531	135851	195949	183338	270519	534879	0	3307068	0
Average Total Receipts **9**	2604	31759	278	519	2227	6793	7257	61113	33815	76411	•	330707	•
Operating Costs/Operating Income (%)													
Cost of Operations **10**	5.1	•	•	•	19.7	1.2	0.4	22.5	17.1	0.1	•	5.2	•
Salaries and Wages **11**	15.7	20.7	•	33.7	7.7	30.1	16.7	4.8	23.4	7.2	•	17.5	•
Taxes Paid **12**	1.9	0.9	0.2	3.6	2.1	2.7	1.7	1.1	4.3	2.7	•	1.9	•
Interest Paid **13**	7.0	2.1	0.5	4.5	2.8	0.4	2.6	0.1	1.3	4.1	•	10.5	•
Depreciation **14**	2.8	0.3	0.4	0.7	4.2	1.7	1.5	0.3	3.8	1.3	•	3.8	•
Amortization and Depletion **15**	3.3	0.1	0.6	1.8	0.3	0.1	1.8	1.1	1.4	4.0	•	4.6	•
Pensions and Other Deferred Comp. **16**	0.3	•	•	0.0	0.0	1.5	0.9	0.4	•	0.1	•	0.3	•
Employee Benefits **17**	1.4	0.3	0.4	4.4	0.6	0.6	1.5	0.0	0.4	0.6	•	1.9	•
Advertising **18**	2.8	0.8	17.2	1.1	3.8	0.8	4.7	•	1.6	3.0	•	1.2	•
Other Expenses **19**	30.5	53.9	45.4	61.7	28.2	34.7	47.5	15.0	18.5	26.7	•	26.2	•
Officers' Compensation **20**	2.7	0.6	•	11.8	9.4	13.7	4.0	3.6	3.4	1.1	•	2.1	•
Operating Margin **21**	26.3	20.3	35.3	•	21.3	12.5	16.9	51.1	24.8	49.0	•	24.8	•
Operating Margin Before Officers' Comp. **22**	29.0	20.9	35.3	•	30.7	26.2	20.9	54.7	28.2	50.2	•	26.9	•

Selected Average Balance Sheet ($ in Thousands)

Net Receivables 23	511	0	18	0	288	732	5300	6671	1766	12961	78304
Inventories 24	•	•	•	•	•	•	•	•	•	•	•
Net Property, Plant and Equipment 25	484	•	19	8	382	520	1541	377	4145	9837	83966
Total Assets 26	9802	0	171	667	1663	6852	16867	28072	69886	164004	1835844
Notes and Loans Payable 27	2854	0	9	458	573	689	2997	703	5154	131110	495062
All Other Liabilities 28	2099	0	55	69	1050	1443	3503	6205	8267	24081	401679
Net Worth 29	4849	0	107	139	39	4720	10366	21165	56465	8813	939103

Selected Financial Ratios (Times to 1)

Current Ratio 30	1.4	•	3.1	3.3	0.7	2.0	3.1	3.1	4.0	1.2	1.3
Quick Ratio 31	0.9	•	1.7	3.3	0.7	1.0	2.3	3.0	1.0	1.2	0.8
Net Sales to Working Capital 32	3.7	•	3.2	3.2	4.8	5.0	1.2	5.0	2.2	5.8	3.6
Coverage Ratio 33	4.7	10.5	66.9	•	8.7	34.3	7.5	494.2	19.3	12.9	3.3
Total Asset Turnover 34	0.3	•	1.6	0.8	1.3	1.0	0.4	2.2	0.5	0.5	0.2
Inventory Turnover 35	•	•	•	•	•	•	•	•	•	•	•
Receivables Turnover 36	•	•	•	•	•	•	•	•	•	•	•
Total Liabilities to Net Worth 37	1.0	•	0.6	3.8	41.3	0.5	0.6	0.3	0.2	17.6	1.0
Current Assets to Working Capital 38	3.4	•	1.5	1.4	•	2.0	1.5	1.5	1.3	5.3	4.3
Current Liabilities to Working Capital 39	2.4	•	0.5	0.4	•	1.0	0.5	0.5	0.3	4.3	3.3
Working Capital to Net Sales 40	0.3	•	0.3	0.3	•	0.2	0.9	0.2	0.5	0.2	0.3
Inventory to Working Capital 41	0.0	•	•	•	•	0.0	0.0	•	0.0	0.1	0.0
Total Receipts to Cash Flow 42	2.0	1.4	1.2	5.1	3.1	2.4	1.7	1.5	2.5	1.3	2.3
Cost of Goods to Cash Flow 43	0.1	•	•	•	0.6	0.0	0.0	0.0	0.4	0.0	0.1
Cash Flow to Total Debt 44	0.3	3.5	0.2	0.2	0.4	1.4	0.7	5.8	1.0	0.4	0.2

Selected Financial Factors (in Percentages)

Debt Ratio 45	50.5	•	37.2	79.1	97.6	31.1	38.5	24.6	19.2	94.6	48.8
Return on Total Assets 46	8.9	•	58.3	•	32.2	12.7	8.4	111.5	12.6	24.9	6.3
Return on Equity Before Income Taxes 47	14.1	•	91.4	•	1206.1	17.9	11.8	147.6	14.8	426.9	8.7
Return on Equity After Income Taxes 48	10.2	•	91.2	•	1176.6	12.8	11.5	137.1	12.9	355.2	5.3
Profit Margin (Before Income Tax) 49	26.3	20.3	35.3	•	21.3	12.5	16.9	51.1	24.7	49.2	24.7
Profit Margin (After Income Tax) 50	19.0	10.8	35.1	•	20.8	8.9	16.5	47.5	21.6	41.0	15.0

Table II

Corporations with Net Income

LESSORS OF NONFINAN. INTANGIBLE ASSETS (EX. COPYRIGHTED WORKS)

MONEY AMOUNTS AND SIZE OF ASSETS IN THOUSANDS OF DOLLARS

Item Description for Accounting Period 7/09 Through 6/10	Total	Zero Assets	Under 500	500 to 1,000	1,000 to 5,000	5,000 to 10,000	10,000 to 25,000	25,000 to 50,000	50,000 to 100,000	100,000 to 250,000	250,000 to 500,000	500,000 to 2,500,000	2,500,000 and over
Number of Enterprises 1	975	4	848	4	64	•	18	0	•	4	0	•	0
Revenues ($ in Thousands)													
Net Sales 2	4576075	251329	434432	15924	142531	•	369787	0	•	412518	0	•	0
Interest 3	41585	1502	0	0	23	•	458	0	•	9216	0	•	0
Rents 4	953	0	0	0	0	•	0	0	•	16	0	•	0
Royalties 5	2289445	0	55137	0	6640	•	31405	0	•	329472	0	•	0
Other Portfolio Income 6	93295	0	0	0	18018	•	412	0	•	3182	0	•	0
Other Receipts 7	2150797	249827	379295	15924	117850	•	337512	0	•	70632	0	•	0
Total Receipts 8	4576075	251329	434432	15924	142531	•	369787	0	•	412518	0	•	0
Average Total Receipts 9	4693	62832	512	3981	2227	•	20544	•	•	103130	•	•	•
Operating Costs/Operating Income (%)													
Cost of Operations 10	5.0	•	•	•	19.7	•	11.3	•	•	•	•	•	•
Salaries and Wages 11	12.7	16.6	•	•	7.7	•	9.6	•	•	5.2	•	•	•
Taxes Paid 12	1.8	0.6	0.2	•	2.1	•	1.3	•	•	2.8	•	•	•
Interest Paid 13	5.4	2.2	0.1	•	2.8	•	1.4	•	•	5.1	•	•	•
Depreciation 14	3.0	0.2	0.4	•	4.2	•	0.8	•	•	1.2	•	•	•
Amortization and Depletion 15	2.7	•	0.5	•	0.3	•	1.3	•	•	0.7	•	•	•
Pensions and Other Deferred Comp. 16	0.3	•	•	•	0.0	•	0.7	•	•	•	•	•	•
Employee Benefits 17	1.1	•	0.2	•	0.6	•	0.8	•	•	0.4	•	•	•
Advertising 18	3.0	0.5	15.7	•	3.8	•	2.5	•	•	3.0	•	•	•
Other Expenses 19	24.2	51.9	44.3	•	28.2	•	22.7	•	•	7.0	•	•	•
Officers' Compensation 20	2.4	0.2	0.2	•	9.4	•	3.3	•	•	0.3	•	•	•
Operating Margin 21	38.7	27.8	38.7	100.0	21.3	•	44.4	•	•	74.4	•	•	•
Operating Margin Before Officers' Comp. 22	41.0	28.0	38.7	100.0	30.7	•	47.7	•	•	74.7	•	•	•

Selected Average Balance Sheet ($ in Thousands)

Net Receivables 23	862	0	30		288	2360	17912
Inventories 24							
Net Property, Plant and Equipment 25	924	0	6		382	2326	3264
Total Assets 26	11945	0	187	740	1663	19034	179458
Notes and Loans Payable 27	3871	0	17	0	573	3973	198216
All Other Liabilities 28	3067	0	6	5988	1050	5442	27818
Net Worth 29	5007	0	164	-5248	39	9619	-46575

Selected Financial Ratios (Times to 1)

Current Ratio 30	3.1		7.0		0.7	1.6	1.2
Quick Ratio 31	2.4		6.9		0.7	1.2	1.2
Net Sales to Working Capital 32	1.7		4.5			8.0	5.8
Coverage Ratio 33	8.2	13.8	394.3		8.7	32.1	15.6
Total Asset Turnover 34	0.4		2.7	5.4	1.3	1.1	0.6
Inventory Turnover 35							
Receivables Turnover 36							
Total Liabilities to Net Worth 37	1.4		0.1		41.3	1.0	
Current Assets to Working Capital 38	1.5		1.2			2.7	5.6
Current Liabilities to Working Capital 39	0.5		0.2			1.7	4.6
Working Capital to Net Sales 40	0.6		0.2			0.1	0.2
Inventory to Working Capital 41	0.0		0.0			0.0	
Total Receipts to Cash Flow 42	1.7	1.3		1.0	3.1	1.2	1.5
Cost of Goods to Cash Flow 43	0.1				0.6	0.2	
Cash Flow to Total Debt 44	0.4		18.5		0.7	1.4	0.4

Selected Financial Factors (in Percentages)

Debt Ratio 45	58.1		12.2	809.4	97.6	49.5	126.0
Return on Total Assets 46	17.3		106.2	538.2	32.2	49.4	45.4
Return on Equity Before Income Taxes 47	36.2		120.6	1206.1	94.7		
Return on Equity After Income Taxes 48	27.8		120.3	1176.6	90.4		
Profit Margin (Before Income Tax) 49	38.6	27.8	38.7	100.0	21.3	44.4	74.0
Profit Margin (After Income Tax) 50	29.6	18.1	38.5	100.0	20.8	42.3	63.3

Table I

Corporations with and without Net Income

LEGAL SERVICES

MONEY AMOUNTS AND SIZE OF ASSETS IN THOUSANDS OF DOLLARS

Item Description for Accounting Period 7/09 Through 6/10		Total	Zero Assets	Under 500	500 to 1,000	1,000 to 5,000	5,000 to 10,000	10,000 to 25,000	25,000 to 50,000	50,000 to 100,000	100,000 to 250,000	250,000 to 500,000	500,000 to 2,500,000	2,500,000 and over
Number of Enterprises	1	111536	19577	84832	4163	2506	•	138	38	19	0	•	0	0
Revenues ($ in Thousands)														
Net Sales	2	92305297	2726635	42456139	9862291	14409494	•	7073908	3783475	3551748	0	•	0	0
Interest	3	33980	158	11220	2204	4579	•	2206	3662	4672	0	•	0	0
Rents	4	30215	0	4625	12239	4143	•	1300	3265	595	0	•	0	0
Royalties	5	2827	0	1902	722	0	•	0	49	154	0	•	0	0
Other Portfolio Income	6	120600	76743	14751	566	1227	•	1540	294	2623	0	•	0	0
Other Receipts	7	2332792	-2838	1440331	190019	255153	•	92975	129784	42304	0	•	0	0
Total Receipts	8	94825711	2800698	43928968	10068041	14674596	•	7171929	3920529	3602096	0	•	0	0
Average Total Receipts	9	850	143	518	2418	5856	•	51970	103172	189584	•	•	•	•
Operating Costs/Operating Income (%)														
Cost of Operations	10	5.8	4.1	4.7	9.4	9.0	•	1.5	1.9	1.6	•	•	•	•
Salaries and Wages	11	29.5	12.3	22.1	29.7	32.0	•	51.5	55.6	44.8	•	•	•	•
Taxes Paid	12	3.3	3.1	3.5	3.3	3.4	•	3.4	3.6	2.8	•	•	•	•
Interest Paid	13	0.5	0.4	0.3	0.4	0.5	•	0.5	0.5	0.7	•	•	•	•
Depreciation	14	0.9	2.6	0.6	0.5	0.8	•	1.4	1.3	1.3	•	•	•	•
Amortization and Depletion	15	0.1	0.0	0.0	0.0	0.0	•	0.0	0.1	0.1	•	•	•	•
Pensions and Other Deferred Comp.	16	1.8	2.4	1.8	2.2	1.1	•	2.8	2.3	1.8	•	•	•	•
Employee Benefits	17	2.1	1.0	1.8	2.9	2.1	•	2.8	2.5	2.0	•	•	•	•
Advertising	18	2.4	5.0	2.2	1.2	5.5	•	1.1	0.9	0.7	•	•	•	•
Other Expenses	19	26.8	39.3	29.4	21.8	21.1	•	21.5	22.6	37.6	•	•	•	•
Officers' Compensation	20	18.4	12.5	23.1	22.7	16.5	•	10.5	8.2	2.6	•	•	•	•
Operating Margin	21	8.4	17.3	10.3	6.0	8.1	•	3.0	0.4	4.2	•	•	•	•
Operating Margin Before Officers' Comp.	22	26.7	29.8	33.4	28.7	24.6	•	13.5	8.7	6.7	•	•	•	•

Selected Average Balance Sheet ($ in Thousands)

Net Receivables 23	14	0	3	7	124	1390	4123	6219
Inventories 24	1	0	0	0	1	161	0	2033
Net Property, Plant and Equipment 25	34	0	13	58	383	3552	8941	11432
Total Assets 26	211	0	70	632	1830	15485	33889	71247
Notes and Loans Payable 27	73	0	32	210	609	4677	7398	20307
All Other Liabilities 28	94	0	29	338	626	5943	12886	33388
Net Worth 29	45	0	9	83	595	4865	13605	17552

Selected Financial Ratios (Times to 1)

Current Ratio 30	1.2	•	1.3	1.0	1.4	1.4	1.7	1.5
Quick Ratio 31	0.8	•	1.0	0.5	1.1	0.7	1.1	0.9
Net Sales to Working Capital 32	33.4	•	48.6	•	17.0	19.7	11.7	17.0
Coverage Ratio 33	23.8	48.8	40.7	22.6	22.2	9.5	9.6	9.4
Total Asset Turnover 34	3.9	•	7.1	3.7	3.1	3.3	2.9	2.6
Inventory Turnover 35	75.9	•	10790.1	892.7	396.2	4.8	•	1.4
Receivables Turnover 36	57.3	•	129.2	262.1	51.6	40.3	•	33.0
Total Liabilities to Net Worth 37	3.7	•	6.7	6.6	2.1	2.2	1.5	3.1
Current Assets to Working Capital 38	5.2	•	4.4	•	3.3	3.6	2.4	3.1
Current Liabilities to Working Capital 39	4.2	•	3.4	•	2.3	2.6	1.4	2.1
Working Capital to Net Sales 40	0.0	•	0.0	•	0.1	0.1	0.1	0.1
Inventory to Working Capital 41	0.0	•	0.0	•	•	0.1	•	0.1
Total Receipts to Cash Flow 42	3.2	1.9	2.7	4.2	3.9	5.2	5.4	2.7
Cost of Goods to Cash Flow 43	0.2	0.1	0.1	0.4	0.4	0.1	0.1	0.0
Cash Flow to Total Debt 44	1.6	•	3.0	1.0	1.2	0.9	0.9	1.3

Selected Financial Factors (in Percentages)

Debt Ratio 45	78.8	•	87.1	86.8	67.5	68.6	59.9	75.4
Return on Total Assets 46	45.4	•	100.8	31.9	32.7	16.4	13.4	16.3
Return on Equity Before Income Taxes 47	205.5	•	760.1	231.2	95.9	46.8	30.0	59.0
Return on Equity After Income Taxes 48	199.4	•	753.7	230.0	93.8	45.8	27.6	48.3
Profit Margin (Before Income Tax) 49	11.1	20.0	13.8	8.1	9.9	4.4	4.1	5.5
Profit Margin (After Income Tax) 50	10.8	19.9	13.7	8.1	9.7	4.3	3.8	4.5

Table II

Corporations with Net Income

LEGAL SERVICES

MONEY AMOUNTS AND SIZE OF ASSETS IN THOUSANDS OF DOLLARS

Item Description for Accounting Period 7/09 Through 6/10	Total	Zero Assets	Under 500	500 to 1,000	1,000 to 5,000	5,000 to 10,000	10,000 to 25,000	25,000 to 50,000	50,000 to 100,000	100,000 to 250,000	250,000 to 500,000	500,000 to 2,500,000	2,500,000 and over
Number of Enterprises **1**	84092	12946	65530	3207	2073	178	111	•	15	0	•	0	0
Revenues ($ in Thousands)													
Net Sales **2**	75519322	2342325	35167681	7039612	11691473	4393003	5722213	•	3209127	0	•	0	0
Interest **3**	27293	76	9479	433	3158	3675	1912	•	4011	0	•	0	0
Rents **4**	14237	0	3585	2350	443	3995	4	•	595	0	•	0	0
Royalties **5**	907	0	0	722	0	0	0	•	136	0	•	0	0
Other Portfolio Income **6**	119462	76741	14728	331	695	14470	1393	•	2621	0	•	0	0
Other Receipts **7**	2132297	-6256	1298031	190757	254970	35628	92082	•	10838	0	•	0	0
Total Receipts **8**	77813518	2412886	36493504	7234205	11950739	4450771	5817604	•	3227328	0	•	0	0
Average Total Receipts **9**	925	186	557	2256	5765	25004	52411	•	215155	•	•	•	•
Operating Costs/Operating Income (%)													
Cost of Operations **10**	6.6	4.0	5.2	11.7	10.7	1.2	1.9	•	0.0	•	•	•	•
Salaries and Wages **11**	27.9	13.7	21.1	28.9	30.6	41.0	49.6	•	41.5	•	•	•	•
Taxes Paid **12**	3.1	3.3	3.3	3.1	3.2	3.3	3.3	•	2.7	•	•	•	•
Interest Paid **13**	0.5	0.5	0.3	0.3	0.5	0.4	0.4	•	0.3	•	•	•	•
Depreciation **14**	0.9	2.9	0.6	0.5	0.7	0.9	1.3	•	1.2	•	•	•	•
Amortization and Depletion **15**	0.1	0.0	0.0	0.0	0.0	0.2	0.0	•	0.1	•	•	•	•
Pensions and Other Deferred Comp. **16**	1.8	2.1	1.7	2.1	1.2	2.1	3.1	•	2.0	•	•	•	•
Employee Benefits **17**	1.9	0.5	1.5	2.6	2.0	2.1	2.7	•	1.9	•	•	•	•
Advertising **18**	2.1	5.3	2.1	1.4	3.2	1.8	1.3	•	0.7	•	•	•	•
Other Expenses **19**	26.4	36.9	28.4	20.8	20.5	17.8	21.5	•	39.5	•	•	•	•
Officers' Compensation **20**	17.4	9.5	21.8	19.2	17.1	20.7	10.9	•	2.7	•	•	•	•
Operating Margin **21**	11.3	21.3	13.9	9.2	10.4	8.4	4.0	•	7.2	•	•	•	•
Operating Margin Before Officers' Comp. **22**	28.7	30.8	35.7	28.5	27.5	29.1	14.9	•	9.9	•	•	•	•

Selected Average Balance Sheet ($ in Thousands)

Net Receivables 23	15	0	3	6	67	307	1451	•	7511
Inventories 24	1	0	0	0	2	70	200	•	1471
Net Property, Plant and Equipment 25	36	0	13	65	401	1477	3324	•	13619
Total Assets 26	234	0	77	624	1838	6577	15479	•	69776
Notes and Loans Payable 27	70	0	26	185	539	1765	3742	•	18120
All Other Liabilities 28	98	0	30	336	599	3191	5736	•	28068
Net Worth 29	66	0	21	103	700	1621	6001	•	23588

Selected Financial Ratios (Times to 1)

Current Ratio 30	1.3	•	1.4	1.1	1.4	1.4	1.5	•	1.4
Quick Ratio 31	0.8	•	1.1	0.6	1.1	0.6	0.8	•	0.8
Net Sales to Working Capital 32	26.1	•	36.3	53.4	17.9	19.1	16.7	•	18.6
Coverage Ratio 33	32.7	51.5	62.4	38.0	25.4	24.0	15.6	•	23.6
Total Asset Turnover 34	3.8	•	7.0	3.5	3.1	3.8	3.3	•	3.1
Inventory Turnover 35	114.8	•	9862.4	797.6	381.8	4.2	4.8	•	0.0
Receivables Turnover 36	58.4	•	130.1	227.0	83.6	63.2	38.6	•	43.1
Total Liabilities to Net Worth 37	2.6	•	2.6	5.1	1.6	3.1	1.6	•	2.0
Current Assets to Working Capital 38	4.1	•	3.4	10.2	3.5	3.3	3.0	•	3.3
Current Liabilities to Working Capital 39	3.1	•	2.4	9.2	2.5	2.3	2.0	•	2.3
Working Capital to Net Sales 40	0.0	•	0.0	0.0	0.1	0.1	0.1	•	0.1
Inventory to Working Capital 41	0.0	•	0.0	0.0	•	0.1	0.1	•	0.1
Total Receipts to Cash Flow 42	2.9	1.8	2.5	3.7	3.6	4.5	4.8	•	2.4
Cost of Goods to Cash Flow 43	0.2	0.1	0.1	0.4	0.4	0.1	0.1	•	0.0
Cash Flow to Total Debt 44	1.9	•	3.8	1.1	1.4	1.1	1.1	•	2.0

Selected Financial Factors (in Percentages)

Debt Ratio 45	72.0	•	72.5	83.5	61.9	75.4	61.2	•	66.2
Return on Total Assets 46	56.7	•	125.5	43.3	40.4	37.9	20.3	•	24.6
Return on Equity Before Income Taxes 47	196.3	•	449.0	256.2	102.0	147.3	49.0	•	69.8
Return on Equity After Income Taxes 48	190.8	•	445.4	254.9	99.8	137.7	48.0	•	59.7
Profit Margin (Before Income Tax) 49	14.3	24.3	17.7	12.0	12.7	9.7	5.7	•	7.7
Profit Margin (After Income Tax) 50	13.9	24.2	17.6	11.9	12.4	9.0	5.6	•	6.6

Table I
Corporations with and without Net Income

ACCOUNTING, TAX PREPARATION, BOOKKEEPING, AND PAYROLL SERVICES

MONEY AMOUNTS AND SIZE OF ASSETS IN THOUSANDS OF DOLLARS

Item Description for Accounting Period 7/09 Through 6/10	Total	Zero Assets	Under 500	500 to 1,000	1,000 to 5,000	5,000 to 10,000	10,000 to 25,000	25,000 to 50,000	50,000 to 100,000	100,000 to 250,000	250,000 to 500,000	500,000 to 2,500,000	2,500,000 and over
Number of Enterprises **1**	80702	17821	60427	1171	1146	•	65	19	7	7	•	0	3
Revenues ($ in Thousands)													
Net Sales **2**	98225121	1466172	18550319	4040340	49279751	•	1616684	2387547	441453	570304	•	0	11716176
Interest **3**	742229	99	7526	4082	4333	•	644	1420	6	4740	•	0	713808
Rents **4**	72227	0	0	7601	0	•	0	0	0	0	•	0	64626
Royalties **5**	271951	0	5660	0	0	•	0	0	0	0	•	0	193881
Other Portfolio Income **6**	139682	160	27945	94	10759	•	652	0	0	252	•	0	98933
Other Receipts **7**	1299899	91432	222838	27965	11648	•	32936	37881	-38	4082	•	0	811181
Total Receipts **8**	100751109	1557863	18814288	4080082	49306491	•	1650916	2426848	441421	579378	•	0	13598605
Average Total Receipts **9**	1248	87	311	3484	43025	•	25399	127729	63060	82768	•	•	4532868
Operating Costs/Operating Income (%)													
Cost of Operations **10**	58.5	3.7	8.0	14.3	93.7	•	46.2	66.7	38.2	5.3	•	•	1.5
Salaries and Wages **11**	13.0	17.6	25.6	33.3	2.3	•	21.5	3.3	26.1	39.6	•	•	35.7
Taxes Paid **12**	2.3	3.8	4.0	4.0	0.2	•	4.9	5.6	2.5	3.5	•	•	4.5
Interest Paid **13**	0.7	2.8	0.7	0.6	0.1	•	0.8	0.2	2.1	4.6	•	•	3.3
Depreciation **14**	0.6	1.6	0.6	1.0	0.1	•	1.6	0.1	1.4	1.6	•	•	2.9
Amortization and Depletion **15**	0.5	1.2	0.4	0.1	0.1	•	0.3	0.0	1.3	2.3	•	•	2.4
Pensions and Other Deferred Comp. **16**	0.8	0.9	2.0	1.8	0.1	•	0.6	0.1	0.1	0.1	•	•	2.2
Employee Benefits **17**	2.0	2.5	1.8	2.2	0.2	•	1.8	1.2	2.2	2.4	•	•	8.2
Advertising **18**	0.4	1.8	0.8	0.4	0.1	•	0.2	0.0	0.6	1.0	•	•	1.7
Other Expenses **19**	13.3	39.8	25.1	20.2	2.9	•	13.9	23.9	21.4	34.5	•	•	35.1
Officers' Compensation **20**	5.9	14.4	22.9	18.7	0.7	•	6.9	0.3	0.4	2.8	•	•	0.3
Operating Margin **21**	1.9	9.9	8.2	3.3	•	•	1.2	•	3.8	2.4	•	•	2.2
Operating Margin Before Officers' Comp. **22**	7.8	24.3	31.1	22.0	0.4	•	8.1	•	4.2	5.2	•	•	2.5

Selected Average Balance Sheet ($ in Thousands)

Net Receivables 23	72	0	5	71	215	•	2624	6117	12949	11549	•	1330891
Inventories 24	1	0	0	8	1	•	174	65	471	294	•	5969
Net Property, Plant and Equipment 25	30	0	12	217	123	•	2309	881	2629	6179	•	328359
Total Assets 26	964	0	55	683	1977	•	15531	33069	58431	157304	•	2026561
Notes and Loans Payable 27	123	0	30	302	551	•	3532	3017	17130	41578	•	1956528
All Other Liabilities 28	640	0	11	225	1223	•	9182	25560	22018	84810	•	15627564
Net Worth 29	200	0	15	156	203	•	2817	4492	19284	30916	•	4442468

Selected Financial Ratios (Times to 1)

Current Ratio 30	0.8	•	1.6	1.0	0.9	•	1.2	1.1	1.5	1.1	•	0.7
Quick Ratio 31	0.5	•	1.4	0.7	0.8	•	0.8	0.6	1.4	0.3	•	0.4
Net Sales to Working Capital 32	•	•	32.3	962.0	•	•	17.8	80.7	6.3	15.0	•	•
Coverage Ratio 33	7.4	6.7	15.2	8.0	•	•	5.0	2.7	2.8	1.9	•	6.7
Total Asset Turnover 34	1.3	•	5.5	5.1	21.7	•	1.6	3.8	1.1	0.5	•	0.2
Inventory Turnover 35	1357.3	•	2050.7	62.3	39032.6	•	65.8	1283.8	51.1	14.7	•	9.6
Receivables Turnover 36	16.4	•	48.1	68.9	175.9	•	7.9	25.6	7.6	5.2	•	5.9
Total Liabilities to Net Worth 37	3.8	•	2.8	3.4	8.7	•	4.5	6.4	2.0	4.1	•	4.0
Current Assets to Working Capital 38	•	•	2.8	81.1	•	•	6.6	17.9	2.9	13.1	•	•
Current Liabilities to Working Capital 39	•	•	1.8	80.1	•	•	5.6	16.9	1.9	12.1	•	•
Working Capital to Net Sales 40	•	•	0.0	0.0	•	•	0.1	0.0	0.2	0.1	•	•
Inventory to Working Capital 41	•	•	0.0	2.3	•	•	0.2	0.0	0.1	0.1	•	•
Total Receipts to Cash Flow 42	6.7	2.3	3.5	5.3	45.1	•	7.6	4.2	4.4	2.9	•	2.2
Cost of Goods to Cash Flow 43	3.9	0.1	0.3	0.8	42.2	•	3.5	2.8	1.7	0.2	•	0.0
Cash Flow to Total Debt 44	0.2	•	2.1	1.2	0.5	•	0.3	1.0	0.4	0.2	•	0.1

Selected Financial Factors (in Percentages)

Debt Ratio 45	79.2	•	73.6	77.1	89.7	•	81.9	86.4	67.0	80.3	•	79.8
Return on Total Assets 46	6.6	•	56.9	24.8	•	•	6.6	1.9	6.3	4.4	•	3.9
Return on Equity Before Income Taxes 47	27.5	•	201.4	94.6	•	•	29.2	8.9	12.3	10.6	•	16.3
Return on Equity After Income Taxes 48	22.3	•	199.8	93.3	•	•	24.5	5.6	11.4	5.4	•	10.6
Profit Margin (Before Income Tax) 49	4.5	16.2	9.6	4.3	•	•	3.3	0.3	3.8	4.0	•	18.6
Profit Margin (After Income Tax) 50	3.7	15.9	9.5	4.2	•	•	2.8	0.2	3.5	3.8	•	12.0

ACCOUNTING, TAX PREPARATION, BOOKKEEPING, AND PAYROLL SERVICES

Table II

Corporations with Net Income

MONEY AMOUNTS AND SIZE OF ASSETS IN THOUSANDS OF DOLLARS

Item Description for Accounting Period 7/09 Through 6/10		Total	Zero Assets	Under 500	500 to 1,000	1,000 to 5,000	5,000 to 10,000	10,000 to 25,000	25,000 to 50,000	50,000 to 100,000	100,000 to 250,000	250,000 to 500,000	500,000 to 2,500,000	2,500,000 and over
Number of Enterprises	1	58721	12720	44421	788	697	31	36	13	•	•	0	•	0
Revenues ($ in Thousands)														
Net Sales	2	44128040	1151456	13460118	2419847	3941070	334189	1444328	2363666	•	•	0	•	0
Interest	3	732138	41	5594	2463	1868	970	569	1412	•	•	0	•	0
Rents	4	72227	0	0	7601	0	0	0	0	•	•	0	•	0
Royalties	5	271951	0	5660	0	0	0	0	0	•	•	0	•	0
Other Portfolio Income	6	127564	67	15935	94	10751	886	652	0	•	•	0	•	0
Other Receipts	7	1187718	39607	192386	27642	10661	2711	31479	37411	•	•	0	•	0
Total Receipts	8	46519638	1191171	13679693	2457647	3964350	338756	1477028	2402489	•	•	0	•	0
Average Total Receipts	9	792	94	308	3119	5688	10928	41029	184807	•	•	•	•	•
Operating Costs/Operating Income (%)														
Cost of Operations	10	24.9	0.5	1.5	7.1	39.4	7.2	49.6	67.1	•	•	•	•	•
Salaries and Wages	11	23.7	18.9	27.5	33.3	25.8	35.3	19.6	2.7	•	•	•	•	•
Taxes Paid	12	4.4	3.2	4.2	4.4	2.4	3.3	4.9	5.6	•	•	•	•	•
Interest Paid	13	0.9	1.4	0.8	0.6	0.8	0.2	0.8	0.2	•	•	•	•	•
Depreciation	14	1.2	1.2	0.7	1.0	0.4	1.2	1.6	0.1	•	•	•	•	•
Amortization and Depletion	15	0.9	1.2	0.4	0.0	0.7	0.2	0.2	0.0	•	•	•	•	•
Pensions and Other Deferred Comp.	16	1.4	0.8	1.8	2.7	0.7	1.8	0.2	0.0	•	•	•	•	•
Employee Benefits	17	4.0	1.8	1.9	2.5	2.1	1.7	0.4	0.1	•	•	•	•	•
Advertising	18	0.8	1.5	0.8	0.2	0.5	0.5	0.2	1.1	•	•	•	•	•
Other Expenses	19	22.2	35.4	25.2	22.1	14.3	15.1	11.9	23.2	•	•	•	•	•
Officers' Compensation	20	9.4	12.4	22.6	19.8	8.2	17.2	5.4	0.3	•	•	•	•	•
Operating Margin	21	6.1	21.7	12.8	6.3	4.6	16.4	3.9	•	•	•	•	•	•
Operating Margin Before Officers' Comp.	22	15.5	34.0	35.4	26.1	12.8	33.6	9.3	•	•	•	•	•	•

Selected Average Balance Sheet ($ in Thousands)

Net Receivables 23	56	0	7	92	179	1847	4482	8657
Inventories 24	0	0	0	0	2	0	0	95
Net Property, Plant and Equipment 25	36	0	14	226	167	472	2789	883
Total Assets 26	1103		64	653	2300	6558	16892	31965
Notes and Loans Payable 27	94	0	29	295	766	390	5623	4372
All Other Liabilities 28	755	0	9	147	975	1240	8265	21815
Net Worth 29	254	0	26	211	559	4929	3004	5778

Selected Financial Ratios (Times to 1)

Current Ratio 30	0.8	•	1.9	1.0	1.1	4.0	1.2	1.1
Quick Ratio 31	0.4	•	1.7	0.7	0.8	3.4	1.0	0.8
Net Sales to Working Capital 32	•	•	20.7	•	44.3	3.3	19.6	59.4
Coverage Ratio 33	13.2	18.7	19.0	14.4	7.6	110.0	8.6	7.6
Total Asset Turnover 34	0.7	•	4.7	4.7	2.5	1.6	2.4	5.7
Inventory Turnover 35	660.8	•	523.3	1232.8	1342.2	•	•	1285.1
Receivables Turnover 36	9.7	•	37.0	48.1	19.3	•	7.4	•
Total Liabilities to Net Worth 37	3.3	•	1.5	2.1	3.1	0.3	4.6	4.5
Current Assets to Working Capital 38	•	•	2.1	•	10.0	1.3	5.6	8.5
Current Liabilities to Working Capital 39	•	•	1.1	•	9.0	0.3	4.6	7.5
Working Capital to Net Sales 40	•	•	0.0	•	0.0	0.3	0.1	0.0
Inventory to Working Capital 41	•	•	0.0	•	0.0	•	•	0.0
Total Receipts to Cash Flow 42	3.5	2.0	3.0	4.1	6.5	3.5	7.1	4.2
Cost of Goods to Cash Flow 43	0.9	0.0	0.0	0.3	2.5	0.2	3.5	2.8
Cash Flow to Total Debt 44	0.3	•	2.6	1.7	0.5	1.9	0.4	1.7

Selected Financial Factors (in Percentages)

Debt Ratio 45	77.0	•	59.4	67.7	75.7	24.8	82.2	81.9
Return on Total Assets 46	8.5	•	71.6	39.8	14.8	29.4	16.4	7.9
Return on Equity Before Income Taxes 47	34.3	•	167.0	114.6	52.8	38.7	81.7	38.0
Return on Equity After Income Taxes 48	28.7	•	165.7	113.1	52.1	38.1	73.8	34.2
Profit Margin (Before Income Tax) 49	11.6	25.1	14.4	7.9	5.2	17.7	6.1	1.2
Profit Margin (After Income Tax) 50	9.7	24.8	14.3	7.8	5.2	17.4	5.5	1.1

PROFESSIONAL, SCIENTIFIC, AND TECHNICAL SERVICES
541315

Table I
Corporations with and without Net Income

ARCHITECTURAL, ENGINEERING, AND RELATED SERVICES

MONEY AMOUNTS AND SIZE OF ASSETS IN THOUSANDS OF DOLLARS

Item Description for Accounting Period 7/09 Through 6/10	Total	Zero Assets	Under 500	500 to 1,000	1,000 to 5,000	5,000 to 10,000	10,000 to 25,000	25,000 to 50,000	50,000 to 100,000	100,000 to 250,000	250,000 to 500,000	500,000 to 2,500,000	2,500,000 and over
Number of Enterprises **1**	103611	19401	74923	3445	4334	766	430	130	64	56	23	29	9
Revenues ($ in Thousands)													
Net Sales **2**	211916650	5223793	40425825	8415860	22833234	12742779	13364877	7532853	7346117	11661382	9321429	20338964	52709536
Interest **3**	390557	3765	10196	4339	13051	7887	13786	8848	12900	15472	43956	108666	147692
Rents **4**	202873	6684	7014	4737	14576	5930	1313	9054	5127	10629	13121	7797	116891
Royalties **5**	49500	8856	0	0	2062	11	1322	2672	3526	5125	2689	5250	17986
Other Portfolio Income **6**	820437	67838	59027	2152	29681	18542	15330	130698	8527	101691	42486	37325	307141
Other Receipts **7**	1803993	74355	110621	124101	73468	151763	140300	81146	37001	143564	194883	195996	476794
Total Receipts **8**	215184010	5385291	40612683	8551189	22966072	12926912	13536928	7765271	7413198	11937863	9618564	20693998	53776040
Average Total Receipts **9**	2077	278	542	2482	5299	16876	31481	59733	115831	213176	418198	713586	5975116
Operating Costs/Operating Income (%)													
Cost of Operations **10**	44.3	43.5	16.1	34.5	34.4	40.1	32.4	38.1	52.4	43.4	55.1	48.2	72.5
Salaries and Wages **11**	18.6	14.4	24.5	19.0	20.4	23.4	25.9	24.7	17.2	21.1	15.9	16.2	10.8
Taxes Paid **12**	2.9	3.8	4.1	3.1	3.5	3.2	3.4	3.5	2.8	2.7	2.2	2.0	1.7
Interest Paid **13**	0.8	1.1	0.6	0.5	0.6	0.5	0.5	0.7	0.8	1.0	1.2	2.9	0.6
Depreciation **14**	1.7	1.7	1.0	1.4	1.5	1.7	2.0	2.2	1.4	2.2	2.9	3.9	1.1
Amortization and Depletion **15**	0.5	0.4	0.0	0.1	0.1	0.1	0.3	0.4	0.5	0.8	0.8	1.2	0.8
Pensions and Other Deferred Comp. **16**	1.0	0.9	1.1	1.3	1.1	1.2	1.3	1.5	0.9	1.1	1.1	0.5	0.8
Employee Benefits **17**	2.5	1.9	2.3	2.7	1.9	2.8	2.6	3.3	2.7	3.4	2.8	2.3	2.6
Advertising **18**	0.3	0.3	0.5	0.3	0.4	0.3	0.3	0.3	0.1	0.2	0.2	0.3	0.0
Other Expenses **19**	18.9	23.6	26.6	22.1	21.7	17.9	25.0	20.3	15.3	20.0	16.7	29.5	6.0
Officers' Compensation **20**	6.3	5.4	18.9	10.4	7.3	4.9	5.1	3.6	2.8	2.2	1.5	1.1	0.8
Operating Margin **21**	2.2	3.0	4.3	4.6	6.9	4.0	1.3	1.3	3.3	2.1	•	•	2.3
Operating Margin Before Officers' Comp. **22**	8.5	8.4	23.2	15.0	14.3	8.9	6.4	4.9	6.0	4.2	1.2	•	3.1

Selected Average Balance Sheet ($ in Thousands)

Net Receivables 23	278	0	9	202	691	2315	5412	11102	20938	39746	85773	189168	880649
Inventories 24	35	0	0	35	86	462	548	1280	2146	5978	12153	14653	130755
Net Property, Plant and Equipment 25	131	0	18	106	351	1326	2558	5992	5843	20740	33785	95372	265390
Total Assets 26	1133	0	64	677	2144	6944	15613	35820	68769	155360	345455	761025	4564612
Notes and Loans Payable 27	267	0	55	274	570	1552	3628	7222	13274	33992	77963	211209	643081
All Other Liabilities 28	407	0	16	197	601	2374	4876	15756	29395	55939	131178	242493	1849058
Net Worth 29	458	-7	206	973	3018	7109	12843	26101	65429	136314	307323		2072473

Selected Financial Ratios (Times to 1)

Current Ratio 30	1.5	•	1.4	1.8	2.0	2.1	1.8	1.5	1.6	1.5	1.7	1.7	1.2
Quick Ratio 31	1.1	•	1.2	1.5	1.6	1.6	1.4	1.2	1.2	1.1	1.2	1.4	0.7
Net Sales to Working Capital 32	10.6	•	57.8	12.7	7.0	6.3	6.5	7.7	7.3	8.1	5.7	5.4	20.7
Coverage Ratio 33	5.5	6.5	9.1	14.6	14.5	12.1	6.3	7.7	6.6	5.9	3.5	•	9.2
Total Asset Turnover 34	1.8	•	8.4	3.6	2.5	2.4	2.0	1.6	1.7	1.3	1.2	0.9	1.3
Inventory Turnover 35	25.9	•	349.8	23.7	21.0	14.4	18.4	17.3	28.0	15.1	18.4	23.1	32.5
Receivables Turnover 36	7.1	•	60.2	10.8	7.2	8.3	5.9	4.8	4.8	4.7	3.9	3.6	6.7
Total Liabilities to Net Worth 37	1.5	•	•	2.3	1.2	1.3	1.2	1.8	1.6	1.4	1.5	1.5	1.2
Current Assets to Working Capital 38	3.0	•	3.6	2.2	2.0	1.9	2.2	3.0	2.8	3.1	2.5	2.4	7.3
Current Liabilities to Working Capital 39	2.0	•	2.6	1.2	1.0	0.9	1.2	2.0	1.8	2.1	1.5	1.4	6.3
Working Capital to Net Sales 40	0.1	•	0.0	0.1	0.1	0.2	0.2	0.1	0.1	0.1	0.2	0.2	0.0
Inventory to Working Capital 41	0.2	•	0.0	0.1	0.1	0.2	0.1	0.1	0.1	0.2	0.1	0.1	0.6
Total Receipts to Cash Flow 42	5.3	4.0	3.9	4.1	4.0	5.1	4.3	4.8	6.4	5.0	6.3	5.0	13.5
Cost of Goods to Cash Flow 43	2.4	1.7	0.6	1.4	1.4	2.0	1.4	1.8	3.3	2.2	3.4	2.4	9.8
Cash Flow to Total Debt 44	0.6	•	2.0	1.3	1.1	0.8	0.9	0.5	0.4	0.5	0.3	0.3	0.2

Selected Financial Factors (in Percentages)

Debt Ratio 45	59.5	•	110.5	69.6	54.6	56.5	54.5	64.1	62.0	57.9	60.5	59.6	54.6
Return on Total Assets 46	8.5	•	45.0	24.1	19.9	14.2	6.1	8.2	8.5	7.5	5.1	•	6.5
Return on Equity Before Income Taxes 47	17.2	•	•	73.9	40.7	30.0	11.2	19.9	19.0	14.7	9.2	•	12.8
Return on Equity After Income Taxes 48	13.5	•	•	72.0	38.1	27.1	8.0	15.1	14.4	9.6	4.7	•	8.9
Profit Margin (Before Income Tax) 49	3.9	6.1	4.8	6.2	7.5	5.4	2.6	4.4	4.3	4.6	3.1	•	4.5
Profit Margin (After Income Tax) 50	3.0	5.7	4.7	6.1	7.0	4.9	1.8	3.3	3.3	3.0	1.6	•	3.2

Table II
Corporations with Net Income

ARCHITECTURAL, ENGINEERING, AND RELATED SERVICES

MONEY AMOUNTS AND SIZE OF ASSETS IN THOUSANDS OF DOLLARS

Item Description for Accounting Period 7/09 Through 6/10	Total	Zero Assets	Under 500	500 to 1,000	1,000 to 5,000	5,000 to 10,000	10,000 to 25,000	25,000 to 50,000	50,000 to 100,000	100,000 to 250,000	250,000 to 500,000	500,000 to 2,500,000	2,500,000 and over
Number of Enterprises 1	66916	11301	48686	2483	3332	598	304	82	46	42	17	16	9
Revenues ($ in Thousands)													
Net Sales 2	180109441	3928904	31778747	5980204	19195839	10163689	10553385	5470106	6199738	9795538	8116727	16217028	52709536
Interest 3	275276	422	4096	2818	7611	4648	8449	5335	9904	12651	39956	31695	147692
Rents 4	161883	100	131	4737	1487	714	176	7420	5034	10099	13121	1973	116891
Royalties 5	28493	136	0	0	0	11	45	2672	0	5125	1335	1183	17986
Other Portfolio Income 6	720608	22638	48370	789	24548	18457	5241	129628	6582	100884	35216	21113	307141
Other Receipts 7	1675870	32714	114304	118861	143576	129018	126674	59385	34903	122931	222929	93780	476794
Total Receipts 8	182971571	3984914	31945648	6107409	19373061	10316537	10693970	5674546	6256161	10047228	8429284	16366772	53776040
Average Total Receipts 9	2734	353	656	2460	5814	17252	35178	69202	136004	239220	495840	1022923	5975116
Operating Costs/Operating Income (%)													
Cost of Operations 10	45.6	34.9	14.5	23.8	35.0	41.5	31.6	41.2	54.0	38.5	57.1	50.1	72.5
Salaries and Wages 11	17.7	16.6	24.4	22.2	19.3	20.9	25.0	20.3	16.2	23.3	13.0	15.8	10.8
Taxes Paid 12	2.7	4.5	3.9	3.0	3.2	3.0	3.3	3.6	2.7	2.8	2.0	1.9	1.7
Interest Paid 13	0.6	0.6	0.5	0.3	0.4	0.5	0.3	0.5	0.5	0.6	0.9	1.5	0.6
Depreciation 14	1.4	1.6	0.8	1.3	1.4	1.5	1.7	2.0	1.2	2.0	2.7	1.8	1.1
Amortization and Depletion 15	0.4	0.0	0.0	0.2	0.0	0.0	0.1	0.1	0.2	0.4	0.6	0.6	0.8
Pensions and Other Deferred Comp. 16	1.0	0.4	1.1	1.5	1.1	1.3	1.4	1.6	1.0	1.2	0.9	0.5	0.8
Employee Benefits 17	2.3	1.3	2.1	2.5	1.8	2.4	2.4	3.4	2.5	3.3	2.5	1.8	2.6
Advertising 18	0.2	0.3	0.5	0.3	0.4	0.3	0.3	0.3	0.1	0.2	0.1	0.2	0.0
Other Expenses 19	16.5	24.7	24.8	23.8	19.1	16.7	24.0	18.2	13.4	21.2	15.3	20.2	6.0
Officers' Compensation 20	6.0	4.7	19.7	12.6	7.1	4.6	5.1	3.7	2.5	2.3	1.5	1.1	0.8
Operating Margin 21	5.5	10.5	7.8	8.4	11.1	7.2	4.8	5.1	5.8	4.2	3.3	4.5	2.3
Operating Margin Before Officers' Comp. 22	11.6	15.1	27.5	21.0	18.2	11.9	9.9	8.8	8.3	6.5	4.8	5.5	3.1

Selected Average Balance Sheet ($ in Thousands)

Net Receivables 23	362	7	189	744	2440	5988	12592	23608	43879	100984	253871	880649
Inventories 24	43	0	32	83	401	534	1137	1995	5920	13213	18976	130755
Net Property, Plant and Equipment 25	141	19	115	375	1213	2229	6216	6355	19951	34525	61479	265390
Total Assets 26	1408	69	680	2129	7028	15662	35529	70660	157923	352143	828770	4564612
Notes and Loans Payable 27	261	39	222	393	1347	2689	5694	11708	22212	70313	196026	643081
All Other Liabilities 28	522	17	154	565	2431	4881	13448	32765	61294	132341	300699	1849058
Net Worth 29	626	13	304	1171	3250	8092	16387	26187	74416	149488	332044	2072473

Selected Financial Ratios (Times to 1)

Current Ratio 30	1.5	•	1.6	2.4	2.5	2.3	2.2	1.8	1.6	1.5	1.8	1.7	1.2
Quick Ratio 31	1.1	•	1.4	2.2	2.0	1.7	1.7	1.5	1.2	1.2	1.3	1.4	0.7
Net Sales to Working Capital 32	10.3	•	47.8	10.0	6.1	5.9	5.8	6.3	7.4	8.0	6.1	6.0	20.7
Coverage Ratio 33	13.1	19.3	19.1	32.6	29.2	18.9	21.5	19.9	15.2	13.6	8.7	4.6	9.2
Total Asset Turnover 34	1.9	•	9.5	3.5	2.7	2.4	2.2	1.9	1.5	1.4	1.2	1.3	
Inventory Turnover 35	28.3	•	851.9	17.8	24.3	17.6	20.6	24.2	36.5	15.2	20.6	26.8	32.5
Receivables Turnover 36	7.1	•	83.0	12.3	7.8	8.3	5.9	4.8	5.0	4.6	4.1	3.5	6.7
Total Liabilities to Net Worth 37	1.3	•	4.4	1.2	0.8	1.2	0.9	1.7	1.7	1.1	1.4	1.5	1.2
Current Assets to Working Capital 38	2.9	•	2.7	1.7	1.7	1.8	1.9	2.3	2.7	3.0	2.3	2.5	7.3
Current Liabilities to Working Capital 39	1.9	•	1.7	0.7	0.7	0.8	0.9	1.3	1.7	2.0	1.3	1.5	6.3
Working Capital to Net Sales 40	0.1	•	0.0	0.1	0.2	0.2	0.2	0.1	0.1	0.1	0.2	0.2	0.0
Inventory to Working Capital 41	0.2	•	0.0	0.0	0.1	0.2	0.2	0.1	0.1	0.2	0.1	0.1	0.6
Total Receipts to Cash Flow 42	5.0	3.1	3.5	3.3	3.6	4.5	3.8	4.4	6.0	4.2	5.2	4.5	13.5
Cost of Goods to Cash Flow 43	2.3	1.1	0.5	0.8	1.3	1.9	1.2	1.8	3.3	1.6	3.0	2.3	9.8
Cash Flow to Total Debt 44	0.7	•	3.3	2.0	1.7	1.0	1.2	0.8	0.5	0.7	0.5	0.5	0.2

Selected Financial Factors (in Percentages)

Debt Ratio 45	55.6	•	81.6	55.4	45.0	53.8	48.3	53.9	62.9	52.9	57.5	59.9	54.6
Return on Total Assets 46	15.0	•	82.7	38.6	33.7	22.3	14.1	17.5	13.7	11.2	11.1	8.5	6.5
Return on Equity Before Income Taxes 47	31.1	•	425.4	83.8	59.1	45.7	26.0	36.0	34.6	21.9	23.2	16.5	12.8
Return on Equity After Income Taxes 48	26.9	•	420.1	82.0	56.3	42.2	22.0	30.0	28.2	15.9	17.7	13.2	8.9
Profit Margin (Before Income Tax) 49	7.2	11.9	8.3	10.6	12.0	8.7	6.1	8.8	6.7	7.0	7.3	5.4	4.5
Profit Margin (After Income Tax) 50	6.3	11.4	8.2	10.3	11.4	8.1	5.1	7.4	5.5	5.1	5.5	4.3	3.2

Table I

Corporations with and without Net Income

SPECIALIZED DESIGN SERVICES

MONEY AMOUNTS AND SIZE OF ASSETS IN THOUSANDS OF DOLLARS

Item Description for Accounting Period 7/09 Through 6/10	Total	Zero Assets	Under 500	500 to 1,000	1,000 to 5,000	5,000 to 10,000	10,000 to 25,000	25,000 to 50,000	50,000 to 100,000	100,000 to 250,000	250,000 to 500,000	500,000 to 2,500,000	2,500,000 and over
Number of Enterprises **1**	38315	8017	29368	476	327	87	24	12	0	3	0	0	0
Revenues ($ in Thousands)													
Net Sales **2**	16404799	658237	10571974	786337	1094710	912918	367748	406415	0	1606461	0	0	0
Interest **3**	8143	7	3010	301	3217	296	230	461	0	621	0	0	0
Rents **4**	744	0	5	19	721	0	0	0	0	0	0	0	0
Royalties **5**	19582	0	0	0	0	0	0	0	0	19582	0	0	0
Other Portfolio Income **6**	10215	6089	815	0	3010	0	205	96	0	0	0	0	0
Other Receipts **7**	189726	18065	142737	1786	1775	8966	7649	5078	0	3668	0	0	0
Total Receipts **8**	16633209	682398	10718541	788443	1103433	922180	375832	412050	0	1630332	0	0	0
Average Total Receipts **9**	434	85	365	1656	3374	10600	15660	34338	•	543444	•	•	•
Operating Costs/Operating Income (%)													
Cost of Operations **10**	44.7	48.4	46.5	44.1	55.5	60.3	40.0	53.0	•	14.4	•	•	•
Salaries and Wages **11**	13.3	5.5	9.8	19.4	16.0	11.9	14.7	30.4	•	31.2	•	•	•
Taxes Paid **12**	2.2	2.2	2.1	2.4	1.8	2.7	2.0	2.3	•	3.3	•	•	•
Interest Paid **13**	0.7	0.7	0.5	1.0	0.3	0.2	0.1	0.6	•	2.6	•	•	•
Depreciation **14**	1.1	0.8	0.7	0.5	1.1	1.6	0.8	4.2	•	3.3	•	•	•
Amortization and Depletion **15**	0.2	•	0.1	0.2	0.3	0.2	0.0	0.7	•	0.6	•	•	•
Pensions and Other Deferred Comp. **16**	0.6	0.8	0.6	1.4	0.9	0.3	0.4	0.1	•	0.2	•	•	•
Employee Benefits **17**	1.3	0.5	0.9	0.1	1.3	2.2	1.3	3.9	•	3.8	•	•	•
Advertising **18**	0.8	0.8	0.6	2.6	1.9	0.6	0.8	0.1	•	0.6	•	•	•
Other Expenses **19**	24.7	35.7	24.0	24.2	21.6	15.1	15.8	5.6	•	39.1	•	•	•
Officers' Compensation **20**	8.1	7.9	10.2	4.9	6.1	3.5	4.4	3.1	•	1.2	•	•	•
Operating Margin **21**	2.4	•	4.0	•	•	1.3	19.7	•	•	•	•	•	•
Operating Margin Before Officers' Comp. **22**	10.4	4.5	14.3	4.0	•	4.8	24.2	•	•	0.9	•	•	•

Selected Average Balance Sheet ($ in Thousands)

Net Receivables 23	21	0	11	166	288	661	2656	6842	•	41785
Inventories 24	19	0	4	219	805	443	4508	1387	•	26837
Net Property, Plant and Equipment 25	23	0	12	91	192	394	1082	6007	•	104522
Total Assets 26	145	0	70	698	2241	8513	17204	35559	•	286673
Notes and Loans Payable 27	55	0	40	878	700	1280	381	3532	•	40383
All Other Liabilities 28	63	0	23	291	1610	5601	7679	5963	•	101589
Net Worth 29	28	0	7	-471	-68	1632	9144	26065	•	144701

Selected Financial Ratios (Times to 1)

Current Ratio 30	1.5	•	1.4	2.1	1.5	1.5	1.6	2.8	•	1.2
Quick Ratio 31	1.0	•	1.2	0.9	0.8	0.8	0.8	2.4	•	0.5
Net Sales to Working Capital 32	15.4	•	30.5	5.5	7.7	8.6	3.8	2.3	•	29.9
Coverage Ratio 33	6.3	1.4	11.9	0.4	•	11.5	256.6	•	•	1.4
Total Asset Turnover 34	3.0	•	5.1	2.4	1.5	1.2	0.9	1.0	•	1.9
Inventory Turnover 35	10.0	•	38.1	3.3	2.3	14.3	1.4	12.9	•	2.9
Receivables Turnover 36	18.5	•	42.2	4.9	8.8	16.1	4.9	•	•	•
Total Liabilities to Net Worth 37	4.2	•	8.9	•	•	4.2	0.9	0.4	•	1.0
Current Assets to Working Capital 38	2.9	•	3.5	1.9	3.0	2.9	2.8	1.5	•	6.2
Current Liabilities to Working Capital 39	1.9	•	2.5	0.9	2.0	1.9	1.8	0.5	•	5.2
Working Capital to Net Sales 40	0.1	•	0.0	0.2	0.1	0.1	0.3	0.4	•	0.0
Inventory to Working Capital 41	0.6	•	0.3	1.0	0.5	0.5	1.1	0.1	•	1.5
Total Receipts to Cash Flow 42	4.4	3.2	4.2	7.1	9.8	8.6	2.9	•	•	2.9
Cost of Goods to Cash Flow 43	2.0	1.5	1.9	3.1	5.4	5.2	1.2	•	•	0.4
Cash Flow to Total Debt 44	0.8	•	1.4	0.2	0.1	0.2	0.7	•	•	1.3

Selected Financial Factors (in Percentages)

Debt Ratio 45	80.8	•	89.9	167.5	103.1	80.8	46.8	26.7	•	49.5
Return on Total Assets 46	13.1	•	30.5	1.0	•	3.1	19.6	•	•	7.1
Return on Equity Before Income Taxes 47	57.3	•	275.6	2.2	302.5	14.7	36.7	•	•	4.3
Return on Equity After Income Taxes 48	56.4	•	274.9	2.2	309.5	12.6	36.0	•	•	4.2
Profit Margin (Before Income Tax) 49	3.7	0.3	5.4	•	•	2.3	21.9	•	•	1.1
Profit Margin (After Income Tax) 50	3.7	0.0	5.4	•	•	2.0	21.5	•	•	1.1

Table II
Corporations with Net Income

SPECIALIZED DESIGN SERVICES

MONEY AMOUNTS AND SIZE OF ASSETS IN THOUSANDS OF DOLLARS

Item Description for Accounting Period 7/09 Through 6/10	Total	Zero Assets	Under 500	500 to 1,000	1,000 to 5,000	5,000 to 10,000	10,000 to 25,000	25,000 to 50,000	50,000 to 100,000	100,000 to 250,000	250,000 to 500,000	500,000 to 2,500,000	2,500,000 and over
1 Number of Enterprises	19946	3627	15775	329	167	•	17	•	0	•	•	0	0
Revenues ($ in Thousands)													
2 Net Sales	11653987	266400	7418994	511260	854258	•	304915	•	•	•	•	0	0
3 Interest	3265	0	1989	291	667	•	0	•	0	•	•	0	0
4 Rents	726	0	5	0	721	•	0	•	0	•	•	0	0
5 Royalties	19582	0	0	0	0	•	0	•	0	•	•	0	0
6 Other Portfolio Income	7680	6089	742	0	638	•	205	•	0	•	•	0	0
7 Other Receipts	78835	18065	41876	25	1188	•	7356	•	0	•	•	0	0
8 Total Receipts	11764075	290554	7463606	511576	857472	•	312476	•	0	•	•	0	0
9 Average Total Receipts	590	80	473	1555	5135	•	18381	•	•	•	•	•	•
Operating Costs/Operating Income (%)													
10 Cost of Operations	42.6	41.3	46.2	44.2	65.7	•	38.1	•	•	•	•	•	•
11 Salaries and Wages	12.4	6.3	7.7	14.4	11.9	•	15.5	•	•	•	•	•	•
12 Taxes Paid	2.0	1.5	1.7	2.1	1.2	•	1.8	•	•	•	•	•	•
13 Interest Paid	0.7	0.3	0.5	1.1	0.2	•	0.1	•	•	•	•	•	•
14 Depreciation	1.0	0.6	0.5	0.5	0.7	•	0.6	•	•	•	•	•	•
15 Amortization and Depletion	0.1	•	0.0	0.4	0.3	•	0.0	•	•	•	•	•	•
16 Pensions and Other Deferred Comp.	0.7	1.9	0.8	2.1	0.5	•	0.4	•	•	•	•	•	•
17 Employee Benefits	1.3	1.2	0.7	0.1	0.8	•	1.5	•	•	•	•	•	•
18 Advertising	0.7	0.4	0.6	0.0	2.2	•	1.0	•	•	•	•	•	•
19 Other Expenses	22.2	27.7	21.3	17.1	12.0	•	12.3	•	•	•	•	•	•
20 Officers' Compensation	7.1	10.0	9.2	6.6	3.4	•	2.5	•	•	•	•	•	•
21 Operating Margin	9.1	8.7	10.9	11.3	1.1	•	26.1	•	•	•	•	•	•
22 Operating Margin Before Officers' Comp.	16.2	18.7	20.1	17.9	4.5	•	28.6	•	•	•	•	•	•

Selected Average Balance Sheet ($ in Thousands)

Net Receivables 23	28	0	13	192	477	•	2003
Inventories 24	22	0	4	148	1215	•	3303
Net Property, Plant and Equipment 25	28	0	13	117	76	•	1416
Total Assets 26	164	0	86	659	2479	•	17085
Notes and Loans Payable 27	49	0	35	221	1139	•	538
All Other Liabilities 28	51	0	25	101	1222	•	9086
Net Worth 29	63	0	27	338	118	•	7461

Selected Financial Ratios (Times to 1)

Current Ratio 30	1.7	•	1.7	5.6	1.3	•	1.3
Quick Ratio 31	1.2	•	1.5	3.5	0.8	•	0.6
Net Sales to Working Capital 32	14.7	65.5	25.1	3.9	13.2	•	6.8
Coverage Ratio 33	14.6		26.4	11.0	9.2	•	400.5
Total Asset Turnover 34	3.6	•	5.5	2.4	2.1	•	1.0
Inventory Turnover 35	11.2	•	58.7	4.6	2.8	•	2.1
Receivables Turnover 36	20.8	•	48.1	5.4	11.1	•	9.3
Total Liabilities to Net Worth 37	1.6	•	2.2	0.9	20.0	•	1.3
Current Assets to Working Capital 38	2.4	•	2.5	1.2	4.1	•	4.5
Current Liabilities to Working Capital 39	1.4	•	1.5	0.2	3.1	•	3.5
Working Capital to Net Sales 40	0.1	•	0.0	0.3	0.1	•	0.1
Inventory to Working Capital 41	0.5	•	0.2	0.3	1.1	•	2.4
Total Receipts to Cash Flow 42	3.7	2.5	3.6	3.9	10.7	•	2.6
Cost of Goods to Cash Flow 43	1.6	1.0	1.7	1.7	7.0	•	1.0
Cash Flow to Total Debt 44	1.6	•	2.2	1.2	0.2	•	0.7

Selected Financial Factors (in Percentages)

Debt Ratio 45	61.2	•	68.9	48.7	95.2	•	56.3
Return on Total Assets 46	38.3	•	65.6	29.5	3.5	•	30.1
Return on Equity Before Income Taxes 47	92.0	•	203.0	52.3	64.9	•	68.7
Return on Equity After Income Taxes 48	91.2	•	202.7	52.2	57.0	•	67.5
Profit Margin (Before Income Tax) 49	10.0	17.8	11.5	11.4	1.5	•	28.6
Profit Margin (After Income Tax) 50	9.9	17.1	11.5	11.3	1.3	•	28.1

Table I

Corporations with and without Net Income

COMPUTER SYSTEMS DESIGN AND RELATED SERVICES

MONEY AMOUNTS AND SIZE OF ASSETS IN THOUSANDS OF DOLLARS

Item Description for Accounting Period 7/09 Through 6/10		Total	Zero Assets	Under 500	500 to 1,000	1,000 to 5,000	5,000 to 10,000	10,000 to 25,000	25,000 to 50,000	50,000 to 100,000	100,000 to 250,000	250,000 to 500,000	500,000 to 2,500,000	2,500,000 and over
Number of Enterprises	1	135467	29588	94586	3524	5540	904	717	275	148	99	35	42	9
Revenues ($ in Thousands)														
Net Sales	2	220809159	11890204	29283680	7474951	31268007	11392315	18250333	14438582	10091986	11849546	7938847	30405665	36525042
Interest	3	848767	14632	11460	5010	21440	15004	21288	21499	21533	41088	45120	184475	446217
Rents	4	91778	135	10658	3083	4322	551	1603	5753	4901	8980	3888	8323	39582
Royalties	5	1006627	136185	30	27	17672	274	8145	21159	39510	25586	92526	196859	468654
Other Portfolio Income	6	825762	86596	76336	19839	65473	42026	15278	43845	122737	76299	33978	179465	63893
Other Receipts	7	2479320	118965	532534	94406	361076	4435	120562	115128	294910	75573	113553	210085	438090
Total Receipts	8	226061413	12246717	29914698	7597316	31737990	11454605	18417209	14645966	10575577	12077072	8227912	31184872	37981478
Average Total Receipts	9	1669	414	316	2156	5729	12671	25686	53258	71457	121991	235083	742497	4220164
Operating Costs/Operating Income (%)														
Cost of Operations	10	29.1	17.3	18.5	40.4	37.3	35.4	43.7	48.5	38.0	33.4	39.7	32.1	6.2
Salaries and Wages	11	26.4	37.6	22.6	23.3	26.6	30.9	24.1	22.1	23.7	28.0	24.2	20.7	33.5
Taxes Paid	12	3.7	4.2	3.3	3.3	3.2	3.2	2.6	3.1	2.9	2.7	2.4	2.4	7.0
Interest Paid	13	1.9	0.6	0.6	0.9	0.7	1.1	0.9	1.0	1.1	1.6	1.9	3.1	4.9
Depreciation	14	1.9	1.3	1.1	1.2	0.6	1.2	1.6	1.7	1.5	2.7	2.5	2.6	3.3
Amortization and Depletion	15	1.5	1.2	0.2	0.3	0.5	0.4	0.9	1.1	1.7	1.8	3.6	2.0	3.4
Pensions and Other Deferred Comp.	16	0.9	0.6	1.1	0.2	0.8	0.6	0.7	0.3	0.4	0.3	0.3	0.9	1.7
Employee Benefits	17	2.6	1.8	1.5	1.6	2.1	2.8	2.2	2.3	1.8	2.7	2.0	3.4	4.3
Advertising	18	0.8	0.4	0.6	0.8	0.7	1.3	1.8	1.0	1.3	1.0	0.9	0.5	0.2
Other Expenses	19	25.7	29.5	29.8	18.6	21.8	22.6	19.2	18.2	24.9	22.9	20.7	26.3	34.8
Officers' Compensation	20	4.7	4.7	16.7	7.3	6.5	5.2	2.7	2.4	2.5	1.5	1.2	0.6	0.6
Operating Margin	21	1.0	0.8	4.0	1.9	•	•	•	•	0.2	1.2	0.7	5.5	0.2
Operating Margin Before Officers' Comp.	22	5.7	5.5	20.7	9.2	5.7	0.3	2.2	0.6	2.7	2.8	1.9	6.0	0.8

Selected Average Balance Sheet ($ in Thousands)

Net Receivables **23**	422	0	10	163	816	2146	5000	9471	16526	27806	54555	142063	3324680
Inventories **24**	15	0	2	29	68	174	367	638	945	1067	4975	7226	9822
Net Property, Plant and Equipment **25**	100	0	9	47	140	397	1092	2458	3030	6460	18081	87166	501376
Total Assets **26**	1606	0	61	755	2214	7009	16011	34700	67723	159289	340426	1058684	9703152
Notes and Loans Payable **27**	415	0	53	349	714	1769	3124	8523	11368	26214	55702	240229	2620081
All Other Liabilities **28**	663	0	23	260	1032	3400	8031	17067	26867	54513	136340	327797	4389872
Net Worth **29**	528	0	-15	146	469	1840	4856	9109	29488	78562	148384	490658	2693199

Selected Financial Ratios (Times to 1)

Current Ratio **30**	1.3	•	1.4	1.6	1.6	1.5	1.4	1.3	1.5	1.4	1.7	1.5	1.0
Quick Ratio **31**	1.1	•	1.2	1.4	1.4	1.4	1.2	1.0	1.1	1.1	1.5	1.1	0.9
Net Sales to Working Capital **32**	10.2	•	25.8	11.0	8.9	7.3	8.2	12.2	5.7	5.8	4.0	7.1	30.7
Coverage Ratio **33**	2.9	7.7	10.5	4.9	1.9	•	1.5	0.8	5.9	3.1	3.4	3.7	2.0
Total Asset Turnover **34**	1.0	•	5.1	2.8	2.5	1.8	1.6	1.5	1.0	0.8	0.7	0.7	0.4
Inventory Turnover **35**	30.8	•	27.1	30.0	30.9	25.7	30.4	40.0	27.5	37.5	18.1	32.1	25.7
Receivables Turnover **36**	3.9	•	32.2	13.3	6.4	6.4	4.9	6.1	4.6	4.2	4.0	4.8	1.3
Total Liabilities to Net Worth **37**	2.0	•	•	4.2	3.7	2.8	2.3	2.8	1.3	1.0	1.3	1.2	2.6
Current Assets to Working Capital **38**	4.7	•	3.5	2.6	2.7	2.8	3.5	4.7	3.0	3.3	2.3	3.2	31.5
Current Liabilities to Working Capital **39**	3.7	•	2.5	1.6	1.7	1.8	2.5	3.7	2.0	2.3	1.3	2.2	30.5
Working Capital to Net Sales **40**	0.1	•	0.0	0.1	0.1	0.1	0.1	0.1	0.2	0.2	0.2	0.1	0.0
Inventory to Working Capital **41**	0.1	•	0.2	0.2	0.1	0.1	0.1	0.2	0.1	0.1	0.1	0.1	0.1
Total Receipts to Cash Flow **42**	3.9	3.3	3.1	5.2	5.1	6.5	5.9	6.5	3.7	4.6	4.5	3.1	3.0
Cost of Goods to Cash Flow **43**	1.1	0.6	0.6	2.1	1.9	2.3	2.6	3.2	1.4	1.5	1.8	1.0	0.2
Cash Flow to Total Debt **44**	0.4	•	1.3	0.7	0.6	0.4	0.4	0.3	0.5	0.3	0.3	0.4	0.2

Selected Financial Factors (in Percentages)

Debt Ratio **45**	67.1	•	125.4	80.7	78.8	73.7	69.7	73.7	56.5	50.7	56.4	53.7	72.2
Return on Total Assets **46**	5.5	•	34.5	12.3	3.7	•	2.0	1.2	6.2	3.7	4.3	7.7	4.1
Return on Equity Before Income Taxes **47**	11.0	•	•	50.9	8.3	•	2.1	•	11.9	5.0	6.9	12.2	7.4
Return on Equity After Income Taxes **48**	8.0	•	•	46.8	5.5	•	•	•	9.3	3.5	4.7	9.0	5.0
Profit Margin (Before Income Tax) **49**	3.6	4.0	6.1	3.5	0.7	•	0.4	•	5.1	3.3	4.5	8.3	4.9
Profit Margin (After Income Tax) **50**	2.6	2.2	6.1	3.2	0.5	•	•	•	4.0	2.3	3.1	6.1	3.3

Table II

Corporations with Net Income

COMPUTER SYSTEMS DESIGN AND RELATED SERVICES

MONEY AMOUNTS AND SIZE OF ASSETS IN THOUSANDS OF DOLLARS

Item Description for Accounting Period 7/09 Through 6/10	Total	Zero Assets	Under 500	500 to 1,000	1,000 to 5,000	5,000 to 10,000	10,000 to 25,000	25,000 to 50,000	50,000 to 100,000	100,000 to 250,000	250,000 to 500,000	500,000 to 2,500,000	2,500,000 and over
Number of Enterprises 1	80142	13434	59318	2619	3537	456	412	149	•	61	24	•	35
Revenues ($ in Thousands)													
Net Sales 2	173294914	9268608	20577348	6061651	26314930	7315217	13583420	8005078	•	7944294	6155348	•	27483735
Interest 3	728512	5240	5435	2695	8396	6337	5157	10266	•	29356	34396	•	167050
Rents 4	70264	135	0	3017	60	448	1192	5399	•	4184	3767	•	8323
Royalties 5	878493	124099	0	0	17336	14	6308	17224	•	19891	81808	•	103867
Other Portfolio Income 6	705990	77622	73334	19556	52688	41905	12387	5263	•	61079	29666	•	155395
Other Receipts 7	1931700	88860	511541	77132	161802	15487	58440	85105	•	65591	27635	•	136741
Total Receipts 8	177609873	9564564	21167658	6164051	26555212	7379408	13666904	8128335	•	8124395	6332620	•	28055111
Average Total Receipts 9	2216	712	357	2354	7508	16183	33172	54553	•	133187	263859	•	801575
Operating Costs/Operating Income (%)													
Cost of Operations 10	27.3	13.6	15.4	42.5	37.7	37.3	45.3	42.7	•	28.6	39.5	•	30.0
Salaries and Wages 11	25.1	38.7	19.8	20.3	23.4	25.6	20.4	20.8	•	29.0	24.1	•	21.2
Taxes Paid 12	3.7	4.2	2.9	3.0	3.0	2.9	2.3	3.1	•	2.8	2.3	•	2.3
Interest Paid 13	1.7	0.4	0.3	0.3	0.3	0.5	0.4	0.7	•	1.6	1.2	•	2.7
Depreciation 14	1.7	1.1	0.6	0.6	0.3	0.8	1.3	1.5	•	1.8	2.6	•	2.7
Amortization and Depletion 15	1.3	0.9	0.1	0.2	0.3	0.2	0.6	1.0	•	1.8	2.3	•	1.8
Pensions and Other Deferred Comp. 16	1.0	0.5	1.3	0.2	0.9	0.9	1.0	0.4	•	0.4	0.3	•	1.0
Employee Benefits 17	2.6	1.9	1.0	1.3	1.9	2.4	1.9	2.2	•	2.5	1.9	•	3.5
Advertising 18	0.7	0.3	0.5	0.6	0.5	1.2	1.9	0.9	•	0.9	1.0	•	0.5
Other Expenses 19	24.0	26.9	28.4	14.3	18.0	14.5	15.2	17.2	•	23.3	18.4	•	26.6
Officers' Compensation 20	4.3	3.7	16.7	6.7	6.1	5.6	2.2	2.5	•	1.3	1.2	•	0.6
Operating Margin 21	6.6	7.8	13.1	9.9	7.6	8.0	7.4	6.8	•	5.9	5.2	•	7.1
Operating Margin Before Officers' Comp. 22	10.9	11.6	29.8	16.6	13.7	13.6	9.7	9.3	•	7.2	6.3	•	7.7

Selected Average Balance Sheet ($ in Thousands)

Net Receivables 23	584	0	9	160	1025	2278	5518	10579	•	27360	65326	152879
Inventories 24	16	0	3	34	54	126	337	562	•	631	4090	7356
Net Property, Plant and Equipment 25	130	0	8	24	97	365	1111	2236	•	6327	22177	96584
Total Assets 26	2131	0	64	736	2267	7141	16073	34258	•	156806	343091	1123090
Notes and Loans Payable 27	484	0	21	161	414	961	2237	7881	•	28720	47748	225765
All Other Liabilities 28	843	0	15	222	1017	3154	7135	14941	•	52297	123896	353155
Net Worth 29	803	0	27	354	836	3027	6702	11436	•	75789	171446	544171

Selected Financial Ratios (Times to 1)

Current Ratio 30	1.3	•	3.0	2.5	1.8	1.7	1.7	1.4	•	1.5	1.7	1.5
Quick Ratio 31	1.1	•	2.6	2.2	1.6	1.5	1.4	1.2	•	1.2	1.5	1.2
Net Sales to Working Capital 32	9.5	•	11.2	7.4	8.5	7.6	7.3	9.1	•	5.9	4.3	6.5
Coverage Ratio 33	6.4	32.6	56.2	35.3	27.7	19.4	23.0	12.8	•	6.2	7.7	4.5
Total Asset Turnover 34	1.0	•	5.4	3.1	3.3	2.2	2.1	1.6	•	0.8	0.7	0.7
Inventory Turnover 35	37.8	•	19.7	29.1	52.0	47.5	44.3	40.8	•	58.9	24.8	32.0
Receivables Turnover 36	4.1	•	33.6	15.1	6.8	7.0	5.8	5.9	•	4.7	4.0	5.0
Total Liabilities to Net Worth 37	1.7	•	1.3	1.1	1.7	1.4	1.4	2.0	•	1.1	1.0	1.1
Current Assets to Working Capital 38	4.3	•	1.5	1.7	2.2	2.4	2.5	3.5	•	3.1	2.4	3.0
Current Liabilities to Working Capital 39	3.3	•	0.5	0.7	1.2	1.4	1.5	2.5	•	2.1	1.4	2.0
Working Capital to Net Sales 40	0.1	•	0.1	0.1	0.1	0.1	0.1	0.1	•	0.2	0.2	0.2
Inventory to Working Capital 41	0.1	•	0.1	0.1	0.1	0.1	0.1	0.1	•	0.0	0.1	0.1
Total Receipts to Cash Flow 42	3.3	2.8	2.4	4.2	4.2	4.8	4.7	4.3	•	3.7	4.3	3.0
Cost of Goods to Cash Flow 43	0.9	0.4	0.4	1.8	1.6	1.8	2.1	1.8	•	1.0	1.7	0.9
Cash Flow to Total Debt 44	0.5	•	3.9	1.4	1.2	0.8	0.8	0.6	•	0.4	0.3	0.5

Selected Financial Factors (in Percentages)

Debt Ratio 45	62.3	•	57.1	51.9	63.1	57.6	58.3	66.6	•	51.7	50.0	51.5
Return on Total Assets 46	11.3	•	88.2	37.4	29.0	21.1	17.3	14.4	•	8.3	7.1	8.5
Return on Equity Before Income Taxes 47	25.2	•	202.0	75.5	75.7	47.3	39.6	39.8	•	14.3	12.3	13.6
Return on Equity After Income Taxes 48	21.8	•	201.0	73.3	73.2	42.5	35.4	35.5	•	11.8	9.5	10.2
Profit Margin (Before Income Tax) 49	9.3	11.2	15.9	11.5	8.5	8.9	8.1	8.5	•	8.3	8.2	9.4
Profit Margin (After Income Tax) 50	8.1	8.9	15.8	11.2	8.2	8.0	7.2	7.6	•	6.9	6.4	7.0

340

Table I

Corporations with and without Net Income

MANAGEMENT, SCIENTIFIC, AND TECHNICAL CONSULTING SERVICES

MONEY AMOUNTS AND SIZE OF ASSETS IN THOUSANDS OF DOLLARS

Item Description for Accounting Period 7/09 Through 6/10		Total	Zero Assets	Under 500	500 to 1,000	1,000 to 5,000	5,000 to 10,000	10,000 to 25,000	25,000 to 50,000	50,000 to 100,000	100,000 to 250,000	250,000 to 500,000	500,000 to 2,500,000	2,500,000 and over
Number of Enterprises	1	233894	50277	169787	7041	5264	640	480	167	104	73	30	23	8
Revenues ($ in Thousands)														
Net Sales	2	185202316	3326832	43852447	18131157	19853254	8918314	10570761	5317904	7913149	9659841	7374191	18350129	31934336
Interest	3	391650	7162	33448	10907	22898	10817	22935	21971	18230	16189	35953	161475	29666
Rents	4	59554	67	639	0	1294	122	2278	904	1389	17905	2601	10266	22088
Royalties	5	464603	961	461	0	10333	0	98	277	4584	19752	28311	30700	369125
Other Portfolio Income	6	627344	34917	46522	9024	45889	12899	14262	21098	2582	27290	26280	205435	181149
Other Receipts	7	3870903	74812	1118766	307980	375579	138081	316200	192118	757176	242791	105242	-436094	678250
Total Receipts	8	190616370	3444751	45052283	18459068	20309247	9080233	10926534	5554272	8697110	9983768	7572578	18321911	33214614
Average Total Receipts	9	815	69	265	2622	3858	14188	22764	33259	83626	136764	252419	796605	4151827
Operating Costs/Operating Income (%)														
Cost of Operations	10	26.4	9.6	20.3	38.6	19.6	28.5	38.4	23.9	25.9	28.2	27.0	22.4	31.2
Salaries and Wages	11	26.3	12.1	20.3	25.0	23.2	28.1	21.2	36.5	38.8	28.5	28.4	35.4	28.8
Taxes Paid	12	3.2	5.0	2.9	3.2	2.8	3.0	2.4	3.8	3.7	3.1	3.5	3.2	3.5
Interest Paid	13	0.9	1.0	0.5	0.4	0.6	0.4	0.8	1.3	1.1	1.3	2.2	1.5	1.6
Depreciation	14	1.3	1.8	0.9	0.8	0.8	1.1	1.8	2.3	2.1	2.3	2.1	1.7	1.4
Amortization and Depletion	15	0.6	0.3	0.0	0.0	0.2	0.1	0.6	1.0	0.7	1.0	2.1	1.9	0.6
Pensions and Other Deferred Comp.	16	1.4	2.1	1.5	0.9	0.9	1.0	0.8	1.5	0.7	1.2	0.5	1.8	2.5
Employee Benefits	17	2.3	1.3	1.8	0.7	2.2	1.7	2.0	3.0	2.1	2.6	2.5	5.9	1.9
Advertising	18	0.6	1.1	1.2	0.4	0.4	0.3	0.4	0.5	1.1	0.5	0.2	0.4	0.2
Other Expenses	19	27.7	45.0	27.1	20.2	35.2	24.6	22.0	24.7	26.7	28.6	28.4	32.6	26.2
Officers' Compensation	20	7.0	14.6	15.1	7.4	9.1	9.7	3.6	3.5	3.2	2.3	1.3	3.1	0.4
Operating Margin	21	2.4	6.1	8.3	2.3	5.2	1.4	6.1	•	•	0.4	1.8	•	1.9
Operating Margin Before Officers' Comp.	22	9.4	20.7	23.4	9.7	14.2	11.1	9.7	1.6	•	2.7	3.1	•	2.2

Selected Average Balance Sheet ($ in Thousands)

Net Receivables 23	127	0	5	138	444	2102	3636	8442	13640	38341	65386	229827	1209064
Inventories 24	11	0	1	12	39	90	427	517	1531	2007	3928	47675	45407
Net Property, Plant and Equipment 25	48	0	9	134	246	720	1802	4517	7198	14390	27789	50159	206762
Total Assets 26	543	0	51	712	2029	7535	15652	35890	68357	151480	357696	1086414	3802275
Notes and Loans Payable 27	169	0	48	288	549	2080	3850	9617	19250	35894	96112	218627	1127958
All Other Liabilities 28	194	0	14	201	568	2946	4688	9100	22448	57580	95750	434712	1683694
Net Worth 29	180	0	-12	223	912	2509	7115	17173	26659	58006	165834	433075	990622

Selected Financial Ratios (Times to 1)

Current Ratio 30	1.5	•	2.1	1.6	2.1	1.6	1.7	1.5	1.3	1.5	1.5	1.5	1.3
Quick Ratio 31	1.2	•	1.7	1.2	1.7	1.1	1.3	1.1	0.9	1.2	1.1	1.0	1.1
Net Sales to Working Capital 32	8.7	•	16.3	15.6	6.5	8.6	7.0	6.3	10.4	5.0	5.5	5.3	9.2
Coverage Ratio 33	6.7	10.6	25.4	11.4	14.6	9.2	13.3	3.1	4.4	3.8	3.0	•	5.0
Total Asset Turnover 34	1.5	•	5.1	3.6	1.9	1.8	1.4	0.9	1.1	0.9	0.7	0.7	1.0
Inventory Turnover 35	18.3	•	63.2	81.7	19.0	44.3	19.8	14.7	12.9	18.6	16.9	3.7	27.4
Receivables Turnover 36	6.0	•	53.8	19.8	9.0	6.2	5.9	3.8	5.1	3.4	3.6	3.0	3.3
Total Liabilities to Net Worth 37	2.0	•	•	2.2	1.2	2.0	1.2	1.1	1.6	1.6	1.2	1.5	2.8
Current Assets to Working Capital 38	2.9	•	2.0	2.6	1.9	2.8	2.5	3.1	4.4	2.8	2.9	3.2	4.3
Current Liabilities to Working Capital 39	1.9	•	1.0	1.6	0.9	1.8	1.5	2.1	3.4	1.8	1.9	2.2	3.3
Working Capital to Net Sales 40	0.1	•	0.1	0.1	0.2	0.1	0.1	0.2	0.1	0.2	0.2	0.2	0.1
Inventory to Working Capital 41	0.1	•	0.1	0.1	0.0	0.1	0.1	0.1	0.2	0.0	0.0	0.3	0.1
Total Receipts to Cash Flow 42	3.5	2.0	2.9	5.5	2.7	4.0	3.7	4.3	3.7	3.5	3.4	7.0	3.5
Cost of Goods to Cash Flow 43	0.9	0.2	0.6	2.1	0.5	1.1	1.4	1.0	1.0	1.0	0.9	1.6	1.1
Cash Flow to Total Debt 44	0.6	•	1.4	1.0	1.3	0.7	0.7	0.4	0.5	0.4	0.4	0.2	0.4

Selected Financial Factors (in Percentages)

Debt Ratio 45	66.9	•	123.9	68.7	55.1	66.7	54.5	52.2	61.0	61.7	53.6	60.1	73.9
Return on Total Assets 46	9.3	•	58.6	16.2	14.9	6.5	14.3	3.5	5.6	4.5	4.7	•	8.2
Return on Equity Before Income Taxes 47	23.8	•	•	47.3	30.9	17.3	29.1	5.0	11.0	8.6	6.8	•	25.1
Return on Equity After Income Taxes 48	19.7	•	•	46.1	29.8	14.7	27.6	2.8	7.7	5.5	3.5	•	15.5
Profit Margin (Before Income Tax) 49	5.4	9.7	11.0	4.1	7.5	3.1	9.4	2.7	3.8	3.8	4.6	•	6.2
Profit Margin (After Income Tax) 50	4.5	8.8	10.9	4.0	7.2	2.7	8.9	1.5	2.7	2.4	2.4	•	3.9

MANAGEMENT, SCIENTIFIC, AND TECHNICAL CONSULTING SERVICES

Table II
Corporations with Net Income

MONEY AMOUNTS AND SIZE OF ASSETS IN THOUSANDS OF DOLLARS

Item Description for Accounting Period 7/09 Through 6/10	Total	Zero Assets	Under 500	500 to 1,000	1,000 to 5,000	5,000 to 10,000	10,000 to 25,000	25,000 to 50,000	50,000 to 100,000	100,000 to 250,000	250,000 to 500,000	500,000 to 2,500,000	2,500,000 and over
Number of Enterprises 1	134644	19642	106201	4571	3357	359	275	87	61	46	•	•	20
Revenues ($ in Thousands)													
Net Sales 2	145181545	2477893	35684029	14877425	14228204	5876127	7182730	3428928	6250013	7296363	•	14120197	•
Interest 3	266243	2291	7742	6880	14200	6959	18651	18868	8741	5972	•	137313	•
Rents 4	36997	0	625	0	6	117	45	693	976	4971	•	8748	•
Royalties 5	427916	961	48	0	0	0	0	58	4584	3963	•	30700	•
Other Portfolio Income 6	573472	34392	43045	7854	43927	2911	8164	7991	1787	21598	•	201891	•
Other Receipts 7	4119648	85928	1071262	281131	496657	116854	183284	154371	722928	188578	•	361252	•
Total Receipts 8	150605821	2601465	36806751	15173290	14782994	6002968	7392874	3610909	6989029	7521445	•	14860101	•
Average Total Receipts 9	1119	132	347	3319	4404	16721	26883	41505	114574	163510	•	743005	•
Operating Costs/Operating Income (%)													
Cost of Operations 10	25.5	10.1	22.0	37.1	19.3	30.6	31.7	14.1	25.1	26.5	•	20.5	•
Salaries and Wages 11	26.1	10.4	19.2	23.6	23.4	28.8	19.5	38.9	38.8	27.7	•	36.1	•
Taxes Paid 12	3.2	4.4	2.6	3.1	2.8	3.2	2.4	3.9	3.9	3.1	•	3.3	•
Interest Paid 13	0.8	0.4	0.3	0.2	0.4	0.3	0.5	1.2	0.9	1.3	•	1.4	•
Depreciation 14	1.1	0.9	0.8	0.5	0.7	0.5	1.5	1.3	1.6	1.5	•	2.1	•
Amortization and Depletion 15	0.4	0.0	0.0	0.0	0.2	0.1	0.3	0.5	0.5	0.6	•	1.7	•
Pensions and Other Deferred Comp. 16	1.5	0.8	1.3	0.9	1.1	0.5	1.0	1.6	0.7	1.1	•	2.1	•
Employee Benefits 17	2.0	1.0	1.7	0.5	2.4	2.1	1.9	3.6	2.0	2.5	•	3.8	•
Advertising 18	0.4	0.4	0.5	0.3	0.3	0.3	0.3	0.3	1.0	0.4	•	0.5	•
Other Expenses 19	23.8	34.1	22.7	20.5	27.5	17.8	20.6	25.6	25.2	25.0	•	23.7	•
Officers' Compensation 20	6.9	12.9	14.4	8.4	10.2	6.7	3.3	3.5	3.3	2.0	•	4.0	•
Operating Margin 21	8.5	24.5	14.6	4.8	11.8	9.1	16.9	5.5	•	8.3	•	0.8	•
Operating Margin Before Officers' Comp. 22	15.4	37.4	28.9	13.2	22.0	15.9	20.2	9.0	0.3	10.3	•	4.8	•

Selected Average Balance Sheet ($ in Thousands)

Net Receivables 23	168	0	5	126	414	2187	3911	10998	14130	44188	210319
Inventories 24	12	0	1	12	39	68	524	467	1150	1119	32365
Net Property, Plant and Equipment 25	51	0	8	83	209	548	1532	3129	7613	12637	53356
Total Assets 26	659	0	55	698	1994	7713	15544	35944	67795	154602	1096759
Notes and Loans Payable 27	151	0	21	189	391	1421	3433	10448	17041	37281	169741
All Other Liabilities 28	246	0	11	199	495	2321	4684	8585	25438	57999	391449
Net Worth 29	262	0	23	310	1108	3971	7427	16910	25316	59322	535569

Selected Financial Ratios (Times to 1)

Current Ratio 30	1.6	•	3.2	2.0	2.3	1.7	1.9	1.8	1.3	1.6	1.5
Quick Ratio 31	1.3	•	2.9	1.5	1.9	1.2	1.4	1.5	0.9	1.3	1.1
Net Sales to Working Capital 32	8.4	•	13.1	15.3	6.0	7.7	6.0	4.7	11.7	5.2	5.1
Coverage Ratio 33	17.2	79.2	61.2	30.1	38.7	37.1	38.2	10.4	11.1	9.6	5.4
Total Asset Turnover 34	1.6	•	6.1	4.7	2.1	2.1	1.7	1.1	1.5	1.0	0.6
Inventory Turnover 35	22.0	•	133.2	101.2	20.8	73.2	15.8	11.9	22.4	37.5	4.5
Receivables Turnover 36	6.5	•	59.4	26.8	10.9	5.5	5.9	3.6	6.3	•	3.4
Total Liabilities to Net Worth 37	1.5	•	1.4	1.2	0.8	0.9	1.1	1.1	1.7	1.6	1.0
Current Assets to Working Capital 38	2.7	•	1.5	2.0	1.7	2.4	2.1	2.2	3.9	2.8	3.0
Current Liabilities to Working Capital 39	1.7	•	0.5	1.0	0.7	1.4	1.1	1.2	2.9	1.8	2.0
Working Capital to Net Sales 40	0.1	•	0.1	0.1	0.2	0.1	0.2	0.2	0.1	0.2	0.2
Inventory to Working Capital 41	0.1	0.0	0.0	0.1	0.0	0.0	0.1	0.0	0.1	0.0	0.3
Total Receipts to Cash Flow 42	3.1	1.7	2.7	4.8	2.5	3.8	2.8	3.1	3.2	3.0	4.1
Cost of Goods to Cash Flow 43	0.8	0.2	0.6	1.8	0.5	1.2	0.9	0.4	0.8	0.8	0.8
Cash Flow to Total Debt 44	0.9	•	3.9	1.7	1.9	1.2	1.2	0.7	0.7	0.6	0.3

Selected Financial Factors (in Percentages)

Debt Ratio 45	60.3	•	58.3	55.5	44.4	48.5	52.2	53.0	62.7	61.6	51.2
Return on Total Assets 46	21.5	•	109.4	32.9	34.1	24.6	34.2	13.2	14.7	13.1	5.0
Return on Equity Before Income Taxes 47	50.8	•	258.0	71.4	59.9	46.6	69.7	25.3	35.8	30.5	8.4
Return on Equity After Income Taxes 48	46.0	•	256.2	70.2	58.5	43.7	67.1	21.1	29.8	25.7	5.8
Profit Margin (Before Income Tax) 49	12.4	29.5	17.7	6.8	15.6	11.3	19.8	10.9	8.8	11.4	6.4
Profit Margin (After Income Tax) 50	11.2	28.4	17.6	6.7	15.3	10.6	19.1	9.0	7.4	9.6	4.4

Table I

Corporations with and without Net Income

SCIENTIFIC RESEARCH AND DEVELOPMENT SERVICES

MONEY AMOUNTS AND SIZE OF ASSETS IN THOUSANDS OF DOLLARS

Item Description for Accounting Period 7/09 Through 6/10		Total	Zero Assets	Under 500	500 to 1,000	1,000 to 5,000	5,000 to 10,000	10,000 to 25,000	25,000 to 50,000	50,000 to 100,000	100,000 to 250,000	250,000 to 500,000	500,000 to 2,500,000	2,500,000 and over
Number of Enterprises	1	16735	2637	10223	609	2020	490	403	129	100	70	23	31	0
Revenues ($ in Thousands)														
Net Sales	2	37850956	211153	3368196	755607	6272711	2058205	2400307	2467989	2488386	3410142	3501376	10916884	0
Interest	3	372604	5649	1452	2036	17409	11014	30039	21642	37372	51314	34745	159932	0
Rents	4	14132	0	0	0	2620	14	1517	516	2792	2175	1367	3131	0
Royalties	5	1675409	181	0	0	30368	16322	46901	57750	91472	203234	47386	1181795	0
Other Portfolio Income	6	1036035	15669	13	1041	40578	18088	18737	20344	45744	215644	28602	631577	0
Other Receipts	7	5296831	38222	105669	30315	274943	189669	270077	228655	169430	299276	144687	3545888	0
Total Receipts	8	46245967	270874	3475330	788999	6638629	2293312	2767578	2796896	2835196	4181785	3758163	16439207	0
Average Total Receipts	9	2763	103	340	1296	3286	4680	6867	21681	28352	59740	163398	530297	•
Operating Costs/Operating Income (%)														
Cost of Operations	10	25.2	15.6	8.3	9.4	31.9	26.1	34.8	27.2	30.5	23.3	30.4	22.8	•
Salaries and Wages	11	35.4	65.1	29.1	27.7	28.1	48.4	49.2	37.8	37.1	37.6	28.0	36.8	•
Taxes Paid	12	3.9	9.7	2.7	5.4	3.8	4.7	6.3	4.5	4.9	4.0	3.5	3.1	•
Interest Paid	13	3.9	5.1	1.0	1.6	2.6	5.7	6.0	3.5	6.1	3.5	3.2	4.8	•
Depreciation	14	4.7	7.0	0.8	2.2	2.9	5.7	8.5	5.9	4.5	4.5	4.3	6.0	•
Amortization and Depletion	15	3.3	15.1	0.6	2.9	1.6	3.3	4.5	4.3	7.1	4.6	2.0	3.5	•
Pensions and Other Deferred Comp.	16	2.0	2.7	2.6	3.1	0.9	1.8	1.1	1.0	0.4	1.1	0.9	3.9	•
Employee Benefits	17	4.3	7.5	2.7	1.8	3.6	4.7	5.2	3.6	4.2	3.8	4.1	5.5	•
Advertising	18	1.5	0.9	3.5	0.4	0.7	2.8	1.8	1.0	1.3	2.1	0.5	1.5	•
Other Expenses	19	52.3	166.1	44.6	83.5	48.5	75.1	89.4	54.6	71.6	68.6	38.0	34.5	•
Officers' Compensation	20	6.5	11.3	13.8	13.0	9.3	10.5	11.2	5.5	6.8	4.7	2.0	2.3	•
Operating Margin	21	•	•	•	•	•	•	•	•	•	•	•	•	•
Operating Margin Before Officers' Comp.	22	•	•	3.9	•	•	•	•	•	•	•	•	•	•

Selected Average Balance Sheet ($ in Thousands)

Net Receivables 23	469	0	9	138	453	686	1432	3492	4302	12820	38080	103039
Inventories 24	171	0	1	34	106	309	440	777	1504	3921	10792	49209
Net Property, Plant and Equipment 25	585	0	14	70	384	1070	2102	5037	6298	13518	40568	138872
Total Assets 26	5155	0	87	664	2336	7481	15836	35856	69657	144919	373714	1286625
Notes and Loans Payable 27	1453	0	94	255	983	4643	3509	7402	13748	19713	91709	377712
All Other Liabilities 28	1520	0	44	320	939	2976	4368	13419	30665	51043	115098	279244
Net Worth 29	2182	0	-51	88	414	-138	7959	15035	25244	74163	166907	629669

Selected Financial Ratios (Times to 1)

Current Ratio 30	2.1	•	1.0	1.6	1.4	1.4	2.5	2.1	2.2	2.9	1.3	2.6
Quick Ratio 31	1.3	•	0.8	1.3	1.2	1.2	2.0	1.5	1.5	1.9	0.8	1.2
Net Sales to Working Capital 32	1.5	•	189.3	7.5	7.1	3.3	1.0	1.6	1.0	0.9	3.6	0.9
Coverage Ratio 33	•	•	•	•	•	•	•	•	•	•	•	6.9
Total Asset Turnover 34	0.4	•	3.8	1.9	1.3	0.6	0.4	0.5	0.4	0.3	0.4	0.3
Inventory Turnover 35	3.3	•	42.1	3.4	9.3	3.6	4.7	6.7	5.0	2.9	4.3	1.6
Receivables Turnover 36	4.8	•	62.9	6.6	6.4	5.2	4.3	4.8	5.1	3.7	4.2	3.7
Total Liabilities to Net Worth 37	1.4	•	6.5	4.6	1.0	•	1.0	1.4	1.8	1.0	1.2	1.0
Current Assets to Working Capital 38	1.9	•	30.1	2.8	3.4	3.3	1.6	1.9	1.9	1.5	4.0	1.6
Current Liabilities to Working Capital 39	0.9	•	29.1	1.8	2.4	2.3	0.6	0.9	0.9	0.5	3.0	0.6
Working Capital to Net Sales 40	0.6	•	0.0	0.1	0.1	0.3	1.0	0.6	1.0	1.1	0.3	1.1
Inventory to Working Capital 41	0.1	•	0.7	0.2	0.3	0.2	0.1	0.1	0.1	0.1	0.3	0.1
Total Receipts to Cash Flow 42	4.5	•	3.5	3.6	8.5	•	•	8.5	59.3	4.9	4.6	1.9
Cost of Goods to Cash Flow 43	1.1	•	0.3	0.3	2.7	•	•	2.3	18.1	1.1	1.4	0.4
Cash Flow to Total Debt 44	0.2	•	0.7	0.6	0.2	•	0.1	0.1	0.0	0.1	0.2	0.3

Selected Financial Factors (in Percentages)

Debt Ratio 45	57.7	•	158.8	86.7	82.3	101.8	49.7	58.1	63.8	48.8	55.3	51.1
Return on Total Assets 46	•	•	•	•	•	•	•	•	•	•	•	9.1
Return on Equity Before Income Taxes 47	•	•	43.3	•	•	2360.9	•	•	•	•	•	15.8
Return on Equity After Income Taxes 48	•	•	44.3	•	•	2400.6	•	•	•	•	•	10.8
Profit Margin (Before Income Tax) 49	•	•	•	•	•	•	•	•	•	•	•	28.3
Profit Margin (After Income Tax) 50	•	•	•	•	•	•	•	•	•	•	•	19.3

Table II

Corporations with Net Income

SCIENTIFIC RESEARCH AND DEVELOPMENT SERVICES

MONEY AMOUNTS AND SIZE OF ASSETS IN THOUSANDS OF DOLLARS

Item Description for Accounting Period 7/09 Through 6/10		Total	Zero Assets	Under 500	500 to 1,000	1,000 to 5,000	5,000 to 10,000	10,000 to 25,000	25,000 to 50,000	50,000 to 100,000	100,000 to 250,000	250,000 to 500,000	500,000 to 2,500,000	2,500,000 and over
Number of Enterprises	1	6761	345	5034	157	887	135	88	37	19	30	9	19	0
Revenues ($ in Thousands)														
Net Sales	2	25844532	71181	2977268	492627	4360928	1277253	1340332	1436535	1212273	2300866	2503591	7871678	0
Interest	3	178692	83	519	17	1790	3085	6478	9780	18217	23286	8519	106918	0
Rents	4	7363	0	0	0	2471	0	253	221	175	1111	0	3131	0
Royalties	5	1407552	0	0	0	19899	23	42467	12240	65333	125110	37716	1104765	0
Other Portfolio Income	6	886885	0	0	0	29944	3199	11525	343	1007	202809	18889	619169	0
Other Receipts	7	4230165	24062	89449	2561	82656	113006	79376	212934	122717	132175	32782	3338448	0
Total Receipts	8	32555189	95326	3067236	495205	4497688	1396566	1480431	1672053	1419722	2785357	2601497	13044109	0
Average Total Receipts	9	4815	276	609	3154	5071	10345	16823	45191	74722	92845	289055	686532	•
Operating Costs/Operating Income (%)														
Cost of Operations	10	23.1	•	4.6	•	25.7	23.9	34.0	22.6	36.4	22.7	27.6	25.0	•
Salaries and Wages	11	27.6	36.8	26.8	8.6	24.0	29.7	21.7	24.9	16.3	24.4	23.0	36.4	•
Taxes Paid	12	3.1	11.1	2.2	3.5	3.2	2.9	3.3	3.6	2.9	2.8	2.9	3.5	•
Interest Paid	13	1.7	6.9	0.1	•	0.4	0.5	0.3	1.0	3.5	0.6	1.4	3.9	•
Depreciation	14	3.5	8.3	0.5	0.0	1.8	1.8	3.4	2.8	1.5	2.9	3.3	6.7	•
Amortization and Depletion	15	1.5	28.8	0.1	0.0	0.3	0.8	0.6	1.1	1.0	1.1	0.9	3.4	•
Pensions and Other Deferred Comp.	16	1.4	•	2.9	4.5	1.1	2.7	1.2	1.2	0.1	1.4	0.9	1.2	•
Employee Benefits	17	3.4	5.3	2.4	0.2	2.8	3.1	2.2	2.9	2.0	2.9	4.1	4.8	•
Advertising	18	1.3	0.1	3.9	•	0.4	0.8	0.7	1.0	0.7	2.3	0.3	1.2	•
Other Expenses	19	30.1	4.6	32.0	72.6	28.3	23.8	23.4	38.1	28.6	28.3	31.9	28.8	•
Officers' Compensation	20	4.4	2.2	12.7	5.7	6.0	5.6	3.9	2.8	1.5	3.1	1.5	2.4	•
Operating Margin	21	•	•	11.8	4.8	5.9	4.4	5.2	•	5.5	7.4	2.3	•	•
Operating Margin Before Officers' Comp.	22	3.2	•	24.5	10.6	11.9	10.0	9.2	0.7	7.0	10.5	3.8	•	•

Selected Average Balance Sheet ($ in Thousands)

	1	2	3	4	5	6	7	8	9	10	11	
Net Receivables 23	684	12	455	735	1392	3729	6213	9707	22187	46819	95985	•
Inventories 24	285	1	62	113	487	249	771	2609	2898	15151	74976	•
Net Property, Plant and Equipment 25	727	23	21	376	693	2421	6639	3809	11918	43931	162430	•
Total Assets 26	6630	122	507	2381	7374	15735	37056	64637	147080	407462	1524244	•
Notes and Loans Payable 27	1614	65	0	461	1865	1636	3518	17814	8681	45901	454641	•
All Other Liabilities 28	1622	25	0	628	3860	3269	16969	27268	46236	158214	290428	•
Net Worth 29	3393	31	507	1291	1649	10830	16568	19554	92163	203347	779174	•

Selected Financial Ratios (Times to 1)

	1	2	3	4	5	6	7	8	9	10	11	
Current Ratio 30	2.5	2.7	•	2.7	1.5	4.3	1.8	1.6	2.9	1.8	2.6	•
Quick Ratio 31	1.3	2.1	•	2.2	1.2	3.3	1.4	0.7	2.0	1.2	1.0	•
Net Sales to Working Capital 32	1.9	14.1	6.5	4.9	6.0	2.0	4.1	4.2	1.4	3.5	0.9	•
Coverage Ratio 33	15.9	259.0	5.3	22.9	29.4	61.5	15.4	7.7	52.1	5.5	14.3	•
Total Asset Turnover 34	0.6	4.9	•	6.2	2.1	1.3	1.0	1.0	0.5	0.7	0.3	•
Inventory Turnover 35	3.1	21.2	•	11.2	4.6	20.7	11.4	8.9	6.0	5.1	1.4	•
Receivables Turnover 36	5.8	86.8	•	5.5	7.2	5.1	4.5	6.4	7.0	6.2	4.3	•
Total Liabilities to Net Worth 37	1.0	2.9	•	0.8	3.5	0.5	1.2	2.3	0.6	1.0	1.0	•
Current Assets to Working Capital 38	1.7	1.6	1.0	1.6	3.1	1.3	2.3	2.5	1.5	2.3	1.6	•
Current Liabilities to Working Capital 39	0.7	0.6	•	0.6	2.1	0.3	1.3	1.5	0.5	1.3	0.6	•
Working Capital to Net Sales 40	0.5	0.1	0.2	0.2	0.2	0.5	0.2	0.2	0.7	0.3	1.1	•
Inventory to Working Capital 41	0.1	0.1	•	0.2	0.2	0.0	0.1	0.2	0.1	0.2	0.2	•
Total Receipts to Cash Flow 42	2.1	2.5	8.6	3.0	3.1	2.9	2.1	2.1	2.2	3.1	1.5	•
Cost of Goods to Cash Flow 43	0.5	0.1	•	0.8	0.7	1.0	0.5	0.8	0.5	0.9	0.4	•
Cash Flow to Total Debt 44	0.6	2.6	363672.0	1.5	0.5	1.1	0.9	0.7	0.6	0.4	0.4	•

Selected Financial Factors (in Percentages)

	1	2	3	4	5	6	7	8	9	10	11	
Debt Ratio 45	48.8	74.6	0.0	77.6	45.8	31.2	55.3	69.7	37.3	50.1	48.9	•
Return on Total Assets 46	15.8	72.5	33.1	18.3	19.4	15.2	16.1	26.6	15.1	5.2	15.1	•
Return on Equity Before Income Taxes 47	28.9	284.7	33.1	78.9	34.3	21.7	33.6	76.4	23.7	8.4	27.5	•
Return on Equity After Income Taxes 48	23.7	281.3	33.1	66.8	32.8	18.7	28.8	69.6	21.5	6.6	20.9	•
Profit Margin (Before Income Tax) 49	25.7	29.8	14.8	5.4	13.7	9.0	15.5	14.3	23.4	28.5	6.2	51.7
Profit Margin (After Income Tax) 50	21.0	29.8	14.7	5.4	11.6	8.6	13.3	12.3	21.3	25.9	4.8	39.2

Table I
Corporations with and without Net Income

ADVERTISING AND RELATED SERVICES

MONEY AMOUNTS AND SIZE OF ASSETS IN THOUSANDS OF DOLLARS

Item Description for Accounting Period 7/09 Through 6/10	Total	Zero Assets	Under 500	500 to 1,000	1,000 to 5,000	5,000 to 10,000	10,000 to 25,000	25,000 to 50,000	50,000 to 100,000	100,000 to 250,000	250,000 to 500,000	500,000 to 2,500,000	2,500,000 and over
Number of Enterprises 1	52234	9454	38541	1702	1922	342	135	55	34	31	4	9	5
Revenues ($ in Thousands)													
Net Sales 2	78172755	609069	19546011	2627601	11723550	4606920	2855432	2733297	2385899	6268903	999973	6754186	17061915
Interest 3	1133703	195	7282	5288	3651	7584	2446	2784	3516	7673	858	12965	1079460
Rents 4	98341	1037	2346	422	932	12	2679	794	103	692	197	510	88615
Royalties 5	45116	0	0	0	31	0	0	33145	0	43	0	10109	1789
Other Portfolio Income 6	638146	65088	18276	9649	27765	4193	2014	7088	5226	2133	6	7211	489495
Other Receipts 7	1266205	-1610	134656	87222	90772	155309	10808	55825	21889	54924	-456	135583	521286
Total Receipts 8	81354266	673779	19708571	2730182	11846701	4774018	2873379	2832933	2416633	6334368	1000578	6920564	19242560
Average Total Receipts 9	1557	71	511	1604	6164	13959	21284	51508	71077	204334	250144	768952	3848512
Operating Costs/Operating Income (%)													
Cost of Operations 10	40.4	28.7	45.5	37.6	54.2	65.9	61.3	44.4	51.4	61.0	64.9	38.8	4.9
Salaries and Wages 11	20.1	9.0	8.9	18.4	12.9	11.9	16.0	17.1	19.7	14.5	11.9	23.3	43.2
Taxes Paid 12	2.4	2.2	1.8	2.7	2.0	1.3	1.7	1.9	1.9	1.6	1.1	3.1	4.1
Interest Paid 13	4.2	2.5	0.6	0.5	0.5	0.3	0.2	1.0	1.4	1.8	2.5	7.6	14.0
Depreciation 14	1.6	5.8	0.7	2.5	0.7	0.6	1.0	1.3	1.5	1.4	0.6	3.3	2.9
Amortization and Depletion 15	1.3	0.7	0.1	0.2	0.3	0.1	0.3	1.0	1.3	1.8	0.8	2.2	3.4
Pensions and Other Deferred Comp. 16	0.5	0.8	0.4	1.6	0.4	0.4	0.3	0.4	0.3	0.3	0.6	0.3	0.9
Employee Benefits 17	1.4	0.9	0.9	1.8	0.9	0.6	1.1	1.6	1.0	1.2	0.9	2.9	2.1
Advertising 18	3.7	0.9	4.9	3.9	6.5	4.6	0.5	14.6	0.7	1.7	0.2	3.7	0.2
Other Expenses 19	22.1	54.0	27.1	29.6	14.1	12.2	12.1	17.0	17.6	14.2	14.9	14.3	31.7
Officers' Compensation 20	4.5	12.8	7.6	8.1	6.0	3.8	4.3	2.8	1.9	1.3	1.0	0.8	2.9
Operating Margin 21	•	•	1.5	•	1.5	•	1.3	•	1.2	•	0.5	•	•
Operating Margin Before Officers' Comp. 22	2.3	•	9.1	1.4	7.5	2.2	5.6	•	3.1	0.5	1.5	•	0.6

Selected Average Balance Sheet ($ in Thousands)

Net Receivables 23	346	0	11	127	742	1991	6434	9682	17830	34131	58993	170821	2091608
Inventories 24	32	0	2	10	115	336	137	934	823	3088	2177	12114	189563
Net Property, Plant and Equipment 25	135	0	17	236	320	294	1652	5766	5772	10446	6556	140956	582442
Total Assets 26	2326	0	67	726	2326	7028	15623	35425	68661	156236	310669	1272426	17375240
Notes and Loans Payable 27	414	0	75	370	445	806	1059	8630	13996	43421	74603	539157	1873840
All Other Liabilities 28	914	0	31	255	1446	3200	10862	13350	34056	62156	126844	393075	6579414
Net Worth 29	999	0	-39	101	435	3022	3702	13444	20609	50659	109222	340195	8921986

Selected Financial Ratios (Times to 1)

Current Ratio 30	0.9	•	0.9	1.3	1.3	1.9	1.2	1.4	1.3	1.1	1.0	1.3	0.7
Quick Ratio 31	0.7	•	0.8	1.2	1.1	1.6	1.1	1.2	1.0	0.8	0.8	0.9	0.5
Net Sales to Working Capital 32	•	•	15.7	17.7	5.1	14.0	8.8	6.5	50.7	75.5	11.1	•	•
Coverage Ratio 33	1.5	•	4.8	5.9	7.6	12.7	1.4	2.8	1.1	1.3	1.3	1.3	1.3
Total Asset Turnover 34	0.6	•	7.6	2.1	2.6	1.9	1.4	1.4	1.0	1.3	0.8	0.6	0.2
Inventory Turnover 35	18.8	•	135.0	59.3	28.9	26.4	94.8	23.7	43.9	39.9	74.5	24.0	0.9
Receivables Turnover 36	4.2	•	49.6	13.9	9.3	5.7	3.0	4.5	4.2	5.9	3.2	3.9	1.6
Total Liabilities to Net Worth 37	1.3	•	6.2	•	4.3	1.3	3.2	1.6	2.3	2.1	1.8	2.7	0.9
Current Assets to Working Capital 38	•	•	•	4.1	4.3	2.1	7.6	3.6	3.9	16.3	28.6	4.6	•
Current Liabilities to Working Capital 39	•	•	•	3.1	3.3	1.1	6.6	2.6	2.9	15.3	27.6	3.6	•
Working Capital to Net Sales 40	•	•	•	0.1	0.1	0.2	0.1	0.1	0.2	0.0	0.0	0.1	•
Inventory to Working Capital 41	•	•	•	0.1	0.3	0.1	0.0	0.1	0.1	0.9	0.1	0.2	•
Total Receipts to Cash Flow 42	5.1	3.3	3.9	5.1	7.4	8.7	9.4	6.8	5.8	8.2	6.9	7.5	3.8
Cost of Goods to Cash Flow 43	2.1	0.9	1.8	1.9	4.0	5.7	5.7	3.0	3.0	5.0	4.5	2.9	0.2
Cash Flow to Total Debt 44	0.2	1.2	0.5	0.5	0.4	0.4	0.2	0.3	0.3	0.2	0.2	0.1	0.1

Selected Financial Factors (in Percentages)

Debt Ratio 45	57.1	•	157.5	86.1	81.3	57.0	76.3	62.0	70.0	67.6	64.8	73.3	48.7
Return on Total Assets 46	4.1	•	21.9	8.1	4.2	2.9	2.0	4.1	2.5	2.6	5.8	•	3.5
Return on Equity Before Income Taxes 47	3.3	•	•	36.1	8.5	11.3	8.8	•	•	•	1.5	5.1	1.5
Return on Equity After Income Taxes 48	2.2	•	•	33.7	7.5	10.5	6.9	•	•	•	0.7	1.1	0.8
Profit Margin (Before Income Tax) 49	2.2	•	2.3	2.6	1.9	2.0	0.4	2.6	0.2	0.7	1.6	2.3	4.0
Profit Margin (After Income Tax) 50	1.5	•	2.3	2.4	1.7	1.8	•	2.0	•	0.5	0.7	•	2.0

Table II
Corporations with Net Income

ADVERTISING AND RELATED SERVICES

Money Amounts and Size of Assets in Thousands of Dollars

Item Description for Accounting Period 7/09 Through 6/10	Total	Zero Assets	Under 500	500 to 1,000	1,000 to 5,000	5,000 to 10,000	10,000 to 25,000	25,000 to 50,000	50,000 to 100,000	100,000 to 250,000	250,000 to 500,000	500,000 to 2,500,000	2,500,000 and over
Number of Enterprises **1**	26977	3576	20932	748	1265	273	98	32	23	21	0	9	0
Revenues ($ in Thousands)													
Net Sales **2**	49289732	328664	12137506	1268264	8274573	3935454	2546612	2164146	1710710	3492203	0	13431601	0
Interest **3**	842236	0	3588	5154	1852	4634	1490	1208	2493	5490	0	816327	0
Rents **4**	72042	0	0	422	0	12	68	406	103	692	0	70339	0
Royalties **5**	43359	0	0	0	0	0	0	33145	0	43	0	10172	0
Other Portfolio Income **6**	507141	65085	14845	9649	20307	4032	886	801	4835	2139	0	384560	0
Other Receipts **7**	981873	1	56893	64652	105605	39411	3366	50965	12489	44526	0	603965	0
Total Receipts **8**	51736383	393750	12212832	1348141	8402337	3983543	2552422	2250671	1730630	3545093	0	15316964	0
Average Total Receipts **9**	1918	110	583	1802	6642	14592	26045	70333	75245	168814	•	1701885	•
Operating Costs/Operating Income (%)													
Cost of Operations **10**	40.0	26.7	40.7	28.0	51.4	70.9	64.8	42.2	49.4	43.4	•	17.5	•
Salaries and Wages **11**	18.2	6.4	7.1	27.7	11.9	8.5	12.9	14.3	20.0	19.6	•	35.5	•
Taxes Paid **12**	2.3	1.4	1.5	3.7	2.2	1.0	1.4	1.8	1.5	2.1	•	3.9	•
Interest Paid **13**	3.7	0.0	0.3	0.3	0.4	0.1	0.1	0.7	1.2	1.9	•	12.2	•
Depreciation **14**	1.1	8.4	0.4	1.9	0.7	0.4	0.6	1.0	0.9	1.6	•	1.9	•
Amortization and Depletion **15**	0.9	0.1	0.0	0.0	0.1	0.1	0.1	0.4	0.8	1.6	•	2.7	•
Pensions and Other Deferred Comp. **16**	0.6	1.0	0.5	2.2	0.4	0.4	0.4	0.5	0.4	0.4	•	0.8	•
Employee Benefits **17**	1.1	0.4	0.5	2.4	0.7	0.3	0.9	1.6	0.8	1.4	•	2.0	•
Advertising **18**	3.2	1.0	2.3	0.4	7.7	0.7	0.1	18.4	0.4	2.0	•	0.9	•
Other Expenses **19**	21.4	29.2	31.9	21.0	11.1	9.8	8.5	15.3	15.8	19.5	•	26.3	•
Officers' Compensation **20**	4.4	7.5	6.9	8.7	5.9	3.6	4.2	2.5	1.8	1.7	•	2.2	•
Operating Margin **21**	3.1	17.9	7.9	3.5	7.5	4.4	6.0	1.3	7.1	4.6	•	•	•
Operating Margin Before Officers' Comp. **22**	7.5	25.5	14.8	12.1	13.4	7.9	10.2	3.8	8.9	6.4	•	•	•

Selected Average Balance Sheet ($ in Thousands)

Net Receivables 23	443	0	10	183	862	1824	6348	10432	21947	36429	•	865135
Inventories 24	41	0	1	9	153	411	108	1336	982	2877	•	36329
Net Property, Plant and Equipment 25	99	0	13	223	355	229	1194	5983	4303	11135	•	119845
Total Assets 26	1774	0	58	836	2400	6865	14977	36771	67551	182021	•	3675320
Notes and Loans Payable 27	398	0	38	227	450	573	854	9184	10664	38448	•	844748
All Other Liabilities 28	818	0	19	263	1530	2875	11013	13518	40375	73941	•	1639491
Net Worth 29	558	0	1	346	420	3417	3110	14070	16512	69632	•	1191081

Selected Financial Ratios (Times to 1)

Current Ratio 30	1.2	•	1.0	1.7	1.5	2.1	1.1	1.4	1.3	1.1	•	1.0
Quick Ratio 31	0.9	•	1.0	1.6	1.3	1.9	1.1	1.2	1.0	0.9	•	0.7
Net Sales to Working Capital 32	16.7	•	402.5	7.7	11.6	5.0	20.0	11.2	7.3	26.6	•	23.4
Coverage Ratio 33	3.3	2585.5	34.8	29.3	24.7	90.5	48.0	9.1	7.9	4.3	•	1.8
Total Asset Turnover 34	1.0	•	10.0	2.0	2.7	2.1	1.7	1.8	1.1	0.9	•	0.4
Inventory Turnover 35	18.0	•	254.3	53.7	21.9	24.9	155.6	21.4	37.4	25.1	•	7.2
Receivables Turnover 36	3.8	•	56.4	9.7	8.5	6.1	3.7	5.5	4.4	•	•	3.0
Total Liabilities to Net Worth 37	2.2	•	98.6	1.4	4.7	1.0	3.8	1.6	3.1	1.6	•	2.1
Current Assets to Working Capital 38	7.5	•	24.9	2.4	2.9	1.9	9.3	3.5	4.6	10.8	•	22.7
Current Liabilities to Working Capital 39	6.5	•	23.9	1.4	1.9	0.9	8.3	2.5	3.6	9.8	•	21.7
Working Capital to Net Sales 40	0.1	•	0.0	0.1	0.1	0.2	0.1	0.1	0.1	0.0	•	0.0
Inventory to Working Capital 41	0.3	•	0.6	0.1	0.2	0.1	0.1	0.2	0.2	0.5	•	1.0
Total Receipts to Cash Flow 42	3.9	1.7	2.7	4.5	5.9	7.7	8.4	5.4	4.7	4.4	•	3.4
Cost of Goods to Cash Flow 43	1.6	0.5	1.1	1.3	3.0	5.4	5.5	2.3	2.3	1.9	•	0.6
Cash Flow to Total Debt 44	0.4	•	3.7	0.8	0.6	0.5	0.3	0.6	0.3	0.3	•	0.2

Selected Financial Factors (in Percentages)

Debt Ratio 45	68.5	•	99.0	58.6	82.5	50.2	79.2	61.7	75.6	61.7	•	67.6
Return on Total Assets 46	12.6	•	87.6	20.5	25.7	11.6	11.1	11.0	10.5	7.3	•	9.1
Return on Equity Before Income Taxes 47	28.2	•	8478.4	47.8	140.9	23.1	52.3	25.6	37.4	14.7	•	12.8
Return on Equity After Income Taxes 48	24.4	•	8439.6	42.6	137.2	22.0	51.1	23.2	33.9	11.8	•	8.6
Profit Margin (Before Income Tax) 49	8.6	377.7	8.5	9.8	9.0	5.5	6.3	5.3	8.3	6.1	•	10.2
Profit Margin (After Income Tax) 50	7.5	37.4	8.5	8.7	8.8	5.2	6.1	4.8	7.5	5.0	•	6.9

Table I

Corporations with and without Net Income

OTHER PROFESSIONAL, SCIENTIFIC, AND TECHNICAL SERVICES

MONEY AMOUNTS AND SIZE OF ASSETS IN THOUSANDS OF DOLLARS

Item Description for Accounting Period 7/09 Through 6/10	Total	Zero Assets	Under 500	500 to 1,000	1,000 to 5,000	5,000 to 10,000	10,000 to 25,000	25,000 to 50,000	50,000 to 100,000	100,000 to 250,000	250,000 to 500,000	500,000 to 2,500,000	2,500,000 and over
Number of Enterprises 1	92310	15221	69812	3763	2771	338	227	75	50	27	13	13	0
Revenues ($ in Thousands)													
Net Sales 2	85830903	3429549	28600343	6471876	9205223	4090023	6618719	2980860	5042685	4499637	4333479	10558510	0
Interest 3	149129	870	5291	3538	11412	3400	14130	9360	12876	15020	7562	65669	0
Rents 4	38288	182	0	1954	2581	1032	0	0	1583	4576	15498	10881	0
Royalties 5	232417	39	0	7	0	0	0	3441	0	227	53980	174725	0
Other Portfolio Income 6	103499	26172	10724	1436	25954	782	11732	13315	5468	4542	1201	2172	0
Other Receipts 7	1344550	-23795	216454	33118	170300	487963	70878	31966	67213	85763	13959	190732	0
Total Receipts 8	87698786	3433017	28832812	6511929	9415470	4583200	6715459	3038942	5129825	4609765	4425679	11002689	0
Average Total Receipts 9	950	226	413	1731	3398	13560	29584	40519	102596	170732	340437	846361	•
Operating Costs/Operating Income (%)													
Cost of Operations 10	29.3	7.8	20.5	25.6	42.2	50.1	62.3	34.6	43.1	27.1	27.4	16.2	•
Salaries and Wages 11	19.8	9.5	20.6	27.2	16.8	17.3	13.0	25.6	12.9	25.4	15.4	25.5	•
Taxes Paid 12	3.0	1.8	3.6	3.6	2.5	2.5	2.3	3.2	2.0	2.4	2.3	3.2	•
Interest Paid 13	1.4	0.2	0.7	0.5	0.6	0.6	0.9	1.8	1.5	2.2	1.9	5.3	•
Depreciation 14	1.6	1.6	1.3	0.8	1.3	1.2	1.2	2.1	1.6	4.0	1.7	2.6	•
Amortization and Depletion 15	0.8	0.2	0.3	0.2	0.4	0.3	0.5	1.3	0.8	1.1	1.7	2.6	•
Pensions and Other Deferred Comp. 16	0.9	2.2	1.0	0.4	0.9	0.5	0.5	0.7	0.6	0.4	0.7	1.7	•
Employee Benefits 17	1.6	0.6	1.2	1.1	1.4	5.1	1.2	2.4	1.4	1.6	2.5	2.4	•
Advertising 18	0.7	0.5	0.9	0.4	0.9	0.7	0.4	0.5	0.7	1.0	1.2	0.5	•
Other Expenses 19	30.7	66.2	30.0	26.7	19.7	27.9	19.1	23.7	32.9	32.4	44.8	36.3	•
Officers' Compensation 20	6.6	8.8	10.8	8.4	11.0	3.7	2.1	2.3	1.4	2.1	1.1	1.1	•
Operating Margin 21	3.4	0.7	9.2	5.1	2.3	•	•	1.7	1.0	0.5	•	2.7	•
Operating Margin Before Officers' Comp. 22	10.0	9.4	20.0	13.5	13.3	•	•	4.0	2.4	2.6	0.4	3.8	•

Selected Average Balance Sheet ($ in Thousands)

Net Receivables 23	87	0	7	112	398	2289	3958	7504	18832	25107	54513	110947	•
Inventories 24	12	0	3	22	34	465	578	744	856	963		6532	•
Net Property, Plant and Equipment 25	68	0	21	120	311	707	2120	3084	7843	22148	20009	96558	•
Total Assets 26	642	0	86	630	1906	7216	16007	37017	72866	171418	345286	1840357	•
Notes and Loans Payable 27	279	0	54	281	606	2555	4680	12153	18069	77912	99847	933032	•
All Other Liabilities 28	206	0	29	106	654	2203	5902	13453	25575	52423	124328	566956	•
Net Worth 29	157	0	4	244	646	2458	5425	11411	29222	41083	121111	340370	•

Selected Financial Ratios (Times to 1)

Current Ratio 30	1.4	•	1.1	2.9	1.7	1.9	1.4	1.6	1.3	0.9	1.6	1.4	•
Quick Ratio 31	1.1	•	0.9	2.6	1.6	1.5	1.1	1.3	1.1	0.6	1.2	0.8	•
Net Sales to Working Capital 32	13.2	•	95.9	9.1	7.2	6.0	11.5	5.6	11.0	•	5.6	8.0	•
Coverage Ratio 33	4.9	4.1	16.3	12.4	8.3	4.5	•	3.1	2.8	2.4	1.7	2.3	•
Total Asset Turnover 34	1.4	•	4.7	2.7	1.7	1.7	1.8	1.1	1.4	1.0	1.0	0.4	•
Inventory Turnover 35	22.0	•	25.7	19.9	41.2	13.0	31.4	18.5	50.8	4.9	94.8	20.1	•
Receivables Turnover 36	10.5	•	63.9	13.9	8.9	5.2	7.3	4.8	5.3	6.6	•	4.4	•
Total Liabilities to Net Worth 37	3.1	•	19.7	1.6	1.9	1.9	2.0	2.2	1.5	3.2	1.9	4.4	•
Current Assets to Working Capital 38	3.3	•	8.6	1.5	2.3	2.2	3.4	2.7	4.1	•	2.7	3.4	•
Current Liabilities to Working Capital 39	2.3	•	7.6	0.5	1.3	1.2	2.4	1.7	3.1	•	1.7	2.4	•
Working Capital to Net Sales 40	0.1	•	0.0	0.1	0.1	0.2	0.1	0.2	0.1	•	0.2	0.1	•
Inventory to Working Capital 41	0.2	•	0.8	0.1	0.1	0.3	0.2	0.1	0.1	•	0.0	0.1	•
Total Receipts to Cash Flow 42	3.2	1.6	3.0	4.0	5.1	4.1	7.0	4.1	3.0	3.2	2.3	2.5	•
Cost of Goods to Cash Flow 43	0.9	0.1	0.6	1.0	2.2	2.1	4.4	1.4	1.3	0.9	0.6	0.4	•
Cash Flow to Total Debt 44	0.6	•	1.6	1.1	0.5	0.6	0.4	0.4	0.8	0.4	0.7	0.2	•

Selected Financial Factors (in Percentages)

Debt Ratio 45	75.5	•	95.2	61.3	65.9	66.1	66.1	69.2	59.9	76.0	64.9	81.5	•
Return on Total Assets 46	10.2	•	50.4	16.8	9.2	4.5	•	6.0	5.9	5.0	3.1	5.4	•
Return on Equity Before Income Taxes 47	33.1	•	980.3	40.0	23.8	10.4	•	13.2	9.4	12.0	3.8	16.6	•
Return on Equity After Income Taxes 48	30.3	•	971.8	38.6	22.7	8.8	•	9.2	6.3	8.8	0.2	13.5	•
Profit Margin (Before Income Tax) 49	5.6	0.8	10.0	5.7	4.6	2.1	3.8	2.7	3.0	1.4	6.9		•
Profit Margin (After Income Tax) 50	5.1	0.6	9.9	5.5	4.4	1.8	2.7	1.8	2.2	0.1	5.7		•

OTHER PROFESSIONAL, SCIENTIFIC, AND TECHNICAL SERVICES

Table II

Corporations with Net Income

MONEY AMOUNTS AND SIZE OF ASSETS IN THOUSANDS OF DOLLARS

Item Description for Accounting Period 7/09 Through 6/10	Total	Zero Assets	Under 500	500 to 1,000	1,000 to 5,000	5,000 to 10,000	10,000 to 25,000	25,000 to 50,000	50,000 to 100,000	100,000 to 250,000	250,000 to 500,000	500,000 to 2,500,000	2,500,000 and over
Number of Enterprises **1**	58950	10251	44484	2194	1607	•	116	38	31	17	9	•	0
Revenues ($ in Thousands)													
Net Sales **2**	63712196	1181490	22127672	5390196	6694112	•	3521279	1886493	3469090	3390239	3724844	•	0
Interest **3**	108913	267	2048	1660	6498	•	5668	5005	8155	5119	6816	•	0
Rents **4**	32939	182	0	1954	2538	•	0	0	1547	226	15498	•	0
Royalties **5**	205848	0	0	7	0	•	0	3441	0	223	27452	•	0
Other Portfolio Income **6**	94047	26124	8131	586	25361	•	11684	10506	3776	4303	1201	•	0
Other Receipts **7**	1225836	38824	211190	32432	131908	•	72040	15876	44471	70503	11631	•	0
Total Receipts **8**	65379779	1246887	22349041	5426835	6760417	•	3610671	1921321	3527039	3470613	3787442	•	0
Average Total Receipts **9**	1109	122	502	2473	4207	•	31126	50561	113775	204154	420827	•	•
Operating Costs/Operating Income (%)													
Cost of Operations **10**	25.0	18.6	17.1	20.3	43.4	•	57.5	29.0	34.3	15.0	18.8	•	•
Salaries and Wages **11**	19.9	15.6	19.9	28.1	14.8	•	13.7	27.3	10.5	28.8	13.9	•	•
Taxes Paid **12**	3.0	3.5	3.3	3.5	2.3	•	2.3	3.2	1.9	2.6	2.5	•	•
Interest Paid **13**	1.5	0.4	0.6	0.2	0.4	•	0.7	0.8	1.3	2.0	2.0	•	•
Depreciation **14**	1.4	0.9	1.0	0.5	1.2	•	1.1	1.3	1.5	3.7	1.4	•	•
Amortization and Depletion **15**	0.8	0.2	0.3	0.0	0.4	•	0.1	1.2	0.6	1.0	1.5	•	•
Pensions and Other Deferred Comp. **16**	0.8	0.2	1.1	0.4	0.5	•	0.4	0.8	0.8	0.4	0.8	•	•
Employee Benefits **17**	1.6	1.3	1.0	1.2	1.2	•	1.2	2.3	1.4	1.7	2.7	•	•
Advertising **18**	0.7	1.1	0.9	0.3	0.6	•	0.2	0.3	1.0	1.2	0.7	•	•
Other Expenses **19**	30.1	27.4	29.7	26.9	16.4	•	16.1	21.3	40.0	37.1	50.2	•	•
Officers' Compensation **20**	6.6	16.5	11.0	8.7	9.3	•	2.7	2.3	1.4	1.7	0.8	•	•
Operating Margin **21**	8.6	14.4	14.0	9.9	9.5	•	4.0	10.1	5.4	4.7	4.8	•	•
Operating Margin Before Officers' Comp. **22**	15.2	30.8	25.1	18.6	18.8	•	6.7	12.4	6.8	6.4	5.6	•	•

Selected Average Balance Sheet ($ in Thousands)

Item		•	•	•	•	•	•	•	•	•	•	•
Net Receivables	23	88	0	8	148	252	•	5188	9399	16513	25999	71345	•
Inventories	24	10	0	4	25	34	•	849	792	239	530	1391	•
Net Property, Plant and Equipment	25	70	0	22	91	377	•	1941	2421	5515	19661	23328	•
Total Assets	26	743	0	100	639	1952	•	16057	38271	71945	172524	365309	•
Notes and Loans Payable	27	315	0	51	137	492	•	4076	6212	17302	63081	89130	•
All Other Liabilities	28	220	0	32	89	693	•	5950	14931	24241	55964	136712	•
Net Worth	29	207	0	17	413	767	•	6030	17128	30401	53479	139466	•

Selected Financial Ratios (Times to 1)

Item		•	•	•	•	•	•	•	•	•	•	•	•
Current Ratio	30	1.6	•	1.3	5.3	1.6	•	1.6	1.9	1.4	1.1	1.4	•
Quick Ratio	31	1.2	•	1.1	5.0	1.3	•	1.3	1.6	1.1	0.9	1.2	•
Net Sales to Working Capital	32	11.8	•	44.5	8.5	10.6	•	7.6	4.3	10.8	24.6	9.0	•
Coverage Ratio	33	8.5	51.0	26.0	43.3	29.9	•	10.0	17.0	6.3	4.5	4.2	•
Total Asset Turnover	34	1.5	•	5.0	3.8	2.1	•	1.9	1.3	1.6	1.2	1.1	•
Inventory Turnover	35	27.3	•	19.7	20.0	52.4	•	20.6	18.2	160.8	56.3	56.0	•
Receivables Turnover	36	12.6	•	73.8	16.7	13.4	•	5.8	5.0	7.9	7.1	•	•
Total Liabilities to Net Worth	37	2.6	•	4.8	0.5	1.5	•	1.7	1.2	1.4	2.2	1.6	•
Current Assets to Working Capital	38	2.7	•	4.1	1.2	2.7	•	2.6	2.1	3.3	7.8	3.4	•
Current Liabilities to Working Capital	39	1.7	•	3.1	0.2	1.7	•	1.6	1.1	2.3	6.8	2.4	•
Working Capital to Net Sales	40	0.1	•	0.0	0.1	0.1	•	0.1	0.2	0.1	0.0	0.1	•
Inventory to Working Capital	41	0.1	•	0.4	0.0	0.1	•	0.2	0.1	0.0	0.1	0.0	•
Total Receipts to Cash Flow	42	2.7	2.5	2.6	3.4	4.3	•	5.0	3.3	2.2	2.5	1.8	•
Cost of Goods to Cash Flow	43	0.7	0.5	0.4	0.7	1.9	•	2.9	1.0	0.8	0.4	0.3	•
Cash Flow to Total Debt	44	0.7	•	2.3	3.2	0.8	•	0.6	0.7	1.2	0.7	1.0	•

Selected Financial Factors (in Percentages)

Item		•	•	•	•	•	•	•	•	•	•	•	•
Debt Ratio	45	72.1	•	82.8	35.4	60.7	•	62.4	55.2	57.7	69.0	61.8	•
Return on Total Assets	46	18.5	•	78.2	41.6	26.2	•	13.6	16.8	13.1	10.4	9.6	•
Return on Equity Before Income Taxes	47	58.6	•	437.4	62.9	64.6	•	32.6	35.3	26.0	26.3	19.2	•
Return on Equity After Income Taxes	48	55.3	•	434.2	61.5	63.0	•	28.6	30.1	21.3	22.4	14.7	•
Profit Margin (Before Income Tax)	49	11.2	19.9	15.0	10.6	12.1	•	6.5	12.2	7.1	7.0	6.5	•
Profit Margin (After Income Tax)	50	10.6	19.4	14.9	10.3	11.8	•	5.7	10.4	5.8	6.0	5.0	•

Table I

Corporations with and without Net Income

OFFICES OF BANK HOLDING COMPANIES

MONEY AMOUNTS AND SIZE OF ASSETS IN THOUSANDS OF DOLLARS

Item Description for Accounting Period 7/09 Through 6/10	Total	Zero Assets	Under 500	500 to 1,000	1,000 to 5,000	5,000 to 10,000	10,000 to 25,000	25,000 to 50,000	50,000 to 100,000	100,000 to 250,000	250,000 to 500,000	500,000 to 2,500,000	2,500,000 and over
Number of Enterprises **1**	4948	43	5	3	101	24	170	509	867	1495	850	712	170
Revenues ($ in Thousands)													
Net Sales **2**	213373855	243045	5756	43937	162950	18693	51616	278323	1200517	3763035	3680025	8283453	195642505
Interest **3**	505373179	541546	0	0	106770	83627	197023	456586	2033791	6588453	9407687	25931975	460025721
Rents **4**	17508703	3694	9	0	47	71	1171	1297	9636	23083	43014	209667	17217015
Royalties **5**	293159	0	0	0	0	0	8	20	149	465	81	4736	287699
Other Portfolio Income **6**	33065698	90814	151	1549	3161	3400	7856	52913	175090	721701	821384	2082401	29105278
Other Receipts **7**	118055291	42124	17372	16481	301270	185416	163467	540478	1648079	4022641	4470608	7163396	99483958
Total Receipts **8**	887669885	921223	23288	61967	574198	291207	421141	1329617	5067262	15119378	18422799	43675628	801762176
Average Total Receipts **9**	179400	21424	4658	20656	5685	12134	2477	2612	5845	10113	21674	61342	4716248
Operating Costs/Operating Income (%)													
Cost of Operations **10**	2.8	•	•	•	•	•	•	•	0.1	0.0	0.0	0.1	3.0
Salaries and Wages **11**	59.5	55.2	48.6	15.8	25.8	93.2	94.6	57.6	55.6	57.3	75.8	87.5	58.1
Taxes Paid **12**	7.0	10.0	8.0	2.6	6.1	5.8	14.1	12.8	10.6	10.6	12.9	13.5	6.5
Interest Paid **13**	98.1	160.4	149.5	107.9	83.6	402.8	224.0	118.4	118.3	110.7	142.1	151.4	94.5
Depreciation **14**	14.5	6.8	11.6	2.3	4.4	18.4	17.7	9.7	12.4	11.0	13.4	16.1	14.6
Amortization and Depletion **15**	5.0	0.1	0.2	0.8	0.4	0.3	3.6	1.1	2.0	1.4	1.7	2.8	5.3
Pensions and Other Deferred Comp. **16**	5.5	2.0	•	0.0	0.8	0.4	2.9	3.3	2.8	3.6	4.4	4.9	5.6
Employee Benefits **17**	6.6	4.4	9.4	1.9	4.7	13.9	23.2	13.4	10.2	10.5	11.5	11.0	6.2
Advertising **18**	3.7	1.4	0.6	1.2	1.5	15.3	4.6	3.8	3.4	3.8	3.8	4.7	3.7
Other Expenses **19**	230.7	677.8	721.1	369.7	406.2	2930.2	1485.3	296.5	492.3	154.8	217.7	227.6	229.5
Officers' Compensation **20**	3.6	9.7	14.2	1.5	9.7	22.2	56.9	45.7	30.7	28.5	26.9	19.5	1.7
Operating Margin **21**	•	•	•	•	•	•	•	•	•	•	•	•	•
Operating Margin Before Officers' Comp. **22**	•	•	•	•	•	•	•	•	•	•	•	•	•

Selected Average Balance Sheet ($ in Thousands)

Net Receivables 23	1195465	0	20	371	0	8891	21963	45101	102550	217326	583059	30059735
Inventories 24	7	0	0	0	0	0	0	0	1	0	3	191
Net Property, Plant and Equipment 25	23456	0	41	567	182	278	593	1411	3532	7165	19208	525753
Total Assets 26	3567430	0	140	2720	8042	18394	37855	74577	164186	351155	992395	95962337
Notes and Loans Payable 27	790544	0	1122	1449	0	1524	1067	3140	8434	20611	68963	22521432
All Other Liabilities 28	2171055	0	55	5390	54987	15324	33155	64631	141922	304160	841892	56440262
Net Worth 29	605831	0	-1037	-4119	-46945	1547	3632	6805	13830	26383	81540	17000643

Selected Financial Ratios (Times to 1)

Current Ratio 30	0.9	•	1.6	0.4	0.3	1.0	1.0	1.0	1.0	1.0	0.9	0.9
Quick Ratio 31	0.8	•	1.5	0.4	0.0	0.9	1.0	1.0	0.9	0.9	0.9	0.8
Net Sales to Working Capital 32	•	•	37.9	•	•	3.3	0.6	2.1	•	•	•	•
Coverage Ratio 33	0.8	•	•	0.6	0.2	•	1.0	•	1.0	0.8	0.8	0.8
Total Asset Turnover 34	0.0	•	8.2	16.1	•	0.0	0.0	1.0	0.0	0.0	0.0	0.0
Inventory Turnover 35	161.7	•	•	•	•	5.6	•	•	5.1	•	2.5	181.6
Receivables Turnover 36	0.0	•	115.1	8.2	•	•	•	•	0.0	•	•	0.0
Total Liabilities to Net Worth 37	4.9	•	•	•	•	10.9	9.4	10.0	10.9	12.3	11.2	4.6
Current Assets to Working Capital 38	•	•	2.8	•	•	154.6	34.9	99.0	•	•	•	•
Current Liabilities to Working Capital 39	•	•	1.8	•	•	153.6	33.9	98.0	•	•	•	•
Working Capital to Net Sales 40	•	•	0.0	•	•	0.3	1.7	0.5	•	•	•	•
Inventory to Working Capital 41	•	•	0.0	•	•	0.0	0.0	0.5	•	•	•	•
Total Receipts to Cash Flow 42	0.5	•	•	0.8	0.2	0.5	1.9	0.7	0.7	0.7	0.5	•
Cost of Goods to Cash Flow 43	0.0	•	•	•	•	0.0	0.0	0.0	0.0	0.0	0.0	•
Cash Flow to Total Debt 44	0.0	•	•	0.3	0.1	0.0	0.0	0.0	0.0	0.0	0.0	•

Selected Financial Factors (in Percentages)

Debt Ratio 45	83.0	•	841.9	251.4	683.8	91.6	90.4	90.9	91.6	92.5	91.8	82.3
Return on Total Assets 46	0.9	•	•	•	0.3	•	•	•	1.7	1.5	1.5	0.9
Return on Equity Before Income Taxes 47	•	•	622.9	3040.8	201.0	•	32.3	75.5	201.0	•	•	•
Return on Equity After Income Taxes 48	•	•	622.9	3040.8	201.0	•	32.3	75.5	201.0	•	•	•
Profit Margin (Before Income Tax) 49	•	•	•	•	•	•	•	•	•	•	•	•
Profit Margin (After Income Tax) 50	•	•	•	•	•	•	•	•	•	•	•	•

Table II

Corporations with Net Income

OFFICES OF BANK HOLDING COMPANIES

MONEY AMOUNTS AND SIZE OF ASSETS IN THOUSANDS OF DOLLARS

Item Description for Accounting Period 7/09 Through 6/10	Total	Zero Assets	Under 500	500 to 1,000	1,000 to 5,000	5,000 to 10,000	10,000 to 25,000	25,000 to 50,000	50,000 to 100,000	100,000 to 250,000	250,000 to 500,000	500,000 to 2,500,000	2,500,000 and over
Number of Enterprises **1**	3238	22	0	0	70	9	103	325	613	1025	531	449	91
Revenues ($ in Thousands)													
Net Sales **2**	92686055	10987	0	0	151502	0	32686	190245	781963	2973347	2598168	5939551	80007606
Interest **3**	168882624	60356	0	0	1153	0	68249	202681	907483	3998568	5336472	14953429	143354234
Rents **4**	7221919	170	0	0	0	0	211	441	6878	14468	24312	120235	7055204
Royalties **5**	2087	0	0	0	0	0	0	6	148	313	80	884	656
Other Portfolio Income **6**	12930742	4897	0	0	331	2337	3855	33990	129540	501854	577796	1319421	10356717
Other Receipts **7**	35126908	4592	0	0	1397	0	18719	271988	872678	2677003	2396994	4681411	24202128
Total Receipts **8**	316850335	81002	0	0	154383	2337	123720	699351	2698690	10165553	10933822	27014931	264976545
Average Total Receipts **9**	97854	3682	•	•	2205	260	1201	2152	4402	9918	20591	60167	2911830
Operating Costs/Operating Income (%)													
Cost of Operations **10**	0.7	•	•	•	•	•	•	•	0.2	0.0	0.0	0.0	0.8
Salaries and Wages **11**	47.9	99.8	•	•	5.8	•	47.4	44.1	45.3	47.5	65.1	73.8	45.5
Taxes Paid **12**	7.0	18.4	•	•	4.6	•	10.5	10.8	9.8	9.5	11.8	12.4	6.3
Interest Paid **13**	59.0	126.2	•	•	0.8	•	96.8	90.5	85.6	87.7	113.0	115.6	51.7
Depreciation **14**	14.0	15.1	•	•	2.0	•	6.8	6.7	7.8	9.4	11.5	13.7	14.4
Amortization and Depletion **15**	2.8	0.5	•	•	•	•	0.3	0.7	0.9	1.0	1.6	2.7	2.9
Pensions and Other Deferred Comp. **16**	5.6	6.5	•	•	•	•	2.3	3.5	3.3	3.6	4.3	5.0	5.8
Employee Benefits **17**	5.7	16.8	•	•	3.4	•	13.9	12.7	10.5	9.4	10.6	10.0	5.0
Advertising **18**	3.9	4.0	•	•	0.4	•	2.6	3.0	3.1	3.4	3.6	4.2	4.0
Other Expenses **19**	143.2	204.8	•	•	18.4	•	79.7	83.2	82.9	83.3	100.1	122.8	149.4
Officers' Compensation **20**	5.6	28.7	•	•	10.1	•	65.0	43.4	32.6	26.4	24.7	18.8	2.9
Operating Margin **21**	•	•	•	•	54.5	•	•	•	•	•	•	•	•
Operating Margin Before Officers' Comp. **22**	•	•	•	•	64.6	•	•	•	•	•	•	•	•

Selected Average Balance Sheet ($ in Thousands)

Line Item	1	2	3	4	5	6	7	8	9	10	11
Net Receivables 23	761314	504	•	0	10418	23108	44636	102611	215095	574197	21449989
Inventories 24	7	0	0	0	0	0	0	1	0	5	226
Net Property, Plant and Equipment 25	15535	438	•	0	201	464	1264	3321	6760	18976	371549
Total Assets 26	1961659	3014	9453	9453	19922	38231	74078	164341	348819	971384	60459843
Notes and Loans Payable 27	199964	340	•	0	639	641	2485	7317	18168	61578	6602945
All Other Liabilities 28	1450898	1070	•	0	15889	32375	63512	140385	297373	818512	43709129
Net Worth 29	310797	1604	9453	9453	3394	5216	8081	16639	33279	91295	10147768

Selected Financial Ratios (Times to 1)

Line Item	1	2	3	4	5	6	7	8	9	10	11
Current Ratio 30	0.9	1.9	•	1.0	1.0	1.0	1.0	1.0	1.0	0.9	0.8
Quick Ratio 31	0.8	1.8	•	0.9	1.0	1.0	1.0	1.0	0.9	0.9	0.8
Net Sales to Working Capital 32	•	2.2	•	0.5	0.4	1.0	1.9	•	1.5	•	1.8
Coverage Ratio 33	1.7	68.1	2.6	1.5	1.6	1.6	1.6	1.5	1.5	•	1.8
Total Asset Turnover 34	0.0	0.7	•	0.0	0.0	0.0	0.0	0.0	0.0	0.0	0.0
Inventory Turnover 35	27.5	•	•	•	•	5.6	0.5	5.1	0.4	•	32.1
Receivables Turnover 36	0.0	8.1	•	0.0	0.0	0.0	0.0	0.0	0.0	0.0	0.0
Total Liabilities to Net Worth 37	5.3	0.9	•	4.9	6.3	8.2	8.9	9.5	9.6	9.6	5.0
Current Assets to Working Capital 38	•	2.1	•	1.0	26.4	21.4	49.6	94.8	•	•	•
Current Liabilities to Working Capital 39	•	1.1	•	•	25.4	20.4	48.6	93.8	•	•	•
Working Capital to Net Sales 40	•	0.4	•	•	2.0	2.7	1.0	0.5	•	•	•
Inventory to Working Capital 41	•	•	•	•	•	•	0.0	0.0	0.0	0.0	•
Total Receipts to Cash Flow 42	0.6	1.4	0.3	0.8	0.7	0.7	0.7	0.6	0.6	0.5	0.6
Cost of Goods to Cash Flow 43	0.0	•	•	•	0.0	0.0	0.0	0.0	0.0	0.0	0.0
Cash Flow to Total Debt 44	0.0	1.1	•	0.0	0.0	0.0	0.0	0.0	0.0	0.0	0.0

Selected Financial Factors (in Percentages)

Line Item	1	2	3	4	5	6	7	8	9	10	11
Debt Ratio 45	84.2	46.8	•	83.0	86.4	89.1	89.9	90.5	90.6	•	83.2
Return on Total Assets 46	1.5	41.0	2.7	2.3	2.3	2.3	2.4	2.4	2.4	•	1.3
Return on Equity Before Income Taxes 47	4.0	75.9	2.7	4.3	6.4	7.9	8.5	8.8	9.1	•	3.6
Return on Equity After Income Taxes 48	2.7	75.9	2.7	3.8	5.7	7.0	7.3	7.0	6.9	•	2.4
Profit Margin (Before Income Tax) 49	43.4	204.6	56.2	46.4	57.0	50.3	48.9	59.6	62.9	•	41.1
Profit Margin (After Income Tax) 50	29.8	136.0	56.2	40.4	51.0	44.5	41.6	47.8	47.8	•	27.2

Table I

Corporations with and without Net Income

OFFICES OF OTHER HOLDING COMPANIES

MONEY AMOUNTS AND SIZE OF ASSETS IN THOUSANDS OF DOLLARS

Item Description for Accounting Period 7/09 Through 6/10		Total	Zero Assets	Under 500	500 to 1,000	1,000 to 5,000	5,000 to 10,000	10,000 to 25,000	25,000 to 50,000	50,000 to 100,000	100,000 to 250,000	250,000 to 500,000	500,000 to 2,500,000	2,500,000 and over
Number of Enterprises	1	42781	9187	22639	2430	4863	1267	1163	504	310	232	95	77	15
Revenues ($ in Thousands)														
Net Sales	2	1939915	3615	1323	0	14035	143682	463952	49766	24547	303135	50572	72456	812834
Interest	3	3268583	559159	19329	13327	81315	36233	79685	79008	165852	166153	381456	1205179	481887
Rents	4	539205	368388	107	1433	23727	28593	11267	5372	28731	12719	18845	40024	0
Royalties	5	118089	15125	1312	9	3562	7921	516	10095	10668	29426	8790	13881	16785
Other Portfolio Income	6	5732778	848526	163380	109732	295792	79640	224647	209598	242003	253368	488617	1236412	1581061
Other Receipts	7	14125301	600787	128101	308721	761372	543966	1024783	347030	1173716	1480019	478556	3766630	3511618
Total Receipts	8	25723871	2395600	313552	433222	1179803	840035	1804850	700869	1645517	2244820	1426836	6334582	6404185
Average Total Receipts	9	601	261	14	178	243	663	1552	1391	5308	9676	15019	82267	426946
Operating Costs/Operating Income (%)														
Cost of Operations	10	31.6	47.6	•	•	1.4	99.0	47.5	•	7.6	38.5	46.6	18.7	11.4
Salaries and Wages	11	57.5	243.4	548.7	•	957.4	12.2	45.0	62.4	1013.9	70.0	119.9	103.4	13.4
Taxes Paid	12	42.3	1121.6	832.2	•	251.6	12.3	13.4	67.4	191.9	28.1	43.4	123.0	45.6
Interest Paid	13	226.9	10453.7	2315.9	•	294.4	23.3	27.0	314.9	935.6	110.5	864.2	1929.7	151.8
Depreciation	14	10.3	427.3	42.4	•	53.4	3.5	6.2	21.0	86.5	6.4	28.5	34.4	6.2
Amortization and Depletion	15	38.2	2501.5	33.3	•	63.7	2.0	17.2	26.5	288.8	14.1	77.2	534.2	0.7
Pensions and Other Deferred Comp.	16	4.0	•	117.0	•	22.0	1.5	1.2	4.6	14.3	0.9	4.5	5.2	6.3
Employee Benefits	17	7.6	55.9	1690.1	•	224.9	2.7	2.4	5.3	89.1	2.4	9.8	11.0	3.9
Advertising	18	1.3	•	•	•	•	0.9	0.3	3.9	1.6	2.5	1.4	0.9	1.4
Other Expenses	19	902.5	28531.4	•	•	4239.2	276.4	217.2	1484.7	4473.0	441.9	4369.6	6951.0	81.7
Officers' Compensation	20	21.7	17.3	998.0	•	498.9	14.3	14.0	43.6	115.3	7.1	33.6	129.8	7.6
Operating Margin	21	•	•	•	•	•	•	•	•	•	•	•	•	•
Operating Margin Before Officers' Comp.	22	•	•	•	•	•	•	•	•	•	•	•	•	•

Selected Average Balance Sheet ($ in Thousands)

Item	1	2	3	4	5	6	7	8	9	10	11	12	13
Net Receivables 23	518	0	7	25	90	154	555	1337	3254	6123	17442	24575	934785
Inventories 24	6	0	0	0	2	4	12	50	61	419	224	290	2192
Net Property, Plant and Equipment 25	124	0	0	6	73	167	296	929	2189	2668	12029	17190	10483
Total Assets 26	7699	0	101	685	2169	7086	16095	34839	70824	150440	342257	1085094	6447021
Notes and Loans Payable 27	1790	0	52	171	467	1011	2421	6547	10580	43112	75132	269359	1610277
All Other Liabilities 28	1069	0	13	336	249	657	2426	3654	14861	21470	53469	116254	951848
Net Worth 29	4841	0	36	178	1452	5417	11248	24638	45383	85859	213656	699481	3884896

Selected Financial Ratios (Times to 1)

Item	1	2	3	4	5	6	7	8	9	10	11	12	13
Current Ratio 30	1.8	•	2.0	7.1	2.9	3.8	1.6	2.1	1.7	1.7	2.7	1.7	1.6
Quick Ratio 31	1.4	•	1.0	4.1	2.0	1.6	1.1	1.2	1.1	1.1	2.3	0.9	1.5
Net Sales to Working Capital 32	0.1	•	0.0	•	0.0	0.1	0.3	0.0	0.0	0.1	0.0	0.0	0.1
Coverage Ratio 33	2.1	•	•	•	6.8	7.1	0.9	•	0.4	1.2	•	0.7	7.9
Total Asset Turnover 34	0.0	•	0.0	•	0.0	0.0	0.0	0.0	0.0	0.0	0.0	0.0	0.0
Inventory Turnover 35	2.5	•	•	•	0.0	31.8	15.5	•	0.1	1.2	1.1	0.6	2.8
Receivables Turnover 36	0.1	•	0.0	•	0.0	•	0.7	0.1	0.6	0.2	0.0	0.0	0.1
Total Liabilities to Net Worth 37	0.6	•	1.8	2.9	0.5	0.3	0.4	0.4	0.6	0.8	0.6	0.6	0.7
Current Assets to Working Capital 38	2.2	•	2.0	1.2	1.5	1.4	2.6	1.9	2.4	2.3	1.6	2.4	2.6
Current Liabilities to Working Capital 39	1.2	•	1.0	0.2	0.5	0.4	1.6	0.9	1.4	1.3	0.6	1.4	1.6
Working Capital to Net Sales 40	15.1	•	632.6	•	137.8	11.1	3.1	36.8	75.6	9.0	70.4	67.0	10.1
Inventory to Working Capital 41	0.0	•	•	•	0.0	0.0	0.0	0.0	0.0	0.1	0.0	0.0	0.0
Total Receipts to Cash Flow 42	0.2	•	0.0	•	0.0	0.3	0.5	0.2	0.0	0.2	0.5	0.0	0.2
Cost of Goods to Cash Flow 43	0.1	•	•	•	0.0	0.3	0.2	•	0.0	0.1	0.2	0.0	0.0
Cash Flow to Total Debt 44	0.1	•	0.1	0.3	0.2	0.2	0.2	0.1	0.1	0.1	0.0	0.1	0.1

Selected Financial Factors (in Percentages)

Item	1	2	3	4	5	6	7	8	9	10	11	12	13
Debt Ratio 45	37.1	•	64.6	74.1	33.0	23.5	30.1	29.3	35.9	42.9	37.6	35.5	39.7
Return on Total Assets 46	2.9	•	•	•	2.7	2.7	0.6	•	0.4	1.2	•	1.2	10.1
Return on Equity Before Income Taxes 47	2.4	•	•	•	3.4	3.0	•	•	•	0.3	•	•	14.6
Return on Equity After Income Taxes 48	•	•	•	•	1.9	2.3	•	•	•	•	•	•	9.7
Profit Margin (Before Income Tax) 49	259.5	•	•	1709.5	933.8	143.0	•	•	22.4	•	•	•	1047.5
Profit Margin (After Income Tax) 50	•	•	•	•	111.5	•	•	•	•	•	•	•	694.6

Table II
Corporations with Net Income

OFFICES OF OTHER HOLDING COMPANIES

MONEY AMOUNTS AND SIZE OF ASSETS IN THOUSANDS OF DOLLARS

Item Description for Accounting Period 7/09 Through 6/10	Total	Zero Assets	Under 500	500 to 1000	1,000 to 5,000	5,000 to 10,000	10,000 to 25,000	25,000 to 50,000	50,000 to 100,000	100,000 to 250,000	250,000 to 500,000	500,000 to 2,500,000	2,500,000 and over
Number of Enterprises 1	10344	1836	4019	948	2207	426	442	168	106	91	44	45	12
Revenues ($ in Thousands)													
Net Sales 2	1601484	8	1245	0	8795	140266	440643	1638	4735	135400	35847	20074	812834
Interest 3	2123754	142401	12617	6378	38536	16422	52805	34607	76349	103141	258313	902098	480089
Rents 4	92481	12518	0	129	22437	22415	8439	3185	4440	364	18402	153	0
Royalties 5	83400	8507	1249	0	1973	7647	516	9910	4538	23312	0	8965	16785
Other Portfolio Income 6	4696993	263434	139834	76091	222532	64855	188518	189405	185569	110354	466933	1208409	1581061
Other Receipts 7	15373800	807070	270881	303099	772999	598095	1090884	635417	1151383	1573179	871937	3787228	3511618
Total Receipts 8	23971912	1233938	425826	385697	1067272	849700	1781805	874162	1427014	1945750	1651432	5926927	6402387
Average Total Receipts 9	2317	672	106	407	484	1995	4031	5203	13462	21382	37533	131709	533532
Operating Costs/Operating Income (%)													
Cost of Operations 10	35.0	•	•	•	1.0	101.4	48.7	•	1.6	78.0	•	21.8	11.4
Salaries and Wages 11	26.0	1087.5	174.8	•	107.4	6.5	29.7	99.7	96.6	67.4	109.1	94.9	13.4
Taxes Paid 12	40.1	342475.0	456.0	•	275.9	8.7	7.2	988.3	633.9	38.3	32.0	289.8	45.6
Interest Paid 13	154.3	724725.0	600.6	•	143.5	3.5	7.5	4413.9	1575.1	72.5	516.3	3465.9	151.1
Depreciation 14	6.7	21875.0	0.1	•	43.2	0.5	3.0	84.6	32.4	8.5	33.6	56.4	6.2
Amortization and Depletion 15	28.9	347575.0	33.0	•	25.7	1.0	3.9	446.9	221.9	2.2	19.0	1894.5	0.7
Pensions and Other Deferred Comp. 16	3.8	•	124.3	•	5.9	0.0	0.8	10.2	58.4	0.1	0.5	5.8	6.3
Employee Benefits 17	2.5	6350.0	65.6	•	4.4	0.6	0.0	20.6	15.1	0.9	1.8	12.0	3.9
Advertising 18	1.0	•	•	•	•	0.9	0.1	6.2	0.1	0.5	1.6	2.6	1.4
Other Expenses 19	150.4	2909675.0	1941.2	•	991.5	48.2	58.8	6725.5	9728.2	103.8	283.2	572.6	81.7
Officers' Compensation 20	16.5	2575.0	931.3	•	493.0	7.0	9.4	315.2	185.2	3.5	4.1	379.7	7.6
Operating Margin 21	•	•	•	•	•	•	•	•	•	•	•	•	•
Operating Margin Before Officers' Comp. 22	•	•	•	•	•	•	•	•	•	•	•	•	•

Selected Average Balance Sheet ($ in Thousands)

Net Receivables 23	1638	0	10	1	49	285	532	1278	2411	8448	13113	13353	1168481
Inventories 24	12	0	0	0	4	11	21	1	1	329	476	377	2705
Net Property, Plant and Equipment 25	214	0	0	0	31	183	268	267	761	2111	10030	23046	13104
Total Assets 26	18424	0	150	652	2196	6944	16486	34998	71097	151341	346836	1124491	6767937
Notes and Loans Payable 27	4163	0	43	341	250	610	1363	6242	7912	26038	58580	225963	2012846
All Other Liabilities 28	2527	0	12	69	87	828	1290	3198	8315	18769	51088	117077	1188965
Net Worth 29	11733	0	94	242	1859	5505	13833	25558	54870	106533	237169	781451	3566127

Selected Financial Ratios (Times to 1)

Current Ratio 30	2.0	•	16.6	15.4	7.5	3.5	2.4	2.7	3.8	2.6	3.8	1.7	1.6
Quick Ratio 31	1.5	•	4.6	10.7	4.5	1.6	1.8	1.7	2.3	1.8	3.2	0.9	1.5
Net Sales to Working Capital 32	0.1	•	0.0	•	0.0	0.2	0.5	0.0	0.0	0.1	0.0	0.0	0.1
Coverage Ratio 33	9.9	17.0	50.3	1548.9	70.4	127.4	32.7	10.3	12.2	15.9	8.9	8.2	7.9
Total Asset Turnover 34	0.0	•	0.0	•	0.0	0.0	0.1	0.0	0.0	0.0	0.0	0.0	0.0
Inventory Turnover 35	4.6	•	•	•	0.0	31.8	23.2	•	1.1	3.5	•	0.3	2.9
Receivables Turnover 36	0.1	•	•	0.1	0.0	•	1.6	0.0	0.0	0.1	0.0	0.0	0.1
Total Liabilities to Net Worth 37	0.6	•	0.6	1.7	0.2	0.3	0.2	0.4	0.3	0.4	0.5	0.4	0.9
Current Assets to Working Capital 38	2.0	•	1.1	1.1	1.2	1.4	1.7	1.6	1.4	1.6	1.4	2.5	2.6
Current Liabilities to Working Capital 39	1.0	•	0.1	0.1	0.2	0.4	0.7	0.6	0.4	0.6	0.4	1.5	1.6
Working Capital to Net Sales 40	12.6	•	705.3	•	137.7	5.0	1.8	456.6	237.6	10.9	55.6	142.3	10.1
Inventory to Working Capital 41	0.0	•	•	•	0.0	0.0	0.0	•	•	0.0	0.0	0.0	0.0
Total Receipts to Cash Flow 42	0.1	0.0	•	0.0	0.2	0.2	0.4	0.0	0.1	0.1	0.0	0.0	0.2
Cost of Goods to Cash Flow 43	0.0	•	•	0.0	0.0	0.2	0.2	•	0.0	0.1	•	0.0	0.0
Cash Flow to Total Debt 44	0.3	•	1.5	0.9	1.1	1.0	1.0	0.4	0.7	0.4	0.3	0.3	0.1

Selected Financial Factors (in Percentages)

Debt Ratio 45	36.3	•	36.8	62.9	15.3	20.7	16.1	27.0	22.8	29.6	31.6	30.5	47.3
Return on Total Assets 46	12.8	•	62.5	38.3	18.3	20.9	14.9	12.7	12.1	11.3	10.8	11.2	12.0
Return on Equity Before Income Taxes 47	18.1	•	97.0	103.2	21.4	26.2	17.2	15.7	14.4	15.0	14.0	14.2	19.9
Return on Equity After Income Taxes 48	13.9	•	88.1	83.6	18.7	24.2	15.3	13.5	12.4	12.0	10.9	11.7	13.2
Profit Margin (Before Income Tax) 49	1374.9	11616450.0	29583.2	•	9962.8	437.5	239.1	41091.2	17639.8	1077.3	4076.1	24876.0	1048.0
Profit Margin (After Income Tax) 50	1055.8	9077225.0	26862.0	•	8724.9	405.3	212.4	35403.2	151197.4	859.3	3185.4	20570.3	695.0

EMPLOYMENT SERVICES

Table I
Corporations with and without Net Income

MONEY AMOUNTS AND SIZE OF ASSETS IN THOUSANDS OF DOLLARS

Item Description for Accounting Period 7/09 Through 6/10	Total	Zero Assets	Under 500	500 to 1,000	1,000 to 5,000	5,000 to 10,000	10,000 to 25,000	25,000 to 50,000	50,000 to 100,000	100,000 to 250,000	250,000 to 500,000	500,000 to 2,500,000	2,500,000 and over
Number of Enterprises 1	30132	8904	18202	1348	1287	182	117	32	15	13	14	13	3
Revenues ($ in Thousands)													
Net Sales 2	127350478	1332477	24828546	6894935	18277419	2633657	8473393	4353418	4480041	8443512	8091125	36889460	2652494
Interest 3	124949	236	1968	2720	6895	1814	2883	504	1026	13370	4830	81826	6877
Rents 4	7805	0	4800	0	293	0	65	0	0	1691	0	956	0
Royalties 5	250026	0	0	0	0	0	0	0	22	0	45621	32333	172050
Other Portfolio Income 6	97497	30039	3400	1256	3758	0	3792	2859	9120	1337	1925	20868	19144
Other Receipts 7	1438362	56572	40793	3996	15510	38410	18618	21440	19253	16829	116851	656075	434015
Total Receipts 8	129269117	1419324	24879507	6902907	18303875	2673881	8498751	4378221	4509462	8476739	8260352	37681518	3284580
Average Total Receipts 9	4290	159	1367	5121	14222	14692	72639	136819	300631	652057	590025	2898578	1094860
Operating Costs/Operating Income (%)													
Cost of Operations 10	48.8	37.3	26.4	64.2	33.4	58.0	41.7	70.1	64.1	47.9	57.8	62.7	66.9
Salaries and Wages 11	25.7	28.4	22.5	15.3	46.6	17.5	34.4	13.9	22.4	40.1	18.2	18.4	18.6
Taxes Paid 12	5.7	6.0	9.2	4.8	2.5	3.6	6.3	4.5	6.2	5.0	4.5	5.3	7.7
Interest Paid 13	0.5	1.8	0.2	0.2	0.2	1.5	0.6	1.2	0.7	0.5	0.8	0.3	4.5
Depreciation 14	0.4	1.9	0.1	0.1	0.3	0.4	0.3	0.3	0.3	0.3	0.7	0.5	1.3
Amortization and Depletion 15	0.5	1.1	0.1	0.1	0.0	0.4	0.2	0.6	0.7	0.9	1.6	0.7	1.5
Pensions and Other Deferred Comp. 16	0.2	0.1	0.3	0.7	0.2	0.1	0.3	0.1	0.1	0.0	0.2	0.2	0.2
Employee Benefits 17	2.5	3.7	1.7	0.6	2.4	4.0	2.3	1.8	1.7	2.4	1.9	3.4	3.7
Advertising 18	0.4	1.2	0.3	0.4	0.2	0.4	1.8	0.2	0.1	0.2	0.4	0.2	0.3
Other Expenses 19	14.6	26.4	34.7	11.7	12.6	13.2	11.4	7.6	4.6	3.1	12.9	7.9	15.1
Officers' Compensation 20	1.7	4.1	4.8	2.2	1.4	2.3	1.3	0.6	0.4	0.2	0.9	0.3	1.2
Operating Margin 21	•	•	•	0.0	0.0	0.9	0.7	•	•	•	0.1	0.1	•
Operating Margin Before Officers' Comp. 22	0.9	•	4.4	2.0	1.4	0.9	0.7	•	•	•	1.0	0.4	•

Selected Average Balance Sheet ($ in Thousands)

Net Receivables **23**	405	0	20	143	639	2221	6535	10268	33658	58724	85646	251636	1196810
Inventories **24**	2	0	0	0	1	1	136	47	374	166	0	2228	1490
Net Property, Plant and Equipment **25**	112	0	8	37	261	311	841	1564	2441	11149	12259	53891	523402
Total Assets **26**	1450	85	676	1999	6241	15128	34601	71437	167260	337939	1076435		4229340
Notes and Loans Payable **27**	375	40	368	969	2281	6038	17450	26675	54280	48244	93708		1379487
All Other Liabilities **28**	494	25	220	771	1837	5091	12043	37098	67664	106221	365836		1379489
Net Worth **29**	582	20	89	258	2123	3999	5108	7664	45316	183473	616891		1470363

Selected Financial Ratios (Times to 1)

Current Ratio **30**	1.3	•	1.3	0.9	1.3	1.5	1.4	1.5	1.0	1.4	2.1	1.8	0.8
Quick Ratio **31**	1.1	•	1.2	0.7	1.0	1.3	1.1	1.2	0.8	1.2	1.7	1.5	0.8
Net Sales to Working Capital **32**	27.5	117.0	•	•	47.3	11.4	22.6	17.5	1045.3	24.9	7.3	13.8	•
Coverage Ratio **33**	2.6	•	•	0.2	1.7	1.0	0.7	0.6	0.2	0.4	3.9	9.7	2.2
Total Asset Turnover **34**	2.9	16.1	7.6	7.1	4.8	2.3	3.9	3.9	4.2	3.9	1.7	2.6	0.2
Inventory Turnover **35**	1059.4	•	5929.9	•	11747.0	221.3	2022.1	511.7	1875.5	•	798.0	•	397.1
Receivables Turnover **36**	9.9	63.5	19.2	25.7	6.5	11.2	14.9	8.6	11.8	5.6	8.2	1.0	
Total Liabilities to Net Worth **37**	1.5	3.3	6.7	•	1.9	2.8	5.8	8.3	2.7	0.8	0.7	1.9	
Current Assets to Working Capital **38**	4.3	4.6	4.4	•	2.9	3.3	3.0	163.3	3.4	1.9	2.3	•	
Current Liabilities to Working Capital **39**	3.3	3.6	3.4	•	1.9	2.3	2.0	162.3	2.4	0.9	1.3	•	
Working Capital to Net Sales **40**	0.0	•	0.0	0.0	0.0	0.1	0.0	0.0	0.1	0.0	0.1	0.1	•
Inventory to Working Capital **41**	0.0	•	0.0	•	0.0	0.0	0.0	0.0	0.1	0.0	•	0.0	•
Total Receipts to Cash Flow **42**	7.3	3.1	9.9	9.0	8.3	10.8	16.0	33.1	48.2	8.3	11.4	7.3	
Cost of Goods to Cash Flow **43**	3.6	0.8	6.3	3.0	4.8	4.5	11.2	21.2	23.1	4.8	7.1	4.9	
Cash Flow to Total Debt **44**	0.7	6.9	0.9	0.9	0.6	0.6	0.3	0.1	0.1	0.4	0.5	0.0	

Selected Financial Factors (in Percentages)

Debt Ratio **45**	59.9	•	76.7	86.9	87.1	66.0	73.6	85.2	89.3	72.9	45.7	42.7	65.2
Return on Total Assets **46**	3.7	•	•	0.3	2.9	3.6	2.0	3.1	0.6	0.9	5.1	6.7	2.1
Return on Equity Before Income Taxes **47**	5.6	•	•	•	9.4	0.4	•	•	•	•	7.0	10.4	3.4
Return on Equity After Income Taxes **48**	3.3	•	8.5	•	•	•	•	•	•	•	5.3	7.1	2.2
Profit Margin (Before Income Tax) **49**	0.8	•	0.2	0.2	•	•	•	•	0.1	0.0	2.2	2.3	5.6
Profit Margin (After Income Tax) **50**	0.5	•	•	0.2	•	•	•	•	•	•	1.7	1.5	3.7

Table II

Corporations with Net Income

EMPLOYMENT SERVICES

MONEY AMOUNTS AND SIZE OF ASSETS IN THOUSANDS OF DOLLARS

Item Description for Accounting Period 7/09 Through 6/10		Total	Zero Assets	Under 500	500 to 1,000	1,000 to 5,000	5,000 to 10,000	10,000 to 25,000	25,000 to 50,000	50,000 to 100,000	100,000 to 250,000	250,000 to 500,000	500,000 to 2,500,000	2,500,000 and over
Number of Enterprises	1	13097	3538	8106	488	801	72	46	16	5	6	10	6	3
Revenues ($ in Thousands)														
Net Sales	2	76832755	766264	19073004	3486180	9334904	1003341	2843089	2305324	2371061	3843937	6049094	23104062	2652494
Interest	3	86273	0	141	831	5921	813	295	74	44	883	3615	66779	6877
Rents	4	925	0	0	0	293	0	65	0	0	6	0	561	0
Royalties	5	226371	0	0	0	0	0	0	0	0	0	32727	21594	172050
Other Portfolio Income	6	73032	30039	0	1039	3610	0	196	106	0	447	223	18227	19144
Other Receipts	7	1185014	46596	17662	2648	9421	8844	11673	18800	4754	934	116233	513436	434015
Total Receipts	8	78404370	842899	19090807	3490698	9354149	1012998	2855318	2324304	2375859	3846207	6201892	23724659	3284580
Average Total Receipts	9	5986	238	2355	7153	11678	14069	62072	145269	475172	641034	620189	3954110	1094860
Operating Costs/Operating Income (%)														
Cost of Operations	10	49.0	36.9	22.7	71.0	40.4	29.9	66.4	74.2	82.9	83.3	62.4	52.5	66.9
Salaries and Wages	11	20.2	18.9	20.0	5.9	35.6	23.2	10.0	6.9	4.7	7.1	14.0	24.5	18.6
Taxes Paid	12	6.3	2.8	10.6	0.7	3.7	2.6	4.9	6.3	6.6	2.4	4.3	6.1	7.7
Interest Paid	13	0.4	1.8	0.1	0.1	0.2	3.6	0.8	0.1	0.4	0.5	0.7	0.1	4.5
Depreciation	14	0.4	0.2	0.1	0.1	0.4	0.9	0.4	0.1	0.1	0.4	0.7	0.5	1.3
Amortization and Depletion	15	0.3	0.8	0.1	0.1	0.1	0.9	0.1	0.1	0.2	0.7	1.2	0.2	1.5
Pensions and Other Deferred Comp.	16	0.3	0.0	0.4	0.6	0.1	0.0	0.0	0.1	0.1	0.0	0.3	0.2	0.2
Employee Benefits	17	2.4	3.4	1.3	0.5	0.5	5.3	2.9	2.0	0.4	1.1	1.7	4.5	3.7
Advertising	18	0.4	0.8	0.2	0.5	0.2	0.7	4.5	0.1	0.1	0.2	0.4	0.2	0.3
Other Expenses	19	16.9	13.4	37.5	14.0	15.1	22.3	6.0	6.3	2.3	2.9	12.0	8.8	15.1
Officers' Compensation	20	1.8	4.3	4.7	2.8	1.1	3.6	1.1	0.7	0.4	0.3	1.0	0.2	1.2
Operating Margin	21	1.6	16.6	2.2	3.8	2.7	6.9	3.0	3.0	1.8	1.2	1.4	2.1	•
Operating Margin Before Officers' Comp.	22	3.4	20.9	7.0	6.6	3.7	10.5	4.0	3.7	2.2	1.5	2.4	2.3	•

Selected Average Balance Sheet ($ in Thousands)

Item	C1	C2	C3	C4	C5	C6	C7	C8	C9	C10	C11	C12	C13
Net Receivables 23	585		16	102	552	1177	8405	12306	28871	53728	91452	232879	1196810
Inventories 24	2		0	0	1	2	161	0	13	232	0	2291	1490
Net Property, Plant and Equipment 25	186		4	33	191	466	901	1057	2205	8898	12128	63683	523402
Total Assets 26	2209		96	678	1750	6441	13352	36464	73535	165475	338850	1221050	4229340
Notes and Loans Payable 27	502		35	279	572	4258	5304	7832	17377	46771	47867	6525	1379487
All Other Liabilities 28	731		28	149	488	2449	4385	7074	50610	66637	106340	422408	1379489
Net Worth 29	976		33	250	690	-267	3663	21559	5548	52067	184643	792117	1470363

Selected Financial Ratios (Times to 1)

Item	C1	C2	C3	C4	C5	C6	C7	C8	C9	C10	C11	C12	C13
Current Ratio 30	1.3		•	2.1	2.2	1.1	1.6	2.2	1.2	1.6	2.1	1.8	0.8
Quick Ratio 31	1.2		•	1.7	1.8	0.8	1.4	1.8	0.8	1.3	1.8	1.6	0.8
Net Sales to Working Capital 32	28.7		•	34.2	20.0	37.9	15.2	8.8	50.8	21.3	6.8	18.0	•
Coverage Ratio 33	9.9		23.3	36.6	15.8	3.2	5.9	59.3	5.8	3.3	6.8	52.0	2.2
Total Asset Turnover 34	2.7	15.9	24.6	10.5	6.7	2.2	4.6	4.0	6.4	3.9	1.8	3.2	0.2
Inventory Turnover 35	1320.0		•	•	3665.2	2309.6	255.3	•	30945.1	2298.1	•	883.0	397.1
Receivables Turnover 36	8.3		96.8	17.9	15.2	6.2	6.0	•	9.5	12.1	•	7.7	1.0
Total Liabilities to Net Worth 37	1.3		1.9	1.7	1.5	•	2.6	0.7	12.3	2.2	0.8	0.5	1.9
Current Assets to Working Capital 38	4.5		4.0	1.9	1.8	10.3	2.8	1.8	5.6	2.8	1.9	2.3	•
Current Liabilities to Working Capital 39	3.5		3.0	0.9	0.8	9.3	1.8	0.8	4.6	1.8	0.9	1.3	•
Working Capital to Net Sales 40	0.0		0.0	0.0	0.0	0.0	0.1	0.1	0.0	0.0	0.1	0.1	•
Inventory to Working Capital 41	0.0		•	•	0.0	0.0	•	•	•	0.0	•	•	•
Total Receipts to Cash Flow 42	5.2	2.7	2.6	5.9	5.9	3.5	12.1	10.5	26.7	29.7	7.6	8.1	7.3
Cost of Goods to Cash Flow 43	2.5	1.0	0.6	4.2	2.4	1.0	8.0	7.8	22.2	24.7	4.8	4.2	4.9
Cash Flow to Total Debt 44	0.9		14.5	2.8	1.9	0.6	0.5	0.9	0.3	0.2	0.5	1.1	0.0

Selected Financial Factors (in Percentages)

Item	C1	C2	C3	C4	C5	C6	C7	C8	C9	C10	C11	C12	C13
Debt Ratio 45	55.8		65.7	63.2	60.6	104.1	72.6	40.9	92.5	68.5	45.5	35.1	65.2
Return on Total Assets 46	11.2		59.8	42.9	20.4	25.0	21.1	15.3	15.4	6.7	8.2	15.4	2.1
Return on Equity Before Income Taxes 47	22.8		166.9	113.4	48.5	•	63.9	25.4	168.8	14.9	12.9	23.3	3.4
Return on Equity After Income Taxes 48	19.6		163.3	113.1	47.9	•	59.7	25.3	164.3	10.6	10.5	17.7	2.2
Profit Margin (Before Income Tax) 49	3.8	26.6	2.3	4.0	2.9	7.9	3.8	3.8	2.0	1.2	3.9	4.8	5.6
Profit Margin (After Income Tax) 50	3.3	26.5	2.3	4.0	2.8	7.1	3.5	3.8	1.9	0.9	3.2	3.6	3.7

Table I

Corporations with and without Net Income

TRAVEL ARRANGEMENT AND RESERVATION SERVICES

MONEY AMOUNTS AND SIZE OF ASSETS IN THOUSANDS OF DOLLARS

Item Description for Accounting Period 7/09 Through 6/10	Total	Zero Assets	Under 500	500 to 1,000	1,000 to 5,000	5,000 to 10,000	10,000 to 25,000	25,000 to 50,000	50,000 to 100,000	100,000 to 250,000	250,000 to 500,000	500,000 to 2,500,000	2,500,000 and over
Number of Enterprises **1**	17735	4314	12102	608	552	30	40	29	19	20	11	9	0
Revenues ($ in Thousands)													
Net Sales **2**	31706392	709352	7809671	1767602	2127021	868767	1133485	1537164	1461094	3630879	2187541	8473815	0
Interest **3**	191910	6	282	739	2879	374	6137	2058	10859	9794	25451	133332	0
Rents **4**	55998	0	7	0	0	107	304	35	3226	5518	4249	42552	0
Royalties **5**	87841	0	0	0	0	0	0	0	781	0	69597	17463	0
Other Portfolio Income **6**	201473	5108	3473	0	65843	89	6891	9308	29540	9436	43469	28313	0
Other Receipts **7**	1865397	24745	22855	4029	36778	1574	41703	122358	175515	204577	898803	332463	0
Total Receipts **8**	34109011	739211	7836288	1772370	2232521	870911	1188520	1670923	1681015	3860204	3229110	9027938	0
Average Total Receipts **9**	1923	171	648	2915	4044	29030	29713	57618	88474	193010	293555	1003104	•
Operating Costs/Operating Income (%)													
Cost of Operations **10**	45.6	48.0	69.2	67.6	47.1	63.1	43.6	76.0	36.7	61.4	20.5	12.7	•
Salaries and Wages **11**	15.8	8.1	5.9	11.6	17.2	18.5	26.5	10.9	23.6	13.2	40.6	18.6	•
Taxes Paid **12**	2.2	1.3	1.2	1.4	1.9	1.8	4.1	1.1	2.6	1.6	3.9	3.2	•
Interest Paid **13**	2.1	2.5	0.3	0.2	0.3	0.1	0.3	0.9	1.8	0.3	4.2	5.4	•
Depreciation **14**	1.3	1.7	0.4	0.6	2.2	0.4	1.3	0.9	2.2	1.7	2.7	1.7	•
Amortization and Depletion **15**	0.8	0.9	0.0	0.0	0.4	0.2	0.9	0.3	0.7	0.7	1.3	1.8	•
Pensions and Other Deferred Comp. **16**	0.6	•	0.1	0.5	0.4	0.0	0.3	0.3	0.5	1.2	3.3	0.6	•
Employee Benefits **17**	1.7	0.7	0.8	0.8	0.9	1.2	1.7	1.0	2.6	1.8	4.3	2.1	•
Advertising **18**	3.6	0.2	1.0	0.4	1.3	4.1	2.9	3.1	2.0	1.2	5.6	8.5	•
Other Expenses **19**	29.5	32.8	18.2	12.7	24.3	11.3	16.0	12.7	39.1	20.1	56.9	46.6	•
Officers' Compensation **20**	1.7	1.6	2.9	1.7	4.1	1.1	3.6	0.9	1.6	0.8	1.1	0.6	•
Operating Margin **21**	•	2.2	•	2.6	•	•	•	•	•	•	•	•	•
Operating Margin Before Officers' Comp. **22**	•	3.8	2.8	4.2	3.9	•	2.5	•	•	•	•	•	•

Selected Average Balance Sheet ($ in Thousands)

Net Receivables 23	148	0	6	28	450	2223	3559	5807	7017	35903	28194	82771
Inventories 24	8	0	1	0	81	58	90	67	1044	308	1558	2766
Net Property, Plant and Equipment 25	138	0	10	118	201	501	1485	3849	12614	22806	25685	108421
Total Assets 26	1665	58	619	1710	7286	17058	34792	70050	152689	367464	1909012	
Notes and Loans Payable 27	523	0	45	102	220	837	1272	5168	22357	9926	103148	728359
All Other Liabilities 28	690	0	28	196	1029	5806	15777	28128	34023	74227	142206	655615
Net Worth 29	453	0	-15	321	461	643	9	1497	13670	68535	122111	525039

Selected Financial Ratios (Times to 1)

Current Ratio 30	0.8	•	1.8	1.9	1.6	1.0	0.8	0.7	1.1	1.4	0.7	0.6
Quick Ratio 31	0.6	•	1.4	1.7	1.3	0.7	0.6	0.6	0.7	1.0	0.4	0.4
Net Sales to Working Capital 32	•	•	31.5	13.6	7.2	•	•	•	43.6	8.3	•	•
Coverage Ratio 33	2.3	3.6	1.8	17.0	15.2	14.9	1.8	2.0	9.5	1.8	1.9	
Total Asset Turnover 34	1.1	•	11.2	4.7	2.3	4.0	1.7	1.5	1.1	1.2	0.5	0.5
Inventory Turnover 35	108.3	397.2	•	22.5	315.8	137.8	599.2	27.0	362.1	26.2	43.2	
Receivables Turnover 36	12.1	108.7	66.5	10.8	10.3	8.3	7.0	8.5	6.2	11.0	9.3	
Total Liabilities to Net Worth 37	2.7	•	0.9	2.7	10.3	1994.0	22.2	4.1	1.2	2.0	2.6	
Current Assets to Working Capital 38	•	2.2	2.1	2.5	•	•	15.3	3.5	•	•		
Current Liabilities to Working Capital 39	•	1.2	1.1	1.5	•	•	14.3	2.5	•			
Working Capital to Net Sales 40	•	0.0	0.1	0.1	•	•	0.0	0.1	•	•		
Inventory to Working Capital 41	•	0.0	•	0.2	•	0.7	0.0	•				
Total Receipts to Cash Flow 42	3.4	2.9	6.4	7.3	3.9	6.2	8.5	2.7	4.9	1.9	2.1	
Cost of Goods to Cash Flow 43	1.6	1.4	4.5	4.9	1.8	2.7	6.5	1.0	3.0	0.4	0.3	
Cash Flow to Total Debt 44	0.4	•	1.4	1.3	0.8	0.3	0.2	0.5	0.4	0.4	0.3	

Selected Financial Factors (in Percentages)

Debt Ratio 45	72.8	•	126.0	48.2	73.0	91.2	99.9	95.7	80.5	55.1	66.8	72.5
Return on Total Assets 46	5.1	•	5.4	14.2	11.6	•	6.6	2.5	3.9	3.0	4.1	5.0
Return on Equity Before Income Taxes 47	10.5	•	•	25.8	40.0	•	12369.0	25.2	9.9	6.1	5.3	8.7
Return on Equity After Income Taxes 48	7.5	•	•	24.7	37.1	•	10421.3	9.6	3.8	4.1	3.4	5.6
Profit Margin (Before Income Tax) 49	2.7	6.4	0.2	2.9	4.8	•	3.7	0.7	1.8	2.3	3.2	4.8
Profit Margin (After Income Tax) 50	1.9	6.4	0.1	2.7	4.4	3.1	3.1	0.3	0.7	1.6	2.1	3.1

TRAVEL ARRANGEMENT AND RESERVATION SERVICES

Table II

Corporations with Net Income

MONEY AMOUNTS AND SIZE OF ASSETS IN THOUSANDS OF DOLLARS

Item Description for Accounting Period 7/09 Through 6/10	Total	Zero Assets	Under 500	500 to 1,000	1,000 to 5,000	5,000 to 10,000	10,000 to 25,000	25,000 to 50,000	50,000 to 100,000	100,000 to 250,000	250,000 to 500,000	500,000 to 2,500,000	2,500,000 and over
Number of Enterprises **1**	8913	2309	5597	500	395	23	31	18	11	16	8	5	0
Revenues ($ in Thousands)													
Net Sales **2**	23277469	254664	6093911	1568841	1375618	775198	962090	1042361	941530	3220162	1863689	5179406	0
Interest **3**	75633	6	97	739	2347	366	5077	1329	9923	8675	20409	26664	0
Rents **4**	46604	0	7	0	0	64	304	35	3226	5453	2269	35246	0
Royalties **5**	86819	0	0	0	0	0	0	0	781	0	69597	16441	0
Other Portfolio Income **6**	174056	5108	3473	0	65841	22	5983	9308	9995	7589	42196	24537	0
Other Receipts **7**	1362232	24554	19552	0	10241	1573	36413	76098	156776	141310	910169	-14449	0
Total Receipts **8**	25022813	284332	6117040	1569580	1454047	777223	1009867	1129131	1122231	3383189	2908329	5267845	0
Average Total Receipts **9**	2807	123	1093	3139	3681	33792	32576	62730	102021	211449	363541	1053569	•
Operating Costs/Operating Income (%)													
Cost of Operations **10**	47.5	20.5	66.7	76.1	42.4	62.3	41.2	73.2	22.7	62.2	19.2	18.1	•
Salaries and Wages **11**	14.8	0.3	4.8	8.6	14.0	19.5	27.1	10.1	25.8	12.1	42.9	16.9	•
Taxes Paid **12**	2.2	1.0	1.2	0.9	1.6	1.9	4.2	1.1	3.2	1.5	4.2	3.3	•
Interest Paid **13**	1.2	0.4	0.1	0.1	0.1	0.1	0.3	1.2	2.1	0.1	3.8	3.0	•
Depreciation **14**	1.3	1.9	0.5	0.6	2.6	0.4	1.4	0.8	1.9	1.3	2.6	1.6	•
Amortization and Depletion **15**	0.7	1.6	•	0.0	0.2	0.2	1.0	0.3	0.2	0.8	1.2	1.6	•
Pensions and Other Deferred Comp. **16**	0.5	•	0.1	0.5	0.6	0.1	0.4	0.2	0.7	0.7	3.0	0.1	•
Employee Benefits **17**	1.5	0.5	0.8	0.4	0.5	1.2	1.6	0.8	2.7	1.5	4.5	1.9	•
Advertising **18**	3.8	0.3	1.1	0.1	1.4	2.9	2.0	2.3	1.7	0.9	6.2	10.8	•
Other Expenses **19**	26.6	54.9	18.9	7.7	27.2	9.3	15.3	13.2	49.3	19.7	61.9	34.7	•
Officers' Compensation **20**	1.9	•	3.4	1.3	4.7	1.2	4.1	1.0	1.9	0.7	1.0	0.5	•
Operating Margin **21**	•	18.4	2.4	3.8	4.8	1.0	1.5	•	•	•	•	7.3	•
Operating Margin Before Officers' Comp. **22**	0.1	18.4	5.8	5.1	9.5	2.2	5.6	•	•	•	•	7.8	•

Selected Average Balance Sheet ($ in Thousands)

	1	2	3	4	5	6	7	8	9	10	11	12	13
Net Receivables 23	201	0	9	0	452	2361	3834	8268	3381	33451	34364	77781	•
Inventories 24	8	0	2	0	73	75	70	40	202	362	536	3440	•
Net Property, Plant and Equipment 25	177	0	14	62	137	599	1600	2382	12612	18647	27499	131558	•
Total Assets 26	2077	0	87	578	1794	7388	16361	34974	66534	155687	375548	1899339	•
Notes and Loans Payable 27	352	0	44	33	164	443	1053	5367	12328	7369	75386	362103	•
All Other Liabilities 28	990	0	29	154	908	6284	15389	27505	32217	72556	169517	847609	•
Net Worth 29	735	0	14	391	722	661	-80	2102	21988	75762	130646	689627	•

Selected Financial Ratios (Times to 1)

	1	2	3	4	5	6	7	8	9	10	11	12	13
Current Ratio 30	0.9	•	3.3	2.7	2.5	0.9	0.8	0.8	1.2	1.5	0.7	0.6	•
Quick Ratio 31	0.6	•	2.6	2.4	2.0	0.6	0.6	0.6	0.7	1.0	0.6	0.3	•
Net Sales to Working Capital 32	•	•	21.8	10.0	3.8	•	•	•	20.5	7.8	•	•	•
Coverage Ratio 33	5.8	73.0	23.6	74.6	180.9	16.4	25.5	4.5	4.4	25.0	2.4	4.0	•
Total Asset Turnover 34	1.3	•	12.6	5.4	1.9	4.6	1.9	1.7	1.3	1.3	0.6	0.5	•
Inventory Turnover 35	148.2	•	339.8	•	20.3	278.3	183.5	1056.0	96.2	345.8	83.6	54.5	•
Receivables Turnover 36	14.4	•	138.7	•	9.8	10.0	10.6	•	10.8	6.5	11.4	14.2	•
Total Liabilities to Net Worth 37	1.8	•	5.4	0.5	1.5	10.2	•	15.6	2.0	1.1	1.9	1.8	•
Current Assets to Working Capital 38	•	•	1.4	1.6	1.7	•	•	•	6.5	3.0	•	•	•
Current Liabilities to Working Capital 39	•	•	0.4	0.6	0.7	•	•	•	5.5	2.0	•	•	•
Working Capital to Net Sales 40	•	•	0.0	0.1	0.3	•	•	•	0.0	0.1	•	•	•
Inventory to Working Capital 41	•	•	0.0	•	0.1	•	•	•	0.1	0.0	•	•	•
Total Receipts to Cash Flow 42	3.4	1.2	5.3	9.4	2.9	11.6	5.4	6.4	1.9	4.6	1.7	2.4	•
Cost of Goods to Cash Flow 43	1.6	0.3	3.5	7.2	1.2	7.2	2.2	4.7	0.4	2.9	0.3	0.4	•
Cash Flow to Total Debt 44	0.6	•	2.8	1.8	1.1	0.4	0.4	0.3	1.0	0.5	0.6	0.4	•

Selected Financial Factors (in Percentages)

	1	2	3	4	5	6	7	8	9	10	11	12	13
Debt Ratio 45	64.6	•	84.4	32.3	59.8	91.1	100.5	94.0	67.0	51.3	65.2	63.7	•
Return on Total Assets 46	8.7	•	36.6	21.3	20.5	6.2	12.6	9.2	11.7	4.8	5.7	6.7	•
Return on Equity Before Income Taxes 47	20.2	•	224.7	31.0	50.6	65.5	•	118.4	27.5	9.5	9.6	13.8	•
Return on Equity After Income Taxes 48	16.5	•	216.6	29.8	47.9	63.2	•	100.5	20.9	7.3	7.2	9.5	•
Profit Margin (Before Income Tax) 49	5.7	30.1	2.8	3.9	10.5	1.3	6.4	4.3	7.1	3.6	5.4	9.2	•
Profit Margin (After Income Tax) 50	4.6	30.0	2.7	3.7	9.9	1.2	5.7	3.6	5.4	2.8	4.0	6.3	•

Table I

Corporations with and without Net Income

OTHER ADMINISTRATIVE AND SUPPORT SERVICES

MONEY AMOUNTS AND SIZE OF ASSETS IN THOUSANDS OF DOLLARS

Item Description for Accounting Period 7/09 Through 6/10	Total	Zero Assets	Under 500	500 to 1,000	1,000 to 5,000	5,000 to 10,000	10,000 to 25,000	25,000 to 50,000	50,000 to 100,000	100,000 to 250,000	250,000 to 500,000	500,000 to 2,500,000	2,500,000 and over
Number of Enterprises **1**	208976	48504	147792	5502	5799	677	326	157	85	57	28	40	7
Revenues ($ in Thousands)													
Net Sales **2**	205673349	3694081	61013569	9597889	29153166	10448107	11113886	6974326	6741289	7760322	9326885	34676805	15173024
Interest **3**	705827	613	12009	5243	10788	7649	5548	9731	19504	16080	13877	299353	305432
Rents **4**	85797	0	5242	5148	8047	20	5729	1406	9010	1917	9072	33806	6400
Royalties **5**	199459	0	178	0	0	0	199	0	5886	852	261	109928	82155
Other Portfolio Income **6**	818920	152119	148291	5227	61779	25725	8799	11580	30370	23810	30188	182287	138745
Other Receipts **7**	4604339	213939	232346	42959	249995	315138	223947	214640	527788	369227	343388	937594	933377
Total Receipts **8**	212087691	4060752	61411635	9656466	29483775	10796639	11358108	7211683	7333847	8172208	9723671	36239773	16639133
Average Total Receipts **9**	1015	84	416	1755	5084	15948	34841	45934	86281	143372	347274	905994	2377019
Operating Costs/Operating Income (%)													
Cost of Operations **10**	37.2	25.1	31.7	42.2	53.5	48.7	43.0	46.4	37.9	23.4	40.3	39.0	11.8
Salaries and Wages **11**	20.7	13.5	20.2	17.1	14.5	21.7	21.3	18.5	24.8	24.0	22.9	23.0	28.3
Taxes Paid **12**	3.3	3.2	3.4	3.4	2.7	2.4	4.0	3.2	3.8	3.0	3.4	3.4	3.8
Interest Paid **13**	2.4	1.2	0.7	0.7	0.9	0.7	0.9	1.7	2.6	2.8	3.7	3.4	11.6
Depreciation **14**	2.3	4.7	1.7	2.1	1.9	1.8	1.6	2.1	2.4	3.0	2.9	2.6	4.0
Amortization and Depletion **15**	1.2	0.6	0.1	0.1	0.2	0.2	0.5	1.1	1.3	1.9	2.0	2.3	6.6
Pensions and Other Deferred Comp. **16**	0.5	0.1	0.3	0.6	0.2	0.5	0.3	0.4	0.3	0.3	0.9	0.7	0.7
Employee Benefits **17**	2.1	1.1	0.9	1.9	2.0	2.5	2.2	2.3	2.5	2.2	3.1	2.9	4.0
Advertising **18**	1.6	4.1	1.5	1.2	1.0	0.8	2.6	1.2	3.2	1.3	1.1	1.9	1.1
Other Expenses **19**	25.1	42.2	26.7	21.9	16.8	17.0	22.4	21.8	24.7	37.9	20.8	26.1	35.7
Officers' Compensation **20**	4.1	10.7	7.9	6.9	4.3	3.6	1.9	2.1	2.2	1.3	1.0	0.7	0.3
Operating Margin **21**	•	•	4.9	1.8	1.8	0.2	•	•	•	•	•	•	•
Operating Margin Before Officers' Comp. **22**	3.8	4.2	12.8	8.7	6.1	3.8	1.1	1.3	•	0.3	0.7	•	0.3

Selected Average Balance Sheet ($ in Thousands)

Net Receivables 23	103	0	10	105	474	1512	4327	7153	17955	24156	67285	160410	297136
Inventories 24	11	0	2	33	60	236	586	626	2664	2572	4652	5947	22844
Net Property, Plant and Equipment 25	112	0	20	229	526	1433	2665	3654	10486	18516	62618	112533	781671
Total Assets 26	672	0	76	678	2078	6720	15021	35206	67643	152972	331932	976506	5089351
Notes and Loans Payable 27	321	0	58	326	1064	2071	6716	13389	25497	55249	112568	381095	3012265
All Other Liabilities 28	173	0	19	131	503	2518	6199	10511	25122	42520	104257	231953	1079910
Net Worth 29	178	0	-1	220	511	2132	2106	11306	17023	55203	115106	363458	997176

Selected Financial Ratios (Times to 1)

Current Ratio 30	1.3	•	1.1	2.0	1.4	1.4	1.2	1.3	1.4	1.2	1.6	1.3	1.4
Quick Ratio 31	1.0	•	1.0	1.4	1.1	1.0	1.0	0.9	1.0	0.8	1.2	1.0	0.8
Net Sales to Working Capital 32	16.8	•	92.7	10.3	14.4	13.9	27.3	11.0	8.3	12.9	6.7	12.9	11.1
Coverage Ratio 33	2.2	3.9	8.7	4.2	4.3	6.2	2.5	2.5	2.3	2.5	2.0	0.5	1.3
Total Asset Turnover 34	1.5	•	5.4	2.6	2.4	2.3	2.3	1.3	1.2	0.9	1.0	0.9	0.4
Inventory Turnover 35	34.4	•	55.4	22.6	45.1	31.9	25.0	33.0	11.3	12.4	28.8	56.9	11.1
Receivables Turnover 36	8.7	•	44.5	14.8	9.9	9.4	7.4	7.2	4.5	5.0	5.2	4.3	6.9
Total Liabilities to Net Worth 37	2.8	•	•	2.1	3.1	2.2	6.1	2.1	3.0	1.8	1.9	1.7	4.1
Current Assets to Working Capital 38	3.9	•	8.4	2.0	3.3	3.6	6.4	4.0	3.7	5.5	2.7	4.1	3.5
Current Liabilities to Working Capital 39	2.9	•	7.4	1.0	2.3	2.6	5.4	3.0	2.7	4.5	1.7	3.1	2.5
Working Capital to Net Sales 40	0.1	•	0.0	0.1	0.1	0.1	0.0	0.1	0.1	0.1	0.1	0.1	0.1
Inventory to Working Capital 41	0.2	•	0.5	0.2	0.2	0.1	0.6	0.2	0.2	0.2	0.1	0.1	0.1
Total Receipts to Cash Flow 42	4.2	2.7	3.6	5.2	6.5	5.8	4.9	4.8	4.0	2.6	5.3	4.8	2.9
Cost of Goods to Cash Flow 43	1.6	0.7	1.1	2.2	3.5	2.8	2.1	2.2	1.5	0.6	2.2	1.9	0.3
Cash Flow to Total Debt 44	0.5	•	1.5	0.7	0.5	0.6	0.5	0.4	0.4	0.5	0.3	0.3	0.2

Selected Financial Factors (in Percentages)

Debt Ratio 45	73.5	•	101.5	67.5	75.4	68.3	86.0	67.9	74.8	63.9	65.3	62.8	80.4
Return on Total Assets 46	7.7	•	34.2	8.1	9.4	9.8	5.3	5.3	6.9	6.3	5.6	1.8	6.2
Return on Equity Before Income Taxes 47	16.0	•	•	19.1	29.3	25.9	22.9	9.8	15.3	10.6	8.3	•	6.6
Return on Equity After Income Taxes 48	12.9	•	•	18.2	27.6	24.1	20.9	8.0	11.8	8.9	5.8	•	2.3
Profit Margin (Before Income Tax) 49	2.9	3.4	5.6	2.4	3.0	3.6	1.4	2.5	3.3	4.3	2.9	•	3.0
Profit Margin (After Income Tax) 50	2.3	2.6	5.5	2.3	2.8	3.3	1.3	2.0	2.5	2.0	2.0	•	1.0

357

OTHER ADMINISTRATIVE AND SUPPORT SERVICES

Table II

Corporations with Net Income

MONEY AMOUNTS AND SIZE OF ASSETS IN THOUSANDS OF DOLLARS

Item Description for Accounting Period 7/09 Through 6/10	Total	Zero Assets	Under 500	500 to 1,000	1,000 to 5,000	5,000 to 10,000	10,000 to 25,000	25,000 to 50,000	50,000 to 100,000	100,000 to 250,000	250,000 to 500,000	500,000 to 2,500,000	2,500,000 and over
Number of Enterprises 1	130992	26752	95758	3463	4092	475	212	98	59	33	19	27	4
Revenues ($ in Thousands)													
Net Sales 2	148115538	2318590	43271752	7122265	24206751	8932895	8160854	5283595	5284429	5204505	8211104	23994747	6124051
Interest 3	257106	471	6663	2633	4629	6308	1600	6332	12947	6510	11537	179340	18136
Rents 4	44505	0	4482	4764	1892	15	5441	732	7744	531	8776	5177	4951
Royalties 5	166256	0	178	0	0	0	0	0	84	852	261	92615	72267
Other Portfolio Income 6	656142	96009	141558	3917	47909	25716	2313	3421	22124	21654	25680	158095	107745
Other Receipts 7	3694500	200250	191307	22200	256986	291909	120079	201511	262527	247115	325863	805790	768964
Total Receipts 8	152934047	2615320	43615940	7155779	24518167	9256843	8290287	5495591	5589855	5481167	8583221	25235764	7096114
Average Total Receipts 9	1168	98	455	2066	5992	19488	39105	56077	94743	166096	451748	934658	1774028
Operating Costs/Operating Income (%)													
Cost of Operations 10	37.7	19.2	29.5	43.3	55.7	48.4	44.4	44.1	36.1	25.4	37.7	38.8	1.1
Salaries and Wages 11	20.3	9.1	18.9	14.4	13.1	20.7	20.2	18.9	21.0	27.4	23.8	26.6	34.5
Taxes Paid 12	3.3	3.0	3.2	3.3	2.5	2.2	3.9	3.5	3.6	3.1	3.7	4.0	5.1
Interest Paid 13	1.4	0.7	0.6	0.5	0.7	0.5	0.5	1.0	1.9	1.4	2.0	2.9	7.4
Depreciation 14	2.1	3.9	1.4	1.6	1.5	1.6	1.4	1.8	2.2	2.9	3.0	2.9	4.9
Amortization and Depletion 15	0.8	0.3	0.1	0.1	0.2	0.1	0.3	1.0	0.9	1.4	1.5	2.1	3.5
Pensions and Other Deferred Comp. 16	0.4	0.0	0.2	0.7	0.2	0.5	0.3	0.4	0.3	0.4	0.9	0.7	1.0
Employee Benefits 17	1.7	0.7	0.7	1.8	1.8	2.4	1.9	2.0	2.3	2.0	3.0	2.2	3.1
Advertising 18	1.3	1.0	1.6	1.1	1.1	0.8	2.7	1.4	3.5	0.3	1.2	0.6	0.6
Other Expenses 19	21.7	36.6	25.7	18.2	14.5	16.7	17.7	20.3	24.8	30.7	20.8	17.2	42.4
Officers' Compensation 20	4.2	10.9	7.6	7.6	4.0	3.7	2.0	2.3	2.0	1.5	1.0	0.8	0.6
Operating Margin 21	5.1	14.6	10.3	7.4	4.7	2.4	4.8	3.2	1.5	3.4	1.5	1.0	•
Operating Margin Before Officers' Comp. 22	9.3	25.4	18.0	15.0	8.7	6.1	6.8	5.4	3.5	4.9	2.5	1.8	•

Selected Average Balance Sheet ($ in Thousands)

Net Receivables 23	118	0	9	126	521	1618	4753	7040	19768	25365	83587	177958	300482
Inventories 24	11	0	2	35	56	173	655	1247	2403	3062	2667	5203	410
Net Property, Plant and Equipment 25	122	0	20	217	593	1255	2755	3636	10753	19228	70817	128652	799017
Total Assets 26	650	0	80	685	2176	6728	14538	35468	68285	144069	347030	951747	3841117
Notes and Loans Payable 27	248	0	42	191	980	2097	3719	11098	23313	38302	109144	344709	1739902
All Other Liabilities 28	163	0	15	126	462	1944	4974	9615	27695	36840	103714	259330	716278
Net Worth 29	238	0	23	367	734	2687	5845	14755	17277	68926	134172	347708	1384937

Selected Financial Ratios (Times to 1)

Current Ratio 30	1.5	1.6	•	2.7	1.4	1.6	1.4	1.6	1.4	1.5	1.8	1.5	1.2
Quick Ratio 31	1.2	1.4	•	2.0	1.2	1.2	1.2	1.1	1.0	1.0	1.3	1.3	0.8
Net Sales to Working Capital 32	13.5	29.5	•	8.1	17.3	12.5	15.0	7.8	8.4	8.1	6.7	9.5	19.6
Coverage Ratio 33	7.0	18.8	38.7	18.0	9.1	13.2	13.8	8.0	5.0	6.9	4.0	3.2	3.0
Total Asset Turnover 34	1.7	5.7	•	3.0	2.7	2.8	2.6	1.5	1.3	1.1	1.2	0.9	0.4
Inventory Turnover 35	40.2	61.8	•	25.8	59.0	52.8	26.1	19.1	13.4	13.1	61.0	66.2	42.9
Receivables Turnover 36	8.8	51.4	•	16.8	10.9	11.1	7.9	•	5.1	6.2	•	4.0	•
Total Liabilities to Net Worth 37	1.7	2.5	•	0.9	2.0	1.5	1.5	1.4	3.0	1.1	1.6	1.7	1.8
Current Assets to Working Capital 38	2.9	2.6	•	1.6	3.4	2.6	3.3	2.6	3.6	3.0	2.3	3.0	6.5
Current Liabilities to Working Capital 39	1.9	1.6	•	0.6	2.4	1.6	2.3	1.6	2.6	2.0	1.3	2.0	5.5
Working Capital to Net Sales 40	0.1	0.0	•	0.1	0.1	0.1	0.1	0.1	0.1	0.1	0.1	0.1	0.1
Inventory to Working Capital 41	0.1	0.1	•	0.2	0.1	0.1	0.3	0.2	0.2	0.1	0.0	0.0	0.0
Total Receipts to Cash Flow 42	3.8	3.1	1.7	4.6	6.0	5.1	4.7	4.2	3.4	2.8	4.6	4.8	2.0
Cost of Goods to Cash Flow 43	1.4	0.9	0.3	2.0	3.3	2.5	2.1	1.8	1.2	0.7	1.7	1.9	0.0
Cash Flow to Total Debt 44	0.7	2.6	•	1.4	0.7	0.9	0.9	0.6	0.5	0.7	0.4	0.3	0.3

Selected Financial Factors (in Percentages)

Debt Ratio 45	63.4	71.5	•	46.4	66.3	60.1	59.8	58.4	74.7	52.2	61.3	63.5	63.9
Return on Total Assets 46	17.4	66.6	•	25.1	18.4	18.2	18.3	12.4	12.1	11.0	10.0	8.8	8.7
Return on Equity Before Income Taxes 47	40.7	221.0	•	44.1	48.6	42.2	42.2	26.2	38.3	19.6	19.4	16.6	16.1
Return on Equity After Income Taxes 48	37.0	219.3	•	43.3	46.9	40.2	41.1	24.0	33.4	17.3	16.1	11.7	10.6
Profit Margin (Before Income Tax) 49	8.6	11.1	27.4	7.9	6.0	6.0	6.4	7.2	7.4	8.6	6.0	6.5	14.6
Profit Margin (After Income Tax) 50	7.8	11.0	26.1	7.7	5.8	5.7	6.2	6.6	6.4	7.6	5.0	4.6	9.6

Table I

Corporations with and without Net Income

WASTE MANAGEMENT AND REMEDIATION SERVICES

MONEY AMOUNTS AND SIZE OF ASSETS IN THOUSANDS OF DOLLARS

Item Description for Accounting Period 7/09 Through 6/10	Total	Zero Assets	Under 500	500 to 1,000	1,000 to 5,000	5,000 to 10,000	10,000 to 25,000	25,000 to 50,000	50,000 to 100,000	100,000 to 250,000	250,000 to 500,000	500,000 to 2,500,000	2,500,000 and over
Number of Enterprises **1**	17057	2308	10175	1620	2325	327	176	46	30	22	9	12	5
Revenues ($ in Thousands)													
Net Sales **2**	64892164	328399	6115150	1646665	10580318	4071479	4101808	1239142	2017450	2631088	2115725	6163431	23381509
Interest **3**	95366	9	585	1168	3877	514	4825	2508	2135	4540	491	28932	45782
Rents **4**	66461	0	0	97	417	0	965	1820	3360	1542	11	692	57555
Royalties **5**	11690	0	0	0	0	0	1	0	393	0	0	10685	612
Other Portfolio Income **6**	653534	4777	92	5175	50551	4717	7040	11442	8503	1135	1774	60211	498117
Other Receipts **7**	646659	1	4284	10055	67310	76240	23910	11192	13311	10785	55074	57747	316751
Total Receipts **8**	66365874	333186	6120111	1663160	10702473	4152950	4138549	1266104	2045152	2649090	2173075	6321698	24800326
Average Total Receipts **9**	3891	144	601	1027	4603	12700	23514	27524	68172	120413	241453	526808	4960065
Operating Costs/Operating Income (%)													
Cost of Operations **10**	39.0	32.0	30.5	28.3	43.0	57.0	53.2	50.2	49.6	38.4	40.9	25.3	36.6
Salaries and Wages **11**	14.9	22.0	13.8	15.1	10.7	8.0	9.5	11.1	11.5	16.0	19.1	19.4	17.9
Taxes Paid **12**	3.1	4.2	3.1	3.6	2.7	2.1	2.3	2.5	2.3	2.9	2.2	3.3	3.7
Interest Paid **13**	3.0	0.9	0.7	1.4	1.1	1.6	1.3	2.8	2.5	4.5	6.6	4.4	4.3
Depreciation **14**	6.6	4.0	3.0	7.5	4.7	4.0	6.5	7.6	6.8	7.6	7.2	6.5	8.6
Amortization and Depletion **15**	1.7	1.9	0.1	0.2	0.2	0.1	0.4	0.8	1.3	2.0	2.2	4.2	2.7
Pensions and Other Deferred Comp. **16**	0.4	0.1	0.4	0.5	0.3	0.5	0.7	0.5	0.2	0.4	0.2	1.0	0.3
Employee Benefits **17**	1.8	2.6	1.0	1.7	1.5	0.7	1.9	1.8	2.2	2.4	2.4	3.2	1.9
Advertising **18**	0.5	2.4	1.5	1.2	0.4	0.3	0.5	0.4	0.2	0.3	0.2	0.3	0.3
Other Expenses **19**	22.6	31.2	30.6	28.9	26.6	17.9	17.4	23.3	23.5	26.1	27.1	29.4	17.1
Officers' Compensation **20**	2.4	9.7	8.5	7.5	2.8	4.3	2.7	2.0	1.3	3.1	1.4	1.1	0.2
Operating Margin **21**	4.1	•	6.9	4.2	6.0	3.5	3.5	•	•	•	•	1.9	6.4
Operating Margin Before Officers' Comp. **22**	6.5	•	15.3	11.7	8.8	7.8	6.2	•	•	•	•	2.9	6.6

Selected Average Balance Sheet ($ in Thousands)

Net Receivables 23	470	0	13	98	427	2594	2803	4293	10943	18874	32991	69074	663978
Inventories 24	44	0	3	36	37	216	386	998	1734	1840	1465	8589	38109
Net Property, Plant and Equipment 25	1888	0	45	277	938	1915	6983	14281	22361	50099	97718	297298	4077334
Total Assets 26	4939	0	103	667	1994	6937	16341	36365	67751	162309	346399	975882	10046919
Notes and Loans Payable 27	1929	0	80	304	964	2377	6443	16766	30128	66798	196104	347529	3671569
All Other Liabilities 28	1431	0	15	90	628	1735	4145	16314	23738	36278	105960	253113	3019187
Net Worth 29	1580	0	8	274	402	2825	5752	3285	13886	59234	44335	375241	3356163

Selected Financial Ratios (Times to 1)

Current Ratio 30	1.1	•	2.0	3.0	1.2	2.1	1.8	1.0	1.7	1.4	0.6	1.0	0.9
Quick Ratio 31	0.9	•	1.9	2.2	0.9	1.7	1.4	0.9	1.3	1.0	0.5	0.6	0.8
Net Sales to Working Capital 32	33.9	•	26.6	4.7	31.1	5.5	8.3	61.8	6.6	11.2	•	•	•
Coverage Ratio 33	3.1	•	10.8	4.7	7.4	4.5	4.2	0.7	1.0	0.4	•	2.1	3.4
Total Asset Turnover 34	0.8	•	5.8	1.5	2.3	1.8	1.4	0.7	1.0	0.7	0.7	0.5	0.5
Inventory Turnover 35	33.4	•	64.3	8.0	53.0	32.8	32.1	13.6	19.2	24.9	65.7	15.1	45.8
Receivables Turnover 36	7.4	•	45.2	11.9	11.2	5.7	9.4	4.7	5.9	6.2	6.3	4.3	6.7
Total Liabilities to Net Worth 37	2.1	•	12.4	1.4	4.0	1.5	1.8	10.1	3.9	1.7	6.8	1.6	2.0
Current Assets to Working Capital 38	8.9	•	2.0	1.5	5.6	1.9	2.3	21.7	2.5	3.6	•	•	•
Current Liabilities to Working Capital 39	7.9	•	1.0	0.5	4.6	0.9	1.3	20.7	1.5	2.6	•	•	•
Working Capital to Net Sales 40	0.0	•	0.0	0.2	0.0	0.2	0.1	0.0	0.2	0.1	•	•	•
Inventory to Working Capital 41	0.4	•	0.1	0.2	0.3	0.1	0.2	1.1	0.2	0.2	•	•	•
Total Receipts to Cash Flow 42	4.3	8.3	3.3	3.4	3.5	5.7	5.6	6.1	5.4	5.8	6.5	3.5	4.8
Cost of Goods to Cash Flow 43	1.7	2.7	1.0	1.0	1.5	3.3	3.0	3.1	2.7	2.2	2.6	0.9	1.8
Cash Flow to Total Debt 44	0.3	•	1.9	0.8	0.8	0.5	0.4	0.1	0.2	0.2	0.1	0.2	0.1

Selected Financial Factors (in Percentages)

Debt Ratio 45	68.0	•	92.5	59.0	79.8	59.3	64.8	91.0	79.5	63.5	87.2	61.5	66.6
Return on Total Assets 46	7.2	•	44.7	10.1	18.9	12.8	8.1	1.5	2.5	1.2	•	4.8	6.9
Return on Equity Before Income Taxes 47	15.4	•	542.7	19.4	80.9	24.3	17.7	•	•	•	•	6.4	14.6
Return on Equity After Income Taxes 48	12.1	•	539.5	19.1	78.5	23.6	16.1	•	•	•	•	4.9	10.3
Profit Margin (Before Income Tax) 49	6.4	•	6.9	5.2	7.2	5.5	4.4	•	•	•	•	4.7	10.3
Profit Margin (After Income Tax) 50	5.0	•	6.9	5.1	6.9	5.4	4.0	•	•	•	•	3.5	7.2

Table II

Corporations with Net Income

WASTE MANAGEMENT AND REMEDIATION SERVICES

MONEY AMOUNTS AND SIZE OF ASSETS IN THOUSANDS OF DOLLARS

Item Description for Accounting Period 7/09 Through 6/10		Total	Zero Assets	Under 500	500 to 1,000	1,000 to 5,000	5,000 to 10,000	10,000 to 25,000	25,000 to 50,000	50,000 to 100,000	100,000 to 250,000	250,000 to 500,000	500,000 to 2,500,000	2,500,000 and over
Number of Enterprises	1	11702	1285	7253	1166	1599	214	110	27	17	17	0	8	5
Revenues ($ in Thousands)														
Net Sales	2	52341785	145894	4495375	1261655	7504581	3129749	3081967	809718	1448735	2284357	0	4298246	23881509
Interest	3	83645	0	422	1165	2438	499	2388	1563	972	4074	0	24342	45782
Rents	4	64198	0	0	97	417	0	103	1719	2763	1542	0	0	57555
Royalties	5	11314	0	0	0	0	0	1	0	17	0	0	10685	612
Other Portfolio Income	6	617847	4777	0	5170	36974	2223	4918	794	7709	904	0	56260	498117
Other Receipts	7	538763	0	1951	2837	61722	74892	21578	7202	5437	9344	0	37050	316751
Total Receipts	8	53657552	150671	4497748	1270924	7606132	3207363	3110955	820996	1465633	2300221	0	4426583	24800326
Average Total Receipts	9	4585	117	620	1090	4757	14988	28281	30407	86214	135307	•	553323	4960065
Operating Costs/Operating Income (%)														
Cost of Operations	10	37.0	1.2	26.4	19.0	36.0	55.1	52.1	46.8	58.0	40.7	•	23.1	36.6
Salaries and Wages	11	14.9	37.6	14.3	14.4	10.2	7.7	8.3	10.2	8.7	13.5	•	20.0	17.9
Taxes Paid	12	3.1	7.5	2.7	3.2	2.7	2.1	2.0	2.3	2.1	3.0	•	3.3	3.7
Interest Paid	13	2.8	0.3	0.5	1.2	0.8	0.6	0.8	2.1	2.0	2.3	•	4.1	4.3
Depreciation	14	6.6	2.2	1.8	8.8	4.6	3.2	5.8	8.3	4.9	6.5	•	6.4	8.6
Amortization and Depletion	15	1.8	•	0.1	0.3	0.0	0.0	0.2	0.5	1.1	1.5	•	5.0	2.7
Pensions and Other Deferred Comp.	16	0.4	•	0.5	0.4	0.0	0.6	0.5	0.6	0.2	0.5	•	1.2	0.3
Employee Benefits	17	1.8	4.1	0.8	1.7	1.4	0.7	1.8	1.7	1.9	2.6	•	3.5	1.9
Advertising	18	0.4	0.6	1.0	1.2	0.4	0.3	0.5	0.4	0.2	0.2	•	0.3	0.3
Other Expenses	19	21.8	26.3	30.4	32.3	30.7	18.1	17.7	17.2	15.9	22.9	•	27.5	17.1
Officers' Compensation	20	2.2	17.4	9.0	6.6	2.7	5.1	3.0	2.0	1.2	1.7	•	1.2	0.2
Operating Margin	21	7.3	2.7	12.6	11.1	10.0	6.7	7.3	7.9	3.7	4.7	•	4.4	6.4
Operating Margin Before Officers' Comp.	22	9.5	20.2	21.6	17.7	12.7	11.7	10.2	9.8	4.9	6.4	•	5.6	6.6

Selected Average Balance Sheet ($ in Thousands)

Net Receivables 23	531	0	16	109	406	2067	2803	3559	12278	21170	•	73435	663978
Inventories 24	50	0	3	0	29	239	467	1316	2909	2075	•	5314	40166
Net Property, Plant and Equipment 25	2358	0	43	308	808	1688	7480	15054	19908	51694	•	304414	4077334
Total Assets 26	6136		105	671	1890	6606	16688	38810	65421	167501	•	1093341	10046919
Notes and Loans Payable 27	2207	0	53	281	697	1401	5559	17582	22226	65102	•	346311	3671569
All Other Liabilities 28	1752	0	13	78	523	1814	3313	12179	16206	34690	•	305701	3019187
Net Worth 29	2177	0	40	313	671	3391	7815	9048	26989	67710	•	441328	3356163

Selected Financial Ratios (Times to 1)

Current Ratio 30	1.1	•	3.2	3.6	1.3	1.8	1.9	1.6	1.7	1.4	•	1.0	0.9
Quick Ratio 31	0.9	•	3.0	3.3	1.0	1.5	1.6	1.3	1.3	1.0	•	0.5	0.8
Net Sales to Working Capital 32	33.2	•	18.4	5.5	22.6	7.9	8.4	7.4	9.4	11.3	•	•	•
Coverage Ratio 33	4.6	22.3	26.4	11.1	15.2	17.4	10.9	5.5	3.4	3.4	•	2.9	3.4
Total Asset Turnover 34	0.7	•	5.9	1.6	2.5	2.2	1.7	0.8	1.3	0.8	•	0.5	0.5
Inventory Turnover 35	33.1	•	61.3	•	58.5	33.8	31.3	10.7	17.0	26.4	•	23.4	43.5
Receivables Turnover 36	7.7	•	38.5	•	13.3	8.2	11.7	5.7	6.3	6.3	•	6.3	•
Total Liabilities to Net Worth 37	1.8	•	1.6	1.1	1.8	0.9	1.1	3.3	1.4	1.5	•	1.5	2.0
Current Assets to Working Capital 38	8.7	•	1.5	1.4	4.1	2.2	2.1	2.6	2.5	3.8	•	3.8	•
Current Liabilities to Working Capital 39	7.7	•	0.5	0.4	3.1	1.2	1.1	1.6	1.5	2.8	•	2.8	•
Working Capital to Net Sales 40	0.0	•	0.1	0.2	0.0	0.1	0.1	0.1	0.1	0.1	•	0.1	•
Inventory to Working Capital 41	0.4	•	0.1	•	0.2	0.2	0.2	0.0	0.3	0.1	•	0.1	•
Total Receipts to Cash Flow 42	3.9	3.3	2.7	2.6	4.8	2.7	4.6	4.6	6.2	4.3	•	3.3	4.8
Cost of Goods to Cash Flow 43	1.4	0.0	0.7	0.5	1.0	2.6	2.4	2.1	3.6	1.7	•	0.8	1.8
Cash Flow to Total Debt 44	0.3	•	3.5	1.2	1.4	0.9	0.7	0.2	0.4	0.3	•	0.2	0.1

Selected Financial Factors (in Percentages)

Debt Ratio 45	64.5	•	62.1	53.4	64.5	48.7	53.2	76.7	58.7	59.6	•	59.6	66.6
Return on Total Assets 46	9.2	•	77.7	20.9	30.1	21.5	15.1	8.7	8.9	6.1	•	5.8	6.9
Return on Equity Before Income Taxes 47	20.3	•	197.2	40.8	79.2	39.4	29.3	30.6	15.2	10.7	•	9.4	14.6
Return on Equity After Income Taxes 48	16.8	•	196.4	40.4	77.1	38.5	27.4	25.8	13.9	8.6	•	7.4	10.3
Profit Margin (Before Income Tax) 49	9.9	6.0	12.7	11.8	11.3	9.1	8.2	9.2	4.8	5.4	•	7.7	10.3
Profit Margin (After Income Tax) 50	8.2	5.9	12.6	11.7	11.0	8.9	7.7	7.8	4.4	4.3	•	6.1	7.2

Table I

Corporations with and without Net Income

EDUCATIONAL SERVICES

MONEY AMOUNTS AND SIZE OF ASSETS IN THOUSANDS OF DOLLARS

Item Description for Accounting Period 7/09 Through 6/10	Total	Zero Assets	Under 500	500 to 1,000	1,000 to 5,000	5,000 to 10,000	10,000 to 25,000	25,000 to 50,000	50,000 to 100,000	100,000 to 250,000	250,000 to 500,000	500,000 to 2,500,000	2,500,000 and over
Number of Enterprises 1	55309	12430	39769	956	1722	159	124	56	31	33	13	10	5
Revenues ($ in Thousands)													
Net Sales 2	55914157	1405851	10415117	1456386	6072624	1411519	2106443	2762478	2548099	5217582	3647818	7159819	11710422
Interest 3	139206	564	3548	137	3684	2604	4024	7862	4380	8276	2430	16007	85689
Rents 4	37782	0	1176	0	1608	1663	3	1682	1692	13637	29	4228	12065
Royalties 5	95638	0	0	0	0	0	806	1448	106	2725	30730	36036	23786
Other Portfolio Income 6	180961	294	12193	0	21636	235	131	13514	5441	23637	50791	8298	44790
Other Receipts 7	858022	8539	100806	24555	147611	6921	114186	48202	32245	71348	49852	180585	73173
Total Receipts 8	57225766	1415248	10532840	1481078	6247163	1422942	2225593	2835186	2591963	5337205	3781650	7404973	11949925
Average Total Receipts 9	1035	114	265	1549	3628	8949	17948	50628	83612	161733	290896	740497	2389985
Operating Costs/Operating Income (%)													
Cost of Operations 10	12.8	33.1	14.8	22.9	12.7	12.0	16.4	22.9	8.9	15.8	6.8	10.0	7.5
Salaries and Wages 11	29.0	12.8	23.7	26.7	31.5	31.4	33.8	25.8	30.9	30.9	28.3	26.7	34.7
Taxes Paid 12	3.2	2.4	3.4	3.9	4.2	4.2	3.6	3.0	3.9	3.3	4.1	2.6	2.3
Interest Paid 13	1.4	1.3	0.8	0.3	0.5	0.6	0.9	2.5	1.3	1.8	1.5	0.4	3.1
Depreciation 14	3.0	2.5	1.3	0.7	1.7	2.6	2.4	4.1	4.2	3.1	3.8	3.0	4.7
Amortization and Depletion 15	0.9	0.6	0.3	0.0	0.1	0.2	0.8	1.1	1.4	1.9	1.1	0.9	1.4
Pensions and Other Deferred Comp. 16	0.4	0.0	0.6	0.2	0.4	0.7	0.2	0.4	0.6	0.4	0.4	0.5	0.2
Employee Benefits 17	2.3	0.7	1.5	2.2	1.3	2.1	1.8	3.0	2.0	2.4	2.4	4.5	2.3
Advertising 18	5.8	4.1	1.6	1.8	3.4	4.1	5.0	5.8	6.0	5.6	5.5	11.4	8.7
Other Expenses 19	29.3	44.4	37.8	27.5	32.3	29.1	28.5	23.1	27.6	27.9	33.0	25.1	22.5
Officers' Compensation 20	4.0	2.4	11.6	5.3	6.0	5.0	3.9	1.8	1.1	1.7	1.1	0.8	1.2
Operating Margin 21	7.9	•	2.7	8.4	6.0	7.9	2.5	6.7	12.2	5.4	11.9	14.1	11.4
Operating Margin Before Officers' Comp. 22	11.9	•	14.3	13.7	12.0	12.9	6.4	8.5	13.3	7.0	13.0	14.9	12.6

Selected Average Balance Sheet ($ in Thousands)

Net Receivables 23	94	0	5	75	432	1396	2671	6049	8514	19398	53804	62187	213552
Inventories 24	10	0	3	3	41	271	139	1581	1190	1857	2778	2274	12181
Net Property, Plant and Equipment 25	158	0	16	261	537	1187	2833	7749	16412	31470	72946	109836	469425
Total Assets 26	943	0	60	628	2075	6860	15588	34554	68017	148045	327563	807448	4264349
Notes and Loans Payable 27	285	0	45	160	927	1162	2769	15669	14452	42164	79011	132681	1321230
All Other Liabilities 28	293	0	27	235	761	4611	6131	12790	24062	43483	94626	194171	1208587
Net Worth 29	365	0	-12	234	387	1087	6689	6095	29503	62398	153926	480596	1734531

Selected Financial Ratios (Times to 1)

Current Ratio 30	1.3	•	1.1	1.6	1.6	1.2	1.5	1.4	1.3	1.2	1.3	1.4	1.3
Quick Ratio 31	1.0	•	0.8	1.3	1.4	0.9	1.3	1.1	1.0	1.0	1.0	1.0	0.7
Net Sales to Working Capital 32	12.2	•	89.0	12.1	8.2	15.4	5.8	11.1	14.4	16.1	11.8	10.2	8.5
Coverage Ratio 33	8.2	•	5.9	30.9	19.5	14.4	10.2	4.7	12.0	5.4	11.9	43.1	5.4
Total Asset Turnover 34	1.1	•	4.4	2.4	1.7	1.3	1.1	1.4	1.2	1.1	0.9	0.9	0.5
Inventory Turnover 35	13.1	•	14.5	131.7	11.0	3.9	20.1	7.2	6.1	13.5	6.9	31.5	14.4
Receivables Turnover 36	11.8	•	51.3	19.9	8.5	6.7	6.5	9.1	9.8	8.2	5.3	11.9	15.9
Total Liabilities to Net Worth 37	1.6	•	•	1.7	4.4	5.3	1.3	4.7	1.3	1.4	1.1	0.7	1.5
Current Assets to Working Capital 38	4.1	•	9.8	2.8	2.8	6.1	2.8	3.8	4.6	5.6	4.5	3.4	4.4
Current Liabilities to Working Capital 39	3.1	•	8.8	1.8	1.8	5.1	1.8	2.8	3.6	4.6	3.5	2.4	3.4
Working Capital to Net Sales 40	0.1	•	0.0	0.1	0.1	0.1	0.2	0.1	0.1	0.1	0.1	0.1	0.1
Inventory to Working Capital 41	0.1	•	0.9	0.0	0.1	0.4	0.0	0.4	0.2	0.2	0.1	0.0	0.1
Total Receipts to Cash Flow 42	3.2	3.7	3.3	3.3	3.2	3.4	3.3	3.8	3.0	3.4	2.4	2.8	3.3
Cost of Goods to Cash Flow 43	0.4	1.2	0.5	0.7	0.4	0.4	0.5	0.9	0.3	0.5	0.2	0.3	0.3
Cash Flow to Total Debt 44	0.6	•	1.1	1.2	0.6	0.5	0.6	0.5	0.7	0.5	0.7	0.8	0.3

Selected Financial Factors (in Percentages)

Debt Ratio 45	61.3	•	120.8	62.8	81.4	84.2	57.1	82.4	56.6	57.9	53.0	40.5	59.3
Return on Total Assets 46	12.6	•	20.3	25.2	15.8	12.0	9.8	16.8	18.4	10.2	14.8	16.0	9.1
Return on Equity Before Income Taxes 47	28.5	•	•	65.6	80.6	70.6	20.7	74.9	38.9	19.6	28.9	26.2	18.2
Return on Equity After Income Taxes 48	21.7	•	•	63.0	78.9	69.1	18.9	67.8	30.9	14.8	21.6	17.0	11.8
Profit Margin (Before Income Tax) 49	10.3	•	3.8	10.1	8.8	8.7	9.3	8.1	14.0	7.7	15.8	17.6	13.5
Profit Margin (After Income Tax) 50	7.8	•	3.8	9.7	8.7	8.5	7.4	11.1	5.9	7.7	•	11.4	8.7

361

Table II

Corporations with Net Income

EDUCATIONAL SERVICES

MONEY AMOUNTS AND SIZE OF ASSETS IN THOUSANDS OF DOLLARS

Item Description for Accounting Period 7/09 Through 6/10	Total	Zero Assets	Under 500	500 to 1,000	1,000 to 5,000	5,000 to 10,000	10,000 to 25,000	25,000 to 50,000	50,000 to 100,000	100,000 to 250,000	250,000 to 500,000	500,000 to 2,500,000	2,500,000 and over
Number of Enterprises 1	26914	3421	21143	781	1298	69	88	43	24	24	•	7	•
Revenues ($ in Thousands)													
Net Sales 2	47629750	1061555	6751045	1317570	5182789	1178034	1608303	2388343	2141721	4357708	•	7013089	•
Interest 3	67749	564	2224	29	2697	2063	1689	2682	3831	5811	•	15873	•
Rents 4	31422	0	959	0	1599	1663	3	1682	626	8865	•	4228	•
Royalties 5	91148	0	0	0	0	0	0	1448	106	1246	•	34158	•
Other Portfolio Income 6	164298	275	12193	0	21636	235	8	425	5307	22124	•	8298	•
Other Receipts 7	624979	362	72789	23825	54732	6968	119531	32421	36816	64456	•	179309	•
Total Receipts 8	48609346	1062756	6839210	1341424	5263453	1188963	1729534	2427001	2188407	4460210	•	7254955	•
Average Total Receipts 9	1806	311	323	1718	4055	17231	19654	56442	91184	185842	•	1036422	•
Operating Costs/Operating Income (%)													
Cost of Operations 10	12.5	40.6	15.6	25.1	8.5	14.4	17.9	24.8	10.0	16.3	•	9.1	•
Salaries and Wages 11	27.9	7.3	18.7	25.8	32.1	29.8	30.1	23.6	27.5	28.9	•	27.0	•
Taxes Paid 12	2.9	1.7	2.5	3.6	3.9	3.6	3.4	2.9	3.8	3.1	•	2.6	•
Interest Paid 13	0.9	0.3	0.3	0.1	0.4	0.2	0.6	1.7	1.2	1.1	•	0.4	•
Depreciation 14	3.0	2.1	0.9	0.3	1.7	1.6	2.7	3.7	3.8	3.1	•	3.1	•
Amortization and Depletion 15	0.7	0.0	0.2	0.0	0.1	0.1	0.2	0.5	0.6	1.2	•	0.9	•
Pensions and Other Deferred Comp. 16	0.4	0.0	0.5	0.3	0.4	0.8	0.3	0.4	0.6	0.2	•	0.5	•
Employee Benefits 17	2.2	0.4	1.1	2.2	1.4	2.3	1.2	2.3	1.9	2.0	•	4.6	•
Advertising 18	6.1	2.4	0.9	1.6	3.4	4.1	4.8	5.6	6.4	6.6	•	11.5	•
Other Expenses 19	27.7	38.3	36.1	26.8	31.2	23.0	28.0	21.1	26.2	27.5	•	25.1	•
Officers' Compensation 20	3.8	2.3	13.7	3.4	6.6	5.5	4.3	1.7	1.0	1.4	•	0.7	•
Operating Margin 21	11.9	4.7	9.5	10.9	10.4	14.5	6.6	11.6	16.9	8.5	•	14.6	•
Operating Margin Before Officers' Comp. 22	15.7	6.9	23.2	14.2	17.0	20.0	10.9	13.3	17.9	10.0	•	15.3	•

Selected Average Balance Sheet ($ in Thousands)

Net Receivables 23	151	0	5	92	411	2150	2914	6174	8616	16780	76482
Inventories 24	14	0	3	3	38	494	75	2027	1164	747	2634
Net Property, Plant and Equipment 25	275	0	18	222	633	822	3618	7701	16533	36798	150037
Total Assets 26	1481	0	68	634	2229	7134	15251	34197	69684	144669	896150
Notes and Loans Payable 27	370	0	28	110	1152	865	2134	15199	14945	28802	103419
All Other Liabilities 28	467	0	22	282	659	3174	6277	11934	24854	42601	224055
Net Worth 29	644	0	17	242	418	3095	6839	7063	29885	73267	568676

Selected Financial Ratios (Times to 1)

Current Ratio 30	1.4	•	1.7	1.5	1.8	1.6	1.6	1.4	1.2	1.3	1.3
Quick Ratio 31	1.0	•	1.2	1.2	1.6	1.4	1.3	1.1	1.0	1.1	0.9
Net Sales to Working Capital 32	11.1	•	20.7	12.5	7.2	8.6	5.3	10.2	18.1	12.6	14.4
Coverage Ratio 33	16.0	18.8	34.2	207.7	33.9	82.8	23.2	8.8	16.5	11.3	44.5
Total Asset Turnover 34	1.2	•	4.7	2.7	1.8	2.4	1.2	1.6	1.3	1.3	1.1
Inventory Turnover 35	15.3	•	17.0	150.6	8.9	5.0	43.6	6.8	7.7	39.7	34.5
Receivables Turnover 36	12.8	•	58.2	29.3	9.2	7.8	6.9	9.6	•	10.6	•
Total Liabilities to Net Worth 37	1.3	•	2.9	1.6	4.3	1.3	1.2	3.8	1.3	1.0	0.6
Current Assets to Working Capital 38	3.7	•	2.5	3.0	2.3	2.7	2.7	3.3	5.2	3.9	4.1
Current Liabilities to Working Capital 39	2.7	•	1.5	2.0	1.3	1.7	1.7	2.3	4.2	2.9	3.1
Working Capital to Net Sales 40	0.1	•	0.0	0.1	0.1	0.1	0.2	0.1	0.1	0.1	0.1
Inventory to Working Capital 41	0.1	•	0.2	0.0	0.1	0.2	0.0	0.4	0.2	0.1	0.0
Total Receipts to Cash Flow 42	2.9	3.6	2.6	3.1	3.1	3.2	2.8	3.4	2.7	3.1	2.8
Cost of Goods to Cash Flow 43	0.4	1.5	0.4	0.8	0.3	0.5	0.5	0.9	0.3	0.5	0.3
Cash Flow to Total Debt 44	0.7	•	2.4	1.4	0.7	1.3	0.8	0.6	0.8	0.8	1.1

Selected Financial Factors (in Percentages)

Debt Ratio 45	56.5	•	74.4	61.8	81.3	56.6	55.2	79.3	57.1	49.4	36.5
Return on Total Assets 46	17.8	•	52.2	33.9	22.0	37.4	17.7	24.2	26.2	15.1	20.7
Return on Equity Before Income Taxes 47	38.4	•	198.1	88.5	114.1	85.1	37.7	103.8	57.4	27.2	31.9
Return on Equity After Income Taxes 48	30.4	•	196.7	85.4	112.1	83.9	35.3	95.8	47.1	21.7	20.8
Profit Margin (Before Income Tax) 49	14.0	4.8	10.8	12.7	11.9	15.4	14.1	13.2	19.2	11.0	18.1
Profit Margin (After Income Tax) 50	11.1	4.1	10.8	12.3	11.7	15.2	13.2	12.2	15.8	8.7	11.8

Table I

Corporations with and without Net Income

OFFICES OF PHYSICIANS

MONEY AMOUNTS AND SIZE OF ASSETS IN THOUSANDS OF DOLLARS

Item Description for Accounting Period 7/09 Through 6/10		Total	Zero Assets	Under 500	500 to 1,000	1,000 to 5,000	5,000 to 10,000	10,000 to 25,000	25,000 to 50,000	50,000 to 100,000	100,000 to 250,000	250,000 to 500,000	500,000 to 2,500,000	2,500,000 and over
Number of Enterprises	1	154471	16592	128201	5342	3871	205	154	45	33	18	3	6	0
Revenues ($ in Thousands)														
Net Sales	2	246899994	3296479	144315513	17523590	44063553	5571007	8854828	3731866	4343047	3393354	1110021	10696738	0
Interest	3	100238	796	22933	2756	15265	3379	5065	3563	5589	8461	1306	31127	0
Rents	4	179815	0	90242	2729	26825	9846	1775	18952	9892	13727	1206	4620	0
Royalties	5	10023	0	9689	4	0	0	330	0	0	0	0	0	0
Other Portfolio Income	6	223664	62311	55420	8959	18852	6623	13976	3924	8936	28460	335	15868	0
Other Receipts	7	6927278	775420	3799955	390775	894788	157062	60877	114931	309965	60367	9208	353927	0
Total Receipts	8	254341012	4135006	148293752	17928813	45019283	5747917	8936851	3873236	4677429	3504369	1122076	11102280	0
Average Total Receipts	9	1647	249	1157	3356	11630	28039	58032	86072	141740	194687	374025	1850380	•
Operating Costs/Operating Income (%)														
Cost of Operations	10	5.1	10.6	3.6	9.5	4.9	5.6	10.3	16.2	10.4	9.4	4.5	3.9	•
Salaries and Wages	11	29.2	21.2	24.7	25.4	34.3	40.8	43.0	43.5	39.5	45.5	23.2	45.5	•
Taxes Paid	12	3.0	3.9	3.0	3.4	3.0	3.2	2.7	2.9	2.8	2.7	2.0	3.2	•
Interest Paid	13	0.4	0.4	0.2	0.5	0.4	0.4	0.5	0.6	0.9	1.6	2.0	1.3	•
Depreciation	14	1.0	1.1	0.7	1.1	1.7	2.0	2.0	1.5	1.8	2.3	2.3	0.7	•
Amortization and Depletion	15	0.1	0.1	0.0	0.1	0.1	0.1	0.1	0.2	0.4	0.5	0.5	0.7	•
Pensions and Other Deferred Comp.	16	3.6	2.2	3.8	3.0	2.8	2.8	2.1	4.1	1.6	2.3	1.4	7.6	•
Employee Benefits	17	2.6	2.6	1.9	1.8	2.4	3.2	3.1	10.7	10.5	3.7	2.5	5.8	•
Advertising	18	0.5	0.3	0.5	0.3	0.6	0.2	0.4	0.2	0.4	1.3	0.2	0.1	•
Other Expenses	19	30.4	39.9	29.7	26.4	31.1	34.7	34.0	22.0	36.6	32.3	60.6	32.3	•
Officers' Compensation	20	21.7	30.6	28.3	19.9	16.4	8.1	3.1	1.6	1.0	0.8	0.5	0.5	•
Operating Margin	21	2.6	•	3.5	8.6	2.2	•	•	•	•	•	0.3	•	•
Operating Margin Before Officers' Comp.	22	24.2	17.6	31.9	28.6	18.6	6.8	1.8	•	•	•	0.7	0.7	•

Selected Average Balance Sheet ($ in Thousands)

	•	•	•	•	•	•	•	•	•	•	•	•
Net Receivables 23	27	0	2	48	284	1382	3090	6378	16804	26049	32095	79886
Inventories 24	2	0	0	5	9	47	121	432	327	622	1024	15837
Net Property, Plant and Equipment 25	68	0	26	144	774	2152	4880	11625	17748	31150	43185	74714
Total Assets 26	269	0	89	664	1900	6917	14393	37577	68099	146087	311523	1358718
Notes and Loans Payable 27	114	0	49	363	913	2918	8772	13652	17649	36463	136326	271365
All Other Liabilities 28	130	0	33	258	720	3275	5551	9606	27576	61311	37599	1246182
Net Worth 29	26	0	7	42	268	724	70	14318	22874	48314	137599	-158828

Selected Financial Ratios (Times to 1)

	•	•	•	•	•	•	•	•	•	•	•	•
Current Ratio 30	1.1	•	1.0	1.6	0.9	0.8	1.0	1.1	1.2	1.2	1.9	1.5
Quick Ratio 31	0.9	•	0.9	1.2	0.8	0.7	0.7	0.9	1.1	1.1	1.7	1.1
Net Sales to Working Capital 32	172.0	•	631.9	24.9	•	•	119.6	22.7	20.4	12.8	17.8	•
Coverage Ratio 33	15.0	34.3	26.8	24.2	10.7	6.0	0.3	1.3	2.9	1.5	1.7	2.8
Total Asset Turnover 34	5.9	•	12.6	4.9	6.0	3.9	4.0	2.2	1.9	1.3	1.2	1.3
Inventory Turnover 35	43.2	•	92.2	57.2	61.6	32.6	48.7	31.2	41.7	28.4	16.4	4.4
Receivables Turnover 36	56.2	•	602.8	74.5	40.6	14.9	19.8	10.9	9.2	7.4	4.3	22.2
Total Liabilities to Net Worth 37	9.4	•	12.5	14.8	6.1	8.6	204.0	1.6	2.0	2.0	1.3	•
Current Assets to Working Capital 38	11.7	•	24.4	2.6	•	•	20.8	5.7	5.5	2.1	3.2	•
Current Liabilities to Working Capital 39	10.7	•	23.4	1.6	•	•	19.8	4.7	4.5	1.1	2.2	•
Working Capital to Net Sales 40	0.0	•	0.0	0.0	•	•	0.0	0.0	0.0	0.1	0.1	•
Inventory to Working Capital 41	0.2	•	0.2	0.0	•	•	0.7	0.1	0.1	0.0	0.2	•
Total Receipts to Cash Flow 42	3.3	2.2	3.2	3.3	3.4	3.2	3.6	5.2	2.9	3.5	1.7	3.4
Cost of Goods to Cash Flow 43	0.2	0.2	0.1	0.3	0.2	0.2	0.4	0.8	0.3	0.3	0.1	0.1
Cash Flow to Total Debt 44	2.0	•	4.2	1.6	2.0	1.4	1.1	0.7	1.0	0.6	1.3	0.3

Selected Financial Factors (in Percentages)

	•	•	•	•	•	•	•	•	•	•	•	•
Debt Ratio 45	90.4	•	92.6	93.7	85.9	89.5	99.5	61.9	66.4	66.9	55.8	111.7
Return on Total Assets 46	35.3	•	82.1	56.5	28.9	8.6	0.5	1.8	5.0	3.1	4.0	4.6
Return on Equity Before Income Taxes 47	343.3	•	1064.5	853.8	185.8	68.7	•	1.0	9.8	3.0	3.5	•
Return on Equity After Income Taxes 48	336.3	•	1057.4	851.0	184.0	66.1	•	•	6.4	2.6	•	•
Profit Margin (Before Income Tax) 49	5.6	12.5	6.3	11.0	4.4	1.8	0.2	•	1.7	0.8	1.3	2.2
Profit Margin (After Income Tax) 50	5.4	12.4	6.2	10.9	4.3	1.8	•	•	1.1	•	1.0	1.3

Table II

Corporations with Net Income

OFFICES OF PHYSICIANS

MONEY AMOUNTS AND SIZE OF ASSETS IN THOUSANDS OF DOLLARS

Item Description for Accounting Period 7/09 Through 6/10		Total	Zero Assets	Under 500	500 to 1,000	1,000 to 5,000	5,000 to 10,000	10,000 to 25,000	25,000 to 50,000	50,000 to 100,000	100,000 to 250,000	250,000 to 500,000	500,000 to 2,500,000	2,500,000 and over
Number of Enterprises	1	103658	9101	87186	4439	2693	104	76	19	21	14	0	3	0
Revenues ($ in Thousands)														
Net Sales	2	15204209	2066715	92617649	11927118	29773175	2258589	5291334	1886880	2912524	3750381	0	1719846	0
Interest	3	56688	742	8602	1145	9451	919	4115	997	4544	6426	0	19747	0
Rents	4	131806	0	73225	1323	21641	8399	1024	15272	4971	4806	0	1146	0
Royalties	5	9905	0	9575	0	0	0	330	0	0	0	0	0	0
Other Portfolio Income	6	147470	62296	43947	8956	16715	2858	7261	709	1163	1723	0	1840	0
Other Receipts	7	5109864	570534	2829001	357505	606964	103848	88776	38622	229179	44134	0	241300	0
Total Receipts	8	159659942	2700287	95581999	12296047	30427946	2374613	5392840	1942480	3152381	3807470	0	1983879	0
Average Total Receipts	9	1540	297	1096	2770	11299	22833	70958	102236	150113	271962	•	661293	•
Operating Costs/Operating Income (%)														
Cost of Operations	10	6.0	3.9	4.1	12.6	5.2	7.5	8.1	25.9	12.7	9.6	•	24.4	•
Salaries and Wages	11	24.9	10.8	22.4	18.2	28.5	40.0	44.5	29.0	33.4	39.2	•	36.7	•
Taxes Paid	12	2.9	3.3	2.9	3.1	2.9	3.7	2.7	2.2	2.6	2.4	•	3.6	•
Interest Paid	13	0.4	0.3	0.3	0.6	0.4	0.4	0.4	0.9	1.0	1.6	•	4.0	•
Depreciation	14	1.0	1.3	0.7	1.3	1.5	2.6	1.9	1.3	1.9	1.9	•	1.6	•
Amortization and Depletion	15	0.1	0.1	0.0	0.1	0.0	0.1	0.2	0.3	0.6	0.4	•	2.9	•
Pensions and Other Deferred Comp.	16	2.9	1.5	3.1	3.2	2.6	2.7	2.4	2.7	1.9	2.1	•	0.3	•
Employee Benefits	17	2.3	1.0	1.8	1.1	2.1	2.7	2.9	15.9	14.3	3.3	•	2.7	•
Advertising	18	0.5	0.3	0.5	0.3	0.6	0.4	0.4	0.2	0.5	0.2	•	0.4	•
Other Expenses	19	30.6	48.8	30.6	24.3	32.4	26.6	32.0	17.8	34.4	36.5	•	19.8	•
Officers' Compensation	20	21.4	30.5	26.1	20.5	17.9	7.6	3.4	1.8	1.1	0.7	•	1.9	•
Operating Margin	21	7.0	•	7.7	14.7	6.0	5.8	1.3	2.0	•	2.1	•	1.8	•
Operating Margin Before Officers' Comp.	22	28.4	28.7	33.7	35.3	23.9	13.4	4.7	3.8	•	2.8	•	3.7	•

Selected Average Balance Sheet ($ in Thousands)

Net Receivables 23	•	54609	32282	13205	7328	2043	1079	248	29	2	0	22
Inventories 24	•	32733	924	290	481	126	65	2	6	1	0	2
Net Property, Plant and Equipment 25	•	54949	34447	18602	15272	5000	2108	683	150	25	0	64
Total Assets 26	•	743675	169422	68563	41242	14362	6791	1780	668	92	0	236
Notes and Loans Payable 27	•	317180	58041	15127	23561	6584	2017	704	291	40	0	95
All Other Liabilities 28	•	-32226	64703	22473	9774	4015	1137	475	169	26	0	60
Net Worth 29	•	458721	46678	30963	7907	3763	3636	601	208	26	0	80

Selected Financial Ratios (Times to 1)

Current Ratio 30	•	2.4	1.2	1.4	0.7	1.0	2.3	1.1	1.9	1.3	•	1.3
Quick Ratio 31	•	1.3	1.1	1.0	0.6	0.8	2.2	1.0	1.4	1.3	•	1.1
Net Sales to Working Capital 32	•	4.1	24.9	15.1	•	535.9	12.5	319.0	16.6	90.6	•	57.1
Coverage Ratio 33	•	5.3	3.2	4.9	6.2	9.2	27.4	21.4	31.5	40.5	86.4	25.7
Total Asset Turnover 34	•	0.8	1.6	2.0	2.4	4.8	3.2	6.2	4.0	11.5	•	6.3
Inventory Turnover 35	•	4.3	27.8	60.7	53.5	44.6	25.3	297.2	52.4	84.1	•	42.3
Receivables Turnover 36	•	•	8.2	11.1	11.8	30.2	•	47.5	90.7	610.9	•	67.3
Total Liabilities to Net Worth 37	•	0.6	2.6	1.2	4.2	2.8	0.9	2.0	2.2	2.5	•	1.9
Current Assets to Working Capital 38	•	1.7	5.3	3.4	•	46.0	1.8	20.1	2.1	3.9	•	3.9
Current Liabilities to Working Capital 39	•	0.7	4.3	2.4	•	45.0	0.8	19.1	1.1	2.9	•	2.9
Working Capital to Net Sales 40	•	0.2	0.0	0.1	•	0.0	0.1	0.0	0.1	0.0	•	0.0
Inventory to Working Capital 41	•	0.2	0.1	0.0	•	0.9	0.0	0.1	0.0	0.0	•	0.1
Total Receipts to Cash Flow 42	•	3.4	2.7	2.8	5.3	3.5	3.4	2.9	2.7	2.8	1.4	2.8
Cost of Goods to Cash Flow 43	•	0.8	0.3	0.4	1.4	0.3	0.3	0.2	0.3	0.1	0.1	0.2
Cash Flow to Total Debt 44	•	0.6	0.8	1.3	0.6	1.9	2.1	3.2	2.1	5.8	•	3.4

Selected Financial Factors (in Percentages)

Debt Ratio 45	•	38.3	72.4	54.8	80.8	73.8	46.5	66.2	68.9	71.4	•	65.9
Return on Total Assets 46	•	16.3	8.3	10.0	14.1	17.2	36.2	53.4	74.0	128.3	•	69.3
Return on Equity Before Income Taxes 47	•	21.4	20.8	17.6	61.5	58.7	65.2	150.7	230.1	437.4	•	195.1
Return on Equity After Income Taxes 48	•	14.0	15.1	13.6	55.6	52.7	64.1	149.6	229.4	434.8	•	191.8
Profit Margin (Before Income Tax) 49	•	17.2	3.6	3.9	4.9	3.2	10.9	8.2	17.8	10.9	28.9	10.5
Profit Margin (After Income Tax) 50	•	11.2	2.6	3.0	4.4	2.9	10.7	8.1	17.8	10.8	28.8	10.4

Table I

Corporations with and without Net Income

OFFICES OF DENTISTS

MONEY AMOUNTS AND SIZE OF ASSETS IN THOUSANDS OF DOLLARS

Item Description for Accounting Period 7/09 Through 6/10		Total	Zero Assets	Under 500	500 to 1,000	1,000 to 5,000	5,000 to 10,000	10,000 to 25,000	25,000 to 50,000	50,000 to 100,000	100,000 to 250,000	250,000 to 500,000	500,000 to 2,500,000	2,500,000 and over
Number of Enterprises	1	74120	5217	61469	6138	1269	10	5	0	4	5	3	0	0
Revenues ($ in Thousands)														
Net Sales	2	63290802	2944844	45317923	9122496	2952427	360421	196016		225009	986127	1185539	0	0
Interest	3	11537	160	7362	2882	516	0	100		49	48	419	0	0
Rents	4	1079	0	1079	0	0	0	0		0	0	0	0	0
Royalties	5	0	0	0	0	0	0	0		0	0	0	0	0
Other Portfolio Income	6	174632	27006	143970	1135	1560	0	254		692	16	0	0	0
Other Receipts	7	1511409	65	1136423	311786	43619	0	2558		10406	4265	2288	0	0
Total Receipts	8	64989459	2972075	46606757	9438299	2998122	360421	198928		236156	990456	1188246	0	0
Average Total Receipts	9	877	570	758	1538	2363	36042	39786	•	59039	198091	396082	•	•
Operating Costs/Operating Income (%)														
Cost of Operations	10	5.7	0.4	5.4	6.3	12.8	1.4	14.4	•	11.1	7.1	2.7	•	•
Salaries and Wages	11	24.8	43.3	22.7	24.2	27.8	33.3	49.6	•	39.2	33.7	41.6	•	•
Taxes Paid	12	3.6	3.8	3.7	3.5	3.9	1.8	3.7	•	2.4	3.4	4.2	•	•
Interest Paid	13	1.3	0.3	0.9	2.3	2.4	0.0	0.0	•	3.5	3.7	3.8	•	•
Depreciation	14	2.0	1.0	1.9	2.2	2.7	0.4	0.5	•	3.4	3.9	3.5	•	•
Amortization and Depletion	15	0.6	0.0	0.4	1.0	1.3	•	•	•	1.7	2.4	3.6	•	•
Pensions and Other Deferred Comp.	16	2.1	1.0	2.2	2.2	1.2	0.4	13.6	•	0.1	1.5	0.1	•	•
Employee Benefits	17	1.2	0.4	1.2	1.7	1.1	0.0	4.2	•	1.6	1.4	0.8	•	•
Advertising	18	1.5	4.3	1.3	1.2	1.2	1.8	0.7	•	1.2	3.2	2.3	•	•
Other Expenses	19	32.0	38.4	33.0	24.2	30.4	58.8	9.4	•	28.4	37.3	33.0	•	•
Officers' Compensation	20	18.4	3.6	20.5	21.9	7.8	•	1.4	•	1.1	0.5	0.7	•	•
Operating Margin	21	6.9	3.4	6.8	9.4	7.5	2.2	2.6	•	6.2	1.6	3.8	•	•
Operating Margin Before Officers' Comp.	22	25.3	7.0	27.4	31.3	15.3	2.2	4.0	•	7.4	2.2	4.4	•	•

Selected Average Balance Sheet ($ in Thousands)

	•	•	•	•	•	•	•	•	•	•	•
Net Receivables 23	12	0	3	51	15	5271	5141	•	20342	3921	57145
Inventories 24	1	0	1	4	0	30	0	•	2055	1656	846
Net Property, Plant and Equipment 25	77	0	54	182	695	372	654	•	8439	30704	53026
Total Assets 26	230	0	138	666	1568	5688	18095	•	70955	162674	404388
Notes and Loans Payable 27	150	0	97	455	1043	77	520	•	33036	90670	162613
All Other Liabilities 28	57	0	27	279	173	6316	8609	•	27063	38079	79181
Net Worth 29	22	0	14	-67	352	-705	8967	•	10856	33925	162594

Selected Financial Ratios (Times to 1)

	•	•	•	•	•	•	•	•	•	•	•
Current Ratio 30	1.0	•	1.3	0.6	0.9	0.8	1.5	•	1.9	0.6	2.0
Quick Ratio 31	0.9	•	1.2	0.5	0.9	0.8	1.5	•	1.6	0.3	1.5
Net Sales to Working Capital 32	452.0	•	61.9	•	•	9.6	•	•	3.8	•	8.2
Coverage Ratio 33	8.6	14.0	11.6	6.6	4.8	229.6	7902.0	•	4.2	1.6	2.0
Total Asset Turnover 34	3.7	•	5.3	2.2	1.5	6.3	2.2	•	0.8	1.2	1.0
Inventory Turnover 35	40.5	•	55.5	22.6	698.5	16.8	•	•	3.0	8.5	12.8
Receivables Turnover 36	76.2	•	274.5	34.1	78.7	5.9	•	•	5.5	47.7	•
Total Liabilities to Net Worth 37	9.3	•	8.6	3.5	•	•	1.0	•	5.5	3.8	1.5
Current Assets to Working Capital 38	34.9	•	3.9	•	•	•	3.1	•	2.1	•	2.0
Current Liabilities to Working Capital 39	33.9	•	2.9	•	•	•	2.1	•	1.1	•	1.0
Working Capital to Net Sales 40	0.0	•	0.0	•	•	•	0.1	•	0.3	•	0.1
Inventory to Working Capital 41	0.6	•	0.1	•	•	•	•	•	0.1	•	0.0
Total Receipts to Cash Flow 42	2.9	2.7	2.8	3.2	3.1	1.7	8.2	•	3.0	3.1	3.3
Cost of Goods to Cash Flow 43	0.2	0.0	0.2	0.2	0.4	0.0	1.2	•	0.3	0.2	0.1
Cash Flow to Total Debt 44	1.4	•	2.1	0.6	0.6	3.4	0.5	•	0.3	0.5	0.5

Selected Financial Factors (in Percentages)

	•	•	•	•	•	•	•	•	•	•	•
Debt Ratio 45	90.3	•	89.6	110.1	77.6	112.4	50.4	•	84.7	79.1	59.8
Return on Total Assets 46	40.3	•	56.6	33.8	17.0	13.7	8.7	•	11.6	7.0	7.6
Return on Equity Before Income Taxes 47	366.2	•	496.3	•	60.0	•	17.6	•	58.0	12.1	9.7
Return on Equity After Income Taxes 48	362.5	•	493.6	•	59.1	•	17.6	•	38.6	7.6	7.5
Profit Margin (Before Income Tax) 49	9.6	4.4	9.7	12.9	9.1	2.2	4.0	•	11.2	2.1	4.0
Profit Margin (After Income Tax) 50	9.5	4.4	9.6	12.8	8.9	2.2	4.0	•	7.4	1.3	3.1

Table II

Corporations with Net Income

OFFICES OF DENTISTS

MONEY AMOUNTS AND SIZE OF ASSETS IN THOUSANDS OF DOLLARS

Item Description for Accounting Period 7/09 Through 6/10	Total	Zero Assets	Under 500	500 to 1,000	1,000 to 5,000	5,000 to 10,000	10,000 to 25,000	25,000 to 50,000	50,000 to 100,000	100,000 to 250,000	250,000 to 500,000	500,000 to 2,500,000	2,500,000 and over
Number of Enterprises **1**	54249	2627	45704	4827	1080	•	0	•	•	•	0	0	0

Revenues ($ in Thousands)

Item	Total	Zero Assets	Under 500	500 to 1,000	1,000 to 5,000	5,000 to 10,000	10,000 to 25,000	25,000 to 50,000	50,000 to 100,000	100,000 to 250,000	250,000 to 500,000	500,000 to 2,500,000	2,500,000 and over
Net Sales **2**	49940927	2266281	35644693	7559536	2531737	•	0	•	•	•	0	0	0
Interest **3**	4038	0	2976	206	358	•	0	•	•	•	0	0	0
Rents **4**	0	0	0	0	0	•	0	•	•	•	0	0	0
Royalties **5**	0	0	0	0	0	•	0	•	•	•	0	0	0
Other Portfolio Income **6**	24200	17787	5522	139	42	•	0	•	•	•	0	0	0
Other Receipts **7**	1289428	65	926465	311553	44392	•	0	•	•	•	0	0	0
Total Receipts **8**	51258593	2284133	36579656	7871434	2576529	•	0	•	•	•	0	0	0
Average Total Receipts **9**	945	869	800	1631	2386	•	•	•	•	•	•	•	•

Operating Costs/Operating Income (%)

Item	Total	Zero Assets	Under 500	500 to 1,000	1,000 to 5,000	5,000 to 10,000	10,000 to 25,000	25,000 to 50,000	50,000 to 100,000	100,000 to 250,000	250,000 to 500,000	500,000 to 2,500,000	2,500,000 and over
Cost of Operations **10**	6.4	0.3	6.2	7.0	14.3	•	•	•	•	•	•	•	•
Salaries and Wages **11**	24.5	45.2	22.6	22.5	28.4	•	•	•	•	•	•	•	•
Taxes Paid **12**	3.6	4.5	3.6	3.5	4.0	•	•	•	•	•	•	•	•
Interest Paid **13**	1.2	0.0	0.8	2.1	2.2	•	•	•	•	•	•	•	•
Depreciation **14**	1.6	0.1	1.4	1.8	2.2	•	•	•	•	•	•	•	•
Amortization and Depletion **15**	0.5	•	0.3	0.9	0.8	•	•	•	•	•	•	•	•
Pensions and Other Deferred Comp. **16**	2.0	1.3	2.1	2.3	1.4	•	•	•	•	•	•	•	•
Employee Benefits **17**	1.1	0.2	1.1	1.4	1.0	•	•	•	•	•	•	•	•
Advertising **18**	1.5	5.5	1.4	0.9	1.2	•	•	•	•	•	•	•	•
Other Expenses **19**	29.6	33.7	31.1	22.9	25.5	•	•	•	•	•	•	•	•
Officers' Compensation **20**	17.2	3.0	18.4	22.7	8.0	•	•	•	•	•	•	•	•
Operating Margin **21**	10.8	6.1	11.1	12.0	11.0	•	•	•	•	•	•	•	•
Operating Margin Before Officers' Comp. **22**	27.9	9.1	29.6	34.7	19.0	•	•	•	•	•	•	•	•

Selected Average Balance Sheet ($ in Thousands)

Net Receivables 23	12	0	3	54	17
Inventories 24	1	0	1	3	0
Net Property, Plant and Equipment 25	79	0	52	158	743
Total Assets 26	249	0	142	660	1579
Notes and Loans Payable 27	140	0	82	405	936
All Other Liabilities 28	42	0	28	109	54
Net Worth 29	67	0	33	147	589

Selected Financial Ratios (Times to 1)

Current Ratio 30	1.6	•	1.6	1.6	1.7
Quick Ratio 31	1.4	•	1.5	1.4	1.7
Net Sales to Working Capital 32	32.4	•	39.4	21.2	17.4
Coverage Ratio 33	12.4	144.0	17.5	8.8	6.7
Total Asset Turnover 34	3.7	•	5.5	2.4	1.5
Inventory Turnover 35	55.2	•	66.3	40.3	1754.4
Receivables Turnover 36	86.7	•	239.1	33.9	101.6
Total Liabilities to Net Worth 37	2.7	•	3.3	2.6	1.7
Current Assets to Working Capital 38	2.7	•	2.7	2.6	2.4
Current Liabilities to Working Capital 39	1.7	•	1.7	1.6	1.4
Working Capital to Net Sales 40	0.0	•	0.0	0.0	0.1
Inventory to Working Capital 41	0.0	•	0.0	0.1	0.0
Total Receipts to Cash Flow 42	2.7	2.9	2.6	3.0	3.2
Cost of Goods to Cash Flow 43	0.2	0.0	0.2	0.2	0.5
Cash Flow to Total Debt 44	1.9	•	2.7	1.0	0.8

Selected Financial Factors (in Percentages)

Debt Ratio 45	73.1	•	76.9	77.8	62.7
Return on Total Assets 46	53.9	•	80.0	43.0	22.2
Return on Equity Before Income Taxes 47	184.6	•	326.9	171.7	50.7
Return on Equity After Income Taxes 48	182.9	•	325.3	170.8	50.1
Profit Margin (Before Income Tax) 49	13.4	6.9	13.8	16.1	12.7
Profit Margin (After Income Tax) 50	13.3	6.9	13.7	16.0	12.6

Table I

Corporations with and without Net Income

OFFICES OF OTHER HEALTH PRACTITIONERS

MONEY AMOUNTS AND SIZE OF ASSETS IN THOUSANDS OF DOLLARS

Item Description for Accounting Period 7/09 Through 6/10	Total	Zero Assets	Under 500	500 to 1,000	1,000 to 5,000	5,000 to 10,000	10,000 to 25,000	25,000 to 50,000	50,000 to 100,000	100,000 to 250,000	250,000 to 500,000	500,000 to 2,500,000	2,500,000 and over
Number of Enterprises **1**	109835	17902	88842	2007	907	66	50	27	21	11	4	0	0
Revenues ($ in Thousands)													
Net Sales **2**	70126625	1433323	40309235	5809140	6476564	1915641	1659839	1181923	2075649	2872132	6393179	0	0
Interest **3**	99784	0	2603	279	773	1008	2426	2913	1795	11610	76377	0	0
Rents **4**	53339	0	27153	0	11	0	252	7924	4015	3671	10312	0	0
Royalties **5**	33013	0	0	0	0	0	0	0	0	0	33013	0	0
Other Portfolio Income **6**	87674	0	58586	646	324	62	12084	810	8576	163	6422	0	0
Other Receipts **7**	1651276	38975	178972	1124	18501	6564	78965	34353	85826	655145	552851	0	0
Total Receipts **8**	72051711	1472298	40576549	5811189	6496173	1923275	1753566	1227923	2175861	3542721	7072154	0	0
Average Total Receipts **9**	656	82	457	2895	7162	29141	35071	45479	103612	322066	1768038	•	•
Operating Costs/Operating Income (%)													
Cost of Operations **10**	16.0	5.1	13.8	20.1	6.9	20.0	50.3	41.6	22.1	42.0	9.8	•	•
Salaries and Wages **11**	19.0	7.2	16.8	25.1	20.8	38.9	24.8	32.3	26.4	29.0	11.5	•	•
Taxes Paid **12**	2.5	2.6	2.7	3.3	2.3	2.9	2.7	3.8	2.1	1.7	1.1	•	•
Interest Paid **13**	0.7	0.2	0.5	0.6	0.5	1.0	0.6	1.5	1.8	1.2	2.0	•	•
Depreciation **14**	1.1	0.9	1.0	1.5	0.8	1.3	1.6	1.7	1.6	1.5	0.6	•	•
Amortization and Depletion **15**	0.3	0.0	0.1	0.7	0.3	0.1	0.3	0.2	1.0	0.7	0.9	•	•
Pensions and Other Deferred Comp. **16**	0.7	2.6	0.6	1.4	0.5	0.7	0.1	0.6	0.2	0.2	0.4	•	•
Employee Benefits **17**	1.5	0.6	1.0	1.9	1.5	2.0	2.6	3.2	3.0	6.2	1.1	•	•
Advertising **18**	1.1	1.2	1.5	0.9	0.5	0.4	1.4	0.4	0.3	0.5	0.6	•	•
Other Expenses **19**	43.3	38.8	41.0	23.6	59.7	27.4	18.8	21.5	44.7	37.7	77.9	•	•
Officers' Compensation **20**	9.0	20.4	12.3	14.6	2.0	1.9	1.4	1.9	0.5	0.2	0.3	•	•
Operating Margin **21**	4.6	20.4	8.7	6.3	4.0	3.6	•	•	•	•	•	•	•
Operating Margin Before Officers' Comp. **22**	13.6	40.7	21.0	20.9	6.0	5.5	•	•	•	•	•	•	•

Selected Average Balance Sheet ($ in Thousands)

Net Receivables 23	21	0	5	70	302	1650	1670	11190	8647	28089	106325
Inventories 24	4	0	2	21	46	19	396	508	970	945	15384
Net Property, Plant and Equipment 25	34	0	22	210	343	1793	2269	6057	14003	12805	49517
Total Assets 26	164	0	73	740	1667	7118	13937	34407	70915	152760	817013
Notes and Loans Payable 27	74	0	38	423	649	3595	4994	11049	35481	42735	322266
All Other Liabilities 28	44	0	15	124	407	2094	5193	11840	17891	69719	257028
Net Worth 29	46	0	20	193	611	1429	3750	11517	17544	40306	237719

Selected Financial Ratios (Times to 1)

Current Ratio 30	1.4	•	1.6	1.4	1.5	1.4	1.3	1.5	1.2	0.8	1.3
Quick Ratio 31	1.1	•	1.4	1.3	0.9	1.3	1.0	1.2	0.8	0.6	1.1
Net Sales to Working Capital 32	32.3	•	35.9	32.4	22.8	21.3	23.1	7.5	25.1	•	20.5
Coverage Ratio 33	10.8	151.8	18.6	12.0	9.3	5.2	3.0	•	1.7	2.9	3.2
Total Asset Turnover 34	3.9	•	6.2	3.9	4.3	4.1	2.4	1.3	1.4	1.7	2.0
Inventory Turnover 35	28.1	•	30.2	27.5	10.8	305.8	42.1	35.9	22.5	116.2	10.2
Receivables Turnover 36	28.7	•	81.1	51.7	24.5	10.9	•	4.1	11.8	9.2	•
Total Liabilities to Net Worth 37	2.6	•	2.7	2.8	1.7	4.0	2.7	2.0	3.0	2.8	2.4
Current Assets to Working Capital 38	3.7	•	2.7	3.6	3.0	3.4	4.5	3.0	6.2	•	4.1
Current Liabilities to Working Capital 39	2.7	•	1.7	2.6	2.0	2.4	3.5	2.0	5.2	•	3.1
Working Capital to Net Sales 40	0.0	•	0.0	0.0	0.0	0.0	0.0	0.1	0.0	•	0.0
Inventory to Working Capital 41	0.2	•	0.2	0.3	0.1	0.0	0.3	0.1	0.2	•	0.2
Total Receipts to Cash Flow 42	2.2	1.9	2.3	4.1	1.6	4.3	6.1	7.4	2.3	2.8	1.2
Cost of Goods to Cash Flow 43	0.4	0.1	0.3	0.8	0.1	0.9	3.1	3.1	0.5	1.2	0.1
Cash Flow to Total Debt 44	2.4	•	3.6	1.3	4.2	1.2	0.5	0.3	0.8	0.8	2.2

Selected Financial Factors (in Percentages)

Debt Ratio 45	71.9	•	72.7	73.9	63.4	79.9	73.1	66.5	75.3	73.6	70.9
Return on Total Assets 46	31.4	•	61.2	26.8	20.8	20.3	4.0	•	4.2	5.9	12.1
Return on Equity Before Income Taxes 47	101.5	•	212.1	94.3	50.6	81.6	9.7	•	7.2	14.5	28.5
Return on Equity After Income Taxes 48	98.2	•	211.4	92.8	48.6	79.0	1.9	•	3.9	10.6	19.3
Profit Margin (Before Income Tax) 49	7.3	23.1	9.4	6.3	4.3	4.0	1.1	•	1.3	2.2	4.2
Profit Margin (After Income Tax) 50	7.1	23.1	9.3	6.2	4.2	3.9	0.2	•	0.7	1.6	2.9

Table II
Corporations with Net Income

OFFICES OF OTHER HEALTH PRACTITIONERS

MONEY AMOUNTS AND SIZE OF ASSETS IN THOUSANDS OF DOLLARS

Item Description for Accounting Period 7/09 Through 6/10	Total	Zero Assets	Under 500	500 to 1,000	1,000 to 5,000	5,000 to 10,000	10,000 to 25,000	25,000 to 50,000	50,000 to 100,000	100,000 to 250,000	250,000 to 500,000	500,000 to 2,500,000	2,500,000 and over
Number of Enterprises **1**	81644	10893	68082	1798	746	53	38	•	13	•	•	0	0
Revenues ($ in Thousands)													
Net Sales **2**	56735608	1126097	33789700	5716977	3137129	1625060	1439104	•	1714609	•	•	0	0
Interest **3**	75505	0	1986	32	101	487	2259	•	307	•	•	0	0
Rents **4**	37906	0	20256	0	0	0	203	•	228	•	•	0	0
Royalties **5**	33013	0	0	0	0	0	0	•	0	•	•	0	0
Other Portfolio Income **6**	75221	0	48224	646	324	62	10812	•	8576	•	•	0	0
Other Receipts **7**	1507849	38975	175584	1124	18234	6442	64931	•	600	•	•	0	0
Total Receipts **8**	58465102	1165072	34035750	5718779	3155788	1632051	1517309	•	1724320	•	•	0	0
Average Total Receipts **9**	716	107	500	3181	4230	30793	39929	•	132640	•	•	•	•
Operating Costs/Operating Income (%)													
Cost of Operations **10**	14.4	4.3	13.2	20.4	12.8	9.1	57.5	•	18.0	•	•	•	•
Salaries and Wages **11**	18.7	5.4	14.4	25.1	39.4	43.7	19.3	•	25.7	•	•	•	•
Taxes Paid **12**	2.5	2.5	2.5	3.2	4.4	3.2	2.3	•	1.9	•	•	•	•
Interest Paid **13**	0.7	0.2	0.5	0.5	1.0	0.8	0.6	•	1.2	•	•	•	•
Depreciation **14**	1.0	0.7	0.9	1.4	1.4	1.5	1.5	•	1.2	•	•	•	•
Amortization and Depletion **15**	0.3	0.1	0.1	0.5	0.6	0.0	0.3	•	0.7	•	•	•	•
Pensions and Other Deferred Comp. **16**	0.7	1.9	0.7	1.4	1.1	0.8	0.0	•	0.1	•	•	•	•
Employee Benefits **17**	1.5	0.7	0.8	2.0	2.4	2.2	1.6	•	2.7	•	•	•	•
Advertising **18**	1.2	0.6	1.5	0.9	1.0	0.4	1.6	•	0.4	•	•	•	•
Other Expenses **19**	42.4	31.3	42.1	23.4	22.2	30.0	12.9	•	44.6	•	•	•	•
Officers' Compensation **20**	9.3	21.5	11.8	14.7	4.0	2.2	1.4	•	0.5	•	•	•	•
Operating Margin **21**	7.2	30.7	11.5	6.4	9.6	6.2	0.9	•	3.1	•	•	•	•
Operating Margin Before Officers' Comp. **22**	16.6	52.2	23.3	21.1	13.6	8.3	2.3	•	3.6	•	•	•	•

Selected Average Balance Sheet ($ in Thousands)

Net Receivables 23	22	0	6	74	309	1937	1406	11809
Inventories 24	4	0	2	24	46	24	520	329
Net Property, Plant and Equipment 25	35	0	21	225	372	2218	2439	11822
Total Assets 26	173	0	79	741	1590	7616	13597	71243
Notes and Loans Payable 27	68	0	33	399	758	3245	3553	24995
All Other Liabilities 28	42	0	14	136	175	1375	5086	24973
Net Worth 29	62	0	32	206	658	2996	4957	21275

Selected Financial Ratios (Times to 1)

Current Ratio 30	1.5	•	1.8	1.4	1.8	2.9	1.5	1.1
Quick Ratio 31	1.3	•	1.5	1.2	1.4	2.5	1.1	0.9
Net Sales to Working Capital 32	25.9	•	29.5	35.7	13.1	10.0	19.7	62.4
Coverage Ratio 33	15.2	178.4	25.0	14.3	11.4	9.4	11.9	4.1
Total Asset Turnover 34	4.0	•	6.3	4.3	2.6	4.0	2.8	1.9
Inventory Turnover 35	23.9	•	27.6	27.5	11.7	118.5	41.9	72.1
Receivables Turnover 36	31.3	•	92.7	66.1	15.3	10.2	18.4	13.2
Total Liabilities to Net Worth 37	1.8	•	1.5	2.6	1.4	1.5	1.7	2.3
Current Assets to Working Capital 38	2.9	•	2.3	3.8	2.3	1.5	3.2	13.7
Current Liabilities to Working Capital 39	1.9	•	1.3	2.8	1.3	0.5	2.2	12.7
Working Capital to Net Sales 40	0.0	•	0.0	0.0	0.1	0.1	0.1	0.0
Inventory to Working Capital 41	0.2	•	0.2	0.3	0.1	0.0	0.3	0.2
Total Receipts to Cash Flow 42	2.1	1.7	2.1	4.1	3.5	3.7	6.2	2.2
Cost of Goods to Cash Flow 43	0.3	0.1	0.3	0.8	0.4	0.3	3.5	0.4
Cash Flow to Total Debt 44	3.0	•	5.0	1.4	1.3	1.8	0.7	1.2

Selected Financial Factors (in Percentages)

Debt Ratio 45	63.8	•	59.5	72.3	58.7	60.7	63.5	70.1
Return on Total Assets 46	44.3	•	80.1	29.6	29.5	29.7	19.3	9.2
Return on Equity Before Income Taxes 47	114.5	•	189.8	99.1	65.1	67.4	48.5	23.5
Return on Equity After Income Taxes 48	111.2	•	189.1	97.5	62.8	65.9	40.6	19.0
Profit Margin (Before Income Tax) 49	10.3	34.2	12.2	6.4	10.2	6.6	6.3	3.8
Profit Margin (After Income Tax) 50	10.0	34.2	12.2	6.3	9.8	6.4	5.3	3.1

Table I

Corporations with and without Net Income

OUTPATIENT CARE CENTERS

MONEY AMOUNTS AND SIZE OF ASSETS IN THOUSANDS OF DOLLARS

Item Description for Accounting Period 7/09 Through 6/10	Total	Zero Assets	Under 500	500 to 1,000	1,000 to 5,000	5,000 to 10,000	10,000 to 25,000	25,000 to 50,000	50,000 to 100,000	100,000 to 250,000	250,000 to 500,000	500,000 to 2,500,000	2,500,000 and over
Number of Enterprises **1**	7448	1157	5028	654	479	50	31	13	10	8	6	8	3
Revenues ($ in Thousands)													
Net Sales **2**	34566885	124511	2486065	1238517	6035509	825035	935983	1606979	1489767	1173743	2351583	3919198	12379993
Interest **3**	135033	760	31	1331	6008	644	1849	2851	3354	3342	15622	84854	14388
Rents **4**	16807	1135	0	0	95	230	189	449	793	205	2461	4387	6866
Royalties **5**	0	0	0	0	0	0	0	0	0	0	0	0	0
Other Portfolio Income **6**	69530	3012	0	4392	23578	7695	0	180	2557	451	6605	14107	6953
Other Receipts **7**	2121934	4375	19187	5317	12981	1688	2419	37222	6732	55740	1045292	272950	658029
Total Receipts **8**	36910189	133793	2505283	1249557	6078171	835292	940440	1647681	1503203	1233481	3421563	4295496	13066229
Average Total Receipts **9**	4956	116	498	1911	12689	16706	30337	126745	150320	154185	570260	536937	4355410
Operating Costs/Operating Income (%)													
Cost of Operations **10**	24.9	10.9	4.4	26.3	7.6	0.8	41.6	82.6	15.3	10.1	53.0	2.8	34.6
Salaries and Wages **11**	23.8	26.6	18.9	29.4	31.8	14.8	29.3	6.5	12.4	19.8	23.4	43.2	18.5
Taxes Paid **12**	3.0	4.1	3.2	3.4	2.7	1.5	2.2	0.7	1.8	2.2	2.6	4.3	3.6
Interest Paid **13**	3.3	2.5	0.4	0.6	0.4	0.7	1.6	0.6	1.1	2.1	1.3	10.0	4.9
Depreciation **14**	2.4	5.8	0.9	1.1	0.4	1.0	3.0	0.9	1.3	3.5	1.0	3.2	4.0
Amortization and Depletion **15**	1.7	•	0.1	0.0	0.0	0.3	0.9	0.2	0.6	2.1	1.1	4.5	2.7
Pensions and Other Deferred Comp. **16**	0.9	•	0.8	0.0	3.7	0.1	0.8	0.1	0.2	0.3	0.2	0.1	0.2
Employee Benefits **17**	4.7	1.4	1.3	1.8	3.1	1.7	1.9	0.5	1.1	40.8	3.0	3.0	5.4
Advertising **18**	0.3	0.2	0.4	0.3	0.2	0.3	0.4	0.6	0.5	0.8	0.2	0.5	0.1
Other Expenses **19**	34.0	69.9	51.6	21.1	43.0	83.7	17.2	6.0	62.9	22.1	51.8	36.4	22.2
Officers' Compensation **20**	2.1	1.9	9.3	2.2	5.1	1.0	2.0	0.3	0.8	0.9	0.8	0.8	0.3
Operating Margin **21**	•	•	8.7	13.8	1.9	•	•	0.9	2.1	•	•	•	3.6
Operating Margin Before Officers' Comp. **22**	0.9	•	18.0	16.0	7.1	•	1.2	1.2	2.8	•	•	•	3.9

Selected Average Balance Sheet ($ in Thousands)

Net Receivables 23	543	0	4	180	881	2332	2415	2824	7584	10908	48684	76111	730285
Inventories 24	60	0	1	43	75	10	19	146	883	1024	555	948	123874
Net Property, Plant and Equipment 25	677	0	18	180	427	982	3383	4930	16364	26885	35115	160988	843286
Total Assets 26	6270	0	61	761	2136	7255	13424	40978	69879	159512	361215	1016943	10426672
Notes and Loans Payable 27	3704	0	78	458	919	2297	7051	5145	26750	60282	83435	512159	6901910
All Other Liabilities 28	1247	0	19	52	955	3978	4053	21065	29088	59493	81429	194080	1764840
Net Worth 29	1319	0	-36	251	261	980	2320	14768	14042	39737	196352	310703	1759922

Selected Financial Ratios (Times to 1)

Current Ratio 30	1.1	•	0.4	1.9	1.0	0.8	1.2	1.4	0.9	0.5	1.8	0.9	1.1
Quick Ratio 31	0.8	•	0.3	1.4	0.8	0.6	0.8	1.3	0.6	0.4	1.0	0.7	0.9
Net Sales to Working Capital 32	75.5	•	•	9.0	•	•	32.8	16.8	•	•	7.5	•	21.1
Coverage Ratio 33	2.7	•	22.3	24.3	7.9	•	0.8	6.4	3.7	1.2	6.2	1.1	2.9
Total Asset Turnover 34	0.7	•	8.1	2.5	5.9	2.3	2.2	3.0	2.1	0.9	1.1	0.5	0.4
Inventory Turnover 35	19.2	•	16.7	11.6	12.8	12.8	675.9	696.9	25.8	14.5	374.3	14.2	11.5
Receivables Turnover 36	8.2	•	131.1	14.1	13.8	6.9	12.8	49.7	15.3	16.9	10.0	•	•
Total Liabilities to Net Worth 37	3.8	•	•	2.0	7.2	6.4	4.8	1.8	4.0	3.0	0.8	2.3	4.9
Current Assets to Working Capital 38	19.7	•	•	2.1	•	•	6.9	3.4	•	•	2.3	•	8.3
Current Liabilities to Working Capital 39	18.7	•	•	1.1	•	•	5.9	2.4	•	•	1.3	•	7.3
Working Capital to Net Sales 40	0.0	•	•	0.1	•	•	0.0	0.1	•	•	0.1	•	0.0
Inventory to Working Capital 41	1.0	•	•	0.2	•	•	0.0	0.0	•	•	0.0	•	0.6
Total Receipts to Cash Flow 42	2.9	3.0	2.0	3.4	2.3	1.4	8.1	11.5	1.6	5.4	1.9	3.0	4.0
Cost of Goods to Cash Flow 43	0.7	0.3	0.1	0.9	0.2	0.0	3.4	9.5	0.2	0.5	1.0	0.1	1.4
Cash Flow to Total Debt 44	0.3	•	2.5	1.1	2.9	1.9	0.3	0.4	1.7	0.2	1.3	0.2	0.1

Selected Financial Factors (in Percentages)

Debt Ratio 45	79.0	•	159.2	67.0	87.8	86.5	82.7	64.0	79.9	75.1	45.6	69.4	83.1
Return on Total Assets 46	6.6	•	80.2	38.0	17.9	•	2.7	12.4	8.4	2.2	9.1	5.2	5.6
Return on Equity Before Income Taxes 47	19.9	•	•	110.5	127.6	•	•	29.0	30.6	1.3	14.0	1.4	21.5
Return on Equity After Income Taxes 48	14.2	•	•	110.4	113.7	•	•	23.7	16.6	1.3	9.4	•	14.3
Profit Margin (Before Income Tax) 49	5.6	9.5	•	14.7	2.6	•	•	3.5	2.9	0.3	7.0	0.9	9.1
Profit Margin (After Income Tax) 50	4.0	9.4	•	14.7	2.4	•	•	2.8	1.6	•	4.7	•	6.1

Table II
Corporations with Net Income

OUTPATIENT CARE CENTERS

MONEY AMOUNTS AND SIZE OF ASSETS IN THOUSANDS OF DOLLARS

Item Description for Accounting Period 7/09 Through 6/10	Total	Zero Assets	Under 500	500 to 1,000	1,000 to 5,000	5,000 to 10,000	10,000 to 25,000	25,000 to 50,000	50,000 to 100,000	100,000 to 250,000	250,000 to 500,000	500,000 to 2,500,000	2,500,000 and over
Number of Enterprises **1**	4571	389	3402	461	254	•	17	•	•	4	•	3	3
Revenues ($ in Thousands)													
Net Sales **2**	28432579	24934	2171943	880703	3702906	•	740496	•	•	791403	•	2518932	12379993
Interest **3**	102642	0	1	1331	2022	•	42	•	•	2336	•	63399	14388
Rents **4**	10039	0	0	0	95	•	0	•	•	0	•	169	6866
Royalties **5**	0	0	0	0	0	•	0	•	•	0	•	0	0
Other Portfolio Income **6**	61714	0	0	16	23578	•	0	•	•	223	•	14107	6953
Other Receipts **7**	1892626	0	759	3389	22668	•	1976	•	•	35495	•	132192	658029
Total Receipts **8**	30499600	24934	2172703	885439	3751269	•	742514	•	•	829457	•	2728799	13066229
Average Total Receipts **9**	6672	64	639	1921	14769	•	43677	•	•	207364	•	909600	4355410
Operating Costs/Operating Income (%)													
Cost of Operations **10**	27.8	54.2	5.0	21.0	3.8	•	52.1	•	•	8.1	•	0.5	34.6
Salaries and Wages **11**	23.0	•	12.6	23.6	46.3	•	23.0	•	•	10.1	•	43.2	18.5
Taxes Paid **12**	3.1	•	2.6	2.9	3.7	•	1.5	•	•	1.3	•	4.8	3.6
Interest Paid **13**	2.9	•	0.1	0.6	0.2	•	0.9	•	•	1.5	•	6.3	4.9
Depreciation **14**	2.5	•	0.8	1.1	0.6	•	2.9	•	•	2.1	•	3.6	4.0
Amortization and Depletion **15**	1.6	•	0.1	0.0	0.0	•	0.7	•	•	0.1	•	3.4	2.7
Pensions and Other Deferred Comp. **16**	0.9	•	0.7	•	5.6	•	0.9	•	•	0.2	•	0.2	0.2
Employee Benefits **17**	5.4	•	1.3	2.0	4.8	•	1.3	•	•	59.6	•	3.5	5.4
Advertising **18**	0.2	0.4	0.4	0.2	0.2	•	0.4	•	•	0.3	•	0.5	0.1
Other Expenses **19**	29.1	34.5	51.0	24.7	24.7	•	13.3	•	•	12.7	•	33.7	22.2
Officers' Compensation **20**	2.0	9.4	9.8	1.7	6.4	•	1.6	•	•	1.1	•	0.7	0.3
Operating Margin **21**	1.3	1.6	15.5	22.2	3.7	•	1.4	•	•	3.1	•	•	3.6
Operating Margin Before Officers' Comp. **22**	3.3	10.9	25.4	23.8	10.1	•	3.0	•	•	4.2	•	0.5	3.9

Selected Average Balance Sheet ($ in Thousands)

Net Receivables 23	682	•	0	5	503	•	2658	•	10647	•	110797	730285
Inventories 24	89	•	0	0	127	•	5	•	652	•	0	123874
Net Property, Plant and Equipment 25	964	•	26	219	516	•	4269	•	32794	•	342068	843286
Total Assets 26	8778	•	57	680	2433	•	14445	•	157824	•	1411313	10426672
Notes and Loans Payable 27	5160	•	9	322	736	•	5434	•	60872	•	552527	6901910
All Other Liabilities 28	1618	•	8	13	1023	•	5795	•	48988	•	226575	1764840
Net Worth 29	2000	•	40	345	674	•	3216	•	47964	•	632211	1759922

Selected Financial Ratios (Times to 1)

Current Ratio 30	1.2	•	1.5	4.1	1.2	•	1.1	•	0.7	•	1.3	1.1
Quick Ratio 31	0.9	•	1.1	2.7	0.9	•	1.0	•	0.6	•	0.9	0.9
Net Sales to Working Capital 32	21.8	•	110.8	9.6	51.2	•	66.8	•		•	22.9	21.1
Coverage Ratio 33	4.0	•	281.7	39.6	25.9	•	2.9	•	6.4	•	2.3	2.9
Total Asset Turnover 34	0.7	•	11.2	2.8	6.0	•	3.0	•	1.3	•	0.6	0.4
Inventory Turnover 35	19.4	•	16.7	944.0	4.4	•	4823.1	•	24.6	•	•	11.5
Receivables Turnover 36	9.0	•	44325.4	737.0	16.8	•	•	•	37.2	•	•	11.3
Total Liabilities to Net Worth 37	3.4	•	0.4	1.0	2.6	•	3.5	•	2.3	•	1.2	4.9
Current Assets to Working Capital 38	5.7	•	3.1	1.3	5.8	•	9.8	•	•	•	4.5	8.3
Current Liabilities to Working Capital 39	4.7	•	2.1	0.3	4.8	•	8.8	•	3.5	•	3.5	7.3
Working Capital to Net Sales 40	0.0	•	0.0	0.1	0.0	•	0.0	•	0.0	•	0.0	0.0
Inventory to Working Capital 41	0.3	•	0.7	0.0	0.1	•	0.0	•	•	•	•	0.6
Total Receipts to Cash Flow 42	3.1	4.0	1.8	2.6	3.6	•	8.3	•	5.3	•	2.6	4.0
Cost of Goods to Cash Flow 43	0.9	2.2	0.1	0.5	0.1	•	4.4	•	0.4	•	0.0	1.4
Cash Flow to Total Debt 44	0.3	•	20.4	2.2	2.3	•	0.5	•	0.3	•	0.4	0.1

Selected Financial Factors (in Percentages)

Debt Ratio 45	77.2	•	30.2	49.3	72.3	•	77.7	•	69.6	•	55.2	83.1
Return on Total Assets 46	8.1	•	174.9	65.4	31.5	•	7.6	•	11.7	•	8.6	5.6
Return on Equity Before Income Taxes 47	26.7	•	249.7	125.8	109.4	•	22.4	•	32.5	•	10.9	21.5
Return on Equity After Income Taxes 48	20.6	•	249.1	125.7	99.2	•	21.2	•	30.1	•	7.3	14.3
Profit Margin (Before Income Tax) 49	8.6	1.6	15.6	22.7	5.1	•	1.7	•	7.9	•	8.2	9.1
Profit Margin (After Income Tax) 50	6.6	1.6	15.5	22.7	4.6	•	1.6	•	7.3	•	5.5	6.1

Table I

Corporations with and without Net Income

MISC. HEALTH CARE AND SOCIAL ASSISTANCE

MONEY AMOUNTS AND SIZE OF ASSETS IN THOUSANDS OF DOLLARS

Item Description for Accounting Period 7/09 Through 6/10	Total	Zero Assets	Under 500	500 to 1,000	1,000 to 5,000	5,000 to 10,000	10,000 to 25,000	25,000 to 50,000	50,000 to 100,000	100,000 to 250,000	250,000 to 500,000	500,000 to 2,500,000	2,500,000 and over
Number of Enterprises 1	65466	16293	44039	2735	1812	264	127	70	51	38	21	15	0
Revenues ($ in Thousands)													
Net Sales 2	101613667	2742296	26447230	6261192	7040329	4238738	4289988	4379806	4589928	7449369	7512910	2666882	0
Interest 3	116344	40	2720	473	1969	3108	3348	4369	6185	15243	8228	70661	0
Rents 4	19740	0	2665	1959	4261	1433	1401	294	1790	1264	3990	683	0
Royalties 5	73675	0	0	0	0	0	0	191	36757	29008	2940	4778	0
Other Portfolio Income 6	514472	2688	65943	26322	16385	35108	1198	2746	17400	167588	103912	75183	0
Other Receipts 7	1843313	20563	550241	29237	144689	170477	31762	75684	79133	126769	187828	426928	0
Total Receipts 8	104181211	2765587	27068799	6319183	7207633	4448864	4327697	4463090	4731193	7789241	7819808	27240115	0
Average Total Receipts 9	1591	170	615	2310	3978	16852	34076	63758	92768	204980	372372	1816008	•
Operating Costs/Operating Income (%)													
Cost of Operations 10	15.5	1.3	7.0	11.3	15.3	18.8	22.1	27.7	31.1	26.2	7.9	19.4	•
Salaries and Wages 11	32.3	19.6	38.5	34.7	38.0	34.7	21.4	29.1	29.0	26.0	38.4	27.8	•
Taxes Paid 12	4.1	2.9	5.0	4.4	4.7	3.5	3.0	4.3	3.3	4.0	3.8	3.6	•
Interest Paid 13	2.0	0.2	0.4	1.7	1.1	0.6	1.2	1.2	1.8	2.9	3.9	3.7	•
Depreciation 14	2.4	1.4	1.1	1.6	1.9	2.6	2.2	2.1	2.1	3.0	4.4	3.5	•
Amortization and Depletion 15	0.8	0.2	0.1	0.3	0.1	0.5	0.9	0.7	1.2	1.9	1.0	1.6	•
Pensions and Other Deferred Comp. 16	0.4	•	0.6	0.2	0.5	0.7	0.6	0.3	0.5	0.2	0.4	0.3	•
Employee Benefits 17	3.2	0.3	1.5	1.1	2.1	3.9	16.5	2.4	3.0	2.1	3.0	4.4	•
Advertising 18	0.5	0.4	0.6	0.5	0.5	0.8	0.5	0.4	0.4	0.7	0.4	0.5	•
Other Expenses 19	31.0	56.5	30.0	33.1	28.8	28.0	29.5	29.7	26.3	30.6	39.5	29.1	•
Officers' Compensation 20	4.9	17.9	11.6	5.5	4.4	4.7	2.1	1.8	1.3	1.1	0.8	0.7	•
Operating Margin 21	2.8	•	3.6	5.5	2.6	1.3	0.1	0.3	0.0	1.3	•	5.5	•
Operating Margin Before Officers' Comp. 22	7.7	17.2	15.2	10.9	7.0	6.0	2.2	2.1	1.3	2.5	6.2	6.2	•

Selected Average Balance Sheet ($ in Thousands)

Net Receivables 23	135	0	6	137	257	1823	2729	8766	16610	28765	59391	206400	•
Inventories 24	11	0	1	6	17	297	465	561	1037	2277	4388	14445	•
Net Property, Plant and Equipment 25	170	0	30	259	742	1515	3127	4076	6542	21291	76265	262202	•
Total Assets 26	954	0	88	699	2001	6964	16484	34016	68481	164315	355427	1969201	•
Notes and Loans Payable 27	396	0	52	379	881	1737	7164	9997	24184	74789	185302	734064	•
All Other Liabilities 28	231	0	18	152	296	1777	5339	10700	21289	47839	81229	458833	•
Net Worth 29	327	0	19	168	823	3450	3982	13319	23007	41686	88896	776303	•

Selected Financial Ratios (Times to 1)

Current Ratio 30	1.7	•	2.2	1.3	2.7	2.0	1.3	1.3	1.3	1.6	2.0	1.6	•
Quick Ratio 31	1.3	•	2.0	1.1	2.3	1.7	1.0	1.0	1.0	1.3	1.4	1.2	•
Net Sales to Working Capital 32	12.3	•	25.6	36.4	6.6	7.7	19.0	14.4	12.8	9.1	5.6	11.2	•
Coverage Ratio 33	3.7	1.8	15.3	4.7	5.5	11.1	1.8	2.8	2.7	3.0	1.1	3.1	•
Total Asset Turnover 34	1.6	•	6.8	3.3	1.9	2.3	2.0	1.8	1.3	1.2	1.0	0.9	•
Inventory Turnover 35	22.6	•	65.5	46.5	34.3	10.1	16.0	30.9	27.0	22.6	6.5	23.9	•
Receivables Turnover 36	11.7	•	80.3	17.7	11.2	9.3	11.3	7.9	6.6	7.1	6.0	8.9	•
Total Liabilities to Net Worth 37	1.9	•	3.7	3.2	1.4	1.0	3.1	1.6	2.0	2.9	3.0	1.5	•
Current Assets to Working Capital 38	2.4	•	1.8	4.0	1.6	2.0	4.5	3.9	4.1	2.8	2.0	2.6	•
Current Liabilities to Working Capital 39	1.4	•	0.8	3.0	0.6	1.0	3.5	2.9	3.1	1.8	1.0	1.6	•
Working Capital to Net Sales 40	0.1	•	0.0	0.0	0.2	0.1	0.1	0.1	0.1	0.1	0.2	0.1	•
Inventory to Working Capital 41	0.1	•	0.0	0.1	0.0	0.1	0.3	0.1	0.1	0.1	0.1	0.1	•
Total Receipts to Cash Flow 42	3.2	2.1	3.5	3.1	3.5	3.4	3.7	3.6	3.9	3.1	2.8	3.2	•
Cost of Goods to Cash Flow 43	0.5	0.0	0.2	0.3	0.5	0.6	0.8	1.0	1.2	0.8	0.2	0.6	•
Cash Flow to Total Debt 44	0.8	•	2.5	1.4	0.9	1.4	0.7	0.8	0.5	0.5	0.5	0.5	•

Selected Financial Factors (in Percentages)

Debt Ratio 45	65.8	•	78.9	76.0	58.9	50.5	75.8	60.8	66.4	74.6	75.0	60.6	•
Return on Total Assets 46	11.9	•	43.3	26.7	11.8	15.9	4.4	6.1	6.5	10.5	4.5	10.3	•
Return on Equity Before Income Taxes 47	25.3	•	192.0	87.4	23.5	29.3	8.1	10.2	12.1	27.7	2.3	17.6	•
Return on Equity After Income Taxes 48	19.9	•	188.9	82.7	21.6	25.2	8.4	9.0	17.3	•	11.5	•	
Profit Margin (Before Income Tax) 49	5.3	0.2	5.9	6.4	5.0	6.3	1.0	2.2	3.1	5.9	0.6	7.7	•
Profit Margin (After Income Tax) 50	4.2	0.1	5.8	6.1	4.6	5.4	0.3	1.8	2.3	3.7	•	5.0	•

Table II

Corporations with Net Income

MISC. HEALTH CARE AND SOCIAL ASSISTANCE

MONEY AMOUNTS AND SIZE OF ASSETS IN THOUSANDS OF DOLLARS

Item Description for Accounting Period 7/09 Through 6/10		Total	Zero Assets	Under 500	500 to 1,000	1,000 to 5,000	5,000 to 10,000	10,000 to 25,000	25,000 to 50,000	50,000 to 100,000	100,000 to 250,000	250,000 to 500,000	500,000 to 2,500,000	2,500,000 and over
Number of Enterprises	1	41054	7500	29992	1783	1357	217	83	45	31	24	12	11	0
Revenues ($ in Thousands)														
Net Sales	2	80656318	2404369	20660554	4647012	5546599	3777609	2481666	3705583	3206813	5456311	5804639	22965162	0
Interest	3	87365	0	1644	471	990	1564	2918	1188	3235	8882	3182	63293	0
Rents	4	17998	0	2665	1959	4261	1433	1401	294	498	815	3990	683	0
Royalties	5	15147	0	0	0	0	0	0	0	12218	0	2925	4	0
Other Portfolio Income	6	397715	0	65740	26176	16373	34957	808	1398	10114	157806	9160	75183	0
Other Receipts	7	1504829	12518	432519	7026	131690	170251	26749	56493	30995	110963	126435	399189	0
Total Receipts	8	82679372	2416887	21163122	4682644	5699913	3985814	2513542	3764956	3263873	5734777	5950331	23503514	0
Average Total Receipts	9	2014	322	706	2626	4200	18368	30284	83666	105286	238949	495861	2136683	•
Operating Costs/Operating Income (%)														
Cost of Operations	10	15.0	1.2	5.7	15.1	12.1	17.4	22.7	27.0	35.0	23.0	7.1	19.6	•
Salaries and Wages	11	31.5	17.9	36.8	32.9	38.0	36.3	28.6	29.0	27.3	26.1	38.0	26.6	•
Taxes Paid	12	4.0	2.5	4.7	4.4	4.5	3.4	3.3	4.3	3.2	4.3	3.5	3.5	•
Interest Paid	13	1.5	0.1	0.4	1.8	0.9	0.5	1.2	0.9	1.2	1.5	1.8	3.1	•
Depreciation	14	2.1	1.2	1.0	1.4	1.9	2.7	3.1	1.2	1.3	1.9	2.6	3.4	•
Amortization and Depletion	15	0.7	0.1	0.1	0.0	0.1	0.5	0.5	0.5	0.7	1.4	0.5	1.4	•
Pensions and Other Deferred Comp.	16	0.4	•	0.5	0.3	0.5	0.7	0.3	0.4	0.4	0.2	0.4	0.3	•
Employee Benefits	17	2.5	0.1	1.4	1.1	1.7	4.1	1.5	2.5	3.0	1.8	3.0	4.2	•
Advertising	18	0.5	0.3	0.6	0.5	0.5	0.6	0.6	0.3	0.3	0.4	0.5	0.5	•
Other Expenses	19	30.2	52.0	30.1	26.8	28.5	22.9	28.9	28.0	22.3	31.1	38.4	29.6	•
Officers' Compensation	20	4.7	19.2	11.2	5.9	3.5	4.7	2.0	1.5	1.2	1.0	0.6	0.6	•
Operating Margin	21	6.9	5.4	7.4	9.9	7.7	6.3	7.3	4.4	4.1	7.3	3.4	7.3	•
Operating Margin Before Officers' Comp.	22	11.6	24.6	18.6	15.9	11.2	11.0	9.3	5.9	5.3	8.2	4.0	7.9	•

Selected Average Balance Sheet ($ in Thousands)

Item	C1	C2	C3	C4	C5	C6	C7	C8	C9	C10	C11	C12	C13
Net Receivables 23	169	0	6	114	249	1871	3041	11152	18370	34071	77270	249876	•
Inventories 24	12	0	1	8	11	319	650	388	724	2176	5234	14657	•
Net Property, Plant and Equipment 25	185	0	32	298	582	1542	3803	3573	5070	19535	49239	299432	•
Total Assets 26	1112	0	92	745	1956	6878	16520	32946	66283	164956	363359	2199397	•
Notes and Loans Payable 27	395	0	38	234	702	1788	6189	10145	23783	49482	133676	803597	•
All Other Liabilities 28	270	0	17	144	233	1783	3124	11871	21687	38835	101578	544747	•
Net Worth 29	447	0	37	367	1022	3307	7207	10930	20813	76640	128105	851053	•

Selected Financial Ratios (Times to 1)

Item	C1	C2	C3	C4	C5	C6	C7	C8	C9	C10	C11	C12
Current Ratio 30	1.8	•	2.7	1.4	4.9	1.9	1.8	1.5	1.4	1.9	1.8	1.6
Quick Ratio 31	1.5	•	2.4	1.2	4.3	1.5	1.2	1.1	1.2	1.6	1.3	1.2
Net Sales to Working Capital 32	11.8	•	21.6	40.2	5.1	9.3	8.6	11.7	11.6	7.5	7.5	12.4
Coverage Ratio 33	7.2	68.9	29.1	7.1	12.4	24.1	8.2	7.7	5.8	9.2	4.2	4.1
Total Asset Turnover 34	1.8	•	7.5	3.5	2.1	2.5	1.8	2.5	1.6	1.4	1.3	0.9
Inventory Turnover 35	24.4	•	46.1	46.3	43.3	9.5	10.4	57.4	50.0	24.0	6.6	27.9
Receivables Turnover 36	12.2	•	81.8	22.2	11.8	10.6	10.2	8.9	8.2	6.8	6.1	9.1
Total Liabilities to Net Worth 37	1.5	•	1.5	1.0	0.9	1.1	1.3	2.0	2.2	1.2	1.8	1.6
Current Assets to Working Capital 38	2.2	•	1.6	3.8	1.3	2.1	2.2	3.0	3.4	2.1	2.3	2.8
Current Liabilities to Working Capital 39	1.2	•	0.6	2.8	0.3	1.1	1.2	2.0	2.4	1.1	1.3	1.8
Working Capital to Net Sales 40	0.1	•	0.0	0.0	0.2	0.1	0.1	0.1	0.1	0.1	0.1	0.1
Inventory to Working Capital 41	0.1	•	0.0	0.1	0.0	0.2	0.2	0.0	0.1	0.1	0.1	0.1
Total Receipts to Cash Flow 42	2.9	2.0	3.1	3.3	2.9	3.3	3.1	3.2	3.9	2.5	2.4	2.9
Cost of Goods to Cash Flow 43	0.4	0.0	0.2	0.5	0.4	0.6	0.7	0.9	1.4	0.6	0.2	0.6
Cash Flow to Total Debt 44	1.0	•	4.1	2.1	1.5	1.5	1.0	1.2	0.6	1.0	0.8	0.5

Selected Financial Factors (in Percentages)

Item	C1	C2	C3	C4	C5	C6	C7	C8	C9	C10	C11	C12
Debt Ratio 45	59.8	•	59.5	50.8	47.8	51.9	56.4	66.8	68.6	53.5	64.7	61.3
Return on Total Assets 46	19.2	•	76.3	43.6	23.8	31.1	17.6	17.1	11.1	19.1	10.4	12.1
Return on Equity Before Income Taxes 47	41.2	•	181.9	76.1	41.9	61.9	35.4	44.9	29.3	36.6	22.4	23.6
Return on Equity After Income Taxes 48	34.9	•	179.7	72.8	39.9	56.8	30.8	41.7	23.7	27.6	18.2	16.0
Profit Margin (Before Income Tax) 49	9.4	5.9	9.8	10.7	10.5	11.8	8.5	6.0	5.9	12.3	5.9	9.6
Profit Margin (After Income Tax) 50	7.9	5.8	9.7	10.2	10.0	10.8	7.4	5.5	4.8	9.3	4.8	6.5

Table I

Corporations with and without Net Income

HOSPITALS, NURSING, AND RESIDENTIAL CARE FACILITIES

MONEY AMOUNTS AND SIZE OF ASSETS IN THOUSANDS OF DOLLARS

Item Description for Accounting Period 7/09 Through 6/10	Total	Zero Assets	Under 500	500 to 1,000	1,000 to 5,000	5,000 to 10,000	10,000 to 25,000	25,000 to 50,000	50,000 to 100,000	100,000 to 250,000	250,000 to 500,000	500,000 to 2,500,000	2,500,000 and over
Number of Enterprises 1	18000	1730	12134	1575	1988	200	193	77	31	29	11	22	9
Revenues ($ in Thousands)													
Net Sales 2	125166953	185146	9164248	3928552	12234189	1779736	4864846	4575248	4740674	6395003	3869913	22765027	50664371
Interest 3	890506	398	353	378	2134	752	3473	7323	3742	11537	9005	204303	647109
Rents 4	557457	0	0	0	363	0	8652	8899	3738	53144	26387	161938	294336
Royalties 5	0	0	0	0	0	0	0	0	0	0	0	0	0
Other Portfolio Income 6	335199	5707	6883	23768	27937	31577	25463	4374	7009	9511	304	68491	124174
Other Receipts 7	8017074	41695	5166	22859	557459	14793	79950	98340	51241	556607	205334	630717	5752913
Total Receipts 8	134967189	232946	9176650	3975557	12822082	1826858	4982384	4694184	4806404	7025802	4110943	23830476	57482903
Average Total Receipts 9	7498	135	756	2524	6450	9134	25815	60963	155045	242269	373722	1083203	6386989
Operating Costs/Operating Income (%)													
Cost of Operations 10	4.2	•	9.4	4.5	8.1	3.2	10.6	3.7	7.3	7.4	6.8	5.7	0.1
Salaries and Wages 11	40.1	31.7	38.0	24.0	43.0	41.7	34.6	41.2	38.7	44.6	42.8	43.3	39.4
Taxes Paid 12	5.0	0.9	5.0	4.0	6.8	5.5	6.0	4.9	5.1	6.6	5.9	5.5	4.0
Interest Paid 13	4.8	17.5	0.8	0.7	0.7	1.8	1.5	1.3	1.0	1.7	3.6	5.0	8.2
Depreciation 14	3.1	2.7	0.9	0.6	1.2	4.5	1.7	1.7	2.3	2.5	3.5	3.6	4.2
Amortization and Depletion 15	0.6	1.4	0.0	0.1	0.1	0.4	0.2	0.2	0.5	0.4	0.7	1.0	0.8
Pensions and Other Deferred Comp. 16	0.4	•	0.1	0.1	0.1	0.4	0.4	0.2	0.3	0.3	0.2	0.1	0.8
Employee Benefits 17	4.7	7.0	1.4	2.3	3.0	4.8	4.6	3.3	3.8	4.0	3.7	4.7	6.3
Advertising 18	0.4	0.1	0.7	0.8	0.3	1.3	0.2	0.3	0.4	0.3	0.2	0.3	0.4
Other Expenses 19	39.5	81.5	34.6	60.4	33.5	34.4	39.4	43.0	40.3	38.7	36.1	34.1	42.7
Officers' Compensation 20	1.0	2.7	6.5	2.3	1.3	1.9	0.9	0.8	0.7	0.6	0.5	0.3	0.2
Operating Margin 21	•	2.5	1.8	0.2	1.8	•	•	•	•	•	•	•	•
Operating Margin Before Officers' Comp. 22	•	9.0	2.5	3.1	•	1.8	0.8	0.4	0.2	•	•	•	•

Selected Average Balance Sheet ($ in Thousands)

Net Receivables 23	754	0	14	180	599	1136	3148	6427	19232	33275	37448	115124	676799
Inventories 24	12	0	0	1	2	7	108	219	666	1051	1518	4031	1786
Net Property, Plant and Equipment 25	2495	0	48	175	622	3479	5327	13333	27145	65328	170644	420461	2911049
Total Assets 26	7180	0	109	716	2108	7194	14930	34324	70221	164535	366753	1194063	8709056
Notes and Loans Payable 27	4439	0	197	245	1160	3846	8941	16540	30619	67243	187018	595319	5890044
All Other Liabilities 28	1816	0	49	406	692	1307	6191	10564	31516	71097	94128	286685	1936553
Net Worth 29	924	0	-137	66	257	2041	-202	7220	8087	26194	85608	312059	882459

Selected Financial Ratios (Times to 1)

Current Ratio 30	1.3	•	0.5	1.0	1.8	1.0	1.1	1.4	1.3	1.5	1.3	1.4	1.4
Quick Ratio 31	1.0	•	0.4	0.9	1.5	0.9	0.9	1.1	1.1	1.2	1.0	1.2	1.0
Net Sales to Working Capital 32	19.4	•	•	•	11.1	141.8	34.8	15.8	20.1	11.8	24.4	14.3	16.3
Coverage Ratio 33	1.8	•	4.3	3.1	10.0	2.4	2.5	2.7	1.9	2.5	1.6	1.2	1.8
Total Asset Turnover 34	1.0	•	6.9	3.5	2.9	1.2	1.7	1.7	2.2	1.3	1.0	0.9	0.6
Inventory Turnover 35	23.9	•	1182.3	82.5	232.0	41.6	24.8	10.1	16.8	15.6	15.8	14.7	4.1
Receivables Turnover 36	8.7	•	103.0	12.4	11.0	6.9	6.7	10.2	8.3	6.8	6.3	8.2	7.8
Total Liabilities to Net Worth 37	6.8	•	•	9.9	7.2	2.5	•	3.8	7.7	5.3	3.3	2.8	8.9
Current Assets to Working Capital 38	4.1	•	•	•	2.2	34.4	8.7	3.5	4.4	3.1	4.9	3.4	3.5
Current Liabilities to Working Capital 39	3.1	•	•	•	1.2	33.4	7.7	2.5	3.4	2.1	3.9	2.4	2.5
Working Capital to Net Sales 40	0.1	•	•	0.1	0.0	0.0	0.0	0.1	0.0	0.1	0.0	0.1	0.1
Inventory to Working Capital 41	0.0	•	•	•	0.0	0.1	0.1	0.1	0.1	0.1	0.0	0.0	0.0
Total Receipts to Cash Flow 42	2.7	1.9	3.9	2.0	3.1	3.3	2.8	2.5	3.0	2.9	3.4	3.6	2.2
Cost of Goods to Cash Flow 43	0.1	•	0.4	0.1	0.3	0.1	0.3	0.1	0.2	0.2	0.2	0.2	0.0
Cash Flow to Total Debt 44	0.4	•	0.8	2.0	1.1	0.5	0.6	0.9	0.8	0.5	0.4	0.3	0.3

Selected Financial Factors (in Percentages)

Debt Ratio 45	87.1	•	225.8	90.8	87.8	71.6	101.4	79.0	88.5	84.1	76.7	73.9	89.9
Return on Total Assets 46	8.5	•	24.0	7.3	21.5	5.4	6.2	5.9	4.1	5.7	5.7	5.2	9.3
Return on Equity Before Income Taxes 47	30.2	•	•	54.1	158.8	11.1	•	17.8	17.0	21.6	9.3	3.4	39.9
Return on Equity After Income Taxes 48	22.2	•	•	46.5	157.1	8.3	•	15.3	11.1	18.7	6.7	1.9	26.1
Profit Margin (Before Income Tax) 49	4.0	•	2.7	1.4	6.6	2.6	2.2	2.2	0.9	2.6	2.3	1.0	6.2
Profit Margin (After Income Tax) 50	3.0	•	2.7	1.2	6.6	1.9	1.9	1.9	0.6	2.2	1.6	0.6	4.1

Table II

Corporations with Net Income

HOSPITALS, NURSING, AND RESIDENTIAL CARE FACILITIES

MONEY AMOUNTS AND SIZE OF ASSETS IN THOUSANDS OF DOLLARS

Item Description for Accounting Period 7/09 Through 6/10	Total	Zero Assets	Under 500	500 to 1,000	1,000 to 5,000	5,000 to 10,000	10,000 to 25,000	25,000 to 50,000	50,000 to 100,000	100,000 to 250,000	250,000 to 500,000	500,000 to 2,500,000	2,500,000 and over
Number of Enterprises **1**	9421	827	5777	835	1662	92	121	47	•	19	6	11	•
Revenues ($ in Thousands)													
Net Sales **2**	92907596	169293	4998288	1815198	10790432	1320311	3153716	2827731	•	4311655	2840220	13990537	•
Interest **3**	323228	308	256	192	2113	155	1693	5696	•	11195	3457	41690	•
Rents **4**	391141	0	0	0	363	0	6778	8855	•	12701	3259	140092	•
Royalties **5**	0	0	0	0	0	0	0	0	•	0	0	0	•
Other Portfolio Income **6**	270046	5707	3513	23768	27937	31209	25019	4074	•	5478	304	62771	•
Other Receipts **7**	6716207	4624	795	10469	550799	9310	62534	94492	•	163829	130790	354549	•
Total Receipts **8**	100608218	179932	5002852	1849627	11371644	1360985	3249740	2940848	•	4504858	2978030	14589639	•
Average Total Receipts **9**	10679	218	866	2215	6842	14793	26857	62571	•	237098	496338	1326331	•
Operating Costs/Operating Income (%)													
Cost of Operations **10**	2.7	•	5.5	9.3	5.0	4.1	12.9	5.5	•	8.0	7.3	0.4	•
Salaries and Wages **11**	41.1	33.2	39.6	36.0	44.2	40.7	31.0	40.8	•	42.0	45.5	46.5	•
Taxes Paid **12**	5.0	0.7	4.7	4.4	6.8	5.4	6.4	5.8	•	6.2	6.4	5.9	•
Interest Paid **13**	4.4	5.4	0.6	0.6	0.5	0.8	1.2	1.4	•	1.7	2.5	3.0	•
Depreciation **14**	3.0	1.9	0.8	0.6	1.0	1.9	2.0	1.8	•	2.5	3.3	2.6	•
Amortization and Depletion **15**	0.6	1.4	0.1	0.2	0.0	0.3	0.2	0.2	•	0.5	0.6	0.9	•
Pensions and Other Deferred Comp. **16**	0.5	•	0.1	0.1	0.1	0.3	0.2	0.3	•	0.5	0.2	0.1	•
Employee Benefits **17**	4.9	7.6	1.4	3.8	3.1	5.4	4.2	3.8	•	3.3	3.4	4.0	•
Advertising **18**	0.4	0.1	0.7	0.3	0.3	1.6	0.2	0.3	•	0.3	0.1	0.2	•
Other Expenses **19**	37.9	34.9	30.3	33.3	34.7	33.2	37.3	38.2	•	33.8	30.1	36.2	•
Officers' Compensation **20**	0.9	1.6	7.4	4.0	1.4	1.6	1.2	0.9	•	0.8	0.5	0.3	•
Operating Margin **21**	•	13.1	8.9	7.4	2.8	4.8	3.2	0.8	•	0.4	0.0	•	•
Operating Margin Before Officers' Comp. **22**	•	14.7	16.3	11.3	4.2	6.4	4.4	1.7	•	1.2	0.5	•	•

Selected Average Balance Sheet ($ in Thousands)

Net Receivables 23	1076	0	12	114	578	1661	2940	6728	•	30755	48848	164845
Inventories 24	14	0	0	1	2	4	83	324	•	1459	1983	3080
Net Property, Plant and Equipment 25	3355	0	45	145	514	3292	6251	14719	•	66688	189934	266977
Total Assets 26	10647	0	133	720	2012	7738	15011	35477	•	167924	383478	1244233
Notes and Loans Payable 27	6402	0	94	169	728	3260	7816	17370	•	66427	205627	428578
All Other Liabilities 28	2399	0	27	99	610	2600	4818	9951	•	57773	79580	361609
Net Worth 29	1846	0	12	453	673	1878	2378	8156	•	43723	98270	454046

Selected Financial Ratios (Times to 1)

Current Ratio 30	1.5	•	2.2	3.5	2.1	1.5	1.3	1.5	•	1.4	1.3	1.3
Quick Ratio 31	1.2	•	1.9	3.3	1.7	1.3	1.0	1.3	•	1.2	1.1	1.1
Net Sales to Working Capital 32	15.2	•	21.7	7.5	9.6	13.5	19.8	12.7	•	13.3	23.5	19.0
Coverage Ratio 33	2.5	4.6	15.0	15.6	16.7	11.5	6.3	4.3	•	3.9	2.9	2.3
Total Asset Turnover 34	0.9	•	6.5	3.0	3.2	1.9	1.7	1.7	•	1.4	1.2	1.0
Inventory Turnover 35	19.7	•	•	158.9	157.9	146.3	40.6	10.3	•	12.4	17.4	1.7
Receivables Turnover 36	9.2	•	139.1	10.7	13.4	10.2	6.6	•	•	7.3	7.5	7.8
Total Liabilities to Net Worth 37	4.8	•	10.2	0.6	2.0	3.1	5.3	3.3	•	2.8	2.9	1.7
Current Assets to Working Capital 38	3.1	•	1.8	1.4	1.9	3.2	4.6	3.0	•	3.3	4.3	4.1
Current Liabilities to Working Capital 39	2.1	•	0.8	0.4	0.9	2.2	3.6	2.0	•	2.3	3.3	3.1
Working Capital to Net Sales 40	0.1	•	0.0	0.1	0.1	0.1	0.1	0.1	•	0.1	0.0	0.1
Inventory to Working Capital 41	0.0	•	•	0.0	0.0	0.0	0.0	0.1	•	0.1	0.1	0.0
Total Receipts to Cash Flow 42	2.6	2.1	3.4	2.6	2.9	2.9	2.6	2.6	•	2.9	4.0	3.1
Cost of Goods to Cash Flow 43	0.1	•	0.2	0.2	0.1	0.1	0.3	0.1	•	0.2	0.3	0.0
Cash Flow to Total Debt 44	0.4	•	2.1	3.1	1.7	0.8	0.8	0.8	•	0.6	0.4	0.5

Selected Financial Factors (in Percentages)

Debt Ratio 45	82.7	•	91.1	37.2	66.5	75.7	84.2	77.0	•	74.0	74.4	63.5
Return on Total Assets 46	10.3	•	62.8	29.9	28.0	16.1	13.0	10.6	•	8.9	9.2	7.2
Return on Equity Before Income Taxes 47	36.0	•	657.3	44.5	78.8	60.5	69.0	35.4	•	25.3	23.5	11.1
Return on Equity After Income Taxes 48	28.4	•	656.5	42.4	78.0	53.9	62.6	31.7	•	22.7	19.4	9.1
Profit Margin (Before Income Tax) 49	6.7	19.4	9.0	9.3	8.2	7.9	6.3	4.8	•	4.9	4.9	4.0
Profit Margin (After Income Tax) 50	5.3	14.6	9.0	8.8	8.1	7.1	5.7	4.3	•	4.4	4.0	3.3

Table I

Corporations with and without Net Income

OTHER ARTS, ENTERTAINMENT, AND RECREATION

MONEY AMOUNTS AND SIZE OF ASSETS IN THOUSANDS OF DOLLARS

Item Description for Accounting Period 7/09 Through 6/10	Total	Zero Assets	Under 500	500 to 1,000	1,000 to 5,000	5,000 to 10,000	10,000 to 25,000	25,000 to 50,000	50,000 to 100,000	100,000 to 250,000	250,000 to 500,000	500,000 to 2,500,000	2,500,000 and over
Number of Enterprises **1**	72240	15569	53023	2050	1082	317	87	41	20	21	18	11	0
Revenues ($ in Thousands)													
Net Sales **2**	41873868	1164686	13156025	3417610	3629869	2414395	1524063	812801	1159888	2687981	4151189	7755361	0
Interest **3**	170186	989	1689	1915	3715	1934	681	2485	2208	2850	26332	125388	0
Rents **4**	110939	1911	1296	855	296	2299	0	82	5665	544	40375	57616	0
Royalties **5**	140263	20438	11143	3	0	4	0	1800	60	20037	74899	11878	0
Other Portfolio Income **6**	251943	2808	45527	11190	10252	694	119	5108	2051	11180	21104	141911	0
Other Receipts **7**	268309	16642	519289	27915	97161	352008	27330	175375	248010	267190	748542	208848	0
Total Receipts **8**	45235508	1207474	13734969	3459488	3741293	2771334	1552193	997651	1417882	2989782	5062441	8301002	0
Average Total Receipts **9**	626	78	259	1688	3458	8742	17841	24333	70894	142371	281247	754637	•
Operating Costs/Operating Income (%)													
Cost of Operations **10**	19.2	18.3	5.1	18.3	22.7	17.4	25.1	7.8	35.3	26.1	22.4	36.0	•
Salaries and Wages **11**	17.9	19.8	12.9	12.8	12.5	21.6	19.5	35.2	33.8	33.4	31.9	12.3	•
Taxes Paid **12**	4.0	2.5	2.3	2.5	4.2	3.3	3.0	3.4	3.1	2.7	11.8	4.5	•
Interest Paid **13**	1.7	1.9	0.4	1.1	0.3	1.3	0.8	1.5	1.4	2.9	2.2	4.3	•
Depreciation **14**	3.0	0.9	1.4	1.7	1.1	4.0	2.1	6.8	2.7	3.5	6.6	4.9	•
Amortization and Depletion **15**	1.6	0.5	0.1	0.2	0.2	0.1	5.2	1.6	1.2	3.9	4.0	3.4	•
Pensions and Other Deferred Comp. **16**	1.4	0.8	2.2	1.0	0.6	0.2	0.7	0.5	1.5	3.2	1.7	0.7	•
Employee Benefits **17**	1.3	1.4	0.7	0.3	0.6	0.8	1.5	2.1	2.8	2.2	3.5	1.3	•
Advertising **18**	2.5	3.6	1.0	5.7	1.8	2.4	0.6	2.2	3.2	5.2	1.8	3.7	•
Other Expenses **19**	38.0	57.3	50.4	24.7	26.1	40.7	20.8	66.8	32.8	24.6	33.2	32.8	•
Officers' Compensation **20**	12.3	7.8	20.3	29.5	15.0	15.3	9.1	4.8	2.4	3.4	1.4	1.6	•
Operating Margin **21**	•	•	3.2	2.2	14.8	•	11.7	•	•	•	•	•	•
Operating Margin Before Officers' Comp. **22**	9.5	•	23.5	31.7	29.8	8.2	20.8	•	•	•	•	•	•

Selected Average Balance Sheet ($ in Thousands)

	•	•	•	•	•	•	•	•	•	•	•	•
Net Receivables **23**	32	0	2	21	138	285	2005	5593	6075	13557	28672	57427
Inventories **24**	8	0	3	15	261	12	41	276	1660	1481	2678	2965
Net Property, Plant and Equipment **25**	147	0	9	287	342	1576	3016	7403	12873	44555	107392	451985
Total Assets **26**	508	0	49	682	2003	7733	15314	35206	68642	167033	356187	1276941
Notes and Loans Payable **27**	247	0	71	287	711	3316	4639	14739	20537	84293	105380	596935
All Other Liabilities **28**	164	0	16	144	519	1549	4535	13864	47948	69956	123483	370245
Net Worth **29**	97	0	-38	251	774	2868	6140	6603	158	12783	127324	309761

Selected Financial Ratios (Times to 1)

	•	•	•	•	•	•	•	•	•	•	•	•
Current Ratio **30**	1.3	•	1.6	1.8	2.1	2.2	2.1	1.5	0.8	1.2	1.3	0.9
Quick Ratio **31**	0.8	•	1.1	1.5	1.2	2.1	1.4	1.1	0.6	0.8	0.8	0.3
Net Sales to Working Capital **32**	15.7	•	19.5	14.6	5.5	3.9	3.8	4.0	•	17.0	9.6	•
Coverage Ratio **33**	4.3	•	19.7	4.1	62.0	6.9	18.4	•	2.3	1.1	1.6	1.7
Total Asset Turnover **34**	1.1	•	5.1	2.4	1.7	1.0	1.1	0.6	0.8	0.8	0.6	0.6
Inventory Turnover **35**	13.1	•	4.9	20.6	2.9	109.1	107.9	5.6	12.3	22.6	19.3	85.6
Receivables Turnover **36**	17.3	•	96.5	101.6	28.3	32.5	9.6	3.4	9.9	7.6	7.8	12.1
Total Liabilities to Net Worth **37**	4.2	•	•	1.7	1.6	1.7	1.5	4.3	434.7	12.1	1.8	3.1
Current Assets to Working Capital **38**	5.0	•	2.6	2.2	1.9	1.8	1.9	3.0	•	6.3	4.7	•
Current Liabilities to Working Capital **39**	4.0	•	1.6	1.2	0.9	0.8	0.9	2.0	•	5.3	3.7	•
Working Capital to Net Sales **40**	0.1	•	0.1	0.1	0.2	0.3	0.3	0.3	0.1	0.1	0.1	•
Inventory to Working Capital **41**	0.2	•	0.2	0.2	0.5	0.0	0.0	0.1	•	0.2	0.1	•
Total Receipts to Cash Flow **42**	2.6	2.7	1.9	4.2	2.6	2.2	3.1	2.0	3.4	5.3	3.3	3.4
Cost of Goods to Cash Flow **43**	0.5	0.5	0.1	0.8	0.6	0.4	0.8	0.2	1.2	1.4	0.7	1.2
Cash Flow to Total Debt **44**	0.5	•	1.5	0.9	1.1	0.7	0.6	0.3	0.2	0.2	0.3	0.2

Selected Financial Factors (in Percentages)

	•	•	•	•	•	•	•	•	•	•	•	•
Debt Ratio **45**	80.9	•	177.7	63.2	61.4	62.9	59.9	81.2	99.8	92.3	64.3	75.7
Return on Total Assets **46**	8.1	•	40.8	11.2	30.3	8.9	16.4	•	2.8	2.4	2.3	4.1
Return on Equity Before Income Taxes **47**	32.4	•	•	22.9	77.3	20.4	38.8	•	687.1	2.3	2.5	7.1
Return on Equity After Income Taxes **48**	29.7	•	21.0	75.0	19.8	37.9	•	506.8	•	•	2.5	5.6
Profit Margin (Before Income Tax) **49**	5.4	•	7.6	3.4	17.8	7.7	13.6	•	1.9	0.2	1.4	3.1
Profit Margin (After Income Tax) **50**	5.0	•	7.6	3.2	17.3	7.5	13.3	•	1.4	0.2	•	2.5

Table II
Corporations with Net Income

OTHER ARTS, ENTERTAINMENT, AND RECREATION

MONEY AMOUNTS AND SIZE OF ASSETS IN THOUSANDS OF DOLLARS

Item Description for Accounting Period 7/09 Through 6/10		Total	Zero Assets	Under 500	500 to 1,000	1,000 to 5,000	5,000 to 10,000	10,000 to 25,000	25,000 to 50,000	50,000 to 100,000	100,000 to 250,000	250,000 to 500,000	500,000 to 2,500,000	2,500,000 and over
Number of Enterprises	1	35274	6476	26616	1187	742	147	49	19	11	10	7	0	
		Revenues ($ in Thousands)												
Net Sales	2	30527347	611530	10238540	3006100	3327880	1519746	1249613	569825	489400	1483860	2597349	5433504	0
Interest	3	74699	112	1156	1903	3017	1590	284	339	1871	1800	22837	39791	0
Rents	4	84171	0	1279	855	0	2299	0	0	5665	541	30206	43327	0
Royalties	5	87439	0	0	0	0	0	0	0	60	19987	55514	11878	0
Other Portfolio Income	6	228978	2131	43537	6344	6984	567	28	3934	1182	10670	11688	141911	0
Other Receipts	7	1956480	28946	536089	1956	87468	339192	21669	58702	98984	85871	508381	189221	0
Total Receipts	8	32959114	642719	10820601	3017158	3425349	1863394	1271594	632800	597162	1602729	3225975	5859632	0
Average Total Receipts	9	934	99	407	2542	4616	12676	25951	33305	54287	160273	322598	837090	•
		Operating Costs/Operating Income (%)												
Cost of Operations	10	19.0	13.9	2.9	14.2	19.8	23.8	27.5	5.5	46.4	25.7	23.9	43.5	•
Salaries and Wages	11	15.6	6.4	11.9	13.4	11.5	22.8	16.2	28.4	10.0	25.3	35.2	12.4	•
Taxes Paid	12	3.3	2.1	2.1	2.5	4.1	3.1	2.2	2.1	3.1	2.8	11.2	2.8	•
Interest Paid	13	1.1	0.9	0.1	0.7	0.1	0.2	0.2	0.4	1.8	2.4	1.4	3.7	•
Depreciation	14	2.1	0.3	0.6	1.0	0.9	1.4	0.9	5.7	3.7	2.8	4.1	5.3	•
Amortization and Depletion	15	1.5	0.0	0.0	0.1	0.2	0.0	6.2	1.6	0.9	3.4	2.5	4.6	•
Pensions and Other Deferred Comp.	16	1.2	0.0	1.6	1.1	0.7	0.3	0.4	0.6	0.3	3.1	2.3	0.6	•
Employee Benefits	17	0.9	0.1	0.3	0.4	0.4	0.7	1.2	1.4	0.6	1.9	4.0	0.9	•
Advertising	18	1.9	1.0	0.8	3.1	2.0	3.4	0.3	1.7	3.3	2.0	1.6	3.4	•
Other Expenses	19	33.1	45.0	49.3	24.8	24.1	19.0	14.4	41.5	35.1	23.4	26.0	24.6	•
Officers' Compensation	20	14.0	10.7	19.1	33.4	15.6	22.4	9.6	5.3	2.6	5.2	1.6	1.8	•
Operating Margin	21	6.2	19.7	11.4	5.3	20.5	3.0	20.9	5.9	•	2.0	•	•	•
Operating Margin Before Officers' Comp.	22	20.2	30.4	30.5	38.6	36.1	25.3	30.5	11.2	•	7.2	•	•	•

Selected Average Balance Sheet ($ in Thousands)

	1	2	3	4	5	6	7	8	9	10	11	12
Net Receivables 23	39	0	1	36	179	89	2013	930	3639	19908	30124	71149
Inventories 24	9	0	1	19	213	18	28	353	2242	1587	2669	3434
Net Property, Plant and Equipment 25	177	0	7	224	231	627	2499	2603	16122	38470	86102	561736
Total Assets 26	622	0	53	683	1963	7782	14264	34415	67041	172844	357164	1391471
Notes and Loans Payable 27	181	0	16	201	478	537	2391	3885	21989	105858	69082	443447
All Other Liabilities 28	201	0	15	169	622	607	4817	7972	41755	86060	123556	430341
Net Worth 29	239	0	21	313	864	6638	7056	22558	3297	-19074	164526	517683

Selected Financial Ratios (Times to 1)

	1	2	3	4	5	6	7	8	9	10	11	12
Current Ratio 30	1.7	•	2.6	2.1	2.4	10.2	1.8	2.8	0.9	1.2	1.6	0.9
Quick Ratio 31	1.3	•	1.9	1.8	1.6	9.8	1.4	1.8	0.7	0.9	1.2	0.8
Net Sales to Working Capital 32	9.8	•	16.5	14.6	6.0	1.9	6.1	2.8	•	13.3	5.1	•
Coverage Ratio 33	14.3	27.7	120.4	8.8	162.2	159.8	151.7	47.7	9.1	5.1	8.5	2.7
Total Asset Turnover 34	1.4	•	7.3	3.7	2.3	1.3	1.8	0.9	0.7	0.9	0.7	0.6
Inventory Turnover 35	18.0	•	7.9	18.9	4.2	136.9	252.9	4.7	9.2	24.1	23.3	98.4
Receivables Turnover 36	20.3	•	159.4	103.9	28.4	•	15.0	20.2	14.4	7.8	6.6	•
Total Liabilities to Net Worth 37	1.6	•	1.5	1.2	1.3	0.2	1.0	0.5	19.3	•	1.2	1.7
Current Assets to Working Capital 38	2.5	•	1.6	1.9	1.7	1.1	2.3	1.6	•	5.8	2.6	•
Current Liabilities to Working Capital 39	1.5	•	0.6	0.9	0.7	0.1	1.3	0.6	•	4.8	1.6	•
Working Capital to Net Sales 40	0.1	•	0.1	0.1	0.2	0.5	0.2	0.4	0.1	0.1	0.2	•
Inventory to Working Capital 41	0.1	•	0.0	0.2	0.1	0.0	0.0	0.0	•	0.1	0.0	•
Total Receipts to Cash Flow 42	2.3	1.6	1.6	3.8	2.3	2.3	2.8	1.8	2.2	3.5	3.0	4.3
Cost of Goods to Cash Flow 43	0.4	0.2	0.0	0.5	0.5	0.6	0.8	0.1	1.0	0.9	0.7	1.9
Cash Flow to Total Debt 44	1.0	•	7.6	1.8	1.7	3.9	1.3	1.4	0.3	0.2	0.4	0.2

Selected Financial Factors (in Percentages)

	1	2	3	4	5	6	7	8	9	10	11	12
Debt Ratio 45	61.5	•	59.4	54.2	56.0	14.7	50.5	34.5	95.1	111.0	53.9	62.8
Return on Total Assets 46	21.8	•	126.1	23.5	53.9	34.2	40.7	14.7	10.6	10.6	8.4	5.7
Return on Equity Before Income Taxes 47	52.6	•	308.2	45.5	121.7	39.8	81.7	21.9	192.2	•	16.0	9.6
Return on Equity After Income Taxes 48	50.4	•	306.9	42.8	118.7	39.3	80.4	21.3	176.6	•	11.7	8.2
Profit Margin (Before Income Tax) 49	14.6	24.8	17.1	5.6	23.4	25.6	22.6	16.5	14.2	10.0	10.2	6.4
Profit Margin (After Income Tax) 50	13.9	24.0	17.0	5.3	22.9	25.2	22.3	16.0	13.1	9.3	7.4	5.5

Table I

Corporations with and without Net Income

AMUSEMENT, GAMBLING, AND RECREATION INDUSTRIES

MONEY AMOUNTS AND SIZE OF ASSETS IN THOUSANDS OF DOLLARS

Item Description for Accounting Period 7/09 Through 6/10	Total	Zero Assets	Under 500	500 to 1,000	1,000 to 5,000	5,000 to 10,000	10,000 to 25,000	25,000 to 50,000	50,000 to 100,000	100,000 to 250,000	250,000 to 500,000	500,000 to 2,500,000	2,500,000 and over
Number of Enterprises 1	49985	6866	34717	3877	3501	437	331	141	54	29	14	13	4
Revenues ($ in Thousands)													
Net Sales 2	45180658	281305	8194729	4119632	6326753	2453589	2639116	2570326	1762595	2577213	3967743	6494878	3792778
Interest 3	459792	2456	2798	4143	6506	5390	10047	7541	16475	17187	62616	21361	303273
Rents 4	161173	0	5380	7848	4159	18983	4120	9429	7270	2986	35067	40423	25508
Royalties 5	170658	0	0	31	498	1995	4	0	339	35143	52360	5295	74992
Other Portfolio Income 6	238137	15316	9319	682	10473	1598	11028	6040	14974	50056	449	33168	85032
Other Receipts 7	3168657	-47847	227707	502515	264810	145481	335905	128228	246356	101919	466211	785385	11989
Total Receipts 8	49379075	251230	8439933	4634851	6613199	2627036	3000220	2721564	2048009	2784504	4584446	7380510	4293572
Average Total Receipts 9	988	37	243	1195	1889	6012	9064	19302	37926	96017	327460	567732	1073393
Operating Costs/Operating Income (%)													
Cost of Operations 10	21.8	9.3	25.2	16.0	26.8	17.0	26.0	20.4	10.6	35.9	38.1	6.1	19.8
Salaries and Wages 11	22.5	5.3	15.2	26.6	20.7	30.0	27.3	29.4	29.0	17.3	20.6	29.2	15.9
Taxes Paid 12	8.4	3.6	4.0	5.1	6.1	9.8	6.3	5.2	11.1	5.7	5.8	13.8	21.8
Interest Paid 13	5.1	3.5	0.9	1.2	3.2	3.1	4.0	3.8	3.5	4.9	9.0	8.5	15.9
Depreciation 14	7.8	5.9	4.7	4.6	5.9	8.9	8.5	10.0	8.6	10.7	7.6	10.3	12.7
Amortization and Depletion 15	0.8	0.4	0.3	0.2	0.3	0.6	1.0	0.8	1.1	0.9	2.1	1.0	2.1
Pensions and Other Deferred Comp. 16	0.2	0.6	0.1	0.2	0.3	0.3	0.2	0.2	0.5	0.5	0.4	0.1	0.2
Employee Benefits 17	1.7	0.8	0.8	1.0	2.0	1.4	2.2	1.6	2.4	2.0	1.8	1.9	2.5
Advertising 18	2.4	3.1	1.8	1.8	1.7	2.5	3.0	2.1	2.9	2.6	2.4	3.2	3.9
Other Expenses 19	37.3	61.2	44.8	46.9	34.7	34.7	32.4	32.4	38.0	29.9	36.1	40.0	23.1
Officers' Compensation 20	2.8	6.2	6.2	4.2	3.9	2.8	2.1	1.2	1.8	0.9	0.6	0.8	0.7
Operating Margin 21	•	0.2	•	•	•	•	•	•	•	•	•	•	•
Operating Margin Before Officers' Comp. 22	•	6.3	2.1	•	•	•	•	•	•	•	•	•	•

Selected Average Balance Sheet ($ in Thousands)

Net Receivables 23	50	0	2	46	89	567	797	1374	4412	5879	12832	29169	70727
Inventories 24	21	0	3	12	53	176	251	1074	1869	2550	2676	8050	21085
Net Property, Plant and Equipment 25	746	0	55	387	1127	5235	10453	21063	38390	80635	206914	669136	1301479
Total Assets 26	1349	0	96	725	2072	6937	15189	35712	70311	140679	351328	1134583	3339582
Notes and Loans Payable 27	842	0	157	322	1564	3812	7269	13042	21913	75771	283341	694914	1911339
All Other Liabilities 28	292	0	18	94	393	1201	2734	8805	16763	29519	153961	300155	436382
Net Worth 29	214	0	-79	309	115	1924	5186	13865	31634	35390	-85974	139514	991860

Selected Financial Ratios (Times to 1)

Current Ratio 30	0.9	•	1.1	1.6	1.2	0.8	1.4	1.2	1.4	1.2	0.3	0.5	1.1
Quick Ratio 31	0.6	•	0.8	1.3	0.9	0.7	0.9	0.7	1.0	0.9	0.2	0.3	0.9
Net Sales to Working Capital 32	•	•	102.6	14.3	18.5	•	9.0	19.0	7.5	21.5	•	•	20.8
Coverage Ratio 33	0.7	•	•	4.7	0.7	•	1.2	0.7	3.0	0.4	0.0	0.9	0.7
Total Asset Turnover 34	0.7	•	2.5	1.5	0.9	0.8	0.5	0.5	0.5	0.6	0.8	0.4	0.3
Inventory Turnover 35	9.3	•	18.1	14.4	9.1	5.4	8.3	3.5	1.8	12.5	40.4	3.8	8.9
Receivables Turnover 36	13.0	•	61.9	23.7	16.3	9.4	9.7	11.4	8.8	11.1	24.4	11.4	4.4
Total Liabilities to Net Worth 37	5.3	•	•	1.3	17.1	2.6	1.9	1.6	1.2	3.0	•	7.1	2.4
Current Assets to Working Capital 38	•	•	11.5	2.7	5.2	•	3.5	7.5	3.7	6.0	•	•	9.1
Current Liabilities to Working Capital 39	•	•	10.5	1.7	4.2	•	2.5	6.5	2.7	5.0	•	•	8.1
Working Capital to Net Sales 40	•	•	0.0	0.1	0.1	•	0.1	0.1	0.1	0.0	•	•	0.0
Inventory to Working Capital 41	•	•	1.4	0.2	0.6	•	0.3	0.9	0.6	0.4	•	•	0.4
Total Receipts to Cash Flow 42	4.4	2.8	4.3	2.6	5.0	4.6	3.9	4.4	2.9	7.4	6.4	3.9	8.9
Cost of Goods to Cash Flow 43	1.0	0.3	1.1	0.4	1.3	0.8	1.0	0.9	0.3	2.7	2.4	0.2	1.8
Cash Flow to Total Debt 44	0.2	•	0.3	1.0	0.2	0.2	0.2	0.2	0.3	0.1	0.1	0.1	0.0

Selected Financial Factors (in Percentages)

Debt Ratio 45	84.1	•	181.6	57.4	94.5	72.3	65.9	61.2	55.0	74.8	124.5	87.7	70.3
Return on Total Assets 46	2.4	•	•	8.5	1.8	•	2.5	1.3	4.8	1.2	0.0	3.2	3.1
Return on Equity Before Income Taxes 47	•	•	3.3	15.7	•	•	1.2	•	7.1	•	29.4	•	•
Return on Equity After Income Taxes 48	•	•	3.4	15.6	•	•	0.5	•	6.6	•	31.4	•	•
Profit Margin (Before Income Tax) 49	•	•	•	4.6	•	•	0.8	•	6.9	•	•	•	•
Profit Margin (After Income Tax) 50	•	•	•	4.5	•	•	0.3	•	6.4	•	•	•	•

Table II

Corporations with Net Income

AMUSEMENT, GAMBLING, AND RECREATION INDUSTRIES

MONEY AMOUNTS AND SIZE OF ASSETS IN THOUSANDS OF DOLLARS

Item Description for Accounting Period 7/09 Through 6/10	Total	Zero Assets	Under 500	500 to 1,000	1,000 to 5,000	5,000 to 10,000	10,000 to 25,000	25,000 to 50,000	50,000 to 100,000	100,000 to 250,000	250,000 to 500,000	500,000 to 2,500,000	2,500,000 and over
Number of Enterprises 1	22472	4739	13940	1927	1591	72	115	46	23	10	6	3	0
Revenues ($ in Thousands)													
Net Sales 2	18436007	246343	4067272	2322588	3435851	713370	1262946	995657	983502	894208	581798	2932472	0
Interest 3	108466	2452	890	1672	3827	1833	385	4059	13526	1908	1077	76836	0
Rents 4	65028	0	5	2133	3004	15247	2763	3663	4505	635	4239	28832	0
Royalties 5	37678	0	0	0	498	1995	4	0	339	33744	1097	0	0
Other Portfolio Income 6	74207	15249	7153	274	7314	751	7896	1711	14801	1167	423	17466	0
Other Receipts 7	1660235	13955	61050	117052	316622	19607	116165	31883	171101	10063	335057	467687	0
Total Receipts 8	20381621	277999	4136370	2443719	3767116	752803	1390159	1036973	1187774	941725	923691	3523293	0
Average Total Receipts 9	907	59	297	1268	2368	10456	12088	22543	51642	94172	153948	1174431	•
Operating Costs/Operating Income (%)													
Cost of Operations 10	20.0	8.0	23.0	22.4	29.8	27.4	26.7	11.8	9.3	15.8	20.9	6.4	•
Salaries and Wages 11	19.5	3.7	11.6	22.7	17.6	23.7	20.1	22.2	27.1	21.6	29.2	24.4	•
Taxes Paid 12	9.3	2.0	3.5	4.6	6.6	4.8	6.0	5.2	13.1	7.5	5.8	28.7	•
Interest Paid 13	2.8	4.0	0.9	1.0	2.1	1.3	3.2	1.9	1.9	2.2	11.9	6.5	•
Depreciation 14	6.1	5.0	3.3	4.0	3.5	5.8	6.8	10.1	7.8	7.5	16.4	10.4	•
Amortization and Depletion 15	0.5	0.1	0.2	0.2	0.1	0.3	0.1	0.1	0.6	1.2	0.6	1.7	•
Pensions and Other Deferred Comp. 16	0.3	0.7	0.2	0.2	0.4	0.3	0.1	0.4	0.7	0.5	0.7	0.1	•
Employee Benefits 17	1.7	0.6	0.8	1.1	2.3	2.2	2.2	2.0	1.7	2.6	3.1	2.1	•
Advertising 18	2.2	3.4	1.2	1.7	1.8	2.3	3.0	3.6	2.3	4.0	6.4	2.4	•
Other Expenses 19	31.9	52.4	39.4	29.0	30.8	25.3	25.0	32.7	33.4	29.9	41.3	25.7	•
Officers' Compensation 20	3.7	7.0	6.3	5.1	4.7	2.2	2.6	1.5	1.7	1.6	2.0	0.4	•
Operating Margin 21	2.0	13.1	9.5	8.2	0.3	4.4	4.1	8.6	0.3	5.7	•	•	•
Operating Margin Before Officers' Comp. 22	5.6	20.1	15.8	13.3	5.0	6.6	6.7	10.1	1.9	7.3	•	•	•

Selected Average Balance Sheet ($ in Thousands)

Net Receivables 23	41	0	3	24	102	645	701	1768	3315	4984	5177	103914	•
Inventories 24	14	0	3	10	61	56	121	1197	498	1089	1856	11870	•
Net Property, Plant and Equipment 25	525	0	47	425	1058	3524	9042	19551	38141	73098	160983	1290207	•
Total Assets 26	1022	0	94	722	2228	6380	14406	38203	68677	133791	303862	2699250	•
Notes and Loans Payable 27	463	0	51	213	1071	1821	5991	8647	19902	41481	128777	1568529	•
All Other Liabilities 28	149	0	11	91	308	1470	2117	5559	7814	28057	73396	336845	•
Net Worth 29	410	0	32	418	848	3088	6298	23997	40961	64253	101688	793876	•

Selected Financial Ratios (Times to 1)

Current Ratio 30	1.6	•	2.3	1.9	1.6	1.2	1.7	1.5	1.3	1.1	1.3	2.0	•
Quick Ratio 31	1.3	•	1.9	1.4	1.1	1.1	1.2	1.0	1.0	0.9	0.9	1.5	•
Net Sales to Working Capital 32	9.5	•	15.3	13.0	9.5	27.4	7.7	8.0	12.5	31.8	10.2	4.5	•
Coverage Ratio 33	5.5	7.5	13.1	14.5	5.7	8.5	5.4	7.6	11.9	6.4	2.7	2.8	•
Total Asset Turnover 34	0.8	•	3.1	1.7	1.0	1.6	0.8	0.6	0.6	0.7	0.3	0.4	•
Inventory Turnover 35	11.9	•	25.8	25.9	10.5	48.9	24.4	2.1	7.9	12.9	10.9	5.3	•
Receivables Turnover 36	16.3	•	41.2	34.3	14.3	•	16.2	11.9	13.8	8.7	12.1	•	•
Total Liabilities to Net Worth 37	1.5	•	2.0	0.7	1.6	1.1	1.3	0.6	0.7	1.1	2.0	2.4	•
Current Assets to Working Capital 38	2.6	•	1.8	2.2	2.8	5.8	2.5	3.1	4.7	11.3	4.2	2.1	•
Current Liabilities to Working Capital 39	1.6	•	0.8	1.2	1.8	4.8	1.5	2.1	3.7	10.3	3.2	1.1	•
Working Capital to Net Sales 40	0.1	•	0.1	0.1	0.1	0.0	0.1	0.1	0.1	0.0	0.1	0.2	•
Inventory to Working Capital 41	0.2	•	0.1	0.2	0.4	0.2	0.1	0.2	0.1	0.4	0.3	0.1	•
Total Receipts to Cash Flow 42	2.9	1.4	2.9	2.8	3.3	3.7	3.1	2.6	2.2	3.1	1.9	3.3	•
Cost of Goods to Cash Flow 43	0.6	0.1	0.7	0.6	1.0	1.0	0.8	0.3	0.2	0.2	0.4	0.2	•
Cash Flow to Total Debt 44	0.5	•	1.6	1.4	0.5	0.8	0.4	0.6	0.7	0.4	0.2	0.2	•

Selected Financial Factors (in Percentages)

Debt Ratio 45	59.8	•	66.3	42.1	61.9	51.6	56.3	37.2	40.4	52.0	66.5	70.6	•
Return on Total Assets 46	12.3	•	37.5	24.0	11.7	17.3	13.3	8.3	14.4	9.3	10.3	6.5	•
Return on Equity Before Income Taxes 47	25.1	•	102.9	38.5	25.3	31.5	24.7	11.5	22.1	16.3	19.5	14.0	•
Return on Equity After Income Taxes 48	23.0	•	102.2	38.3	24.7	29.5	23.1	10.0	21.2	15.4	15.6	9.7	•
Profit Margin (Before Income Tax) 49	12.5	26.0	11.2	13.4	10.0	9.8	14.2	12.7	21.1	11.7	20.4	11.4	•
Profit Margin (After Income Tax) 50	11.5	26.0	11.1	13.3	9.7	9.2	13.2	11.1	20.3	11.0	16.4	7.8	•

Table I

Corporations with and without Net Income

ACCOMMODATION

MONEY AMOUNTS AND SIZE OF ASSETS IN THOUSANDS OF DOLLARS

Item Description for Accounting Period 7/09 Through 6/10	Total	Zero Assets	Under 500	500 to 1,000	1,000 to 5,000	5,000 to 10,000	10,000 to 25,000	25,000 to 50,000	50,000 to 100,000	100,000 to 250,000	250,000 to 500,000	500,000 to 2,500,000	2,500,000 and over
Number of Enterprises **1**	34347	4820	16263	4107	7415	1018	427	129	69	34	23	27	14
Revenues ($ in Thousands)													
Net Sales **2**	78250277	1614672	4529255	1796768	7434161	2723111	3920846	3055399	4209775	4535700	3638581	6548380	34243629
Interest **3**	1592513	2735	268	607	8931	2405	6492	8377	26680	19270	12817	287355	1216577
Rents **4**	928662	43041	237	4277	2857	1758	6104	8944	14107	11929	16599	72573	746235
Royalties **5**	1647035	4562	0	0	0	0	1126	0	2398	2465	199725	29137	1407623
Other Portfolio Income **6**	1722082	424703	9362	0	3722	5120	3455	13396	18820	5509	585	7408	1230004
Other Receipts **7**	8652163	-116644	70664	24610	64134	94792	121741	79932	52183	374073	74418	-9558	7821814
Total Receipts **8**	92792732	1973069	4609786	1826262	7513805	2827186	4059764	3166048	4323963	4948946	3942725	6935295	46665882
Average Total Receipts **9**	2702	409	283	445	1013	2777	9508	24543	62666	145557	171423	256863	3333277
Operating Costs/Operating Income (%)													
Cost of Operations **10**	15.4	7.1	9.0	8.3	15.3	13.6	33.6	18.1	23.8	21.8	20.4	15.4	12.5
Salaries and Wages **11**	27.6	14.7	18.1	12.0	18.3	21.8	13.3	14.6	10.4	18.5	19.4	22.7	40.8
Taxes Paid **12**	7.7	5.9	9.5	8.1	6.5	7.3	4.2	5.1	4.3	3.5	4.5	11.8	9.1
Interest Paid **13**	11.5	6.8	1.5	8.3	9.7	10.2	4.9	4.4	2.5	2.0	3.2	13.5	18.0
Depreciation **14**	8.4	7.9	3.3	7.5	9.1	12.3	5.5	7.4	4.2	5.2	8.7	12.0	9.4
Amortization and Depletion **15**	1.1	0.4	0.1	0.5	0.7	0.5	0.3	0.5	0.2	0.2	0.7	0.9	2.0
Pensions and Other Deferred Comp. **16**	0.5	0.4	0.1	0.2	0.1	0.1	0.1	0.2	0.2	0.1	0.8	0.3	0.9
Employee Benefits **17**	2.9	1.1	0.4	0.9	1.2	2.5	1.5	1.0	1.5	1.6	1.6	2.3	4.7
Advertising **18**	3.2	2.7	1.9	1.7	1.8	1.3	2.2	1.5	5.5	3.2	3.0	4.3	3.7
Other Expenses **19**	47.5	75.0	65.6	52.9	38.9	39.3	44.9	57.0	55.1	59.5	46.8	36.6	45.0
Officers' Compensation **20**	1.2	2.4	2.4	5.3	2.9	2.4	0.6	0.8	0.6	0.4	1.4	0.8	0.6
Operating Margin **21**	•	•	•	•	•	•	•	•	•	•	•	•	•
Operating Margin Before Officers' Comp. **22**	•	•	•	•	•	•	•	•	•	•	•	•	•

Selected Average Balance Sheet ($ in Thousands)

Net Receivables 23	283	0	1	9	74	184	740	1821	4836	7633	26754	59708	397558
Inventories 24	118	0	2	2	16	20	134	467	874	1922	3142	21703	211125
Net Property, Plant and Equipment 25	3365	0	111	587	1686	5059	10499	21580	43252	83830	189092	538997	4406740
Total Assets 26	7588	0	171	738	2159	6549	14936	35918	74649	169295	338875	917764	12689580
Notes and Loans Payable 27	4448	0	171	584	1935	5419	10116	21242	32334	61135	134978	507785	7109901
All Other Liabilities 28	1564	0	25	54	147	603	2154	6336	15179	48372	61991	153043	2956106
Net Worth 29	1576	0	-26	99	77	527	2666	8341	27136	59788	141906	256936	2623573

Selected Financial Ratios (Times to 1)

Current Ratio 30	1.1	•	0.8	1.6	1.7	1.0	1.6	1.5	1.3	0.8	1.5	1.2	1.0
Quick Ratio 31	0.8	•	0.4	1.0	1.1	0.8	1.0	1.1	1.0	0.6	1.2	0.7	0.7
Net Sales to Working Capital 32	30.6	•	12.3	12.3	9.2	138.5	9.9	8.9	15.5	•	6.6	9.2	•
Coverage Ratio 33	0.3	0.7	•	0.5	0.7	0.3	•	•	•	•	0.4	•	0.5
Total Asset Turnover 34	0.3	•	1.6	0.6	0.5	0.4	0.6	0.7	0.8	0.8	0.5	0.3	0.2
Inventory Turnover 35	3.0	•	11.0	19.7	9.8	18.4	23.1	9.2	16.6	15.1	10.3	1.7	1.4
Receivables Turnover 36	8.3	•	167.0	64.4	12.5	10.6	11.2	12.9	13.6	15.0	6.0	3.8	6.8
Total Liabilities to Net Worth 37	3.8	•	•	6.4	27.1	11.4	4.6	3.3	1.8	1.8	1.4	2.6	3.8
Current Assets to Working Capital 38	13.4	•	•	2.7	2.4	32.1	2.7	2.9	4.7	•	3.0	6.3	•
Current Liabilities to Working Capital 39	12.4	•	1.7	1.7	1.4	31.1	1.7	1.9	3.7	•	2.0	5.3	•
Working Capital to Net Sales 40	0.0	•	0.1	0.1	0.1	0.0	0.1	0.1	0.1	•	0.2	0.1	•
Inventory to Working Capital 41	1.5	•	•	0.1	0.1	1.1	0.1	0.2	0.2	•	0.1	1.0	•
Total Receipts to Cash Flow 42	4.2	2.2	5.0	3.5	3.9	5.6	4.5	4.2	4.1	4.1	3.2	7.2	4.1
Cost of Goods to Cash Flow 43	0.6	0.2	0.5	0.3	0.6	0.8	1.5	0.8	1.0	0.9	0.7	1.1	0.5
Cash Flow to Total Debt 44	0.1	•	0.3	0.2	0.1	0.1	0.2	0.2	0.3	0.3	0.2	0.1	0.1

Selected Financial Factors (in Percentages)

Debt Ratio 45	79.2	•	115.2	86.5	96.4	92.0	82.1	76.8	63.6	64.7	58.1	72.0	79.3
Return on Total Assets 46	1.1	•	•	2.6	2.9	1.1	•	•	•	•	0.6	•	1.7
Return on Equity Before Income Taxes 47	•	•	107.4	•	•	•	•	•	•	•	•	•	•
Return on Equity After Income Taxes 48	•	•	108.6	•	•	•	•	•	•	•	•	•	•
Profit Margin (Before Income Tax) 49	•	•	•	•	•	•	•	•	•	•	•	•	•
Profit Margin (After Income Tax) 50	•	•	•	•	•	•	•	•	•	•	•	•	•

Table II

Corporations with Net Income

ACCOMMODATION

MONEY AMOUNTS AND SIZE OF ASSETS IN THOUSANDS OF DOLLARS

Item Description for Accounting Period 7/09 Through 6/10	Total	Zero Assets	Under 500	500 to 1,000	1,000 to 5,000	5,000 to 10,000	10,000 to 25,000	25,000 to 50,000	50,000 to 100,000	100,000 to 250,000	250,000 to 500,000	500,000 to 2,500,000	2,500,000 and over
Number of Enterprises **1**	10806	1256	4433	1728	2809	364	130	36	23	•	8	8	•
Revenues ($ in Thousands)													
Net Sales **2**	26862752	229174	1901963	805170	3651752	847105	1744179	499775	833310	•	1346076	3095831	•
Interest **3**	563321	1391	117	6	8240	1159	1775	1496	13029	•	6439	157000	•
Rents **4**	130460	4546	19	0	194	1186	2462	4164	7138	•	3451	33824	•
Royalties **5**	1061323	4562	0	0	0	0	1126	0	177	•	199725	63	•
Other Portfolio Income **6**	1100350	414828	9362	0	2864	77	1867	6552	13720	•	481	669	•
Other Receipts **7**	1868106	53276	5703	19077	15797	71186	11608	44101	33845	•	42373	109332	•
Total Receipts **8**	31586312	707777	1917164	824253	3678847	920713	1763017	556088	901219	•	1598545	3396719	•
Average Total Receipts **9**	2923	564	432	477	1310	2529	13562	15447	39183	•	199818	424590	•
Operating Costs/Operating Income (%)													
Cost of Operations **10**	16.7	9.6	11.4	7.2	17.8	9.9	51.3	10.9	17.1	•	25.3	12.2	•
Salaries and Wages **11**	31.5	15.4	15.8	12.7	15.8	19.6	12.4	26.5	22.1	•	20.8	24.7	•
Taxes Paid **12**	6.3	9.0	6.8	8.0	5.2	10.7	4.0	10.6	5.0	•	4.3	16.1	•
Interest Paid **13**	5.9	6.2	1.1	6.4	6.2	11.1	3.5	4.7	4.7	•	3.0	11.5	•
Depreciation **14**	7.0	10.8	2.0	6.5	7.4	10.2	3.9	9.4	7.3	•	7.9	11.3	•
Amortization and Depletion **15**	0.4	0.4	0.0	0.1	0.4	0.3	0.1	0.5	0.5	•	0.9	•	•
Pensions and Other Deferred Comp. **16**	0.6	2.8	0.0	0.4	0.1	0.3	0.1	0.5	0.3	•	1.5	0.4	•
Employee Benefits **17**	3.2	2.1	0.8	0.9	1.3	0.8	0.3	1.9	2.6	•	1.4	1.7	•
Advertising **18**	3.4	4.5	1.8	1.6	1.5	1.1	0.7	2.4	10.6	•	6.0	3.6	•
Other Expenses **19**	32.5	43.3	48.4	35.3	32.3	30.3	19.0	30.1	29.9	•	32.3	24.3	•
Officers' Compensation **20**	1.7	4.0	4.0	8.8	3.3	3.9	0.6	1.5	1.4	•	3.0	0.6	•
Operating Margin **21**	•	•	7.8	12.1	8.8	1.7	4.2	1.0	•	•	•	•	•
Operating Margin Before Officers' Comp. **22**	•	•	11.9	20.9	12.0	5.7	4.8	2.5	•	•	•	•	•

Selected Average Balance Sheet ($ in Thousands)

Net Receivables 23	220	0	2	11	110	293	1382	2514	6511	•	40107	36232	•
Inventories 24	217	0	3	3	31	26	72	263	1091	•	4401	25213	•
Net Property, Plant and Equipment 25	2325	0	123	583	1539	4958	10506	21715	39928	•	167220	728452	•
Total Assets 26	4744	0	204	737	2089	6381	15220	35611	73291	•	346283	1135186	•
Notes and Loans Payable 27	2099	0	122	449	1446	4557	9273	16303	30838	•	116787	539173	•
All Other Liabilities 28	1177	0	23	58	118	906	991	3639	13636	•	89824	171451	•
Net Worth 29	1468	0	59	230	526	919	4956	15669	28818	•	139672	424563	•

Selected Financial Ratios (Times to 1)

Current Ratio 30	1.2	•	2.5	0.8	2.7	2.8	2.7	3.7	2.5	•	1.3	1.3	•
Quick Ratio 31	0.7	•	1.8	0.8	2.2	2.2	2.0	2.7	2.0	•	1.2	0.7	•
Net Sales to Working Capital 32	23.5	12.6	•	6.0	6.0	6.7	1.8	3.2	•	•	9.2	10.0	•
Coverage Ratio 33	2.6	33.1	9.2	3.3	1.9	2.5	3.6	2.4	0.5	•	5.0	1.4	•
Total Asset Turnover 34	0.5	2.1	0.6	0.6	0.4	0.9	0.4	0.5	0.0	•	0.5	0.3	•
Inventory Turnover 35	1.9	17.1	11.7	7.5	8.8	96.1	5.8	5.7	•	•	9.7	1.9	•
Receivables Turnover 36	7.7	216.3	63.2	10.0	11.0	8.2	4.1	6.3	•	•	4.3	7.6	•
Total Liabilities to Net Worth 37	2.2	2.4	2.2	3.0	5.9	2.1	1.3	1.5	•	•	4.0	1.7	•
Current Assets to Working Capital 38	7.0	1.7	1.6	1.6	1.6	1.6	1.4	1.7	•	•	4.0	3.9	•
Current Liabilities to Working Capital 39	6.0	0.7	•	0.6	0.6	0.6	0.4	0.7	•	•	3.0	2.9	•
Working Capital to Net Sales 40	0.0	0.1	0.1	0.2	0.2	0.2	0.0	0.5	•	•	0.1	0.1	•
Inventory to Working Capital 41	1.7	0.1	•	0.1	0.1	0.1	0.0	0.0	•	•	0.2	0.6	•
Total Receipts to Cash Flow 42	3.1	3.2	2.5	2.8	2.8	2.8	4.8	2.8	3.2	•	2.5	4.2	•
Cost of Goods to Cash Flow 43	0.5	0.0	0.2	0.5	0.3	0.3	0.3	0.3	0.5	•	0.6	0.5	•
Cash Flow to Total Debt 44	0.2	•	0.9	0.4	0.3	0.1	0.3	0.2	0.3	•	0.6	0.1	•

Selected Financial Factors (in Percentages)

Debt Ratio 45	69.1	•	70.9	68.8	74.8	85.6	67.4	56.0	60.7	•	59.7	62.6	•
Return on Total Assets 46	8.1	•	20.4	13.2	9.8	7.8	6.6	6.6	5.6	•	7.5	5.7	•
Return on Equity Before Income Taxes 47	16.2	•	62.3	29.3	23.4	26.4	14.3	10.8	8.3	•	14.8	4.6	•
Return on Equity After Income Taxes 48	13.5	•	60.4	28.9	23.2	25.6	13.1	8.8	7.3	•	10.3	3.6	•
Profit Margin (Before Income Tax) 49	9.6	200.7	8.6	14.5	9.5	10.4	5.3	12.2	6.6	•	12.3	5.1	•
Profit Margin (After Income Tax) 50	8.0	200.1	8.4	14.2	9.4	10.1	4.8	10.0	5.8	•	8.5	3.9	•

Table I

Corporations with and without Net Income

FOOD SERVICES AND DRINKING PLACES

Money Amounts and Size of Assets in Thousands of Dollars

Item Description for Accounting Period 7/09 Through 6/10	Total	Zero Assets	Under 500	500 to 1,000	1,000 to 5,000	5,000 to 10,000	10,000 to 25,000	25,000 to 50,000	50,000 to 100,000	100,000 to 250,000	250,000 to 500,000	500,000 to 2,500,000	2,500,000 and over
Number of Enterprises 1	263639	40128	197741	13560	10539	978	376	128	72	45	29	30	13
Revenues ($ in Thousands)													
Net Sales 2	334650023	4337990	102730325	25090126	43482153	13167014	9369318	6990710	8997126	10532955	13822457	30097248	66032600
Interest 3	635081	984	9409	5464	15094	5765	8951	11826	4868	8566	29639	111704	422811
Rents 4	661065	10753	17204	1248	8891	1857	7423	4995	10666	32327	68707	258864	238130
Royalties 5	4333081	26685	10819	311	1629	23859	56630	61876	76274	175889	585417	841206	2472487
Other Portfolio Income 6	2410874	62996	80553	2813	44460	10407	24797	2093	7156	17000	18007	660340	1480254
Other Receipts 7	8773013	59337	722724	159231	598829	153695	288959	112140	87715	203175	158958	1326948	4901302
Total Receipts 8	351463137	4498745	103571034	25259193	44151056	13362597	9756078	7183640	9183805	10969912	14683185	33296310	75547584
Average Total Receipts 9	1333	112	524	1863	4189	13663	25947	56122	127553	243776	506317	1109877	5811353
Operating Costs/Operating Income (%)													
Cost of Operations 10	41.6	37.3	41.8	38.1	41.5	40.5	43.2	40.6	38.5	41.6	43.2	39.6	44.3
Salaries and Wages 11	19.2	19.9	17.4	20.2	18.5	18.3	20.9	19.0	18.8	22.3	19.9	25.2	18.7
Taxes Paid 12	4.1	6.1	4.2	4.1	3.7	3.3	4.2	4.3	3.3	4.0	4.1	3.8	4.3
Interest Paid 13	1.8	1.2	0.6	0.9	1.3	1.3	1.7	1.8	2.0	2.5	3.5	2.2	3.8
Depreciation 14	3.1	4.2	1.9	2.9	2.7	3.1	3.5	4.1	3.4	4.6	3.6	5.4	3.7
Amortization and Depletion 15	0.6	1.0	0.3	0.4	0.6	0.5	0.6	0.6	0.5	1.0	0.9	0.7	1.1
Pensions and Other Deferred Comp. 16	0.2	0.0	0.1	0.1	0.0	0.1	0.3	0.1	0.1	0.1	0.2	0.3	0.5
Employee Benefits 17	1.3	0.1	0.5	0.8	0.8	0.9	1.0	1.4	1.4	1.4	1.7	1.6	3.1
Advertising 18	2.3	1.3	1.6	2.8	3.0	3.6	3.2	3.1	2.2	2.4	2.4	2.7	2.2
Other Expenses 19	24.5	38.7	26.2	23.9	23.9	25.9	21.4	25.6	30.2	24.5	22.6	21.7	22.8
Officers' Compensation 20	2.4	4.0	4.8	3.3	2.5	1.1	1.7	1.1	0.9	0.9	0.9	0.8	0.5
Operating Margin 21	•	•	0.5	2.5	1.6	1.3	•	•	•	•	•	•	•
Operating Margin Before Officers' Comp. 22	1.1	5.2	5.2	5.8	4.1	2.4	0.1	•	•	•	•	•	•

Selected Average Balance Sheet ($ in Thousands)

Net Receivables 23	40	0	3	32	83	157	825	1905	4554	5293	14042	32495	467033
Inventories 24	21	0	7	29	43	192	488	816	1798	3493	9542	19288	116956
Net Property, Plant and Equipment 25	299	0	63	354	883	3465	6838	16182	34414	82157	126365	471828	1552442
Total Assets 26	810	0	126	688	1782	6890	14788	33271	71203	153287	342404	967167	7158432
Notes and Loans Payable 27	368	0	97	388	1046	3600	7420	16464	32708	75680	184027	338002	2463764
All Other Liabilities 28	240	0	25	129	377	1513	3262	9205	23341	45401	109279	362903	2388589
Net Worth 29	202	0	5	171	359	1776	4106	7601	15153	32206	49098	266262	2306080

Selected Financial Ratios (Times to 1)

Current Ratio 30	0.9	•	1.2	1.4	1.1	1.1	1.1	1.0	0.7	0.6	0.8	0.8	0.8
Quick Ratio 31	0.6	•	0.8	0.9	0.7	0.7	0.8	0.6	0.4	0.4	0.6	0.5	0.6
Net Sales to Working Capital 32	•	•	83.6	35.6	94.0	97.1	61.1	•	•	0.6	•	•	•
Coverage Ratio 33	3.3	•	3.0	4.3	3.4	3.2	2.5	1.6	1.4	1.4	1.9	4.2	3.9
Total Asset Turnover 34	1.6	•	4.1	2.7	2.3	2.0	1.7	1.6	1.8	1.5	1.4	1.0	0.7
Inventory Turnover 35	25.7	•	31.2	24.7	39.7	28.5	22.0	27.2	26.7	27.8	21.6	20.6	19.3
Receivables Turnover 36	29.1	•	239.3	50.0	36.9	77.0	27.9	32.3	26.6	39.6	31.4	•	10.9
Total Liabilities to Net Worth 37	3.0	•	25.4	3.0	4.0	2.9	2.6	3.4	3.7	3.8	6.0	2.6	2.1
Current Assets to Working Capital 38	•	•	5.6	3.8	10.3	12.3	9.6	•	•	•	•	•	•
Current Liabilities to Working Capital 39	•	•	4.6	2.8	9.3	11.3	8.6	•	•	•	•	•	•
Working Capital to Net Sales 40	•	•	0.0	0.0	0.0	0.0	0.0	•	•	•	•	•	•
Inventory to Working Capital 41	•	•	1.1	0.5	1.0	1.5	1.1	•	•	•	•	•	•
Total Receipts to Cash Flow 42	5.4	7.9	6.0	5.5	5.5	5.2	6.2	5.6	4.3	7.0	5.8	5.3	4.6
Cost of Goods to Cash Flow 43	2.3	3.0	2.5	2.1	2.3	2.1	2.7	2.3	1.6	2.9	2.5	2.1	2.0
Cash Flow to Total Debt 44	0.4	•	0.7	0.6	0.5	0.5	0.4	0.4	0.5	0.3	0.3	0.3	0.2

Selected Financial Factors (in Percentages)

Debt Ratio 45	75.1	•	96.2	75.1	79.9	74.2	72.2	77.2	78.7	79.0	85.7	72.5	67.8
Return on Total Assets 46	9.2	•	7.9	10.9	10.2	8.0	7.2	4.8	4.9	2.3	9.2	9.9	10.5
Return on Equity Before Income Taxes 47	25.5	•	139.3	33.9	35.8	21.4	15.6	7.9	6.5	•	30.9	27.4	24.3
Return on Equity After Income Taxes 48	18.7	•	132.3	32.8	34.5	20.8	13.5	5.7	3.6	•	23.1	18.5	15.9
Profit Margin (Before Income Tax) 49	4.1	•	1.3	3.1	3.1	2.8	2.6	1.1	0.8	•	3.2	7.3	11.0
Profit Margin (After Income Tax) 50	3.0	•	1.2	3.0	3.0	2.7	2.2	0.8	0.4	•	2.4	4.9	7.2

Table II

Corporations with Net Income

FOOD SERVICES AND DRINKING PLACES

MONEY AMOUNTS AND SIZE OF ASSETS IN THOUSANDS OF DOLLARS

Item Description for Accounting Period 7/09 Through 6/10

Item	Total	Zero Assets	Under 500	500 to 1,000	1,000 to 5,000	5,000 to 10,000	10,000 to 25,000	25,000 to 50,000	50,000 to 100,000	100,000 to 250,000	250,000 to 500,000	500,000 to 2,500,000	2,500,000 and over
Number of Enterprises **1**	129280	8390	104681	8257	6763	738	256	79	42	•	22	24	•
Revenues ($ in Thousands)													
Net Sales **2**	249929056	1555692	66022800	17787786	32248666	10503198	6741284	4605397	6022132	•	10807361	26750002	•
Interest **3**	550892	830	5884	4767	12354	4308	7498	5894	2078	•	28532	99176	•
Rents **4**	521292	52	8418	1248	4355	1606	5156	2591	3014	•	58652	248388	•
Royalties **5**	3920323	1569	7569	311	55	19977	39017	22451	48444	•	546768	735209	•
Other Portfolio Income **6**	2345108	40614	74973	2696	25268	10314	17065	1334	6894	•	17885	658089	•
Other Receipts **7**	7607634	9912	540504	127778	402454	109246	258588	92072	76344	•	135721	1263550	•
Total Receipts **8**	264274305	1608669	66660148	17924586	32913152	10648649	7068608	4729739	6158906	•	11594919	29754414	•
Average Total Receipts **9**	2044	192	637	2171	4867	14429	27612	59870	146641	•	527042	1239767	•
Operating Costs/Operating Income (%)													
Cost of Operations **10**	41.8	34.3	40.7	38.6	42.0	41.7	40.5	42.4	35.8	•	46.5	39.8	•
Salaries and Wages **11**	18.8	22.4	17.2	19.8	17.3	16.7	22.6	16.7	19.3	•	19.0	24.9	•
Taxes Paid **12**	4.0	6.4	4.2	4.1	3.5	3.0	4.1	4.2	3.2	•	4.1	3.8	•
Interest Paid **13**	1.7	0.8	0.5	0.7	1.1	1.0	1.3	1.4	1.0	•	2.8	1.8	•
Depreciation **14**	2.8	1.1	1.3	1.6	2.0	2.5	3.3	3.4	2.9	•	3.9	5.7	•
Amortization and Depletion **15**	0.6	0.3	0.3	0.2	0.6	0.6	0.4	0.7	0.3	•	0.8	0.4	•
Pensions and Other Deferred Comp. **16**	0.2	•	0.0	0.1	0.0	0.0	0.4	0.1	0.1	•	0.2	0.3	•
Employee Benefits **17**	1.4	0.3	0.6	0.8	0.8	0.5	1.0	1.3	1.4	•	1.6	1.6	•
Advertising **18**	2.3	0.7	1.5	2.2	3.0	3.6	3.0	3.5	2.2	•	2.5	2.7	•
Other Expenses **19**	22.8	26.2	23.6	22.1	22.5	25.3	20.0	22.9	31.4	•	20.4	21.6	•
Officers' Compensation **20**	2.2	4.0	4.8	2.9	2.6	0.8	1.9	1.0	0.9	•	0.5	0.8	•
Operating Margin **21**	1.3	3.6	5.3	6.9	4.6	4.1	1.4	2.5	1.5	•	•	•	•
Operating Margin Before Officers' Comp. **22**	3.5	7.6	10.1	9.8	7.2	4.9	3.3	3.5	2.4	•	•	•	•

Selected Average Balance Sheet ($ in Thousands)

Net Receivables 23	64	0	3	44	96	149	927	1379	5639	•	11997	31279
Inventories 24	30	0	7	29	45	159	466	726	2082	•	8581	21716
Net Property, Plant and Equipment 25	438	0	60	310	834	3291	6813	15969	33826	•	140172	553703
Total Assets 26	1274	0	133	687	1842	6655	14943	33823	70705	•	331101	997655
Notes and Loans Payable 27	489	0	67	317	918	3357	6788	15376	26829	•	159533	341313
All Other Liabilities 28	365	0	24	111	341	1439	2795	7787	19258	•	110254	280896
Net Worth 29	421	0	41	259	583	1859	5359	10660	24618	•	61314	375446

Selected Financial Ratios (Times to 1)

Current Ratio 30	1.0	•	1.6	1.9	1.4	1.1	1.3	1.1	1.0	•	0.8	0.8
Quick Ratio 31	0.7	•	1.1	1.3	1.0	0.8	1.0	0.8	0.7	•	0.5	0.5
Net Sales to Working Capital 32	226.3	•	41.4	19.0	34.3	140.3	29.0	67.9	•	•	•	5.8
Coverage Ratio 33	5.6	9.9	12.7	12.2	6.5	6.3	5.9	4.6	4.7	•	2.8	5.8
Total Asset Turnover 34	1.5	•	4.7	3.1	2.6	2.1	1.8	1.7	2.0	•	1.5	1.1
Inventory Turnover 35	27.0	•	39.0	28.4	44.5	37.3	22.9	34.0	24.7	•	26.6	20.4
Receivables Turnover 36	27.8	•	256.5	50.7	32.2	84.1	28.2	42.0	•	•	41.7	34.8
Total Liabilities to Net Worth 37	2.0	•	2.2	1.7	2.2	2.6	1.8	2.2	1.9	•	4.4	1.7
Current Assets to Working Capital 38	27.4	•	2.8	2.2	3.8	13.4	4.6	8.4	•	•	•	•
Current Liabilities to Working Capital 39	26.4	•	1.8	1.2	2.8	12.4	3.6	7.4	•	•	•	•
Working Capital to Net Sales 40	0.0	0.0	0.0	0.1	0.0	0.0	0.0	0.0	0.0	•	•	•
Inventory to Working Capital 41	3.5	•	0.5	0.2	0.4	1.5	0.5	0.8	•	•	•	•
Total Receipts to Cash Flow 42	4.8	4.2	4.8	4.8	5.0	4.7	5.3	4.8	3.4	•	5.7	5.0
Cost of Goods to Cash Flow 43	2.0	1.4	2.0	1.9	2.1	2.0	2.1	2.1	1.2	•	2.6	2.0
Cash Flow to Total Debt 44	0.5	•	1.4	1.0	0.8	0.6	0.5	0.5	0.9	•	0.3	0.4

Selected Financial Factors (in Percentages)

Debt Ratio 45	67.0	•	69.1	62.3	68.4	72.1	64.1	68.5	65.2	•	81.5	62.4
Return on Total Assets 46	14.3	•	32.2	26.3	18.4	13.9	13.3	11.4	9.8	•	11.5	11.5
Return on Equity Before Income Taxes 47	35.5	•	96.0	64.0	49.2	41.9	30.9	28.4	22.1	•	39.8	25.2
Return on Equity After Income Taxes 48	28.9	•	94.4	62.8	47.9	41.2	28.5	25.7	19.1	•	31.6	17.4
Profit Margin (Before Income Tax) 49	7.8	7.0	6.3	7.7	6.0	5.5	6.3	5.2	3.8	•	5.0	8.5
Profit Margin (After Income Tax) 50	6.3	6.4	6.2	7.6	5.8	5.4	5.8	4.7	3.3	•	3.9	5.8

Table I

Corporations with and without Net Income

AUTOMOTIVE REPAIR AND MAINTENANCE

MONEY AMOUNTS AND SIZE OF ASSETS IN THOUSANDS OF DOLLARS

Item Description for Accounting Period 7/09 Through 6/10	Total	Zero Assets	Under 500	500 to 1,000	1,000 to 5,000	5,000 to 10,000	10,000 to 25,000	25,000 to 50,000	50,000 to 100,000	100,000 to 250,000	250,000 to 500,000	500,000 to 2,500,000	2,500,000 and over
Number of Enterprises **1**	108317	15772	82550	6685	3066	153	58	15	8	5	4	0	0
Revenues ($ in Thousands)													
Net Sales **2**	63677172	2112081	37053388	9223303	8590171	1058334	1476683	737909	935173	671348	1818784	0	0
Interest **3**	29204	2046	5111	6127	1732	1184	1264	1777	1191	527	8244	0	0
Rents **4**	15312	344	1994	342	1735	7388	551	401	0	112	2445	0	0
Royalties **5**	102618	0	0	0	0	0	1480	0	1557	47043	52538	0	0
Other Portfolio Income **6**	167674	39045	48896	6941	5525	20657	18039	6061	18842	1881	1787	0	0
Other Receipts **7**	306409	7878	154206	24273	19175	47055	9123	6266	6067	10508	21859	0	0
Total Receipts **8**	64298389	2161394	37263595	9260986	8618338	1134618	1507140	752414	962830	731419	1905657	0	0
Average Total Receipts **9**	594	137	451	1385	2811	7416	25985	50161	120354	146284	476414	•	•
Operating Costs/Operating Income (%)													
Cost of Operations **10**	49.2	35.8	47.1	51.7	56.4	52.4	52.5	42.2	60.3	45.1	56.6	•	•
Salaries and Wages **11**	13.4	13.4	13.8	10.9	13.6	11.8	14.7	20.7	15.7	19.9	9.0	•	•
Taxes Paid **12**	3.4	4.0	3.5	2.9	3.6	1.9	3.4	3.3	2.6	3.4	1.8	•	•
Interest Paid **13**	1.3	0.9	0.9	2.0	1.5	3.4	0.5	2.0	0.8	6.7	3.9	•	•
Depreciation **14**	2.0	3.1	1.5	2.7	2.2	3.1	2.7	5.5	2.2	2.7	2.1	•	•
Amortization and Depletion **15**	0.5	0.2	0.3	0.5	0.7	0.5	0.2	2.4	0.5	3.6	2.8	•	•
Pensions and Other Deferred Comp. **16**	0.1	0.0	0.1	0.1	0.1	0.1	0.1	0.1	0.3	0.2	0.4	•	•
Employee Benefits **17**	1.2	0.4	1.2	1.9	0.8	1.4	1.1	1.0	2.2	2.0	1.9	•	•
Advertising **18**	1.6	0.6	1.4	2.3	1.2	3.2	1.5	1.6	0.5	1.0	4.8	•	•
Other Expenses **19**	20.0	40.3	20.5	18.2	15.2	19.9	21.6	22.0	13.5	19.9	20.0	•	•
Officers' Compensation **20**	5.9	4.6	7.6	5.0	3.5	3.9	1.4	1.0	0.9	1.2	0.9	•	•
Operating Margin **21**	1.4	•	2.2	1.8	1.1	•	0.3	•	0.5	•	•	•	•
Operating Margin Before Officers' Comp. **22**	7.3	1.2	9.8	6.8	4.6	2.5	1.7	•	1.3	•	•	•	•

Selected Average Balance Sheet ($ in Thousands)

Net Receivables 23	20	0	9	63	162	1033	1503	2377	11155	13265	11407
Inventories 24	19	0	11	61	114	646	885	2421	2413	4019	40349
Net Property, Plant and Equipment 25	83	0	33	323	793	2214	6272	16746	20246	36422	99183
Total Assets 26	215	0	95	688	1690	6830	15229	34042	71608	186333	420942
Notes and Loans Payable 27	134	0	74	476	942	3064	4002	15817	18577	95592	209639
All Other Liabilities 28	49	0	29	115	312	1127	1079	7054	26286	45750	94957
Net Worth 29	31	0	-8	97	436	2639	10148	11171	26745	44991	116346

Selected Financial Ratios (Times to 1)

Current Ratio 30	1.4	•	1.3	1.5	2.0	1.9	1.2	1.0	1.0	1.2	1.0
Quick Ratio 31	0.9	•	0.9	0.9	1.4	1.2	0.9	0.6	0.6	0.8	0.3
Net Sales to Working Capital 32	27.0	•	44.5	19.9	10.5	6.2	34.3	•	5.9	24.6	122.2
Coverage Ratio 33	2.8	•	4.1	2.1	2.0	2.7	5.9	1.0	5.9	1.6	1.2
Total Asset Turnover 34	2.7	•	4.7	2.0	1.7	1.0	1.7	1.4	1.6	0.7	1.1
Inventory Turnover 35	15.2	•	19.1	11.6	13.8	5.6	15.1	8.6	29.2	15.1	6.4
Receivables Turnover 36	30.0	•	52.2	23.9	19.2	4.4	20.5	13.7	8.9	10.5	41.1
Total Liabilities to Net Worth 37	5.8	•	•	6.1	2.9	1.6	0.5	2.0	1.7	3.1	2.6
Current Assets to Working Capital 38	3.4	•	4.2	3.0	2.0	2.1	6.7	•	•	5.5	21.2
Current Liabilities to Working Capital 39	2.4	•	3.2	2.0	1.0	1.1	5.7	•	•	4.5	20.2
Working Capital to Net Sales 40	0.0	•	0.0	0.1	0.1	0.2	0.0	•	•	0.0	0.0
Inventory to Working Capital 41	0.9	•	1.1	0.9	0.4	0.6	1.3	•	•	0.7	11.7
Total Receipts to Cash Flow 42	6.6	3.7	6.3	7.0	9.1	5.5	6.2	8.8	9.3	7.6	6.9
Cost of Goods to Cash Flow 43	3.2	1.3	3.0	3.6	5.2	2.9	3.2	3.7	5.6	3.4	3.9
Cash Flow to Total Debt 44	0.5	•	0.7	0.3	0.2	0.3	0.8	0.2	0.3	0.1	0.2

Selected Financial Factors (in Percentages)

Debt Ratio 45	85.4	•	108.2	85.8	74.2	61.4	33.4	67.2	62.7	75.9	72.4
Return on Total Assets 46	10.1	•	17.2	8.4	4.9	9.2	4.7	3.0	7.4	7.7	4.9
Return on Equity Before Income Taxes 47	44.1	•	•	31.4	9.4	15.1	5.8	0.3	16.3	12.1	2.4
Return on Equity After Income Taxes 48	42.3	•	•	30.5	9.0	13.0	5.0	0.3	14.9	10.0	•
Profit Margin (Before Income Tax) 49	2.4	•	2.8	2.2	1.5	5.7	2.3	0.1	3.7	4.1	0.6
Profit Margin (After Income Tax) 50	2.3	•	2.7	2.2	1.4	5.0	2.0	0.1	3.4	3.3	•

Table II

Corporations with Net Income

AUTOMOTIVE REPAIR AND MAINTENANCE

MONEY AMOUNTS AND SIZE OF ASSETS IN THOUSANDS OF DOLLARS

Item Description for Accounting Period 7/09 Through 6/10		Total	Zero Assets	Under 500	500 to 1,000	1,000 to 5,000	5,000 to 10,000	10,000 to 25,000	25,000 to 50,000	50,000 to 100,000	100,000 to 250,000	250,000 to 500,000	500,000 to 2,500,000	2,500,000 and over
Number of Enterprises	1	63267	7611	50058	3886	1729	126	41	•	•	•	0	0	0
Revenues ($ in Thousands)														
Net Sales	2	43130470	805487	26517391	5055892	6503059	854028	1357416	•	•	•	•	•	•
Interest	3	13890	1888	2958	3119	1349	946	1264	•	•	•	•	•	•
Rents	4	10579	0	1032	6	1735	7388	5	•	•	•	•	•	•
Royalties	5	50080	0	0	0	0	0	1480	•	•	•	•	•	•
Other Portfolio Income	6	138841	39045	44464	2053	3314	20657	2963	•	•	•	•	•	•
Other Receipts	7	238789	6988	123690	26498	16875	41694	6730	•	•	•	•	•	•
Total Receipts	8	43582649	853408	26689535	5087568	6526332	924713	1369858	•	•	•	•	•	•
Average Total Receipts	9	689	112	533	1380	3775	7339	33411	•	•	•	•	•	•
Operating Costs/Operating Income (%)														
Cost of Operations	10	47.9	20.6	45.6	47.5	58.9	50.1	53.6	•	•	•	•	•	•
Salaries and Wages	11	14.0	14.0	14.1	13.6	12.9	11.9	14.1	•	•	•	•	•	•
Taxes Paid	12	3.3	2.5	3.4	3.1	3.6	1.8	3.1	•	•	•	•	•	•
Interest Paid	13	1.0	2.2	0.7	1.8	0.9	3.9	0.4	•	•	•	•	•	•
Depreciation	14	1.5	1.9	1.2	1.7	1.7	2.6	2.4	•	•	•	•	•	•
Amortization and Depletion	15	0.2	0.3	0.1	0.3	0.1	0.6	0.2	•	•	•	•	•	•
Pensions and Other Deferred Comp.	16	0.1	•	0.1	0.1	0.1	•	0.1	•	•	•	•	•	•
Employee Benefits	17	1.2	•	1.1	2.4	0.9	0.5	1.2	•	•	•	•	•	•
Advertising	18	1.4	0.7	1.4	1.6	1.3	3.3	1.3	•	•	•	•	•	•
Other Expenses	19	17.7	43.3	18.8	14.2	12.1	22.3	19.5	•	•	•	•	•	•
Officers' Compensation	20	6.1	4.8	7.5	5.7	3.4	3.8	1.5	•	•	•	•	•	•
Operating Margin	21	5.6	9.8	5.9	8.2	4.1	•	2.7	•	•	•	•	•	•
Operating Margin Before Officers' Comp.	22	11.6	14.5	13.5	13.9	7.5	3.1	4.2	•	•	•	•	•	•

Selected Average Balance Sheet ($ in Thousands)

Net Receivables 23	25	0	11	76	230	1079	2016
Inventories 24	17	0	10	51	116	588	865
Net Property, Plant and Equipment 25	81	0	30	314	787	2182	6143
Total Assets 26	212	0	98	679	1642	7162	14610
Notes and Loans Payable 27	103	0	56	373	670	3259	3456
All Other Liabilities 28	48	0	22	102	406	1170	4540
Net Worth 29	62	0	21	204	566	2732	6614

Selected Financial Ratios (Times to 1)

Current Ratio 30	1.7	•	1.8	1.7	2.3	2.0	1.2
Quick Ratio 31	1.2	•	1.3	1.1	1.7	1.4	1.0
Net Sales to Working Capital 32	19.0	•	25.0	16.5	9.6	5.8	26.6
Coverage Ratio 33	7.5	8.1	10.4	5.9	5.8	3.0	11.2
Total Asset Turnover 34	3.2	•	5.4	2.0	2.3	0.9	2.3
Inventory Turnover 35	18.8	•	24.7	12.9	19.1	5.8	20.5
Receivables Turnover 36	29.6	•	60.2	20.9	18.6	3.9	20.9
Total Liabilities to Net Worth 37	2.4	•	3.7	2.3	1.9	1.6	1.2
Current Assets to Working Capital 38	2.4	•	2.3	2.5	1.8	2.0	5.1
Current Liabilities to Working Capital 39	1.4	•	1.3	1.5	0.8	1.0	4.1
Working Capital to Net Sales 40	0.1	•	0.0	0.1	0.1	0.2	0.0
Inventory to Working Capital 41	0.5	•	0.5	0.7	0.3	0.5	1.0
Total Receipts to Cash Flow 42	5.6	2.0	5.4	5.3	8.6	4.6	5.9
Cost of Goods to Cash Flow 43	2.7	0.4	2.5	2.5	5.1	2.3	3.2
Cash Flow to Total Debt 44	0.8	•	1.3	0.5	0.4	0.3	0.7

Selected Financial Factors (in Percentages)

Debt Ratio 45	70.7	•	78.7	70.0	65.5	61.9	54.7
Return on Total Assets 46	24.5	•	39.3	21.5	12.4	10.8	9.0
Return on Equity Before Income Taxes 47	72.6	•	166.9	59.5	29.9	18.8	18.1
Return on Equity After Income Taxes 48	71.0	•	165.6	58.7	29.2	16.5	16.3
Profit Margin (Before Income Tax) 49	6.6	15.7	6.6	8.8	4.5	7.6	3.6
Profit Margin (After Income Tax) 50	6.5	15.7	6.5	8.7	4.4	6.6	3.3

Table I

Corporations with and without Net Income

OTHER REPAIR AND MAINTENANCE

Money Amounts and Size of Assets in Thousands of Dollars

Item Description for Accounting Period 7/09 Through 6/10		Total	Zero Assets	Under 500	500 to 1,000	1,000 to 5,000	5,000 to 10,000	10,000 to 25,000	25,000 to 50,000	50,000 to 100,000	100,000 to 250,000	250,000 to 500,000	500,000 to 2,500,000	2,500,000 and over
Number of Enterprises	1	58959	9691	45563	1815	1577	154	109	26	14	9	0	3	0
Revenues ($ in Thousands)														
Net Sales	2	36954439	880957	14882582	3638009	6219415	1859939	2799203	1557459	1433102	1844408	0	1839366	0
Interest	3	150078	1367	2345	3160	5625	2794	1742	461	7290	2142	0	123151	0
Rents	4	25171	0	20258	630	1345	150	1948	809	0	0	0	30	0
Royalties	5	75532	0	0	0	0	0	0	0	294	0	0	75239	0
Other Portfolio Income	6	52593	16659	4122	289	10539	2293	3884	604	1807	4520	0	7876	0
Other Receipts	7	424737	517	21003	102062	11665	4730	21939	2593	9429	13863	0	236938	0
Total Receipts	8	37682550	899500	14930310	3744150	6248589	1869906	2828716	1561926	1451922	1864933	0	2282600	0
Average Total Receipts	9	639	93	328	2063	3962	12142	25952	60074	103709	207215	•	760867	•
Operating Costs/Operating Income (%)														
Cost of Operations	10	52.0	36.4	42.3	55.4	57.3	60.2	61.2	69.6	57.2	65.0	•	59.9	•
Salaries and Wages	11	13.0	10.3	16.5	11.1	8.8	10.6	13.6	13.5	11.6	10.0	•	9.3	•
Taxes Paid	12	2.7	2.2	3.1	3.0	2.3	2.0	2.2	3.0	2.0	2.8	•	2.7	•
Interest Paid	13	2.1	0.5	0.8	0.7	1.1	1.0	0.6	0.9	2.6	2.4	•	22.5	•
Depreciation	14	1.9	2.5	1.6	1.8	1.6	2.9	3.1	1.4	3.3	2.1	•	1.5	•
Amortization and Depletion	15	0.5	0.0	0.1	0.2	0.3	0.0	0.1	0.2	0.7	2.5	•	5.0	•
Pensions and Other Deferred Comp.	16	0.4	0.0	0.4	0.7	0.2	1.2	0.5	0.7	0.2	0.2	•	0.3	•
Employee Benefits	17	1.7	0.8	0.8	2.5	2.0	1.8	1.6	4.6	3.0	3.0	•	2.5	•
Advertising	18	0.7	1.3	0.9	0.8	0.5	0.4	0.4	1.5	0.2	0.1	•	1.4	•
Other Expenses	19	17.0	36.5	21.9	16.1	11.8	12.6	13.3	•	18.3	10.4	•	17.8	•
Officers' Compensation	20	6.1	10.1	8.6	7.9	6.5	3.3	2.0	2.0	1.0	1.1	•	1.0	•
Operating Margin	21	1.8	•	3.1	•	7.5	3.8	1.4	4.1	•	0.3	•	•	•
Operating Margin Before Officers' Comp.	22	7.9	9.5	11.7	7.6	13.9	7.2	3.4	6.0	1.0	1.4	•	•	•

Selected Average Balance Sheet ($ in Thousands)

Net Receivables 23	65	0	9	171	373	1774	3353	9729	15967	38924	346353	•
Inventories 24	44	0	12	105	426	1114	4429	8917	11111	5203	32145	•
Net Property, Plant and Equipment 25	46	0	18	115	295	1235	4336	5186	12384	20508	32068	•
Total Assets 26	383	0	66	721	1749	6538	16160	32438	67524	199456	3056694	•
Notes and Loans Payable 27	186	0	42	220	742	2652	4626	5391	27551	71460	1787024	•
All Other Liabilities 28	97	0	23	128	338	1505	3918	14499	19924	43879	725642	•
Net Worth 29	101	0	0	373	669	2381	7617	12548	20049	84117	544028	•

Selected Financial Ratios (Times to 1)

Current Ratio 30	1.8	•	1.7	2.2	2.1	1.9	2.3	2.1	1.3	1.9	1.4	•
Quick Ratio 31	1.2	•	1.2	1.2	1.3	1.3	1.2	1.1	0.7	1.2	1.1	•
Net Sales to Working Capital 32	8.5	•	21.0	7.7	6.9	5.5	4.4	5.0	14.2	4.7	4.0	•
Coverage Ratio 33	2.8	4.4	5.2	4.7	8.0	5.2	5.3	5.8	1.5	1.7	1.0	•
Total Asset Turnover 34	1.6	•	5.0	2.8	2.3	1.8	1.6	1.8	1.5	1.0	0.2	•
Inventory Turnover 35	7.4	•	11.9	10.6	5.3	6.5	3.6	4.7	5.3	25.6	11.4	•
Receivables Turnover 36	9.5	•	32.6	11.7	9.8	8.3	6.5	4.8	5.7	6.6	2.0	•
Total Liabilities to Net Worth 37	2.8	•	504.7	0.9	1.6	1.7	1.1	1.6	2.4	1.4	4.6	•
Current Assets to Working Capital 38	2.2	•	2.4	1.8	1.9	2.1	1.7	1.9	4.3	2.1	3.7	•
Current Liabilities to Working Capital 39	1.2	•	1.4	0.8	0.9	1.1	0.7	0.9	3.3	1.1	2.7	•
Working Capital to Net Sales 40	0.1	•	0.0	0.1	0.1	0.2	0.2	0.2	0.1	0.2	0.2	•
Inventory to Working Capital 41	0.6	•	0.7	0.5	0.6	0.6	0.7	0.8	1.2	0.1	0.2	•
Total Receipts to Cash Flow 42	6.1	3.2	5.0	7.2	6.0	7.0	7.7	78.4	7.3	9.9	6.8	•
Cost of Goods to Cash Flow 43	3.2	1.1	2.1	4.0	3.4	4.2	4.7	54.6	4.2	6.4	4.0	•
Cash Flow to Total Debt 44	0.4	•	1.0	0.8	0.6	0.4	0.4	0.0	0.3	0.2	0.0	•

Selected Financial Factors (in Percentages)

Debt Ratio 45	73.7	•	99.8	48.2	61.7	63.6	52.9	61.3	70.3	57.8	82.2	•
Return on Total Assets 46	9.5	•	21.1	9.5	20.5	10.0	4.9	9.7	5.9	4.2	4.5	•
Return on Equity Before Income Taxes 47	23.3	•	8620.4	14.3	46.7	22.2	8.4	20.8	6.6	3.9	0.1	•
Return on Equity After Income Taxes 48	21.3	•	8509.1	13.2	44.5	18.4	6.6	16.0	4.4	2.5	•	•
Profit Margin (Before Income Tax) 49	3.7	1.6	3.4	2.7	7.9	4.4	2.5	4.4	1.3	1.6	0.1	•
Profit Margin (After Income Tax) 50	3.4	1.4	3.4	2.5	7.5	3.6	2.0	3.4	0.9	1.0	•	•

Table II

Corporations with Net Income

OTHER REPAIR AND MAINTENANCE

MONEY AMOUNTS AND SIZE OF ASSETS IN THOUSANDS OF DOLLARS

Item Description for Accounting Period 7/09 Through 6/10		Total	Zero Assets	Under 500	500 to 1,000	1,000 to 5,000	5,000 to 10,000	10,000 to 25,000	25,000 to 50,000	50,000 to 100,000	100,000 to 250,000	250,000 to 500,000	500,000 to 2,500,000	2,500,000 and over
Number of Enterprises	1	31122	4638	23955	1101	1196	127	70	20	•	•	•	0	0
Revenues ($ in Thousands)														
Net Sales	2	27205016	384586	10160755	2416221	5792563	1649927	2316966	1118866	•	•	•	0	0
Interest	3	27255	295	1622	3011	4354	1831	1018	221	•	•	•	0	0
Rents	4	21737	0	19207	0	899	150	1106	375	•	•	•	0	0
Royalties	5	295	0	0	0	0	0	0	0	•	•	•	0	0
Other Portfolio Income	6	29365	0	1414	272	9683	1412	3782	604	•	•	•	0	0
Other Receipts	7	176239	76	19977	7530	9910	4600	8885	1932	•	•	•	0	0
Total Receipts	8	27459907	384957	10202975	2427034	5817409	1657920	2331757	1121998	•	•	•	0	0
Average Total Receipts	9	882	83	426	2204	4864	13054	33311	56100	•	•	•	•	•
Operating Costs/Operating Income (%)														
Cost of Operations	10	50.8	30.2	39.1	52.3	57.8	58.3	58.4	68.3	•	•	•	•	•
Salaries and Wages	11	12.4	1.1	17.4	6.3	7.9	11.3	14.9	9.0	•	•	•	•	•
Taxes Paid	12	2.6	1.8	3.0	3.1	2.2	1.9	2.3	1.8	•	•	•	•	•
Interest Paid	13	0.9	0.4	0.5	0.6	1.1	1.1	0.3	0.8	•	•	•	•	•
Depreciation	14	1.6	1.0	1.2	1.9	1.6	2.9	2.4	1.0	•	•	•	•	•
Amortization and Depletion	15	0.3	0.1	0.0	0.1	0.3	0.0	0.1	0.2	•	•	•	•	•
Pensions and Other Deferred Comp.	16	0.4	•	0.3	1.0	0.2	1.3	0.6	0.3	•	•	•	•	•
Employee Benefits	17	1.6	0.7	0.6	2.8	1.9	1.7	1.5	1.5	•	•	•	•	•
Advertising	18	0.5	2.4	0.4	0.6	0.5	0.4	0.5	2.0	•	•	•	•	•
Other Expenses	19	16.2	42.8	20.9	16.4	10.9	11.9	13.0	7.0	•	•	•	•	•
Officers' Compensation	20	6.0	7.6	8.1	9.0	6.7	3.4	2.2	1.7	•	•	•	•	•
Operating Margin	21	6.6	12.0	8.3	6.1	8.9	5.9	3.9	6.5	•	•	•	•	•
Operating Margin Before Officers' Comp.	22	12.6	19.6	16.5	15.1	15.6	9.3	6.1	8.1	•	•	•	•	•

Selected Average Balance Sheet ($ in Thousands)

Net Receivables 23	92	0	11	178	454	1787	3895	9253
Inventories 24	58	0	14	50	437	1139	4623	9817
Net Property, Plant and Equipment 25	59	0	22	96	344	1324	3551	3578
Total Assets 26	350	0	81	739	1790	6359	16379	32436
Notes and Loans Payable 27	140	0	36	131	875	2563	1973	4780
All Other Liabilities 28	88	0	27	85	361	1518	4173	12302
Net Worth 29	123	0	19	523	554	2277	10233	15354

Selected Financial Ratios (Times to 1)

Current Ratio 30	2.3	•	2.4	3.5	2.1	1.9	2.6	2.2
Quick Ratio 31	1.5	•	1.7	2.0	1.3	1.3	1.5	1.1
Net Sales to Working Capital 32	7.2	•	16.5	5.9	8.0	5.9	4.7	4.0
Coverage Ratio 33	9.6	31.3	18.2	12.2	9.6	6.9	15.2	10.0
Total Asset Turnover 34	2.5	•	5.2	3.0	2.7	2.0	2.0	1.7
Inventory Turnover 35	7.7	•	11.8	22.9	6.4	6.6	4.2	3.9
Receivables Turnover 36	9.8	•	36.3	17.5	11.5	8.5	6.8	4.5
Total Liabilities to Net Worth 37	1.8	•	3.4	0.4	2.2	1.8	0.6	1.1
Current Assets to Working Capital 38	1.8	•	1.7	1.4	1.9	2.1	1.6	1.8
Current Liabilities to Working Capital 39	0.8	•	0.7	0.4	0.9	1.1	0.6	0.8
Working Capital to Net Sales 40	0.1	•	0.1	0.2	0.1	0.2	0.2	0.2
Inventory to Working Capital 41	0.5	•	0.5	0.2	0.7	0.6	0.6	0.8
Total Receipts to Cash Flow 42	5.0	2.1	4.0	5.7	5.7	6.5	6.7	8.1
Cost of Goods to Cash Flow 43	2.6	0.6	1.6	3.0	3.3	3.8	3.9	5.5
Cash Flow to Total Debt 44	0.8	•	1.7	1.8	0.7	0.5	0.8	0.4

Selected Financial Factors (in Percentages)

Debt Ratio 45	64.8	•	77.1	29.2	69.0	64.2	37.5	52.7
Return on Total Assets 46	21.0	•	48.2	21.1	28.3	15.2	9.9	12.9
Return on Equity Before Income Taxes 47	53.4	•	198.9	27.4	82.0	36.3	14.8	24.6
Return on Equity After Income Taxes 48	50.3	•	197.4	26.1	78.3	31.5	12.7	19.5
Profit Margin (Before Income Tax) 49	7.5	12.1	8.7	6.5	9.4	6.4	4.6	6.7
Profit Margin (After Income Tax) 50	7.1	11.8	8.7	6.2	5.5	5.5	3.9	5.4

Table I

Corporations with and without Net Income

PERSONAL AND LAUNDRY SERVICES

MONEY AMOUNTS AND SIZE OF ASSETS IN THOUSANDS OF DOLLARS

Item Description for Accounting Period 7/09 Through 6/10	Total	Zero Assets	Under 500	500 to 1,000	1,000 to 5,000	5,000 to 10,000	10,000 to 25,000	25,000 to 50,000	50,000 to 100,000	100,000 to 250,000	250,000 to 500,000	500,000 to 2,500,000	2,500,000 and over
Number of Enterprises 1	160308	38692	110320	6441	4274	325	161	43	26	9	5	12	0
Revenues ($ in Thousands)													
Net Sales 2	72510568	2619558	27351229	7647886	10304690	4197722	2271748	1723727	1948101	983097	1539400	11923412	0
Interest 3	93919	1470	5642	1785	7526	1250	4762	6015	3136	2515	2677	57142	0
Rents 4	60285	229	1079	2751	2271	1581	6733	942	1799	4771	7248	30883	0
Royalties 5	131577	0	0	0	1	312	1499	0	2766	0	0	126999	0
Other Portfolio Income 6	224210	61019	30402	15680	36633	1859	5065	8340	1906	10716	4711	47877	0
Other Receipts 7	1733929	125118	391163	80762	446616	103763	86791	26032	50584	83075	19531	320492	0
Total Receipts 8	74754488	2807394	27779515	7748864	10797737	4306487	2376598	1765056	2008292	1084174	1573567	12506805	0
Average Total Receipts 9	466	73	252	1203	2526	13251	14761	41048	77242	120464	314713	1042234	•
Operating Costs/Operating Income (%)													
Cost of Operations 10	28.9	12.8	25.6	30.2	22.8	52.6	30.4	41.2	38.5	29.6	35.3	31.4	•
Salaries and Wages 11	20.5	18.7	19.0	19.2	28.1	14.6	22.1	15.8	19.8	17.8	23.0	21.3	•
Taxes Paid 12	3.9	4.1	3.5	3.8	5.3	3.0	2.9	2.1	3.4	3.2	3.1	4.7	•
Interest Paid 13	2.0	1.7	1.2	1.6	1.9	0.7	2.1	1.8	2.1	3.3	3.2	4.4	•
Depreciation 14	3.4	4.2	2.2	3.6	3.1	3.8	5.4	5.1	3.6	3.9	5.5	5.2	•
Amortization and Depletion 15	1.2	0.9	0.5	0.6	0.6	0.2	0.6	0.8	1.5	2.0	7.7	3.7	•
Pensions and Other Deferred Comp. 16	0.5	0.0	0.4	0.4	0.5	0.3	0.4	0.4	0.3	0.4	1.2	0.8	•
Employee Benefits 17	1.4	0.8	0.8	1.2	1.6	0.6	3.2	2.1	2.9	3.3	2.6	1.9	•
Advertising 18	1.7	1.8	1.5	2.7	1.7	0.9	1.7	1.2	2.4	0.4	0.4	1.8	•
Other Expenses 19	31.0	60.3	35.1	27.8	32.7	17.1	27.9	25.9	26.1	41.2	19.5	23.6	•
Officers' Compensation 20	5.7	7.0	9.2	8.9	4.7	1.5	2.2	1.6	1.5	2.1	0.6	0.6	•
Operating Margin 21	•	•	1.1	0.0	•	4.6	1.0	1.9	•	•	•	0.6	•
Operating Margin Before Officers' Comp. 22	5.5	•	10.3	8.9	1.6	6.2	3.2	3.5	•	•	•	1.2	•

Selected Average Balance Sheet ($ in Thousands)

Net Receivables 23	25	0	3	50	232	1124	2246	5434	8593	15558	48074	72796
Inventories 24	13	0	3	28	42	335	611	1895	3604	3324	16798	56278
Net Property, Plant and Equipment 25	111	0	28	335	834	2400	4559	8444	24536	24347	101968	484599
Total Assets 26	343	71	718	1837	7077	14967	35378	76220	163626	433968		1898455
Notes and Loans Payable 27	141	0	55	365	1003	1295	5267	10745	20970	48840	117835	553817
All Other Liabilities 28	120	0	15	157	473	2533	4391	16657	28330	82734	164466	835321
Net Worth 29	82	0	2	197	360	3248	5308	7977	26921	32051	151667	509318

Selected Financial Ratios (Times to 1)

Current Ratio 30	1.3	•	1.0	1.5	1.6	1.5	1.5	1.3	0.9	1.3	1.0	1.3
Quick Ratio 31	0.8	•	0.8	1.0	1.2	1.2	1.1	0.7	0.6	0.8	0.6	0.6
Net Sales to Working Capital 32	23.4	•	307.3	16.9	11.0	12.5	8.2	11.9	•	13.3	•	14.3
Coverage Ratio 33	2.4	•	3.1	1.9	1.8	10.8	3.7	3.4	1.4	2.0	1.0	2.3
Total Asset Turnover 34	1.3	•	3.5	1.7	1.3	1.8	0.9	1.1	1.0	0.7	0.7	0.5
Inventory Turnover 35	9.7	•	25.0	12.6	13.1	20.3	7.0	8.7	8.0	9.7	6.5	5.5
Receivables Turnover 36	16.1	•	99.9	23.5	10.1	13.2	6.3	7.0	9.9	5.1	5.8	11.2
Total Liabilities to Net Worth 37	3.2	•	43.3	2.7	4.1	1.2	1.8	3.4	1.8	4.1	1.9	2.7
Current Assets to Working Capital 38	4.4	•	25.0	3.1	2.7	3.0	2.9	4.8	•	4.9	•	4.3
Current Liabilities to Working Capital 39	3.4	•	24.0	2.1	1.7	2.0	1.9	3.8	•	3.9	•	3.3
Working Capital to Net Sales 40	0.0	•	0.0	0.1	0.1	0.1	0.1	0.1	0.1	0.1	•	0.1
Inventory to Working Capital 41	0.7	•	3.0	0.4	0.2	0.3	0.4	0.4	•	0.2	•	1.2
Total Receipts to Cash Flow 42	4.5	3.0	4.2	5.3	4.5	5.4	4.4	6.1	5.2	5.2	5.6	4.9
Cost of Goods to Cash Flow 43	1.3	0.4	1.1	1.6	1.0	2.8	1.3	2.5	2.0	1.5	2.0	1.6
Cash Flow to Total Debt 44	0.4	•	0.9	0.4	0.4	0.6	0.3	0.2	0.3	0.2	0.2	0.1

Selected Financial Factors (in Percentages)

Debt Ratio 45	76.2	•	97.7	72.6	80.4	54.1	64.5	77.5	64.7	80.4	65.1	73.2
Return on Total Assets 46	6.5	•	13.7	4.8	4.7	14.4	7.2	6.9	3.0	4.4	2.4	5.3
Return on Equity Before Income Taxes 47	16.0	•	413.3	8.1	10.7	28.5	14.8	21.6	2.6	11.0	0.3	11.2
Return on Equity After Income Taxes 48	13.5	•	407.7	7.5	9.7	27.0	12.7	19.3	0.8	8.9	0.3	7.3
Profit Margin (Before Income Tax) 49	2.9	•	2.7	1.3	1.6	7.2	5.6	4.3	0.9	3.2	0.1	5.8
Profit Margin (After Income Tax) 50	2.4	•	2.6	1.2	1.4	6.8	4.8	3.8	0.3	2.6	0.1	3.8

Table II
Corporations with Net Income

PERSONAL AND LAUNDRY SERVICES

MONEY AMOUNTS AND SIZE OF ASSETS IN THOUSANDS OF DOLLARS

Item Description for Accounting Period 7/09 Through 6/10	Total	Zero Assets	Under 500	500 to 1,000	1,000 to 5,000	5,000 to 10,000	10,000 to 25,000	25,000 to 50,000	50,000 to 100,000	100,000 to 250,000	250,000 to 500,000	500,000 to 2,500,000	2,500,000 and over
Number of Enterprises **1**	82487	16580	59159	4103	2208	271	114	23	16	6	0	7	0

Revenues ($ in Thousands)

	Total	Zero Assets	Under 500	500 to 1,000	1,000 to 5,000	5,000 to 10,000	10,000 to 25,000	25,000 to 50,000	50,000 to 100,000	100,000 to 250,000	250,000 to 500,000	500,000 to 2,500,000	2,500,000 and over
Net Sales **2**	51025896	1587405	16466302	5882825	7250046	3965770	1740572	1299732	1369595	1288170	0	10175479	0
Interest **3**	59462	1446	4289	1584	4571	1005	2241	2292	2780	690	0	38564	0
Rents **4**	25584	229	240	2084	1746	1136	4817	873	706	264	0	13490	0
Royalties **5**	127321	0	0	0	1	312	1459	0	3	0	0	125546	0
Other Portfolio Income **6**	152118	46460	8184	8845	33850	229	4100	7299	1226	1964	0	39959	0
Other Receipts **7**	1025946	90770	346337	34543	39191	86799	67752	5273	18826	68574	0	267882	0
Total Receipts **8**	52416327	1726310	16825352	5929881	7329405	4055251	1820941	1315469	1393136	1359662	0	10660920	0
Average Total Receipts **9**	635	104	284	1445	3319	14964	15973	57194	87071	226610	•	1522989	•

Operating Costs/Operating Income (%)

	Total	Zero Assets	Under 500	500 to 1,000	1,000 to 5,000	5,000 to 10,000	10,000 to 25,000	25,000 to 50,000	50,000 to 100,000	100,000 to 250,000	250,000 to 500,000	500,000 to 2,500,000	2,500,000 and over
Cost of Operations **10**	27.9	12.0	21.1	31.9	18.4	53.1	27.9	46.4	38.6	14.9	•	33.9	•
Salaries and Wages **11**	20.6	13.3	19.9	17.0	26.1	14.4	24.0	15.9	18.3	28.2	•	22.6	•
Taxes Paid **12**	3.9	4.2	3.5	3.4	5.5	2.9	2.6	1.7	3.0	3.1	•	4.7	•
Interest Paid **13**	1.6	1.7	1.1	1.3	1.2	0.4	0.8	1.5	1.3	1.7	•	3.3	•
Depreciation **14**	2.8	2.6	1.9	2.5	1.7	3.8	5.0	3.6	3.2	3.2	•	4.6	•
Amortization and Depletion **15**	1.1	0.6	0.5	0.5	0.5	0.2	0.4	0.6	0.7	1.9	•	3.5	•
Pensions and Other Deferred Comp. **16**	0.5	0.0	0.2	0.4	0.7	0.3	0.3	0.5	0.3	1.3	•	0.9	•
Employee Benefits **17**	1.3	0.8	0.8	1.1	1.5	0.5	3.3	2.5	2.8	2.7	•	1.9	•
Advertising **18**	1.6	1.1	1.6	3.1	1.0	0.8	1.8	1.1	1.1	0.6	•	2.1	•
Other Expenses **19**	28.2	49.6	33.8	24.2	34.0	16.3	27.4	18.6	25.7	39.9	•	18.8	•
Officers' Compensation **20**	5.2	7.8	8.6	9.6	4.9	1.5	1.6	1.4	1.2	1.8	•	0.5	•
Operating Margin **21**	5.2	6.3	7.0	4.9	4.6	5.9	4.8	6.2	4.0	0.7	•	3.3	•
Operating Margin Before Officers' Comp. **22**	10.4	14.1	15.6	14.6	9.5	7.4	6.4	7.6	5.1	2.5	•	3.8	•

Selected Average Balance Sheet ($ in Thousands)

Net Receivables 23	33	0	3	50	240	1185	2451	7362	9458	29075	95076	•
Inventories 24	18	0	2	34	38	344	587	2806	4897	5399	114962	•
Net Property, Plant and Equipment 25	138	0	29	320	806	1966	3726	7999	20225	58941	680502	•
Total Assets 26	449	0	80	728	1992	6858	14385	36694	75774	269248	2533203	•
Notes and Loans Payable 27	151	0	44	344	870	927	3187	11118	16873	68018	705088	•
All Other Liabilities 28	144	0	13	88	461	2293	4050	18476	26618	88304	1043332	•
Net Worth 29	154	0	23	296	661	3638	7148	7100	32283	112926	784783	•

Selected Financial Ratios (Times to 1)

Current Ratio 30	1.5	•	1.7	2.0	1.9	1.6	2.0	1.2	1.1	1.1	1.3	•
Quick Ratio 31	1.0	•	1.3	1.5	1.4	1.3	1.5	0.7	0.7	0.8	0.6	•
Net Sales to Working Capital 32	15.3	•	26.7	12.3	8.8	11.8	5.7	19.1	31.4	47.0	16.3	•
Coverage Ratio 33	6.1	9.7	9.2	5.3	5.6	19.2	12.4	6.1	5.4	4.7	3.5	•
Total Asset Turnover 34	1.4	•	3.5	2.0	1.6	2.1	1.1	1.5	1.1	0.8	0.6	•
Inventory Turnover 35	9.9	•	25.2	13.5	16.1	22.6	7.2	9.4	6.7	5.9	4.3	•
Receivables Turnover 36	16.5	•	86.0	25.9	13.0	•	6.9	6.4	•	•	•	•
Total Liabilities to Net Worth 37	1.9	•	2.4	1.5	2.0	0.9	1.0	4.2	1.3	1.4	2.2	•
Current Assets to Working Capital 38	2.9	•	2.4	2.0	2.1	2.7	2.0	6.4	8.0	14.0	4.7	•
Current Liabilities to Working Capital 39	1.9	•	1.4	1.0	1.1	1.7	1.0	5.4	7.0	13.0	3.7	•
Working Capital to Net Sales 40	0.1	•	0.0	0.1	0.1	0.1	0.2	0.1	0.0	0.0	0.1	•
Inventory to Working Capital 41	0.5	•	0.2	0.4	0.1	0.3	0.2	0.6	1.8	1.2	1.3	•
Total Receipts to Cash Flow 42	3.8	2.0	3.2	4.7	3.8	5.3	3.8	5.4	4.1	3.3	4.9	•
Cost of Goods to Cash Flow 43	1.1	0.2	0.7	1.5	0.7	2.8	1.1	2.5	1.6	0.5	1.7	•
Cash Flow to Total Debt 44	0.5	•	1.5	0.7	0.6	0.9	0.6	0.4	0.5	0.4	0.2	•

Selected Financial Factors (in Percentages)

Debt Ratio 45	65.7	•	71.0	59.3	66.8	47.0	50.3	80.7	57.4	58.1	69.0	•
Return on Total Assets 46	13.2	•	35.6	13.8	11.3	18.3	10.9	13.7	7.9	6.4	6.6	•
Return on Equity Before Income Taxes 47	32.1	•	109.4	27.6	28.1	32.7	20.2	59.0	15.1	11.9	15.4	•
Return on Equity After Income Taxes 48	29.5	•	108.7	27.0	27.0	31.1	18.0	54.3	12.6	11.0	11.1	•
Profit Margin (Before Income Tax) 49	8.0	15.1	9.1	5.7	5.7	8.1	9.5	7.4	5.7	6.3	8.3	•
Profit Margin (After Income Tax) 50	7.3	14.8	9.1	5.6	5.4	7.7	8.4	6.8	4.7	5.8	6.0	•

Table I

Corporations with and without Net Income

RELIGIOUS, GRANTMAKING, CIVIC AND PROFESSIONAL ORGANIZATIONS

MONEY AMOUNTS AND SIZE OF ASSETS IN THOUSANDS OF DOLLARS

Item Description for Accounting Period 7/09 Through 6/10		Total	Zero Assets	Under 500	500 to 1,000	1,000 to 5,000	5,000 to 10,000	10,000 to 25,000	25,000 to 50,000	50,000 to 100,000	100,000 to 250,000	250,000 to 500,000	500,000 to 2,500,000	2,500,000 and over
Number of Enterprises	1	47474	4935	35661	4198	2342	222	84	23	9	0	0	0	0
Revenues ($ in Thousands)														
Net Sales	2	9902582	224355	4067863	1509233	2075383	839504	608805	307233	270206	0	0	0	0
Interest	3	160146	355	38950	37825	62386	10300	4257	4475	1598	0	0	0	0
Rents	4	36464	1	16550	3224	10811	3501	422	189	1767	0	0	0	0
Royalties	5	2530	0	3	2526	0	0	0	2	0	0	0	0	0
Other Portfolio Income	6	34693	0	13465	4368	3420	1584	3837	3342	4676	0	0	0	0
Other Receipts	7	3227117	6132	721466	488490	654879	145099	113739	55207	1042104	0	0	0	0
Total Receipts	8	13363532	230843	4858297	2045666	2806879	999988	731060	370448	1320351	0	0	0	0
Average Total Receipts	9	281	47	136	487	1198	4504	8703	16106	146706	•	•	•	•
Operating Costs/Operating Income (%)														
Cost of Operations	10	12.3	3.1	8.8	7.6	16.1	17.6	27.0	16.3	15.4	•	•	•	•
Salaries and Wages	11	12.8	4.1	6.3	9.9	18.4	17.2	23.6	31.9	33.4	•	•	•	•
Taxes Paid	12	2.4	1.4	2.0	1.8	3.1	1.9	3.6	4.9	3.8	•	•	•	•
Interest Paid	13	1.0	0.0	1.1	0.7	0.7	0.9	1.3	2.3	0.8	•	•	•	•
Depreciation	14	1.9	2.2	0.6	1.4	2.4	4.0	3.8	6.6	5.0	•	•	•	•
Amortization and Depletion	15	0.1	•	0.1	0.0	0.1	0.1	0.0	1.1	0.1	•	•	•	•
Pensions and Other Deferred Comp.	16	0.2	•	0.1	0.0	0.0	0.6	0.2	1.3	1.2	•	•	•	•
Employee Benefits	17	1.4	0.4	0.4	0.8	2.5	1.8	3.2	5.0	2.5	•	•	•	•
Advertising	18	1.5	0.8	2.8	0.1	0.5	0.1	0.7	1.0	3.4	•	•	•	•
Other Expenses	19	100.2	95.5	95.7	114.3	92.1	75.1	48.4	48.2	409.6	•	•	•	•
Officers' Compensation	20	1.3	3.1	1.8	0.5	0.3	0.2	2.5	2.0	4.2	•	•	•	•
Operating Margin	21	•	•	•	•	•	•	•	•	•	•	•	•	•
Operating Margin Before Officers' Comp.	22	•	•	•	•	•	•	•	•	•	•	•	•	•

Selected Average Balance Sheet ($ in Thousands)

Net Receivables 23	21	0	5	30	79	268	1301	5020	25734
Inventories 24	1	0	0	0	12	14	92	600	233
Net Property, Plant and Equipment 25	73	0	10	74	437	2350	7220	13872	33953
Total Assets 26	319	0	89	703	1967	6161	15562	33616	109511
Notes and Loans Payable 27	40	0	21	48	183	1085	1583	4479	4294
All Other Liabilities 28	74	0	18	110	397	1021	4077	12408	70616
Net Worth 29	205	0	50	546	1387	4054	9902	16729	34601

Selected Financial Ratios (Times to 1)

Current Ratio 30	3.2	•	4.0	6.7	4.1	1.9	1.8	1.5	0.9
Quick Ratio 31	2.8	•	3.7	6.3	3.7	1.6	1.1	1.2	0.5
Net Sales to Working Capital 32	1.4	•	2.1	0.7	0.9	2.6	2.8	2.5	•
Coverage Ratio 33	0.6	•	0.5	•	•	0.4	4.9	0.8	12.4
Total Asset Turnover 34	0.7	•	1.3	0.5	0.5	0.6	0.5	0.4	0.3
Inventory Turnover 35	20.6	•	103.5	61.7	12.4	48.5	21.2	3.6	19.8
Receivables Turnover 36	9.4	•	19.4	10.3	7.6	13.0	5.7	3.9	1.6
Total Liabilities to Net Worth 37	0.6	•	0.8	0.3	0.4	0.5	0.6	1.0	2.2
Current Assets to Working Capital 38	1.5	•	1.3	1.2	1.3	2.1	2.2	3.0	•
Current Liabilities to Working Capital 39	0.5	•	0.3	0.2	0.3	1.1	1.2	2.0	•
Working Capital to Net Sales 40	0.7	•	0.5	1.4	1.2	0.4	0.4	0.4	•
Inventory to Working Capital 41	0.0	•	0.0	0.0	0.0	0.0	0.0	0.0	•
Total Receipts to Cash Flow 42	1.2	1.4	1.3	1.1	1.3	1.4	2.2	2.5	0.2
Cost of Goods to Cash Flow 43	0.1	0.0	0.1	0.1	0.2	0.3	0.6	0.4	0.0
Cash Flow to Total Debt 44	1.5	•	2.3	2.1	1.1	1.2	0.6	0.3	1.6

Selected Financial Factors (in Percentages)

Debt Ratio 45	35.6	•	43.4	22.5	29.5	34.2	36.4	50.2	68.4
Return on Total Assets 46	0.4	•	0.7	•	•	0.2	3.0	0.8	2.7
Return on Equity Before Income Taxes 47	•	•	•	•	•	•	3.7	•	7.9
Return on Equity After Income Taxes 48	•	•	•	•	•	•	2.6	•	6.1
Profit Margin (Before Income Tax) 49	•	•	•	•	•	•	5.1	•	9.1
Profit Margin (After Income Tax) 50	•	•	•	•	•	•	3.5	•	7.1

RELIGIOUS, GRANTMAKING, CIVIC AND PROFESSIONAL ORGANIZATIONS

Table II
Corporations with Net Income

MONEY AMOUNTS AND SIZE OF ASSETS IN THOUSANDS OF DOLLARS

Item Description for Accounting Period 7/09 Through 6/10	Total	Zero Assets	Under 500	500 to 1,000	1,000 to 5,000	5,000 to 10,000	10,000 to 25,000	25,000 to 50,000	50,000 to 100,000	100,000 to 250,000	250,000 to 500,000	500,000 to 2,500,000	2,500,000 and over
Number of Enterprises **1**	22850	1689	16231	2916	1839	90	61	•	•	0	0	0	0

Revenues ($ in Thousands)

Item Description for Accounting Period 7/09 Through 6/10	Total	Zero Assets	Under 500	500 to 1,000	1,000 to 5,000	5,000 to 10,000	10,000 to 25,000	25,000 to 50,000	50,000 to 100,000	100,000 to 250,000	250,000 to 500,000	500,000 to 2,500,000	2,500,000 and over
Net Sales **2**	5492168	73862	1629476	773214	1643519	341972	545099	•	•	0	0	0	0
Interest **3**	127751	13	31990	32223	49348	7349	2810	•	•	0	0	0	0
Rents **4**	16930	1	2479	2301	9801	98	422	•	•	0	0	0	0
Royalties **5**	2516	0	0	2514	0	0	0	•	•	0	0	0	0
Other Portfolio Income **6**	16625	0	4062	2442	1827	5	732	•	•	0	0	0	0
Other Receipts **7**	2125658	2208	341990	302460	265528	41982	102029	•	•	0	0	0	0
Total Receipts **8**	7781648	76084	2009997	1115154	1970023	391406	651092	•	•	0	0	0	0
Average Total Receipts **9**	341	45	124	382	1071	4349	10674	•	•	0	0	0	•

Operating Costs/Operating Income (%)

Item Description for Accounting Period 7/09 Through 6/10	Total	Zero Assets	Under 500	500 to 1,000	1,000 to 5,000	5,000 to 10,000	10,000 to 25,000	25,000 to 50,000	50,000 to 100,000	100,000 to 250,000	250,000 to 500,000	500,000 to 2,500,000	2,500,000 and over
Cost of Operations **10**	12.8	9.6	8.5	14.9	12.7	5.3	24.7	•	•	•	•	•	•
Salaries and Wages **11**	14.5	•	5.3	10.7	17.9	13.5	23.2	•	•	•	•	•	•
Taxes Paid **12**	2.5	1.5	2.0	2.2	2.2	1.8	3.5	•	•	•	•	•	•
Interest Paid **13**	0.5	•	0.2	0.2	0.6	0.0	1.1	•	•	•	•	•	•
Depreciation **14**	1.7	•	0.7	0.6	1.9	1.8	3.1	•	•	•	•	•	•
Amortization and Depletion **15**	0.0	•	•	0.0	0.0	0.0	0.0	•	•	•	•	•	•
Pensions and Other Deferred Comp. **16**	0.2	•	•	•	0.0	0.3	0.2	•	•	•	•	•	•
Employee Benefits **17**	1.5	0.7	0.1	0.3	2.3	2.3	3.0	•	•	•	•	•	•
Advertising **18**	0.9	2.5	1.4	•	0.5	0.1	0.8	•	•	•	•	•	•
Other Expenses **19**	100.7	71.0	98.0	111.1	78.0	82.1	50.1	•	•	•	•	•	•
Officers' Compensation **20**	1.2	9.3	1.4	•	0.3	0.0	2.7	•	•	•	•	•	•
Operating Margin **21**	•	5.5	•	•	•	•	•	•	•	•	•	•	•
Operating Margin Before Officers' Comp. **22**	•	14.8	•	•	•	•	•	•	•	•	•	•	•

Selected Average Balance Sheet ($ in Thousands)

Net Receivables 23	31	0	5	20	64	402	1764
Inventories 24	2	0	0	0	11	8	112
Net Property, Plant and Equipment 25	77	0	10	37	329	861	6850
Total Assets 26	449	0	121	701	1865	5918	15222
Notes and Loans Payable 27	24	0	6	15	114	123	1473
All Other Liabilities 28	106	0	17	83	364	1493	4208
Net Worth 29	319	0	98	603	1386	4302	9541

Selected Financial Ratios (Times to 1)

Current Ratio 30	3.7	•	7.9	7.8	5.0	2.9	1.6
Quick Ratio 31	3.3	•	7.6	7.5	4.6	2.9	1.1
Net Sales to Working Capital 32	1.0	•	1.1	0.5	0.8	1.4	4.1
Coverage Ratio 33	12.4	•	30.2	17.5	7.5	156.5	7.3
Total Asset Turnover 34	0.5	•	0.8	0.4	0.5	0.6	0.6
Inventory Turnover 35	15.5	•	172.8	85.8	9.9	26.4	19.8
Receivables Turnover 36	8.3	•	18.7	10.8	10.3	•	5.3
Total Liabilities to Net Worth 37	0.4	•	0.2	0.2	0.3	0.4	0.6
Current Assets to Working Capital 38	1.4	•	1.1	1.1	1.3	1.5	2.7
Current Liabilities to Working Capital 39	0.4	•	0.1	0.1	0.3	0.5	1.7
Working Capital to Net Sales 40	1.0	•	0.9	2.0	1.2	0.7	0.2
Inventory to Working Capital 41	0.0	•	0.0	0.0	0.0	0.0	0.1
Total Receipts to Cash Flow 42	1.1	1.4	1.2	1.0	1.5	1.1	2.1
Cost of Goods to Cash Flow 43	0.1	0.1	0.1	0.2	0.2	0.1	0.5
Cash Flow to Total Debt 44	1.7	•	3.6	2.6	1.2	2.1	0.8

Selected Financial Factors (in Percentages)

Debt Ratio 45	28.8	•	18.9	14.0	25.7	27.3	37.3
Return on Total Assets 46	3.0	•	5.0	1.7	2.0	4.7	4.7
Return on Equity Before Income Taxes 47	3.9	•	6.0	1.8	2.3	6.4	6.4
Return on Equity After Income Taxes 48	3.4	•	5.5	1.6	2.0	6.1	4.8
Profit Margin (Before Income Tax) 49	5.2	8.5	5.8	4.1	3.6	7.3	6.9
Profit Margin (After Income Tax) 50	4.5	7.5	5.3	3.5	3.1	6.9	5.1

Index

Index